CLINICAL ASSESSMENT of MALINGERING and DECEPTION

CLINICAL ASSESSMENT of MALINGERING and DECEPTION

THIRD EDITION

Edited by
RICHARD ROGERS

THE GUILFORD PRESS
New York   London

Last digit is print number: 9   8   7   6   5   4   3   2   1

Library of Congress Cataloging-in-Publication Data

Clinical assessment of malingering and deception / edited by Richard Rogers.—3rd ed.
   p. ; cm.
   Includes bibliographical references and index.
   ISBN 978-1-59385-699-1 (hardcover : alk. paper)
   1. Malingering—Diagnosis. 2. Deception. I. Rogers, Richard, 1950–
   [DNLM: 1. Malingering—diagnosis. 2. Deception. 3. Mental Disorders—diagnosis.
   W 783 C641 2008]
   RA1146.C57 2008
   616.85′2—dc22

                                                        2007042846

About the Editor

Richard Rogers, PhD, ABPP, is Professor of Psychology at the University of North Texas. His contributions to research on malingering and other response styles have been recognized by national awards from the American Academy of Forensic Psychologists, the American Psychiatric Association, the American Psychological Association, and the Society of Clinical Psychology.

Contributors

R. Michael Bagby, PhD, is Professor of Psychiatry at the University of Toronto and Director of the Clinical Research Department at the Centre for Addiction and Mental Health in Toronto, Ontario, Canada.

Scott D. Bender, PhD, is Assistant Professor in the Department of Psychiatry and Neurobehavioral Sciences and a Consulting Neuropsychologist for the Departments of Surgery and Physical Medicine and Rehabilitation at the University of Virginia School of Medicine in Charlottesville, Virginia.

David T. R. Berry, PhD, is Professor of Psychology and Director of Graduate Studies at the University of Kentucky in Lexington, Kentucky.

Daniel C. Condit, PhD, is a postdoctoral resident in Clinical Neuropsychology (2006–2008) in the Neuropsychology Service of Evanston Northwestern Healthcare, Evanston, Illinois.

Cody Crawford, BA, is an advanced doctoral student at the Pacific Graduate School of Psychology in Palo Alto, California.

Alan J. Cunnien, MD (deceased), was a Consultant in Psychiatry at Mayo Clinic Scottsdale, Scottsdale, Arizona, and Assistant Professor of Psychiatry at the Mayo Medical Center in Rochester, Minnesota.

Marc D. Feldman, MD, is Clinical Professor of Psychiatry in the Department of Psychiatry and Behavioral Medicine at the University of Alabama, Tuscaloosa, Alabama.

Elke Geraerts, PhD, was a postdoctoral fellow at Harvard University and Maastricht University, the Netherlands, and is now a lecturer at the University of St. Andrews, Scotland, United Kingdom.

Robert P. Granacher, Jr., MD, MBA, is Clinical Professor of Psychiatry at the University of Kentucky College of Medicine and Director of the Lexington Forensic Institute in Lexington, Kentucky.

Roger L. Greene, PhD, is Professor of Psychology at the Pacific Graduate School of Psychology in Palo Alto, California.

James C. Hamilton, PhD, is Associate Professor of Clinical Psychology in the Department of Psychology and coordinator of the Clinical Health Psychology Doctoral Training Program at the University of Alabama, Tuscaloosa, Alabama.

William G. Iacono, PhD, is Distinguished McKnight University Professor of Psychology at the University of Minnesota, Minneapolis, Minnesota.

Rebecca L. Jackson, PhD, is Director of the Forensic Psychology Program at the Pacific Graduate School of Psychology in Palo Alto, California.

James L. Knoll, IV, MD, is Associate Professor of Psychiatry and Director of the Division of Forensic Psychiatry at State University of New York Upstate Medical University in Syracuse, New York.

Franz A. Kubak, MA, is a doctoral student at the University of Alabama, Tuscaloosa, Alabama.

Richard I. Lanyon, PhD, ABPP, is Professor of Psychology at Arizona State University in Tempe, Arizona.

Zina Lee, PhD, is a postdoctoral fellow at the University of Alabama, Tuscaloosa, Alabama.

Richard J. McNally, PhD, is Professor and Director of Clinical Training in the Department of Psychology at Harvard University, Cambridge, Massachusetts.

Nathaniel W. Nelson, PhD, is Assistant Professor of Physical Medicine and Rehabilitation at the Neuropsychology Laboratory of the University of Minnesota, Minneapolis, Minnesota.

Randy K. Otto, PhD, ABPP, is Associate Professor in the Department of Mental Health Law and Policy at the Florida Mental Health Institute, University of South Florida, Tampa, Florida, and an adjunct faculty member at Stetson University College of Law, St. Petersburg, Florida.

Christopher J. Patrick, PhD, is Starke R. Hathaway Distinguished Professor of Psychology at the University of Minnesota, Minneapolis, Minnesota.

Joshua W. Payne, MA, is an advanced doctoral student at the University of North Texas, Denton, Texas.

Phillip J. Resnick, MD, is Professor of Psychiatry and Director of the Division of Forensic Psychiatry at Case Western Reserve University School of Medicine, Cleveland, Ohio, and Director of the Court Psychiatric Clinic for Cleveland.

Richard Rogers, PhD, ABPP (see "About the Editor").

Randall T. Salekin, PhD, is Associate Professor of Psychology at the University of Alabama, Tuscaloosa, Alabama, and Associate Director of the Center for the Prevention of Youth Behavior Problems.

Lindsey J. Schipper, MA, is a doctoral student in the clinical psychology program at the University of Kentucky, Lexington, Kentucky.

Martin Sellbom, PhD, is a postdoctoral research associate in the Department of Psychology at Kent State University, in Kent, Ohio, and a psychology resident at the Psycho-Diagnostic Clinic in Akron, Ohio.

Kenneth W. Sewell, PhD, is Professor of Psychology and Director of Clinical Training at the University of North Texas, Denton, Texas.

Glenn P. Smith, PhD, is Chief of the Posttraumatic Stress Disorder (PTSD) Clinical Team at the James A. Haley Veterans Administration Hospital, Tampa, Florida.

Lynda A. R. Stein, PhD, is Assistant Professor of Psychology at the University of Rhode Island; Director of Research, Rhode Island Training School; Director, Juvenile Forensic Psychology Postdoctoral Training Program; and Senior Research Associate, Department of Psychiatry and Human Behavior, Brown University, Providence, Rhode Island.

Jerry J. Sweet, PhD, is Professor of Psychiatry and Behavioral Sciences at Northwestern University Feinberg School of Medicine, Chicago, Illinois, and Director of the Neuropsychology Service at Evanston Northwestern Healthcare, Evanston, Illinois.

Michael L. Thomas, MA, is an advanced doctoral student in clinical psychology at Arizona State University, Tempe, Arizona.

Michael J. Vitacco, PhD, is Associate Director of Research at Mendota Mental Health Institute in Madison, Wisconsin.

Sara West, MD, is a fourth-year psychiatry resident at University Hospitals, Case Medical Center, in Cleveland, Ohio.

Preface

The first edition of *Clinical Assessment of Malingering and Deception* achieved its overriding goal of integrating clinical practice and applied research in its critical examination of malingering and other response styles. It was largely successful in meeting the needs of both seasoned practitioners and applied researchers. Among its accolades, the first edition was recognized by the Manfred S. Guttmacher Award of the American Psychiatric Association as an outstanding contribution to forensic psychiatry. After an 8-year interval, the second edition was published, capturing the major advances in the assessment of response styles and the burgeoning of clinical literature.

This third edition emerges after a decade of intensive research on response styles and important advances in research methods. Focusing on malingering alone, the phenomenal growth from 1997 through 2007 is measured by its inclusion in 714 journal articles, 156 dissertations, and 126 chapters.[1] This scholarly output exceeds the cumulative efforts of the past century (1896–1996). Beyond the virtual explosion of scholarly activity, assessment methods continue to be developed and refined. Moreover, research on response styles is increasingly sophisticated in its design and applications. A major contribution to the third edition is its formal examination of detection strategies that bridge both measures and relevant populations.

Not all revised editions are created equal. My goal was a complete revision, including new contributors, new chapters, and new coverage. No pages and very few paragraphs remain unchanged. It is my hope that the third edition, like its predecessors, will become an authoritative text used widely by clinical practitioners and response-style researchers.

RICHARD ROGERS

NOTE

1. These numbers are based on a PsycINFO search using only the word *malingering* and ending in September 2007.

Contents

IV. Specialized Methods

V. Specialized Applications

VI. Summary

CLINICAL ASSESSMENT of MALINGERING and DECEPTION

I

Conceptual Framework

1

An Introduction to Response Styles

RICHARD ROGERS, PhD

Complete and accurate self-disclosure is a rarity even in the uniquely supportive context of a psychotherapeutic relationship. The most involved clients may intentionally conceal and distort important data about themselves. Issues of sexuality, procreation, and body image are rarely discussed fully in the therapeutic context (Farber, 2003; Farber & Hall, 2002). Even in intimate relationships, willingness for self-disclosure is variable and multidetermined (Laurenceau, Barrett, & Rovine, 2005). Beyond therapy and intimacy, decisions to disclose or deceive are also common in health care and social settings. Most individuals, including mental health professionals, are selective about how much they share with others; their concealments may be either passive omissions or active distortions.

A national survey of professionals and managers by Ellison, Russinova, MacDonald-Wilson, and Lyass (2003) has important implications for understanding individuals' disclosures and deceptions regarding mental disorders. The majority of these employees had disclosed their psychiatric conditions to their supervisors and coworkers. However, many disclosures were not entirely voluntary (e.g., pressure to explain health-related absences), and about one-third regretted their decisions because of negative repercussions. Moreover, the degree of self-disclosure (e.g., diagnosis, symptoms, or impairment) and the timing of the disclosures were highly variable. Nondisclosing employees

were typically motivated by fears of job security and concerns about stigma. What are the implications of the Ellison and colleagues study? First, decisions about response styles (to disclose or to deceive) are often rational and multidetermined; this theme is explored later in the context of the adaptational model. Second, these decisions are often individualized responses to interpersonal variables (e.g., a good relationship with a coworker) or situational demands (e.g., explanation of poor performance). This openness to individualized decisions directly counters a popular misconception that response styles are inflexible, trait-like characteristics of certain individuals. For example, malingerers are sometimes misconstrued as having an invariant response style, unmodified by circumstances and personal motivations.[1]

Most individuals engage in a variety of response styles that reflect their personal goals in a particular setting. Certain behaviors, such as substance abuse, may be actively denied in one setting and openly expressed in another. Social desirability and impression management may prevail during the job application process but later be abandoned once hiring is completed.

In personal injury cases, claimants may use two response styles in the same evaluation. They may minimize psychological problems (i.e., defensiveness) prior to the accident but grossly exaggerate their symptoms (i.e., malingering) following it. As noted, response styles should not be considered to be intrinsic attributes, because of their potential to change depending on an individual's differing goals and circumstances.

Clients in an evaluative context may experience internal and external influences on their self-reporting. Within a forensic context, for example, clients may respond to the adversarial effects of litigation in which their credibility is implicitly questioned (Rogers & Payne, 2006). As observed by Rogers and Bender (2003), these same clients may also be influenced internally by their diagnosis (e.g., borderline personality disorder), identity (e.g., avoidance of stigmatization), or intentional goals e.g., malingering). By necessity, most chapters in this volume focus on one or more response styles within a single domain (e.g., mental disorders, cognitive abilities, or medical complaints). Beyond the assessment of specific response styles, practitioners may wish to consider the effects of internal and external influences on self-reporting. However, they are limited by the lack of standardized measures to systematically evaluate such idiosyncratic factors.

In summary, all individuals fall short of full and accurate self-disclosure, irrespective of the social context. Clinically, mental health professionals are often not fully forthcoming about their assessment and treatment methods (Bersoff, 2003). Consider for a moment how providing a complete description of MMPI-2 validity scales to clients might limit the effectiveness of these indicators in the assessment of malingering (see, e.g., Rogers, Bagby, & Chakraborty, 1993). Such revelations could be deemed tantamount to coaching clients on how to foil the MMPI-2 detection strategies.

The evidence is compelling that some degree of deception, be it omission or commission, is a part of most extended communications. Although most individuals are likely to judge acts of deception more harshly than those of omission (Haidt & Baron, 1996), both can be equally important. Rather than consider the type of deception, I advance the argument that only *consequential* deceptions and distortions should be considered in the context of response styles. As an illustrative case, a male client seeking services was administered the Personality Assessment Inventory (PAI; Morey, 1991). His elevated score on the Rogers Discriminant Function (RDF; Rogers, Sewell, Morey, & Ustad, 1996) indicated a strong likelihood of feigning (Morey, 2003; see also Chapter 11, this volume); however, none of his clinical

scales were elevated. If we were to consider these findings in isolation,[2] should we report the likelihood of *failed* malingering? Whatever his intention, an argument could be put forth that the client did *not* malinger and that the reporting of "likelihood of failed malingering" is both unhelpful and unnecessary. Beyond this unusual case, mental health professionals must decide whether any evidence of response styles, however equivocal, should be routinely included in clinical and forensic reports. Guided by professional and ethical considerations, these decisions are likely to be influenced by at least two dimensions: (1) accuracy versus completeness of reports and (2) use versus misuse of clinical findings by others.

As an introduction to response styles, this chapter has the primary goal of familiarizing practitioners and researchers with general concepts associated with malingering and deception. It operationalizes response styles and outlines common misconceptions associated with malingering and other forms of dissimulation. Conceptually, it distinguishes explanatory models from detection strategies. Because research designs affect the validity of clinical findings, a basic overview is provided. Finally, this chapter outlines the content and objectives of the subsequent chapters.

FUNDAMENTALS OF RESPONSE STYLES

Basic Concepts and Definitions

Since the second edition, considerable progress has been made in the standardization of terms and operationalization of response styles. Such standardization is essential to any scientific endeavor. This section is organized conceptually into four categories: nonspecific terms, overstated pathology, simulated adjustment, and other response styles.

Nonspecific Terms

Practitioners and researchers seek precision in the description of response styles. Why, then, begin the consideration of response styles with nonspecific terms? It is my hope that moving from general to specific categories will limit the decisional errors in the determination of response styles. As a consultant on malingering and related response styles, I find that the most common error appears to be the *overspecifica-*

tion of response styles. For instance, criminal offenders are frequently miscategorized as malingerers simply because of their manipulative behavior, which may include asking for special treatment (e.g., overuse of medical call for minor complaints) or displaying inappropriate behavior (e.g., a relatively unimpaired inmate exposing his genitals). When disabled clients express ambivalence toward clinical or medical interventions, their less-than-wholehearted attitudes are sometimes misconstrued as prima facie evidence of secondary gain (see Rogers & Payne, 2006).

The working assumption about errors in the *overspecification of response styles* is that practitioners approach this diagnostic classification by trying to determine which specific response style best fits the clinical data. Often, this approach results in the specification of a response style, even when the data are inconclusive or even conflicting. Instead, I recommend a two-step approach:

1. Do the clinical data support a nonspecific (e.g., "unreliable informant") description?
2. If yes, are there ample data to determine a specific response style?

This model asks practitioners to make an explicit decision between nonspecific descriptions and specific response styles. Such direct comparisons may help to reduce errors of overspecification.

Nonspecific terms are presented with a brief commentary in a bulleted format as an easily accessible reference:

1. *Unreliability* is a very general term that raises questions about the accuracy of reported information. It makes no assumption about the individual's intent or the reasons for inaccurate data. This term is especially useful in cases of conflicting clinical data.

2. *Nondisclosure* simply describes a withholding of information (i.e., omission). Similar to unreliability, it makes no assumptions about intentionality. An individual may freely choose not to disclose or may feel compelled by internal demands (e.g., command hallucination) to withhold information.

3. *Self-disclosure* refers to how much individuals reveal about themselves (Jourard, 1971). A person is considered to have high self-disclosure when he or she evidences a high degree of openness. A lack of self-disclosure does not imply dishonesty but simply an unwillingness to share personal information.

4. *Deception* is an all-encompassing term used to describe any consequential attempts by individuals to distort or misrepresent their self-reporting. As operationalized, deception includes acts of deceit, often accompanied by nondisclosure. Deception may be totally separate from the patient's described psychological functioning (see *dissimulation*).

5. *Dissimulation* is a general term to describe an individual who is deliberately distorting or misrepresenting psychological symptoms. Practitioners find this term useful because some clinical presentations are difficult to classify and clearly do not represent malingering, defensiveness, or any specific response style.

Overstated Pathology

Important distinctions must be realized between *malingering* and other terms used to describe overstated pathology. For example, the determination of malingering requires the exclusion of factitious presentations (see Chapter 3, this volume). This subsection addresses three recommended terms: *malingering, factitious presentations*, and *feigning*. It also includes three quasi constructs (secondary gain, overreporting, and suboptimal effort) that should be avoided in most clinical and forensic evaluations.

Following are recommended terms for categorizing overstated pathology:

1. *Malingering* has been consistently defined by DSM nosology as "the intentional production of false or grossly exaggerated physical or psychological symptoms, motivated by external incentives" (American Psychiatric Association, 2000, p. 739). An important consideration is the magnitude of the dissimulation; it must be the fabrication or gross exaggeration of multiple symptoms. The presence of minor exaggerations or isolated symptoms does not qualify as malingering. Its requirement of external incentives does not rule out the co-occurrence of internal motivations.

2. *Factitious presentations* are characterized by the "intentional production or feigning" of symptoms that is motivated by the desire to assume a "sick role" (American Psychiatric Association, 2000, p. 517). As discussed further in Chapter 3, this volume), the diagnosis of factitious disorders is excluded if any external in-

centives are found. This categorical exclusion can be problematic because most patient roles also involve concomitant modifications of work and family responsibilities (Rogers, Jackson, & Kaminski, 2004).

3. *Feigning* is the deliberate fabrication or gross exaggeration of psychological or physical symptoms without any assumptions about its goals (Rogers & Bender, 2003). This term was introduced because standardized measures of response styles (e.g., psychological tests) have not been validated for assessment of an individual's specific motivations. Therefore, determinations can often be made for feigned presentations but not their underlying motivations. To underscore this point, psychological tests can be used to establish feigning, but not malingering.

Several terms, common to clinical and forensic practice, lack well-defined and validated descriptions. This absence stems either from (1) the lack of clear inclusion criteria or (2) the presence of multiple and conflicting definitions. Three terms to be avoided in clinical and forensic practice are summarized:

1. *Suboptimal effort* (also referred to as "incomplete" or "submaximal" effort) is sometimes used as a proxy for malingering (Rogers & Neumann, 2003). However, this term lacks precision and could be applied to nearly any client or professional (see Rogers & Shuman, 2005). The "best" effort of any individual may be affected by a variety of internal (e.g., an Axis I disorder or fatigue) and external (e.g., a stressful evaluation) factors.

2. *Overreporting* simply refers to an unexpectedly high level of item endorsement, especially on multiscale inventories. Practitioners sometimes erroneously equate it with feigning. However, this descriptive term lacks clarity with respect to its content (i.e., socially undesirable characteristics, as well as psychopathology). Moreover, it has been used to describe both deliberate and unintentional acts (Greene, 2000).

3. *Secondary gain,* unlike the other unacceptable terms, does have clear definitions. Its inherent problem for professional practice, however, is the presence of conflicting meanings (Rogers & Reinhardt, 1998). From a psychodynamic perspective, secondary gain is part of an unconscious process to protect the individual that is motivated by intrapsychic needs and defenses. From a behavioral medicine per-

spective, illness behaviors are perpetuated by the social context (e.g., health care providers), not by the individual. From a forensic perspective, individuals deliberately use their illness to gain special attention and material gains.

Mental health professionals bear an important responsibility to use professional language that is clearly defined. Ambiguous terminology (e.g., *suboptimal effort, overreporting,* and *secondary gain*) adds unnecessary confusion to clinical assessments. Moreover, the misuse of professional language may lead to grievous errors in adjudicative settings, such as the courts.

Simulated Adjustment

Three closely related terms are used to describe specific response styles that are associated with simulated adjustment. *Defensiveness* is operationalized as the masking of psychological difficulties, whereas the other two terms apply more broadly to the concealment of undesirable characteristics.

1. *Defensiveness* is defined as the polar opposite of malingering (Rogers, 1984b). Specifically, this term refers to the deliberate denial or gross minimization of physical and/or psychological symptoms. Defensiveness must be distinguished from "ego defenses," which involve intrapsychic processes that distort perceptions.

2. *Social desirability* is the pervasive tendency for certain individuals to "present themselves in the most favorable manner relative to social norms and mores" (King & Bruner, 2000, p. 80). It involves both the denial of negative characteristics and the attribution of positive qualities (Carsky, Selzer, Terkelson, & Hurt, 1991). Not limited to psychological impairment, social desirability is a far more encompassing construct than defensiveness. Social desirability and its concomitant measurement should be carefully distinguished from defensiveness.

3. *Impression management* refers to deliberate efforts to control others' perceptions of an individual; its purpose may range from maximizing social outcomes to the portrayal of a desired identity (Leary & Kowalski, 1990). Impression management is often construed as more situationally driven than social desirability, which may reflect a characteristic style of presentation. Although research studies often assume that impression management involves

only a prosocial perspective, individuals may use this response style for a variety of purposes that are not necessarily prosocial (e.g., "playing dumb"; see Thornton, Audesse, Ryckman, & Burckle, 2006).

Preferred terms for simulated adjustment are likely to vary by the professional setting. Clinically, *defensiveness* is often the more precise term with which to describe an individual's minimization of psychological difficulties. In many professional contexts that include clinical settings, efforts at self-presentation are likely to involve social desirability and impression management. For research on social interactions, *impression management* is the most versatile term for describing different roles on a continuum from prosocial to antisocial.

Other Response Styles

Several additional response styles are not as well understood as malingering, defensiveness, and other approaches previously described. Four other response styles are outlined:

1. *Irrelevant responding* refers to a response style in which the individual does not become psychologically engaged in the assessment process (Rogers, 1984b). The given responses are not necessarily related to the content of the clinical inquiry. This process of disengagement, although more prevalent in psychological testing, is also observed in clinical interviews when a particular patient makes no effort to respond accurately to clinical inquiries.

2. *Random responding* is a subset of irrelevant responding based entirely on chance factors. A likely example would be the completion of the MMPI-2 in less than 5 minutes. In this instance, the individual has probably read only a few of its 567 items and completed the remainder without any consideration of their content.

3. In *role assumption,* individuals may occasionally assume the role or character of another person in responding to psychological measures. For example, Kroger and Turnbell (1975) asked undergraduates to simulate the role of commissioned officers in the air force. This response style is poorly understood and is included only for research purposes.

4. *Hybrid responding* is a term used to describe an individual's use of more than one response style in a particular situation. For example, clients may evidence honest responding

about most facets of their lives but engage in defensiveness with respect to substance abuse. Hybrid responding underscores the importance of considering response styles as adaptable and potentially transitory.

Domains of Dissimulation

Response styles are almost never pervasive. For example, malingerers do not feign everything from viral infections to mental retardation. A convenient framework for understanding and assessing response styles is the concept of domains. As described in detail in Chapter 2, in this volume, three broad domains that encompass most attempts at dissimulation are mental disorders, cognitive abilities, and medical complaints. These domains are essential to assessment of response styles, because detection strategies (see Rogers, Chapter 2) are rarely effective across domains.

Common Misconceptions of Malingering

Malingering is unique among response styles in its number of associated myths and misconceptions. Rogers (1998; Rogers & Bender, 2003) outlined common fallacies about malingering held by both practitioners and the public. Common misconceptions are summarized:

• *Malingering is very rare.* Some clinicians simply ignore the possibility of malingering, perhaps equating infrequency with inconsequentiality. Large-scale surveys of more than 500 forensic experts (Rogers, Duncan, & Sewell, 1994; Rogers, Salekin, Sewell, Goldstein, & Leonard, 1998) suggest that malingering is not rare in either forensic or clinical settings.[3] When the outcome of an evaluation has important consequences, malingering should be systematically evaluated. Its neglect is a serious omission.

• *Malingering is a static response style.* Some practitioners use the flawed logic "once a malingerer, always a malingerer." On the contrary, most efforts at malingering appear to be related to specific objectives in a particular context. For example, descriptive data by Walters (1988) suggest that inmates rarely feign except when hoping to achieve a highly desired goal (e.g., obtaining a single cell for psychological reasons); among those applying for parole, many inmates manifest the opposite response style (i.e., defensiveness).

• *Deception is evidence of malingering.* This fallacy is apparently based on the erroneous notion that "malingerers lie; therefore, liars malinger." Egregious cases have been observed in which the clients' marked minimization of symptoms (i.e., defensiveness) was misreported by a practitioner as evidence of malingering. More commonly, deceptions by manipulative inpatients are mistakenly equated with malingering.

• *Malingering precludes genuine disorders.* An implicit assumption is that malingering and genuine disorders are mutually exclusive. This common misconception can sometimes be detected by a careful record review. The typical two-step sequence begins with a description of all symptoms as genuine. After the determination of malingering, all symptoms are dismissed as bogus.

• *Malingering is an antisocial act by an antisocial person.* This common misperception is perpetuated by DSM-IV, which attempts to use the presence of antisocial personality disorder as a screening indicator for malingering. As detailed in Chapter 2 in this volume (see the section on conceptual issues), this serious error arises from confusing *common characteristics* (e.g., criminality in criminal settings) with *discriminating characteristics,* which consistently differentiate malingerers from nonmalingerers.

• *Malingering is similar to the iceberg phenomenon.* This misconception appears to be based on the theory that any evidence of malingering is sufficient for its classification. The erroneous assumption appears to be that any observable feigning, similar to the visible tip of an iceberg, represents a pervasive pattern of malingering.

• *Malingering has stable base rates.* As reported by Rogers, Salekin, and colleagues (1998), marked variations are observed in the base rates (i.e., *SD* = 14.4%) for malingering across forensic settings. Even within the same setting, marked variations are likely to occur depending on the referral question and individual circumstances. Within the forensic context, the motivation to malinger is substantially greater for an insanity case than a child-custody determination. Moreover, the assessment process itself will also affect applicable base rates. When malingering measures are used with all referrals, the base rate is likely to be relatively low (e.g., 10–30%), even in forensic settings. However, when validated screens (e.g., the Miller Forensic Assessment of Symp-

toms Test [M-FAST]) are used to identify possible malingerers, the base rate is likely to exceed 50%. Finally, efforts to "correct" base rates in malingering studies often make tenuous assumptions, such as the stability of sensitivity.[4]

Other misconceptions include the naïve idea that malingerers often engage an indiscriminant effort that is easily detectable by practitioners (Rogers, 1998). Although not empirically tested, the additive effects of multiple misconceptions may fundamentally damage clinicians' abilities to evaluate malingering and render sound judgments. The effects of inadequate evaluations can be profound for misclassified malingerers and other affected parties. When unvalidated hunches supersede science, then the professional standing of mental health specialties is called into question.

CLINICAL AND RESEARCH MODELS

Motivational Basis of Response Styles

This section introduces a clinical framework for understanding response styles such as malingering. Because most response styles are conceptualized as deliberate efforts, individual motivations become a central concern. The motivational basis for response styles, sometimes referred to as explanatory models, has far-reaching implications for clinical and forensic practice. As summarized in the subsequent paragraphs, the predominant motivation found in most theoretical work is best conceptualized as *predicted utility.* In other words, the selection of most response styles can be understood as a comparative decision based on predicted utilities.

The general category of simulated adjustment is likely the most common constellation of response styles, and it encompasses defensiveness, impression management, and social desirability. For example, the minimization of suicidal ideation may serve twin goals, each with its own predicted utility: the maintenance of a positive image and the minimization of social sanctions (e.g., civil commitment). Predicted utilities may focus on others or be predominantly self-focused. As an example of the latter, a male executive may not want to acknowledge his depression because it would be a sign of personal weakness. Although it is possible that such defensiveness is unconscious (see, e.g., the Self-Deceptive Enhancement scale; Paulhus, 1998), data suggest that individuals can deliberately modify their "self-deceptive" responses to achieve a desired goal (see Rogers & Bender, 2003).

General deception constitutes a broad category that involves various forms of dishonesty and nondisclosure. Like simulated adjustment, the predominant motivation is based on predicted utility. For instance, the nondisclosure of socially unacceptable behaviors (e.g., anomalous sexual acts) likely involves a consideration of potential risks (e.g., legal consequences) that overshadow any transient benefits (e.g., titillation at recounting these behaviors). Even the telling of "white lies" serves the deceiver by minimizing unpleasant conflict and preserving his or her likeability.

Within the general category of overstated pathology, conceptual and empirical work has focused primarily on malingering. Again, the prevailing model relies on expected utility. In what is described as the adaptational model, malingerers attempt to engage in a cost–benefit analysis in choosing to feign psychological impairment. In an analysis of malingering cases from 220 forensic experts, the cost–benefit analyses within adversarial contexts were prototypical of malingerers (Rogers, Salekin, et al., 1998). Unlike other general categories, two additional explanatory models have been posited for malingering: pathogenic and criminological (American Psychiatric Association, 2000).

The pathogenic model conceptualizes an underlying disorder as motivating the malingered presentation (Rogers & Bender, 2003). The malingerers, in an ineffectual effort to control their genuine impairment, voluntarily produce symptoms. As their condition deteriorates, they presumably become less able to control the feigned disorders. A distinctive feature of the pathogenic model is this prediction of further deterioration. Although immediate recovery following litigation is uncommon (i.e., accident neurosis; see Resnick, 1997), research does not support this "further deterioration" hypothesis. Prototypical analysis (Rogers, Salekin, et al., 1998) of the pathogenic model indicated that it is not representative of most malingerers, especially those found in a forensic context.

DSM classifications (American Psychiatric Association, 1980, 1987, 1994, 2000) have adopted the criminological model to explain the primary motivation for malingering. Its underlying logic is that malingering is typically an antisocial act that is likely to be committed by antisocial persons. Whether this logic is persuasive, empirical data (Rogers, 1990a) strongly question whether its current operationalization in DSM-IV as four indicators (i.e., forensic context, antisocial background, uncooperativeness, and discrepancies with objective findings) is useful. When DSM indices are evaluated in a criminal forensic setting, they are wrong approximately four out of five times. According to Rogers and Shuman (2005), the DSM indicators should not be used even as a screen for potential malingering because they produce an unacceptable error rate.

The fundamental problem with the criminological model is that it relies on common rather than distinguishing characteristics of malingering (see Chapter 2, this volume). Most malingerers in criminal forensic settings have antisocial backgrounds and are participating in a forensic consultation. However, the same conclusion is true about nonmalingering individuals with genuine disorders. Therefore, the criminological model is not useful with criminal–forensic and correctional settings. It has yet to be tested with other populations in which it may be less common, yet still not able to distinguish characteristics of malingerers.

Returning to the predominant predicted-utility model, Lanyon and Cunningham (2005) provide an elegant example of how this model can apply across both domains and response styles. Simulators may attempt to maximize the predicted utility of their efforts by using both overstated pathology (e.g., malingering Axis I symptoms and health problems) and simulated adjustment (e.g., exaggerating their personal virtues). The latter response style may serve two related goals: (1) to enhance the credibility of the disability claim (e.g., good citizens do not file false insurance reports) and (2) to emphasize the magnitude of the purported loss (e.g., the avoidable suffering of an upstanding citizen).

Overview of Research Designs

Many skilled practitioners and researchers benefit from a quick overview of research designs as they relate to response styles. This brief section highlights key differences in designs and their relevance to clinical practice; for a more extensive treatment of response styles, please see Chapter 24. Together with Chapter 2, this summary should facilitate the sophisticated use of response-style measures that are presented in subsequent chapters.

Four basic research designs are used in most studies of response styles (see Table 1.1). Two basic designs complement each other with their respective strengths: Simulation designs can provide unparalleled control over internal validity, whereas known-group comparisons are unequaled in their consideration of exter-

nal validity. Because of the challenges in establishing the independent categorization required for known-group comparisons, two other designs have been introduced. These designs differ markedly in methodological rigor, from patently simplistic (i.e., differential prevalence design) to generally sophisticated (i.e., bootstrapping comparisons). The following paragraphs describe these four basic designs and

TABLE 1.1. Researching Response Styles: An Overview of Basic Designs

Simulation research

Description. Analogue research randomly assigns participants to different experimental conditions. Results are typically compared with those from relevant clinical groups.

Internal validity. Strong: Procedures include standardized instructions, conditions, incentives, and manipulation checks.

External validity. Weak: Participants do not face the often grave circumstances and consequences of succeeding or failing at a particular response style.

Classification. Effectively tested: With cross-validation, the accuracy of classification can be evaluated against the experimental condition for specific response styles.

Known-groups comparison

Description. With the use of independent experts, individuals can be classified in real-world conditions according to specific response styles.

Internal validity. Weak: Researchers have no control over experimental assignment or other standardized procedures.

External validity: Strong: The participants, settings, issues, and incentives fit real-world considerations.

Classification. Effectively tested: With cross-validation, the accuracy of classification can be evaluated for specific response styles as established by independent experts.

Differential prevalence design

Description. Based on assumed incentives, greater numbers of a broadly defined group (e.g., litigants) are presumed to have a specific response style when compared with a second group (e.g., nonlitigants).

Internal validity. Weak: Researchers have no control over experimental assignment or other standardized procedures.

External validity. Moderate: Participants are often involved in real-world consultations facing important consequences for successful and unsuccessful adoption of a specific response style. However, the lack of ground truth (i.e., independent classification of response styles) militates against knowing which participants are attempting to engage in which response styles.

Classification. Untestable: Without knowing group membership, the accuracy of classification is impossible to establish.

Bootstrapping comparisons

Description. By using multiple detection strategies, stringent cut scores can be applied that maximize specificity (e.g., no genuine patients are classified as malingerers) and preserve moderate sensitivity (e.g., the majority of feigners are classified as malingerers).

Internal validity. Weak: Researchers have no control over experimental assignment or other standardized procedures.

External validity. Moderately strong: The participants, settings, issues and incentives fit real-world considerations. Researchers typically have a high level of confidence for one relevant group.

Classification. Variable: The greatest risk is false positives, because an unknown percentage of the assigned group (e.g., "feigning") do not warrant this classification. Careful application of external indicators with well-established utility estimates can make this design a valuable contribution to the study of response styles.

provide salient examples of how each design can be misused by clinicians.

Simulation Design

Most research on response styles relies on simulation designs using an analog design, which may be augmented by additional samples. As noted in Table 1.1, this research often has excellent internal validity, using standardized methods and relying partly on an experimental design, with the random assignment of participants to different experimental conditions. In most malingering studies, for example, community participants are randomly assigned to feigning and control (honest) conditions. To address the critical issue (genuine vs. feigned disorders), the feigning group is typically compared with a nonrandom clinical sample of convenience. Interestingly, the use of relevant comparison samples is generally omitted from defensiveness research. If applied, researchers would compare defensive individuals to persons with above-average to superior adjustment. Such refined comparisons, missing from current research, would ensure that high-functioning persons are not routinely being miscategorized as defensive.

• *Flawed use of simulation designs:* Conclusions about malingering without samples of genuine patients are confounded. Abnormal findings for the feigning group could apply equally well to a genuine patient group.

Known-Groups Comparisons

This design, underutilized in dissimulation research, uses independently established groups to evaluate specific response styles. It provides very strong evidence of external validity for cases drawn from similar professional settings (see Table 1.1). Methodologically, the two critical issues are (1) the use of the most accurate classification of a specific response style that is available and (2) the complete masking of this classification from researchers administering the target measures (i.e., avoidance of criterion contamination).

• *Flawed use of known-groups comparisons:* Studies using inaccurate or unreliable independent categorization will yield erroneous classifications. For example, cut scores on the MMPI-2 should be not be used as an external

criterion for malingering or defensiveness because its validity scales have wide-ranging cut scores that yield strong but variable utility estimates.

Differential Prevalence Design

Because of challenges in establishing known-groups comparisons, this design attempts to address external validity by assuming that differences in types of referrals can be used as an expedient proxy for known groups. Such simplistic thinking should not be tolerated in clinical research, although it may play a marginal role in advancing theory.[5] The fundamental and fatal weaknesses of differential prevalence design can be convincingly illustrated by a consideration of Axis I diagnoses. Extensive gender research (e.g., Hartung & Widiger, 1998) has firmly established differential prevalence rates for depression and schizophrenia. Any facile efforts to equate depression with women and schizophrenia with men would never be tolerated. Applied to response styles, parallel errors are easily observed: Litigation equals faking (especially malingering), and nonlitigation equals honest responding.

Why should the differential prevalence design be categorically excluded from the classification of response styles? Even when base rates and results are very favorable, the fundamental and fatal weaknesses of this design prevent its clinical use. For example, using a high estimate of malingering for forensic referrals (32%) and a low estimate for nonforensic (1%) referrals[6] does not help. Even in the best-case scenario, when identical percentages (i.e., 32% of the forensic referrals and 1% of the nonforensic referrals) exceed the malingering cut score on any feigning test, no valid conclusions can be drawn. It is possible but unlikely that 0.0% of malingerers were identified (i.e., that all high scores are false positives); it is also as possible but even less likely that 100% of malingerers were identified. This example clearly illustrates the invalidity of differential prevalence design for most clinical classification of response styles.

• *Flawed use of differential prevalence design.* Any specific conclusions about individual or group classification of response styles based on differential prevalence designs lack sufficient empirical basis. To avoid risks of serious misinterpretation, studies with differential prevalence designs should not report utility estimates.

Bootstrapping Comparisons

Researchers on feigned cognitive impairment are acutely aware of the challenges in establishing known groups (e.g., malingerers) and have sought an alternative approach to independent classifications. In a design described by Rogers and Bender (2003) as "bootstrapping comparisons," researchers use previously established measures to classify high-probability groups of feigners and genuine patients. Slick, Sherman, and Iverson (1999) provide an example of an elaborate model for probable malingering. A more direct approach would be the use of several well-validated scales based on specific detection strategies to establish two groups: feigning and genuine. Stringent cut scores could be applied for each group to increase the probability of accurate classification.[7]

• *Flawed use of bootstrapping comparisons.* Clinical conclusions often extend far beyond focused criterion measures and are empirically untested. For example, many well-established measures of cognitive feigning focus on short-term memory; extrapolations to other cognitive abilities, such as mental retardation, are unwarranted.

Determination of response styles represents a complex, multifaceted process that includes domains, detection strategies, and measures. A critical first step in mastering assessment methods is the accurate identification of the four basic designs for dissimulation research. Knowledge of these designs allows practitioners to have a most sophisticated appreciation of empirical findings and their clinical relevance. In addition to understanding their respective strengths, mental health professionals must also be able to recognize faulty designs for clinical classification (i.e., the differential prevalence design) and flawed applications to dissimulation research.

LOOKING FORWARD

This book is organized into six major parts that provide a logical progression in the examination of malingering and other forms of deception. Although chapters vary substantially in their content and scope, a unifying theme is the integration of research, theory, and clinical practice. As will become evident, chapters vary in their success at achieving this integration. This variability accurately reflects the strengths and weaknesses in our knowledge of response styles. For example, hundreds of studies have examined feigned mental disorders. In contrast, denial of medical complaints is a vast but largely uncharted territory. Understandably, the integration of research and clinical practice will be substantively different between well-established (e.g., feigned mental disorders) and recently considered (e.g., denial of medical complaints) areas of dissimulation research.

The overriding goal of most chapters is the provision of clear, usable information that will have a direct impact on professional practice and clinical research. Whenever possible, specific guidelines are provided regarding the clinical applications of particular measures, scales, and detection strategies. Some dissimulation scales are especially useful for the *ruling-in* (i.e., identification and classification) of specific response styles. Other scales can serve an important purpose for the *ruling-out* of one or more response styles. When accomplished efficiently, such measures are very useful as screens. Despite our positive focus on advances in the assessment of response styles, we also consider common missteps and inaccuracies that can lead to grievous errors in the determination of dissimulation.

The book, as previously noted, is organized into six major parts that introduce, examine, and summarize the relevant theory and clinical data on response styles. Part I is composed of the first two chapters, which operationalize response-style terms and provide a conceptual basis for the remaining chapters. Chapter 2 is especially important in providing the critical distinction between *common* and *distinguishing* characteristics; only the latter can be used effectively in clinical classification. However, the centerpiece of Chapter 2 is the description of detection strategies that are organized by response styles and domains. This examination of detection strategies provides the essential template for the remaining chapters.

Malingering and other response styles pose singular challenges, depending on the clinical presentation and purported disorders. Part II consists of seven chapters that address a range of disorders and syndromes for which dissimulation can become a central concern. Chapter

3 provides a broad and valuable overview of specific syndromes and clinical conditions that are frequently associated with dissimulation. Chapters 4 through 7 examine specific diagnostic categories in which response styles are often considered, especially when consultations have significant financial or forensic relevance. Of these, Chapter 6 is essential to most professional practices, given the endemic nature of substance abuse and its widespread denial. Chapter 8 exemplifies the importance of near-neighbor comparisons. For example, can sophisticated practitioners reliably distinguish factitious presentations from the closely related construct of malingering? Chapter 9 introduces mental health professionals to the important but often neglected topic of feigned medical presentations.

Parts III and IV address the assessment of response styles. Part III concerns psychometric methods, in which the breadth and sophistication of dissimulation research has been particularly impressive in two areas: multiscale inventories and feigned cognitive impairment. As a result, each area is subdivided into two chapters: inventories (MMPI-2, Chapter 10; other inventories, Chapter 11) and cognitive feigning (memory, Chapter 13; other cognitive abilities, Chapter 14). Chapter 12 covers the controversies and clinical data concerning response styles and the use of projective methods. Part IV addresses specialized methods. The usefulness of physiological and other standardized measures are considered in relationship to lie detection (Chapter 15) and sexual deviation (Chapter 17). Controversies continue to surround recovered memories; Chapter 16 examines the usefulness and limitations of clinical methods used for the recovery of early memories. Finally, structured interviews (Chapter 18) and specialized screens (Chapter 19) make substantial contributions to the assessment of response styles.

Beyond diagnostic and assessment issues, professionals must also consider specialized applications. Part V considers three critically important applications: youths (Chapter 20), forensics (Chapter 21), and law enforcement (Chapter 22). These chapters also serve an integrative function by bringing together measures and detection strategies from earlier chapters in drawing conclusions about specialized applications.

Researchers and clinicians often struggle with the process, specifically focusing on the question of how to proceed. Part VI distills clinical data and underscores critical issues. Chapter 23 summarizes the key findings and provides useful guidelines for conducting evaluations of response styles. Chapter 24 highlights key issues for conducting research on response styles. It is intended to offer general suggestions for addressing overlooked areas of response styles and to address these areas with improved methodology.

NOTES

1. As an implicit example, a report of malingering during adolescence was used as "evidence" decades later to corroborate the current classification of malingering.
2. In this particular case, no other evidence of feigning was observed either on the PAI or other measures (e.g., the SIRS).
3. The two surveys yielded similar data for forensic (Ms of 15.7% and 17.4%) and nonforensic (Ms of 7.2% and 7.4%) referrals. The percentages for nonforensic cases may be higher than among other clinicians because forensic experts are often consulted on nonforensic issues that are highly consequential to clients (e.g., independent evaluations of insurance claims).
4. These efforts implicitly assume that sensitivity is a stable estimate, whereas positive predictive power (PPP) is not. Although PPP does vary in relationship to base rates, sensitivity also evidences nonsystematic variability (see Rogers & Sewell, 2007).
5. More precisely, this design would be best used to discount a hypothesized relationship if predicted findings are not observed.
6. Rogers, Salekin, et al. (1998) used estimates from 221 highly experienced forensic experts. For this hypothetical example, the differences were strongly accentuated: (1) for forensic referrals, the 32% prevalence assumes a rate that is approximately 1 standard deviation *above* the Rogers, Salekin, et al. average (M = 17.44%, SD = 14.44%); and (2) for nonforensic referrals, the 1% prevalence assumes a rate that is close to 1 standard deviation *below* the average (M = 7.16%, SD = 7.09%).
7. Researchers sometimes focus closely on the feigning group and simply assume that the remaining group is genuine. Instead of group membership by default, cut scores can also be applied to increase the probability that "genuine samples" are composed of bona fide patients with little likelihood of feigning (i.e., hybrid response style).

2

Detection Strategies for Malingering and Defensiveness

RICHARD ROGERS, PhD

This chapter introduces detection strategies and provides a conceptual framework for understanding their development and validation. In this context, five essential criteria of detection strategies are examined. The second major section provides an overview of detection strategies as they are applied to specific response styles. This latter section is intended as a template for understanding the specific contributions provided in subsequent chapters.

CONCEPTUAL ISSUES

The modern era for the systematic assessment of response styles was heralded by the empirical development of the Minnesota Multiphasic Personality Inventory (MMPI; Hathaway & McKinley, 1940). Seminal efforts on the MMPI relied on discriminating items that were uncharacteristic of normative populations. Simplest in construction was the F scale, which merely relies on MMPI items infrequently endorsed by the Minnesota normative samples. Lacking any conceptual underpinnings, interpretations of F-scale elevations cover the gamut from attentional difficulties and poor reading comprehension to psychotic interference, hostile noncompliance, and deliberate feigning (Dahlstrom, Welsh, & Dahlstrom, 1972). In contrast, the L scale was developed with a specific detection strategy to detect falsification. Modeling it after Hartshone and May (1928), Hathaway and McKinley (1940) constructed 15 items that involved the denial of personal faults and foibles. As evidence that these faults are widely observed, normative samples typically endorse two-thirds of them as "true." Subsequent studies (Baer, Wetter, & Berry, 1992) tended to narrow the interpretation of L-scale elevations from general falsification to defensiveness, specifically the denial of personal shortcomings. Because many patients with obvious psychopathology failed to show clinical elevations (i.e., "within normal limits" profile), discriminating items were selected to constitute the K scale. Unlike the earlier validity scales, those items were chosen that differentiated between two clinical samples, those acknowledging psychopathology and those denying psychopathology.

What lessons can be learned from the MMPI validity scales? First, the initial conceptualization of the detection strategy is paramount to subsequent interpretation. The clarity of the K-scale development and interpretation is easily contrasted with the interpretational challenges faced by the F scale, which lacks sufficient conceptual underpinnings. Second, the selection of criterion groups dictates the precision of subsequent interpretations. Using the F scale as an example, scales developed simply on normative samples are confounded as measures of malingering; in other words, elevations could result from either feigned or genuine psychopathology.

Despite its limitations, the MMPI represents the first critical stage in the development of empirically based detection strategies for response styles. Prior to the MMPI, most assessments of malingering and other response styles relied on unproven methods. In many instances, the "salient" characteristics of feigning were identified in a particular population, such as the Ganser syndrome in prison samples. In such instances, two major pitfalls can easily arise. First, without systematic investigations, clinicians can unwittingly engage in a tautological exercise: "Salient" characteristics of malingering are identified with reference to suspected malingerers, who are thus identified on the basis of these "salient" characteristics (i.e., a confirmatory bias; Borum, Otto, & Golding, 1993). Second, common features of malingering can be mistaken for discriminating characteristics. In the case of the Ganser syndrome, a common but not discriminating characteristic was the correctional setting. The misuse of a common characteristic for the classification of response styles may result in catastrophic errors, with false positives dwarfing accurate classifications.

Clinicians are likely to believe that the confusion of common and discriminating characteristics is a historical problem, resolved by the introduction of empirically validated detection strategies. This is not so. DSM screening indices for malingering,[1] first established two decades ago (American Psychiatric Association, 1980), continue to use two common features of malingering as if they were discriminating characteristics (American Psychiatric Association, 2000). Although malingerers are commonly found in forensic evaluations and often have antisocial backgrounds, the use of these two indices can produce disastrous inaccuracies. In criminal forensic evaluations, all individuals are involved in a forensic evaluation, with the large majority warranting the diagnosis of antisocial personality disorder (APD). For the purpose of discussion, let us make two simple assumptions: (1) the prevalence of APD is 50% and (2) the prevalence of malingering is 15–17%, based on extensive surveys (see Chapter 1, this volume). Even if the common characteristic of APD *always* occurred with malingerers, the false-positive rate (e.g., 50% [APD] − 17% [malingering] = 33%) would be approximately 200% higher than the true-positive rate (e.g., 17%). Available data suggest that the actual false-positive rate is much higher than 200% (see Rogers, 1990a). This analysis demonstrates the devastating consequences of confusing common features with discriminating characteristics.

The key distinction between common and distinguishing characteristics is illustrated by the following descriptions:

- Common characteristics, often described as "clinical correlates," are often observed in individuals with a specific response set. Even when frequencies exceed 50%, common characteristics or correlates do *not* assist in clinical classification.
- Distinguishing characteristics refer to specific clinical features that reliably differentiate between relevant groups. They can be used in clinical classification.

The earlier example regarding APD and malingering in criminal forensic evaluations clearly illustrates why common characteristics should not be used for clinical classifications. In addition, most clinical correlates are relatively modest (e.g., $rs < .40$) and cannot be used for classification. Even when correlates are high (e.g., $rs > .70$), they do not assist in clinical classification because certain diagnoses or other response styles may have correlations of similar magnitude.

An outgrowth of discriminating characteristics is the formulation of detection strategies. The remainder of the chapter is devoted to the description of detection strategies for common response styles and a critical examination of their applicability to professional practice.

Description of Detection Strategies

Discriminating characteristics are typically specific to a particular scale and cannot be generalized to other assessment methods. For example, early research on the MMPI L scale suggested that the denial of personal shortcomings and foibles may be useful in the assessment of defensiveness. Would this finding qualify as a detection strategy? The conditional answer is only when the strategy has been formalized and tested with multiple measures across multiple settings. Built on earlier conceptualizations (e.g., Rogers & Bender, 2003; Rogers, Harrell, & Liff, 1993), the description of detection strategies is as follows:

• *A detection strategy is a standardized method that is conceptually based and empirically validated for systematically differentiating a specific response style (e.g., malingering or defensiveness) from other response styles (e.g., honest responding).*

This description includes five critical criteria, specifically: (1) standardized method, (2) conceptual basis, (3) empirical validation, (4) systematic differentiation, and (5) a specific response style. Each component is briefly examined, as follows.

1. *Standardized methods* are essential to all scientific endeavors. Detection strategies must be operationalized to provide uniform items, scoring, and administration so that their results can be rigorously tested and cross-validated.

2. The absence of a well-defined construct limits the usefulness and the interpretability of research findings (see the subsequently described "forced-choice testing"). Therefore, a *conceptual basis* must be described in order to test a specific detection strategy and evaluate competing hypotheses.

3. *Empirical validation* focuses on the use of proven methodology to establish the validity of a specific detection strategy. As summarized in Chapter 1, the empirical validation of detection strategies optimally includes both simulation designs and known-group comparisons. It avoids flawed methodology (e.g., differential prevalence rates) and inappropriate comparisons (e.g., contrasting feigned and unimpaired protocols). Other important methodological considerations are summarized in Rogers and Cruise (1998) and Chapter 24.

4. *Systematic differentiation* is simply the estimation of accuracy. Statistical significance is an inadequate proxy for accuracy. Many studies of response styles yield results with a high probability of statistical significance that have very little utility in professional practice. Instead, the magnitude of difference is the critical issue (Wilkinson & Task Force on Statistical Inference, 1999). Because of its clarity, Cohen's *d* is used in this volume as the standard measure of effect sizes.[2] Beyond effect sizes, the *sine qua non* of accuracy is level of individual classification. Utility estimates are used to calculate the probabilities that individuals are or are not engaging in a specific response style (see Streiner, 2003).

5. The delineation of a *specific response style* is essential to the accurate interpretation of results. For example, some research on malingered cognitive impairment attempts to substitute "suboptimal effort" for malingering. This construct drift (i.e., broadening the conceptualization of malingering to embrace any manifestation of inadequate motivation) is unacceptable. Researchers and clinicians must verify that criterion groups and instructional sets correspond to the specific response styles under consideration.

What is a good detection strategy? In meeting the five criteria, the detection strategy should be cross-validated with different measures and should consistently produce large effect sizes and accurate classifications. If it is not effective across different measures, then the detection strategy is not sufficiently established and may be capitalizing on idiosyncratic features of one particular scale. If the effect sizes are only moderate, then the detection strategy is comparatively ineffective and should be avoided. Importantly, detection strategies for response styles must be targeted, focusing on a specific response style within a particular domain. The next section examines the focused nature of detection strategies.

Focused Nature of Detection Strategies

A fundamental principle is that detection strategies are not universal but must be considered within specific response styles and general domains. Unquestionably, different detection strategies are needed for the evaluation of specific response styles. For example, the assessment of malingering on the MMPI-2 (Rogers, Sewell, Martin, & Vitacco, 2003) uses very different detection strategies than does the evaluation of defensiveness (Baer & Miller, 2002). Although an inverse relationship between malingering and defensiveness can occur (see, e.g., the bipolarity hypothesis; Greene, 1997), detection strategies focused on a specific response style have proven to be the most effective. To illustrate this point with the MMPI-2, Rogers, Sewell, and colleagues (2003) found large to very large effect sizes for validity scales based on detection strategies for malingering. In stark contrast, the absence of defensiveness (i.e., low scores on scales using its detection strategies) generally produced only small to moderate effect sizes.

Detection strategies must also take into account the broad domains in which specific response styles commonly occur. The three broadest domains include mental disorders, cognitive abilities, and medical complaints (Rogers & Bender, 2003). Consider malingering. Individuals feigning a schizophrenic disorder are faced with a very different task than are those feigning mental retardation. With feigned schizophrenia, malingerers must create believable sets of symptoms and associated features. They must decide on the course of the current episode, its concomitant impairment, and their level of insight into their disorder. In contrast, persons feigning mental retardation must put forth a convincing effort while failing on intellectual and cognitive measures. They must also decide on how badly to fail and how such failures should affect their day-to-day functioning. Because the tasks of malingerers are dissimilar, different detection strategies are needed.

The medical domain is far more complex than either mental disorders or cognitive abilities. With medical malingering, patients can specialize in one debilitating symptom (e.g., pain), portray a constellation of common but distressing ailments (e.g., headaches, fatigue, and gastrointestinal difficulties), or specialize in complex syndromes (e.g., fibromyalgia). In light of this complexity, detection strategies for the medical domain face formidable challenges in their development and validation.

Two parameters are essential in evaluating the usefulness of detection strategies: effect sizes and utility estimates. Effect sizes provide a standardized method for evaluating the comparative value of different detection strategies in distinguishing between relevant criterion groups. Utility estimates examine the effectiveness of particular cut scores for individual and group classification of response styles.

Effect Sizes and Detection Strategies

Cohen's (1962) seminal work on effect sizes was designed to consider relatively small differences as relevant to research. For example, he recommended that effect sizes of 0.80 be considered "large," even though differences were substantially less than one pooled standard deviation (Cohen, 1988). More rigorous standards are needed for professional practice, especially when the presence of a response

style may serve to invalidate an individual's clinical presentation. For the assessment of malingering, Rogers, Sewell, and colleagues (2003) proposed more rigorous standards for Cohen's d: "moderate" ≥ 0.75; "large" ≥ 1.25; and "very large" ≥ 1.75. Based on the meta-analysis of defensiveness by Baer and Miller (2002), the recommended standard for "very large" effect sizes (≥ 1.50) is slightly lower than the standard for malingering. As a ready reference, the following standards are used in categorizing effect sizes (Cohen's d) for the evaluation of response styles:

- Moderate ≥ 0.75
- Large ≥ 1.25
- Very large ≥ 1.50

Accuracy and Detection Strategies

Mental health professionals need to know the accuracy of cut scores and more complex decision rules in clinical determinations, such as a specific response style. Even our very best psychometric measures are often imprecise and are sometimes simply inaccurate. As evidence of imprecision, consider for the moment the Wechsler Adult Intelligence Scale (WAIS-III), a superb psychometric measure. When taking into account its standard error of measurement (i.e., SEM = 2.30), we can say with 95% certainty that a tested IQ of 100 (presumably the 50th percentile) falls somewhere between the 39th and 61st percentiles[3] (see Wechsler, 1997, Appendix A). Imprecision is also evident on measures of psychopathology, such as the MMPI-2. Taking into account the SEM on standard MMPI-2 clinical scales (conservatively 6T points; see Rogers & Sewell, 2006), a marginal elevation at 65T has a 95% likelihood of falling between 53T (normal) and 77T (moderate elevation). The point of this discussion is that some clinicians are overly confident in the precision of their results. Especially when making consequential decisions about response styles, clinicians should take great care to be prudent in their conclusions by taking into account the imprecision of measurement.

In the critical evaluation of detection strategies, clinicians should consider at least four utility estimates. Least helpful is the overall hit rate, which may obscure important weaknesses. As an extreme example, a cut score could miss every single person with a factitious disorder but could still achieve a 90% hit rate because of the very low prevalence of factitious disorders. In establishing a specific response style (SRS), two utility estimates should be considered at a particular cut score:

- Sensitivity is the proportion of persons with the SRS correctly identified by the cut score. If 18 of 20 malingerers are identified by a particular cut score (e.g., 65T on the MMPI-2 F scale), then the sensitivity is .90.
- Positive predictive power (PPP) is the likelihood that persons meeting a particular cut score will be correctly identified with the SRS. If the same cut score correctly identifies 18 of 20 malingerers but misclassifies 60 genuine patients, then the PPP (18/78) is .23.

This example clearly illustrates the importance of considering both sensitivity and PPP in evaluating the accuracy of particular cut scores. Extremely high sensitivity can be achieved at the expense of PPP. However, error rates (e.g., false positives) are very important and have been recognized by the Supreme Court as a critical component for the admissibility of expert testimony (see *Daubert v. Merrell Dow Pharmaceuticals, Inc.*, 1993).

Use of utility estimates is discussed more extensively in subsequent chapters (see also Streiner, 2003). For the purpose of establishing the construct validity of detection strategies, the minimum guidelines across different measures should be .75 for PPP and .50 for sensitivity.[4] In some cases the presence of a very high PPP may justify a lower sensitivity. As an example from feigned cognitive impairment, symptom validity testing can achieve a very high PPP (e.g., .99) but is effective in only a small minority of cases. Moreover, lower sensitivities can be justified only if other detection strategies are also employed. In summary, the effectiveness of utility estimates must be considered individually for specific measures as they pertain to particular cut scores or decision rules. This general consideration of minimal guidelines for detection strategies is simply to provide evidence of construct validity.

Practitioners sometimes review research studies that do not provide complete utility estimates; PPP and negative predictive power (NPP) are often omitted. Fortunately, these are simple calculations that are readily available via Internet sites. One highly reputable site is maintained by the Society of Personality Assessment via its instructions to authors and reviewers for the *Journal of Personality Assessment*.

DETECTION STRATEGIES FOR SPECIFIC RESPONSE STYLES

Detection strategies form two general categories that capitalize either on unlikely presentations or on amplified presentations. For unlikely presentations, detection strategies emphasize the *presence* of unusual and atypical characteristics that are not generally observed in genuine populations. For amplified presentations, detection strategies evaluate the *frequency* and *intensity* of characteristics commonly found in genuine populations. This categorization has been tested with feigned mental disorders (Rogers, Jackson, Sewell, & Salekin, 2005) and presented as a useful heuristic for feigned cognitive impairment (Rogers & Bender, 2003). At present, unlikely and amplified presentations provide us with a general conceptual framework for evaluating the comprehensiveness of detection strategies.

Research on detection strategies has focused intensively on two domains: mental disorders and cognitive abilities. For mental disorders, the emphasis has been divided between malingering and defensiveness. For cognitive abilities, the focus has been solely on malingering, with defensiveness being largely neglected. In the latter case, mental health professionals have assumed that clients could not perform better than their actual abilities. Although mainly true, some individuals are able to conceal their cognitive deficits while performing work-related responsibilities. Concealed deficits could be either chronic (e.g., cognitive decline) or temporary (e.g., hangover effects for pilots; Bates, 2002). In light of the current research, the next three subsections examine (1) malingering and mental disorders,[5] (2) defensiveness and mental disorders, and (3) malingering and cognitive abilities. Despite fewer studies of detection strategies, the final section summarizes the current data on malingering and medical syndromes.

Malingering and Mental Disorders

Rogers (1984b) provided the original analysis of detection strategies, which combined empirical and heuristic models of malingering. From this earliest analysis, detection strategies have gradually evolved and been subjected to rigorous examination (Rogers, 1997d; Rogers & Bender, 2003). As summarized in Table 2.1, 10 detection strategies for malingered mental disorders have been validated. Five strategies are based on unlikely presentations: (1) rare symptoms, (2) quasi-rare symptoms, (3) improbable symptoms, (4) symptom combinations, and (5) spurious patterns of psychopathology. The first three strategies examine the legitimacy of individual symptoms and features. Of these, the rare-symptoms strategy is the "workhorse" for assessing feigned mental disorders; it frequently appears on many multiscale inventories and specialized measures of malingering. As evidence of its usefulness, this strategy typically produces large to very large effect sizes. Importantly, rare symptoms must be distinguished from quasi-rare symptoms. In

the latter case, scales were developed by examining what clinical characteristics were uncommon among community participants. The method of scale development is faulty because items may reflect either genuine disorders or feigned disorders. As a case in point, only 25.0% of the F-scale items (a quasi-rare strategy) were also uncommon in clinical populations.[6] Quasi-rare symptoms, although they produce large to very large effect sizes, are difficult to interpret. They may result in unacceptable levels of false positives (i.e., the misclassification of a genuine patient as simply malingering).

The final detection strategy devoted to individual symptoms and features involves improbable symptoms. Virtually by definition, endorsements of improbable symptoms cannot be veridical. However, improbable symptoms

TABLE 2.1. Detection Strategies for Feigned Mental Disorders

Rare symptoms

1. *Description:* This strategy capitalizes on symptoms or features that are very infrequently reported (e.g., <5.0%) by bona fide clinical populations. Malingerers are often detected because they overreport these infrequent psychological problems.

2. *Strengths:* This detection strategy has been widely applied to different psychological measures; it tends to yield large to very large effect sizes.

3. *Limitation:* None is noted.

4. *Examples:*
   a. SIRS RS (Rare Symptoms) scale
   b. MMPI-2 Fp (F-psychiatric) scale
   c. Personality Assessment Inventory (PAI) NIM (Negative Impression) scale
   d. Miller Forensic Assessment of Symptoms (M-FAST) UH (Unusual Hallucinations) scale

Quasi-rare symptoms

1. *Description:* This strategy uses symptoms and features that are infrequently found in normative samples. It is considered a "quasi" strategy because infrequent items could reflect either genuine or malingered disorders.

2. *Strength:* This detection strategy produces large to very large effect sizes.

3. *Limitations:* Because infrequent problems in normative samples often occur in clinical samples, the interpretation of these results is confounded. For example, clients with schizophrenia or posttraumatic stress disorder (PTSD) routinely have marked elevations (e.g., *M* scores ≥ 80T) on the MMPI-2 F and Fb scales (see Rogers, Sewell, et al., 2003). This confound also contributes to a wide array of cut scores.

4. *Examples:*
   a. MMPI-2 F scale
   b. MMPI-2 Fb (F-back) scale

Improbable symptoms

1. *Description:* This strategy is an extreme variant of Rare Symptoms. It utilizes symptoms or features that have a fantastic or preposterous quality.

2. *Strength:* Because of their fantastic nature, most of its items could not possibly be true. Therefore, substantial endorsement of improbable symptoms is less open to alternative explanations than some other detection strategies.

(continued)

TABLE 2.1. (*continued*)

3. *Limitation:* The extremeness of improbable symptoms may limit its usefulness with sophisticated malingerers, who can identify the unlikelihood that these represent genuine symptoms.

4. *Examples:*
   a. SIRS IA (Improbable and Absurd Symptoms) scale
   b. Validity Index of the Miller Clinical Multiaxial Inventory (MCMI-III)

Symptom combinations

1. *Description:* This strategy utilizes symptoms and features that are common to clinical populations but that rarely occur together. Malingerers often endorse a substantial number of infrequent pairs (e.g., grandiosity and increased sleep).

2. *Strengths:* This strategy is sophisticated and should be resistant to coaching and other forms of preparation. It is also easily adaptable to structured interviews and multiscale inventories. It produces large effect sizes.

3. *Limitation:* At present, it has been tested only with structured interviews.

4. *Examples:*
   a. SIRS SC (Symptom Combinations) scale
   b. M-FAST RC (Rare Combinations) scale

Spurious patterns of psychopathology

1. *Description:* This strategy is an extensive elaboration of symptom combinations. It relies on certain scale configurations that are characteristic of malingering but that are very uncommon in clinical populations.

2. *Strength:* Its complexity minimizes the possibility that malingerers could prepare for and foil its detection strategy.

3. *Limitation:* Because of its complexity, Spurious Patterns of Psychopathology requires extensive cross-validation to ensure that its results are not capitalizing on chance variance. Care must also be taken against overinterpretation (e.g., drawing conclusions in the absence of clinical elevations).

4. *Examples:*
   a. PAI Malingering Index
   b. PAI Rogers Discriminant Function (RDF)

Indiscriminant symptom endorsement

1. *Description:* This strategy relies on the finding that some malingerers, unlike genuine clients, tend to endorse a large proportion of symptoms.

2. *Strength:* The overall proportion of endorsed symptoms is easy to calculate and can be applied to all psychological measures.

3. *Limitations:* It has been tested only with structured interviews. Care must be taken that measures cover a broad array of symptoms; otherwise, its use may lead to false positives.

4. *Examples:*
   a. SIRS SEL (Symptom Selectivity) scale
   b. Schedule of Affective Disorders and Schizophrenia (SADS) SEL (Symptom Selectivity) scale

Symptom severity

1. *Description:* This strategy capitalizes on the finding that even severely impaired patients experience only a discrete number of symptoms as "unbearable" or "extreme" in intensity. Malingerers often endorse a wide array of psychological problems with extreme severity.

2. *Strengths:* This strategy is easily adaptable to a wide range of structured interviews and clinical scales. It produces large effect sizes.

3. *Limitation:* At present, symptom severity is considered only across entire scales. Further research may improve its effectiveness by identifying which psychological problems are almost never characterized as "extreme" in clinical populations.

4. *Examples:*
   a. SIRS SEV (Symptom Severity) scale
   b. MMPI-2 LW (Lachar–Wrobel Critical Items) scale
   c. M-FAST ES (Extreme Symptomatology) scale

(*continued*)

TABLE 2.1. (*continued*)

Obvious symptoms

1. *Description:* This strategy relies on the idea that malingerers are likely to report or endorse prominent symptoms that are clearly indicative of serious mental disorders. Obvious symptoms are either considered alone or in relationship to subtle symptoms (i.e., "everyday" problems that are not necessarily indicative of a major mental disorder).

2. *Strength:* This strategy produces large to very large effect sizes.

3. *Limitation:* Researchers debate whether obvious symptoms should be considered alone or in relationship to subtle symptoms. In the latter case, both obvious and subtle symptoms work best if converted to standard scores (e.g., MMPI-2 T scores).

4. *Examples:*
   a. SIRS BL (Blatant Symptoms) scale
   b. MMPI-2 O-S (Obvious–Subtle Difference) scale

Reported versus observed symptoms

1. *Description.* This strategy uses marked discrepancies between the person's own account of his or her noticeable symptoms and clinical observations. Malingerers can often be identified by the direction of these discrepancies (i.e., lack of clinical observations for reported symptoms that should be conspicuous).

2. *Strength:* With standardized observations, this strategy provides independent verification of reported symptoms.

3. *Limitation:* Because many genuine patients lack insight about their psychopathology, standardization is essential for accurate discrimination.

4. *Examples:*
   a. SIRS RO (Reported vs. Observed) scale
   b. M-FAST RO (Reported vs. Observed) scale

Erroneous stereotypes

1. *Description:* This strategy capitalizes on the finding that many persons, including mental health professionals, have common misconceptions about which clinical characteristics are commonly associated with mental disorders. Malingerers are often identifiable by their overendorsement of erroneous stereotypes.

2. *Strength:* This strategy appears resistant to preparation because even mental health professionals have difficulty detecting erroneous stereotypes.

3. *Limitations:* It has been tested only with the MMPI-2 and PSI; it varies by scale in the magnitude of the effect sizes.

4. *Examples:*
   a. MMPI-2 Ds (Dissimulation) Scale
   b. Psychological Screening Inventory (PSI) EPS (Erroneous Psychiatric Stereotype) scale

Requiring further validation: Close approximations to genuine symptoms

1. *Description:* This strategy uses apparently bogus symptoms that parallel genuine symptoms except for some important detail.

2. *Strength:* None are noted.

3. *Limitations:* Genuine patients may respond to the gist of the item and be misclassified. It has been tested only with one measure; its item content is considered proprietary.

4. *Example:*
   a. Malingering Probability Scale (MPS) MAL (Malingering) scale

Requiring further validation: Overly specified symptoms

1. *Description:* This strategy assumes that malingerers may be willing to endorse symptoms with an unrealistic level of precision.

2. *Strength:* It produces moderate effect sizes (e.g., 0.91 and 1.06).

3. *Limitations:* It lacks the conceptual basis of other detection strategies. It has been tested with only one measure.

4. *Example:*
   a. SIRS OS (Overly Specified) symptoms

represent a trade-off. On the one hand, their fantastic quality increases the likelihood that endorsements are feigned. On the other hand, the high face validity of these items (i.e., recognizability as bogus symptoms) may decrease their effectiveness, especially with sophisticated malingerers.

The remaining five detection strategies utilize amplified presentations, with an emphasis on degree (e.g., frequency and intensity) rather than presence or absence. The two clearest examples are indiscriminant symptom endorsement and symptom severity. In the first instance, malingerers can be identified simply by the sheer number of reported symptoms. In the second instance, the proportion of symptoms with extreme severity is used to classify malingering. In both instances, the magnitude (i.e., frequency and proportion) is the decisive factor without any consideration of items themselves or their specific content. The remaining three strategies focus on content that may appear plausible to malingerers. Because obvious symptoms are easy to recognize and appear to be clinically significant, malingerers often endorse them in greater numbers than do their genuine counterparts. Although each symptom is plausible, the detection strategy capitalizes on the number or proportion of obvious symptoms. Interestingly, malingerers do not necessarily endorse more obvious than subtle symptoms[7]; the detection strategy relies primarily on the proportion of obvious symptoms. Reported versus observed symptoms is a detection strategy that incorporates the clinician's standardized perceptions of the patient's self-described symptoms. Although the reported symptoms may be plausible, the detection strategy uses marked discrepancies in the direction of greater reported than observed psychopathology.

The final detection strategy, erroneous stereotypes, deserves an extended comment. Especially on multiscale inventories (e.g., the MMPI-2), with their complex array of clinical and content scales, persons may mistakenly assume that certain clinical characteristics are common among patient populations. When these misassumptions are widespread, erroneous stereotypes can be used to detect likely malingerers. The MMPI-2 Ds scale is a singularly good example, because even mental health professionals make misassumptions about erroneous stereotypes. Similarly, the Erroneous Psychiatric Stereotype scale (EPS) for the Psycho-

logical Screening Inventory (PSI; Lanyon, 1993b) uses common misassumptions about persons with mental disorders. Although community participants and inpatients have comparable scores on the EPS ($d = .18$), simulators do not recognize these stereotypes. Their overendorsements result in very large effect sizes ($ds > 2.00$). This detection strategy deserves further investigation because of its amplified presentation and possibility for excellent discriminability.

Two detection strategies lack sufficient validation, which limits their use in clinical practice. The use of "close approximations to genuine symptoms" needs to be cross-validated by other investigators and tested on different measures. Although the insertion of incorrect details may be an effective approach, it requires extensive investigation to demonstrate that patient populations are not misled by the gist of the items to overlook inaccurate details. A second strategy without sufficient validation is "overly specified symptoms." Although it yields moderate effect sizes, it has a weak conceptual basis (i.e., unrealistic precision is not necessarily evidence of feigning) and has been tested only with the Structured Interview of Reported Symptoms (SIRS).

In summary, clinicians have a wealth of detection strategies relying on both unlikely and amplified presentations. These strategies generally produce large to very large effect sizes, which are critical to accurate classifications. As noted in subsequent chapters, many scales designed to measure these detection strategies remain effective, even when malingerers are coached or otherwise prepared.

Malingering and Cognitive Abilities

The past decade has observed an exponential increase in malingering research using neuropsychological measures (Reynolds, 1998; Rogers & Bender, 2003). The research has been divided between assessment methods adapted from standardized tests, such as tests of intelligence and memory, and specialized measures designed specifically to assess feigned cognitive impairment. Use of standardized tests has several advantages: (1) efficiency (i.e., test data are useful with all referrals, including genuine patients), (2) direct applicability (i.e., unlike some specialized measures, no extrapolations are needed between feigned abilities and test results), and (3) low face validity (i.e., malingerers are not "cued" about the possible detection of feigned abilities). Despite these major advantages, adaptations from standardized tests sometimes have less success than specialized measures. The simple reason is that test items on standard tests were not developed to assess detection strategies. Although they lack the other advantages, the main strength of specialized measures is the operationalization of detection strategies to maximize the discriminability between criterion groups. As described by Bender (Chapter 5), Sweet, Condit, and Nelson (Chapter 13), and Berry and Schipper (Chapter 14) in this volume, clinicians may wish to combine adaptations of standardized tests with specialized measures in the assessment of feigned cognitive impairment.

Rogers, Harrell, and Liff (1993) provided the first systematic review of detection strategies for feigned cognitive abilities. These strategies continue to be refined and tested with diverse clinical populations. However, two problematic trends have emerged. First, a few detection strategies (e.g., floor effect) have gained unwarranted popularity at the expense of other sound detection strategies. Second, many researchers have concentrated their efforts with detection strategies on short-term learning and have consequently neglected other facets of cognitive functioning. Awareness of these trends is important to practitioners so that they (1) select detection strategies based on effectiveness rather than popularity and (2) utilize methods appropriate to the purported deficits.

Detection strategies for cognitive abilities can be conceptualized within two general categories: unlikely presentations and excessive impairment. Paralleling feigned mental disorders, unlikely presentations focus on response patterns that are unusual and atypical for patients with genuine neuropsychological impairment. The simple presence of unlikely presentations is often indicative of malingering. Corresponding to amplified presentations with feigned mental disorders, excessive impairment[8] reflects the magnitude of the assessed deficits. With excessive impairment, the general performance of malingerers is much lower than expected for cognitively impaired populations.

Three detection strategies are based on unlikely presentations that are uncharacteristic of genuine patients (see Table 2.2). Although not as extensively researched as strategies for excessive impairment, they are conceptually sound and can provide compelling data regarding feigned cognitive impairment. Magni-

tude of error is a very effective detection strategy from the general category of unlikely presentations. The overriding thrust of cognitive assessment is the measurement of correct responses (i.e., incorrect, partially correct, and correct); therefore, practitioners and patients alike pay little attention to the level of inaccuracy. Because of this inattention, the magnitude-of-error strategy is effective even when feigners are coached about its strategy. As an additional detection strategy, the performance curve was first recognized by Goldstein (1945); it examines comparative success, taking into account item difficulty. This strategy is simple yet sophisticated because malingerers are unlikely to consider gradations of difficulty in determining their success rate. The performance is likely to be more effective when the items are not organized by difficulty or provided in a paper-and-pencil format.[9]

Violation of learning principles differs from other detection strategies in its conceptual complexity. While representing a general construct, this strategy is a constellation of well-established learning concepts with diverse measures of these concepts. The most common learning principle for feigned cognitive impairment involves the comparative advantage of recognition over recall, which has consistently yielded differences across measures. For example, the Word Memory Test (WMT; Green, Astner, & Allen, 1996) allows delayed recognition (approximately 30 minutes) to be compared with immediate recall, delayed recall, and long delayed recall. As expected, effect sizes vary by specific comparisons. For 315 compensation cases evidencing good effort, a comparison of delayed recall to delayed recognition yielded a very large effect size ($d = 3.09$); the effect size, although still very large, was significantly less for compensation cases with poor motivation ($d = 2.35$; Green, Astner, & Allen, 1997). In general, the WMT surpasses other feigning measures in its use of this strategy to identify potential malingerers with its sophisticated comparisons (e.g., cued vs. uncued recall). As an important caution, the application of certain learning principles is complex (e.g., serial position curves; Tan & Ward, 2000) and cannot be readily applied to detection strategies. In most cases, mental health professionals will limit their use of this strategy to well-researched comparisons (e.g., recognition vs. recall) on psychometrically sound measures.

TABLE 2.2. Detection Strategies for Feigned Cognitive Impairment

Magnitude of error

1. *Description:* This strategy relies on data indicating that genuine patients often make predictable errors. Most malingerers do not focus on *which* incorrect answers are common; they are frequently detectable by choosing incorrect responses that are unlikely among genuine patients.

2. *Strengths:* It is less transparent than most cognitive detection strategies and less vulnerable to coaching (Bender & Rogers, 2004). It produces large effect sizes. This strategy could easily be adapted to the forced-choice formats of standardized tests, such as the Matrix Reasoning subtest of the WAIS-III.

3. *Limitation:* None is noted.

4. *Examples:*
   a. Multiple-choice format applied to the Wechsler Memory Scale—Revised (WMS-R) Visual Reproduction and Logical Memory subtests
   b. Test of Cognitive Abilities (TOCA) Magnitude of Error (MOE) scale
   c. "d errors" on the "b Test"

Performance curve

1. *Description:* This strategy is based on the finding that genuine patients produce predictable patterns (i.e., fewer successes and more frequent errors) with increased item difficulty. When plotted, this "rate of decay" forms a characteristic "performance curve." Malingerers, unaware of this pattern, typically produce much less discrimination between easy and difficult items.

2. *Strength:* It is a sophisticated strategy that could prove to be resistant to coaching.

3. *Limitation:* It is challenging to implement this strategy, which requires a broad range of item difficulty.

4. *Examples:*
   a. Rate of decay on the Raven Standard Progressive Matrices (see Gudjonsson & Shackleton, 1986; McKinzey, Podd, Krehbiel, & Raven, 1999)
   b. TOCA Performance Curve (PC) scale

Violation of learning principles

1. *Description:* This strategy is a specialized application of performance curve; some malingerers are unaware of underlying learning principles.

2. *Strength:* It is conceptually superior to most strategies in that specific testable hypotheses about learning principles are rigorously evaluated. At present, examples of the following learning principles have been tested: (a) recognition versus recall, (b) cued recall versus uncued recall, (c) immediate versus delayed recall, (d) simple recall versus cognitive transformation, and (e) priming effect (Haines & Norris, 1995).

3. *Limitations:* Violation of certain learning principles produces only modest group differences. This approach is applicable only to purported problems with current learning.

4. *Examples:*
   a. WMT Immediate Recognition versus Delayed Recognition
   b. WMT Delayed Recall versus Delayed Recognition
   c. WMT Paired Associates (i.e., cued recall) versus Immediate Recognition
   d. Rey Auditory Verbal Learning Test (RAVLT; see Sullivan, Deffenti, & Keane, 2002)

Floor effect

1. *Description:* This strategy capitalizes on the finding that some malingerers do not recognize that simple cognitive tasks can be completed by most impaired persons.

2. *Strength:* It is easily adaptable to many cognitive measures.

3. *Limitation:* When the strategy is used in a stand-alone measure, malingerers can easily be coached (e.g., "just succeed").

4. *Examples:*
   a. Rey-15
   b. TOMM
   c. WMT
   d. Letter Memory Test (LMT)

Symptom validity testing (SVT)

1. *Description:* This strategy uses a forced-choice paradigm to test whether an individual's failure rate is significantly below chance. When give two equiprobable choices, even the most impaired individuals should succeed approximately 50% of the time (i.e., chance levels).

(continued)

TABLE 2.2. (*continued*)

2. *Strength:* Failures significantly below chance provide definitive evidence of feigning.

3. *Limitation:* Most malingerers do not need to fail at such an unlikely level to achieve their objectives. Therefore, the strategy is typically successful in less than 25% of feigned cases.

4. *Examples:*
    a. Portland Digit Recognition Test (PDRT)
    b. Computerized Assessment of Response Bias (CARB)
    c. Victoria Symptom Validity Test (VSVT)

Forced-choice testing (FCT)

1. *Description:* This strategy is based on the observation that some malingerers evidence greater "deficits" than genuine patients with cognitive impairment.

2. *Strength:* None is noted.

3. *Limitations:* FCT is a conceptually weak detection strategy. It relies simply on poor performance without specifying *how* that performance differs from genuine efforts. Other limitations for most FCT measures include (1) not being tested with a full range of clinical conditions and (2) not being tested with comorbid Axis I and II disorders that may confound results.

4. *Examples:*
    a. PDRT (revised scoring)
    b. 21-Item Test (Iverson, Franzen, & McCracken, 1991)

Requiring further validation: Consistency across comparable items

1. *Description:* Genuine patients with stable mental status tend to perform consistently across comparable items. Some malingerers are much more variable in their performance and can be identified by their inconsistencies.

2. *Strength:* With rigorous testing, discrepancies can be effective in distinguishing between criterion groups (feigners vs. genuine patients). At present, only the Validity Indicator Profile (VIP) has been rigorously tested for consistency across comparable items.

3. *Limitations:* Most research simply addresses group differences without looking at intraindividual performances on comparable items. Because of unknown effects of comorbidity, the presence of Axis I and II disorders is a potential confound.

4. *Example:*
    a. VIP EIP (Equivalent Item Pairs) scale

Requiring further validation: Atypical test pattern

1. *Description:* This strategy is based on the finding that some test patterns occur infrequently in genuine populations. In its clearest form, these patterns are identified statistically without any consideration of their theoretical bases.

2. *Strength:* None is noted.

3. *Limitations:* It is a conceptually weak approach; it lacks the conceptual clarity of other detection strategies (e.g., SVT and floor effect). Use of discriminant analysis requires extensive cross-validation. Some paired comparisons appear to be loosely based on the performance curve strategy in their differential requirements of cognitive abilities.

4. *Examples:*
    a. General Memory vs. Attention/Concentration on WMS
    b. Vocabulary versus Digit Span on the WAIS-III (Mittenberg, Aguila-Pentes, et al., 2002)

Requiring further validation: Symptom frequency

1. *Description:* This strategy is based on the idea that some malingerers may report symptoms associated with cognitive impairment at a much higher rate than genuine populations.

2. *Strength:* With cross-validation, this strategy extends beyond cognitive performance to examine patients' reported symptoms and their potential interference in day-to-day functioning.

3. *Limitations:* This approach has been systematically evaluated with only a single measure. A major concern is whether its results will be confounded by Axis I and Axis II comorbidity.

4. *Example:*
    a. NSI (Gelder et al., 2002) total score; most feigners endorse more than 25% of the total possible score.

Three detection strategies involve claims of excessive impairment. The most popular of these strategies is floor effect, which has been adapted to dozens of measures. Simply put, malingerers sometimes claim impairment on simple cognitive tasks that are successfully completed by most cognitively compromised populations. With some measures (e.g., the Test of Memory Malingering [TOMM]; Tombaugh, 1996), it may be important to rule out dementias[10] and other severe conditions prior to the classification of feigned cognitive impairment. A major drawback of this simple strategy is that malingerers can easily be educated about how to defeat it. Comorbidity may also be an important consideration. For example, persons with severe depression may lack the motivation and attentional abilities required to complete more extensive floor-effect measures; even a modest decrement in functioning (e.g., 10–15% errors) may meet the feigning criterion for the floor-effect strategy (see, e.g., the second trial on the TOMM).

Symptom validity testing (SVT) is unique among detection strategies in its ability to accurately estimate false-positive rates. In two-choice paradigms using equiprobable alternatives, binomial probabilities can be calculated to approximate the likelihood that a particular below-chance performance could occur in a nonfeigning individual. At extremely low scores (e.g., ≤ 25 on the 72-item Portland Digit Recognition Test; Binder, 1993), the probability of feigning exceeds 99%, with a false-positive rate below 1%. The strength of symptom validity testing (i.e., certainty at extremely low scores) is also its inherent limitation. Catastrophic failures on psychometric measures are unnecessary in most clinical and forensic settings, in which they are most likely indicative of feigned cognitive impairment. Therefore, only a minority of malingerers meet the extreme requirement for its classification. However, clinicians continue to use the symptom-validity-testing strategy because of the unparalleled certainty that can be achieved (i.e., PPP), albeit in a small proportion of cases.

Forced-choice testing was intended as a solution to the inaccuracies (i.e., false negatives) of symptom validity testing in classifying feigned cognitive impairment. Rather than insisting on "below chance" performance, this strategy simply requires "below expected" performance. How is below-expected performance assessed? Typically using clinical samples of convenience, the lower range of scores for genuine patients is used to establish the cut scores for malingering. This expediency, characteristic of the forced-choice-testing strategy, lacks the conceptual basis underlying most established detection strategies. Without extensive normative data, including Axis I and Axis II comorbidities, the rate of false positives cannot be established. Despite its widespread use, clinicians are likely to be divided on whether it should be classified as a detection strategy or simply as a "potential method" requiring further validation. In keeping with past reviews (e.g., Rogers & Bender, 2003), forced-choice testing has been retained as a detection strategy. In practice, however, other detection strategies should be considered first.

As an important caution, Rogers, Harrell, and Liff (1993) carefully operationalized SVT and forced-choice testing (or FCT). In the domain of feigned cognitive impairment, some researchers have been careless in their use of these terms. In particular, researchers and practitioners must verify that studies reporting the use of SVT are based on binomial probabilities.

In summary, clinicians have several well-established detection strategies for both general categories (i.e., unlikely presentation and excessive impairment). Selection of strategies from both categories is strongly recommended. Practitioners should be guided by the general effectiveness of each detection strategy and its applicability to the purported impairment. To capitalize on their respective advantages, practitioners may also wish to combine adaptations of standard tests with specialized measures in their evaluations of feigned cognitive impairment.

Defensiveness and Mental Disorders

The prevalence of defensiveness among mentally disordered samples is unknown but likely exceeds malingering and other forms of dissimulation. Baer and Miller (2002) estimated the base rate of defensiveness at .30 in job applicant and child custody referrals. Applying the three most effective scales of Baer and Miller to Greene's (2000) analysis of Caldwell's data set, estimates of defensiveness range from 16 to 33% of clinical referrals. Despite its greater prevalence, the development of detection strategies for defensiveness is less advanced when compared with the assessment of malingering.

Defensive detection strategies effectively address only one of the two general categories, namely amplified presentations (see Table 2.3). Even the most obvious strategies (i.e., affirmation of idealized attributes and denial of personal faults) are expected to occur, albeit less frequently, among clinical populations responding forthrightly. Therefore, all these strategies focus on magnitude, rather than presence, in their operationalization of defensiveness. Could defensive detection strategies be developed that utilize the other general category—unlikely presentations? Quite simply, the answer is yes. Analogous to symptom combinations, *pairs of positive attributes* could be identified that are very infrequent in general and clinical populations. In addition, logical inconsistencies could be explored. For instance, thoughtfulness and decisive action could be construed as positive characteristics, yet they appear logically inconsistent as primary modes of addressing setbacks. Patterns of logical inconsistencies might also yield an effective detection strategy.

This section focuses on defensiveness as it relates specifically to mental disorders and psychological maladjustment (see Table 2.2). The mixed success of detection strategies may be due to their different purposes, which do not focus on the denial of psychological maladjustment. The L scale, as the name denotes, was intended to measure general dishonesty rather than the minimization of psychological problems and symptoms. Despite their diverse purposes, considerable success has been achieved in assessing defensiveness in the domain of mental disorders. Multifaceted scales (i.e., blends of "affirmation of virtuous behavior" and "denial of nonvirtuous behavior") appear to be more effective than denial alone. However, further research is needed to understand what elements of each contribute to this effectiveness.[11] Conceptually, these strategies should be relatively ineffective for assessing denied psychological maladjustment, given both their broad focus and attention to idealized attributes.

Two defensive detection strategies have a strong conceptual basis for the evaluation of denied psychological maladjustment: denial of patient characteristics and social desirability. The MMPI K scale best represents the denial of patient characteristics in its empirical development of test items common in clinical populations. The main advantage of this approach is that the strategy focuses specifically on the denial of psychological maladjustment. Despite its conceptual strength, effect sizes for the K scales are comparatively modest for defensive patients (Baer & Miller, 2002) and do not appear to be effective when simulators are coached (Baer & Sekirnjak, 1997). As a detection strategy, social desirability involves an attempt to create a favorable impression on others. By avoiding idealized attributes, this detection strategy appears to be particularly effective at detecting individuals who deny maladjustment. Using Wiggins's (1959) social desirability (Wsd) scale, MMPI-2 research has demonstrated its superior effect sizes, even when individuals are coached in advance regarding this strategy (Baer & Miller, 2002).

A complex strategy, exemplified by Personality Assessment Inventory (PAI) indexes, is described as "spurious patterns of simulated adjustment." The strategy assumes that genuinely adjusted persons will evidence characteristic patterns of well-being that cannot be easily replicated by defensive responders. It has yielded mixed success (see Sellbom & Bagby, Chapter 11, this volume). As a caveat, this strategy should not be applied to protocols with marked elevations (i.e., evidence of psychological impairment) because they fail to meet the threshold for patterns of simulated adjustment.

In summary, detection strategies for denied psychological maladjustment lack some of the sophistication found with malingering strategies. Still, several detection strategies have proven successful in classifying defensiveness. In particular, social desirability has a sound conceptual basis and superior empirical data.

Response Styles and Specific Clinical Domains

The development and validation of detection strategies has largely been limited to three domains (i.e., malingering and mental disorders, malingering and cognitive impairment, and defensiveness and mental disorders) described in previous sections. The purpose of this section is to provide brief summaries of detection strategies for three other domains: (1) defensiveness and cognitive impairment, (2) malingering and medical presentations, and (3) defensiveness and medical presentations. These descriptions are very brief because detection strategies are in their early stage of develop-

TABLE 2.3. Detection Strategies for Defensiveness and Social Desirability

Denial of personal faults

1. *Description:* This strategy is based on the idea that persons minimizing maladjustment will take this to the extreme and deny any shortcomings or nonvirtuous behaviors
2. *Strength:* None is noted.
3. *Limitations:* The complete denial, as contrasted with comparative statements (e.g., "better than most") is unnecessary for clients denying maladjustment. It tends to produce moderate effect sizes and can be vulnerable to coaching.
4. *Example:*
   a. MMPI-2 Lie (L) scale

Blended strategy with affirmation of virtuous behavior and denial of personal faults

1. *Description:* This strategy combines the affirmation of overly positive attributes with the denial of common foibles.
2. *Strength:* It produces moderate to large effect sizes.
3. *Limitation:* As a blended strategy, it is difficult to know which component (i.e., affirmation or denial) is more effective.
4. *Examples:*
   a. Marlowe–Crowne
   b. Paulhus Deception Scales (PDS) Self-Deceptive Enhancement (SDE)
   c. PDS Impression Management (IM)
   d. MMPI-2 Superlative (S) scale

Spurious patterns of simulated adjustment

1. *Description:* This strategy relies on certain scale configurations that are characteristic of defensiveness but are very uncommon in clinical and community populations.
2. *Strength:* Its complexity minimizes the possibility that defensive responders could prepare and foil its detection strategy.
3. *Limitations:* Because of its complexity, Spurious Patterns of Simulated Adjustment requires extensive cross-validation to ensure that its results are not capitalizing on chance variance. Care must also be taken against overinterpretation (e.g., drawing conclusions when clinical elevations are present).
4. *Examples:*
   a. PAI Defensiveness Index
   b. PAI Cashel Discriminant Function (CDF)

Denial of patient characteristics

1. *Description:* This strategy capitalizes on research demonstrating that certain attributes are commonly endorsed by clinical populations.
2. *Strength:* It is designed specifically to evaluate patients who do not acknowledge their psychological problems. Its items may be less transparent than those rationally based on idealized attributes.
3. *Limitation:* Scales produce moderate effect sizes and are vulnerable to coaching.
4. *Examples:*
   a. MMPI-2 K scale
   b. MMPI-2 Edward's Social Desirability (Esd)[a]
   c. SADS Commonly Reported Symptoms (CRS)

Social desirability

1. *Description:* This strategy attempts to identify persons denying maladjustment by assessing the adoption of a positive role that is intended to create a very favorable image to most persons.
2. *Strengths:* It produces larger effect sizes than most other defensive strategies. It also appears to be effective even when persons are coached about the strategy.
3. *Limitation:* The term *social desirability* has been defined and operationalized in several different ways. This definition has been examined via the use of a single scale (Wsd).
4. *Example:*
   a. MMPI-2 Wsd

---

[a]Despite its name, the Esd focuses on the denial of common psychological problems.

ment. At present, most work on detection strategies is more conceptual than empirical.

Defensiveness and Cognitive Abilities

Traditionally, practitioners have assumed that clinical populations could not mask their cognitive weaknesses because testing measured optimal functioning. Simply put, patients could not do better than their best. Because of this assumption, research has largely neglected the question of whether cognitive problems can be concealed via preparation and coaching. Is the assumption accurate? Research has generally found that performance on standardized aptitude tests can be substantially enhanced by practice and preparation (Kulik, Bangert-Drowns, & Kulick, 1984), especially when identical tests are used (Kulik, Kulick, & Bangert-Drowns, 1984). As evidence for the "benefits" of practice effects, WAIS-III Performance IQ increases an average of 11 points after only a single readministration, even after a lengthy interval (i.e., 3 or 6 months; Basso, Carona, & Lowery, 2002). For job selection (i.e., law enforcement positions), readministrations after 12 months significantly enhanced performances on tests of both cognitive abilities and oral communication (Hausknecht, Trevor, & Farr, 2002). With the ease and availability of Web-based information, individuals can practice and prepare for enhanced performances on cognitive measures. The other critical question remains unaddressed: Can preparation successfully mask cognitive deficits and their concomitant impairment?

Cognitive defensiveness can involve either the masking of cognitive deficits or the false portrayal of cognitive strengths. In the former case, successful individuals may wish to conceal even minor decrements in cognitive abilities. Commercial pilots, for instance, may wish to mask even the slightest declines in cognitive abilities. Rebok, Li, Baker, Grabowski, and Willoughby (2002) surveyed 1,310 airline pilots and found that almost none rated their own cognitive skills as diminished; on the contrary, a common pattern was to claim enhanced cognitive abilities. In the latter case, the false presentation of cognitive strengths may be viewed as an "asset" in securing a highly competitive position. Examples include selections for executive training, highly sought promotions, and acceptances into graduate school.

In computer searches of the neuropsychological literature, I was unable to identify any empirically validated detection strategies for defensiveness and cognitive abilities. A potential detection strategy for this issue would be "practice-effect gains." Readministrations of brief measures should produce predictable patterns: substantial improvements on some scales and negligible differences on others. For example, Bird, Papadopoulou, Ricciardelli, Rossor, and Cipolotti (2004) found that several very brief scales evidence substantial improvement (e.g., 11.2% for verbal fluency in generating words beginning with *s*), whereas one subscale (i.e., Digit Symbol) evidences a slight decrement in performance (−3.2%). Conceptually based strategies, such as practice-effect gains, need to be carefully developed and rigorously validated. The effectiveness of detection strategies must be evaluated for both the concealment of cognitive deficits and the false presentation of cognitive strengths.

Malingering and Medical Presentations

Illness behavior is far more complex than malingering per se (Halligan, Bass, & Oakley, 2003). Beyond malingered and factitious presentations, patients with chronic medical complaints can adopt one of several maladaptive responses to their illnesses. According to Radley and Green (1987), these maladaptive patterns can include *accommodation* and *resignation*. With *accommodation*, the illness becomes incorporated into the patient's identity, thereby complicating assessment and treatment. With *resignation*, patients become overwhelmed by their diseases and may passively accept their illness status. Such maladaptive responses may be mistaken as deliberate efforts by patients to malinger by prolonging their medical conditions and thwarting treatment efforts (Rogers & Payne, 2006).

The importance of empirically validated detection strategies for feigned medical presentations is underscored by recent investigations of Waddell's classic signs for nonorganic pain. The presence of these signs was interpreted as either malingering or psychological stress (Kiester & Duke, 1999). However, Fishbain and colleagues (2003) conducted a comprehensive review of Waddell signs and the validity of chronic pain. Despite early claims, they found that Waddell signs generally did not discriminate between (1) organic and nonorganic pain and (2) genuine presentation and secondary gain. In a further analysis, Fishbain, Cutler, Rosomoff, and Rosomoff (2004) found that the Waddell signs do not provide credible evidence of malingering or secondary gain. Their impressive work strongly questions the use of Waddell signs to assess "sincerity of effort," as recently touted by other investigators (Lechner, Bradbury, & Bradley, 1998). This careful analysis of Waddell signs is especially instructive. Without conceptually sound and rigorously tested detection strategies, tragic errors in the misclassification of malingering are likely to be perpetuated for decades on hundreds of misclassified patients.

Tearnan and Lewandowski's (1997) original work on feigned medical complaints resulted in the development of the Life Assessment Questionnaire (LAQ), which was intended to evaluate preliminary detection strategies. These strategies included (1) unusual symptom endorsement (i.e., nonsensical items, rare items, and unusual pairings), (2) breadth of physical complaints (e.g., cardiovascular, neurological, musculosketal, gastrointestinal, and dermatological ailments), and (3) unrealistic display of public virtue. Despite its early promise, research on the LAQ and its detection strategies was not sustained.[12] In this section, this seminal work is used as a template for examining preliminary detection strategies for feigned medical complaints.

Detection strategies for malingered medical presentations, similar to other domains, can be conceptualized in two general categories: unlikely presentations and amplified presentations (see Table 2.4). Unlikely presentations, basically corresponding to the LAQ's unusual symptom

TABLE 2.4. Initial Detection Strategies for Malingered Medical Presentations

Rare medical complaints

1. *Description:* This strategy capitalizes on reported symptoms and ailments that are infrequently described by genuine populations.

2. *Potential strengths:* Within the general category of unlikely presentations, it has received the most attention in the initial development of two specialized measures and the recent adaptation of a standardized test, the MMPI-2. The initial empirical data are promising.

3. *Examples:*
   a. MMPI-2 Fs (Infrequent Somatic Complaints) scale
   b. TIPS (Costa, 2000) RS (Rare Symptom) scale (see postconcussional symptoms)
   c. LAQ Rare Items

Improbable medical complaints

1. *Description:* This strategy is an extreme variant of Rare Medical Complaints. It utilizes symptoms or features that have fantastic or preposterous quality.

2. *Potential strength:* If established, its items call into question the genuineness of the reported complaints.

3. *Examples:*
   a. TIPS Implausibility (IMP) scale (see somatoform pain and postconcussional symptoms)
   b. LAQ Nonsense Items

Symptom combinations

1. *Description:* This strategy relies on complaints and symptoms that are common to medical populations but that rarely occur together. Malingerers are unlikely to be aware of their low co-occurrence.

2. *Potential strength:* With extensive validation, this strategy is a sophisticated approach to malingered medical presentations.

3. *Examples:*
   a. LAQ Unusual Pairings scale
   b. TIPS Symptom Association (SA) scale (see headache symptoms)

Indiscriminant endorsement of health problems

1. *Description:* This strategy is based on the finding that some malingerers report a broad array of physical symptoms and complaints when provided with extensive checklists.

(continued)

TABLE 2.4. (*continued*)

2. *Potential strength:* If systemic diseases (e.g., lupus) can be ruled out, the breadth of health-related complaints may provide excellent discrimination between genuine and malingered medical presentations.

3. *Examples:*
   a. LAQ Physical Complaints
   b. PSI HPO (Health Problem Overstatement) scale

Intensity of medical complaints

1. *Description:* This strategy relies on observations that persons who malinger medical problems are likely to overstate the frequency, duration, and severity of their physical complaints.

2. *Potential strengths:* It combines several parameters (e.g., frequency and severity) to create a composite strategy. Some results have produced very large effect sizes.

3. *Examples:*
   a. MSPQ
   b. BHI-2 Self-Disclosure scale
   c. NSI

Reported versus observed symptoms

1. *Description.* This strategy uses marked discrepancies between the person's own account of his or her medical complaints and corresponding observations. Malingerers can often be identified by systematic discrepancies (i.e., medical complaints unsupported by clinical observations).

2. *Potential strength:* With standardized observations, this strategy provides independent verification of reported symptoms.

3. *Example:*
   a. Consistency score between Pain Rating Scale (PRS) and Pain Behavior Checklist (PBC)

Dependency on medical complaints

1. *Description:* This strategy is based on the idea that malingerers may be willing to acknowledge positive attributes of their physical condition or disability status.

2. *Potential strength:* None is noted. The willingness to acknowledge any potential motivation to malinger appears counterintuitive.

3. *Example:*
   a. BHI-2 Symptom Dependency scale

Endorsement of excessive virtue

1. *Description:* This strategy relies on the finding that some malingerers attempt to obfuscate response style issues (e.g., malingering) by falsely claiming overly positive attributes.

2. *Potential strength:* In combination with other detection strategies, it may augment the discrimination between genuine and feigned medical complaints.

3. *Examples:*
   a. PSI EEV (Endorsement of Excessive Virtue) scale
   b. BHI-2 Perseverance scale

Note. The limitations of these initial detection strategies are not listed separately. All strategies require extensive validation and cross-validation.

endorsement, are composed of three detection strategies. Of these, the greatest attention has been paid to rare symptoms. As an initial conceptual effort, Costa (2000) and Tearnan and Lewandowski (1997) developed examples of rare medical complaints. On an empirical basis, Wygant, Ben-Porath, Berry, and Arbisi (2006) identified uncommon symptoms by reviewing MMPI-2 protocols for more than 55,000 medical and chronic pain patients. Despite their lenient criterion of infrequency (i.e., <25% prevalence) for item inclusion, their Infrequent Somatic Complaints (F_s) scale produced large to very large effect sizes. In summary, the strategy of rare medical complaints shows strong promise for feigned medical presentations.

Two other strategies for unlikely presentations (i.e., improbable medical complaints and symptom combinations) have received comparatively less attention than rare medical complaints. The early conceptual work remains unpublished but provides the impetus for systematic research. At present, these approaches and the resulting scales (e.g., the LAQ and the Toronto Interview for Posttraumatic Symptoms [TIPS]; Costa, 2000) lack the necessary work on empirical validation. Therefore, they should be considered preliminary detection strategies for research purposes.

Five detection strategies for malingered medical presentations rely on amplified presentations for which the classification is based on the magnitude rather than the presence of specific indicators. Indiscriminant endorsement of health problems is the strategy best researched. An early study (Furnham & Henderson, 1983) found that persons who feigned medical illnesses endorsed a broad range of somatic and psychological symptoms. More recently, McGuire and Shores (2001) compared simulators with chronic pain patients on the Symptom Checklist 90—Revised (SCL-90-R; Derogatis, 1992). They found that simulators were indiscriminant in their reporting of somatic and psychological symptoms, with marked elevations on each of the clinical scales.[13] Lanyon (2003) developed the Health Problem Overstatement (HPO) scale as a specialized scale on the PSI that measures how respondents "overstate their health problems in general" (p. 2). The majority of items involve physical complaints, fatigue, and overall poor health. Persons simulating severe physical problems had a much higher endorsement level than medical inpatients (Cohen's $d = 2.10$).

A second established strategy for amplified presentation is the intensity of medical complaints. This strategy is operationalized in terms of time (e.g., frequency and duration) and severity, which is often focused on distress and impairment. For example, an adaptation of the Neuropsychological Symptom Inventory (NSI; Dean, 1982) concentrates on the frequency of medical and psychological symptoms. Gelder, Titus, and Dean (2002) found that persons feigning neurological conditions reported frequent symptoms across a broad

spectrum. At the extreme (i.e., "most often") ratings, certain symptom pairs (e.g., ringing in the ears and dizzy spells, changes in vision and reading problems) could also be tested for their co-occurrences. In other words, marked discrepancies in frequencies of conceptually related symptom pairs could be explored as a variant of the intensity of medical complaints strategy. This strategy can also be operationalized in terms of severity and distress. In comparing likely malingerers with genuine pain patients, Larabee (2003c) found that the intensity of pain by itself did not effectively differentiate the groups, largely due to ceiling effects for both groups. Instead, the severity of somatic and autonomic perceptions on the Modified Somatic Perception Questionnaire (MSPQ; Main, 1983) produced very large effect sizes. In summary, the general intensity of medical complaints strategy shows great promise in distinguishing malingered and genuine medical presentations. A current challenge to its implementation is that most measures combine breadth and intensity of medical complaints into a composite score. This challenge is easily addressed. The intensity of medical complaints could be simply scored by averaging the endorsed characteristics.[14]

The strategy of reported versus observed symptoms parallels the detection of malingered mental disorders. With operationally defined characteristics and systematic methods, correspondence between medical complaints and health care observations can be standardized. For example, Dirks, Wunder, Kinsman, McElhinny, and Jones (1993) compared pain ratings by patients with parallel ratings by health care personnel. Patients who were deliberately exaggerating pain had very frequent discrepancies (64.6%) that were very different from genuine pain patients (14.2%). The chief consideration with this strategy is that sufficient groundwork is done to establish normative data on what is expected from heterogeneous clinical populations.

Two strategies have yielded promising results, although their conceptual basis is less precise than other strategies. The strategy dependency on medical complaints expects that malingerers would acknowledge the undeserved benefits of their feigning. Conceptually, this strategy appears counterintuitive. The second strategy, endorsement of excessive virtue (Lanyon, 2003), does have merit because some malingerers want to strengthen their cases for achieving their desired goals (e.g., compensation or a favorable outcome in the criminal justice system). The concern is its nonspecific nature. This strategy is potentially confounded by defensiveness (i.e., affirmation of virtuous behavior) or narcissistic personality traits. As noted in Table 2.4, the endorsement of excessive virtue strategy might best be conceptualized as an ancillary strategy that could augment the discriminability of other detection strategies.

In summary, the current literature provides an excellent conceptual framework for the further study of detection strategies in the medical malingering domain. Within unlikely presentations, work on rare medical complaints has demonstrated the feasibility of this detection strategy. More research is needed on improbable medical complaints and symptom combinations to augment strategies based on unlikely presentations. Within amplified presentations, considerable progress has been made with two detection strategies: indiscriminant endorsement of health problems and the intensity of medical complaints. In addition, reported versus observed symptoms has good potential, whereas the final two strategies (i.e., dependency on medical complaints and endorsement of excessive virtue) may require refinement on their conceptual basis. Overall, malingered medical presentations represent a critically important domain of response styles that is poised for further scale development and empirical validation.

Defensiveness and Medical Presentations

The denial and gross minimization of medical complaints is rampant in North America and represents an immense public health problem (Kortte & Wegener, 2004). For example, the leading cause of death is cardiovascular illness (Hoyert, Heron, Murphy, & Hsiang-Ching, 2006), which is often treatable at the early stages of the disease. Nonetheless, defensiveness is common in medical patients, even at the end stages of heart (Williams et al., 2000) and lung (Putzke, Williams, Daniel, & Boll, 1999) disease. Defensiveness plays a similar role with other common diseases, including cancer, diabetes, and substance abuse. It contributes to treatment noncompliance, estimated to be between 35 and 50% for chronic medical conditions. Poor outcomes from untreated conditions add astronomically to health costs (Sokol, McGuigan, Verbrugge, & Epstein, 2005).

The public dissemination of medical information has been an important step in increasing awareness of medical conditions and health-risk behaviors (e.g., smoking and unprotected sexual practices). However, defensiveness plays an important role in how media campaigns are processed. For example, smokers are likely to minimize or simply reject media presentations against smoking, while maintaining an "illusion of personal immunity" (Freeman, Hennessy, & Marzullo, 2001, p. 425). Moreover, public awareness addresses only one facet of defensiveness. Health care professionals and their consultants assess many patients who actively hide their medical symptoms (e.g., failing to disclose angina) or minimize their investment in treatment (Fowers, 1992). According to Bullard (2003), 95% of patients concealed relevant information from medical staff, including symptoms and unhealthy practices (e.g., poor diet or no exercise). Most deceptions in the medical context involve concealments and equivocations rather than direct lying (Burgoon, Callister, & Hunsaker, 1994). The critical issue is whether mental health professionals have anything to contribute to the determination of medical defensiveness. In particular, can accurate detection strategies be established to identify those patients actively masking their medical symptoms?

Early research has demonstrated the obvious with respect to medical defensiveness. Furnham and Henderson (1983) found that defensive individuals simply did not report prominent medical symptoms; they admitted to less than half the symptoms acknowledged by a presumably healthy community sample of young adults. This finding raises an interesting question: Are some physical symptoms so common that their absence could be used to identify medical defensiveness? Lees-Haley and Brown (1993) found that patients in a group family practice often report (i.e., > 50%) headaches, fatigue, nervousness, and sleeping problems. More extensive research might uncover a predictable pattern of common physical symptoms that could be used as a potential detection strategy for medical defensiveness.[15]

A second potential approach would be the systematic evaluation of health attitudes, which may provide an unobtrusive measure of medical defensiveness. Rather than query patients' symptoms directly, questions could focus on their attitudes toward physicians, health, and illness. For instance, does a fatalistic approach to illness predict medical defensiveness? In addition, a normative approach (e.g., "What do most people think . . . ") to health-related attitudes may be even less obtrusive. Extrapolating from Rogers, Vitacco, and colleagues (2002), expressed beliefs about how most people view antisocial behavior were useful for identifying psychopathic youths. When youths attempted to deny their own psychopathy, their expressed attitudes about others made them *more* identifiable. How might a normative approach be applied to medical defensiveness? Items about general health attitudes (e.g., "doctors care more about profit than patients" or "illness is a sign of personal weakness") could be tested for their potential discriminability between genuine disclosures and medical defensiveness.

Bruns, Disorbio, and Copeland-Disorbio (1996) developed the Defensiveness scale for the Battery for Health Improvement—2 (BHI-2) to assess physically injured patients who are unwilling to disclose medical complaints and personal problems. Its detection strategy relies on general complaints and psychological problems and does not appear to be specific to medical symptoms and physical ailments. Although it discriminates genuine patients from those faking good, it lacks conceptual clarity needed for distinguishing medical defensiveness from the underreporting of psychological disorders.

In summary, clinical researchers have neglected medical defensiveness in their studies of response styles. Several potential strategies appear conceptually sound and deserve empirical validation. Critical to the validation is the identification of criterion groups that either deny medical symptoms or conceal their seriousness. As with other domains, detection strategies for medical defensiveness require the operationalization and systematic testing of potential methods.

SUMMARY

Detection strategies provide the structural framework for the systematic assessment of response styles. Three domains (malingering and mental disorders, malingering and cognitive impairment, and defensiveness and mental disorders) have been subjected to intensive investigations. As a result, detection strategies and concomitant scales were developed that are conceptually sound and empirically validated. Three additional domains (defensiveness and cognitive impairment, malingering and medical presentations, and defensiveness and medical presentations) are conceptually based and await the intensive investigations in the first three domains.

NOTES

1. Please note that the presence of these two indices alone is considered sufficient for malingering to be "strongly suspected" (American Psychiatric Association, 2000, p. 739).
2. Cohen's d examines the difference between two criterion groups (e.g., feigning and genuinely disordered) in standardized units based on the pooled standard deviations.
3. These percentiles are based Table A.5 (Wechsler, 1997) that reports IQs of 96 and 104 as representing the 95% confidence level. When calculated on the SEM ($M = 2.30$; Wechsler, 1997), the true 95% confidence level is ± 4.51 (i.e., IQs from 95 to 105) with an extended range from the 37th to 63rd percentiles.
4. Because specific response styles generally occur in only a minority of cases, a higher PPP is warranted to ensure that its accuracy will typically exceed 50%.
5. The term *mental disorders* is used as shorthand for the feigning of psychological and emotional difficulties that may include mental disorders and syndromes.
6. Specifically, 15 of the 60 F-scale items were retained on the Fp scale, which represents a true rare-symptom strategy.
7. For example T-score transformations, but not raw scores, produce the highly significant differences on the MMPI-2 O-S scale.
8. This term is preferable to *amplified presentations* because purported deficits are sometimes extreme and, therefore, not plausible.
9. Oral and computer-based administrations provide malingerers with only a limited opportunity to compare item difficulty.
10. Tombaugh (1996) found a false-positive rate of 27.0% for dementias (see Table 3.7, p. 14), even when nonstandardized procedures (e.g., additional cuing) were used.
11. For instance, the S scale has three affirmation and two denial factors (Butcher & Han, 1995); arguably, Contentment with Life should be a

strong predictor of those denying psycho-logical maladjustment, whereas Beliefs in Human Goodness may have little bearing on this facet of defensiveness.

12. Recent searches of PsycINFO and Medline have failed to yield any published research on the LAQ.

13. However, effect sizes were small because patients with chronic pain also evidence substantial elevations (M T scores >60) across clinical scales.

14. A minimum number of endorsed items (e.g., ≥ 10) would need to be established; presence of one or two severe items is likely to be an unreliable indicator of this detection strategy.

15. An initial design could use those persons who openly acknowledge that they disregard key medical symptoms (e.g., chest pains and breathlessness). Even with socialized medicine in Great Britain, more than 10% ignore these symptoms (Prior & Wood, 2003).

II

Diagnostic Issues

3

Syndromes Associated with Deception

MICHAEL J. VITACCO, PhD

In traditional therapeutic settings, honesty is taken for granted, as the client enters therapy with a specific agenda aimed at improving mental health functioning or interpersonal relationships. In other clinical settings, persons seeking services may view mental health professionals as serving multiple goals that are not always consistent with the clients' best interests. Disparities in goals and perceived allegiances are further accentuated in potentially adversarial settings. A common theme of these settings is the inclusion of a formal proceeding that is consequential to the client. Examples include employment (e.g., disability), military (e.g., medical discharge), school (e.g., placement in special programs), and forensic (e.g., personal injury). In these settings, the stakes may be quite high, which make it understandable that an individual might make a conscious decision to distort his or her presentation (e.g., malingering or defensiveness). The same individual may have different motivations at different times. In a correctional setting, a person may malinger to obtain a preferred placement on a mental health unit (Vitacco & Rogers, 2005). At the point of parole decisions, the motivation may be entirely opposite (i.e., defensiveness) in an attempt to appear well adjusted and ready for community placement.

The next section underscores the challenges to accurate classification, using malingering as a principal example. The primary focus of the chapter involves an overview of mental disorders and other clinical phenomena that are of-

ten associated with response styles and general deception. The chapter continues with an examination of clinical applications, which provides general guidelines for the assessment of response styles. It concludes with a consideration of ethical issues that arise in assessments of dissimulation.

CHALLENGES TO THE ASSESSMENT OF MALINGERING

The DSM-IV-TR (American Psychiatric Association, 2000) describes malingering as the "intentional production of false or grossly exaggerated physical or psychological symptoms, motivated by external incentives" (p. 739). The DSM-IV-TR provides additional criteria and suggests that clinicians should suspect malingering if *any combination* of the following are present: (1) medicolegal context of presentation, (2) marked discrepancy between the person's claimed stress or disability and the objective findings, (3) lack of cooperation during the diagnostic evaluation and in complying with the diagnostic evaluation, and (4) the presence of antisocial personality disorder. Criticisms have been leveled at these criteria because of their ineffectiveness and limited conceptualization of malingering. Simply put, these guidelines should not be used to classify malingering because they result in a misclassification rate of over 80% (Rogers & Vitacco, 2002). The failure rate is unacceptable in any setting, but especially when potential misdiagnosis can have deleterious effects, such as being labeled a malingerer and being denied needed mental health services. Unfortunately, many clinicians rely exclusively on these unvalidated DSM-IV-TR indices when making conclusions about malingering. Instead, clinicians should use one or more validated instruments (e.g., the Structured Interview of Reported Symptoms [SIRS]; Rogers, Bagby, & Dickens, 1992) and multiple sources of independent data to confirm or disconfirm feigning.

Determinations of response styles rely on the assessment of conscious motivations for deception. This problem is highlighted by the crucial distinction between malingering (conscious motivations) and factitious disorders (unconscious motivations). Although courts have clearly rejected claims of disability and mental disorder based on conscious malingering (Weintraub, 2006), other forms of deception present a less clear picture. Judging whether deception is a conscious decision or underpinned by subconscious motivations is a complicated endeavor. As noted by Rogers, Bagby, and Dickens (1992), the behaviors of those individuals who are malingering and those with factitious disorders are often indistinguishable.

The assessment of malingering can be conceptualized as extending beyond its presence or absence. Resnick (1997; see also Resnick, West, & Payne, Chapter 7, this volume) described three distinct types of malingering: false imputation, partial malingering, and full malingering. *False imputation* occurs when an individual attributes symptoms to an etiologically unrelated cause. For example, a male client seeking to be exempted from college math courses might attribute his problems with concentration to a learning disorder rather than to daily substance abuse. *Partial malingering* occurs when patients describe past symptoms that they no longer have or exaggerate actual symptoms, otherwise known as "gilding the lily." For instance, a female client may describe past depression in describing her current "disability." As a further example, a male individual with a psychotic disorder may overreport hallucinations with constant symptoms of a high intensity either as a call for help or to ensure that his symptoms are not overlooked. Finally, *full malingering* is what clinicians generally classify. It refers to the fabrication and gross exaggeration of a mental disorder for ex-

ternal purposes. These types of malingering should be considered in assessments; they add complexity to evaluating response styles.

An additional complication in the assessment of malingering is the introduction of similar terms, such the concept of secondary gain (see Rogers, Chapter 1, this volume). Clinicians must be able to distinguish malingering, which is a well-researched construct, from other constructs that have limited empirical basis. Focusing on secondary gain, Rogers and Reinhardt (1998) warned against believing that an individual is deceiving just because there is potential for secondary gain. This serious bias is akin to forensic evaluators approaching malingering evaluations with the mantra, "I know it is there, I just need to find it." This approach increases the likelihood that clinicians will make facile interpretations based on the potential for secondary gain. Quite simply, the potential for gain is present with most individuals undergoing evaluations in criminal or civil settings. Due to its high level of ambiguity and risk of misinterpretation, Vitacco and Rogers (2005) recommended that clinicians do not use the term *secondary gain*.

This section has illustrated the challenges and complexities in the assessment of malingering. Different but equally complex challenges face the assessment of defensiveness and its variants (e.g., social desirability). These challenges underscore the importance of developing a full appreciation of each response style prior to conducting assessments.

DSM-IV-TR DIAGNOSES ASSOCIATED WITH DECEPTION

The aforementioned issues are often crucial to the conceptualization of malingering, and clinicians must have an awareness of how factors of secondary gain and overreliance on the DSM may negatively affect impartiality and objectivity. Failure to acquire awareness of these issues may lead to improper assessment and might even be unethical (Iverson, 2006). Unfortunately, many clinicians facilely interpret any deception as an indicator of malingering. To the contrary, several legitimate DSM diagnoses include deception as either a central or peripheral aspect. Adding to the discussion, it must be realized that syndromes exist in which deception is voluntary or even planned (e.g., psychopathy), whereas in other syndromes deception appears to be much less under the control of the patient (e.g., false-memory syndrome).

This section aims to elucidate the forms of deception and dissimulation as they relate to DSM-IV-TR disorders in both children and adults. Its primary goal is to improve the understanding of response styles and how they potentially manifest in clinical disorders. Response styles can be conceptualized as a dimensional construct, with complete denial on one end of the spectrum and full malingering at the other end (Greene, 2000). Disorders discussed in this section include those associated with various types of deception, such as (1) conduct and oppositional defiant disorders and (2) personality disorders and psychopathy. It also covers several diagnostic categories in which defensiveness is common: (1) substance abuse, (2) eating disorders, and (3) paraphilias. The section also examines several other diagnoses in which more focused dissimulation is common: (1) reactive attachment disorder and

(2) factitious disorders and factitious disorder by proxy. For those disorders covered extensively in other chapters, this section provides an important overview. For other disorders, it provides additional detail. Deception extends beyond diagnoses per se and can be an important component of syndromes and other clinical phenomena. Such syndromes include false-memory, and chronic fatigue. For clinical phenomena, practitioners must consider such issues as pathological lying.

Explanatory models of response styles were discussed in Chapter 1 in this volume. One feature of this section is a systematic effort to consider multiple explanatory models as they apply to specific disorders and syndromes. Table 3.1 offers distilled descriptions of how the explanatory model might be expressed with diagnostic categories, disorders, and selected syndromes. Researchers and practitioners may find this distillation to be useful in understanding the multideterminants of motivation.

TABLE 3.1. Disorders and Syndromes Associated with Dissimulation: Explanatory Models of Motivation

Disorder	Explanatory model	Characteristics associated with deception
Conduct disorders	Criminological	Instrumental/poor impulse control
Reactive attachment	Pathogenic	Secondary to extreme abuse and abandonment
	Adaptational	Compensatory mechanism in social situations
Factitious disorders	Criminological	Secondary to antisocial behavior/psychopathy
	Pathogenic	Rigidity
	Adaptational	Financial motivations
Substance abuse	Criminological	Secondary to antisocial behavior/psychopathy
	Pathogenic	Self-medication/comorbidity
	Adaptational	Avoiding adult responsibilities/escapism
Eating disorders	Pathogenic	Maintaining control/rigidity, distorted body image
Paraphilias	Criminological	Luring victims/maintaining offending
	Pathogenic	Own abuse history leads to poor boundaries
Psychopathy	Criminological	Instrumental/game-playing/poor impulse control
False-memory syndrome	Criminological	Secondary to antisocial behavior/psychopathy
	Pathogenic	Regression/repression/avoiding responsibilities
	Adaptational	Financial motivations (evaluating malingering)
Child custody	Criminological	Extortion/lying to turn child against parent
	Pathogenic	Rigidity/pathological denial or acknowledgment
	Adaptational	Denial of problems to remain with child
Chronic fatigue syndrome	Criminological	Secondary to antisocial behavior/psychopathy
	Pathogenic	Secondary to mental illness/comorbidity
	Adaptational	Financial motivations/receiving disability

The goals for the remainder of this chapter are threefold:

1. To present information regarding the presentation of deception in several DSM-IV-TR diagnoses.
2. To present information on other syndromes associated with deception that often occur in the context of forensic and other potentially adversarial settings.
3. To emphasize how ethical assessments place demands on clinicians and the importance of considering various motivations when evaluating deception.

Oppositional Defiant and Conduct Disorders

The diagnoses of oppositional defiant disorder (ODD) and conduct disorder (CD) are often considered precursors to the development of more serious antisocial behavior in adulthood. Deceitfulness is part of the core diagnostic criteria in both disorders. In CD, for instance, deceitfulness and theft are core symptoms and are subsumed under the description "often lies to obtain goods or favors or to avoid obligations (i.e., 'cons' others)" (American Psychiatric Association, 2000, p. 99). For ODD, lying and deception relate to an overarching negativistic attitude toward authority. Although deception is not a formal criterion in ODD, it is still common. Frick, Lahey, Loeber, and Stouthamer-Loeber (1991) evaluated the covariation of symptoms between CD and ODD in a sample of 177 clinic-referred boys. A multitude of symptoms were evaluated with factor analysis, and lying loaded strongly on both CD and ODD when both teacher and parent ratings were factor analyzed. Although lying manifests differently between ODD and CD, the deception negatively affects social relationships (Hughes & Hill, 2006).

Beyond diagnoses, deception is central to understanding childhood development of broad-based antisocial behaviors, including sex offending. In looking at the development of antisocial behaviors, Waldman, Singh, and Lahey (2006) highlighted how early engagement in less severe types of conduct problems, such as lying, often is a developmental marker that indicates more severe types of violent behavior yet to come. Deception can also take the form of denial and minimization in adolescent sex offenders (Barbaree, Marshall, & Hudson,

1993; Curwen, 2003). Beyond individual deception, children's prevarications can sometimes be understood within the family context. Baker, Tabacoff, Tornusciolo, and Eisenstadt (2003) compared sexually abused children with others on child welfare. A factor of "family deception" was identified, which was composed of family myths and active lying. This factor increased the likelihood that sexually abused children would eventually engage in sexual offending.

In summary, several key issues are relevant to deception in relation to CD and ODD. In both disorders, the deception is both conscious and voluntary. For both disorders, deception often has both proximal and distal effects. In the short term, deception interferes with the development of positive peer and family relationships, and in the long term, early deception is sometimes the precursor to more severe antisocial behavior. The perpetuation of any criminal behavior typically requires some skill at prevarication to avoid suspicion (e.g., explanations for "acquired" property). Clinicians must assess the magnitude and type of deception when evaluating children and adolescents with potential ODD and CD diagnoses.

Reactive Attachment Disorder

Reactive attachment disorder (RAD) is defined by "markedly disturbed and developmentally inappropriate social relatedness in most contexts that begins before age 5 years and is associated with grossly pathological care" (American Psychiatric Association, 2000, p. 127). Two subtypes of RAD can be diagnosed: inhibited and disinhibited. A review of available literature demonstrates a clear link between RAD and deceptive behaviors. For example, S. L. Wilson (2001, p. 42) characterized RAD as a disorder of early attachment in which the child often presents with "sociopathic behavior which includes deception" (see also Reber, 1996). Hoksbergen and Laak (2000) found that adolescents with a history of attachment problems engaged in a greater number of antisocial behaviors, including lying, cheating, and vandalism, when compared with controls without a history of attachment problems.

Awareness of early home environments of evaluated children and adolescents is important so as not to confuse attachment disorder with ODD or CD on the basis of deceptive behaviors. Although the deception might appear similar, it is clear that the motivations for deception are quite different. Far from using deception for instrumental purposes (e.g., deceiving for money), children with RAD try to overcome early abuse through the use of superficial charm and manipulation. Certainly, handling social relationships in this superficial and deceptive manner can be an adaptive strategy. Although the underpinnings of RAD remain controversial and confusing (Zilberstein, 2006), it is clear that additional research is needed so that clinicians and researchers can gain a better understanding of the etiology and pathogenesis of deception and manipulation in children and adolescents diagnosed with RAD.

Factitious Disorders

Besides malingering, factitious disorders (FD) are most often characterized as deceptive behaviors that involve the feigning of symptoms and impairment (see Hamilton, Feldman, & Cunnien, Chapter 8, this volume). As described in the DSM-IV-TR (American Psychiatric Association, 2000) the "essential feature of Factitious Disorder is the intentional production of physical or psychological signs or symptoms" (p. 513). DSM-IV-TR (American Psychiatric Association, 2000) does not provide specific criteria for FD diagnosis. In its description, DSM-IV acknowledges the complexity of the disorder. Characteristics may include (1) atypical or dramatic presentation that does not conform to an identifiable general medical condition or mental disorder, (2) symptoms or behaviors present only when the individual is being observed, (3) pseudologia fantastica (i.e., pathological lying), (4) disruptive behavior on an inpatient unit, (5) arguing excessively with nurses and physicians, (6) covert use of substances, (7) evidence of multiple treatment interventions, (8) extensive history of traveling, (9) few, if any, hospital visitors, and (10) fluctuating hospital course.

Consistent with malingering, the feigning of symptoms is within the patient's control; however, a primary difference is motivation. Unlike malingering, the primary motivation for the feigning is to assume a sick role in the absence of other external incentives (American Psychiatric Association, 2000). Far from straightforward, no guidelines or psychological measures are available to directly assess different motivations. Moreover, patients with factitious disorders are frequently uncooperative with diagnostic procedures. Instead, clinicians must rely on their professional judgment and explore evidence of an intrapsychic need to maintain a sick role. The lack of objective findings limits the ability to effectively diagnose factitious disorder.

There are a wide range of symptoms that have been suggested that might be associated with FD diagnoses. In addition to the DSM, Cunnien (1997) added the following: (1) strong masochistic needs exist, (2) sickness allows regression and avoidance of adult responsibilities, (3) illness is symbolic of anger or conflict with authority figures, (4) illness fulfills dependency needs, or (5) illness symbolizes attempts at mastery of past trauma. Therefore, the diagnosis of FD can be difficult due to the range of possible symptoms coupled with the challenges of assessing voluntariness and intentionality. No diagnostic tool is available that evaluates the intrapsychic need to take on the sick role. Difficulties with differential diagnosis are further magnified because these individuals may be misclassified as malingering on psychological measures. As a rule, clinicians must first determine that feigning is occurring and then attempt to ascertain motivation (Rogers, Bagby, & Dickens, 1992).

Factitious presentations vary dramatically according to the disorder being feigned. Cunnien (1997) identified several types of factitious presentations related to psychological and physical disorders. Within the psychological domain, he noted that factitious symptoms could be associated with (1) psychosis, (2) posttraumatic stress disorder (PTSD), (3) bereavement, (4) dissociative identity disorder, and (5) false claims of child abuse. In examining factitious psychosis, Pope, Jonas, and Jones (1982) described nine patients who demonstrated voluntary control over their psychotic symptoms. They were women with chronic personality disorders. Regarding factitious PTSD, Sparr and Pankratz (1983) described cases in which military records contradicted specific claims of traumatic events. A close evaluation of these patients found diverse reasons for factitious PTSD, most unrelated to any type of external gain. The range and depth of symptoms associated with FD underscores the need for considering multiple motives.

Deceptions associated with FDs are varied in motivation, severity, and magnitude (Rogers, 2004). It is likely that individuals with FD utilize more beds in inpatient hospitals than previously thought (Gregory & Jindal, 2006); clinicians must be on the lookout for patients who present with a varied symptom pattern and be alert to the possibility that the individual might not be malingering but fulfilling deep-seated psychological needs (see Hamilton et al., Chapter 8, this volume).

Factitious Disorder by Proxy

A variant of FD is factitious disorder by proxy (FDBP), in which caretakers either exaggerate or make up psychological or physical symptoms in others, often in their own children (see also Munchausen by proxy, or MBP). Case studies were first described by Meadow (1977) involving parents who induced serious medical conditions in their children. Cases of FDBP and MBP are not rare, and it has been suggested that they constitute approximately 10% of all FD cases (Reich & Gottfried, 1983).

Feldman (2004a) described another variant of this disorder referred to as *malingering by proxy,* whereby individuals engage in FDBP or MBP to obtain a reward or receive a financial settlement. As an illustrative example, a parent may exaggerate the nature of his or her child's illness to seize on the charity of individuals who donate to assist families in need. I was part of a team that evaluated a mother who claimed her child had a rare form of leukemia and sought financial assistance. The ruse was exposed when well-wishers were unable to find the child at the hospital and began to question the veracity of the claim. Clinicians involved in the assessment of maladaptive parenting often will have cases in which evidence suggests that parents or caretakers are responsible for the ills ailing their children. The key distinction is whether the parental actions are simply neglect or purposeful efforts to fabricate or induce a disorder.

The etiology of FDBP and MPB remains to be established (Mart, 2002). As one step in this direction, Rogers (2004) evaluated the usefulness of applying explanatory models of malingering to FDBP. In a comprehensive review, he found three explanatory models of malingering (i.e., pathogenic, criminological, and adaptational) that have potential utility in explaining the motivations for FDBP. For example, some explanations of the pathogenic model include overattachment with the child or rigid

defensive style. Criminological explanations may possibly include psychopathy and previous criminal convictions. Finally, the adaptational model includes motivations of financial gain or attempts to resolve family conflict (for a complete review, see Rogers, 2004). Applying an explanatory model represents a forward step toward understanding FDBP disorders. Subsequent research is needed to clarify the causes and diagnostic picture of FDBP and MBP. Such research is especially salient as more than 110 symptoms have been associated with FDBP (see Rogers, 2004; Seibel & Parnell, 1998).

Substance Abuse

Society, and the government by extension, has taken a strong stand against illicit drug use. In 1986, as part of its "war on drugs," Congress enacted mandatory minimum sentences to target high-level drug dealers. However, many users have been caught up in these sweeping sentencing reforms, as evidenced by the 723,000 marijuana-related arrests in 2001 (Erlen & Spillane, 2004). The use and abuse of alcohol and illicit drugs has long been associated with denial and misrepresentation. Recently, the spotlight has focused on professional athletes for use of disallowed performance-enhancing drugs. Professional leagues are now sanctioning players with lengthy suspensions and bans following positive tests for prohibited substances. Criminal and noncriminal sanctions provide strong motivations for individuals to deny or minimize their substance abuse.

Regardless of social policy, individuals engaged in substance abuse frequently lie, deny, or minimize in order to continue their ability to abuse substances. Deception is used to conceal the fact that a "great deal of time is spent in activities necessary to obtain the substance . . . , use the substance . . . , or recover from its effect" (American Psychiatric Association, 2000, p. 197). At this level, deception becomes a critical tool used to justify lengthy time away from home and work. Studies have supported this relationship between deception and substance abuse. Klein (2000) found a significant correlation between scores on the SIRS (Rogers, Bagby, & Dickens, 1992) and the Substance Abuse Subtle Screening Inventory (SASSI; Miller, 1994a). Substance abuse is also found in greater levels in college students who self-report unethical academic behavior, including cheating on exams or having lied to avoid an examination (Blankenship & Whitley, 2000).

The evaluation of individuals with substance abuse is often complicated by inconsistent presentations because of different response styles (see Stein & Rogers, Chapter 6, this volume). Richards and Pai (2003) evaluated response styles in 312 inmates sentenced in the Maine Department of Corrections for substance abuse. The results were very informative: 22% "faked good" (i.e., denial and minimization) and 14.7% "faked bad" (e.g., exaggerating psychopathology). Consistent with the adaptational model (see Rogers, Chapter 1, this volume), inmates adopted the response style they believed would be most beneficial to them. Likewise, Pierre, Wirshing, and Wirshing (2003) found that many veterans with substance abuse problems would malinger when it was perceived as the only way to receive mental health treatment within the Veterans Administration.

Application of Rogers's explanatory models of malingering to deception in substance abusers provides useful information. The pathogenic model might partially apply to persons with substance dependence for highly addictive drugs. The criminological model may apply as part of a broader pattern of antisocial behavior. Finally, the adaptational model may explain how deception is used by substance abusers to cope with adversarial circumstances, such as medications for simulated pain when the actual problem may be an Axis II disorder. Clinicians must remain cognizant of the potential reasons for deceptions among substance abusers. Awareness of multiple motivations should be a central aspect of assessment and treatment models, especially if the ultimate goal is to effectively intervene in problematic substance-abusing behavior.

Eating Disorders

Patients with diagnoses of anorexia nervosa and bulimia nervosa engage in a variety of deceptive practices aimed at enabling them to continue their obsessive and compulsive behavior centered on their weight and body image. Deception in eating disorders can occur in a variety of ways, including:

• Hiding food in order to engage in bingeing behavior

• Secretly exercising, even when under close observation
• Stealing laxatives and diet supplements to avoid the embarrassment of purchasing them
• Traveling long distances to use drugstores outside of one's typical neighborhood to avoid family and friends while purchasing diet aids
• Lying about weight gain and minimizing weight loss

Lacey (1993) evaluated a group of 112 individuals who were suffering from bulimia but were also diagnosed with other impulse control disorders. In this study, 21% of the patients repeatedly stole, 28% abused drugs, and over one-third chronically abused alcohol. These results confirm how deception can be manifested within eating disorders and that eating disorders have a high comorbidity with other disorders in which deception is central (e.g., substance abuse).

Family deceptiveness has been identified as a factor in the etiology of eating disorders (Dalzell, 2000; Roberto, 1993), much as it is for adolescents who engage in sexual misbehavior. Often these families have histories of nondisclosure among their members, accentuated by denial of basic flaws and the desire for the outward appearance of perfection. Within individuals with eating disorders, deception and lying are often designed to allow the individual to maintain a feeling of control. From that perspective, the deceptive practices involved in eating disorders go hand in hand with pathology and thus may be best understood using the pathogenic model.

Paraphilias and Sexual Abuse

According to the DSM-IV-TR (American Psychiatric Association, 2000), paraphilias are referred to as sexual deviations or perversions with behaviors or sexual urges focusing on unusual objects, activities, or situations. Such deviations present in many forms (i.e., exhibitionism, fetishism, frotteurism, pedophilia, masochism, transvestitism, and voyeurism), with the common theme being maladapted sexual behavior. Given their deviant and often illegal status, these behaviors lead to the possibility of long-term prison sentences. Recently, convicted sex offenders have faced the ominous possibility of civil commitment to a secure facility for an indefinite period of time after serving their sentences (Doren, 2002). These severe sanctions, coupled with social stigmas, provide strong motivation for defensiveness.

A predominant feature of paraphilias and sexually abusive behavior is the presence of defensiveness, minimization, and lying. Defensiveness and lying refer to voluntary actions typically based on a desired objective. In contrast, cognitive distortions (e.g., rationalizations) may represent characteristic patterns of thinking that are potentially less voluntary. For example, a male perpetrator may justify incestuous behavior as "educational" at a sentencing evaluation, even though this obvious lack of insight may hurt rather than help his desired objective (i.e., avoiding incarceration). Treatment interventions must address both response styles and cognitive distortions as integral components of treatment (Ward, Gannon, & Keown, 2006). Schneider and Wright (2004) posited that denial of past sexual offending behavior interferes with accepting responsibility and serves to continue the abusing behavior. Combining denial and cognitive distortions, they concluded that denial is "best understood as the acceptance of explanations that reduce accountability and are reinforced by distorted beliefs and self-deceptive thinking process" (p. 3). Various forms of deception and cognitive distortions are highly prevalent in individuals engaging in sexually deviant acts.

Kennedy and Grubin (1992) used cluster analysis to study 102 sex offenders engaged in deceptive practices. Two groups used defensiveness in their denials of sexual offenses or minimization of its effects on survivors. Two groups used cognitive distortions whereby they admitted to the offenses and either (1) blamed others for their actions or (2) offered excuses or mitigating reasons for their offending behavior.

We must understand that motivations for deception among sexual offenders can be varied and complex. Consistent with the criminological model, many offenders will use deceptive practices to lure victims or to prey on compromised individuals. Other explanations exist for deceptive practices in sex offenders. An offender may deny offenses if faced with a lengthy sentence or the prospect of civil commitment and if he or she views deception as the only option for maintaining freedom (i.e., adaptational model) or has a significant history of abuse and has failed to develop appropriate

social skills and the ability to form age-appropriate interpersonal relationships (i.e., pathogenic model).

The assessment of deception regarding sexual deviations is especially challenging (see Lanyon & Thomas, Chapter 17, this volume). In postconviction treatment, polygraph testing has been used to minimize current lying by sex offenders and for the possible detection of those offenders engaging in deceptive practices (Kokish, Levenson, & Blasingame, 2005). Possibly its best use is to encourage sex offenders to be more forthright about past and current problems. As discussed by Iacono and Patrick in Chapter 15 (this volume), controversy continues regarding the effectiveness of the polygraph to accurately detect deception.

Personality Disorders and Psychopathy

Personality disorders are defined by a chronic, maladaptive pattern of thoughts and behaviors. Proneness to lying or deceptive behaviors is a common feature of many personality disorders. The personality disorder primarily associated with lying and deception is antisocial personality disorder (APD), which is associated with aliases, persistent lying, and manipulating others. Deception is also present in other DSM-IV-TR Cluster B syndromes—borderline, histrionic, and narcissistic disorders, as well as obsessive–compulsive personality disorder. Deception in other Axis II disorders appears under control of the individual, although not to the degree found in APD, in which the lying is voluntary, conscious, and frequently instrumental.

Psychopathy is a syndrome associated with APD that warrants our attention. Psychopathy is a constellation of personality and behavioral traits that includes affective deficits (e.g., callousness), interpersonal characteristics (e.g., glibness and superficial charm), and lifestyle components (e.g., impulsivity), in conjunction with antisocial behavior (Vitacco, Neumann, & Jackson, 2005). Psychopathy has been linked to a large number of deceptive behaviors, ranging from manipulation at work (Babiak, 2000) to full-blown malingering (Gacono, Meloy, Sheppard, Speth, & Roske, 1995). It appears that a subgroup of psychopaths, mainly those with high levels of the interpersonal features, can lie easily and have few qualms about it. However, this finding does not mean that typical psychopaths are especially good at deception or malingering (see Rogers & Cruise, 2000). In particular, Kropp and Rogers (1993) found that most psychopaths are no more effective than other offenders at malingering or defensiveness.

Kucharski, Duncan, Egan, and Falkenbach (2006) reported mostly negative findings regarding the relationship between psychopathy and malingering in a sample of criminal defendants. They found group differences between malingerers and nonmalingerers on certain personality characteristics associated with psychopathy. However, receiver operator curves suggested that the utility estimates for psychopathy with regard to malingering were low. The authors advised that psychopathy was mostly unrelated to malingering and warned that using psychopathy as a criterion for malingering would result in high levels of false positives. In summary, psychopathy is certainly related to a variety of deceptive and antisocial behaviors; however, psychopathy should not be substituted for malingering and should not be used as either a symptom or a predictor of malingering.

OTHER CLINICAL PHENOMENA ASSOCIATED WITH DECEPTION

Clinicians must be aware of how deception can manifest itself beyond formalized disorders, as deception is frequently found in several other areas of clinical attention. This section focuses on three specific areas: false-memory syndrome, child custody evaluations, and chronic fatigue syndrome. In each of these clinical areas, deception can be prominent and can have large effects on how clinicians view symptoms and the manner in which evaluations are conducted. The goals for this section are to elucidate how deception occurs in these clinical phenomena and to provide specific information regarding the application of explanatory models of deception.

False-Memory Syndrome

The idea of false-memory syndrome (FMS) was first advanced in 1992 by an organization with the same name. Since the criteria were set forth 14 years ago, the number of theoretical and scientific articles devoted to FMS has substantially increased. Many articles are characterized by a social and political debate

regarding the validity of FMS (see Geraerts & McNally, Chapter 16, this volume). FMS consists of a cluster of symptoms that expands beyond the presence of a false memory. Instead, the syndrome focuses on the degree to which the trauma-based memories remain present in the absence of any objective evidence and the degree to which these memories define the individual's life, leading to an inability to handle adult responsibilities. In this way, FMS acts similarly to the psychodynamic concepts of regression and repression. Such repressed memories have been the impetus behind criminal prosecution and lawsuits aimed at the alleged perpetrators of the abuse (Wakefield & Underwager, 1992).

Memory itself is highly problematic in legal settings. The work of Dr. Elizabeth Loftus has been highly influential in demonstrating the malleability of memory and identifying the relationship of certain therapeutic techniques to the creation of false memories (for a review, see Loftus & Davis, 2006). Such techniques include hypnotic age regression and intense interrogation techniques. Persinger (1992) reported on six cases of questionable recall for sex abuse in which the patients were subjected to hypnosis as part of treatment. As Persinger (1994) later noted, it is unclear whether the memories were genuine or secondary to misattribution of the perpetration of abuse. Moreover, memories can be simply forgotten. Williams (1994) found that approximately 38% of women who were brought to the hospital for sexual abuse as children did not recall the abuse many years later. Pope and Hudson (1995) conducted a thorough review of studies of amnesia and attempted to develop alternative hypotheses (e.g., forgetting or denial) to repressed memories of sexual abuse.

The concept of FMS has become highly contentious, with advocates on both sides becoming forceful proponents for their respective positions. Davis (2005) described the constructivist process by which accusers have withdrawn their complaints, often resulting from personal distress and disbelief surrounding uncovering repressed memories. Given that often memories are not "recovered" without the aid of hypnosis or therapy, the recovered memories are often subjected to a great deal of skepticism. In contrast, Whitfield (2001) suggested that perpetrators will claim their victims have FMS in attempts to discredit their victims and minimize their own criminal behavior. Others (e.g., Raitt & Zeedyk, 2003) have suggested that trauma-based memories are problematic not because of the unreliability of recovering memories but because of the low credibility traditionally afforded to women.

Often, judges or juries are required to determine the veracity of abuse claims years after their onset and discontinuation. Unfortunately, studies of FMS have not focused on reliability and validity of the memory; instead, articles are often politicized and promote a partisan agenda (for a review, see Olio, 2004). In Chapter 16 in this volume, Geraerts and McNally critically examine the research data as they relate to FMS and other memory claims.

Clinicians should continue to consider the broad array of possibilities when dealing with sudden-onset memories. Included in these possibilities are the potential for malingering and factitious disorders. As noted by Cunnien (1997), dissimulation should be considered in litigated cases of alleged abuse. He wrote, "Factitious claims should be suspected when psychological evaluation reveals a substantial likelihood that revenge, displacement of anger, or recent abandonment triggered the abuse allegations" (p. 40).

Child Custody and Parental Alienation Syndrome

In custody evaluations, parents often have two complementary goals. First, they seek to make themselves out to be as virtuous as possible, extolling their positive qualities and minimizing any difficulties. Second, they often attempt to make the other parent appear less fit or even incapable of performing parental responsibilities, even when this is not the case. The first response style is characterized by defensiveness. The second response style is a type of deception (i.e., maligning others) that is commonly observed in custody evaluations.

A high level of defensiveness is a common feature of custody litigants. Their conscious goals are to minimize psychopathology and maladaptive traits (Erickson, Lilienfeld, & Vitacco, 2007) in an effort to gain custody. Given that defensiveness is the norm in contested custody cases, it is critical that clinicians consider defensiveness in the context of the evaluation. Competing hypotheses exist, including (1) outright lying or intentional distortion and (2) personality symptoms that could be mistaken for lying.

Clinicians should recognize that defensiveness is pervasive in custody cases and has little utility per se in custody determinations. Empirical research confirms that defensiveness is the normative response style (see Otto, Chapter 21, this volume). For example, Strong, Greene, Hoppe, Johnston, and Olesen (1999) evaluated defensive responding in 206 pairs of parents undergoing custody evaluations. The results indicated both intentional distortion (defensiveness) and "positivity," a trait-like phenotype whereby the examinee is extremely positive but apparently unaware of his or her self-distortions, which could be mistaken as defensiveness. Research with the Minnesota Multiphasic Personality Inventory (MMPI-2; Ackerman & Ackerman, 1997; Medoff, 1999) has found defensiveness to be very common in parents undergoing custody evaluations. Similar findings (McCann et al., 2001) have been found for the Millon Clinical Multiaxial Inventory—Third Edition (MCMI-III; Millon, 1994).

Parental alienation syndrome (PAS) is a controversial clinical construct that does not appear to be widely accepted. PAS is thought to occur when a dominant parent exerts undue influence on the child, making him or her an ally of that parent. Deception can occur by the child in complying with the dominant parent's expectations. It can also occur with the dominant parent (e.g., lying to limit the other parent's access). Emery (2005) suggested that in the absence of objective standards, PAS should be considered a hypothetical construct.

In a survey of 106 custody evaluators, Baker (2007) assessed the evaluator's knowledge of and attitudes toward PAS. Several notable findings were revealed. First, 75% of the respondents were aware of the symptoms associated with PAS and believed that one parent can attempt to turn his or her child against the other parent. Second, a large majority of the respondents had personally evaluated custody cases in which they believed PAS occurred. Nonetheless, the respondents noted several problems with PAS, including failing to meet evidentiary admissibility standards, as well as criticisms for its subjectivity and lack of norms. The validity of PAS remains far from settled.

Chronic Fatigue Syndrome and Other Related Disorders

Chronic fatigue syndrome (CFS) is characterized by extreme fatigue and exhaustion whereby basic tasks of daily living become extremely difficult to accomplish. In addition, several "minor" symptoms of CFS have been identified, including musculoskeletal pain, infections, and slight neurological abnormalities (Janal, Ciccone, & Natelson, 2006). Abbey (1996) outlined the multitude of mental health symptoms that can accompany CFS. Such symptoms include problems with mood, anxiety, somatoform disorders, substance abuse, eating disorders, and obsessive–compulsive disorder. In addition, Abbey listed factitious disorder and malingering as potential issues associated with CFS. Cantor and Heads (2004) added problems with sleep, difficulties concentrating, and irritability as potential symptoms.

The majority of patients who present with CFS symptoms are likely legitimate. However, skepticism surrounds the diagnosis. Beaulieu (2000) interviewed a group of patients, their family members, insurance providers, and physicians and found that patients had genuine impairment but often suffered from stigmatization attached to the disorder. A great deal of the stigmatization has evolved from associations of CFS with malingering. In this regard, Cantor and Heads (2004) cautioned against the association of malingering with CFS and similar disorders. They posited that heightened concerns about malingering created the possibility of unhealthy mistrust between doctors and patients. Even the term *chronic fatigue syndrome* carries a negative connotation. On this point, Jason, Taylor, Stepanek, and Plioplys (2001) surveyed 100 undergraduates and 100 medical school students and found that symptoms of CFS had less credibility than when these same symptoms were attributed to other medical disorders (i.e., myalgic encephalopathy or Florence Nightingale disease).

CFS lacks a definitive test for diagnosis. Instead, physicians and psychologists are guided by the patient's self-report and description of his or her own symptoms. Moreover, CFS has no clearly defined etiology, so clinicians lack a clear understanding regarding its onset and development. Given the potential incentives associated with CFS (e.g., time off work and disability payments), the potential for deception is certainly present. However, research is very limited. Complicating the diagnostic picture for CFS is the large overlap with symptoms of other mental disorders. For instance, Fink (1992) found that 18% of somatizers had also been hospitalized for a mental illness.

In explaining CFS, both the pathogenic and adaptational models are well suited for the understanding of CFS. Given the high degree of comorbidity, it would be easy to apply the pathogenic model, and this model is likely most appropriate in the large majority of cases. However, the adaptational model could apply in cases in which symptoms serve to protect the individual from stress or involve financial gain.

CLINICAL APPLICATIONS

Four important conclusions are identified in this chapter. First, deception is common among a variety of diagnoses spanning from childhood through adulthood. Second, the criteria for evaluating deception are often not well defined and lack standardized methods. Third, feigned and genuine symptoms are often present in the same individuals. Many individuals with bona fide mental disorders feign and exaggerate for a variety of reasons, including access to needed services. Fourth, evaluating the level of voluntariness of deception is often made difficult by the presence of conflicting motivations within the same individual. Such complications can become highly challenging for clinicians.

Two models are helpful when evaluating various types of deception: threshold and clinical-decision models. The threshold model functions as a screen for identifying potential cases of dissimulation that require further evaluation. In contrast, the clinical-decision model represents a definite conclusion about the presence of a specific response style or general deception. Such models are especially relevant in rendering determinations between closely aligned clinical constructs. For example, malingering is best understood as a nonpathological condition, which is often characterized by a sudden onset consistent with an external goal. In contrast, FD may have a more variable presentation that appears to be affected by the doctor–patient relationship (Cunnien, 1997).

In making such differentiations, clinicians must look for evidence of voluntariness, which is often indicated by significant change in presentation during the time of the evaluation compared with other times when the clinician is not present. Finally, evidence of a desire to play the sick role cannot explain the totality of the current symptoms. In Chapter 8 in this volume, Hamilton and colleagues address the diagnosis of FD in more detail. In differentiating FD from malingering, a critical issue is the establishment of the individual's desire to assume a sick role. On this point, Cunnien (1997) provided three useful indicators: (1) persistent, inappropriate efforts to remain a patient; (2) persistent, inappropriate behavioral regression in the presence of health care providers; and (3) clinical certainty that the illness allows psychological avoidance of a significant personal, marital, or occupational conflict.

ETHICAL ISSUES IN EVALUATING DECEPTION

This final section provides an outline of ethical issues to consider during the course of evaluation of syndromes associated with deception. It is vital for practitioners to recognize the far-reaching consequences associated with classifications of response styles. For instance, the determination of either malingering or FD frequently leads to the withdrawal or severe restriction of health care services. In the case of FMS, such determinations could lead to discounted reports of abuse. Conclusions about deception in custody evaluations could lead to substantial changes in child custody arrangements. As such, the accurate evaluation of deception must be a priority and should include:

• A recognition that the application of explanatory models of deception may serve to minimize countertransference and other negative perceptions about the evaluated person. For instance, adaptational and pathogenic explanations may engender greater understanding when compared with a purely criminological model. In this respect, the DSM model is very limited in its conceptualization of malingering (Rogers & Vitacco, 2002).
• The use of standardized methods based on validated detection strategies (see Rogers,

Chapter 2, this volume) is essential to the accurate assessment of syndromes associated with deception. For many syndromes, systematic methods and strategies have yet to be developed. In these cases, clinicians need to be forthright about the limitations of their methods. This is fully consistent with the ethical guidelines set for by the American Psychological Association (2002) in its section 9.02(b) that states "Psychologists use assessment instruments whose validity and reliability have been established for use with members of the population tested. When such validity or reliability has not been established, psychologists describe the strengths and limitations of test results and interpretation" (see also "Specialty Guidelines for Forensic Psychology," for which a draft is available at *www.ap-ls.org*).
• A sophisticated understanding is needed that both genuine and deceptive presentations are very heterogeneous. In addition, deception and response styles are often dimensional and are best understood in gradients (Rogers, Bagby, & Dickens, 1992).
• A full appreciation that (1) malingering and other forms of dissimulation and (2) genuine mental disorders are not mutually exclusive. Clinical evaluation of mental disorders should continue even in the presence of malingering and deception (Vitacco, Rogers, Gabel, & Munizza, 2007).

Following basic guidelines when evaluating malingering and deception provides a greater understanding of deception across diagnostic categories and takes into account varying complexities and motivations related to deceptive responding. Full consideration of explanatory models and how they relate to deceptive practices across settings and individuals allows greater understanding and may ultimately minimize countertransference associated with deception.

4

Malingered Psychosis

PHILLIP J. RESNICK, MD
JAMES L. KNOLL, IV, MD

> Though this be madness, yet there is method in it.
> —SHAKESPEARE, *Hamlet* (Act 2, Scene 2)

The detection of malingered psychosis is a complex endeavor that requires the clinician to take a specialized, systematic approach and to consider multiple collateral sources of data. The degree of difficulty involved will depend on the skill and knowledge of the malingerer. Malingerers with relatively poor understanding of the phenomenology of genuine psychotic symptoms may be readily detected. In contrast, malingerers who possess shrewdness and detailed knowledge of psychosis may deceive even seasoned forensic clinicians. For example, reputed Mafia leader Vincent "The Chin" Gigante was alleged to have deceived "the most respected minds in forensic psychiatry" by malingering, among other things, schizophrenia (Newman, 2002). Mr. Gigante ultimately admitted to deceiving multiple psychiatrists during evaluations of his competency to stand trial from 1990 to 1997. One of the psychiatrists who concluded that Mr. Gigante was malingering observed, "When feigning is a consideration, we must be more critical and less accepting of our impressions when we conduct and interpret an examination than might

otherwise be the case in a typical clinical situation" (J. D. Brodie, personal communication, September 12, 2005).

Many clinicians are reluctant to classify malingering even when presented with compelling data (Yates, Nordquist, & Schultz-Ross, 1996). Reasons for this reluctance include fears of litigation and assault. Although rare, physicians have even been murdered for classifications of malingering by a vengeful examinee (Parker, 1979). In addition, misclassifications of malingering may have disastrous effects on those misclassified, including the denial of needed care, stigma, and legal sanctions (Kropp & Rogers, 1993). Therefore, it is particularly important for clinicians to use a systematized approach to the detection of malingering, as opposed to merely forming a global impression (Kucharski, Ryan, Vogt, & Goodloe, 1998).

The true prevalence of malingering is not known but varies substantially across settings (see Rogers, Chapter 1, this volume) and referral issues. Regarding the latter, Mittenberg, Patton, Canyock, and Condit (2002) found higher frequencies in civil than criminal forensic cases. With reference to malingered psychosis, Cornell and Hawk (1989) found that 8% of defendants referred for pretrial assessments attempted to feign psychosis. Importantly, the accuracy of such prevalence estimates is questionable, because only unsuccessful malingerers (i.e., those detected) are included. Those who successfully fake psychosis are never included in the statistics. The apparently low prevalence of malingering in nonforensic populations may be due to a lack of external motivation coupled with a decreased emphasis on its detection.

Regardless of the true prevalence, the frequency of malingered psychosis is likely to increase in the foreseeable future. The deinstitutionalization of persons with severe mental disorders was often not successful in terms of community resources and treatment. As a result, many persons with chronic disorders have entered the criminal justice system (Knoll, 2006a) or been subjected to homelessness and/or marginal living conditions in the community (Lamb & Weinberger, 2005; Travin & Protter, 1984). Recently, state prisoners with severe mental problems were 200% more likely to be homeless than other inmates in the year before their arrest (James & Glaze, 2006). At the same time, many states are reducing expenditures on community mental health programs and social programming (National Alliance on Mental Illness, 2006). Together, these factors may induce many individuals with mental disorders to grossly exaggerate their symptoms in order to obtain needed treatment or shelter (Rogers, 1992). Persons with schizophrenia have shown the ability to present themselves as either sick or healthy, depending on their goals (Braginsky & Braginsky, 1967).

OVERVIEW OF CONCEPTUAL ISSUES

Conceptualizing Response Styles

During the peak of psychoanalytic influence, malingering was believed to be a form of mental illness. Eissler (1951, p. 252), for example, stated, "It can be rightly claimed that malingering is always a sign of disease often more severe than a neurotic disorder because it concerns an arrest of development at an early phase." Others have found less merit to this view. For example Wertham (1949, p. 49) noted, "There is a strange, entirely unfounded superstition even among psychiatrists that if a man

simulates insanity there must be something mentally wrong with him in the first place. As if a sane man would not grasp at any straw if his life were endangered by the electric chair." At the present time, the criminological model (DSM-IV; American Psychiatric Association, 1994, 2000) model has largely supplanted the earlier pathogenic model of malingering (Rogers, 1997d).

Malingering is described in DSM-IV-TR (American Psychiatric Association, 2000) as a condition that is not attributable to a mental disorder. It is defined as the intentional production of false or grossly exaggerated physical or psychological symptoms motivated by *external* incentives (American Psychiatric Association, 2000). Despite its clear-cut definition, the classification of malingering is fraught with difficulty. Malingering requires differentiation from a factitious disorder, which also involves the intentional production of symptoms. However, in factitious disorders the motivation is to assume the sick role, which can be thought of as an *internal* or psychological incentive.

The term *pseudo malingering* has been used to describe a prodromal phase of genuine psychosis in which the individual allegedly feigns psychosis in a desperate attempt to ward off decompensation into genuine psychosis. A number of early authors (Berney, 1973; Bustamante & Ford, 1977; Folks & Freeman, 1985; Hay, 1983; Pope, Jonas, & Jones, 1982; Schneck, 1970) have suggested that pseudo malingering should be carefully considered before making a classification of malingering. In the novel *The Dilemma* by Leonid Andreyev (1902), a male physician committed murder with a premeditated plan to feign insanity. When the physician later began to have true hallucinations, he realized that he was genuinely psychotic. This story represents a fictionalized account of pseudo malingering.

The idea that malingering may precipitate a genuine disorder is extremely rare in clinical or forensic practice. In a case study, Hay (1983) concluded that simulated schizophrenia was likely a prodromal phase of genuine psychosis. Four of five patients originally thought to have feigned psychosis were subsequently reevaluated years later with genuine schizophrenia. Although they may have pseudo malingered, an alternative explanation is that with time and practice they had improved their ability to malinger psychosis to the point that they were undetectable.

Motivations to Malinger

The motives to malinger psychosis fall into two general categories: (1) to circumvent difficult situations or punishment (i.e., avoiding pain), and (2) to obtain compensation or desired medications (i.e., seeking pleasure). Examples of pain being avoided include criminal prosecutions or military service. Examples of pleasures being sought include medications and unwarranted disability payments.

Criminals may seek to avoid punishment by feigning incompetence to stand trial or insanity at the time of the act. Psychotic disorders may also be malingered in an effort to mitigate sentencing. Malingerers may seek to avoid military duty, undesirable military assignments, or combat. In the civil arena, the motive to malinger psychosis is often to obtain unwarranted financial assistance in such forms as social security disability, veterans' benefits, workers' compensation, or personal injury compensation. More generally, malingerers may seek inpatient admissions to obtain free room and board, to secure social services, or to "pave the way" for future disability claims. In correctional settings, inmates may malinger to do "easier time" (e.g., better jail conditions or prescription drugs).

Malingering may be an adaptive coping strategy in certain circumstances. According to the DSM-IV-TR, "Under some circumstances, malingering may represent adaptive behavior—for example, feigning illness while a captive of the enemy during wartime" (American Psychiatric Association, 2000, p. 739). For example, a 14-year-old girl feigned hallucinations in order to be hospitalized so that she could escape from sexual harassment by her mother's new boyfriend (Greenfeld, 1987). She had previously observed an older cousin's genuine psychosis. When her family situation became intolerably chaotic, she was institutionalized on the basis of a feigned psychosis. She eventually acknowledged to hospital staff that she had faked her psychotic symptoms.

RESEARCH ON MALINGERED PSYCHOSIS

If sanity and insanity exist, how shall we know them?
—ROSENHAN (1973)

The research literature on detecting malingered psychosis without standardized methods remains sparse. Little research has examined the ability of clinicians to accurately detect malingered psychosis in their daily practice. In contrast, extensive research has documented the usefulness of psychological measures for detecting malingered psychosis. Examples of specialized measures include the Structured Interview of Reported Symptoms (SIRS; Rogers, Bagby, & Dickens, 1992; see Rogers, Chapter 18, this volume), and the Miller Forensic Assessment of Symptoms Test (M-FAST; Miller, 2001; see Smith, Chapter 19, this volume). General tests also have effective validity scales, including the Minnesota Multiphasic Personality Inventory (MMPI-2; see Greene, Chapter 10, this volume) and the Personality Assessment Inventory (PAI; see Sellbom & Bagley, Chapter 11, this volume). As noted, these instruments are addressed in other chapters. This chapter investigates potential detection strategies that can be used by skilled practitioners.

Rosenhan's (1973) classic study evaluated eight pseudo patients who feigned very atypical auditory hallucinations. When admitted to psychiatric hospitals, they ceased simulating any psychotic symptoms, yet all were diagnosed with schizophrenia and remained hospitalized from 9 to 52 days. Despite its methodological limitations, this study has been used to question clinicians' ability to detect feigned psychosis.

Several studies have examined clinical differences between genuine patients and those simulating severe disorders. For example, Sherman, Trief, and Strafkin (1975) instructed a group of Veterans Administration day-care psychiatric patients to present themselves as (1) severely mentally ill and (2) mentally healthy. Not surprisingly, the more disturbed patients manifested greater differences between the two interviews. In the "malingered" condition, patients more frequently claimed recurrent senseless thoughts, hallucinated noises, and suicidal ideas. The primary differences involved their reported symptoms rather than their interview behavior. Using a known-groups comparison, Cornell and Hawk (1989) studied the characteristics of 39 criminal defendants classified with malingered psychosis by experienced forensic psychologists. Malingerers were more likely to claim bogus symptoms, suicidal ideas, visual hallucinations, and memory problems. Furthermore, their symptoms did not cluster into any known diagnostic entities. With reference to Chapter 2 in this volume, these studies suggest that rare symptoms and indiscriminant symptom endorsement are potentially effective detection strategies.

Anderson, Trethowan and Kenna (1959) studied *vorbeirden* (i.e., giving an approximate answer), which is a core symptom of the Ganser syndrome. Simulators were compared with normal controls and two comparison groups: (1) patients with organic dementia and (2) patients with pseudo dementia (primary diagnosis of hysteria with conversion symptoms). The simulators most often chose to feign depression or paranoid disorders; their efforts did not closely resemble well-defined mental disorders. Two feigned mental retardation by maintaining an air of obtuseness, vagueness, and poverty of content. The simulators experienced difficulty, however, in suppressing correct answers to questions. This difficulty was attributed to a "pull of reality" that they felt throughout the interviews. Fatigue or difficulty sustaining the response style apparently caused simulators to become increasingly normal during the prolonged interviews.

Many simulators in the Anderson and colleagues (1959) study gave approximate answers because they believed they should not give the right answers. In an effort to avoid the impression of spuriousness, they gave nearly correct answers in contrast to the more obvious errors by patients with actual dementia. This pattern corresponds to the "magnitude of error" that has been mostly researched with reference to feigned cognitive impairment (see Chapter 2, this volume). Patients with genuine organic dementia demonstrated substantial perseveration (e.g., giving the same response to sequential questions). In contrast, malingerers demonstrated no significant perseveration. The authors concluded that the perseveration could be used to *rule out* feigned organic impairment. The fact that the simulators gave approximate answers lends indirect support to the theory that the Ganser syndrome is a form of malingering.

Other researchers have used purported deficits on cognitive measures to evaluate feigned psychosis. For example, Powell (1991) compared 40 mental health facility employees instructed to malinger schizophrenia with 40 inpatients with genuine schizophrenia. Using the Mini-Mental Status Examination (MMSE; Folstein, Folstein, & McHugh, 1975), malingerers were significantly more likely than patients with genuine schizophrenia to give one or more approximate answers on the MMSE. In addition, malingerers reported a higher occurrence of visual hallucinations, particularly with dramatic and atypical content (e.g., not ordinary human beings). Finally, the malingerers more often called attention to their delusions.

Pollock (1998) compared three groups of prisoners: genuinely psychotic, psychotic simulators, and malingerers with past psychotic histories. A detailed inquiry of 40 questions was made about hallucinations. Prisoners faking psychosis are more likely to have the following characteristics:

- *Presentation:* vague and unintelligible; few words; lack of accent; continuous hallucinations; more than an hour in duration
- *Impairment:* uncontrollable, unbearable
- *Command hallucinations:* greater frequency, more often obeyed, more often related to a criminal offense
- *Relative absence of other psychotic symptoms:* delusions, other sensory hallucinations, and thought broadcasting

Previously psychotic prisoners who faked psychosis were more likely to resemble prisoners with genuine psychosis (Pollock, 1998). It is not surprising that they would be harder to detect because they could draw on their own prior psychotic experience rather than rely on media caricatures of mentally disordered persons. This study supported several hypotheses put forth about malingered hallucinations in earlier editions of this book.

The next section focuses on differences between genuine and feigned hallucinations. Hallucinations and other perceptual disturbances provide a unique opportunity to examine the genuineness of reported psychotic disorders.

Characteristics of Feigned Hallucinations

Persons presenting with atypical hallucinations should be questioned about them in great detail. Before discussing current hallucinations and their effects on present functioning, the person should be asked to describe past hallucinations and their responses to them. Specifically, patients should be questioned about content, vividness, and other characteristics of the hallucinations (Seigel & West, 1975). Table 4.1 gives a list of potential topics of clinical inquiry

TABLE 4.1. Topics of Inquiry for Suspect Auditory Hallucinations

Source	Inside or outside head, above or behind, heard in one or both ears
Gender	Male or female
Age	Child or adult
Vocal characteristics	Single or multiple voices; clear, vague, or inaudible; loudness
Frequency/timing	Continuous or intermittent, time of day, during sleep
Familiarity	Known or unknown person, familiar or unfamiliar
Type of language	Commands, stilted language, speaking in second or third person
Response	Degree of insight, ability to disregard, and emotional response; converses with them
Associated characteristics	Hallucinations in other sensory modalities or delusions Other psychotic symptoms

when malingered auditory hallucinations are suspected.

The detection of malingered disorders can be conceptualized as an advanced clinical skill, because clinicians must possess a detailed knowledge about the phenomenology of genuine psychiatric symptoms. In the case of malingered psychosis, a thorough understanding of how genuine psychotic symptoms present themselves is the clinician's greatest asset in recognizing simulated hallucinations.

Common characteristics of genuine hallucinations are:

- *Co-occurrence.* Hallucinations are usually (88%) associated with delusions (Lewinsohn, 1970; Pollock, 1998).
- *Frequency.* Genuine hallucinations are much more likely to be intermittent than continuous (Goodwin, Anderson, & Rosenthal, 1971; Nayani & David, 1996; Pollack, 1998).
- *Rare symptoms.* Olfactory and tactile hallucinations are uncommon except when associated with general medical causes or late-onset schizophrenia (onset after age 45; see Pearlson et al., 1989).
- *Response to treatment.* Immediate improvement is unlikely; the median number of days for hallucinations to clear after the first initiation of antipsychotic medication is 27 (Gundez-Bruce et al., 2005).

Auditory Hallucinations

Goodwin and colleagues (1971) conducted the classic study of genuine phenomenology using 116 hallucinating patients. Most patients heard voices of both genders (75%) and *both* familiar and unfamiliar voices (88%), providing helpful data on the characteristics of genuine hallucinations. In contrast, auditory hallucinations are rarely vague (7%) or inaudible; rather, the message is usually clear.

Early research (e.g., Goodwin et al., 1971) suggested that genuine hallucinations were most often perceived as originating outside of the head. However, Junginger and Frame (1985) reported that only 50% of patients with schizophrenia reported auditory hallucinations as originating from outside of the head. Recent research evidence (Copoloy, Trauer, & Mackinnon, 2004) suggests that many psychotic patients hear voices both internally and externally. The location of hallucinations should not be used to determine their genuineness. One possibility is that persons with chronic schizophrenia may have gained sufficient insight to attribute hallucinated voices to an internal source.

Baethge and colleagues (2005) studied hallucinations in 4,972 psychiatrically hospitalized patients. The prevalence of hallucinations by disorder at admission was: schizophrenia, 61.1%; bipolar mixed, 22.9%; bipolar manic, 11.2%; bipolar depressed, 10.5%; and unipolar depressed, 5.9%. Across all diagnoses, hallucinations, particularly olfactory, were significantly associated with delusions.

Clinicians should be aware that the content of auditory hallucinations may vary with the individual's culture. For example, Kent and Wahass (1996) found that the auditory hallucinations of Saudi patients were of a religious and superstitious nature, whereas instructional themes and running commentary were common in British patients.

Patients may have different perceptions of their hallucinations. One common theme is to view hallucinated voices as omnipotent and omniscient (Chadwick & Birchwood, 1994; Pollock, 1998). Evidence that voices are omniscient is based on the voices knowing that person's thoughts and being able to predict the person's future. In addition, hallucinated voices can be perceived as benevolent or malevolent (Chadwick & Birchwood, 1994). Patients commonly said that evil commands were evidence that the voice was bad and kind, protective words were evidence that the voice was good. Malevolent voices evoke negative emotions (anger, fear, depression, or anxiety). Patients often respond by arguing, shouting, noncompliance, and avoidance of cues that trigger voices. Benevolent voices usually provoke positive emotions (amusement, reassurance, calm, or happiness). Patients often respond to benevolent voices by elective listening, willing compliance, and doing things to bring on the voices.

Most persons with genuine auditory hallucinations (81%) report that they are worried or upset by their hallucinations (Carter, Mackinnon, & Copoloy, 1996; Pollock, 1998). The major themes of auditory hallucinations in schizophrenia are usually persecutory or instructive (Small, Small, & Andersen, 1966). The voices are often threatening, obscene, accusatory, or insulting (Sadock & Sadock, 2003). Schizophrenic hallucinations tend to consist of ego-dystonic, derogatory comments about the patient or the activities of others (Goodwin et al., 1971; Leudar, Thomas, McNally, & Glinski, 1997; Oulis, Mavreas, Mamounas, & Stefanis, 1995). Genuine hallucinated questions tend to be chastising rather than simply information seeking. The negative content may also focus on sexuality. Nayani and David (1996) found that hallucinations may be experienced as derogatory, with women described as immoral (e.g., "slut") and men as gay (e.g., "queer"). Such voices are not likely to be faked because the content is often stigmatizing.

Certain hallucinations are rare in patients with schizophrenia but are observed in those with brain pathology. For example, hallucinations of music are rare with psychotic disorders but not organic pathology (Fischer, Marchie, & Norris, 2004). If the origin is due to brain disease, insight is more common than if the hallucination is the result of a mental disorder (Berrios, 1991).

Command auditory hallucinations are easy to fabricate and may be used to excuse behavior (e.g., a bogus insanity defense). However, command hallucinations are common in genuine patients with Axis I disorders. Hellerstein, Frosch, and Koenigsberg (1987) found in a retrospective chart review that 38.4% of patients with auditory hallucinations reported hearing commands. Approximately one-half of patients with mood disorders (Goodwin et al., 1971), and schizophrenia (Zisook, Byrd, Kuck, & Jeste, 1995) reported experiencing command hallucinations. Command hallucinations occurred in 30% (Goodwin et al., 1971) to 40% (Mott, Small, & Andersen, 1965) of persons with alcoholic withdrawal hallucinosis.

Genuine patients with command hallucinations often exhibit other psychotic symptoms, such as noncommand hallucinations (85%) and delusions (75%; see Thompson, Stuart, & Holden, 1992). Furthermore, compliance with command hallucinations is often the combined effect of psychological variables (e.g., beliefs about the voices and coexisting delusions) that mediate the process (Braham, Trower, & Birchwood, 2004). Therefore, someone who claims an isolated command hallucination in the absence of other psychotic symptoms should be evaluated closely (Pollock, 1998). Compliance with command hallucinations per se does not distinguish between genuine and feigned symptoms.

Research has produced conflicting data on the percentage of patients who obey command hallucinations. Junginger (1990) reported that 39% of patients with command hallucinations obeyed them. Kasper, Rogers, and Adams (1996) found that 84% of nonforensic psychotic inpatients with command hallucinations had obeyed them within the preceding 30 days. Rogers, Gillis, Turner, and Frise-Smith (1990) found that 44% of a forensic population with command hallucinations reported that they frequently responded with unquestioning obedience. McNeil, Eisner, and Binder (2000) found that 30% of psychiatric inpatients reported having had command hallucinations to harm others during the previous year, yet only 22% reported that they had complied with such commands. Compliance with *dangerous* commands is less likely (Junginger, 1995; Kasper et al., 1996). Pollock (1998) found that prisoners instructed to malinger mental illness were far more likely than genuinely psychotic prisoners to allege command hallucinations and to claim that they had to obey them. In a review of the research over the past decade, Braham and colleagues (2004) concluded that the weight of the evidence suggests that some individuals who hear commands will in fact act on them. However, the strength of the link between commands and actions is unclear at the present time.

Persons suffering from genuine schizophrenia typically develop a variety of coping strategies to deal with their hallucinations. Genuine hallucinations of schizophrenia tend to diminish when patients are involved in activities (Falloon & Talbot, 1981; Goodwin et al., 1971). Carter and colleagues (1996) found that the majority (66%) of patients with auditory hallucinations reported that they had ways of managing their voices; many (69%) described at least some success using one or more strategies. Coping strategies may involve engaging in activities (e.g., working, listening to a personal stereo, watching TV), changes in posture (e.g., lying down, walking), seeking out interpersonal contact, or taking medications (Falloon & Talbot, 1981; Kanas & Barr, 1984). Patients with malevolent voices are likely to have developed a strategy, whereas those with benevolent voices may not be motivated to reduce their voices. Therefore, persons suspected of malingered auditory hallucinations, especially with negative content, should be asked what they do to make the voices go away or diminish in intensity.

One potentially adaptive response is to engage in an internal dialogue with their hallucinations. Leudar and colleagues (1997) found that many patients cope with chronic hallucinations by incorporating them into their daily lives as a kind of internal advisor. They considered their advice in the context of the moment. Interestingly, sometimes patients reported that their hallucinated voices would insist on certain actions after the patient refused to carry them out. They would rephrase their requests, speak louder, or curse the patient for being noncompliant. In contrast, malingerers are more likely to claim that they were compelled to obey commands without further discussion.

Nearly all patients (98%) reported experiencing significant adverse effects from their hallucinations (Miller, O'Connor, & DiPasquale, 1993), such as difficulty holding a job, emotional distress, and feeling threatened. However, approximately one-half of patients also reported some positive effects of their hallucinations, such as companionship, relaxation, and more ease in receiving disability benefits. Therefore, reported effects of hallucinations appear unhelpful for discriminating between genuine and malingered hallucinations.

An important consideration is what factors intensify hallucinations. Most persons (80%) with genuine hallucinations reported that being alone worsened their hallucinations (Nayani & David, 1996). Hallucinated voices were also made worse by listening to the radio and watching television (Leudar et al., 1997). TV news programs were particularly hallucinogenic.

Genuine auditory hallucinations are characterized by a wide range of intensity, from whispers to shouting. This range is sometimes experienced within the same patient; however, the cadence of the speech is typically normal. In contrast, malingerers may report auditory hallucinations that consist of stilted or implausible language (Pollock, 1998). For example, a malingerer charged with attempted rape alleged that voices said, "Go commit a sex offense." Malingerers may also allege implausible or far-fetched commands, such as a bank robber who alleged that voices kept screaming, "Stick up, stick up, stick up!" Both examples contain language that is very questionable for genuine hallucinations, in addition to providing "psychotic justification" for an illegal act.

Visual Hallucinations

The incidence of visual hallucinations in psychotic individuals varies markedly, from 24% (Mott et al., 1965) to 30% (Kanas & Barr, 1984) to 54.4% (Duncan, 1995) of patients with symptoms of active schizophrenia. Genuine visual hallucinations are usually of normal-sized people and are seen in color (Goodwin et al., 1971). On rare occasions, genuine visual hallucinations of small people ("Lilliputian hallucinations") may be associated with (1) alcohol use and organic disease (Cohen, Alfonso, & Haque, 1994) or (2) toxic psychosis (Lewis, 1961) such as anticholinergic toxicity (Assad, 1990) In contrast, persons with schizophrenia rarely see Lilliputian hallucinations (Leroy, 1922).

Other characteristics of visual hallucinations must be considered. Genuine visual hallucinations do not typically change if the eyes are closed or open. In contrast, drug-induced hallucinations are more readily seen with the eyes closed or in darkened surroundings (Assad & Shapiro, 1986). Unformed hallucinations, such as flashes of light, shadows, or moving objects, are typically associated with neurological disease and substance use (Cummings & Miller, 1987; Mitchell & Vierkant, 1991). Visual hallucinations occurring in persons over age 60 are suggestive of eye pathology, particularly cataracts (Beck & Harris, 1994).

Dramatic or atypical visual hallucinations should definitely arouse suspicions of malingering (Powell, 1991). For example, the author (P. J. R.) saw a defendant charged with bank robbery was evaluated for competence to stand trial. During the evaluation, he calmly reported experiencing visual hallucinations consisting of a "thirty foot tall, red giant smashing down the walls" of the interview room. When he was asked further detailed questions about his hallucinations, he frequently replied, "I don't know." He subsequently admitted to malingering.

Distinctive Hallucinations

Alcoholic hallucinosis following the cessation or reduction of alcohol intake often involves quite vivid hallucinations. Auditory hallucinations are most common, but the likelihood of noise, music, or unintelligible voices is greater than with schizophrenia. The auditory hallucinations of an alcohol-induced psychotic disorder are usually maligning, reproachful, or threatening and generally last a week or less (Sadock & Sadock, 2003). Persons with alcohol-induced hallucinations discuss them more easily than do those with hallucinations due to schizophrenia (Alpert & Silvers, 1970). Mott and colleagues (1965) found that persons hospitalized due to alcohol misuse had an 84% prevalence of hallucinations (75% auditory and 70% visual). The major themes of the alcoholic auditory hallucinations were spirituality, persecution, and instructions concerning the management of everyday affairs. The majority of patients thought the hallucinations were real at the time but later recognized their unreality. Whereas alcoholics are typically frightened by their hallucinations, persons with schizophrenia often become more comfortable with them over the course of their disorder.

Hallucinations due to a general medical or neurological disorder can often be distinguished

from schizophrenia due to the higher prevalence of prominent visual hallucinations and the lower prevalence of thought disorder, bizarre behavior, negative symptoms, and rapid speech (Cornelius et al., 1991). Tactile hallucinations are frequently seen in cocaine-induced psychosis (e.g., "cocaine bugs") and involve sensations of cutaneous or subcutaneous irritation (Ellinwood, 1972), sometimes leading the individual to excoriate the skin with excessive scratching (Sadock & Sadock, 2003). Unlike persons with schizophrenia, individuals with cocaine-induced psychosis do not generally report delusions of identity, grandiosity, or beliefs that their families are imposters (i.e., Capgras syndrome; Mitchell & Vierkant, 1991).

Certain neurological syndromes can produce striking and relatively stereotyped complex visual hallucinations that often involve animals and human figures in bright colors and dramatic settings. The most common causes of complex visual hallucinations are epileptic disorders, brain stem lesions, and visual pathway lesions (Manford & Andermann, 1998). Peduncular hallucinosis is a syndrome of hallucinations and neurological symptoms due to a brain stem lesion. In this rare disorder, patients were unable to discriminate their hallucinations from reality (Benke, 2006).

Cenesthetic hallucinations are unfounded sensations of altered states in bodily organs. For example, a psychotic patient may report a pushing sensation in the blood vessels or a cutting sensation in the bone marrow (Sadock & Sadock, 2003). The bizarre and obscure nature of cenesthetic hallucinations make them an unlikely choice for a malingerer to feign.

Delusions

Genuine delusions vary in content, theme, degree of systemization, and relevance to the person's life. Most delusions involve the following general themes (Spitzer, 1992): disease (somatic delusions), grandiosity, jealousy, love (erotomania), persecution, religion, and being possessed. Persecutory delusions are more likely to be acted on than other types of delusions (Wessely et al., 1993). Generally, delusional systems will reflect the intelligence level of the individual in terms of complexity and sophistication. Delusions of nihilism, poverty, disease, and guilt are commonly seen in depression. Higher levels of psychomotor retardation, guilt, feelings of worthlessness, and increased suicidal ideation and intent are found more commonly in psychotic as compared with nonpsychotic depression (Thakur, Hays, Ranga, & Krishnan, 1999). Delusions of technical content (e.g., computer chips, telephones, telepathy) occur seven times more frequently in men than women (Kraus, 1994).

Malingerers may claim the sudden onset or disappearance of a delusion. In reality, systematized delusions usually take weeks to develop and much longer to disappear. The median length of time for delusions to fully clear after the first initiation of antipsychotic medication is 73 days (Gundez-Bruce et al., 2005). Typically, the delusion will become somewhat less relevant, and the individual will gradually relinquish its importance over time after adequate treatment (Sachs, Carpenter, & Strauss, 1974). Feigned delusions are generally persecutory, occasionally grandiose, but seldom (except in depression) self-deprecatory (Davidson, 1952a; East, 1927).

Most individuals with schizophrenia and other psychotic disorders who demonstrate disordered speech also show strange nonverbal behavior and odd beliefs (Harrow et al., 2003). For genuine delusions, more bizarre content is often associated with more disorganized thinking. Therefore, when suspect delusions are alleged, the clinician should carefully consider the associated behavior and speech patterns. Table 4.2 gives a list of suspect hallucinations and delusions.

With genuine delusions, the individual's behavior often conforms to the content of the delusions. For example, Russell Weston made a deadly assault on the capital building in Washington, DC. His delusional history was consistent with this behavior; several years before, he had approached Central Intelligence Agency headquarters and voiced the same delusional concerns. Reports of persecutory delusions without any corresponding paranoid behaviors should arouse the clinician's suspicion of malingering. One exception to this principle is the person with long-standing schizophrenia who has grown accustomed to his delusions and may no longer behave in a corresponding manner. Harrow and colleagues (2004) found that patients with schizophrenia and affective disorders who had a high emotional commitment to their delusions showed significantly poorer work functioning and were significantly more likely to be hospitalized. Thus persons who vigorously claim a firm conviction of

TABLE 4.2. Atypical Hallucinations and Delusions

Atypical hallucinations
- Continuous
- Vague, inaudible
- Not associated with delusions
- Stilted language
- No strategies to diminish malevolent voices
- Non-context-dependent
- Unbearably distressing
- Unpredictable
- All commands obeyed
- Visual in black and white
- Visual alone in schizophrenia

Atypical delusions
- Abrupt onset or termination
- Conduct inconsistent with delusions
- Bizarre content without disorganization
- Eagerness to discuss
- High conviction without adverse effects on work or community functioning

their delusion should be carefully assessed for work performance and community functioning.

The delusions seen with Alzheimer's dementia frequently involve paranoid beliefs about caregivers stealing or being deceitful (Trabucchi & Bianchetti, 1996). In a large study of 771 patients with Alzheimer's disease, Mizrahi and Starkstein (2006) found delusions in one-third and hallucinations in approximately 7%. Most patients with hallucinations also had delusions. Delusions were significantly associated with depression, anosognosia (unawareness of illness), overt aggression, and agitation.

Malingered Mutism

Mutism and mental illness have had a long-standing historical relationship to the issue of competence to stand trial (Daniel & Resnick, 1987). During the early colonial period, persons who refused to enter a plea were considered to be either "mute by malice" or mute by "visitation of God." If a defendant remained mute and did not put forth a plea, he was "pressed" for a plea by gradually increasing poundage placed on his chest. Malingered mutism may occur as a solitary symptom or as part of a malingered psychosis. It is a difficult task to give up speech for a lengthy period, and it is not usually attempted unless the individual is facing a severe penalty or anticipating a large reward (Davidson, 1952b).

Genuine mutism may occur in patients with or without catatonia. Mutism with catatonic stupor is recognized by the presence of posturing, negativism, automatic obedience, waxy flexibility, and other features typical of schizophrenia. For unclear reasons, the catatonic type of schizophrenia has become rare in the United States and Europe over the past several decades (Sadock & Sadock, 2003). Mutism without catatonia may be seen in patients with paranoid schizophrenia who are unwilling to communicate due to paranoid distrust. Mutism may also be seen in patients with chronic schizophrenia who have been isolated in long-term settings. Corticosteroids (Kalambokis, Konitsiotis, Pappas, & Tsianos, 2006) and antihypertensive agents (Altshuler et al., 1986) have been described as producing mutism without catatonia.

Catatonic mutism can also occur in severe depression, mania, and brief dissociative states. Medical etiologies include neurological disease, such as head injury, herpes encephalitis, tertiary syphilis, frontal lobe lesions, PCP use, postictal states, akinetic mutism, and Wernicke's encephalopathy (Altshuler et al., 1986). It is extremely common for mutism due to stroke to produce other neurological impairments. Only one case report of stroke-induced mutism without other neurological findings has been reported in the literature (Evyapan, 2006).

Because mutism and/or catatonia are difficult states to simulate for long periods, observation of the suspected malingerer should ideally take place in an inpatient setting. Clinicians should consider a comprehensive evaluation including the following: neurological exam, repeat interviews, observation at unsuspected times for communicative speech with peers, handwriting samples, and collateral nursing documentation. Feigned mutism may sometimes be exposed by suddenly arousing the individual from a deep sleep and immediately asking a simple question. A malingerer may reflexively reply before remembering to continue the feigned mutism (Davidson, 1952a; East, 1927).

Daniel and Resnick (1987) reported the case of a defendant who remained mute for 10 months in an effort to malinger incompetence to stand trial. The 53-year-old defendant was charged with raping and murdering an 11-year-old girl. The day after the crime, he was admitted voluntarily to a state hospital and complained of hearing voices. He stopped talking completely when told he was charged with murder. In his room, he would lay curled up and would not respond to attending clinicians. When he did not know he was being observed, he appeared to initiate conversations with fellow patients. No signs of catatonia or depression were observed. A thorough neurological workup and laboratory studies were negative. With the permission of the defendant and his attorney, a sodium amobarbital interview was conducted. The defendant described the offense and spoke for about 90 minutes but did not utter a word afterward. A careful review of collateral data revealed a pattern of voluntary admission to psychiatric hospitals after several prior offenses, with the charges against him being dismissed.

CLINICAL INDICATORS OF MALINGERED PSYCHOSIS

The best liar is he who makes the smallest amount of lying go the longest way.

—SAMUEL BAUTLER

Malingerers may be detected when they have inadequate or incomplete knowledge of the disorders they are faking. Indeed, malingerers are like actors who can only portray a role as best they understand it (Ossipov, 1944). However, they often overact their parts (Wachpress, Berenberg, & Jacobson, 1953) or mistakenly believe that the more bizarre their behavior, the more convincing they will be. Conversely, "successful" malingerers are more likely to endorse a fewer number of symptoms and to avoid endorsing overly bizarre or unusual symptoms (Lowensteien, 2001). Jones and Llewellyn (1917, p. 80) have observed that the malingerer "sees less than the blind, he hears less than the deaf, and he is more lame than the paralyzed. Determined that his insanity shall not lack multiple and obvious signs, he, so to speak, crowds the canvas, piles symptom upon symptom and so outstrips madness itself, attaining to a but clumsy caricature of his assumed role."

Malingerers are more likely to volunteer symptoms of their illness, in contrast to genuine

patients with schizophrenia who are often reluctant to discuss them (Powell, 1991; Ritson &
Forest, 1970). For example, one malingerer
proffered in a forensic evaluation that he was an
"insane lunatic" when he killed his parents. He
claimed the hallucinations "told me to kill in my
demented state." A malingerer may also attempt
to take control of the interview and behave in
an intimidating or hostile manner. The clinician
should avoid the temptation to prematurely terminate the interview and may consider having
security personnel present in the exam room.

As an interesting stratagem, a malingerer may
even accuse the clinician of suggesting that he or
she is faking. However, such accusations are
rarely seen in genuinely psychotic individuals.

The presence of antisocial personality disorder (APD) should not be used as evidence
of malingering. Although the DSM-IV-TR
(American Psychiatric Association, 2000) states
that the mere presence of APD should arouse
suspicions of malingering, studies have failed to
show this relationship. The presence of psychopathic traits has been associated with malingering in one study (Edens, Buffington, & Tomicic,
2000); however, most persons with APD do not
warrant the classification of psychopathy. Studies (Poythress, Edens, & Watkins, 2001; Rogers
& Cruise, 2000) have suggested that antisocial
or psychopathic persons are no more adept than
others at malingering. These data questioned
the usefulness of APD as a "risk factor" for malingering in the DSM (see Rogers, Chapter 2,
this volume).

Malingerers with feigned psychotic symptoms often simulate cognitive impairment as
well (Bash & Alpert, 1980; Lowensteien, 2001;
Powell, 1991; Schretlen, 1988). These malingerers give a greater number of evasive answers
than patients with genuine schizophrenia (Powell, 1991). Malingerers may also repeat questions or answer questions slowly to give themselves time to think about how to successfully
deceive the evaluator. Malingerers are more
likely to give vague or hedging answers to
straightforward questions. For example, when
asked whether an alleged voice was male or female, one malingerer replied "It was *probably*
a man's voice." Feigned cognitive impairment
is addressed by Bender (Chapter 5), Sweet,
Condit, and Nelson (Chapter 13), and Berry
and Schipper (Chapter 14) in this volume.

Malingerers have more difficulty imitating
the form and process of psychotic thinking than

the content of a bogus delusion (Sherman et
al., 1975). Symptoms of formal thought disorders, such as derailment, neologisms, loose associations, and word salad, are rarely simulated. If the malingerer is asked to repeat an
idea, he may do it exactly, whereas the genuine
patient with schizophrenia will often become
tangential. Regarding speech, malingerers rarely
show perseveration, which is more likely to
suggest brain pathology or, conversely, a well-
prepared malingerer.

Malingerers are unlikely to imitate the subtle
signs of schizophrenia, such as negative symptoms that include flat affect, alogia, avolition,
and impaired interactions. In contrast, they find
the positive symptoms (e.g., hallucinations,
delusions) easier to feign because of their more
obvious nature. Malingerers' alleged symptoms
may not fit into any known diagnostic category,
instead representing symptoms from various
disorders. Therefore, malingering should always be considered before making a diagnosis
of "psychosis not otherwise specified." Table
4.3 lists a number of clinical factors suggestive
of malingering.

Persons with genuine schizophrenia may also
malinger additional symptoms to avoid criminal responsibility or seek an increase in disability compensation. For example, a man with
genuine schizophrenia in partial remission
killed his mother because she would not give
him money to purchase cocaine. He then alleged that the murder was due to a command

---

**TABLE 4.3. Interview-Based Characteristics
Suggestive of Malingering**

- Absence of active or subtle signs of psychosis
- Marked inconsistencies, contradictions
- Unlikely psychiatric symptoms (see also Chapter 2)
  - Contradictory symptoms
  - Overly dramatic symptom presentation
  - Rare symptoms and improbable symptoms
- Evasiveness or noncooperation in discussing psychotic symptoms
  - Excessively guarded or hesitant
  - Frequently repeats questions
  - Frequently replies, "I don't know" to simple questions
  - Hostile, intimidating; seeks to control interview or refuses to participate

hallucination from God. Such cases are very difficult to accurately assess for several reasons. First, clinicians usually have a lower index of suspicion because of the individual's documented history of genuine psychotic symptoms. Second, these malingerers are able to draw on their own previous experience of psychotic symptoms and observations of other patients while in a psychiatric hospital. In essence, they know what questions to expect from the clinician and may be better equipped to successfully provide deceptive answers. Third, there is an inherent tendency among some clinicians toward a dichotomous categorization of patients into either "mad" or "bad." Therefore, it is important that clinicians not conceptualize malingering and genuine psychosis as an "either–or" situation (Rogers, Sewell, & Goldstein, 1994).

The following case illustrates clinical indicators of feigned psychosis. Mr. B was a 36-year-old man charged with murder and referred for an evaluation of a possible insanity defense. Mr. B reported that he had had his brother killed based on Mr. B's beliefs that his brother had betrayed the family and violated his honor. On evaluation, Mr. B was found to have no psychiatric history, no unusual beliefs about his brother, and nothing that suggested insanity at the time of his offense. After being informed of these findings, Mr. B's attorney referred him for a second forensic evaluation. Mr. B told the second evaluator "Some people who wanted to destroy the family business replaced my brother with a robot." Mr. B claimed to believe that "springs and wires would pop out" when his brother was destroyed. The second expert accepted the robot story at face value. Mr. B went on to tell the same robot story to a third expert. Interviews with family members revealed that the defendant had never told them that his brother had been replaced by a robot. Upon arrest, Mr. B denied any involvement in his brother's killing and made no mention of the robot story. The third expert concluded that Mr. B was malingering. Mr. B showed the following clinical indicators of malingering: (1) absence of past psychotic symptoms, (2) an atypical delusion, (3) nonpsychotic alternative motives of anger and greed, (4) absence of behavior consistent with his alleged delusion, (5) contradictions in his story, (6) absence of any negative symptoms of schizophrenia, and (7) psychiatric symptoms that fit no known diagnostic entity.

CLINICAL INTERVIEW APPROACH

Do you smile at my childish deception?
—Clara Schumann

Good interviewing technique is critical to the accurate detection of malingering. When malingering is suspected, the clinician should refrain from showing suspicion and proceed in conducting an objective evaluation. An annoyed or incredulous response is likely to result in the client becoming more defensive, thus decreasing the ability of the clinician to evaluate malingering (Sadock & Sadock, 2003). It is important to begin the evaluation by asking open-ended questions that will allow clients to report symptoms in their own words. In the initial stage, inquiries about symptoms should be carefully phrased to avoid leading questions that will give clues to the nature of genuine psychotic symptoms. Later in the interview, the clinician can proceed to more detailed questions of specific symptoms, as discussed later. The clinician should also attempt to ascertain whether the client has ever had the opportunity to observe persons with psychosis (e.g., during employment or in prior hospitalizations).

The review of collateral data is most helpful when conducted prior to the interview. The clinician should consider any information that will assist in supporting or refuting the alleged symptoms, such as prior treatment records, insurance records, police reports, and interviews with close friends or family members. The client interview may be prolonged, as fatigue may diminish a malingerer's ability to maintain feigned symptoms (Anderson et al., 1959). In very difficult cases, inpatient assessment should be considered, because feigned psychotic symptoms are extremely difficult to maintain 24 hours a day (Broughton & Chesterman, 2001).

Clinicians should be on watch for individuals who endorse *rare* or *improbable* symptoms (see Rogers, Chapter 2, this volume). Improbable symptoms are almost never reported, even in severely disturbed patients (Thompson, LeBourgeois, & Black, 2004). Malingerers may be asked about improbable symptoms to see if they will endorse them. For example, "Do you ever have periods when you experience upside-down vision?" Some clinical strategies are controversial but may assist the clinician in very difficult cases. For example, one detection strategy is to mention, within earshot of the suspected malingerer, some easily imitated symptom that is not present. The rapid endorsement of that symptom would suggest malingering. Another strategy is to ask clients a relevant question at the moment that they have "let down their guard," such as during a break or an otherwise relaxed moment during the evaluation. This strategy was used in the Gigante case to conclude that he was malingering a severe dementia. In addition to alleging symptoms of schizophrenia, Gigante also claimed to be disoriented to time. During a break in the exam, Gigante was asked in an offhand manner if he knew what time it was. Without hesitation, Gigante reflexively responded with the correct time (J. D. Brodie, personal communication, September 12, 2005).

Inconsistencies

Lying is like alcoholism. You are always recovering.
—STEVEN SODERBERGH

The clinician should pay close attention to evidence of inconsistency or contradiction in evaluating a suspected malingerer. Inconsistencies may be classified as either internal or external to the individual's presentation. Table 4.4 lists examples of important internal and external inconsistencies.

Internal inconsistencies may exist when malingerers report severe symptoms, such as mental confusion or memory loss, but clearly articulate multiple examples of confusion or memory loss. Another type of internal inconsistency occurs when malingerers give markedly

TABLE 4.4. Inconsistencies Often Observed in Malingerers

1. *Internal*
- In person's own report of symptoms: a clear and articulate explanation of being confused
- In person's own reported history: markedly conflicting versions

2. *External*
- Between person's reported and observed symptoms
- Between person's reported level of functioning and observed level of functioning
- Between person's reported symptoms and the nature of genuine symptoms
- Between person's reported symptoms and psychological testing

conflicting versions of their own history to the same evaluator. External inconsistencies are seen in marked discrepancies between what the subject reports and the symptoms that are observed. For example, a malingerer may allege that he is having active auditory and visual hallucinations yet show no evidence of being distracted.

External inconsistencies can occur between the clients' reported level of functioning and observations of their level of functioning by others. For example, a malingerer may behave in a disorganized or confused manner around the psychiatrist yet play excellent chess with other inpatients. As noted, inconsistencies can arise between reported symptoms and how genuine symptoms actually manifest themselves. For example, a malingerer may report seeing visual hallucinations in black and white, whereas genuine visual hallucinations are typically seen in color.

CLINICAL APPLICATIONS

In a clinical setting, malingering should always be considered when there is the possibility of an external incentive for the patient. Otherwise, small separate clues of feigning may be overlooked that would lead to a more detailed investigation. In suspected cases of malingered psychosis, the clinician should inquire about the specific details of hallucinations and delusions, as the typical characteristics of these symptoms have been well researched. A major focus of this book is the development of clinical decision models to establish malingering. Table 4.5 offers such a model for malingered psychosis.

For the determination of malingering, clinicians must establish that (1) the motivation is conscious and (2) the motivation is an external incentive, as opposed to a desire to be in a sick role. Furthermore, to reach a firm conclusion of malingered psychosis, the clinician must observe (1) inconsistent or contradictory presentations, (2) improbable or incongruous clinical presentations, and (3) supportive collateral data.

The following case illustrates the importance of detecting malingering in a clinical setting. Mrs. C had successfully malingered chronic schizophrenia over a 12-year period in order to receive social security disability payments. Whenever Mrs. C went to her disability evaluations or a disability hearing, she alleged "constant" auditory hallucinations, dressed bizarrely,

TABLE 4.5. Criteria for the Assessment of Malingered Psychosis

A. Clear external incentive to malinger (established, not inferred)

B. Marked variability of presentation as evidenced by at least one of the following:
   1. Marked discrepancies in interview and noninterview behavior
   2. Gross inconsistencies in reported psychotic symptoms
   3. Blatant contradictions between reported prior episodes and documented psychiatric history

C. Unlikely psychiatric symptoms as evidenced by one or more of the following:
   1. Elaborate psychotic symptoms that lack common paranoid, grandiose, or religious themes
   2. Sudden emergence of alleged psychotic symptoms to explain criminal behavior
   3. Atypical hallucinations or delusions (see Table 4.2)

D. Confirmation of malingered psychosis by either:
   1. Admission of malingering
   2. Strong corroborative data (e.g., findings from psychological measures with very low false-positive rates)

and gave absurd answers to questions. She alleged confusion so severe that she was unable to drive or meet her own basic needs. At her disability hearing, she testified that her entire family was dead and refused to give any telephone numbers of third parties. Mrs. C and her husband, Mr. C, acted together as partners in feigning her mental disorder and defrauding the government. They worked together on a number of other disability frauds using false social security numbers, claiming benefits for nonexistent children, and making false workers' compensation claims. They were ultimately caught when it was discovered that Mrs. C was pursuing a PhD; she was videotaped by federal agents appropriately dressed and attending graduate classes.

FORENSIC APPLICATIONS

There were no real demons, no talking dogs, no satanic henchmen. I made it all up via my wild imagination so as to find some form of justification for my criminal acts against society.

—"Son of Sam" serial killer DAVID BERKOWITZ
(in Samenow, 1984, p. 130)

Concerns about defendants feigning mental disorders to avoid criminal responsibility date

back to at least the 10th century (Brittain, 1966; Collinson, 1812; Resnick, 1984). By the 1880s, many Americans considered physicians generally impious, mercenary, and a cynical lot who might participate in the "insanity dodge" (Rosenberg, 1968). After the verdict on John Hinckley, who attempted to assassinate President Ronald Reagan, columnist Carl Rowan (1982, p. 10B) stated, "It is about time we faced the truth that the 'insanity' defense is mostly the last gasp legal maneuvering, often hoaxes, in cases where a person obviously has done something terrible." In cases that capture national attention, a finding of insanity often results in a public outcry that forensic mental health professionals are paid "excuse makers."

Clinical Assessment of Criminal Defendants

When evaluating criminal defendants in a forensic setting, the clinician must always consider malingering. Prior to evaluating a defendant, the clinician should be equipped with as much background information as possible, such as police reports, witness statements, autopsy findings, past psychiatric records, statements of the defendant, and observations of correctional staff. Consultations with family members, social contacts, or witnesses are often helpful prior to the clinician's examination. The clinician should attempt to learn some relevant information about the defendant or crime that the defendant does not know the clinician knows. This approach provides a method of assessing veracity, in that the information can be compared with the defendant's self-report upon questioning. For example, will the defendant honestly report past criminal activity as recorded on his "rap sheet"? How does the defendant's version of the offense compare to victim or witness accounts (Hall, 1982)?

An attempt should be made to evaluate the defendant who raises psychiatric issues as a defense as soon as possible after the crime. An early evaluation reduces the likelihood that the defendant will have been coached or will have had sufficient time to observe genuine psychotic symptoms in a forensic hospital setting. The more quickly the defendant can be seen, the less time he or she will have to plan deceptive strategy, craft a consistent story, and rehearse fabrications. Normal memory distortions are also less likely to occur. Moreover, prompt examination enhances the clinician's credibility in court.

Defendants who present with a mixed picture of schizophrenia and antisocial features may pose difficulties for the clinician due to negative countertransference. The clinician should not focus on the antisocial traits to the exclusion of a genuine comorbid illness (Travin & Protter, 1984). The clinician must guard against the temptation to accept a psychotic version at face value, as well as the temptation to dismiss it out of hand. Any facile attempt to dichotomize a defendant into "mad" (assuming the credibility of the psychotic symptoms) or "bad" (assuming an antisocial person has fabricated psychotic symptoms) may reduce the accuracy of the forensic assessment.

The farsighted clinician will record in detail the defendant's early account of the crime, even if issues of competency and sanity have not been raised. Once defendants are placed in a jail or a forensic hospital, they may learn how to modify their stories to avoid criminal responsibility (Samenow, 1984). Recording the early version also reduces the likelihood of being misled later by a defendant's unconscious memory distortions. The clinician should take a careful history of past mental disorders, including details of prior hallucinations, before eliciting an account of the current crime. Malingerers are less likely to be on guard because they infrequently anticipate the relevance of such information. If a defendant should subsequently fake hallucinations to explain his or her criminal conduct at the time of the offense, it will be too late to falsify past symptoms to lend credence to the deception. Whenever possible, a defendant's report of prior hallucinations and delusions should be confirmed by a review of past hospital records. The lack of any history may be informative; Kucharski and colleagues (1998) found that malingerers with no prior history of psychiatric hospitalization or treatment were likely to present with atypical hallucinations and an implausible level of impairment.

The following example of Mr. K provides helpful insights into the thinking of a defendant who repeatedly feigned psychosis for the explicit purpose of avoiding trial. Charged with aggravated robbery, he had successfully feigned incompetency to stand trial on three prior occasions. Observations of Mr. K by police and correctional officers revealed no abnormal behavior. During his evaluation, however, Mr. K rocked back and forth and sang songs. He spoke rapidly and repeatedly interrupted the evaluator. He eagerly reported that he had ESP powers and was being tormented by the government as a political prisoner. He answered nearly all questions with questions and often refused to explain his symptoms. Mr. K alleged that all courtroom personnel were against him, due to a government plot. He stated explicitly that he was too sick to stand trial and should be hospitalized. When the clinician left the room, Mr. K stopped rocking and was quiet.

Mr. K had written to his girlfriend, an incarcerated codefendant, with instructions on how to malinger. The following three excerpts (K. Quinn, personal communication, August 6, 1985) are instructive:

1. "When the doctors see you, they only hold you for a little while. All the time you are with them, don't hold a normal conversation with them. When they start asking you a question, interrupt them before they can finish asking. You can always use scriptures from the Bible to interrupt them with; make up your own scriptures, stare a lot at the floor, turn your head away from them and mumble to yourself."

2. "Start talking about any- and everything. Keep changing subjects. Don't complete sentences with them. You don't know the judge from the bailiff or prosecutor. You don't fully understand what you are charged with. You never see eye to eye with your lawyer. Accuse him of being a communist. You don't understand the regular courtroom procedures; the voices told you that the courtroom was like a circus or zoo. . . . Talk stupid, dumb, and crazy to even your social worker."

3. "Let me give you a real-life example. Today, a doctor talked to me for an hour and a half. During my competency test, the psychiatrist said I would make a good actor. He just made remarks to see how I would respond. My reply was more mumbling to myself and saying things he didn't understand. You just have to act like most of the time you're in your own little world. Just make like a real baby, meaning you don't even know the English language. You just answer like you think a crazy woman would. No matter how many times someone calls you a con or a fake, just keep up the act."

Several indicators were observed in ascertaining that Mr. K was malingering. He over-acted his part and was eager to call attention to his disorder. He showed no negative signs of schizophrenia. He did not maintain his psychotic behavior. He answered many questions with "I don't know" and refused to give details. He pretended both to be psychotic and to have low intelligence. The diagnosis of malingering was confirmed by his letters to his girlfriend.

Insanity evaluations add an additional dimension to the assessment of feigned psychosis. Defendants may malinger for the time of the offense but not the present time. In assessing defendants for criminal responsibility, clinicians must determine whether they are malingering psychosis at the time of the offense only or are alleging continued psychosis at the time of the examination (Hall, 1982; see also Table 4.6). Some malingerers mistakenly believe that they must show ongoing symptoms of psychosis in order to succeed with an insanity defense. When defendants present with current psychiatric symptoms, the clinician has the opportunity to see whether the alleged symptoms are consistent with contemporaneous psychological testing.

Clinical indicators of feigned psychosis should take into account the criminal conduct in forensic evaluations. Table 4.6 provides potential characteristics of defendants attempting to excuse their criminal behaviors as part of a mental health defense. A psychotic explanation for a crime should be questioned if the crime fits the same pattern as established in previous criminal convictions.

Malingerers may attempt to "retro-fit" the facts of the crime to be consistent with a mental disorder. For example, one male malingerer with prior armed robbery convictions claimed that he robbed only on commands of auditory hallucinations and gave away all the stolen money to homeless people. Malingering should be suspected if a partner was involved in the crime because most accomplices will not participate in a crime that is motivated by psychotic or bizarre beliefs. In such cases, the clinician may assess the validity of the alleged insanity by questioning the codefendant. Thompson and colleagues (1992) found that 98% of successful insanity acquittees acted alone.

Malingering should be carefully considered in the case of a defendant who alleges a sudden or irresistible impulse. The clinician should be skeptical of an impulse that is not a frequent symptom associated with a recognized mental disorder. If a defendant denies any previous

TABLE 4.6. Malingered Psychosis: Criminal Forensic Applications

A. Types of malingering

1. Feigning psychosis while actually committing the crime (very infrequent)
2. Feigning "psychosis during the crime" but now claiming to be well
3. Feigning "psychosis during the crime" and continuing to feign for the current time
4. Genuinely psychotic at the time of the crime but feigning exculpatory symptoms

B. Clinical indicators

1. A nonpsychotic, rational motive for the crime
2. Suspect hallucinations or delusions (see Table 4.2)
3. Current offense fits a pattern of prior criminal conduct
4. Absence of active or negative symptoms of psychosis during evaluation
5. Report of a sudden, irresistible impulse
6. Presence of a partner in the crime
7. "Double denial" of responsibility (disavowal of crime plus attribution to psychosis)
8. Far-fetched story of psychosis to explain crime
9. Alleged intellectual deficit coupled with alleged psychosis

knowledge of an impulse, lying should be suspected. Experience has shown that it is extremely improbable for an obsessional impulse to be uncontrollable at its first appearance (East, 1927). Genuine obsessions are characterized by a pathological persistence of a thought or feeling that is experienced as ego-dystonic (Sadock & Sadock, 2003). They are often accompanied by anxiety symptoms and feelings of anxious dread that lead the individual to take specific countermeasures against the thoughts. Clinicians should be suspicious of allegations of obsessional impulses that are unaccompanied by anxiety symptoms, that are ego-syntonic, or that do not fit common themes of obsessions and compulsions.

Malingering defendants may present themselves as doubly blameless within the context of their feigned disorders. This strategy was demonstrated by a defendant, Mr. Y, who pled insanity to a charge of murder involving a 7-year-old boy stabbed 60 times with an ice pick. One week prior to the homicide, Mr. Y claimed to be constantly pursued by an "indistinct, human-like, black blob." He stated that he was sexually excited and intended to force homosexual acts on the victim but abandoned his plan when the boy began to cry. When he started to leave, Mr. Y alleged that "10 faces in the bushes" began chanting, "Kill him, kill him, kill him." He yelled, "No," and repeatedly struck out at the faces with an ice pick. He alleged that the next thing he knew, "the victim was covered with blood." The autopsy revealed a tight cluster of stab wounds to the victim's head and neck—inconsistent with the defendant's claim that he struck out randomly at multiple faces in the bushes. The defendant's version of the offense demonstrates a double avoidance of responsibility: (1) The faces told him to kill, and (2) he claimed to have attacked the faces and not the victim. After his conviction for the offense, he confessed to six unsolved, sexually sadistic murders.

MALINGERING IN CORRECTIONAL SETTINGS

The incidence of malingering in correctional settings is unclear. Furthermore, the accuracy of clinicians' classifications is unclear, given the brevity of most mental health consultations in jails and prisons. Pollock, Quigley, Worley, and Bashford (1997), using the SIRS and MMPI-2, reported a 32% rate of malingering among prisoners referred to a medium-security mental health unit. Rogers, Ustad, and Salekin (1998) found 20.0% rate of malingering on consecutive evaluations on emergency psychiatric referrals to a large metropolitan jail. Once an individual has been sentenced to prison, the incentives to malinger become more complex. The shift of chronically mentally ill persons into the correctional system has resulted in mental health needs far outstripping resources (Knoll, 2006a). Mentally disordered inmates must sometimes exaggerate their symptoms simply to ensure that needed treatment will be provided (Kupers, 2004).

An incorrect classification of malingering may have seriously detrimental and long-lasting effects for genuinely disordered inmates. Genuine patients, miscategorized as malingering, may be subjected to a variety of adverse outcomes, including the denial of needed treatment and disciplinary actions.

DSM-IV-TR screening indices for suspected malingering are inaccurate in correctional settings and should not be applied (Vitacco & Rogers, 2005). The DSM-IV-TR cautions that "under some circumstances, malingering may represent adaptive behavior—for example, feigning illness while a captive of the enemy during wartime" (American Psychiatric Association, 2000, p. 739). As the correctional environment has become increasingly violent and punitive, it becomes more difficult to distinguish malingering from "adaptive" coping strategies. For example, some inmates may correctly observe that staff members will generally ignore their requests for mental health treatment unless those requests are greatly amplified. Inmates with genuine, serious mental disorders may exaggerate symptoms to avoid a decompensation and prolonged isolation. Certainly, not all inmate patients malinger for such adaptive reasons. Some inmates do indeed have such motives as obtaining medications to abuse or avoiding disciplinary actions.

Vitacco and Rogers (2005) have recommended a comprehensive three-stage model for the detection of malingering in a correctional setting. Step 1 consists of an initial clinical screening evaluation. Step 2 involves a systematic screening using brief instruments such as the M-FAST or Structured Inventory of Malingered Symptomatology (SIMS). Step 3 calls for a comprehensive evaluation consisting of a review of records, validated measures (SIRS, PAI, or MMPI-2), and several interviews. Although this approach is highly commendable, many correctional institutions will not possess the resources needed to carry out the three stages on a regular basis.

The finding that an inmate patient has malingered one or more symptoms of psychosis does not rule out the presence of true mental disorders. Therefore, a determination of malingering should not exclude the inmate from receiving further mental health services. Kupers (2004) and Knoll (2006b) have suggested some clinical indicators that caution against classifications of malingering (see Table 4.7). Inmates evidencing several of these indicators are likely to have a genuine disorder, irrespective of response style issues.

Many prisons have special disciplinary segregation units, called secure housing units or segregated housing units (SHU). In an SHU, the inmate serves disciplinary time in a single cell and under highly restrictive conditions. This solitary confinement, sometimes called "the hole" by inmates, typically requires inmates to spend no less than 23 hours per day

TABLE 4.7. Cautions against Malingering Classifications in Correctional Settings

1. No clear external incentive
2. Extensive history of psychiatric treatment
3. High number of objective suicide risk factors
4. Frequently requires special observations
5. Shows improvement on psychotropic medications
6. Does well or improves in a mental health unit
7. Not self-referred
8. Defensive, minimizes illness, or opposes treatment
9. History of serious traumatic brain injury

alone in a cell. Some experts have referred to an "SHU syndrome" arising from notorious conditions of solitary confinement (see *Madrid v. Gomez*, 1995; *Jones'El v. Barge*, 2001). This informal term has been used to describe a set of psychological symptoms experienced by some inmates, particularly those with preexisting mental illness, who are confined in highly restrictive conditions for long periods (Ferrier, 2004). Some of the symptoms of SHU syndrome are pervasive anxiety, agitation, percep-tual distortions (e.g., hallucinations), aggressive fantasy, and suicidal ideation. Thus clinicians evaluating inmates who are, or have recently been, in the SHU should be aware of this phenomenon, as it may look like a picture of atypical psychosis.

CONCLUSIONS

The correct identification of malingered psychosis is necessary to bring accuracy to forensic assessments, to avoid miscarriages of justice, and to prevent misuse of limited health care resources. The detection of malingered psychosis can be difficult and requires a systematic approach. To confidently conclude that an individual is malingering psychotic symptoms, the clinician must have a detailed understanding of genuine psychotic symptoms and must review data from multiple sources. The clinician must assemble valid indicators from a thorough evaluation, clinical records, collateral data, and psychological assessment. Although special effort is required, the clinician bears considerable responsibility to assist society in differentiating true psychosis from malingering.

5

Malingered Traumatic Brain Injury

SCOTT D. BENDER, PhD

The virtual explosion of malingering research in neuropsychological assessment likely stems from at least two sources. First, clinical neuropsychologists were previously criticized as being incapable of detecting malingering (e.g., Faust & Guilmette, 1990; Faust, Hart, & Guilmette, 1988; Heaton, Smith, Lehman, & Vogt, 1978). Second and more generally, forensic neuropsychology has grown in prominence and publications. Between 1990 and 2000, this specialty has seen a threefold increase in the number of publications (Sweet, King, Malina, Bergman, & Simmons, 2002). The vast majority of forensic cases involve issues of contested mild traumatic brain injury (mTBI) in which feigning must be considered. Moreover, it is almost universally accepted that all forensic neuropsychological assessments should include methods for the detection of malingering. Forensic neuropsychologists have an increased awareness that a broad array of dissimulated behaviors can masquerade as neurocognitive dysfunction. In addition, there is a great deal of symptom overlap between certain conditions arising from mental disorders and mTBI. This lack of symptom specificity poses a major challenge for clinicians asked to make differential diagnoses involving brain injuries, particularly when faced with the rigorous standards of legal admissibility.

This chapter reviews the concept of malingering and provides descriptions of traumatic brain injury (TBI) subtypes and their typical course. Malingering is not the same construct as other response-style constructs: deception, feigning, faking, incomplete/suboptimal/poor effort, uncooperativeness, exaggeration, or dissimulation. Most cognitive tests of "malingering" are actually tests of effort. This chapter provides detection strategies for the assessment of *malingering*. Although this process often involves the assessment of suspect effort, poor effort is neither necessary nor sufficient for a determination of malingering to be made in TBI cases.

The main foci of this chapter are fourfold: (1) the detection of malingered TBI through analysis of inconsistencies (both test-related and contextual), (2) the utility of combining tests of neuropsychological functioning with specific tests of response bias, (3) the special problem of postconcussional syndrome, and (4) pitfalls in differential diagnosis. Due to its prevalence in forensic settings, special emphasis is placed on mTBI. The chapter ends with an illustrative case study. Reviews of neuropsychological feigning more generally can be found in Hom and Denney (2002a, 2002b), Iverson and Binder (2000), Larrabee (2005b), Nicholson and Martelli (2007), and Sweet (1999a).

MALINGERING

Definition and Subtypes

The DSM-IV-TR (American Psychiatric Association, 2000) defines malingering as the intentional production of false or grossly exaggerated physical or psychological symptoms motivated by external gain. Malingering is not a diagnosis, but a classification of behavior, hence its status as a V-code (V65.2). According to Lipman (1962), four types of malingering occur:

1. Invention: No genuine symptoms present; patient fabricates symptoms.
2. Perseveration: Genuine symptoms existed but have resolved; the patient alleges their continuance.
3. Exaggeration: Genuine symptoms currently exist but have been magnified beyond their true severity.
4. Transference: Genuine symptoms exist but are not related to the injury in question.

The first type of malingering is the only subtype that involves outright fabrication of symptoms, and it is the rarest form. The other three types involve conscious manipulation of genuine symptoms.

Characteristics of Malingered Neurocognitive Deficits

Prior to Slick, Sherman, and Iverson's (1999) comprehensive "diagnostic" criteria for possible, probable, and definite malingering of cognitive dysfunction, no systematic criteria were specific to clinical neuropsychology. In essence, the Slick and colleagues classification of definite malingering requires clear and compelling evidence of volitionally exaggerated or fabricated cognitive dysfunction in the absence of a plausible alternative explanation. Clinical diagnoses that could explain response patterns must be ruled out, and the behavior should not be the result of diminished mental capacity. Probable malingering requires similar features (e.g., volitional production of symptoms) but with comparatively less evidence (e.g., less than clear and compelling but still strongly suggestive evidence). The Slick and colleagues classification system has produced much needed research, but for forensic practice, the criteria for definite malingering may be too narrow. Moreover, "possible" malingering does not appear to be particularly helpful as a construct; with almost no data a clinician could argue that the patient is "possibly" malingering. This and other constraints of the Slick criteria are reviewed in Rogers and Bender (2003).

It is almost always easier to detect dissimulation than it is to determine the underlying motivation. No single score (or set of scores) can be considered "diagnostic" of malingering. A determination of malingering must include careful examination of contextual (i.e., nontest) factors. Nevertheless, certain scores and patterns are highly indicative of feigned or purposely biased performance. Selected examples are discussed in subsequent sections of this chapter. Importantly, the daunting task of determining whether a certain test performance represents an intentional attempt to obtain material gain requires much more consideration than simply deriving a score within the "malingering range."

Prevalence

The true prevalence of malingering is unknown because successful malingerers go undetected and uncounted. Past surveys of forensic experts suggested that feigning occurred in 7–17% of mental health assessments, with the higher estimate referring to forensic cases (Cornell & Hawk, 1989; Rogers, Salekin, Sewell, Goldstein, & Leonard, 1998; Rogers, Sewell, & Goldstein, 1994). More recent surveys suggest that the rate is much higher, at least for mTBI cases, and approaches 40% when the category is broadened to include symptom exaggeration (e.g., Mittenberg, Patton, Canyock, & Condit, 2002). This is highly consistent with Larrabee's (2003a) review of 11 neuropsychological studies involving mTBI. Studies tend to establish the prevalence of malingering by calculating the percentage of patients who performed below generally accepted cut scores on tests of feigning. However, very few studies have proven that the individuals in question were motivated exclusively by external gain. Thus the prevalence rates of "malingering" may better be thought of as the prevalence of "feigning."[1] Accurate classification of malingering is further compromised by the multiple conditions that can resemble malingering.

TRAUMATIC BRAIN INJURY

Mild Traumatic Brain Injury and Related Conditions

In the United States, roughly 1.5 million new cases of traumatic brain injury occur each year

(Sosin, Sniezek, & Thurman, 1996). Though almost 80% of TBIs are classified as "mild," this percentage is likely an underestimate due to the significant number of cases that are not reported. The vast majority of epidemiological studies on mTBI rely on emergency department records and, therefore, exclude the mTBI cases that went untreated. Mild TBI patients also represent the majority of cases seen in forensic neuropsychological practice, and, as will be seen, they pose significant clinical challenges.

The terms *concussion* and *mTBI* are sometimes used interchangeably, but many neuropsychologists agree that concussion refers to particularly mild TBI. The diagnoses of both remain muddy and controversial; currently there are at least 27 gradation systems of concussion alone (Bender, Barth, & Irby, 2004).

Generally speaking, TBI is defined by the presence of (1) trauma to the brain either through blunt force to the skull or by acceleration–deceleration forces and (2) resultant signs and symptoms. In contrast to moderate and severe TBI, mTBI is usually undetectable on traditional neuroimaging. In fact, structural evidence of brain injury is often viewed as exclusion criteria, or as a reason to subclassify the injury (i.e., "complicated mTBI"). Despite the lack of evidence on computerized tomography (CT) and magnetic resonance imaging (MRI), studies have shown that diffuse physiological and chemical changes can occur with mTBI (e.g., Giza & Hovda, 2004; see also Barth, Freeman, & Broshek, 2002). Diffuse axonal injury via shear-strain effects has also been documented (Bigler, 1990b). Clinical evidence of the sequelae of mTBI can be wide-ranging and variable in presentation. To date, clinical correlations of these physiological changes and imaging have been lacking, which limits their diagnostic utility.

The best method for operationalizing the signs and symptoms of mTBI has been debated, but some consensus has been achieved for scores of 13–15 on the Glasgow Coma Scale (GCS; American Congress of Rehabilitation Medicine, 1993; Jennett, 2002; Rowley & Fielding, 1991; Teasdale & Jennett, 1974). Others (e.g., Dikmen, Machamer, Winn, & Temkin, 1995) have suggested that the elapsed time before commands are followed is a sensitive indicator. Ruff and Richardson (1999) operationalized mTBI in terms of loss of consciousness (LOC) and posttraumatic amnesia (PTA). Table 5.1 provides their operationalized criteria and three gradations of mTBI.

The DSM-IV-TR (American Psychiatric Association, 2000) includes a diagnosis of dementia due to head trauma. This diagnosis appears to best characterize moderate and severe TBI; however, its criteria lack specificity. The current DSM nosology may actually hamper diagnosis of milder forms of brain injury, particularly when there is a question of psychogenic overlay (Goodyear, 2006). For example, the available criteria do not fully describe the role of neuropsychological impairment in making diagnostic decisions about somatoform, factitious, or dissociative disorders. Also, the only DMS-IV diagnostic criteria for concussion (i.e., postconcussional disorder) are experimental and are therefore of limited utility.

Natural Course of mTBI

Approximately 90% of patients with mTBI recover and are asymptomatic 3 months postinjury (Alexander, 1995; Binder, 1997). Thus a reliable profile of neuropsychological deficits beyond that time has not been forthcoming and may not exist. Even within the 3-month window, no single profile is available to clinicians trying to distinguish feigned from genuine deficits. However, both acute (i.e., less than 24 hours postinjury) and postacute (i.e.,

TABLE 5.1. Ruff and Richardson's Classifications of mTBI

If the patient experiences . . .	Then diagnose . . .
1. No LOC but is confused or has altered mental status *and* PTA of 1–60 seconds	Type 1 mTBI
2. Definite LOC <5 minutes *and* has PTA of 60 seconds–12 hours	Type 2 mTBI
3. LOC of 5–30 minutes *and* PTA of >12 hours	Type 3 mTBI

Note. All gradations involve at least one neurological sign or symptom. LOC, loss of consciousness; PTA, posttraumatic amnesia.

7–10 days postinjury) symptoms of mTBI are well described (see Alexander, 1995; Barth, Macciocchi, Boll, Giordani, & Rimel, 1983; Landre, Poppe, Davis, Schmaus, & Hobbs, 2006; Levin et al., 1987). Salient symptoms include: dizziness, headache, disorientation, amnesia (usually transient), attention deficits, and slowed cognitive processing speed. A challenging issue facing forensic neuropsychologists involved in mTBI litigation is the fact that the symptoms are not specific to mTBI. Issues pertaining to differential diagnoses are discussed later in this chapter.

Course of Moderate to Severe TBI

Severe TBI is typically defined by GCS scores of 3–8 and/or posttraumatic amnesia of >48 hours. In general, TBI follows a dose–response curve, meaning that the more severe the TBI, the longer the recovery period and the poorer the outcome. Penetrating injuries, subdural hematoma, and diffuse axonal injury are more often associated with severe TBI than with milder injuries. Severe TBI often involves frank neurological signs (e.g., nonreactive pupils) and other traumatic injuries (e.g., spinal cord injury). Neurosurgical intervention and higher complication rates are also common in severe cases (Dikmen et al., 1995).

Groups of severely brain-injured individuals produce highly variable scores on neuropsychological tests. Deficits tend to be wide-ranging and include (1) impaired learning and memory, (2) attention and concentration deficits, (3) slowed mental processing speed, and (4) dysexecutive syndromes (e.g., poor cognitive flexibility). Length of coma (i.e., time until the patient follows commands) predicts degree of cognitive impairment (Dikmen et al., 1995; Jennett & Bond, 1975). For severe TBI, between 20 and 40% achieve "good" recovery (Millis et al., 2001). Although cognitive deficits due to moderate to severe TBI can persist indefinitely, they do not worsen over time. However, secondary psychological disturbances such as depression can worsen or prolong cognitive dysfunction.

The clinical issue of whether severe TBI can be malingered has been subject to far less scrutiny than feigned TBI, partly due to one or two assumptions: (1) that patients with documented brain damage cannot successfully feign cognitive deficits or (2) that they are not motivated to do so. Evidence that questions these assumptions is presented in the section on detection methods for feigned TBI.

Postconcussive Syndrome Controversy

Postconcussive syndrome (PCS) is a term used to describe the neuropsychological and physical problems that some TBI patients continue to report well beyond the expected time frame (i.e., beyond 1–3 months). PCS is a controversial construct. It has been difficult to (1) distinguish acute psychological effects of injury (e.g., anxiety and other impediments to attention span) from neurocognitive deficits, (2) know how to interpret neuroimaging in concussion, and (3) determine whether the disability is due to the neurological injury itself or to disruptions in routines of daily living (Davies & McMillan, 2005). PCS is difficult to define because its symptoms can be equally well explained by psychological or neurological problems or both. Without a full consensus, most clinicians agree that PCS involves various nonspecific somatic, emotional, and cognitive sequelae to mTBI that last 3 months or more.

Critics have underscored the conceptual limitations of the PCS construct. For instance, Gouvier, Uddo-Crane, and Brown (1988) noted that the diagnostic validity of PCS is suspect due to the high base rate of PCS symptoms in the general population. They found that symptoms such as "difficulty becoming interested" and "often irritable" were endorsed at comparable rates by normal controls and PCS patients. Only one self-reported symptom ("subjective sense of restlessness") differed significantly between these groups. Iverson and McCracken (1997) noted a similar problem of symptom overlap when comparing symptoms of PCS with those of chronic pain without a history of mTBI. These problematic results are further confirmed by Lees-Haley and Brown (1993; see also Fox, Lees-Haley, Earnest, & Dolezal-Wood, 1995), who found a very high incidence of PCS-like symptoms in litigants without a neurological injury or claim.

The ICD-10 (World Health Organization, 1992) offers nine diagnostic criteria for PCS, but they appear to have little clinical utility. Kashluba, Casey, and Paniak (2006) recently found that endorsement of ICD-10 criteria correctly classified just 67% of patients at 1 month post-mTBI. Only one symptom (increased susceptibility to fatigue) showed superior discrimination at 1 month postinjury, and none of the symptoms successfully discriminated at the 3-month postinjury interval.

PCS also evidences significant diagnostic overlap with depressive disorders. Iverson (2006) recently studied 64 patients with a depressive disorder and found that 89% had at least three "mild or greater" symptoms of PCS; most of these symptoms were of at least moderate severity; and 72% of the sample endorsed the same number of "moderate to severe" symptoms of PCS. Iverson cautioned that depression, chronic pain, sleep problems, litigation stress, and malingering can cause a patient to report PCS symptoms. As a result, the examiner must carefully consider several factors, including the probability of each potential diagnosis (e.g., PCS vs. depression) occurring at that particular time. In general, the further the patient is from the injury date, the lower the probability of neurogenic PCS.

Suhr and Gunstad (2002) and Ruff (1996) have noted that patients' expectations about mTBI can affect neuropsychological test performance and clinical outcome. Ruff (2005) has since promoted a patient-based view of mTBI and PCS, emphasizing the individual phenomenology and treatment of the condition, rather than an etiological polarity (i.e., neurogenic vs. psychogenic). Attempts to dichotomize these symptoms have led to diagnostic problems and probably contribute to biases against patients who "only have psychological problems."

In summary, the constellation of symptoms known as PCS lacks clear diagnostic boundaries. PCS is at risk of becoming a pejorative term. It has the potential for mislabeling symptoms and causing iatrogenic problems (Larrabee, 1997; Wood, 2004). Forensic neuropsychologists are urged to carefully evaluate other potential symptom etiologies before concluding that they are likely due to PCS. However, it is equally important not to rule out a priori, due to personal biases, the possibility of genuine PCS.

EFFECT SIZES FOR MALINGERED mTBI

Binder, Rohling, and Larrabee (1997) conducted a meta-analysis of neuropsychological test scores among patients with mTBI compared with healthy controls; the average effect size of impairment was small ($d = 0.12$). In contrast, feigners (i.e., suspected malingerers and simulators) showed a moderately large effect size on neuropsychological tests ($d = 1.13$; Vickery, Berry, Inman, Harris, & Orey, 2001). As Iverson (2003) observed, these meta-analytic findings suggest that neuropsychological tests are rather poor indicators of mTBI and strong indicators of probable malingering. The effect size of malingered performance on testing appears to be more commensurate with severe TBI. The strategy of "severity indexing" uses this type of information to help identify malingering and is discussed later in a case study.

Litigation and the possibility of considerable financial gain can have profound effects on the patient, including his or her neuropsychological test performance. Binder and Rohling (1996) found that such incentives potentially lower test scores on average by nearly one-half standard deviation ($d = .47$), which is much more than the decrement associated with mTBI. This is a potentially misleading statistic, as it may persuade clinicians and attorneys to believe that litigation is a unitary entity that is solely responsible for the patient's deficits (e.g., "accident neurosis"; Miller, 1961). Importantly, litigation involves a number of stress-producing components that may be completely unrelated to any attempts at malingering. For instance, Weissman (1990) noted that protracted litigation lowers morale, reduces effectiveness of treatment, and fosters iatrogenic conditions. Such effects can lower test performance and can be mistaken for malingering. Furthermore, the repeated recounting of symptoms during litigation likely leads to some "drift" and at least minor fictionalization of symptoms (see Lishman, 1988). In summary, the complex set of psychological factors that accompany litigation may increase the likelihood of malingering but cannot be equated with it.

MASQUERADING SYNDROMES AND THE DIFFERENTIAL DIAGNOSIS OF mTBI

Multiple factors influence the symptomatology of mTBI. Mooney, Speed, and Sheppard (2005) cogently underscored this point in their prospective study of 67 mTBI patients with poor recovery, most of whom were in litigation. They found that postinjury depression, but not premorbid depression, was a strong predictor of poor outcome. Fully one-half of the sample met diagnostic criteria for three conditions: PCS, a new Axis I diagnosis, and pain. The authors concluded that attributing poor outcome to the mTBI alone is overly simplistic and misleading.

The accurate diagnosis of mTBI is not simply a matter of excluding malingering; several other diagnoses and conditions must be ruled out as well. Neuropsychologists are cautioned against an unsophisticated differential diagnosis consisting simply of mTBI versus malingering. Other diagnostic considerations include depression, posttraumatic stress disorder (PTSD), and pain.

Depressive disorders occur in almost 14% of mTBI patients 12 months postinjury (Deb, Lyons, Koutzoukis, Ali, & McCarthy, 1999), which is 4 times the rate in the general adult (nonelderly) population. Depressive symptoms can mimic symptoms of mTBI both clinically and on neuropsychological test scores. Depressed patients typically have low motivation, which traditionally is considered a correlate of malingering in the cognitive domain. Decreased attention and concentration and slowed cognitive processing speed are common both in patients with depression and those with brain injury. Fortunately, not all symptoms overlap; patients with depression have more memory problems on effortful tests but have fewer problems on more structured versions of the same test (Weingartner, Cohen, Murphy, Martello, & Gerdt, 1981).

Differential diagnosis of mTBI and depression relies on multiple indicators. Obviously, the presence of physical trauma is necessary for a determination of mTBI. Beyond that, a preexisting history of depression and cognitive deficits that fluctuate appreciably with mood changes are suggestive of depression, whereas deficits that slowly resolve over time with less fluctuation are indicative of mTBI. Practitioners should be careful in their diagnosis because mTBI can include behavioral and emotional dysregulation that lowers cognitive efficiency, especially during times of irritability.

Differentiating depression from mTBI is more difficult in the postacute stages, when symptom overlap increases and the true source of symptoms is blurred. Nevertheless, epidemiological data indicate that the greater the intervals from the time of injury, the less likely the symptoms are due to mTBI itself. In the end, a thorough clinical interview is usually required to make this important differentiation.

Mild TBI must also be differentiated from PTSD. The essential feature of PTSD is the development of disabling symptoms following exposure to a potentially life-threatening traumatic event (e.g., being a victim or witness of violence). Patients with PTSD alone often have neuropsychological complaints such as attention, concentration, memory, and organization problems (see Kay, 1999). These symptoms overlap with those of mTBI and therefore pose obvious difficulties when trying to determine the source of deficits in the context of mTBI.

Recent studies suggest that PTSD may be more common following mTBI than originally thought (Harvey & Bryant, 1998; Koren et al., 2005). The presence of bodily trauma appears to increase the risk of PTSD (Koren, Hemel, & Klein, 2006). PTSD symptoms and subclinical features also are more common in patients whose symptoms have been slow to resolve. PTSD has a similar course to PCS, leading to the suggestion that PTSD is a variant of PCS (Davidoff, Kessler, Laibstain, & Mark, 1988). Cases in which the patient has witnessed a death or suffered a personal attack without retrograde amnesia may increase his or her vulnerability to symptoms of PTSD. Kay (1999) has provided four key points for forensic neuropsychologists working with patients with PTSD:

1. PTSD can co-occur with genuine symptoms of TBI.
2. Neuropsychological deficits must be carefully evaluated with reference to the nature and severity of the injury. Deficits that are out of proportion to the injury raise the probability of psychological versus neuropsychological disorder.
3. Regardless of the severity of injury and context, all plausible diagnoses must be considered, including PTSD.
4. Exaggeration by the patient does not rule out legitimate psychological conditions or mTBI.

These points can be applied to almost all differential diagnosis involving TBI, and, as will be seen, are important components for the strategic detection of malingering.

Like depression and PTSD, pain can produce symptoms and deficits similar to those of mTBI. Pain is subjective and is an accessible means of expressing psychological distress in patients who are not psychologically minded (e.g., symptoms of a somatoform disorder). Given its subjectivity, pain is also an accessible symptom for malingerers. Neuropsychologists must be aware of and account for the neuropsychological effects of pain. Unfortunately, neuropsychological evaluations are not designed to detect pain directly. Therefore, the veracity of pain symptoms must be inferred from performance on tests of other constructs, including tests of malingered cognitive impairment, and from behavioral observations. This determination is troubling given that (1) pain is a common comorbid condition with mTBI, (2) chronic pain patients without a history of concussion often have several symptoms of PCS, and (3) the prevalence of malingered pain has been estimated to be as high as 34% (Mittenberg, Patton, Canyock, & Condit, 2002). As a further complication, over 80% of chronic pain patients without TBI report three or more symptoms of PCS (Iverson & McCracken, 1997). Chronic pain complaints may be over 4 times more common in mTBI than in moderate to severe TBI (Uomoto & Esselman, 1993).

Attempts to improve the ability to detect malingered pain are under way. Bianchini, Greve, and Glynn (2005) recently outlined proposed criteria for malingered pain-related disability, largely based on Slick and colleagues' (1999) criteria for malingered neurocognitive deficits. Interestingly, the criteria include poor effort on purely neuropsychological tests, a criterion that may improve specificity but may be of questionable benefit otherwise as less than one-third of litigating pain patients may be expected to fail neurocognitive "validity checks" (Meyers & Diep, 2000). Though the utility of the criteria has not yet been established, Bianchini and colleagues (2005) present a logical methodology for the criteria and are the first to use a systematic and testable approach to this complex diagnostic problem.

Pain is naturally distracting but also seems to produce a separate state of psychological distress that interferes with cognitive efficiency (Kewman, Vaishampayan, Zald, & Han, 1991). Clinicians working with mTBI patients must be aware of pain syndromes and somatoform disorders and carefully consider the role of pain when questions of adequate effort are raised.[2]

Resnick (1997) has suggested that clinicians watch for several characteristics that can differentiate pain and conversion symptoms from malingering. For instance, malingerers tend to be less eager to be examined or treated, whereas patients with pain disorders welcome the opportunity to obtain an explanation for their symptoms. Whereas genuine mTBI and pain patients often avoid the details of the accident that caused the symptoms, malingerers typically go into great detail. Such willingness may reveal the lack of genuine emotional salience of the purported trauma.

Despite the fact that neuropsychological tests are not tests of pain per se, some cognitive measures may assist in determining the genuineness of reported pain. Etherton, Bianchini, Greve, and Ciota (2005) found that the Test of Memory Malingering (TOMM) is insensitive to the effects of pain, suggesting that a failed TOMM score results from something other than pain, such as poor effort. Recent work by the same group (Etherton, Bianchini, Ciota, Heinly, & Greve, 2006; Etherton, Bianchini, Heinly, & Greve, 2006) showed that the Working Memory Index (WMI) and the Processing Speed Index (PSI) from the Wechsler Adult Intelligence Scale—III (WAIS-III) are only modestly affected by either experimentally induced or chronic pain. In contrast, many of those feigning pain had low WMI scores. Using a WMI cut score of <65 yielded a positive predictive power of 100% in identifying feigned pain, even when the base rate of feigning was conservative (10%). The PSI yielded only slightly less impressive classification rates. These cognitive tests are not designed to assess the validity of pain complaints but appear to hold utility because they measure pain-related complaints.

In sum, depression, PTSD, and pain represent the most common differential diagnoses when considering mTBI (see Table 5.2). In addition, each diagnosis can be feigned in its own right, meaning that there are at least three possible outcomes from a neuropsychological evaluation: The patient may (1) have a genuine brain injury, (2) have a genuine mental disorder masquerading as TBI, or (3) be malingering. Combinations of the three alternatives are possible as well. The forensic neuropsychologist must establish the veracity not only of the primary complaint (e.g., mTBI) but also of the competing diagnoses. The accuracy of this determination is essential. It is not difficult to imagine how disastrous the consequences would be for a patient who is incorrectly classified as a malingerer.

TABLE 5.2. Specialized Measures of Feigned mTBI with Comparisons to Specific Conditions

Measure	Representative studies	Feigners vs. specific conditions (Cohen's ds)		
		TBI	Dep	Pain
TOMM (Retention trial)	Etherton, Bianchini, Greve, & Ciota (2005)			4.65
	Gierok, Dickson, & Cole (2005)[a]		.95	
	Rees, Tombaugh, Gansler, & Moczynski (1998)	1.42		
	Weinborn, Orr, Woods, Conover, & Feix (2003)[b]		.71	
Reliable Digit Span (RDS)	Axelrod, Fichtenberg, Millis, & Wertheimer (2006)	1.21		
	Babikian, Boone, & Arnold (2006)[c]	1.05		
	Etherton, Bianchini, Greve, & Heinly (2005)			1.27
21-Item Test	Vickery et al. (2001)[c]	1.46		
Category Test	Forrest, Allen, & Goldstein (2004)[c]	1.4		
CVLT-II Trials 1–5 (raw score)	Root et al. (2006)[c]	.82		

Note. Dep, depression.
[a]Differential prevalence design; heterogeneous psychiatric inpatient group
[b]Differential prevalence design; forensic psychiatric inpatients
[c]Heterogeneous clinical group

As summarized in Table 5.2, the comorbidity of mTBI and clinical conditions of depression and pain has not been systematically evaluated with commonly used measures of feigned cognitive impairment. These representative studies underscore the importance of further research for systematically evaluating comorbid conditions. The available data (see Table 5.2) do suggest that measures may have moderate to large effect sizes when compared with these disorders. Further work is needed on the ability of these measures to yield accurate individual classifications.

STRATEGIC IDENTIFICATION OF FEIGNED TBI

The clinical history, context of injury, and other background information are critical parts of the determination of injury severity. The patient's performance on neurocognitive testing should match that expected given the characteristics of the injury. Forensic neuropsychologists must use their knowledge both of symptomatology and of the natural course of TBI to identify neuropsychological inconsistencies. Iverson and Binder (2000) have recommended a systematic assessment of such inconsistencies during each evaluation. Reported symptoms should match observed behavior. If, for example, the patient is reportedly "almost blind" but grasps a pen from the examiner without difficulty, there is an inconsistency between report and observation. If the patient reports severe anterograde amnesia but recalls the route to your office, then there is a mismatch between report and observation. Many possible comparisons can be made using this approach. Although it is highly accessible, it is qualitative and subject to biases in clinical judgment.

The second type of assessment involves the inferential technique of "syndrome analysis" (Walsh, 1985). With this technique, the clinician compares features of the current presentation with the known syndrome. An exhaustive review is beyond the scope of this chapter, but an example would be a reported decline in functioning in the postacute stages of mTBI (in the absence of an evolving bleed). Such an exacerbation would be inconsistent with the known course of mTBI and raises questions of feigning. Likewise, a newly acquired aphasia in the context of TBI without well-documented damage to the temporal lobe is highly unusual and deserving of a comprehensive assessment for possible response biases. Neither observation by itself is pathognomic of malingering; other diagnoses such as depression and the somatoform disorders must be ruled out. This approach is a necessary part of malingering detection, but because atypical but genuine cases do not always fit the syndrome in question, it is not sufficient by itself.

A third method is the assessment of intertest inconsistency. Generally consistent performances are expected on tests of similar abilities (e.g., Arithmetic and Digit Span subtests; Finger Tapping and Grooved Pegboard), and significant deviations are difficult to explain syndromally. However, a word of caution is warranted: Significant scatter on the WAIS-III subtests is the norm, not the exception.[3] The base rate of a difference between two tests must be considered before rendering an opinion about the likelihood that the inconsistency represents actual feigning.

The fourth and final method is "severity indexing," which can be used to compare the current patient's characteristics (including demographic data, injury characteristics, test scores, etc.) with those of previously studied patient groups. This approach is similar to the traditional use of norms but incorporates norms from impaired populations rather than healthy controls.

Rohling, Meyers, and Millis (2003) have proposed the Overall Test Battery Mean (OTBM) as such a measure of severity inconsistency. Basically, the authors transformed raw scores from neuropsychological tests into T scores and then calculated an overall average (i.e., the OTBM). They then compared the patients' OTBM with data sets from samples of neurocognitively impaired individuals. The authors used the outcome data from Dikmen and colleagues (1995) and from Volbrecht, Meyers, and Kater-Bundgaard (2000) as benchmarks for impaired performances. The comparison of OTBMs to these data sets allows clinicians "to determine the relative congruity between acute injury and residual cognitive deficits" (p. 299). An OTBM that falls outside of the range expected in light of the patient's length of loss of consciousness should be considered suspect.

This approach is promising because it provides unique clinical information; it yields an empirical index of the expected severity of neurocognitive deficits given the characteristics of the injury. Symptoms and ostensible deficits that do not fit within the expected

course and severity of injury raise the likelihood of dissimulation. However, it is a fairly new approach, and there is a paucity of data at this point. Also, there are limited data regarding the prevalence of genuine but atypical neurocognitive profiles that do not fit with the existing estimates of severity. Clinicians are encouraged both to explore this technique conceptually and to use data from Dikmen and colleagues (1995) or from Volbrecht and colleagues (2000) for specific comparisons. However, they are also cautioned not to rely on this approach alone when making determinations of malingering.

Severe TBI and Malingering

Very few case studies have investigated the feigning of severe TBI. As an exception, Boone and Lu (2003) described noncredible performance in two cases of severe TBI. They noted that both patients underwent numerous multidisciplinary workups but that the possibility of malingering was not considered. In their subsequent evaluation, the authors documented "odd" and "nonsensical" fluctuations in neurocognitive test performance. For instance, one patient had shown good neuropsychological recovery 6 months postinjury and had reenrolled part time in high school, but her neurocognitive scores declined significantly in the next 2 months. There was no identifiable brain mechanism to explain this unexpected decline.

Bianchini, Greve, and Love (2003) reported three cases of litigating patients, each with documented severe TBI. Each patient performed significantly below chance on symptom validity tests and had clear incentive to fake deficits. The investigators' published classification of "definite malingering" appears to be the first for feigned severe TBI. They reiterated Boone and Lu's (2003) contention that tests of effort and feigning be included in all cases with potential material gain (see also Ju & Varney, 2000).

SELECTED NEUROPSYCHOLOGICAL TESTS USED IN TBI

Multiple studies have demonstrated (to varying degrees) that certain neuropsychological tests can be used simultaneously as tests of genuine neurocognitive dysfunction and as tests of malingering. The chief advantage of using tests in this way is time efficiency, but they may also be less recognizable as tests of malingering and may be more resistant to coaching. A brief review of some commonly administered "double-duty" tests is provided here. However, see Van Gorp and colleagues (1999) and Curtiss and Vanderploeg (2000) for dissenting opinions.

California Verbal Learning Test

The recognition trial of the California Verbal Learning Test (CVLT) and CVLT-II provides an opportunity for forced-choice testing of response bias during a test of true neurocognitive dysfunction. Although several studies have demonstrated the utility of the CVLT in detecting dissimulation (e.g., Ashendorf, O'Bryant, & McCaffrey, 2003; Millis, Putnam, Adams, & Ricker, 1995; Slick, Iverson, & Green, 2000), it is difficult to synthesize the findings due to the differing criteria used to define the malingering groups. Among TBI patients, Bauer, Yantz, and Ryan (2005) used the Word Memory Test (WMT; Green, Iverson, & Allen, 1999) as the criterion for malingering (defined as performance below 82.5% on one of three WMT scores). A discriminant function using five CVLT-II variables correctly classified 75.8% of their sample. Specificity was an impressive 95.6%, but sensitivity was just 13.5%.

Root, Robbins, Chang, and van Gorp (2006) evaluated the utility of the Critical Item Analysis (CIA) procedure as well as the forced-choice recognition indices from the CVLT-II. Basically, CIA relies on the performance curve strategy (see Rogers, Chapter 2, this volume) in comparing performance on easy versus difficult items. Using a bootstrapping comparison (see Rogers, Chapter 1, this volume), they divided the entirely forensic sample into adequate- and inadequate-effort groups as defined by performance on the Validity Indicator Profile (VIP) and/or TOMM. They found that the CIA—Recognition index yielded exceptionally good specificity (100%) and positive predictive power (PPP; 100% at base rates of 15, 30, and 48%). The other indices performed similarly and were in line with prior studies. In other words, the CVLT-II appears to be a strong indicator of inadequate effort, but it lacks sensitivity (4–60%). Although combining indices from the CVLT-II seems to improve incremental validity somewhat, clinicians are advised

not to rely solely on the CVLT-II for malingering detection.

Digit Span and Reliable Digits

Because only 5% of the normative sample (both healthy and clinical samples) score below the 5th percentile on the Digit Span subtest of the WAIS-III, some authors (e.g., Greiffenstein, Baker, & Gola, 1994; Iverson & Tulsky, 2003) have argued that it is a useful measure of effort. As such, it is an example of the floor effect strategy. Axelrod, Fichtenberg, Millis, and Wertheimer (2006) recently reported that a cut score of 7 on the Digit Span subtest correctly classified 75% of probable malingerers and 69% of patients with mTBI. Though studies report specificities ranging from 90 to 100%, the degree of forensic utility is limited by small samples and lack of replication.

Greiffenstein and colleagues (1994) introduced Reliable Digits (RD) as a measure of effort. At least eight studies have provided estimates of specificity, with results ranging from 57 to 100%, but sensitivity is often too low to be useful. Moreover, RD may not be appropriate for individuals with borderline IQs. The reader is referred to Babikian, Boone, Lu, and Arnold (2006) for a summary of sensitivities and specificities of RD.

Category Test

The Category Test (CT) also employs the floor effect to detect malingered responding. Bolter, Picano, and Zych (1985) determined that certain items of the CT were so easy that individuals with brain injuries rarely missed them. Tenhula and Sweet (1996) later developed six validity indicators for the CT that in some combinations correctly classified 88.9% with a specificity of 92.6%. Adding a group of difficult items lowered specificity; clinicians are urged to avoid use of these items. Sweet and King (2002) provide a comprehensive review of the CT and recommendations for its use in forensic practice.

As can be seen, tests of genuine neuropsychological dysfunction can also be used to assess suboptimal effort. However, none should be used in isolation. Studies have demonstrated the benefit of using multiple measures of relatively independent constructs to increase incremental validity (e.g., Bender & Rogers, 2004; Nelson et al., 2003).

In this volume, Greene (Chapter 10) and Sellbom and Bagby (Chapter 11) provide details regarding the use of multiscale inventories to evaluate malingering and other response styles. Rogers and Bender (2003) advanced a strong argument (see also Rogers, Chapter 2, this volume) for addressing malingering differently for feigned cognitive impairment than for other domains (i.e., mental disorders and medical complaints). In essence, each domain places unique demands on malingerers and has its own detection strategies. Nonetheless, some researchers have persisted in using detection strategies for feigned mental disorders to assess malingered cognitive deficits. These studies rely mostly on simulation designs and have not included known-groups comparisons. One possibility is that simulators do not discriminate between psychological and neurocognitive impairment. Alternatively, they may believe that most traumatic injuries result in personality changes and psychological impairment.

The Minnesota Multiphasic Personality Inventory–2 (MMPI-2) and Personality Assessment Inventory (PAI) are commonly examined in suspected cases of feigned cognitive impairment. They are summarized briefly in the next two subsections.

Minnesota Multiphasic Personality Inventory–2

Among the most commonly administered tests both in clinical and forensic cases is the MMPI-2. Lees-Haley, Iverson, Lange, Fox, and Allen (2002) point out that part of the appeal of the MMPI-2 is that it not only characterizes emotional distress and the effects of mood disturbance on cognitive functioning but also yields data regarding effort and exaggeration. It is critical to note that the MMPI-2 validity scales were in no way designed to provide information about the veracity of an individual's *cognitive* complaints. Nonetheless, its utility for that very purpose has been scrutinized with some potentially surprising results.

In a recent meta-analysis of 19 studies, Nelson, Sweet, and Demakis (2006) summarized the effect sizes of the most commonly used validity scales from the MMPI-2 (e.g., L, F, K, Fp, F-K, O-S, Ds2, FBS) when used to differentiate "overresponders" from honest groups. Nelson and colleagues found that several validity scales yielded large effect sizes, with the Fake Bad Scale (FBS; Lees-Haley, English, & Glenn,

1991) yielding the largest ($d = .96$). Both insufficient cognitive effort ($d = 1.50$) and TBI ($d = 1.21$) produced large effect sizes. This suggests that FBS taps something unique about cognitive functioning. The Fake Bad Scale has also shown promise in specific neuropsychological studies, as it appears to correlate more with tests of feigned cognitive impairment (the Victoria Symptom Validity Test; VSVT) than with F, F-K, and Fp (Slick, Hopp, Strauss, & Spellacy, 1996).

FBS accurately classifies mildly head-injured litigants putting forth poor effort (Ross, Millis, Krukowski, Putnam, & Adams, 2004). Larrabee (2003b) found that FBS scores of patients with moderate to severe TBI were well below the scores of litigants who had failed the Portland Digit Recognition Test (PDRT) with an effect size of 1.81 (see also Larrabee, 2003b, for effect sizes when using MMPI-2 clinical scales). Similarly, Dearth, Berry, and Vickery (2005) found that the effect size of the FBS scale between honest patients with TBI and patients with TBI instructed to feign deficits was substantial: $d = 1.39$. Others have questioned the construct validity of the FBS (Arbisi & Butcher, 2004). Lees-Haley and colleagues (2002) caution that, although the MMPI-2 certainly meets the Daubert standard of general acceptance within the scientific community, its reliability and validity may not be as high as many clinicians assumed. As a component of Daubert, its error rate may also be problematic.

Gervais, Ben-Porath, Wygant, and Green (2007) recently developed the Response Bias Scale (RBS) for the MMPI-2. In short, they used multiple regression analyses to predict failure on one or more cognitive feigning tests in an archival sample of over 1,200 disability claimants without head injury. The resultant 28-item scale yielded excellent specificity (95% overall; 100% for chronic pain patients), but very poor sensitivity (25%) when using a cutoff of 17. Cutoffs ranging from 16 to 20 resulted in hit rates ranging from 63 to 68%. The authors note that they intentionally chose a cut score that favored specificity in order to minimize the risks of false positives. Cross-validation appears warranted.

Personality Assessment Inventory

The PAI (Morey, 1991) is newer to the forensic realm than the MMPI-2 but appears to be gaining acceptance in forensic and clinical practice. A PsycINFO search conducted in March 2007 yielded more than 35 studies of the PAI, many of which appear to have been conducted in the forensic arena. The PAI appears to hold advantages over other multiscale inventories. These advantages include (1) a fourth-grade reading level, (2) a shorter length than some other inventories (e.g., the MMPI-2), (3) nonoverlapping scales that aid differential diagnosis, and (4) a larger range of response options (i.e., "false," "slightly true," "mainly true," and "very true"). The PAI includes four validity scales: Inconsistency (ICN), Infrequency (INF), Positive Impression Management (PIM), and Negative Impression Management (NIM). Response bias can be assessed both in terms of defensiveness (PIM) and malingering (NIM). The Malingering Index (Morey, 1996) and the Rogers Discriminant Function (RDF; Rogers, Sewell, Morey, & Ustad, 1996) were developed later for added malingering detection power and have shown good preliminary discriminability (Morey & Lanier, 1998).

Rogers, Sewell, and colleagues (1996) found that the PAI was quite effective at discriminating bona fide psychiatric patients from simulators (with a sensitivity of 96.4% and a hit rate of 92.2%). However, almost 20% of genuine patients were incorrectly classified as fakers. Feigned depression was particularly well detected by the PAI, among both naive and sophisticated simulators. To date, the research on the PAI's classificatory accuracy for feigned PTSD is mixed (e.g., Calhoun, Earnst, Tucker, Kirby, & Beckham, 2000; Eakin, Weathers, & Benson, 2006). Its utility with actual criminal defendants was found to have both strengths and limitations that may temper somewhat the aforementioned findings in simulators (Kucharski, Toomey, Fila, & Duncan, 2007).

To date, only two studies have examined the PAI in TBI populations. Demakis and colleagues (2007) found that genuine TBI was associated with elevations on the Somatic Complaints, Depression, Borderline Features, Paranoia, and Schizophrenia scales, which is generally in line with similar studies using the MMPI-2 (Warriner, Rourke, Velikonja, & Metham, 2003). The social isolation and confused thinking items associated with Cluster 8 profiles (Morey, 1991) were endorsed by almost 20% of the sample, suggesting that the PAI includes items that are at least somewhat

sensitive to symptoms of TBI. Perhaps not surprisingly, the NIM scale had one of the highest elevations in the study, with over 24% of the sample scoring 2 standard deviations or more above the standardization sample's mean. Such marked elevations raise a critical concern about whether genuine TBI patients might be misclassified as feigners on the PAI NIM scale. The authors did not control for litigation status, and it is unclear whether or not the NIM scale holds utility for classifying feigners of TBI.

The second study of the PAI involving patients with TBI (Kurtz, Shealy, & Putnam, 2007) examined whether or not PAI scales yield the "paradoxical severity effect" noted on the MMPI-2. Previous research has shown that milder head injuries are associated with higher scale elevations on the MMPI-2, especially on the "neurotic triad" (Youngjohn, Davis, & Wolf, 1997). Kurtz and colleagues (2007) replicated the paradoxical severity effect on four scales of the MMPI-2 but noted a different result on the PAI. Only two PAI scales (Somatization and Depression) were elevated among mTBI patients. Moreover, among patients with mTBI, the mean scale elevation was significantly higher on the MMPI-2 than on the PAI. These and other data led the authors to conclude that the PAI is both valid and useful "for psychodiagnostic assessment of head injury" (p. 71). They also noted that the PAI was developed using a construct validation strategy that may reduce interpretive uncertainty in cases involving head injury. The extent to which this may be true requires further study.

Unlike the MMPI-2, the PAI has few published studies on its efficacy for identifying feigned TBI. In a study of claims for worker's compensation, Sumanti, Boone, Savodnik, and Gorsuch (2006) found that correlations between the PAI validity scales and cognitive effort tests were modest (rs from .02 to .30). At present, the usefulness of the PAI with feigned TBI and other feigned neurocognitive deficits has not been established.

FOUR TESTS DESIGNED TO DETECT FEIGNED COGNITIVE DEFICITS

No neuropsychological battery is complete without a measure designed expressly to detect feigned neurocognitive dysfunction. Dozens of tests are available; only four are included here, based on their familiarity to most clinicians and their forensic utility. Interested readers are encouraged to review Chapters 13 and 14 in this volume, as well as other reviews (see Nies & Sweet, 1994; Rogers & Bender, 2003). The four tests cover both verbal and nonverbal domains, thereby theoretically improving incremental validity when used in combination. The degree to which this is true empirically deserves more research.

The 21-Item Test is ostensibly a test of verbal recall but has been shown to be insensitive to bona-fide memory disorders, making it a good candidate for assessing effort (Iverson, Wilhelm, & Franzen, 1993). Among other things, the 21-Item Test uses a normative measure of inconsistency that reveals violations of learning principles. If the number of words recalled on the free-recall portion is significantly greater than the number of words correctly endorsed during the recognition trial, then feigning is suspected. The VIP (Frederick & Crosby, 2000) is also commonly used in forensic cases. It is unique in at least two ways: First, it employs multiple detection strategies, making it difficult for the examinee to know which strategy is being used for which items; second, it assesses feigning in multiple cognitive domains (e.g., conceptualization, attention, and memory). The value of domain-specific malingering assessment has been discussed (Larrabee, 2005). The Performance Curve strategy of the VIP visually depicts any misjudgments the feigner may have made as to *when* to miss items. Missing items too soon (i.e., comparatively easy items) will be shown in the curve as a premature dip in performance, as compared with the curves of both normal and clinical samples. The subsequent flattening out or even rise of the curve (indicating improved performance) as items become more difficult may not be obvious to the examinee. It is virtually impossible to explain improved performance in terms other than feigning. The Digit Memory Test (DMT; Hiscock & Hiscock, 1989) uses both symptom validity testing (SVT) and floor effect strategies. The DMT requires the examinee to recognize the correct sequence of digits when provided with two choices. It has shown very good classification rates but may be vulnerable to discovery as a detection strategy by sophisticated malingerers. Finally, the TOMM is a test of visual recognition memory that relies primarily on the floor effect. It is a commonly used test of neurocognitive feigning with ex-

cellent classification rates in a number of studies. Unfortunately, suggested cut scores and sample reports have found their way to several websites, which raises questions about test security (Bauer & McCaffrey, 2006).

Vickery and colleagues (2001) conducted a meta-analysis on the aforementioned tests of feigned cognitive impairment, as well as the PDRT (Binder, 1993) and the Dot Counting Test (Rey, 1941). The DMT yielded the largest effect size ($M d = 1.95$), which falls within the "very large" range (see Rogers, Chapter 2, this volume). The 21-Item Test showed an impressive average specificity of 100% but a low sensitivity of 22%. The meta-analysis also revealed large effect sizes for both the 21-Item Test ($M d = 1.46$) and the PDRT ($M d = 1.26$). In contrast, the 15-Item Test (Rey, 1964) has been shown to be relatively insensitive to subtle feigning (Guilmette, Hart, Giuliano, & Leininger, 1994) and overly sensitive to genuine neurocognitive disorders, including mental retardation (Goldberg & Miller, 1986; Schretlen, Brandt, Krafft, & van Gorp, 1991). Although the authors did not discuss the positive and negative predictive powers (PPP and NPP) of these measures, these estimates are critically important to clinical and forensic neuropsychologists (see Rogers, Chapter 2, this volume). The reader is directed to O'Bryant and Lucas (2006) for a good example of how these scores are derived.

It is worth noting that the aforementioned measures and the vast majority of all malingering tests measure effort via tests of recognition memory.[4] It is reasonable to question the degree to which such tests measure effort in other cognitive domains. Indeed, their clinical utility rests solely on the premise that they do. Constantinou, Bauer, Ashendorf, Fisher, and Mc-Caffery (2005) provide a preliminary answer to this question in the mTBI population. They found that poor performance on the TOMM correlated significantly with multiple domain scores from the WAIS-R and the Halstead–Reitan Neuropsychological Test Battery. However, with the exception of the General Neuropsychological Deficit Score (GNDS; $r^2 = .47$), the amount of variance in neuropsychological performance accounted for by the TOMM was small ($r^2 = .19$–$.30$). There appear to be grounds for further exploration of this important question.

In 2002, the *Journal of Forensic Neuropsychology* devoted two issues to detection of response bias in forensic neuropsychology. The articles provide an excellent empirical review of the most common tests of feigning and a clear distillation of important conceptual issues regarding forensic assessment in general and malingering detection specifically.[5]

EVALUATION OF FEIGNED TBI: A CASE EXAMPLE

Case Findings

A 43-year-old right-handed man (FM) was involved in a slow-moving (< 5 mph) motor vehicle accident at work. FM was exiting his pickup truck when another pickup struck his vehicle from behind. The patient stated that the door frame struck him in the back of the head. Witnesses noted that, though there was no loss of consciousness, he was slightly confused and slow to respond to their questions. When paramedics arrived 15 minutes later, his GCS score was 15, and he was following commands without difficulty. His past medical history is noncontributory, and subsequent CT of the head was negative. When he presented for neuropsychological assessment 12 months later as part of a worker's compensation evaluation, he reported that he experienced posttraumatic amnesia of 5–7 days. FM claimed disabling attention deficits, memory problems, anxiety, and insomnia. He noted that he had never experienced any of these symptoms before the accident. He later sought medical advice from his primary care physician and was told that he was probably suffering from a postconcussive syndrome. During the neuropsychological interview, he complained that his cognitive symptoms were worsening and that he began having flashbacks shortly after his appointment with his primary care physician.

FM was administered a comprehensive neuropsychological battery. He was urged to put forth his best effort and was cautioned that less than complete effort would likely compromise the results. There were no signs of fatigue or of difficulty with comprehension. To assess the possibility of feigned memory impairment, the TOMM was administered. Based on the floor effect strategy, scores below the 90th percentile on the second trial and retention phase are likely to be indicative of feigning. The patient's scores were at the 67th percentile. Applying Bayes's Theorem to conservative estimates of sensitivity and specificity of the TOMM and assuming a base rate of 30% yields a PPP of 94.3% and an NPP of 87.4%. The VIP was also administered because it provides a visual depiction of performance across items of increasing difficulty. Contrary to well-known learning principles, FM's performance curve revealed a slight improvement in performance in the middle of the curve. This finding indicates that he mistimed when to appear impaired on the test and missed more easy items relative to difficult items. Finally, the NIM scale from the PAI was suggestive of symptom exaggeration.

Data from Volbrecht and colleagues (2000) can be used to compare the patient's scores with the scores that would be expected given the severity of the TBI. For illustration, Table 5.3 compares FM's transformed scores to the

TABLE 5.3. Severity Indexing of Selected Scores from Neuropsychological Testing in the Case of FM

Test	FM's T scores	T scores from Volbrecht et al. (2000)			
		LOC < 60 min	LOC = 25 hours to 6 days	LOC = 14 to 28 days	LOC > 29 days
RAVLT—Total	22	40	34	26	19
Trails A (Time)	32	43	43	34	33
Trails B (Time)	40	46	48	32	37
WAIS-III PIQ	35	49	46	36	35
RCFT—Immediate	36	46	42	37	25
RCFT—Delayed	18	44	39	36	23

Note. Data are distilled from the case and Volbrecht et al. (2000). LOC, loss of consciousness; WAIS-III, Wechsler Adult Intelligence Scale, 3rd Edition; PIQ, performance IQ; RAVLT, Rey Auditory Verbal Learning Test; RCFT,= Rey Complex Figure Test.

T scores and standard deviations from selected tests taken by genuine TBI patients. As can be seen, the severity of deficits increases in a dose–response curve as LOC increases.[6] Comparison of FM's T scores and injury characteristics with mean T scores at each level of severity proved to be a powerful indicator of feigned impairment. His T score of 22 on the Rey Auditory Verbal Learning Test (RAVLT) falls within the range of patients whose LOC was beyond 2 weeks. This is clearly incongruent with what was reported both by the paramedics and by the patient. Also, his performance IQ (PIQ) would suggest that he was either unable to follow commands or was unconscious for at least 2 weeks, and possibly for over 1 month. The other indicators in the table reveal similar incongruities between observed scores and the expected level of performance.[7]

Case Conceptualization

In FM's case, the claimant stands to gain monetarily if he is found to be disabled. The neuropsychological evaluation included specific tests of feigning and analyzed patterns of performance within the test battery to assess response bias. The medical history was carefully reviewed in order to identify incongruities between reported and observed symptoms. Finally, the claimant's test scores were compared to known groups of patients with brain injury.

Tests of neurocognitive feigning do not directly address the validity of Mr. FM's psychological complaints (e.g., insomnia and PTSD). Though not especially common, PTSD can result from mTBI, can include flashbacks, and can impair cognition. It could possibly be argued that FM suffered a potentially life-threatening event. However, at no time was his life in actual danger, and, with the exception of flashbacks after being told by his physician that he suffered a concussion, at no time in the acute and postacute periods did he experience shock or complain of reexperiencing the event. Moreover, he did not change his driving habits. FM reported that his symptoms (both cognitive and psychological) had worsened over time, which is inconsistent with the course of recovery from mTBI. The clinical profile from the PAI was consistent with a preoccupation with physical functioning and with several features of PTSD. However, the NIM scale revealed a clear tendency to exaggerate symptoms. Even if these symptoms were legitimate,

they cannot fully account for the number or degree of poor performances on neurocognitive testing.

FM stated in the interview that he had never experienced attention or memory problems of any kind prior to his injury. This kind of blanket dismissal is consistent with research suggesting that mTBI patients often overestimate their premorbid functioning (Greiffenstein, Baker, & Johnson-Greene, 2002), which leads to inflated and unrealistic expectations and subsequent dissatisfaction with cognitive performance following concussion. Although such a bias certainly does not equate with malingering, it provides supportive evidence in this case, especially given the strong evidence of malingering from other sources. Also, the patient was educated by his primary care physician about the expected symptoms of PCS. Questions remain about whether or not providing such information increases or decreases symptomatology. Mittenberg, DiGuilio, Perrin, and Bass (1992) have demonstrated that psychoeducation about the course of mTBI can decrease recovery time and increase satisfaction with outcome. However, when malingering is concerned, it is not difficult to imagine how the good intentions of a health care professional could inadvertently amount to coaching, thereby improving the malingerer's chances of going undetected (see Greub & Suhr, 2006; Johnson & Lesniak-Karpiak, 1997).

FM was provided feedback about his performance and was reminded of our cautionary statement at the beginning of the assessment. He denied any intentional response bias and later insisted that his poor performance was due to fatigue. He was provided with a referral to a clinical psychologist for any psychological distress he may be experiencing as a result of the accident or litigation.

CLINICAL APPLICATIONS

According to the National Academy of Neuropsychology, assessment of response bias is a critical part of assessment; moreover, the burden of proof lies with the clinician to justify why such testing would *not* be conducted (Bush et al., 2005). Despite this requirement, assessment methods are not standardized. On the contrary, the methods of detection (e.g., observation, multiscale inventories, indices, intra- and intertest performance) vary markedly across practitioners and settings. There are dozens of published "malingering tests," but in reality there is no such thing as a "malingering test." These tests are largely tests of effort, and effort can be suboptimal for a number of reasons. It is the task of the forensic neuropsychologist to link poor effort with the intent to fake deficits.

Use of Utility Estimates

In the assessment of feigned cognitive impairment, the most useful question is typically something akin to, "Given this test score, how likely is it that the patient is malingering?" As noted, this question is addressed by PPP, which is influenced by the base rate of malingering. Greve and Bianchini (2004) have stated that PPP and specificity should be emphasized above other utility estimates in order to reduce the number of false positive errors. Rogers (1997c) has cautioned clinicians not to confound litigation status with malingering (e.g., differential prevalence designs); meta-analysis of the MMPI-2 and malingering (Rogers, Sewell, Martin, & Vitacco, 2003) illustrates this point nicely. Litigation status played a minor role in producing relatively small effect sizes that were overshadowed by diagnostic differences (e.g., genuine profiles of schizophrenia vs. depression). Ross, Putnam, and Adams (2006) make the same case with brain-injured patients; although both incomplete effort and psychological disturbance were good predictors of neuropsychological performance, compensation-seeking status was not.

Incremental Validity

Studies have shown that using more than one test of feigning (Iverson & Franzen, 1996) and multiple detection strategies (Bender & Rogers, 2004) can improve detection. To the extent possible, each feigning-detection test should measure largely independent constructs and should have good classification rates in and of themselves. For example, the TOMM (Tombaugh, 1997) is a test of visual recognition memory with very good classification rates that primarily uses the floor effect strategy. Ideally, the forensic neuropsychologist should complement such a feigning measure with an equally accurate feigning test of something other than recognition memory, such as the VIP (Frederick & Foster, 1991). Using an additional test

with a lower hit rate will likely lower the aggregate classification accuracy of a single test.

Multistep Approach to the Evaluation of Malingered TBI

Many of the decisions during an evaluation of mTBI must be made on a case-by-case basis. Nevertheless, all cases should involve a determination of the source or sources of the symptoms. At the outset the clinician must try to answer the question, Was there a concussion? This determination may be difficult in itself, but probably the most difficult step is deciding whether or not the symptoms are actually attributable to the reported injury (Ruff & Richardson, 1999). The determination that the injury did not cause the symptoms is a multistep process that involves both qualitative and quantitative methods (see Table 5.4). Poor effort does not equate to malingering, and other alternative explanations for the lack of effort must be addressed. The Slick and colleagues (1999) criteria provide a useful heuristic for classifying individuals as malingerers but may be both too conservative and too liberal in places (see Rogers & Bender, 2003). Table 5.5 summarizes the signs to consider when assessing the possibility of malingering.

Forensic neuropsychologists face major challenges with regard to mTBI, PCS, and malingering. Mild TBI is the most common diagnosis seen in forensic cases, and most of the features of PCS are nonspecific. Mild TBI is difficult to diagnose partly because the most easily identified markers of injury (radiological evidence of contusion or hematoma) are exclusionary. Multiple conditions can masquerade as PCS, and there are many reasons for a patient to put forth questionable effort during testing. Pain, depression, and symptoms of PTSD must be ruled out as potential causes for low scores on testing. Each of these conditions can also be malingered and may require an evaluation of their veracity.

The question of whether or not a brain injury actually occurred should remain at the forefront of the forensic neuropsychologist's mind. In cases of suspected malingering, it is equally important to assess one's reasons for attributing poor effort specifically to malingering. Familiarity with the utility estimates of the test in question is critical to the malingering detection process. As noted, PPP and specificity hold particular importance.

TABLE 5.4. Sequential Decision Model for Malingering Detection

1. Determine whether or not there is a brain injury. Evaluate the following:
   a. Does the symptom constellation fit with a known neurological syndrome?
   b. Are medical workups (e.g., imaging) suggestive?
   c. Are the neuropsychological evaluation results suggestive?
   d. Are patient and collateral reports consistent and congruent with the syndrome in question?

2. If Step 1 indicates a neurological cause, whether or not the reported symptoms are attributable to the injury must be determined. Evaluate the following:
   a. History and course/time gradient of the symptoms
      i. Did symptom onset coincide with the injury? Did their evolution follow the known course?
   b. The impact of preexisting symptoms and comorbid mental disorders such as depression and somatoform disorders
   c. Whether any symptoms are being malingered (i.e., exaggeration or prolongation of genuine symptoms)
      i. Results of validity tests
      ii. See Table 5.5

3. If Step 1 does not indicate a neurological injury, then the clinician may conclude that symptom etiology is "nonneurological"
   a. Therefore, symptoms are associated with a psychological disturbance or with malingering.
   b. However, duration and degree of debilitation are critical here:
      i. For instance, symptoms of PCS at 72 hours can be clinically debilitating but can exist without frank neurological signs.
      ii. In contrast, PCS symptoms at 6 months without evidence of trauma strongly suggest nonneurological mechanisms.

Neurocognitive malingering may occur in up to 40% of cases involving litigation, although these estimates include a broader category of symptom exaggeration. Though it could be argued that many would-be malingerers do not know enough about neuropsychological syndromes and performance expectations to go undetected, even the most naive malingerer can evade detection if the forensic neuropsychologist does not employ valid and reliable detection techniques.

TABLE 5.5. General Signs of Neurocognitive Malingering

1. The degree of cognitive impairment is beyond that expected given the severity of the injury.

2. The degree of impairment is inconsistent with degree of functional disability.

3. Reported symptoms and/or cognitive profile(s) do not make neurological sense.

4. Test performance does not fit known cognitive profiles (e.g., better performance on free recall than on recognition).

5. Discrepant performance on tests of similar ability.

6. Frequent near misses.

7. Failing on easy items, and passing more difficult ones.

8. Quick to say, "I don't know."

Given the significance of malingering in legal cases, intensive study will likely continue for the foreseeable future. The application of conceptually based strategies to malingering detection (see Rogers, Harrell, & Liff, 1993, and Rogers, Chapter 2, this volume) appears already to have improved detection accuracy. However, there is room for further improvement. Whether explicitly stated or not, fairly simple applications of the floor effect strategy have predominated in the literature, largely because it is easy to understand and use. More sophisticated applications appear promising. Backhaus, Fichtenberg, and Hanks (2004) demonstrated the potential in their archival study that used a normative floor effect to detect suboptimal effort. In essence, they applied standards expected in moderate to severe brain injury to the performances of patient with mTBI. This approach (which is similar to severity indexing) resulted in excellent classification rates.

Tests and strategies emphasizing incremental validity are also receiving more attention and are important elements of effective malingering detection. Empirical studies have begun to show that hit rates improve when certain feigning detection scales are combined (e.g., Bender & Rogers, 2004; Nelson et al., 2003). However, this area is still fairly new and warrants more validation. Finally, future research should include more sophisticated methods of distinguishing malingered mTBI from genuine neurological and psychiatric conditions. To date, the vast majority of research has compared feigned mTBI with genuine mTBI, whereas less attention has been paid to the performances of patients with other bona fide disorders. To achieve maximum clinical utility, measures of the future must be able to rule out these other conditions, as well.

Summary guidelines for forensic neuropsychologists follow.

- Be knowledgeable about the injury characteristics present at the time of the injury.
- Be familiar with the natural recovery curves of the different severities of TBI and the expected outcomes at various points in time.
- Systematically evaluate the role of psychological and litigation factors, including those unrelated to external or material gain.
- Be familiar with PCS and its masquerading syndromes.
- Use multiple tests of feigning (both embedded and free-standing tests).
- Ensure incremental validity of tests before including them in the battery.
- Do not rule out a priori, via one's own biases, the possibility of genuine mTBI and/or PCS.

NOTES

1. In this chapter, *malingering* refers to cases of feigning in which motivation to obtain some external gain can be presumed. *Feigning* (or a similar term) is used to denote performance that may be indicative of malingering but in which the motivation for the performance has not yet been established.
2. Even with a sound working knowledge of pain syndromes, a referral to a pain specialist is often warranted.
3. See Tables B.3–5 in the WAIS-III Scoring and Administration Manual (Wechsler, 1997) for frequencies of differences between subtests and indexes.
4. As a major exception, the VIP assesses other domains, as well.
5. Publication of the *Journal of Forensic Neuropsychology* ceased in January 2007.
6. According to their article, Volbrecht et al. (2000) used LOC synonymously with TFC (time to follow commands).
7. Like all feigning detection strategies, this method is not foolproof. Some of the standard deviations in the Volbrecht et al. (2000) study are quite large. It is included here to illustrate the concept of severity indexing and to demonstrate its utility as an adjunct to other detection strategies.

6

Denial and Misreporting of Substance Abuse

LYNDA A. R. STEIN, PhD
RICHARD ROGERS, PhD

Substance use is often associated with severe penalties, including social sanctions and stigmatization. This association is illustrated by recently increased penalties for driving under the influence (Hingson, Heeren, & Winter, 1999; Popkin & Wells-Parker, 1994) and by the widespread adoption of drug-testing policies in work settings (Mastrangelo & McDonald, 2001). Research suggests that dissimulation about substance use is common and can occur under a variety of conditions. For example, adolescents whose families were present during interviews reported much lower frequency of substance use than those adolescents who were interviewed alone (Friedman, Johnson, & Brett, 1990; Needle, McCubbin, Lorence, & Hochhauser, 1983). Stigma and sanctions associated with a particular drug also seem to influence response styles; for example, Fendrich and Vaughn (1994) found more underreporting of cocaine than of marijuana use. Treatment status may also affect rates of underreporting: Weissfeld, Holloway, and Kirscht (1989) found that more persons completing a cigarette-smoking treatment had underreported their smoking when compared with those seeking assistance for smoking-related illness. However, both groups minimized their smoking to a greater degree than the general population.

Despite social sanctions and stigma, nonmedical use of substances is widespread. A substantial proportion of adults and adolescents have used illicit drugs (Johnson, O'Malley, & Bachman, 1994; Substance Abuse and Mental Health Services Administration, 1996). Lifetime prevalence for substance use disorder is about 27% for adults (Kessler et al., 1994). Adolescents are also affected; the number of adolescents entering public substance abuse treatment grew by 53% from 1992 to 1998 in the United States (Dennis, Funk, Godley, Godley, & Waldron, 2004). Individuals may minimize reports of their substance use in order to avoid legal consequences and to enhance social desirability (see Buchan, Dennis, Tims, & Diamond, 2002).

Survey data of young adolescents suggest that they are likely to minimize their substance abuse despite assurances of confidentiality. O'Malley, Johnston, Bachman, and Schulenberg (2000) surveyed 18,667 eighth graders under confidential and anonymous conditions in a between-subjects design. They found that even after controlling for demographic differences, youths under anonymous conditions reported significantly more illicit substance use. For example, rates of illicit substance use in the preceding 30 days were 13.1% and 16.2% under confidential and anonymous conditions, respectively. Although this represents a difference of only 3.1%, it does illustrate the potential impact of whether or not young respondents believe endorsements are truly confidential.

Criminalization of substance abuse confounds estimates of its use. Persons are unlikely to be entirely forthright when faced with potential consequences of criminal sanctions, as well as sanctions imposed in civil proceedings. The latter may include proceedings involving parenting (e.g., child negligence, fitness to parent, and child custody) and employment (e.g., revocation of professional licensure and torts arising from drug-related work injuries). It is well known that in legal settings (e.g., detention centers or correctional facilities) self-reports underestimate substance involvement, as compared with biological testing (Knight, Hiller, Simpson, & Broome, 1998; Mieczkowski, 2002; Mieczkowski, Newel, & Wraight, 1998). On the opposite end of the spectrum, offenders arrested for very serious crimes may be motivated to report, overreport, or fabricate drug use as a mitigating factor in sentencing (Rogers & Mitchell, 1991). Similarly, even in nonlegal settings, adolescents may overreport in an effort to enhance an image of rebelliousness (Palmer, Dwyer, & Semmer, 1994), and persons may overreport in an effort to access treatment (Midanik, 1982).

OVERVIEW

Specific Terminology

Specific terms have been developed to describe response styles related to substance abuse. These terms include *disacknowledgment, misappraisal, denial,* and *exaggeration.*

1. *Disacknowledgment:* The person disclaims knowledge (e.g., "I don't know" and "I don't remember") of either the drug usage or its behavioral consequences. Whether this disacknowledgment is sincere is often open to question.

2. *Misappraisal:* This refers to an honest error in reporting of substance abuse. Distortions are based on misinformation rather than a deliberate attempt to deceive. This concept is widely understood; it appears that even children and adolescents ranging in age from 12 to 19 years old understand that honest misappraisals of substance use sometimes occur (Stein et al., 2002).

3. *Denial:* This is a generally accepted term for defensiveness in substance abuse clinical practice and research. Substance use or its consequences are purposely minimized for specific reasons, including social desirability, desire to avoid unwanted consequences (e.g., treatment), and unwillingness to accept responsibility for ensuing behavior (e.g., driving while intoxicated).

4. *Exaggeration:* Defined as the magnification of substance use or its effects. An important distinction must be made between *exaggeration* and *malingering.* According to the *Diagnostic and Statistical Manual of Mental Disorders* (DSM-IV; American Psychiatric Association, 2000), malingering involves intentional production or marked overreporting of symptoms motivated by external incentives, such as financial gain or avoiding legal consequences. In contrast, exaggeration involves intentional production or overreporting but with motivation not necessarily linked to external incentives.

Prevalence of Dissimulation among Substance Abusers

The prevalence of defensiveness and denial among drug users has not been well established. Winters, Stinchfield, Henly, and Schwartz (1991) examined general defensiveness (i.e., the Marlowe–Crowne) among large samples of adolescent drug users and controls. For defensiveness, they found moderate levels in 44.5% of drug users, which was unexpectedly lower than in controls (61.6%). As a general measure of defensiveness, these estimates do not directly address denied or minimized substance abuse.

Stein, Colby, Barnett, Monti, and Lebeau (2006) conducted a large study of incarcerated adolescents ($N = 180$), most of whom had frequently used alcohol and marijuana. They found that about one-third purposely underreported alcohol and marijuana use or their effects. Interestingly, nearly the same percentage deliberately overreported alcohol (30%) and marijuana (32%) use or concomitant problems, respectively. Despite assurances of confidentiality, 46% indicated some concern that the information was not private, and 5% admitted to not paying good attention when answering the questionnaires (i.e., inconsistent responding).

Williams and Nowatzki (2005) studied 367 adolescents referred for substance use assessment by parents, social services, courts, and pediatricians. They found that 26% denied substance use, although its presence was confirmed via biochemical testing. An equal percentage reported drug use that was inconsistent with highly reliable laboratory testing. These data suggest that some adolescents may have been misled about what substance was provided to them during consumption, may have had poor memory concerning recent drug use, or may have deliberately fabricated their reports of use. These authors indicated that an unspecified number of adolescents later admitted to overreporting use as either a cry for help or as a boast. Among clinical populations, Winters and colleagues (1991) reported low percentages of adolescents in treatment (up to 6.3%) who exaggerated their drug use. No attempt was made to address inconsistent or random responding; therefore, this percentage may be inflated by adolescents responding erratically on the surveys. Fabricated drug use, observed in the endorsement of fictitious drugs, also appears to be relatively rare in nonclinical adolescent populations (Petzel, Johnson, & McKillip, 1973).

Several observations temper our use of these prevalence data. First, the studies are limited to only adolescent populations. Second, the crucial difference between "drug" defensiveness and "general" defensiveness is often not considered (see also Smart & Jarvis, 1981). Third, some studies use adolescents' self-appraisals of honesty after the study as a manipulation or validity check; however, participants may continue to misrepresent their substance use or, alternatively, to deny accurate past reports. Fourth, these studies do not consistently differentiate between response styles, such as misappraisal versus underreporting versus outright denial. In summary, denied and underreported substance use is likely to be very widespread in adolescent populations. In addition, overreported and exaggerated use may also occur but is less well understood. In general, we lack accurate prevalence estimates for both adult and adolescent populations in a variety of contexts, including clinical and legal settings.

Types of Distortion

Distortions regarding substance abuse may occur on three dimensions: (1) amount and type of substance abuse, (2) immediate behavioral

and psychological effects of substance abuse, and (3) consequent impairment and psychological sequelae from cumulative substance abuse. Laboratory procedures focus principally on the amount and type of substance abuse for varying intervals: immediate (e.g., Breathalyzer), short term (e.g., urinalysis), and long term (e.g., hair analysis). In contrast, psychometric methods tend to focus on long-term effects and sequelae of substance abuse. Examples arising from chronic substance abuse include syndromes and disorders (e.g., alcohol dependence), cognitive deficits (e.g., patterns of memory impairment on neuropsychological tests), and clinical correlates (e.g., personality characteristics, such as delinquency, commonly associated with substance abusers). For instance, versions of the Substance Abuse Subtle Screening Inventory (SASSI; Miller, 1985, 1994a, 1994b; Miller & Lazowski, 2001; Miller, Roberts, Brooks, & Lazowski, 1997) have been employed to evaluate unacknowledged chemical dependency based on clinical correlates; however, this psychometric method offers no data on the amount and usage of alcohol and drugs.

In an effort to study distortion on the aforementioned dimensions, Stein and colleagues (2006) asked incarcerated adolescents directly about their misreported substance use. The adolescents (1) were enrolled in treatment targeting alcohol and marijuana use and (2) were assessed at multiple points regarding frequency and amount of alcohol and marijuana use, as well as the effects of use (e.g., becoming ill, losing money, or impairing relationships). Using extensive questioning at the time of the debriefing with assurances of anonymity, results indicate that 7% endorsed having overreported the number of drinks (8% underreported the number of drinks); 6% endorsed overreporting how often they drank (8% underreported how often they drank); and 7% overreported the number of problems related to alcohol (6% underreported problems). For marijuana, results indicate that 11% endorsed having overreported amount of marijuana used (11% underreported); 9% endorsed overreporting frequency of marijuana use (8% underreported); and 9% overreported problems related to marijuana (9% underreported). Although differences were small, these data tentatively suggest that (1) more misreports occurred regarding marijuana than alcohol and (2) small but significant percentages either over- or underreported their substance abuse and its effects. Despite assurances that all information was confidential and private, 46% of the sample had some concern that answers would be shared with others. We can only assume that had most adolescents in this setting thought responses would have legal consequences, the frequency of their misreports would be substantially increased.

Distortions in the immediate behavioral and psychological effects of substance abuse are generally not systematically investigated. Closely related research, although not ideal, involves the Comprehensive Drinker Profile (CDP; Miller & Marlatt, 1984), which examines characteristic patterns of alcohol abuse (including estimates of blood alcohol concentrations, or BACs) with reasons and effects of drinking and certain situational variables. The authors indicate that much clinical judgment goes into the interview process and that it is possible to both under- and overreport on this instrument. Given the limitations of the CDP, we have no standardized measures for assessing the immediate behavioral consequences of substance use. More specifically, a patient may be accurate and forthright about both the amount of drug abuse and its long-term effects, yet we have no standardized data about the accuracy of self-reporting as it relates to specific incidents. This gap is particularly salient to forensic evaluations, in which issues of impaired judgment and erratic behavior are often more relevant to a specific incident rather than general usage (e.g., BAC) or diagnosis.

Scales such as the Alcohol Sensation Scale (Maisto, Connors, Tucker, McCollam, & Adesso, 1980), the Biphasic Alcohol Effects Scale (Martin, Earleywine, Musty, Perrine, & Swift, 1993), and the Selective High Assessment Scale (Judd, Hubbard, Huey, & Attewell, 1977) have been developed to measure subjective intoxicating effects of alcohol. However, the relationship of blood alcohol to intoxicated behavior and psychological effects is highly variable. Even the same individual can respond differently to identical BACs, depending on mood state and other situational factors (de Wit, Uhlenhuth, Pierri, & Johanson, 1987). As observed by Rogers and Mitchell (1991), investigators are highly divergent in their conclusions about BAC and its relationship to clinical intoxication. Likewise, the relationship between the amount of any drug in the body and its con-

sequences (i.e., intoxicated behavior and psychological effects) is also highly variable.

Subsequent Sections

The following sections organize the assessment of substance abuse into two major components, specifically, clinical and laboratory methods. In clinical methods, brief screens, such as the Alcohol Use Disorders Identification Test (AUDIT; Saunders, Aasland, Babor, De La Fuents, & Grant, 1993) and the Drug Abuse Screening Test (DAST; Skinner, 1982), offer rapid and relatively effective means of evaluating self-acknowledged substance abuse. Given the simplicity of these screens, they should be used as a basis of comparison for questioning discrepancies. In cases of denied or exaggerated drug use, more elaborate procedures with greater discriminant validity than screening may be particularly useful. Other clinical methods include structured interviews and multiscale inventories; these methods adopt a broad-spectrum approach toward psychological impairment and incorporate syndromes and scales for substance abuse. Finally, specialized methods have been developed specifically for the comprehensive assessment of substance abuse.

CLINICAL METHODS

The validation of substance abuse measures is predicated on the accurate measurement of the external criterion, namely the use or misuse of alcohol and drugs (see Table 6.1). However, many studies are satisfied simply to use uncorroborated self-reporting as an external criterion measure. Practitioners can quickly recognize the nonindependence and paradoxical nature of this approach. Other research has relied on informants and convergent indicators from other measures. Although they are a modest improvement over the "self-report by self-report" validity, such studies are still largely dependent on secondary sources of self-report. In contrast to these approaches, two types of external validity are generally effective: (1) treatment history for establishing drug-related disorders and (2) laboratory methods for confirming the use or nonuse of alcohol and drugs. However, even these methods are limited because they do not provide a good indication of amounts consumed over a specific

TABLE 6.1. Types of Test Validation for Substance Abuse Measures and their Relevance to Honesty and Dissimulation

1. *Self-report by self-report.* Acknowledged use or nonuse is employed as the criterion. The paradox is that honesty is assumed for the self-described use or nonuse to assess forthrightness on the substance abuse measure.

2. *Self-report by informant report.* Often a family member is used as an informant to satisfy this criterion. This approach assumes that the user will be more honest with family members than with clinicians. It is suggested that informants provide a rating of how confident they are in their reports.

3. *Self-report by treatment history.* Documented history of treatment provides an excellent criterion for a longitudinal perspective of substance abuse. Substance abusers are likely to know that denial of use will be detected; therefore, they are likely to be more forthright than the target group (i.e., individuals for whom substance abuse has not been established).

4. *Self-report by laboratory methods.* Laboratory methods can accurately establish current (urine analysis) and long-term (hair analysis) drug use. This approach is an effective means of verifying drug use, although not its behavioral effects.

5. *Self-report by convergent indicators.* The degree of association between two or more substance abuse measures is evaluated. Because the external validity of most measures is based on methods 1 or 2, the convergence of measures also remains vulnerable to response styles.

6. *Self-report by simulation design.* Users and nonusers are asked to simulate on substance abuse measures. Although rarely used, the simulation design provides direct information on the vulnerability of substance abuse measures to distortion.

---

time period. As noted in subsequent sections, research can easily demonstrate the vulnerability of substance abuse measures to denial and exaggeration. Therefore, studies should combine treatment history, laboratory methods, and corroborated self-reports (e.g., via significant others) as external criteria with simulation studies of denial and exaggeration. Babor, Stephens, and Marlatt (1987) provide a thoughtful review of criterion measures and the relevant literature.

Screens for Substance Abuse

Screens for substance abuse are widely used because they are easily administered and scored. From the perspective of substance abuse, their simplicity is a liability. In most instances, the items are face-valid, making them especially vulnerable to distortion. In addition, many screens make no effort whatsoever to determine over- or underreporting of substance abuse (see Table 6.2).

Alcohol Screeners Primarily for Adults

Michigan Alcoholism Screening Test

The Michigan Alcoholism Screening Test (MAST; Selzer, 1971) is one of the earliest and most widely used screens for alcohol abuse. An abbreviated 13-item version is called the SMAST (Selzer, Vinokur, & van Rooijen, 1975). The MAST consists of 25 descriptive statements that are given by the clinician as a screen for alcohol abuse and concomitant impairment. It is apparently effective in classifying alcohol abuse and dependence among inpatients seeking treatment for self-acknowledged problems (e.g., Moore, 1972; Ross, Gavin, & Skinner, 1990). However, its usefulness among patients denying substance use is brought into question. Because of its high face validity, data (Otto & Hall, 1988; Otto, Lang, Megargee, & Rosenblatt, 1988) have suggested that patients can easily fake the MAST by denying alcohol abuse. Nochajski and Wieczorek (1998) tested the MAST with convicted drunk drivers in a treatment program. The group whose results were shared with program instructors (i.e., creating the perceived potential for negative consequences) appeared to intentionally suppress their MAST scores when compared with the group whose scores were kept confidential. Clearly, the MAST is vulnerable to faking.

Self-Administered Alcoholism Screening Test

Swenson and Morse (1975) modified the MAST to produce a self-report version that is referred to as the Self-Administered Alcoholism Screen-

TABLE 6.2. Brief Summary of Substance Abuse Screens

Measure[a]	Number of items	Substance covered	Population	Face validity	Response style scales
MAST	25	Alcohol	Adults	Yes	No
SAAST	34	Alcohol	Adults	Yes	No
CAGE	4–16	Alcohol	Adults	Yes	No
AUDIT	10	Alcohol	Adults	Yes	No
SIP	15	Alcohol	Adults	Yes	No
AAIS	14	Alcohol	Adolescents	Yes	No
ADI	24	Alcohol	Adolescents	Yes	No
RAPI	23	Alcohol	Adolescents	Yes	No
SIP-AD	15	Alcohol/drugs	Adults	Yes	No
PESQ	18	Alcohol/drugs	Adolescents	Yes	Yes
DUSI	152	Alcohol/drugs	Adults/adolescents	Yes	Yes
DAST	10–28	Drugs	Adults/adolescents	Yes	No

Note. Population reflects *general* use of the measure.
[a]See text for full measure names.

ing Test (SAAST). The SAAST is composed of 34 items that are presented in a yes–no format. Employing the SAAST, Swenson and Morse discovered 9 of 100 controls with elevated scores; 6 of these were later revealed to have significant histories of alcohol abuse. In addition, 16 of 100 participants in the alcoholic group, despite their current involvement in inpatient alcohol treatment, were characterized as defensive, based on their low SAAST scores. These data would suggest that the SAAST, like the MAST, is fakable. Vickers-Douglas and colleagues (2005) revised the instrument to create the SAAST-R. Its improvements include updated language, a consideration of recent use-related problems, better assessment of lifetime-use problems, and fuller assessment of alcohol dependence and abuse. However, no attempt was made to reduce its vulnerability to faking.

CAGE Questionnaire

Mayfield, McLeod, and Hall (1974) developed the CAGE questionnaire as a measure of covert problem drinking. Inquiries are made regarding whether the respondent feels that he or she should Cut down; whether he or she has been Annoyed regarding criticisms of use; whether he or she has felt Guilty about use; and whether he or she uses drinking in the morning as an Eye-opener. To decrease the face validity of the CAGE, they embedded 6 alcohol-content questions in a screening interview of 16 inquiries. Four of the six alcohol-content questions addressed pathological alcohol use. Mayfield and colleagues found that, of 142 in-

patients with alcoholism, 19 (13.4%) denied alcohol-related problems (i.e., a score of 0 or 1). In order to avoid denial, it is recommended that persons not be asked about the quantity and frequency of alcohol use prior to administration of the CAGE questions (Sokol, Ager, & Martier, 1992). Steinweg and Worth (1993) found that rates of persons identified with a potential alcohol problem dropped from 20 to 7% when this recommendation was not followed. Even in a self-report format, persons seeking Web-based smoking cessation treatment appear to be underidentified for potential alcohol problems when this recommendation is not followed (Etter, 2004). As with other screens, the generalizability of the CAGE to nondisclosing individuals should be further investigated.

Alcohol Use Disorders Identification Test

The AUDIT (Saunders et al., 1993) consists of 10 questions about alcohol-related symptoms. Since its inception, various studies (Donovan, Kivlahan, Doyle, Longabaugh, & Greenfield, 2006; Reinert & Allen, 2002; Shields & Caruso, 2003) in hospitals and other settings have demonstrated its reliability and validity. Recent work by Maisto, Carey, Carey, Gordon, and Gleason (2000) has demonstrated its usefulness with inpatients; a cut score of ≥ 7 provides adequate sensitivity (SN = .79), specificity (SP = .79), positive predictive power (PPP = .76), and negative predictive power (NPP = .88) in detecting presence of past-year alcohol use disorder. However, its face validity leaves this brief screen vulnerable to faking.

Short Index of Problems

The Short Index of Problems (SIP; Miller, Tonigan, & Longabaugh, 1995) is composed of 15 items that assess lifetime consequences of alcohol use. The SIP was developed for use when time does not permit completion of the DrInC (i.e., Drinker Inventory of Consequences; discussed later). Five subscales assess alcohol-related problem areas: Physical, Social Responsibility, Intrapersonal, Impulse Control, and Interpersonal. Feinn, Tennen, and Kranzler (2003) studied 153 problem drinkers in treatment; their results indicate marginal internal consistency, which is affected by the brevity of scales (Cronbach α's ranged from .56 to .64). For concurrent validity, the SIP scales correlated with the longer DrInC parent scales, and SIP total score modestly correlated with number of alcohol dependence criteria (r = .36). No data are presented regarding susceptibility of the SIP to under- or overreported drinking.

Adolescent Alcohol Screeners

Adolescent Alcohol Involvement Scale

The Adolescent Alcohol Involvement Scale (AAIS; Mayer & Filstead, 1979) is a 14-item multiple-choice scale for the assessment of alcohol use and resulting problems. Although severity of scores appeared associated with criterion groups, the authors supply no data on response styles. Rather, they assume that adolescents minimizing alcohol problems might still be detected, based on an entirely unrelated study of adult drunken drivers.

Adolescent Drinking Index

Harrell and Wirtz (1989) constructed the Adolescent Drinking Index (ADI) as a 24-item self-report for the assessment of problem drinking. Items are rated on their accuracy of self-description (e.g., *like me a lot*) or their frequency (i.e., *never* to *4 or more times*). Although the ADI appears to discriminate effectively among criterion groups (e.g., Maag, Irvin, Reid, & Vasa, 1994), no research has investigated its usefulness with adolescents who are

minimizing or exaggerating their alcohol use and resulting impairment.

Rutgers Alcohol Problem Index

White and Labouvie (1989) developed the Rutgers Alcohol Problem Index (RAPI) for the rapid screening of alcoholism among adolescents. The RAPI contains 23 face-valid items, presented in a questionnaire, regarding the potential negative effects of problem alcohol use. The authors have experimented with different time frames (e.g., "last 3 years" or "ever") and different response categories. In addition, the authors acknowledge the potential for denial or exaggeration, neither of which has been researched with the RAPI.

Adult Alcohol and Drug Screener

Short Index of Problems—Alcohol and Drug

The Inventory of Drug Use Consequences (InDUC; see later in the chapter) was shortened to create a 15-item measure called the Short Index of Problems—Alcohol and Drug (SIP-AD; Blanchard, Morgenstern, Morgan, Labouvie, & Bux, 2003). The InDUC, which assesses consequences of both alcohol and drugs, was developed using the DrInC as a template. Therefore, the SIP-AD is similar to the SIP (which was based on the DrInC) in content and format. Like the SIP, data on the SIP-AD indicate adequate reliability and validity as a screen; however, this instrument also appears susceptible to under- and overreported problems.

Adolescent Alcohol and Drug Screener

Personal Experience Screening Questionnaire

Winters (1992), the first author of the Personal Experience Inventory (PEI; see later in the chapter), developed a screening version that was named the Personal Experience Screening Questionnaire (PESQ). The PESQ is composed of 18 face-valid items that are scored on a 4-point scale of frequency in order to screen for alcohol or drug use. The Defensiveness (five items) and Infrequency (three items) scales are designed to detect response distortion. Although data suggested that approximately 15% of the

PESQ protocols were invalid because of compromised self-reporting, no formal studies have been conducted to determine efficacy of scales to detect response distortion.

Adult and Adolescent Alcohol and Drug Screener

Drug Use Screening Inventory

Tarter and Hegedus (1991) developed the Drug Use Screening Inventory (DUSI) for use with both adolescents and adults reporting alcohol or other drug abuse. As the longest of the screens (152 items on 10 domains), the items extend beyond substance abuse to address general functioning (behavior patterns, physical and mental health, social and family functioning, and adjustment at school or work). A revised version exists (DUSI-R; Kirisci, Hsu, & Tarter, 1994) that includes a Lie Scale. High scores on this scale indicate potential denial of use. Dalla-Déa, De Micheli, and Formigoni (2003) researched the adolescent Brazilian version of the DUSI (De Micheli & Formigoni, 2000, 2002b) and provided the questionnaire to 655 adolescents. The validity of the Lie Scale is called into question because (1) over half the sample was classified as underreporting and (2) groups with and without confidentiality did not differ. Simulation research is needed on the use of the DUSI to detect denial and underreporting.

Adult and Adolescent Drug Screener

Drug Abuse Screening Test

The Drug Abuse Screening Test (DAST; Skinner, 1982) parallels the MAST with questions regarding nonprescribed drug use. Several versions exist, including a 10-item version (Cocco & Carey, 1998) and a 27-item adolescent version (DAST-A; Martino, Grilo, & Fehon, 2000). At a cut score of ≥ 2, the DAST-10 has shown good SN (.80), SP (.88), PPP (.73), and NPP (.93) for screening psychiatric outpatients with past-year drug use disorder symptoms (Maisto et al., 2000). The 28-item DAST is composed of self-report items as a quantitative index of problems associated with substance abuse. The content of the items reflects frequency of drug use and interpersonal, legal, and medical problems associated with drug use. Skinner (1982) compared DAST results for 223 referred indi-

viduals with the Basic Personality Inventory (BPI; Jackson, 1976) validity scales. Correlations with denial (−.28) and social desirability (−.38) were found, suggesting that scores may have been influenced by these response styles. Skinner suggested that the DAST is only "minimally influenced by response style biases of denial and social desirability" (Skinner, 1982, p. 369). This interpretation must be tempered by two observations: First, the study was composed of persons voluntarily seeking treatment and may not generalize to other populations. Second, the BPI scales reflect general denial and social desirability and were not intended to evaluate undisclosed drug use and attendant problems. Although the correlation for social desirability (−.38) is not large, it is similar to those correlations found for the primary criterion measure, namely the frequency of drug use (rs range from .19 to .55; mdn r = .35).

The DAST-A was tested by Martino and colleagues (2000) with 194 adolescent inpatients and yielded good utility estimates. It also demonstrated a very low correlation (r = −0.11) with social desirability. It is difficult to ascertain whether the correlation would have been higher had undisclosed substance use or related problems been measured rather than general social desirability. In summary, versions of the DAST appear vulnerable to denial and exaggeration, just as the MAST and other face-valid screens do.

Structured Interviews

Rogers (1995, 2001) articulated the methodological advantages of structured interviews for differential diagnosis. One particular advantage is the standardization of clinical inquiries and responses so that direct comparisons can be accomplished between the patient and significant others. Generally speaking, the level of patient–informant agreement tends to be relatively modest, even when no evidence of dissimulation is found. Therefore, a lack of agreement does not signify deception. In this section, we review (1) Axis I interviews that contain substance abuse components and (2) targeted substance abuse interviews.

Axis I Interviews

Each of the primary Axis I interviews includes sections on substance abuse: Schedule of Affective Disorders and Schizophrenia (SADS), Diagnostic Interview Schedule (DIS), and Structured Clinical Interview of DSM-IV Disorders (SCID). The SADS (Spitzer & Endicott, 1978), for example, exhibits very good interrater reliability but only modest test–retest reliability when used with substance-abusing patients (e.g., Hasin & Grant, 1987; Rounsaville, Cacciola, Weissman, & Kleber, 1981). The DIS-III-A (Robins et al., 1985) focuses extensively on substance abuse and dependence (i.e., alcohol, barbiturates, opioids, cocaine, amphetamines, hallucinogens, cannabis, and tobacco). The DIS substance abuse sections have considerable evidence of concurrent and convergent validity (e.g., Gavin, Ross, & Skinner, 1989; Griffin, Weiss, Mirin, Wilson, & Bouchard-Voelk, 1987; Ross et al., 1990). The DIS-IV reflects DSM-IV diagnostic criteria and has good test–retest reliability (kappas range from .53 to .86) for substance abuse dependence and abuse diagnoses (Compton & Cottler, 2004).

The most extensive coverage of substance abuse is found on the SCID (Spitzer, Williams, Gibbon, & First, 1990) and its subsequent revisions, on which eight drug classes are rated on as many as 15 symptoms and associated features. Williams and colleagues (1992) found that the interrater reliability of the SCID for drug and alcohol abuse fluctuated widely across clinical settings. A large sample ($N = 592$) of inpatients, outpatients, and nonpatients yielded good test–retest reliabilities, with kappas of .75 and .84 for alcohol and substance use disorders, respectively. In a study of participants recruited from substance abuse inpatient and day treatment programs ($N = 100$), the SCID showed good concurrent, discriminant, and predictive validity for substance use disorders (Kranzler, Kadden, Babor, Tennen, & Rounsaville, 1996). The SCID has been updated to reflect DSM-IV disorders, and several changes have been made (First, Spitzer, Gibbon, & Williams, 2002a, 2002b), including the following alterations to the substance disorders module: Marijuana withdrawal may now be assessed; polysubstance dependence is now assessed more consistently with DSM criteria; age of onset is now specified; and 10 different drug classes may now be assessed. In a sample of patients recruited from community treatment facilities ($N = 164$), concordance between raters trained on the updated SCID for DSM-IV and clinical chart review yielded only modest results, with kappas averaging .29

for alcohol and drug diagnoses (Shear et al., 2000).

No studies have examined the vulnerability of Axis I interviews to the denial or exaggeration of substance abuse. Although these measures have varying degrees of face validity for other sections, items that address substance abuse are very direct and easily identified. Therefore, clinical and nonclinical populations should have no difficulties in modifying their reported substance abuse, either through exaggeration or denial.

Targeted Interviews

Increased interest in substance abuse disorders has led to the development of targeted interviews. In the following sections four targeted interviews are described that focus on substance abuse.

Comprehensive Drinker Profile

Miller and Marlatt (1984) developed the Comprehensive Drinker Profile (CDP) as a structured interview for the assessment of alcoholism and treatment potential. Because persons with alcoholic disorders are frequently inaccurate in their accounts of current drinking, an elaborate schedule is constructed for the preceding week, and consumption is related to estimates of BAC across days and episodes. Although fakable, the elaborate structure discourages blatant denial of alcohol use. As an additional precaution against misreporting, a corroborative form of the CDP is available. Surprisingly, research by Miller, Crawford, and Taylor (1979) concluded that informants were as likely to overestimate as to underestimate alcohol consumption. As expected, patients who were mandated to treatment were less likely to be forthright about alcohol use than self-referred patients.

Rogers (1995) wondered whether the knowledge that informants would be employed might affect the honesty and completeness of alcoholics' self-reporting. Initial research by Graber and Miller (1988) found no significant differences. Depending on the clinical setting, however, practitioners may wish to inform patients that collateral interviews are an important component of the assessment process. Of course, such a warning may encourage certain patients to become more circumspect in their defensiveness or denial.

Addiction Severity Index and Teen Addiction Severity Index

McLellan, Luborsky, Woody, and O'Brien (1980) developed the Addiction Severity Index (ASI) for the assessment of seven domains in which persons with substance disorders usually have difficulty (medical, work, alcohol, drugs, family/social, legal, psychiatric). The ASI, chiefly validated using male Veterans Administration (VA) patients, emphasizes the treatment needs of individual patients. McLellan and colleagues reported that only 11 of 750 (1.5%) interviews produced invalid information; however, the basis of this estimate was not reported. Given this minuscule percentage, it is suspected that these investigators did not systematically screen patients for response styles but reported only very blatant cases of dissimulation.

A recent within-subjects study found that self-administered ASIs (whether Web-based or telephone-based using voice-response technology) produce significantly higher drug composite scores than clinician-administered ASIs (Brodey et al., 2004). Interestingly, respondents reported that they were more likely to be honest when reporting to an interviewer than to technology-driven ASIs. It is noteworthy that Gresnigt, Breteler, Schippers, and Van den Hurk (2000) have proposed that the ASI can be adapted to measure substance abuse severity on the day of an offense; however, psychometric limitations of the ASI include lack of standardized scores and low criterion-validity indices (Mäkelä, 2004; Melberg, 2004).

Kaminer, Bukstein, and Tarter (1991) developed the Teen Addiction Severity Index (T-ASI) as a parallel measure to the ASI. This modified interview has been tested on small samples of adolescent inpatients (see also Kaminer, Wagner, Plummer, & Seifer, 1993), but no data are provided on response styles, either exaggeration or denial. Using a within-subjects design, Brodey and colleagues (2005) found that adolescents did not differ in reported substance use between interviewer or self-report (i.e., Web-based or telephone-based with voice-response technology) conditions. However, adolescents indicated that they were more honest using the Web-based format than in the interview.

Global Appraisal of Individual Needs

The Global Appraisal of Individual Needs (GAIN; Dennis, 1999) is a structured interview

administered in 90–120 minutes. The GAIN is a standardized biopsychosocial interview that has eight main sections covering areas in which adolescents with substance disorders usually have difficulty (background, substance use, physical health, risk behaviors, mental health, environment, legal, and vocational). The 20-item GAIN–Short Screener (GSS; Dennis, Chan, & Funk, 2006) may be used for quick assessment when time precludes the lengthier GAIN. There are also adult (see Dennis et al., 2006) and parent (see Dennis et al., 2004) versions. The GAIN is a versatile instrument that maps onto diagnosis, placement, treatment planning, outcome, and economic analyses. It has over 100 scales and subscales. Adequate internal consistency (Dennis, Dawud-Noursi, Muck, & McDermett, 2003), test–retest reliability (Dennis et al., 2002), and indicators of validity have been documented (Godley, Godley, Dennis, Funk, & Passetti, 2002; Shane, Jasiukaitis, & Green, 2003). This family of measures is extremely versatile, has a relatively low cost, and is psychometrically very sound; furthermore, ample technical support is provided. The GAIN has no scales for assessing response style. Given its face-valid questions, the GAIN measures are likely to be vulnerable to faking.

Scales on Multiscale Inventories

Many multiscale inventories include scales for the assessment of substance abuse and its behavioral correlates. We focus on two that have considerable substance abuse research: versions of the Minnesota Multiphasic Personality Inventory (MMPI; see Greene, Chapter 10, this volume) and versions of the Millon Clinical Multiaxial Inventory (MCMI; see Sellbom & Bagby, Chapter 11, this volume).

MMPI Scales

The MacAndrew Alcoholism Scale (MAC; MacAndrew, 1965) of the MMPI (Hathaway & McKinley, 1940) was developed to differentiate alcoholic from nonalcoholic psychiatric patients. MacAndrew (1981) reviewed more than two dozen studies that demonstrated the ability of the MAC to differentiate alcoholic from nonalcoholic persons. Despite its early promise, however, the MAC has come under increasing attack. Gottesman and Prescott (1989) reviewed 74 MAC studies and concluded that it was not suitable for clinical practice. More specifically, they were concerned with its insufficient positive predictive power of .15 (i.e., only 1 in 7 alcoholic disorders was correctly identified). Other problems with the MAC include its potential confound with antisocial features and modest discriminability among criterion groups. Wolf, Schubert, Patterson, Grande, and Pendleton (1990) found that individuals with antisocial personality disorder (APD) received higher MAC scores than did substance abusers (see also Rathus, Fox, & Ortins, 1980). Other research (e.g., Levinson et al., 1990; Moore, 1984) had demonstrated only modest group differences among criterion groups, with nonusers often achieving elevations beyond the cut score (e.g., Miller & Streiner, 1990), particularly for minorities (Greene, 1991).

In contrast, Gripshover and Dacey (1994) found that the MAC scale had excellent sensitivity with substance abusers (≥ .90 across conditions) but very poor specificity (≤ .20). Likewise, Otto and colleagues (1988) established a very high sensitivity (.98) but modest specificity (.30). Even with these latter results, the clinical utility of the MAC as a screen is called into question unless the base rate of suspected substance abuse is very high. Otto and colleagues also examined the usefulness of the MAC scale to detect white adult males denying their alcohol dependence. They found that 47.5% eluded detection on the MAC. In contrast, they found that the MMPI Mp scale (Positive Malingering Scale; Cofer, Chance, & Judson, 1949) identified 75.0% of the defensive profiles. Although not directly tested, this finding provides a tantalizing hypothesis that the combined use of a specialized scale of substance abuse (e.g., the MAC) and a general measure of defensiveness (e.g., Mp) may produce effective classification rules.

For adolescents, Gantner, Graham, and Archer (1992) demonstrated that different raw MAC cut scores from ≥ 25 to ≥ 28 were optimal, depending on the criterion groups, to establish even a moderate sensitivity (≥ .55). As with adults, results for adolescents indicate that the MAC is less than satisfactory in discriminating between psychiatric adolescents with conduct disorder and substance-abusing adolescents (Gantner et al., 1992; Wolfson & Erbaugh, 1984). Stein and Graham (2001) examined the usefulness of the revised MAC (MAC-R; raw score ≥ 26) in a sample of incarcerated adolescents (N = 123; 56% had a sub-

stance use problem) that had taken the Minnesota Multiphasic Personality Inventory—Adolescent (MMPI-A; Butcher et al., 1992). They found that the MAC-R was ineffective in distinguishing substance-abusing from non-abusing groups. Similarly, the MAC-R was also developed for the MMPI-2 (Butcher, Dahlstrom, Graham, Tellegen, & Kaemmer, 1989). Investigations have provided mixed results on the effectiveness of MAC-R in accurately detecting adult substance abuse (Clements & Heintz, 2002; Greene, Weed, Butcher, Arredondo, & Davis, 1992; Stein, Graham, Ben-Porath, & McNulty, 1999; Weed, Butcher, McKenna, & Ben-Porath, 1992).

MacAndrew (1986) also constructed a 36-item Substance Abuse Proclivity (SAP) scale for differentiating young males (ages 16 to 22) with substance abuse problems from normal and clinical samples. As noted by Greene (1991), the SAP produced very similar results to the MAC, thus questioning its incremental validity. In its application to the MMPI-2, Greene and colleagues (1992) found negligible differences between substance abusers and non-substance abusers on the SAP.

Weed and colleagues (1992) developed two new scales for the assessment of substance abuse on the MMPI-2: (1) the Addiction Acknowledgement Scale (AAS), a 13-item face-valid measure of which nine items address the misuse of alcohol or drugs; and (2) the Addiction Potential Scale (APS), a 39-item scale with a varied content unrelated to substance abuse. They found similar elevations on the APS (raw Ms from 28.4 to 30.7) across both gender and type of abuse (alcohol, drug, or both) that were somewhat higher than nonabusing criterion groups (Ms from 23.3 to 23.9). However, Greene and colleagues (1992) found only modest differences between abusers (Ms from 26.8 to 27.6) and nonabusers (Ms from 23.6 to 23.8). Interestingly, Fantoni-Salvador and Rogers (1997) found the AAS to be superior to the MAC and APS in identifying Hispanic patients with alcohol dependence. In summary, the APS and the AAS evidence modest improvements over the MAC and MAC-R but have not been tested in simulation research in which known substance abusers are instructed to minimize or exaggerate their drug use.

Adolescent versions of the AAS and APS are named the Alcohol/Drug Problem Acknowledgement scale (ACK; Weed, Butcher, & Williams, 1994) and the Alcohol/Drug Problem Proneness scale (PRO; Weed et al., 1994). Weed and colleagues (1994) found that ACK and PRO discriminated between substance abusers and both clinical and nonclinical adolescents, although PRO performed best. Clinical adolescents with and without substance use problems were best distinguished by PRO as compared with ACK (Weed et al., 1994). Stein and Graham (2001) found in the previously described study of incarcerated adolescents that both ACK and PRO significantly distinguished among substance abusing and nonabusing adolescents. ACK (T score ≥ 55) produced the best classification rates with SN (.68), SP (.67), PPP (.72), and NPP (.62).

Stein and Graham (2005) studied the ability of ACK and PRO to detect underreported substance use in incarcerated adolescents ($N = 126$), about half of whom had a substance disorder. In a counterbalanced design, respondents took the test under standard and fake-good instructions. Under standard instructions, substance scales correctly classified about 60–85% of adolescents. Under fake-good instructions, substance-abusing and non-substance-abusing juveniles produced lower scores on substance scales. However, the Lie scale (T score ≥ 56) was able to detect over 75% of deceptive profiles and about 77% of honest profiles. When the Lie scale and the best substance scale (ACK T score ≥ 55) were used in combination, 82% of faking substance abusers were identified as either substance abusers or as underreporting. Interpretation of these results must be tempered, as the faking instructions were for general psychological problems and behavioral disturbance and not specific to substance abuse.

MCMI Scales

The MCMI (Millon, 1983) and its revisions (MCMI-II, Millon, 1987; MCMI-III, Millon, 1994) have two scales for the assessment of substance abuse. The MCMI-III Scale B, the Alcohol Dependence scale, consists of 15 items; Scale T, Drug Dependence, is composed of 14 items. The adolescent version is named the Millon Adolescent Clinical Inventory (MACI; Millon, 1993) and has a 35-item Substance Abuse Proneness scale (Scale BB). As compared with the MMPI, relatively little research has been conducted on the Millon measures. Because Scales B and T vary markedly in content

across revisions of the inventory, comparisons between MCMI versions have very limited value.

The discriminability of the original Scales B and T, even with acknowledged substance abusers, has been called into question. Craig and Weinberg (1992) reviewed 16 MCMI studies of substance abuse. Of these, three studies reported classification rates; none of the sensitivity rates exceeded .50. For instance, Miller and Streiner (1990) found poor sensitivity for Scale B for both current (.36) and lifetime (.33) diagnosis in a sample of 175 inpatients and outpatients. On the MCMI-II, Flynn and colleagues (1997) studied Scale T with acknowledged drug users and found the scale to be ineffective (e.g., SN = .59; SP = .30). If the MCMI scales are unsuccessful with acknowledged substance abusers, many of whom were actively involved in treatment, how can it be expected to detect unacknowledged or misreported substance abuse?

The MCMI scales appear to be vulnerable to faking. Millon (1983) instructed participants to appear psychologically disturbed. Both scales B and T were markedly elevated (BR >85). On the MCMI-II, Craig, Kuncel, and Olson (1994) investigated the effectiveness of the substance abuse scales in detecting denied drug use. They found that 52% of drug abusers were able to successfully deny drug or alcohol abuse. On a more positive note, those unable to elude detection tended to be persons with more severe addictions.

In summary, the MCMI appears to have very modest discriminant validity for the detection of substance abusers. At best, its results should be viewed as a screening measure. In other words, if high scores are recorded, then further investigation is warranted. On the other hand, the presence of low scores does not signify the absence of substance abuse. Certainly more work is required to evaluate the MCMI-III and MACI regarding their susceptibility to under- and overreporting of substances.

Specialized Measures for the Determination of Substance Abuse

Specialized measures have been developed for the determination of substance abuse. These measures typically focus on pathological patterns rather than formal diagnoses. For a summary, please see Table 6.3.

TABLE 6.3. Brief Summary of Specialized Measures for Substance Abuse

Measure[a]	Number	Substance covered	Population	Face validity	Response style scales
AUI	147	Alcohol	Adults	Yes	Yes
DrInC	45	Alcohol	Adult	Yes	Yes
InDUC	50	Alcohol/drug	Adult	Yes	Yes
PEI	300	Alcohol/drug	Adolescent/adult	Yes	Yes
SASSI	~90[b]	Alcohol/drug	Adult/adolescent	Variable[c]	Yes
TLFB	Variable	Alcohol/drug	Adult/adolescent	Yes	No

Note. Population reflects *general* use of the measure.
[a]See text for full measure names.
[b]Approximately 90 items, depending on which of the five versions is used.
[c]Scales are included that are face-valid, whereas other scales are specifically designed to be less face-valid.

Specialized Alcohol Measures for Adults

Alcohol Use Inventory

The Alcohol Use Inventory (AUI; Horn, Wanberg, & Foster, 1990; Wanberg, Horn, & Foster, 1977) is a well-designed measure of 147 items that address three domains: styles of alcohol use, unfavorable consequences of drinking, and perceived beneficial consequences of drinking. The 16 scales evidence little overlap, appear conceptually related to treatment status (outpatient, acute inpatient, and chronic inpatient), are relatively stable across ethnic groups, and have excellent reliability (see Horn et al., 1990; Rohsenow, 1982; Wanberg et al., 1977; Wanberg, Lewis, & Foster, 1978). The AUI has a scale designed to measure deterioration and disruption as a result of chronic alcohol use. A second scale is designed as a cross-check on the first; individuals who differ more than 3 sten scores are considered to be invalid. However, the effectiveness of this index has not been empirically demonstrated. In a cluster-analytic approach, Kline and Snyder (1985) identified one subtype of alcoholics with clinical elevations on the MMPI F scale (used to detect faking bad) but found remarkably little differences between it and other groups on the AUI scales. The actual meaning of this finding is obscure; perhaps an F scale elevation was more associated with confusion and psychopathology than with exaggerated alcohol use. In summary, the AUI is a well-validated measure that may serve as a useful adjunct to the assessment of suspected substance abuse.

Drinker Inventory of Consequences

The 45-item DrInC (Miller et al., 1995) was designed to measure drinking consequences while avoiding the direct measurement of dependence, pathological drinking, and help seeking. Normative data and acceptable validity information exist on a large sample of alcohol-dependent treatment-seeking adults. Five subscales (see the SIP, discussed earlier) and a total score are derived for lifetime and past-6-month problems. Scale internal consistency ranged from .61 to .91, and test–retest reliability ranged from .79 to .96. This measure has also been validated for use with intravenous drug users who drink heavily (Anderson, Gogineni, Charuvastra, Longabaugh, & Stein, 2001). The DrInC contains five items to assess honest responding. Although this measure has promise in establishing a pattern of behavioral consequences associated with alcohol use for a specified time period, no published studies examine the utility of the honest responding scale for misreported substance abuse.

Specialized Alcohol and Drug Measure for Adults

Inventory of Drug Use Consequences

The 50-item InDUC (Tonigan & Miller, 2002) was derived from the DrInC using treatment-seeking substance users. It assesses both alcohol and drug consequences and includes a reverse-scaled five-item Control scale to detect careless or preservative responding. Again, this measure has promise in establishing a pattern of behavioral consequences associated with drug use for a specified time period, nevertheless no studies have examined the utility of its Control scale to detect errant responding.

Specialized Alcohol and Drug Measure for Adolescents

Personal Experience Inventory

The PEI (Winters & Henly, 1989) is composed of 33 scales and 300 items that are organized into two broad dimensions that address the severity of drug use and associated psychosocial problems. The PEI is intended for use with adolescents ages 12–18 who have a minimum reading level of grade 6 and are cooperative with the assessment (Dahmus, Bernardin, & Bernardin, 1992). A parent version exists, demonstrating significant convergence between mother and child reports (PEI-PV; Winters, Anderson, Bengston, Stinchfield, & Latimer, 2000). A 270-item adult version exists as well (PEI-A; Winters, 1999). Although no work has been done on the PEI-A response distortion scales, the PEI-A drug involvement scale strongly correlated ($r = .62$) with significant-other reports of substance use.

PEI research has demonstrated good reliability (see Winters & Henly, 1989; Winters et al., 1991; Winters, Stinchfield, & Latimer, 2004), consistent evidence of diagnostic validity (e.g., Henly & Winters, 1988; Kennedy & Minami, 1993; Winters, Stinchfield, & Henly, 1993; Winters et al., 2004), and little or no evidence of ethnic bias (Winters et al., 2004). The validity data are limited to general constructs (e.g., severity of abuse) rather than specific drugs or patterns of drug use. Importantly, most research has used treatment history as the external criterion for establishing substance abuse.

Two PEI scales specifically address response styles. The Infrequency scale (7 items) is intended to measure faked drug use by the endorsement of fictitious drugs and improbable statements related to drug use and procurement. The Defensiveness scale (11 items) was derived from Marlowe–Crowne and designed to measure general defensiveness. Winters and colleagues (1991) imposed a categorization on these two scales that was rational (i.e., inspection of frequency distributions) rather than empirically based. Participants with raw scores ≥ 3 were judged to be "faking bad" on the Infrequency scale. On the Defensiveness scale,

raw scores of ≥ 4 and ≤ 8 were deemed to be moderately defensive and >8 to be highly defensive. For 886 delinquents receiving treatment for drug abuse, approximately 5.7% were placed into the faking-bad category, in contrast to 2.6% of high school controls. As previously noted, the Defensiveness scale is not specific to drug use. Therefore, the large percentages classified as moderately defensive (44.5% of drug users and 61.6% of controls) is not surprising. Several later studies, mostly on adolescents in drug treatment, indicate general response distortion rates of about 5–7% (Stinchfield & Winters, 2003; Winters et al., 2004; Winters, Latimer, Stinchfield, & Henly, 1999).

Winters and colleagues (1993) adopted a different standard for ruling PEI protocols to be invalid. Participants who scored in the 90th percentile on either the Infrequency or Defensiveness scales of the normative sample for drug users were classified as invalid. Based on this standard, 18.9% of delinquents were declared invalid. Again the rationale for this decision rule was not made explicit.

In summary, the authors have produced a highly valuable series of instruments with consideration to response style. However, much research is left to be accomplished, particularly on the discriminant validity of the PEI with respect to dissimulation. To date, we have no systematic comparisons of criterion groups (defensive, exaggerating, and control). Without such comparisons, optimum cut scores cannot be established. For the present, marked elevations on the Infrequency scale should trigger a more complete evaluation of exaggeration or careless responding. Marked elevations on the Defensiveness scale should not be interpreted as denial or minimization of drug use, as these elevations are more common among nonusers than users.

Specialized Alcohol and Drug Measures for Adults and Adolescents

Substance Abuse Subtle Screening Inventory

Adult versions of the Substance Abuse Subtle Screening Inventory (SASSI) include the original SASSI (Miller, 1985), SASSI-2 (Miller, 1994a), and SASSI-3 (Miller & Lazowski, 1999), whereas adolescent versions include the SASSI-A (Miller, 1990) and SASSI-A2 (Miller & Lazowski, 2001).

In order to facilitate research comparisons and to allow continued use of accumulated clinical information, the purpose and overall structure of the SASSI revisions are comparable to the original SASSI (Lazowski, Miller, Boye, & Miller, 1998; Miller & Lazowski, 2001). These measures were intended to be effective with both acknowledged and unacknowledged substance abuse. From this perspective, versions of the SASSI offer several advantages over other substance abuse measures: (1) scales for the assessment of denied or minimized use, (2) coverage of both alcohol and drug use, and (3) assessment specific to adolescents.

The original SASSI study of denial asked 50 polydrug abusers and 36 alcoholics to conceal all chemical use and to make the best impression possible. Results were compared with the same sample and other criterion groups under instructions to be honest. Provisional subscales and decision rules were generated that likely represented an overfitting of the data. These provisional decision rules appeared to be highly successful with defensive male alcoholics (92%) and moderately successful with defensive substance abusers (73 to 82%). As acknowledged by the author, no attempt had been made to identify exaggerated substance abuse (see Miller, 1985, 1994a, 1994b).

Svanum and McGrew (1995) examined the usefulness of the SASSI in screening 495 students, 57 of whom met DSM-III-R (American Psychiatric Association, 1987) criteria for substance abuse. They found that the SASSI rules were ineffective at detecting most substance abusers with SN of .33. When the SASSI did classify a person as a substance abuser, the PPP was very modest (.25), which meant that only one of four persons classified as substance abusers met the DSM-III-R criteria. Interestingly, the MAST outperformed the SASSI as a screening measure. Similarly, other researchers have found that adult versions of the SASSI have limited psychometric properties and ability to identify problematic substance use (see Clements, 2000; Gray, 2001). On the other hand, Schwartz (1998), in collaboration with the SASSI Institute, found that the SASSI effectively identified substance abuse and prior criminal involvement. Similarly, Lazowski and colleagues (1998) studied almost 2,000 participants and found very high SN (.97) and SP (.95).

Myerholtz and Rosenberg (1998) studied 164 college students randomly assigned to complete the SASSI under standard, fake-good, and fake-bad instructions in a between-subjects design. Faking instructions were specific to substance use. They found that few scales evidenced significant differences under fake-good versus standard instructions. The proportion of students classified as chemically dependent was similar under standard and fake-good instructions. With fake-bad instructions, mean scores were markedly elevated in comparison with standard instructions, and more students were classified as chemically dependent under fake-bad than standard instructions. These data suggest that the SASSI has limited value for detecting overreported substance abuse in college students.

Myerholtz and Rosenberg (1997) studied 46 offenders convicted for driving under the influence (DUI) who took the SASSI under various conditions. The standard-instruction SASSI was administered first; then participants took the SASSI two more times under counterbalanced fake-good and fake-bad instructions that were specific to substance abuse. When instructed to fake good, 71% of participants successfully hid their substance abuse. When instructed to fake bad, 63% of participants successfully modified their responses to appear chemically dependent. Importantly, few simulators were detected as invalid in either the fake-good (26%) or fake-bad (30%) condition. Moreover, on a scale designed to be less vulnerable to denied substance abuse, means did not differ between standard and fake-good conditions. In total, these results indicate that for DUI offenders, the SASSI may be vulnerable to faking.

In the original validation of the SASSI-A (Miller, 1990), decision rules appeared to be moderately successful at identifying chemically dependent adolescents (83%) and marginally successful at classifying adolescents without substance abuse (72%) or denying substance abuse (69%). The SASSI-A2 manual (Miller & Lazowski, 2001) presents SN, SP, PPP, and NPP of .95, .85, .97, and .72, respectively, for adolescent offenders with an 86% base rate for substance problems. Several researchers (Piazza, 1996; Risberg, Stevens, & Graybill, 1995) have found promising results when the SASSI was used to classify adolescent substance abusers and nonabusers (overall classification rates as high as .90); however, others (see Bauman, Merta, & Steiner, 1999) have obtained less favorable results.

Rogers, Cashel, Johansen, Sewell, and Gonzalez (1997) studied 319 adolescent offenders in residential treatment on a dual-diagnosis unit. For substance abusers openly acknowledging their alcohol and drug problems, the SASSI-A, as expected, was highly accurate. For the 82 adolescents who minimized their abuse, the hierarchical decision rules identified 75.6%. The greatest concern was the misclassification of nonusers as abusers. Of the 19 nonusers in the study, the decision rules incorrectly classified more than two-thirds (68.4%) as abusers. Rogers and colleagues also reported initial data that questioned the SASSI-A's generalizability with Hispanic populations. When controlling for the level of substance abuse, significant differences were found on several SASSI scales.

Stein and colleagues (2005) studied a sample of 178 incarcerated adolescents with a high prevalence of problematic alcohol use. The decision rules were moderately effective with self-acknowledged alcohol problems. As with Rogers and colleagues (1997), the results indicate potential ethnic bias on the SASSI. Acceptable classification rates for drug use were not found.

Many of the SASSI items appear to have an antisocial or delinquent content. Given the concordance between antisocial behavior and substance abuse, this strategy of capitalizing on antisocial attitudes and behavior to identify substance abusers is likely to be effective in some settings. We would caution, however, that the use of the SASSI in court-referred populations may actually be stymied by this strategy. In these cases, the diagnostic task is to differentiate abusing and nonabusing offenders. The danger is that the SASSI, as found by Rogers and colleagues (1997), may misclassify nonabusing offenders based on this underlying strategy.

Timeline Followback

Timeline Followback (TLFB) uses a calendar method to evaluate daily patterns of alcohol and drug use (Fals-Stewart, O'Farrell, Freitas, McFarlin, & Rutigliano, 2000; Sobell & Sobell, 1996). It has been used with adults and adolescents. Good reliability and validity data exist (see Fals-Stewart et al., 2000). An abbreviated version of TLFB, the Form-90 (Miller, 1996; Miller & Del Boca, 1994), is also available. Memory aids (lists of holidays, news events, personally relevant dates, etc.) are used to assist in accurate recall, and recall covering 365 days is not uncommon. TLFB has been used to establish quantity (difficult to establish for illicit substances) and frequency of substance use, as well as other significant events, such as hospitalizations and arrests. A collateral form can be used where extensive face-to-face contact and knowledge of use patterns has been established (see Fals-Stewart et al., 2000). Validity has been established with biological testing, record review, and collateral reports (Fals-Stewart et al., 2000; O'Farrell & Langenbucher, 1988).

TLFB can be used to establish substance use and behavioral patterns. In this sense, it may be used to establish a link between use and subsequent behavior. The face-valid nature of the interview questions makes it fakable; however, the detailed nature of TLFB may make it hard for respondents to reliably fabricate a pattern of use over multiple interviews covering a specified time period. It must be cautioned that little research has addressed this issue. On a promising note, Fals-Stewart and colleagues (2000) found no correlation between TLFB substance use indices and a general measure of social desirability in adults seeking drug treatment.

LABORATORY METHODS

We review three very common laboratory methods of detecting substance use, including Breathalyzer, urinalysis, and hair analysis. However, it should be pointed out that other methods also exist, including blood sampling (and use of mean corpuscular volume, gamma-glutamyl transferase, and carbohydrate-deficient transferin; see Schwan et al., 2004), wearable electronic devices to sense metabolism via skin perspiration (see Swift & Swette, 1992), and saliva (Dolan, Rouen, & Kimber, 2004). Biological detection of drug use usually involves screening, which, if positive, is followed by confirmatory testing (Dolan et al., 2004). It is important to note that drug concentrations in various specimens are highly variable and depend on many factors, such as amount of drug consumed, time since use, metabolism rate, body fat, and consumption of liquids (see Jaffee, Trucco, Levy, & Weiss, in press).

Dolan and colleagues (2004) provide *general* benchmarks for windows of detection based on different laboratory methods:

- Saliva, 1–36 hours
- Urinalysis, 1–3 days
- Hair analysis, 7–100 or more days
- Sweat via continuous monitoring, 1–14 days.

Breathalyzer

Sobell, Sobell, and VanderSpek (1979) demonstrated the potential usefulness of Breathalyzer data in multiple samples of alcoholic patients. They administered the Breathalyzer under one of two conditions: either routinely to patients involved in treatment or selectively to patients in treatment suspected of drinking. The results were very similar across groups; approximately half the patients who had been drinking denied their ongoing alcohol use. Certainly, the treatment potential of selective Breathalyzer use has not been fully tested.

Most mental health professionals have access to Breathalyzer data following the arrest of a person on charges of driving while intoxicated (DWI; Jalazo, Steer, & Fine, 1978). It may also be used in some employment screenings (Cohen, 1984). Because different BACs are employed to define intoxication, clinicians must be careful to distinguish between *legal* intoxication (BACs ranging in levels from 80–100 mg/dl) and *clinical* intoxication, for which BACs are highly variable. With clinical intoxication, behavioral observations likely include one or more of the following: slurred speech, poor coordination, unsteady gait, nystagmus, attention and memory problems, and stupor/coma (see American Psychiatric Association, 2000). Chronic alcoholics with increased tolerance may show no evidence of intoxication with BAC levels ≥ 100 mg/dl (American Psychiatric Association, 2000). As observed by Mikkelsen (1985), marked variations in BAC have been associated with clinical intoxication, with the majority becoming visibly intoxicated at levels between 100 and 200 mg/dl.

The standard for most Breathalyzers, according to Kapur (1994), is the 2100:1 alveolar breath:blood conversion; this ratio is conservative and tends to underestimate the actual BAC. Although Simpson (1987) concurred that most BACs are underestimates, he asserted that a substantial minority (19–23%) of those tested may have overestimates of their BAC.

Potential errors in Breathalyzer results are possible if the test is administered directly after the person has been drinking. Because of residual alcohol vapor in the mouth, artificially high readings are possible if readings are taken within 20 minutes of alcohol consumption. Few technical problems occur in Breathalyzer administration, particularly with the widely adopted computer-based models. Although concerns have been raised regarding the effective maintenance of Breathalyzers (Trichter, McKinney, & Pena, 1995), these concerns can easily be addressed through documentation and service records.

The relationship of alcohol consumption to BAC is highly variable. In testing BAC with 64 male participants who had fasted for 4 hours, O'Neill, Williams, and Dubowski (1983) found that a low dose (0.5 g/kg, or approximately 27 oz. of beer for a 150-lb male) had dramatic effects on BAC levels (range from 32 to 109 mg/dl). High doses (1.0 g/kg) also had marked ranges (99–180 mg/dl). On average, low dosages peaked 31 minutes after drinking, whereas high dosages peaked 51 minutes following alcohol consumption. In addition, Breathalyzer technology is not suitable for continuous long-term measurement of alcohol. It also requires the individual's cooperation (Swift & Swette, 1992).

Exposure to methyl tert-butyl ether (MBTE) may result in false positives on commercial Breathalyzers (Buckley, Pleil, Bowyer, & Davis, 2001). This may be particularly germane for persons working with gasoline and other fuels oxygenated with MBTE (e.g., auto mechanics, gas station attendants). Use of newer Breathalyzer technology (that employs infrared and electrochemical detectors) can mitigate this concern.

Urinalysis

Urinalysis is the most widely used method in drug detection (Dolan et al., 2004), and as such, we review methods of tampering with urinalysis, as well as methods to combat tampering. Urinalysis may be used to screen for a number of drugs, including amphetamine, barbiturates, benzodiazepines, cocaine metabolites, methadone, phencyclidine (PCP), morphine, ethanol, and cannabinoids (Morgan, 1984). Urinalysis is a generally effective measure within a rather narrow window of detection, typically ranging from 1 to 3 days. The notable exception is cannabis, which is sometimes detected after an 8-week period.

Because ethanol is rapidly metabolized and eliminated from the body, methods that depend on sampling breath, blood, urine, and saliva are somewhat limited to detection of alcohol consumption within the past few hours (Jones, 1993). One notable exception to this is testing urine for concentrations of 5-hydroxy-tryptophol (5HTOL) and 5-hydroxyindole-3-acetic acid (5HIAA). The ratio of 5HTOL to 5HIAA can provide a sensitive method of detecting even moderate amounts of alcohol (roughly 50 g, or a little less than about five bottles of beer) within approximately 24 hours (Helander et al., 1999).

Three types of urinalysis are readily available for the assessment of suspected substance abuse: immunoassay, chromatographic, or chromatography-mass-spectrometry methods (Kapur, 1994). Immunoassay procedures are comparatively less expensive and therefore widely used, despite their potential for misclassification. They may be divided into laboratory-based and on-site tests (Dolan et al., 2004). Immunoassay techniques (Mieczkowski, Landress, Newel, & Coletti, 1993) are based on antigen–antibody reactions, with the antibody being radioisotope-, fluorescence-, or enzyme-labeled. In the first two procedures, the labeled antibody is introduced into a urine sample. If a sample is drug-positive, a binding with the labeled antibody will occur, and the amount of radioactivity or fluorescence will be measured. If the antibody is enzyme labeled, it will bind with a drug-positive sample, and the enzyme will cause some measurable reaction. Immunoassay methods are the first step in evaluating suspected urine samples.

Chromatography or chromatography/mass spectrometry should be used to verify any positive findings on immunoassay methods. These methods involve the separating, typically with gas or fluid, and, in the case of mass spectrometry, the "fingerprinting" of a drug or its metabolites (Kapur, 1994). The technical expertise required for sample preparation is fairly sophisticated, but a positive result via gas chromatography/mass spectrometry (GC/MS) is considered to be extremely accurate.

The accuracy of urinalysis can be affected by several environmental factors that extend beyond the laboratory procedures and that may result in either false positives or false negatives. These factors include (1) common over-the-counter medications that may lead to positive test results for drugs (e.g., Alka-Seltzer Plus and Sudafed; Potter & Orfali, 1990); (2) ingestion of poppy seeds that may result in false positives for cocaine use (Baer, Baumgartner, Hill, & Blahd, 1991); (3) ingestion of large amounts of water prior to testing (i.e., flushing) that may result in false negatives (Baumgartner, Hill, & Blahd, 1989); and (4) contamination of urine (e.g., mixing with toilet water) that can result in false negatives (Kapur, 1994). Direct observation of the urine collection, although intrusive, can minimize this risk.

With the popularity of the Internet, many persons have access to a plethora of compounds, products, and methods to tamper with urinalysis. Jaffee and colleagues (2007) reviewed research indicating that there are a number of commercial and household products that can effectively produce false-negative urines depending on factors such as type of urine detection method used, concentration of adulterant added to the sample, and type of drug being detected (marijuana, amphetamine, opioids, cocaine, hallucinogens, or barbiturates). In addition, the studies reviewed by Jaffee and colleagues indicate that some household products (e.g., soap, ammonia) may cause false positives as well when added to urine samples. Ingesting adulterants to avoid detection does not seem to be more effective than simple ingestion of excessive amounts of water in order to avoid detection; however, some ingested adulterants contain products that aid in avoiding detection of dilution or flushing (Jaffe et al., 2007).

In their review of urinalysis tampering methods, Jaffee and colleagues (2007) also describe various methods of urine substitution. External urine storage may be difficult to detect, even with direct observation and urine temperature checks, since the specimen can be concealed in or near a body cavity and expelled via a channel (e.g., tube or prosthetic penis) near the genitals. Obviously, more invasive observation methods may reveal use of such techniques. On the other hand, another technique is urine substitution *within* the bladder, in which a person will void his or her bladder and then use a catheter to refill the bladder with new urine. Understandably, this technique is more difficult to detect by observation.

In most cases, ingesting or adding adulterants and urine substitution can be minimized or detected (Jaffee et al., 2007). During specimen collection, the collector must remain in the presence of the donor (a stall may be used) and outer garments must be removed. Urines should be inspected for unusually cloudy, bubbly, clear, or orange appearance, for presence of undissolved crystals, for fluorescent glow under black light, and for temperature outside of about 90–100°F. Several products are marketed and effective in detecting adulterants, and among them Intect 7 appears most effective (see Jaffee et al., 2007) for on-site analysis. Finally, laboratory tests can be used to detect whether or not creatinine, specific gravity, and pH levels are within expected parameters, and they can detect the presence of oxidizing adulterants.

Urinalysis may play a useful adjunctive role in the treatment of substance abusers. Treatment Alternatives to Street Crime (TASC; Hirschel & McCarthy, 1983), a comprehensive treatment program for persons arrested on drug charges, employs urine testing as an essential component of the treatment. Its purpose is the verification of patient reports of drug abstinence. Clinicians likely differ in their views of whether urinalysis is an intervention or an outcome measure. We prefer to conceptualize urinalysis as an intervention with the threat of detection serving as a temporary, albeit externally imposed, treatment. In this light, the goal of treatment would be the replacement of this external threat with more internalized motivations. Moreover, the disavowal of drug use in the presence of a drug-positive screen provides useful data on denial and defensiveness.

Hair Analysis

Kelly and Rogers (1996) reviewed the literature on hair analysis as it applies to misreported drug use. The procedure involves radioimmunoassay of hair (RIAH) to determine current (within past 4 weeks) and past drug use. Because metabolites of illicit drugs are embedded in the hair shaft, the shaft becomes a chronology of drug use or nonuse. Depending on the hair length, laboratories are able to estimate patterns of drug use based on (1) the relative position of positive results and (2) the relatively stable growth of scalp hair (approximately 0.5 inches per month). Concentrations of these metabolites are proportional to drug use, which allows laboratories to estimate not only their presence but also the extent of their use. Currently, no on-site tests exist for hair analysis (Dolan et al., 2004).

The efficacy of hair analysis has been investigated through animal models that have demonstrated a nearly perfect linear relationship between amount ingested and residue in hair samples. Ethical and legal constraints have limited its testing in humans using experimental designs. Although several investigators have administered compounds chemically associated with illegal drugs (e.g., Baumgartner et al., 1989; Nakahara, Shimamine, & Takahashi, 1992) and measured residue in scalp hair, most researchers have employed indirect and less precise methods, with self-reporting of drug use as the external criterion. A further validation is performed by confirming RIAH results with a more sensitive technique, such as GC/MS. Employing GC/MS as a criterion, RIAH has proven more than twice as effective as urinalysis in testing for commonly abused drugs (e.g., cocaine, PCP, and opiates; Feucht, Stephens, & Walker, 1994; Mieczkowski, Barzelay, Gropper, & Wish, 1991). The difficulty in reviewing this literature (see Kelly & Rogers, 1996) is that classificatory accuracy is not expressed in the form of interpretable estimates, such as specificity and sensitivity. Of crucial importance, investigators have found few cases of false positives. In the published literature, positive results on the RIAH are confirmed by a more accurate technique such as GC/MS. As a precaution, we recommend that positive RIAH findings in clinical practice be confirmed, either by acknowledgement of the suspected user or through GC/MS.

The RIAH has several important limitations. First, generally, RIAH has not been useful for suspected alcohol abuse, although more recent work has indicated that fatty acid ethyl esters and ethyl glucuronide in hair are suitable markers for alcohol abuse (Pragst & Balikova, 2006). Second, different laboratories use different extraction procedures (e.g., solvent-based, acid-base, or antibody extraction), which precludes precise comparisons across laboratories. Third, external contamination (e.g., marijuana or crack cocaine smoke) may possibly alter drug estimates, although many researchers believe the proper washing of hair samples prior to extraction obviates this potential problem. In addition, detection of drug-specific metabolites in hair reduces concern regarding external contamination (Pragst & Balikova, 2006). Similarly, use of pubic hair may mitigate exposure to some environmental contaminants (Gaillard, Vayssette, & Pepin, 2000). Despite exposure to the same drug concentration in blood, the concentration of drugs in pigmented as compared with white hair appears to be ten-fold higher (see Pragst & Balikova, 2006). In addition, exposure to sunlight, especially for cannabinoids, may result in degradation of the sample and produce false negatives (see Pragst & Balikova, 2006). Furthermore, there is increased risk for false-positive results in hair analysis of bleached and permanent waved hair (Skopp, Potsch, & Moeller, 1997).

From a treatment perspective, RIAH offers an unequaled opportunity to assess types and patterns of substance abuse. Whether a patient is decreasing or increasing drug use is critical to measuring treatment success. For validation of psychometric measures, RIAH can provide a close approximation to "ground truth" in establishing clear criteria between abusers and nonabusers. The chief limitation of RIAH, as with all laboratory procedures, is that it provides little data on behavioral responses. Its primary use by clinicians is likely to be for the confirmation or questioning of reported ingestion rather than the effects of drug use.

In summary, we believe that RIAH with appropriate confirmation is the assessment method of choice for several clinical and research situations, including (1) *retrospective accounts* (at a specified period in the past, whether the patient ingested specific drugs), (2) *longitudinal questions* (patterns of drug use that can be documented in the past year), (3) *behavioral correlates of drug use* (patterns of symptoms and associated features that are related to specific drug use), and (4) *criterion-related validity* (identifying criterion groups of specific users and nonusers and examining differences on designated instruments' scales).

CLINICAL APPLICATIONS

Many, if not most, diagnoses of substance abuse disorders are missed simply because patients are not asked about these disorders (see Moore et al., 1989). In both medical and psychiatric populations, substance abuse and associated problems must be addressed systematically. Health professionals may simply assume that they will be able to detect intoxicated patients among those in treatment, thereby obviating the need for a more systematic investigation. In a classic study of 705 alcoholic patients, Sobell and colleagues (1979) found that clinicians were not particularly effective at de-tecting those who were under the influence of alcohol. Of those patients denying intoxication, clinicians correctly identified between 50 and 67% as verified by breath analysis of blood alcohol level. False positives ranged across samples from 0 to 17%. Clearly, clinical observation alone is insufficient for the detection of ongoing substance abuse.

A relevant but virtually unexplored issue is the misuse of prescribed medications in clinical populations. An early cross-sectional study by Ballinger, Simpson, and Stewart (1974) suggested that substantial numbers (11.9%) of psychiatric inpatients ingested nonprescribed medications. Another 6.4% had undetectable levels of the prescribed medication, suggesting treatment noncompliance. Although nursing staff medication errors may account for a few inaccuracies, these variations among inpatients raises considerable concern.

Screens and many specialized measures assume forthrightness and complete self-disclosure, not only about the type and frequency of substance abuse but also about its short- and long-term sequelae. Such assumptions, in light of our current knowledge of widespread denial, are likely to be naive. Still, the systematic use of screens is likely to be helpful in discovering undiagnosed cases of substance abuse. Toward this objective, we recommend the systematic use of screens, such as the AUDIT and the DAST.

Minimized substance use may be evidenced in marked discrepancies among a variety of sources. These include (1) acknowledgment of use with peers but denial with authority figures, (2) minimized history of use in contradiction to treatment or arrest records, (3) denial of use in contradiction to performance on face-valid measures of substance use, (4) elevations on SASSI defensive scales for nonminorities, and (5) computation of use levels based on CDP or TLFB, partially verifiable from other sources, that are much higher than self-reports. Because inconsistencies in reported drug use may have many determinants (e.g., confusion secondary to drug use, unawareness of consumed drugs, and contradictory accounts by co-users), we should not assume that discrepancies per se are evidence of dissimulation.

Similarly, exaggerated substance use may be evidenced in marked discrepancies among a variety of sources. These include (1) denial of substance use with peers but exaggeration with authorities, (2) gross exaggeration of past substance use in contradiction to past treatment or arrest records, (3) elevation of the PEI Infrequency scale, (4) endorsement of fictitious drugs, (5) ascribing very atypical behavioral effects from known drug use (e.g., prolonged hallucinatory experiences from the use of marijuana), and (6) computation of use levels based on CDP or TLFB, partially verifiable from other sources, that are much lower than self-reports. In certain settings, persons may be motivated to fabricate drug use as an explanation or excuse for misconduct. For example, many sex offenders imply that alcohol or drugs clouded their judgment, distorted their sexual interests, or impeded their "normal" self-control. Some offenders will report a "blackout" after ingesting some "bad" or laced marijuana. Careful inquiry into atypical effects may be helpful in distinguishing purely self-serving explanations from more believable descriptions. For instance, use of hallucinogens is unlikely to produce command hallucinations focused solely on execution of a well-planned bank robbery. We caution against drawing any immediate conclusions about the endorsement of fictitious drugs and deliberate exaggerations. Drug users may be motivated to appear knowledgeable or may simply be confused by the myriad of street and scientific terms. Clinicians can easily test the limits of credibility by associating uncommon effects (e.g., accelerated hair growth) with different fictitious drugs.

Clinical decision models provide the basis for determining whether patients reporting on substance use are engaging in some form of dissimulation. Unfortunately, our ability to make accurate classifications is substantially curtailed. For denied or minimized drug use, several sources provide useful information in clinical decision making. These include the following:

- Independent witnesses that disconfirm patient's denial or minimization of substance use for a specific event
- Positive alcohol Breathalyzer results covering a very limited time period (2–12 hours), which depends on level of intoxication and metabolism rates
- Positive urinanalysis results covering a circumscribed period of time (36–72 hours), although chronic use of cannabinoid substances can be detected for a more extended period (2–8 weeks)

- hair analysis covering an extended period of time (minimum time is 4 weeks; maximum is dependent on hair length but could extend to several years)
- Observed data (biochemical concentrations or behavioral observations) that disconfirm patient's minimization of substance use for a specific event or period of time

The limitation of the preceding data sources is that they do not address the immediate or long-term behavioral effects of drug use. Large-scale normative research is urgently needed on what symptoms and correlates should be expected with specific drug use, verified through laboratory procedures. At present, highly skilled clinicians with extensive experiences with drug users are likely to have some knowledge based on associated features with particular drug patterns. Their ability to distinguish bogus from genuine drug effects has not been empirically tested.

We have intentionally not included psychometric data in the clinical decision model. More specifically, the PEI Defensiveness scale is a measure of social desirability and does not appear to have discriminant validity with respect to denied drug use. In the same vein, the SASSI scales capitalize on their delinquency content (limiting their usefulness in forensic, court, or correctional settings) and lack demonstrated validity with minority populations. These measures should not be used in the determination of denied drug use.

It is difficult to propose a clinical decision model for exaggerated drug use because of the paucity of research on accurate classification. Of course, the absence of laboratory data may provide a convincing argument for exaggerated drug use. For example, Moeller, Fey, and Sachs (1993) reported that forensic cases may include fabricated substance abuse as a mitigating or exculpatory factor. In this regard, hair analysis may be useful in certain retrospective evaluations. For exaggerated drug use, several sources provide useful information in clinical decision making. These include the following:

- Independent witnesses who disconfirm patient's exaggeration of substance use for a specific event
- Negative alcohol Breathalyzer results covering a very limited time period (2–12 hours),

which depends on level of intoxication and metabolism rates

- Negative urinanalysis results covering a circumscribed period of time (36–72 hours), although for chronic use of cannabinoids the period of time can be extended (2–8 weeks)

- Negative hair analysis covering an extended period of time (4 weeks to several years)

- Observed data (biochemical concentrations or behavioral observations) that disconfirm patient's exaggeration of substance use for a specific event or period of time

7

Malingering of Posttraumatic Disorders

PHILLIP J. RESNICK, MD
SARA WEST, MD
JOSHUA W. PAYNE, MA

The detection of malingered posttraumatic stress disorder (PTSD) is one of the most difficult tasks faced by clinicians. Whereas the nuances of the phenomenology of genuine memory disorders and psychoses are fairly well established, the symptoms of PTSD are virtually all subjective and widely disseminated to the public.

DEFINING THE DISORDERS

Posttraumatic Stress Disorder

Posttraumatic stress disorder, or PTSD as it is commonly known, is a relatively new term in the field of psychiatry. However, the concept has existed for at least 100 years. In the 1880s, epithets such as "nervous shock" and "posttraumatic neurosis" were coined to describe the psychological phenomena resulting from exposure to trauma (Adamou & Hale, 2003; Hausotter, 1996; Sparr, 1990). In 1889, Clevenger proposed the idea that such diagnoses, including "railroad spine" and "compensation neurosis," were related to an accidental concussion resulting in abnormalities in the central nervous system (Clevenger, 1889; Hall, 2005; Thomann & Rauschmann, 2003, 2004). According to Hamilton (1906), the disorder was seized on by dishonest litigants seeking compensation after accidents. Prior to the concept of traumatic neuroses, personal injury cases were based on obvious injuries (e.g., loss of a limb) with objective and incontrovertible evidence that the physical injury had occurred (Trimble, 1982).

The psychological ramifications of trauma were revisited in relation to combat in the 20th century. It was called "shell shock" in World War I and "battle fatigue" in World War II. In 1952, the first edition of the *Diagnostic and Statistical Manual of Mental Disorders* (DSM; American Psychiatric Association, 1952) included "gross stress reaction," which was later subsumed within the category of "adjustment reaction to adult life" in the DSM-II (American Psychiatric Association, 1968). Societal awareness of these symptoms intensified with the return of the veterans from the Vietnam War. The debut of "posttraumatic stress disorder" occurred in 1980 with the publication of DSM-III (American Psychiatric Association, 1980).

The DSM-IV (American Psychiatric Association, 1994) modified the criteria used to diagnose PTSD. Criterion A, which defines the traumatic event, was changed from the DSM-III's *objective* standard (an event that would be markedly distressing to almost anyone) to a *subjective* standard (an event that the victim found intensely distressing). This broadening of the definition led to a 39% increase in the number of individuals who meet diagnostic criteria for PTSD (Breslau & Kessler, 2001). Table 7.1 contains the most recent diagnostic criteria for PTSD (American Psychiatric Association, 2000). The DSM-IV also introduced the diagnosis of "acute stress reaction," which is a time-limited precursor to PTSD involving dissociative symptoms (American Psychiatric Association, 1994).

The diagnosis of PTSD stands alone among disorders in specifying a causal link to an external event. Its criteria have been criticized for producing "illusory objectivity" in the legal arena (Stone, 1993). Plaintiffs' attorneys have found the diagnosis to be a boon due to the fact that the DSM criteria specifically attribute their clients' symptoms to the traumatic event. The symptoms are based almost entirely on the client's subjective report. Furthermore, once the PTSD diagnosis is raised, it tends to preclude consideration of other potential causal factors (Slovenko, 1994).

Breslau, Davis, Andreski, and Petersen (1991) described five risk factors for exposure to traumatic events. They include low education, male gender, early conduct problems, extraversion, and a family history of mental disorder or substance problems. Because exposure to trauma leads to PTSD in only a minority of cases, Davidson (1993) identified 11 pretrauma characteristics that cause an individual to be more vulnerable to PTSD (see Table 7.2). Increased vulnerability was due to background factors, childhood antecedents, and prior psychiatric problems. Ozer, Best, Lipsey, and Weiss (2003) found in an extensive meta-analysis of 476 studies that the single best predictor of PTSD was peritraumatic dissociation. Addi-

---

TABLE 7.1. A Distillation of DSM-IV-TR Criteria for PTSD

A. Exposed to a traumatic event with both:
   1. Actual or threatened death or serious injury or a threat to the physical integrity.
   2. A response with intense fear, helplessness, or horror.

B. The traumatic event is persistently reexperienced by:
   1. Recurrent and intrusive distressing recollections (e.g., images, thoughts, or perceptions).
   2. Recurrent distressing dreams.
   3. Acting or feeling as if the traumatic event was recurring (e.g., reliving the experience, illusions, hallucinations, and dissociative flashback episodes).
   4. Intense psychological distress at exposure to internal or external cues that symbolize or resemble an aspect of the traumatic event.
   5. Physiological reactivity upon exposure to internal or external cues that symbolize or resemble an aspect of the traumatic event.

C. Persistent avoidance of stimuli associated with the trauma and numbing of general responsiveness (not present before the trauma), as indicated by at least three of the following:
   1. Efforts to avoid thoughts, feelings, or conversations associated with the trauma.
   2. Efforts to avoid activities, places, or people that arouse recollections of the trauma.
   3. Inability to recall an important aspect of the trauma.
   4. Markedly diminished interest or participation in significant activities.
   5. Feeling of detachment or estrangement from others.
   6. Restricted range of affect (e.g., unable to have loving feelings).
   7. Sense of foreshortened future (e.g., does not expect to have a career, marriage, children, or a normal life span).

D. Persistent symptoms of increased arousal (not present before the trauma), as indicated by at least two of the following:
   1. Difficulty falling or staying asleep.
   2. Irritability or outbursts of anger.
   3. Difficulty concentrating.
   4. Hypervigilance.
   5. Exaggerated startle response.

E. Duration of the disturbance (symptoms in B, C, and D) is more than 1 month.

F. The disturbance causes clinically significant distress or impairment in social, occupational, or other important areas of functioning.

Note. Several criteria for children are different; please refer to DSM-IV-TR (American Psychiatric Association, 2000). From American Psychiatric Association (2000). Copyright 2000 by the American Psychiatric Association. Adapted by permission.

TABLE 7.2. Pretrauma Characteristics That Increase the Likelihood of Developing PTSD

Background

1. Female gender
2. History of psychiatric illness in first-degree relatives

Childhood antecedents

1. Parental poverty
2. Separation or divorce of parents before the age of 10
3. Trauma in childhood (may be of a sexual nature)
4. Behavior disorder in childhood or adolescence
5. Poor self-confidence in adolescence

Prior psychiatric problems

1. Prior psychiatric disorders
2. Introversion
3. Life stress prior to and following the trauma
4. High neuroticism

Note. Data from Davidson (1993).

tional predictors of PTSD were prior trauma, prior psychological maladjustment, family history of psychopathology, perceived life threat during the trauma, lack of posttrauma social support, and peritraumatic emotional responses.

Clinical predictions have also been applied to the chronicity of PTSD. According to DSM-IV (American Psychiatric Association, 2000), PTSD can be categorized as "acute" (symptoms lasting less than 3 months) or "chronic" (symptoms occurring for longer than 6 months). According to Breslau and Davis (1992), risk factors for chronicity include Axis I comorbidity (additional anxiety or mood disorders), comorbid medical conditions, family history of antisocial behavior, and female gender.

The neurobiology of PTSD has been more clearly defined in recent years. Dysfunction in both the hippocampus and the amygdala has been linked to PTSD. Increased stress is believed to lead to increased systemic glucocorticoids, which in turn interfere with the biochemical process of long-term potentiation in the hippocampus (McEwen, 1997). This process is hypothesized to be the origin of the memory disturbance seen in PTSD. A number of studies have been performed comparing the size of hippocampi in persons with PTSD with that in normal controls; the results have been varied (Grossman, Buchsbaum, & Yehuda, 2002). The amygdala is involved in processing fear and the accompanying autonomic re-

sponses. An overactive amygdala may play a role in the inability to extinguish classical fear conditioning and the hyperarousal symptoms of PTSD.

The prevalence of PTSD varies with the type of trauma that is experienced. Those who experience trauma of a sexual nature tend to be more likely to develop PTSD (Hapke, Schumann, Rumpf, John, & Meyer, 2006). PTSD has been reported in up to 80% of rape victims, whereas 15–30% of individuals involved in car accidents develop PTSD (Hall, Hall, & Chapman, 2006). In an examination of 66 participants exposed to either battlefield trauma, civilian terrorism, or work or auto accidents, those experiencing combat-related trauma were more severely affected with PTSD symptoms (Amir, Kaplan, & Kotler, 1996). The lifetime prevalence of PTSD is approximately 9% (Breslau et al., 1991). However, diagnosing the disorder may prove difficult because of the high degree of comorbid psychopathology. Brown, Campbell, Lehman, Grisham, and Mancill (2001) found in a large study of treatment-seeking outpatients with a primary diagnosis of PTSD that 92% had another active Axis I diagnosis. For the clinician, the challenge lies in determining whether the comorbid disorder was present prior to the trauma and its contribution to the claimant's current symptoms.

Malingering

Malingering is defined by the American Psychiatric Association (2000, p. 739) as "the intentional production of false or grossly exaggerated physical or psychological symptoms, motivated by external incentives." This external gain may take the form of financial rewards, relief of responsibilities at a job or at home, avoiding military service, or evading criminal responsibility (American Psychiatric Association, 2000). The definition was carefully constructed to avoid labeling as malingerers those who are prone to mild exaggerations with no intent to deceive (Wiley, 1998).

Malingering can be further categorized into (1) pure malingering, (2) partial malingering, and (3) false imputation. When an individual feigns a disorder that does not exist at all, this is referred to as *pure malingering*. When an individual has actual symptoms but consciously exaggerates them, it is called *partial malingering*. *False imputation* refers to the attribution of actual symptoms to a cause consciously recognized by the individual as having no relationship to the symptoms. For example, a male claimant who is aware that he is suffering from PTSD due to an earlier trauma may falsely ascribe the symptoms to a car accident in order to gain monetary compensation. False imputation is more difficult to identify as malingering because the individual can, from personal experience, accurately describe the symptoms. In addition, some individuals fail to recognize that consecutive events do not necessarily have a causal relationship (Collie, 1971). Such misattribution can be genuine and must be differentiated from malingering. Of these response styles, partial malingering that uses existing symptoms is the most common pattern (Kleinman & Stewart, 2004). Pure malingering is much less common (Trimble, 1981).

In the differential diagnosis for malingering, the clinician must also consider factitious and conversion disorders. Factitious disorder is similar to malingering in that the diagnosis requires the intentional, conscious production of false symptoms. They differ, however, in the motivation to report symptoms. Unlike malingering, those with factitious disorder produce symptoms in order to enjoy the patient role. In contrast, conversion disorders involve the unconscious production of symptoms.

Malingering should be considered in all referrals seeking compensation after a personal injury. Mittenberg, Patton, Canyock, and Condit (2002) surveyed clinicians regarding the prevalence of probable malingering and symptom exaggeration, with rates of 29% for personal injury and 30% for disability cases. These rates, although substantial, should not be equated with confirmed rates of malingering. Nonetheless, they underscore the importance of closely evaluating feigning in compensation cases. Feigned impairment is also a key issue. A follow-up study of individuals deemed 100% disabled showed that 40% had no disability 1 year after their disabilities were determined (Maloney, Glasser, & Ward, 1980). Although some cases were likely legitimate, others probably reflected a feigning of impairment.

Evaluators should be aware that disreputable attorneys may coach their clients about psychological symptoms following trauma; this may be especially true in the case of a large accident with multiple plaintiffs (Rosen, 1995). Legally, malingering often constitutes fraud, but to convict an individual of perjury requires that the trier of fact be convinced beyond a reasonable doubt that conscious lying under oath occurred. Because this is the highest standard of proof, there is frequently not enough evidence to support the criminal charge. Often, the trier of fact simply will not grant an award to a plaintiff believed to be malingering.

Clinicians are hesitant to diagnose malingering for at least three reasons (Burges & McMillan, 2001). First, a wide range of diagnoses must be ruled out prior to the classification of malingering (Pollack, 1982). Second, a misclassification of malingering may lead to stigmatization and subsequent inability to receive appropriate care (Kropp & Rogers, 1993). Third, the clinician may fear being sued for defamation of character or being physically assaulted due to labeling an individual as a liar.

Public hostility toward the suspected malingerer is understandable, especially in view of the fact that the malingerer's undeserved financial gain is necessarily associated with another's underserved loss (Braverman, 1978). Suspicions of malingering help to explain why damages awarded for posttraumatic psychological symptoms are substantially less than those for physical injury, in spite of the fact that limitations on the claimant's life may actually be greater (Trimble, 1981).

Two methods of identifying malingering can provide strong evidence with considerable certainty. The first occurs when individuals participate in activities for which they claim incapacity. For example, a woman may allege that she is terrified of men following a rape but then be surreptitiously videotaped dancing with multiple male partners. The second occurs when an individual confesses to malingering. However, occasional cases have been observed in which the claims of malingering were false. Given the infrequency of these two methods, most assessments of malingering involve the integration of multiple pieces of evidence following a thorough investigation.

MALINGERING OF SPECIFIC DISORDERS

Malingering PTSD

PTSD is an easy disorder to fake. The diagnosis is based almost entirely on the individual's subjective report of symptoms, which are very difficult to verify independently. Furthermore, in an effort to educate the public, the diagnostic criteria have been made widely available in print and on the Internet, allowing unscrupulous individuals to familiarize themselves with which symptoms to falsely report. Even individuals naive to the criteria of PTSD could qualify for the diagnosis on a checklist when asked to do so 86–94% of the time (Burges & McMillan, 2001; Lees-Haley & Dunn, 1994; Slovenko, 1994).

The primary motivation to malinger PTSD is financial gain. Indeed, it is a rare individual who is not influenced to some degree by the possibility that an injury may lead to monetary gain (Keiser, 1968). After PTSD was included in DSM-III, personal injury lawsuits in federal court increased by more than 50% over the next decade (Olson, 1991). Mental stress-related disorders became the most rapidly increasing type of worker's compensation claim, and insurance costs for stress claims began to outstrip costs for physical injury claims (De Carteret, 1994). By the late 1990s, 14% of all workers' compensation claims were based on stress-related disorders (Gureil & Fremouw, 2003).

Financial gain may be the sole motive to malinger PTSD, or personal psychological reasons may also contribute. For example, an "official" determination of disability may provide a "face-saving" solution for personal life crises or other issues (e.g., substance use or interpersonal problems) that are separate from the alleged trauma (Drukteinis, 2003). Thus adverse or shameful consequences arising from personal decisions may be transformed into sympathy and support for a disability. Furthermore, financial compensation can take on different meanings for different people. For one claimant, money may represent security; for another, revenge against a hated employer or perceived aggressor. In some cases, malingered PTSD may represent a last-ditch effort for a claimant whose physical injury claims have been unsuccessful.

Once an individual takes on the role of personal-injury or workers' compensation claimant, the nature of the litigation may alter the claimant's attitudes and the course of the illness. The attorney for the plaintiff may overdramatize the client's impairment, whereas the defense attorney may imply that the plaintiff is a pure malingerer. As a result, litigants may easily become angry or worry that they will be cheated out of justified compensation (Enelow, 1971). Such scenarios may have a negative impact on the claimant's overall mental health. Claimants may feel it is necessary to exaggerate their claims in order to obtain what they believe they fairly deserve.

Beyond civil forensic issues, PTSD is rarely the basis for a finding of not guilty by reason of insanity (NGRI). According to Appelbaum, Jick, and Grisso's (1993) study, only 0.3% of defendants used PTSD in their insanity pleas. These individuals were more likely to be found competent to stand trial, to have a jury trial, and to be found guilty than those with other diagnoses. In addition, alleging PTSD can result in a reduction of charges or mitigation of penalties (Pittman & Sparr, 1998).

Other Trauma-Related Disorders and Feigning

Patients may experience persistent pain or loss of motor or sensory functioning after an injury that cannot be explained by organic pathology. The differential diagnosis includes malingering, conversion disorder, and pain disorder. Otis, Pincus, and Keane (2006) report that between 20 and 34% of patients referred for chronic pain had significant PTSD symptoms. Research indicates that patients experiencing both chronic pain and PTSD have more intense pain and affective distress (Geisser, Roth, Bachman, & Eckert, 1996) and greater disability (Sherman, Turk, & Okifuji, 2000) than pain patients without PTSD. The distinction between conversion disorder and malingering can be extremely difficult. In both conditions, clinicians are confronted with similar discrepancies between laboratory findings and self-report, objective signs, and subjective symptoms. Tests for malingering that are valid with reference to organic diseases are invalid in conversion disorders (Lipman, 1962; Smith, 1967). The differential diagnosis is further complicated by the fact that individuals with conversion disorders may also malinger.

Both malingerers and patients with conversion disorder may avoid unpleasant activity (e.g., disliked work) and seek support (e.g., financial) from the environment. The critical element that distinguishes conversion disorder from malingering is that conversion symptoms are not under voluntary control. Patients with conversion disorders deceive themselves as well as others; malingerers consciously deceive others, but not themselves:

- Malingerers use symptoms for gain and are *aware* of their purpose.
- Patients with conversion disorders also use symptoms for gain but are *unaware* of their purpose.

Disability due to conversion disorder may serve a wide range of psychological needs. It may (1) legitimize latent dependent needs, (2) allow punitive retaliation against an employer or a spouse, (3) provide exemption from societal and domestic obligations, (4) accomplish temporary resolution of preexisting life conflicts, or (5) simply allay anxiety (Hurwitz, 2004; Martin, 1970).

In contrast to the malingerer, a person with conversion disorder is genuinely disordered. If the disorder can be shown to be caused by a particular injury, it is compensable. For example, if a man developed hysterical paralysis of the legs (i.e., a conversion disorder) after a frightening auto accident in which he was not physically injured, the disability would be a direct result of the accident. The paralysis would not be voluntary or a conscious choice for the injured victim.

Clinicians' ability to distinguish conversion disorder from malingering depends on their ability to assess consciousness, an extremely difficult task. With respect to consciousness, Rosanoff (1920, p. 310) wrote, "It is strange that so futile a consideration, one so obviously belonging to the domain of metaphysics and not science, as the question of degree of consciousness of a mental process should . . . be chosen as a criterion of clinical diagnosis!"

Table 7.3 summarizes the key clinical characteristics for the differential diagnosis between malingering and conversion disorder. These characteristics are described next.

Interpersonal Characteristics

Malingerers often present as sullen, ill at ease, suspicious, uncooperative, resentful (Huddleston, 1932), aloof, secretive, and unfriendly (Engel, 1970). They may appear angry and indignant about their symptoms and the pejorative effects that these symptoms have had on their lives (Kaplan & Sadock, 2003). Malingerers often exist in a chaotic social situation (Hollander & Simeon, 2002), but they may be unwilling to share personal information given that it could reveal the reasons for their presentations (e.g., recent unemployment or loss of disability payments). Patients with conversion disorder are more likely to be cooperative (Trimble, 1981), appealing, clinging, and dependent (Engel, 1970). It is worthwhile to search for the reason behind the development of the symptoms, which these patients most likely will share willingly, given that they themselves do not recognize the underlying connection between the symptoms and the traumatic event. Conversion symptoms may also be displayed in a dramatic and exaggerated fashion using vibrant, colorful language. In some cases, personality disorders (most commonly histrionic and dependent personality disorders) are evident and may predispose individuals to conversion symptoms (Kaplan & Sadock, 2003; Yutzy, 2002).

Attitude toward the Evaluation

Malingerers may try to avoid examination, unless it is required as a condition for receiving some financial benefit (Engel, 1970; Soniat, 1960). They may be preoccupied with the possibility of receiving compensation rather than a cure (Kaplan & Sadock, 2003). The patient with conversion disorder welcomes examinations (Hofling, 1965; Rosanoff, 1920). Whereas the malingerer may decline to cooperate with recommended diagnostic or therapeutic procedures, patients with conversion disorder are typically eager for an organic explanation for their symptoms (Trimble, 1981) and are anxious to be cured (Rosanoff, 1920; Hofling, 1965). While *la belle indifference* (a patient's lack of apparent concern about his or her symptoms) was traditionally considered to be associated with conversion disorder, a meta-analysis showed

TABLE 7.3. Differential Diagnosis between Malingering and Conversion Disorder Following Trauma

Malingering	Conversion disorder
Uncooperative, suspicious, aloof	Cooperative, appealing, dependent
Avoids examination	Welcomes examination
Refuses employment with partial disability	Accepts employment with partial disability
Describes accident in full detail	Describes accident with gaps and inaccuracies

that the frequency of this symptom in patients with conversion disorder was actually less than in those with organic disease (Stone, Boone, Back-Madruga, & Lesser, 2006).

Attitude toward Employment

The malingerer is more likely than the patient with conversion disorder to refuse employment that could be handled in spite of some disability (Davidson, 1952a).

Description of the Accident

Malingerers are likely to give every detail of the accident and its sequelae (Huddleston, 1932). However, by doing so, they may reveal an inconsistent history and unexpected symptoms. There is often some incongruity between the provided history, their claimed distress, and the objective data (Hollander & Simeon, 2002). The patient with conversion disorder is more likely to give an account that contains gaps, inaccuracies (Huddleston, 1932; Kaplan & Sadock, 2003), and vague generalized complaints (Chaney, Cohn, Williams, & Vincent, 1984). Patients from rural areas with little formal education, low IQs, low socio-economic status, and unsophisticated psychological and medical knowledge appear predisposed to conversion symptoms. Patients with existing neurological disorders may also present with conversion symptoms. This finding has been attributed to "modeling," the idea that these patients may mimic their own neurological symptoms (or the symptoms of others close to them) during a conversion reaction (Kaplan & Sadock, 2003; Yutzy, 2002).

Comorbidity as Challenge to the Assessment of Malingered PTSD

The diagnosis of PTSD following a trauma may prove more challenging if the clinical picture is complicated by pain, physical symptoms, or other psychological symptoms and neurological sequelae. DSM-IV (American Psychiatric Association, 2000) proposed the diagnosis of postconcussive syndrome (PCS) to describe emotional, cognitive, and physical symptoms that occur for longer than 3 months following a cerebral concussion (see Table 7.4). The diagnosis requires evidence from neuropsychological testing that identifies impairment in attention or memory. PCS and PTSD both require

TABLE 7.4. Research Criteria for Postconcussional Syndrome

A. Head trauma that has caused a significant cerebral concussion

B. Evidence from neuropsychological testing or quantified cognitive assessment of difficulty in attention or memory

C. Three or more occur shortly after the trauma and last for at least 3 months:
1. Easily fatigued
2. Disordered sleep
3. Headache
4. Vertigo or dizziness
5. Irritability or aggression with little to no provocation
6. Anxiety, depression, or affective lability
7. Changes in personality
8. Apathy or lack of spontaneity

D. Symptoms have their onset following the head trauma or experience a substantial worsening

E. Disturbance causes significant impairment

F. Symptoms do not meet criteria for dementia due to head trauma and are not better accounted for by another diagnosis

Note. From American Psychiatric Association (2000). Copyright 2000 by the American Psychiatric Association. Adapted by permission.

an antecedent traumatic experience and share several criteria for their diagnosis. Some of the overlapping symptoms may include amnesia for some element of the traumatic event, features of depression, sleep disturbance, irritability, decreased concentration, and inability to tolerate loud noises.

A trauma victim can develop PTSD (or acute stress disorder) and PCS in response to the same injury (McAllister, 1994). Price (1994) has erroneously argued that the two entities are logically incompatible because an individual who suffered a head injury with loss of consciousness cannot have reexperiencing phenomena for that event. Price suggested that the individual's diagnosis should be PCS or malingering, but not PTSD. However, the moment of impact does not constitute the only portion of the traumatic event that can meet Criterion A of PTSD (American Psychiatric Association, 1994). With partial or complete clearing of the short retrograde amnesia associated with a head injury, trauma victims may develop reexperiencing symptoms due to a frightening experience preceding the loss of consciousness (e.g., a car speeding toward him or her).

CLASSIFICATION OF MALINGERED PTSD

Clinical Indicators

Every malingerer is an actor playing a role, and the performance will mirror the individual's preparation (Ossipov, 1944). A lack of detailed knowledge regarding PTSD will likely result in a poor performance during the clinical evaluation. Malingerers may overact their parts by giving excessively dramatic reports of their symptoms. They may be overly eager to share information; alternatively, they may adopt a globally evasive posture, hesitating to discuss their return to work or their potential for monetary compensation (Powell, 1991). To avoid being specific, malingerers may state that their responses to clinical inquiries would take too long or be too complicated. Conversely, successful malingerers often endorse fewer symptoms and avoid those that are unusual or dramatic (Lowensteien, 2001).

Malingerers may "go on the offensive" and attempt to control the interview by intimidating or being hostile toward their evaluators. They may even accuse interviewers of implying that they are malingering. The presence of antisocial traits (Hollander & Simeon, 2002) and psychopathic traits (Edens, Buffington, & Tomicic, 2000) in civil litigation may signal the need to evaluate malingering. A person who has consistently been a contributing member of society is less likely to malinger (Davidson, 1952a). Rather, the malingerer is often the type of person who has poor social and occupational functioning prior to the trauma (Braverman, 1978). This might include sporadic employment with long absences from work or previous incapacitating injuries.

Amnesia may play a role in both PTSD and PCS and can certainly be feigned. It is important to note, however, that some memory distortion can be expected over time in patients with genuine PTSD (Buckhout, 1974; Loftus, 1979). The following criteria may help to distinguish feigned memory alterations from true memory deficits:

1. Overplaying memory deficits
2. Inability to recall overlearned data
3. Alleged impairment of procedural memory
4. Poor performance on tests labeled "memory testing"
5. Performing worse than chance on memory testing (see Chapter 13, this volume)

6. Clear recollection of trauma with alleged memory loss

Malingerers tend to overplay their memory deficits. They may allege inability to recall overlearned data, such as their name, gender, or social security number (Brandt, 1992; Levin, Lilly, Papanicolau, & Eisenberg, 1992). Even with a legitimate history of head trauma, procedural memory is rarely impaired. Therefore, malingering should be suspected in an individual who alleges an inability to drive. As discussed by Sweet, Condit, and Nelson in Chapter 13, this volume, malingering can also be assessed with a variety of assessment measures.

The clinician should look for evidence of inconsistency in the symptoms of a suspected malingerer. Inconsistencies may be thought of as either internal or external to the individual's presentation. Internal inconsistencies may occur when a malingerer reports severe symptoms such as an inability to concentrate or gross memory loss yet is able to clearly articulate multiple examples of poor concentration and memory loss. Another type of internal inconsistency occurs when a malingerer gives grossly conflicting versions to the same evaluator.

External inconsistencies can occur between what clients report and the symptoms that are observed. For example, a malingerer may allege severe distraction due to "flashbacks" yet appear consistently calm and show no evidence of being distracted. There may also be an external inconsistency between reported levels of functioning and the observations of others. For example, a malingerer may allege social detachment from others yet eagerly engage in a variety of social and recreational activities. Finally, inconsistencies may occur between self-reports and hospital or police records of the traumatic event.

Collateral Information

Obtaining collateral information is crucial to validating the subjective report of symptoms when differentiating genuine and malingered PTSD. It is more helpful when collateral data are available prior to the evaluation, so that the examiner may clarify any inconsistencies that arise in the examination. Evaluators may begin by reviewing police reports or other witness accounts of the trauma in order to gain an objective view of the events that occurred. Reports written at the time of the incident also help to curtail biased retrospective recalls, in which claimants may amplify their memories of the traumatic event (Harvey & Bryant, 2000; Koch, O'Neill, & Douglas, 2005). In a similar vein, it is best to insist on reviewing complete past mental health records rather than accepting a treating clinician's summary letter. Many treating clinicians become conscious or unconscious advocates for their patients. Employee files, school grades, and tax returns may provide insight into the claimant's daily functioning prior to the trauma and should be compared with the claimant's subjective report.

The persons most helpful in providing collateral data are those who are in close contact with the claimant but do not stand to gain from the litigation. Information obtained from collateral sources helps to establish the individual's baseline level of functioning prior to the trauma. For example, an individual may claim a loss in concentration since a traumatic accident, but a coworker may report that the claimant has always been easily distractible.

Observational data (e.g., sleep patterns and avoidance behavior) can be confirmed or disconfirmed in a collateral interview. The reliability of family's or friends' reporting must be taken into account, as it is possible that they may benefit from the outcome (Drukteinis, 2003) or are influenced by the nature of their relationship to be "helpful" to the claimant. Access to relatives will vary depending on the jurisdiction and whether one is employed by the plaintiff or the defense attorney. If denied direct access, the clinician can request that close relatives be deposed by the attorney.

The Interview

The interview, when conducted in a careful and thorough manner, is a key component in differentiating genuine from malingered PTSD. During the interview, evaluators must take care not to reveal the criteria used to define PTSD or to convey any bias regarding the diagnosis. If interviewers adopt a confrontational style, claimants may feel compelled to exaggerate symptoms in order to justify their impairment. Interviewers should initially adopt an open-ended questioning style and avoid leading questions that give clues to correct responses.

Almost any person is capable of reciting the criteria for PTSD. Consequently, evaluators should insist on a detailed account of the symptoms that the individual is claiming. Falsified symptoms often have a vague or artificial quality (Pitman, Sparr, & Saunders, 1996) and lack the convincing nuances inherent in personally experienced symptoms. Statements such as "I have nightmares" cannot be accepted at face value. Details, including circumstances, degree, frequency, and context, must be explored. For example, malingerers may claim that their nightmares are repetitive and have occurred without variation over the past several months. However, genuine civilian (not combat-related) posttraumatic nightmares have been shown to change over time and involve variations on a theme related to the traumatic event (Garfield, 1987). For example, a woman who was raped may dream about another situation in which she feels helpless. Genuine traumatic dreams usually begin to diminish within several weeks after the trauma, especially with psychotherapy. Conversely, traumatic dreams usually increase in frequency due to reminders of the event, such as giving a deposition.

During an interview with an individual malingering PTSD, evaluators may note the absence of behavioral manifestations of the disorder, which include irritability, inability to focus, or exaggerated startle response. Interviewers may also find that PTSD malingerers minimize other possible causes of their symptoms or portray their pretrauma level of functioning in an overly complimentary light (Layden, 1966). Careful consideration must be given to the temporal course of symptom development in relationship to the trauma. It may also be useful to inquire about a claimant's capacity to work versus his or her ability to enjoy recreational activities. A malingerer may assert that he or she is incapable of remaining employed but acknowledge active participation in hobbies. A person with genuine PTSD would be likely to withdraw from both work and personal activities.

Third parties should not be present during the interview. Informants might alter their stories, consciously or not, based on the claimant's reports. Furthermore, if interviewers confront the claimant about his or her suspected malingering, he or she will be far less willing to admit this with others in the room.

In some instances, evaluators may believe that the situation warrants the use of subterfuge to expose a potential malingerer. Prior to starting the interview, evaluators could converse with a colleague about PTSD within

earshot of the claimant and mention some specific symptoms clearly not associated with the
disorder (e.g., grandiosity, rapid speech, or impulsive traveling). Evaluators can then observe
whether the individual volunteers these symptoms of his or her disorder. In rare cases, inpatient hospitalization may be required to monitor alleged symptoms such as sleep disturbance,
social withdrawal, and exaggerated startle responses.

PSYCHOLOGICAL TESTING AND MALINGERING PTSD

Psychological assessment of individuals who
have experienced traumatic events is a complex endeavor. Specifically, this complex presentation may be reflected by extreme symptom
endorsements and diffuse clinical elevations on
psychological tests (Frueh, Hamner, Cahill,
Gold, & Hamlin, 2000). Common characteristics of genuine trauma patients include multiple comorbid disorders (Kessler, Sonnega,
Bromet, & Hughes, 1995) and high levels of
symptom reporting (Keane, Buckley, & Miller,
2003, p. 122). Additionally, the heterogeneity
of trauma populations (e.g., combat exposure
and victims of rape) may contribute to dissimilar clinical profiles among different trauma
samples (Elhai, Frueh, Gold, Gold, & Hamner,
2000). These characteristics may be responsible for atypical profile configurations and uncommon scale elevations on psychological
tests (Wilson, 2004).

Elevations on the validity indices of psychological tests are commonly observed in pre-
sumptively honest trauma samples (Rogers,
Sewell, Martin, & Vitacco, 2003). Thus a key
concern is that persons with genuine PTSD will
be misclassified as malingered PTSD. As is
outlined in the following sections, many commonly utilized feigning scales have a propensity to misclassify genuine PTSD patients.
Therefore, the standard practice of considering multiple data sources, including but not exclusively relying on feigning scales, should be
performed by clinicians when evaluating for
malingered PTSD (for a review of comprehensive malingering PTSD evaluations, see also Simon, 2003).

The following sections provide a brief summary of feigning scales contained within
psychological tests commonly used in evaluations of PTSD (Gureil & Fremouw, 2003). We
used the standards in Chapter 2 in this volume
for detection strategies as a benchmark for including studies in our review. Malingering studies were used only if they had both: (1) a genuine PTSD comparison group and (2) feigners
(i.e., simulators or known malingerers).

Minnesota Multiphasic Personality Inventory

The Minnesota Multiphasic Personality Inventory (MMPI-2) is currently the psychological test most widely utilized by practicing
mental health professionals (Greene, 2000).
The MMPI-2 contains a variety of validity
scales useful in the assessment of response
styles (for a comprehensive review of MMPI-2
scales, see Greene, Chapter 10, this volume).
One strength of the MMPI-2 is its inclusion
of multiple detection strategies (see Rogers,
Chapter 2, this volume, for descriptions).

A recent meta-analysis of the MMPI-2 and
malingering (Rogers, Sewell, et al., 2003) indicated that the MMPI-2 rare symptom and erroneous stereotype detection strategies were the
most useful for the assessment of malingering.
Specifically, the rare symptom (Fp) and erroneous stereotype (Ds) scales demonstrated substantial ability to differentiate between genuine
PTSD patients and malingerers. As observed by
Rogers, Sewell, and colleagues (2003), a major
problem in the evaluation of feigned PTSD is
that genuine patients with PTSD also have very
high elevations on standard MMPI-2 validity
scales, especially F and Fb.

Since Rogers, Sewell, and colleagues' (2003)
meta-analysis, studies of malingered PTSD on
the MMPI-2 have expanded. Table 7.5 summarizes the effect sizes and average elevations
for eight PTSD studies.

This table confirms Rogers, Sewell, and colleagues' (2003) conclusion about the effectiveness of rare symptoms (i.e., Fp) for malingered
PTSD. It outperformed F and Fb with lower
clinical elevations for genuine PTSD groups
and larger effect sizes. These studies also revealed that there is a 91% likelihood that a person is feigning when scores exceeded a cut
score of Fp >8 (raw score).[1] Correspondingly,
using this cut score Fp labeled true PTSD patients as malingerers only 9% of the time.

A specialized scale for feigned PTSD (Fptsd)
has recently been created. At the time of this
review, two studies have provided preliminary
support for its utility within evaluations of

TABLE 7.5. Effect Sizes and Scale Elevations for MMPI-2 Feigning Scales and PTSD

Detection strategy	Quasi-rare symptoms			Rare symptoms		Erroneous stereotypes	
Feigning Scale	F	Fb	F-K	Fp	Fptsd	Ds	FBS
Bury & Bagby (2002)[a]	1.06	1.37	0.97	1.24		1.39	0.02
Eakin et al. (2006)	0.89	1.04		0.97		0.84	
Elhai, Frueh, et al. (2000)	0.93		1.10	1.01		0.87	–0.09
Elhai, Gold, Sellers, & Dorfman (2001)	1.10		1.37	1.41		1.03	0.47
Elhai, Ruggiero, Frueh, Beckham, & Gold (2002)	0.91	0.75		1.31			
Elhai, Naifeh, et al. (2004)	0.53			1.21	0.81		
Marshall & Bagby (2006)	1.17	1.38		1.53	1.32		
Wetter, Baer, et al. (1993)	1.52	1.13	1.60			1.73	
M effect size	1.01	1.13	1.26	1.24	1.07	1.17	0.13
M PTSD patient elevation	84.98	82.77	5.19	66.61	65.90	77.71	82.00
M PTSD patient SD	22.33	23.83	10.53	19.75	15.92	14.45	14.68
M feigner elevation	102.35	107.67	20.47	89.74	84.85	96.64	83.30
M feigner SD	19.97	19.08	14.48	23.85	23.68	18.24	14.46
PTSD screening cut (M + 1 SD)	107.31	106.60	15.72	86.36	81.82	92.16	96.68
PTSD intermediate cut (M + 1.5 SD)	118.48	118.52	20.99	96.24	89.78	99.39	104.02
PTSD conservative cut (M + 2 SD)	129.64	130.43	26.25	106.11	97.74	106.61	111.36

Note. All effect sizes are reflected as Cohen's *d* values. Total PTSD patients in review (*N* = 839); total feigners in review (*N* = 257). Mean PTSD patient–feigner elevations and *SD*s based only on samples in this review.
[a]Only the symptom-coached simulator group was used to provide uniform comparisons with other studies.

feigned trauma. Similarly, the standard F and Fb scales demonstrated a moderate ability to differentiate between honest and feigned MMPI-2 protocols. However, patients with PTSD also scored very highly on F and Fb, with averages exceeding 80T. The danger of misclassifying genuine patients as feigning is very real. Taking into account the standard deviation (*SD*), we should expect that significant numbers of patients with genuine PTSD should easily exceed 100T on these scales (see Table 7.5).

Two MMPI-2 validity scales address the detection strategy of erroneous stereotypes. Gough's Ds scale appears the most promising, with substantial effect sizes between genuine and feigned PTSD groups. We found that a Ds cut score of >35 (raw score) identified a 74% likelihood of feigning but had a false positive rate of 26%.[2] The FBS scale was not able to substantially differentiate between honest PTSD and malingered protocols. This finding may be due to the relatively high average elevations noted on the FBS scale by genuine PTSD patients (*M* = 82.00). It should be noted, however, that the FBS was designed specifically for personal injury settings (Greiffenstein, Baker, Axelrod, Peck, & Gervais, 2004; Lees-Haley, English, & Glenn, 1991) and its effectiveness outside of that specific setting remains questionable (Arbisi & Butcher, 2004; Rogers, Sewell, et al., 2003). A recent meta-analysis of the FBS demonstrated support for its ability to differentiate malingered and nonmalingered protocols within forensic settings (Nelson, Sweet, & Demakis, 2006). This review, however, contained a limited number of studies that utilized patients with PTSD and therefore has limited applicability to the current discussion.[3]

Gough's F-K index was found to be surprisingly effective with PTSD populations, despite cautions about its use (Greene, 2000; Rogers, Sewell, et al., 2003). The criticisms of F-K have relied mostly on the wide variability among cut scores in malingering studies (i.e., −8 to +32 for raw scores). Considering the marked variability of F-K scores for patients with PTSD, a high cut score seems prudent. One possibility would be F-K >21, which would eliminate the misclassification of most cases of genuine PTSD (see Table 7.5).

In summary, the current review lends support to the positive results obtained by Rogers, Sewell, and colleagues (2003) concerning the MMPI-2 rare symptom and erroneous stereotype detection strategies. Specifically, Fp and Ds scales appear to be the most effective MMPI-2 validity scales for evaluations of malingering PTSD.

Personality Assessment Inventory

The Personality Assessment Inventory (PAI; Morey, 1991) is a multiscale inventory that assesses a variety of psychological domains including psychopathology, treatment needs, interpersonal functioning, and response styles. It has demonstrated excellent psychometric properties and support for its use within inpatient, outpatient, and correctional settings (Morey & Boggs, 2004). The PAI has also received support for its use in the assessment of PTSD (Cherepon & Prinzhorn, 1994). The PAI possesses three scales useful for the detection of malingering. These scales capitalize on two different detection strategies: (1) rare symptoms (i.e., Negative Impression, or NIM) and (2) spurious patterns of pathology (i.e., the Malingering Index, or MAL, and Rogers Discriminant Function Index, or RDF).

Four studies have utilized the PAI to address malingered PTSD (see Table 7.6). Using rare symptoms, NIM had a moderate effect size (M $d = .85$) between genuine and malingered PTSD. Reassuringly, patients with genuine PTSD tended not to have elevated NIM scores ($M = 58.60$). However, in a study of combat veterans with PTSD, Calhoun, Earnst, Tucker, Kirby, and Beckham (2000) found substantial false positive rates of malingering (35%) at the NIM cut score >13.

TABLE 7.6. Effect Sizes and Scale Elevations for PAI Feigning Scales and PTSD

Detection strategy	Rare symptom	Spurious patterns of pathology	
Feigning scale	NIM	MI	RDF
Eakin (2005)[a]	0.99	1.05	0.68
Eakin et al. (2006)	0.19	0.04	0.36
Liljequest, Kinder, & Schinka (1998)	1.06		
Scragg, Bor, & Mendham (2000)	1.17	0.96	0.21
M effect size	0.85	0.68	0.41
M PTSD patient elevation	58.60	56.70	50.25
M PTSD patient SD	13.64	12.10	10.00
M feigner elevation	78.88	65.15	58.5
M feigner SD	20.93	15.7	12.25
PTSD screening cut ($M + 1\ SD$)	72.24	68.80	60.25
PTSD intermediate cut ($M + 1.5\ SD$)	79.06	74.85	65.25
PTSD conservative cut ($M + 2\ SD$)	85.88	80.90	70.25

Note. All effect sizes are reflected as Cohen's d values. Total PTSD patients in review ($N = 94$); total feigners in review ($N = 103$). Mean PTSD patient–feigner elevations and SDs based only on samples in this review.
[a]Doctoral dissertation.

The PAI's use of spurious symptom patterns produces only modest results. Overall, the MAL and RDF demonstrated only a modest ability to discriminate between genuine and malingered PTSD protocols. Although individuals with genuine PTSD have low scores on these scales, feigners' scores are also similarly low (see Table 7.6).

In a comparative study between the PAI and MMPI-2, Eakin, Weathers, and Benson (2006) found that all PAI validity indicators including NIM were relatively ineffective at identifying PTSD feigners. In contrast, several MMPI-2 validity scales (see Table 7.5) were moderately effective. Further investigation of the PAI's validity scales for evaluations of PTSD is clearly needed. The potential for false positives (i.e., the classification of genuine PTSD patients) is a major concern. At present, the MMPI-2 may be the preferred measure when evaluating feigned PTSD.

Trauma Symptom Inventory

The Trauma Symptom Inventory (TSI; Briere, 1995) is a 100-item self-report questionnaire. The TSI contains 10 clinical scales assessing various symptom clusters associated with trauma and three validity scales that assess response styles. Of these validity scales, the Atypical Response Scale (ATR) is the most relevant to malingering. The ATR relies on a quasi-rare symptom detection strategy to screen for the possibility of symptom overreporting.

Most studies investigating the ability of the ATR scale to detect malingering have used college and not clinical samples (Edens, Otto, & Dwyer, 1998; Guriel et al., 2004; Rosen et al., 2006). As the sole exception, Elhai and colleagues (2005) examined ATR's usefulness when compared with a PTSD sample. Unfortunately, ATR's ability to differentiate between patients with PTSD and malingerers was marginal at best. Although a cut score of $T > 61$ was able to identify almost two-thirds of feigners, the false-positive rate was substantial (34%). The TSI manual recommends using a more conservative cut score of $T > 90$ to protect against the misclassification of malingering (Briere, 1995). When applying this conservative cut score, Elhai and colleagues reported a false positive rate of less than 5%. Unfortunately, additional utility estimates were not reported. Currently, research has demonstrated significant limitations of the ATR scale when utilized within genuine trauma populations.

Structured Interview of Reported Symptoms

The Structured Interview of Reported Symptoms (SIRS; Rogers, Bagby, & Dickens, 1992) is a 172-item specialized structured interview designed specifically to assess feigning and related response styles. The SIRS has consistently demonstrated excellent psychometric properties and support for its discriminability within a number of different clinical populations (Rogers, 2001; see also Rogers, Chapter 18, this volume). However, few investigations of the SIRS have focused specifically on PTSD. An early study by Rogers, Kropp, Bagby, and Dickens (1992) produced large effect sizes on SIRS primary scales when PTSD simulators were compared with a mixed clinical sample of psychiatric patients. More recently, Eakin (2005) compared PTSD simulators with individuals with mild to moderate symptoms of PTSD. Marked differences were observed between feigned and genuine PTSD. For classification purposes, PTSD simulators averaged three scales in the probable feigning range versus none for the genuine PTSD group.

Rogers, Payne, Berry, and Granacher (2007) are currently undertaking a large SIRS study of 497 disability referrals. Importantly, referrals with genuine PTSD were generally comparable to the normative data on genuine patients (Rogers, Kropp, et al., 1992).

Conclusions about Psychological Tests

The current review reveals several important findings about the assessment of malingered PTSD by psychological testing. First and foremost, a number of commonly utilized feigning scales have been found to be susceptible to misclassifications of malingering when administered to patients with genuine PTSD. False-positive rates on these popular feigning scales ranged from 9% to as high as 65%. Establishment of PTSD specific cut scores may be needed to protect against false-positive classification of malingering. Tables 7.5 and 7.6 provide suggested cut scores based on expected elevations of patients with PTSD (i.e., M plus 1 SD). Use of these scores for screening purposes only can help clinicians identify what cases may need further and more thorough consideration of malingering (e.g., SIRS administration). More conservative cut scores (e.g., M plus 2 SD) would minimize false-positive classifications and provide evidence of possible feigning when making malingering determinations.

Extreme elevations for genuine PTSD for common validity indicators are very concerning. Clinicians should always consider the typical elevations on these scales and interpret scales as evidence of feigned PTSD only when most genuine cases can be excluded (e.g., M plus 2 SD).

Psychophysiological Assessment

Measurement of the body's responses to trauma may serve as one of the few objective means of discriminating genuine from malingered PTSD. A positive response would fulfill Criterion B, physiological reactivity to cues related to the traumatic event (Pittman, Saunders, & Orr, 1994). Several studies have been performed to determine the success of evaluators in diagnosing PTSD based on psychophysiological assessment. Blanchard, Kolb, Pallmeyer, and Gerardi (1982) played an audiotape of combat sounds and measured the heart rate, systolic blood pressure, and muscle tension in the forehead of veterans with PTSD and a control group. The two groups responded differently to the combat sounds in terms of heart rate, blood pressure, and forehead electromyography (EMG). Based on the heart rate response, 95.5% of the combined samples were correctly classified.

Lang (1985) improved on the stimuli used to trigger physiological changes by using recorded sounds of combat, such as machine-gun fire. It allowed for a more accurate re-creation of an individual's unique stressors in a given traumatic event. For example, gunfire may have little meaning to a medic, who may instead have a strong physiological response to the sounds of a helicopter. Pittman and colleagues (1994) requested that 16 combat veterans without PTSD attempt to simulate the physiological profile of a patient with PTSD. They found that only 25% were successful in feigning the physical symptoms.

In the largest study on the psychophysiology of PTSD, Keane and colleagues (1998) subjected Vietnam veterans with (1) a current diagnosis of PTSD ($n = 778$), (2) a past diagnosis of PTSD ($n = 181$), and (3) no diagnosis of PTSD ($n = 369$) to autobiographical scripts and neutral scripts. Veterans with PTSD exhibited increased heart rate, skin conduction, and muscle tension to autobiographical scripts as compared with those with no diagnosis. The patients with a past diagnosis of PTSD formed an intermediate group. However, one-third of veterans with current PTSD did not react physiologically; this limits the usefulness of this assessment method.

Persons without PTSD may show physiological reactions to an upsetting experience. Patients claiming to be abducted by space aliens (i.e., who did not meet Criterion A for PTSD) were exposed to a narrative script similar to their own reported experiences. Their psychophysiological responses were at or above those of the veterans with PTSD in Keane and colleagues' (1998) study (McNally, 2006). Thus a genuine physiological response cannot confirm or disconfirm the presence of PTSD.

In order to gain insights into some of the discrepancies with psychophysiological testing for PTSD, Pole (2006) conducted a metaanalysis to determine which variables influence effect sizes between PTSD and control groups. The effect sizes were the greatest between the two groups when (1) the control group had not been exposed to trauma, (2) the PTSD group had severe symptoms, and (3) the PTSD group was diagnosed on the stricter DSM-III criteria rather than DSM-IV criteria. These findings are commonsensical. Removing any trauma from the control group increases the observed differences. The latter findings simply indicate that more salient cases based on the severity of the symptoms (2) or trauma (3) will increase the observed differences.

In summary, psychophysiological testing does provide an objective but flawed method of differentiating genuine and malingered PTSD. A significant minority of persons with genuine PTSD have negative findings that may lead to false positives (i.e., being misclassified as malingering). Conversely, psychophysiological testing can be positive for persons without PTSD with the possibility of false negatives (i.e., being misclassified as genuine cases of PTSD). Given the conflicting evidence concerning its accuracy, psychophysiological testing of PTSD may or may not be admitted as evidence in court depending on the jurisdiction.

A MODEL FOR THE DIAGNOSIS OF MALINGERED PTSD

No one piece of data is pathognomonic for malingered PTSD. Rather, the diagnosis requires careful scrutiny of all the evidence gathered, including a meticulously detailed history of symptoms, past and present social and occupational functioning, and careful corroboration of symptoms. A clinical decision model for establishing malingered PTSD is presented in Table 7.7. The model requires the establishment of (1) the individual's motivation for feigning his or her symptoms, (2) the presence of at least two common characteristics associated with malingered PTSD, and (3) strong collateral information supporting malingering.

Confronting the Malingerer

After a thorough investigation has caused the examiner to conclude that malingering is probably present, the clinician may decide to confront the examinee. The clinician should avoid direct accusations of lying. A more fruitful approach asks the examinee for clarification of inconsistencies. The clinician could also convey a sympathetic understanding of the temp-

---

TABLE 7.7. Clinical Decision Model for Establishing Malingered PTSD

A. Understandable motive to malinger PTSD

B. At least two of the following criteria:
  1. Irregular employment or job dissatisfaction
  2. Prior claims for injuries
  3. Capacity for recreation, but not work
  4. No nightmares or, if nightmares, exact repetitions of the civilian trauma
  5. Antisocial personality traits (not applicable to criminal–forensic cases)
  6. Evasiveness or contradictions
  7. Noncooperation in the evaluation

C. Confirmation of malingering by one of the following criteria:
  1. Confession of malingering
  2. Unambiguous psychometric evidence of malingering
  3. Strong corroborative evidence of malingering (e.g., videotape contraindicating alleged symptoms)

---

tation to exaggerate symptoms of PTSD, which may offer the examinee an easier forum to acknowledge malingering. Inducing shame is likely to increase feelings of anger and opposition in the examinee. Once an examinee feels accused of malingering and has denied it, subsequent acknowledgment of malingering is very unlikely.

Thus affective responses of shame and indignation should be avoided, and the suspected malingerer should be given every opportunity to "save face." For example, it is preferable to say "I don't think that you have told me the whole truth," rather than "You have been lying to me" (Inabu & Reid, 1967). This approach is more likely to be both productive and safe for the examiner. It is sometimes wise to confront certain individuals with a history of violence in the presence of adequate security personnel.

In one case, a federal appellate court determined that malingering was equivalent to obstruction of justice and could result in an enhancement of a defendant's penalty (Knoll & Resnick, 1999). Thus, in certain cases in which a criminal defendant is malingering, the clinician may consider whether there is an ethical obligation to notify the defendant that malingering may result in an enhancement of the penalty. Of course, such a notification may result in the defendant clinging more fiercely to his or her malingered symptoms.

Prognosis after Trauma

When an individual fails to recover after a traumatic injury, some clinicians may conclude that he or she is malingering. This is not always the case. Some factors may contribute to this lack of progress. Physical injury, pain, and stress may cause a regression in the person's ability to cope, leading to the use of less mature defense mechanisms. Examinees may then become increasingly dependent on their social support system, thus sacrificing their autonomy, which may lead to decreased self-worth. Depression can delay recovery by causing a lack of interest and motivation to return to the premorbid state. Blaming others following a severe accident was found to be an indicator of poor coping (Bulman & Wortman, 1977). Other factors associated with a poor prognosis following an injury include old age, low-back injury, and loss of libido (Mendelson, 1982).

Finally, an inability to return to work at the conclusion of the settlement indicates a poor prognosis (Kelly & Smith, 1981).

MALINGERED PTSD IN COMBAT VETERANS

PTSD in Combat Veterans

Over the past four decades, United States military forces have been involved in a number of countries: Vietnam, Somalia, Lebanon, the Persian Gulf, and Iraq. In 1980, the Veterans' Administration (VA) began to accept PTSD as a diagnosis for purposes of assigning service-connected benefits to veterans (Bitzer, 1980). Following this, veterans became exposed to the diagnostic criteria for PTSD in a number of ways: distributed literature (Atkinson, Henderson, Sparr, & Deale, 1982), contact with other veterans diagnosed as having PTSD (Lynn & Belza, 1984), and the Internet. Recently, numerous Internet sites have been developed that detail PTSD symptoms and how to present oneself so as to maximize the chances of receiving service-connected benefits (*ncptsd.va.gov; vva.org/benefits/ptsd/htm*). Some sites even provide step-by-step instructions for writing "stress letters" to be submitted to the VA ratings board (*ptsd.support.net*).

Though multiple studies regarding military PTSD have been performed, some issues have been raised concerning the quality of those studies. Often the diagnosis is based only on the veterans' subjective reports of both their symptoms and combat experiences. Estimates of the prevalence of PTSD in Vietnam veterans have ranged from 20 to 70% (Ashlock, Walker, Starkey, Harmand, & Michel, 1987; Friedman, 1981; Wilson & Zigelbaum, 1983). In the differential diagnosis of combat PTSD, one must also consider malingering, factitious disorder, antisocial personality disorder, and genuine PTSD due to a non-combat-related cause.

Motivations to Malinger Combat-Related PTSD

The motives for veterans to malinger PTSD generally fall into three categories: (1) to obtain financial compensation, (2) to reduce criminal culpability, and (3) to obtain admission to a VA hospital. Veterans who successfully malinger PTSD may be well rewarded. Individuals qualifying for a 100% "service connected" disability due to PTSD may be eligible for lifelong, tax-free compensation in the range of $36,000 to $40,000 per year, in addition to other military-related benefits (Burkett & Whitley, 1998). Once individuals have qualified for PTSD-related disability, there is an ongoing financial incentive to remain disabled regardless of their true status (Mossman, 1994).

If former military personnel are in current legal trouble, a diagnosis of PTSD confirmed by the VA may serve as an excusing or a mitigating factor. Though PTSD is not often successful as a basis of an insanity plea, some situations occur in which it might play a role: (1) a veteran may experience a dissociative state and resort to survival skills learned in military training (e.g., killing); (2) a veteran with survivor guilt may take measures to have himself killed (e.g., threatening a police officer to accomplish "suicide by cop") in order to rejoin fallen comrades; and (3) a veteran may engage in sensation-seeking behavior (e.g., drug trafficking) in order to relive combat excitement (Wilson, 1981). When assessing the relationship of PTSD to a crime, evaluators should consider whether the crime scene recreated a traumatic event and whether the veteran experienced dissociative symptoms at the time that the crime was committed.

The Office of the Inspector General of the Department of Veterans Affairs conducted a survey of 2,100 veterans who were receiving at least 50% service-connected PTSD disability. They concluded that 25.1% were misdiagnosed and thus were not entitled to their benefits. Extrapolating these results to all veterans who are service connected for PTSD, they estimated that $19.8 billion had been erroneously paid out over a lifetime to those who did not meet diagnostic criteria (Department of Veterans Affairs Office of the Inspector General, 2005). In addition, a sample of 92 veterans with alleged PTSD continued to make regular mental health care visits until they received a 100% service connection. Their symptoms "worsened" over time despite the treatment. However, once 100% service connection was achieved, 39% of the patients reduced mental health visits by an average of 82%; some veterans then received no mental health care at all (Department of Veterans Affairs Office of the Inspector General, 2005).

Given the easy opportunity for monetary gain, some veterans fraudulently claim symptoms of PTSD from combat even though they were never exposed to battle (Lynn & Belza, 1984). Some individuals who never even served in military combat have successfully acquired service-connected benefits for PTSD (Burkett & Whitely, 1998). A key step in either supporting or discrediting a veteran's account is the collection of collateral data about the veteran's combat experiences.

Collateral Information

Military records, including discharge papers, often identify stressors to which a veteran has been exposed, but the clinician should be aware that these documents can easily be forged (Burkett & Whitley, 1998). Forgeries may be avoided by obtaining the documents directly from the U.S. Department of Defense (Sparr & Atkinson, 1986). Individuals malingering PTSD may state that their records do not reflect their covert missions or "black ops"; hence no evidence of their experiences exists. Although there may be no written record of the event, examiners should look for the special training required for these missions in a veteran's file; the term *classified assignment* will appear next to the date of the mission (Burkett & Whitley, 1998). Eyewitness accounts, though difficult to come by, can also provide evidence to validate the veteran's claim.

Collaboration with employees at the VA or experienced combat veterans may help to elucidate false claims (Lynn & Belza, 1984). Although malingerers may fabricate stories that are as vivid and horrifying as the experiences of true combat veterans (Burkett & Whitley, 1998; Hamilton, 1985), they may reveal their dishonesty by incorrectly identifying certain details, including the geography and culture of the area, the military terminology used at the time, and dates related to specific events (Burkett & Whitley, 1998). Family and friends of combat veterans may be interviewed to determine both the validity of the symptoms and the social functioning of veterans prior to their service in the military.

Frueh and colleagues (2005) performed an archival study on 100 consecutive cases of men who reported combat trauma related to their experiences in Vietnam. Almost all (94%) had received a diagnosis of PTSD. For 41% of the veterans, archival data verified their stories. One-third had served in Vietnam, but the records indicated that they held positions in which exposure to trauma would have been highly unlikely. Five percent had not been in Vietnam or had not served in the military at all. Finally, those without any combat experience reported twice the rate (28% vs. 12%, respectively) of battlefield atrocities when compared with those with verified combat exposure.

Interview Style for Combat-Related PTSD

Evaluating genuine versus malingered combat PTSD requires special attention to maintaining objectivity and equanimity. Due to the fact that war typically evokes strong feelings, evaluators must recognize the potential for powerful and potentially biasing emotions during the evaluation. In particular, examinees may recount horrific combat experiences, producing a highly charged, affect-laden interview that can be stressful for both parties (McAllister, 1994). In the face of powerful emotions or outbursts of anger, the clinician may feel moved to diagnose PTSD in the absence of objective data out of a sense of moral responsibility for the combat veteran as "victim" (Lynn & Belza, 1984; Pankratz, 1985).

Evaluators should be aware that some Vietnam and Gulf War veterans may regard the federal government with animosity and suspicion, which may adversely affect the evaluation (McAllister, 1994). In this sense, a strong authoritarian approach by the clinician is unlikely to be productive. An interview style that is composed, impartial, and respectful is recommended.

The presence of antisocial personality disorder does not rule out PTSD; however, it should increase the clinician's index of suspicion for malingering. Unfortunately, there is significant overlap between the two conditions, particularly in areas such as inconsistent work pattern, having had poor parenting as a child, repeated legal difficulties, interpersonal difficulties, irritability, failure to honor financial obligations, and impulsive behavior. In addition, veterans with genuine combat-related PTSD frequently engage in substance abuse and reckless behaviors. Thus it is important to search for early developmental evidence of antisocial personality in school records, family interviews, and juvenile offender records.

Clinical Indicators of Malingered Combat-Related PTSD

The clinical indicators for malingered combat-related PTSD are based primarily on individual case reports and anecdotal descriptions (see Table 7.8). Thus they should be considered tentative and must be weighed along with the totality of the available data.

The evaluator should pay attention to how the examinees attribute blame for their stressors and symptoms. Veterans with genuine PTSD are more likely to feel intense guilt and to perceive themselves as the cause of their problems. They are more likely to express "survivor's shame" for having lived while others who fought alongside them died (Burkett & Whitely, 1998). They are generally hesitant to blame their problems directly on their combat experience (Melton, 1984) and often seek help as a result of the insistence of family members. In contrast, malingerers are more likely to present as "victims" and emphasize how their problems are a direct result of alleged war experiences. The malingerer is more likely to dwell on themes of condemnation of war and authority.

Malingerers of combat-related PTSD are more likely to give a chief complaint of fear of "losing control" and harming others (Melton, 1984). This complaint is commonly used by malingerers to gain admission to a psychiatric inpatient unit. Malingerers also have a tendency to overplay their war experience or claim improbable combat heroics. For example, the clinician should be particularly suspicious of the examinee who alleges overly dramatic exploits such as escaping from a prisoner of war camp by fighting off enemy forces in hand-to-hand combat.

Individuals who recite DSM criteria or introduce psychiatric jargon such as "I have intrusive recollections" should be viewed with suspicion due the likelihood that they have received coaching. Malingerers are more likely to make gratuitous, conclusory statements such as "I've got PTSD. I've got flashbacks and nightmares" (Merback, 1984, p. 6). Veterans with genuine PTSD are more likely to downplay their combat experiences or to make statements such as "Lots of men had it worse than me."

Veterans' posttraumatic nightmares take on a pattern that is distinct from those in civilian PTSD, although the reasons for this are unclear. The nightmares of veterans with PTSD take the form of an encapsulated traumatic combat scene that may become isolated. When activated, the dream proceeds in an almost identical fashion for many years. A veteran with genuine posttraumatic nightmares may wake up terrified and report having a dream of the combat stressor exactly or almost exactly as it occurred in reality (Atkinson et al., 1982). It is possible that this phenomenon may represent nighttime flashbacks as opposed to actual dream states.

The dreams of veterans with genuine PTSD generally contain themes of helplessness regarding the combat stressor as opposed to the themes of grandiosity and power sometimes seen in malingerers (Merback, 1984, p. 6). Regarding the intrusive distressing recollections of Criterion B, veterans with genuine PTSD often report experiencing themes of helplessness, guilt, or rage. Conversely, the themes of intrusive recollections in malingered combat PTSD often consist of anger toward authority.

The clinician should make note of how emotions are handled and expressed by the examinee. The veterans with genuine PTSD often deny or have been numbed by the emotional impact of combat. In contrast, the malingerers will often make special efforts to impress evaluators with how emotionally traumatizing the war was for them. Such efforts may include "acting out" of alleged feelings. Veterans with genuine PTSD are more likely to downplay symptoms, such as trying not to call attention to hyperalertness or suspicious eye movements. On the other hand, malingerers are more likely to overplay their alleged symptoms

TABLE 7.8. Clinical Indicators of Malingered Combat-Related PTSD

Genuine PTSD	Malingered PTSD
Minimize relationship of problems to combat	Emphasize relationship of problems to combat
Blame self	Blame others
Dreams: themes of helplessness, guilt	Dreams: themes of grandiosity, power
Deny emotional impact of combat	"Act out" alleged feelings
Reluctant to discuss combat memories	"Relish" discussing combat tales
Survivor guilt relates to specific incidents	Generalized guilt over surviving war
Avoidance of environmental stimuli	No avoidance of environmental stimuli
Anger over helplessness	Anger toward authority

and may present them with a dramatic, attention-seeking quality. Similarly, the malingerers sometimes dwell on their alleged war experiences and seem to relish relating combat tales and memories (Merback, 1984).

Veterans with genuine PTSD will acknowledge appropriate instances in which they avoided the associated environmental conditions (Criterion C of PTSD). For example, a combat veteran with PTSD may stay at home on hot, rainy days because of the resemblance to weather in Vietnam. Camping or boat rides may be avoided due to the resemblance to military terrain or circumstances. Individuals who attempt to malinger combat PTSD are less likely to report having such postcombat reactions to environmental stimuli (Merback, 1984).

In summary, military veterans have easy access to websites that offer instruction on how to fake PTSD to obtain unearned service-connected disability pensions. Collateral data must be obtained to confirm actual combat trauma. Malingering veterans are more likely to present themselves as victims, to overplay their heroics, and to use PTSD jargon. Malingerers are more likely to report dreams of grandiosity rather than helplessness and to emphasize reliving symptoms rather than psychic numbing.

data and careful evaluation of the individual to differentiate between genuine and malingered PTSD. Clinicians charged with the task of evaluating PTSD must be well versed in both the phenomenology of the disorder and the common differences between genuine and malingered PTSD.

In summary, in order to improve the likelihood of recognizing malingered PTSD, the evaluator should:

- Establish an external gain for malingering
- Collect collateral information from a variety of sources prior to the evaluation
- Approach the interview with a nonjudgmental attitude
- Ask open-ended questions during the interview to avoid revealing the symptoms of PTSD to the examinee
- Evaluate the veracity of the reported symptoms based on familiarity with the phenomenology of genuine PTSD
- Consider the utility of psychological and physiological testing
- Clarify inconsistencies in the examinee's account
- Provide the examinee with the opportunity to admit to malingering without inducing shame

CONCLUSIONS

Most clinicians would agree that malingering is difficult to diagnose, no matter what disorder is feigned. It requires an assessment of whether false symptoms are intentionally produced and what an individual gains by having those symptoms. Given that the diagnosis of PTSD is primarily based on a subjective report of psychological symptoms, it is an easy disorder to successfully simulate. Despite a complex and lengthy process, it is often possible through meticulous collection of collateral

NOTES

1. Fp classification percentages are reflected as average positive predictive power and false-positive rates obtained from three studies that had utility estimate data available.
2. Ds classification percentages are reflected as average positive predictive power and false-positive rates obtained from two studies that had utility estimates available.
3. This review contained limited comparisons of actual individuals diagnosed with PTSD with simulators, and several studies utilized a differential prevalence design.

8

Factitious Disorder in Medical and Psychiatric Practices

JAMES C. HAMILTON, PhD
MARC D. FELDMAN, MD
ALAN J. CUNNIEN, MD

The late Dr. Alan J. Cunnien (1997) contributed an outstanding chapter on factitious disorder and related syndromes to this book's second edition. Since that time, major advances have occurred in the conceptualization of illness behavior and deception. Several developments were presaged and, indeed, inspired by Dr. Cunnien's insights and analyses. We (Hamilton and Feldman) are honored to coauthor this chapter with Dr. Cunnien, whose words and ideas are an important part of this effort. Dr. Cunnien's original chapter was encompassing in its scope. In contrast, this contribution is more focused on factitious disorder and related conditions.

OVERVIEW OF ILLNESS BEHAVIOR AND DECEPTION

The scholarly study of medical and psychiatric deception is rooted in hundreds of carefully documented cases, providing irrefutable evidence that patients intentionally exaggerate, lie about, simulate, aggravate, or induce disease, injury, or functional disability, either in themselves or in persons under their care. The existence of such cases has been widely accepted for over a century, and these clinical phenomena have been codified since DSM-III

(American Psychiatric Association, 1980). Cases of intentional feigning are organized into factitious disorder (FD) and malingering. The latter is not a formal diagnosis but rather a condition of clinical concern. Factitious disorder is coded into three subtypes, officially referred to as FD with primarily physical signs and symptoms (herein called factitious physical disorders), FD with primarily psychological signs and symptoms (herein called factitious psychological disorders), and FD with mixed physical and psychological symptoms. More recently, factitious disorder by proxy (also called Munchausen by proxy, or MBP for purposes of this chapter) has been recognized as a variant of factitious illness behavior in which a caregiver feigns or creates an illness or injury in a person under his or her care (Meadow, 1977). In each of these conditions, the medical or psychiatric falsification is presumed to be intentional. In FD and MBP, the motivation for doing so is presumed to be "internal," whereas in malingering the incentives for the deception are considered to be more tangible, instrumental, or external.

In the current nosological systems, the intentional quality of the false "sick role" enactments in FD and malingering is used as the basis for distinguishing these disorders from behaviorally similar ones, including the somatoform disorders (e.g., somatization, pain, and conversion disorders) and functional somatic syndromes (e.g., chronic fatigue syndrome and fibromyalgia). In the somatoform disorders and functional somatic syndromes, excessive illness behavior is regarded as the unintended result of unconscious cognitive processes. However, as we have argued elsewhere (J. C. Hamilton & Feldman, 2007), there is no empirical support for the use of consciousness and intentionality to categorically distinguish factious disorder and malingering from other excessive illness behavior phenomena.

There is no scientifically based reason to reject the alternative assumption that most instances of excessive illness behavior reflect the operation of both cognitive and motivational factors. The implications of this view are (1) that illness deception may be a more significant public health issue than it currently appears to be and, more important, (2) that motivational influences on excessive illness behavior can be meaningfully studied in patient populations that are generally more agreeable to research participation than are frank malingerers and patients with factitious disorders.

Empirical Basis of Factitious Disorders

Little empirical research exists on factitious disorder, its epidemiology, and its psychopathology. This lack of research is certainly not due to a lack of professional interest. There are nearly 1,300 papers indexed in Medline that contain *factitious* or *Munchausen* in their titles. However, fewer than 20 of these articles are empirical. The situation is similar for the MBP literature. For both conditions, the vast majority of published articles are case reports, selective reviews of the literature, or papers offering clinical guidance. Many more articles address factitious physical disorders than factitious psychological disorders. In stark contrast, malingering research is devoted to mental disorders and cognitive impairment with relatively little attention to medical complaints (see Rogers, Chapter 2, this volume).

The pattern of research on factitious disorders illuminates some of the unique barriers faced by scientists who try to study medical and psychiatric deception. The most fundamental barrier is the unwillingness of persons to report honestly about their current or past deceptions. Regardless of the specific motivations behind the deception, honest self-disclosure of decep-

tion would defeat its purpose and perhaps expose the deceiver to civil or criminal liability. Because few openly admit to illness deception, the only way to establish with reasonable certainty that a person is falsely enacting the sick role is to assemble supportive evidence from collateral sources (e.g., medical records, accounts by others, physical evidence, and surveillance). These efforts are made difficult by the patients' right to confidentiality and protections against unauthorized investigations into patients' personal lives. In contradistinction, malingering cases typically provide greater access to clinical data. In advancing legal claims, patients often forfeit their right to confidentiality and allow themselves to be examined by medical, psychiatric, and forensic experts whose explicit goal is to determine the authenticity of the patients' claims.

The strategies used to detect deception and their likelihood of success vary according to the nature of the unexplained illness. Subjective medical and psychiatric complaints, such as pain, fatigue, depression, or anxiety, are very difficult to authenticate. For more verifiable medical problems, such as hematuria, the question is not whether the medical signs are present but whether they occurred naturally or were created artificially. In contrast, many malingering cases permit the collection of extensive documentation of impairment and the administration of standardized measures of psychological functioning and neuropsychological performance. Many of the tests include empirically validated algorithms for detecting feigned impairment.

In summary, most research data on illness deception rely on malingering research within specific legal contexts. As a comparison, FD arises mostly from clinical settings in which practitioners have more limited access to data and fewer standardized measures. Although some of the same strategies employed in the detection of malingering might be useful for identifying FD, their application ultimately rests on factors outside of their predictive validity; their usefulness depends on when and how the strategies will be used in low base-rate contexts and on the willingness of patients to cooperate with them.

The Potential Burden of Medical and Psychiatric Deception

Factitious disorders and malingering are a part of a larger problem concerning excessive illness behavior. Studies in primary medical care of unexplained medical complaints (e.g., Nimnuan, Hotopf, & Wessely, 2001) suggest that 30–50% of all patient-initiated visits are for medical complaints with no identifiable physical cause (Nimnuan et al., 2001). Functional somatic syndromes (e.g., fibromyalgia and chronic fatigue syndrome), in which excessive illness behavior is regarded as an important feature, represent 1–3% of primary care patients (Kim, Shin, & Won, 2005; Nampiaparampil & Shmerling, 2004; Prins, van der Meer, & Bleijenberg, 2006; Wessely, Chalder, Hirsch, Wallace, & Wright, 1997). Excessive illness behavior is common in somatoform disorders, in which it is judged to create distress or problems with adaptive functioning in 15–20% of primary care patients (Arnold, de Waal, Eekhof, & Van Hemert, 2006; Grabe et al., 2003), or even at a higher percentage (Fink, Steen Hansen, & Sondergaard, 2005).

For the purposes of this chapter, a key question is what proportion of the costs is associated with factitious disorder and malingering. We have no data on direct and indirect health care costs of intentional illness deception. However, even very conservative estimates, such as 1% of visits for unexplained medical complaints, suggest that factitious disorder and malingering place a great economic burden on society. The next major sections address key diagnoses associated with factitious symptoms.

FACTITIOUS DISORDERS

The DSM-IV-TR diagnostic criteria for factitious disorder (FD) are: "A. Intentional production or feigning of physical or psychological signs or symptoms; B. The motivation for the behavior is to assume the sick role; C. External incentives for the behavior (such as economic gain, avoiding legal responsibility, or improving physical well-being, as in Malingering) are absent" (American Psychiatric Association, 2000, p. 517). In addition, there are qualifications that FD should not be diagnosed when sick role behavior or self-injury is better explained by another disorder, such as an eating disorder or borderline personality disorder.

There are two peculiarities about the FD diagnosis that are worth pointing out. First, the DSM-IV-TR criteria do not specify any thresholds of severity or chronicity that a case must meet in order to receive an FD diagnosis. Similarly, the DSM does not require the usual standard of subjective distress or interference with the patient's social or occupational functioning. The reasons for these omissions are unclear.

Second, the inclusion criteria are devised in a manner that is strongly biased against the FD diagnosis and in favor of a somatoform-disorder diagnosis. The criteria for the somatoform disorders suggest that unexplained medical complaints should be regarded as unconsciously produced unless there is affirmative evidence that they are intentionally falsified. There is no requirement of affirmative evidence that the symptom is unconsciously produced. In contrast, FD requires definitive evidence of intentional illness deception. Taken together, these criteria sets make a somatoform disorder the default diagnosis in cases of unexplained medical complaints owing to the difficulty of proving intentional deception.

Even if evidence for intentional illness falsification is obtained, the presence of any external incentives for the patient's sick role enactment excludes the FD diagnosis. As external incentives are inherent to the sick-role experience (e.g., time off from work or school; obtaining narcotic analgesic medicines), FD would be excluded on this basis from most cases of illness deception.

Given the way the criteria for FD and related diseases have been crafted, it is not surprising that FD is rarely diagnosed and that, when it is, the case is usually spectacular with regard to the severity or chronicity of the medical deceptions involved. The question, of course, is whether the impression of FD as a severe and rare form of psychopathology is an accurate portrayal of the prevalence of psychologically motivated sick-role enactments in medicine and psychiatry.

In the following section and subsections we describe the major subtypes of FD defined by the DSM-IV-TR. Most of the clinical applications are discussed within each of the subsections.

Factitious Disorder with Predominantly Psychological Signs and Symptoms

In FD with predominantly psychological signs and symptoms (factitious psychological disorder), individuals feign or produce psychiatric and/or behavioral ailments motivated by internal incentives. Surprisingly, this category is gaining in complexity as developments in neuropsychiatry blur the lines between central nervous system dysfunction and features that are primarily "psychological" or "emotional" in origin. As Parker (1996) writes, "[T]he distinction of psychological from physical is becoming increasingly artificial in the face of neurophysiologic advances pointing to the interplay between psychology and neurobiology" (p. 38). This finding is evidenced by explanations of behavior, which are increasingly understood in terms of neurotransmitters. Today, however, psychological symptoms still lack the biological markers that might be available in the patient with factitious physical disorder, and the resources needed to confirm psychosocial data are not nearly as available in clinical practice as is the laboratory for obtaining physiological data.

The complexities of factitious psychological disorders have long been recognized (e.g., Gavin, 1843). Merrin, Van Dyke, Cohen, and Tusel (1986), for example, argued that factitious psychological and physical disorders should be a single diagnosis carrying a modifying statement rather than being split into separate disorders. Rogers, Bagby, and Vincent (1994) questioned the diagnostic legitimacy of factitious psychological disorders; the observed patterns of bogus symptoms were very similar to malingering.

Factitious psychological disorders may mimic any genuine disorder or syndrome. Symptom presentations are so varied as to defy a unitary formulation. Carney and Brown (1983) estimated that this specific diagnosis may account for up to 40% of all factitious illness presentations, even though many cases are probably missed due to inherent difficulties in objective assessment (Popli, Masand, & Dewan, 1992). Examples of particularly difficult factitious presentations include alcohol abuse (Caradoc-Davies, 1988; Mitchell & Francis, 2003), hallucinations (Yildiz & Torun, 2003), and suicidal or homicidal ideation (Thompson & Beckson, 2004). Links, Steiner, and Mitton (1989) found a remarkable 13% incidence of factitious psychotic symptoms in inpatients with borderline personality disorder. As a striking contrast, admissions to inpatient units evidence much lower rates of factitious psychological disorders, ranging from 0.14% (Nicholson & Roberts, 1994) to 6.0% (Gregory & Jindal, 2006). Patients with factitious psychological disorders tend to manifest traits that resemble those seen in Munchausen syndrome.

They generally have few visitors and discharge themselves from the hospital if confronted (Parker, 1996). Other characteristics include itinerancy, lawlessness, self-destructiveness, problems with developing and maintaining relationships, open hostility, and pseudologia fantastica (Feldman, 2004; see the subsequent section on pseudologia fantastica). In addition, the symptoms are often more pronounced when the physician and hospital staff members are present. Clues are often buried in discrepancies between what patients say and their actual appearances or behavior.

The classic findings of a well-defined mental disorder are unlikely in factitious psychological disorders. Instead, the patients' symptoms will typically represent their concepts of mental disorders. Likewise, medications indicated for the factitious condition may appear inexplicably ineffective. An important distinction is that patients with factitious psychological disorders are willing to accept psychiatric hospitalization unlike those with factitious physical disorders. Parker (1996) explained that "[a] common pattern for the factitious disorder patient with physical symptoms is to leave the hospital against medical advice when referred to the psychiatric unit; the patient with factitious psychological symptoms, however, seeks hospitalization on the psychiatric unit" (p. 41). She also noted that, "[i]f the patient is willing to provide valid psychological data, traits of psychopathic deviation, paranoia, hysteria, depression, and hypochondriasis may be present" (p. 41). However, her remarks are based on very small numbers of patients; patients generally will not provide valid psychological data. In addition, other authors (e.g., Taskaynatan et al., 2005) have found no comorbid disorders for many factitious patients assessed with psychological evaluations.

Misuse of drugs and/or alcohol is common among patients with factitious psychological disorders. They may secretly use psychoactive substances to produce actual signs that suggest a mental disorder. Feldman (2004) reported:

> stimulants such as amphetamines, cocaine, or caffeine may be used to produce restlessness or insomnia. Illegal drugs such as LSD . . . , mescaline, and marijuana might be used to induce altered levels of consciousness and perception. Heroin and morphine . . . may be employed to induce euphoria. . . . Hypnotics such as barbiturates can be used to create lethargy. Combinations of these

substances often produce extraordinarily bizarre presentations. The main difference between factitious and actual drug abusers is that the factitious disorder patient induces an altered state not as an end in itself, but as a way to mislead caregivers and others. (p. 109)

Factitious Psychosis

Along with factitious bereavement and factitious posttraumatic stress disorder (see subsequent sections), factitious psychotic symptoms are particularly common among published reports (Limosin, Loze, & Rouillon, 2002). For almost a century, the term *hysterical psychosis* defined a condition characterized by brief psychotic symptoms with onset during stress, dramatic personality traits, and a rapid return to baseline functioning. Patients with this condition were suggestible and usually hypnotizable (Spiegel & Fink, 1979), raising questions of voluntary control over symptoms. Ritson and Forrest (1970) were the first to evaluate these patients; all presented clear signs of deception though several had previous diagnoses of schizophrenia. Without evidence of voluntary control over symptoms, these patients would currently be diagnosed with acute stress disorder (American Psychiatric Association, 2000). Hysterical features and characteristics akin to somatoform disorders were found in 56 cases reviewed by Bishop and Holt (1980). This group seemed to represent a "good prognosis" factitious syndrome with regression under stress.

Another form of factitious psychosis implies a more ominous prognosis. Pope, Jonas, and Jones (1982) analyzed phenomenological and outcome data on nine patients with voluntary control over psychotic symptoms. Most patients were females with severe personality disorders and no family history of psychosis. Strikingly, long-term follow-up revealed this group to perform more poorly on measures of global assessment and social functioning than did patients with bipolar and schizophrenic disorders. For this characterologically disturbed subgroup, the investigators concluded that "acting crazy may bode more ill than being crazy" (p. 1483). A similar phenomenon was noted by Hay (1983), who found that 5 of 6 patients with feigned psychosis eventually developed schizophrenia. Feigned psychosis apparently entails several possible motivations: a coping strategy for acute stress, a justification of care for incipient "legitimate" psychosis, or a mechanism for permissible regression.

Factitious Posttraumatic Stress Disorder (PTSD)

The introduction of PTSD as a diagnostic entity in DSM-III provided potentially duplicitous veterans and pseudo veterans with another avenue to psychological care or financial gain, though false claims of other forms of posttraumatic injury have been made for decades (Resnick, 1997). Sparr and Pankratz (1983) described differential diagnostic difficulties in Vietnam veterans with false claims of combat-related PTSD; review of military records revealed that none experienced the alleged traumas. Diagnoses included factitious psychological disorder, combined factitious disorder with Munchausen features, and malingering. Diverse diagnoses were also noted by Lynn and Belza (1984) and by Hamilton (1985); such cases reinforce the need to distinguish external motives that are characteristic of malingering from the unique, personalized, psychological motivation to be sick as seen in factitious disorders (Lacoursiere, 1993).

Any trauma will provide opportunities for malingering or factitious presentation. Two books, *Stolen Valor* (Burkett & Whitley, 1998) and *Fake Warriors* (Holzer & Holzer, 2003), are devoted to cases in which persons who never even served have falsely claimed military heroism and battle-related injuries, apparently to garner attention and enhance self-perception. Genuine PTSD related to military action (Feldman, 2004; see also Resnick, West, & Payne, Chapter 7, this volume) is characterized by the following: (1) attempts to minimize the relationship between one's symptoms and the trauma experience, (2) self-blame, (3) dreams about traumatic events, 4) denial of the emotional impact of combat, (5) an unwillingness to recount combat stories, (6) guilt about having survived, (7) avoidance of environments that resemble the combat situation, and (8) anger at the personal inability to overcome PTSD. Counterfeit war heroes often fail to present this complete picture.

Factitious Bereavement

Snowdon, Solomons, and Druce (1978) described 12 patients whose chief complaints were the fabricated loss of a loved one with resulting depression or suicidality. Most patients were male, with previous use of aliases, factitious physical symptoms, and sudden departures from the hospital. Phillips, Ward, and Ries (1983) reported a similar group of 20 factitious mourners with high rates of feigned physical illness, suicide attempts, felonious acts, substance abuse, and pathological lying. Feldman (2004) noted that the allegedly bereaved often report especially tragic or gruesome deaths (e.g., the individual was decapitated or impaled) that may involve multiple individuals, including children and adolescents.

Factitious mourners differ from the genuinely bereaved in both their moods and their actions. Factitious mourners manifest variable or angry affect, report suicidal ideation, demand hospitalization, fail to produce corroboration of the death, and resist treatment efforts. These features are often shared with malingering and Munchausen syndrome. Despite the small number of reported cases, these simulators serve to remind the clinician of the protean nature of factitious symptoms, the fluidity of deceptive behavior across affective and somatic boundaries, and the likelihood that patients readily traverse the artificial limits among factitious disorder, malingering, and simple lying.

Factitious Dissociative Identity Disorder

Dissociative identity disorder (DID), formerly multiple personality disorder (MPD), is a dramatic and unusual dissociative condition reported with increasing frequency since its legitimization in DSM-III. Its clinical features, described by Putnam, Guroff, Silberman, Barban, and Post (1986), include high rates of personality pathology, history of trauma, chemical dependency, hypnotizability, and suggestibility. Malingered DID was reviewed by Kluft (1987) and might occur fairly frequently in view of the ease of claiming amnesia and child abuse. Few case reports describe factitious DID (Coons, 1993; Friedl & Draijer, 2000) in nonforensic settings. It is reasonable to wonder whether strong advocates of the DID diagnosis, by criticizing clinicians who question the diagnosis (e.g., Dell, 1988), have discouraged investigation regarding the veracity of DID reports.

Patients with apparent DID report personal histories and comorbid conditions frequently seen in factitious disorder patients (see Jonas & Pope, 1985). Borderline personality pathology is common, and self-hypnosis or autogenic dissociation may serve the purpose of nurturance or avoidance of pain (Buck, 1983). This observation raises the interesting interpreta-

tion that factitious behavior (perhaps the voluntary production of dissociation to serve regressive needs) is part and parcel of DID. Toth and Baggaley (1991) described a patient in whom treatment for DID led to a reduction of factitious behavior. As with other conditions whose diagnostic popularity has increased, devoted advocates and staunch opponents heatedly disagree (e.g., Foote, Smolin, Kaplan, Legatt, & Lipschitz, 2006). The prudent clinician will recall that any disorder can be feigned and that highly subjective states, such as DID, may be prone to deception. The inability of the various identity states to produce a consistent response set on special scales of the MMPI appears to be one mechanism that is helpful in this regard (Coons, 1993).

Factitious Claims of Child Abuse

The tragic consequences of child abuse need no elaboration. Unfortunately, false claims of child sexual abuse are a reality and require investigators to be aware of motivations behind both false denials and false accusations (Goodwin, Sahd, & Rada, 1978). In a survey of more than 1,200 reports of child sexual abuse, Everson and Boat (1989) estimated 4.7–7.6% to be false. They found that only 56% of sexual abuse allegations were substantiated, with most of the remaining cases being unresolved. It suggests that the percentage of false claims may be substantially higher. Recently, Malloy, Lyon, and Quas (2007) examined 257 cases of alleged child sexual abuse; 23.1% of the children later recanted their accusations, although an unknown number may have felt pressured to do so.

Mikkelsen, Gutheil, and Emens (1992) emphasized the importance of assessing abuse allegations in context. False accusations may arise out of child custody disputes, through iatrogenic factors, by conscious manipulation on the child's part, or out of psychological needs. Only the last group of complaints could properly be called factitious.

Most false allegations are made by parents or other caretakers (Cantwell, 1981), sometimes out of delusional beliefs but more commonly because attention to the child enhances the reporter's perceptions of being a good parent and meets dependent or narcissistic needs or desires for retaliation (see the later section on factitious disorder by proxy for further exploration of the psychological needs prompting false claims). The presence of monetary issues in child custody and divorce proceedings makes psychologically based false reports difficult to distinguish from mere greed or fraud. When children themselves initiate false reports without prompting or coaching, factitious behavior appears motivated by fear of abandonment, attention seeking, or regressive needs (Everson & Boat, 1989)—the same motivations seen in other types of FD. Though most reports of child abuse are valid and possibly underreported in general (Jensen, Gulbrandsen, Mossige, Reichelt, & Tjersland, 2005), investigators and evaluators should remain aware of the myriad motivations behind false reporting, particularly in the context of custody proceedings. In addition to the invention of sexual abuse histories, individuals have made false victimization claims that have involved stalking, sexual harassment, emotional and physical abuse and neglect, and countless other crimes.

Factitious Disorder with Predominantly Physical Signs and Symptoms

Factitious physical disorder in medical contexts is considered to be rare, but this assumption may well be mistaken. Epidemiological data are difficult to obtain because population surveys are ineffective for determining the prevalence of disorders, such as factitious disorder, in which secretiveness and intentional deceit are central features. One alternative to surveys is the review of case series regarding psychiatric referrals. In a German sample of 995 inpatient and outpatient psychiatric referrals, Fliege, Scholler, Rose, Willenberg, and Klapp (2002) reported a 3% rate for factitious medical disorders. Earlier studies have yielded lower rates:

- 0.6% for German inpatient psychiatry referrals (Kapfhammer, Rothenhausler, Dietrich, Dobmeier, & Mayer, 1998)
- 0.8% for Canadian inpatient psychiatric referrals
- 0.3% for German inpatient neurological referrals (Bauer & Boegner, 1996)

Unfortunately, none of these reports includes the rate of psychiatric or neurological referrals, so it is impossible to extrapolate the reported rates to all hospitalized patients. In more refined samples of particularly puzzling cases, the reported rates of factitious medical disorders are higher. For example, the prevalence rates in cases of fever of unknown origin range from 2 to 9% (Aduan, Fauci, Dale, Herzberg, & Wolff, 1979; Rumans & Vosti, 1978).

Attempts to use large health care databases to determine the prevalence of factitious medical disorders are unlikely to be accurate. Krahn, Li, and O'Connor (2003) studied occurrences of FD in a general medical inpatient population. Of the 93 patients with FD ultimately identified, only 20 were identified by their official discharge diagnosis. An alternate approach is to survey physicians about their experiences with patients with FD. Fliege and colleagues (2007) surveyed 83 physicians, who observed FD in 1.3% of their patients, though the range of estimates was very wide. Finally, in a compelling but seldom-cited outpatient study, Sansone, Weiderman, Sansone, and Mehnert-Kay (1997) asked primary care patients to complete a confidential questionnaire related to medical self-sabotage. They found that 6.6% of patients admitted to actively and intentionally causing, prolonging, or exacerbating an illness.

Medical patients with FD may appear in primary care settings, emergency departments, hospitals, or any number of specialty care settings. They are most frequently encountered in dermatology (Fliege et al., 2007), with rashes, burns, infections, or nonhealing wounds; endocrinology, with dysregulation of thyroid hormones, blood glucose, and insulin; and neurology (Bauer & Boegner, 1996), with seizures, dizziness, sensory deficits, and paralysis. In general practice, bleeding problems, such as coughing up blood (Kokturk, Ekim, Aslan, Kanbay, & Acar, 2006), blood in the urine (Lazarus & Kozinn, 1991), and anemia (Hirayama et al., 2003) are often encountered, as are infections, including sepsis (Lazarus & Kozinn, 1991). However, the voluminous case literature on factitious physical disorders suggests that almost any medical problem can be falsified.

The clinical presentation of factitious physical disorders is highly variable, so relying on stereotypes based on bizarre reports may cause clinical errors. By definition, medical falsification can come in multiple forms: (1) exaggerated symptoms or medical history, (2) outright lies about symptoms or medical history, (3) simulations of medical illnesses through the production of compelling signs, (4) manipulations to prolong or exacerbate an existing illness, or (5) actual self-induction of disease (American Psychiatric Association, 2000). Rarely does a factitious medical patient use only one method of deception. Rather, typical patients with FD employ multiple forms of deception, such as simulated signs of disease (e.g., rashes), feigned symptoms (e.g., joint pain), and false history (e.g., tick bites) to create the full medical picture of a known disease (e.g., Lyme disease). Because the diagnosis relies on conclusive evidence of intentional medical deception, FD is more likely to be uncovered in cases that include simulation or self-induction of medical signs: Patients are caught tampering with blood or urine samples, found to be in possession of syringes, drugs, or mechanical devices, or observed harming themselves. Cases of FD that involve only false histories and feigned or exaggerated symptoms are likely to go undiscovered. Thus the requirement of affirmative proof of intentional illness falsification almost certainly creates a biased view that factitious physical disorders are limited to rare and severe cases (Hamilton & Feldman, 2007).

The few available published case series on factitious physical disorders suggest that the majority of patients are women, with a significant representation of persons with medical training, such as nurses and lab technicians (Goldstein, 1998; Kapfhammer et al., 1998; Krahn et al., 2003). Most patients with FD are reasonably well educated, employed or in school (Krahn et al., 2003), and are at least marginally connected to a network of family and social contacts (Goldstein, 1998). All of the larger case series report substantial comorbidity with other mental disorders, but none reports comparison rates from the populations from which the FD cases were drawn, so it is difficult to interpret these findings (Goldstein, 1998; Kapfhammer et al., 1998; Krahn et al., 2003) Borderline personality disorder appears to be common in patients with FD (Goldstein, 1998; Kapfhammer et al., 1998), along with other cluster B personality disorders, eating disorders, and substance abuse (Feldman, Hamilton, Deemer, & Phillips, 2001; Fliege et al., 2002).

The course of factitious physical disorders is extremely difficult to ascertain. Patients with FD cannot be relied on to provide an accurate history or access to past medical records. As such, we know little about the onset and development of their factitious illness behavior or about their long-term outcomes. Large case series indicate that, typically, patients with FD are 30–40 years old at the time they are first recognized (Goldstein, 1998; Kapfhammer et al., 1998; Krahn et al., 2003; Reich & Gottfried, 1983). It would seem reasonable to suspect that patients with FD typically progress (1) from less to more extreme modes of medical deception and (2) from an episodic to a chronic pattern. Data from at least one study supports this view (Kapfhammer et al., 1998). Also, there is reason to believe that medical deception in adulthood sometimes follows being the victim of Munchausen-by-proxy maltreatment in childhood (Libow, 1995).

Considerable morbidity and mortality are associated with factitious physical disorders. Medical deceptions associated with factitious physical disorders can lead directly to permanent disease or disability (Salvo, Pinna, Milia, & Carta, 2006). In other cases, patient deceptions have led physicians to perform unnecessary and irreversible surgeries, including mastectomies (Feldman, 2001), adrenalectomies (Cook & Meikle, 1985), pancreatectomies (Hirshberg et al., 2002), and other permanent procedures. In a report by Fliege and colleagues (2002), approximately 50% of patients with apparent FD experienced iatrogenic harm or placed themselves at imminent risk of iatrogenic harm. Simulations or self-induced disease can also be deadly (Croft, Racz, Bloch, & Palmer, 2005; Hirayama et al., 2003; Kansagara, Tetrault, Hamill, Moore, & Olson, 2006). In addition, mortality can be caused by heroic treatment measures that are misguided by dissimulation or false information provided by the patient (Eisendrath & McNiel, 2004). Finally, there may be cases in which the disease simulation was so crude or so badly miscalculated that the patient's death was not connected with FD and was regarded instead as an accidental death or suicide (Croft et al., 2005).

The etiology of factitious physical disorder remains a mystery. As with the somatoform disorders, early formulations were dominated by psychoanalytic theories. Menninger (1934) viewed the willingness to undergo surgery as a way of representing a sadistic parent projected onto the physicians. Asher (1951) suggested motives spanning the conceptual spectrum between FD and malingering, such as desire for attention, a grudge against doctors, and a desire for drugs or free lodging (Cramer, Gershberg, & Stern, 1971). Spiro (1968) was the first to suggest psychodynamic consistencies in patients with chronic FD. He noted such features as (1) imposture to compensate for ego and super-ego deficits, (2) choice of the hospital as a stage on which to enact masochistic conflicts because of the ready availability of suffering and caretaking, (3) masochistic transference reenactment of early parental conflicts, and (4) masochistic identification with the pain-inflicting doctor. The focus of psychodynamic thinking has shifted from classical dynamic formulations to those centered on pre-oedipal and object-relations problems. For example, Bursten (1965) suggested that patients with factitious physical disorders act out with doctors and nurses their need for, and fear of, closeness and caring.

More recently, the strong connection between FD and borderline and narcissistic personality disorders has led some to suggest that FD provides a way of coping with poor interpersonal attachments and identity problems. Ehlers and Plassmann (1994) studied the personality profiles of 14 patients with factitious physical disorders and found high scores of narcissistic and borderline personality functioning. Consistent with these formulations, rigorous empirical studies of hypochondriacal and somatizing patients suggest that these patients are characterized by insecure adult attachment (Noyes et al., 2002, 2003; Stuart & Noyes, 1999, 2006). In a similar line of thinking, Hamilton and colleagues (Hamilton et al., 2003; Hamilton & Janata, 1997) have used social psychological models of self-esteem to suggest that factitious illness behavior can be used to compensate for a low self-appraisal or poorly defined self-concepts.

Etiological models based on poor early attachments are consistent with clinical anecdotes that collectively suggest high prevalence of child abuse in patients with factitious physical disorders (Brown & Scheflin, 1999). However, these clinical data must be interpreted with great caution given the predilection of patients with FD for telling lies that cast them as hapless victims.

Detection of factitious physical disorders rests entirely on the awareness and skill of the patient's primary medical treatment team. The most important barrier to the detection of a factitious physical disorder is the failure of medical treatment teams to consider the FD as a differential diagnosis. Physicians will often overlook the possibility of factitious physical disorders, as they instead explore hypotheses

about extraordinarily rare, even unprecedented, physical diseases. Thus the first and most important step in detecting factitious physical disorders is to promote a higher level of suspicion in cases in which the first and second most likely diagnoses have been ruled out.

There are several aspects of patient behavior that should raise suspicions of factitious physical disorder. Patients with factitious physical disorder may try to exert an unusual degree of control over medical decision making, such as what tests should be performed and how and when they should be performed. They often have an impressive command of medical knowledge that might lead physicians to be more open to their input. Although the stereotype of the patient with FD in medical contexts is focused on their willingness to undergo a large number of unnecessary procedures, a more important clue may be the patient's attempt to avoid basic definitive medical tests. Patients have successfully feigned HIV/AIDS and cancers of various sorts in this way (Savino & Fordtran, 2006). The patient might insist that the test was done recently and report the results verbally or may insist that his or her case is terminal and beg the physician to spare him or her the further indignities of additional tests.

A second, related indicator of factitious physical disorder is confusion or evasiveness in the patient's account of his or her medical history. In addition, the patient may resist attempts to secure records of previous treatments. The patient might claim that the records were lost in a fire or a major natural disaster, such as Hurricane Katrina. The goal of this obfuscation is to keep the current treatment team unaware of the patient's extensive history of suspicious medical problems, especially any records in which the suspicions of previous physicians are explicit.

Patients with factitious physical disorders often do not respond to effective medical treatments. They may even fail to respond to highly effective palliative measures aimed at reducing their pain and discomfort. If a treatment seems to work, unexplained relapse may occur, particularly as the medical team begins to discuss discharge plans with the patient. Although patients with FD may complain about pain or discomfort, they often show an unusual willingness to undergo invasive diagnostic or treatment procedures and may even propose these if the physician suggests a more conservative approach. The patient may become angry and confrontational when presented with negative test results.

None of these features nor the presence of all of them constitutes proof of a factitious physical disorder. However, they should serve to heighten suspicion and prompt the treatment team to devise a plan for gathering affirmative proof of medical deception. Many patients with factitious physical disorders use methods of simulating or causing diseases that are easily detected if the treatment staff is open to the possibility that the patient may be intentionally deceiving them. Patients with unexplained blood in their urine can be examined for pinpricks and asked to provide urine samples while a nurse observes. Blood and urine samples can be assayed for the presence of substances that are not part of routine blood and urine screens. The status of the patient can be compared with and without continuous observation, and a nonhealing wound can be compared across conditions of soft bandaging and a hard cast. Factitious physical disorder is confirmed if the patient's condition worsens only when he or she has the opportunity to injure him- or herself.

Consultation from a psychiatrist or psychologist is usually requested after factitious physical illness is confirmed or shortly before. The primary goals of consultation are ultimately (1) to help protect the patient from further self-harm and (2) to protect the patient from iatrogenic harm. Self-harm can be prevented by closer observation of the patient or by arranging to separate the patient from his or her personal effects (among which the patient may have hidden chemicals or devices used to simulate medical signs). Iatrogenic harm can be prevented by urging the medical team to assume a more conservative approach to diagnosis and to retrace their steps, making sure to correct any deviations from standard care that the patient may have persuaded them to make.

Consultation services are probably most effective if they are requested before the medical team has confronted the patient with their suspicions. The consulting mental health professional may serve several important functions to a treatment team as suspicions are beginning to develop, such as: (1) providing an objective view of the evidence so far collected, (2) helping the physicians and nurses deal with their feeling of disbelief, anger, and betrayal, (3) helping to repair any rifts that may have developed between staff members who are advo-

cating the FD hypothesis and those who regard the patient's medical problem as genuine, and (4) developing a viable plan for managing the case.

Once FD has been established beyond a reasonable doubt, a decision must be made about whether to confront the patient. Although there may be dire medical emergencies in which direct confrontation is unavoidable, it appears that confrontation is seldom effective (Eisendrath, 1989). Patients who are directly accused of medical deception may become indignant, accuse medical staff of negligence and incompetence, and ultimately discharge themselves from the hospital. Although the hospital staff might be relieved to see the patient depart, their goals for the patient have not been met: The patient is likely to continue to expose him- or herself to self-harm and iatrogenic risks at another hospital.

An alternative approach is to more gently suggest that the patient has a serious illness but that it is a psychological illness, not a medical one. The response to this approach is also generally unfavorable. In Krahn and colleagues' (2003) case series, only 12% of inpatients and 9% of outpatients with FD accepted psychiatric referrals. Plassman's (1994) report of an inpatient treatment with long-term psychoanalytic outpatient follow-up treatment is the most encouraging treatment outcome report to date. He reports that 12 of 24 patients accepted treatment and that 10 remained in treatment long enough to observe improvement.

Eisendrath (1989) and others have advocated nonconfrontational, face-saving approaches that give patients with FD a way to relinquish the sick role without admitting to having falsified their illness (Eisendrath, 1989; Klonoff, Youngner, Moore, & Hershey, 1983; Servan-Schreiber, Tabas, & Kolb, 2000). Patients' problems can be framed according to a broad biopsychosocial perspective in which physical and psychological factors combine to determine health outcomes. By emphasizing the connection between stress and genuine physical illness, patients with FD may be able to engage in psychosocial interventions in a way that does not threaten their sick-role claims. Klonoff and colleagues (1983) report on a case in which this framework was used as a rationale for employing biofeedback therapy with a patient with psychogenic nonepileptic seizures. The ostensibly successful biofeedback treatment gave the patient a way to achieve a "cure" that did not challenge the patient's claim of having a genuine seizure disorder.

Munchausen Syndrome

Asher (1951) coined the term *Munchausen syndrome* to describe what is now thought to be a rare, archetypal, and largely untreatable form of factitious physical disorder. For these cases, illness induction seems to maintain a lifestyle revolving around hospitalizations, surgeries, and contentious battles with physicians. Unlike the typical patient with factitious physical disorder, Asher's patient with Munchausen syndrome was a male, who was admitted to the hospital after sudden onset of neurological, abdominal, or hematological symptoms. As objective information fails to corroborate complaints or when falsification of illness is suspected, belligerence, evasiveness, and stepped-up demands for drugs or surgery ensue. These patients are typically uncooperative, often present with pseudologia fantastica (see later section), often are found to have had prior admissions using aliases, and frequently discharge themselves against medical advice.

Factitious Disorder with Combined Psychological and Physical Signs and Symptoms

Eagerness to assume the sick role may lead to seemingly random choices to enact physical, psychological, or combined symptoms. For example, AIDS and cancer provide ample opportunities for fabrication of both physical complaints and depression. Merrin, Van Dyke, Cohen, and Tusel (1986) remarked on the pitfall of ignoring the possibility of factitious psychological complaints in the face of dramatic physical symptoms and personal histories. They emphasized the need to focus on inconsistencies in both spheres. The psychological need to be a patient does not respect traditional boundaries between physical and mental disorders.

False claims of rape (e.g., Feldman, 2000; Gibbon, 1998) are socially relevant examples of combined factitious illness behavior. Kanin (1994) found that 41% of forcible rape complaints over a 9-year period in a small community were fabricated. Over half served an alibi function (malingering to avoid undesirable consequences), but the remainder were interpreted to be false allegations in the service of revenge, sympathy, or attention-getting. Kanin

parenthetically noted that 50% of forcible rape complaints from two large university campuses were false. Feldman, Ford, and Stone (1994) hypothesized that factitious claims of sexual harassment or rape serve multiple psychological functions, such as nurturance, search for rescue from actual current abuse, dissociation from past abuse, or projection of anger (see preceding discussion of masochism and projection in Munchausen syndrome). For exhaustive, recent coverage, see the book, *Playing Sick?* (Feldman, 2004).

Pseudologia Fantastica

Compulsive lying, pathological lying, and pseudologia fantastica refer to repetitive, quasi-compulsive, sometimes patently ridiculous lies with no clear external goal orientation (see Weston & Dalby, 1991). Everyday lying is so common and nonpathological, moral implications aside, as to be outside the scope of this chapter; instead, the reader is referred to Ford (1996). Falsification is by definition a conscious act, though it may serve multiple unconscious motivations (e.g., revenge, mastery, self-aggrandizement, or humiliation).

In her classic paper, Deutsch (1982) noted that normal lies are goal-directed, whereas pseudologia fantastica serves as its own gratification. Via psychoanalytic formulation, Deutsch asserted that pathological lies appeared to represent daydreams, distortions of past events, or an admixture. Analogous to a verbal conversion reaction, the lie allows fulfillment of a disguised, otherwise forbidden libidinal wish. In contrast to the profit motive discerned in professional liars (e.g., con men) and the nonsensical quality of organically based confabulation, the perpetration of pseudologia fantastica seems designed to bolster self-esteem and promote admiration by others. Unlike the common braggart, however, the pseudologue falsifies a substantial amount of information with bearing on activities, acquaintances, or personal identity (Green, James, Gilbert, & Byard, 1999).

King and Ford (1988) reviewed 72 cases of pseudologia fantastica. They found a strong comorbidity with imposture, disease simulation, and peregrination—suggesting overlap with Munchausen syndrome and antisocial personality disorder. King and Ford emphasized the matrix of truth in the pseudologue's tale, the narcissistic gratification inherent in lies, the absence of monetary profit, and the similar characteristics of the lies (i.e., containing elements of revenge, vanity, and exaggeration). Surprisingly, 40% of their cases demonstrated apparent central nervous system abnormalities on neuropsychological testing. Modell, Mountz, and Ford (1992) found hemithalamic dysfunction in a patient with pseudologia fantastica by use of positron emission scanning. Similarly, Ford, King, and Hollender (1988) gave a thoughtful analysis of biological, developmental, social, and psychological determinants of pseudologia fantastica. They noted complex and sometimes overlapping motivations behind pseudologia: assertion of power (oral aggression), wish fulfillment, wishes for autonomy, denial or repression, and regulation of self-esteem.

In summary, lies (fantastic or not) may exist either in isolation or in the presence of another entity, such as factitious disorder or borderline personality disorder. Their presence, rather than implying the existence of a distinct syndrome of compulsive lying, should prompt a search for underlying psychopathology and for disorders associated with deception. To reemphasize this point, *pseudologia fantastica* is a descriptive term for deceitful behavior that is sometimes associated with specific syndromes. By itself, this term should not be invoked as an explanatory mechanism for falsehoods or be used to imply the absence of volition in the production of such falsehoods.

Factitious Disorder by Proxy

Meadow (1977) applied the term *Munchausen by proxy* (MBP) to describe a unique situation in which parents or other caretakers falsified health information or produced factitious disease in children principally to garner emotional satisfaction. In Appendix B in the DSM-IV-TR (American Psychiatric Association, 2000) includes research criteria for what it terms *factitious disorder by proxy* but also includes it in the factitious disorder chapter as the sole example of factitious disorder, not otherwise specified. Confusion in nomenclature has predictably followed, with the terms *pediatric condition falsification* (Ayoub et al., 2002) and *fabricated and induced illness* advocated by others (e.g., Foreman, 2005). For purposes of this chapter, the term MBP will be applied. Controversy has also raged about "whether [MBP] should be viewed as a form of abuse, a

mental disorder of the caretaker, the resulting emotional consequences to the victim, or a combination" (von Hahn et al., 2001, p. 129). However, most authors believe that the behavior constitutes abuse and/or neglect at a minimum. Therefore, we discuss MBP as a form of maltreatment.

A PubMed search yielded more than 500 professional articles dealing with MBP. The authors are aware of more than 200 additional cases supplied by colleagues, victims, and even perpetrators. These reports come from industrialized as well as developing countries such as Nigeria and Sri Lanka (Feldman & Brown, 2002). Analogous to factitious disorder proper, proxy behavior implies assumption of the vicarious sick role by intentional production or feigning of disease in a second person. The victim is usually a preschool child but could be a disabled adult or even a fetus in utero (Feldman & Hamilton, 2006; Jureidini, 1993). In many cases, a mother either falsely claims that her child is medically or psychiatrically ill or actually makes the child sick. She then presents the child for treatment while disclaiming knowledge of the origin of the problem. The child may then undergo immense numbers of diagnostic tests, medication trials, and surgeries. For instance, one of us (Feldman) is aware of a case in which a 3-year-old had had 11 known physicians who saw him more than 130 times and performed 18 surgical procedures during 15 hospitalizations in five different states. Diagnoses included upper respiratory infection, asthma, sinusitis, fever, diarrhea, gastroesophageal reflux, milk intolerance, food allergies, chronic intestinal pseudo obstruction, and irritable colon. Notably, only two medical contacts took place in the first 6 months after custody was assumed by the state, and both were routine follow-up visits.

Frequency data for MBP are constrained by both the elusive nature of the diagnosis, with "successful" cases never being identified, and clinicians' lack of familiarity with the diagnosis (Ostfeld & Feldman, 1996). Also, no databases are available to systematically collect and analyze MBP data appropriately. Like FD, MBP is more frequent in highly specialized treatment settings, with estimates of 1.5% to an astounding 33% among children with apparent life-threatening events (Rahilly, 1991; Truman & Ayoub, 2002). In addition, Sheridan's (2003) review of 451 MBP cases published in the professional literature found that 25% of the siblings were known to be dead, suggesting that earlier maltreatment had been unrecognized. Commonly induced signs or symptoms include bleeding, apnea (induced by suffocation), diarrhea or vomiting (induced by laxatives or ipecac), fever (falsified or induced by pathogens), seizures (falsified or induced by insulin overdose), abnormal levels of consciousness (caused by benzodiazepines), rash (caused by caustic agents), hypernatremia (due to salt poisoning), and false or exaggerated psychiatric or behavioral abnormalities (e.g., Ayoub, Schreier, & Keller, 2002; Schreier, 1996, 2000). In many cases, central venous catheters are eventually placed, which then become the sources of "medical chaos" (Feldman & Hickman, 1998), with mothers contaminating or blowing into them to sicken the child. Acetone added to a urine specimen can create the illusion of uncontrolled diabetes while a panoply of medications or poisons are used (see Holstege & Dobmeier, 2006) to induce dizziness (diuretics), vomiting (ipecac), respiratory distress (opioids), diarrhea (laxatives), hypoglycemia (insulin), or cardiac arrhythmias (tricyclic antidepressants). Children may even learn to gratify the mother by feigning symptoms under her tutelage (Croft & Jervis, 1989; Stutts, Hickey, & Kasdan, 2003).

Rosenberg (1987) reviewed 117 reported cases of MBP. The perpetrators were biological mothers in 98% of cases, and mortality rates for children approached 9%, a figure supported by Sheridan's (2003) later review of published cases. These statistics reveal MBP to be perhaps the most lethal form of child maltreatment. In contrast to Rosenberg, Sheridan's analysis indicated that only 75% of perpetrators were biological mothers; she found that other relatives, including fathers and stepmothers, or day-care providers or even health professionals were culpable in the remaining 25%. Importantly, FD syndrome and related abnormal illness behaviors were present in 24% of mothers in Rosenberg's (1987) study; other investigators (Feldman, Feldman, Grady, Burns, & McDonald, 2007) provide empirical support.

Researchers (Adshead & Bluglass, 2005; Gray & Bentovim, 1996) have described psychodynamic features of MBP: Mothers appeared to have primitive forms of character pathology, deprived or abusive childhoods, feelings of insecurity, early loss or bereavement, insecure attachment representations, and chronic conflicts with passive, ineffectual partners (when present). Through projective identification, the child becomes a receptacle of the mother's conflicts translated into factitious symptoms, and the mother gains security from nurturing hospital or outpatient personnel. Clinicians may question the statement of Sigal, Gelkopf, and Meadow (1989) that "the parent usually has no intention of killing or maiming the child" (p. 532), particularly in cases in which the parent overtly covets bereavement rituals (Firstman & Talan, 1997). Criminal intent aside, no evidence exists to suggest that this form of maltreatment is undertaken with anything other than full understanding about its potential consequences for the child.

Griffith and Slovik (1989) described clinical features common to MBP. These features included a symbiotic mother–child relationship and a laissez-faire attitude on the mother's part toward the child's illness. However, there have been concerns that the subjectivity of some of these features or the use of a personal "profile" heightens risk for a false-positive diagnosis (Ayoub et al., 2002; Rand & Feldman, 1999). Although clinical methods for the assessment of MBP are not well developed (Rogers, 2004), Feldman (2004b) proposed criteria that focus on objective observation:

1. Episodes of illness begin when the mother is or has recently been alone with the child.
2. Illness abates when the child is separated from the mother.
3. Other children in the family have had unexplained illnesses.
4. The mother has provided false information in other areas.
5. Physiological or laboratory parameters are consistent with induced illness.
6. The suspected disease or disease pattern is extremely rare.
7. Signs and symptoms do not respond to appropriate treatment.
8. The child has been to numerous caregivers without a cure or even a clear diagnosis.
9. The mother has medical or nursing training or access to illness models.
10. The mother has a personal history of factitious or somatoform disorders.
11. The mother is unresponsive to the child when unaware of being observed.

Detection of MBP cases is complicated by the fact that gross evidence of child abuse (e.g., bruises, fractures, burns) is uncommon. Another challenge is to balance general trust toward the family members of patients with the recognition of factors pointing to MBP in a given case. MBP is a diagnosis usually established by a meticulous review of clinical information; there are no pathognomonic findings on psychiatric or psychological evaluations. However, covert video surveillance (CVS) can provide proof if the parent engages in MBP behavior during hospitalization (e.g., (Hall, Eubanks, Meyyazhagan, Kenney, & Johnson, 2000). Every hospital should develop a CVS protocol well in advance of encountering such a case, and models exist (e.g., Patterson, Taylor, & Wells, 2005). It is helpful to involve not only medical and psychiatric professionals but also the local child protection agency, an attorney, law enforcement personnel, community representatives, an individual well versed in MBP, and possibly an ethicist. Decisions will need to be made as to whether CVS is to be viewed as a clinical, research, or criminal procedure, because the choice has implications, for example, for whether hospital personnel or police place the cameras (Bauer, 2004). Though legal and ethical concerns about CVS have arisen, it should be pointed out that it can help exonerate an innocent parent as well as impugn a guilty one.

Feldman (1997), Munro and Thrusfield (2001), and Milani (2006) noted interesting MBP variants, such as disease induction in pets. More controversially, these authors also classified overly zealous or naive professionals who fail to include MBP in the differential diagnosis of difficult cases as "professional participants" (Jureidini, Shafer, & Donald, 2003; Zitelli, Seltman, & Shannon, 1987). Direct clinician culpability is found in the cases of nurses or other hospital personnel who serially sicken and/or murder patients through mechanisms such as surreptitious succinylcholine or epinephrine injections (Yorker, 1996) because they enjoy crisis situations.

Physicians and other mandated reporters of abuse must alert child protection agencies if there is reasonable cause to suspect MBP maltreatment. Separation of parent and child is almost always necessary in the detection of MBP, even if only temporarily. The child should be safeguarded from further invasive procedures, and siblings must also be protected. Subsequent care should be consolidated at a single medical center while the doctors who initially diagnosed the MBP remain involved to counter the skepticism or disbelief that can emerge over time. Relevant personnel must cooperate with the courts, provide education, and dispel myths about MBP (e.g., that it is "faddish"). They should also be prepared to discuss the aspects of investigation, methodology, criteria for its confirmation, intervention, case planning, and case and legal management that are unique to MBP.

Decisions about the investigation, diagnosis, and case management are best handled by a multiagency, multidisciplinary team (Holstege & Dobmeier, 2006). If clear and compelling evidence is available, the child can be removed from the home on an emergency basis for up to 72 hours. Subsequent court actions will include a justification of removal hearing, motions hearings, an evidentiary hearing, and a dispositional hearing if maltreatment is found. The reader is referred to the excellent practical text by Lasher and Sheridan (2004) for much more detailed information about the steps involved.

Questions inevitably arise as to whether, and when, the child or children can be safely reunified with the parent with MBP. A general guideline is that the perpetrator and her or his partner should acknowledge that a pattern of MBP behavior occurred and do not claim any ongoing unexplained problems in the child. Criteria for possible return include: (1) a child over the age of 5, (2) only mild abuse, (3) the absence of active and serious maternal psychopathology, (4) an understanding on caretakers' part as to why the MBP took place, (5) identification of trigger situations, and (6) an understanding of any partner complicities. Everyone in the extended family should be committed to victim safety, and long-term monitoring must be provided by the court and a child protection agency (Lasher & Sheridan, 2004).

Without intervention, adult survivors of MBP suffer emotional disturbances. Libow (1995) summarized observations from 10 self-identified survivors: problems in adulthood included insecurity, reality-testing issues, avoidance of medical treatment, and posttraumatic stress symptoms. Some survivors expressed considerable residual anger toward the abusing mothers but a surprising degree of sympathy for the fathers who passively colluded or failed to protect. Some of the parents with MBP have continued fabricating their own medical illnesses or harassing their adult children with fabricated dramas even decades later.

The dearth of empirical research on MBP is partly responsible for its historical controversies. Among the areas needing attention is the consolidation of reports to detect patterns, perhaps through a national or international data collection system. Further public and professional education would enhance recognition of MBP and related conditions. Research from psychological and neuropsychological testing of abusive parents may eventually assist both in diagnosis and intervention. The field as a whole needs to study alternate ways to address the persistent denial among MBP perpetrators, even when faced with incontrovertible evidence (Feldman, 1994). Longitudinal study of outcomes with and without reunification of parent and child is needed. Finally, as in all forms of maltreatment, keys to preventing MBP behavior need to be identified.

CLINICAL APPLICATIONS

DSM-IV-TR inclusion criteria for disorders characterized by medical and psychiatric deception are not based on easily observed clinical features, and therefore they are difficult to apply. The distinction between FD and malingering on the one hand and the somatoform disorders on the other is difficult to make clinically and may not even be valid. The same is true about distinctions between internally versus externally motivated intentional deception. By requiring these distinctions, the DSM pushes clinicians toward categorical thinking about cases involving excessive illness behavior. In this section, we discuss some of the clinical disadvantages of categorical thinking and highlight some advantages of an alternative multidimensional model of excessive illness behavior.

The greatest disadvantage of categorical thinking derives from the fact that the categories of disorders related to excessive illness behavior are distinguished on the basis of poorly understood psychological processes rather than observable characteristics. Segregating patients into distinct and mutually exclusive categories has the unintended effect of setting apart these psychological processes as well. Cases of somatoform disorders, functional somatic syndromes, or medically unexplained symptoms generally are presumed to

reflect the operation of unconscious conflicts or cognitive distortions (Brown, 2004). Motivational issues are almost never discussed in these cases, and when they are it usually comes in the form of vacuous and dismissive references to secondary gain. FD and malingering, on the other hand, are defined by motivational processes. Because these cases are usually identified only after they have progressed to severe illness deception, the role of subtle cognitive processes in their development is seldom considered. In short, the categorical approach of the DSM disinclines clinicians to think about cases of excessive illness behavior as a complex product of both cognitive and motivational processes.

The second and related disadvantage of the DSM approach is that it advocates an artificial demarcation of FD and malingering. It limits the scope of malingering by emphasizing attempts to evade legal prosecution, avoid work or military service, or achieve illicit financial gains. The emphasis on bald-faced cheating is reinforced by the association drawn in the DSM between malingering and antisocial personality disorder and by the bias in the malingering literature toward forensic populations. This focus casts the malingerer in a decidedly unfavorable light, and the consequence is that both medical and mental health professionals are more intent on discovering malingerers than on understanding them. This approach does a disservice to persons who revert to sick-role enactments as means of coping with situational stresses or to compensate for modifiable psychological problems.

We would like to endorse two new ways of approaching cases of excessive illness behavior that might help avoid the clinical problems outlined here. The first approach is to apply a functional analysis to cases of excessive illness behavior. This is not a new idea by any means; Rogers's adaptational model of malingering (Rogers, Salekin, et al., 1998), Stone's conceptual model of functional neurological complaints (Stone, Carson, & Sharpe, 2005; Stone & Sharpe, 2006), and the vast multidisciplinary literature on the treatment of chronic pain (Fernandez & McDowell, 1995; Sullivan, 2006; Turk & Burwinkle, 2005) exemplify this approach. It is predicated on the working hypothesis that excessive illness behavior serves one or more purposes in the patient's life. If the functions of illness behavior can be determined, the clinician can begin to search for deficits that prevent the patient from achieving his or her goals in more healthy and adaptive ways. The main advantage of this approach is that it leads the clinician to ask important questions beyond those specified by the DSM-IV-TR. For example, imagine four patients who present to the emergency department feigning chest pain in order to secure admission to the hospital because they want to avoid going to work the following day. One of them might fit the stereotype of the shiftless, greedy, antisocial malingerer. However, another might be a painfully shy person who is desperately seeking to avoid making a scheduled speech to an important group of business clients. Another might be trapped in an unhealthy romantic relationship with her boss, and she feels unable to face him another day. The fourth patient might be trying to show his coworkers how indispensable he is to his work team. Applying a categorical, descriptive analysis to these patients might lead a clinician to conclude that each is a malingerer and that none is a candidate for further care. In contrast, a functional approach encourages the clinician to look beyond the fact that the patient is trying to get something to which he or she is not entitled and to ask why. In our example, taking this approach might lead to the identification of the three patients with genuine and treatable psychological problems.

In examining the functional role of illness behavior in each of these cases, it becomes clear that there is no natural demarcation between internal and external incentives, and thinking categorically about a patient's motivations serves no clinical purpose. If clinicians accept this assertion, it follows that the distinction between malingering and FD is clinically useless (though it may be an important distinction in medicolegal contexts).

The second advantage of applying a thorough functional analysis in cases of excessive illness behavior is that the functional approach allows for the possibility that the sick-role enactment may serve multiple functions in a patient's life. For example, the patient who feigns chest pain to get out of work might be pleasantly surprised that his sickness has, in addition, resulted in a decrease in conflicts between him and his wife. A mother who falsifies a chronic illness in her child may do so as a pretext for quitting her job but also because her child's putative illness allows her to connect to a nurturing social support network. Motives usually associated with malingering can operate contemporaneously with motives typically associated with FD. Whereas the current DSM approach orients clinicians to focus on one of these and ignore the other, the functional approach encourages a comprehensive search for all of the contingencies that might be maintaining factitious illness behavior.

Finally, the functional approach is useful for understanding not only the functions served by excessive illness behavior but also the extent to which sick-role behavior is interfering with the patient's social or occupational adaptation. As we alluded to earlier, the DSM definitions of FD and malingering do not include any consideration of the severity or chronicity of the patient's illness deceptions or of the degree to which excessive illness behavior interferes with the ability of the patient to lead a meaningful and productive life. Beyond limiting the reliability of these clinical definitions, omitting these parameters reinforces several beliefs that (1) patients with FD or malingering are not suffering, (2) they are hopeless cases, or (3) they do not deserve help.

The second approach that we wish to encourage is attention to the development of excessive illness behavior over time. It is doubtful that a person with a factitious physical disorder wakes up one day and decides to simulate kidney disease by ingesting rat poison. It is much more plausible that excessive illness behavior arises in the context of unintended experiences with the sick role through which the patient experiences adventitious reinforcement. These experiences in a person with personality vulnerabilities may represent the start of a pattern of increasing reliance on excessive illness behavior. For instance, the shy person learns that the sick role can be used to avoid social encounters, whereas the insecure person learns that the sick role provides a buffer against criticism and rejection.

The available data indicate that as few as two or three unexplained medical complaints may predict the eventual development of significant psychological impairment related to excessive illness behavior (Kroenke & Rosmalen, 2006; Little, Williams, Puzanovova, Rudzinski, & Walker, 2007; Nakao & Yano, 2003; Terre, Poston, Foreyt, & St. Jeor, 2003). These findings suggest that with the proper awareness and training, it should be possible for medical and mental health professionals to prevent chronic and disabling illness behavior problems through early detection and intervention (Hamilton & Feldman, 2006). At this early stage of treatment development, intervention may be as simple as explaining to the patients and their family members about the seductions of the sick role. It may also provide them with reasonable expectations about the limitations associated with the patient's medical or mental health problem and educating them about the anticipated time course for recovery.

Although the most precipitous increase in sick-role behavior might occur in early adulthood, it is likely that the roots of excessive illness behavior problems can be found in the way illness behavior is modeled and reinforced during childhood and adolescence (Bijttebier & Vertommen, 1999; Brace, Scott Smith, McCauley, & Sherry, 2000). Accordingly, pediatricians and primary school teachers might be in a particularly good position to aid in the early identification of children at risk for becoming too dependent on the sick role.

The importance of prevention of and early intervention in chronic and severe FD is particularly important in light of the poor treatment response reported for these cases. Once illness deceptions have reached that point, there are few face-saving ways of relinquishing the sick role. However, for cases that are detected earlier, psychosocial interventions can be presented to the patient using frameworks such as stress and coping. Treatment approaches that are focused on improving daily functioning, as opposed to curing disease, provide a context for engaging patients in a thorough functional analysis of their strengths and weaknesses. On the basis of this assessment, the clinician can help the patient develop sufficient skills so that he or she no longer needs to use sick-role enactments as a coping strategy. This approach allows patients a way out of their sick-role enactments that does not require confrontation about the veracity of their illness claims.

9

Feigned Medical Presentations

ROBERT P. GRANACHER, Jr., MD, MBA
DAVID T. R. BERRY, PhD

Mental health professionals with diverse training are increasingly consulted by health care providers regarding response styles among medical patients. This chapter reviews clinical data on feigning during various medical presentations. It also presents as a paradigm empirical data from nearly 200 evaluations of purported traumatic brain injury (TBI). These data provide practitioners with a data-based understanding regarding the frequency and significance of malingering by persons claiming a medical disorder. The centerpiece of this chapter is the development of a clinical framework useful for assessing feigned medical presentations. Where possible, the use of empirically validated detection strategies is emphasized.

Malingerers may present to their physicians with a variety of feigned complaints. There are three basic ways to malinger a medical examination: (1) presentations of false cognitive or neuropsychological signs and symptoms, (2) presentations of false psychiatric signs and symptoms, and (3) presentations of false somatic signs and symptoms. Hall and Poirer (2001) have summarized the response styles that malingerers may present to medical examiners in order to produce false cognitive, neuropsychological, or psychiatric symptoms.

1. *Presenting realistic symptoms:* The malingerer may employ a commonsense or popularly understood schema of what cognitively impaired or psychiatrically impaired persons are thought to be like.

2. *Distributing errors:* Malingers tend to make a deliberate number of mistakes throughout their evaluation, rather than miss only difficult items of cognitive effort tests (see Rogers, Chapter 2, this volume, on performance curves). They attempt to seek balance between missing too few items and appearing too impaired by missing too many items on the test.

3. *Protesting the tasks that are too difficult or feigning confusion and frustration:* Malingerers may appear confused or angry or they may display other emotions that are superimposed on reasonably adequate cooperation and task compliance.

4. *Performing at a crudely estimated fraction of their actual ability:* Speed of thought and speed of task effort may be deliberately decreased. Because many neuropsychological assessments have a timed component, this is an efficient way to malinger the examination.

5. *Employing errant affective style:* Malingerers may employ changes in affect as part of their malingering strategy. Depression or posttraumatic stress disorder may be common themes.

The preceding response styles fairly describe common strategies of individuals malingering cognitive or psychiatric presentations.

Persons malingering physical presentations present a particular diagnostic challenge. For instance, it is difficult to separate conversion disorder from physical malingering. As commonly defined by neurologists, conversion disorders refer to temporary disorders involving mental, voluntary motor, or sensory functions that mimic neurological disease. However, conversion disorders are caused by unconscious determinants, not by organic lesions in the neuroanatomical sites that should produce the dysfunction being presented (DeMyer, 2004). Since the time of Charcot and Freud, classic psychoanalytical theory has held that hysteria (conversion disorder) arises from unconscious mental mechanisms that relieve overwhelming anxiety by converting it into physical symptoms. These symptoms provide primary and secondary gain (Weintraub, 1995). The primary gain in conversion disorders is the relief of anxiety. Secondary gain consists of a manipulative control over the expressed emotional responses, the attention received from others, and the actions of other persons. In addition, the relief of responsibility is frequently a secondary gain. It is apparently the primary and secondary gains that make the symptoms more acceptable to the patient, more so than the anxiety that the symptoms relieve.

CLASSIFICATIONS AND BASE RATES

When reviewing response styles of cognitive, psychological, and physical presentations, health care professionals must distinguish between conversion disorders, factitious disorders, and malingering. The *Diagnostic and Statistical Manual of Mental Disorders*, 4th edition (DSM-IV-TR; American Psychiatric Association, 2000) clarifies the differences found with these three presentations. In conversion disorder, the dysfunction and the purpose it serves seem to arise at a subconscious level, but the patients experience the illnesses as genuine. At the opposite pole of this presentation is the frank malingerer. This individual consciously fakes an illness to achieve some tangible external goal, such as unwarranted compensation in a lawsuit or avoiding criminal prosecution. Factitious disorder (such as Munchausen syndrome) is the midpoint presentation; it is the deliberate production of false signs and symptoms in an effort to assume the role of a sick person. Although the production of symptoms is deliberate, the motivation for the sick role may involve presentations to medical practitioners to gain attention and concern generally accorded to those who are ill. Examples of fac-

titious disorders include individuals who have multiple surgical procedures that have failed to disclose any organic lesions or to effect cures.

Mental health professionals who are consultants to medical professionals should strive where possible to measure response rates of possible malingering using the best instruments available. In providing these consultations, it is important to understand base rates of biased responding among various presentations to medical professionals. The largest review of base rates of malingering and symptom magnification in medical disorders to date has been provided by Mittenberg, Patton, and colleagues (2002). This survey of the American Board of Clinical Neuropsychology yielded estimated base rates of probable malingering and symptom exaggeration for 22,121 medical consultations with additional estimates for personal injury ($n = 6,371$), disability ($n = 3,688$), and criminal ($n = 1,341$) referrals. Importantly, base rates did not differ significantly among geographical regions or practice settings. Diagnostic impressions of probable malingering were reported in 39% of mild head injury, 35% of fibromyalgia/chronic fatigue, 31% of chronic pain, 27% of neurotoxic, and 22% of electrical injury claims. The classification of malingering was supported by multiple sources of evidence, including reported severity, illness patterns, cognitive impairment inconsistent with the purported condition, and discrepancies among records, self-report, and observed behavior. Test data used (1) cut scores for symptom validity testing and other detection strategies and (2) validity scales for multiscale inventories. Marked discrepancies were also considered for repeat administrations of standardized tests that yielded implausible changes.

An important development in the detection of medical feigning is the extensive work by Slick, Sherman, and Iverson (1999) to develop diagnostic criteria for malingered neurocognitive dysfunction, which have been proposed as a standard for clinical practice. These criteria are being increasingly applied to the evaluation of medical conditions wherein cognitive disorders may be presented (Bianchini, Greve, & Love, 2003). The Slick model organizes neurocognitive malingering into three categories based on the level of certitude: (1) *definite* malingering of neurocognitive dysfunction (MND), (2) *probable* MND, and (3) *possible* MND. Definite MND is indicated by the presence of clear and compelling evidence of volitional exaggeration or fabrication of cognitive dysfunction and the absence of plausible alternative explanations (i.e., significantly below chance performance on a test of symptom validity testing (SVT; see Rogers, Chapter 2, this volume). Probable MND is indicated by the presence of evidence strongly suggesting volitional exaggeration or fabrication of cognitive dysfunction in the absence of plausible alternative explanations. Such evidence typically includes performance consistent with fabrication on one or more well-validated psychometric measures designed to measure feigning. Possible MND, according to Slick and colleagues, is indicated by the presence of evidence suggesting volitional exaggeration or fabrication of cognitive dysfunction and the absence of plausible alternative explanations. Alternatively, they report that possible MND is indicated by the presence of criteria necessary for either definite or probable MND except that other primary etiologies cannot be ruled out. In medical evaluations *possibilities* should not be considered, as they are not consistent with evidence-based practice. If MND cannot be stated as *definite* or *probable,* it is best not to make a diagnosis of feigning.

Slick and colleagues (1999) also developed four basic criteria that are used to evaluate MND. Criterion A is the presence of a substantial external incentive for exaggeration or fabrication of symptoms (e.g., personal injury settlement, disability pension, evasion of criminal prosecution, and release from military service). However, it should be remembered that the presence of a potential incentive to feign is not equivalent to established malingering. Criterion B is evidence from neuropsychological testing of exaggeration or fabrication of cognitive dysfunction during the neuropsychological assessment. The evidence for malingering detection while using various neuropsychological test instruments is provided further by other chapters in this volume (see Sweet, Condit, & Nelson, Chapter 13, and Berry & Schipper, Chapter 14). Criterion C is evidence of MND from self-reports. Such evidence includes (1) self-reported history discrepant with documented history, (2) self-reported symptoms discrepant with known patterns of brain functioning, (3) self-reported symptoms discrepant with behavioral observations, (4) self-reported symptoms that are inconsistent with information obtained from collateral informants and where there is evidence

of exaggerated or fabricated psychological dysfunction. Criterion D is a rule-out criterion wherein behaviors meeting necessary criteria from groups B or C are not fully accounted for by genuine psychiatric, neurological, or developmental factors. These four criteria for neurocognitive malingering provide the most systematic approach to malingered presentations during medical evaluations. Systematic models for psychological and/or physical malingering are less well developed.

Within the domain of psychological malingering, virtually any known psychiatric condition can be feigned. The detection of malingering rests primarily on the documentation of observable behaviors consistent with malingering that are confirmed by psychological measures using established detection strategies and validated scales of response bias. Such measures include the MMPI-2 (Butcher, Graham, Ben-Porath, Tellegen, Dahlstrom, & Kaemmer, 2001; see Greene, Chapter 10, this volume), the Personality Assessment Inventory (PAI; Morey, 1991; see Sellbom & Bagby, Chapter 11, this volume), and the Structured Interview of Reported Symptoms (SIRS; Rogers, Bagby, & Dickens, 1992; see Rogers, Chapter 18, this volume).

Resnick (2002) has described the observable behaviors commonly associated with psychological malingering. These behaviors typically include malingerers who (1) present as sullen, ill at ease, suspicious, uncooperative, resentful, aloof, secretive, and unfriendly; (2) may try to avoid examinations, unless required as a condition for receiving some financial benefit; (3) are more likely than persons with conversion disorders to refuse opportunities for employment; and (4) are more likely to give every fact of the accident or injury and its sequelae with an acute memory for detail. These behavioral observations, when combined with confirmatory medical and psychological test data, offer the greatest promise for detecting psychological malingering during medical presentations.

One issue often posed to mental health professionals is whether a person with a true medical condition can be detected if he or she is also feigning concomitant psychological or cognitive symptoms. For instance, can an individual with a real medical illness also malinger depression, anxiety, or PTSD? The answer seems affirmative. Berry and Granacher (2007) have documented that individuals can feign psychiatric symptoms within the context of a documented severe brain injury while preserving an acceptable level of motivation on concurrent neuropsychological testing. These persons passed screening tests for cognitive effort while providing invalid MMPI-2 profiles regarding psychological symptoms. Other common questions raised by health care staff include the following:

• *Can clinicians differentiate feigning of brain injury in a person who had a blow to the head?* Bianchini, Houston, and colleagues (2003) reported data in individuals who met the Slick criteria for a diagnosis of definite malingered neurocognitive dysfunction and who performed significantly below chance on at least one cognitive forced-choice symptom validity test. These individuals demonstrated a deliberate attempt to appear cognitively impaired.

• *Can conversion disorder be differentiated from cognitive malingering?* Boone and Lu (1999) evaluated participants presenting with cognitive complaints and conversion symptoms. They found MMPI/MMPI-2, 1-3/3-1 code types (conversion/somatization) with no conclusive evidence of psychological feigning However, most participants did show evidence of cognitive feigning on neuropsychological tests. Together, these results suggest that somatization/conversion personality orientations can be differentiated from cognitive feigning. With careful psychological consultation, physicians can parse out these apparently confounding medical presentations. Moreover, Vickery and colleagues (2004) reported significant evidence that individuals feigning brain injury can be detected even in persons with alleged blunt-trauma head injuries. Their study revealed that persons with head injuries are no more able to feign neuropsychological deficits successfully than persons without head injuries.

The third and last domain of malingered medical presentations is physical or somatic malingering. For mental health professionals providing services to physicians and other medical personnel, this domain proves to be the most difficult form of malingering to evaluate with valid detection strategies. Most important, with physical malingering, physicians must exclude all genuine conditions that could produce the suspected presentations before mental health professionals attempt to evaluate response styles. Beyond medical disorders

causing apparent symptoms, consideration must be given to potential conversion disorders, as previously discussed. Table 9.1 lists psychogenic physical disorders that may be produced by malingering.

SOMATIC MALINGERING

Somatic malingering is often presented as a disorder of neurological functioning. However, any physical condition can be malingered. For a more detailed analysis regarding the medical detection of somatic malingering and its physical manifestations, the reader is referred to the

TABLE 9.1. Potential Psychogenic Presentations of Somatic Malingering

A. Oculomotor signs
   • Blinking, squinting (blepharospasm), volitional eye crossing, volitional eyelid drooping

B. Dysfunctions of voice, swallowing, and breathing
   • Mutism
   • Spasmodic hoarseness (dysphonia)
   • Choking (dysphagia)
   • Hyperventilation with apnea

C. Vomiting

D. Disturbances of station (standing) and gait
   • Inability to stand (astasia)
   • Inability to walk (abasia)
   • Incomplete paralysis on one side (hemiparesis)
   • Complete paralysis on one side (hemiplegia)
   • Dragging one leg (monoplegia)
   • Apparent paralysis of arms and legs (paraplegia)

E. Tremors

F. Disorders of vision
   • Blindness (monocular or binocular)
   • Visual field defects
   • Double vision (diplopia)
   • Pain in eyes with light exposure (photophobia)

G. Disorders of sensation
   • Deafness
   • Nonanatomic sensory loss
   • Inability to smell (anosmia)
   • Inability to taste (ageusia)

H. Seizures (pseudoepilepsy)

I. Fevers

J. Pain
   • Headaches
   • Backaches

texts by DeMyer (2004) and Gorman (1993). Detection methods employed by physicians are part of the art form of medicine; they are based on identification of nonanatomical or non-physiological presentations of apparent neurological and physical disorders. Physiological or pharmacological tests may be applied in some instances to confirm a diagnosis of somatic malingering. As noted by Bogduk (2004), malingering is not a diagnosis but is a behavioral pattern for which there are no established diagnostic criteria. Particularly for patients who present with pain, malingering cannot be proved, but it can be refuted if a genuine source of a pain can be established. For example, a positive response to pharmacological diagnostic blocks by needle insertion demonstrates that the complaint of pain is genuine and, by implication, refutes the hypothesis that the patient is malingering. When positive, diagnostic blocks provide objective data on whether or not a patient is malingering pain. When negative, responses to blocks do not exclude a genuine complaint of pain, because bona fide patients may have a source of pain that is not amenable to testing with diagnostic blocks.

Beyond feigned pain and neurological presentations, somatic malingering can often present with diverse medical complaints. Examples of challenging presentations include the following:

• A formidable challenge to physicians and mental health professionals alike is somatic malingering involving the injection or ingestion or substances to produce infection. Some patients will malinger by repeated subcutaneous or intravenous self-injection of an irritant or contaminant (Sorin, April, & Ward, 2006).
• Upper-extremity and hand disorders frequently present to orthopedic physicians as factitious disorders (Louis, Doro, & Hayden, 2006).
• Electrical injury is commonly encountered as part of somatic malingering in workers' compensation claims. Bianchini, Love, Greve, and Adams (2005) found about a 50% rate of somatic malingering using the Slick and colleagues (1999) criteria.
• The prevalence of neurotoxic malingering following exposure to putative toxic environmental substances has been found to have a base rate of about 40% when applying the Slick and colleagues (1999) criteria (Greve, Bianchini, Black, et al., 2006).

Potential Indicators of Somatic Malingering

Physicians conducting neurological assessments may observe, upon physical examination, potential signs and symptoms of somatic malingering (see Table 9.1). Importantly, these indicators are considered "potential" because their lack of anatomical or physiological correlation must be confirmed by physical laboratory testing or psychological consultation for motivational testing.

Detection of Feigned Visual Deficits

As noted in Table 9.1, patients can intentionally learn to appear cross-eyed. This simulated condition can be detected by having the patient look to one side. Also, a volitional attempt to cross the eyes will cause the pupils to simultaneously constrict. This finding is not seen in organic sixth-nerve palsy, as the failure of the abducens nerve does not cause pupilloconstriction. In a patient with true organic inability to lift the eyelid (ptosis), the person lifts the eyebrow using actions of the frontalis muscle. In malingered ptosis of the eyelids, the patient voluntarily contracts the muscles surrounding the eye (orbicularis oculi), which causes the eyebrow to descend. Sometimes the malingerer will place drops in the eye, which cause the pupil to dilate, which further mimics a third-nerve palsy (paralysis). However, blepharospasm (squinting or constriction of the eyelids) occurs commonly in patients with true dystonias or inflammation to the eye.

Detection of Feigned Dysfunctions of Voice, Swallowing, and Breathing

Patient feigning mutism or an inability to speak at a normal voice volume are mimicking laryngal dysfunction. Via laryngoscopic examination, normal vocal cord action can be determined. Moreover, normal movement of the palate is noted with feigned mutism, and the patient with malingered dysphonia will breathe and swallow normally and may whisper with perfect articulation of words. This observation will prove the presence of intact motor innervation to the vocal cords.

Most patients with a psychogenic breathing disorder will not demonstrate cyanosis (blue color to the lips or nail beds due to reduced oxygenation of hemoglobin), and they will have normal arterial oxygen partial pressures with blood gas determination. However, they may present to an emergency department with apnea (cessation of breathing) in association with a Valsalva maneuver, and they may hyperventilate and produce weak or shallow breathing. These patients usually avoid eye contact or have theatrical gagging with guttural noises, high-frequency breath sounds as if the larynx is in spasm (stridor), and rolling of the head and trunk with demonstratively expressive eyes (Walker, Alessi, & Digre, 1989). On a neurological basis, most physicians would conclude that these presentations are intentional, However, they could be manifestations of a conversion disorder if confirmed by psychological consultation and testing.

Detection of Feigned Disturbances of Posture and Gait

Patients presenting with malingered astasia and abasia (see Table 9.1) will often attempt to "walk" at the examiner's suggestion (Keane, 1989). These patients will often show wild gyrations of the trunk when standing or walking. They rarely fall. If they do fall, they will fall into the examiner's arms or into a chair without suffering bodily injury. The flamboyant gyrations of the body and arms without falling demonstrates eloquently the intactness of the patient's motor system and balance system.

In psychogenic hemiplegia, the lower part of the face on the same side of the alleged paralysis is not involved. Moreover, paradoxically, the protruded tongue, if it deviates at all, deviates toward the normal side (Keane, 1986). When the patient is at rest, the arm and the leg on the alleged affected side do not assume true hemiplegic postures. In true hemiparesis, the leg swings outward in a circular movement. However, a malingering patient typically walks with the good leg forward and drags the other leg behind. The foot may be turned out or inverted or everted (Stone, Zeman, & Sharpe, 2002). In a patient who presents as if both arms and legs are paralyzed (quadriplegia), on neurological examination the abdominal muscle stretch reflexes will be normal, and in males the cremasteric (scrotal) reflexes will be present. In psychogenic paraplegia, muscle tone and re-tention of bowel and bladder control are normal (Baker & Silver, 1987).

Sensory changes are highly variable in false presentations of movement. Specifically, the dermatomes do not match the motor level and do not demonstrate the sacral sparing of sensation that may characterize organic paraplegia. Multiple-crossed motor tests can be preformed during neurological examination, such as the "Double-Crossed-Arm-Pull Test" for psychogenic arm monoparesis or the "Make-a-Fist Test" for psychogenic wrist drop (DeMyer, 2004).

Detection of Feigned Visual Deficits

For patients malingering neurological blindness, the pupillary light reactions are present, and the fundi will appear normal. On neuroimaging, no cerebral lesions in the visual pathway will be noted in the malingerer. By careful observation, the examiner can often detect that the patient may swiftly glance at a moving object that appears in the visual field unexpectedly. Such glances would not occur in a truly blind person. Placing a mirror directly in front of the patient and moving it toward the person may cause the patient's eyes to pursue his or her reflection. In addition, the patient may show optokinetic nystagmus (railroad electrical pole nystagmus while looking out the window of a moving train) when exposed to a rotating drum of moving stripes (DeMyer, 2004). In hysterical blindness, the typical visual field defect consists of constriction of the diameter of the field, thereby producing tunnel or tubular vision, as if the patient were looking through a tunnel. For patients presenting with photophobia, the pain in the eyes on exposure to light will require careful ophthalmological consultation and possible slit-lamp examination to rule out organic disease.

Detection of Feigned Sensory Deficits

In humans, tactile sensation is mapped on the human body in a particular dermatomal pattern conforming to sensory nerve distributions. Usually, the malingerer will report loss of sensation from head to foot on one side of the body. In organic hemianesthesia, the sensory loss fades gradually at the midline of the patient, particularly for the sensation of vibration. The malingerer usually has an abrupt loss of sensation at the midline, with no crossing slightly to the opposite side, as would be expected in genuine patients. Also, in patients claiming hemianesthesia, the motor functions usually remain normal, which is impossible without proprioception ability. Organic anesthesia can be ruled out when the stretch reflexes are preserved and there is an absence of hypotonia, atrophy, and dystaxia. In genuine cases, complete sensory loss must concurrently produce loss of reflexes, loss of muscle tone (hypotonia), and unsteady gait (dystaxia) due to loss of sensation to the joint receptors of the feet and legs (i.e., the loss of proprioceptive ability).

Detection of Feigned Seizures

For those patients presenting with psychogenic (pseudoepileptic or nonepileptic) seizures, the most accurate method of detection is for a neurologist to place the patient into an electroencephalogram (EEG) laboratory with video recording. This method enables the neurologist to provide split-screen monitoring of the patient. In other words, the EEG can be demonstrated on one-half of the electronic screen while the patient's body is observed on the other half. Observed "seizures" should correlate directly with observed electrical activity of the brain. When they do not, the diagnosis of pseudoepilepsy or nonepileptic seizures can be made. However, approximately 40% of patients with nonepileptic seizures also have epilepsy (Bruni, 2000). Nonepileptic seizures may be a manifestation of conversion disorder or malingering, and psychological testing should help differentiate conversion disorder seizures from the intentional production of nonepileptic seizures.

The challenges to nonphysician mental health professionals are great in assisting physicians to detect the malingered presentation of a physical disorder. As noted by Larrabee (1998), standard procedures such as the MMPI-2 are often ineffective in assessing feigned somatic complaints, such as pain, paresthesia, and malaise. However, Larrabee demonstrated that the Lees–Haley Fake Bad Scale (FBS) scale was the most effective scale to detect somatic malingering; other validity scales (F, Fb, and Fp) did not appear to be useful. Likewise, Boone and Lu (1999) found that somatic malingering in forensic examinations was not adequately identified by traditional MMPI-2 validity scales, although the FBS showed promise.

Nelson, Sweet, and Demakis (2006) conducted a meta-analysis on 19 MMPI-2 studies from forensic practices that met rigorous inclusion criteria. These selections by their inclusion criteria resulted in a pooled sample of 1,615 dissimulators and 2,049 genuine patients. For MMPI-2 validity scales, the largest effect sizes were observed for FBS (0.96) and O-S (0.88), with smaller effect sizes noted for Dsr2 (0.79), F-K (0.69), and F (0.63). On present evidence from multiple studies, the FBS appears to be the best validated MMPI-2 scale for detecting somatic malingering (Berry & Schipper, in press).

ARCHIVAL ANALYSIS OF BRAIN TRAUMA REFERRALS

As director of the Lexington Forensic Clinic, I (R. P. G.) have instituted a battery of standardized measures that are routinely administered in forensic referrals regarding brain trauma. This standardized approach is supplemented by case-specific procedures as dictated by specific issues in the clinical presentation. Based on results from the formal assessment of cognitive effort, participants were classified into one of three groups: honest (HON), indeterminate (IND), and probable cognitive feigning (PCF).

Methodology

Sample

Participants were compensation-seeking adults undergoing forensic neuropsychiatric evaluations to determine the presence and extent of brain dysfunction from a variety of causes, predominantly TBI. All had been referred either by an attorney or by the workers' compensation system. Participants were provided with the option of consenting to allow their results to be used anonymously for research. One hundred and ninety-eight individuals consented.

This sample of referrals for brain injury (N = 198) had a mean age of 40.8 (SD = 13.2), had mean education of 12.3 years (SD = 2.8), and were mostly European American (98.5%). They were also predominantly right-handed (90%) and male (70.2%). They were evaluated an average of 19.5 months after injury or disease onset (SD = 9.1). Presumed causes of brain injury included trauma (70%), exposure to solvents (5%) and other neurotoxic chemicals (5%), and hypoxic episodes (2%).

Evaluation Process

The evaluation included clinical interview, neuropsychiatric examination, background questionnaire, and a battery of motivational, neuropsychological, and psychological tests determined by the neuropsychiatrist and supervising psychologist. However, examination of individuals who were blatantly feigning was terminated as soon as the inadequate motivation was objectively documented.

The clinical interview followed the format described by Granacher (2003). It included the following components: chief complaint, additional problems, current treatments, activities of daily living, past medical and neuropsychiatric history, and family and social history. The formal neuropsychiatric examination included evaluation of psychiatric symptoms, mental status, cranial nerves, and motor and sensory functions (Granacher, 2003). Available records were reviewed for each patient and, where indicated, additional diagnostic procedures were ordered (e.g., computerized tomography [CT] or magnetic resonance imaging [MRI]).

Neuropsychological Assessment

Objective evaluation of neurocognitive functions was undertaken with a battery of neuropsychological tests administered by psychometrists following standardized procedures, as indicated in the relevant manuals. Most examinees received the Wechsler Adult Intelligence Scale—Third Edition (WAIS-III), and the Wechsler Memory Scale—Third Edition (WMS-III), the Wisconsin Card Sorting Test (WCST), and the Wide Range Achievement Test 3 (WRAT-3) Reading subtest. Other, more specialized measures were also administered: the Boston Naming Test, the Brief Test of Attention, the Controlled Oral Word Association Test, the Finger Oscillation Test, the Grooved Pegboard Test, the Hand Dynamometer Test, the Ruff 2 and 7 Test, the Trail Making Test, and the Wechsler Test of Adult Reading (WTAR). Where appropriate, raw scores were converted to T scores using the Heaton, Grant, and Matthews (1991) norms correcting for age, sex, and education. Remaining procedures were converted to standard scores as indicated in their manuals.

Psychological Assessment

Standardized assessment of psychopathology included the Minnesota Multiphasic Personality Inventory—Second Edition (MMPI-2; Butcher et al., 2001). The Miller Forensic Assessment of Symptoms Test (M-FAST; Miller, 2001) and the Structured Interview of Reported Symptoms (SIRS; Rogers, Bagby, & Dickens, 1992) were administered to detect feigned psychiatric symptoms.

Motivational Testing

Objective motivational measures included the Victoria Symptom Validity Test (VSVT; Slick, Hopp, Strauss, & Thompson, 1997), the Test of Memory Malingering (TOMM; Tombaugh, 1996), the Letter Memory Test (LMT; Inman et al., 1998), and the Digit Span subtest from the WAIS-III (Babikian, Boone, Lu, & Arnold, 2006).

VSVT

The VSVT is a computer-administered forced-choice digit recognition procedure that has 48 trials, including 24 "easy" and 24 "difficult" items presented in three blocks of 16 with delays increasing across blocks from 5 to 10 to 15 seconds. Three summary indices are derived, including the total percent correct across all trials, the percent correct on "Easy" trials, and the percent correct for "Difficult" trials. Test–retest reliabilities at a 1-month interval are .84 for total score, .83 for the Easy score and .78 for the Difficult score (Slick et al., 1997). Several cross-validation studies have supported the VSVT's ability to discriminate adequate from inadequate effort (Doss, Chelune, & Naugle, 1999; Grote et al., 2000; Strauss et al., 2000). Initially, performances were classified with reference to a confidence interval around the 50% correct performance expected due to chance. However, Grote and colleagues (2000) found that a cut score of < 90% (i.e., floor effect strategy) on Total or Difficult scores increased sensitivity without lowering specificity. The VSVT is apparently used in about 17% of forensic examinations (Slick, Tan, Strauss, & Hultsch, 2004).

TOMM

The TOMM (Tombaugh, 1996) is a forced-choice recognition-memory test that uses line drawings as stimuli. It consists of two learning trials and a delayed trial (see Sweet et al., Chapter 13, this volume, for a description). Most published studies have been generally supportive of the accuracy of the TOMM (Rees, Tombaugh, Gansler, & Moczynski, 1998; Tombaugh, 1997; Weinborn, Orr, Woods, Conover, & Feix, 2003), as well as its insensitivity to depression (Rees, Tombaugh, & Boulay, 2001). Vallabhajosula and Van Gorp (2001) and Tombaugh (2002a, 2002b) concluded that the procedure is well validated and appropriate for forensic evaluations. Slick and colleagues (2004) found that the TOMM was the most commonly used motivational test in forensic neuropsychological examinations. However, Green, Lees-Haley, and Allen (2002) present data suggesting that the TOMM is less accurate than certain other motivational tests.

LMT

The LMT (Inman et al., 1998) also uses the forced-choice recognition-memory format. Its apparent difficulty is manipulated on two dimensions: (1) the number of letters to be recalled (three, four, or five) and (2) the number of choices presented (two, three, or four). Nine blocks of five trials each provide a total of eight increases in apparent difficulty level, each potentially cuing a suppression of performance as the feigner attempts to demonstrate "realistic" deficits. Internal consistency reliability has been reported at .93 (Inman et al., 1998). Using a floor effect strategy, a cut score of <93% correct has been shown to be effective in both simulation and known-groups studies of college students with mild TBI, community volunteers, patients with depression, patients with moderate to severe TBI, simulators, and forensic neuropsychiatric examinees (Inman & Berry, 2002; Orey, Cragar, & Berry, 2000; Vagnini et al., 2006; Vickery et al., 2004).

Digit Span

The Digit Span subtest of the WAIS-III is used as a screen for poor effort (Iverson & Tulsky, 2003). Babikian and colleagues (2006) compared multiple indices derived from Digit Span scores between likely malingerers and genuine patients; they found that a cut score <6 on the Digit Span age-corrected scaled score had the best overall hit rate, with sensitivity of .42 and a specificity of .93.

Forensic Reports

Forensic reports were prepared by the neuropsychiatrist following completion of all testing and scoring. Research assistants coded selected information from these reports. As a check on interrater reliability, a subset of records (10%) was independently coded by two raters, with a high level of correspondence (≥ 90%) for coded variables.

Classification of Response Styles

Three groups were identified using the LMT, TOMM, and VSVT, plus, when available, the age-corrected Digit Span scales score. Examinees were classified into the following groups: honest (HON), indeterminate (IND), and probable cognitive feigning (PCF). Using the recommended cut scores, six indicators of motivational impairment were summed to create a cognitive malingering index (CMI) score: LMT Total % correct, TOMM 2nd Learning Trial % correct, TOMM Delayed Retention Trial % correct, VSVT Total % correct, VSVT Difficult % correct, and WAIS-III age-corrected Digit Span scaled score. With scores ranging from 0 to 6, 58 examinees with a CMI score of 0 were classified in the HON group. Those with CMI scores of 3 or more (i.e., ≥ 3 objective signs of questionable effort) were placed in the PCF group ($n = 55$). Examinees with CMI scores of 1 and 2 were classified in the IND group ($n = 85$), as the objective evidence regarding effort was judged inadequate to place them in either the HON or PCF group with complete confidence. Their data were removed from subsequent analysis. This conservative group assignment yielded a base rate of PCF of 27.8%.

Similarities in Background

An examination of demographic and background characteristics for the HON and PCF groups revealed no significant differences. Compared with the HON group, the PCF group had smaller percentages of abnormal CT (36% vs. 48%) and MRI (20% vs. 30%); however, these differences were not statistically different. Moreover, comparable percentages were documented with loss of consciousness. In addition, results from the WTAR, an index of premorbid level of function, were quite similar for the two groups. Data from the abnormal

TABLE 9.2. Comparisons of Glasgow Coma Scale for Honest and Probable Cognitive Feigning Groups

	HON group		PCF group				
	M	SD	M	SD	t	p	d
EMS GCS	12.8	3.6	13.7	2.4	1.01	.32	.29
ER GCS	11.8	4.7	12.6	4.3	.52	.61	.18

Note. HON, honest group; PCF, probable cognitive feigning group; EMS GCS, Glasgow Coma Scale Total score from EMS report; ER GCS, GCS Total score from ER report.

scans suggest that some feigners may have experienced brain trauma but are grossly exaggerating the effects of this trauma. Differences on the Glasgow Coma Scale (GCS) were examined for the HON and PCG groups (see Table 9.2). Interestingly, the two groups scored at the boundary between moderate and minor comas on both EMS and ER ratings. As noted in Table 9.2, their results were comparable.

Turning to results from neuropsychological testing, 23 of the 55 initial PCF participants had their evaluations terminated early due to failure on all three motivational tests. Therefore, cognitive data were available on only 32 of the PCF group. The lack of data from the most obvious malingerers limits the generalizability of neuropsychological results to some extent; more pronounced differences would likely be observed had the most blatant malingerers been included.

Differences for selected cognitive measures between PCF and HON groups are summarized in Table 9.3. Interestingly, even these less pronounced feigners evidenced marked deficits on broad measures of intellect and memory that resulted in moderately large effect sizes. Differences were substantially less for specific measures. Interestingly, the PCF group evidenced substantial impairment on the Trail Making Tests (Ms < 40T) in contrast to the genuine patients.

An interesting question is whether cognitive feigners in the context of disability evaluations also exaggerate their psychopathology in an effort to achieve unwarranted compensation. As preliminary data, we compared data for MMPI-2 validity scales, the M-FAST total score, and the SIRS total score (see Table 9.4). The two traditional feigning scales, F and Fb, evidenced moderate effect sizes, suggesting the possibility of feigned mental disorders. However, the mean elevation for the PCF group is lower than the averages for genuine patients with major depression and PTSD (see Rogers,

TABLE 9.3. Comparisons on Cognitive Measures between Honest and Probable Cognitive Feigning Groups

Selected cognitive measures		HON group		PCF group				
Scale	Score	M	SD	M	SD	t	p	d
WAIS-III	Full IQ	94.6	11.3	83.8	13.4	3.90	.001	.89
WMS-III	General memory	96.4	17.6	75.8	26.7	4.18	.001	.97
WCST	Total perseverative errors (T scores)	48.2	14.6	43.2	19.0	1.31	.19	.31
Trail-Making	Part A (T scores)	46.2	9.6	38.0	11.7	3.36	.001	.79
Trail-Making	Part B (T scores)	45.7	10.7	38.0	14.1	2.77	.007	.64
Grip-strength	Dominant hand (T scores)	36.4	10.5	27.5	15.4	3.07	.003	.72

Note. WAIS, Wechsler Adult Intelligence Scale; WMS, Wechsler Memory Scale: WCSI, Wisconsin Card Sorting Test; HON, honest group; PCF, probable cognitive feigning group. The PCF group excludes the more blatant feigners who failed on all three cognitive feigning measures.

TABLE 9.4. Effect Sizes for Measures of Feigned Psychopathology Applied to Feigned Cognitive Impairment

Measure	Scale	HON group		PCF group		t	p	d
		M	SD	M	SD			
MMPI-2	F	7.7	4.9	11.8	5.5	3.62	.001	.79
MMPI-2	Fb	5.3	5.1	9.7	6.4	3.49	.001	.77
MMPI-2	Fp	2.4	7.8	2.2	2.3	.22	.82	.03
MMPI-2	FBS	22.3	6.2	25.6	72	2.53	.01	.49
M-FAST	Total score	2.3	2.5	4.6	3.7	3.77	.001	.75
SIRS	Total score[a]	20.9	18.9	40.6	24.6	4.39	.001	.90

Note. HON, honest group; PCF, probable cognitive feigning group; MMPI, Minnesota Multiphasic Personality Inventory; M-FAST, Miller Forensic Assessment of Symptoms Test; SIRS, Structured Interview of Reported Symptoms. Numbers for the PCF group vary slightly: MMPI-2 ($n = 50$); M-FAST ($n = 45$); SIRS ($n = 55$).
[a]SIRS classifications are based on primary scales, which have the best discrimination; the total score is included as a general benchmark.

Sewell, et al., 2003). Interestingly, the touted FBS scale performed less well with this particular population, whereas the Fp scale evidenced no meaningful differences. Regarding interview-based approaches, both the M-FAST and the SIRS yielded significant findings. Of special note, the SIRS total score, which is generally less discriminating than primary scale elevations, outperformed the other measures, with a Cohen's *d* of .90.

SUMMARY AND CONCLUSIONS

Data reviewed in this chapter suggest that base rates of probable malingering and symptom exaggeration are quite high in many instances. In Mittenburg, Patton, and colleagues' (2002) survey, approximately two-thirds of the more than 33,000 annual cases included issues of medical illness or injury. Using categories broader than malingering per se, roughly one-third of the total cases resulted in diagnostic impressions of symptom exaggeration and probable malingering. Based on this categorization, the rate for mild head injuries was reported at almost 40%. Consulting mental health professionals must be aware of its frequency along a continuum from symptom exaggeration to probable and definite malingering.

Mental health professionals providing services to physicians should be aware of the potential for malingering during medical evaluations across three domains (see Rogers, Chapter 2, this volume): cognitive, psychological, and physical. Of these domains, the most concerted work has been the development of explicit criteria for malingered neurocognitive dysfunction as standards for clinical practice (Slick et al., 1999). However, psychological malingering and physical malingering can be detected by numerous empirically validated detection strategies.

The original data presented in this chapter on 198 disability referrals have important implications for physicians and consulting health care professionals. These implications include the following:

1. The presence of medical findings, such as CT, MRI, and GCS ratings, do not rule out the feigning of medical or cognitive conditions. For example, the GCS ratings from both EMS and ER were comparable for genuine patients and those claimants likely feigning cognitive dysfunction. Clearly, the presence of genuine brain dysfunction does not preclude the possibility of malingering.

2. Malingering within the cognitive domain is not necessarily pervasive. In the current investigation, cognitive feigners appeared to do nearly as well as genuine patients on the WCST. Between-test discrepancies (e.g., severe impairment on the WMS-III vs. slight impairment on the WCST) may be useful in the evaluation of feigned cognitive impairment.

3. Different domains of malingering must be evaluated by different measures with their own specific detection strategies. Although it is

possible that some claimants are feigning in multiple domains (e.g., cognitive and psychological), the current results suggest that tests for one domain cannot be used to evaluate other domains. In particular, the MMPI-2 has often been used to evaluate cases presenting with cognitive or medical complaints. In the current study, the FBS ($d = .49$) and other MMPI-2 scales (ds from .03 to .79) yielded only moderate results. These findings make sense in light of the different detection strategies for each malingering domain.

III

Psychometric Methods

10

Malingering and Defensiveness on the MMPI-2

ROGER L. GREENE, PhD

This chapter focuses on the Minnesota Multiphasic Personality Inventory—2 (MMPI-2; Butcher, Dahlstrom, Graham, Tellegen, & Kraemmer, 1989; Butcher et al., 2001), which is the most widely used and researched multiscale inventory. Frequent references are made to the original MMPI (Dahlstrom, Welsh, & Dahlstrom, 1972, 1975), because much research on malingering and defensiveness was conducted on the original MMPI and extended directly to the MMPI-2, often without any further validation. The reader should be familiar with the clinical interpretation of the MMPI-2. Interpretive information on the MMPI-2 can be found in Fowler, Butcher, and Williams (2000), Friedman, Lewak, Nichols, and Webb (2001), Graham (2006), Greene (2000), and Nichols (2001). In addition, the reader is urged to consult the classic references on the original MMPI (Dahlstrom et al., 1972, 1975).

An important facet of this chapter is the inclusion of frequency tables for the MMPI-2 Malingering and Defensiveness scales. The frequency data from the MMPI-2 normative group (Butcher et al., 1989) are integrated with clinical data from 161,239 patients with mental disorders in inpatient and outpatient treatment settings (Caldwell, 2003). Profiles with excessive omissions ("Cannot Say" [?] >20) and inconsistent profiles (VRIN >14) were removed prior to the development of the frequency tables for the Malingering and Defensiveness scales.

DEVELOPMENT OF VALIDITY SCALES

In the development of the MMPI, Meehl and Hathaway (1946) were convinced of the necessity of assessing two dichotomous categories of test-taking attitudes: plus-getting ("faking bad") and defensiveness ("faking good"). Consistent with other chapters in this text, these two categories are designated, respectively, as *malingering* and *defensiveness*. Meehl and Hathaway (1946) considered three different methods to assess malingering and defensiveness: inconsistent responses to similarly worded items, extremely desirable but infrequently endorsed items, and empirically identified items.

The first methodological approach provided an opportunity for individuals to distort their responses, which could result in observed inconsistencies on items of similar or opposite content. A large number of inconsistent responses suggests that persons were either incapable of or unwilling to respond consistently. Although Meehl and Hathaway rejected this solution, the MMPI group booklet form included 16 identical repeated items (Test–Retest [TR] Index; Dahlstrom et al., 1972); Greene (1978) developed the Carelessness (CLS) scale, both of which can be used for detecting inconsistent responding. Because there are no repeated items on the MMPI-2, the TR Index cannot be utilized. However, two new MMPI-2 scales were developed that are variations on the CLS scale: the Variable Response Inconsistency scale (VRIN) and the True Response Inconsistency scale (TRIN). These two scales are discussed later in this chapter.

The second methodological approach of Meehl and Hathaway (1946) involves the development of items that have a low probability of being true. One set of items contained extremely desirable but very rare human qualities. If persons endorse a large number of these items, the probability is very high that their responses would be dishonest. The Lie (L) scale was developed specifically for this purpose. Items for the L scale, based on the work of Hartshorne and May (1928), reflect socially desirable but rarely true attributes. A large number of endorsements on the L scale indicates defensiveness.

The second approach was also operationalized by the endorsement of items that are often indicative of psychopathology but are rarely observed in the normative samples. As noted by Rogers in Chapter 2 of this volume, this approach is characterized as a *quasi-rare strategy*. An infrequency (F) scale was developed as a variant of this second approach. Because the content of this scale is so varied, individuals are unlikely to have undergone the breadth of these experiences; therefore, a high number of endorsements is unlikely to be true and often signals an impaired presentation, such as malingering. The quasi-rare strategy was extended on the MMPI-2 with the creation of the Back F scale (Fb; Butcher et al., 1989) that consists of items that were endorsed infrequently in the preceding 300 items. Arbisi and Ben-Porath (1995) refined this approach with the Infrequency Psychopathology scale (Fp); it consists of items infrequently endorsed by a patient population, resulting in a true *rare-symptom strategy* (see Rogers, Chapter 2, this volume).

The third methodological approach of Meehl and Hathaway (1946) used an empirical procedure to identify items that elicit different responses from persons instructed to malinger than from those with standard instructions. Gough's Dissimulation scale (Ds; Gough, 1954) is based on this procedure of *erroneous stereotypes*. Meehl and Hathaway adopted a variant of this third approach with the K scale, which was developed to differentiate inpatients with normal profiles from putatively normal individuals with abnormal profiles.

Meehl and Hathaway (1946) empirically determined the proportions of K that, when added to a clinical scale, would maximize the discrimination between the criterion group and the normative group. Because Meehl and Hathaway (1946) determined the optimal weights of K in an inpatient population, they warned that other weights of K might serve to maximize the identification of individuals in other clinical settings. This issue of the optimal weights for different populations has received little attention (see Greene, 1980; Wooten, 1984). Moreover, several investigators have questioned the usefulness of the K correction procedure (Colby, 1989; McCrae, Costa, & Dahlstrom, 1989). Despite these warnings and almost nonexistent research, the K correction procedure was continued on the MMPI-2 without further validation.

Assessing the validity of an individual MMPI-2 profile is a multistep process that must be carried out in a sequential manner. An overview of these steps is provided in Figure 10.1. This process for the assessment of response styles involves three main steps: completeness (i.e., item omissions), consistency, and accuracy (e.g., malingering and defensiveness).

ITEM OMISSIONS

The first step in assessing the validity of an MMPI-2 profile is to evaluate the number of items omitted (see Figure 10.1). The term "item omissions" is a misnomer because it includes not only unendorsed items but also items endorsed as both true and false and items endorsed on the answer sheet other than in the allotted spaces. Persons completing the MMPI-2 occasionally make comments about the items on the answer sheet that the clinician may miss unless it is checked carefully. Consequently, clinicians need to check the answer sheet meticulously and tabulate the number of "item omissions."

The number of items usually omitted is very small in both normative and clinical samples. More than 70% of each sample omitted no items, and 85% omitted two or fewer items. Even among patients, less than 1% omit more than 30 items. The restandardization of the MMPI-2 improved its item content by removing most items with objectionable content and outdated terminology that had caused item omissions in the original MMPI (Butcher & Tellegen, 1966).

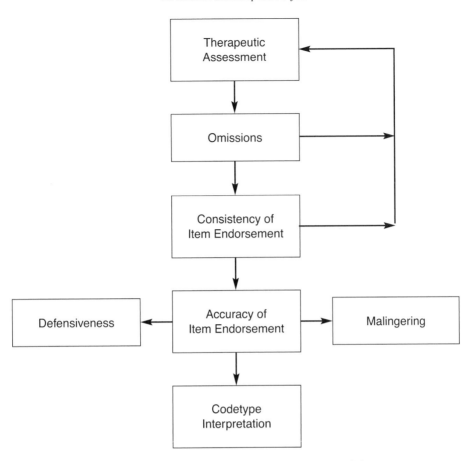

FIGURE 10.1. Flowchart for assessing MMPI-2 validity.

Omission of a large number of items on the MMPI-2 is an infrequent problem in most clinical assessments. They are detected easily by a careful check of the answer sheet. Occasionally, a very defensive or possibly paranoid person will be encountered who refuses to endorse most of the items. These personality characteristics are readily apparent in a clinical interview and easily recognized by the clinician. Omission of items is not typically an issue when malingering is involved, as the person must endorse the items in order to malinger. Occasionally, feigners may omit a large number of items because they claim that they are too impaired to complete the MMPI-2. Any time there is a large number of omissions—typically defined as more than 20 or 30 items—interpretation of the MMPI-2 stops. The reason for the large number of omissions should be determined and, if the issue can be resolved, the person can either complete the omitted items or the entire MMPI-2 can be administered in an evaluation at a later date.

CONSISTENCY OF ITEM ENDORSEMENT

The next step in assessing the validity of the person's responses, after item omissions have been checked and found to be in the acceptable range, is to assess the consistency of item endorsement (see Figure 10.1). Consistency of item endorsement verifies that the person has endorsed the items in a reliable manner. Response consistency must be evaluated before any assessment of accuracy (e.g., defensiveness or malingering) is made. To highlight this difference, *consistency* of item endorsement may be conceptualized as being independent of item content, whereas *accuracy* of item endorsement is dependent on item content. Thus measures of consistency assess whether the individual has provided a reliable pattern of responding to the items throughout the inventory regardless of their content, whereas measures of the accuracy of item endorsement assess whether the individual has attempted to distort his or her responses to the items in some specific manner.

Random MMPI-2 Profiles

One method of trying to simulate inconsistent patterns of item endorsement has utilized random MMPI-2s (i.e., "true" and "false" responses are assigned randomly). Even a cursory inspection of these profiles (see Graham, 2006, pp. 40–41; Greene, 2000, p. 125) arouses the clinician's suspicions of a random response style. Subsequent examination of several validity indices confirms the high probability of such a response pattern. In general, validity scales with large numbers tend to be especially effective. For example, a random sort of the F scale, with 60 infrequently endorsed items, should result in approximately 30 endorsed items (i.e., a T score >120). Thus, the F scale tends to be one of the most reliable indicators of random MMPI-2s (Sewell & Rogers, 1994).

A second method of simulating inconsistent responses involves generating groups of profiles based on patterns of item endorsements such as TFTF, TTFTTF, FFTFFT, and so on.

These profiles are identified almost as easily as random sorts. Again, longer scales facilitate detection of these inconsistent patterns of responding (Dahlstrom et al., 1972; Nichols, Greene, & Schmolck, 1989). Huba (1986) has developed a statistical test that examines specific sequences of stereotyped responses to assess whether the individual switches between "true" and "false" responses more or less often than would be expected by chance (see Table 10.1). Only 4.2% of the normal men and 5.2% of the normal women had revised Z scores with absolute values greater than 1.96 (i.e., greater than 2 standard deviations in either direction). The percentages are slightly larger for clinical populations. The revised Z statistic appears to reflect accurately the typical pattern of inconsistent endorsement because of their nonrandom order. The revised Z statistic is particularly promising because it does not correlate with VRIN and TRIN (see Table 10.3) and, therefore, provides an independent measure for the consistency of item endorsement.

Inconsistency Scales

Individuals may endorse the items inconsistently by a variety of methods. Rather than focusing on how they generate inconsistent responses, two MMPI-2 scales focus directly on assessing the consistency of item endorsement: VRIN and TRIN. VRIN uses item pairs that

TABLE 10.1. Distribution of Z Scores for Runs Test in Assessing Inconsistency of Item Endorsement

Range	Percentages for normative data				Percentages for clinical data			
	Men		Women		Men		Women	
	M	SD	M	SD	M	SD	M	SD
Less than −2.50	2.99	0.53	3.76	0.00	2.14	0.60	2.80	0.51
−2.24–2.49	1.58	0.35	3.28	0.55	1.19	0.30	1.83	0.32
−1.96–2.23	2.37	0.79	3.56	1.44	1.99	0.59	2.85	0.68
−1.64–1.95	4.49	2.20	6.09	2.33	3.52	1.36	4.86	1.59
−1.15–1.63	12.93	6.07	15.53	7.05	9.17	4.79	10.96	5.26
1.14–1.14	67.81	80.56	60.74	76.33	67.65	75.87	63.31	70.72
1.63–1.15	3.43	5.01	3.83	6.57	6.18	8.15	5.40	9.17
1.95–1.64	1.76	1.93	1.30	2.53	2.39	2.84	2.08	3.74
2.23–1.96	0.35	0.53	0.62	1.23	1.31	1.43	1.24	2.08
2.49–2.24	0.44	0.35	0.34	0.68	0.85	0.86	0.80	1.30
Greater than 2.50	1.85	1.67	0.96	1.30	3.59	3.21	3.86	4.62

have similar or opposite content. VRIN consists of 49 pairs of unique items; because two separate response patterns are scored for 18 pairs, the total is 67 item pairs.

The last columns of Table 10.2 illustrate the distribution of scores on VRIN if the person randomly "endorsed" the MMPI-2 items. Because only one of the four possible combinations of "true" and "false" response patterns is scored on each of the 67 pairs of items on VRIN, the average score in such random sorts is 16.75 (i.e., 67 item pairs/4 alternatives).

Butcher and colleagues (1989) recommended a cutting score of 13 (T score of 80). Some 14.9% of these random responses are missed by this cut score. In addition, patients in clinical settings with VRIN scores of as high as 13 or 14 appear to have endorsed the items consistently (see Table 10.2).

Research is needed to determine empirically the optimal cutting score on VRIN. Various cut scores for random profiles have been proposed: 10 (Greene, 2000), 13 (Butcher et al., 1989), and 14 (Berry, Wetter, et al., 1991). Given this

TABLE 10.2. Percentages of VRIN and |F-FB| Scores for the Normative, Clinical, and Random Data

	MMPI-2 normative		Mentally disordered		Random profiles	
	VRIN%	F-FB%	VRIN%	F-FB%	VRIN%	F-FB%
0	1.4	10.4	3.0	9.7	0.0	1.0
1	4.9	24.4	6.6	19.3	0.0	2.5
2	9.1	21.0	9.3	18.6	0.0	3.0
3	14.4	17.0	11.3	15.6	0.0	3.2
4	15.1	11.8	12.7	11.6	0.0	3.7
5	15.4	6.2	13.0	8.2	0.0	4.3
6	13.7	4.0	11.9	5.7	0.0	5.6
7	9.7	2.2	10.0	3.9	0.1	6.7
8	6.7	1.5	7.7	2.6	0.2	7.2
9	3.7	0.7	5.5	1.6	0.6	8.0
10	2.5	0.4	3.5	1.1	1.1	8.2
11	1.8	0.3	2.2	0.7	2.8	8.7
12	1.0	0.1	1.4	0.5	3.9	7.5
13	0.4	0.0	0.8	0.3	6.2	7.1
14	0.0	0.0	0.5	0.2	8.1	5.6
15	0.0	0.1	0.3	0.1	10.8	4.0
16	0.1		0.2	0.1	12.1	4.3
17			0.0	0.1	12.6	2.7
18			0.0	0.1	11.4	2.1
19			0.0	0.0	10.0	1.5
20			0.0	0.0	7.8	1.0
21			0.0	0.0	5.2	1.0
22			0.0	0.0	3.2	0.4
23			0.0	0.0	1.9	0.3
24					1.2	0.2
25					0.8	0.2
26					0.6	
27					0.2	
28					0.0	

variation in optimal cutting scores, some general guidelines that can be followed for ranges of scores on VRIN are:

1. *7 or lower:* There is a high probability that the patient has endorsed the items consistently.

2. *8 to 15:* It is not clear whether the patient has endorsed the items consistently or inconsistently. The clinician is encouraged to examine the indexes described in the next section. These indexes may be useful even in cases in which VRIN is low to ensure that the items have been endorsed consistently, particularly during the later portions of the MMPI-2.

3. *16 or higher:* There is a high probability that the patient has endorsed the items inconsistently.

Infrequency Scales

Several infrequency scales are available for the MMPI-2 that also can be used to assess the consistency of item endorsement. The F scale and the Back F (Fb) scale are composed of items that were endorsed less than 10% of the time by the normative sample on the MMPI and MMPI-2, respectively. Three additional infrequency scales have been developed: Fake Bad (FBS; Lees-Haley, English, & Glenn, 1991), Infrequency Psychopathology (Fp; Arbisi & Ben-Porath, 1995), and Inconsistent Response (IR; Sewell & Rogers, 1994). FBS consists of 43 items endorsed infrequently by disability claimants who were assessed to have bona fide claims; Fp consists of 27 items endorsed infrequently in patient samples; and IR consists of 16 items, 8 of which are scored on Fp, endorsed infrequently in patient samples. The in-tercorrelations for these infrequency scales, except for FBS, average approximately .75 (see Table 10.3). The correlations of the inconsistency scales with the infrequency scales tend to be fairly low (<.30), which suggests that they are measuring different aspects of the consistency of item endorsement.

One advantage of VRIN over infrequency scales in assessing random profiles is that VRIN is not affected by the presence of psychopathology. In contrast, elevations on infrequency scales can represent either (1) an inconsistent pattern of item endorsement; (2) less often, the person's acknowledgment of the presence of psychopathology; or (3) the person's malingering of psychopathology (see the later section, "Accuracy of Item Endorsement"). As noted, VRIN is relatively unaffected by the type and severity of psychopathology, with similar means and standard deviations in the MMPI-2 normative and clinical samples. VRIN also is not affected by malingering or defensiveness because the person has to endorse the items consistently to alter their responses. In fact, a potential indicator of a defensive MMPI-2 profile is one in which the person has been more consistent than would be expected. Consequently, VRIN can provide an independent estimate of the consistency of item endorsement.

VRIN detects some inconsistent profiles that would be considered consistent by infrequency scales. It also can demonstrate that the person has been endorsing the items consistently despite elevated scores on the F and Fb scales (see Evans & Dinning, 1983; Gallucci, 1985; Maloney, Duvall, & Friesen, 1980; Wetter, Baer, Berry, Smith, & Larsen, 1992). These findings indicate that VRIN and infrequency scales are not measuring identical processes in test-tak-

TABLE 10.3. Intercorrelations of Inconsistency and Infrequency Scales in Normative and Clinical Data

Scale	Normative data					Clinical data				
	F	Fb	Fp	FBS	IR	F	Fb	Fp	FBS	IR
VRIN	.36	.38	.25	.15	.22	.38	.36	.30	.30	.25
TRIN	.14	.23	.11	−.04	.13	.20	.24	.19	.04	.21
Z′	.17	.18	.05	.05	.07	.14	.15	.05	.14	.04
F		.59	.58	.14	.41		.85	.72	.53	.65
Fb			.53	.26	.49			.66	.55	.65
Fp				.08	.58				.28	.75
FBS					.01					.23

ing attitudes (Fekken & Holden, 1987) and consequently cannot be simply substituted for one another.

Because the items on the F and Fb scales are endorsed infrequently, persons would be expected to endorse comparable numbers of items on each scale. Consequently, the absolute value of the difference between F and Fb (i.e., |F-Fb|) can be used as a measure of the consistency of item endorsement. Table 10.2 provides the distribution of this measure of the consistency of item endorsement for the MMPI-2 normative group, Caldwell's (2003) clinical data, and 2,600 randomly endorsed MMPI-2s. Exactly 70.0% of random profiles have a score of 7 or higher on this index, with a mean of 10.0 (*SD* = 5.0). Less than 26% of these random sorts with VRIN scores in the intermediate range (8–15) had scores of 6 or lower on this index. Thus the clinician can be fairly confident that the person has endorsed the items consistently if |F-Fb| is 6 or lower when VRIN is in the intermediate range of 8–15.

Clinicians typically assume that patients follow the same pattern of item endorsement for all 567 items. This assumption may not always be appropriate, because patients' motivation and ability to concentrate may change as they complete the test. For example, a patient could endorse the first 400 items consistently and then endorse the remainder of the items inconsistently. Berry and his colleagues (Berry, Wetter, et al., 1991; Berry et al., 1992) have examined the ability of measures of consistency of item endorsement to detect persons who were instructed to respond randomly after completing 100, 200, 300, 400, or 500 items appropriately. They found that F, Fb, and VRIN were effective at detecting persons who

endorsed the items randomly and that these measures were more accurate as the number of items endorsed randomly increased.

All items for the MMPI-2 standard validity and clinical scales occur in the first 370 items. If inconsistent responding is observed to begin somewhere after item 370, clinicians could still score and interpret the standard scales. If blocks or groups of items rather than the entire 567 items could be assessed for inconsistency, those items up to the point at which the patient started responding randomly could be scored. One advantage of hand scoring VRIN is that the clinician can evaluate whether inconsistent responses tend to be distributed evenly throughout the MMPI-2 or begin to occur after some specific point.

As shown in Table 10.4, the VRIN and F and Fb items are distributed throughout the MMPI-2 so clinicians can determine when individuals start to make inconsistent responses. This approach might be particularly appropriate for intermediate scores on VRIN, as it is more difficult to make an assessment of the consistency of item endorsement.

TRIN consists of 23 pairs of items and is very similar to VRIN except that the scored response is either "true" or "false" to both items in each pair. TRIN has virtually no published research and negligible information on its use clinically, other than that very high (>13; i.e., true biased) or very low (< 5; i.e., false biased) scores (Butcher et al., 1989) may reflect inconsistent item endorsement.

Although VRIN is useful in identifying inconsistent patterns of item endorsement, the clinician should keep in mind that an acceptable score indicates only that the person has endorsed the items consistently and not necessar-

TABLE 10.4. Distribution of Validity Scale Items by Blocks of One Hundred

Blocks	Inconsistency scales		Infrequency scales				
	VRIN	TRIN	F	Fb	Fp	FBS	IR
1–100	4	4	16	0	5	14	3
101–200	6	7	17	0	6	6	2
201–300	9	3	16	2	8	9	2
301–400	9	5	11	13	5	5	4
401–500	10	1	0	11	1	5	2
501–567	11	3	0	14	2	3	3

ily accurately, because the person can consistently malinger or be defensive. Moreover, because VRIN assesses only the consistency of the person's responses, it will not detect "all true" (VRIN = 5) or "all false" (VRIN = 5) response sets that are consistent but nonveridical test-taking sets. These response sets are detected easily by TRIN (scores of 23 and 0, respectively).

Reaction Time

The advent of computer-administered MMPI-2s enables clinicians to examine the reaction time for each item response. Very rapid reaction times would suggest that the person has not taken sufficient time to read the items carefully and is indicative of inconsistent item endorsement. Research that evaluates such a hypothesis and provides guidelines for interpreting the obtained reaction times is needed. In addition, any changes in the person's reaction time across the 567 items could be measured easily by blocks of items. Research to test other response styles also is feasible. For example, persons who have very slow reaction times may be trying to malinger or be defensive because they are trying to make sure that they are providing the "correct" response to each item (see Holden & Kroner, 1992).

Clinical Applications

The importance of assessing consistency of item endorsement before trying to assess accuracy of item endorsement cannot be overstressed. Otherwise, inconsistent patterns of item endorsement may be labeled inappropriately as malingering (e.g., Rogers, Dolmetsch, & Cavanaugh, 1983; Wetter et al., 1992). A variety of reasons explain why a person may endorse the items inconsistently on any multiscale personality inventory. These potential reasons are summarized in Table 10.5, as well as strategies for how each of them may be resolved.

ACCURACY OF ITEM ENDORSEMENT

The third step in the process of assessing the MMPI-2 validity, after item omissions (Step 1) and consistency of item endorsement (Step 2) have been checked and found to be good enough to proceed, is to verify the accuracy of item endorsement (see Figure 10.1). Accuracy of item endorsement evaluates whether the person has adopted a response set to either malinger or be defensive. As a caution, the MMPI-2 can be used to determine a response set but not an individual's motivation for that response set.

Although the point should be self-evident, any measure of malingering or defensiveness is likely to be confounded with measures of psychopathology because the person is being evaluated on those dimensions (Schretlen, 1988). Clinicians and researchers should not be surprised that measures of malingering are related

TABLE 10.5. Potential Causes of and Solutions for Inconsistent Item Endorsement

Causes	Solutions
Client has not been told why the MMPI-2 is being administered	Explain why the MMPI-2 is being administered and how the data are to be used.
Inadequate reading ability or comprehension, inadequate educational opportunity, or limited intellectual ability	Present the MMPI-2 orally by CD or cassette tape. Dahlstrom et al. (1972) reported that audiotape administrations are effective with reading and educational levels as low as the third grade and with IQs as low as 65.
Too confused psychiatrically or neuropsychologically	Readminister the MMPI-2 when the patient is less confused.
Still toxic from substance abuse	Readminister the MMPI-2 when the client is detoxified.
Noncompliant or uncooperative	Be sure patient understands the importance of the MMPI-2 for treatment and intervention and readminister the MMPI-2. If the client is still noncompliant, that issue becomes the focus of treatment.

positively to measures of psychopathology, whereas measures of defensiveness are related inversely to measures of psychopathology. In evaluating the probability that the person is malingering or being defensive, the clinician must evaluate the base rate with which malingering or defensiveness occurs in his or her specific setting in order to have an appropriate estimate of positive predictive power[1] (i.e., the probability that a person said to be malingering or defensive is classified accurately).

Several basic issues about malingering and defensiveness must be made explicit before the scales and indexes for assessing accuracy of item endorsement are discussed. First, researchers often assume that malingering and defensiveness represent a single continuum characterized by malingering at one end and defensiveness at the other (see Figure 10.2). Consequently, accurate patterns of item endorsement gradually will shade into malingering or defensiveness as one moves across this continuum; no exact point exists at which the person's performance suddenly reflects either malingering or defensiveness. Instead, a probability statement can be made that this person's performance reflects either malingering or defensiveness. Second, given that malingering and defensiveness exist on a continuum, numerous scales can be used to assess both response sets, with high scores reflecting malingering and low scores reflecting defensiveness. Scales with dual purposes are reviewed first, followed by scales limited to a single purpose (malingering or defensiveness). Third, many persons, when they decide to malinger, attempt to do so by "faking bad" in a global and extreme manner

that is easily detected in most circumstances. The issues of persons malingering specific disorders and the effects of coaching (e.g., being given information about validity indicators used to detect malingering and defensiveness) are explored following examination of global dissimulation. Fourth, the presence of malingering or defensiveness does not rule out actual psychopathology. A person who actually has a specific mental disorder also can malinger or be defensive about the presence of psychopathology. The scales and indexes to assess accuracy of item endorsement cannot determine whether the person actually has psychopathology, only whether the person has provided an accurate self-description.

MALINGERING AND DEFENSIVENESS: ENDPOINTS ON A CONTINUUM

A number of scales and indexes are used to assess malingering and defensiveness, with high scores reflecting malingering and low scores reflecting defensiveness. These MMPI-2 scales and indexes tend to be biased toward "true" responses when reflecting malingering, because items that are endorsed "true" on the MMPI-2 have a high probability of reflecting significant psychopathology. Thus clinicians and researchers should be alert to the possibility that a malingered profile actually reflects a "yea-saying" bias to endorse the items "true." The exception to this generalization is those MMPI-2 items assessing somatic functioning, on which "false" is typically the deviant response. As sum-

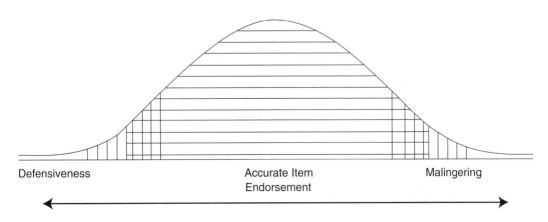

Defensiveness   Accurate Item   Malingering
                         Endorsement

FIGURE 10.2. Accuracy of item endorsement conceptualized as a single dimension.

TABLE 10.6. Intercorrelations of Malingering Scales for Clinical (Above the Diagonal) and Normative (Below the Diagonal) Data

	F	Ds	KB	LW	F-K	O-S	True
F		.84	.84	.85	.91	.82	.70
Ds	.61		.90	.91	.90	.90	.85
KB-Sum	.66	.80		.97	.89	.93	.80
LW-Sum	.66	.84	.92		.89	.93	.78
F-K	.75	.77	.79	.79		.92	.87
O-S	.58	.79	.82	.82	.84		.83
True	.46	.76	.74	.72	.80	.78	

Note. For specialized indices: KB-Sum, total number of Koss and Butcher (1973) critical items; LW-Sum, total number of Lachar and Wrobel (1979) critical items; F-K, Gough Dissimulation Index (1950); O-S, total T score difference between the obvious and subtle subscales (Wiener, 1948); True, proportion scored "true."

marized in Table 10.6, the intercorrelations among these measures are high, and sometimes virtually interchangeable. The reader should realize that it is not necessary to score all of these scales to assess malingering or defensiveness for every person. A number of different scales will be illustrated that are sensitive to malingering and defensiveness. The reader will need to determine the scale(s) most appropriate for his or her specific setting and type of patients.

Several reviews of the MMPI assessment of malingering and defensiveness are available to the interested reader (Franzen, Iverson, & McCracken, 1990; Greene, 1997; Schretlen, 1988). In addition, one meta-analysis of malingering was conducted on the MMPI (Berry, Baer, & Harris, 1991) and three on the MMPI-2 (Nelson, Sweet, & Demakis, 2006; Rogers, Sewell, Martin, & Vitacco, 2003; Rogers, Sewell, & Salekin, 1994). Berry, Baer, and Harris (1991) found that the F scale, Gough Dissimulation (Ds) scale, and the Gough Dissimulation index (F-K) had the largest effect sizes on the MMPI. For the MMPI-2, Rogers, Sewell, and Salekin (1994) found that the F scale, F-K, and O-S (i.e., the total T score difference on the obvious and subtle subscales; Wiener, 1948) had the largest effect sizes on the MMPI-2. Rogers, Sewell, and colleagues (2003) categorized the results of their meta-analysis by the types of comparisons that were made, which helps to clarify some of the contradictory findings in past research. All validity scales were effective at identifying simulators when compared with nonclinical samples (e.g., students); however, these differences have only a marginal relevance to clinical assessments

that focus on the differences between feigned and genuine psychopathology. For more relevant comparisons, as simulators were compared with clinical samples, the effect sizes decreased substantially, but they are still very large compared with most psychological research. Key findings from Rogers, Sewell, and colleagues can be summarized as follows:

1. Litigation status had very limited impact on these validity scales, with effect sizes in the range of 0.03 (Ds) to 0.83 (O-S); this finding questions the use of differential prevalence designs based on litigation status.
2. Ds had a remarkably consistent cutting score of 35 across all seven studies.
3. Fp had relatively consistent cutting scores (4–9) and worked better than most indicators with potentially problematic diagnoses (i.e., schizophrenia and posttraumatic stress disorder [PTSD]).

Nelson and colleagues (2006) limited their meta-analysis to the Fake Bad Scale (FBS; Lees-Haley et al., 1991) in forensic practice. FBS is an infrequency scale whose current use is limited to disability claimants or similar types of forensic settings. They found that FBS had the largest effect size (0.96) and appeared to perform as well as or better than the other validity scales in these studies.

The initial studies of dissimulation provided the participants with general or global instructions to either malinger or be defensive with a variety of normal populations: students (Bagby, Rogers, & Buis, 1994; Graham, Watts, & Timbrook, 1991; Wetter et al., 1992), professionals (Gough, 1954); and community samples (Wetter, Baer, Berry, Robison, & Sumpter, 1993). Clinical samples included patients with mental disorders (Bagby, Rogers, Buis, & Kalemba, 1994; Graham et al., 1991; Rogers, Sewell, & Ustad, 1995); and correctional/forensic patients (Bagby, Rogers, & Buis, 1994; Iverson, Franzen, & Hammond, 1995; Walters, 1988; Walters, White, & Greene, 1988).[2] These studies typically reported that the malingering or defensive group could be successfully distinguished from the group taking the test honestly, although the specific scale or index employed and the optimal cut score tended to vary widely across studies.[3] As expected, research has greater difficulty in making the relevant comparison of simulators with actual patients than comparisons between simulators and normal individuals. Global instructions have little external validity (Rogers, 1988; Sivec, Lynn, & Garske, 1994; Wetter, Baer, Berry, & Reynolds, 1994). To parallel real-world circumstances, researchers have suggested that participants must have or be given specific knowledge of the psychopathology to be simulated.

A series of studies made disorder-specific criteria available to the participants, who were then instructed to feign the following disorders: borderline personality disorder (Sivec, Hilsenroth, & Lynn, 1995; Wetter, Baer, Berry, Robison, & Sumpter, 1993; Wetter et al., 1994); closed head injury (Lamb, Berry, Wetter, & Baer, 1994); depression (Bagby, Rogers, Buis, et al., 1997; Steffan, Clopton, & Morgan, 2003; Walters & Clopton, 2000); paranoia (Sivec et al., 1994); PTSD (Fairbank, McCaffrey, & Keane, 1985; Wetter, Baer, Berry, Robison, & Sumpter, 1993); schizophrenia (Bagby, Rogers, Buis, et al., 1997; Bagby et al., 1997b; Rogers, Bagby, & Chakraborty, 1993; Wetter, Baer, Berry, Robison, & Sumpter, 1993); and somatoform disorders (Sivec et al., 1994). Two generalizations can be formulated from this series of studies. First, validity scales usually have good success at detecting those disorders, such as schizophrenia (Rogers, Bagby, & Chakraborty, 1993) and borderline personality disorder (Sivec et al., 1995; Wetter et al., 1994), that are characterized by extensive and severe psychopathology. Again, the specific scale or index that is most successful varies by study, as does the optimal cut score. Second, persons feigning a specific disorder that is characterized by circumscribed and less severe psy-

chopathology are able to do so quite readily and are fairly difficult to detect (Lamb et al., 1994; Wetter, Baer, Berry, Robison, & Sumpter, 1993). Third, clinical training and experience did not seem to facilitate graduate students or psychiatry residents in malingering schizophrenia (Bagby et al., 1997a).

A second series of studies investigated the effects of providing the participants with information about the validity scales that would be used to detect malingering or defensiveness (Baer, Wetter, & Berry, 1995; Bagby, Nicholson, Bacchiochi, Ryder, & Bury, 2002; Lamb et al., 1994; Rogers, Bagby, & Chakraborty, 1993; Storm & Graham, 2000; Walters & Clopton, 2000), sometimes in combination with diagnostic-specific information. Most studies found that information about the validity scales helped simulators to avoid detection (Storm & Graham, 2000; Walters & Clopton, 2000), but Bagby and colleagues (2002) did not. In general, having more information about the validity scales enables simulators to feign without being detected (Baer et al., 1995; Rogers, Bagby, & Chakraborty, 1993). Information about the validity scales also was more valuable in avoiding detection as malingering than were diagnostic-specific criteria (Rogers, Bagby, & Chakraborty, 1993).

The ethics of providing participants with specific information about the disorders to be assessed, as well as the role of validity scales in assessing malingering or defensiveness, have been debated (Ben-Porath, 1994; Berry, Lamb, Wetter, Baer, & Widiger, 1994). These ethical issues are quite complex, and anyone who is contemplating research on coached dissimulation should consult these articles.

Infrequency Scales

The F scale is the traditional measure of malingering on the MMPI-2 because its items were selected to detect unusual or atypical ways of endorsing (Dahlstrom et al., 1972). As noted earlier, four other infrequency scales on the MMPI-2 can be scored: Fb, FBS, Fp, and IR. This discussion is limited to the Fp scale, which is based on the *rare symptoms* strategy, because it is less sensitive to the presence of psychopathology per se and yields more consistent cutting scores in meta-analyses (Rogers, Sewell, & Martin, 2003). High scores on the Fp scale can occur for three reasons: (1) inconsistent patterns of item endorsement, (2) severe psychopathology, or (3) malingering. Low scores can occur for two reasons: (1) the absence of actual psychopathology or (2) defensiveness. Thus the reasons for a high or low score on the Fp scale are very difficult to ascertain without considering the other indicators of the consistency and accuracy of item endorsement. Clinicians are probably safe to conclude that a raw score greater than 6 or 7 (T score >100) on the Fp scale does not reflect actual psychopathology but could reflect either inconsistent responding or malingering. Similarly, a raw score of 0 (T score = 41) could reflect either the absence of psychopathology or defensiveness. Because different clinical decisions will be made depending on the reason for the specific score on the Fp scale, clinicians should use the other validity indicators described in this chapter to make this discrimination. Thus the best use of the Fp scale and other infrequency scales is in conjunction with other validity indicators.

Tables 10.7 and 10.8 provide normative data on a variety of validity indicators, including the Fp scale for normal individuals and patients, respectively. Clinical samples endorse nearly the same number of items on the Fp scale as normal individuals, and neither group endorses more than one or two of these items. This fact shows that the presence of psychopathology per se does not elevate the Fp scale. Clinicians do need to be aware that the Fp scales contain four L (Lie) items that measure defensiveness and four familial items, either of which can produce false-positive elevations on the Fp scale (>70 T). Because no one, either clinical patients or normal individuals, typically endorses more than one or two of the Fp items, the scale does not measure defensiveness.

The optimal cutting score on the Fp scale to identify persons who are malingering within clinical samples has ranged from 5 to 9 and yielded good (~84%) classification rates (Rogers, Sewell, & Martin, 2003). A cutting score of 6 would classify nearly 5% of the patients in Table 10.8 as malingering, whereas a cutting score of 7 would classify about 2% as malingering.

Critical Items

Clinicians attempt to discern information from individual MMPI items, despite the considerable problems with such efforts that provided the original impetus for the empirical selection of items on the MMPI. Grayson (1951) constructed the original set of "critical" items (i.e., problems that require careful scrutiny); his efforts were followed by the development of other sets of critical items (Caldwell, 1969; Koss & Butcher, 1973; Lachar & Wrobel, 1979).[4] Because critical items have obvious (i.e., face-valid) content, they provide another means of assessing the accuracy of item endorsement. Large numbers of critical items are endorsed by persons malingering or experiencing extensive, severe psychopathology. Conversely, very few critical items are endorsed by persons who are defensive or experiencing no psychopathology. The Lachar and Wrobel (1979) critical items are used here to illustrate this procedure, although any critical item set could be used to assess accuracy of item endorsement.

Lachar and Wrobel (1979) developed their critical items to be face-valid (obvious) descriptors of psychological concerns. They first identified 14 categories of symptoms that (1) motivate people to seek psychological treatment and (2) assist the clinician to make diagnostic decisions. A group of 14 clinical psychologists reviewed each MMPI item and nominated items as face-valid indicators of psychopathology in one of these 14 categories. These items were validated empirically by contrasting item-response frequencies for normal controls and clinical samples matched for gender and race. Lachar and Wrobel were able to validate 130 of the 177 items nominated. After eliminating 19 duplicative items, a final list of 111 (20.2%) critical items was established. In the restandardization of the MMPI, four items were deleted; there are 107 Lachar and Wrobel critical items on the MMPI-2.

The total number of critical items can indicate the accuracy of item endorsement based on large (malingering) or small (defensiveness) numbers. Tables 10.7 and 10.8 summarize the total number of Koss and Butcher's (1973) and Lachar and Wrobel's (1979) critical items that are endorsed by normal individuals and patients, respectively. On average, patients with mental disorders endorse about twice as many critical items as normal individuals. The fact that the typical normal individual endorses 10 of the Koss and Butcher and 15 of the Lachar and Wrobel critical items may suggest that at least some of these items are not as "critical" as originally thought. Surprisingly, about 25% of patients endorse fewer total critical items than the average normal individual.

F-K Index (Gough Dissimulation Index)

The F-K index (Gough, 1950) utilizes the relationship between the standard validity scales of F and K to assess both malingering and defensiveness. The reader is cautioned not to confuse the F-K index (Gough Dissimulation index) with the Gough Dissimulation scale (Ds) described later. Gough (1950) suggested that the raw score difference between F and K scales would be useful in screening MMPI profiles for accuracy of item endorsement. If the F-K index was greater than +9, the profile was designated as malingering. If the F-K index was less than zero, the profile was classified as being defensive. Intermediate scores on the F-K index (0–9) indicated accurate item endorsement (i.e., valid profiles). Gough reported that the F-K index readily detected malingering; in one sample, it accurately classified 97% of the authentic profiles and 75% of those malingered.

Most MMPI and MMPI-2 studies of the F-K index have utilized normal persons instructed to feign psychopathology. Numerous investigators (e.g., Graham et al., 1991) have confirmed the ability of the F-K index to identify students instructed to malinger. They also noted that the F scale alone identified malingering as well as or more accurately than the F-K index. The optimal cut scores for the F-K index has ranged from 6 (Sivec et al., 1994) to 17 (Graham et al., 1991).

Higher cutting scores on the F-K index are required to distinguish between feigners and genuine patients. Optimal cutting scores have ranged from 12 (Iverson et al., 1995) to 27 (Graham et al., 1991). Rothke and colleagues (1994) have provided extensive tables of the distribution of the F-K index in samples of patients with mental disorders and head injuries, disability claimants, job applicants for police and priest positions, and substance abusers, as well as the MMPI-2 normative group. Substantial differences were observed in the F-K index for these various samples. Rothke and colleagues suggested that clinicians using the F-K index consider both gender and specific diagnostic groups.

Tables 10.7 and 10.8 summarize the distribution of scores for the F-K index in normal individuals and patients, respectively. Normal individuals achieve mean scores of nearly −12 on this index, whereas the psychiatric patients achieve mean scores of −11. If F-K scores greater than +9 are labeled as malingering,

about 10% of the patients would be so classified. Because the F scale also may reflect the presence of actual psychopathology, use of this cutting score would yield an unacceptably high false-positive rate (i.e., the misclassification of genuine patients as malingerers). A cutting score much higher than +9 would be needed on the F-K index to decrease the number of false positives; available studies are not clear whether a more appropriate cutting score can be identified for this index, partially because the F scale also is elevated by actual psychopathology.

Obvious and Subtle Items

Comparison of subtle versus obvious items has shown some promise in the detection of malingering and defensiveness. In the early research, Wiener and Harmon (Wiener, 1948) performed a rational inspection of MMPI items, identifying obvious items (i.e., easy to detect as indicating emotional disturbance) and subtle items (i.e., difficult to detect as reflecting emotional disturbance). Although Wiener and Harmon had intended to develop subtle and obvious subscales for each clinical scale, they succeeded for only five scales: scales 2 (D), 3 (Hy), 4 (Pd), 6 (Pa), and 9 (Ma). The other clinical scales were composed primarily of obvious items, so it was not possible to develop subtle and obvious subscales. These clinical scales also include the scales that require the most K-correction (scales 1 [Hs], 7 [Pt], and 8 [Sc]).

The available research on the Wiener and Harmon subtle and obvious subscales does not suggest explicit criteria for defining malingering or defensiveness. Clinicians are probably safe to assume that a person who achieves T scores greater than 80 on all five obvious subscales and T scores near 40 on all five subtle subscales is trying to malinger. The converse relationship between scores on the obvious and subtle subscales should arouse the suspicion of defensiveness. If we assume that malingering and defensiveness are global response styles, one method for creating a criterion to assess malingering and defensiveness would be the subtraction of T scores for all obvious from all subtle subscales. This subtraction yields a single score, O-S. Raw scores on the obvious and subtle scales must be converted to T scores before computing this difference score because they do not have the same number of items. In interpreting O-S, an extreme difference score of +250 strongly suggests malingering. In contrast, a difference score of –100 strongly suggests defensiveness.

Three issues must be addressed before the use of this difference score to assess accuracy of item endorsement is explored. First, other obvious and subtle scales could be used to assess accuracy of item endorsement (Greene, 2000, pp. 128–132). The Wiener and Harmon (Wiener, 1948) obvious and subtle subscales were selected because of their long history of research, but item overlap and high correlations suggest that other versions of obvious and subtle scales could work equally well (Dubinsky, Gamble, & Rogers, 1985). Second, the usefulness of large differences on the individual clinical scales has not been explored. For example, it is not clear whether a difference of +30 points on Scale 2 (D) has the same meaning as +30 points on Scale 9 (Ma). Third, obvious and subtle subscales should not be used to predict specific clinical criteria because research has established that obvious scales are better than subtle scales for these predictions (Jackson, 1971). As noted, the O-S index is used solely to assess accuracy of item endorsement.

A renewed debate has emerged during the past decade over the usefulness of obvious and subtle scales as a measure of malingering and defensiveness. Researchers have advocated both the pros (Brems & Johnson, 1991; Dush, Simons, Platt, Nation, & Ayres, 1994; Greene, 1997) and cons (Schretlen, 1990; Timbrook, Graham, Keiller, & Watts, 1993; Weed, Ben-Porath, & Butcher, 1990). Timbrook and colleagues (1993) concluded that the total T score difference between the obvious and subtle subscales provided no additional information beyond that provided by the traditional validity scales.

The correlations between the total T score difference on the obvious and subtle subscales and the other measures of malingering reported in Table 10.6 would suggest that all of these measures of malingering are essentially interchangeable. What remains to be established is whether any particular scale or index works more effectively in a given setting or with a specific population. The work of Dush and colleagues (1994) might suggest, however, that the total T score difference on the obvious and subtle subscales could provide additional information in pain patients when the keyed direction ("true") of the obvious items is opposite from the deviant response ("false") for most somatic items on the MMPI-2.

The optimal cutting scores on the O-S index have been extremely variable. The range of cutting scores include +106 (Rogers, Bagby, & Chakraborty, 1993), +160 (Sivec et al., 1994), +169 (Bagby, Rogers, & Buis, 1994), +179 (Bagby, Rogers, Buis, & Kalemba, 1994), and +200 (Fox, Gerson, & Lees-Haley, 1995).

Tables 10.7 and 10.8 present the distribution of the total T score difference between the Wiener and Harmon (Wiener, 1948) obvious and subtle subscales for normal individuals and patients with mental disorders, respectively. The 50th percentile for the O-S index is –6 in normal samples and +17 in patient samples. Patients score higher than nonclinical samples because their acknowledged psychopathology increases their scores on the obvious subscales. Based on the data presented in Tables 10.7 and 10.8, the clinician can decide what percentage of persons should be labeled as malingering. Clearly, O-S indexes in the +250 to +300 range are strongly suggestive of malingering. However, the clinician must decide the lower limit for classifying a person's responses as indicative of malingering. For example, if the O-S index was set at +140 or higher for malingering, 15% of the patients would be so classified. The optimal cutting scores on this index, reported previously, that ranged from +106 to +200 suggest that a lower cutting score would be appropriate in most clinical settings.

The cut score for O-S index for malingering must be used as a threshold rather than as a clinical decision. Clinicians always must verify that the person is malingering rather than actually experiencing severe psychopathology. When the O-S index exceeds +250 to +300, an interview and other collateral sources should easily confirm whether the person is malingering or experiencing pervasive and severe psychopathology. Occasionally in an inpatient setting, difference scores above 200 will be seen in a nonmalingering person. In an outpatient setting, it is extremely unlikely for difference scores in this range to reflect actual psychopathology.

MALINGERING-ONLY SCALES

Gough Dissimulation Scale (Ds)

The Gough (1954) Dissimulation (Ds) scale consists of 74 items that significantly differentiated neurotic persons from college students and professional psychologists instructed to feign neuroses on the MMPI. The items pertain not to neuroticism but to the prevailing stereotypes about neuroticism, that is, it is based on *erroneous stereotypes*. The psychologists and students scored three to four times higher than neurotic persons on the Ds scale and were easily identified.

Research has been somewhat limited because the Ds is not a standard scale that is scored routinely. However, Berry, Baer, and Harris (1991) in their meta-analysis of the MMPI, found that Ds had one of the largest effect sizes, and Rogers, Sewell, and colleagues (2003) found that the Ds scale had the most consistent cutting score (>35 items endorsed) across all seven studies that used the scale. Rogers, Sewell, and colleagues concluded that "the Ds scale appears to be a premier specialized validity scale with its sophisticated strategy and minimal risk of false positives" (p. 173).

Tables 10.7 and 10.8 summarize the range of scores that are seen on Ds for normal individuals and patients with mental disorders, respectively. Raw scores greater than 26 occur in 1% of the normal individuals and 10% of the psychiatric patients. If a raw score of 38 or higher on the Ds scale were used to indicate malingering, 1% of the patients would be classified as endorsing the items inaccurately, whereas none of the normal adults would be so classified.

Clinical Applications of the MMPI-2

Five different scales/indexes are described to assess malingering. The reader will need to select the scale or index that is most appropriate for specific populations and treatment settings. When a global response style of malingering is present, clinicians will not find it necessary to use several scales or indexes simultaneously, because they are correlated highly and likely redundant (see Table 10.6). However, when a specific form of psychopathology is being simulated, a scale such as Ds may be more appropriate (Peterson & Viglione, 1991).

A point worthy of emphasis is that a malingered profile cannot be interpreted as a valid profile. The person's specific reasons for malingering should be ascertained by a clinical interview, and the profile can be described as reflecting such a process. However, neither the MMPI-2 codetype (the highest clinical scale or the high-point pair) nor the individual scales can be interpreted. Importantly, once an MMPI-2 is characterized as malingered, the interpretive process stops. Although the MMPI-2 could be readministered, this procedure may not result in a valid profile. Once a person is motivated, for whatever reason, to malinger, he or she may have difficulty responding to the items accurately in subsequent administrations. Researchers have not established whether malingering is likely to persist across treatment settings for a particular person, although Audubon and Kirwin (1982) found at least some situational influences on response style.

Although malingering profiles cannot be interpreted, several empirical correlates of such profiles have been identified in a manner similar to Marks, Seeman, and Haller's (1974) description of a K+ profile. Both Greene (1988) and Hale, Zimostrad, Duckworth, and Nicholas (1986) found that persons who malingered were very likely to terminate treatment within the first few sessions; frequently they did not return after the initial session. The finding that these persons terminate treatment quickly is almost exactly the opposite of what might be anticipated, because these persons were historically described as "pleading for help" and would be expected to remain in treatment longer than most persons. Additional research is needed to determine whether other empirical correlates of malingering can be validated.

DEFENSIVENESS

The use of infrequency scales, critical items, the F-K index, and the Wiener and Harmon (Wiener, 1948) obvious and subtle subscales to assess malingering was described earlier. Low scores on these same scales and indexes can be used to assess defensiveness. The only information that is covered in this section is the research on optimal cutting scores and the data presented in Tables 10.7 and 10.8.

Baer, Wetter, and Berry (1992) reported the results of a meta-analysis of MMPI measures of defensiveness. The largest effect sizes were found for two scales not scored routinely on the MMPI: Wiggins's (1959) Social Desirability scale (Sd), the Wiener (1948) obvious subscales, and the Positive Malingering (Mp; Cofer, Chance, & Judson, 1949) scale. The effect sizes for these three scales averaged nearly 1.50; in contrast, effect sizes for the L and K scales averaged 1.00, whereas the effect size for F-K averaged only .71.

Infrequency Scales

Little research on infrequency scales addresses their effectiveness in isolation as measures of defensiveness, other than simply to note that low scores will be encountered. Typically, the F scale is considered in conjunction with the K scale (i.e., the F-K index) to assess defensiveness. Because the typical normal individual (50th percentile) endorses three F scale items (Table 10.7), clinicians could assume that patients who endorse three or fewer items are being defensive. Using this criterion, more than 25% of psychiatric patients would be classified as being defensive (Table 10.8).

Critical Items

The total number of the Koss and Butcher (1973) or Lachar and Wrobel (1979) critical items that are endorsed can be used as another index of defensiveness. A person who is trying to be defensive would be expected to endorse few of these items because their item content is obvious (face valid) and unambiguously reflective of psychopathology. Tables 10.7 and 10.8 summarize the total number of critical items that were endorsed by normal individuals and patients with mental disorders, respectively. Using a typical normal individual (50th percentile) who endorses 10 of the Koss and Butcher critical items and 15 of the Lachar and Wrobel critical items as a criterion, more than 25% of the psychiatric patients endorsed fewer total critical items than the normal individuals. This percentage for defensiveness is similar to what is found with other scales and indexes.

F-K Index: Gough Dissimulation Index

Gough's (1950) initial reservations about the efficiency of the F-K index in detecting defensiveness have been corroborated by numerous investigators. Most MMPI-2 studies have found extensive overlap in the distributions of the F-K index under honest and defensive conditions. Consequently, clinicians have problems in establishing a consistent cutting score

TABLE 10.7. Percentiles for Measures of Malingering and Defensiveness in Normal Data

%tile	T score	F	Fp	KB-Sum	LW-Sum	F-K	O-S	Ds	True %
99	79	14	5	38	49	6	161	26	57
98	75	12	4	36	46	4	138	24	54
95	68	10	3	30	37	0	105	20	50
90	63	8		23	31	−3	78	17	47
85		7	2	21	27	−5	60	16	45
80	58	6		18	25	−6	44	14	43
75		5	1	16	23	−8	34	13	42
50	49	3	0	10	15	−12	−6	9	37
25		2		5	10	−16	−41	6	33
20	42	1		4	8	−17	−49	5	32
15		0		3	7	−18	−57	4	31
10	38			2	6	−20	−66	4	30
5	36			1	4	−21	−80	3	28
2	33			0	3	−23	−93	2	27
1	32				2	−24	−99	1	25

Note. Data from Butcher et al. (1989). High scores are suggestive of malingering, whereas low scores are suggestive of defensiveness. F, Infrequency; Fp, Infrequency psychopathology (Arbisi & Ben-Porath, 1995); KB-Sum, total number of Koss and Butcher (1973) critical items endorsed; LW-Sum, total number of Lachar and Wrobel (1979) critical items endorsed; F-K, Gough Dissimulation index (1950); O-S, total T score difference between the obvious and subtle subscales (Wiener, 1948); Ds, Gough Dissimulation scale (Gough, 1954); True %, percentage of scale items endorsed "True."

TABLE 10.8. Percentiles for Measures of Malingering and Defensiveness in Patients with Mental Disorders

%tile	T score	F	Fp	KB-Sum	LW-Sum	F-K	O-S	Ds	True %
99	79	29	9	61	79	21	266	38	63
98	75	25	7	57	74	17	242	35	60
95	68	19	5	50	65	10	203	31	55
90	63	15	4	44	56	5	167	26	50
85		12	3	39	51	2	140	23	48
80	58	10		35	46	−1	117	20	45
75		9	2	32	41	−3	97	18	43
50	49	5	1	16	24	−11	17	11	36
25		2	0	6	11	−17	−47	6	31
20	42			5	9	−19	−58	5	30
15		1		3	8	−20	−70	4	29
10	38			2	6	−21	−82	3	28
5	36			1	4	−23	−97	2	25
2	33	0		0	2	−24	−110	1	23
1	32				1	−25	−117	0	22

Note. Data from Caldwell (2003). High scores are suggestive of malingering, whereas low scores are suggestive of defensiveness. F, Infrequency; Fp, Infrequency psychopathology (Arbisi & Ben-Porath, 1995); KB-Sum, total number of Koss and Butcher (1973) critical items endorsed; LW-Sum, total number of Lachar and Wrobel (1979) critical items endorsed; F-K, Gough Dissimulation index (1950); O-S, total T score difference between the obvious and subtle subscales (Wiener, 1948); Ds, Gough Dissimulation scale (Gough, 1954); True %, percentage of scale items endorsed "True."

on the F-K index that reliably identifies defensive profiles. The optimal cutting scores on the F-K index ranged from −11 (Bagby, Rogers, Buis, & Kalemba, 1994), −12 (Baer et al., 1995), −13 (Austin, 1992), to −15 (Bagby, Rogers, & Buis, 1994).

One problem with the F-K index in identifying defensiveness is that anyone who is (1) acknowledging the capability to handle his or her own problems, (2) well adjusted (high raw score on K), and (3) not experiencing stress or conflict (low raw score on F) will most likely be defined as being defensive rather than honestly responding by this index. Thus normal persons often will be inappropriately classified as being defensive on the MMPI-2 F-K index.

The F-K index is a questionable measure of defensiveness. If scores of < −12 are used (50th percentile in normal individuals; see Table 10.7), then nearly 50% of patients would be classified as defensive (see Table 10.8). Because normal individuals routinely achieve negative scores on this index (see Table 10.7), the F-K

index will not distinguish between normal individuals scoring in this range and defensive patients.

Obvious and Subtle Scales

Low scores, usually negative scores, on the Wiener and Harmon O-S index can be used as a measure of defensiveness. Few studies have reported optimal cutting scores for this measure; the results have been highly variable, ranging from +17 (Bagby, Rogers, Buis, & Kalemba, 1994) and −24 (Bagby, Rogers, & Buis, 1994), to −79 (Austin, 1992).

Because normal individuals typically score −6 on the O-S index (see Table 10.8), a clinician could decide that any person in a treatment setting who scores less than −6 is being defensive. By this criterion, more than 25% of the patients would be classified as being defensive. With the exception of F-K, the O-S index classifies a similar percentage of patients as being defensive.

DEFENSIVENESS-ONLY SCALES

Five scales have been developed to assess defensiveness: Lie (L); Correction (K); Positive Malingering (Mp); Superlative (S; Butcher & Han, 1995); and Wiggins's Social Desirability (Sd; 1959) scale. The scorable responses for most items on these scales are "false"; in fact, L, K, and S virtually are totally false-endorsement scales. The intercorrelations among these measures are much more variable (see Table 10.9) than was seen in the measures of malingering (see Table 10.6).

Lie (L) Scale

The Lie (L) scale consists of 15 items selected to identify persons who are deliberately trying to be defensive. Although denial and defensiveness are characteristic of most high scorers on the L scale (Fowler et al., 2000; Friedman et al., 2001; Graham, 2006; Greene, 2000, Nichols, 2001), persons with any psychological sophistication will not be detected. Because low scores on the L scale can occur with defensive individuals, the usefulness of the L scale for detecting defensiveness is constrained. The distributions for the L scale in normal individuals (Table 10.10) and patients with mental disorders (Table 10.11) are very similar, which confirms its limitations as a measure of defensiveness.

Correction (K) Scale

The Correction (K) scale is a traditional measure of defensiveness on the MMPI-2, with high scores (T scores > 59) in patients with mental disorders indicating defensiveness and the unwillingness to acknowledge any type of psychological distress. These persons typically lack insight into their own functioning, which makes prognosis for any type of psychological intervention very poor. The actual behaviors and symptoms about which the person is being defensive probably will not be discernible from the clinical scales because they are likely to be within the normal range.

The distributions for the K scale in normal individuals (Table 10.10) and patients with mental disorders (Table 10.11) also are very strikingly similar despite the different qualities tapped by this scale in normal individuals and patients (Fowler et al., 2000; Friedman et al., 2001; Graham, 2006; Greene, 2000; Nichols, 2001).

Positive Malingering (Mp) Scale

The Positive Malingering scale (Mp) was developed to identify defensiveness. Cofer and colleagues (1949) asked groups of college students to endorse the MMPI items the way an emotionally disturbed person might (malingering) or so as to make the best possible impression (defensiveness). They then identified 34 items that were insensitive to malingering and yet susceptible to defensiveness ("positive malingering"). They found that a cutting score of > 20 correctly identified 96% of the honest and 86% of the defensive MMPIs. They also noted that scores on the Mp scale tended to be correlated positively with scores on the Wiener (1948) subtle scales.

TABLE 10.9. Intercorrelations Among Scales Measuring Defensiveness for Clinical (Above the Diagonal) and Normative (Below the Diagonal) Data

	L	K	S	ODecp	Sd	False %
L		.43	.47	.59	.46	.45
K	.32		.88	.48	.23	.83
S	.40	.82		.55	.29	.85
ODecp	.55	.32	.40		.85	.37
Sd	.46	.03	.11	.80		.09
False %	.34	.81	.83	.19	−.14	

Note. L, Lie; K, Correction; S, Superlative (Butcher & Han, 1995); ODecp, Other Deception (Nichols & Greene, 1991); Sd, Social Desirability (Wiggins, 1959); False %, percentage of items endorsed "False."

TABLE 10.10. Percentiles for Measures of Defensiveness in Normal Individuals

%tile	T score	L	K	ODecp	S	Sd	False %
99	79	10	25	23	44	21	73
98	75	9	24	21	42	20	72
95	68	7	22	19	39	17	70
90	63	6	21	17	36	16	68
85		5	20	16	34	15	67
80	58	5	19	15	32	15	66
75		4	18	14	31	14	65
50	49	3	15	11	25	12	61
25		2	11	9	19	9	56
20	42	1	11	8	17	9	55
15		1	10	7	16	8	53
10	38	1	9	6	13	8	51
5	36	0	7	5	11	7	48
2	33	0	5	4	8	6	43
1	32	0	4	3	7	5	41

Note. Data from Butcher et al. (1989). High scores are indicative of defensiveness. L, Lie; K, Correction; ODecp, Other Deception (Nichols & Greene, 1991); S, Superlative (Butcher & Han, 1995); Sd, Social Desirability (Wiggins, 1959); False %, percentage of all 567 items endorsed "False."

TABLE 10.11. Percentiles for Measures of Defensiveness in Patients with Mental Disorders

%tile	T score	L	K	ODecp	S	Sd	False %
99	79	11	26	25	47	22	76
98	75	10	25	24	46	21	74
95	68	9	24	22	44	19	72
90	63	8	23	20	41	18	71
85		7	22	18	39	17	69
80	58		21	17	37	16	68
75		6	20	16	35	15	67
50	49	4	16	13	27	12	62
25		3	12	9	19	10	54
20	42	2	11	8	17	9	52
15			9	7	15	8	50
10	38	1	8	6	12	7	47
5	36		7	5	10	6	43
2	33	0	5	4	7	5	38
1	32		4	3	6	4	35

Note. Data from Caldwell (2003). High scores are indicative of defensiveness. L, Lie; K, Correction; ODecp, Other Deception (Nichols & Greene, 1991); S, Superlative (Butcher & Han, 1995); Sd, Social Desirability (Wiggins, 1959); False %, percentage of all 567 items endorsed "False."

Baer and colleagues (1992) found in their meta-analysis that Mp had one of the largest effect sizes between defensive and honest conditions. The optimal cutting score for Mp ranged from +9 (Bagby, Rogers, Buis, & Kalemba, 1994) to +13 (Baer et al., 1995) and +14 (Bagby, Rogers, & Buis, 1994). Nichols and Greene (1991) have updated the Mp scale for the MMPI-2 and renamed the scale Other Deception (ODecp).

Tables 10.10 and 10.11 summarize the range of scores that were found on the ODecp scale in normal individuals and patients, respectively. Raw scores of 19 or higher were found in about 5% of the normal individuals and 10% of the patients.

Superlative (S) Scale

Butcher and Han (1995) developed the Superlative (S) scale to assess persons who present themselves as outstanding individuals; these idealized presentations are encountered in personnel settings, especially with high-status positions. As noted, most items on the S scale are scored as "false," with very high correlations (.82 to .88) with the K scale (see Table 10.9). As expected, normal individuals (Table 10.10) achieve higher scores on the S scale than patients with mental disorders (Table 10.11), but the distributions become fairly similar at marked elevations (raw scores > 35).

Wiggins's Social Desirability (Sd) Scale

Wiggins (1959) developed his Social Desirability scale (Sd) to discriminate MMPIs taken under a socially desirable condition from those taken under standard instructions. As noted earlier, Sd has one of the largest effect sizes in identifying students directed to be defensive (Baer et al., 1992). The distribution of scores of the normal individuals (Table 10.10) and patients with mental disorders (Table 10.11) are very similar throughout the entire range.

Clinical Applications of the MMPI-2

The selection of scales and indexes for defensiveness is more difficult than for malingering because they appear to be measure different aspects of defensiveness, as indicated by their relatively low intercorrelations (see Table 10.9). Research is needed that examines which of these scales or indexes of defensiveness is most

appropriate in a particular clinical setting by validating these scales and indexes with independent measures of defensiveness.

When extreme defensiveness is observed, the standard profile is no longer interpretable because it reflects an invalid response set. In such cases, a clinician will have little reason to try to interpret such a profile because extreme defensiveness usually results in no clinical elevations, even at marginal levels (e.g., T scores of 60). The clinician should describe the person's style of defensiveness, determine the potential causes for this response set, and assess its implications for treatment and interventions.

Once defensiveness is identified in a clinical setting, the empirical correlates of such a response set can be studied. Persons who are defensive are likely to see their problems as less troubling to themselves and hence be less motivated to change. Their problems also may be more chronic in nature, and consequently they may be more difficult to treat if they remain in treatment. Duckworth and Barley (1988) have provided a valuable summary of the correlates of persons who produce such MMPI profiles.

CONCLUSION

Tables 10.12 and 10.13 summarize the scales and indexes that can be used to assess item omissions, consistency of item endorsement, and accuracy of item endorsement on the MMPI-2. They provide possible cutting scores that might be used with normal individuals and individuals in a clinical setting, respectively. Clinicians should proceed through each step in order: (1) item omissions should be checked before examining consistency of item endorsement and (2) consistency of item endorsement should be checked before considering accuracy of item endorsement. Clinicians need to determine which scale or index of malingering and defensiveness is the most appropriate for their particular settings and whether raising or lowering the cutting scores would facilitate the identification of malingering or defensiveness. The establishment of the base rates with which malingering and defensiveness are encountered in a specific clinical setting and the consequences of misidentifying (false positives) or not identifying (false negatives) malingering or defensiveness are important in deciding what cutting scores should be used or modified. Clinicians also need to establish the empirical

TABLE 10.12. Cutting Scores for Assessing MMPI-2 Validity in Normal Individuals

I. Item omissions

	Percentile										
	1	2	5	10	25	50	75	90	95	98	99
?							0	2	5	10	15

II. Consistency of item endorsement

	Percentile										
	Consistent									Inconsistent	
	1	2	5	10	25	50	75	90	95	98	99
VRIN		0	1		3	4	6	8	9	11	12
TRIN	5	6		7	8		9	10	11	12	13
|F-Fb|			0	1	2	3	5	6	8	9

III. Accuracy of item endorsement

	Percentile										
	Defensiveness									Malingering	
	1	2	5	10	25	50	75	90	95	98	99
F				0	1	3	5	8	10	12	14
Fb				0	1	2	5	7	9	11
Fp				0	1	2	3	4	5
IR					0		1		2	3	4
FBS	4	5	6	7	10	12	15	18	20	22	24
KB-Sum		0	1	2	5	10	16	23	30	36	38
LW-Sum	2	3	4	6	10	15	23	31	37	46	49
F-K	−24	−23	−21	−20	−16	−12	−8	−3	0	4	6
O-S	−99	−93	−80	−66	−41	−6	34	78	105	138	161
Ds	1	2	3	4	6	9	13	17	20	24	26
True %	25	27	28	30	33	37	42	47	50	54	57
L	10	9	7	6	4	3	2	1	0		
K	25	24	22	21	18	15	11	9	7	5	4
ODecp	23	21	19	17	14	11	8	6	5	4	3
S	44	42	39	36	31	25	19	13	11	8	7
Sd	21	20	18	17	14	12	9	8	7	6	5
False %	73	72	70	68	65	61	56	51	48	43	41

Note. Data from Butcher et al. (1989). ?, Cannot Say; VRIN, Variable Response Inconsistency; TRIN, True Response Inconsistency; \|F-Fb\|, absolute value of F (raw) – Fb (raw); F, Infrequency; Fb, Back Infrequency; Fp, Infrequency Psychopathology; FBS, Fake Bad Scale; IR, Inconsistent Response; KB-Sum, Total number of Koss and Butcher (1973) critical items endorsed; LW-Sum, Total number of Lachar and Wrobel (1979) critical items endorsed; F-K, Gough (1950) Dissimulation index; O-S, Total T score difference on the Wiener and Harmon obvious and subtle subscales; Ds, Gough (1954) Dissimulation scale; True %, percentage of items endorsed "True;" L, Lie; K, Correction; ODecp, Other Deception (Nichols & Greene, 1991); S, Superlative (Butcher & Han, 1995); Sd, Wiggins (1959) Social Desirability; False %, percentage of items endorsed "False." Scores on L, K, ODecp, S, Sd, and False % are inverted because higher scores indicate defensiveness.

TABLE 10.13. Cutting Scores for Assessing MMPI-2 Validity in Clinical Settings

I. Item omissions

	Percentile										
	1	2	5	10	25	50	75	90	95	98	99
?						0	1	4	9	22	29

II. Consistency of item endorsement

	Percentile										
	Consistent										Inconsistent
	1	2	5	10	25	50	75	90	95	98	99
VRIN		0		1	3	5	7	9	10	12	14
TRIN	5		6	7	8	9		10	11	12	13
|F-Fb|				0	1	2	4	6	8	10	12

III. Accuracy of item endorsement

	Percentile										
	Defensiveness										Malingering
	1	2	5	10	25	50	75	90	95	98	99
F			0	1	2	5	9	15	19	25	29
Fb					0	1	5	12	17	21	24
Fp					0	1	2	4	5	7	9
IR					0	1	2	4	5		6
FBS	6	7	8	10	12	16	23	28	31	34	35
KB-Sum		0	1	2	6	16	32	44	30	57	61
LW-Sum	1	2	4	6	11	24	41	56	65	74	79
F-K	−25	−24	−23	−21	−16	−11	−3	5	10	17	21
O-S	−117	−110	−97	−82	−47	16	97	167	203	242	266
Ds		1	2	3	6	11	18	26	30	35	38
True %	22	23	25	27	31	36	43	51	55	60	63
L	11	10	9	8	6	4	3	2	1	0	
K	27	26	24	23	20	16	12	8	7	5	4
ODecp	25	24	22	20	16	13	9	6	5	4	3
S	47	46	44	41	35	27	19	13	10	7	6
Sd	22	21	19	18	15	12	10	8	6	5	4
False %	76	74	72	71	67	62	54	47	43	38	35

Note. Data from Caldwell (2003). ?, Cannot Say; VRIN, Variable Response Inconsistency; TRIN, True Response Inconsistency; |F-Fb|, absolute value of F (raw) − Fb (raw); F, Infrequency; Fb, Back Infrequency; Fp, Infrequency Psychopathology; FBS, Fake Bad Scale; IR, Inconsistent Response; KB-Sum, Total number of Koss and Butcher (1973) critical items endorsed; LW-Sum, Total number of Lachar and Wrobel (1979) critical items endorsed; F-K, Gough (1950) Dissimulation Index; O-S, Total T score difference on the Wiener and Harmon obvious and subtle subscales; Ds, Gough (1954) Dissimulation scale; True %, percentage of items endorsed "True;" L, Lie; K, Correction; ODecp, Other Deception (Nichols & Greene, 1991); S, Superlative (Butcher & Han, 1995); Sd, Wiggins (1959) Social Desirability; False %, percentage of items endorsed "False." Scores on L, K, ODecp, S, Sd, and False % are inverted because higher scores indicate defensiveness.

correlates of malingering and defensiveness so that better assessments, treatments, and interventions can be made when these response sets are encountered in clinical settings. Finally, clinicians should understand that, although this chapter has emphasized the MMPI-2, the same rationale for assessing consistency and accuracy of item endorsement and the need for extensive validation is applicable to all multiscale inventories.

NOTES

1. The reader who needs more information on the effects of base rates on positive and negative predictive power should consult Baldesserini, Finkelstein, and Arona (1983).
2. Research in this area is very prolific; in the interest of conserving space, there has been no attempt to be exhaustive in citing references. Several citations have been provided for all major issues so that the interested reader will have easy access to the literature. In addition, emphasis has been placed on MMPI-2 research, even though most of these issues arose with the MMPI.
3. Although clinicians would find it comforting if more similarity existed in optimal cutting scores, given the heterogeneity of patient samples, settings, and the base rates with which malingering and defensiveness occur, there is little reason to expect a high degree of convergence. Regardless of the differences in optimal cut scores, the discrimination between malingering and actual psychopathology should be easier as higher cut scores are utilized, because the clinician will have access to the person's background and reasons for being evaluated.
4. For a thorough discussion of critical items, the interested reader should see Graham (2006) or Greene (2000).

11

Response Styles on Multiscale Inventories

MARTIN SELLBOM, PhD
R. MICHAEL BAGBY, PhD

Accurate assessment of personality and psychopathology on multiscale inventories depends on the respondent's ability and motivation to provide accurate responses. For various reasons, individuals undergoing clinical assessments may over- or underreport their psychological problems. Common examples of overreporting include individuals who feign psychopathology to receive financial compensation or avoid criminal prosecution. Conversely, others may cover up psychological difficulties in preemployment evaluations or child custody determinations. As the stakes involved in a psychological evaluation increase, so does the likelihood that the individual will distort his or her responses (Rogers, 1997b).

Early critics (see Allport, 1937; Ellis, 1946, 1953) of self-report measures argued that their susceptibility to intentional and unintentional response distortion constituted a major weakness. However, all clinical methods, including interviews, are susceptible to this problem, regardless of their psychometric validity (Ben-Porath, 2003). An advantage of multiscale inventories, compared with most other methods, is their *potential* for directly evaluating response styles. This chapter addresses four commonly researched multiscale inventories and their utility in detecting response distortion.

TYPES OF INVALID RESPONSE STYLES

We begin by discussing various types of response distortion or protocol invalidity.[1] Ben-Porath (2003) recommended an organization of response styles directly linked to multiscale inventories. This model serves as a foundation for our review of the various inventories. These types of invalid response styles fall into two broad domains, based on the applicability of content.

Non-Content-Based Invalid Responding

This response style refers to the *inability* or unwillingness of test takers to comprehend or otherwise process the test questions; their responses are independent of the actual content (Ben-Porath, 2003). Because test takers are not responding to the actual items, it is impossible to ascertain their true responses. Three specific styles are observed:

1. *Nonresponding.* Responses cannot be scored (e.g., no response or multiple responses).
2. *Random responding.* Unsystematic response patterns are not based on the item content. This may occur unintentionally because of

reading difficulties, language problems, or cognitive processing.

3. *Fixed responding.* Systematic response patterns are not based on item content. Examples include acquiescent (or yea-saying) or counteracquiescent (or nay-saying) response styles.

Content-Based Invalid Responding

According to Ben-Porath (2003), this invalid response style occurs when the test taker misrepresents his or her answers to test items, resulting in a distorted picture of the constructs being measured. Ben-Porath describes these response styles as underreporting (e.g., minimizing psychological difficulties) and overreporting (e.g., exaggerating psychological difficulties). Although we acknowledge that these terms may provide neutral descriptions, standardization of terminology is essential. Consistent with all chapters in this book, we use the terms *malingering* and *defensiveness* to describe response styles. In using these terms, our focus is on intentional distortions. The cited research, unless otherwise noted, is based on simulation designs and known-group comparisons that focus solely on intentional distortions.

OVERVIEW

In this chapter, we examine the literature concerning the assessment of invalid response styles on four widely used and well-researched multiscale inventories: Millon Clinical Multiaxial Inventory (MCMI; Millon, 1983), Personality Assessment Inventory (PAI; Morey, 1991), revised NEO Personality Inventory (NEO-PI-R; Costa & McCrae, 1992a), and Trauma Symptom Inventory (TSI; Briere, 1995). The basic requirement for inclusion in this chapter was that each inventory have validity scales that have been examined empirically in at least four studies, with at least two studies reporting on the measure's classification accuracy. These minimal criteria were employed to ensure that at least some preliminary conclusions could be generated on the usefulness of each measure to detect specific response styles. We acknowledge that other well-established inventories have validity scales, such as the Schedule for Nonadaptive and Adaptive Personality (SNAP; Clark, 1993),

Multidimensional Personality Questionnaire (MPQ; Tellegen, in press), Basic Personality Inventory (BPI; Jackson, 1989), and Sixteen Personality Factors Inventory (16PF; Cattell, Eber, & Tatsuoka, 1970). However, their validity scales have not been studied widely enough to generate broad conclusions.

We begin the discussion of each multiscale inventory with three main sections. The first section introduces each measure and its validity scales. It also considers the detection strategies for malingering (i.e., overreporting) or defensiveness (i.e., underreporting) based on the categorizations in Chapter 2 in this volume. For malingering, detection strategies rely on *unlikely symptom presentations* (i.e., rare symptoms, improbable symptoms, rare symptom combinations, and unlikely patterns of psychopathology) and *plausible presentations* (i.e., symptom severity, indiscriminant symptom endorsement, obvious symptoms, and erroneous stereotypes). For defensiveness, detection strategies include denial of nonvirtuous attitudes and behavior, blended (affirmation of virtuous and denial of nonvirtuous behavior), denial of patient characteristics, and social desirability.

The second section evaluates specific response styles by examining three categories of research: group differences, correlational studies, and classification accuracy. As outlined in Chapter 2 in this volume, we focus on the following:

- *Group differences.* For each response style, effect sizes (Cohen's *d*) are reported to assess the magnitude of the difference as it applies to simulation designs and known-group comparisons (see Rogers, Chapter 1, this volume). Group differences based on differential prevalence designs (see Chapter 1) make tenuous assumptions about group membership; these studies are avoided when sufficient research is available using sound research designs (see Rogers, Chapter 24, this volume). When available, the effects of coaching are also considered.

- *Correlational studies.* Relationships between specific measures of response distortion are considered for each response style.

- *Classification accuracy.* For each response style, classification accuracy is considered. As defined in Chapter 2 in this volume, five major utility estimates are used: positive predictive power (PPP), negative predictive power (NPP), sensitivity (SN), specificity (SP), and overall correct classification (OCC). As a benchmark, the threshold of .80 is deemed acceptable for PPP and NPP (Bagby, Rogers, & Buis, 1994).

MILLON CLINICAL MULTIAXIAL INVENTORY

The Millon Clinical Multiaxial Inventory (MCMI; Millon, 1983) and its revisions, MCMI-II (Millon, 1987) and MCMI-III (Millon, 1994; Millon, Davis, & Millon, 1997), is one of the most frequently used multiscale inventories in clinical (Camara, Nathan, & Puente, 2000) and forensic (Archer, Buffington-Vollum, Stredney, & Handel, 2006) practice. The most recent version, the MCMI-III, was developed to measure personality pathology consistent with Millon's typology (Craig, 1999), in addition to assessing features of DSM-IV Axis I mental disorders. MCMI-III items are intended to discriminate general clinical groups from specific diagnostic groups.

The original MCMI contained two modifying indices related to response styles: the Validity Index and the Weight Factor Composite Score. When the MCMI-II (Millon, 1987) was developed, the Weight Factor Composite Score was revised and renamed the Disclosure Scale, and two additional modifying indices were added, the Desirability Scale and the Debasement Scale. The MCMI-III (Millon, 1994; Millon et al., 1997) retained these four indices but modified their composition. The MCMI-III validity scales are summarized in Table 11.1 and are described in the next paragraphs:

• *Validity Index (V).* The current version V scale adheres to the improbable symptoms detection strategy and consists of only three (four for the MCMI and MCMI-II) highly unlikely statements (e.g., "I have not seen a car in ten years") designed to assess random responding or confusion (Craig, 1999). Responding "true" to two or more statements invalidates the test protocol, whereas one statement indicates a protocol of questionable validity.

• *Disclosure Scale (X).* The X scale represents the degree of deviation from midrange with respect to an adjusted composite raw score derived from the 10 Clinical Personality Pattern Scales (i.e., scales 1–8). This scale represents a revision of the Weight Factor Composite Score originally developed for use with the MCMI. Low scores represent secretiveness; high scores constitute unlikely levels of self-disclosure.

• *Desirability Scale (Y).* The Y scale uses the denial of nonvirtuous attitudes and behavior detection strategy. The Y scale was constructed

TABLE 11.1. Scales for the Assessment of Response Styles and Their Detection Strategies

Measure	Scale	Response style	Detection strategy
MCMI-II and -III	V	Inconsistent	Improbable symptoms
	X	High: questionable	Indiscriminant symptom endorsement
	X	Low: secretive	Denial of patient characteristics
	Y	Defensive	Denial of nonvirtuous attitudes
	Z	Feigned	Derivative rare symptoms
PAI	INF	Random	Improbable symptoms
	INC	Inconsistent	Inconsistency
	PIM	Defensive	Denial of nonvirtuous attitudes
	DEF	Defensive	Blended
	CDF	Defensive	N/A
	NIM	Feigned	Rare symptoms
	MAL	Feigned	Unlikely patterns of psychopathology
	RDF	Feigned	Unlikely patterns of psychopathology
NEO-PI-R	INC	Inconsistent	Inconsistency
	PPM	Social desirability	Blended
	NPM	Negative impression	Rare symptoms and denial of common virtues
	NPM–PPM	High: Feigned	Rare symptoms and denial of common virtues
	NPM–PPM	Low: defensive	Blended
TSI	ATR	Feigned	Rare symptoms

Note. MCMI, Millon Clinical Multiaxial Inventory; PAI, Personality Assessment Inventory; NEO-PI-R, Revised NEO Personality Inventory; TSI, Trauma Symptom Inventory.

by asking graduate students to exaggerate positive traits and deny faults (Millon, 1987). Modified for MCMI-III, the Y scale is a 21-item scale designed to detect defensive response styles, with high scores reflecting overreporting of virtues and the denial of psychological symptoms. Scoring adjustments are made for elevated scales that correlate with the Y scale; nonelevated scores are not interpreted.

• *Debasement Scale (Z)*. The Z scale was developed for the MCMI-II using graduate student responses to selected items that identify individuals who are deliberately self-debasing far beyond feigned mental disorders to "create an image of personal unattractiveness" (Millon, 1987, p. 119). Its detection strategy is considered a derivative of rare symptoms. Unlike true rare symptoms that occur very infrequently (e.g., ≤ 10%) among bona fide populations, the Z scale uses items with much higher endorsement levels among genuine patients. With 46 MCMI-II items, median endorsements for genuine patients are 22.8% for males and 38.0% for females. Less gender disparity is observed with the MCMI-III 33-item Z scale (25.8% and 28.9%, respectively). As noted by Craig (1999), high Z scale scores can also represent acute emotional turmoil; thus Z elevations may be conflated by genuine psychopathology.

Detection of Random Responding

The V scale has some utility in discriminating random profiles from genuine protocols. Bagby, Gillis, and Rogers (1991) demonstrated that students instructed to respond randomly produced significantly higher MCMI-II V scales than did psychiatric inpatients under standard instructions, which were comparable to the normative sample. As expected, random responders achieved approximately chance levels. Bagby and colleagues found that the MCMI-II decision rule (i.e., V > 1 for invalid profiles) missed many random pro-files with a high false-negative rate of 37.9%; they recommended V ≥ 1 to identify invalid protocols. Retzlaff, Sheehan, and Fiel (1991) used computer-generated random profiles under the assumption that inconsistent or careless test takers would produce truly random profiles. The expected elevations were found. A serious oversight is the absence of any validation research for the revised 3-item MCMI-III V scale.

Detection of Defensiveness

Group Differences

The most replicated finding is higher elevations on the MCMI-II Y scale for student simulators "faking good" than other experimental (standard or "faking bad") conditions (see Bagby, Gillis, & Dickens, 1990; Bagby, Gillis, Toner, & Goldberg, 1991; Retzlaff et al., 1991). Research also indicates some evidence that the MCMI-II Y scale can make similar distinctions in clinical samples instructed to fake good (Craig, Kuncel, & Olson, 1994; Fals-Stewart, 1995). For instance, Fals-Stewart (1995) reported that the Y scale differentiated between defensive and nondefensive substance-dependent patients. However, the Y scale failed to differentiate defensive substance abusers from a group of substance-dependent patients referred from the criminal justice system.

Only one simulation study (Daubert & Metzler, 2000) examined defensiveness on the MCMI-III. The Y scale yielded a moderate effect size (Cohen's $d = .93$) in an outpatient sample. Steffan, Morgan, Cicerello, and Birmingham (2005) yielded equivocal results (Cohen's $d = .31$) in a differential prevalence design using forensic patients. Unfortunately, these designs are inherently weak, rendering these results inconclusive.

Practitioners might assume that defensiveness would produce low scores on the Z scale, used to evaluate feigning, but results of such studies are clearly mixed. Although defensiveness appears to produce lower Z scores than students or inpatients under standard instructions (Bagby et al., 1990; Bagby, Gillis, Toner, & Goldberg, 1991; Retzlaff et al., 1991), this finding does not hold for substance abusers (Craig et al., 1994; Fals-Stewart, 1995).

Correlational Studies

MCMI-II studies have yielded modest correlations for the Y scale and corresponding scales: .23 with the MMPI-2 L scale (Blais, Benedict, & Norman, 1995) and .25 with the 16PF Fake Good scale (Grossman & Craig, 1995). For the MCMI-III, Morgan, Schoenberg, Dorr, and Burke (2002) reported that the Y scale was moderately correlated with the MMPI-2 L (.42) and K (.56) and negatively correlated with F (–.71) in a sample of 202 inpatients. Using virtually the same data, Schoenberg, Dorr, Morgan, and Burke (2004) reported similar results.

Classification Accuracy

Table 11.2 provides a summary of the classification accuracy of MCMI-II and MCMI-III modifying indices in detecting defensiveness. Overall, the research is sparse and scattered on the clinical utility of the MCMI-II and MCMI-III for the classification of defensiveness. Applying a discriminant function with MCMI-II validity scales (X, Y, Z, and V), Bagby and colleagues (1990) initially produced overall correct classification (OCC) of .84 for defensiveness, standard, and malingering conditions with a relatively small false-positive rate (.15). As often occurs with discriminant analysis, the cross-validation was disappointing for OCC (.67) and false positives (.33), which were approximately double compared to the initial analysis. In a separate discriminant analysis, Bagby, Gillis, Toner,

and Goldberg (1991) yielded a cross-validated OCC of .74 that warrants further investigation. Applying a cut score of Y >75, Fals-Stewart (1995) yielded a modest OCC rate of .59 for defensive substance abusers. Given its very poor positive predictive power (PPP = .19), the cut score appears to have little utility in substance-abusing populations.

The MCMI-III Y scale, subject to cross-validation, appears to be potentially useful with outpatients. Daubert and Metzler (2000) tested two cut scores: Y >85 yielded an OCC of .64, whereas an optimized cut score of Y > 74 had a slightly improved OCC of .69. Using Y > 74 produced moderate values: PPP = .73; NPP = .66; sensitivity = .60; and specificity = .78. As an optimized cut score, cross-validation is critical in confirming these utility estimates.

TABLE 11.2. Summary of Classification Accuracy Statistics for the MCMI-II and MCMI-III Modifying Indices

Scale and cut score	Study (first author/ authors)	Experimental group	Comparison	BR	OCC	SN	SP	PPP	NPP
Defensiveness									
DFA (V, Y, Z)	Bagby (1990)	Students	Students	.50	.76	.85	.69	.69	.85
DFA Cross-validated		Students	Students	.50	.57	.67	.47	.56	.58
DFA (X, Y, Z)	Bagby, Gillis, Toner, & Goldberg (1991)	Students	Students	.50	.70	.76	.64	.68	.73
DFA Cross-validated		Students	Students	.50	.74	.80	.68	.71	.77
Y ≥ 75	Fals-Stewart (1995)	Students	SD clients	.50	.59	.19	.98	.92	.55
Y ≥ 75	Daubert (2000)	Outpatient	Outpatient	.50	.69	.60	.78	.73	.66
Y ≥ 86		Outpatient	Outpatient	.50	.64	.35	.93	.82	.59
Malingering[a]									
DFA (V, Y, Z)	Bagby, Gillis, Toner, & Goldberg (1991)	Students	Inpatients	.40	.79	.68	.87	.77	.80
DFA Cross-validated				.40	.73	.64	.78	.67	.77
X ≥ 80	Daubert (2000)	Outpatient	Outpatient	.50	.74	.76	.71	.73	.75
X ≥ 85	Schoenberg (2003)	Students	Inpatients	.37	.65	.52	.73	.56	.72
X ≥ 90		Students	Inpatients	.37	.69	.35	.88	.64	.70
Z ≥ 81	Daubert (2000)	Outpatient	Outpatient	.50	.71	.64	.78	.74	.68
Z ≥ 83	Schoenberg (2003)	Students	Inpatients	.37	.63	.59	.66	.50	.73

Note. DFA, discriminant function analysis; BR, base rate; OCC, overall correct classification; SN, sensitivity; SP, specificity; PPP, positive predictive power; NPP, negative predictive power; SD, substance dependence.
[a]Only studies that include a patient comparison group.

Detection of Malingering

Group Differences

Several MCMI-II studies found that Z and X scales discriminated college feigners from standard "fake-good" instructions (Bagby et al., 1990; Bagby, Gillis, Toner, & Goldberg, 1991; Retzlaff et al., 1991) and a clinical comparison sample of inpatients (Bagby, Gillis, Toner, & Goldberg, 1991). Surprisingly, Z was only slightly better than X for differentiating between criterion groups in terms of effect sizes.

Two simulation studies have directly examined the utility of the MCMI-III for feigned protocols across different settings. Using a within-subjects design with psychiatric outpatients, Daubert and Metzler (2000) found moderately large effect sizes in comparing feigned and standard conditions for Z ($d = 1.12$) and X ($d = 1.13$). For a similar comparison with student analogue participants and psychiatric inpatients, Schoenberg, Dorr, and Morgan (2003) found substantially lower effect sizes ($ds = .81$ and $.59$, respectively). An unexpected finding was that Z did not outperform X despite its intended focus on feigning. On the contrary, X was greater than Z in the Schoenberg and colleagues study.

The V scale, with its improbable symptoms detection strategy, has been applied to feigning with variable success. As a potential confound, this scale is also used to assess confusion and lack of understanding. Wierzbicki (1993) reported higher V scales for feigning than for honest and defensive conditions. Unfortunately, this study did not employ a patient comparison group, rendering it inconclusive, at least in a clinical context, and there have been no attempts to replicate these findings using the MCMI-III with patient samples.

Correlational Studies

Few studies have examined correlates of feigning with Z and X scales. For the MCMI-II, Blais and colleagues (1995) found moderate correlations with the MMPI-2 F scale ($rs = .54$ and $.49$, respectively) in an inpatient sample; interestingly, these scales evidenced strong negative correlations with K ($-.64$ and $-.78$, respectively). Similarly, Grossman and Craig (1995) reported moderate correlations for Z ($.41$) and X ($.42$) with the 16PF Fake Bad scale. Overall, the two studies provide only modest evidence of convergent validity

and their results cannot be applied to the MCMI-III.

Classification Accuracy

Table 11.2 provides a summary of the classification accuracy of MCMI-II and MCMI-III modifying indices in detecting malingering. Using the MCMI-II, both Bagby and colleagues (1990) and Wierzbicki (1997) examined the effectiveness of separate discriminant function analyses (using V, Y, and Z scales) to classify honest, feigned, and defensive responding. As described earlier, the discriminant function produced disappointing results in the cross-validation phase. Unfortunately, these studies did not employ clinical comparison groups, which substantially reduces the clinical implications of the findings. On the other hand, Bagby, Gillis, Toner, and Goldberg (1991) did use a clinical comparison group and found that a discriminant function composed of X, Y, and Z scale scores correctly classified 79.4% of protocols produced by students instructed to overreport versus psychiatric inpatients responding to standard instructions with cross-validation in the 70% range and was thus only modestly useful. Predictive powers were modest at best.

Several well-designed studies of feigning have been conducted with the MCMI-III. Daubert and Metzler (2000) found that a cut score of X scale ≥ 80 correctly classified 74% of outpatient feigners (SN = .76, SP = .71). Even with a high base rate of .50, the PPP of .73 is only moderately effective. With much lower base rates that are commonly found in clinical and forensic evaluations, the PPP is likely to drop below .50 (Streiner, 2003), thereby limiting the clinical usefulness of this cut score. The optimal cut score Z scale ≥ 81 produced very similar results with an OCC rate of .71 (SN = .64, SP = .78, PPP = .74, and NPP = .68).

Using a base rate of .37 for feigning, Schoenberg and colleagues (2003) reported that X scale >89 was optimal with an OCC of .69 (SN = .35, SP = .88, PPP = .64, and NPP = .70). Likewise, Z scale >82 had an OCC of .63 (SN = .59, SP = .66, PPP = .50, and NPP = .73).

Conclusions and Future Directions

Several important conclusions can be drawn from studies that have examined the MCMI-II and MCMI-III scales designed to assess defensiveness and malingering. First, the Y scale seems generally inadequate as a screening measure for defensiveness. It does not reach the large effect sizes found for other measures (e.g., MMPI-2 or PAI). Even at low cut scores (i.e., BR >75), it does not identify many individuals who respond defensively. At high cut scores (i.e., BR >85), it generates a significant number of false positives. However, Fals-Stewart's (1995) study reported a high PPP (.92) at a cut score of 75, indicating a low false-positive prediction error rate, but the SN was .19, suggesting that the majority of defensive individuals would be incorrectly classified as nondefensive. Thus, at this juncture, it is recommended that the MCMI-III Y scale be used as neither a "screening out" nor a "screening in" measure of defensiveness. More research is clearly needed, however, before this becomes a firm recommendation.

Second, the Z scale was intended to assess feigning, based on a derivative rare symptom strategy. The evidence is clear that this strategy was relatively unsuccessful. Scale X produced comparable or even better results than Scale Z, which is intended as a measure of disclosure. The error rates at varying base rates and cut scores are unimpressive. Moreover, these scales have limited effectiveness in correctly classifying individuals, even when cut scores are optimized to maximize classification in a particular setting. Thus, at this point, we do not recommend routine use of these scales in ruling in or ruling out malingering.

The most salient limitation regarding the MCMI-II and MCMI-III validity scales is the shortage of studies attempting to cross-validate previously published results. This shortage precludes the use of these scales for the classification of defensiveness and malingering. As noted, an examination of response styles is critical to clinical interpretation. Unfortunately, different versions of the test (e.g., MCMI-II and MCMI-III), compounded by methodological differences, limit cross-study comparisons. Moreover, studies have primarily relied on analogue simulation designs, which provide some threats to external validity. More studies, including those that utilize known-groups designs, are needed to further elaborate on the operating characteristics of these modifying indices.

No studies have examined incremental validity of the X and Z scales on the MCMI-III. Therefore, practitioners do not know whether examining both scales in conjunction provides any additional information. Research should examine whether classification accuracy would improve based on both scales.

No MCMI-II and MCMI-III studies have examined the effects of coaching. Research with other measures demonstrated that coaching may compromise the effectiveness of detection strategies. This finding holds true for both defensiveness (see, e.g., Butcher, Atlis, & Fang, 2000; Butcher, Morfitt, Rouse, & Holden, 1997; Cigrang & Staal, 2001) and feigning (see, e.g., Bury & Bagby, 2002; Rogers, Bagby, & Chakraborty, 1993; Storm & Graham, 2000). This critical oversight constrains significantly the clinical utility of the MCMI-II and MCMI-III.

PERSONALITY ASSESSMENT INVENTORY

The Personality Assessment Inventory (PAI; Morey, 1991) is a widely used multiscale inventory that has become increasingly popular in forensic settings (Archer et al., 2006). The PAI is composed of 344 items, and it includes 11 clinical scales, 5 treatment-based scales, and 2 interpersonal scales. The PAI corresponds mostly to DSM-IV conceptualizations of psychopathology; each clinical scale includes subscales that focus on specific aspects within each broader syndrome scale. Validational data of these clinical scales have begun to generate support for its utility with both clinical and correctional samples (e.g., Edens, Cruise, & Buffington-Vollum, 2001; Edens & Ruiz, 2005; Morey & Quigley, 2002).

The PAI includes specific scales and indexes for the assessment of inconsistent responding, defensiveness, and malingering. Several validity indices were developed subsequent to the original publication (Morey, 1991). They are presented in subsequent texts (Morey, 1996, 2003). Synopsized in Table 11.1, PAI scales and indexes are described in more detail in the following.

• *Infrequency* (*INF*). According to Morey (1991), INF was designed to measure random or otherwise careless or incomprehensive responding. The scale utilizes the improbable symptoms detection strategy; it was rationally derived, with eight items that are extremely unusual in content for most test takers regardless of the setting. Items are balanced, with four "false" and four "very true" scores for most genuine test takers capable of focusing on the content.

• *Inconsistency* (INC). The INC scale is an empirically derived scale that measures random responding (Morey, 1991). The scale consists of 10 highly correlated item pairs that share similar content (both in the same and opposite directions). The INC does not adhere to a formal detection strategy beyond its self-described purpose.

• *Positive Impression Management* (PIM). The PIM scale uses a denial of nonvirtuous attitudes and behavior detection strategy (see Chapter 2, this volume, and Rogers et al., 2005) to assess defensiveness. PIM items were endorsed infrequently in both the normal and clinical samples used to develop the PAI (Morey, 2003).

• *Defensiveness Index* (DEF). DEF is an index based on the presence or absence of eight characteristics across 12 PAI clinical scales and subscales for assessing defensiveness (Morey, 2003). Not corresponding directly to the detection strategies for defensiveness (see Chapter 2, this volume), it resembles the "blended" strategy in that it draws clinical data from multiple sources. High DEF scores can reflect more sophisticated attempts to deny problems, attitudes, or symptoms of psychopathology but are also moderately related to "true" mental health status (Morey, 2003).

• *Cashel's Discriminant Function* (CDF). The CDF (Cashel, Rogers, Sewell, & Martin-Cannici, 1995) is a discriminant function index consisting of six PAI scales that best differentiate standard and defensive conditions. It includes a sample of inmates coached about the PAI validity scales. The CDF does not employ a formal detection strategy for defensiveness (see Rogers et al., 2005), but instead it utilizes a purely empirical approach that maximizes the differences between honest and defensive individuals. Scores on the CDF index are less related to "true" mental health status than are scores on DEF (Morey, 2003), which may assist in the classification of defensiveness.

• *Negative Impression Management* (NIM). The NIM consists of nine items that use the rare symptoms detection strategy, capitalizing on infrequent psychological and personal problems (Morey, 1991). High NIM scores can reflect fabrication or exaggeration of psychopathology via the endorsement of rare symptoms. As with all feigning scales, inconsistent responding must be ruled out first (see LePage & Mogge, 2001).

• *Malingering Index* (MAL). The MAL (Morey, 1993, 1996) uses a similar methodology to the DEF and is based on the presence or absence of eight characteristics across the NIM and 11 PAI clinical scales and subscales more frequently associated with simulators than bona fide clinical profiles completed under standard instructions (Morey, 2003). It adheres to the unlikely patterns of psychopathology detection strategy, which involves an elaboration of symptom combinations (see Chapter 2, this volume; Rogers et al., 2005). MAL is designed to be used with the NIM scale for increased accuracy in the detection of feigning.

• *Rogers Discriminant Function* (RDF). The RDF (Rogers, Sewell, Morey, & Ustad, 1996) is a discriminant function index composed of 20 PAI scales and subscales that best distinguish simulators instructed to feign specific disorders, given different levels of preparation. The RDF corresponds to the unlikely patterns of psychopathology detection strategy, although it was derived in a purely empirical approach that maximizes the differences between honest and malingered responding.

Detection of Random Responding

Morey (1991) conducted the first study of the PAI and random responding, which is reported in the test manual. Morey (1991) generated 1,000 random protocols and compared the frequency distributions of INF and INC with those of normal and clinical participants. He found that the distributions for these scales were negatively skewed in normal and clinical samples but appeared normally distributed among random protocols. A cut score of 71T on INF correctly classified 93.0% as random protocols, whereas only 5.0% normal and 5.4% clinical participants scored above this cut score. Increasing the cut score to 75T somewhat decreased the predictive power of INF and only marginally decreased false-positive rates. The data on INC were less impressive. Although a cut score of 64T correctly classified 84% of random protocols, it misclassified as random 11.7% of normal and 16.4% of clinical participants. Increasing the INC cut score to 73T substantially decreased the number of false positives but detected only 50.5% of random profiles. Importantly, the combined use of

INF and INC did not increase predictive utility. Therefore, an INF cut score of 71T appears to be the best predictor of random responding.

Three studies have examined the issue of random responding on the second half of the PAI protocol, based on the untested assumption that clinical samples will become more inconsistent during the latter administration of the PAI. LePage and Mogge (2001) hypothesized that rates of random responding would be lower for the PAI than the MMPI-2 because of its shorter length. However, they found no differences in a clinical sample.

Clark, Gironda, and Young (2003) examined the effects of back random responding (BRR) on the PAI, replacing 50 to 300 (in blocks of 50) responses with random data in a sample of 785 Veterans Administration patients. They found that PAI scales were susceptible to BRR even at low to moderate levels. Moreover, INC and INF were poor predictors of BRR when at least one-third of the items were random.

To address Clark and colleagues' (2003) negative findings, Morey and Hopwood (2004) designed a study to develop a strategy that would be superior to INF and INC. They examined differences on full-instrument and short-form versions of Suicidal Ideation (SUI) and Alcohol Problems (ALC), two scales apparently sensitive to BRR based on Clark and colleagues' data. Replicating Clark and colleagues' procedures with 1,000 community

participants, Morey and Hopwood found reasonable sensitivity and specificity even at low levels of BRR. For instance, using a difference score of greater than 5 T score points between the two scale versions, they demonstrated an SN of .86 and an SP of .72 at detecting BRR when using either SUI or ALC as the decision rule. However, PPP was generally weak when base rates of BRR were low ($\leq 25\%$) and did not become acceptable until the base rate of BRR was 50%, an unlikely phenomenon in most assessment settings.

Detection of Defensiveness

The utility of the PAI validity scales in detecting defensive responding has been examined in seven published studies. Each study used analog simulation designs (Baer & Wetter, 1997; Baity, Siefert, Chambers, & Blais, 2007; Cashel et al., 1995; Fals-Stewart, 1996; Fals-Stewart & Lucente, 1997; Morey & Lanier, 1998; Peebles & Moore, 1998); two of these same studies also included differential prevalence samples in which the denial of substance-abuse problems was suspected (Fals-Stewart, 1996; Fals-Stewart & Lucente, 1997).

Group Differences

Table 11.3 shows the effect sizes for studies that examined the PAI defensiveness validity scales. Several studies demonstrated signifi-

TABLE 11.3. PAI and Defensiveness: Effect Sizes for Simulation Designs

Study (first author/authors)	Simulation design		Effect sizes (Cohen's *d*)		
	Experimental group	Comparison	PIM	DEF	CDF
Baer & Wetter (1997)	Students–NC	Students[a]	2.56	1.62	—
	Students–C	Students[a]	0.49	0.20	—
Baity (2007)	Inpatients	Inpatients	1.74	1.71	0.54
Cashel (1995)	Inmates	Inmates	—	0.77	—
	Students	Students	—	0.51	—
Fals-Stewart (1996)	SD patients[b]	SD patients	2.79	—	—
	SD patients[b]	Students	1.84	—	—
Fals-Stewart (1997)	SD patients[c]	SD patients	2.22	—	—
	SD patients[c]	Students	1.37	—	—
Morey (1998)	Students	Students	1.48	1.47	0.71
Peebles (1998)	Students	Students	1.98	1.89	—
Mean effect size			1.83	1.17	0.63

Note. Effect sizes were either (1) directly reported or (2) calculated from results (i.e., means, standard deviation, and *n*s for each group). Groups with same superscript are identical. PIM, positive impression management; DEF, defensiveness index; CDF, Cashel discriminant function; Students–NC, students with noncoaching instructions; students–C, students with coaching instructions; SD, substance dependent.

cantly higher scores on the PIM and DEF scales under defensive than standard conditions (Baer & Wetter, 1997; Morey & Lanier, 1998; Peebles & Moore, 1998). Importantly, all effect sizes were large to very large (e.g., 1.48 for PIM and 1.47 for DEF; see Morey & Lanier, 1998). Large differences were also found for individuals concealing drug abuse (Fals-Stewart, 1996; Fals-Stewart & Lucente, 1997), for psychiatric inpatients denying impairment (Baity et al., 2007), and for jail inmates minimizing maladjustment (Cashel et al., 1995). The average effect sizes across all studies were 1.83 (PIM; range from 0.49 to 2.79) and 1.17 (DEF; range from 0.20 to 1.89).

A few studies have examined defensiveness via the CDF index; however, their results are generally weaker for the CDF than for the PIM and DEF in simulation designs. Cashel and colleagues (1995) showed initial evidence that the CDF index could discriminate between defensive and standard conditions. Subsequent research has found only low to moderate effect sizes. Morey and Lanier (1998) yielded a Cohen's d of .71, whereas Baity and colleagues (2007) produced a lower effect size ($d = .54$) with inpatients.

Correlational Studies

Several studies have examined correlations between underreporting scales on the PAI and corresponding scales from other measures. For instance, Morey (1991) found moderate PIM correlations with MMPI-2 L ($r = .41$) and K ($r = .47$) scales, and the Marlowe–Crowne Social Desirability Scale in both community ($r = .44$) and college ($r = .56$) samples. In evaluations of parental capacity, even higher correlations were observed for PIM with L ($r = .66$) and K ($r = .73$; Carr, Moretti, & Cue, 2005).

Classification Accuracy

Table 11.4 displays the classification statistics for optimal cut scores across each study. Morey's (1991) recommended cut score of 57T for PIM appears the most effective at classifying defensiveness (see Baer & Wetter, 1997; Baity et al., 2007; Cashel et al., 1995; Fals-Stewart, 1996; Peebles & Moore, 1998). Although Morey and Lanier's (1998) receiver operating characteristic (ROC) curve analysis suggested that a cut score of 61T was most optimal, 57T was nearly as accurate (see Table

11.4). The OCC for the 57T ranged from .73 (Cashel et al., 1995) to .88 (Baer & Wetter, 1997) with a good balance of PPP and NPP. In the Cashel and colleagues (1995) study, however, the PPP was modest (.53). As expected, PPP is negatively affected by low base rates (e.g., .51 at base rate of .20; Morey & Lanier, 1998), which may result in a large number of false-positive errors in low base rate settings. Moreover, false-positive rates substantially decrease at a higher cut score of 68T (0–12%), including settings in which substance abuse is concealed, indicating greater confidence of defensiveness at this level. However, the majority of defensive individuals are misclassified as nondefensive using this score.

Practitioners are likely concerned whether scoring the DEF index will improve their classifications of defensiveness. Although Baity and colleagues (2007) found that DEF did not add to the accuracy of PIM in a discriminant analysis, other studies found that the DEF index ≥ 5 raw score was most accurate in identifying defensiveness (e.g., Morey & Lanier, 1998). OCC for these studies ranged from .76 (Baer & Wetter, 1997) to .90 (Morey & Lanier, 1998). Estimates of PPP were smaller than those reported for PIM, with a range from .57 to .87.

One potential advantage of the CDF is its sensitivity and PPP, which compare favorably with most defensiveness scales on multiscale inventories. PPP ranges from .77 (Morey & Lanier, 1998) to .83 (Cashel et al., 1995), with an unweighted average of .81 at a base rate of .43 or higher (PPP was only .45 at a base rate of .20; see Morey & Lanier, 1998). As a result, the CDF can potentially serve as a useful complement to PIM and DEF in that it accurately classified many defensive individuals (particularly at a cut score of 148), whereas the other scales are superior in classifying nondefensive individuals. Thus, although it lacks in overall classification, the CDF may yield some useful data when elevated.

Coaching

A critical issue in clinical and forensic assessments is whether coaching will foil the defensiveness scales and their underlying detection strategies. Baer and Wetter (1997) found that classifications for both PIM and DEF were substantially decreased with coaching. Although they identified lower optimal cut scores for

TABLE 11.4. Summary of Classification Accuracy Statistics for the PAI Defensiveness Validity Scales

Scale and cut score	Study (first author/ authors)	Experimental group	Comparison	BR	OCC	SN	SP	PPP	NPP
PIM ≥ 50T	Baity (2007)	Inpatients	Inpatients	.50	.81	.90	.71	.76	.88
PIM ≥ 50T	Baer & Wetter (1997)	Students–C	Students	.31	.64	.54	.73	.65	.63
PIM ≥ 57T	Baity (2007)	Inpatients	Inpatients	.50	.81	.76	.86	.84	.78
PIM ≥ 57T	Baer & Wetter (1997)	Students–NC	Students	.31	.88	.92	.85	.85	.92
PIM ≥ 57T	Cashel (1995)	Correctional	Correctional	.43	.73	.52	.88	.77	.71
PIM ≥ 57T	Cashel (1995)	Students	Students	.64	.58	.43	.81	.83	.46
PIM ≥ 57T	Fals-Stewart (1996)	SD patients	SD patients	.50	.84	.88	.81	.82	.87
PIM ≥ 57T	Morey (1998)	Students	Students	.20	.81	.93	.78	.51	.97
PIM ≥ 57T	Morey (1998)	Students	Students	.50	.86	.93	.78	.80	.92
PIM ≥ 57T	Peebles (1998)	Students	Students	.50	.85	.81	.89	.88	.83
PIM ≥ 61T	Morey (1998)	Students	Students	.20	.91	.82	.93	.75	.95
PIM ≥ 61T	Morey (1998)	Students	Students	.50	.88	.82	.93	.92	.83
PIM ≥ 68T	Cashel (1995)	S/C	S/C	.52	.55	.17	.98	.88	.51
PIM ≥ 68T	Fals-Stewart (1996)	SD patients	SD patients	.50	.72	.49	.95	.91	.65
PIM ≥ 68T	Peebles (1998)	Students	Students	.50	.70	.41	1.0	1.0	.63
DEF ≥ 3	Cashel (1995)	Correctional	Correctional	.43	.66	.57	.71	.61	.69
DEF ≥ 3	Cashel (1995)	Students	Students	.64	.67	.73	.55	.74	.54
DEF ≥ 4	Baer & Wetter (1997)	Students–C	Students	.31	.58	.54	.62	.57	.59
DEF ≥ 5	Baer & Wetter (1997)	Students–NC	Students	.31	.76	.71	.81	.77	.75
DEF ≥ 5	Morey (1998)	Students	Students	.20	.88	.93	.87	.63	.98
DEF ≥ 5	Morey (1998)	Students	Students	.50	.90	.93	.87	.87	.92
DEF ≥ 5	Peebles (1998)	Students	Students	.50	.83	.81	.86	.78	.82
DEF ≥ 6	Peebles (1998)	Students	Students	.50	.80	.67	.94	.71	.74
CDF—no cut score[a]	Cashel (1995)	Correctional	Correctional	.43	.84	.79	.88	.83	.85
CDF—no cut score[a]	Cashel (1995)	Students	Students	.64	.75	.87	.54	.77	.70
CDF >148	Morey (1998)	Students	Students	.20	.77	.98	.71	.45	.99
CDF >148	Morey (1998)	Students	Students	.50	.85	.98	.71	.77	.96

Note. Values for the optimal cut score in each sample are presented in **boldface**. PIM, positive impression management; DEF, defensiveness index; CDF, Cashel discriminant function; BR, base rate; OCC, overall correct classification; SN, sensitivity; SP, specificity; PPP, positive predictive power; NPP, negative predictive power; S/C, student and correctional samples combined; SD, substance dependent. [a]Development sample.

both scales—PIM (50T) and DEF (4 raw)—the OCCs were considerably lower (.64 and .58, respectively). Clinicians are therefore faced with a quandary. Using the lower scores reduces the effectiveness of the defensiveness scales with uncoached participants, whereas employing the higher scores misses most coached simulators. More research is clearly needed, including with the CDF, which should

theoretically be less susceptible to coaching, to determine the most effective use of validity scales when coaching is suspected.

Detection of Malingering

The PAI scales designed to detect malingering (i.e., NIM, MAL, and RDF) have been extensively studied, with a total of 15 published articles addressing the validity and predictive capacity of these scales. A particular strength of the PAI over other multiscale inventories is its use of both known-groups comparisons and simulation designs (see Tables 11.5 and 11.6). Six studies used known-groups designs, which are rare in malingering research, whereas the remainder used simulation designs. One study included both simulation and known-groups designs (Edens, Poythress, & Watkins-Clay, 2007).

Group Differences

Results from analogue designs revealed that nonclinical respondents instructed to feign bad or feign specific disorders (Bagby, Nicholson, Bacchiochi, Ryder, & Bury, 2002; Liljequist, Kinder, & Schinka, 1998; Morey & Lanier, 1998; Rogers, Ornduff, & Sewell, 1993; Rogers, Sewell, et al., 1996; Scragg, Bor, & Mendham, 2000) and clinical or forensic patients instructed to feign (Baity et al., 2007; Blanchard, McGrath, Pogge, & Khadivi, 2003) always score significantly higher on NIM, MAL, and RDF than do individuals in clinical samples responding to standard instructions. Table 11.5 displays the effect size differences for these studies. RDF clearly had the highest average effect size across studies (mean = 1.87; range from 1.20 to 2.61) relative to both NIM (mean = 1.30; range from 0.44 to 2.48) and MAL (mean = 1.21; range from 0.05 to 2.48). Bagby and colleagues (2002) reported the lowest effect size for both NIM and MAL and concluded that these scales are ineffective in differentiating feigners from honest test takers. Other studies, however, have shown more promise.

The results of these studies can be contrasted to those of known-groups designs. The six such studies (Boccaccini, Murrie, & Duncan, 2006; Edens et al., 2007; Kucharski, Toomey, Fila, & Duncan, 2007; Rogers, Sewell, Cruise, Wang, & Ustad, 1998; Rogers, Ustad, & Salekin, 1998; Wang et al., 1997) used the Structured Interview of Reported Symptoms (SIRS; Rogers, Bagby, & Dickens, 1992) to identify "known" feigning and honest groups. Of these studies, only three examined actual group differences (Boccaccini et al., 2006; Kucharski et al., 2007; Wang et al., 1997; the remaining focused on correlational analyses and classification accuracies; see next sections) and revealed that both NIM and MAL scores successfully differentiated those who were identified as malingerers from those who were determined to be non-

malingerers in each of the studies. The RDF, however, failed to significantly differentiate these groups in each of the three studies. The average effect sizes for both NIM (1.47; range from 1.05 to 1.87) and MAL (1.00; range from 0.68 to 1.21) were remarkable similar to those identified in simulation designs.

Correlational Studies

Several studies have reported correlations between the PAI overreporting scales and parallel scales from other measures. For instance, the PAI scales have generally large correlations with the MMPI-2F, Back Infrequency (Fb), and Infrequency Psychopathology (Fp) scales. Correlations for NIM have ranged from .53 to .78 with these scales (Bagby et al., 2002; Blanchard, McGrath, et al., 2003; Boccaccini et al., 2006), whereas both MAL (.35 to .61) and RDF (.17 to .59) have generally correlated at a weaker magnitude with these scales.

Three studies in correctional settings have reported correlations between PAI overreporting scales and the SIRS (Edens et al., 2007; Kucharski et al., 2007; Wang et al., 1997). Edens and colleagues (2007) and Kucharski and colleagues (2007) report correlations between the SIRS Total Score and PAI scales. For NIM, they were .75 and .76; for MAL, .57 and .58; and for RDF, .40 and .04, respectively. Wang and colleagues (1997) found that NIM correlated moderately with all SIRS scales, ranging from .32 to .52 (mdn r = .42), whereas MAL was significantly and moderately correlated with four of the eight SIRS scales (rs = .32 to .41 for those scales). However, RDF was not significantly correlated with any of the SIRS scales, ranging from –.23 to .11. Edens and colleagues also reported correlations between the PAI overreporting scales and the Structured Inventory of Malingered Symptomotology (SIMS; Smith & Burger, 1997). NIM (r = .84) had the strongest correlation, followed by MAL (r = .68) and RDF (r = .45).

In summary, NIM appears most strongly correlated with external measures of feigning, including other inventories and structured interviews. MAL is moderately to strongly associated with these measures. The RDF appears consistently least correlated with external measures of overreporting and is uncorrelated in two of three studies with what is generally considered to be the "gold standard" of feigned mental disorders, the SIRS.

TABLE 11.5. PAI and Malingering: Effect Sizes for Simulation and Known-Group Designs

Simulation design			Effect sizes (Cohen's d)		
Study (first author/authors)	Experimental group	Comparison	NIM	MAL	RDF
Bagby (2002)	Students–NC	Patients	0.53	0.48	1.55
	Students–C	Patients	0.44	0.05	1.87
Baity (2007)	Inpatients	Inpatients	1.61	1.30	1.20
Blanchard, McGrath (2003)	Forensic/Psychiatric	Patients	2.48	2.48	2.61
Liljequist (1998)	Students	PTSD patients	1.08	—	—
Morey (1998)	Students	Patients	1.63	1.75	1.96
Average simulation designs			1.30	1.21	1.84

Known-groups design			Effect sizes (Cohen's d)		
Study (first author/authors)	Criterion variable[a]	Setting	NIM	MAL	RDF
Boccaccini (2006)	SIRS	Forensic	1.54	1.10	—[b]
Kucharski (2007)	SIRS	Forensic	1.82	1.21	–0.09
Wang (1997)	SIRS	Correctional/Psychiatric	1.05	0.68	—[b]
Average known-groups designs			1.47	1.00	–0.09

Note. Effect sizes displayed for those studies that either (a) directly reported them or (b) reported sufficient information to calculate them (i.e., means, standard deviation, and n for each group). NIM, negative impression management; MAL, malingering index; RDF, Rogers discriminant function; SIRS, Structured Interview of Reported Symptoms; Students–NC, students with noncoaching instructions; Students–C, students with coaching instructions.
[a]Criterion used to determine group membership.
[b]Not statistically significant (and not reported).

Classification Accuracy

Table 11.6 shows these classification statistics for simulation designs. The classification rates for NIM across eight simulation studies vary from 73T (recommended in the PAI manual; Morey, 1991) to 110T (Blanchard, McGrath, et al., 2003; Rogers, Sewell, et al., 1996). Five of the eight studies (Baity et al., 2007; Edens et al., 2007; Morey & Lanier, 1998; Rogers, Ornduff, & Sewell, 1993; Rogers, Sewell, et al., 1996) used optimal cut scores that fell in a narrow range of 73T to 81T (i.e., 3 raw score points). These studies reported OCCs from .59 (Calhoun, Earnst, Tucker, Kirby, & Beckham, 2000) to .89 (Morey & Lanier, 1998) with a mean of .76.[2] The predictive powers were generally low (<.80; see Bagby, Rogers, & Buis, 1994) with the exception of Baity and colleagues (2007) and Morey and Lanier (1998), who both showed acceptable PPPs (.82–.88) at 50% base rates. Across all studies, sensitivity is a problem, especially when higher cut scores

are used (range from .54 to .90, with 50% of studies being below .70). The Blanchard, McGrath, and colleagues (2003) study is unique because of its low base rate (10.7%) of simulators; its findings are most applicable to clinical settings in which malingering is infrequent. Both Blanchard, McGrath, and colleagues and Rogers, Sewell, and colleagues (1996) report excellent specificity and PPP at a cut score of 110T, but as expected, this very high cut score missed the majority of simulators (sensitivity = .10–.54).

Several research studies have examined the utility of NIM in classifying malingering of specific forms of psychopathology. In two separate studies, Rogers, Ornduff, and Sewell (1993) and Rogers, Sewell, and colleagues (1996) studied the effectiveness of the NIM and other PAI feigning scales in an elaborate simulation design that involved the feigning of specific disorders (schizophrenia, depression, and generalized anxiety) and two types of simulators: (1) sophisticated (doctoral psychology

TABLE 11.6. Summary of Classification Accuracy Statistics for the PAI Overreporting Validity Scales in Simulation Designs

Scale and cut score	Study (first author/ authors)	Experimental group	Comparison	BR	OCC	SN	SP	PPP	NPP
NIM ≥ 73T	Baity (2007)	Inpatient	Inpatient	.50	.82	.78	.86	.82	.82
NIM ≥ 73T	Calhoun (2000)	Students	PTSD	.50	.59	.83	.35	.56	.67
NIM ≥ 77T	Baity (2007)	Inpatients	Inpatients	.50	.79	.67	.90	.88	.73
NIM ≥ 77T	Edens (2007)	Correctional	C/P	.49	.63	.76	.50	.59	.68
NIM ≥ 77T	Morey (1998)	Students	Patients	.20	.88	.91	.87	.63	.97
NIM ≥ 77T	Morey (1998)	Students	Patients	.50	.89	.91	.87	.87	.91
NIM ≥ 77T	Rogers, Sewell (1996)	Correctional	Correctional	.46	.69	.56	.81	.70	.69
NIM ≥ 81T	Morey (1998)	Students	Patients	.20	.89	.89	.89	.67	.97
NIM ≥ 81T	Morey (1998)	Students	Patients	.50	.89	.89	.89	.88	.89
NIM ≥ 84T	Calhoun (2000)	Students	PTSD	.50	.59	.74	.43	.57	.63
NIM ≥ 84T	Scragg (2000)	Students	PTSD	.43	.83	.55	1.0	1.0	.79
NIM ≥ 92T	Calhoun (2000)	Students	PTSD	.50	.63	.61	.65	.64	.63
NIM > 110T	Blanchard, McGrath (2003)	F/P	Patients	.11	.94	.54	.99	.85	.95
NIM ≥ 110T	Rogers, Sewell (1996)	Correctional	Correctional	.46	.58	.10	.98	.82	.57
MAL ≥ 3	Calhoun (2000)	Students	PTSD	.50	.67	.57	.78	.72	.64
MAL ≥ 3	Liljequist (1998)	Students	PTSD	.23	.84	.59	.92	.70	.88
MAL ≥ 3	Morey (1998)	Students	Patients	.20	.91	.81	.93	.75	.95
MAL ≥ 3	Morey (1998)	Students	Patients	.50	.88	.81	.93	.92	.84
MAL ≥ 3	Rogers, Sewell (1996)	Correctional	Correctional	.46	.64	.32	.90	.74	.62
MAL ≥ 3	Scragg (2000)	Students	PTSD	.43	.77	.70	.95	.88	.86
MAL ≥ 4	Liljequist (1998)	Students	PTSD	.23	.86	.44	.99	.92	.85
MAL ≥ 5	Blanchard, McGrath (2003)	F/P	Patients	.11	.94	.60	.99	.89	.95
MAL ≥ 5	Calhoun (2000)	Students	PTSD	.50	.65	.61	.70	.67	.64
MAL ≥ 5	Edens (2007)	Correctional	C/P	.49	.63	.52	.73	.65	.61
MAL ≥ 5	Rogers, Sewell (1996)	Correctional	Correctional	.46	.58	.07	.99	.92	.56
RDF ≥ 50T	Baity (2007)	Inpatients	Inpatients	.50	.67	.86	.48	.62	.77
RDF ≥ 60T	Baity (2007)	Inpatients	Inpatients	.50	.76	.81	.79	.74	.76
RDF ≥ 70T	Edens (2007)	Correctional	C/P	.49	.81	.90	.80	.65	.88
RDF ≥ 80T	Baity (2007)	Inpatients	Inpatients	.50	.62	.29	.95	.86	.57
RDF ≥ 0.06	Scragg (2000)	Students	PTSD	.43	.86	.70	.95	.88	.86
RDF > 0.12[a]	Rogers, Sewell (1996)	Correctional	Correctional	.46	.86	.84	.89	.91	.87
RDF ≥ 0.57	Morey (1998)	Students	Patients	.20	.95	.95	.96	.84	.99
RDF ≥ 0.57	Morey (1998)	Students	Patients	.50	.96	.95	.96	.96	.95
RDF ≥ 1.80	Blanchard, McGrath (2003)	F/P	Patients	.11	.95	.48	1.0	.96	.94

Note. Values for the optimal cut score in each sample are presented in **boldface**. NIM, negative impression management; MAL, malingering index; RDF, Rogers discriminant function; C/P, correctional/psychiatric; F/P, forensic/psychiatric; PTSD, patients with post-traumatic stress disorder; BR, base rate; OCC, overall correct classification; SN, sensitivity; SP, specificity; PPP, positive predictive power; NPP, negative predictive power.
[a]Development sample.

students with 1 week preparation) and (2) naive (undergraduates with several minutes of preparation). In the 1996 study, a NIM cut score ≥ 77T accurately predicted most naive simulators feigning depression (PPP = .82) and many feigning schizophrenia (PPP = .69). However, this cut score was ineffective with sophisticated simulators across all conditions and naive simulators feigning anxiety disorders. Although it yielded generally disappointing results, this design illustrates the complexities of malingering research in assessing across the type of simulators and targeted disorders.

Feigned posttraumatic stress disorder (PTSD) is an important consideration in clinical (e.g., Veterans Administration) and forensic (e.g., personal injury) cases. For a NIM cut score of ≥ 92T, Calhoun and colleagues (2000) reported an overall .63 OCC rate in distinguishing coached PTSD simulators from veterans diagnosed with combat-related PTSD. Using the recommended cut score of NIM ≥ 73T resulted in a moderate drop in OCC rates to .59. Scragg and colleagues (2000) reported much higher utility estimates in their study of feigned PTSD, using a NIM cut score of ≥ 84T. With an OCC of .83, it yielded a PPP of 1.00 and an NPP of .79. Differences between the two studies may be attributable to coaching and to differences in the reference groups (combat vs. civilian PTSD). In general, higher cut scores for NIM may be necessary when malingered PTSD is suspected.

As noted, a major strength of the PAI feigning research is its inclusion of known-groups comparisons, which maximizes the ecological validity of its findings. The primary focus has been on psychiatric correctional inmates, using the SIRS as the external criterion. Within corrections, the samples varied substantially regarding their mental health status: general population (Edens et al., 2007), referrals for mental health treatment (Boccaccini et al., 2006; Edens et al., 2007; Kucharski et al., 2007; Rogers, Ustad, & Salekin, 1998), and inpatient treatment (i.e., a subsample of Rogers, Sewell, et al., 1998).[3] The optimal cut score varied across these studies: 77T (Edens et al., 2007; Rogers, Sewell, et al., 1998), 80T (Rogers, Ustad, & Salekin, 1998), 88T (Kucharski et al., 2007), and 92T (Boccaccini et al., 2006).

The OCCs for these studies ranged from .61 (Rogers, Sewell, et al., 1998) to .85 (Kucharski et al., 2007) with a mean of .76. The selected cut scores emphasized ruling out genuine PAI

profiles from further consideration. As a result, the NPPs were uniformly high (> .80) in each of these studies, with an overall average of .87. With the emphasis on NPP, the PPP rate was only moderate, ranging from .67 to .83 with a mean of .72. With four of five optimal cut scores having a PPP < .80, the NIM scale should be used only as a screen. For the actual classification of malingering, its false-positive rate (> 20%) is not acceptable. Similar to the simulation designs, Rogers, Sewell, and colleagues (1998) found that a cut score of 110T had excellent SP and PPP (.98 and .93, respectively) but misses a lot of malingers (SN = .24).

Optimal cut scores for MAL in analogue simulation designs (see Table 11.6) are generally consistent with four of seven studies using ≥ 3; the remaining studies use either ≥ 4 or ≥ 5. The OCC rates across the analogue design studies ranged from .58 to .94, with a mean of .76. On average, PPP was .82 and NPP was .76 for optimal cut scores, suggesting that the MAL is best used as a screen; however, an 18% false-positive rate is high given the high stakes associated with labeling someone a malingerer. When following Morey's (1996) recommendation that ≥ 3 be used as a screen for possible malingering, the sensitivity was .60, indicating that 40% of malingerers would be incorrectly classified as honest.

As indicated earlier, a few studies have examined the detection of malingered PTSD. Whereas Calhoun and colleagues (2000) found that a low OCC of .67 in differentiated symptom-coached simulators from actual PTSD patients, Liljequist and colleagues (1998) found that a MAL cut score of ≥ 4 was effective, yielding an OCC of .86. It had excellent PPP (.92) and a very good NPP (.85). Scragg and colleagues (2000) found similar corroborating results (PPP = .89, NPP = .86). With further cross-validation, MAL may prove to be especially useful in evaluating feigned PTSD.

For three known-groups comparisons in correctional settings (see Table 11.7), MAL produced only mediocre results, with OCC rates for optimal cut scores ranging from .63 to .75. The PPP ranged from .59 to .77, and the NPP ranged from .63 to .81. Sensitivity was a major concern, with utility estimates ranging from .47 to .53, indicating that MAL is generally ineffective at classifying malingerers as determined by the SIRS. The MAL also failed to add incrementally to NIM in a logistic regression analysis (Kucharski et al., 2007). Note-

TABLE 11.7. Summary of Classification Accuracy Statistics for the PAI Overreporting Validity Scales in "Known-Groups" Designs

Scale and cut score	Study (first author/ authors)	Criterion variable[a]	Sample	BR	OCC	SN	SP	PPP	NPP
NIM ≥ 77T	Edens (2007)	SIRS	C/P	.45	.73	.80	.68	.67	.81
NIM ≥ 77T	Rogers, Sewell (1998)	SIRS	C/P	.50	.79	.84	.74	.76	.83
NIM ≥ 80T	Rogers, Ustad (1998)	SIRS	Correctional	.27	.64	.63	.95	.83	.87
NIM ≥ 84T	Boccaccini (2006)	SIRS	Forensic	.30	.78	.89	.73	.59	.94
NIM ≥ 84T	Kucharski (2007)	SIRS	Forensic	.27	.83	.84	.82	.63	.93
NIM ≥ 88T	Kucharski (2007)	SIRS	Forensic	.27	.85	.81	.86	.68	.92
NIM ≥ 92T	Boccaccini (2006)	SIRS	Forensic	.30	.82	.78	.84	.68	.90
NIM ≥ 110T	Rogers, Sewell (1998)	SIRS	C/P	.50	.61	.23	.98	.93	.56
MAL ≥ 3	Boccaccini (2006)	SIRS	Forensic	.30	.75	.53	.84	.59	.81
MAL ≥ 3	Rogers, Sewell (1998)	SIRS	C/P	.50	.67	.47	.86	.77	.63
MAL ≥ 5	Boccaccini (2006)	SIRS	Forensic	.30	.73	.13	.97	.67	.72
MAL ≥ 5	Edens (2007)	SIRS	C/P	.45	.63	.52	.77	.65	.67
MAL ≥ 5	Rogers, Sewell (1998)	SIRS	C/P	.50	.58	.16	1.0	1.0	.55
RDF ≥ 70T	Edens (2007)	SIRS	C/P	.45	.55	.36	.71	.50	.58
RDF—no cut score	Rogers, Sewell (1998)	SIRS	C/P	.50	.62	.51	.72	.64	.60

Note. Values for the optimal cut score in each sample are presented in **boldface**. NIM, negative impression management; MAL, malingering index; RDF, Rogers discriminant function; SIRS, Structured Interview of Reported Symptoms; C/P, correctional/psychiatric; BR, base rate; OCC, overall correct classification; SN, sensitivity; SP, specificity; PPP, positive predictive power; NPP, negative predictive power.
[a]Criterion used to determine group membership.

worthy, however, is that Rogers, Sewell, and colleagues (1998) had an SP and PPP of 1.0 at a MAL cut score of ≥ 5, but this level of specificity came with a sensitivity of .16.

Rogers, Sewell, and colleagues (1996) conducted the original study of the RDF using large calibration and cross-validation samples that included sophisticated and naive simulators. The OCC was .86 in the calibration sample and .80 in the cross-validation sample, with the majority of "successful" simulators being from the sophisticated group of doctoral psychology students. The RDF is the least frequently examined validity index. Subsequent simulation studies (Baity et al., 2007; Blanchard, McGrath, et al., 2003; Edens et al., 2007; Morey & Lanier, 1998; Scragg et al., 2000) and two known-groups design studies (Edens et al., 2007; Rogers, Sewell, et al., 1998) have been conducted, with various cut scores being recommended. On a positive note, the OCCs

across these studies have generally been good, ranging from .76 to .96 with a mean of .87 for the optimal cut score across five studies (see Table 11.6). Consistent with Rogers, Sewell, and colleagues (1996), the PPP was exceptionally good (PPP ≥ .88) in three studies but only moderate in the remaining two (.79, Baity et al., 2007; .65, Edens et al., 2007).

Consistent with the group differences and correlational findings, the RDF has performed poorly in known-groups designs (see Table 11.7). It failed to add incrementally to NIM in both a discriminant analysis (Boccaccini et al., 2006) and a logistic regression (Kucharski et al., 2007). Rogers, Sewell, and colleagues (1998) found modest utility estimates in applying the RDF to a correctional sample; the OCC was .62 (sensitivity = .51, specificity = .72, PPP = .64, and NPP = .60). In a recent study, Edens and colleagues (2007) reported even worse results with an OCC of .55. These findings support

Rogers, Sewell, and colleagues cautions that the RDF should be avoided in forensic/correctional settings.

In summary, the RDF is clearly the best index for identifying malingering in simulation studies. This is not unexpected because the RDF was developed to maximize differential prediction among these two conditions. However, because its development relied so heavily on empirical differentiation between these types of conditions, it is at a disadvantage when a different methodology is applied (known-groups comparisons). In addition, these data come exclusively from correctional settings; we have no data on how the RDF would perform on known-groups comparisons from general clinical settings.

Coaching Studies

Several studies have examined the effects of coaching on the detection of feigning via the NIM scale and other PAI validity indices. Despite the simulators' having been warned about validity indices and educated about disorders, Blanchard, McGrath, and colleagues (2003) found higher scores for simulators than for psychiatric inpatients. On the other hand, simulators educated about PTSD were much more able to avoid detection (Calhoun et al., 2000) relative to studies in which simulators had not been educated (e.g., Scragg et al., 2000). Using doctoral students with training in psychopathology and psychometrics, Rogers, Ornduff, and Sewell (1993) and Rogers, Sewell, and colleagues (1996) reported that most simulators were able to elude detection. However, these studies should be viewed as a very rigorous examination of coaching; most "self-taught" simulators are not likely to have this level of training.

Determinations of Feigned Presentations

Some preliminary research has indicated that an examination of response pattern on the PAI can help determine the type of malingered presentation in which the test taker is engaging. Hopwood, Morey, Rogers, and Sewell (2007) found that the discrepancy between NIM-predicted clinical scale scores and actual clinical scale scores in the profile could help identify the type of disorder (e.g., schizophrenia, major depressive disorder, or general-ized anxiety disorder) being feigned with promising accuracy. However, replication of these findings is in order before any recommendations can be generated.

Conclusions and Future Directions

In terms of random responding, practitioners should be advised that an INF cut score of 71T appears to be the best predictor of random responding, whereas INC generally has poor classification accuracy. However, neither of these scales is effective in detecting partially random responding until a large portion of the protocol has been randomized.

The PAI shows promise as a screening measure for defensive responding, but false positives are generally too high to accurately classify defensiveness. Nevertheless, data on various cut scores suggest a three-tier decision approach (modeled after Rogers, Sewell, et al.'s 1996 approach to detecting malingering).

1. *Low likelihood of defensiveness* (i.e., interpretation of PAI profile is unlikely to be confounded by defensive responding).
   a. PIM < 57T, DEF < 5, and CDF < 148
2. *Defensiveness should be further explored* (i.e., there is substantial risk for defensiveness, and interpretation of PAI profile is possibly affected by such responding).
   a. PIM between 58T and 67T or DEF ≥ 5
3. *Defensiveness is very likely* (i.e., extreme scores indicative of defensiveness; however, sole reliance on these scores will miss many defensive individuals. Further independent corroboration is recommended.).
   a. PIM ≥ 68T
   b. CDF > 148 corroborates defensiveness, but should not be used in isolation, due to high false-positive rates

The PAI also shows significant promise particularly in *screening out* malingering, but the validity scales generally perform worse in terms of *screening in* malingering. High false-positive rates (except for extreme cut scores) negate accurate classification of malingering. We propose the following three-tier approach (modeled after Rogers, Sewell, et al., 1996) to assist practitioners in decision making:

1. *Low likelihood of malingering* (i.e., interpretation of PAI profile is unlikely to be confounded by feigning).

a. Nonforensic: NIM < 73T, MAL < 3, and low RDF

b. Forensic: NIM < 77T

2. *Malingering should be further evaluated* (i.e., there is substantial risk that the profile is confounded by malingering).

a. Nonforensic: NIM ≥ 73T, MAL ≥ 3, or high RDF

b. Forensic: NIM ≥ 77T

3. *Malingering is very likely* (i.e., extreme scores are indicative of malingering, but sole reliance on these scores will miss the majority of malingerers. Further independent corroboration is required.).

a. Nonforensic: NIM ≥ 110T or very high RDF (≥ 1.80 raw)

b. Forensic: NIM ≥ 110T or MAL ≥ 5

The PAI validity scales are the best-researched scales of the inventories reviewed in this chapter. Nonetheless, they would benefit from more studies in a wider range of clinical samples. Only Baity and colleagues (2007) used nonforensic psychiatric inpatients as the over- and underreporting conditions. Unfortunately, no malingering study has examined psychiatric outpatients. These types of samples are particularly important for generating conclusions about both civil and criminal forensic evaluations in which many individuals who malinger likely have some underlying psychological difficulties that they are exaggerating. Moreover, for reasons just mentioned, simulation design studies are needed in forensic settings, whereas known-groups design studies are sorely needed in nonforensic settings. The latter design can help determine whether the RDF low predictive validity with SIRS as the criterion is method-specific or setting-specific.

A number of strengths are associated with the PAI validity scales. First, unlike most other multiscale inventories, the PAI has made use of a variety of research designs, including known groups. Even the MMPI-2, which has a far greater number of validation studies relative to the PAI validity scales (e.g., Bagby, Marshall, Bury, Bacchiochi, & Miller, 2006), has not been as extensively studied with this methodology. Second, the PAI also employs a wide range of detection strategies, which incorporate rare symptoms (e.g., NIM) and various methods to detect unlikely patterns of psychopathology (e.g., MAL and RDF). Similar strengths are noted for detecting defensiveness. Finally, the PAI validity scales have a relative narrow range of optimal cut scores compared with other inventories (e.g., MMPI-2; see Rogers, Sewell, Martin, & Vitacco, 2003, although this is not true for the Fp scale; see Greene, Chapter 10, this volume). For both PIM and NIM, a clear pattern was observed indicating that 57T of PIM and 77T for NIM were the optimal cut scores.

Although a few known-groups comparisons and one of the simulation studies report incremental validity in terms of classification accuracy, more studies need to examine whether combining validity indicators adds incremental information above each individual indicator. More information about the relationships among the scales is also needed. For example, what is a clinician to infer if NIM is elevated but MAL is not? Or vice versa? Thus more research that indicates the incremental utility of each scale or index is needed.

Finally, although a few coaching studies are available, more research is needed, particularly with the CDF and RDF. The CDF has the most promise in being the least susceptible to coaching compared with the other defensiveness scales, but it has not been examined in this regard. It is recommended that a design that uses various types of coaching be employed. These conditions would include (1) uncoached; (2) coached: symptom information about feigned disorders; (3) coached: detection strategies; and (4) coached: combined #2 and #3. These comparisons will best help identify the types of coaching to which the PAI validity scales are most vulnerable.

REVISED NEO PERSONALITY INVENTORY

The revised NEO Personality Inventory (NEO-PI-R; Costa & McCrae, 1992a) has become the most well-known and widely used instrument to assess the five-factor model (FFM) of personality. The NEO-PI-R provides five domain scores that correspond to the five basic factors of personality: neuroticism (N), extraversion (E), openness to experience (O), agreeableness (A), and conscientiousness (C). The NEO-PI-R consists of 240 self-report items answered on a 5-point Likert format with separate scales for each of its five domains. Each scale consists of six correlated facets or subscales with 8 items for a total of 48 items. A factor-analytic study (Bagby et al., 1999) revealed that the same five factors and the 30 facets extend from normal to clinical samples. The stability estimates for the domains and facets are substantial in both "normal" (see, e.g., Costa & McCrae, 1992a) and patient samples (Costa, Bagby, Herbst, & McCrae, 2005; De Fruyt, Van Leeuwen, Bagby, Rolland, & Rouillon, 2006; Santor, Bagby, & Joffe, 1997). The traits and facets of the FFM, as measured by the NEO-PI-R, are culturally universal (McCrae & Terracciano, 2005; Terracciano & McCrae, 2006).

The topic of validity scales has been controversial for the NEO-PI-R. Ben-Porath and Waller (1992) expressed concern that its lack of validity scales might limit its clinical utility. However, Costa and McCrae (1992b) argued that there is no evidence that correction adjustments based on validity scales increase the predictive validity of personality scales (see also McCrae, Costa, & Dahlstrom, 1989; Ones, Viswesvaran, & Reiss, 1996; Piedmont, McCrae, Riemann, & Angleitner, 2000). However, the logic is compelling that test profiles will not accurately reflect personality constructs when test takers deliberately distort their responses. Moreover, studies (e.g., Caldwell-Andrews, Baer, & Berry, 2000; Paulhus, Bruce, & Trapnell, 1995; Scandell, 2000; Yang, Bagby, & Ryder, 2000) have found that response styles, such as social desirability or feigned maladjustment, produce very different profiles on NEO-PI-R (or NEO-FFI, an abbreviated form of the instrument). In addition, the psychometric validity of NEO-PI-R scales is significantly weaker with feigned and defensive conditions relative to standard conditions (Ballenger, Caldwell-Andrews, & Baer, 2001; Caldwell-Andrews et al., 2000).

Despite the test authors' negative stance on validity scales, Schinka, Kinder, and Kremer (1997) developed research validity scales for the NEO-PI-R. They constructed scales to measure three response styles: random responding, defensiveness, and feigning.

• The *Inconsistency* (*INC*) scale was developed to detect random responding on purely an empirical basis. Schinka and colleagues (1997) selected 10 item pairs that correlated, positively or negatively, at .40 or greater. They chose 5 pairs with positive correlations and 5 pairs with negative correlations.
• The *Positive Presentation Management* (*PPM*) scale was developed to identify test takers

who "in a statistically uncharacteristic manner, claimed uncommon virtues and/or denied common faults" (Schinka et al., 1997, p. 129), thus adhering to the *blended* detection strategy for defensiveness (see Rogers, Chapter 2, this volume). Schinka and colleagues (1997) chose items through examining the mean item scores for the overall sample. They selected items that deviated from the mean by at least .5 standard deviations. The PPM scale consists of 10 overly positive items that are distributed across all five domains.
• The *Negative Presentation Management* (*NPM*) scale is based partly on Rogers and colleagues' (2005) rare symptoms detection strategy in using rare faults to identify feigners. However, it also includes denied common virtues. Similarly to PPM, Schinka and colleagues (1997) selected items that deviated from the mean, had the appropriate content, and represented the five domains.

Detection of Random Responding

Schinka and colleagues (1997) conducted the only NEO-PI-R study on random responding. They compared randomly generated profiles with those taken under standard, defensive, and feigning instructions. The INC was significantly higher for random than other conditions when compared with the standard administration. NPM was also significantly higher for random responding, which is not surprising given that most items on NPM are infrequently endorsed. Unfortunately, the descriptive statistics presented by Schinka and colleagues were not adequate to calculate effect sizes.

Detection of Defensiveness

Six published studies examine the utility of the NEO-PI-R in detecting defensiveness. Four (Ballenger et al., 2001; Caldwell-Andrews et al., 2000; Reid-Seiser & Fritzsche, 2001; Schinka et al., 1997) use only simulation designs. Of the remaining two studies, one combined simulation and differential prevalence designs (Bagby & Marshall, 2003) and the other employed a bootstrapping comparison with the PAI PIM scale used as the independent criterion (Young & Schinka, 2001).

Group Differences

Studies (Ballenger et al., 2001; Caldwell-Andrews et al., 2000; Reid-Seiser & Fritzsche,

2001; Schinka et al., 1997) generally have shown that PPM scores are significantly higher for defensive than for honest conditions. The average effect sizes were $d = .80$ for college and $d = .74$ for clinical samples. Clinically, Ballenger and colleagues (2001) found only a moderate effect size for PPM ($d = .74$). Unexpectedly, PPM was overshadowed by *low* scores on NPM that produced a large effect size ($d = 1.21$). They also examined an NPM–PPM index, analogous to the MMPI-2 F-K index, but it offered no advantage over NPM alone (Cohen's $d = 1.23$). One study (Bagby & Marshall, 2003) did not conform to this pattern of results; however, it used a highly unusual sample of actors trying to become finalists on a reality show, which may have introduced defensiveness even within the honest condition.

Correlational Studies

Three studies report correlations between PPM and validity scales from other measures. For male veterans seeking substance-abuse treatment, Young and Schinka (2001) reported moderate correlations between PPM and PAI validity scales (PIM, $r = .62$; NIM, $r = -.41$). Reid-Seiser and Fritzsche (2001) examined the relationships between PPM and the Balanced Inventory for Desirable Responding (Paulhus, 1991a) under defensive and honest conditions. For defensiveness, PPM was significantly correlated with both Impression Management (IM; $r = .41$) and Self-Deception (SD; $r = .58$). Interestingly, PPM and SD were also significantly correlated in the honest condition ($r = .25$). In contrast to these positive findings, Morey and colleagues (2002) found very modest correlations ($rs < .20$) between PPM and the Schedule for Nonadaptive and Adaptive Personality (Clark, 1993) defensiveness scales in a longitudinal sample study of personality disorders.

Classification Accuracy

Only two studies evaluate the effectiveness of the NEO-PI-R validity scales in correctly classifying defensiveness. Caldwell-Andrews and colleagues (2000) reported that a cut score of 22 on PPM best differentiated defensive and honest conditions. It is moderately effective with an OCC of .79 (sensitivity = .77, specificity = .81, PPP = .79, NPP = .79). In a clinical sample, Ballenger and colleagues (2001) used a slightly lower PPM cut score ≥ 20; how-

ever, it produced only modest results with an OCC of .63 when patients comprised the control group. Differentiation of defensive patients from honest students was even less accurate, yielding an OCC of .57. They further found that low scores on NPM (cutoff ≤ 10) was the most effective with an OCC of .82 and good predictive powers (PPP = .81, NPP = .83) when patients composed the honest control group. However, when students composed the control group, NPM yielded the worst classification accuracies of all scales. This disparity is possibly explained by the fact that patients tend to score very low on the PPM in general more than nonclinical student samples; thus, the absolute difference between defensive patients and defensive controls might be disproportionally greater relative to the difference between defensive patients and honest students.

Detection of Malingering

Only four studies have examined the utility of the NEO-PI-R in evaluating malingering. These studies, described earlier for defensiveness, used either a simulation design (Berry et al., 2001; Caldwell-Andrews et al., 2000; Schinka et al., 1997) or a boot-strapping comparison (Young & Schinka, 2001).

Group Differences

Research indicates that individuals who are instructed to overreport score significantly higher than both psychiatric patients (Berry et al., 2001) and college students (Caldwell-Andrews et al., 2000; Schinka et al., 1997) taking the test under standard instructions. However, malingering research can be validly interpreted only if simulators are compared with clinical samples. Sole reliance on student or community samples does not allow the critical comparison between feigned and genuine psychopathology. As a result, Berry and colleagues (2001) conducted two studies in which they compared college students who were instructed to overreport with actual psychiatric patients who took the NEO-PI-R under standard instructions. In both studies, they found that NPM significantly differentiated student overreporters from honest psychiatric patients (Cohen's $d = .81$ and 1.74). They found that the NPM–PPM index performed better with Cohen's ds of 1.54 and 2.27, respectively, in these two studies. Finally, Young and Schinka (2001) used NIM as an imprecise classification of possible feigners. In this bootstrapping comparison with treatment-seeking substance abusers, they found that NPM was higher among the NIM invalid participants relative to the NIM valid participants. No effect size could be calculated based on the available data.

Correlational Studies

Correlations between NPM and corresponding validity scales have yielded mostly disappointing results. In Young and Schinka (2001), NPM correlations were low for NIM ($r = .31$) and PIM ($r = -.29$). In Morey and colleagues (2002), a moderate correlation was found with SNAP Deviance ($r = .54$).

Classification Accuracy

Berry and colleagues' (2001) study is the only one that generated clinically meaningful classification statistics in an analogue simulation design for the NEO-PI-R validity scales. They showed that a cut score of 21 on NPM was optimal in differentiating overreporting students from actual patients. Classification accuracies in their study yielded an OCC of .81 with SN = .41, SP = .95, PPP = .72, and NPP = .82. Thus, 59% of simulators were misclassified as genuine patients at this cut score. The PPP became increasingly worse at lower base rates of overreporting, indicating that in settings in which overreporting is less prevalent, NPM is unlikely to be effective is detecting such individuals. Berry and colleagues found stronger evidence for the utility of the NPM–PPM index. At a cutoff of ≥ -1, it yielded an OCC of .92 and SN = .76, SP = .98, PPP = .93, and NPP = .92. PPP remained adequate even at very low base rates. Finally, in their bootstrapping comparison with the PAI NIM scale as the criterion for overreporting, Young and Schinka (2001) revealed that a cut score of 70T (T scores derived from their normative sample; see Schinka et al., 1997) had an OCC of .70 in classifying those scoring greater than 70T on the PAI as overreporters. As discussed by Rogers in Chapter 24, this volume, bootstrapping comparisons generally lack precision in their identification of groups. Therefore, utility estimates should be interpreted with caution when using this design.

Conclusion and Future Directions

Despite the controversy discussed earlier, the preponderance of evidence indicates that NEO-PI-R scale scores are susceptible to over- and underreporting, suggesting the need for validity scales to detect such response styles. Despite their development after test construction, the NEO-PI-R validity scales appear promising in detecting such response styles. Although it is too early to make far-reaching conclusions (relative to instruments such as the MMPI-2 or the PAI), we nonetheless believe that some tentative guidelines are in order.

Defensiveness

The PPM shows some promise in nonclinical samples for screening out defensiveness. A cut score of < 22 yields adequate specificity and NPP and suggests that low-scoring individuals are unlikely to be defensive. Because the false-positive rates are greater than 20%, it is not advisable for practitioners to rule in defensiveness. Profiles in which PPM scores are 22 or higher should be viewed with caution, and other sources should be considered before any conclusions about defensiveness are reached.

Malingering

The NPM has shown promise as a measure to detect feigning. Berry and colleagues (2001) recommends a cut score of 21. At this cut score, the NPM does an adequate job of screening out potential malingerers, as both sensitivity and NPP are acceptable. Berry and colleagues' data also indicate that a cut score of 27 would yield a 0% false-positive rate. Such extreme scores should raise serious concerns about malingering; however, only 13% of malingerers are correctly classified at this score, which makes it relatively ineffective at the determination (i.e., ruling in) of malingering. Furthermore, the NPM–PPM index showed greater promise relative to the NPM alone. In fact, at a cutoff score ≥ -1, it yielded an OCC of .92 with excellent predictive powers (PPP = .93 and NPP = .92). Thus individuals who meet this cut score have profiles that should be seriously questioned in terms of malingering. With greater confidence, individuals who score below this cut score are unlikely to be malingerers. However, these results require extensive replication in a variety of settings (including forensic) and using known-groups designs before these scores can be used in routine practice.

More research needs to be conducted with these scales. The INC scale has only one study supporting its validity, from which no effect sizes or classification accuracies could be derived. In other words, there is preliminary evidence that it can detect random protocols, but we cannot ascertain how well. Studies also need to be conducted using a true known-groups design. Elevations on validity scales, even from well-established multiscale inventories, are very imprecise and do not qualify as known groups. The SIRS has been used effectively to establish known groups for malingering because of its very low false-positive rates.

Future research needs to evaluate the effects of coaching. As mentioned earlier, studies examining both underreporting (e.g., Baer & Wetter, 1997; Butcher et al., 2000) and overreporting (e.g., Bury & Bagby, 2002; Storm & Graham, 2000) suggest that the effectiveness of validity scales in detecting overreported protocols is substantially compromised when test takers are coached about the presence and operating characteristics of validity scales.

TRAUMA SYMPTOM INVENTORY

The Trauma Symptom Inventory (TSI; Briere, 1995) is more specific than the broadband personality and psychopathology inventories just discussed. It is a 100-item self-report inventory specifically designed to measure clinical reactions to traumatic events, including various forms of abuse and violence, combat situations, accidents, and natural disasters. The instrument includes 10 clinical scales that measure a wide range of psychological impacts to trauma, including symptoms directly associated with PTSD, but also other interpersonal and behavioral difficulties. It is the only measure of posttraumatic stress that includes validity scales (Guriel & Fremouw, 2003), an important feature given that such measurement often occurs in litigious settings.

The TSI has three validity scales that were developed to detect random responding, overreporting, and underreporting.

• Inconsistent Response (INC) and Response Level (RL) were designed to detect random responding and underreporting, respectively. However, they have not been tested explicitly for these purposes in any peer-reviewed publication. We therefore focus primarily on the scale developed to detect overreporting, which has been researched.

• The Atypical Response (ATR) scale consists of the most rarely endorsed unusual, bizarre, and aberrant items on the TSI. Although the scale clearly used the rare symptoms approach as a detection strategy for overreporting (see Rogers et al., 2005), little is known from the TSI professional manual about the ATR development or the retention of its items based on their infrequency in either normative or clinical samples.

Detection of Malingering

Four studies using analogue simulation designs have examined the utility of the TSI in detection of overreporting (Edens, Otto, & Dwyer, 1998; Elhai et al., 2005; Guriel et al., 2004; Rosen et al., 2006). Each of these studies reported group differences and classification accuracies, but none of them reported correlations with external validity scales.

Group Differences

Edens and colleagues (1998) reported a within-subject design in which 155 college students who were instructed to overreport PTSD on the TSI scored significantly higher on ATR than when they took the test under standard instructions (Cohen's $d = 1.93$). These participants also scored significantly higher on INC and lower on RL. Guriel and colleagues (2004) followed up with a between-subjects design including college student participants across four conditions: standard instructions ($n = 10$), overreporting PTSD ($n = 19$), overreporting PTSD coached with symptom information ($n = 23$), and overreporting PTSD coached with both symptom information and validity scale strategies ($n = 16$). They found that the ATR, but not other scales, were significantly higher among participants given malingering instructions compared with standard instructions. There were no significant differences across malingering conditions. In this same vein, Rosen and colleagues (2006) replicated these findings, showing that students overreporting PTSD scored significantly higher on ATR than students who took the TSI honestly. However, each of these studies used only college students as their honest controls, which is of limited value because their findings tell nothing of how effective ATR is in differentiating overreporting individuals from those with bona fide PTSD.

Elhai and colleagues (2005) is the first study that used 47 participants with PTSD as the clinical comparison group with whom they compared 63 student simulators who were provided symptom information regarding PTSD. Simulators were also screened for absence of PTSD. Elhai and colleagues found that the ATR was only modestly higher (Cohen's $d = .48$) in the simulation compared to the genuine PTSD group. Thus, the results for the ATR are unimpressive when making the real-world discrimination between simulators and bona fide patients with PTSD.

In a more recent simulation study, Efendov, Sellbom, and Bagby (in press) found that the ATR significantly differentiated between remitted trauma patients asked to feign PTSD and carefully diagnosed PTSD claimants undergoing evaluations for work injury compensation. The magnitude of the difference was only moderate (Cohen's $d = .76$). When the simulation group was coached on how the validity scales operate, any appreciable effect of the ATR disappeared (Cohen's $d = .14$). Moreover, Efendov and colleagues showed that the ATR failed to add incremental predictive utility over the MMPI-2 F scales in predicting feigned PTSD regardless of coaching.

Classification Accuracy

Edens and colleagues (1998) reported that the optimal cut score for ATR was greater than 61T, which had an OCC of .85 of classifying college student participants as either overreporting or honest. Realizing that error rates would likely not be as low for patients with bona fide PTSD, Edens and colleagues examined the specificity in various samples that included individuals with PTSD and other emotional difficulties. The specificities ranged from .45 to .94, with a median of .85 in nine samples. The specificities expectedly increased slightly when a higher cutoff score of 65T was applied. However, these results revealed nothing about sensitivity of the ATR in detecting malingered PTSD relative to the patient samples. Guriel and colleagues (2004) and Rosen and colleagues (2006) both used students as

honest controls; thus we do not report the classification accuracies of these studies due to their limited value in clinical applications of the ATR. Elhai and colleagues (2005) conducted two discriminant function analyses (DFA) with ATR as the only predictor of group classifications for PTSD simulators and PTSD patients. In the first DFA, they examined continuous scores on ATR across four different base rates (.50, .21, .16, .07) based on previous findings in malingering research. The OCC ranged from .59 to .73; its SN was modest (.48) and SP was moderately good (.75). PPP ranged from .13 to .71 from low to high base rate, whereas NPP ranged from .51 to .95 from high to low base rate. Thus, all classification statistics were unacceptably low across base rates with the exception of NPP. The second DFA was conducted with ATR as a dichotomous variable with those who met the manual's recommended cut score of 90T for feigned PTSD and those who scored below this cutoff. The classification accuracies decreased substantially, with OCC ranging from .54 through .60 across the aforementioned base rates. Despite the high cut score, PPP met acceptable standards at only a .50 base rate level, and NPP was less than .55 across all base rate levels. Finally, Efendov and colleagues (in press) found that the ATR demonstrated poor OCC rates of .57 and .73 at cut scores of 61T and 90T, respectively. PPPs were extremely poor at each cut score (.34 and .48, respectively), resulting in unacceptably high false-positive rates.

Conclusions and Future Directions

Currently, no firm conclusions can be drawn regarding the ATR's ability to differentiate malingerers from patients with genuine disorders. The most useful studies to date (Efendov et al., in press; Elhai et al., 2005) found a poor effect size in differentiating simulators from actual patients with PTSD and quite inadequate classifications. These results recommend against using the ATR even as a screen for malingered PTSD.

The ATR clearly needs more research before it can be routinely used as a validity scale. No research with known-groups design or bootstrapping comparisons has been conducted. A challenge for the former is the establishment of an external criterion, specifically for feigned PTSD. An alternative perspective would be to focus on the range of disorders commonly found with disability cases. In this instance, data with the SIRS appears promising (see Rogers, Chapter 18, this volume). In addition, bootstrapping comparisons are quite feasible using stringent scores on scales such as the Fp. For example, Rogers, Payne, and Granacher (2007) used Fp >7 for likely feigners and Fp <4 for likely genuine patients based on a recent meta-analysis that examined PTSD as a separate diagnosis (Rogers, Sewell, Martin, & Vitacco, 2003).

In terms of simulation research, more studies need to incorporate bona fide patients with PTSD as the clinical comparison group. Use of presumably healthy participants produce generally nonmeaningful results. The Elhai and colleagues (2005) and Efendov and colleagues (in press) studies represent a first step toward this goal. These studies clearly show, however, that the ATR would be quite susceptible even to minimal PTSD coaching.

Studies should also examine a range of cut scores to determine the optimal cut score for clinical settings. The 61T cut score is based on irrelevant comparisons (malingerers with healthy controls). Edens and colleagues (1998) recognized this problem and at least published some specificity rates across various trauma samples, but there was no information on the ability to differentiate simulators from patients with PTSD. Elhai and colleagues (2005) used only the manual's recommended cutoff score of 90T, which proved to be clearly too high. Efendov and colleagues (in press) did not find support for either cut score.

Guriel and colleagues (2004) attempted to study the effects of coaching on the ATR's utility; the absence of a bona fide patient group with PTSD thwarted their efforts. More rigorous studies need to compare the scale's utility in differentiating both uncoached and coached simulators from patients with PTSD. As noted, Elhai and colleagues' (2005) and Efendov and colleagues' (in press) studies demonstrated the vulnerabilities of ATR to coaching. Still, research on the TSI may produce refinements of ATR or other scales that are less susceptible to the effects of coaching.

SUMMARY AND GENERAL CONCLUSIONS

This chapter reviewed the validity and utility of four multiscale inventories for assessment of specific response styles: inconsistent responding, defensiveness, and feigning. The results showed generally poor to modest utility, especially for the MCMI and TSI validity scales, which were decidedly unimpressive. Practitioners would be wise *not* to rely on these scales to make decisions about defensiveness or malingering. Extreme scores on the MCMI-III scales might invalidate the actual profile at hand, but no decisions that expand past the actual instrument can be warranted. The NEO-PI-R validity scales show promise, particularly the NPM–PPM index, but it would also benefit from more research in clinical settings with varied methodology. The PAI performs best in simulation designs, with RDF being particularly promising in such studies. However, the RDF's lack of association with the SIRS, often labeled the "gold standard" of feigned mental disorders, is troublesome. Thus NIM and potentially MAL, despite its somewhat poor sensitivity and susceptibility to coaching, are preferred in forensic settings. Practitioners should refer to the "Summary and Conclusions" section for each instrument to obtain more direct guidelines for the use of validity scales for each individual instrument. Here is a recap:

1. MCMI-III
   a. The modifying indices are not sufficiently supported to make conclusions about defensiveness or malingering. Extreme scores (e.g., BR >85) could potentially invalidate a specific protocol, but conclusions should not be extended past such protocols.
   b. Under no circumstances should practitioners use this measure in forensic evaluations to determine response styles.
2. PAI
   a. The validity scales are effective in ruling out both defensiveness and malingering but are inadequate to confidently rule in such response styles. Extreme scores (e.g., PIM >68T or NIM >110T) are likely indicative of defensiveness or malingering, but sole reliance on such scores will lead to poor classification and decision making.
   b. The PAI is recommended for use in forensic settings; however, it behooves the practitioner to be intimately familiar with the weaknesses of these scales in classification of response styles.
3. NEO-PI-R
   a. PPM and NPM–PPM seem promising in ruling out defensiveness and malinger-

ing. However, more research is clearly needed.

b. At this juncture, the NEO-PI-R validity scales are not recommended for use in forensic evaluations.

4. TSI

a. Practitioners would be wise not to use the ATR to make any determinations about individual protocol validity at this point, particularly in settings in which coaching is suspected.

Practitioners are often faced with key decisions regarding which psychological measures to use with particular clients for a variety of reasons, including time and cost. It would not be surprising should the relative ability of the tests to detect certain response styles play an important role in these decisions, particularly in settings in which clients have a higher prevalence of distorting their responses (e.g., civil and criminal forensic evaluations, preemployment screening). Although it was not the intention of this chapter to compare these multiscale inventories with other tests, we used the same evaluative framework as two previous reviews (Bagby & Marshall, 2005; Bagby et al., 2006) of the MMPI-2 and MCMI instruments. Readers may wish to examine these reviews and other chapters in drawing their own conclusions about the best measures for their own professional settings.

If clinicians were to consider the multiscale inventories discussed in this chapter (especially the PAI vs. MCMI-III because of their broad range in psychopathology assessment), it becomes very clear that the PAI would be the choice. Its validity scales have been rigorously tested in more research studies and the overall conclusions are generally more positive than those for the MCMI-III modifying indices.

From a forensic perspective, the PAI is the only test reviewed in this chapter that can generate sufficiently valid information about response styles that would likely withstand a challenge or a rigorous cross-examination in court.

NOTES

1. Per Ben-Porath's (2003) recommendations, we differentiate between instrument validity and protocol validity. The former refers to the psychometric validity of scale, whereas the latter refers to the test protocol generated by an individual test taker. It is theoretically possible for an instrument to be 100% valid but for an individual's protocol to be 100% invalid. For instance, if an individual responds randomly to all questions on a scale, it becomes 100% uninterpretable, even if the scale itself has excellent psychometric validity.

2. Edens et al. (2007) reported sensitivity and specificity for several groups. To maintain continuity with the other analogue studies, we focused on simulators versus clinical patients. This comparison had a sensitivity of .76 ($n = 29$) and specificity of .50 ($n = 30$), which were used to calculate the utility estimates for this study (i.e., OCC = .62; SN = .76, SP =.50, PPP = .59, NPP = .68).

3. It should be noted, however, that two of these studies (Boccaccini et al., 2006; Kucharski et al., 2007) used samples from the same population, the United States penitentiary in Atlanta. Although the amount of participant overlap across the two studies is unknown (neither study referenced the other), it is likely large. Boccaccini et al. (2006) used a final sample of 154 adult male defendants who were evaluated at this facility between 1992 and 2001, whereas Kucharski et al. (2007) used a final sample of 117 adult male defendants who were evaluated at the same facility between 1990 and 2004.

12

Dissimulation on Projective Measures

KENNETH W. SEWELL, PhD

This chapter provides an overview of the clinical and research literature investigating dissimulation (both malingering and defensiveness) on the group of psychological measures traditionally called *projectives*. Projective measures have usually been defined as those psychological instruments that present the respondent with an ambiguous stimulus, such that the content of the response must represent a projection of the respondent's personality rather than simply a cognitively chosen answer. A questionable dichotomy has arisen between *projective* and *objective* tests. Certainly, most meanings of the term *objective* do not constitute an opposite to the concept of *projective* as just described. In this review, I consider projective measures to be those tests that elicit a free response from the examinee on the basis of an incompletely structured stimulus. This definition is used to distinguish projective measures from rating scales, multiple-choice tests, or self-report measures, which are usually dubbed *objective measures.*

The distinction between projective and objective measures has less significance than once assumed for the determination of malingering and defensiveness. Historically, the concept of *projection* was viewed as an important protection against the deliberate faking of test results. Based on the earliest thinking (see, e.g., Frank, 1939), responses were seen as projecting unconscious motives and therefore were not subject to conscious distortion. Based on subsequent investigations, this perspective is now disputed. As observed by Exner (1991), ambiguous stimuli per se do not necessarily lead to projection. Moreover, many elements of the Rorschach, for example, are far less ambiguous than once assumed. Taken together, Exner (p. 109) properly concluded that "projection is only a possibility in the Rorschach."

Practitioners may wonder whether response ambiguity plays any significant role in ensuring the accuracy of clients' responses. Interestingly, measures with high face validity (see Rogers & Kelly, 1997) have been criticized for the ease with which clients can modify their responses (e.g., denying suicidal thoughts when asked directly). Beyond this obvious problem, research has not examined the relationship between level of ambiguity and modifiability of responses.

Projective measures and other scales that provide for open-ended responses complicate the assessment of response styles. With more structured formats, researchers can devise specific items and scales (e.g., the validity scales of the Minnesota Multiphasic Personality Inventory [MMPI-2]) for the determination of malingering and defensiveness. Even in the absence of specialized scales, specific patterns of responses (see, e.g., Berry & Schipper, Chapter 14, this volume) can be easily identified and tested. For projective measures, specific patterns of responses are possible, although the myriad of response possibilities is daunting. For example, extensive Rorschach research would be needed to identify (1) common responses on malingered profiles that would be subsequently tested to discover (2) differentiating characteristics between malingered and genuine protocols in clinical populations.

A practical alternative to development of response-based scales is the application of well-validated detection strategies utilizing current scoring systems. For the Exner system, could patterns of responses be used to test detection strategies for malingering, such as (1) rare symptoms, (2) symptom combinations, (3) symptom severity, and (4) spurious patterns of psychopathology? Similarly, could defensiveness on the Exner system be categorized using detection strategies, such as (1) denial of patient characteristics, (2) social desirability, and (3) spurious patterns of simulated adjustment? The application of detection strategies to projective measures is considered further after reviewing the available dissimulation research.

This chapter is intended to cover research on all projective measures that address malingering and defensiveness. However, its focus is predominantly on the Rorschach Inkblot Test (or, simply termed, the Rorschach). This focus is dictated by the current status of research; nearly all investigations utilize only the Rorschach. Scoring systems for the Rorschach vary substantially in their criteria and coverage (Exner, 1969). Although all studies are included, research on the Exner scoring system is emphasized given its predominance in current Rorschach practice. Beyond the Rorschach, research data on other projectives are included. Each section presents the Rorschach studies first, followed by any available research on non-Rorschach projectives.

Two recent reviews (i.e., Elhai, Kinder, & Frueh, 2004; Schretlen, 1997) of response distortion on projective measures have adopted a chronological/historical approach to organizing the literature. Such an approach highlights the criticisms that have arisen in response to early assertions that the projectives (particularly the Rorschach) were not "fakable" and thus not a source of concern for clinicians evaluating response distortion. In this chapter, key issues are framed as a set of sequential questions, applicable to both malingering and defensiveness studies. In this way, the early and recent research can be evaluated side by side; such direct comparisons provide an opportunity to critically evaluate the methodology and conclusions irrespective of publication date. This review covers mostly peer-reviewed research; unpublished dissertations are included only if their methodology or results represent

a significant departure from what is found in the published literature.[1] The next two major sections address a series of questions first applied to malingering and then to defensiveness.

A major objective of this book is to evaluate systematically differences in test data because of response styles. Table 12.1 summarizes the available effect sizes (see Rogers, Chapter 2, this volume) on feigning for the major Rorschach studies and recent dissertations. When means and standard deviations were not available for the direct computation of Cohen's d, Wilson's (2001) program was used to estimate Cohen's ds from available reported data (e.g., F values or proportions).

Elements of Table 12.1 are discussed in subsequent sections. As an overview, readers will likely note the overuse of college (i.e., presumably healthy) samples, the diversity of indicators, and the preponderance of negligible effect sizes. For the few large to very large effect sizes, potential indicators have yet to be replicated.

MALINGERING ON PROJECTIVE MEASURES

Modifiability of Projective Scores

The first and most fundamental question regarding malingering on projective measures is simply: Can clients and research participants alter their projective test results when attempting to feign psychopathology? Obviously, clients choose how to respond to projectives and are capable of choosing different content for their responses depending on their motivations and situational variables. However, the critical issue is whether such alterations in their responses reflect concomitant changes in the scoring of projective measures. Because the readership of this book is diverse in its professional training, this section begins with a brief introduction to the Exner system of the Rorschach.

As noted, Rorschach scoring systems vary substantially in scope and complexity. Focusing on the Exner system, Rorschach responses are scored along a variety of dimensions, including content of the response (e.g., human, anatomical, food), the popularity of a particular response, and the extent to which the shape characteristics of the response conform to those of the stimulus. In addition, its scoring addresses the issues of which aspects of the inkblot have prompted the response (referred to as *determinants*), the sophistication of the

TABLE 12.1. Effects of Feigned Psychopathology on Rorschach Scoring

First author	Year	Sample	Design	Negligible < .20	Moderate ≥ .75	Large ≥ 1.25	Very Large ≥ 1.75
		Study		Effect sizes (Cohen's d)			
Batchelder	1995	Clinical	Known-groups malingerers versus patients	R, Con+Alog, DV+DR, WSum6			
Batchelder	1995	Clinical	Known-groups malingerers versus controls	Lambda, F+%, DV+DR, WSum6			
Caine	1995	College and clinical	Simulators versus patients	C, S-Con			
Caine	1995	College	Simulation between-groups	R, DEPI, S-Con		Morbid	
Carp	1950	College	Simulation within-groups	D, Dd, Light, F+, F, C, A+Ad, R, T/R			
Easton	1967	College	Simulation between-groups		P, R, D, F, Obj		
Feldman	1954	College	Simulation between-groups		P		
Feldman	1954	College	Simulation within-groups		R, W, Achrom, Sex	FC, FC>CF +C, A	F, P, A+Ad
Frueh	1994	College	Simulation within-groups	H, X-%, Wsum6, SumY, Dscore, DEPI, CDI	FC+C, X+%, Dramatic		
Frueh	1994	College and clinical	Simulators versus patients	Dscore, Wsum6, MOR, S-Con	M-, X+%, X-%, SumC		
Labott	2002	College	Simulation between-groups	FM+M+m, CF+C>FC			
McDougall	1996	Normals and clinical	Simulators versus clinical comparison	SCZI, M-, P on Card X, Card IV Spoil, R, Special Score Card VI, Fire, Ell	Total PSV, Phonemic PSV	Stuck PSV	Malingering Index
Meisner	1988	College	Simulation between-groups	ΣC'YTV, 3r+(2)			
Miles	1989	College	Simulation between-groups	Fqu>FQ-	Sum6		
Netter	1994	Normals	Simulation between-groups	M-	SCZI, Modified SCZI, #Modified,	Wsum6	
Netter	1994	Normals and clinical	Simulators versus clinical comparison	M-	Modified SCZI, Modified Wsum6, #Modified, Reaction Time, #Good-Derepressed		
Perry	1990	College	Simulation between-groups	R-Ratio, PER, CF+C	RT, R, Wsum6, P, X+%	X-%, M-%	Dramatic, SCZI
Seamons	1981	Inmates with and without psychosis	Simulation within-groups	Nonsignificant findings are not listed	dramatic		

Note. Netter and Viglione (1994) and McDougall (1996) used a variety of nonstandard indices, including "modified" versions of standard indices. Some studies did not report statistical values for nonsignificant differences; thus the list of negligible effect sizes is likely incomplete.

response, and the extent to which the response incorporates all or only part of the inkblot. Usually, these scores are then expressed as simple counts (e.g., P refers to the number of popular responses provided) or percentages of the total number of responses (e.g., F% refers to the percentage of responses determined by form characteristics, X-% refers to the percentage of responses containing poor form quality). Given that the respondent can supply more than one response per stimulus, the overall number of responses (R) is also used as a variable. A variety of special scores are applied to response types that are thought to carry particular interpretive significance, such as fabulized combinations of response components fused into a single response (FabCom) or expression of anomalous logic (Alog). Individual count and percentage scores can have specific interpretations; however, scores may also be combined into composite or *index* scores. Examples of common index scores include the Depression Index (DEPI), which is the count of several scores in excess of specified thresholds, and the Wsum6, which is a weighted sum of six special scores associated with severe psychopathology.

Most Rorschach studies on the modifiability of Rorschach scoring are designed as simple within-subjects research on nonclinical samples. Participants, often college students with presumably little psychopathology, are administered the Rorschach twice, once under standard instructions and once under feigning instructions. This design has two major limitations. First, the absence of any retesting under standard (honest) instructions is problematic because some of the observed differences or absence of differences may simply occur when the Rorschach is readministered to nonclinical samples at short intervals. Second, the absence of clinical comparison samples limits the interpretability of any significant findings; we cannot determine whether faked Rorschach protocols are distinguishable from the protocols of genuine patients.

Fosberg (1938, 1941, 1943) conducted the original simulation research on the alterability of Rorschach scoring using the Klopfer system on mixed samples of patients and presumably healthy persons. He did not find significant differences between protocols generated under standard and feigning instructions. These findings led to the assertion that the Rorschach was not susceptible to feigning and could therefore

be used as a valid clinical measure even when the examinee was attempting to feign psychopathology. Fosberg's analytic approach utilized test–retest correlations, which have been justly criticized (e.g., Cronbach, 1949) as being unable to detect important mean differences as long as the rank orders remain comparable. Fosberg also utilized chi-squared analyses to compare multiple protocols generated by individual participants. Likewise, this approach was criticized by Cronbach (1949) as confounded by the extreme frequency differences that are characteristic of various Rorschach scores. Despite these analytic limitations, Carp and Shavzin (1950) did find some significant differences using a similar methodology. In applying the Beck scoring system, they found that F+ was lower in those feigning bad and that large individual differences in both directions "balanced out in the analyses" (p. 232) such that the group means did not differ even though the individual simulators altered their responses broadly. Possible explanations for these disparate results include differing instructional sets (i.e., Carp and Shavzin included realistic scenarios rather than simple admonitions to "make the best/worst impression") and a more detailed analysis of individual variability.

Feldman and Graley (1954) improved the statistical analysis by adopting Cronbach's (1949) guidelines for adjusting chi-squared values. In a sample of students using a combination of the Klopfer and Hertz scoring systems, they found that feigned Rorschach protocols were lower than genuine protocols on several determinants—m, CF + C, and FC—and on two content scores, Sexual Anatomy and Dramatic. In contrast, feigned protocols were lower on R and P. The lack of popular responses (P) is likely attributable to malingerers' efforts to appear abnormal via the denial of nonambiguous responses. Subsequently, Easton and Feigenbaum (1967) replicated the fewer responses (R) and fewer popular responses (P) among individuals feigning psychopathology. However, their report did not evaluate form quality or dramatic content. These investigators also did not report which scoring system they used on their modest sample of 22 students.

Seamons, Howell, Carlisle, and Roe (1981) improved on earlier simulation studies by using clinical samples, specifically forensic inpatients. Using a within-subjects design, clients completed the Rorschach under two instructional sets: malingering and defensive conditions. In the absence of a standard condition, differences are accentuated by using polar-opposite instructions. Although feigners gave fewer popular responses (5.25 vs. 6.35), the difference is too small to be clinically relevant (Cohen's $d = .53$). More promising was the use of dramatic content. Patients gave many more responses with dramatic content in the feigning ($M = 6.13$) than defensive ($M = 1.77$) condition, producing a large effect size ($d = 1.11$).

A criticism of Rorschach dissimulation research is that the number of responses can markedly affect Rorschach scoring, potentially confounding observed differences in various indicators between feigned protocols and genuine protocols. This issue can be particularly problematic given that feigned protocols tend to have fewer responses. Perry and Kinder (1992) addressed this problem by using only the first or second response to each card, thus equalizing the number of responses between a group of undergraduates under standard conditions and a group of undergraduates instructed to feign schizophrenia. Even after equalizing number of responses, they found that the simulators had higher scores on Wsum6, SCZI, X-%, and M-% and lower P and X+% than the honest controls. Similarly, Frueh and Kinder (1994) showed that post-traumatic stress disorder (PTSD) simulators generated higher X-%, higher SumC, more Dramatic content, and lower X+% than honest controls. Diverging from these studies, Labott and Wallach (2002) found that women simulating dissociative identity disorder did not differ significantly from honest controls on Rorschach indices.

Several investigators have examined the modifiability of scoring on non-Rorschach projectives by individuals attempting to feign pathology. For example, Timmons, Lanyon, Almer, and Curran (1993) evaluated different response sets on a 136-item sentence completion test developed for use in psychiatric disability evaluations. They found that undergraduate students produced elevated scores consistent with feigning instructions (angry negativity, disability exaggeration, and excessive virtue) compared with their own scores under instructions to simulate successful recovery from an accident. In the absence of a clinical comparison group, these findings remain difficult to interpret. The Thematic Apperception Test (TAT; Morgan & Murray, 1935) is commonly used as a projective measure to assess person-

ality, social motives and needs, and problem solving. However, only a few studies have examined whether people can feign psychological impairment and conflict on the TAT. For instance, Kaplan and Eron (1965) compared undergraduate and graduate students on differences between honest TAT responses and those generated with instructions to portray hostile/aggressive impulses. They found that instructions did elicit more hostile/aggressive content, although graduate students showed even higher levels than undergraduates.

The findings from the studies reviewed here are diverse and mixed. Some consistencies appear to emerge from the Rorschach studies: Persons attempting to feign pathology tend to produce popular responses less frequently (lower P) and more frequent responses that do not conform well to the shapes represented on the inkblots (as reflected in form quality indices such as X+%, X-%, M-%, etc.). Thus it appears clear that persons attempting to feign psychopathology do indeed produce results on projective measures that are different than would be produced without the attempt to feign. This conclusion provides the basis for further questions.

Pathology Production and Exaggeration: Effects of Feigning on Clinical Interpretation

People often can and do alter their projective test results when attempting to feign psychopathology. The question remains as to whether such alterations affect the likelihood that a clinician would interpret the results as representing either the presence or greater severity of psychopathology. Asked more simply, do changes in results produced by attempts to feign psychopathology have the intended impact on clinical interpretation? Although this question appears straightforward, its answer is more complex. Specifically, the question itself assumes that projective measures are administered and interpreted for the purpose of diagnostic categorization. Although that is often the case, projective measures and their derived indices are commonly used to *generate* clinical hypotheses (e.g., How might this person handle affectively charged stimulation? What social stances might this person be inclined to assume?) rather than to *test* them (e.g., Is this person depressed? Is this person dangerous? Is this person psychotic?).

The feigning of psychopathology (and the attempt to detect such feigning) in psychological assessments assumes that the examiner will ultimately utilize the test data (which are often continuous and multidimensional) to make a categorical decision, such as whether the respondent is to be diagnosed with major depression. Even when the notion of diagnosis is broadened to include the identification of problem behaviors, projective techniques often show marginal diagnostic efficiency (e.g., Hunsley & Bailey, 1999, 2001). Wood, Nezworski, Garb, and Lilienfeld (2001) have criticized the most widely applied norms for diagnostic use of the Rorschach (Exner's Comprehensive System; Exner, 1974; see also Exner & Erdberg, 2005) for generating unacceptably high false-positive rates in generating clinical diagnoses. If the Rorschach generates a large proportion of false positives, can clinicians necessarily interpret "impaired findings" as successful malingering? Feigning is, at its core, an attempt to engineer a false positive. Certainly, caution is warranted in concluding that a person is feigning based on an elevated test score when the test is known to produce large proportions of false positives under nonfeigning conditions. Although research that includes comparison groups can assist in separating error variance from changes produced intentionally, the caution stands with regard to the clinical application of any research findings. With these cautions in mind, the studies addressing the diagnostic impact of feigned psychopathology are reviewed next.

Meisner (1988) coached 29 undergraduate participants to simulate depression, comparing them with 29 undergraduates taking the Rorschach under standard instructions. Results of this study are only partially comparable to the other studies reviewed earlier, because Meisner evaluated only Rorschach indices thought to be relevant to depression. Nonetheless, simulators showed lower R (consistent with other studies) and more content containing Blood or other Morbid elements. Also evaluating the feigning of depression, Caine, Kinder, and Frueh (1995) compared 20 nonpsychotic depressed women with 20 undergraduate and 20 graduate female students simulating depression. With the exception of patients showing more Morbid content, simulators were not significantly different on the multiple indicators evaluated. Showing a similar pattern with PTSD as the diagnostic focus, the PTSD simulators of

Frueh and Kinder (1994) generated higher X-%, higher SumC, more Dramatic content, and lower X+% than a group of actual patients with PTSD. However, no significant differences were observed on 17 other indices.

Bash and Alpert (1980) introduced a known-groups design to this area of research, comparing persons independently evaluated as malingering a mental disorder with genuine patients on Rorschach. Malingerers showed several differences from the patient groups (including greater number of rejected cards, lower P, and lower F%). However, the overall research design combined the Rorschach indices with scores on nonprojective instruments to evaluate overall differentiation between the two groups. Thus the only interpretation that can be made specifically about the Rorschach in their study is that malingerers do not look exactly like genuine patients.

The studies reviewed in this section thus far offer evidence that feigning pathology can result in a profile of Rorschach results that is not significantly different from those of genuine patients. However, only a few studies have directly reported the extent to which feigned psychopathology resulted in interpretations of pathology presence in the feigner.

Albert, Fox, and Kahn (1980) compared small groups of coached simulators, uncoached simulators, and genuine patients with paranoid schizophrenia (*n* = 6 in each group) by having their Rorschach responses scored and interpreted by fellows of the Society for Personality Assessment. Here is a summary of the key findings;

- 48% of genuine patients with schizophrenia were correctly diagnosed with psychotic disorders.
- 46% of naive simulators were misdiagnosed with psychotic disorders.
- 72% of coached simulators (i.e., a 25-minute audiotaped description of paranoid schizophrenia) were misdiagnosed with psychotic disorders.

Thus persons trained in the Rorschach identified feigned pathology as legitimate pathology as frequently as, or more frequently than, they identified bona fide pathology. Attempts to reanalyze these and other unpublished data by using prescored protocols, computerized interpretation, and updated SCZI, DEPI, and CDI measures have shown mixed results in improving the rate at which feigners are diagnosed as pathological (see Exner, 1987, 1991; Kahn, Fox, & Rhode, 1988). Despite small improvements in some reanalyses, Exner (1991) concluded that "nonpatient subjects may be able to approximate serious disturbance if set to do so" (p. 495).

Netter and Viglione (1994) compared 20 simulators and 20 patients with schizophrenia on multiple Rorschach indicators, including the SCZI. Using the established cut score of 4 or more on the SCZI as the criterion for likely schizophrenia, they found a false-positive rate of 45% (i.e., simulators misclassified with likely schizophrenia). However, the false-negative rate was also substantial at 30% (i.e., genuine patients with schizophrenia scoring below 4). These findings suggest that the SCZI is relatively ineffective for the accurate diagnostic classification (i.e., genuine patients with schizophrenia) and the assessment of feigning (i.e., the detection of uncoached simulators).

Taken together, the limited research in this area (all confined to the Rorschach) leads to a straightforward conclusion: The altered results achievable by attempting to feign pathology on a projective measure often do lead to an interpretive conclusion of categorical pathology. Simply put, skilled practitioners often misclassify simulators as impaired patients.

Detection of Malingering on Projective Measures

Earlier sections demonstrated attempts to feign psychopathology on projective measures that often result in altering the assessment findings to be consistent with an interpretation of pathology. The critical question remains: Can feigned projective measures be accurately detected? This section examines research relevant in addressing this critical question.

Elhai, Kinder, and Frueh (2004) conducted an extensive review of feigning studies. They noted that most studies of feigning on projective measures have relied on between-subjects and within-subjects analyses of variance approaches to determine whether groups were statistically different or similar. They suggested that more sophisticated approaches, such as discriminant function analyses (DFAs), might offer greater insight into the possibilities for distinguishing the presentations of feigned versus genuine pathology on projectives. Even apart from sophisticated discriminative statistical techniques, straightforward cut scores for

distinguishing groups are rarely tested in these studies. Moreover, efforts to characterize the few distinguishing features into empirically based detection strategies (see Rogers, 1984b and Chapter 2, this volume) are largely missing. In reviewing the few studies that directly evaluate the ability of the Rorschach to detect dissimulation, this section attempts to characterize the detection strategies implicit in the findings.

Batchelder (1995) conducted a DFA to determine the utility of several Rorschach indices (P, R, Con+Alog, DV+DR, WSum6, Lambda, and F+%) in discriminating known malingerers ($n = 23$) from psychotic patients ($n = 30$) and nonpsychotic patients ($n = 30$). The results would likely have greater clarity had two-group discriminations (e.g., feigned vs. non-feigned) been conducted rather than the more cumbersome three-group DFA. Nonetheless, Batchelder reported a significant first function that was completely accounted for by differences in P across the three groups. P, or the number of popular responses, can be thought of as reflecting the detection strategy of *erroneous stereotypes*. When feigning pathology, persons appear to assume, incorrectly, that disordered persons would be unable to generate common responses. When Batchelder reformulated the function based solely on P, 74% of malingerers were correctly identified. However, false positives were unacceptably high: (1) 37% of the psychotic patients were incorrectly classified as malingerers, and (2) 50% of the nonpsychotic patients were also misclassified. Given the low positive predictive power shown in this study that relies solely on P, even a cross-validation of these results would yield little clinical usefulness.

McDougall (1996) used a similar analytic method, logistic regression, to evaluate the ability of a putative set of malingering indicators and a corresponding set of nonmalingering (genuine patient) indicators to correctly classify schizophrenia patients ($n = 40$) and simulators ($n = 80$). An extensive set of 11 variables were identified as malingering indicators, and a smaller set of 3 variables were selected as nonmalingering indicators. Some of the variables chosen were standard Rorschach indices, whereas others were ratings of extra-test behavior and specially derived indices. McDougall's indicators and their respective implicit detection strategies are shown in Table 12.2.

TABLE 12.2. McDougall's (1996) Indicators and Implicit Detection Strategies

Indicator type	Indicator definition	Detection strategy
Indicators of malingering	2 or more instances of circumstantiality	Rare symptoms
	2 or more instances of the card coming "alive" in some way	Quasi-rare symptoms
	2 or more distress comments	Symptom severity
	WSum6 >5 + ModWSum6	Symptom combinations
	2 or more simple responses (Wo Fo or Do Fo) containing multiple special scores	Symptom combinations
	Card V reaction time >10 sec	Rare symptoms
	Card V popular with special score	Symptom combinations
	2 or more FabCom	Rare symptoms
	No unspoiled P on Cards IV or V	Rare symptoms
	At least 4 more special scores on Cards IV, V, and VI than on Card I	Symptom combinations
	3 or more Dramatic content scores (Mor, Ag, blood, fire, explosion, sex)	Rare symptoms
Indicators of nonmalingering	D1 popular on Card VIII with no special score	Absence of rare symptoms
	D1 popular on Card X with no special score	Absence of rare symptoms
	2 or more insecure responses (acknowledgment that the response might not be plausible)	Acknowledgment of an unlikely response

Before conducting the logistic regression, McDougall (1996) simply compared the groups based on a simple score computed as the total number of malingering minus the total number of nonmalingering indicators for each participant. As expected, the index was much higher for simulators than for patients (Cohen's $d = 1.16$). Entering the indicators of malingering and indicators of nonmalingering separately into a logistic regression, McDougall achieved an overall correct classification rate of 78.3%. Treating malingering as the criterion being classified, the approach yielded a very low false-negative rate of 11.3% (simulators misclassified as schizophrenic). However, the false-positive rate (schizophrenia patients misclassified as malingerers) was quite high at 42.5%. If cross-validated, this approach could be said to function marginally well as a *screen* for malingering (i.e., a test with high sensitivity regardless of its marginal positive predictive power). Given the laborious nature of scoring many indices not used routinely for clinical assessment, McDougall's approach seems unlikely to gain popularity in general clinical use. However, its utility as a screen in forensic contexts that incorporate Rorschach assessments should be further evaluated.

McDougall's (1996) preliminary work on detection strategies is a major contribution to research on feigned projective measures (see Table 12.2). He attempted to conceptualize very

atypical responses for genuine patients that likely reflect a rare-symptom strategy. Of even greater interest, McDougall pioneered a variant of symptom combinations. For example, he hypothesized on Card V that popular responses would not be combined with special scores. Whether such unexpected pairings represent a potential detection strategy could be tested empirically. Researchers need to follow McDougall's lead in their a priori conceptualization of potential detection strategies.

To date, methods for identifying feigned Rorschach protocols as reliably distinct from those of genuine patients have not proven useful. This appraisal represents a disappointing picture when combined with the conclusions of the previous sections. Simply stated, many simulators are successful at feigning psychopathology, and there are no validated methods for detecting feigned projective measures.

Studies investigating malingering on projective measures[2] have been subject to several general difficulties. First, the diagnostic efficiency of projective measures (discussed earlier) provides something of a ceiling for their accuracy in the assessment of response styles. If high rates of false positives are common in genuine clinical samples, then these rates also pose an upper limit in the assessment of malingering. Second, research on feigned projective measures is constrained by the multitude of indices that are derivable from projective measures (particularly from the Rorschach). With studies using different and usually multiple indices, systematic reviews are difficult to conduct in a cumulative fashion, and family-wise error rate in the individual studies is often ignored. Because of these two general constraints, no efficient and replicated indicators of feigning are reported on projective measuress, despite single studies that appear to generate promising results. Beyond the initial work by McDougall (1996), the current state of the literature offers little basis for employing projective measures with empirically validated methods to identify feigned psychopathology.

The conscientious clinician who desires to employ the Rorschach in contexts sensitive to malingered presentations must ensure that other tests or procedures are administered to evaluate for malingering. Then, if malingering is suspected on the basis of these other assessment tools, the interpretability of the Rorschach findings should be treated with extreme caution.

DEFENSIVENESS ON PROJECTIVE MEASURES

Defensiveness, as used here, refers to an individual's efforts to protect certain aspects of the self (e.g., psychological impairment) from being revealed to others. This term is distinct from the concept of *ego defenses,* which are seen to operate outside of conscious awareness. In the current use, defensiveness involves responses on the part of a test taker that are designed to keep pathology from being revealed on the test. When tests are used to identify pathology, efforts to conceal that pathology are of obvious clinical importance. Much less attention has been paid to defensive concealment of pathology on projective measures than to feigning pathology. Nonetheless, similar questions can be asked of the existing literature. First, do persons alter their test results when attempting to simulate the absence of present pathology?

Hamsher and Farina (1967) demonstrated that TAT results differ significantly when participants are instructed to appear "open" versus to appear "guarded" in their responding. However, it is unclear that asking presumably healthy persons to appear guarded is an adequate simulation (or even an analogue) of patients attempting to conceal their pathology.

Krieger and Levin (1976) administered an abbreviated version of the Holtzman Inkblot Test to 23 patients with schizophrenia under honest conditions and under instructions to appear well adjusted (i.e., as a hospital employee rather than as a patient). Under the defensiveness condition, patients showed significantly fewer pathology indicators. Compared with standard conditions, they exhibited fewer Pathognomonic Verbalizations, better Form Appropriateness, better Integration, more Rejections, and more Movement.

As noted in an earlier section, Timmons and colleagues (1993) showed that persons coached to adopt various response sets, including defensiveness, could produce the desired results on a sentence completion test. When asked to simulate a full recovery from an accident, students produced their lowest levels of angry negativity and disability exaggeration.

Taken together, these findings do suggest that results on projective measures are likely to be altered by defensive attempts to conceal pathology. But do such alterations influence the clinical interpretation?

Grossman, Wasyliw, Benn, and Gyoerkoe (2002) utilized a quasi-known-groups design, identifying persons as "minimizers" or "non-minimizers" based on MMPI indicators. Then, employing an implicit rare symptoms hypothesis, they evaluated the extent to which pathology indicators on both the MMPI and the Rorschach appeared suppressed by the minimizing response style. Grossman and colleagues concluded that minimizers were able to suppress their presentation of psychopathology on the MMPI but that those same persons appeared less able to do so on the Rorschach. The frequency of pathology indicators on the Rorschach (D, AdjD, Wsum6, X+%, X-%, Intellectualization, SCZI, SCon, CDI, and DEPI) appeared comparable between persons responding defensively (minimizers) and their nondefensive counterparts. This study suggests that defensiveness on the Rorschach might not effectively mask pathology. Alternatively, it may simply indicate the weaknesses of the MMPI-2 in evaluating defensiveness, especially as the investigators did not use the most effective scales (i.e., Wiggins Sd and Cofer's Mp; see Greene, Chapter 10, this volume). Moreover, accused sex offenders may engage in selective defensiveness about their alleged offenses that is not adequately captured by general defensiveness on the MMPI-2.

Although a few other studies investigate potential concealment of pathology on the Rorschach (e.g., Moncho, 2004; Wasyliw, Benn, Grossman, & Haywood, 1998), they utilize differential prevalence designs. In other words, there is no way to know which persons in these studies were masking pathology or accurately presenting the absence of pathology. Therefore, their findings are not relevant to the crucial issue of evaluating differences between defensive and nondefensive Rorschach protocols.

The current literature lacks compelling evidence to suggest that pathology concealment results in consistent and clinically relevant masking of pathology on projective measures. Therefore, it is premature to evaluate the potential effectiveness of projective measures to detect defensiveness. Clinicians utilizing projective measures in contexts sensitive to defensive response styles have no choice but to rely on pathology indicators. However, suspicions of defensive concealment of pathology must be evaluated through the use of other assessment tools. Of critical importance, neither the presence nor the absence of pathology indicators on projective measures can be used to evaluate defensiveness.

MULTIPLE-CHOICE FORMATS FOR RESPONSE DISTORTION ON STIMULI FROM PROJECTIVE MEASURES

A few studies have investigated response distortion using measures that borrow their stimuli from projective measures but then utilize those stimuli in a multiple-choice format. For example, Pettigrew, Tuma, Pickering, and Whelton (1983) devised a multiple-choice test composed of miniaturized inkblots from the Rorschach as stimuli and various response possibilities. Participants were provided with four response options: (1) good form with bizarre wording, (2) good form with nonbizarre wording, (3) poor form with lengthy but nonbizarre wording, and (4) poor form with concise, nonbizarre wording. They found that simulators choose more responses with good form and bizarre wording than did honest or patient groups. This is a variant of symptom combinations. Although ignored for the past 15 years, the multiple-choice format is potentially relevant to clinical practice. One possibility would be to test its effectiveness for feigned psychopathology after a standardized administration of the Rorschach. This design would minimize its potential contamination of Rorschach interpretation.

Other examples include studies of the so-called Group Personality Projective Test (GPPT). Despite its name, the GPPT is a multiple-choice test involving human stick-figure drawings as stimuli and various descriptions of what might be going on as response choices. Brozovich (1970), as well as Cassel and Brauchle (1959) have performed studies utilizing within-subjects designs involving administrations with honest, fake bad, and fake good instructions with normal adults. Utilizing an implicit rare symptoms strategy, both studies identified significant differences based on instructional sets. Feigning produced higher tension-reduction quotients, succorance needs, and total scores; defensiveness yielded lower total scores and neuroticism.

FINAL COMMENTS

The Rorschach and other projective measures appear to be easily vunerable to response distortion, almost certainly when examinees attempt to feign pathology and probably when they attempt to conceal pathology. Both Stermac (1988) and Schretlen (1997), in earlier editions of this book, concluded that research to date did not support the development of a clinical decision model for the detection of dissimulation via the Rorschach. That is still the case. Certainly the few findings from non-Rorschach projectives require the same hesitance. Elhai, Kinder, and Frueh (2004), focusing exclusively on malingering, echoed the conclusions that the Rorschach could not be used as a method to detect malingering. They went even further to suggest that all future research attempting to develop projective-based indices to identify dissimulation be evaluated for incremental validity over that which can be achieved via objective measures. This review of the literature endorses this suggestion. Given the innovations and successes demonstrated in recent years in detecting dissimulation with objective measures (e.g., scales from the MMPI-2 and Personality Assessment Inventory, as well as specialized measures), it is likely that the more laborious tasks involved in administering and scoring most projective measures for the purpose of dissimulation detection would be justifiable only if the resulting information could add incrementally to that which can easily be achieved from objective tests.

Projective measures often produce misleading results, with test takers successfully feigning or concealing pathology. Moreover, there are no reliable methods to detect either malingering or defensiveness. Thus the choice to employ a projective measure likely needs to involve a complex evaluation of the context (e.g., likely perceived as adversarial vs. cooperative), the consequences of diagnostic errors (e.g., false positives and false negatives), and even the benefits of whatever valid information might be obtained. These issues should not categorically rule out the use of projective measures in forensic contexts, but it places the onus on the evaluator to demonstrate the probable validity of the results based on other (likely objective) indicators and to have a clear rationale for the use of the information to be inferred from any putatively valid results of the projective measure.

Future research endeavors in the area of response styles with projective measures should attend to the following recommendations in order to facilitate the possible identification of useful and replicable detection strategies. Several priorities are outlined:

1. Studies should be conducted in specific contexts in which the demand characteristics lend themselves to likely response styles (e.g., custody determinations and disability evaluations). The studies should focus on a small number of variables that fall into two categories: (1) variables closely related to the most useful clinical inferences in the population of interest and (2) variables identified a priori as the best candidates for potential detection strategies (e.g., consideration of specific response styles, testable methods, and well-defined principles). Focusing on small variable sets increases the likelihood of clinical applicability and research replicability while concomitantly reducing the risk of spurious findings based on inflated family-wise error.

2. Studies should employ robust design for response styles (see Rogers, Chapter 24, this volume), using either known-groups comparisons or sophisticated simulation designs with appropriate clinical samples and other methodological considerations (e.g., manipulation checks and use of negative incentives). With known-groups comparisons, gold-standard assessments that are independent of projective data are preferred over marginal indicators (e.g., MMPI-2 indicators with far-ranging cut scores; see Rogers, Sewell, Martin, & Vitacco, 2003).

NOTES

1. The decision to exclude most dissertation research in this review was made for several reasons. First, the vast majority of dissertation research surveyed in preparation for this chapter contained results derivative of and consistent with that which is presented in the published literature. Second, the surveyed dissertations showed a marked variability in methodological soundness and analytic clarity. To present such work without comment would risk apparent endorsement, but to offer a full critical evaluation of such research would tilt the entire review. Some of these problems are remedied (or at least filtered) by the peer-review process. Thus dissertations were included only when the approach or the results were divergent from the published literature. Nonetheless, when relevant effect sizes could be extracted from recent dissertations, they are included in Table 12.1.

2. Some published studies are not even reviewed in the current context because of idiosyncratic design variations that make the results virtually uninterpretable (e.g., within-subjects designs using instructions to appear "good" and "bad" with no honest condition, retest instructions to "improve" without specification of what that means, differential prevalence studies, using an MMPI F cutting score as a sole criterion for malingering, etc.). However, such problems are not seen as endemic to the entire research field.

13

Feigned Amnesia and Memory Loss

JERRY J. SWEET, PhD
DANIEL C. CONDIT, PhD
NATHANIEL W. NELSON, PhD

Complaints of memory impairment in civil litigation involving claims of personal injury are so common that the domain of learning and memory is usually a focus of forensic evaluations. Reported amnesia for important events related to criminal litigation is frequent enough that memory testing is also common in evaluations of those accused of crimes. There is an obvious and strong motivation, in this instance a disincentive to perform normally, for civil litigants[1] and criminal defendants to appear unable to recall information. We can refer to the situation in which civil litigants and criminal defendants are evaluated as involving a *secondary gain context*.[2] For the civil litigant, the potential secondary gain is receiving compensation for injury; for the criminal defendant, the potential secondary gain is avoiding responsibility or creating the appearance of not being guilty. The powerful contingencies in these secondary gain contexts raise the risk of feigning of memory impairment and/or amnesia.

The common inclusion of formal psychological and neuropsychological testing in forensic evaluations is easy to understand. As an example, the increasing involvement of clinical neuropsychologists as consultants or evaluators in forensic cases has in turn increased the energy and productivity of clinical researchers (see Sweet, King, Malina, Bergman, & Simmons, 2002). The number of peer-reviewed publica-

tions related to forensic activity of neuropsychologists has increased dramatically, and, from 1990 to 2000, it represents an average of 10% of the published articles in the three most widely read clinical neuropsychology journals (i.e., *Archives of Clinical Neuropsychology, Journal of Clinical and Experimental Neuropsychology, The Clinical Neuropsychologist*). Most pertinent to this book, the proportion of these articles related to the topic of malingering is very high. Of a total of 139 forensic articles, 120, or 86%, pertained to the topic of malingering and malingering detection methods (Sweet et al., 2002). As a result of increased demand for services and increased clinical research, the practice of forensic neuropsychology has become a major activity for many clinical neuropsychologists (see Sweet, Ecklund-Johnson, & Malina, 2007).

Estimates of the base rates of exaggeration or complete feigning of memory impairment among civil litigants have been of considerable interest. Of special note, Mittenberg, Patton, Canyock, and Condit (2002) surveyed practice data from board-certified clinical practitioners based on more than 33,000 forensic cases. Estimates varied by practice setting (e.g., private practice, academic medical center), type of alleged disorder (e.g., mild head injury vs. moderate or severe head injury), and type of litigation context (i.e., civil vs. criminal). Mittenberg and colleagues' findings suggested that the base rates of "probable malingering or symptom exaggeration" were approximately 29% in personal injury cases and 30% of disability cases and ranging as high as 41% for mild head injury. Also in keeping with most prior research (e.g., Frederick & Denney, 1998), the base rate estimate was substantially higher for civil than for criminal cases, with the majority of the civil case estimates near 30% and the majority of criminal case estimates near or below 20%.

Ardolf, Denney, and Houston (2007) examined comparative rates of feigned cognitive impairment using current methods of detection and applying the Slick criteria (Slick, Sherman, & Iverson, 1999; see also Bender, Chapter 5, this volume). They found the base rate of probable and definite malingering among criminal defendants to be higher (i.e., approximately 54%) than among civil litigants. If confirmed via follow-up studies, this base rate would indeed surpass most malingering base-rate estimates among civil litigants. For example, Larrabee (2003a) combined the results of 11 separate studies and found a 40% of malingering among civil litigants.

Slick, Tan, Strauss, and Hultsch (2004) also published survey data that in part addressed the base rate of malingering. These investigators surveyed "experts" on malingering, who were defined by having published at least twice on the topic and being actively involved in evaluations of litigants. Estimates of the proportion of *possible* and *probable* malingerers vary considerably. Though clinical researchers vary in their estimates of base rates, the literature as a whole has amply demonstrated that malingering among civil litigants and claimants and among criminal defendants occurs regularly and requires *proactive* steps by the clinician in order to improve the probability of detecting it when present and accurately ruling it out when not present (Sweet, 1999b).

In this chapter, we explore the current state of the art related to detection of feigned amnesia and memory loss. We begin with an examination of genuine memory disorders.

IDENTIFICATION OF GENUINE MEMORY DISORDERS

Clinicians and neuroscientists have studied the domain of memory, both in terms of normal functioning and related disorders of memory,

for many years, precisely because learning and remembering information is essential to most human endeavors. Without some ability to learn and remember, most individuals would be at a decided disadvantage in our complex society and might even be unable to function independently and safely. From a different perspective, individuals with substantial memory disorders may not be held accountable for their actions. Historically, genuine memory disorders have been divided into those caused by medical and by psychological conditions. Both types need to be distinguished from malingered memory disorders.

Amnesia and Memory Loss Due to Neurological/Medical Causes

The terms *amnesic* and *amnestic* are synonymous in the literature; both are used to describe human memory disturbances. Though, technically speaking, all disturbances of memory can be termed amnestic disturbances, the term *amnesia* is often reserved as a descriptive term for patients whose compromised anterograde memory (i.e., capacity for new learning after a salient point in time) is quite severe and predominantly more severe than other cognitive impairments, if any are also present. Within this chapter, we use the term *memory loss* to indicate instances of amnestic disturbance that are less severe than amnesia.

The literature has employed numerous terms to refer to the category of neurological/medical causes of amnesia. Years ago, the term *organic* was popular in reference to brain-based disorders; the polar opposite of the presumed dichotomy was *functional,* which implied nonphysical cause. More recently, biological research has questioned the assumption of "functional disorders" with growing evidence of brain dysfunction, instead assuming that all psychiatric conditions were associated with mental disorders. However, even when originally used, the term *organic* was an odd misnomer because all parts of the human body, not just the brain, are organic (i.e., physically alive). In this chapter we use the term *neurogenic* to refer to all causes of amnesia and memory loss that are fundamentally brain-based and are believed to be occurring as a result of a primary neurological disorder or a nonneurological medical disorder that secondarily impairs brain function.

Several excellent treatises (Bauer, Grande, & Valenstein, 2003; Kopelman & Stanhope, 2002) are available concerning genuine neurogenic amnesia. It can result from various neurological and medical conditions that affect mesial temporal or diencephalic brain systems. Salient to the current topic of detecting feigned amnestic symptoms, many stable, genuine neurological conditions demonstrate a substantial difference between free-recall performance and recognition performance in well-designed memory studies (Kopelman & Stanhope, 2002) that are not confounded by floor or ceiling effects (i.e., tasks either too easy or too difficult that do not allow for a wide range of performances). Characteristics of preserved nonmemory functions are also commonly present in individuals with even dense amnesia. For example, preserved preillness memory may be present in the form of intellectual, social, and language information and skill, as well as previously acquired motor and cognitive skills (Bauer et al., 2003). These characteristics, relatively unknown to lay persons, can be useful in the development of procedures that differentiate feigned from genuine brain-based amnestic disturbances.

Amnesia and Memory Loss Due to Psychogenic Causes

Some examples of common (1) neurological and medical disorders and (2) psychological/psychiatric disorders that are capable of causing temporary or persistent memory disorder are listed in Table 13.1. It is readily apparent that very few conditions of a psychological or psychiatric nature are associated with frank amnesia or memory loss. As described by Kopelman (2002), psychogenic (dissociative) amnesia can be *global,* which refers to a profound loss of past memory and may even include on very rare occasions loss of personal identity. It can also be *situation-specific,* such as memory loss that might be reported for the commission of a crime in which the victim experiences events as emotionally traumatic or stressful.

The current clinical nomenclature of mental disorders associated with memory disturbance (American Psychiatric Association, 2000) presents *dissociative fugue* as a separate condition in which an individual demonstrates a sudden, unexpected departure from normal life activities, with inability to recall his or her past, as well as confusion regarding personal identity. This condition is distinguished from *dissociative identity disorder* (formerly multiple personality disorder), which is characterized by "two or more distinct personalities or psychological states that recurrently take control of the individual's behavior accompanied by an inability to recall important personal information" (American Psychiatric Association, 2000, p. 519). Finally, *factitious disorder* is characterized by the deliberate feigning of a clinical condition for the purpose of meeting a psychological need (primary gain). It must be contrasted with malingering, which has an external motivation.

Grossman (2005) notes some salient discriminating features of neurogenic and psychogenic memory disorders. Dissociative amnesia involves an inability to recall particular events, most often of a psychologically traumatic nature, rather than an ongoing inability to learn new information, as is often seen in neurogenic memory disorders. Unrelated to physical trauma, an individual with dissociative amnesia may be unable to recall either a specific time interval or specific events that occurred within a particular time interval. Though physical trauma can induce amnesia for a limited time interval, the duration of the time interval is a marker of the severity of brain injury. At more severe levels, trauma is also associated with anterograde learning and memory disturbance that can continue long after recovery from acute confusional effects of the initial brain injury (see Bender, Chapter 5, this volume). The course of the dissociative amnesia is also different in that abrupt, dramatic recovery followed by completely accurate recall of the initial amnestic time interval is possible. Risk factors described by Grossman for development of dissociative amnesia include preexisting heightened suggestibility, previous development of a hysterical or conversion disorder in response to stress, and an emotional personality style that might increase the probability of a conversion disorder, which by implication would involve overreliance on repression as a defense against unwanted feelings. According to Grossman, an amobarbital interview can help distinguish psychogenic from neurogenic amnesia, with the former producing more lucid and detailed memory and the latter more prone to development of a transient delirium.

In the sections that follow, we consider stand-alone and embedded feigning measures in civil and criminal litigation. These measures generally apply to memory loss, with

TABLE 13.1. Examples of Neurogenic[a] and Psychogenic[b] Causes of Amnestic Conditions

Neurogenic causes	Psychogenic causes
Alcohol or drug intoxication	Dissociative amnesia (previously "psychogenic amnesia")
Anoxia or hypoxia	Dissociative fugue (previously "psychogenic fugue")
Delirium	Dissociative identity disorder (previously "multiple personality disorder")
Alcohol/drug withdrawal syndrome	Factitious disorder
Medical illness (e.g., urinary tract infection)	
Concussion/traumatic brain injury	
Cerebrovascular disorder (e.g., stroke)	
Dementia (e.g., Alzheimer's, Lewy-body, and Parkinson's diseases)	
High-altitude illness	
Hypothermia	
Infection of the brain (e.g., herpes encephalitis)	
Intracranial tumor	
Metabolic disorder	
Seizures	
Thromboembolic stroke	
Viral encephalitis	
Vitamin deficiency (e.g., Wernicke's encephalopathy)	

[a]Brain-based neurological/medical disorders.
[b]Psychological/psychiatric disorders.

stand-alone measures often assessing anterograde memory.

APPLICATION OF FEIGNING MEASURES IN CIVIL LITIGATION

A neuropsychological evaluation may be the primary source of evidence regarding claims of brain dysfunction in compensation-seeking civil litigation (Guilmette, Hart, & Giuliano, 1993). This observation is especially true in cases of mild injury in which objective neuroimaging techniques fail to reveal confirmatory evidence. The need to evaluate effort led to the development of procedures that are objectively easy but that may not appear so to the examinee (commonly known as the "floor effect" detection strategies). These effort measures can be referred to as cognitive feigning measures (CFM). CFMs can vary in content (verbal vs. nonverbal stimuli; recall vs. recognition), format (paper and pencil vs. computerized), actual degree of difficulty, transparency (i.e., obviousness of the test's purpose), and length of administration time. Table 13.2 lists

CFMs related to memory that have been subjected to peer review and enjoy widespread acceptance.

Many instruments have been scrutinized as to whether they meet evidentiary standards required by the Supreme Court in *Daubert v. Merrell Dow Pharmaceuticals* (1993). On the issue of admissibility, the edited volume by Hom and Denney (2002a) reviews many of the common CFMs and embedded validity indicators, and they specifically address the Daubert criteria.

CFMs frequently make use of a forced-choice, often two-choice, recognition paradigm in which there is a known probability of success based on random responding (e.g., 50%). Just as performance significantly above chance indicates intact recognition memory, performance significantly below chance strongly suggests intact recognition but with purposeful failure. This detection strategy, based on the probability of obtaining a given score, is referred to as *symptom validity testing* (SVT). The advantage of such statistical evaluation of performance (i.e., below-chance cut scores, rather than norm-referenced cut scores) is that

TABLE 13.2. Stand-Alone Measures with Demonstrated Utility for Identifying Feigned Memory Loss

Measures	Key reference	Detection strategies
Amsterdam Short-Term Memory Test (ASTM test)	Schagen, Schmand, de Sterke, & Lindeboom (1997)	FCT, FE
b Test	Boone et al. (2000)	FE
Computerized Assessment of Response Bias (CARB)	Green & Iverson (2001)	FCT
Digit Memory Test[a]	Vickery, Berry, Inman, Harris, & Orey (2001)	FCT
Letter Memory Test	Vagnini et al. (2006)	FCT
Medical Symptom Validity Test	Richman et al. (2006)	FCT
Memory for 16 Item Test (modified Rey MFIT)	Fisher & Rose (2005)	FE, VLP
Portland Digit Recognition Test (PDRT)	Greve & Bianchini (2006)	FCT
Rey Memory for 15 Item Test (Rey MFIT) and variants	Boone et al. (2002)	FE, VLP
Rey Word Recognition List	Nitch, Boone, Wen, Arnold, & Alfano (2006)	FE, VLP
Victoria Symptom Validity Test (VSVT)	Thompson (2002)	FCT
Test of Memory Malingering (TOMM)	Greve, Beauchini, & Doche (2006)	FCT
Word Completion Memory Test (WCMT)	Hilsabeck & Gouvier (2005)	VLP
Word Memory Test (WMT)	Green et al. (2002)	FCT, VLP

Note. FE, floor effect; FCT, forced-choice test; VLP, violation of learning principles.
[a]Also known as Multi-Digit Memory Test and Hiscock Forced-Choice Procedure.

the influence of the malingering base rates is removed, and positive results can be interpreted with greater confidence (Bianchini, Mathias, & Greve, 2001). SVTs are designed to be very simple; individuals with actual brain injury and cognitive impairment, as well as psychiatric patients, are able to achieve near-perfect performance. However, for this reason, SVTs may be relatively "transparent" (i.e., recognized as an easy task by the malingerer, who may temper or withhold biased responding on these measures to avoid detection). Moreover, below-chance performance as an operational definition of malingering tends to lack sensitivity, as deliberately reduced performances, even though at or above-chance performances are not identified as malingering. To address this problem, researchers have attempted to improve sensitivity by developing performance criteria based on administering the measures to well-documented patient groups, including patients with brain injuries, memory disorders, and psychiatric illnesses. Such scores obtained by nonlitigants with severe cognitive impairments can be used to define the lower bound-

aries of credible performance. This strategy (i.e., floor effect) has been adapted to several CFMs currently in use. Scores obtained by litigating patients, especially those with less severe injuries, can be compared with genuine clinical performances that frequently show a *clinical floor* (i.e., a point in the distribution of scores below which legitimate patient performance is not expected). Scores that are well below those obtained by individuals with well-documented disorders can be viewed as noncredible and very likely to reflect insufficient effort.

Sharland and Gfeller (2007) surveyed clinical neuropsychologists to rate the frequency with which they use various indicators of effort. Results showed the following: 75% of neuropsychologists used the Test of Memory Malingering (TOMM), 41% the Word Memory Test (WMT), and 18% the Victoria Symptom Validity Test (VSVT). In an earlier survey, Essig, Mittenberg, Petersen, Strauman, and Cooper (2001) reported that 56% of clinical neuropsychologists use the Rey Memory for 15 Item Test (RMFIT). Slick and colleagues

(2004) surveyed forensic experts and found that most used the RFMIT (75%) and TOMM (71%). Due to space constraints and the quantity of literature on this topic, we limit our discussion to a relatively small number of illustrative studies involving commonly used measures that differ in their content and format.

Test of Memory Malingering

The TOMM (Tombaugh, 1996; see Tombaugh, 2002, for a review) is a 50-item visual recognition test for the differentiation of actual versus malingered memory impairment. Two learning trials are administered in which examinees are shown 50 pictures for 3 seconds each. Each trial is then followed by a forced-choice recognition trial, with feedback provided for every response. After a short delay, a third recognition trial is administered. Each recognition trial contains unique foils.

The original validation studies provided support for its use as an instrument to detect exaggerated or feigned claims of memory impairment (Rees, Tombaugh, Gansler, & Moczynski, 1998; Tombaugh, 1997). More recently, Teichner and Wagner (2004) provided normative data for cognitively intact, cognitively impaired, and demented elderly patients. The rate of misclassification was high for the patients with dementia using the recommended cut score. However, the TOMM correctly identified 100% of cognitively intact and 92.7% of cognitively impaired patients, with an overall correct classification rate of 94.7%. Greve, Bianchini, and Doane (2006) examined the classification accuracy of the TOMM in a sample with traumatic brain injury (TBI), which included patients meeting Slick's strict criteria for malingered neurocognitive dysfunction (MND; Slick et al. 1999), and patients with memory disorders who had no external incentive to perform poorly. Using the original cut scores, specificity was greater than 95%, and sensitivity was over 45%. Within the subset of patients with mild TBI, none of the likely genuine patients (i.e., without MND) were misclassified by the original cut scores; for feigning, 60% of the patients with malingered mild TBI were correctly classified. Consistent with previous studies, suggested cut scores produced higher rates of misclassification with patients with memory disorders (primarily dementia) and moderate to severe TBI.

Word Memory Test

The Word Memory Test (WMT; Green, Allen, & Astner, 1996) is a stand-alone measure designed to measure both verbal memory and suboptimal effort. The test begins with two learning trials in which the examinee is twice presented with the same list of 20 word pairs. Immediate Recognition (IR) is then administered, in which the participant must identify the original words from a series of 40 target-foil word pairs in a forced-choice recognition format. The IR score equals the percentage of words correctly identified. Without warning, Delayed Recognition (DR) is administered after a 30-minute interval, and the examinee must identify the original words from a series of target-foil pairs containing new foils. The DR score equals the percentage of words correctly identified. The consistency of responses between the 40 paired IR and DR trials is then calculated (CNS). The CNS score equals the percentage of words correctly identified on both IR and DR trials. The WMT manual (Green, 2003) recommends that suboptimal effort or biased responding be considered if any of the three IR, DR, or CNS scores fall at or below a specific cut score. These portions of the WMT may be administered either orally or by computer; the two administration versions appear equivalent (Green, Lees-Haley, & Allen, 2002).

The WMT has been shown to have good sensitivity and specificity. In the original validation study, Green and colleagues (1996) gave the WMT to 15 uninjured simulators and 15 litigants with moderate to severe TBI. The simulators, mainly psychologists, were warned that the WMT was designed to detect feigned impairment and were instructed to simulate deficits without being detected. Only one simulator produced a passing DR score.

Green, Iverson, and Allen (1999) examined WMT performance in 298 consecutive patients referred for clinical assessment in connection with head injury litigation. Patients had moderate to severe TBI ($n = 64$) or mild head injuries (MHI; $n = 234$). Patients in the TBI group had serious injuries and successful disability claims; they were viewed as having no reason to exaggerate their cognitive impairment. By contrast, the MHI group had a greater incentive to demonstrate impairment, because many seeking disability benefits would likely be denied. Using a differential prevalence design, the moderate-to-severe TBI group performed significantly better than the MHI group on all three WMT effort measures. Mean scores for the patients with TBI were above the recommended cut scores.

The WMT performs well when compared with other commonly used CFMs. Gervais, Rohling, Green, and Ford (2004) compared the sensitivity of the WMT, the forced-choice digit recognition procedure known as the Computerized Assessment of Response Bias (CARB; Allen, Conder, Green, & Cox, 1997), and the TOMM. The 519 participants were involved in workers' compensation, long-term disability, or personal injury claims. Failure rates for each test were determined using the cut scores recommended by the tests' authors. Sensitivity of the instruments varied widely, with failure rates of 32% for the WMT, 17% for the CARB, and 11% for the TOMM. Each of these effort measures could be used to create a bootstrapping comparison (see Rogers, Chapter 24, this volume). However, in a comparison of the sensitivities of multiple effort measures, the experimental design used in this study more closely approximates a differential prevalence design, which can be suggestive rather than conclusive regarding effectiveness of malingering detection. Base rate estimates in relevant literature suggest that the WMT may be the most sensitive of these three effort measures.

Victoria Symptom Validity Test

The Victoria Symptom Validity Test (VSVT; Slick, Hop, Strauss, & Thompson, 1997) is a stand-alone measure of effort that involves recognition of digits using a computerized forced-choice format. Validity of performance is judged by the number of items correct and by mean response latencies. Binomial probability estimates and interpretive classification labels are generated by the computerized scoring program. Performances below the level of chance are classified as "invalid"; scores above chance level are considered "valid"; chance-level scores are classified as "questionable." The initial validation study (Slick et al., 1997) compared four groups: controls, simulators, compensation-seeking, and nonlitigating neurological groups. All controls and nonlitigants, some of whom had profound memory impairment, performed above the chance level. For simulators, the classifications were 19% valid, 51% questionable, and 30% invalid. For the litigating group, 85% were valid, 11% ques-

tionable, and 3% invalid. Within the limitations of a differential prevalence design, these results suggest good sensitivity with simulators and a modest degree of sensitivity with civil litigants.

The VSVT has been found to be insensitive to genuine neurologically based memory impairment. For example, six nonlitigating neurological patients with *profound* memory impairment were able to obtain perfect or near-perfect scores on the VSVT (Slick et al., 2003).

To address possibly high false-negative rates, Macciocchi, Seel, Alderson, and Godsall (2006) assessed the sensitivity of the VSVT in a homogeneous sample of acute, severely brain-injured patients. Their sample performed well above the suggested cut scores for accuracy; however, mean response latencies were longer. They concluded that individuals in the acute phase of severe TBIs can be expected to perform well on the VSVT in terms of number correct but not mean response latencies.

Clinicians interpreting the VSVT should be aware that the computer output is based on binomial probabilities for the purpose of identifying only individuals scoring below chance. It uses SVT, which is consistent with the Slick criteria for definite malingering. This standard reflects a very conservative view toward identifying individuals who are deliberately withholding effort and therefore are designated as malingerers. This interpretive stance is viewed as too limited by many forensic experts. In fact, if clinicians were to label as malingerers only those individuals whose performances were significantly below chance, numerous false negatives would occur. Many relevant forced-choice studies, including those performed with *comparable* digit-recognition procedures, such as the Digit Memory Test (DMT; e.g., Guilmette et al., 1993; Prigatano & Amin, 1993; Prigatano, Smason, Lamb, & Bortz, 1997), as well as with the VSVT (e.g., Grote et al., 2000) itself, have found that insufficient effort and malingering can be identified at performance levels that are well above chance. These studies and others find that nonlitigant neurological samples generally complete the VSVT and similar digit recognition procedures with very few errors, which has allowed for the development of a much higher cut score to identify those who are withholding effort.

Rey Memory for 15 Items Test

The Rey Memory for 15 Items Test (RMFIT; Rey, 1964) is a brief and easily administered test, available in the public domain; it is de-signed to detect exaggerated or feigned memory impairment. The test involves brief exposure to and immediate reproduction of a visual stimulus. The stimulus contains 15 items in a simple 3×5 arrangement, with three columns and five rows (A B C, 1 2 3, a b c, □ ○ △, I II III). The test is often presented as a difficult memory test but is in fact fairly easy due to the redundancy of the items. The RMFIT has been criticized in several studies (e.g., Bernard, Houston, & Natoli, 1993; Schretlen, Brandt, Krafft, & van Gorp, 1991) for limited sensitivity and specificity problems with select populations (Arnett, Hammeke, & Schwartz, 1995). Nonetheless, the RMFIT continues to be one of the most commonly used measures of insufficient effort (Sharland & Gfeller, 2007). Likely, this popularity is related to expediency, specifically its brevity and availability in the public domain.

A recent meta-analysis of the RMFIT (Reznek, 2005) examined 13 studies with a pooled sample size of 983 participants. Applying a commonly used cut score of less than nine items recalled, specificity was 85% and sensitivity was 36%. Adopting a lower cut score of less than eight improved specificity (92%), although sensitivity decreased to 9%. Classification improved when participants with IQs below 70 were excluded from the analyses. Excluding these participants, the customary cut score yielded a specificity of 90%; use of the more conservative cut score yielded a specificity of 95%.

Citing limitations of the RMFIT, one group of investigators (Boone, Salazar, Lu, Warner-Chacon, & Razani, 2002) developed a procedure to enhance its sensitivity and specificity. Based on observations that malingerers tend to suppress recognition more than actual patients do, the researchers appended a brief recognition procedure to the standard test administration. The procedures were administered to four groups: (1) patients with independent evidence of suspect effort, (2) nonlitigant referrals, (3) learning-disabled college students, and (4) normal controls. Boone and colleagues (2002) presented means, standard deviations, and ranges for each group. These investigators found that the use of a combined recall and recognition score yielded high specificity (92%) and produced substantially increased sensitivity (71%). Because the addition of the recognition trial adds almost no additional adminis-

tration time and substantially increases its sensitivity, we recommend that clinicians using the RMFIT incorporate the recognition procedure.

Because multiple studies have demonstrated specificity problems and low sensitivity in its original format, it has been recommended that use of the RMFIT be limited. The RMFIT can be used with populations that have *not* demonstrated reduced performance outside of a secondary gain context, such as mild TBI (Greiffenstein, Baker, & Gola, 1996). As noted, we recommend use of the recognition format in all RMFIT applications.

Conclusions

Poor performance on stand-alone CFMs has been associated with poorer performance on neuropsychological testing in general (see Iverson, 2005, for a comparison of effect sizes caused by various neurological and medical conditions versus effect sizes for insufficient effort). A substantial literature concerning the TOMM, WMT, VSVT, RMFIT, and additional CFMs has accumulated. Such measures are now a standard of practice in forensic cases in which cognitive integrity is at issue.

VALIDITY INDICATORS EMBEDDED WITHIN CLINICAL MEMORY TESTS

Performance patterns on actual tests of ability can also be examined, when applicable, for detection strategies, such as magnitude of error, performance curve, violation of learning principles, and floor effect. There are a number of benefits to having indices of effort embedded in standard neuropsychological tests. Unlike stand-alone CFMs, they may be applied retrospectively to test results contained in case records (Mittenberg, Aguila-Puentes, Patton, Canyock, & Heilbronner, 2002). They are more time efficient than external validity measures, as they do not require additional time to administer. Effort can vary over the course of the evaluation; reliance on stand-alone CFMs as the sole indicator of effort may result in effort being assessed over too small a portion of the examination. In contrast, embedded validity indicators allow more continuous assessment of effort, rather than relying on a discrete point in the evaluation. Moreover, a single failed CFM is considered insufficient evidence for a classification of malingering (Slick et al.,

1999), which requires examination of multiple types of information. Embedded measures permit identification of specific performance patterns or ranges of severity that are very unlikely to reflect the specific type of brain dysfunction alleged and, minimally, should raise alternative hypotheses that include malingering. Finally, multiple validity checks are less obtrusive than stand-alone CFMs, thereby decreasing the likelihood that examinees will be able to learn or be coached successfully regarding how to present credibly.

A number of methods for detecting feigned memory impairment have been developed with such commonly used instruments as the Wechsler Memory Scale, revised and third editions (WMS-R and WMS-III, respectively), the original and second editions of the California Verbal Learning Test (CVLT and CVLT-II), and the Rey Auditory Verbal Learning Test (RAVLT). This is not an exhaustive list by any means; an impressive body of literature is now available on embedded validity indicators. The reader is referred to Morgan and Sweet (2008) for a more comprehensive listing of relevant research concerning embedded CFMs.

Wechsler Memory Scale—Third Edition

Differences between the WMS-R index scores have been established as useful markers for identifying insufficient effort (Mittenberg, Azrin, Millsaps, & Heilbronner, 1993). However, some of the subtests and indexes were restructured for the WMS-III, and these methods may not generalize. Discrepancies between the Working Memory Index (WMI) and other WMS-III memory index scores have been examined with mixed results as potential indicators of suspect effort. Using the WMS-III, Langeluddecke and Lucas (2003) failed to replicate the findings of Mittenberg and colleagues (1993), who found that poor WMS-R attentional abilities relative to immediate memory effectively classified head-injured nonlitigants and healthy analogue malingerers. Lange, Iverson, Sullivan, and Anderson (2006) examined the clinical utility of WMS-III memory minus Working Memory Index (memory–WMI) discrepancy scores in an Australian sample of 145 personal injury litigants (19 with insufficient effort and 126 with adequate effort). Specifically, they examined memory–WMI discrepancies using the Auditory Immediate Index (AII), Immediate Memory Index (IMI),

Auditory Delayed Index (ADI), and General Memory Index (GMI). They found that the insufficient-effort group obtained statistically significantly lower WMS-III index scores than the adequate-effort group. Statistically significant group differences were also observed on three of four memory–WMI discrepancy scores examined (i.e., ADI–WMI, IMI–WMI, and GMI–WMI). The insufficient-effort group obtained significantly lower WMS-III memory indexes and demonstrated larger memory–WMI discrepancy scores. Memory–WMI discrepancies had high specificity and negative predictive power (NPP) values, ranging from 95 to 98% and .86 to .88, respectively. However, sensitivity and positive predictive power (PPP) were unacceptably low. Only a small percentage of individuals with insufficient effort obtained unusually high memory–WMI differences (sensitivity ranged from 0 to 11%); furthermore, such scores were not predictive of group membership (PPP ranged from .0 to .40). However, Lange and colleagues acknowledged that the base rate of insufficient effort observed in their sample (13.1%) was lower than published estimates of malingering base rates in North American samples (which tend to be higher), possibly resulting in PPP values that underestimate the clinical utility of memory–WMI discrepancy scores.

Killgore and DellaPietra (2000) examined item responses on the WMS-III Logical Memory Delayed Recognition (LMDR) subtest in a sample of 50 healthy volunteers who had no prior exposure to the content of the Logical Memory stories. Interestingly, these researchers found that six items were correctly answered above chance probabilities; each of the six items was correctly answered by 70–80% of the naive respondents. A weighted combination of the six items was summed to form the Rarely Missed Index (RMI). On the assumption that examinees *with* prior exposure to the stories should perform as well as the naive participants, it was hypothesized that the RMI could be used to identify malingered memory impairment on the LMDR subtest. The researchers compared the performances of 36 simulators and 51 neurologically impaired patients and found that the RMI accurately classified 98.9% of the participants, with 97% sensitivity and 100% specificity. Statistical cross-validation using the jackknife procedure produced identical classification accuracies. Acknowledging the influence of base rates on classification accuracy, the investigators reanalyzed the data after manually adjusting prior odds of malingering at five different base rates (i.e., 50%, 30%, 10%, 5%, and 1%). The overall proportion of correct classification did not significantly decline until the base rate of malingering was dropped to 1%, which produced a sensitivity of 87%. However, specificity remained at 100%, suggesting that the RMI is unlikely to misclassify sufficient effort. Subsequent studies have yielded mixed results. Miller, Ryan, Carruthers, and Cluff (2004) examined the specificity of the RMI in a mixed group of clinical patients diagnosed with either alcohol abuse, polysubstance abuse, or TBI. They obtained low rates of misclassification for genuine patients, with error rates of 3%, 5%, and 7%, respectively, for the three clinical groups. A more recent investigation into the clinical utility of the RMI (Lange, Sullivan, & Anderson, 2005) utilized a mixed sample of 78 nonlitigating patients and 158 personal injury litigants. The litigant group comprised 20 suspected exaggerators, 12 borderline exaggerators, and 126 genuine responders, yielding an overall sample base rate of 12.7% for probable malingered neurocognitive dysfunction, based on the Slick criteria. Although specificity ranged from 91 to 95%, sensitivity was only 25%. PPP ranged from .50 to .71; NPP ranged from .68 to .83. These results suggest, as has been found by a number of other investigators, that embedded validity indicators may have less sensitivity than standalone CFMs, and therefore their findings must be viewed in a broader context.

Langeluddecke and Lucas (2003) compared the WMS-III performances of 25 litigants with mild TBI with those of 50 patients with severe TBI not involved in litigation. All litigants with mild TBI met the Slick criteria for probable MND. The investigators defined malingering cut scores based on the minimum subtest scores of the severely injured group; scores below the cut scores were considered to reflect biased responding. Two subtests emerged as effective in differentiating between the groups: Auditory Recognition Delayed (sensitivity = 80%) and Word Lists II Recognition (sensitivity = 81%); specificities were 91.8% and 95.6%, respectively. The Faces I and II subtests demonstrated good specificity (96% and 98%, respectively), although sensitivity was much lower (32% and 28%, respectively).

Digit Span

The Digit Span subtest, which appears on the current and prior editions of both the WMS-III and the Wechsler Adult Intelligence Scale—Third Edition (WAIS-III), has been the subject of much research. The subtest's application in the current context is mentioned only briefly. Digit Span, which requires the examinee to repeat auditorily presented strings of numbers in the same and reverse order, has the appearance of a memory test. In actuality, individuals with memory disorders perform about as well as unimpaired individuals. Digit Span is robust and relatively insensitive to many forms of brain damage and dysfunction (Axelrod, Fichtenberg, Millis, & Wertheimer, 2006). Malingerers and research participants simulating brain injury tend to perform poorly on this test, presumably because it appears to test memory functioning. Researchers have taken advantage of this and have developed a number of well-validated procedures for ascertaining the validity of Digit Span performance. Examples of Digit Span–based indices of suspect effort include but are not limited to (1) Vocabulary minus Digit Span (Mittenberg, Theroux-Fichera, Zielinski, & Heilbronner, 1995; Mittenberg et al., 2001), (2) Reliable Digit Span (Greiffenstein, Baker, & Gola, 1994), and (3) longest string of digits correctly recited forward and backward compared with the WMS-III normative sample (Iverson & Tulsky, 2003).

California Verbal Learning Test—Second Edition

The California Verbal Learning Test—Second Edition (CVLT-II; Delis, Kramer, Kaplan, & Ober, 2000) is one of the most commonly used memory measures by neuropsychologists in North America (Rabin, Barr, & Burton, 2005). Its research builds on a substantial body of research on the original version (California Verbal Learning Test; CVLT). New to the second edition is the optional Forced-Choice Recognition trial (FCR), in which the examinee is asked to choose which of two words appeared on the original word list. List words are paired with concrete and abstract foils. The manual provides normative data for the FCR, including a cut score below which no individuals scored in the normative sample (i.e., the floor-effect detection strategy). The manual also includes normative data for Critical Item Analysis (CIA); it is composed of two indices: CIA Recall, which compares items missed on FCR but recalled on earlier free recall trials; and CIA Recognition, which compares items missed on FCR but recognized earlier on Yes/No Recognition. CIA is based on the idea that items recalled on the more difficult free-recall task should be correctly identified later on easier recognition tasks (i.e., violation of learning principles detection strategy).

Moore and Donders (2004) compared the performances of the CVLT-II FCR and the TOMM in detecting insufficient effort for rehabilitation referrals assessed within 1 year of sustaining a TBI (72 mild TBI and 59 moderate–severe TBI cases). Results revealed that 20 (15%) patients obtained invalid scores; 15 of these patients obtained CVLT-II FCR scores below cut score, and 11 of these obtained invalid TOMM scores. Agreement between the CVLT-II FCR and TOMM was approximately 89%. Six patients were classified as providing insufficient effort by both tests, all of whom had sustained mild injuries (i.e., meaningful response to verbal commands within 24 hours postinjury and no positive neuroimaging findings). The authors also assessed the impact of secondary gain and psychiatric history on validity of test performance. Both compensation seeking and positive psychiatric histories were predictive of an invalid test performance; injury severity and substance abuse history did not substantially improve classification accuracy.

Bauer, Yantz, Ryan, Warden, and McCaffrey (2005) sought to extend previous research on the utility of the original CVLT as an effort measure. Discriminant analysis was performed using five variables from the CVLT-II (i.e., Immediate Recall Total 1–5, Long-Delay Recognition Discriminability, Long-Delay Recognition Hits, Long-Delay Cued Recall, and Long-Delay Forced-Choice Recognition Hits) to discriminate between groups with sufficient and insufficient effort. Participants with postacute mild to moderate TBI were assigned to either incomplete-effort ($n = 29$) or adequate-effort ($n = 91$) groups based on WMT performance. Results revealed high specificity (95.6%) but low sensitivity (13.8%). Though useful when positive results are obtained, this CVLT-II formula should not be used in isolation because of a high false-negative rate.

A more recent retrospective study by Root, Robbins, Chang, and van Gorp (2006) examined the utility of the FCR and CIA indices of the CVLT-II in clinical referrals, forensic referrals with adequate effort, and forensic referrals with insufficient effort as defined by cut scores on freestanding effort measures. Various FCR cut scores were examined:

- FCR Total ≤ 15 produced the best classification accuracy, with 60% sensitivity and 81% specificity. Assuming a malingering base rate of .30, PPP was .58, and NPP was .83.
- FCR Total ≤ 11, the first cut score at which 100% specificity was achieved, unfortunately produced a sensitivity of only 12%, which at a base rate of .30 results in a PPP of 1.00 and an NPP of .73.
- CIA Recall ≥ 2 produced the best classification accuracy, with sensitivity of .24 and specificity of .96. At a base rate of .30, PPP was .72, and NPP was .75.
- CIA Recognition ≥ 2 produced the best classification accuracy, with sensitivity of 16% and specificity of 100%. At a base rate of .30, PPP was 1.00, and NPP was .74.

Memory impairment was not correlated with FCR performance, indicating that the learning and memory demands on the task are minimal. Clinicians should note that both FCR and CIA indices are conservative, making positive results much more meaningful than negative results.

Wolfe and colleagues (2007) examined the ability of several CVLT-II variables to differentiate between (1) individuals with moderate to severe TBI and (2) litigants with mild injuries (i.e., brief or no loss of consciousness, normal neuroimaging findings, and no focal neurological deficits) who failed at least one feigning test (i.e., TOMM, WMT, or VSVT). Bayesian model averaging was used to derive a multivariable logistic regression model for classification of participants with Total Recall Discriminability, Total Recognition Discriminability (d-prime), and Long-Delay Free Recall as predictor variables. The best model showed an area under the receiver operating characteristic (ROC) curve of .82, which indicates excellent group discrimination. The authors also produced a range of probability cut scores and associated diagnostic efficiency statistics. The results demonstrate that the CVLT-II variably differentiates between genuine TBI and individuals exhibiting insufficient effort.

In summary, following years of productive malingering research on the original CVLT (e.g., Sweet et al., 2000), which resulted in widespread usage by forensic experts, the CVLT-II malingering literature is still developing. The extant research clearly indicates that the CVLT-II also contains data that will inform clinical judgments on malingering; specific cut scores and formulae are still being validated. At present, minimally, clinicians can rely on the numerous studies that established the test component in both CVLT and CVLT-II known as Recognition Hits (Yes–No format; typically cut score ≤ 10) as effective in identifying insufficient effort (see Curtis, Greve, Bianchini, & Brennan, 2006).

FEIGNING OF AMNESIA AND MEMORY LOSS IN CRIMINAL CONTEXT

Reliable and accurate assessment of amnesia within the criminal setting is essential for several reasons. A criminal defendant's claim of amnesia for crimes committed may influence decisions related to *mens rea* (i.e., criminal intent), the insanity defense, and the death penalty (Hermann, 1986). Evaluation of amnesia is also important given that amnesia for a criminal act may affect competency to stand trial (Schacter, 1986b). That is, a defendant without memories for a crime may be unable to consult meaningfully with counsel (Porter, Birt, Yuille, & Herve, 2001). In addition, amnesia for criminal activity is commonly reported. Research estimates from 25 to 45% (Kopelman, 1987) to as many as 65% (Bradford & Smith, 1979) of individuals who commit murder report amnesia for their crimes.

Recent studies have attempted to compare general characteristics among amnesic and nonamnesic criminals. Cima, Merckelbach, Hollnack, and Knauer (2003) examined characteristics of 62 male inmates from a German psychiatric correctional institute, 17 (27%) of whom claimed amnesia for their alleged crimes. Compared with others, amnesic criminals had lower IQ scores, more frequent diagnoses of antisocial personality, greater executive dysfunction, and greater frequency of possible feigning on the Structured Inventory of Malingered Symptomatology (SIMS) (see Smith, Chapter 19, this volume). The authors suggested that these findings supported the following conclusion: "because of their low intelligence, and lack of executive control, these [amnesic] individuals engage in violent behavior and later try to avoid responsibility by claiming amnesia" (p. 279).

In a separate study, Cima, Nijman, Merckelbach, Kremer, and Hollnack (2004) examined 308 forensic male inpatients from Germany and the Netherlands. Similar to prior reports (e.g., Cima et al., 2003; Kopelman, 1987, 1995), 72 (23%) of the participants claimed at least partial amnesia for their crimes. The amnesic group was significantly older, had more prior convictions, and had a greater likelihood of substance abuse histories. The groups did not differ on whether the crime committed was a homicide or in their frequencies of psychotic or personality disorders. Contrary to the previous study (Cima et al., 2003), no significant differences were found in the level of intelligence between the amnesic and comparison groups.

Pyszora, Barker, and Kopelman (2003) examined characteristics associated with amnesia for criminal offenses in a sample of 207 English and Welsh inmates who had been imprisoned for various crimes in 1994. Twenty-nine percent of the group claimed amnesia for the offenses, with 31.4% of participants convicted of homicide claiming amnesia. Similar to Cima and colleagues (2004), amnesic offenders were significantly older and more likely to have histories of alcohol abuse than nonamnesic offenders. Unlike Cima and colleagues, the amnesic group was more likely to have histories of mental disorders than the nonamnesic group.

In summary, these studies suggest that within the criminal context, base rates of at least partial amnesia for crime approximate 25% or more (Cima et al., 2003, 2004; Kopelman, 1987, 1995; Pyszora et al., 2003). Relative to nonamnesic criminals, amnesic groups have been found to be somewhat older, to have histories of more convictions, and to have more significant substance abuse histories (Cima et al., 2004). There is evidence that amnesic criminals may have more frequent antisocial tendencies and have greater executive dysfunction (Cima et al., 2003). Level of overall intellectual ability may not differ between amnesic and nonamnesic criminal groups (cf. Cima et al., 2003, 2004).

What classifications of amnesia are most relevant to the criminal litigant? In a now-classic paper addressing genuine versus simulated amnesia, Schacter (1986b) suggested the possibility of at least four distinct types of amnesia:

chronic "organic" (i.e., neurogenic) amnesia (e.g., as a result of various brain-based conditions), functional retrograde amnesia (e.g., memory loss for autiobiographical information as a result of trauma), multiple personality amnesia (now designated *dissociative identity disorder*), and limited amnesia (or the inability to recall a specific, critical event or events). Schacter suggests that within the criminal forensic context, limited amnesia tends to be the most relevant, as it pertains to memory for a specific crime-related event (e.g., murder). Nevertheless, neuropsychologists may be asked to discriminate whether the criminal litigant's amnesia for a crime is most consistent with: (1) neurogenic amnesia, (2) psychogenic (dissociative) amnesia, or (3) feigned amnesia (Cima, Merckelbach, Nijman, Knauer, & Hollnack, 2002).

Neurologically Based Amnesia in Criminal Context

TBI, stroke, epilepsy, or any other neurological condition may represent the primary etiology of amnesia for crime, though this appears as a relatively infrequent cause of amnesia within the criminal setting. Only 3 of the 72 forensic patients (4.2%) in the Cima and colleagues (2004) study who claimed amnesia for their crimes had the amnesia attributed to a serious neurological disorder (e.g., TBI or epilepsy). Pyszora and colleagues' (2003) study reported that a higher percentage (15%) of the purported amnesic criminals had a history of neurological involvement, with 68% of this group reporting a previous head injury and 16% a history of epilepsy. However, the authors observe that "although organic pathology is relatively common in the offender population, it accounts for only a very small minority of cases of amnesia" (Pyszora et al., 2003, p. 486).

One of the more salient and potentially confounding examples of a neurologically based amnesia for crime is alcohol or other substance intoxication (Cunnien, 1986; Denney & Wynkoop, 2000; Rogers & Shuman, 2000). Alcohol "blackouts" represent the effect of alcohol's interference with the usual acquisition of memory (Cunnien, 1986), whereby a perpetrator may develop amnesia for an event without having diminished awareness or consciousness during the time of alcohol consumption itself. To illustrate the impact that intoxication

may have on memory loss, consider the findings of Rogers and Shuman (2000), who summarize frequencies of moderate, severe, and extreme memory loss for an offense by intoxication status in a group of clinically evaluated "sane" and "insane" defendants. When intoxicated litigants were excluded, frequencies of sane litigants with severe or extreme amnesia for a crime decreased significantly (as low as 1.0% frequency for severe and 1.4% for extreme memory loss), whereas frequencies of amnesia for the insane group remained relatively stable.

Psychogenic/Dissociative Amnesia in Criminal Context

Dissociative amnesia, previously designated as psychogenic amnesia in DSM-III and DSM-III-R, is a topic of ongoing controversy within the criminal forensic setting. Porter and colleagues (2001) noted that the North American legal system has responded to claims of dissociative amnesia inconsistently; some courts recognize it as a valid phenomenon, and others assign "limited credibility" to such claims. Within the psychological community, Rogers and Shuman (2000) comment on sharply divided views: "the polarization of professional views regarding dissociative amnesia provides a surplus of rhetoric and a shortage of empiricism" (p. 124). In spite of this controversy, Rogers and Shuman provide a very useful summary of symptoms and features that are presumed to discriminate psychogenic amnesia from neurogenic amnesia. Unlike neurogenic amnesia, psychogenic amnesia is (1) ostensibly related to psychic trauma, rather than brain-based causes, such as brain injury or disease, (2) more likely to affect personal memory only, and (3) more likely to be reversible. Moreover, dissociative amnesia memory loss is more likely restricted to *posttrauma* memory loss, whereas neurogenic amnesia may involve memory loss for events immediately before, as well as subsequent to, a certain event that is physical in nature.

Cercy, Schretlen, and Brandt (1997) suggest that dissociative amnesia is more likely than other forms of amnesia to be associated with: (1) a significant psychological stressor, (2) loss of autobiographical information or personal identity, (3) preexisting psychopathology, and (4) absence of brain involvement as demonstrated by neuroimaging. Regarding (3), subsequent to neurological insult (e.g., TBI), memory loss tends to be inversely proportionate to the age of memories, a principle known as Ribot's law of regression (Loring, 1999). In other words, remote memories are presumed to be less vulnerable to insult than more recent memories in the context of neurological brain injury. Kopelman (1994) found, for example, that individuals with dementia-related amnesia showed relative sparing for biographical facts and incidents. In contrast, patients with dissociative amnesia were more likely to show a disproportionate impairment in remote autobiographical memory. Likewise, Rubinsky and Brandt (1986, p. 43) state, "we know of no instance in the literature on organic [neurogenic] memory disorders where a patient with a pure amnesic syndrome loses his personal identity." Thus one feature that often discriminates dissociative from neurogenic amnesia is that the former consists of greater memory loss for remote forms of personal information than the latter, which is more likely to affect episodic memory (i.e., memory for contextually specific information and events, including one's conversations, appointments, activities, etc.).

Porter and colleagues (2001) reviewed the nature of memory for murder as it relates to dissociative amnesia. They discriminated between dissociative amnesia (a psychologically based amnesia subsequent to a traumatic experience), a dissociative state (altered consciousness after a traumatic experience), and dissociation (a general term that includes both dissociative amnesia and dissociative state). Porter and colleagues also noted two mechanisms that may underlie dissociative amnesia: repression and state-dependent memory. With regard to repression, although "there have been no studies that convincingly demonstrate the validity of repression" (p. 28), Porter and colleagues found that a number of North American courts have nevertheless upheld repression as the underlying mechanism for the amnesia.

State-dependent memory as an explanation for dissociative amnesia relates to the suggestion that the extreme nature of emotional involvement associated with violent acts (e.g., Kopelman, 1995) diminishes subsequent retrieval of crime-related events. Pyszora and colleagues (2003), for example, reported that significantly more amnesic than nonamnesic criminals claimed "provocation" as a defense; amnesic crimes often could be characterized as "crimes of passion" (e.g., cases of infidelity).

Pyszora and colleagues concluded that these crimes were "likely to reflect an association between extreme emotional arousal, on the one hand, and dissociation with accompanying amnesia, on the other" (2003, p. 486).

As noted, dissociative amnesia is controversial and somewhat "polarized" in professional circles (Rogers & Shuman, 2000). In partial support of dissociative amnesia as a genuine phenomenon, it should be noted that some amnesic perpetrators acknowledge committing their crimes and do not take steps to avoid apprehension (e.g., Kopelman, 1987, 1995; Porter et al., 2001; Pyzsora et al., 2003). Such admissions appear to eliminate an obvious external motivation (i.e., avoidance of punishment) for feigned amnesia. In this vein, Pyzsora and colleagues (2003) concluded that these admissions controverted the common assumption that "a claim of amnesia is used as an easy way of denying the offense or responsibility for it" (p. 487).

Cima and colleagues (2002) questioned this reasoning and suggested that the motivation for a claim of dissociative amnesia may be to make a more *sympathetic* impression during trial. They also questioned the assumption that most forms of dissociative amnesia are associated with intense emotional reactions. If this assumption is correct, then others who experience emotionally intense events (e.g., incarceration in a concentration camp) should show similar forms of amnesia, which is not usually the case. Cima and colleagues contended that dissociative amnesia should be considered a "rare phenomenon" and that most claims of dissociative amnesia should be considered instances of feigned amnesia.

Feigned Amnesia in Criminal Context

In contrast to civil litigants, criminal defendants may feign amnesia to avoid or minimize legal responsibility (van Oorsouw & Merckelbach, 2004). Porter and colleagues (2001) suggest the following as more specific potential motivations for "malingered memory impairment" in criminal groups: to (1) support a legal defense, (2) elicit sympathy from the jury or family, (3) instill doubt regarding crime-related involvement, or (4) avoid the "cognitively taxing" approach associated with explicit deception, such as developing a plausible alibi. Whereas 25–45% of individuals who commit murder subsequently claim amnesia for the act (Kopelman, 1987), base rates of *feigned* amnesia for other criminal acts are less clear. Interestingly, in the Pyszora and colleagues (2003) study, only 2.4% of the amnesic offenders were suspected of feigned memory loss based on psychiatric assessments or a trial judge's conclusions. However, this percentage likely represents an underestimate of feigned amnesia.

One of the challenges in the evaluation of feigned amnesia for crime relates to the issue of *intention*. By definition, malingered amnesia entails an intentional production of memory loss to obtain an external incentive (e.g., in the criminal arena, to avoid punishment or sentencing). With the exception of severe dementias, intention as it pertains to amnesia is extremely difficult to assess (Rogers & Shuman, 2000). Boone and colleagues (2001) go so far as to suggest that neuropsychologists "can only observe and measure behavior, not intent" (p. 17). To complicate matters, mental health professionals have fared relatively poorly in discriminating genuine from simulated amnesia. Schacter (1986b), for example, demonstrated that experienced psychiatrists, psychologists, and neuropsychologists classified feigned and genuine amnesic participants at near-chance levels (i.e., only 53% accuracy).

Most research addressing amnesia for crime employs a simulation strategy, often through inclusion of undergraduates who are instructed either to simulate amnesia for a given crime or to recollect the crime in a genuine manner. The strengths of simulation studies include enhanced internal validity (Arnett et al., 1995) and the ease of sample recruitment, though what might be gained in the way of internal validity is often at the expense of external validity (Haines & Norris, 1995). That is, it is not clear that simulators' experiences and behaviors reflect accurately those of malingerers in a criminal context. Nevertheless, simulation studies in which simulators are debriefed following participation to ensure that they adhered to instructions are able to identify with confidence those participants who are *not* putting forth genuine performances on memory tasks. Obviously, short of confession, such information can be extraordinarily difficult to obtain within the "real world" criminal setting.

Analogue Research on Feigned and Genuine Memory

Wiggins and Brandt (1988) were among the first researchers to examine the lay person's

naive assumptions regarding the nature of genuine amnesia. Using simulators, genuine amnesics, and normal controls, they conducted a series of experimental tasks (e.g., autobiographical interview, word-stem completion task, word association tasks). Simulators were divided into different conditions based on putative etiology (i.e., head injury, psychological trauma, or no specified cause). Simulators performed similarly irrespective of their assigned conditions. Key findings include the following: First, simulators demonstrated greater retrograde memory impairment relative to the amnesic group and only mild anterograde memory impairment. Second, simulators may not be aware that certain memory processes (implicit memory) are rather automatic in nature.

In a second study, Wiggins and Brandt (1988) added a 20-item forced-choice recognition procedure to the list of experimental tasks administered to the three groups. None of the participants in any of the three groups demonstrated below-chance performance on the forced-choice task. Differences were observed in performance at chance levels: 1.7% of normal controls, 8.0% of amnesics, 20.8% of the simulators. In summarizing both studies, Wiggins and Brandt (1988, p. 75) concluded that lay persons do not fully understand the nature of amnesia, a fact that may lead to useful detection methods. In other words, lay persons are vulnerable to the detection strategy of violation of learning principles when attempting to feign amnesia.

Recent simulation studies have also been conducted to explore the nature of amnesia for crime (e.g., Bylin & Christianson, 2002; Christianson & Bylin, 1999; Jelicic, Merckelbach, & van Bergen, 2004; Merckelbach, Hauer, & Rassin, 2002; van Oorsouw & Merckelbach, 2004, 2006). One compelling set of findings on crime-related amnesia is that simulation of amnesia may genuinely distort later recall of an episode (Bylin & Christianson, 2002; Christianson & Bylin, 1999). In the Bylin and Christianson (2002) study, 79 undergraduate students were presented with a story about a motor vehicle accident involving a drunk driver who killed a young woman. The students were assigned to one of four groups: (1) genuine memory for the story tested at a second occasion only, (2) genuine memory for the story tested on two occasions, (3) simulated amnesia by omitting details, and (4) simulated amnesia by committing errors in recall. Importantly, all four groups, including the simulators, had a follow-up session in which they were instructed to perform optimally. Both simulating groups performed worse than the genuine respondents after a 1-week delay. Moreover, the type of simulation also affected later recall. The simulation-by-omission group showed worse free recall than simulation-by-commission group; however, the latter group performed better at open-ended questioning. These results, therefore, suggested that the initial simulation of amnesia may result in a genuine "memory-undermining effect."

Van Oorsouw and Merckelbach (2004) attempted to validate these findings by instructing a group of 61 undergraduates to "commit a mock crime" that involved striking a dummy. One group simulated amnesia for the crime on immediate recall but responded honestly on follow-up. This group was compared with two honest groups, one tested both times and one only at follow-up. Similar to Bylin and Christianson's (2002) study, the simulation group recalled significantly less than the honest group tested both times but was comparable to the follow-up-only group. These data suggest that the lack of accurate rehearsal might have contributed to poor recall at a later time.

Symptom Validity Testing for Episodic Memory

Cercy and colleagues (1997) note that the primary constraint in the identification of malingering pertains to criterion-related validity: "simply stated, no 'gold standard' exists to determine with certainty whether a patient is feigning symptoms independent of clinical tests or experimental procedures being investigated" (p. 89). However, SVT remains the closest to an "evidentiary gold standard for malingering" available to neuropsychologists (Slick et al., 1999, p. 551). Most of the research pertaining to feigned amnesia and memory loss has been conducted within the civil, rather than the criminal, forensic arena (Wynkoop & Denney, 1999), but SVT has nevertheless been effective in assessing claims of amnesia for past events in criminal samples as well (Denney & Wynkoop, 2000).

Rogers and Shuman (2000) suggested that feigned dissociative amnesia may be more detectable than feigned neurological amnesia because most assessment methods for malingering examine the ability to acquire new forms of information (i.e., *anterograde* amnesia). In criminal settings, authenticity of amnesia for a specific event (e.g., murder) may be of interest. In such cases, the evaluation of *retrograde* amnesia is likely to be of greater relevance.

Frederick, Carter, and Powel (1995) and Denney (1996) illustrate a modification to SVT in several case examples consisting of claimed amnesia for specific crimes. Standard performance on SVT measures (e.g., Digit Memory Test) does not evaluate amnesia for a specific past event. Frederick and colleagues illustrate a modification of the SVT detection strategy to evaluate "suspicious amnesia" for a prior event. The clinician identifies relevant information that the examinee would know if his or her memory were intact (e.g., weapons used and amount of money stolen) and then provides forced-choice trials (the correct answer and an alternative) to assess the validity of amnesia. The application of at least 25 items is recommended. A potential limitation of this modification is the difficulty in identifying consistent alternatives (i.e., foils) to correct choices that are plausible (Frederick et al., 1995). Still, the authors suggested that the procedure is "inherently valid: performance below chance most likely indicates the presence of memory" (p. 236), and they present three case studies that illustrate the usefulness of the modification.

Denney (1996) provided important recommendations for this SVT modification. An initial step entails a thorough collection of information (from medical records, eyewitnesses, family members) surrounding the event(s) for which the examinee is presumably amnesic. Information should be of sufficient detail to allow the creation of a sufficient number of questions, though "use of too detailed questions lessens the power of the test" (p. 591) because it may increase the likelihood of random responding. Denney provides three case examples with sample test items. For example, in a case of armed bank robbery, the defendant was asked, "What was the teller's gender?" (female, male), and "Did the robber speak to the teller?" (yes, no). Additionally, Denney administered the same test items used in the three case examples to a sample of 60 adults who had no knowledge of the events in order to verify that the items were in accordance with the assumptions of the binomial distribution (i.e., were relatively normally distributed). Results suggested that item selection was satisfactory, and the author concluded that this SVT modification was sound. Frederick and Denney (1998) provide an elaborate overview of developing unbiased test items and applying the methodology to individual cases of feigned amnesia.

Simulation studies (e.g., Jelicic et al., 2004; Merckelbach et al., 2002; van Oorsouw & Merckelbach, 2006) have investigated this SVT modification. Merckelbach and colleagues (2002) examined 20 undergraduate students who committed a mock crime involving theft and were subsequently instructed to feign amnesia for the episode. These simulators were then administered a 15-item forced-choice task that pertained to the theft; these items had been previously tested to ensure that they were unbiased. Results indicated that 40% of the participants performed below chance. Using a similar design, Jelicic and colleagues (2004) found that 59% of simulators performed below chance. These studies provide strong support for the SVT modification as a method of identifying feigned crime-related amnesia.

Van Oorsouw and Merckelbach (2006) attempted to replicate their earlier findings and also to examine whether "memory undermining" effects occurred with respect to the original mock crime. Simulators again showed poorer performances on free-recall trials relative to a comparison group, which provided further evidence that simulating amnesia may have a negative effect on true memory. Although simulators performed worse on the SVT modification than a comparison group, only 7% of the simulators performed significantly below chance. These results question the utility of the SVT modification.

ASSESSMENT OF FEIGNED AMNESIA AND MEMORY WITH THE MMPI-2

Rogers and Bender (2003; see also Rogers, Chapter 2, this volume) examined how the different domains (mental disorders, cognitive impairment, and medical complaints) affect the usefulness of detection strategies. For example, in a criminal context, the simple denial of memory for a specific event is very different from the elaborate fabrication of a schizophrenic disorder. Moreover, in a civil context, minimization of psychological problems often occurs simultaneously with feigned memory impairment. Separate detection strategies are

needed for different domains. Despite this, some forensic experts have attempted to extrapolate from the MMPI-2, intended for malingered psychopathology, to feigned amnesia. It is no longer acceptable, as some forensic experts have done in the past, to infer adequate cognitive effort based on normal-range MMPI-2 validity scales.

As wide as the chasm may appear to be when making a comparison between the typical criminal forensic presentation of a feigned amnesia and the typical civil forensic presentation of a feigned memory disorder, it would be incorrect to assume that within either of these categories there is little variability. In fact, for example, the heterogeneity of presentations of response bias within civil forensic examinees can be rather marked. In an initial study that provided relevant data, Greiffenstein, Gola, and Baker (1995) found that traditional MMPI-2 validity indicators, such as F, F-K, and O-S, loaded on a separate factor from cognitive effort measures.

Lees-Haley, Iverson, Lange, Fox, and Allen (2002) exhaustively reviewed the MMPI-2 literature with regard to use in forensic applications, with an emphasis on the Daubert criteria. These authors state succinctly what many researchers and clinicians have noted: that although the MMPI-2 validity scales "cannot be used as an indicator of cognitive exaggeration, they are often helpful in providing supporting evidence for the exaggeration of psychological distress" (p. 171). This is not to suggest that there is no relationship between MMPI-2 validity scales and cognitive effort as measured by CFMs; rather, the relationships vary and are specific to the particular MMPI-2 validity scale, and even then at best they can be considered moderate (Sweet, Nelson, & Heilbronner, 2005). To be sure, a small minority of malingerers engage in gross feigning that crosses all, or nearly all, domains. However, the majority of malingerers are not so cooperative in ensuring their easy detection.

Nelson, Sweet, Berry, Bryant, and Granacher (2007) conducted an exploratory factor analysis of MMPI-2 validity scales and CFMs in a sample of compensation-seeking claimants, none of whom were evaluated in a criminal setting. Four factors emerged: underreporting of symptoms (MMPI-2 L, K, S), overreporting of neurotic symptoms (MMPI-2 Fake Bad Scale, Response Bias Scale, and Malingered Depression Scale), insufficient cognitive effort (VSVT, TOMM, and Letter Memory Test), and over-reporting of psychotic/rarely endorsed symptoms (MMPI-2 F, Fp, and Dsr2). Results suggested that select "postrelease" MMPI-2 scales (e.g., FBS) were more associated with cognitive effort than some of the traditional scales (e.g., F). This finding is consistent with studies (e.g., Nelson, Sweet, & Demakis, 2006) that have suggested that FBS may have a unique relationship with cognitive effort. Nevertheless, taken together, these results provide an empirical basis for the cautions about the use of feigning measures to bridge multiple domains. Practitioners are advised to administer both cognitive effort measures *and* psychological validity scales when evaluating claims of amnesia or memory disorder (Nelson & Sweet, in press).

SUMMARY

In the decades that have ensued since researchers first expressed concern regarding the limited ability of clinicians to detect feigned amnesia (e.g., Faust, Hart, Guilmette, & Arkes, 1988; Heaton, Smith, Lehman, & Vogt, 1978; Schacter 1986a; Wiggins & Brandt, 1988), the development of various detection strategies has improved identification of feigned amnesia in both criminal and civil contexts. Clinical researchers concerned with the discrimination of genuine and feigned memory disorders and amnesia have followed the general guidance of malingering experts whose interests involved nonmemory neuropsychological domains and mental disorders. That is, these clinical researchers have recommended strongly that clinicians use multiple methods to evaluate response validity with each forensic case and, more specifically, identify possible response bias, whether in the form of overreporting of symptoms or exaggeration or complete fabrication of neuropsychological impairments (e.g., Bender & Rogers, 2004; Bush et al., 2005; Mittenberg, Aguila-Puentes, et al., 2002; Nelson et al., 2003; Nies & Sweet, 1994; Slick et al., 1999; Sweet, 1999b). Not only have forensic experts who publish on malingering for years recommended the use of multiple detection methods, but it is clear that practicing clinicians who make individual case decisions clearly have come to rely on multiple detection

methods, rather than a single score or test, when ruling in or ruling out malingering.

Lally (2003) published a survey of tests used by board-certified forensic psychologists. This survey found that forensic experts used an average of 5.8 tests to evaluate malingering. Similarly, with regard to current practice expectations among neuropsychologists, the survey results of Mittenberg, Patton, and colleagues (2002) show that board-certified neuropsychologists rely on multiple methods when assessing the probability of malingering. Respondents in this latter survey considered an average of 7.53 of 9 indicators. Importantly, when a classification of malingering was supported, board-certified neuropsychologists relied on an average of 4.47 malingering indicators. The percentages of Mittenberg and colleagues' respondents employing each of nine malingering criteria are:

- 65% severity of cognitive impairment inconsistent with condition
- 64% pattern of cognitive test performance inconsistent with condition
- 57% scores below empirical cut scores on forced-choice tests
- 56% discrepancies among records, self-report, and observed behavior
- 46% implausible self-reported symptoms in interview
- 46% scores below empirical cut scores on other malingering tests
- 45% implausible changes in test scores across repeated examinations
- 38% scores above validity scale cut scores on multiscale inventories
- 30% scores below chance on forced-choice tests

This review of civil and criminal contexts for feigning amnesia and memory loss makes it clear that the types of feigned disorders may vary, with feigned memory loss from neurogenic causes more common in civil contexts and feigned amnesia, often of the psychogenic or dissociative type rather than neurogenic type, in criminal contexts. Nevertheless, the procedures relied on in identifying feigned memory conditions are in fact quite similar across contexts. In fact, though, the prototypical manner of presentation in these very different scenarios has additional ramifications. For example, criminal defendants seeking to prove "insanity" as a defense are more likely to overreport psychopathology on measures such as the MMPI-2, whereas it is common for civil litigants pursuing a claim of memory impairment to underreport psychopathology on the MMPI-2. Relatedly, it is important to emphasize that methods of detecting response bias and invalid responding for psychological conditions such as depression have limited utility for detecting feigned cognitive problems such as memory disorder.

NOTES

1. For the purposes of this chapter, the term *civil litigants* refers to all individuals involved in formal litigation and all claimants pursing disability status, workers' compensation claims, special educational accommodations, or other entitlements in some form of administrative review process. Although many of these individuals have not filed lawsuits, the evaluation and proceedings have similarities regarding the potentially adversarial context and external incentives.

2. The term *secondary gain* has been given various meanings in the literature and when used by testifying experts. In fact, the term is very poorly understood by attorneys, resulting in questions to experts regarding whether a person or a person's specific test results is "showing secondary gain." We prefer to minimize confusion by limiting use of this term to the context within which an individual's evaluation takes place. Unlike clinical settings, forensic contexts may include an external incentive, such as a financial reward for physical injury.

14

Assessment of Feigned Cognitive Impairment Using Standard Neuropsychological Tests

DAVID T. R. BERRY, PhD
LINDSEY J. SCHIPPER, MA

Driven partly by increased acceptance of neuropsychological evidence in legal and administrative proceedings, interest in objective methods for detecting feigned cognitive impairment has increased dramatically over the past two decades (Larrabee, 2005b). In addition to development and validation of many new instruments dedicated to identifying false memory deficits (see Sweet, Condit, & Nelson, Chapter 13, this volume), significant strides have been made in conceptual and theoretical understanding of malingered impairment. Although initial interest in detection of feigning focused primarily on false psychiatric symptoms (Rogers, 1984b), later work investigated a second domain of malingering, namely feigned memory deficits (Hiscock & Hiscock, 1989). More recently, Larrabee (1998) proposed investigation of feigned physical complaints as a third area (see also Rogers, Chapter 2, this volume). Bridging the latter two domains, Greiffenstein (2007) argues that yet another type of malingering is encountered in forensic neuropsychological examinations: contrived perceptual and motor deficits. The existence of multiple types of feigning suggests that clinicians evaluating patients in compensation-seeking circumstances must address several possible malingered presentations.

Neuropsychological assessments can rely solely on specialized measures for assessing specific types of feigned memory deficits, as reviewed in Chapter 13 (this volume). However, considerable research has emerged in the past decade exploring the application of standard neuropsychological tests to detection of feigning. Their use has several potential advantages: (1) serving multiple purposes simultaneously (i.e., assessment of both genuine and feigned deficits), (2) allowing retrospective evaluations of response validity in previous examinations (Larrabee, in press), (3) expanding the feigning detection methods employed from the primarily recognition memory format used in most symptom validity tests, and (4) providing some protection against coaching. Regarding the final point, detection strategies embedded in standard neuropsychological measures are less transparent for coaching and other preparation, such as Internet research (see the later section on coaching). Thus there is reason for optimism about the possible contributions of standard neuropsychological tests to detection of cognitive feigning. This chapter first addresses important conceptual and practical issues. It is followed by a review of effect sizes and classification accuracies of available procedures and concludes with recommendations for clinical practice.

BACKGROUND AND CONCEPTUAL ISSUES

Diagnostic Criteria

In the DSM-IV-TR diagnostic system (American Psychiatric Association, 2000), false symptoms are a key feature of several conditions of interest. DSM-IV-TR utilizes two factors to classify individuals feigning symptoms: (1) whether or not feigned symptoms are volitional and (2) whether goals appear to be external (e.g., avoiding criminal charges or obtaining drugs) or intrapsychic (e.g., fulfilling the sick role or resolving unconscious conflicts). Two mental disorders and a V-code may be identified using this system. Relevant mental disorders include factitious disorder (conscious feigning for internal goal; specifically, to achieve the sick role) and conversion disorder (unconscious production of symptoms to resolve internal psychological conflicts). The V-code, Malingering, is defined as conscious feigning for external goals. Thus, in addition to detecting false symptoms, the issues of conscious intent, as well as apparent goals, must also be evaluated to identify malingering.

Unfortunately, this diagnostic framework has been heavily criticized (Rogers, 1990b) and may be of limited applicability to feigned cognitive deficits (Slick, Sherman, & Iverson, 1999). A major concern with the DSM-IV-TR framework for evaluating malingering is the need to make subjective judgments about complex psychological issues such as (1) external versus internal incentives and (2) conscious versus unconscious mechanisms. Additionally, the DSM-IV-TR criteria for malingering provide little guidance for assessing exaggeration or fabrication of cognitive deficits.

To address these limitations in applying the DSM-IV-TR malingering framework to neuropsychological cases, Slick, Sherman, and Iverson (1999, p. 552) defined malingered neurocognitive deficit (MNCD) as "the volitional exaggeration or fabrication of cognitive dysfunction for the purpose of obtaining substantial material gain, or avoiding or escaping formal duty or responsibility." Key terms in this definition were operationalized, and Slick and colleagues also provided gradations of certainty to accompany identification of MNCD: definite, probable, and possible. The two most relevant gradations of MNCD (definite and probable) both require presence of a substantial external incentive for cognitive feigning, as

well as a lack of alternative explanations for the false deficits. In addition to these two criteria, definite MNCD requires performance statistically significantly below chance; this detection strategy is termed *symptom validity test* (SVT; see Rogers, Chapter 2, this volume). In contrast, probable MNCD requires two or more signs from neuropsychological or psychological testing that suggest feigning, such as discrepancy between test results and other information or performance below a patient-norm-based cut score. As discussed in Chapter 2 (this volume), below-norm-based performance is referred to as forced-choice testing (FCT). The Slick and colleagues framework has been increasingly used in the research literature on detecting MNCD (Larrabee, 2005a), although its efficacy has not been empirically evaluated relative to the DSM-IV-TR malingering criteria.

The issue of identifying feigners as "definite" as opposed to "probable" is of importance because of data suggesting that requiring a statistically significantly below-chance performance (definite feigning) results in much lower detection rates in simulation research, which asks participants to fake cognitive problems. Guilmette, Hart, and Giuliano (1993) reported that using a cut score of < 90% correct (i.e., "floor effect" strategy; see Chapter 2) on a forced-choice method resulted in correct classification of 90% of simulators. In contrast, using SVT with its significantly below-chance criterion, correctly classified only 34% of same simulators. This finding led to recommendations that less stringent cut scores be used instead of SVT (Guilmette et al., 1993).

Slick and colleagues (1999) recognized the risks of false positives (i.e., misclassifying genuine patients as malingerers) in adopting less stringent cut scores than those used for SVT. Therefore, they designated as "probable" cognitive feigners those individuals who met at least two other criteria indicative of feigning.

Base Rates of Cognitive Feigning

Prevalence estimates of malingering have thus far been based on two general methods: (1) the administration of validity measures to consecutive series of compensation-seeking neuropsychological examinees and (2) surveys of forensic clinicians to estimate the base rates of feigning in their practices. Both methods fail to incorporate results from "successful" malingerers, who by definition avoid detection, raising the possibility of systematic underestimation of the prevalence of cognitive feigning. Using the nonverbal form of the Validity Indicator Profile (VIP), a specialized measure of feigned cognitive impairment, Frederick, Crosby, and Wynkoop (2000) evaluated 737 pretrial criminal defendants. They reported that 44% were classified as having an "invalid" approach to testing. Interestingly, only 6.1% were classified as *definite* cognitive feigners when using conservative decision rules based on the Slick criteria. In a survey of American Board of Clinical Neuropsychology diplomates, Mittenberg, Patton, Canyock, and Condit (2002) estimated prevalence of probable (*not* definite) malingering and the broader category of "symptom exaggeration" at 41% in patients with mild traumatic brain injury (TBI) undergoing forensic neuropsychological examinations. Pooling data from 11 published studies on the issue, Larrabee (2003a) found that approximately 40% of forensic evaluations of mild TBI (range 15% to 64%) fell below patient-norm-based cut scores on objective motivational tests. This criterion is roughly equivalent to *probable* feigning in the Slick and colleagues (1999) system. Thus probable false cognitive deficits may be present in a substantial minority of forensic examinees. While the prevalence of *definite* malingering remains much smaller and less known, these estimates underscore the importance of objective evaluation for probable feigned cognitive impairments, which may, conservatively, approximate 40% in mild TBI examinations undertaken in compensation-seeking circumstances.

Coaching

Because of the high stakes involved in many forensic examinations, concern has been raised that some interested parties to the evaluations might "coach" plaintiffs to avoid detection (Victor & Abeles, 2004). For example, Wetter and Corrigan (1995) surveyed law students and attorneys and found that the majority believed they had an ethical obligation to warn their clients about validity indices used in psychological assessments. In some instances, detailed warnings may be tantamount to coaching. Although the base rate of coaching is unknown, it may be very common in some settings (Lees-Haley, 1997). For instance, case reports documented attorney coaching in a

personal injury trial (Youngjohn, 1995). Consistent with concern about the effect of coaching on malingering tests, Allen and Green (2001) described a steady decline in detection rates on the Computerized Assessment of Response Bias (CARB), a measure that relies primarily on the floor effect, given to forensic examinees over a 6-year period.

Some authors have used Internet search engines to find information with the potential to compromise the validity of instruments for the detection of feigned symptoms. Ruiz, Drake, Glass, Marcotte, and van Gorp (2002) reported that up to 5% of sites with information on psychological testing were a "direct threat to test security" (p. 294). In a warning to customers, Multi-Health Systems, Inc., publisher of the Test of Memory Malingering (TOMM), suggested hiding the test's acronym from examinees to protect against individuals searching the Internet for information about motivational tests, including the TOMM (Multi-Health Systems, Inc.; personal communication to TOMM users, January 8, 2003).

A brief, informal evaluation of the vulnerability of malingering test security to Internet searches was undertaken for this chapter in January 2007. The Psychological Assessment Resources, Inc., site (http://www3.parinc.com/) was accessed without logging in as a registered customer. In the "Product Search" box, the term "malingering" was entered. Seven products were returned, each with the full name of the test, the associated acronym, and a brief description of the nature of the procedure. Results included several widely used feigning tests, such as the TOMM, the Victoria Symptom Validity Test (VSVT), and the Structured Interview of Reported Symptoms (SIRS). When the entry for the TOMM was clicked, a picture of the manual and the three stimulus booklets appeared with the statement "The TOMM is useful for detecting exaggerated or deliberately faked memory impairment." Lower on the page, the following statement appeared: "Based on research in neuropsychology and cognitive psychology, the TOMM is a 50-item visual recognition test specially designed to help psychologists and psychiatrists discriminate between malingered and true memory impairments." This information would appear to make it possible for forensic examinees or any interested party searching the Internet to identify the TOMM as a test on which it would be wise to exert full effort.

Thus a variety of findings suggests that the validity of widely used dedicated motivational tests may be eroded through diffusion of knowledge about their procedures. Fortunately, using results from standard neuropsychological tests to identify cognitive feigning may mitigate this problem to some extent, as successful malingering requires demonstration of deficits on at least some standard neuropsychological tests to document cognitive impairment.

Methods for Validating Cognitive Malingering Tests

Rogers (1997b) suggested that all feigning measures and their detection strategies be evaluated with both simulation and known-groups validation methodologies prior to clinical use. As described by Rogers in Chapters 1 and 24 in this volume, a simulation design is analogue research that contrasts feigners to clinical comparison samples of honestly responding patients.[1] Simulation designs have several limitations, including their unknown generalizability to actual forensic patients. However, their main strength lies in the ability to draw causal inferences through experimental manipulation by instructional sets. Although important to validation of an MNCD test, simulation research should be supplemented by known-groups comparisons.

The known-groups design involves the use of clinical patients identified by one or more previously validated methods as feigning and comparing them with a group of patients classified as responding honestly. Known-groups comparisons are thought to have higher ecological validity because they use genuine patients in real-world settings and situations. However, the inability to make causal inferences is a weakness, as is the potential for inaccuracy in identifying the two groups. For example, it is possible that only blatant malingerers are identified, resulting in unrepresentative feigning samples. Given the contrasting strengths and weaknesses of the simulation and known-groups designs, Rogers's (1997c) recommendation to evaluate malingering tests using both methods appears appropriate.

Accuracy of Classification

Evaluation of feigning measures and detection strategies requires knowledge of the utility estimates used to assess diagnostic tests. Although they are addressed in detail in Chapter 2 (this volume), we briefly review the relevant issues. Using a recommended cut score on a feigning test, sensitivity indicates the percentage of individuals in the sample known to be malingering who receive a positive test sign (suggestive of feigning). In contrast, specificity represents the percentage of individuals in the sample known to be responding honestly who receive a negative test sign (suggestive of honest responding). Sensitivity and specificity are widely presumed to be fixed properties of the test at a given cut score; this assumption may be tenuous in some cases, such as across groups characterized by differing severity levels of a condition (Kraemer, 1992). The hit rate (i.e., overall percentage of correct classifications) may also be generated to quantify a test's accuracy. A significant limitation of hit rate is that any given value may subsume a wide range of sensitivity and specificity levels. Thus it is not possible to use hit rates alone to estimate the likely accuracy of predictions made using test results.

In combination with sensitivity and specificity, base rate estimates (percentage in the sample with the target condition) are used to determine the clinically relevant statistics of positive predictive power (PPP) and negative predictive power (NPP). PPP estimates the likelihood that an individual with a positive test sign has the condition (e.g., malingering). Conversely, NPP estimates the probability that an individual with a negative test sign does not have the condition (e.g., nonmalingering). PPP and NPP are the most important utility estimates in the real world, as they represent the performance of an assessment method in clinical practice.

It should be noted that, in a given base rate environment, a test may have excellent NPP but modest PPP (or vice versa). Thus these values should be worked out for the selected feigning measure in a given setting using the best available estimates of base rates of feigning. For the purposes of this chapter, PPP and NPP are calculated for each procedure, using the estimated base rate of 40% for feigned cognitive deficits in patients with mild TBI undergoing forensic evaluations. It is important to note that these values will change in other settings and populations having different base rates of MNCD.

Detection Strategies for Feigned Cognitive Impairment Using Standard Neuropsychological Tests

Rogers, Harrell, and Liff (1993) provided one of the first conceptual reviews of detection strategies for identifying feigned cognitive impairment. In Chapter 2 (this volume), Rogers broadly divides cognitive feigning detection strategies into unlikely presentations and excessive impairment. Unlikely presentations involve response patterns that are atypical for patients with genuine neuropsychological impairment and that thus raise the possibility of feigned symptoms. Excessive Impairment involves performances much lower than expected from genuine neuropsychological patients.

Within the category of unlikely presentations are four specific detection strategies:

• Magnitude of error involves analysis of incorrect responses for characteristics unusual in genuine disorder.

• Performance curve analysis capitalizes on the typical failure of malingerers to titrate their incorrect responses accurately against levels of item difficulty.

• Violation of learning principles scrutinizes test performances for differences that contradict known characteristics of cognitive performances, such as the superiority of recognition memory to free-recall memory.

• The atypical pattern strategy compares results from multiple tests or subtests with expectations based on patterns seen in genuine neuropsychological syndromes. Atypical pattern approaches often rely on multivariate methods (e.g., discriminant function analysis, or DFA) applied to results from several subtests or indices.

Three detection strategies are characterized by excessive impairment; these focus on the degree rather than specific type of purported impairment:

• Floor effect, which involves deficits on cognitive tasks typically preserved, or relatively preserved, even in the face of genuine neuropsychological impairment.

• Symptom validity testing is based on determining the probability of a correct response in the face of no retained ability and is most appropriate for a test with a multiple-choice format. Results from SVT are interpretable when a performance falls statistically significantly below chance. These strategies potentially allow identification of "definite" malingering, as performances that are statistically significantly below chance, although seemingly rare in clinical practice, are strongly suggestive of deliberate choice of incorrect answers (Slick et al., 1999).

• Forced-choice testing evaluates performance relative to "normative" samples of patients with neuropsychological disorders who have little motivation to feign (e.g., those evaluated in non-compensation-seeking circumstances). As noted earlier, these strategies generally may be used only to identify "probable" malingering, as volition is not documented by a statistically significantly below-chance performance.

Traditionally, research on detection indices appears to have been rather more inductive than deductive. Studies have tended to contrast honest and feigning groups using multiple instruments without much explicit attention to the underlying detection strategies. To address this issue, this chapter describes the most likely underlying detection strategy, when it has not been articulated.

Criteria for the Evaluation of Feigning Detection Procedures

Feigning measures, including standard neuropsychological tests used for this purpose, vary considerably in the quantity and quality of supporting literature. Clinicians evaluating clients in forensic and other adjudicative settings should seek the best available techniques for the important task of detecting cognitive feigning. Berry and Schipper (2007) suggested quality control standards for feigning instruments as follows:

1. Sufficient peer-reviewed publications should be available on a test's utility estimates to allow an informed evaluation of its classification accuracy. More explicitly, sensitivity and specificity data using the procedure at the recommended cut score should have been derived in well-characterized and appropriate samples and published in peer-reviewed outlets.

2. Reasonable convergence in sensitivity and specificity values at recommended cut scores should be shown across published reports based on comparable samples.

3. Predictive power values in varying base rate environments should have been calculated and determined to provide support for the intended clinical application of the test (e.g., to rule in or rule out feigning).

4. Supportive results should have been based on both high-quality simulation and known-groups methodologies and published in peer-reviewed outlets.

5. Supportive results should have been published in peer-reviewed outlets by at least one research team independent of the test's original developers.

6. Data on clinical comparison groups of psychiatric patients should be available and supportive.

APPLICATION OF STANDARD NEUROPSYCHOLOGICAL TESTS TO DETECTION OF COGNITIVE FEIGNING

To focus attention on the most relevant literature, this review of the use of standard neuropsychological tests to detect feigning addresses only the most thoroughly evaluated procedures. Attention is focused on those instruments that met two criteria: (1) ≥ three published empirical studies of feigning detection with clinical comparison groups and (2) ≥ three published studies with sensitivity and specificity parameters. Altogether, 11 measures met these criteria; 10 of them are summarized individually next. The California Verbal Learning Test-II (CVLT) also met these criteria, but it is summarized by Sweet and colleagues in Chapter 13 of this volume. This review is organized by the domain of neuropsychological functioning thought to be tapped by each test.

Batteries of Global Neuropsychological or Intellectual Functioning

Halstead–Reitan Battery

The Halstead–Reitan Battery (HRB; Reitan & Wolfson, 1985) core includes seven subtests measuring multiple neuropsychological functions. Individual subtests from this battery that meet the inclusion criteria are discussed subsequently. This section examines HRB feigning detection strategies using the atypical-pattern approach across multiple subtests. In the earliest research, Heaton, Smith, Lehman, and Vogt (1978) studied 16 simulators and 16 participants with head injuries who were administered the entire HRB and the Wechsler Adult Intelligence Scale (WAIS; Wechsler, 1997b). Expert judges were relatively ineffective at identifying cases based on examining test results (accuracy of 50.0–68.8%). In contrast, a DFA using HRB and WAIS data classified 100% of participants correctly. However, an attempted cross-validation of this DFA by Thompson and Cullum (1991) using a known-groups comparison (i.e., independently classified as genuine or feigning) with compensation-seeking patients with mild TBI undergoing evaluation failed to produce supporting results.

Mittenberg, Rotholc, Russell, and Heilbronner (1996) tackled the atypical-pattern strategy via a new DFA based on 40 simulators and 40 non-compensation-seeking patients with TBI based on HRB scores. Utility estimates were excellent: .85 for sensitivity (i.e., simulators) and .93 for specificity (i.e., patients with TBI). These estimates remained fairly high on cross-validation (.84 and .80, respectively). However, McKinzey and Russell (1997) evaluated the specificity of the Mittenberg DFA on 796 Veterans' Administration (VA) patients, who were not considered by the authors to have any motivation for feigning cognitive deficits. Their specificity estimate of .73 was lower than in the Mittenberg studies. In response, Mittenberg, Aguila-Puentes, Patton, Canyock, and Heilbronner (2002) found fault with McKinzey and Russell's sample in that it included both neurologically normal participants and neurological conditions other than TBI. In a secondary analysis of the McKinzey and Russell data, Larrabee, Millis, and Meyers (2007) reported that a substantial subset of these VA patients may have been feigning. This conclusion suggests that Mittenberg and colleagues' DFA may have a higher specificity than originally reported by McKinzey and Russell.

Research on the detection of cognitive feigning using the HRB has several strengths. The implicit underlying detection strategy for the DFA approach involves identification of atypical patterns, which has proven useful when applied to cognitive feigning. In addition, these studies used a diverse set of clinical samples and tested cut scores with both simulation and known-groups designs. However, the effectiveness of DFA formulas appears rather variable. Cross-validations have tended to produce lower to substantially lower classification rates when applied to new samples, suggesting that the equations may, to some extent, capitalize on error variance in specific groups. The resulting variability of sensitivity and specificity values on cross-validation effectively precludes establishing consistent PPP and NPP values. Additionally, available DFA studies have not evaluated the effects of Axis I disorders, which may be a serious confound when interpreting the results. Overall, the available evidence on the use of the HRB to detect cognitive feigning suggests great caution in applying the procedures, particularly in forensic practice, as PPP and NPP cannot be confidently estimated based on currently available data. However, further research may identify more robust techniques for detecting feigning on this battery.

Wechsler Adult Intelligence Scale–III

The Wechsler Adult Intelligence Scale—Revised (WAIS-R, Wechsler, 1981) and its successor, the Wechsler Adult Intelligence Scale–III (WAIS-III, Wechsler, 1997b) are among the most commonly administered tests of intellectual functioning and have obvious relevance to the detection of cognitive feigning.

Two variants of atypical test pattern analysis have been used to detect feigning on the WAIS-R and WAIS-III. Mittenberg, Theroux-Fichera, Zielinski, and Heilbronner (1995) derived a DFA from WAIS-R subtests, which was subsequently extended to the WAIS-III by Axelrod and Rawlings (1999) and Mittenberg and colleagues (2001). The second pattern analytic approach to the WAIS-R and WAIS-III involves the relationship between Digit Span (DS) and Vocabulary (V) subtests. Mittenberg and colleagues (1995) observed that many feigners seem to interpret the DS subtest as tapping memory, which they mistakenly believe "should be" impaired following a head injury. In contrast, no such view is thought to be held regarding the V subtest. Thus these authors proposed that contrasting results from the two subtests might offer an index of feigning on the WAIS-R. The Vocabulary minus Digit Span (V – DS) index is calculated by subtracting the DS subtest scaled score, thought to be suppressed by feigners, from the V subtest scaled score, thought to be relatively spared by most feigners.

Review of the methodological issues for research on these two procedures indicates that there are an adequate number of publications with reasonably converging sensitivity and specificity results from both simulation and known-groups designs. Evaluations have been carried out by authors independent of the original researchers. One concern is that the impact of psychiatric disorders on these indices has not yet been evaluated.

Turning to quantitative indicators for these indices, a summary is presented in the first two columns of Table 14.1. Both approaches generate significant effect sizes, although the DFA (median $d = .97$) is much larger than V – DS (median $d = .44$). Cut scores for V – DS and DFA have varied somewhat, particularly for V – DS, but still fall within an acceptable range. For V – DS, the median sensitivity value is .41, whereas the median specificity value is .86. For the DFA, median sensitivity was .66 and specificity was .84. Using the estimated base rate of probable cognitive feigning of .40 in forensic evaluations of mild TBI cases and the median sensitivity and specificity values for the V – DS variable, projected PPP was .66, whereas predicted NPP was .69. Using the same base rate estimate and median sensitivity and specificity values for the DFA variable, projected PPP was .73 and estimated NPP was .79. The estimated predictive values for these two indices are modest, particularly for high-stakes evaluations, suggesting that they should not be used in isolation to identify probable cognitive feigning. However, there is some support for use of the WAIS-III DFA to rule out probable cognitive feigning, as its NPP value was .79.

Attention and Executive Functions

WAIS-R and WAIS-III Digit Span Subtest

The DS subtest of the WAIS-R and WAIS-III, thought to tap attention, has also been widely studied as a malingering detection tool. As noted earlier, malingerers often tend to overestimate the severity of deficits on this test after a brain injury, perhaps believing it taps memory rather than attention. Thus the DS subtest of the revised and third WAIS editions has been proposed as a potential index of cognitive feigning, and it represents an application of the floor-effect detection strategy. A variant of the DS subtest is Reliable Digit Span (RDS), proposed by Greiffenstein, Baker, and Gola (1994). RDS is based on the Wechsler version of the DS but sums the longest string of digits

TABLE 14.1. Wechsler Adult Intelligence Scale: Summary of Cut Scores and Utility Estimates across Studies

	WAIS indicators of feigning				
	V – DS	DFA	DS Fwd	DS Rev.	RDS
Cut scores					
N	6	3	4	3	13
Median	1.77	.21	5.00	3.00	7.00
Range	>1.53–>4	>.105–>.212	≤4–≤5	≤2–≤3	≤6–≤8
SD	.96	.06	.50	.57	.64
Sensitivity					
N	6	6	4	3	13
Median	.41	.66	.63	.53	.57
Range	.18–.72	.36–.88	.21–.95	.16–.53	.27–.86
SD	.24	.20	.40	.21	.19
Specificity					
N	6	6	4	3	13
Median	.86	.84	.95	1.00	.93
Range	.79–.89	.82–.94	.90–1.00	.93–1.00	.57–1.00
SD	.03	.05	.06	.04	.12
Hit rate					
N	6	6	4	3	13
Median	.67	.78	.87	.77	.73
Range	.51–.79	.64–.90	.57–.93	.71–.77	.62–.88
SD	.10	.10	.17	.03	.07
Effect sizes d					
N	3	3	7	6	13
Median	.44	.97	−.96	−.63	−1.19
Range	(.44)–(1.48)	(.97)–(2.10)	(−.44)–(−2.94)	(−.44)–(−1.92)	(−.65)–(−1.81)
SD	.60	.65	.92	.60	.33

Note. Results from patient-controlled studies of the WAIS-R and WAIS-III are combined. *N*, number of studies. For scales: V – DS, Vocabulary minus Digit Span subtests; DFA, Discriminant Function score from Mittenberg et al. (1995); DS Fwd, Digit Span forward raw score; DS Rev, Digit Span reverse raw score; RDS, Reliable Digit Span total score.

completed on both trials for digits forward and digits backward. In this way, information from the forward and backward digit span can be combined into a single malingering indicator, which is less cumbersome than the original use of DS (cut scores from forward and reverse subtests).

Review of the methodological issues with published evaluations of the DS and RDS suggests sufficient evaluation using both simulation and known-groups designs, research independent of the developers of the indices and fair convergence on utility parameters. Limitations include the study primarily of patients with TBI and the lack of information on the effect of Axis I mental disorders.

In the last three columns, Table 14.1 presents results from patient-controlled studies of DS as an indicator of cognitive feigning. Co-

hen's *d* scores for DS Forward Raw (median *d* = −.96) and DS Raw Backward (median *d* = −.63) have been moderate to strong. Median sensitivity and specificity rates for these indices are also adequate (Forward median sensitivity = .63, specificity = .95; Reverse median sensitivity = .53, specificity = 1.00). Using an estimated MNCD base rate of .40, these translate into moderately strong to strong predictive powers: DS Forward PPP = .89, NPP = .79; DS Reverse PPP = 1.00, NPP = .76.

Data from RDS appear in the final column of Table 14.1. This procedure has tended to generate high specificity (median = .93) and moderate sensitivity values (median = .57). At a cognitive feigning base rate of .40, RDS has estimated PPP of .84 and NPP of .79. Overall, these results support the use of the DS subtest and RDS for identifying probable MNCD, as

PPP values are moderately to very strong, particularly for the DS Reverse. However, these procedures have somewhat lower NPP, suggesting that they are not as useful at ruling out probable MNCD. Thus, clinically, if an examinee "fails" indices derived from the DS subtest, suspicion regarding MNCD should be raised, although converging findings from other MNCD procedures are needed to meet the Slick and colleagues (1999) criteria.

Trail Making Test

The Trail Making Test (TMT) is a core subtest of the HRB and includes Form A and the more complex Form B. Form A is thought to measure visual attention, whereas Form B is thought to evaluate both visual attention and sequencing abilities of executive functioning. Results from the TMT have been used primarily as a floor-effect strategy for detecting MNCD using noncompensation-seeking patients to obtain norms. Although a performance-curve approach to detecting cognitive feigning has been proposed (dividing time to complete Form B by time to complete Form A), only two published studies reported sensitivity and specificity values, and thus available information does not meet the selection criteria outlined earlier.

From a methodological perspective, there are multiple published studies of the TMT, including independent evaluations using both simulation and known-groups designs. Specificity values fall in a fairly narrow range, although sensitivity varies more widely. Additionally, the lack of data on psychiatric patients is a concern.

Summary data on published studies using the TMT as a floor-effect strategy appear in the first two columns of Table 14.2. Most effect

TABLE 14.2. Trail Making Test and Wisconsin Card Sorting Test: Summary of Cut Scores and Utility Estimates Across Studies

	Feigning indicators		
	Trails A	Trails B	WCST Disc. Fx
Cut score			
N	2	2	0
Median	≥63	≥200	*
Range	≥63–≥63	≥200–≥200	*
SD	0	0	*
Sensitivity			
N	3	3	4
Median	.17	.19	.84
Range	.11–.40	.07–.56	.70–1.00
SD	.15	.26	.12
Specificity			
N	3	3	4
Median	.98	.95	.92
Range	.92–1.00	.75–1.00	.87–.96
SD	.04	.10	.04
Hit rate			
N	3	3	4
Median	.61	.61	.89
Range	.57–.66	.56–.68	.78–.96
SD	.04	.06	.07
Effect size d			
N	11	11	0
Median	.87	.74	*
Range	(−.53)–2.07	(−1.01)–1.62	*
SD	.76	.71	*

Note. N, number of studies. Trails A, Trail Making Test Form A; Trails B, Trail Making Test Form B; WCST Disc. Fx, Wisconsin Card Sorting Test discriminant function; *, no data available.

sizes for the TMT are respectable; however, it is disconcerting that they vary so widely. Using the median sensitivity and specificity values for Form A and a .40 base rate of MNCD, PPP was estimated at .85, whereas NPP was .64. For Form B, PPP was .72, whereas NPP was .65. From a clinical perspective, this pattern suggests that when an examinee "fails" Form A, concern about the presence of probable MNCD might be raised, although converging evidence is required when using the Slick and colleagues (1999) criteria. In contrast, when Forms A and B are "passed," NPP is fairly modest and does not rule out MNCD.

Wisconsin Card Sorting Test

The Wisconsin Card Sorting Test (WCST) is often used to assess executive function. Results from the WCST have been applied to identification of MNCD using primarily the atypical-pattern strategy. Bernard, McGrath, and Houston (1996) derived an equation to identify feigned cognitive impairment using DFA.

From a methodological standpoint, there are multiple publications that evaluate the DFA, including some independent of the equation's developer. Results using both simulation and known-groups designs are available. Concerns include the nearly exclusive use of patients with TBI and the lack of information on the effects of psychiatric disorders.

The last column of Table 14.2 presents results from application of the WCST to detection of cognitive feigning. Successful cross-validation of the discriminant function equations with reasonably converging sensitivity (median = .84) and specificity (median = .92) values are noteworthy, although effect sizes are not reported. At an MNCD base rate of .40, PPP is estimated to be .88, whereas NPP is .90.

From a clinical standpoint, these robust predictive powers support the use of the WCST DF equation to both rule in (when positive) and rule out (when negative) MNCD. However, as previously noted, to meet the Slick and colleagues (1999) criteria for probable MNCD, converging findings must be present.

Seashore Rhythm Test

The Seashore Rhythm Test (SRT) is another part of the core HRB and measures auditory attention. The SRT relies on the floor-effect strategy for detecting cognitive malingering. At

present, three studies have examined the SRT total errors score as a malingering detection tool. From a methodological standpoint, strengths here include multiple and independent evaluations of the SRT using both major types of study designs and reasonable consistency across recommended cut scores. However, the effects of psychiatric disorders have not apparently been evaluated, and neurological patient groups have been limited to TBI.

Overall, cut scores are reasonably consistent. Effect sizes for specificity and d values appear moderately strong (median specificity = .85; median d = 1.13), whereas sensitivity values are moderate (median = .71). Using an MNCD base rate of .40, projected PPP is .76, whereas NPP is .81. Although not as robust as some of the other tests, these results suggest that the SRT can contribute to ruling out feigning but is not as strong at ruling in the condition.

Memory

Wechsler Memory Scale–III

The Wechsler Memory Scale–Revised (WMS-R; Wechsler, 1987) and its successor, the Wechsler Memory Scale–III (WMS-III; Wechsler, 1997c), are the most commonly administered memory batteries. Because memory deficits are often feigned, great interest has been generated in identifying indices from the WMS-R and WMS-III for detection of cognitive feigning. Both floor-effect and atypical-pattern strategies have been used to derive feigning indices for the WMS. Bernard and colleagues (1993) used DFA to derive a discriminant function in an application of the atypical-pattern analysis. Lange, Sullivan, and Anderson (2005) applied the floor-effect strategy by identifying easy items for the Rarely Missed Index (RMI).

Review of the literature reveals three studies evaluating the WMS discriminant function and four evaluating the WMS RMI. Results from several independent studies using known-groups and simulation designs provide promising support for the WMS discriminant function, with slightly less supportive data available for the RMI. One concern arises from the lack of data on the effects of psychiatric disorders.

Turning to quantitative indices, as shown in the first two columns of Table 14.3, overall cut scores across studies have been consistent for these indices, and d scores, only available for the RMI (median d = –1.02) are strong. Dis-

TABLE 14.3. Wechsler Memory Scale, Rey Auditory Verbal Learning Test, and Recognition Memory Test: Summary of Cut Scores and Utility Estimates Across Studies

	Malingering indicators						
	WMS Disc. Fx	WMS RMI	RAVLT Exagg. Ind.	RAVLT Recogn.	RMT Faces	RMT Words	RMT Discr. Fx.
Cut score							
N	1	4	4	10	3	3	0
Median	<1.87	≤136	>3	≤9	<32.00	<40	*
Range	<1.87–<1.87	≤136–≤136	>3–>3	≤6–≤9	<27–<32	<31–<40	*
SD	0	0	0	1.25	2.89	5.20	*
Sensitivity							
N	3	4	4	10	3	3	4
Median	.79	.25	.66	.38	.93	.95	.80
Range	.77–.90	.25–.25	.59–.72	.09–.67	.44–.93	.70–.95	.78–.88
SD	.07	0	.08	.23	.28	.14	.04
Specificity							
N	3	4	4	10	3	3	4
Median	.90	.93	.95	1.00	.90	.90	.84
Range	.80–.92	.91–.94	.92–.98	.92–1.00	.80–.90	.90–.90	.75–1.00
SD	.06	.02	.03	.04	.06	0	.10
Hit rate							
N	3	4	4	10	3	3	4
Median	.83	.72	.85	.67	.94	.95	.82
Range	.79–.91	.67–.83	.83–.88	.45–.82	.68–.94	.83–.95	.76–.93
SD	.06	.07	.02	.14	.15	.07	.07
Effect size _d_							
N	*	4	0	23	4	4	0
Median	*	−1.02	*	−1.10	−2.61	−2.77	*
Range	*	(−1.04)–.73	*	(−1.88)–.25	(−2.84)–(−.87)	(−3.85)–(−1.25)	*
SD	*	.15	*	.52	.92	1.07	*

Note. Results from patient-controlled studies of the WMS-R and WMS-III are combined. N, number of studies. For scale: Disc. Fx, discriminant function derived from WMS indices; RMI, Rarely Missed Index; RAVLT Exagg. Ind., Exaggeration Index composed of seven RAVLT inconsistency scales (see Barrash et al., 2004, for operational definition); RAVLT Recogn., correct recognition on RAVLT; RMT Discrim. Fx., RMT disriminant function; *, no data available.

criminant function utility values are promising (median sensitivity = .79, median specificity = .90). Sensitivity results for the RMI are lower, although specificity remains strong (median sensitivity = .25, median specificity = .93). At an MNCD base rate of .40, PPP is .83, and NPP is .82 for the discriminant function. Comparable values for the RMI are PPP at .70 and NPP at .65.

These findings suggest that the WMS-R/WMS-III discriminant function appears to be the most promising index from the test. From a clinical standpoint, the discriminant function appears moderately strong at both ruling in and ruling out MNCD. However, converging evidence should be sought from other indices, as both of these predictive values are in the low .80s.

Rey Auditory Verbal Learning Test

The Rey Auditory Verbal Learning Test (RAVLT) is a popular "list learning" procedure for assessing memory abilities. A number of investigators have proposed a tremendous variety of indicators from the RAVLT for detection of cognitive feigning, capitalizing on both the floor-effect and atypical-pattern strategies.

Many published studies attempt to detect MNCD using the RAVLT, with independent evaluation of indices using both simulation and known-groups designs. Varied neurological and psychiatric samples have also been included in this research.

The third and fourth columns of Table 14.3 present published results from two of the most commonly used RAVLT cognitive feigning indicators. Many patient-controlled studies examine the recognition portion of the test. In the Recognition Trial, test takers are asked to pick out the previously presented words from a paragraph or word list. There is some variability across studies in the cut score used (from ≤ 6 to ≤ 9). Additionally, although specificity values are excellent for this indicator (median = 1.00), sensitivity values are modest (median = .38). Using an MNCD base rate of .40 for the recognition trial projected PPP is excellent at 1.00, NPP is moderate at .71.

A promising new index from the RAVLT uses the atypical-pattern strategy as proposed by Barrash, Suhr, and Manzel (2004) and other investigators (Boone, Lu, & Wen, 2005; Suhr, Gunstad, Greub, & Barrash, 2004). For example, Barrash and colleagues (2004) described an Exaggeration Index; it was composed of seven possible indicators of cognitive feigning, such as poor learning across trials and worsening recall, which been supported in several studies. As shown in Table 14.3, four patient-controlled studies have examined the Exaggeration Index, with a moderate sensitivity value of .66 and strong specificity value of .95. At an MNCD base rate of .40, estimated PPP was .90 and NPP was .81.

From the standpoint of clinical application, both the RAVLT Recognition Trial and Exaggeration Index have strong support for ruling in MNCD. However, both indices are less robust at ruling out MNCD.

Recognition Memory Test

The Recognition Memory Test is a forced-choice procedure that taps recognition memory for words and faces. Millis (1992), noting the similarity of the RMT's format to other forced-choice measures, proposed using the test to identify cognitive feigning. He suggested identifying a cut score on both the Words and Faces tests to detect cognitive feigning that utilizes the floor-effect strategy. Incorporating the atypical-pattern approach, Millis (1992) also developed an equation using DFA to identify cognitive feigning.

From a methodological standpoint, three studies are published on the floor-effect detection strategy and four on the atypical-pattern approach; research has been evaluated using simulation and known-groups designs. Neurological patient groups have primarily been those

with TBI, although some data on psychiatric groups have been published.

The last three columns in Table 14.3 present results from published studies on the detection of cognitive feigning using the RMT. For the Words section, sensitivity was .95, and specificity was .90. For the Faces test, sensitivity was .93, whereas specificity was .90. Slightly lower values were seen for the discriminant function: sensitivity at .80 and specificity at .84. At an MNCD base rate of .40, RMT Words had projected PPP of .86 and NPP of .96; RMT Faces had PPP of .86 and NPP of .95; RMT discriminant function had PPP of .77 and NPP of .86.

For clinical application, the PPPs of both the RMT Words and Faces sections are moderately strong. The NPPs for both these tests are outstanding. The RMT discriminant function has moderately strong NPP and moderate PPP. Overall, the RMT Words and Faces subtests have moderately strong support for ruling in MNCD and exceptional support for ruling out cognitive feigning.

Motor Functioning

Finger Oscillation Test

The Finger Oscillation Test (FOT) is part of the core HRB assessing bilateral upper motor speed. Conceptually, it is attractive as a potential feigning indicator in that it is clearly effort-dependent. Additionally, feigners can easily titrate their efforts to produce results below their abilities. Both floor-effect and atypical-pattern strategies have been used to derive feigning indices from the FOT. Floor-effect strategies set cut scores based on dominant, nondominant, or the sum of both hand performances. A simple variant of the performance-curve strategy involves the calculation of a difference score between the dominant and nondominant hands. One potential complication with FOT as a feigning indicator results from gender differences, with males tapping 3 to 4 points faster (Mitrushina, Boone, Razani, & D'Elia, 2005). This difference suggests the need for sex-specific cut scores.

Review of the published literature indicates over a dozen studies on this test, with independent evaluations of proposed indices. Despite the large number of studies, there has been a reasonable convergence in findings. Both simulation and known-groups designs have been used, and the effects of psychiatric disorders have been evaluated.

Table 14.4 presents summary results from both floor-effect and atypical-pattern indices from the FOT. Most effect sizes are strong. For the floor-effect strategies in the first three columns of the table, specificity values are adequate (median = .88 and .88 for dominant hand and nondominant hand, respectively, and higher at a median of .93 for the sum of hands variable). Sensitivity values were less encouraging (median = .50, .36, and .43, respectively). Similar results were found for the atypical-pattern analysis using the difference score (median specificity = .90, median sensitivity = .21).

Using an MNCD base rate of .40, the following utility values were generated: dominant hand PPP = .74, NPP = .73; nondominant hand PPP = .67, NPP = .67; sum of hands PPP = .80,

NPP = .71; difference between hands PPP = .58, NPP = .63. From a clinical perspective, these results suggest that, despite the strong interest in using the FOT as an indicator of feigning, it does not appear to be as effective for this purpose as other instruments. The one possible exception is the PPP for the sum of hands variable.

CONCLUSIONS AND RECOMMENDATIONS

This chapter reviews published data on the use of selected standard neuropsychological tests to detect cognitive feigning. As previously noted, this approach has several potential advantages over dedicated feigning measures, including saving clinical time, less transparency

TABLE 14.4. Finger Oscillation Test: Summary of Cut Scores and Utility Estimates Across Studies

	Malingering indicators for the FOT			
	Dom. hand	Ndom. hand	Sum	Difference
Cut score				
N	12	12	13	12
Median	≤31.50	≤27.50	≤63.00	≤–3.50
Range	≤28–≤35	≤25–≤30	≤58–≤66	≤–5–≤–2
SD	3.66	2.61	4.01	1.54
Sensitivity				
N	13	13	13	12
Median	.50	.36	.43	.21
Range	.36–.61	.36–.36	.40–.55	.21–.21
SD	.08	0	.06	0
Specificity				
N	13	13	12	12
Median	.88	.88	.93	.90
Range	.75–1.00	.76–1.00	.71–1.00	.70–1.00
SD	.08	.08	.10	.08
Hit rate				
N	13	13	12	12
Median	.66	.49	.62	.39
Range	.55–.74	.45–.71	.50–.71	.30–.50
SD	.05	.07	.07	.06
Effect size d				
N	13	13	13	12
Median	–1.02	–.62	–.86	–.46
Range	(–1.61)–(–.39)	(–1.15)–(–.21)	(–2.34)–(–.34)	(–.90)–(–.05)
SD	.36	.32	.57	.29

Note. Dom. hand, dominant hand; Ndom. hand, nondominant hand; Sum, sum of dominant and nondominant hand; Difference, difference between dominant and nondominant hands.

for coaching, greater applicability to specific cognitive abilities, and extending the range of feigning detection methods. To focus attention on the most thoroughly studied tests, it was required that there be at least three published evaluations using neurological controls and providing data on sensitivity and specificity values.

The published literature provides varying support for the use of standard neuropsychological tests to detect cognitive feigning. A weakness common to many procedures was limited or no investigation of the effects of psychiatric disorders on the feigning index. This omission is a significant concern in light of the high comorbidity of psychiatric disorders with neurological conditions, such as TBI (Granacher, 2003). In addition, the large majority of neurological patient groups focused on TBI. Particularly where multivariate statistics are used to derive pattern-analytic indices, it will be important to verify that other types of neurological disorders do not generate excessive false positives on these malingering indicators. Nevertheless, it is possible to provide clinically useful suggestions for identifying feigned cognitive deficits using standard neuropsychological tests based on available literature.

Identifying Definite Cognitive Feigning

Using the Slick and colleagues (1999) framework for diagnosing definite MNCD, it is necessary that a substantial incentive for feigning be present, that there be a lack of alternative explanation for apparent false deficits, and that performance be statistically significantly below chance on a validated cognitive test. To use SVT as a detection strategy, a multiple-choice format for responding is necessary to allow the determination of a significantly below-chance performance. Several subtests from the WMS-III have this format, although sufficient publications are not available to include them in this review. For those procedures reviewed in this chapter, the following allow calculation of a chance level of responding and thus potentially contribute to identification of definite MNCD:

• Seashore Rhythm Test
• Recognition Memory Test—Words
• Recognition Memory Test—Faces

Thus, if a patient meets the other Slick and colleagues (1999) criteria and scores statistically significantly below chance on one or more of these procedures, a diagnosis of definite MNCD may be appropriate.

Identifying Probable Cognitive Feigning

In order to identify probable MNCD using the Slick and colleagues (1999) classification system, it is necessary that there be a substantial incentive for feigning, a lack of alternative explanations for false deficits, and two or more indicators of feigning. Table 14.5 summarizes the projected predictive powers for the tests and procedures reviewed earlier, using an estimated base rate of MNCD of 40% in patients with mild TBI undergoing forensic neuropsychological examinations. Results point to certain instruments as having strong PPP, whereas others have strong NPP. It is important to emphasize that differing base rates and/or the use of different cut scores will alter these values in local settings. To address this issue, the median sensitivity and specificity values at a given cut score may be combined with the local base rate to estimate revised predictive values.

To rule in, or identify, probable cognitive feigning, the three procedures with the highest PPP (all ≥ .90) are:

• Digit Span Reverse
• RAVLT—Exaggeration Index
• RAVLT—Recognition Trial

Thus, if a patient meets the other Slick and colleagues (1999) criteria and "fails" two or more of these procedures, a diagnosis of probable MNCD may be appropriate. These scales use two detection strategies: floor effect and atypical test patterns.

To rule out, or exclude, the possibility of probable cognitive feigning, the three procedures with the highest NPP (all ≥ .90) are:

• WCST discriminant function equation
• Recognition Memory Test—Words
• Recognition Memory Test—Faces

These procedures appear to have the highest available NPP and thus lend themselves to ruling out probable MNCD.

As summarized in Table 14.5, most successful investigations of cognitive feigning on embedded measures have relied heavily on only

TABLE 14.5. Summary of Positive and Negative Predictive Powers at an MNCD Base Rate of 40% and Using Median Sensitivity and Specificity Values from the Published Literature

Test/index	Indicator	PPP	NPP	Strategy
WAIS-R/WAIS-III	V – DS	.66	.69	ATP
	Discriminant function	.73	.79	ATP
Digit Span	Forward	.89	.79	FE
	Reverse	**1.00**	.76	FE
	Reliable Digit Span	.84	.79	FE
Trail Making Test	Form A	.85	.64	FE
	Form B	.72	.65	FE
Wisconsin Card Sort	Discriminant function	.88	**.90**	ATP
Seashore Rhythm Test	# errors	.76	.81	FE
WMS-R/WMS-III	Discriminant function	.83	.82	ATP
	Rarely Missed Index	.70	.65	FE
RAVLT	Exaggeration Index	.90	.81	FE
	Recognition Trial	**1.00**	.71	ATP
Recognition Memory	Words total	.86	**.96**	FE
	Faces total	.86	**.95**	FE
	Discriminant function	.77	.86	ATP
Finger Oscillation	Dominant hand	.74	.73	FE
	Nondominant hand	.67	.67	FE
	Summary of hands	.80	.71	FE
	Hand difference	.58	.63	PC

Note. See text for test names. Predictive values ≥ .90 are presented in boldface. V – DS, Vocabulary subtest score minus Digit Span subtest score; Hand difference, difference in total score between dominant and nondominant hands. For detection strategies, ATP, atypical test pattern; FE, floor effect; PC, performance curve.

two detection strategies (i.e., floor effect and atypical test patterns). In contrast, two more sophisticated test strategies have been virtually ignored. The magnitude-of-error strategy is easily adaptable to measures such as the WCST and WAIS-III Matrix Reasoning and Picture Arrangement. It has proven to be a very effective detection strategy. Likewise, the performance-curve strategy could be implemented with most test batteries. For instance, the WAIS-III Picture Completion items could be divided into two or three categories based on item difficulty. The slope or curve could be examined in cases of cognitive feigning.[2]

Overall, this review finds much promise in the application of standard neuropsychological tests to the detection of cognitive feigning. Significant work remains to be done in extending the empirical basis for many procedures and incorporating additional detection strategies. For clinical and forensic applications, research is needed to evaluate systematically the effects of psychiatric conditions and cognitive disorders beyond TBI. Finally, studies should examine the relative effectiveness of embedded scales and specialized measures for the assessment of cognitive feigning.

NOTES

1. Historically, some simulation studies did not include clinical comparisons. These studies are flawed because differences could represent either feigning or genuine impairment. Such flawed studies are excluded from this chapter.
2. Feigning is most likely to be considered in cases of significantly below-average abilities; this strategy is likely to be effective in those cases in which a substantial number of items are missed.

Appendix 14.1. Studies Used in the Analyses of Detection Strategies and Reported in One or More Tables

- Arnold, Boone, et al. (2005)
- Axelrod & Rawlings (1999)
- Axelrod, Fichtenberg, Millis, & Wertheimer (2006)
- Babikian, Boone, Lu, & Arnold (2006)

- Barrash, Suhr, & Manzel (2004)
- Backhaus, Fichtenberg, & Hanks (2004)
- Bernard (1990)
- Bernard, McGrath, & Houston (1993)
- Bernard, McGrath, & Houston (1996)
- Binder, Kelly, Villaneuva, & Winslow (2003)
- Boone, Lu, & Wen (2005)
- Chouinard & Rouleau (1997)
- Duncan & Ausborn (2002)
- Etherton, Bianchini, Ciota, & Greve (2005)
- Etherton, Bianchini, Ciota, Heinly, & Greve (2006)
- Etherton, Bianchini, Greve, & Heinly (2005)
- Frederick, Crosby, & Wynkoop (2000)
- Gfeller & Craddock (1998)
- Glassmire et al. (2003)
- Goebel (1983)
- Greiffenstein, Baker, & Gola (1994)
- Greiffenstein, Gola, & Baker (1995)
- Haines & Norris (2001)
- Heaton, Smith, Lehman, & Vogt (1978)
- Heinly, Greve, Bianchini, Love, & Brennan (2005)
- Inman & Berry (2002)
- Iverson & Franzen (1994)
- Iverson, Lange, Green, & Franzen (2002)
- Lange, Sullivan, & Anderson (2005)
- Langeluddecke & Lucas (2003)
- Larrabee (2003a)
- Martin, Hoffman, & Donders (2003)
- Mathias, Greve, Bianchini, Houston, & Crouch (2002)
- McKinzey & Russell (1997)
- Meyers & Diep (2000)
- Meyers, Morrison, & Miller (2001)
- Millis (1992)
- Millis (2002)
- Millis & Putnam (1994)
- Millis, Ross, & Ricker (1998)
- Mittenberg, Azrin, Millsaps, & Heilbronner (1993)
- Mittenberg, Rotholc, Russell, & Heilbronner (1996)
- Mittenberg et al. (2001)
- Mittenberg, Theroux-Fichera, Zielinski, & Heilbronner (1995)
- O'Bryant, Hilsabeck, Fisher, & McCaffrey (2003)
- Ross, Putnam, Millis, Adams, & Krukowski (2006)
- Ruffolo, Guilmette, & Willis (2000)
- Sherman, Boone, Lu, & Razani (2002)
- Suhr & Boyer (1999)
- Suhr, Gunstad, Greub, & Barrash (2004)
- Suhr, Tranel, Wefel, & Barrash (1997)
- Thompson & Cullum (1991)
- Trueblood & Schmidt (1993)

IV

Specialized Methods

15

Assessing Deception

Polygraph Techniques and Integrity Testing

WILLIAM G. IACONO, PhD
CHRISTOPHER J. PATRICK, PhD

Outside of clinical settings, deception is often assessed through polygraphic interrogation and standardized questionnaires designed to assess integrity. In this chapter, we tackle both of these topics and include information that should be useful to clinicians who encounter the results of these assessments in their practices.

POLYGRAPHY

Few mental health professionals are likely to ever administer or interpret polygraph tests. Nevertheless, polygraphs are used in many professional settings, including government agencies and the criminal justice system. In particular, most federal government workers with access to classified information must pass polygraph tests to maintain their security clearances. Those applying for jobs in law enforcement often have to pass preemployment polygraph tests reviewing their integrity. Moreover, police departments administer polygraph tests as investigative aids to help solve crimes. Defense attorneys may arrange for their clients to take polygraph tests in hopes that they will pass, thereby providing exculpatory evidence. Polygraph tests are also utilized to combat insurance fraud and sometimes are used in civil

cases in which a question of fact cannot be resolved with physical evidence. In this section, we review what clinicians need to know to evaluate the results of polygraph tests arising from these different venues.

Instrumentation

A polygraph is a multichannel recording device that amplifies physiological signals from the autonomic nervous system, displaying them as tracings on moving chart paper. Three types of physiological information are recorded: respiration, blood pressure, and palmar sweating. Respiration is recorded from two pneumatic belts, one strapped around the chest and the other around the abdomen. Relative blood pressure and heart rate are monitored from a standard sphygmomanometer cuff wrapped around the arm. The cuff is inflated midway between diastolic and systolic pressure, allowing fluctuations in arterial pressure to be recorded as each heartbeat sends a bolus of blood under the cuff. Changes in the electrical conductance of the skin are monitored from electrodes attached to the fingertips. Developments in electronic engineering make it possible to replace the polygraph instrument with a laptop computer that records and digitizes these signals, displaying them as they would appear on chart paper. This computer display can be printed, producing a hard copy identical to the paper output of a field instrument.

Polygraph Methods

Polygraph applications do not satisfy the formal criteria for a psychological test. Polygraph tests are neither objective nor standardized, and they do not have norms. Therefore, it is not possible to derive meaningful estimates of their accuracy that generalize across cases. Rather, polygraphs are interviews administered by skilled interrogators who, assisted by the physiological recording, use the occasion to make an assessment about a person's truthfulness. It is the utility of the polygraph, not its validity, that supports its widespread and continued use. Under the pressure of this assessment, examinees often make revealing admissions that would be undiscoverable through other methods. Many persons confess to crimes that would otherwise go unsolved. It is because polygraph tests provide a tool for gathering incriminating information that their use is growing, despite overwhelming skepticism from the scientific community.

Because no unique physiological response is associated with lying, polygraph examiners make inferences about lying based on the relative size of a person's response to different types of questions. There are many ways to arrange these questions, and thus dozens of terms are used to describe different types of polygraph tests. However, all tests can be categorized as falling into one of the following three categories.

Employee Screening Tests

When an employer wishes to know whether employees are trustworthy, the employees are likely to be examined with a variant of the Relevant–Irrelevant Test (RIT). The RIT was originally used to investigate possible criminal wrongdoing and included *relevant* (e.g., for a case of sexual assault, "Did you force the victim to have sex with you?") and *irrelevant* (e.g., "Is today Wednesday?") questions. Originally, individuals responding more intensely to the relevant questions were deemed guilty. Those with any other pattern were considered truthful. However, the irrelevant question provides a poor psychological control for the emotional impact of the accusatory relevant question. Therefore, the RIT is considered biased against the innocent and thus is rarely used to investigate crimes.

However, variants of the RIT are used in employee screening to investigate possible misbehavior and character flaws of current and prospective employees. In this context, similar irrelevant questions are used along with a series of relevant questions exploring the likelihood that the examinee uses illicit drugs, mishandles classified information, or otherwise behaves in ways that could undermine the employer. The examiner watches for any relevant question that appears to elicit reactions that are more pronounced than those elicited by the other relevant questions. With the physiological record in hand, the examiner might confront the individual with: "It looks like something must be bothering you about your answer to the drug question. I really want to work with you to make sure this test plays to your advantage, but I can't do that if you're holding back on me. Is there something you want to tell me that could help?" The failure to offer a satisfactory explanation typically results in a failed test verdict.

The employee screening polygraph has no theoretical rationale that would suggest that this procedure would be very accurate. No studies in the scientific peer review literature support its use. Although examiners often uncover information that is deemed valuable, the extent to which deceptive or otherwise unfit employees escape detection is unknown. Moreover, these tests are widely believed to have deterrent value despite an absence of empirical evidence to support this claim.

Guilty Knowledge Test

An alternative strategy for detecting liars is based on the knowledge that a triggering of recognition memory elicits a physiological reaction. Almost 50 years ago, David Lykken (1959) developed the Guilty Knowledge Test (GKT; sometimes referred to as a "concealed information test"), a procedure in which participants are asked factual questions about their alleged involvement in a crime. Possible answers to the question are presented in multiple-choice format while physiological reactions are monitored to each alternative. Guilty individuals are expected to respond most strongly to alternatives that reflect their knowledge about the crime. Innocent suspects would respond most strongly to any given alternative only by chance. By including many GKT items, it is unlikely that an innocent person would fail many of them. As more items are failed, it becomes increasingly likely that the examinee has guilty knowledge about the crime. A sample GKT might take the following form:

1. "If you forced Susan to have sex with you, you'd know what weapon you used to gain her cooperation. Was it a (a) box cutter, (b) bowie knife, (c) switchblade, (d) razor, (e) pair of scissors?"
2. "The perpetrator of this crime carved a word on what part of Susan's body? Was it her (a) neck, (b) breast, (c) butt, (d) forearm, (e) thigh?"

A test composed of five or more such questions discriminates well between innocent and guilty individuals in laboratory research in which guilt is established by participating in a mock crime (Iacono, Boisvenu, & Fleming, 1984).

It is ironic that the GKT is virtually never used by North American polygraphers, despite its obvious soundness and an extensive research literature supporting its validity (Ben-Shakar & Elaad, 2003). Among many reasons, the most likely explanation is that polygraph examiners believe their own techniques to be both highly accurate and relatively easy to use. The GKT, unlike conventional polygraphs, requires investigation of crime facts to identify proper items and time-consuming effort to construct these items. Some polygraphers have concerns about possible false-negative outcomes if the constructed items do not effectively capture crime-related guilty knowledge. As evidence to the contrary, GKT procedures are highly developed in Japan, where it is used with apparent success by law enforcement (Nakayama, 2002).

In the United States, an event-related brain potential (ERP) version of the GKT is currently being made available for forensic applications by a Seattle company that advertises its product as "brain fingerprinting" (for a review, see Iacono, 2007). The ERP-GKT offers many advantages over GKTs based on autonomic nervous system recordings; it has a better chance of one day being accepted in legal proceedings as credible scientific evidence.

The GKT may also have untapped potential for various clinical applications. For instance,

it has been used to study amnesia associated with prosopagnosia (Bauer, 1984), hypnosis (Allen, Iacono, Laravuso, & Dunn, 1995), and dissociative identity disorder (Allen & Iacono, 2001). The GKT could also have value as a tool for assessing malingered memory loss, but this potential application has not been developed. Despite its obvious appeal, the forensic and clinical potential of the GKT has yet to be realized.

Control Question Test

The only polygraphic technique that has both been used extensively in real-life cases and been comprehensively studied is the Control Question Test (CQT). Not coincidentally, this procedure is most likely to be made available to mental health providers. Therefore, it warrants critical scrutiny.

Description

The CQT employs the same type of "did you do it" relevant questions that are used on the criminal investigation version of the RIT, as well as irrelevant questions that do not affect the scoring of the test. What distinguishes the CQT is the inclusion of "control" questions, items designed to tap a probable lie. In the case of rape, for example, a control question might take the form "Have you ever engaged in any unusual sexual behavior?" CQT scoring is predicated on the assumption that innocent individuals, presumably because they do engage in unusual sexual practices, will be concerned about their likely lie to the control question when they answer it "no." This concern should cause their response to this question to be stronger than that to the relevant question. In contrast, guilty persons, because they actually committed the sexual assaults, attach more weight to their lies to the relevant questions and thus respond more strongly to them.

Critique of CQT Rationale

Although an improvement over the RIT, the CQT has the same weakness: The control question does not control for the provocative nature of the accusation contained in the relevant question. Readers of this chapter can probably recall an instance when, confronted with an unjust accusation, they responded truthfully "no" but nevertheless felt a wave of sympathetic arousal course through their bodies, perhaps resulting in blushing and sweaty palms. This reaction could stem from any of a number of emotions, including anger, embarrassment, and worry about not being believed. On a CQT, their arousal is compared with that generated by the control question. No sound reasoning explains why the relevant question is not likely to be relevant to the innocent person or why the relatively innocuous matter addressed in the control question should be given more weight by an innocent person than the threatening accusation covered by the relevant question.

Furthermore, how likely is it that the innocent person is actually lying or otherwise disturbed by the control question? In the "pretest" phase of the polygraph interview, control questions are reviewed with the examinee to make sure they can be honestly denied. However, many individuals admit that they have committed an "unusual" sex act (e.g., masturbation or oral sex) and are asked to disclose it to the polygrapher. When this occurs, the question is subsequently modified to state "Other than what you have told me about, have you ever engaged in any unusual sexual behavior?" Taking this step further increases the likelihood that innocent individuals will be answering the control question honestly. Like the RIT, the CQT is biased against the innocent.

Unable to counter this critique, the American Polygraph Association in 1999 changed the name of the CQT to the "Comparison Question Test." However, this name change does nothing to blunt the criticism that the control questions are inadequate. An alternative to the CQT, called the Directed Lie Test (DLT), has been introduced to further combat concerns about the control questions. The relevant question on the DLT is the same, but the probable-lie control question is replaced with a directed lie, such as "Have you ever broken even one rule?" Once the examinee admits that this is true, he or she is told to deliberately think of the rule that was broken while answering the question "no." In this way, the test participant provides a response to an acknowledged lie, which for an innocent person is presumed to elicit a larger response than what would be expected to the relevant question. Again, it is difficult to understand how a directed-lie question can be seen as equivalent in psychological significance to the relevant question. Apparently polygraph examiners remain unconvinced

that the DLT is an improvement over the CQT, because it is not in common use.

The transparent intent of the CQT questions makes it vulnerable to countermeasures, deliberate strategies adopted to manipulate the outcome of the test. Research has shown that with no more than one half-hour of instruction, naive laboratory participants committing a mock crime can defeat a CQT more than half the time (Honts, Hodes, & Raskin, 1985; Honts, Raskin, & Kircher, 1994). Moreover, trained examiners cannot detect when examinees are using countermeasures. The training includes learning to recognize control and relevant questions coupled with adopting strategies to enhance responding to the control questions. These strategies include mental countermeasures such as having the examinee carry out stressful mental arithmetic and physical maneuvers, such as lightly biting the tongue or curling the toes, when asked a control question. These techniques can be learned by reading the cited articles and books on polygraphy or websites such as *antipolygraph.org* or *polygraph.com*. Although the CQT is vulnerable to countermeasures, the DLT would appear more so, because the purpose of its questions is even more transparent.

Any method that enhances the relevance of the control questions increases the likelihood of a passed test. Because it is in the interest of a person taking the CQT to be lying when asked the control questions, those taking the test enhance their chances of passing by not divulging information covered by the control questions, such as instances of unusual sexual behavior. Although this strategy would benefit anyone taking a CQT, it may especially help sex offenders who may have committed many sex offenses prior to being apprehended. Sex offenders with such records would be especially unlikely to divulge such offenses while reviewing control questions for fear of worsening their current predicaments. But by keeping this information secret, they would increase the odds of passing the test, because the control question would be more salient than the relevant question under these circumstances.

Withholding information is a special concern in the testing of sex offenders, as noted by Abrams (1989) in his textbook on polygraphy. Abrams cautions against ever telling sex offenders they have passed; it would imply to a male sex offender that he was "found truthful on the control questions, which he has almost definitely responded to deceptively" (p. 176).

Evaluating the Empirical Evidence

Although the CQT has been used for over half a century, with hundreds of thousands of generated reports, its psychometric properties are largely unknown. This peculiar state of affairs arose primarily because polygraph testing has grown out of professions associated with law enforcement, not academic psychology. In addition, relatively few psychologists have taken an active interest in this important area of applied psychology.

Adequate reliability studies on the CQT do not exist. In particular, test–retest reliability has received little attention. This neglect is unfortunate because it is not known to what degree the outcome of a CQT is dependent on its many facets: (1) construction of control questions, (2) wording of relevant questions, (3) ordering and pairing of questions, and (4) nature of the pretest interview. Interrater reliability has been studied by examining whether analysis of the physiological tracings leads to the same conclusion. These studies indicate high reliability, typically around .90 (e.g., Patrick & Iacono, 1991).

By contrast, CQT validity has received a great deal of attention. Unfortunately, it has been impossible to provide anything approaching a definitive validity study. Although this might also be true for many psychological tests, polygraph test validity would appear, at least superficially, to be straightforward to appraise. First, as noted, chart scoring is highly reliable, so at least one element important to validity has a solid footing. Second, there are only two meaningful outcomes for a CQT: truthful or deceptive. Third, those taking tests are either innocent or guilty. Given the dichotomous nature of the outcome and the criterion, one would think that it would be easy to determine how often the examiner's verdict matches ground truth. Nevertheless, several methodological reasons explain why the validity of polygraph tests has yet to be established.

The easiest way to establish ground truth is to rely on laboratory studies in which volunteers do or do not carry out a mock crime, thereby establishing guilt or innocence. However, this artificial situation does not involve the high-stakes context that accompanies real-life polygraph testing. In the laboratory, the cost of failing a test is relatively inconsequential, and innocent participants will not fear a false-positive outcome. Control questions are likely to be quite disturbing to innocent participants because they will be perceived as privacy invading. Guilty participants will not have the incentive or the time to research the technique and learn about countermeasures. The conflict and shame over lying and getting caught that are present in real life will be minimized in the laboratory, as participants are simply following instructions and no truly dishonest act was carried out. Laboratory studies thus might be expected to overestimate polygraph validity.

In a recent study comparing the physiological reactivity evident in mock crime and real-life CQTs, Pollina, Dollins, Senter, Krapohl, and Ryan (2004) found that electrodermal, cardiovascular, and respiratory responses were more pronounced in field polygraph applications. The authors interpreted these findings as possibly reflecting defensive responses motivated by fear during field polygraph tests and orienting responses that reflect a "fascination with the process and a desire to 'win the game' " (p. 1104) in laboratory situations. Also of interest are two laboratory studies that introduced mock crime circumstances designed to approximate some of those conditions found in real life. Patrick and Iacono (1989) studied incarcerated felons who were told that failing a CQT could lead to reprisals from other inmates who were counting on them to appear innocent on their tests in order for all participants to receive a monetary reward. Forman and McCauley (1986) gave participants the option to decide on their own whether to be innocent or guilty, the latter choice leading to a larger monetary reward if they passed the CQT. In these two studies, the CQT accuracy averaged 73%, considerably lower than the 88% reported for mock crime investigations without such attention to external validity (Kircher, Horowitz, & Raskin, 1988).

Field studies based on real-life polygraph examinations administered by law enforcement do not have the same problems with ecological validity, which limit laboratory investigations. However, establishing ground truth in a manner that is methodologically sound has been problematic. The most commonly accepted approach relies on confessions to identify the guilty while establishing as innocent the cosuspects in the same case. In the typical field study, the only cases selected for inclusion are those in which a failed polygraph test was corroborated by a confession obtained by the examiner once it was obvious the test indicated deception. In the best of these investigations, the polygraph tracings are examined by skilled evaluators who are unaware of the case facts, questions asked, or any details regarding test administration. The results of this independent chart rescoring are then compared with ground truth. Under these circumstances, ground truth (i.e., the confession) and the polygraph test results are not independent. Polygraph chart scoring is highly reliable. If the original examiner decided that the relevant questions produced stronger reactions than the control questions (i.e., deception was indicated), it should be no surprise that the independent evaluator reached the same conclusion. However, because the original examiner used the deceptive charts to interrogate the examinee and elicit the confession, the confession will always be a product of a failed chart. As a result, all the cases chosen in field studies based on confessions can be expected to come from original examiners who were correct almost all the time. This result follows because cases in which the original examiner made an error will not produce a confession and therefore will never become part of the field study. That is, all cases in which the original examiner erred (i.e., judged a guilty person to be nondeceptive or an innocent person to be deceptive) will be excluded from the field study because, absent a confession, these errors will not lead to confessions. Consequently, like laboratory investigations, field studies inflate estimates of accuracy.

Only one field study has attempted to circumvent this problem of inflated estimates. Carried out with the Royal Canadian Mounted Police, Patrick and Iacono (1991) examined police records obtained subsequent to the administration of a polygraph test for evidence of ground truth. They identified all cases in which postpolygraph files maintained by local police departments indicated that individuals being investigated confessed or in which it was later determined that no crime was committed (e.g., lost possessions mistakenly believed to be stolen). When these charts were blindly rescored, they yielded a modest hit rate of 57% (50% reflects chance) for verified innocent individuals. However, a corresponding rate for guilty suspects could not be determined because all but one of the confessions obtained in these local police files were from people whose confessions cleared as innocent the person

who took a polygraph. Consequently, the study could not establish the hit rates for guilty persons. However, the false-positive rate for innocent suspects of 43% is clearly unacceptably large.

In our 20 years of experience, we have found that polygraph examiners assert quite sincerely that the CQT is virtually infallible. They will acknowledge that mistakes are made but argue that those mistakes arise from incompetent examiners. They do not believe that they ever make mistakes. This strongly held opinion follows from the confession-bias problem that plagues field studies. That is, when polygraphers obtain a confession following failed tests, the confession always shows that they were correct. Suspects who are innocent and fail do not confess, nor do those who are guilty and pass. Hence, examiners become aware of their successes while being protected from learning about their failures. This fact explains why the polygraph profession does not take to heart the many reports from scientists that challenge their claims.

Scientific Opinion Regarding CQT Accuracy

To buttress their claims for CQT accuracy, the American Polygraph Association Web page (polygraph.org) cites a report by Forensic Research Incorporated (1997) indicating that "researchers conducted 12 studies of the validity of field examinations, following 2,174 field examinations, providing an average accuracy of 98%" (p. 215). Psychologists who have received training as polygraphers also argue that the CQT has very high accuracy, exceeding 90%. For instance, Raskin and Honts (2002) asserted that hit rates in field studies should be based on the original examination, not on subsequent hit rates by blind chart evaluators. They argue that "independent evaluators rarely testify in legal proceedings, nor do they make decisions in most applied settings. It is usually the original examiner who makes the decision on how to proceed in an actual case and provides court testimony. Thus, accuracy rates based on the decisions of independent evaluators may not be the true figure of merit for legal proceedings" (p. 33). These comments accompany a table that lists the hit rates of original examiners in field studies that show an average accuracy of 97.5%. These studies are all subject to the confession-bias problem that inflates CQT validity. As noted earlier, the nature of case selection in field studies virtually ensures that original examiners will be "correct," so relying on original examiner hit rates is indefensible.

Converging evidence from many sources in the scientific community rejects these inflated claims from the polygraph profession. The most thorough evaluation of polygraph testing was undertaken by the National Research Council (NRC; 2003) of the National Academy of Sciences. The NRC held public hearings, visited government polygraph facilities, and accessed unpublished government reports, including classified material. Their analysis relied mostly on CQT studies.

The NRC had three major criticisms: (1) the theoretical basis for the CQT was weak, (2) research was of low quality (e.g., the majority of studies were not published in scientific peer-reviewed journals), and (3) knowledge had not accumulated in this field in a manner that had strengthened its scientific underpinnings. The NRC did not accept the validity claims of the polygraph profession: "What is remarkable, given the large body of relevant research, is that claims about the accuracy of the polygraph made today parallel those made throughout the history of the polygraph: practitioners have always claimed extremely high levels of accuracy, and these claims have rarely been reflected in empirical research" (p. 107). They also observed that "almost a century of research in scientific psychology and physiology provides little basis for the expectation that a polygraph test could have extremely high accuracy" (p. 212). Noted were the problems with laboratory studies and the biases of field investigations that lead to overestimates of accuracy.

The NRC also criticized the lack of data on moderating variables and polygraph methods. It concluded that the evidence does not "provide confidence that accuracy is stable across personality types, sociodemographic groups, psychological and medical conditions, examiner and examinee expectancies, or ways of administering the test and selecting questions" (p. 214).

An independent review of the CQT literature by German psychologists reached similar conclusions, leading the German Supreme Court to outlaw their use (Fiedler, Schmod, & Stahl, 2002). Surveyed scientific opinion has been similarly damning. In the only published survey of scientist opinion, Iacono and Lykken (1997) found that psychophysiologists and fellows from the Division of General Psychology of the American Psychological Association did not believe that the CQT is standardized, objective, immune to countermeasures, based on sound theory, or as accurate as the polygraph profession asserts. Other scientists (Ben-Shakar, 2002; Oksol & O'Donohue, 2003) have reached similar conclusions.

Alternatives to Conventional Polygraphy

Dissatisfaction with conventional polygraphy, coupled with increased concerns about national security, have served as an impetus for the development of alternative methods of lie detection. One such method is the computer voice-stress analyzer. Although voice-stress analysis has been employed to detect lying since the 1960s, it has been remarketed by the National Institute for Truth Verification (www.cvsa1.com) in portable, handheld computer form as a means of detecting truth through measurement of the stress presumably associated with vocalized lies. There is no empirical evidence that this method works much better than chance (National Research Council, 2003).

Another unobtrusive technique of lie detection is based on thermal imaging of the face. Thermography relies on a high-speed camera to record changes in facial blood flow. The only report to use this technique involved a mock crime study with a total of 20 participants (Pavlidis, Eberhardt, & Levine, 2002). Much more research will be required to place this method on a firm footing.

Methods based on the recording of brain electrical activity have been explored for use in lie detection. Besides ERP-GKT, these methods include monitoring the electrical potential that precedes a dishonest response (Fang, Liu, & Shen, 2003) and measuring motor cortex evoked potentials to magnetic pulses presented before and after questions answered truthfully or with a lie (Lo, Fook-Chong, & Tan, 2003). In addition, electroencephalographic (EEG) studies are being carried out to examine brain processes involved in lying (Johnson, Barnhardt, & Zhu, 2003, 2004). Functional magnetic resonance imaging (fMRI) methods are also being developed for lie detection (for reviews, see Iacono, 2007; Iacono & Patrick, 2006). Most of the research in this area has been devoted to understanding brain mechanisms related to lying, an important undertaking given how little information exists on this topic. However, two companies have been formed that plan to offer fMRI-based lie detector tests (see *www.cephoscorp.com* and *www.noliemri.com*), with the work launching each company initially consisting of a single laboratory study showing that it is possible to classify the brain responses of individual participants as indicative of deception or truthfulness (Kozel et al., 2005; Langleben et al., 2005). Although the different technologies used in these studies is impressive, investigations using these novel methods are burdened with the same problems that have confronted CQT studies. Hence this research is quite preliminary, but over time, it could contribute insights that would lead to the development of improved lie detection technology.

Clinical Applications

Of the various procedures described in this chapter, only employee screening and CQTs are in routine use. Screening tests are the more prevalent of the two, but few psychologists see cases involving such tests unless they are working in personnel evaluation for government agencies. The government exempted itself from the Employee Polygraph Protection Act that banned most private sector personnel screening when it was signed into law in 1988. Psychologists are much more likely to encounter CQTs because they are used widely in forensic settings. As noted, police may use CQTs as investigative aids to gain information and elicit confessions from the accused. Statistics are not available to document the types of crimes most likely to lead to polygraph tests. However, sex crimes probably make up the plurality, if not the majority, of polygraphed cases because often these crimes involve issues surrounding consent or intent, and they may include victims who are too young to provide reliable testimony. Polygraph tests are also used in child custody cases, especially in cases in which allegations have surfaced about possible child abuse.

Polygraph tests are also utilized with those convicted of crimes. Sometimes they are used to verify the accuracy of information provided by plea bargainers who agree to cooperate with prosecutors in return for a reduced sentence. Many states with sex-offender treatment programs now rely heavily on polygraph tests to compel offenders to reveal all of their inappropriate sexual behavior, as well as to monitor their treatment progress.

In a typical polygraph test report, the polygrapher describes the allegations against the suspect, the suspect's explanation for what happened, a list of the relevant questions, and the conclusion about deception. Some examiners will indicate that they used a movement sensor on the examinee's chair to detect physical countermeasures. However, as noted previously, mental countermeasures and physical maneuvers such as tongue biting would remain largely undetectable with any CQT method. Because it is not possible to arrive at a general estimate of CQT validity, there is no way to establish the validity of a particular polygraph examiner and his or her personalized method of administration. This absence of validity limits the usefulness of CQT results. Therefore, the clinical value of the CQT rests primarily on any admissions made by examinees during the examination.

INTEGRITY TESTING

Proclivities toward theft, dishonesty, and other forms of misconduct are an important consideration in selecting individuals for employment positions. According to recent estimates (U.S. Chamber of Commerce, 2005, cited in Perkins, 2006), employee theft alone accounts for as much as $40 billion in annual business losses. Contributing further to corporate losses are other obviously antisocial acts such as sabotage and fraud, as well as more broadly defined "counterproductive" behaviors such as absence or tardiness, misuse of sick leave, and on-the-job substance use. At one time, polygraph tests were used widely in the private sector to identify and screen out job applicants who might be prone to such behaviors. However, the use of polygraph testing for preemployment screening purposes was banned in 1988 by passage of the federal Employee Polygraph Protection Act.

The major alternative that has emerged in subsequent years is integrity testing, which entails the administration of paper-and-pencil instruments to index traits or behaviors associated with job dishonesty or counterproductivity. The use of integrity testing (originally termed *honesty testing*) for personnel selection originated, along with many other psychological assessment procedures, during World War II. Betts (1947) developed the Biographical Case History (BCH) scale as the first face-valid honesty test. The BCH was used at first to screen out undesirable military recruits and then, subsequently, for personnel selection. The first honesty test to gain widespread use was the Reid Report, developed in the late 1940s by police polygraph examiner John Reid. This test was originally validated against polygraph results. As a further development, the first "veiled purpose" honesty test was developed in the 1950s, named the Personnel Reaction Blank (PRB). The PRB included more subtle questions about attitudes and self-perceptions that were designed to assess the resistance to "wayward impulse" (Gough, 1971).

Since the federal polygraph act was passed, the use of integrity tests for personnel selection has mushroomed in the United States, with millions of tests now administered annually. Reflecting the importance of this phenomenon, the U.S. Congressional Office of Technology Assessment (1990) and the American Psychological Association (Goldberg, Grenier, Guion, Secrest, & Wing, 1991) both released significant position papers on integrity testing in the early 1990s. Academic investigators have since become increasingly active in research on this topic. This section reviews the major categories and types of integrity tests. It summarizes the evidence concerning their reliability and criterion-related and construct validity. The chapter concludes with a discussion of controversies and legal issues surrounding their use, clinical applications, and future trends in the field.

An Overview of Integrity Tests

Integrity tests are most frequently used as a preemployment assessment tool to screen out applicants who are likely to be dishonest or irresponsible on the job. In a smaller proportion of cases, integrity tests are administered to current employees to (1) guide decisions about promotion, (2) assist in specific-incident investigations (e.g., theft or loss), or (3) "encourage" continuing awareness on the part of employees of company standards for honesty and productivity. Tests developed specifically for use with current employees include the Employee Attitude Inventory (London House, Inc.; reviewed by Schmitt, 1985), the Phase II Profile/Current Employee Version (Lousig-

Nont & Associates, Inc.), the Reid Survey III (Reid Psychological Systems), the Stanton Inventory (The Stanton Corporation; reviewed by Wheeler, 1985), and the Wilkerson Employee Input Survey (Team Building Systems).

Sackett, Burris, and Callahan (1989) distinguished between two types of preemployment integrity tests. *Overt integrity tests* (or "clear purpose" tests) comprise questions that ask directly about attitudes toward dishonesty and the applicant's own past involvement in illegal activities. This type of test includes instruments such as the Personnel Selection Inventory (see Craig, 1986), the Phase II Profile (see Kleinmuntz, 1989), the Reid Report (see Willis, 1986), and the Stanton Survey (see Wheeler, 1985). These instruments are aimed at assessing a job applicant's potential for theft and other wrongdoing. Examples of overt integrity test questions (cited in U.S. Congressional Office of Technology Assessment, 1990, pp. 31–32) include the following:

- "How often do you tell the truth?"
- "Do you feel guilty when you do something you should not do?"
- "In any of your other jobs, was it possible for a dishonest person to take merchandise if a dishonest person had your job?"

Personality-oriented tests (or "veiled purpose" tests) consist of items not obviously related to theft or dishonesty but rather to personality characteristics such as dependability, conventionality, impulsiveness, and emotional stability. Personality-oriented integrity tests are more concerned with the prediction of broadly defined counterproductivity and occupational adjustment than with theft or dishonesty per se. Tests of this type include Gough's PRB (1971), the Inwald Personality Inventory (see Waller, 1992), the Personnel Decisions, Inc. (PDI) Employment Inventory (see Johnson, 1986), and the reliability scale of the Prospective Employee Potential Inventory, formerly known as the Hogan Personnel Selection Series (see Leung, 1992). Representative test items include the following true–false formatted questions: "I like to take chances" and "I am usually confident about myself" (U.S. Congressional Office of Technology Assessment, 1990, p. 32); "You work steady and hard at whatever you undertake" and "You never would talk back to a boss or a teacher" (Sackett et al., 1989, p. 493).

Reliability

The available literature indicates that integrity tests generally demonstrate acceptable reliability according to most standard psychometric criteria (see Goldberg et al., 1991). O'Bannon, Goldinger, and Appleby (1989) reviewed test–retest reliability data for the principal "honesty" scales of several integrity tests. Reliability coefficients ranged from .56 to .97, with most exceeding .80. The lowest figure, .56 for the PRB, was for a lengthy test–retest interval and may reflect changes in the sample over time. Sackett and colleagues (1989) hypothesized that restrictions in the range of scores within different samples may contribute to variations in reported reliabilities across studies.

Sackett and colleagues (1989) cited internal consistency estimates of .85 or higher for several overt integrity tests, including the Personnel Selection Inventory, the Phase II Profile, the Reid Report, and the Stanton Survey. These authors surmised that indices of homogeneity would generally be lower for personality-oriented tests, given their broader scope. In this regard, Sackett and colleagues reported coefficients of .73 and .65 for the PRB in college male and female samples and of .63 overall for the Hogan Reliability Scale.

Validity

In evaluating the validity of integrity tests, the most crucial questions pertain to criterion-related validity and construct validity. Criterion-related validity is concerned with whether integrity tests are effective for their intended purposes (i.e., to identify employees who are likely to engage in theft or other counterproductive behaviors). Construct validity deals with the question of what underlying psychological constructs tests of this kind actually measure.

Criterion-Related Validity

Criterion Measures

Published reviews of the literature have focused on counterproductive behaviors and overall job performance as indices of employee behavior for purposes of assessing the criterion-related validity of integrity tests. Two main indices of employee counterproductivity have been examined: self-report and external criteria. *Self-report* criteria include admissions of theft, past dishonest or illegal activities, and counterproductive behaviors on the job, such as absenteeism or drunkenness (see Ones, Viswesvaran, & Schmidt, 1993a). A limitation of this index of counterproductivity is that the criterion (self-reported wrongdoing) may not be independent of the predictor (integrity testing). Relationships between admissions and integrity test scores may simply reflect a general propensity to disclose or not to disclose indiscretions. This propensity would be expected to inflate validity coefficients in studies of overt integrity tests that include questions about past indiscretions. Some self-report criterion studies have even collected integrity test data and admissions data concurrently within the same protocol.

External criteria have also been used to assess employee counterproductivity. These criteria include recorded incidents of rule breaking on the job, disciplinary actions, and terminations for theft or other forms of dishonesty. A limitation of this approach is criterion sensitivity: Not all dishonest or disruptive behaviors are detected or recorded. However, research is needed on how different external criteria affect validity estimates. Criterion insensitivity could suppress validity correlations to the extent that low-integrity scorers commit transgressions for which they are not caught. On the other hand, validity coefficients would be inflated if high-integrity scorers were systematically more adept at avoiding detection for their misdeeds.

In keeping with the recent trend toward broadening of the integrity concept (Sackett et al., 1989), validation studies have increasingly focused on overall job performance as an outcome criterion. Job performance is most often assessed using supervisory ratings of employees and, in some cases, production records for individual employees. The more common measure, supervisory ratings, could be problematic to the extent that integrity test scores and supervisory ratings are mutually influenced by tendencies toward impression management and socially desirable responding. Individuals skilled at conveying a false image may score well on integrity tests and also impress job supervisors for reasons that have nothing to do with integrity or productivity.

Research Findings

Traditional qualitative reviews exist that provide summaries of results from earlier studies of integrity test validity (Guastello & Rieke, 1991; O'Bannon et al., 1989; Sackett & Harris, 1984; Sackett et al., 1989; U.S. Congressional Office of Technology Assessment, 1990). In addition, several quantitative meta-analyses have been published. The most comprehensive analysis to date was by Deniz Ones and colleagues (1993a). This meta-analysis incorporated all criterion-related validity studies available at that time, including: (1) empirical studies of integrity testing cited in prior reviews or published in scholarly or trade journals, (2) relevant published or unpublished technical reports available from testing corporations, and (3) raw data and correlational analyses from corporate-sponsored validation studies that had not yet been compiled into technical reports. Twenty-five different integrity tests were represented in the meta-analysis, including two of the five current employee inventories listed earlier (i.e., Employee Attitude Inventory and Reid Survey) and all of the preemployment inventories.

Ones and colleagues (1993a) used interactive meta-analysis procedures (Hunter & Schmidt, 1990) to examine 665 criterion-related validity coefficients obtained from these various sources. They included 389 coefficients for overt integrity tests and 276 for personality-oriented inventories. Approximately two-thirds of the validity coefficients ($k = 443$) employed counterproductive behaviors (i.e., self-report or external measures of theft, violence, drug abuse, absenteeism, etc.) as the criterion, whereas the rest ($k = 222$) employed indices of job performance (i.e., supervisory ratings or production records). Two major meta-analyses were performed. The first evaluated the validity of integrity tests as a whole for predicting the criterion of overall job performance. The mean observed (i.e., raw) validity coefficient across samples ($k = 222$) was .21; the estimated mean true validity (after correcting for statistical artifacts including sampling error, criterion and predictor unreliability, range restriction, and dichotomization of scores) was .34. The second major meta-analysis assessed the validity of integrity tests as a whole for predicting the criterion of counterproductive behaviors, as indexed by admissions-based and external indices. The mean observed validity coefficient across samples ($k = 443$) was .33; the estimated mean true validity (after correcting for statistical artifacts in the data) was .47.

Ones and colleagues (1993a) also assessed the moderating effects of different variables on validity estimates. For estimates based on the criterion of job performance, the variable that most clearly affected validity coefficients was job status, with a mean estimated true validity of .40 for job applicants versus .29 for current employees. In addition, there was some evidence that concurrent validities overestimated predictive validities for employees but not for job applicants. None of the other variables examined was found to systematically affect estimates of test validity based on job performance criteria. These variables included (1) type of integrity test (overt vs. personality oriented), (2) criterion measurement method (supervisory ratings vs. production records), and (3) complexity of job position (high, medium, or low).

For validity estimates based on the criterion of counterproductive behaviors, several moderating factors were identified. Overt integrity tests were found to be more strongly predictive than personality-oriented tests (estimated true validity = .55 and .32, respectively), although comparative data were available only from studies using the broad criterion of counterproductive behavior, which encompasses various forms of misconduct, including substance abuse, aggression, absenteeism, and tardiness. As Sackett and Wanek (1996) have pointed out, the comparative validity of personality-oriented versus overt integrity tests may vary with respect to different forms of counterproductive behavior. For example, there is evidence that personality-oriented tests have a higher prediction of absenteeism (Ones, Viswesvaran, & Schmidt, 2003). Understandably, estimated validity was generally much higher when based on self-report criteria (.58) than on relatively independent external criteria (.32). Employee samples yielded higher validity estimates ($M = .54$) than applicant samples ($M = .44$) for overt tests, but not for personality-oriented tests. Coefficients derived using concurrent validation strategies systematically exceeded predictive validities ($Ms = .56$ vs. .36), particularly in the case of overt tests.

To summarize, the results for validity coefficients based on job performance criteria were quite straightforward. Ones and colleagues (1993a) concluded from these data that (1) the best estimate of integrity test validity for the criterion of job performance in personnel selection settings (i.e., predictive studies of job applicants) is .41, and (2) overt and personality-oriented tests are similarly valid as predictors of supervisory ratings of job performance. On the basis of the latter finding, the authors hypothesized that both types of test may assess a broad construct of conscientiousness linked to "generally disruptive tendencies."

Ones and colleagues (1993a) also drew general conclusions about counterproductive behaviors. They found that integrity test validity is "quite substantial" but moderated by various factors. Most notably, validity coefficients were higher for self-report than for external criteria and for concurrent than for predictive measurements. As noted earlier, these findings may reflect an interdependence between predictor and criterion in studies that assess counterproductivity on the basis of admissions, especially when criterion data are obtained concurrently with the integrity test. Ones and colleagues also concluded that theft behavior is less well predicted from overt integrity test scores than are indices of broad counterproductivity; this finding could not be evaluated for personality-oriented inventories. Despite these mixed findings, the authors advanced the general conclusion that "the validity of integrity tests is positive and in useful ranges for both overall job-performance criteria and counterproductive-behaviors criteria" (p. 694).

Notwithstanding its scope and sophistication, some limitations of Ones and colleagues (1993a) meta-analytic investigation must be acknowledged. One issue is the credibility of the body of data included in the meta-analysis. Much of the available research surveyed by Ones and colleagues was sponsored by test publishers, and only a fraction of the research consisted of published articles in scholarly journals. Although academic researchers have become increasingly active in this domain since publication of this report, the lack of independence of validity studies from test publishers remains a problem. A second issue with the Ones and colleagues meta-analysis is that the authors failed to consider systematic biases that could have inflated validity estimates for the most common outcome criteria, including: (1) the lack of predictor–criterion independence for admissions-based criteria and (2) parallel effects of impression management on integrity measures and supervisory ratings of job performance.

Ones and colleagues (1993a) endorsed the use of integrity testing on the basis of their findings without adequately considering how these results may translate into practice. For one thing, "true validities" computed via meta-analysis greatly overestimate the validity for practical purposes (i.e., "observed validities" in the Ones and colleagues study were substantially smaller than "true validity" estimates). Moreover, in practice, integrity tests are usually evaluated dichotomously using "pass–fail" cut scores (Goldberg et al., 1991). Ones and colleagues presented relationships between integrity test scores and criterion variables in terms of correlation coefficients, and "in cases where no correlations were reported, using the information supplied, [we calculated] the phi correlation and then corrected it for dichotomization" (p. 683). It is not clear how the "true validity" coefficients that Ones and colleagues computed correspond to the predictive validity of decisions based on cut scores for specific integrity tests.

Since publication of the Ones and colleagues (1993a) meta-analysis, other meta-analytic reports have appeared focusing on the validity of integrity tests for predicting specific types of criterion behavior. Schmidt, Viswesvaran, and Ones (1997) evaluated criterion-related validity evidence pertaining to the prediction of drug and alcohol abuse. Data from a total of 50 validity studies were examined. A wide range of overt and personality-oriented integrity tests were represented in the analysis. Integrity test scores correlated substantially (.34 to .51) with admissions of alcohol and drug abuse in student and current employee samples. However, results were less compelling ($M = .21$) for drug abuse in job applicant samples. Alcohol abuse was poorly represented by a single study. Overall, the authors estimated the criterion-related validity of integrity tests for predicting drug and alcohol abuse in the workplace to be about .30. A notable weakness was that all studies included in the analysis employed a concurrent validation (i.e., the predictor and criterion measures were administered contemporaneously); this method inflates validity coefficients.

Ones and Viswesvaran (1998a) reported findings from separate meta-analyses focusing on three other specific job-relevant criteria: training performance, on-the-job accidents, and property damage. Two strengths were noted for training performance: (1) external criteria (objective test scores or supervisory ratings) were used and (2) most studies used predictive rather than concurrent validity. Predictions averaged approximately 120 days after criterion measures. With an overall sample of 2,364 individuals, the average predictive validity was estimated to be .38 based mostly on personality-oriented instruments. For the criterion of job-related accidents (indexed from organizational records), data from five studies (overall $N = 759$) yielded an estimated mean validity of .52. The third criterion was property damage arising from willful acts of destruction, such as vandalism or sabotage. Data were available from 12 studies employing overt integrity tests and 2 studies employing personality-oriented integrity tests. Mean estimated validities were .69 and .48, respectively. Contrary to expectation, validity coefficients were higher (.71) for studies using external criteria than for respondents' self-reports.

Most recently, Ones and colleagues (2003) reported findings from a meta-analysis of 28 studies (overall $N = 13,972$) that examined the comparative validity of overt and personality-oriented integrity tests for predicting job-related absenteeism. All 28 studies used external criteria. Most studies (78.6%) utilized a predictive design. Their analysis revealed higher mean validity for personality-oriented tests (.36) compared with overt integrity tests (.09). As expected, validity coefficients were higher in both types of integrity tests when using a concurrent rather than a predictive design.

Construct Validity

Overt versus Personality-Oriented Tests

An important issue is whether different types of integrity tests (i.e., overt and personality oriented) share common psychological constructs. Studies have directly compared scores for these two types of instruments, providing evidence of construct overlap. For example, Woolley and Hakstian (1992) examined relations between three personality-oriented instruments (i.e., PRB, Hogan Reliability Scale, and the PDI Employment Inventory) and one overt integrity test (i.e., Reid Report). As expected, the personality-oriented tests showed moderate to high intercorrelations. In addition, the Honesty scale of the Reid test evidenced moderate correlations with the three personality-oriented inventories (mean $r = .30$). On the other hand, the Reid Punitive scale, which was designed to index attitudes toward punishing others, was uncorrelated with these other tests.

More comprehensive analyses of relations between overt and personality-oriented tests have been reported by Ones and her colleagues. Ones, Schmidt, and Viswesvaran (1994) administered a variety of overt (i.e., Personnel Selection Inventory, Reid Report, and Stanton Survey) and personality-oriented integrity tests (i.e., Hogan Reliability scale, Inwald Personality Inventory, PDI Employment Inventory, PRB) to a sample of 1,365 college students. Associations among tests within each category were generally high: "True score" correlations (i.e., correcting for unreliability of the measures) averaged .85 among the three overt integrity tests and .75 among the four personality-oriented tests. Raw correlations between the two types of tests ranged from .20 to .55, with an average "true score" correlation of .52. In addition, using factor analysis, Ones and colleagues demonstrated that the two types of tests loaded on a shared general factor.

Ones, Viswesvaran, and Schmidt (1993b; cited in Sackett & Wanek, 1996) used meta-analysis to evaluate correlations among a broader array of overt and personality-oriented integrity tests computed from data provided by test publishers. These authors reported mean corrected ("true score") correlations of .45 among various overt tests, .70 among the available personality-oriented tests, and .39 between tests of the two types. Although the mean correlation among personality-oriented tests in this study was similar to that reported by Ones (1993), the average correlations among overt tests and between overt and personality-oriented tests in this study were notably lower. Sackett and Wanek (1996) postulated that the three integrity tests examined by Ones—the Personnel Selection Inventory, the Reid Report, and the Stanton Survey—may be more similar to one another and to personality-based tests than to other overt integrity tests. Accordingly, these authors recommended that caution be exercised in generalizing findings based on specific overt integrity tests to other overt tests.

More recent research has examined relations between the two types of integrity tests by undertaking item-level analyses that combine data across overt and personality-oriented tests. In an initial effort, Hogan and Brinkmeyer (1997) performed a structural analysis of items from one overt integrity test (Reid Report) and one personality-oriented test (Hogan Reliability Scale). The items from the Hogan scale all loaded on one factor, whereas the items from the Reid inventory loaded on three separate factors (labeled "punitive attitudes," "admissions," and "drug use"). However, a second-order confirmatory analysis of scores on the four factors demonstrated that all of them loaded together on a common higher-order factor, which the authors termed *Conscientiousness*. Wanek, Sackett, and Ones (2003) evaluated relations among items from a wider array of overt (Personnel Selection Inventory, Reid Report, and Stanton Survey) and personality-oriented tests (Employee Reliability Index, PRB, PDI Employment Inventory, and Inwald Personality Inventory). A principal-components analysis yielded evidence of four broad components: (1) antisocial behavior, indicating admissions of wrongful acts and association with deviant peers; (2) socialization, reflecting achievement motivation and internal control orientation; (3) positive outlook, indicating a benign view of people and the world; and (4) orderliness/diligence. Both overt and personality-oriented tests loaded on these four distinctive components, but differences were observed in the magnitude of these loadings.

Relationships with Established Personality Constructs

Considerable progress has been made over the past several years in understanding how scores on integrity tests relate to known personality constructs. Much of the available research has focused on relations between integrity tests and the five-factor ("Big Five") model of personality: *Extraversion* (e.g., sociability, assertiveness, and activity), *Emotional Stability/Neuroticism* (e.g., presence vs. absence of anxiousness, hostility, and insecurity), *Agreeableness* (e.g., soft-heartedness and cooperativeness), *Conscientiousness* (e.g., dependability, ability to plan, and responsibility), and *Openness to Experience* (e.g., originality and broad-mindedness).

Barrick and Mount (1991) conducted a meta-analysis of 117 published and unpublished criterion-related validity studies of personality testing for the purpose of personnel selection. Although this analysis did not focus specifically on integrity tests, it did evaluate relations between the Big Five personality dimensions and various job-related indices, including performance ratings, a criterion that Ones and colleagues (1993a) found to be predicted successfully by integrity tests. Barrick

and Mount found that Conscientiousness, as defined by a range of personality scales, was consistently the best predictor of all job-related criteria, including supervisory ratings of job performance. across all occupational groups. Extraversion was also a significant predictor of job performance but only for two occupational categories (i.e., management and sales). Openness to Experience predicted employee responsiveness to training, but not general job performance. Emotional Stability and Agreeableness did not significantly predict either job performance or training proficiency in this study. Barrick and Mount concluded that traits such as dependability and trustworthiness are most highly predictive of job success. Because validity coefficients for subjective measures of job performance (e.g., supervisory ratings) substantially exceeded objective measures (e.g., employee productivity records), these authors acknowledged that subjective measures could have been biased by employees' social reputations.

Tett, Jackson, and Rothstein (1991) also conducted a meta-analysis to investigate the relationship between personality measures and job performance criteria. This study included data from 86 separate studies and evaluated the validity of eight dimensions of personality, including the Big Five, as predictors of job performance. These authors restricted their analysis of the Big Five personality dimensions to studies that used a confirmatory strategy (i.e., an a priori rationale was given for assessing particular traits as predictors of performance in specific jobs). In contrast with Barrick and Mount (1991), Agreeableness was found to be the best overall predictor (estimated true validity = .33), followed by Openness to Experience (.27), Emotional Stability (−.22), Conscientiousness (.18), and Extraversion (.16).

Ones, Mount, Barrick, and Hunter (1994) challenged the findings of Tett and colleagues (1991) on several grounds. In the first place, the Tett and colleagues meta-analysis included far fewer studies and markedly smaller sample sizes than Barrick and Mount's (1991) analysis. Moreover, Tett and colleagues did not specify the procedures they used to assign scales from different personality inventories to the Big Five categories. According to Ones and colleagues, differences between the two studies could stem from differences in how personality scales were classified. Ones and colleagues also suggested that Tett and colleagues did not adequately consider the potential influence of moderator variables on the relationships they examined.

Ones and her colleagues (Ones, Schmidt, & Viswesvaran, 1994b) undertook a meta-analysis to clarify the degree to which the Big Five personality factors contribute to the relationship between integrity tests and supervisory ratings of job performance. These investigators used the following sources of information to construct the matrix of estimated "true score correlations" between integrity, the Big Five dimensions, and performance ratings: (1) correlations between the Big Five and job performance (from Barrick & Mount, 1991), (2) correlations between integrity tests and job performance (from Ones et al., 1993a), (3) correlations among the Big Five personality dimensions (from the published literature in the field of personality), and (4) correlations between integrity tests and the Big Five dimensions (from the integrity testing literature).

From the meta-analytically derived matrix of intercorrelations, Ones and colleagues (1994b) concluded that both overt and personality-oriented integrity tests were most strongly related to Conscientiousness (mean estimated true score correlations = .39 and .45, respectively), followed by Agreeableness (.34 and .44), and then Emotional Stability (.26, and .37). Correlations for Extraversion (.03 and −.11) and Openness to Experience (.09 and .14) were negligible in comparison. These investigators also found that Conscientiousness, Agreeableness, and Emotional Stability each contributed independently to the prediction of integrity test scores. Thus the findings of this meta-analytic work converged with those of Barrick and Mount (1991) in suggesting that Conscientiousness is a prominent element of integrity tests and also with the findings of Tett and colleagues (1991), which suggested that Agreeableness and Emotional Stability also mediate relationships between integrity scores and job performance. However, Ones and colleagues noted that relations with these three personality dimensions did not account entirely for the association between integrity test scores and job performance: Within a hierarchical regression model, integrity test scores contributed incrementally to the prediction of job performance after scores on the Big Five were first entered as predictors.

Ones and colleagues' (1994b) findings raise an interesting question of what integrity tests measure beyond basic personality traits that contributes to prediction of job performance. Varying perspectives have been offered in this regard. Sackett and Wanek (1996) hypothesized that integrity tests measure important aspects of self-control that fall outside the constructs indexed by the Big Five dimensions. Lee and colleagues (Lee, Ashton, & de Vries, 2005; Marcus, Lee, & Ashton, 2007) have presented empirical evidence that integrity tests tap an "honesty–humility" factor (reflecting attributes such as fairness, sincerity, humility, and lack of greed) not indexed by the Big Five.

Integrity versus Externalizing

In a previous edition of this book (Iacono & Patrick, 1997), we noted similarities between the personality correlates of integrity tests and those of antisocial behavior, defined in terms of DSM criteria for antisocial personality disorder (APD; American Psychiatric Association, 2000) or social deviance associated with the syndrome of psychopathy (Hare, 1991). Since that time, evidence has emerged to indicate that antisocial deviance in childhood and adulthood is part of a broader *externalizing* spectrum that also encompasses addictive behaviors (alcohol and drug abuse/dependence). In this section, we briefly review evidence for a possible association between integrity tests and the general externalizing factor that underlies this spectrum.

It has long been recognized that antisocial behavior problems and substance use disorders co-occur at rates far exceeding chance (see, e.g., Zuckerman, 1999). A potential explanation for this high comorbidity is that disorders of both types reflect the presence of an underlying dispositional factor that confers a general vulnerability to problems of impulse control. This general vulnerability was formally evaluated in a twin study by Krueger and colleagues (2002) that assessed genetic and environmental contributions to the systematic covariance among child and adult antisocial behavior symptoms and symptoms of alcohol and drug dependence. This study confirmed the existence of a broad factor (labeled *externalizing*) on which symptoms of these various disorders all loaded very strongly (factor coefficients ranged from .58 to .78). In addition, a biometric (behavior genetic) analysis of etiological contributions revealed that more than 80% of the phenotypic variance in this broad factor was attributable to additive genetic influences. Parallel results have been reported in other large-scale twin studies (Kendler, Prescott, Myers, & Neale, 2003; Young, Stallings, Corley, Krauter, & Hewitt, 2000). The implication is that a broad dispositional factor, largely heritable in nature, underlies the general vulnerability to disorders of impulse control—encompassing antisocial and addictive behavior problems.

Scores on this broad externalizing factor have been examined in terms of their associations with lower order traits and higher order dimensions indexed by the Multidimensional Personality Questionnaire (MPQ; Tellegen, 1982), an omnibus inventory of normal personality. High scores on the externalizing factor are associated with high scores on the Negative Emotionality dimension of the MPQ (in particular, constituent traits of Alienation and Aggression) and low scores on the Constraint dimension (in particular, its Control vs. Impulsivity facet; see, e.g., Krueger, 1999).

Although the Big Five personality correlates of the externalizing factor have not been studied directly, it is possible to infer their relationships from existing data on the Big Five correlates of antisocial personality and substance use disorders. Using the NEO Personality Inventory (Costa & McCrae, 1985), Trull (1992) found diagnoses of antisocial personality to be associated with low Conscientiousness and Agreeableness and to a lesser degree with high Neuroticism. Likewise, Trull and Sher (1994) reported low Conscientiousness, low Agreeableness, and high Neuroticism to be the common dimensions that differentiated individuals with alcohol use disorders and drug use disorders from individuals without such disorders. Interestingly, drug but not alcohol disorders were also associated with high Openness to Experience. Thus, specific Big Five dimensions are likely to be associated with the broad externalizing factor: Conscientiousness (–), Agreeableness (–), and possibly Neuroticism (+). As described in the preceding section, these are the same Big Five dimensions that relate to integrity test scores.

We previously reported (Iacono & Patrick, 1997) correlations between scores on an abbreviated version of the NEO Inventory and the two factors of Hare's (1991) Psychopathy Checklist—Revised (PCL-R), reflecting (1) core affective–interpersonal features of psychopathy and (2) antisocial deviance features of psychopathy. Using a male prisoner sample (N

= 80), high scores on the antisocial factor were associated with low Conscientiousness, low Agreeableness, and high Neuroticism. Together with other recent work (Patrick, Hicks, Krueger, & Lang, 2005), this result provides further evidence that these dimensions of the Big Five are associated with externalizing. On the other hand, the core affective–interpersonal factor of psychopathy was related only to Agreeableness, and then only as a function of variance shared with the antisocial factor.

In summary, these results are consistent with the hypothesis that integrity test scores reflect individual differences in externalizing—defined as the general, largely heritable vulnerability toward impulse-control problems (Krueger et al., 2002). As noted in the preceding section, integrity test scores contribute to prediction of job performance over and above their association with Big Five personality traits (Ones, 1993). An important avenue for future research will be to evaluate whether this incremental validity derives from the fact that integrity tests tap aspects of externalizing vulnerability not indexed by Big Five personality dimensions. This issue could be directly assessed by collecting diagnostic data relevant to externalizing tendencies along with integrity test measures and Big Five personality scores. Investigators could examine whether integrity test scores predicting job performance independently of Conscientiousness, Agreeableness, and Neuroticism overlap with scores on the externalizing factor. One other implication arising from the last set of findings described here is that integrity tests are poor indicators of the core affective–interpersonal features of psychopathy. Based on this finding, there may be some truth to critics' concerns that these tests fail to detect unprincipled liars who are skilled in impression management.

Controversial Aspects of Integrity Testing

False-Positive Misclassification and Labeling

One issue of concern is the extent to which honest and dependable workers are denied employment because their integrity test scores fall below the established cut scores for hiring. The criterion-related validity of integrity testing is at best moderate (Ones et al., 1993a), and the frequency of false-positive misclassifications will vary with the base rate of dishonesty in an employment setting. Even a test with high validity will misclassify a substantial number of individuals as untrustworthy if the existing base rate of dishonesty is low.

The counterargument is that personnel selection of some kind is always necessary in the employment setting and that any selection technique with proven validity will result in fewer errors of classification than a strictly random selection procedure (Goldberg et al., 1991; Ones et al., 1993a; Sackett & Wanek, 1996). From this viewpoint, the essential issue is the incremental validity of integrity testing, not its absolute validity.

Fakability

The obverse of the false-positive issue is the concern that integrity tests are vulnerable to deliberate distortion (i.e., defensiveness and social desirability) by individuals who are motivated to appear trustworthy. This problem is potentially greater for overt tests, which inquire transparently about attitudes toward and past incidents of wrongdoing (Ryan & Sackett, 1987). Empirically, Alliger and Dwight (2000) reported a meta-analysis that compared test outcomes under conditions in which respondents were instructed to "beat the test" versus to "respond as an applicant"; they reported a mean effect size of .93 for overt integrity tests as compared with .38 for personality-oriented tests. In particular, it appears that overt integrity tests are vulnerable to social desirability. However, Berry, Sackett, and Wiemann (2007) have challenged the findings and conclusions of this report on various methodological grounds and called for additional research on this topic.

Although "faking good" may be easy to accomplish with an overt integrity test, the available data suggest that this response style does not occur routinely (Murphy, 1993; Van Iddekinge, Raymark, Eidson, & Putka, 2003, cited in Berry et al., 2007). Goldberg and colleagues (1991) suggested some reasons why this may be true, including the possibility that prospective employees tend not to perceive integrity tests as crucial to hiring and a "false consensus effect," whereby applicants assume that their own peculiarities and indiscretions are "normal" and hence reportable without negative consequences.

Adverse Impact

Another crucial issue in the use of integrity tests is the extent to which these tests discriminate against legally protected groups. Fairness in hiring is mandated by many federal, state, and local statutes. The Equal Employment Opportunity Act of 1972, for example, explicitly prohibits discrimination in the preemployment screening context. With regard to integrity testing, the key issue is whether legally protected groups (e.g., women, elderly people, and racial minorities) score higher on average on such tests. A significant issue that clouds interpretation of existing work by test publishers is the practice of adjusting integrity test scores for social desirability in summary reports, a practice that could have the effect of masking subgroup differences in integrity scores (Sackett & Wanek, 1996). Ones and Viswesvaran (1998b) addressed this concern by comparing unadjusted scores of various subgroups on three different overt integrity tests (Personnel Selection Inventory, Reid Report, and Stanton Survey). In general, the findings of this study indicated that to the extent that differences existed, they favored protected groups. Specifically, women tended to score higher than men, and older (40+) applicants tended to score higher than younger applicants. No significant differences were found for minority racial groups in comparison with European American applicants. An obvious limitation of this study is that it focused exclusively on overt tests; further research of this kind is needed to address this issue for personality-oriented tests.

The evidence for a lack of adverse impact provides one compelling argument for the use of these tests. Scores on the other major class of personnel selection inventories (i.e., ability tests) do differ systematically as a function of race. Ones and colleagues (1993a) argued convincingly that, because scores on ability tests and integrity tests are uncorrelated, the combined use of integrity testing and ability testing would lead to a substantial increase in predictive validity while reducing adverse impact.

Privacy and Informed Consent

A further issue is whether the types of questions asked on an integrity test constitute an unjustified intrusion into the respondent's private life. This concern has been raised particularly in regard to overt integrity tests, which include blunt questions about personal wrongdoing. Questions of privacy have also arisen because of the historical association between integrity testing and polygraph testing. However, only one privacy case is known to have arisen from the use of an integrity test (*Heins v. Commonwealth of Pennsylvania, Unemployment Compensation Board of Review*, 1987); it was resolved in favor of the employer.

A related issue relates to informed consent. The Standards for Educational and Psychological Testing (1985) approved by the American Psychological Association specify that informed consent can be considered implied when job applicants are tested. However, the APA Task Force (Goldberg et al., 1991) expressed the viewpoint that "[t]he pressure on applicants to submit to testing must be balanced by an obligation on the part of examiners to explain fully the application procedures," an opinion also expressed in the U.S. Congressional Office of Technology Assessment (1990) report on integrity testing. A similar recommendation was made in the Model Guidelines for Preemployment Integrity Testing Programs (Association for Personnel Test Publishers, 1990).

Legal Status of Integrity Testing

To date, only two state legislatures have introduced laws prohibiting or restricting the use of integrity tests. Massachusetts prohibits the practice entirely, and the state of Rhode Island added a less restrictive clause to its Polygraph Act that prohibits the use of written integrity testing as the *primary* basis for an employment decision. One potential basis for more widespread restriction of the use of integrity tests is a legal precedent in the area of privacy violation. For example, in the case of *Saroka vs. Dayton Hudson Corporation* (1991), a California appeals court ruled that a preemployment screening consisting of two well-known personality inventories (Minnesota Multiphasic Personality Inventory [MMPI], California Psychological Inventory [CPI]) violated examinees' right to privacy because of the intrusive content of certain test questions.

Another potential legal challenge to the use of integrity tests is the Americans with Disabilities Act (ADA), passed in 1990, which prohibits medical screening of applicants before the point of a job offer. The intent behind this legislation was to prevent employers from assessing for the presence of disabilities not specifically related to the performance of job duties and screening out employees on that basis. With respect to psychological tests, the Equal Employment Opportunities Commission (EEOC) issued a position statement in 1994 establishing the following criteria for classifying tests as medical examinations under the ADA: (1) the test is administered and/or interpreted by a health care professional in a medical setting; (2) the test is designed to measure psychological health; and (3) the purpose of testing is to determine psychological health. The EEOC noted specifically that a test originally developed to detect mental illness (e.g., such as the MMPI) would qualify as a medical examination according to these criteria. In addition, the EEOC noted that even on tests that do not qualify as medical examinations, specific items dealing with the presence of a disability are not allowable under the Act.

Revisions to integrity test content have occurred in response to the ADA, most notably in terms of deleting items dealing with prior drug use (which are specifically prohibited by the ADA). However, it has been argued that integrity tests as a whole do not qualify as medical examinations under the EEOC guidelines because (1) they were not developed to assess psychological health or illness and (2) they are not used for this purpose (Berry et al., in press). Nonetheless, it is conceivable that this perspective could change as the constructs underlying integrity tests become clearer. To date, the construct validity of integrity testing has been examined mainly in relation to normal personality traits, in particular the Big Five. However, as noted earlier, in the section on construct validity, it seems likely that integrity tests also measure tendencies related to the broad externalizing dimension of psychopathology. From this perspective, a case could be made that integrity tests are designed to assess externalizing tendencies (i.e., propensities toward various forms of misconduct likely to affect job performance) and that they are administered specifically to screen out individuals with such tendencies from employment positions.

Clinical Applications

Overt integrity tests appear to have some validity, although these measures account for considerably less than 20% of the variance in criterion measures. However, even tests with relatively low validity can have utility from the vantage point of personnel screening, in which the focus is on the aggregate of persons screened for employment purposes. Nevertheless, the low validity of and the many problems inherent in these tests make it difficult to utilize them in a clinical setting, in which the assessment of a single person is important. Unfortunately, little information is available concerning the effects of different cut scores on classifica-

tion accuracy. Therefore, it is possible to have confidence in the significance of only extreme scores on these tests. The inability to interpret integrity test scores is exacerbated by the fact that most of the tests and their scoring keys are proprietary. These factors combine to make it difficult to determine how these tests could be used to advantage in a clinical decision-making context. Hence it would be imprudent for clinicians to place much stock in individual scores from these inventories.

16

Assessment of Recovered and False Memories

ELKE GERAERTS, PhD
RICHARD J. McNALLY, PhD

On February 7, 2005, a jury in Cambridge, Massachusetts, convicted Paul Shanley, a defrocked Catholic priest, of having raped Paul Busa approximately two decades earlier. When Busa was 6 years old, Shanley allegedly began removing him from his Sunday school classroom to sodomize him in the boys' restroom. Several of Busa's friends from his elementary school days said they recalled experiencing nearly identical assaults by Shanley. Although other witnesses never recalled Shanley removing any child from the classroom, Busa and his friends said that they had experienced these brutal assaults for years, sometimes on a weekly basis (Lyons, 2003; Rauch, 2005; Wypijewski, 2004).

According to the alleged victims, they were entirely unaware of having been repeatedly traumatized during Sunday school until Shanley's name surfaced in the media during the sexual abuse scandal in the Boston archdiocese. After their memories of childhood rape surfaced, they joined the more than 500 plaintiffs who received financial compensation for childhood sexual abuse (CSA) in the out-of-court settlement with the Church. Busa received $500,000 from the settlement and then testified for the prosecution in the criminal trial.

Busa's testimony strikingly exemplifies what Harvard psychiatrist Judith L. Herman and Emily Schatzow call "massive repression" (Herman & Schatzow, 1987, p. 12) of trauma—the notion that repeated, horrific events are especially likely to be sealed off from conscious awareness, often for many years, yet become accessible once retrieval conditions are favorable. As Stanford psychiatrist David Spiegel (1997) expressed it in the foreword to his edited book titled *Repressed Memories:* "the nature of traumatic dissociative amnesia is such that it is not subject to the same rules of ordinary forgetting; it is more, rather than less, common after repeated episodes; involves strong affect, and is resistant to retrieval through salient cues" (p. 6).

In effect, Spiegel claims that certain kinds of trauma are exempt from the principles that ordinarily govern memory. Indeed, ever since Ebbinghaus (1885/1913), psychologists have known that repetition strengthens memory rather than impairing it. More specifically, central features of a repeated event will be strengthened by virtue of its repetition. A person who has flown on airplanes many times is highly unlikely to develop amnesia for having flown, even though memory for specific flights may meld with memories of other, highly similar flights. Moreover, stress hormones released in response to extremely aversive experiences consolidate the memory for the experience, rendering it resistant to forgetting (McGaugh, 2003).

Although *traumatic dissociative amnesia* theorists acknowledge that most victims remember their trauma all too well, they nevertheless maintain that a significant minority are unable to recall their trauma. As Brown, Scheflin, and Hammond (1998) put it, "when emotional material reaches the point of being traumatic in intensity—something that cannot be replicated in artificial laboratories—in a certain subpopulation of individuals, material that is too intense may not be able to be consciously processed and so may become unconscious and amnesic" (p. 97). That is, according to these authors, some victims are unable, not merely unwilling, to recall their horrific experiences, precisely because the trauma was so overwhelming. Echoing Freud's early work (Breuer & Freud, 1895/1955; Freud, 1896/1962), traumatic dissociative amnesia theorists believe that dissociated (or "repressed") memories of trauma can exert a toxic effect on the mind of the unwitting victim, as expressed in otherwise inexplicable psychological symptoms. Accordingly, they believe that special methods are often needed to help the patient recover and emotionally process the presumably inaccessible memories of trauma (Courtois, 1992; Olio, 1989). As Brown and colleagues (1998, p. 647) say, "Because some victims of sexual abuse will repress their memories by dissociating them from consciousness, hypnosis can be very valuable in retrieving these memories. Indeed, for some victims, hypnosis may provide the only avenue to the repressed memories."

In summary, traumatic dissociative amnesia (or repression) theorists hold that a significant minority of trauma victims are unaware of having been traumatized, precisely because the trauma was so horrific, so frequent, or both.

This perspective on memory and trauma lies at the heart of the "memory wars" (Crews, 1995), the bitter controversy over the reality of repressed and recovered memories of trauma, especially CSA. Certainly this controversy has been among the most vitriolic in the history of the mental health field (McNally, 2003). Unlike most controversies in our field, this one has spread far beyond the clinic and laboratory, influencing legislation and outcomes in civil suits and criminal trials, as the Shanley trial makes clear. The purpose of this chapter is to review forensically relevant clinical research bearing on the issue of recovered and false memories of trauma.

CONFUSIONS ABOUT THE CLINICAL SCIENCE LITERATURE AND MEMORY

A striking feature of the repressed- and recovered-memory controversy is that both believers and skeptics cite abundant data in support of their opposing views. Even more strikingly, they sometimes cite the same studies to support diametrically opposed arguments. Brown and his colleagues have been among the most prominent traumatic dissociative amnesia theorists devoted to documenting their position with abundant citations from the clinical science literature (Brown et al., 1998; Brown, Scheflin, & Whitfield, 1999). This seeming paradox becomes immediately resolved once individuals realize that traumatic dissociative amnesia theorists either (1) misunderstand the studies they cite in support of the phenomenon or (2) misinterpret studies as indicative of repressed memories of trauma when the data are more plausibly interpreted in other ways. In the following section, we discuss the most common confusions.

Misinterpreting Everyday Forgetfulness as Traumatic Dissociative Amnesia

After having experienced a traumatic event, some victims complain about difficulty concentrating and remembering things in everyday life. In fact, this problem was a symptom in the original definition of posttraumatic stress disorder (PTSD) in the third edition of the *Diagnostic and Statistical Manual of Mental Disorders* (DSM-III; American Psychiatric Association, 1980). Although objective psychological tests on individuals with PTSD drawn from epidemiological samples have not confirmed posttraumatic cognitive dysfunction (Zalewski, Thompson, & Gottesman, 1994), a recent meta-analysis involving clinical cases of PTSD did document memory impairment for neutral material (Brewin, Kleiner, Vasterling, & Field, 2007). Of course, complaints about concentration and memory are not confined to individuals with PTSD. For example, depression impairs effortful cognitive processes, such as free recall of neutral material (Hartlage, Alloy, Vázquez, & Dykman, 1993).

Unfortunately, some practitioners misinterpret these problems as relevant to traumatic dissociative amnesia (e.g., Brown et al., 1999). In reality, this symptom refers to everyday forgetfulness that develops after a trauma; it does not refer to difficulty remembering the trauma itself. For example, many survivors of the skywalks collapse at the Kansas City Hyatt Regency Hotel complained about memory difficulties (Wilkinson, 1983). However, most (88%) complained about intrusive memories of the fatal disaster, confirming that they had not repressed the memory of the event. Indeed, the everyday forgetfulness and concentration impairment that develop after a tragedy are likely consequences of intrusive recollections of the trauma rendering it difficult to attend to matters in daily life.

In another example of this misunderstanding, Freyd (1996) wrote that Archibald and Tuddenham's (1965) study on chronic combat-related psychiatric casualties from World War II documented "veterans' amnesia for their combat experiences" (p. 40). Although 65% of these veterans complained about "difficulty in memory," the authors emphasized how these patients "cannot blot out their painful memories" (Archibald & Tuddenham, 1965, p. 480). Hence their memory problems reflected everyday absentmindedness, not an inability to remember that they had been traumatized by combat. Indeed, a control group of psychiatric patients with diagnoses other than persistent combat stress reaction complained about difficulty in memory to nearly the same extent.

In summary, forgetfulness that develops *after* a trauma must not be confused with amnesia *for* the trauma. Indeed, vivid, intrusive recollections of the trauma may partly cause problems with memory and concentration in daily life.

Misinterpreting Psychogenic Amnesia as Traumatic Amnesia

Psychogenic amnesia is a rare syndrome whose hallmark is sudden, massive retrograde memory loss, including some loss of personal identity, which cannot be attributed to a direct physical insult to the brain (Kihlstrom & Schacter, 2000). Neurologists assessing these cases can sometimes identify antecedent stressors, but these are seldom traumatic (e.g., difficulties at work). Moreover, it is unclear whether the stressor precipitated the syndrome or coincidentally preceded it (McNally, 2003, pp. 186–189). The term *psychogenic* implies the absence of an obvious organic cause rather than an identified psychological etiology. Most cases of psychogenic amnesia remit within

hours, days, or weeks, and often without therapeutic intervention.

The striking differences between the syndrome of psychogenic amnesia and reports of traumatic dissociative amnesia mean that they are dissimilar clinical constructs. With traumatic dissociative amnesia, a person is (allegedly) unable to recall a specific traumatic event rather than being entirely unable to recall his or her past. Persons alleged to have repressed memories of trauma do not entirely forget their personal identities.

Misinterpreting Organic Amnesia as Traumatic Dissociative Amnesia

Given that cognition and emotion are mediated by the brain, encoding of any event, traumatic or otherwise, produces changes in the brain. But psychologically traumatic events have their impact by virtue of their meaning, not their physical properties. In contrast, head injury and other nonpsychological traumatic events produce memory impairments by virtue of their physical properties, not their personal emotional meaning. Accordingly, clinicians must not confuse organic amnesia with (alleged) psychologically caused amnesia. Yet occasionally traumatic dissociative amnesia theorists have made this serious mistake. When reviewing the literature on repressed memories of trauma, Brown and colleagues (1998) wrote that "Dollinger (1985) found that 2 of the 38 children studied after watching lightning strike and kill a playmate had no memory of the event" (pp. 609–610). Brown and colleagues, however, forgot to mention that both amnesic children had themselves been hit by side flashes from the main lightning bolt, knocked unconscious, and nearly died. All the children who were not struck by the lightning remember the disaster all too well, and many had marked symptoms of psychological distress. Hence, the physical, not psychological, aspects of the lightning strike were responsible for the amnesia in the two injured children.

Misinterpreting Incomplete Encoding as Traumatic Dissociative Amnesia

According to the DSM-IV-TR (American Psychiatric Association, 2000), one of the criteria for PTSD is "inability to recall an important aspect of the trauma" (p. 468). Some clinicians have adduced this symptom as relevant to traumatic dissociative amnesia (e.g., Gleaves, Smith, Butler, & Spiegel, 2004). Unfortunately, the wording of this criterion is ambiguous. If someone does not remember an aspect of the trauma, one cannot tell whether the person (1) cannot recall something that was encoded into memory or (2) whether the person never encoded the information in the first place. The mind does not operate like a videotape recorder, and not all sensory input arising from an experience, traumatic or otherwise, gets encoded into memory (e.g., Loftus & Loftus, 1980; Schacter, 1996, p. 40). Moreover, under conditions of high arousal, attention often narrows to the most salient feature of an unfolding event such that central aspects get encoded at the expense of peripheral ones. For example, consider the phenomenon of "weapon focus" (Loftus, Loftus, & Messo, 1987). A clerk robbed at gunpoint while working the midnight shift in a convenience store may encode and remember details of the robber's gun yet be incapable of recalling his or her face. This lack of success does not constitute a memory failure (let alone amnesia), but rather an encoding failure. Failing to recall something that was never encoded in the first place does not count as amnesia. Amnesia denotes that the material was encoded but cannot be retrieved. Although this DSM-IV-TR symptom is seldom endorsed by trauma-exposed people (e.g., Breslau, Reboussin, Anthony, & Storr, 2005), it should not be used as evidence that people cannot recall their traumatic experiences.

Misinterpreting Nondisclosure as Traumatic Dissociative Amnesia

Goodman and colleagues (2003) found that most adults with documented childhood abuse histories acknowledged these abuses to interviewers. As a contrasting perspective, several researchers found that a significant minority do not disclose childhood abuses (Widom & Morris, 1997; Williams, 1994). But failure to disclose one's abuse does not necessarily mean that one cannot recall it. As Widom and Morris (1997) point out, there may be several reasons for nondisclosure; clinicians should not automatically interpret nondisclosure as evidence of traumatic dissociative amnesia. In one small but important study, researchers recontacted respondents who had described their abuse during a first interview but had denied it during a second interview (Femina, Yeager, &

Lewis, 1990). When queried about the discrepancy in a follow-up interview, each respondent affirmed having recalled it during the second interview. The nondisclosing respondents gave several reasons for their denial of having been abused during the second interview (e.g., they did not want to talk about an upsetting event or experienced dislike of the interviewer). Therefore, clinicians cannot equate failure to disclose abuse with an inability to remember it. Although it may indicate forgetting, practitioners should first rule out the more parsimonious explanation, namely, a reluctance to disclose.

Misinterpreting Childhood Amnesia for Traumatic Dissociative Amnesia

Most people can remember very few experiences from before 4 or 5 years of age. Few autobiographical memories survive into later childhood, let alone adulthood. Accordingly, a failure to recall an episode of CSA from the preschool years may reflect "childhood amnesia" rather than traumatic dissociative amnesia. For example, several of the respondents in Williams's (1994) classic study had been very young when they were taken to the hospital for suspected, and often confirmed, CSA. Their failure to recall the episode years later was likely a function of childhood amnesia, not traumatic dissociative amnesia.

Misinterpreting Not Thinking About Something for a Long Time as Traumatic Dissociative Amnesia

Briere and Conte (1993) found that nearly 60% of adult patients undergoing psychotherapy for problems related to their CSA responded affirmatively to a questionnaire item asking whether there was ever "a time when you could not remember" (p. 24) the abuse. Briere and Conte interpreted these affirmative replies as evidence for "sexual abuse-related repression" (p. 26). A positive response to this question might imply that the patient had spent a period of time trying unsuccessfully to recall his or her sexual abuse. But if the patient was entirely unaware of having been abused (i.e., had repressed the memory of the experience), why would he or she attempt to recall it in the first place? On the other hand, if patients had interpreted this oddly worded question as asking, "Was there ever a time when you had not thought about your abuse?" then their affirmative replies make sense. Yet not thinking about something for a long time, including CSA, does not mean that the person was incapable of recalling it during the period when it never came to mind. Only an *inability* to remember encoded material should be considered amnesia. Had patients been interviewed during the time of their supposed amnesia, recollections of the abuse may very well have emerged.

FALSE MEMORIES OF TRAUMA

No foolproof method is available for distinguishing true from false memories of trauma, including those associated with CSA. A failure to secure independent verification of the abuse does not mean that the reported memory is false, let alone "implanted" by an inept therapist. For our research (McNally, Perlman, Ristuccia, & Clancy, 2006), we have found it difficult to corroborate memories of abuse, including those the victim never forgot, often because the victim had not disclosed the abuse to other people who could have corroborated it. For example, we have obtained consent from our adult participants who report having been sexually abused during childhood to speak to someone to whom they had disclosed the abuse (e.g., a sibling or a mother) shortly after it had occurred. Although this method of corroboration is not infallible (e.g., a child might lie about being abused), if someone never mentions the abuse to anyone, most routes to corroboration will be closed. Moreover, even if someone happens to recall long-forgotten abuse while in psychotherapy, this recall does not mean that the therapist inadvertently fostered a false memory of abuse. Psychotherapists who encourage reflection on one's past may provide retrieval cues for authentic memories that had been forgotten.

Some indicators can be used in ascertaining whether a trauma account, including a recovered memory of CSA, is unlikely to be authentic. First, the least credible recollections are types of trauma for which there is no convincing evidence. For example, some individuals who experience episodes of isolated sleep paralysis, accompanied by hypnopompic (upon awakening) hallucinations of intruders in the bedroom, "recover" memories during hypnosis of having been abducted and sexually abused

by space aliens (Clancy, 2005; McNally & Clancy, 2005). Given the improbability of alien abduction (McNally, 2005), we can be fairly confident that individuals providing such accounts are mistaken. Likewise, in light of the complete absence of any convincing evidence of satanic cults in contemporary America (Lanning, 1992), contemporary Britain (La Fontaine, 1998), or throughout history (Frankfurter, 2006), we can be reasonably confident that traumatic memories of infant sacrifice, sexual torture, cannibalism, and other satanic rituals are false. To be sure, one can never prove the null hypothesis that alien abductions, satanic ritual abuse, and other bizarre events have never occurred. Nevertheless, the burden of proof lies on those claiming the reality of these phenomena.

An Additional Third Perspective on Recovered Memories

Debates about recovered memories of trauma, especially CSA, have typically involved two polarized positions: the repressed-memory versus the false-memory viewpoints. Yet there is a third perspective that is *not* tantamount to a "middle ground"; it blandly asserts that some recovered memories are formerly repressed and genuine, whereas other recovered memories are false. In our research on memories of CSA (Clancy & McNally, 2005–2006; McNally et al., 2006), the typical individual with recovered memories of CSA reports one or several episodes of having been molested (e.g., fondled) by a trusted adult (e.g., uncle) at about the age of 7 or 8. Baffled, upset, and disgusted by the experience, the child fails to understand what is happening. The experience seldom triggers terror because the perpetrator neither committed violence nor threatened it, and hence it is not encoded as a traumatic event in the original sense of trauma: an overwhelmingly terrifying, often life-threatening experience. The victim manages not to think about the abuse for many years, and such ordinary forgetting is often fostered by absent retrieval cues (e.g., the perpetrator dies). But many years later, the victim encounters salient reminders, usually outside of psychotherapy, and the memories suddenly return. As an adult, the person fully understands what had happened and correctly interprets the experience as sexual abuse. Nearly one-third of our participants with recovered memories qualify for PTSD diagnoses after having remembered their abuse (Clancy & McNally, 2005–2006). Because the abuse was not experienced as terrifying, it was not encoded as a trauma. Moreover, we have not found convincing evidence that the memory was inaccessible, blocked, repressed, and so forth during the years when it apparently never came to mind. Yet it is a recovered memory of abuse, but not of a trauma that had been previously repressed.

Given the highly polarized views of recovered memories, we should like to underscore our viewpoint. The mere fact that an episode of molestation was not experienced as terrifying and encoded as traumatic does not mean that the perpetrator is any less morally reprehensible. In our view, the sexual exploitation of children is a social evil, even if it does not produce terror in the victims or result in psychiatric disorder (e.g., PTSD).

Recovered Memories: A View from the Laboratory

Until recently, no studies had been reported on the cognitive functioning of the people at the center of this recovered-memory debate: specifically, those who report recovered CSA memories. This state of affairs could be due to the fact that few clinicians have expertise in laboratory research and few cognitive psychologists have access to trauma populations (McNally, Clancy, & Barrett, 2004). Recently, psychologists have been applying experimental methods to investigate memory functioning in people reporting recovered memories of CSA (see McNally, 2003).

We examined whether individuals reporting recovered CSA memories are more prone to false-memory effects induced in the laboratory. In one of our studies, we (Clancy, Schacter, McNally, & Pitman, 2000) used the Deese–Roediger–McDermott (DRM) task (Deese, 1959; Roediger & McDermott, 1995), a paradigm that is very effective in eliciting false memories. In this paradigm, participants study a list of words that are strong semantic associates of a word not presented on the list—the *critical lure*. The critical lure is a word that captures the gist, or essence, of the list. For example, participants may study such words as *bed*, *rest*, *awake*, *tired*, and so forth, all of which are strongly related to the nonpresented critical

lure, *sleep*. On a subsequent test, participants often falsely recall and recognize having heard or seen the critical lure (e.g., *sleep*) on the list. Relative to individuals with continuous memories and to control participants who report no history of abuse, individuals reporting recovered CSA memories more often falsely recognized the nonpresented critical lures. In this study, however, the word lists comprised entirely neutral material, not emotional material potentially related to trauma (Clancy et al., 2000). Moreover, the heightened false-memory propensity for neutral critical lures does not confirm that people reporting recovered memories of CSA have false memories of CSA, although it is consistent with that possibility.

Subsequently, we extended these findings to trauma-related material (Geraerts, Smeets, Jelicic, van Heerden, & Merckelbach, 2005). That is, besides using neutral DRM lists (e.g., the critical lure *sleep*), we used trauma-related lists (e.g., the critical lure *assault*). Relative to the nonabused control group and the continuous-memory group, the recovered-memory group had higher rates of false recall and recognition for both neutral and trauma-related material.

A number of researchers have suggested that such susceptibility to false memories may be due to a source monitoring deficit, that is, incorrect judgments about the origin or source of information (Johnson, Hashtroudi, & Lindsay, 1993). For example, participants may think of the nonpresented lure at study, so then at test they must differentiate between memories of internally generated thoughts versus memories of the studied words. Our results (Clancy et al., 2000; Geraerts et al., 2005; McNally, Clancy, Barrett, & Parker, 2005) suggest that individuals reporting recovered CSA memories may have a source monitoring deficit for all types of material, whether the content is neutral or trauma-related. These individuals may tend to confuse an internally generated thought with a genuine memory. That is, they confuse mental contents arising from memory of perceived events with mental contents arising from imagination. This could have serious implications, both in terms of the development of false memories per se and in terms of the development of mistaken beliefs. Thus it may be that a subsample of those with recovered memories developed false memories via a subtle interaction between intrinsic source monitoring difficulties and suggestive therapeutic techniques.

Underestimation of Prior Remembering

Although the previously cited research suggests that recovered memories are likely to be false memories, Jonathan Schooler and coworkers (e.g., Schooler, Bendiksen, & Ambadar, 1997; Shobe & Schooler, 2001) described several case studies of individuals who experienced the "discovery" of apparently long-forgotten memories of abuse. Importantly, Schooler's group corroborated these abuse reports. In two of the cases, the partners of the women who reported full-blown recovered-memory experiences said that the women had discussed the abuse *before* they had the recovered-memory experience. In both cases, the women were surprised to discover that they had mentioned the presumably forgotten abuse prior to the time when they thought they had first recalled it. Schooler and colleagues proposed that these cases illustrate a "forgot-it-all-along" (FIA) phenomenon. That is, they had forgotten their prior rememberings of the abuse, mistakenly believing that it had not come to mind until they had their recovered-memory experience.

Recent studies have provided elegant laboratory analogues of this FIA phenomenon. For example, a series of experiments by Arnold and Lindsay (2002, 2005) required participants to recall material in qualitatively similar or different ways on two occasions. They reasoned that if the retrieval of CSA memories in qualitatively different ways can lead to the underestimation of previous CSA recollections, then this mechanism should transfer to the laboratory. They had participants study a list of homographic target words, each accompanied by a biasing context word (e.g., hand–*palm*). In Test 1, participants were tested on a subset of the study list, with some of the target items cued with the studied-context word (e.g., hand–p**m) and the rest of the items cued with an other-context word (e.g., tree–p**m). In the final test, participants were tested on all of the studied items, and the studied-context cues were always given as recall prompts. Additionally, after recalling each word, participants judged whether they had recalled that word on Test 1. The key result was that participants more often forgot their prior recall of the words when they had been cued with the other-context cue than with the studied-context cue on Test 1. Hence, these results provided compelling evidence that remembering a past event in a different way can result in a fail-

ure to remember a prior instance of recalling that event.

The FIA phenomenon has also been studied by Merckelbach and colleagues (Merckelbach et al., 2006). Based on the pioneering work of Parks (1999), they had undergraduate students try to remember events and facts from their childhood (e.g., "Do you have vivid memories of the first time you were on a plane?"). During the second part of the study (either 1 hour or 2 weeks later in study 1 and study 2, respectively), they were asked how recently they had thought about 18 childhood events, with half of these items drawn from the first autobiographical questionnaire (e.g., "When was the last time you recalled being on a plane for the first time?"). Results indicated that a nontrivial proportion of recent recalls of vivid childhood memories was dated incorrectly. That is, more than half of the participants gave a mean estimate of "several weeks ago" or longer for vivid childhood memories that they in fact had thought about just an hour ago. Similarly, when a longer time interval was involved, almost half of dating estimates for vivid memories were incorrect (e.g., in the range of "several months ago" or longer). Thus these results indicate that people are often highly inaccurate in dating recent recalls, even when salient childhood events are involved for which they claim to have vivid memories. As Schooler argued, this underestimation of prior remembering is typical for at least some cases of recovered memories.

In another study, Merckelbach and colleagues (2006) examined whether individuals reporting recovered CSA memories exhibit an especially strong tendency to underestimate their prior remembering relative to individuals who reported having continuous (i.e., permanently accessible) memories. Using the same procedure as in studies 1 and 2, they found that individuals with recovered memories showed a specific failure to take recent recall into account when they estimated the last time they thought about vivid target memories.

Because individuals with recovered memories exhibited as a group such a strong FIA effect, we conducted a large study employing Arnold and Lindsay's (2002) FIA test (Geraerts et al., 2006). We tested whether individuals reporting recovered CSA memories are more prone to underestimating their prior remembering relative to individuals with continuous CSA memories and controls reporting no history of abuse. In study 1, participants with recovered CSA memories were more prone to forget that they had previously recalled a studied item when they had been cued to think of it differently on two recall tests. That is, the FIA effect was larger in those who reported recovered memories.

In study 2, participants were requested to recall autobiographical events (e.g., being home alone as a child) in an emotionally negative or positive framing across three test sessions over a period of 4 months. In the first session, participants were instructed to recall 25 selected events in either a positive or negative frame. After 2 months, participants were required to recall 16 of the autobiographical target events for a second time. For half of the trials, the framing cue presented with the events corresponded to the negative–positive framing cue presented with the autobiographical events during the first session, whereas for the remaining trials the framing was the opposite from the framing cue presented in the first session (e.g., positive framing if the framing on the first session had been negative). In the third session, again 2 months later, participants were tested on all the target events, accompanied by the framing cues that were presented with the targets during the first session. Again, individuals reporting recovered CSA memories showed an enhanced FIA effect relative to individuals with continuous abuse memories and controls, even for mildly emotional autobiographical material over a period of 4 months. These conditions, however, more closely mirror everyday life than memories of trauma. These findings imply that some of the participants' recovered CSA memories may be fundamentally accurate but that these individuals may have underestimated their prior memories for the abuse.

Discovered Memories or False Memories?

The two basic findings of source monitoring deficits and enhanced FIA suggest radically different interpretations of recovered memories. On the one hand, studies by Clancy and colleagues (2000) and Geraerts and colleagues (2005) show that reports of recovered memories are linked to false-memory effects as measured by the DRM task. Conversely, studies by Merckelbach and colleagues (2006) and Geraerts and colleagues (2006) indicate that recovered-memory reports are closely related to

underestimation of prior remembering. How can these phenomena be integrated? Careful inspection of the precise type of recovered-memory experiences may provide an answer to this question.

Two remarkably different types of recovered-memory experiences have been documented in the literature (e.g., McNally et al., 2004; Shobe & Schooler, 2001). In one type, people come to believe that they are abuse survivors, commonly attributing current life difficulties to their repressed memories of abuse. Here, abuse events are mostly gradually recalled over time, often through suggestions of a therapist. People usually indicate that they have *learned* (e.g., through hypnosis) that the abuse occurred to them. In the other type of recovered-memory experience, people are suddenly *reminded* about events that they believe they had not thought about for many years. They are shocked and surprised by their recollection but not by the content of the memory as such. Stunned, they often say things such as, "I'm amazed that I had forgotten this!" This kind of recollection differs from the one in which the person is gradually recalling the abuse, often in the course of therapy. For this reason, Schooler and coworkers (Schooler, 2001; Schooler et al., 1997) referred to these suddenly recovered memories as *discovered* memories, reflecting situations "in which individuals sincerely perceive themselves to have discovered memories of experiences of which they think they had previously been unaware" (Shobe & Schooler, 2001, p. 100). This term keeps open the possibility that individuals could have discovery experiences corresponding to memories that were not completely forgotten. Hence, the two types of recovered-memory experience are: (1) learned memories gradually recovered during psychotherapy that often involves hypnosis or related techniques and (2) discovered memories that the person suddenly recalls, usually after encountering reminders outside of therapy.

Given the two different types of recovered-memory experiences, clinicians could speculate that people who report CSA memories recovered during therapy may score high on tasks yielding false-memory effects (e.g., the DRM task). Yet they might perform similarly to control participants on tasks tapping the FIA effect. Conversely, researchers would expect that people with spontaneously recovered memories may be especially prone to the FIA effect, whereas they would score similarly to controls on false-memory tasks (e.g., DRM task). A recent study (Geraerts et al., 2007) in our lab examined these hypotheses by recruiting four groups of people. Participants in the *spontaneously recovered memory group* reported that they had previously forgotten and then spontaneously recalled memories of CSA outside of therapy, without prompting from anyone else or even a conscious attempt to seek such memories. Participants in the *recovered in therapy group* stated that they had gradually recovered their memories of abuse during therapy, prompted by suggestive therapeutic techniques, during an active effort to reconstruct their missing past. The *continuous-memory group* comprised participants who said that they had never forgotten their abuse. The *control group* consisted of participants who reported no history of abuse in either childhood or adulthood. To examine our hypothesis about the differing origins of recovered memories, we ran our four participant groups in both the DRM false-memory task and the FIA paradigm. Indeed, as we hypothesized, people with CSA memories recovered in the course of therapy had a significantly higher rate of false recall and recognition of nonpresented critical lures relative to people reporting spontaneously recovered memories, people with continuous memories, or control participants.

For the FIA task, we found that there was a difference among the four groups in how well they could remember their past acts of remembering when the retrieval context had changed. The only measurable difference among the four groups on the FIA task was that participants with spontaneously recovered memories showed a significantly greater tendency to believe that they had never recalled an experience before when retrieval contexts had changed.

These findings indicate that there are important differences in the cognitive profiles of people who recover memories of CSA either through suggestive therapy or spontaneously, without prompting or attempts to reconstruct their past. As a group, people who come to believe they have recovered a memory of CSA only through suggestive therapy generally show a pronounced tendency to incorrectly claim that they have experienced events when they have demonstrably not experienced them. To the extent that this pattern on the DRM task is indicative of a broader deficit in monitoring the source of one's memories, this finding suggests that such reports of recovered memories

should be viewed cautiously, as they may reflect the interaction of suggestive therapy with preexisting source monitoring deficits. In contrast, people who believe they have spontaneously recovered a memory of CSA show no evidence of heightened susceptibility to the creation of false memories. This group does, however, show a striking tendency to forget prior occurrences of remembering when these prior retrievals have taken place in a different retrieval context. To the extent that performance on the FIA task is indicative of a broader susceptibility to forgetting in the face of shifts in context, these findings suggest that this group, as a whole, may simply be failing to remember their prior thoughts about a *genuine* episode of CSA.

Corroborative Evidence

We found support for the view that CSA memories spontaneously recovered outside of therapy are more likely to reflect genuine events relative to memories recovered in therapy. In this study, information was sought to validate the CSA memories. We found that CSA memories discovered outside of therapy are more likely to be corroborated than are those recovered in therapy (Geraerts et al., 2007). In this study, people with recovered CSA memories ($n = 57$) responded to an extensive memory questionnaire. Participants were asked to characterize (1) their prior degree of forgetting, (2) the quality of their memory recovery if they had recovered a memory, (3) the nature and context of the abuse, and (4) the qualities of their current memory. Moreover, we sought information to validate the CSA memories. Memories were characterized as "corroborated" if one or more of the following three criteria were met: (1) another individual reported learning about the abuse soon (i.e., within the next week) after its occurrence, (2) another individual reported having also been abused by the alleged perpetrator, or (3) another individual reported having committed the abuse. The presence of corroborative evidence was evaluated by two raters masked to any additional information associated with each case.

Table 16.1 shows that abuse events recovered during therapy could not be corroborated, whereas 36.6% of the CSA memories discovered outside of therapy were corroborated. Moreover, in this study, 85% of participants reporting recovered memories had failed

TABLE 16.1. Amount of Corroborative Evidence for Abuse Events Recovered Outside and in the Course of Therapy

| | Corroborative evidence | | | |
| | No | | Yes | |
	Frequency	Percentage	Frequency	Percentage
Recovered in therapy	16	100.0	0	0.0
Discovered outside of therapy	26	63.4	15	36.6

to appreciate their abuse as traumatic at the time it occurred, in part due to lack of understanding of the nature of the event. In fact, many of them rated the abuse as being more traumatic now than it was when it occurred. Years later, potent retrieval cues prompt the recollection of the long-forgotten experience, which the person now correctly understands as sexual abuse. This realization is often accompanied by an onrush of emotions, interpreted as the impact of remembering something for the first time. These findings were strikingly consistent with another study by our group that showed that nearly one-third of recovered-memory participants qualified for PTSD diagnoses after having been reminded of their long-forgotten abuse (Clancy & McNally, 2005–2006).

Although such cases undoubtedly qualify as recovered or discovered memories of sexual abuse, they do not constitute cases of traumatic amnesia for two reasons. First, the abuse was not experienced as a trauma when it occurred. Second, there is no convincing evidence that the abuse was inaccessible during the time in which it did not come to mind. The inaccessibility of an encoded memory is the hallmark of amnesia. No special dissociative or repression mechanism needs to be invoked to explain material that is not remembered.

RECOMMENDATIONS FOR PSYCHOTHERAPISTS

Therapists should focus on treating the patient's disorder (e.g., PTSD and depression) rather than focusing on helping patients recall presumably dissociated memories of CSA. There is no convincing evidence that hypnosis can facilitate accurate recall of memories. On the contrary, there is abundant evidence that hypnosis can lead to the generation of imagery

that the patient mistakes for memories (Lynn, Lock, Myers, & Payne, 1997). Individuals who have already spontaneously recalled CSA memories may benefit from cognitive therapy designed to correct distortions that sometimes occur, such as the belief that the patient, when a child, was somehow responsible for the perpetrator's behavior.

RECOMMENDATIONS FOR EVALUATORS

Clinicians working in a forensic context may encounter individuals who report having recovered memories of CSA after a long period of time of not having thought about the abuse. Given that such memories may be either false or true, what indicators increase or decrease the likelihood of their authenticity?

As summarized in Table 16.2, the following factors *decrease* the likelihood of the memory's authenticity: (1) the abuse occurred prior to the age of 4 years; (2) the abuse was repeated many times over the course of years, yet was reportedly entirely forgotten; (3) the abuse involved several perpetrators, especially if organized in a cult; (4) the abuse involved violence; (5) the abuse provoked terror when it occurred; and (6) memory of the abuse surfaced during the course of therapy designed to recover memories of suspected abuse.

The following factors *increase* the likelihood of the memory's authenticity as related to the described abuse: (1) the abuse occurred during the elementary school years; (2) the abuse occurred only once or a few times; (3) the abuse involved a single perpetrator; (4) the abuse did not involve violence or threats of violence; (5) the abuse provoked discomfort, fear, or confusion, but not terror, when it occurred; (6) the person did not understand the experience as sexual abuse when it occurred. Several addi-

TABLE 16.2. Indicators That Decrease or Increase the Likelihood Regarding the Authenticity of the Recovered Memory

Factors	Decrease likelihood	Increase likelihood
Age	Abuse prior to age 4	Abuse during elementary school
Frequency	Repeated abuse events	Abuse occurred only a few times
Perpetrators	Abuse involved several perpetrators	Abuse involved one perpetrator
Violence	Violent abuse	Abuse did not involve violence
Emotions	Terror provoking	Provokes discomfort, fear, or confusion
Retrieval	Gradual recovery during therapy	Spontaneously recovered
Emotional reaction		Shock at recollection
Insight		Experiences were not understood as abuse at the time it occurred; at retrieval, they are understood as abuse

tional factors that increase the likelihood of authentic memories relate to its recall: (7) recollection of the abuse occurred spontaneously outside psychotherapy and in response to reminders; (8) the person experiences shock at the recollection.

CONCLUSIONS

In conclusion, perspectives on trauma and memory have been highly polarized. Research testing these perspectives has often involved study of people who do *not* report recovered memories. For example, the majority of the studies on the creation of false memories have used undergraduates. Recent studies concerning the cognitive psychology of people at the heart of the debate, specifically, people reporting recovered CSA memories, have shown that some people with recovered memories are more vulnerable to developing false memories, at least in the laboratory. On the other hand, research has shown how individuals who were sexually abused as children may forget and then remember their abuse without it ever having been repressed or dissociated. Episodes of abuse that were neither terrifying nor understood by the victim at the time of the crime may be forgotten without having been repressed and yet be recalled years later when the person encounters reminders. Finally, some individuals who report recovered memories of CSA forget their prior rememberings of the experience.

In this chapter, we examined the two main perspectives on recovered memories of CSA: either (1) they are false or (2) they have been previously repressed or dissociated and hence inaccessible to recall. There is evidence to support the first perspective (e.g., sexual abuse by satanic cults) but little convincing evidence in support of the second perspective. Our third perspective shows how CSA victims may forget and then recall abuse episodes without memory of these experiences having been repressed or dissociated.

ACKNOWLEDGMENT

Elke Geraerts was supported by a grant from the Netherlands Organization for Scientific Research (NWO 446-06-002).

17

Detecting Deception in Sex Offender Assessment

RICHARD I. LANYON, PhD
MICHAEL L. THOMAS, MA

The topic of sex offenses has received increasing attention in the United States during the past decade. Several indicators or correlates of this trend can be identified. First, there has been an increase in legislation and case law directed at the control of sexual deviance, such as the "sexually violent predator" (SVP) designation with indefinite commitment. This work has been documented by Miller, Amenta, and Conroy (2005) and by Rogers and Shuman (2005). Second, public awareness has been heightened by the prosecution of deviant sexuality within the Catholic clergy. Third, reports have been publicized and debated regarding adult women with recovered memories of childhood sexual molestation (e.g., American Psychological Association Working Group on Investigation of Memories of Childhood Abuse, 1998). The sentencing and confinement of sex offenders has also been increased. Even when eventually released, sex offenders may receive lifetime probation and community notifications (LaFond, 2003). According to the *New York Times* (June 10, 2006; *www.nytimes.com/2006/06/10/us/10execute.html*), South Carolina and Oklahoma became the fourth and fifth states to allow the death penalty for sex crimes against children.

Consistent with these trends, the psychological literature on assessment related to sex offending has grown rapidly, together with specific techniques and procedures focusing on particular aspects or characteristics of sex offenders and their victims. As with any area of psychological assessment within a forensic context, the question of deliberate misrepresentation for personal gain is a prominent issue. The fact that sex offending is regularly demonized by politicians and the public makes it even more likely that there will be dissimulation by persons facing accusations. Indeed, in a previous edition of this book, Sewell and Salekin's (1997) corresponding chapter recommended that dissimulation should be considered with all accused or admitted sex offenders.

Lanyon (2001) provided a general organizational framework for the assessment of sex offenders. He proposed that six components are critical to these evaluations: (1) general psychological characteristics, (2) deviant sexual interests, (3) risk of reoffending, (4) amenability to treatment, (5) response distortion, and (6) appraisal of formal legal criteria (e.g., SVP). Dissimulation can play an important role in assessing each of these components. The two components that have received the most attention in the literature are the assessment of deviant sexual interests and risk of sexual reoffending. Two other issues that are especially relevant to this chapter include assessment for

285

SVP status and victim truthfulness. The latter topic has received a great deal of attention in the literature since the early 1980s, when the view was popularized that child accusers are always truthful (Summit, 1983), followed by the gradual accumulation of evidence that sometimes they are not (e.g., Ceci & Bruck, 1993).

The assessment of truthfulness regarding specific acts (the question of guilt or innocence) is an issue for the finder of fact, not for the mental health professional. However, it is commonly addressed in the context of treatment in order to determine the offender's full history of sexual deviance. Therefore, it is addressed in this chapter. Some assessment procedures have been specifically designed for use with sex offenders, such as the penile plethysmograph, whereas others (e.g., the Minnesota Multiphasic Personality Inventory–2 [MMPI-2]) are utilized in this endeavor but not specifically designed for this purpose. Both types of procedures are considered in this review. It should also be pointed out that nearly all sex offenders are men and that the relevant literature—including the work reviewed here—is based on men.

METHODOLOGICAL ISSUES

Scientific Standards

Before embarking on a systematic review of the research literature on detecting deception in the context of sex offending, several preliminary comments are in order. First, a primary consideration is the quality of the research from which relevant conclusions are drawn. Thus publication in peer-reviewed journals is considered authoritative. The authoritative standard for evaluating the quality of the assessment instruments is provided by the *Standards for Educational and Psychological Testing* (American Educational Research Association, American Psychological Association, & National Council on Measurement in Education [AERA/APA/NCME], 1999, referred to hereafter as the *Standards*), along with the standards for test development and use promulgated by the American Psychological Association's (APA) journal related to testing, *Psychological Assessment*.

The purpose of the *Standards* is "to provide criteria for the evaluation of tests, testing practices, and the effects of test use" (AERA/APA/NCME, 1999, p. 2). Prominent among its basic themes include the following.

1. "Tests and testing programs should be developed on a sound scientific basis. Test developers and publishers should compile and document adequate evidence bearing on test development" (p. 43).
2. "Validity is . . . the most fundamental consideration in developing and evaluating tests. The process of validation involves accumulating evidence to provide a sound scientific basis for the proposed score interpretations" (p. 9).
3. "Reports of norming studies should include precise specification of the population that was sampled . . . [and] the information provided should be sufficient to enable users to judge the appropriateness of the norms" (p. 55).

These criteria for the acceptability of test development and validation are consistent with the *Daubert* standard (*Daubert v. Merrell Dow Pharmaceuticals, 1993*) established by the U.S. Supreme Court for the admissibility of expert testimony in federal courts and in most state courts (Steinberg, 1993). The *Daubert* standard requires that the expert's testimony be appropriately grounded in scientific method and procedure and be evaluated according to its empirical accuracy.

Admitters and Nonadmitters

Relevant to the preceding statement on scientific standards, a serious methodological difficulty is common to virtually all empirical research in sex offender assessment procedures that involve direct responding by the accused person (Lanyon, 2001; Sewell & Salekin, 1997). The source of this difficulty involves the fact that nearly all studies of the validity of assessment procedures in sex offending have been conducted on male *admitters*—men who have acknowledged their sexually deviant behavior. As pointed out by Murphy and Peters (1992), admitters usually do not need extended assessments because they are likely to provide much of the required information in response to direct questioning. In contrast, nonadmitters require carefully constructed and validated assessment instruments because they do not provide the needed information voluntarily.

Valid assessment procedures that are applicable to nonadmitters are critical in forensic evaluations. Because life-altering consequences frequently rest on the outcome of these cases, denial of deviant sexual interests and offenses is common. In this sense, procedures must be demonstrably valid for nonadmitters. At the present time, however, this issue has been recognized only minimally by researchers. Rather, the trend tends to be avoidance of the topic and/or confusion as to its relevance.

Researchers are confronted with a further complication in their assessment of nonadmitters. The critical comparison for validation purposes must be between *guilty* nonadmitters (men falsely denying their offenses) and *innocent* nonadmitters (men falsely accused). To our knowledge, such comparisons have simply never been conducted. As discussed later in the chapter, the effort required to conduct studies of this comparison is burdensome, but such studies have nevertheless been successfully carried out in other clinical areas.

Other methodological issues must be considered. First, the term *nonadmitter* has been used in two different ways. The generally accepted definition is denial of deviant *behavior* (e.g., Haywood, Grossman, & Cavanaugh, 1990). However, it has also been used more broadly to refer to the denial of sexually deviant *preferences* (e.g., Blanchard, Klassen, Dickey, Kuban, & Blak, 2001), rather than being restricted to only deviant behavior. Whether or not this distinction makes a practical difference, we attempt to be clear in its usage for each given study.

A second issue involves the need for accurate identification of those persons who show deviant interests but who did not commit the crime under investigation. This is an important issue, because it is common for law enforcement to contact all registered sex offenders whenever a sex offense is committed in a particular location. Third, in the interests of reducing complexity, this chapter combines studies of two slightly different groups utilized in various investigations: (1) nonadmitters of deviant behavior regarding a specific offense in question and (2) deniers of any sexually deviant behavior. These two groups obviously overlap considerably; here they are treated as functionally similar.

The settings of sex offender research may affect the obtained responses. Four different settings are common: pretrial, presentence, treatment, and research. Studies also differ in sample characteristics, such as different offenses, paraphilias, and backgrounds (e.g., adults vs. adolescents; first-time vs. repeat offenders). Thus

the assessment task with sex offenders is a complex and heterogeneous. It cannot be meaningfully reduced to a few simple rules or generalizations. We have attempted to respect this complexity in presenting the following sections, although some simplifications were unavoidable in light of the available literature.

The reader is alerted in advance to the somewhat discouraging conclusions drawn in earlier chapters on deception in sex offending. Langevin (1988) concluded that "available research offers no meaningful criteria for distinguishing between reliable and dissimulating individuals suspected of deviant sexual behavior" (p. 289). Sewell and Salekin (1997) offered a similar conclusion: "Given the inconclusive state of the literature on dissimulation, no explicit decision rules are indicated by current empirical knowledge" (p. 350). The truth of the matter is that very little methodologically sound research attention has been paid to the assessment of deception in the domain of sex offending. This review necessarily focuses on what we do know that is useful and attempts to differentiate this knowledge from findings that are interesting but not of relevance in the task of assessing deceptiveness.

Deviant Sexual Interests

The presence of deviant sexual interests has been the most central and general topic in the assessment of sex offending and occupies the lion's share of this chapter. Deviant sexually arousing fantasies, urges, or behaviors that have led to action or that cause marked distress or interpersonal difficulties signal the presence of mental disorders termed *paraphilias* (American Psychiatric Association, 2000). This general definition of the paraphilias is generally taken as the "gold standard" for sexual deviance. It allows making a positive diagnosis purely on the basis of documented overt behaviors. In such cases, an individual's defensiveness does not obscure the diagnosis. But the definition also allows paraphilias to be characterized simply by the presence of *internal* states (e.g., sexually arousing fantasies). Internal states cannot be observed directly, and few persons are likely to admit having them. A variety of assessment procedures have therefore been developed to fill this gap. To repeat, if the person is reliably observed to have engaged in sustained, observable sexually deviant behavior, the diagnostic question of assessment by "indirect" methods does not arise; and so the issue of defensiveness or denial is not pivotal.

ASSESSMENT ISSUES

For each of the five areas of assessment that are addressed in this chapter, we identify relevant assessment instruments or procedures and briefly examine their nature and basic validity. We then consider the literature on deception. In this regard, we ask two key questions:

1. How accurate is the instrument for its intended assessment?
2. Can the instrument itself be deceived or foiled?

Self-Report Instruments

Self-report instruments have become the mainstay of noncognitive assessment in clinical psychology. Various self-report methods have been tried for the assessment of deviant sexual interests.

Sexual Interest Questionnaires

The simplest of these instruments consist of straightforward questionnaires inquiring about a wide range of normal and deviant sexual interests. Examples are the Clarke Sexual History Questionnaire and its revision (Langevin, 1983; Langevin & Paitch, 2005) and the first edition of the Multiphasic Sex Inventory (MSI; Nichols & Molinder, 1984). Related procedures include card sorts in which respondents designate their order of personal preference for a series of statements or pictorial representations of deviant and nondeviant sexual stimuli (e.g., Brownell, Hayes, & Barlow, 1977; Haywood et al., 1990). Except for the MSI, no published literature could be found on the validity of any of these instruments, nor any indication of procedures that were included in order to address or detect response distortion. Because the MSI was designed to be used only with admitters, the question of response distortion and its detection is not directly applicable.

The current revision of the MSI (i.e., MSI-II; Nichols & Molinder, 1996) is also a true–false questionnaire designed primarily for the assessment of admitters. The unpublished manual makes reference to "over 900 test protocols . . . gathered from 45 cities" and refers to elaborate scale development procedures.

However, because none of this work is published or set forth in detail in the manual, it is not available for review and evaluation. In the MSI-II, six scales termed *validity measures* were included "to identify those persons who were defensive or who wanted to manipulate their findings" (1996, p. 53). No systematic account is presented on how these scales were developed or what they were intended to measure. Moreover, there is no published literature on either their development or their validity. As best can be determined from the manual, scale construction involved only admitters and excluded nonadmitters. The manual contains a discussion of possible uses for the MSI-II with nonadmitters and refers to a group of guilty nonadmitters whose scores are stated to be closer to the scores of known sex offenders than to the scores of normal nonoffenders. No published studies could be found on the MSI-II that addressed response distortion or its detection.

An additional self-report questionnaire is found in the first section of the two-part Abel Assessment for Sexual Interest (Abel, Huffman, Warberg, & Holland, 1998); it covers sexual history and related topics. However, it is impossible to assess the validity of the questionnaire because details of its construction and validation remain unpublished. In addition, documentation of its scoring and interpretation are not available. We have no evidence of whether it even considers response distortion.

General Clinical Measures

Attempts have been made to assess deviant sexual interests from measures that were not specifically designed for this purpose, most prominently the MMPI and MMPI-2. The expectation that such an approach could be useful has its roots in the test construction technology and philosophy of a prior generation. Stimulus materials with a wide-ranging content were thought to be useful for evaluating almost all clinical constructs. This viewpoint was applied to the Rorschach Inkblot Test, the Thematic Apperception Test (TAT), and the original MMPI item pool. Of course, the usual purpose in administering a "general" clinical instrument, such as the MMPI/MMPI-2, is to assess whether the person has any significant psychopathology. In this section, we focus on whether the MMPI/MMPI-2 can identify deviant sexual interests and whether such a pattern can be deliberately suppressed.

Is there a consistent sex offender "profile" on the MMPI? Friedrich (1988) extensively reviewed this question and found no such profile. Subsequently, Lanyon (1993c) compared admitters and guilty nonadmitters to direct deviant behavior with a control group who were not sexually deviant but had a comparable degree of other psychopathology. Four scales previously developed from the MMPI item pool for the purpose of identifying sex offenders were evaluated: Pedophile (Pe; Toobert, Bartelme, & Jones, 1958), Sexual Deviation (Sv; Marsh, Hilliard, & Liechti, 1955), Sexual Morbidity (Sm; Cutter, 1964), and Aggravated Sex (Asx; Panton, 1979). All scales had been developed by contrasting groups of known sex offenders with one or more other comparison groups (with varying degrees of appropriateness). The first three of these scales had significantly higher scores (p < .001) for admitters than for controls but not for nonadmitters. However, when the nonadmitters were compared with control group members who were comparably defensive in an overall sense as assessed by the MMPI K scale, the results again showed significant predictive value for the same three scales (p < .001). Thus the results demonstrated some potential utility of the MMPI item pool in contributing to the identification of guilty nonadmitters. However, these findings have not been followed up with the MMPI-2.

An additional use of the MMPI/MMPI-2 is to evaluate the standard validity scales (L, F, K, and others) in order to determine whether the respondent has been generally defensive on this test and possibly defensive for the entire evaluation. Several studies reviewed by Sewell and Salekin (1997) found that general defensiveness scales do show significant differences between admitters and nonadmitters. Indeed, Lanyon and Lutz (1984) showed that guilty nonadmitters could be distinguished from admitters using the raw score index L + K − F with a hit rate of 83%, corresponding to a correlation of .64. Of course, this finding is not specific to defensiveness regarding sexual deviance.

Conclusions

Self-report assessment procedures for sexual interest have not been shown to be valid for this purpose, particularly with nonadmitters. Given their high face validity, there is no reason to suppose that such instruments can detect deviant sexual interests in nonadmitters.

However, the presence of relevant content may be useful in collecting information from admitters. For the MMPI/MMPI-2, validity scales can distinguish between generally defensive and nondefensive groups of sex offenders, although the relationship of general defensiveness to the specific denial of sexual deviance has not been established. Moreover, the critical distinction between guilty and innocent nonadmitters has yet to be evaluated.

Penile Plethysmograph

A great deal of research on the assessment of sex offenders has focused on the use of physiological indicators as the primary approach. In particular, the penile plethysmograph (PPG), also termed *phallometry*, has gained considerable acceptance. Indeed, when erection measurement techniques were first developed in the 1950s (e.g., Freund, 1957), they were hailed as a hopeful sign that valid scientific measurement methods had finally been developed for sexual deviance.

Unfortunately, relatively little research has been conducted on the critical group of nonadmitters. Therefore, the question as to whether the PPG can detect persons attempting to be deceptive cannot be readily addressed in this chapter. A counterargument might be advanced that the PPG does not rely on conscious processes and that, therefore, the question of deceptiveness would be irrelevant. In this vein, the PPG would itself be regarded simply as a procedure for assessing sexual deviant interests, regardless of whether or not they are overtly denied. However, in the absence of empirical support for this position, the PPG, like all measures, is here evaluated first for its validity and second for its susceptibility to faking. Indeed, the few studies that have investigated nonadmitters show somewhat less positive findings than for admitters (discussed later).

In this review, validity studies involving admitters are briefly described and summarized, and then more detailed attention is given to those involving nonadmitters. Unfortunately, many studies do not adequately separate these two types, and some have combined admitters with nonadmitters.

Basic Description and Scoring

Two types of phallometric assessment devices have been used to assess sexual interest.

Freund's (1957) early attempts at diagnosis and prediction of homosexuality in men resulted in the development of a volumetric PPG. This invention, essentially an airtight glass cylinder that measures volumetric changes based on penile tumescence, can detect such small indices of arousal that examinees are often unaware of any physical changes. Early criticisms of the bulkiness of the volumetric PPG led to the common use of circumferential PPGs that measure changes in the diameter of the penis. Mercury strain gauges (Bancroft, Jones, & Pullan, 1966; Fisher, Gross, & Zuch, 1965) and mechanical strain gauges (Barlow, Becker, Leitenberg, & Agras, 1970) quickly found favor with practitioners and researchers because of their less invasive quality. Although these circumferential PPGs are more commonly used than the volumetric type, it is generally accepted that the latter are more sensitive measures of tumescence (Freund, Langevin, & Barlow, 1974).

Recorded phallometric data are based on a change in tumescence during stimulus presentation. Investigators compare measures of tumescence when participants are exposed to neutral stimuli and to a variety of sexually provocative stimuli. Two common methods of scoring participants' responses are Z score transformations and percentage of full erection. The advantage of using Z scores comes from the ability to calculate scores for participants who demonstrate low arousal. However, Z score transformations have been criticized for their susceptibility to accentuating small differences within participants, which can obscure important information concerning the overall magnitude of responses (Howes, 2003).

Percent full erection (PFE; e.g., Murphy, DiLillo, Haynes, & Steere, 2001) is a scoring method commonly used as an alternative to Z score transformations of data (Howes, 1995). For PFE to be a meaningful measure, researchers and practitioners must be able to record participants' full erection scores. The difficulty in doing so has led to an attempt to develop normative data on change scores for full erection (Howes, 2003).

Testing Procedures

PPG assessments are often criticized for the wide variability in testing procedures used by researchers and practitioners alike (Marshall & Fernandez, 2000; Seto, 2001). Howes (1995) surveyed 48 phallometric testing centers

throughout the United States and found considerable variability in the assessments being conducted. Although some have argued that flexibility in testing procedures allows examiners to tailor assessments to individuals, studies have shown that variability in testing procedures can create inconsistent results. Research (e.g., Abel, Blanchard, & Barlow, 1981; Lalumière & Quinsey, 1994) has tended to show that highly "animated" erotic material is more effective at eliciting changes in tumescence. Thus optimal assessment may require the use of very graphic and realistic erotic stimuli. Not surprisingly, a discussion concerning the ethics of using deviant assessment material (e.g., child pornography) for research and treatment purposes is occurring (see Seto, 2001, for a discussion of ethical issues).

Reliability and Validity

A review by Marshall and Fernandez (2000) concluded that the reliability of phallometric assessment has not been studied sufficiently to achieve any definitive conclusions. In a meta-analysis, Hall, Shondrick, and Hirschman (1993) reported a range of test–retest reliability correlations from $r = .26$ to $r = .85$, with lower correlations coming from studies with test–retest intervals greater than 1 day. Preliminary evidence suggests that reliability is greater for pedophiles than for rapists and nonoffenders (Kalmus & Beech, 2005), but this conclusion is speculative until enough research has accumulated.

An exhaustive review regarding the validity of phallometric assessments is beyond the scope of this chapter. Extensive reviews are readily available; see Marshall and Fernandez (2000), Murphy and Barbaree (1994), O'Donohue and Letourneau (1992), and Seto (2001). However, a summary of the pertinent issues is needed in order to set the foundation for discussing deception.

Validity research has typically involved determining how well the PPG can differentiate sexual interests between different types of known sexual offenders versus nonoffenders. Studies have demonstrated that PPG evaluations can sometimes be done successfully with a moderate level of accuracy (e.g., Barbaree & Marshall, 1989; Firestone, Bradford, Greenberg, & Nunes, 2000; Looman & Marshall, 2001; Quinsey & Chaplin, 1988a; Quinsey, Chaplin, & Carrigan, 1979; Travin, Cullen, &

Melella, 1988). Estimates of sensitivity and specificity are considered later in this chapter. However, the face validity of the PPG lures some practitioners into thinking that patterns of sexual arousal can be directly equated with determination of sex offending. The literature does not support this proposition. In addition, the findings are too complex for any facile generalization. For example, familial and nonfamilial pedophiles show different patterns of arousal to adult and child erotic stimuli (Blanchard et al., 2006). In contrast, rapists are difficult to identify through PPG patterns of sexual arousal, as they often show greater preference for erotic stimuli depicting consensual sex than forced sex (Looman, 2000; Looman & Marshall, 2005). Such variations interfere with drawing firm conclusions from PPG findings.

A pervasive issue in phallometric assessment is deciding what to conclude about nonresponders (i.e., participants with less than 10% of full arousal to all stimuli). A substantial minority of research participants, estimated at 30% by Looman, Abracen, Maillet, and DiFazio (1998), are typically discarded from statistical analyses due to nonresponding. Although nonresponding could be due to factors such as possible criminal sanctions or the anxiety created by the testing situation, a conclusion of greater concern would be that nonresponding is due to deliberate deception. In support of this view, Looman and colleagues found that nonresponding correlated (at around $r = .50$) with high scores on the Impression Management scale of the Balanced Inventory of Desirable Responding (Paulhus, 1991a). The idea that examinees' PPG responses might be affected by their concern for social approval suggests that greater arousal might be achieved in the "natural" environment. In a clever use of a portable PPG, Rea, DeBriere, Butler, and Saunders (1998) tested this hypothesis by comparing sexual offenders' arousal in the natural environment and in the laboratory. As predicted, greatest arousal was demonstrated in the natural environment, when offenders were far removed from research assistants.

Some researchers have questioned whether the PPG measures overall sexual arousability rather than specific sexual interest. Hall (1989; Hall, Hirschman, & Oliver, 1995; Hall, Proctor, & Nelson, 1988) found that the arousal of some sex offenders to deviant and nondeviant stimuli were correlated. In addition, men who

were able to inhibit sexual arousal on request demonstrated less sexual arousal in general. Hall and colleagues (1988) suggested that the inconsistent and imprecise patterns of arousal in sex offender populations—rapists in particular—supported the view that the PPG measures only general arousal rather than specific responses to deviant material.

How accurate is the PPG? As established in the preceding paragraphs, this is a complex question. Furthermore, studies that report sensitivity and specificity have often not distinguished between (1) admitters and nonadmitters or (2) deviant behavior and deviant sexual interests. In addition, because determining an individual's specific primary sexual interest (i.e., the accuracy of assessment) is only practical with admitters, studies with nonadmitters have difficulty determining sensitivity and specificity. For a given group of sex offenders, some may have deviant sexual interests and others may not, which makes homogeneous sexual interests rather unlikely. If researchers do not know in advance which men have deviant sexual interests and which men do not, the validity of the PPG cannot be determined with any great precision.

Blanchard and colleagues (2006), for example, examined sensitivity and specificity in identifying deviant sexual interest among offenders, some of whom admitted their offense and some of whom did not; however, all denied deviant sexual interest. They found a sensitivity of .43 and specificity of .92. The authors reported their result as *minimum* sensitivity because it was unlikely that the sexual offenders were homogeneous in deviant sexual interest; thus sensitivity was presumably underestimated.

Several other studies have reported sensitivity and specificity data on sexual interests but are compromised either by combining admitters and nonadmitters and/or by marked variations in the number and ages of the offenders' victims. For example, Blanchard and colleagues (2001) reported sensitivities ranging from .29 to .61 and specificities ranging from .79 to .96; the values vary according to number and type of victims. Seto, Lalumière, and Blanchard (2000) found sensitivity of .42 and specificity of .92 for a combined group of admitter and nonadmitter adolescent sexual offenders. Much earlier, Freund and Watson (1991) examined PPG responses for men convicted of various sexual crimes who denied deviant sexual interest. They found sensitivities ranging from .45 to .89 and specificities ranging from .81 to .97, depending on the offenders' number and type of victims. In general, sensitivity tends to be highest when assessing offenders with multiple child victims.

Lalumière and Quinsey (1993) reviewed published and unpublished data sets comparing PPG assessment with rapists with that of non-rapists and reported the following sensitivities and specificities for different rape stimuli: .67/.90 (Oak Ridge), .69/.94 (Abel), and .14/.95 (Barbaree). It appears that most of the studies reviewed by Lalumière and Quinsey were conducted with admitters who were convicted sexual offenders, although this is difficult to determine because of the inclusion of data from unpublished studies.

The PPG and Deception

The belief that penile tumescence is difficult for males to control seems to bolster professional confidence in phallometric assessment's immunity to faking. However, most relevant research suggests that this assumption is incorrect. Furthermore, when considering deception, it is important to remember that the PPG cannot assess guilt or innocence; rather, it is intended to assess sexual preference. Deviant sexual interest does not necessarily equate with guilt, and a lack of deviant sexual interest does not necessarily equate with innocence. The relevant issue is whether examinees can fake or inhibit sexual arousal and, in doing so, disguise their sexual interests. There are a number of possible explanations for inhibited arousal (i.e., nonresponding), such as anxiety, disgust, disinterest, or old age, but deliberate misrepresentation is potentially the greatest threat to the validity of the procedure.

Freund (1971) concluded early that due to the susceptibility of the PPG to faking, it was only appropriate for use with men who admitted their sexual interests. For example, Freund, Chan, and Coulthard (1979), using the PPG to assess men with pedophilic (attraction to prepubescent children) or hebephilic (attraction to postpubescent adolescents) interests, misdiagnosed more than 30% of nonadmitters but only 5% of admitters. More recently, Seto and colleagues (2000) found that nonadmitters scored significantly lower than admitters on the PPG.

A few studies have reported that the PPG can be used effectively in the assessment of nonad-mitters as well as admitters (e.g., Becker, Hunter, Stein, & Kaplan, 1989; Blanchard, Racansky, & Steiner, 1986; Haywood et al., 1990). However, two problems with these studies make their results difficult to interpret: small sample sizes and/or a failure to report interpretive statistics. Because of small sample size, lack of significance in these studies could be due to the absence of an effect or simply to a lack of statistical power. Compounding this problem, the quantitative data needed for making this distinction were not reported. A likely reason for the absence of such information is that these studies were not designed to answer the question of present interest; that is, whether the PPG can accurately diagnose the sexual interest of nonadmitters as well as admitters.

One method of studying whether the PPG can successfully diagnose the sexual interests of nonadmitters is by asking research participants to deliberately fake sexual interest or disinterest. Hall and colleagues (1988) asked 122 adult male inpatient sex offenders to inhibit all sexual arousal and found that fully 80% were able to do so. A number of other studies on both child molesters and rapists have concluded that many examinees are able to both inhibit sexual arousal to preferred (deviant) stimuli and to create sexual arousal to nonpreferred (prosocial) stimuli (e.g., Hall, 1989; Laws & Holmen, 1978; Wilson, 1998; Wydra, Marshall, Earls, & Barbaree, 1983). Thus most researchers agree that deceiving the PPG is possible. It is of interest whether there might be characteristics within the examinee that relate to the ability to do so, such as general sexual arousability, psychopathy, specific sexual interest, or age. Finally, some researchers have suggested that the volumetric PPG might be less susceptible to deception than the circumferential PPG (Freund et al., 1974; McConaghy, 1999).

Recognizing that faking in PPG assessment is possible and perhaps even common, researchers have examined some of the most common methods examinees use to generate or inhibit arousal. For example, Blanchard (1980; as cited in Langevin, 1988) asked heterosexual male research participants to fake arousal to children and nonarousal to adults. Participants' self-reported methods for faking were described as either avoiding looking at the stimulus or generating alternative thoughts. Quinsey and Chaplin (1988b) used a semantic tracking task to prevent examinees from diverting their attention from the erotic stimuli. Their study demonstrated that faking was much more difficult for participants when being forced to attend to the experimental stimuli in this manner.

Other studies have investigated physical signs that are correlated with faking. Freund, Watson, and Rienzo (1988) observed pedophilic sexual offenders performing abdominal movements referred to as "pumping" when viewing erotic stimuli of adult women. These movements appeared to be self-stimulation that was intended to increase arousal to socially appropriate erotic stimuli. Wilson (1998) found a significant correlation between pulse rate and faking on the PPG in a group of heterosexual participants who were asked to fake pedophilic interests. These studies suggest possible relationships between test responses and physical movement or physiological reactions, which might then be considered to signal faking.

Conclusions

Regarding the validity of the PPG in classifying individuals according to their sexual interest, the conclusion of earlier reviews still stands, namely, that "classification of sex offenders is not particularly accurate using these data" (Sewell & Salekin, 1997, p. 347) and that individual PPG classification rates are insufficient for use in legal settings (Murphy & Peters, 1992). In view of these conclusions, it would seem somewhat irrelevant to consider the accuracy of the PPG under conditions of defensiveness, whether deliberate or nondeliberate. Two of the major limitations of the PPG, recognized years ago (Howes, 1995; Schouten & Simon, 1992), are the lack of standardization and adequate reliability. These limitations still remain to be adequately addressed in the literature. More recently, Marshall and Fernandez (2000, 2001) wrote of the serious limitations due to lack of standardization and reviewed several studies that showed rather unsatisfactory data on reliability. Another serious impediment to accuracy is the relative failure to study different sex offenders separately. The few studies that have done so have shown differences among specific groups, suggesting the potential for improvement in accuracy through a more tailored approach.

In view of the preceding conclusions, it would seem somewhat irrelevant to address the question of success in identifying deception on the PPG. However, we find no reason to disagree with the statements of Marshall and Fernandez, (2000, 2001), who concluded that "numerous studies have shown that rapists and child molesters are able to both inhibit arousal to preferred stimuli and generate arousal to nonpreferred stimuli" (2000, p. 811). Also, although two studies reported procedures aimed specifically at preventing faking, it appears difficult either to prevent it or to detect it when it occurs.

A major limitation is the absence of PPG studies on truthful nonadmitters, as the critical comparison for practical utility is between accused nonadmitters who are truthful and those who are deceptive. Thus the question as to whether the PPG can distinguish guilty and innocent nonadmitters remains unanswered. The methodology for conducting such studies is logically straightforward, though logistically somewhat onerous. Nevertheless, such studies have been successfully performed in other areas of assessment and are discussed later in this chapter.

The authors draw attention to the obvious complexity of performing a PPG assessment, including the need for elaborate instrumentation, extensive training, and an unusual interpersonal interaction. It is also complicated by the lack of standardized procedures for both administration and scoring. When this is compared with the simplicity of most nonphysiological procedures, it would seem clear that the onus is on proponents of the PPG to demonstrate that their method is sufficiently more effective to compensate for its disadvantages.

Abel Assessment of Sexual Interest

The Abel Assessment of Sexual Interest (AASI) involves a two-part procedure that includes both a questionnaire and a behavioral task (Abel et al., 1998; Fischer & Smith, 1999; Krueger, Bradford, & Glancy, 1998). The first part consists of a self-report questionnaire that covers sexual history and related topics. The second part is somewhat analogous to the plethysmograph, but instead of penile arousal, it involves the use of both visual reaction and viewing time. While the computer records viewing time, each person is asked to rate 135 slides on a scale of 1 through 7, according to how each is perceived, from highly sexually disgusting through highly sexually arousing. Two sets of scores are generated: one based on viewing time for each slide and a second based on the individual's subjective ratings of disgust versus arousal.

Scoring and interpretation of the AASI are proprietary and are available only by sending the raw data to the test author. Details are not available on the development, norms, or validity of any section of the test. The process by which the raw data are scored, normed, or converted to clinical interpretations is not accessible for review. Abel and colleagues (1998) compared AASI viewing time with penile plethysmograph and concluded that both methods of assessment had high validity. But in a detailed examination of the viewing time measure, Fischer and Smith (1999) concluded that "its use with adults is tenuous at best" (p. 195). A study on its utility with adolescents also showed negative results (Smith & Fischer, 1999). Two further studies (Abel et al., 2004; Letourneau, 2002) showed results that were not much of an improvement over chance. Overall, these findings indicate that, at the least, further research with the AASI is needed before its potential for assessing deviant sexual interests can be known.

As previously reported for the questionnaire section, no AASI research could be found that (1) utilized accused nonadmitters or (2) examined deliberate faking on the test. Thus the ability of the viewing time procedure to detect deceptive respondents is unknown.

TRUTHFULNESS REGARDING SPECIFIC ACTS

It is never the responsibility of experts to offer forensic opinions as to whether a defendant committed a specific criminal act. Such testimony would rarely, if ever, be permitted. However, there are two separate sets of circumstances under which this question is legitimately asked. One is in a practical situation, in which an attorney, for purposes of case preparation, is seeking information to support the defendant's insistence that he or she is innocent. The other is in formal treatment programs, now operating in many states, that (rightly or wrongly) believe that the resident must "come clean" with regard to all past sexual behaviors, whether deviant or not, in order to make progress toward successful rehabilitation. In both of these settings, and particularly in the second, it is common to employ the traditional polygraph procedure in the hope and/or expectation of establishing the truth.

The Polygraph

In contrast to most of the other assessment procedures described in this chapter, the polygraph is explicitly a test for detecting deception that has been put to use with sex offenders. The polygraph has long been touted to the public as an unfaltering measure of deception. However, its acceptance in the courts and in the scientific community has been decidedly less positive. In Chapter 15 in this volume, Iacono and Patrick provide a critical analysis of the polygraph and its different methodologies. They detail a scientific review conducted by the National Academies of Science (NAS) on its accuracy and usefulness (National Research Council, 2003).

Several writers have questioned the polygraph's ability to detect deception by sex offenders. Ekman (2001) warned that autonomic arousal varies depending on a number of factors, such as the perpetrator's feelings about the crime. It is possible that sex offenders' tendency to rationalize and minimize their offenses (i.e., an anxiety-reducing cognitive strategy) would make them difficult to detect on the polygraph (Cross & Saxe, 1992). However, this suggestion was challenged by Williams (1995), who argued that the minimization strategies of sex offenders are no different nor more effective than those of other criminal offenders.

A less controversial use of the polygraph is for the detection of deception in the postconviction monitoring of offenders. In a wellknown study, Sigall and Page (1971) demonstrated that attaching participants to a fictitious lie detection device with alleged excellent accuracy (i.e., a "bogus pipeline") resulted in more truthful responding. This concept of influencing people to confess via the use of technological subterfuges has become standard practice in many regions of the United States. Bolstered by civil commitment laws for sex offenders passed in 16 U.S. states (Miller et al., 2005), many agencies currently use the polygraph both as a means of deciding whether parole should be granted and in the subsequent monitoring of sex offenders (Branaman & Gallagher, 2005; Grubin & Madsen, 2005).

The polygraph is used in this manner with sex offenders because of its ability to elicit confessions and admissions of additional criminal activity. For example, English, Jones, Pasini-Hill, Patrick, and Cooley-Towell (2000) described the remarkable differences in the responses of 180 offenders before and after postconviction polygraph testing:

- 80% increase in the number of offenders admitting to male victims
- 190% increase in the number of offenders admitting to both male and female victims
- 230% increase in admission of both juvenile and adult victims
- 204% increase in admissions of hands-off offenses
- 196% increase in admission of more than one kind of high-risk behavior.

Thus the monitoring of sex offenders with the aid of the polygraph led to an enormous increase in admission of problematic behavior. A study by Ahlmeyer, Heil, McKee, and English (2000) offered a consistent but more complex conclusion that polygraph monitoring increased postconviction admissions of the number of both sexual offenses and victims.

The implicit assumption underlying this procedure is that greater admission of offenses will result in better therapeutic outcomes for the offenders. However, Kokish (2003) warned that no studies have yet demonstrated that posttreatment recidivism rates are lower for offenders who were monitored with the polygraph than for those who were not.

There is good reason to believe that as long as criminals remain convinced that the polygraph can accurately detect deception (i.e., if the integrity of the "bogus pipeline" is maintained), they will be more likely to admit to their offenses. But some critics have warned that the coercive nature of the polygraph might have the unintended consequence of creating false confessions (Cross & Saxe, 1992, 2001). At least one study (Kokish, Levenson, & Blasingame, 2005) has confirmed the tenability of this suggestion, as an anonymous survey of sex offenders monitored with the polygraph suggested that about 5% had admitted to crimes they had not committed. With these concerns in mind, a number of authors have been cognizant of the potential misuse of postconviction polygraph monitoring and have suggested ethical guidelines for practitioners (Blasingame, 1998; Kokish, 2003).

In conclusion, research on the polygraph as a means of eliciting the truth varies widely in its findings. However, its utility within the framework of a "bogus pipeline" (i.e., the ex-

aminee believes in its accuracy) has been demonstrated in several studies regarding the postconviction rehabilitation of sex offenders.

Can the polygraph itself be foiled? In other words, can deceivers deceive the test designed to detect deception? Reviews of the literature on this topic disagree. For example, Saxe, Dougherty, and Cross (1985) concluded that it was quite possible to do so. On the other hand, Raskin (1989) concluded that the literature showed mixed results. In any case, we were unable to find any relevant studies with sex offenders about their ability to foil the polygraph.

RISK ASSESSMENT: THE PREDICTION OF RECIDIVISM

In the present context, risk assessment refers to the probability that the offender will commit another offense in the future. This question has generated a large volume of research literature over the past 15 years, concentrating on the identification of empirical predictors and their combination into composite variables to be correlated with the presence or absence of another sexual offense within a set length of time, such as 6 or 10 years. Three such instruments are the Sex Offender Risk Appraisal Guide (SORAG; Quinsey, Harris, Rice, & Cormier, 1998), the Minnesota Sex Offender Screening Tool—Revised (MnSOST-R; Epperson, Kaul, Huot, Goldman, & Alexander, 2003), and the Static-99 (Hanson & Thornton, 1999), an extension of the earlier Rapid Risk Assessment for Sexual Offense Recidivism (RRASOR; Hanson, 1997).

These instruments (and the individual items of which they are composed) have become increasingly popular in forensic assessments and are the subject of a considerable amount of research. Indeed, a recent meta-analysis by Hanson and Morton-Bourgon (2005) was able to identify 82 studies with 1,620 findings based on 29,450 offenders. However, the strength of the validity findings tends not to be proportionate to the enthusiasm of the researchers. Correlations vary considerably but overall are quite modest, rarely exceeding .30 (see also Hanson & Thornton, 2000; Nunes, Firestone, Bradford, Greenberg, & Broom, 2002). Reasons for these modest showings and other criticisms of this endeavor have been offered by Rogers and Jackson (2005) and by Sreenivasan, Kirkish, Garrick, Weinberger, and Phenix (2000).

The issue for this chapter is the extent to which these measures can be faked. Because they depend almost entirely on historical or biographical data, they would appear to be impervious to defensiveness, provided the data are collected from sources other than the offenders. The recent interest in including "dynamic" variables (e.g., Thornton, 2002) that can change over time (such as the successful completion of a sex offender treatment program while incarcerated) does not alter this conclusion provided such data are gathered objectively.

SEXUALLY VIOLENT PREDATOR (SVP) EVALUATIONS

The 1997 Supreme Court decision in *Kansas v. Hendricks* (1997) opened an entirely new area of assessment in sex offending. This case upheld a Kansas law establishing postincarceration civil commitment procedures for sex offenders who were considered to be still dangerous. As of 2004, 16 states had adopted legislation of this nature (Miller et al., 2005), and, with some minor variations, they all required the following criteria: (1) conviction of a sexually violent offense; (2) a mental disorder or abnormality that made the person likely to commit further such acts; and (3) based on the mental disorder, lack of ability to control such behaviors (Rogers & Shuman, 2005). A number of sources have provided a detailed analysis of the practical implications of this case in performing what have come to be known as SVP evaluations (e.g., Doren, 2002; Miller et al., 2005; Rogers & Shuman, 2005; Schlank, 2001). We next review methods for evaluating each of the three required elements in regard to their capacity for distortion through defensiveness.

Sexually Violent Offense

The offenses are essentially a matter of record, based on the specifics of the conviction. There can be some ambiguity when the defendant has plea-bargained to a lesser offense, but the decision is still made on the basis of the police and court records, without the opportunity for distorting input from the offender.

Mental Abnormality

SVP determinations generally require the presence of a mental abnormality or, in some states,

a mental disorder (Rogers & Shuman, 2005). The term *abnormality*, rather than *disorder*, is used to dictate a requirement for involuntary commitment that is less stringent than the diagnosis of a formal mental disorder. In this context, abnormality is generally defined in rather vague terms as an emotional or volitional impairment that predisposes the sex offender to reoffend (Doren, 2002). But in the absence of mainstream recognition of this concept or a more workable definition (Rogers & Shuman, 2005), its assessment cannot logically be addressed.

The concept of a formal mental disorder is much more in line with the assessment capabilities of clinicians. SVP designations that refer to mental disorder generally require the assignment of a DSM-IV diagnosis of a paraphilia that relates to a sex crime or a personality disorder. Regarding the latter, the diagnosis of antisocial personality disorder is sometimes used as a basis or partial basis for satisfying this criterion. The fact that rape is not a DSM-IV paraphilia is sometimes dealt with by using the "not otherwise specified" category—a move of doubtful legitimacy but one that tends not to be successfully challenged. To the extent that the criteria for paraphilia are behavioral, observable, and already documented, there is little opportunity for distortion by the offender during this aspect of the assessment procedure; and, clearly, past records play a major role in such diagnoses. The various procedures for assessing deviant sexual interests, discussed earlier, are also directly relevant in this context. It should be obvious that few sex offenders voluntarily acknowledge the presence of the internal (cognitive and affective) criteria that can be diagnostic of pedophilia. The use of the Psychopathy Checklist—Revised (PCL-R; Hare, 1991) is a popular procedure for assessing antisocial personality disorder. The PCL-R, too, can be scored from archival records provided they are comprehensive. However, PCL research suggests that delinquents can substantially lower clinician ratings of both core features and lifestyle traits (Rogers, Vitacco, et al., 2002).

Ability to Control

The volitional requirement was clarified in a subsequent case of the U.S. Supreme Court (*Kansas v. Crane,* 2002) and indicates that the deviant behavior must result from a lack of control based on the mental disorder, rather than being a volitional choice made by the perpetrator. The issue of what constitutes lack of self-control in this context and how to assess it has been discussed by several authors (e.g., Doren, 2002; Janus, 2001; Miller et al., 2005) but without much that is conclusive. Janus (2001) has argued that "inability to control" should be construed very narrowly and carefully, whereas Doren (2002) has taken the position that, at least for some paraphilias, inability to control is simply part of the disorder. Rogers and Shuman (2005) have outlined four issues that should be addressed in the assessment of volition: lack of deliberate choice (i.e., whether the sex offender exercised choices and made plans), disregard for personal consequences, incapacity for delay, and chronicity. They have presented a detailed plan for conducting such assessments.

To establish volitionality, one source of evidence could be the person's historical ability to delay gratification, especially as it relates to delinquent or antisocial behavior. Relevant topics for inquiry could include, on the one hand, ADHD and impulse disorders and, on the other, a history of completing school coursework despite competing pressures or sustaining employment in circumstances in which it was difficult to do so. Another consideration would be the presence of physiological conditions, such as brain injury, which might serve to disinhibit acting-out behaviors. Of course, the crux of the issue is a specific loss of volitionality for sexual reoffending. Rogers and Shuman (2005) have pointed out two fundamental differences between the definitions of volitional impairment in the SVP context and in insanity statutes that include a volitional component: The former typically require a less complete loss of behavioral control and refer to behavior that is repetitive over time.

What about the offender's ability to successfully deceive the evaluator regarding volitionality? As there are no agreed-upon tools or procedures to use in making the assessment of "ability to control" for sex offenders, it is premature to ask the question of whether any such procedures can be successfully circumvented. Practitioners must necessarily rely on general clinical information and historical background, which do not usually offer sufficient empirically based data for the necessary complex judgments regarding deceptiveness in these specific situations. However, it is reasonable to conclude that traditional methods for assessing deceptiveness in general can be of significant use.

VICTIM TRUTHFULNESS

This chapter would not be complete without addressing the other side of the coin—the assessment of truthfulness by those who accuse others of sex offending. The literature on this topic almost exclusively addresses sex offending against children. This literature was spurred by the introduction of the "child sexual abuse accommodation syndrome" (Summit, 1983), which represented the position that children are always truthful in their initial claims that they have been molested but often withdraw accusations in the face of family and other pressures. Summit's (1983) article drew a spate of responses detailing the circumstances in which and possible reasons that a child's report of sexual abuse might indeed be untruthful. An analysis by Ceci and Bruck (1993) of this and other literature on children's truthfulness led to their conclusion that "children sometimes lie when the motivational structure is tilted toward lying" (p. 433). This conclusion applies to both suggestibility and unintentional distortions, as well as to deliberate lying (see Salekin et al., Chapter 20, this volume).

A number of procedures have been proposed for evaluating a child's truthfulness regarding sexual abuse allegations. Bow, Quinnell, Zaroff, and Assemany (2002) presented an elaborate framework for assessing sexual abuse allegations in the context of child custody cases. The most important aspect of this wide-ranging evaluation is the interview of the alleged child victim by a carefully trained interviewer following a highly structured protocol proposed by Kuehnle (1996) and Poole and Lamb (1998). Other relevant sources of data include the nature, sequence, and circumstances of the allegation(s), a careful review of available records, the alleged perpetrator's sexual history, collateral contacts, and psychological testing when appropriate. Lipian, Mills, and Brantman (2004) have offered additional clinical information in this area. Although there is some research literature on the assessment of the truthfulness of children's statements when they are interviewed by an interviewer following a structural protocol (see Lanyon, 1993a), we emphasize that, again, this is ultimately a clinical judgment task to be taken on by professionals who are well-trained both in psychological assessment and in the field of sex offending.

GENERAL DISCUSSION

As stated at the beginning of this chapter, we agree with Langevin (1988) and Sewell and Salekin (1997) about the dearth of methodologically sound research that has generated encouraging conclusions regarding the assessment of deception in the domain of sex offending. Several recent assessment procedures have been reviewed, including the AASI and the MSI-II. Unfortunately, the published research on the AASI is not encouraging, and very little relevant published research is available on the MSI-II. With both measures, details of the development of these instruments remain unpublished. For the AASI, scoring and interpretation procedures are proprietary. This lack of accessibility renders it impossible for other researchers to evaluate these measures rigorously. Likewise, this lack of accessibility is ethically problematic because practitioners cannot determine of the validity of the interpretations (see Ethical Standard 9.09; American Psychological Association, 2002). Regarding the PPG, the lack of standardization of the procedures, noted years ago, remains a serious impediment.

One exception to this otherwise dismal state of affairs is the use of the polygraph in treatment settings to encourage acknowledgment of prior offenses. Whether or not this procedure is helpful in treatment, the client's belief in the accuracy of the instrument (i.e., the bogus pipeline effect) has been shown to lead to acknowledgment of past offenses well beyond what was previously acknowledged.

In general, a comparison of the procedures discussed in this chapter with the *Standards* (AERA/APA/NCME, 1999) shows that most assessment procedures in sex offending fall short of what is considered appropriate practice in psychology. Beyond methodological limitations detailed in the introduction to this chapter, an early and obsolete view of sex offending still has a disproportionate influence on the field, namely, that there is a single underlying cause, a "disease" called sexual psychopathology (Ellis, 1942; Freud, 1953; Krafft-Ebing, 1965). Most persons with the disease are infected at a very young age, whereas others become infected through procedures such as Internet pornography. Although no longer stated explicitly, this view still holds sway. For example, it gives rise to the untenable position that all sex offenders should be studied as a single group, despite the fact that this approach has led to findings that are much less specific than they would be if individual types of offenders were considered separately. Thus the opportunities for higher validities that are potentially available by studying homogeneous groups are lost.

An example of this one-size-fits-all approach can be seen in large-scale recidivism studies in which heterogeneous data are pooled regardless of the nature of the offense (e.g., Hanson & Morton-Bourgon, 2005). Because any assessment tool needs to be understood and validated before its susceptibility to distortion through defensiveness can be studied, research on deceptiveness is also negatively affected by this view. Sewell and Salekin (1997) offered a similar criticism in regard to the validity of PPG assessment, which "must be separately established for specific paraphilias and rape" (p. 341). Some initial steps have recently been taken in this direction (e.g., Blanchard et al., 2001, 2006).

We now return to an issue raised initially in this chapter, namely, that the most important assessment question related to deception in sex offending is whether we can distinguish between guilty and innocent nonadmitters. Several studies illustrate sound designs that could be used for this critical comparison. For detecting malingered psychosis in a court-related setting, Cornell and Hawk (1989) used follow-up information and a retrospective case conference with cases of honest and feigned psychosis. These authors retrospectively coded and analyzed case records and were able to identify characteristics that could have distinguished between the two conditions. A similar strategy was employed by Lanyon (1993b) in constructing a detection procedure for "erroneous psychiatric stereotype"; it distinguished between persons with genuine and feigned disorders. Using a known-groups comparison, Chapman and Brena (1990) adopted a similar strategy in a study on chronic back pain. A retrospective analysis of nursing notes and other available records identified useful discriminators.

Applying this research strategy to sex offenders would involve defining the condition to be studied as the absence of a true condition (e.g., the absence of pedophilic characteristics) rather than the presence of a condition (e.g., chronic pain). Participants would be individuals accused of sexual offenses who deny having the condition (i.e., nonadmitters). As with the Cornell and Hawk (1989) study, many of these participants could eventually be classified as truthful or untruthful based on subsequent data. The two groups would then be retrospectively compared on data that were originally available in order to identify variables that distinguished those who were subsequently determined to have probably been truthful from those who probably were not. Such data could potentially involve questionnaire responses, PPG data, biographical information, or information sources. Studies of this type are completely feasible, but to our knowledge, none has been attempted.

It is important to acknowledge that the level of accuracy achievable by the available procedures for assessing variables relevant to sex offending is quite low, despite some enthusiastic claims to the contrary. Because the public demands that prosecutors and judges make few false-negative errors (i.e., not convicting guilty offenders), cut scores, whether qualitative or quantitative, are set at a low level, thereby miscategorizing many truthful nonadmitters as deceptive and guilty (i.e., false positives). The dire consequences of false accusation and erroneous convictions make it particularly important that improved methods be developed for distinguishing guilty and honest nonadmitters.

THRESHOLD MODEL

The question posed in this section asks what cues or circumstances should be utilized by the clinician in determining that a particular accused man should be assessed for possible deception. Consistent with the conclusions of Langevin (1988) and Sewell and Salekin (1997), it would seem clear that this question should be addressed in all cases of accused sex offending. An exception might be made in cases in which the accused offender admits the offense in question and also acknowledges other deviant sexual interests. The findings of Marshall, Barbaree, and Eccles (1991) are of interest in this regard. These authors used a variety of procedures to increase the validity of self-reports and found that, in contrast to the popular belief that sex offenders have multiple

paraphilias (e.g., Abel, Becker, Cunningham-Rathner, Mittelman, & Rouleau, 1988), most of the men they studied reported only one.

TOWARD A DECISION MODEL

This review has considered five areas of assessment within the general domain of sex offending. Practical suggestions stemming from the review of each are now considered. We repeat that the focus here is on making an accurate assessment of nonadmitters.

1. *Deviant sexual interests.* No evidence was found that self-report questionnaires are valid for nonadmitters. The majority of the literature on this topic concerned the PPG, but the research shows little or no methodologically sound evidence that this procedure enables sufficiently valid assessments even with admitters, let alone nonadmitters. There is evidence that many nonadmitters can "beat" the PPG when specifically motivated to do so. The visual reaction time section of the AASI is a creative attempt to assess responses (relative viewing time) of which the person is probably unaware. But once again, there is inadequate positive research evidence even for admitters, let alone for sexually deviant persons who are attempting to be deceptive.

2. *Truthfulness regarding specific acts.* Putting aside the excessive claims for the accuracy of the polygraph propagated by commercial interests, some initial evidence indicates that respondents who believe in the accuracy of the polygraph procedure do in fact acknowledge many more prior instances of sexual deviance than they do when not connected to this "bogus pipeline." These data were obtained in the context of treatment settings rather than trial-related situations, in which the use of polygraph evidence is subject to significant legal constraints.

3. *Risk assessment.* The procedures developed over the past 15 years or so for the prediction of future sex crimes are based on biographical data and other verifiable aspects of the person's recent life. Therefore, the question of deception arises only minimally, and what relatively modest predictive validity can be obtained using these instruments is not affected by attempts at deception.

4. *SVP evaluations.* In general, there are three relevant aspects to be assessed in this

area. *Conviction of a sexually violent offense* is a matter of public record. *Presence of a mental disorder or abnormality* making the person likely to commit further such acts and the *lack of ability to control* such behavior are primarily a matter of data-based clinical judgment by the evaluator, and the defendant has relatively little control over this process. Attempts at deception are obviously possible; however, traditional methods of assessing deception are applicable and have a reasonable basis in empirical validity.

5. *Victim truthfulness.* Once again, there is reasonable support in the clinical literature, although not backed by empirical data, that deception in claiming to have been the victim of a sex offense can often be accurately detected.

CONCLUSIONS

Aspects of sex offender assessment that rely mainly on general clinical procedures involving structured interviews, standardized tests, and biographical data are difficult to feign, because of mainstream factors such as the application of established validity scales and the detection of internal contradictions through multiple data sources. But these measures are limited in their ability to assess sexual deviance. Unfortunately, instruments developed and tailored specifically for the assessment of deviant sexuality have not fared well, either in demonstrations of basic validity or in their susceptibility to deception. These conclusions are highly consistent with past reviews of the literature.

18

Structured Interviews and Dissimulation

RICHARD ROGERS, PhD

Standardized interview-based assessments are serving an increasingly important role for diagnostic and other clinical purposes (Rogers, 2001). In diagnosing DSM-IV disorders, clinicians have three basic choices: extrapolated, unstandardized, and standardized diagnoses. Although psychological tests yield valuable clinical information, their results yield only extrapolated diagnoses that typically lack sufficient accuracy (Rogers & Shuman, 2005). For example, elevated test scores for depression (e.g., Minnesota Multiphasic Personality Inventory–2 [MMPI-2] Scale 2 and the Rorschach Depression Index) are not specific to depression per se but are observed in a range of DSM-IV disorders. Unstandardized diagnoses based on traditional interviews also have limited accuracy; they have major problems with both misdiagnoses and missed diagnoses (Rogers, 2003). Using major depression again as an example, missed diagnoses are likely to exceed 50% in both medical and mental health settings (Rogers & Shuman, 2005). Because of these limitations of extrapolated and unstandardized diagnoses, the use of structured interviews has gained prominence in the past decade.

Structured interviews standardize the assessment process. Focusing on Axis I and II disorders, these interviews standardize the clinical inquiries and the organization of inquiries (e.g., the order of questions and use of optional probes). In addition, structured interviews standardize the clinical ratings and overall scoring. They provide criteria for rating the presence and severity of symptoms and associated features. This standardization not only facilitates reliable diagnoses but also provides an opportunity for the systematic evaluation of response styles.

INCONSISTENCIES AND DISCREPANCIES IN DATA SOURCES

The major focus of this chapter, consistent with its title, is the assessment of response styles using structured interviews. However, conclusions from structured interviews are often informed by clinical data from two other sources: unstandardized interviews and collateral sources. Therefore, this chapter begins with a consideration of inconsistencies and discrepancies in these sources.

Unstandardized Interviews and Response Styles

Comprehensive evaluations typically combine structured and traditional (i.e., unstandardized) interviews in their assessment of diagnostic and referral issues. Because of their unstandardized nature, traditional interviews provide unmatched flexibility for establishing rapport and gathering relevant background information. In addressing referral issues, the flexibility of traditional interviews is essential in seeking to understand complex issues, such as motivation, treatment amenability, and disability status.

Sources of Inconsistencies

Unstandardized interviews may yield inconsistent information from the same examinee that appears conflicting, if not contradictory. Moreover, such interview-based information may be markedly discrepant with other data sources. How should these inconsistencies and discrepancies be understood?

- Do they represent general deception or a specific response style?
- Alternatively, are these disparities by-products of genuine disorders and their effects on insight and self-appraisal?
- Are they affected by contextual factors?

Before addressing these issues, the section examines the potential sources of inconsistencies that are common to unstandardized interviews. In other words, inconsistencies may be explainable by the methodology. As noted, the greatest strength and limitation of traditional interviews is their flexibility. Rogers (1997a) observed three potential sources of inconsistencies that are inherent in traditional interviews:

1. *Differences in the wording of clinical inquiries.* An examinee may simply misunderstand the meaning of a question. As an obvious example of potential confusion, a literal understanding of the following interview question should always be answered affirmatively: "Do you hear voices?" With this inquiry, however, the question about voices is a shorthand expression regarding perceptual disturbances. Still, the response may be variable depending on the examinee's insight and interpretation (e.g., illusions or hallucinations).

2. *The sequencing of questions.* In the flow of traditional interviews, responses are likely influenced by earlier questions and answers. As an obvious example, personally intrusive questions (e.g., marital compatibility) may yield very different responses if asked at the onset of a consultation or after rapport has been firmly established.

3. *The recording of questions and responses.* Many practitioners do not record verbatim responses but simply their conclusions based on the available information. For the example in #1, "hearing voices" may be recorded as "auditory hallucinations." Summary information may be recorded differently depending on diagnostic impressions (e.g., PTSD flashbacks). Because the questions are almost never recorded, the context of the response is lost.

Reasons for Inconsistencies and Disparities

Inconsistent responding on unstandardized interviews could reflect the imprecision of the clinical inquiries, their sequencing, and the recorded responses. If a prominent pattern of inconsistencies emerges, however, practitioners must collect additional data using detection strategies and closely consider alternative explanations. For instance, the subsequent reporting of previously unmentioned psychotic symptoms could reflect (1) a greater willingness for self-disclosure, (2) additional insight as a result of treatment (e.g., medication or therapy), (3) a genuine exacerbation of symptoms, (4) a response to treatment "cues" from providers (e.g., "your plan only reimburses . . ."), or (5) deliberate feigning. To avoid biased decision making, practitioners should always consider competing hypotheses (see, e.g., *Specialty Guidelines for Forensic Psychologists,* Committee on Ethical Guidelines for Forensic Psychologists, 1991). Rival hypotheses should include genuine (i.e., 1, 2, and 3), contextual (i.e., 4), and intentional (i.e., 5) considerations.

Patients with poor insight into their disorders can often be identified by open-ended inquiries and a concomitant review of clinical records. In contrast, abbreviated consultations, implicitly premised on patient insight, can lead to tragic misconclusions. As an extreme but true example, a mentally disordered male inmate on death row lacked insight into his long-standing mental health problems on a brief, routine check. Despite extensive documentation of unremitting delusions and hallucinations spanning more than two decades, his lack of insight was accepted at face value (i.e., no acknowledged symptoms) and used as key evidence of his "adjustment" that resulted in his eventual execution.

Contextual issues can also significantly affect an examinee's presentation. In disability cases, Samra and Koch (2002) described the "lexogenic effects" of prolonged litigation on the clinical status of claimants. In this same vein, Rogers and Payne (2006) described how some examinees may construe insurance-required evaluations as questioning their credibility. Their clinical presentation may be slanted by their efforts to *prove their disability status* or risk losing their benefits. This slanted presentation is substantively different from malingering; it is not present with treatment providers but is only observed in the context of a mandatory consultation for determining the nature and severity of their disabilities.

Regarding contextual issues, Beck and Strong (1982) conducted a classic study on how clinicians' feedback altered clients' presentations. Using impression management theory, they provided feedback with either positive or negative connotations. For example, *being alone* could be construed negatively as an "avoidance and rejection of others" (p. 553) or positively as "tolerance for solitude and basic self-satisfaction" (p. 554). A follow-up after only two therapy sessions revealed major differences in levels of reported depression on the Beck Depression Inventory (BDI) as a result of positive versus negative feedback.

Clinical inquiries, especially in an unstandardized format, may also yield positive and negative connotations. For example, questions about parenting in a custody evaluation may elicit different responses depending on their connotations. For instance, clinical inquiries about dating could be construed positively (e.g., an important adjustment following the divorce) or negatively (e.g., burdening the children with additional stress). Examinees are likely to be sensitive to these connotations that are often communicated by the clinician's tone and sequencing of inquiries.[1]

Inconsistency Trap

Some practitioners mistakenly assume that all inconsistencies are evidence of malingering or manipulation. They make two implicit assumptions: (1) examinees deliberately distorted their presentations but (2) they were "tripped up" in attempting to keep their "stories" consistent. These assumptions are completely untenable. First, inconsistencies can reflect the imprecision of the assessment process. Second, persons with mental disorders often have poor insight, which leads to inconsistencies. Third, unimpaired individuals often show some inconsistencies. Fourth, the use of inconsistencies is an

ineffective detection strategy for feigning. As an apt illustration of the latter two points, college students were administered the MMPI twice in a 2-week period. Substantial differences in MMPI profiles were observed, with the majority of 2-point codes being different (Ben-Porath & Butcher, 1989). If these individuals have no apparent motivation to feign, the equation of these inconsistencies with malingering would represent a colossal error.

Rogers and Shuman (2000) described the *inconsistency trap*. This trap occurs when (1) any inconsistencies are wrongly equated with feigning and (2) the absence of inconsistencies is equated with extensive preparation (i.e., manipulation) or high functioning (i.e., the lack of Axis I disorders). It is considered a "trap" because the examinee's presentation is always invalidated.

Malingering and Defensiveness on Unstandardized Interviews

The modifiability of patients' responses to traditional interviews was studied extensively during the 1960s and 1970s. In a classic study, Braginsky and Braginsky (1967) established several experimental conditions for chronic inpatients with schizophrenia, including continued placement on an open unit (desirable goal) or immediate discharge (undesirable goal). Psychiatric ratings of audiotaped interviews found that patients could minimize their impairment ($d = 1.67$) and need for hospital restrictions ($d = 1.03$). Sherman, Trief, and Strafkin (1975) used a more refined design that examined which symptoms were the easiest to manipulate when day-treatment patients were asked to malinger a severe mental disorder or to be defensive and respond as a normal person would. Surprisingly, patients with greater impairment were more effective than their healthier counterparts at denying most Axis I symptoms ($d = .58$). For malingering, substantial proportions ($\geq 25\%$) feigned anxiety, suicide, and psychotic symptoms. As an interesting side note, Watson (1975) tested whether Veterans' Administration (VA) patients' adeptness at impression management was associated with secondary gain (i.e., their level of VA compensation). Unexpectedly, the small but significant correlations ($rs < .20$) were in the *opposite* direction, providing no support for this hypothesis.

An extensive body of research has examined the use of impression management during preemployment interviews. Impression management strategies can either be "assertive" (i.e., promoting a favorable impression via ingratiation and self-promotion) or "defensive" (i.e., repairing or protecting one's self-image via excuses and justifications). Testing with structured interview formats, Ellis, West, Ryan, and DeShon (2002) found that assertive tactics were used far more commonly than defensive methods among job applicants. Importantly, trained observers had only moderate correlations ($M r = .56$) with self-reported assertive management strategies. Impression management tactics influence hiring recommendations and decisions; they may even outweigh relevant background variables (e.g., work experience and grade point average). Although personnel selection is beyond the scope of this chapter, its conceptualization of impression management is sophisticated and studied systematically in other professional settings. Ellis and colleagues outlined the key components:

- Assertive tactics
- Self-promotion: Statements emphasize positive personal qualities, exaggerated achievements, and ability to overcome obstacles.
  - Ingratiation: Statements emphasize commonalities (shared beliefs with the interviewer) or affirmation (praise or flattery expressed to the interviewer).
- Defensive tactics
  - Excuses: Statements deny external responsibility for negative outcomes.
  - Justifications: Statements accept responsibility but minimize the effects of negative outcomes.
  - Apologies: Statements accept responsibility and imply both regret and a commitment to change.

Each facet of impression management should be investigated regarding its effectiveness at (1) avoiding detection and (2) modifying the interviewers' conclusions. As discussed in Chapter 2 in this volume, specific detection strategies should be developed and tested for the identification of impression management and its specific facets.

Detection Strategies and Unstandardized Interviews

Traditional interviews, despite their unstandardized format, can still utilize detection strategies for response styles. Seasoned practitioners can embed clinical inquiries into traditional interviews that use detection strategies, such as rare symptoms and symptom combinations. In this regard, Resnick, West, and Payne (Chapter 7, this volume) provide an excellent example of unusual symptom presentations for posttraumatic stress disorder (PTSD) and related disorders. For example, many individuals with genuine PTSD reexperience the traumatic events in the sequence in which they occurred. Other sequences of events (e.g., reverse order) would be very rare. Practitioners will sometimes rely on clinical sources for examples of unusual symptoms. For instance, the Schedules for Clinical Assessment of Neuropsychiatry (SCAN; World Health Organization, 1994) are an excellent source for obtaining questions regarding unusual perceptual disturbances.

A major requirement in using embedded detection strategies is experience and sophistication on the part of the clinician. The ability to differentiate truly rare symptoms (e.g., <5% of the relevant population) from relatively uncommon (e.g., 10 to 20%) symptoms relies on years of specialized experience. As noted previously, these inquiries must be embedded within the general interview format. Otherwise, a sudden shift to oddly sounding questions is likely to alert examinees to a change in objectives.

Discrepancies in Collateral Sources

Collateral data are typically both incomplete and inaccurate. Most symptoms are not directly observable, and inferences about their presence cannot be independently verified. Often collateral sources attempt to recall what they were told by a particular patient. Obviously, these recollections are not independent of the examinee. Their veridicality depends on the patient's accuracy of reporting and collateral sources' accuracy of recall.

Lidz, Banks, Simon, Schubert, and Mulvey (2007) provide an insightful illustration of the challenges in addressing discrepancies between patients and collateral sources. They focus on violent incidents, which are both observable and highly salient behaviors. Their key findings were twofold:

- When patients reported violent acts, collateral sources corroborated these incidents only 25% of the time.

• When collateral sources reported on the patients' violent acts, they agreed with these patients only 34% of the time.

Major errors are likely to occur if only corroborated acts are considered or if we automatically assume the worst about patients (i.e., that any report of violence is always correct). Germane to the current discussion, considerable disagreement can be found even when sources are focused on observable and highly salient behavior. Care must be taken not to assume that such discrepancies necessarily represent deceptive responses.

Collateral data can provide useful perspectives in understanding examinees and the contexts of their evaluations. In considering these sources, clinicians must take into account the nature of the professional relationship, the adequacy of the assessment methods, and the level of documentation. The next section examines the use of collateral data in the appraisal of response styles.

Collateral Data and Defensiveness

The clearest examples of defensiveness occur when the examinee categorically denies any past mental health history, denial that is controverted by extensive documentation of inpatient or outpatient treatment. Such outright denials typically provide strong evidence of defensiveness. Less obvious but still convincing cases are commonly observed with substance abuse. The client denies any past history of substance abuse; however, repeated laboratory testing reveals an extensive pattern of drug use. Importantly, the comparisons reflect the same time period: retrospective reports compared with past findings.

Defensiveness is often revealed in consistent minimizations rather than outright denials. Because many symptoms have a subjective component, the challenge for clinicians is to focus on quantifiable symptoms and associated features. For example, clients may minimize their past suicidal behaviors by deemphasizing their severity (e.g., "superficial cutting" rather than deep lacerations) or lethality (e.g., "extra pills" rather than an entire prescription). For eating and mood disorders, weight loss is easily quantifiable and readily available in medical records. To establish minimizations, clinicians look for patterns of retrospective reporting that claim markedly less than what has been quantifiably assessed in past documentations.

Patients' emotional experiences regarding past episodes are likely to change over time. For instance, the intense affect associated with hopelessness may lessen as a result of time and clinical interventions. Such changes do not necessarily reflect any deliberate efforts to minimize the intensity of emotions or Axis I symptoms. Especially in a therapeutic context, these changes may signal positive adjustments. Clinicians may wish to explore these differences in patient reporting without making any inferences regarding response styles or deliberate misrepresentations.

The assessment of Axis II disorders is particularly challenging, because patients with personality disorders often lack insight into their symptoms and their effects on other persons. Bernstein, Kasapis, Bergman, and Weld (1997) compared patient and informant accounts on the Structured Interview for DSM-III Personality Disorders (SIDP; Pfohl, Blum, & Zimmerman, 1995). As was true in earlier research, they found poor correspondence between the two data sources. For approximately one-fourth of the discrepancies, informant data contributed significantly to resolving diagnostic issues. As subsequently described, the use of structured interviews is strongly recommended for addressing response styles with patients with Axis II disorders. In the absence of research data, however, only consistent and blatant denial of symptoms should be considered as evidence of defensiveness.

Collateral Data and Malingering

Otto (Chapter 21, this volume) provides valuable information on how third-party information can be used to corroborate or question an examinee's reported impairment. Within the disability context, issues arise regarding the genuineness of reported symptoms and the accuracy of reported impairment. Occasionally, a detailed account of the examinee's activities, compared with reports from one or more collateral sources, will reveal highly discrepant accounts. For instance, the examinee may claim marked loss of concentration secondary to depression. However, a collateral review may reveal a highly sustained focus on non-work-related activities.

Persons feigning disorders may enlist the assistance of collateral sources to corroborate their disorders and concomitant impairment. These "collaborations" are difficult to present convincingly, especially when the collateral interviews rely on standardized questioning that is comprehensive in its coverage. Especially in the case of a cohabitant (e.g., significant other or roommate), confusion or uncertainty in response to straightforward questions is highly atypical. For instance, questions about easily observable and salient behaviors (e.g., heightened startle responses or panic reactions) do not need to be mulled over. Questions about highly salient remarks by the examinee to the collateral source, such as threatening suicide, should not evoke uncertainty. When informants appear to be in alliance with the examinees, clinicians must seek to replace them with more objective sources of collateral data.

Many malingerers do not appear to entertain the possibility that their reported symptoms can be disconfirmed by external sources. In an inpatient evaluation, an examinee may claim pervasive auditory hallucinations that occur in the presence of others. Formal thought disorders are especially difficult to feign. For example, loose associations and tangentiality may be claimed by examinees but never observed by those in frequent contact. As with defensiveness, the key issue is a prominent pattern of unmistakable discrepancies. In the case of malingering, this pattern should consist of fabricated or grossly exaggerated symptoms that can be clearly negated by extensive observations from reliable sources.

STANDARDIZED INTERVIEWS AND RESPONSE STYLES

This section progresses from the broadest clinical uses to specialized applications. It begins with diagnostic interviews and proceeds to forensic interviews and malingering-based interviews.

Overview of Diagnostic Interviews

Standardized Axis I and Axis II interviews are vulnerable, as are all clinical measures, to the effects of specific response styles on clinical data and observations. Especially with personality disorders, important steps have been undertaken to reduce response bias via the refinement of clinical inquiries to address social desirability and reduce item transparency. Using the SIDP-IV as a sophisticated example,

Pfohl, Blum, and Zimmerman (1998) devised many clinical inquiries that provided two alternatives (e.g., more or less likely to express feelings) with similar levels of social desirability. Even when examinees are asked to disclose negative personality characteristics, the SIDP-IV attempts to cast these attributes in a relatively positive light. For example, the exploitative use of others is characterized as "a reputation to do whatever it takes" to achieve a desired goal.

Item transparency must be considered in developing clinical inquiries that are less easily manipulated by examinees in pursuit of a specific response style. As an example related to character pathology, the Psychopathy Checklist —Revised (PCL-R; Hare, 2003) is particularly concerned that offenders may deny core psychopathic features. Therefore, clinical ratings of characteristics such as superficial charm and pathological lying are based on very general questions about personal relationships.

Axis I and Axis II interviews have largely neglected any systematic methods for the detection of response styles. Detection strategies could be used to devise specific methods to evaluate persons engaging in feigned or defensive response styles. Instead, some test developers have added collateral interviews to provide greater assurance regarding the accuracy of the reported clinical data. Clearly, the use of collateral interviews may serve an important role in (1) modulating deliberate distortions and (2) providing useful data on blatant attempts to feign or deny mental disorders. The mere knowledge that practitioners will be corroborating reported symptoms may have a salutary effect on an examinee's forthrightness (Rogers, 1995). Although it requires empirical investigation, this point seems commonsensical.

This section features the Schedule of Affective Disorders and Schizophrenia (SADS; Spitzer & Endicott, 1978) because of the systematic efforts to define and test detection strategies (see Rogers, Chapter 2, this volume). These sections are relatively brief because available research tends to focus on whether the interviews can be faked. Specifically, can individuals modify their responses in the appropriate directions when given experimental conditions for malingering and defensiveness? Use of detection strategies for the classification of response styles is rarely researched for general diagnostic interviews other than the SADS.

Schedule of Affective Disorders and Schizophrenia

SADS research has focused primarily on feigned mental disorders with a compilation of item-level data from several studies. Descriptive information offers some preliminary insights regarding the use of the SADS for the assessment of defensiveness.

SADS and Feigned Mental Disorders

In the second edition of this volume, Rogers (1997d) integrated SADS data from three clinical and clinical-forensic samples and compared these data with those from a small sample of probable malingerers. The current edition distills the more robust findings and augments them with data from the SADS—Change (SADS-C) version. For the SADS itself, the following samples were used:

• *Forensic.* SADS data were available on 104 forensic examinees after cases of suspected malingering were removed. These data are from two university-based forensic clinics: the Isaac Ray Center, Rush Medical School in Chicago, and METFORS, Clarke Institute of Psychiatry, Toronto.
• *Patients with schizophrenia.* SADS data were examined for 90 patients in the active phase of schizophrenia. These patients were involved in a partial hospitalization program following their inpatient stays.
• *Genuinely disordered: Jail mental health referrals.* SADS data were analyzed on 50 mentally disordered offenders at a large metropolitan jail. Most cases were emergency referrals for mental health care. The Structured Interview of Reported Symptoms (SIRS), a highly effective interview that is often used as a gold standard for feigned mental disorders (see the subsequent section on the clinical applications of the SIRS), was used to classify these cases as genuinely disordered.
• *Probable malingerers: Jail mental health referrals.* Using the SIRS classification, SADS data on 22 offenders with a high likelihood of malingering were examined.

Rogers (1997d) investigated five detection strategies for the assessment of feigned mental disorders. They included four well-established strategies summarized in Chapter 2 in this vol-ume: rare symptoms, symptom combinations, symptom severity, and indiscriminant symptom endorsement. In addition, contradictory symptoms were considered.

Contradictory Symptoms

Contradictory symptoms include item pairs with opposite content. On occasion, these may legitimately occur with highly unstable patients, but they are generally not observed in most patient populations. In the current analysis, only two pairs of contradictory symptoms evidenced strong promise: (1) psychomotor retardation and agitation and (2) insomnia and hypersomnia. They occurred in more than 25% of probable malingerers but were comparatively rare among genuine samples. Other contradictory symptom pairs were seldom observed in either genuine patients ($M = 1.9\%$) or probable malingerers ($M = 5.4\%$).

Rare Symptoms

As summarized in Table 18.1, two constellations of rare symptoms were observed: current manic symptoms and unusual psychotic symptoms. Very few patients (< 5%) reported or exhibited current manic symptoms, although they were sometimes reported by probable malingerers ($M = 13.6\%$). In general, manic symptoms (e.g., elevated or euphoric moods) are difficult to simulate for any period of time. Therefore, the examinee's reports can be evaluated against clinical observations.

Certain types of psychotic symptoms are generally infrequent in clinical populations. As noted in Table 18.1, however, patients in an active phase of schizophrenia often report such symptoms as thought withdrawal. Therefore, these comparatively rare symptoms should not be used in cases in which there is clear evidence that the examinee is actively psychotic. The one exception appears to be neologisms, which appear to be extremely rare in all clinical and forensic samples.

Symptom Combinations

This strategy utilizes symptoms that are common by themselves but that rarely occur together. For most SADS symptom combinations, pairs were selected if (1) each individual symptom was commonly reported ($\geq 30\%$) in the

TABLE 18.1. Rare Manic and Psychotic Symptoms on the Schedule of Affective Disorders and Schizophrenia

	Genuinely disordered			
	Forensic	Schiz.	Jail MH	Maling.
Current manic symptoms				
354 Elevated mood (past week)	4.0	0.0	1.9	18.2
356 Less sleep (past week)	2.0	2.2	1.9	13.6
360 Increased activity (past week)	3.1	0.0	1.9	9.1
Psychotic symptoms				
427 Thought withdrawal	2.0	30.0	1.9	36.4
432 Somatic delusions	5.0	16.6	0.0	27.3
515 Neologisms	2.0	0.0	0.0	0.0

Note. Forensic, criminal forensic referrals; Schiz., actively psychotic patients with schizophrenia; Jail MH, mentally disordered offenders with genuine Axis I disorders in a jail setting; Maling., probable malingerers in a jail setting.

forensic sample and (2) both symptoms rarely occurred together (i.e., typically ≤ 10%). Unlike contradictory symptoms that can be rationally identified (i.e., opposite content), symptom combinations are based entirely on clinical patterns that may be difficult for malingerers to identify.

Table 18.2 summarizes the data on symptom combinations. Among genuine groups, small but expected differences were observed. Inmates in crises (i.e., emergency referrals) had slightly more symptom combinations involving psychomotor agitation. Actively psychotic patients had slightly more symptom combinations concerning persecutory delusions. Across all genuine samples, reported symptom combinations occurred in less than 15.0% of the cases.

The strategy of symptom combinations can be used as an effective SADS screen for potential feigning. Using the cut score of ≥ 2 symptom combinations for possible feigning yielded the following estimates:

- 81.8% of probable malingerers were retained for further assessment.
- 77.9% of bona fide cases scored below this cut score.

The SADS symptom combinations strategy proved to be the most effective screen. Clinicians may wish to combine this screen with other strategies to ensure that possible cases of malingering are not overlooked.

Indiscriminant Symptom Endorsement

Some malingerers are nonselective in their reporting of Axis I symptoms. A markedly disproportionate number of reported symptoms is likely to reflect feigning. For SADS Part I, the number of symptoms (worst episode and current week) in the clinical range (≥ 3) was tabulated beginning with item #234. The cut score set ≥ 52 symptoms for possible feigning to minimize false positives. Using this cut score yielded the following:

- 45.5% of probable malingerers met or exceeded this cut score.
- 99% of genuine forensic and jail cases fell below this cut score.
- 95% of genuine patients in an active phase of schizophrenia fell below this cut score.

Symptom Severity

Genuine patients tend to report a relatively small proportion of symptoms on the SADS as "severe" or "extreme" (i.e., ratings ≥ 5). In contrast, some malingerers will report an unrealistically high number of severe symptoms. On SADS Part I, the cut score of ≥ 20 symptoms in the *severe* or *extreme* range (≥ 5) was used to reduce false positives:

- 22.7% of probable malingerers met or exceeded this cut score.

TABLE 18.2. Symptom Combinations on the Schedule of Affective Disorders and Schizophrenia

Symptom combinations	Genuinely disordered			Maling.
	Forensic	Schiz.	Jail MH	
317–239 Appetite and current worrying	8.3	2.2	10.0	40.9
317–243 Appetite and current feelings of inadequacy	7.4	4.4	4.0	22.7
317–245 Appetite and current discouragement	6.5	5.6	8.0	36.4
317–266 Appetite and current psychic anxiety	6.5	3.3	10.0	31.8
317–331 Appetite and current anger	6.5	2.2	4.0	40.9
317–419 Appetite and current distrustfulness	8.3	8.9	6.0	22.7
334–245 Agitation and current discouragement	8.3	6.7	12.0	59.1
334–266 Agitation and current psychic anxiety	9.3	6.7	12.0	40.9
428–239 Persecutory delusions and current worrying	9.3	13.3	0.0	36.4
428–245 Persecutory delusions and current discouragement	9.3	13.3	2.0	31.8
428–313 Persecutory delusions and current insomnia	7.4	7.8	2.0	36.4
428–331 Persecutory delusions and current anger	9.3	11.1	0.0	31.8
332–266 Overt irritability and psychic anxiety	>10.0	8.9	4.0	27.3
341–332 Current agitation and overt irritability	>10.0	3.3	8.0	54.5
419–324 Current distrustfulness and indecisiveness	>10.0	7.8	4.0	18.2

Note. Symptom combinations are organized to facilitate rapid checking. If the patient has not described poor appetite, psychomotor agitation, persecutory delusions, or irritability in the clinical range, then very few symptom combinations are likely to be found. Forensic, criminal forensic referrals; Schiz., actively psychotic patients with schizophrenia; Jail MH, mentally disordered offenders with genuine Axis I disorders in a jail setting; Maling., probable malingerers in a jail setting.

- 99% of genuine forensic and jail cases fell below this cut score.
- 99% of genuine patients in an active phase of schizophrenia fell below this cut score.

A more relaxed cut score of ≥ 16 results in approximately 5% false positives but identifies 31.8% of probable feigners. The strength of symptom severity with a cut score of ≥ 20 involves the identification of probable malingerers. Although not effective as a screen (i.e., it misses 77.3% of probable malingerers), it can provide moderate evidence of likely feigning in a minority of cases.

Clinical Applications

A systematic administration of the SADS that includes the full psychotic section (i.e., not using the psychotic screens) can yield valuable diagnostic data and useful information about possible feigning. The simplest and most effective screen for possible feigning uses symptom combinations with the following cut score:

- *SADS Screen:* Symptom combinations ≥ 2 identified 81.8% of possible malingerers for a more comprehensive evaluation.

For clinical evidence of feigning, three cut scores are proposed that have very low false positive rates (≤ 1%) in the clinical and forensic samples. The combination of multiple strategies increases the confidence in making this determination:

- *SADS Clinical Evidence of Feigning:*
  - Symptom combinations >8
  - Indiscriminant symptom endorsement ≥ 52
  - Symptom severity ≥ 20

These decision rules are categorized as "clinical evidence of feigning." Any determination of malingering or factitious disorders requires the use of multiple methods and preferably relies on multiple detection strategies. Although the current data are very strong, further validation is needed before the SADS scales are used as a primary method for the classification of feigning.

SADS-C and Malingering

The SADS-C is an abbreviated version of the SADS used to assess the presence and severity of key Axis I symptoms. Originally designed to measure change over time, the SADS-C is often used as a brief diagnostic measure to cover essential mood and psychotic symptoms. Rogers, Jackson, Salekin, and Neumann (2003) integrated data from several studies to examine the usefulness of the SADS-C in screening for feigned mental disorders. In a large-scale analysis, 45 probable malingerers were compared with 177 mentally disordered offenders with genuine Axis I symptoms.

The rare-symptom strategy could not be tested with the SADS-C because of a lack of highly infrequent symptoms. Like the SADS, the SADS-C proved relatively ineffective (Cohen's d = .55) with probable malingerers averaging less than one symptom.

The SADS-C Symptom Combinations scale was composed of 11 pairs organized into three symptom constellations: appetite disturbance (228–214, 228–217, 228–220, 228–231, and 228–240), psychomotor agitation (233–217 and 233–220), and delusions (241–214, 241–217, 241–223, and 241–231). Symptom combinations were more effective (d = .81) with relatively few genuine patients having three or more symptom combinations. As a screen, however, the cut score ≥ 1 symptom combinations was the most effective, eliminating 108 of the 177 (61.0%) genuine patients from further consideration. This cut score capitalizes on negative predictive power (NPP) at the cost of positive predictive power (PPP):

- Below cut score: Only 11% of probable malingerers are missed (NPP = .89).
- Above cut score: This designates the need for a full assessment, although only about one-third (PPP = .31) are probable malingerers.

SADS-C Symptom Selectivity (d = 1.06) and Symptom Severity (d = .75) scales demonstrated good discriminability. Of these, Symptom Selectivity (i.e., indiscriminant symptom endorsement) proved the most successful. A cut score of ≥ 10 minimized the number of probable malingerers eluding a comprehensive evaluation:

- Below cut score: Only 7% of probable malingerers are missed (NPP = .93).
- Above cut score: This designates the need for a full assessment, although substantially less than half (PPP = .38) are probable malingerers.

In summary, extensive SADS-C data provide solid support for using two interview-based detection strategies (i.e., symptom combinations and symptom severity) with two of the strategies closely paralleling the full SADS. In addition, 10 or more SADS-C items in the clinical range or any symptom combinations can be used as a moderately effective screen for possible feigning.

SADS and Defensiveness

Descriptive data from the SADS provide useful information on what symptoms are very common across diverse clinical and forensic samples. As noted in Chapter 2 in this volume, denial of patient characteristics is a well-established detection strategy; it is exemplified on the SADS as the Commonly Reported Symptoms (CRS) scale. The CRS scale is composed of seven symptoms, which have been described by at least 40% of examinees.

Genuine patients typically report three or more CRS items (see Table 18.3). It is very rare for patients who acknowledge their mental disorders not to report at least one of these seven symptoms. As noted in Table 18.3, patients with urgent treatment needs are likely to report the majority of CRS items. The CRS scale has not been formally tested with defensive patients. Depending on an examinee's history, it may be useful in addressing possible defensiveness in patients reporting only one or two CRS items. In addition, specialized scales on the MMPI-2 can be used to further evaluate defensiveness for examinees who appear to deny even the most common symptoms.

A closely related strategy is the denial of symptoms within common symptom constellations. Rogers (1988b) developed two symptom constellations that occurred in the great majority of patients: (1) six symptoms representative of dysphoric feelings (i.e., subjective feelings of depression, worrying, feelings of discouragement, subjective feelings of anxiety, feelings of self-reproach, and subjective feelings of anger) and (2) six somatic complaints (i.e., somatic anxiety, sleep disturbance, hyper-

TABLE 18.3. Schedule of Affective Disorders and Schizophrenia—Change (SADS-C) Commonly Reported Symptoms (CRS)

	Forensic	Schiz.	Jail MH
234 Subjective feelings of depression	55.2	52.2	83.3
238 Worrying	55.7	55.5	63.0
244 Discouragement	51.5	42.2	64.8
265 Subjective feelings of anxiety	50.0	52.2	64.8
272 Sleep disturbance	51.5	44.4	75.9
330 Subjective feelings of anger	73.1	42.2	74.1
418 Antisocial behavior	55.7	64.4	100.0
Average	56.1	50.4	75.1

Note. Forensic, criminal forensic referrals; Schiz., actively psychotic patients with schizophrenia; Jail MH, mentally disordered offenders with genuine Axis I disorders in a jail setting.

somnia, loss of appetite, increased appetite, and excessive concern with physical health). The following benchmarks were established. For the dysphoric constellation (Items 234, 238, 240, 244, 265, and 330):

- 83.3% of the entire clinical sample (i.e., 244 patients) has at least one symptom.
- The modal response to the dysphoric constellation is 4.

For the somatic complaints constellation (Items 263, 272, 314, 317, 320, and 322):

- 74.9% of the entire clinical sample (i.e., 244 patients) has at least one symptom.
- The modal response to the somatic complaints constellation is 2.

CRS and common symptom constellations are closely related, largely due to item overlap. The use of ≥ 1 CRS item appears to be the most stringent standard for identifying cases of possible defensiveness. Common symptom constellations are unlikely to add incremental validity. However, they may be valuable on a conceptual basis for discussing with defensive patients why their presentations appear to reflect an underreporting of common symptoms.

Denial of patient characteristics can also be evaluated via an examination of the SADS symptoms in the clinical range. As the polar opposite of indiscriminant symptom endorsement, some patients may categorically deny nearly every symptom and associated feature of mental disorders. As a benchmark, 93% of patients report at least seven SADS symptoms in the clinical range. When collateral sources and past history demonstrate significant mental health issues, the disacknowledgment of most symptoms would appear incongruous. In such cases, the absence of SADS symptoms can be used to address possible issues affecting the examinee's forthrightness regarding psychological problems.

STANDARDIZED FORENSIC INTERVIEWS AND RESPONSE STYLES

Forensic consultations and other highly consequential evaluations (see Otto, Chapter 21, this volume) have far-reaching risks and rewards. Honest disclosures may result in punitive sanctions (e.g., for sexually deviant behavior; see Chapter 17, this volume). Unsuccessful attempts to malinger mental disorders or deny substance abuse can markedly affect multiple domains of examinees' lives.

A striking oversight in the development of forensic measures has been the neglect of validity scales using well-validated detection strategies to assess response styles (Rogers, Sewell, Grandjean, & Vitacco, 2002). The untenable assumption appears to be that most forensic examinees will not attempt to "better their circumstances" by either markedly accentuating or deemphasizing legally relevant psychological issues. The next two sections briefly review forensic measures and relevant material on response styles. They are organized into two domains: criminal and civil issues.

Criminal Forensic Measures

Georgia Court Competency Test

The Georgia Court Competency Test (GCCT; Wildman et al., 1979) is a first-generation competency measure that is typically used for screening purposes (Rogers & Shuman, 2005). Gothard, Rogers, and Sewell (1995) demonstrated that both simulators and suspected malingerers could easily feign severe impairment on competency-related abilities. Gothard and colleagues (1995) developed the Atypical Presentation Scale (APS) as a brief screen for feigned incompetency. They tested the APS on simulators, suspected malingerers, competent defendants, and incompetent defendants. A cut score ≥ 6 had a sensitivity of 89.2%, an overall specificity of 91.0%, and a specificity with incompetent defendants of 82.6%. They also tested two other detection strategies (see Chapter 2, this volume) that are used for feigned cognitive impairment: performance curve and floor effect. Both were moderately effective but had lower specificities (< 70%) for incompetent defendants.

Rogers, Sewell, and colleagues (2002), using a known-groups comparison with mentally disordered detainees and probable malingerers, found large differences for the APS (d = 1.16). Using the cut score ≥ 6 had a very good specificity (.89) but only a modest sensitivity (.32). A lower cut score balanced specificity (.78) and sensitivity (.73). The floor effect showed some promise (d = .77), whereas performance curve was unsuccessful (d = .18).

MacArthur Competence Assessment Tool—Criminal Adjudication

The MacArthur Competence Assessment Tool—Criminal Adjudication (MacCAT-CA; Poythress et al., 1999) is a second-generation competency measure. Rogers, Sewell, and colleagues (2002) found that probable malingerers scored significantly lower than genuinely disordered detainees (d = .62); their scores on the Understanding scale were particularly affected (d = .56). Attempts were made to establish floor-effect and performance-curve strategies. However, the mean differences between disordered detainees and probable malingerers were minimal (i.e., raw score differences of 1.03 and 0.17, respectively). Therefore, these strategies proved ineffective

with the MacCAT-CA. At present, the Mac-CAT-CA has no validated method for detecting feigned incompetency.

Evaluation of Competency to Stand Trial—Revised

The Evaluation of Competency to Stand Trial—Revised (ECST-R; Rogers, Tillbrook, & Sewell, 2004a, 2004b) is the first specialized forensic measure to include specific feigning scales in its development. Referred to as Atypical Presentation (ATP), two scales use the rare-symptom strategy to assess Psychotic (i.e., ATP-P) and Nonpsychotic (i.e., ATP-N) content. The third basic ATP scale, based on the symptom severity strategy, assesses the purported impairment (i.e., ATP-I) resulting from these unlikely symptoms. Beyond feigning, low scores on a fourth scale assessing realistic concerns (i.e., ATP-R) is used as a basic screen for defensiveness.

The ATP scales have impressive interrater reliabilities across two sites; Rogers, Tillbrook, and Sewell (2004a, 2004b) found almost perfect agreement, with reliabilities averaging .996 (range from .98 to 1.00). More recently, Vitacco, Rogers, Gabel, and Munizza (2007) produced similarly high reliabilities (M = .98; range from .96 to 1.00). In demonstrating their discriminant validity, ATP scales yielded very large effect sizes for feigners when compared with jail detainees in the general population (M d = 2.50) and hospitalized competency cases (M d = 1.83). In a known-groups comparison with the SIRS as the external criterion, Vitacco, Rogers, and colleagues established very large effect sizes (M d = 2.39; range from 1.81 to 2.79) between genuine and feigned competency referrals.

The ECST-R ATP cut scores appear to be effective as screens for feigned symptoms and impairment associated with competency to stand trial (Rogers, Jackson, Sewell, & Harrison, 2004; Vitacco, Rogers, et al., 2007). In cases in which malingering has been established, the ATP scales can be used to specify whether incompetency is the likely objective of the feigning. The ECST-R is distinguished from other competency measures by its development and validation of feigning screens. Given the prevalence of malingering in competency evaluations, the ECST-R's inclusion of feigning screens is critically important.

Psychopathy Checklist—Revised

The Psychopathy Checklist—Revised (PCL-R; Hare, 1991, 2003) is designed for the assessment of psychopathy and its underlying dimensions. Its Interpersonal facet is characterized by deception that includes pathological lying, conning, and manipulative behavior (Hare, 2003; see also Rogers & Cruise, 2000). Despite their importance, response styles are not systematically evaluated on the PCL-R. Instead, the PCL-R uses several initiatives to minimize or neutralize the effects of deception and defensiveness. Its structure is very general, reducing the transparency of Factor 1 (interpersonal and affective components) PCL-R ratings. Hare (2003, p. 32) provided anecdotal evidence that even possession of the PCL-R manual did not produce much difference in total scores. In resolving discrepancies between different sources of information, clinicians are instructed to consider the credibility of each source. If issues remain, then "the preference is given to the source most suggestive of psychopathy, on the assumption that the majority of people tend to underreport or minimize traits and behaviors that are characteristic of the disorder" (Hare, 2003, p. 19). Some clinicians are likely to be concerned with this scoring procedure on two grounds: (1) basing clinical decisions on untested assumptions, and (2) rendering an improper generalization from "the majority of people" to all examinees.

Rogers, Vitacco, and colleagues (2002) conducted the only study that examines the vulnerability of PCL measures to response styles. They examined the effects of social desirability and social nonconformity on the PCL—Youth Version (PCL-YV; Forth, Kosson, & Hare, 2003). Under the social desirability condition, adolescent offenders were able to reduce their PCL-YV scores by an average of 5 points (Cohen's d = .79), with comparable differences for Factors 1 and 2. As suggested by Hare (2003), adult examinees may have extensive records that could possibly assist with social desirability.[2] For social nonconformity (e.g., appearing tough), the effects were even greater for PCL-YV (8 points; d = 1.10). Given the scoring guidelines that favor greater psychopathy, social nonconformity is likely to exert a substantial effect that is undetected by clinicians.

In summary, the PCL-R and its derivative measures appear vulnerable to response styles.

A priority for PCL-R research is to establish standardized methods for the detection of social desirability and other response styles. Otherwise, PCL measures become almost paradoxical in asking examinees to be honest about their dishonesties.

Civil Forensic Measures

Grisso (2003) provided a scholarly review of forensic measures, including those intended for the civil domain. Interestingly, those measures intended for custody determinations omit structured interviews and pay very little attention to standardized methods of assessing response styles (Otto & Edens, 2003). These oversights are unfortunate because parents engage in impression management, as evidenced by MMPI-2 profiles in child custody cases (Strong, Greene, Hoppe, Johnston, & Olesen, 1999).

Structured interviews are widely used for the assessment of guardianship and conservatorship (Grisso, 2003). For example, the Hopemont Capacity Assessment Interview (HCAI; Edelstein, 1999) assesses decision-making abilities through the use of scenarios. Because most adults are likely to be highly invested in preserving their independence, some response styles (e.g., malingering) are unlikely to be an issue. Defensiveness is also unlikely to play a major role. Although technical descriptions of the HCAI are available, persons with markedly impaired decisional abilities are not likely to gain access to this information or be able to apply it meaningfully to their preparation. Therefore, the lack of attention to response styles may not be particularly consequential to the assessment of basic decisional abilities in the context of guardianships. A similar analysis applies to the MacArthur Competence Assessment Tool for Treatment (MacCAT-T; Grisso & Appelbaum, 1998).

In summary, the civil forensic domain has mostly neglected the use of structured interviews with standardized methods for assessing response styles. This oversight is especially unfortunate for those forensic issues, such as child custody and disability cases, that are commonly associated with different forms of dissimulation. In these determinations, interviews often play a central role in the appraisal of motivation, response styles, and key legal issues.

A SPECIALIZED INTERVIEW FOR RESPONSE STYLES: THE STRUCTURED INTERVIEW OF REPORTED SYMPTOMS

The Structured Interview of Reported Symptoms (SIRS) was developed by Rogers and his colleagues (Rogers, 1992; Rogers, Bagby, & Dickens, 1992) to assess the feigning of mental disorders and to provide additional data about defensiveness, self-appraisal of honesty, and inconsistent responding. This section focuses on the SIRS because it is the only well-validated structured interview for the evaluation of response styles. Interview-based screens, such as the Miller Forensic Assessment of Symptoms Test (M-FAST), are covered in Chapter 19, in this volume.

Description

The SIRS (Rogers, 1992) was first developed in 1985 and has gone through several important revisions. At present, the SIRS is a 172-item structured interview that is composed of (1) Detailed Inquiries, which address specific symptomatology and its severity; (2) Repeated Inquiries, which parallel the Detailed Inquiries and test for response consistency; and (3) General Inquiries, which probe specific symptoms, general psychological problems, and symptom patterns. These items are organized into eight primary scales for the evaluation of feigning.

The SIRS is a fully structured interview that was designed to assess feigning and related response styles. The key difference between a fully structured and a semistructured interview is that the former does not allow clinicians to make their own clinical inquiries to clarify a patient's responses. The rationale for restricting the SIRS to a fully structured interview is the concern that the wording or tone of certain idiosyncratic questions may express disbelief or humor, either of which is likely to alter the patient's presentation.

The eight primary strategies were selected from the empirical literature (Rogers, 1984b). From a pool of potential items, eight experts in malingering selected individual items that assessed a single strategy; the average concordance rate on single strategies for retained items was 88.2%. The next step was the transformation of strategies to scales. To enhance scale homogeneity, item-to-scale correlations were

computed on combined data from seven samples. As a result, three items with item-to-scale correlations <.20 were dropped. Subsequently, alpha coefficients were computed for six of the primary scales; they ranged from .77 to .92, with a mean of .86 (Rogers, Bagby, & Dickens, 1992).

SIRS primary scales utilize eight validated detection strategies (see Chapter 2, this volume) that have proven useful in the key discrimination between feigned and genuine disorders. These scales are briefly summarized:

1. Rare Symptoms (RS; 8 items) uses symptoms and clinical features that are very infrequent among patients with genuine disorders.
2. Symptom Combinations (SC; 10 items) uses common symptoms that are rarely paired together.
3. Improbable and Absurd Symptoms (IA; 7 items) uses purported symptoms that have a fantastic or preposterous quality, which renders them extremely unlikely to be true.
4. Blatant Symptoms (BL; 15 items) uses "obvious" symptoms that untrained persons easily recognize as severe psychopathology.
5. Subtle Symptoms (SU; 17 items) uses characteristics common to mental disorders; some are not immediately recognizable as evidence of major mental disorders.
6. Selectivity of Symptoms (SEL; 32 items) uses the indiscriminant endorsement of symptoms.
7. Severity of Symptoms (SEV; 32 items) considers the proportion of symptoms considered unbearable or potentially incapacitating.
8. Reported versus Observed (RO; 12 items) uses easily perceived behavioral characteristics to examine disparities with patients' descriptions.

Validation: Original Research and Recent Studies

Reliability

Alpha coefficients provide useful estimates regarding the internal reliability of SIRS primary and supplementary scales. Focusing on primary scales, the original research summarized in the test manual (Rogers, Bagby, & Dickens, 1992) produced good to excellent alpha coefficients (i.e., .77–.92). Several recent investiga-

TABLE 18.4. Reliability for Structured Inventory of Reported Symptoms (SIRS) Primary Scales: Data from the SIRS Manual and Recent Studies

Study	Format	Alphas		Interrater reliabilities	
		M	Range	M	range
SIRS manual (Rogers, Bagby, & Dickens, 1992)	Standard	.86	.77–.92	.98	.93–1.00
Goodness (1999)	R-SIRS	.89	.85–.91	1.00	1.00–1.00
	CT-SIRS	.87	.82–.92	1.00	1.00–1.00
Norris & May (1998)	4 scales	.80	.67–.84		
Ustad (1997)	Standard	.79	.72–.90		
Vitacco, Rogers, & Gabel (2007)	Standard	.86	.77–.96	.99	.95–1.00
Recent studies: Unweighted averages		.85	.77–.91	.99	.97–1.00

Note. The R-SIRS and CT-SIRS use the same SIRS questions but specify a previous time period.

tions (see Table 18.4) have generally produced comparable results, even when using retrospective versions of the SIRS or abbreviated formats. In only one instance, the reported alpha was marginal (.67). When the five recent samples are compared with the test manual, the results are virtually identical, with a mean alpha of .85 and a range from .77 to .91. Overall, these data provide strong evidence of good to excellent internal reliability for the SIRS primary scales. In general, the SIRS supplementary scales have alphas in the .7 to .8 range.

Feigning and other response styles are based on an appraisal of the current context and cost–benefit decisions. Therefore, the interrater reliability is the critical issue in establishing the SIRS reliability. With appropriate training, clinicians should be able to achieve very high reliabilities. As summarized in Table 18.4, reliabilities for SIRS primary scales have ranged from .93 to 1.00. Its average interrater reliability of .99 is impressive.

The reliability of individual scales is evaluated via standard error of measurement (SEM; Anastasi, 1988). Using Rogers, Payne, and Granacher's (2007) large database on 498 disability referrals, patients in the likely genuine category had an average standard deviation (SD) of 2.87 on the SIRS primary scales. With an interrater reliability of .99, the average SEM is minuscule (i.e., .29). Even for the highest SD, the SEM is only .60. Therefore, clinicians can be confident that the SIRS primary scales provide a very reliable estimate of the "true" score.

Factor-Analytic Studies

Rogers, Bagby, and Dickens (1992) used principal-components analyses (PCA) to examine the underlying dimensions of the SIRS primary and ancillary scales separately for feigning and honest samples. Both PCA solutions had a very strong *feigning* dimension and a relatively weak *inconsistent/dishonest* dimension; they differed on whether *defensiveness* was represented. Although the primary purpose of the SIRS is the classification of feigned mental disorders, early investigations considered different response styles (Rogers, 1997d).

Recent factor-analytic studies have focused on whether the detection strategies, operationalized as SIRS scales, represent a single or multiple dimensions. For example, McCusker, Moran, Serfass, and Peterson (2003) conducted a PCA on 63 suspected malingerers and established two dimensions that correspond to unlikely (i.e., RS, SC, and IA) and amplified (i.e., BL, SU, SEL, and SEV) presentations. Despite the modest sample, the magnitude of these factor loadings (M = .82) is high and suggests a robust solution.

Rogers, Jackson, Sewell, and Salekin (2005) conducted confirmatory factor analyses on the original validation (n = 403) and recent cross-validation (n = 255) samples. Across these diverse samples (i.e., forensic, correctional, clinical, and community), they established two underlying dimensions of feigning. Using the terms in Chapter 2 (this volume), unlikely presentations were distinguished from amplified presentations. For unlikely presentations, Factor 1 was generally consistent with McCusker and colleagues (2003; unique loadings for RS, SC, and IA; a cross-loading for BL). For Factor 2, Rogers and colleagues (2005) did not include SEL and SEV in their analyses because these items are also used with a different scoring for the BL and SU scales. Their amplified presentation was composed of SU and Defensive Symptoms (DS) plus the BL cross-loading. Considering the heterogeneity of the samples and different research designs, these data, augmented by McCusker and colleagues' findings, provide strong empirical data for two dimensions of detection strategies: unlikely and amplified presentations.

Convergent Validity

Rogers, Bagby, and Dickens (1992) demonstrated strong convergent validity between the SIRS and the MMPI feigning scales. For example, they found high correlations for the F scale ($M r = .76$; range from .71 to .80). High but slightly lower correlations were produced for F-K and Dsr. Recent investigations with the MMPI-2 and Personality Assessment Inventory (PAI) have also yielded robust relationships:

- Heinze (2003) correlated the number of SIRS primary scales in the probable and definite range with MMPI-2 F and F-K. Despite using these less-than-optimal methods, the correlations were moderately strong ($M r = .62$; range from .54 to .68). Story (2000) compared six of the SIRS primary scales with the MMPI-2 validity scales. The highest correlations were found with F ($M r = .72$; range from .64 to .78), followed by Fb ($M r = .62$) and Fp ($M r = .57$).
- In the first investigation with the PAI, Rogers, Ustad, and Salekin (1998) found moderate correlations for the PAI NIM scale (see Chapter 11, this volume, for a description of PAI indicators) and SIRS primary scales ($M r = .58$). More recently, Kucharski, Toomey, Fila, and Duncan (2007) found stronger correlations for the standard NIM scale ($M r = .63$) than for the specialized MAL ($M r = .49$).
- In a large-scale study of disability referrals, Rogers, Payne, and Granacher (2007) found moderate correlations for the SIRS primary scales and MMPI-2 validity scales; averages were in the .50 range for F, Fb, F-K, and Ds. SIRS total scores for these scales were

moderately high, ranging from .69 to .75. When considering Rogers and colleagues and the previously cited studies, the research data provide strong evidence of convergent validity.

Discriminant Validity

As outlined in Chapter 2 (this volume), the crucial test for response style measures is their ability to successfully differentiate between criterion groups. In establishing the discriminant validity, Cohen's ds measure the magnitude of differences between feigning and nonfeigning groups. Rogers (1997d) summarized the effect sizes of the original SIRS validation on 403 participants from multiple samples. When they were compared with clinical samples, he found very large effect sizes for suspected malingerers ($M d = 1.74$) and simulators ($M d = 1.74$).

Additional studies with criminal forensic samples have generally produced very large effect sizes (see Table 18.5). The one exception was Connell's (1991) research on correctional samples that produced mostly moderate to large effect sizes ($M d = .92$). Rogers, Payne, and Granacher (2007) recently conducted large-scale SIRS research on disability referrals. Using MMPI-2 cut scores, groups of likely feigners (i.e., Fp >7 or Ds >35) and likely genuine patients (i.e., Fp <4 or Ds <35) were compared. This approach is considered a bootstrapping design because these cut scores do not result in independently classified samples; they simply signify a high likelihood of feigning and honest responding (see Rogers, Sewell, Martin, et al., 2003). When combined across simulation, known-groups, and bootstrapping designs, the results with varied samples are consistently robust. The overall effect size is very large ($d = 1.89$); it even exceeds the original validation (overall $d = 1.74$; Rogers, 1997d). Two scales (RS and BL) are especially impressive, with Cohen's ds exceeding 2.00.

Goodness (1999) examined two experimental forms of the SIRS that were designed to explore retrospective feigning at the time of the offense among criminal defendants found not guilty by reason of insanity. In feigning mental disorders at the time of the offense, these inpatients produced large effect sizes (ds from 1.03 to 1.74). These promising results have yet to be replicated with larger samples.

TABLE 18.5. Discriminant Validity for the Structured Inventory of Reported Symptoms (SIRS): Summary of Effect Sizes for Feigning versus Clinical Samples

Study		Cohen's d for SIRS primary scales							
Author (year)	Design	RS	IA	SC	BL	SU	SEL	SEV	RO
Rogers (1997d)	KG	2.31	1.67	1.60	2.29	1.40	1.59	1.65	1.44
	Sim	1.83	1.48	1.20	1.87	1.79	1.98	1.95	1.78
Connell (1991)	Sim[a]	1.23	1.20	.98	.57	.59	.50	.58	1.75
Kropp (1992)	Sim[bc]	2.15	1.33	1.77	2.41	1.40	2.29	1.92	1.70
Gothard, Viglione, Meloy, & Sherman (1995)	Sim[d]	2.07	2.47	1.72	2.53	1.65	1.88	2.34	2.10
	Sim[e]	2.60	2.82	2.04	2.80	1.78	2.37	2.15	2.36
	KG[d]	2.10	1.86	2.57	2.30	1.77	1.66	2.12	1.68
	KG[e]	3.37	2.66	3.14	2.50	1.74	2.05	1.99	2.08
Story (2000)	BTS[f]		1.24		2.00	1.48	1.61	1.76	
Rogers, Payne, & Granacher (2007)	BTS[g]	1.67	1.97	1.54	2.87	1.78	1.94	2.43	1.50
Unweighted averages (grand $M = 1.89$)		2.15	1.87	1.84	2.21	1.54	1.79	1.89	1.82
Goodness (1999): retrospective feigning	Sim[h]	1.07	1.36	1.50	1.41	1.06	1.24	1.29	
	Sim[i]	1.74	1.60	1.41	1.64	1.03	1.52	1.14	

Note. Sim, simulation; KG, known groups; BTS, bootstrapping; RS, Rare Symptoms; IA, Improbable and Absurd Symptoms; SC, Symptom Combinations; BL, Blatant Symptoms; SU, Subtle Symptoms; SEL, Selectivity of Symptoms; SEV, Severity of Symptoms; RO, Reported versus Observed.
[a]Clinical sample is correctional inpatients.
[b]Cohen's ds are calculated from F ratios.
[c]Inmates receiving counseling.
[d]Compared with patients incompetent to stand trial.
[e]Compared with patients competent to stand trial.
[f]Only five primary scales were administered. Classifications were based on multiple MMPI-2 indicators, the clinical classification of malingering, or other data, including the diagnosis of APD.
[g]MMPI-2 scales Fp and Ds were used to form a suspected malingering group because they have relatively consistent cut scores that appear to be effective across diagnoses (see Rogers, Sewell, et al., 2003).
[h]Retrospective version of the SIRS; forensic inpatients were asked to feign for the time of their offense. RO is not applicable for past feigning.
[i]Second retrospective version of the SIRS; forensic inpatients were asked to feign for the time of their offense. RO is not applicable for past feigning.

Clinical Applications of the SIRS

The SIRS is widely accepted as a well-validated measure of feigned mental disorders. Lally (2003) surveyed diplomate-level forensic psychologists regarding standardized assessment of malingering. The SIRS was the only specialized measure to be evaluated as acceptable for forensic evaluations by most diplomates (89%) and recommended by the majority of them (58%). More recently, Archer, Buffington-Vollum, Stredny, and Handel (2006) examined the test usage of forensic psychologists for specific issues. The SIRS received the highest scores; 86.2% had used the SIRS in forensic evaluations, and their frequency of use exceeded other measures across both malingered mental disorders and feigned cognitive impairment.

The SIRS has been widely accepted by malingering researchers as a gold standard for the classification of feigned mental disorders. Its use as a gold standard has been applied to both multiscale inventories and specialized measures. A summary of the measures and studies follows:

1. MMPI-2: Gassen, Pietz, Spray, and Denney (2007); Lewis, Simcox, and Berry (2002); McCusker and colleagues (2003)
2. PAI: Boccaccini, Murrie, and Duncan (2006); Kucharski and colleagues (2007); Rogers, Sewell, Cruise, Wang, and Ustad (1998)
3. Structured Inventory of Malingered Symptomatology (SIMS): Lewis and colleagues (2002); Vitacco and colleagues (2007)

4. M-FAST: Guy and Miller (2004); Jackson, Rogers, and Sewell (2005); Miller (2004, 2005); Vitacco, Rogers, and colleagues (2007)
5. ECST-R ATP scales: Rogers, Sewell, and colleagues (2002); Rogers, Tillbrook, and Sewell (2004a, 2004b); Vitacco, Rogers, and Gabel (2007); Vitacco, Rogers, and colleagues (2007b)
6. Feigned hallucinations: Pollock (1998)

The establishment of criterion groups is essential to malingering research using known-groups comparisons. Research use of the SIRS as a gold standard for feigned mental disorders should be seen as very strong evidence of its validity and utility in clinical practice.

Determinations of Feigned Mental Disorders

The primary purpose of the SIRS is the clinical determination of feigned mental disorders. As clearly specified in the SIRS professional manual (Rogers, Bagby, & Dickens, 1992), malingering classifications should always be multimethod and never rely on a single measure. The use of multiple measures based on validated detection strategies provides further empirical data, with the goal of reducing false positives.

Original validation of the SIRS reduced the false-positive rate to a very low percentage even when applied to diverse clinical and forensic samples. For the determination of feigning, the SIRS relies primarily on the following classification rule: three or more scales in the *probable feigning* category. This category was established for primary scales to minimize false positives (i.e., 2.1%). Focusing on individual SIRS scales, the following percentages were found:

- Genuine patients rarely had individual SIRS scales in the probable feigning category. The range across primary scales was 0.0 to 5.9% (average = 3.2%).
- The majority of probable malingerers had individual SIRS scales in *at least* the probable feigning category. The range across primary scales was 35.5 to 76.5% (average = 53.4%).
- The majority of simulators had individual SIRS scales in *at least* the probable feigning category. The range across primary scales was 38.4 to 74.7% (average = 57.8%).

When malingerers and simulators did not have primary scale elevations in *at least* the probable feigning category, they were most likely to fall in the indeterminate range. With the exception of the IA scale, relatively few probable malingerers were classified in the "honest" category on individual SIRS scales (i.e., M with IA = 19.3%; M without IA = 13.4%). These percentages were even lower for simulators (i.e., M with IA = 13.7%; M without IA = 8.1%).

Several studies have confirmed the SIRS classification with its general accuracy and minimal false-positive rate. Gothard, Viglione, Meloy, and Sherman (1995) studied the SIRS cut scores in a simulation study using pretrial defendants. She and her colleagues found the SIRS to be effective at identifying simulators, with a very low false-positive rate of 2.6%. Heinze (2003) checked the specificity of the individual SIRS primary scales for probable feigning. She found high rates ranging from .88 to .96 with an average of .92; this indicates that the individual scales are excellent at excluding honest responders from misclassifications.

Two studies with weak research designs have produced mixed results in using the SIRS classifications. Edens, Poythress, and Watkins-Clay (2007) used a quasi-known-groups comparison to identify 26 suspected malingerers. It is considered "quasi" because of its multiple limitations in attempting to establish independent classifications. Prison psychiatrists were given a list of SIRS strategies, which they apparently applied with little or no training during their routine evaluations. Two additional limitations of the study include (1) the apparent brevity of routine psychiatric evaluations and (2) the unduly broad classification (*any* instance of *any* strategy was classified as suspected malingering; see earlier description of the same data by Poythress, Edens, & Watkins, 2001, p. 571). The fourth limitation of the study was its use of inconsistent responding in 89% of the cases as evidence of suspected malingering; this approach has been proven ineffective in the detection of malingering (see the earlier section on unstandardized interviews and response styles). Ironically, a major goal of the SIRS was to eliminate such unstandardized evaluations based on vague classifications. Moreover, Edens and colleagues tested only the total SIRS score as the *sole* criterion for feigning; not surprisingly, they found poor specificity (.60) when applied to correctional patients. They were apparently unaware that the total SIRS score should be used only with indeterminate cases in which elevated SIRS scales (e.g., one or two scales in the probable feigning range) raise substantial concerns about malingering.

Kucharski, Duncan, Egan, and Falkenbach (2006) used a bootstrapping (BTS) design to evaluate SIRS classifications. Because BTS only approximates independent groups, it has limited value in establishing accurate classifications. For the MMPI-2, they relied on a cut score of F ≥ 106T for suspected feigning; this choice is questionable given the marked variability in F cut scores and the superiority of the Fp scale (see Greene, Chapter 10, this volume). For genuine responders, they used F < 95T, which is higher than many cut scores for malingering (see MMPI-2 meta-analysis; Rogers, Sewell, et al., 2003). Despite these substantial limitations, the SIRS performed well, with a sensitivity of .86 and a specificity of .94.[4]

In summary, the SIRS classification has performed impressively across research designs and diverse samples. With the exception of one flawed study, recent research has also produced very positive results. The next section addresses the SIRS generalizability across diagnostic groups. SIRS classifications are subsequently revisited with respect to potentially problematic diagnoses, such as PTSD and mental retardation.

Generalizability across Diagnostic Groups

The original validation of the SIRS used diagnostically heterogeneous patients with no attempt to consider specific diagnoses. This approach was based on the clinical reality that most patients with mental disorders do not warrant a single diagnosis. Instead, they typically experience multiple Axis I and Axis II disorders (see, e.g., Zimmerman & Mattia, 1999). Moreover, data from the National Comorbidity Survey (NCS) demonstrate that multiple Axis I diagnoses are very common. For example, the majority of persons with PTSD also warranted two additional Axis I diagnoses (Kessler, Sonnega, Bromet, & Hughes, 1995). Moreover, this rate of comorbidity is likely an underestimate because the NCS data covered only 14 Axis I disorders. Likewise, patients with serious mental disorders are often comorbid for

substance abuse and other diagnoses (see Kessler, Chui, Dennier, & Walters, 2005). Beyond diagnosis per se, many patients experience symptoms and clinical features of many disorders at a level below the DSM-IV criterion. Taking into account both diagnostic comorbidity and additional symptomatology, the use of diagnostically heterogeneous samples is highly representative of clinical and forensic practice.

Rogers, Payne, Berry, and Granacher (2007) were able to examine three nonoverlapping diagnostic groups in a large sample of disability referrals. They compared differences in SIRS primary scales for three diagnostic groups (i.e., major depression, PTSD, and other anxiety disorders) evaluated as likely to be genuine responders. They found minimal differences between the diagnostic groups: depression versus PTSD ($M\ d = .24$), depression versus other anxiety disorders ($M\ d = .17$), and PTSD versus other anxiety disorders ($M\ d = .15$). These effect sizes are small and comparatively trivial in light of the very large effect sizes (unweighted $M\ d = 1.89$; see Table 18.5) between feigners and clinical comparison samples.

The use of the SIRS for detecting feigned mental disorders in intellectually challenged populations has produced mixed results. Hayes, Hale, and Gouvier (1996) conducted a small study of 30 genuine patients with mild mental retardation ($M\ IQ = 60.5$). They found that these patients did not produce elevated SIRS profiles and were distinguishable from 9 suspected malingerers. More recently, Hurley and Deal (2006) attempted to study the potential for feigning measures (i.e., Test of Memory Malingering [TOMM], SIRS, Rey-15 Item, and Dot Counting) to produce false positives in intellectually challenged populations with IQs ranging from 50 to 78. Because of their functional incapacities, these participants were placed in residential facilities for mental retardation. They reported a false-positive rate for SIRS classification of 30.8%. This percentage was even higher when the SIRS total score was applied to all cases irrespective of primary scale elevations. The study raises several methodological concerns.[5] The training of the interviewers in the SIRS and structured interviews is unreported. As a related concern, the SIRS appeared to have been administered irrespective of the person's capacity to be meaningfully engaged in the assessment. For example, the authors reported SIRS total scores as high as

238. In the original validation, no malingerer or simulator scored as high as 150. In the absence of any manipulation check, it is impossible to ascertain what percentage of participants remembered and stayed motivated in the research study. Moreover, intellectually challenged residents may not have been given sufficient time to understand and respond to SIRS items. For instance, these intellectually challenged residents were administered the SIRS, the TOMM, and two cognitive screens in as little as 45 minutes, including breaks. These four measures would typically require at least an hour, even with high-functioning individuals.

What conclusions can be gleaned from these two studies?

1. Some persons with mental retardation have the verbal abilities to be meaningfully engaged in a structured interview, such as the SIRS. These abilities cannot simply be equated with a particular IQ score but must be carefully assessed on an individual basis.

2. Unstructured interviews prior to the SIRS are essential to ascertain the possibility of an acquiescent response set.

3. Clinical observations are especially important in administering the SIRS and other psychological measures to persons who are intellectually challenged. Some persons with mental retardation attempt to cover up their comprehension deficits with affirmative responses. Practitioners can easily ascertain whether this is occurring by simply asking the interviewee to repeat or paraphrase the questions.

4. The indiscriminant administration of psychological measures to intellectually challenged persons is substandard practice and should always be avoided.

Rogers, Payne, and colleagues (2007) examined the potential effects of a cognitive disorder (i.e., dementia, amnestic disorder, and cognitive disorder, not otherwise specified) on the SIRS primary scales for disability referrals. When compared with patients with other genuine disorders, individuals with cognitive disorders had slightly *lower* scores ($M d = -.20$). Clearly, the presence of a cognitive disorder is unlikely to invalidate SIRS results. These investigators also considered the potential role of impaired intellectual functioning (IQs <85). For 54 individuals with borderline to mild mental retardation, higher scores were observed for the SIRS primary scales ($M d = .49$). Despite these differences, four SIRS scales remained in the honest-responding range, whereas the other four scales fell in the indeterminate range. Although SIRS classifications are not recommended for bootstrapping designs, possible differences due to intellectual deficits were explored. It revealed a potential false-positive rate of 5.6%, which is in the low range.

SIRS Screen for Feigned Cognitive Impairment

Wyncoop, Frederick, and Hoy (2006) recommended that the SIRS Improbable Failure (IF) scale be used as a screen for feigned cognitive impairment. The IF scale consists of very simple cognitive tasks involving opposites and rhymes. They found high alphas and split-half reliabilities across clinical and forensic samples. They found low scores for patients with mental disorders and those with closed-head injuries. Cognitively impaired patients with focal lesions, encephalopathy, and dementia scored substantially higher.

Using a bootstrapping design, Rogers, Payne, Berry, and colleagues (2007) identified 58 examinees who were likely to be feigning cognitive impairment based on cut scores for the TOMM, the Victoria Symptom Validity Test (VSVT; Slick, Hopp, Strauss, & Thompson, 1997), and the Letter Memory Test (LMT; Inman et al., 1998). A high sensitivity (.86) was achieved with an IF cut score ≥ 1, although the specificity was only moderate (.51). This cut score maximizes the NPP (.95) so that potential feigning cases are not missed at the expense of PPP (.25). Additional analyses will examine individual IF items in an effort to improve utility estimates. Presently, the IF scale can be quickly used to evaluate whether feigned cognitive impairment should be further evaluated.

SIRS Strengths and Limitations

Rogers (2001) summarized important strengths and limitations of the SIRS. Its chief strengths are enumerated:

1. Its validation includes both simulation and known-groups comparisons that capitalize on internal and external validity, respectively. Unlike many measures, its discriminant validity is maintained across both designs.

2. The SIRS primary scales were specifically designed to evaluate explicit detection strategies for feigning. In contrast, many feigning measures lack this strong conceptual basis, relying instead on post hoc inferences regarding detection strategies.

3. Its accuracy of measurement, as exemplified by the SEM, is unparalleled (*M* SEM = .29) among measures of response styles. As a comparison, the widely used MMPI-2 F scale is much higher; even using normative (i.e., nonclinical) data, the SEM for F raw scores is 1.52 for men and 1.62 for women.

4. The interrater reliability for the SIRS primary scales is exceptionally high (*M r* = .996) and surpasses other measures of response styles.

5. The SIRS uses stable cut scores that allow direct comparisons across research studies and clinical samples. This standardized use avoids the marked variability observed with other measures. For example, cut scores for the MMPI-2 have ranged from 61T to 129T; such variability militates against the accurate classification of response styles.

6. The SIRS is designed via its scoring and classification to be highly accurate in the determination of feigned mental disorders. As a result, its low false-positive rate is unmatched for feigning measures of psychopathology.

The SIRS also minimizes problems with literacy and patient recording of responses that are common problems with paper-and-pencil measures. It also provides initial data for distinguishing between malingered and factitious response styles. In summary, the SIRS is a psychometrically sound measure with a high level of discriminant validity.

The SIRS also has several limitations that should be considered in its clinical and forensic applications. These limitations include the following:

1. The SIRS is not intended to evaluate feigned cognitive impairment. Available data indicate the usefulness of its IF scale as a *screen* for faked cognitive abilities. However, the SIRS should not be used in the determination of feigned memory or simulated intellectual deficits.[6]

2. Occasionally, examinees in forensic evaluations will be educated about their failed attempts to feign on the SIRS (Rogers & Shu-

man, 2005). Although the SIRS remains effective with general coaching, review of specific SIRS data is likely to invalidate its classification. Several cases have been observed in which SIRS elevations have dropped precipitously after such exposure. Needless to say, mental health professionals must protect the test security of all psychological measures, including the SIRS.

3. Special care must be taken in the administration of the SIRS to persons with mild mental retardation. Their abilities to comprehend and communicate are critical. Practitioners must be alert to signs of confusion or uncertainty; many persons with mental retardation are reticent to express their lack of comprehension. It is permissible to proactively clarify the meaning of certain words in SIRS inquiries, although these clarifications should be documented on the SIRS protocols.

Several recent lines of research suggest caution in applying the SIRS to dissociative identity disorders (DID). Brand, McNary, Loewenstein, Kolos, and Barr (2006) compared 43 simulators with 20 DID patients. They found that approximately one-third of the DID patients exceeded the classification of ≥ 3 scales in the probable-feigning range. Interestingly, SU and SEL were particularly affected, whereas SC and IA were not. Ongoing research by the author and his research team also suggests that DID combined with multiple traumas may produce false positives in the .20 range. Two significant issues for DID assessments include (1) a shift in alters during the SIRS administrations and, more commonly, (2) one alter attempting to report how other alters would respond. The SIRS should only be used in DID cases when the alter remains consistent during the administration and is restricted to only "self-report" about his or her own personality. Even in these cases, reports should clearly specify the SIRS' reduced accuracy with DID examinees.

SIRS Summary

The SIRS has been widely adopted as the gold standard for malingering research on feigned mental disorders. As noted earlier, it is widely used in clinical and forensic practice. In terms of its conceptualization, reliability, and validity, the SIRS should be considered the strongest measure of feigned mental disorders. Table

TABLE 18.6. Clinical Applications of the Structured Inventory of Reported Symptoms (SIRS)

Application/cautions	Classification	Commentary
Screen for cognitive feigning	Elevated IF scale	Indicator when further assessment is needed
Determination of feigned mental disorders	≥ 3 probable feigning	Strongest indicator of feigning based on multiple detection strategies
	≥ 1 definite feigning	Effective alternative rule based on a single strategy
	> 76 Total SIRS score	This supplementary classification should only be used when there is possible evidence of feigning (e.g., one or two scales in the probable feigning range).
Caution with mental retardation	Mild mental retardation	Case-by-case application with verification that the examinee comprehends the SIRS inquiries and is responding relevantly
	Moderate retardation	SIRS should not be used.
Caution with DID	Stable alter (administration)	The SIRS may be administered if the examinee can be focused on his or her alter only; the report should be explicit about reduced SIRS accuracy.

18.6 summarizes its use as a screen for cognitive feigning and for the determination of feigned psychopathology.

CONCLUSIONS

Structured interviews are playing an increasingly important role in the establishment of DSM-IV disorders and addressing other clinical and forensic issues. As described in this chapter, the SADS remains the centerpiece of Axis I diagnoses for consideration of feigning and defensiveness. Research is urgently needed on other Axis I and II interviews to develop detection-based scales for the assessment of response styles. Recent developments with forensic measures, such as the ECST-R, represent important advances in specialized assessment. Finally, the SIRS demonstrates the effectiveness of detection strategies that combine sound conceptualization with extensive empirical validation.

NOTES

1. Staying with this example, a series of inquiries about the parent's adaptation to single life might signal a possible approval of dating; a sequence of questions about parent–child conflicts might signal a possible disapproval of dating.

2. However, reliance on records alone results in lower scores than typical PCL-R interviews augmented by records (Hare, 2003, p. 19); therefore, the usefulness of the further documentation to counteract the effects of social desirability remains a testable yet unexamined hypothesis.

3. For clarification, this classification categorizes clinical samples with only genuine disorders. It is well recognized that many feigners also have genuine disorders; their inclusion would blur this critical discrimination.

4. If F ≤ 90T were used, the specificity would increase to .97, consistent with the original validation studies.

5. The level of scholarship is also suspect. For instance, the SIRS is referred to as "Structured Interview of *Support* Symptoms" on seven occasions.

6. Rogers, Payne, and colleagues (2007) found moderate to large effect sizes ($M\,d = .94$) for disability referrals likely to be feigning only cognitive impairment when compared with genuine referrals. However, its detection strategies are not designed to evaluate feigned cognitive impairment.

19

Brief Screening Measures for the Detection of Feigned Psychopathology

GLENN P. SMITH, PhD

Malingering is defined by the *Diagnostic and Statistical Manual of Mental Disorders—Fourth Edition* (DSM-IV) as "the intentional production of false or grossly exaggerated physical or psychological symptoms, motivated by external incentives" (American Psychiatric Association, 2000, p. 739). Though easily defined, its detection is far more complicated due to the interactions between three separate but interrelated considerations: (1) the type of feigned symptomatology, (2) different populations and settings, and (3) the heterogeneity of screens and detection strategies.

Early research aimed at measures to detect malingering (e.g., Fay & Middleton, 1941) focused on global response styles such as "simple" deception. More recently, the clinical literature on detection of malingering has emphasized the type of condition being feigned. This chapter focuses on malingering within the domain of feigned psychopathology and, when possible, it examines subdomains of malingered conditions (e.g., feigned posttraumatic stress disorder [PTSD]).

As a second consideration, the selection and use of malingering screens involves differences in populations and settings. For example, the feigning of psychosis may be presented differently in a forensic setting than on an inpatient psychiatric unit. Such differences may result in disparities in the effectiveness of screening measures across studies. Therefore, this chapter considers the generalizability of measures across settings.

A third consideration involves the heterogeneity of malingering screens and the logistical issues that they may introduce. Screens vary markedly in their methods (interviews, observations, and self-reports), the type of detection strategies employed (see Chapter 2, this volume), and their differential sensitivity and specificity. Different methods have logistical implications, including administration time, training of evaluators, and specialized equipment. Varying detection strategies may also have clinical implications (e.g., observational data versus self-reports). Sensitivity and specificity may vary across instruments as clinicians weight the relative costs versus benefits of false-positive or false-negative classifications. Given these complexities, malingering screens play an important role, particularly in the earlier stages of the evaluation process, in providing a threshold decision for determining whether a comprehensive assessment is warranted. Screening instruments may also have utility when used as a source of confirmatory data.

This chapter is organized into four major sections. The first section reviews several well-established malingering screens, including the M Test (Beaber, Marston, Michelli, & Mills, 1985), the Miller Forensic Assessment of Symptoms Test (M-FAST; Miller, 2001), and Structured Inventory of Malingered Symptomatology (SIMS; Widows & Smith, 2005). These screening measures use both simulation design (i.e., research participants instructed to feign pathology) and known-groups comparisons (i.e., suspected malingerers). In these reviews, the nature of the condition being malingered, the population variables, and the methodological factors of the screening measure are considered. The second section examines more recently developed instruments, often in their initial stages of validation. Consistent with the book's objectives, the third section discusses the use of malingering screens in the comprehensive assessment of malingering, taking into account clinical and methodological issues. The fourth and final section addresses future research directions for malingering screens.

ESTABLISHED SCREENING MEASURES

M Test

The M Test (Beaber et al., 1985) is a 33-item, self-report, true–false inventory designed originally to detect malingered schizophrenia. Its scale items include an amalgam of detection strategies, including improbable symptoms and rare symptoms. Beaber and colleagues (1985) hypothesized that individuals feigning schizophrenia would not be able to differentiate actual schizophrenic characteristics on the S (Schizophrenia) scale from symptoms on the M (Malingering) scale.

The M Test is organized into three scales. The C (Confusion) scale is composed of eight items that reflect "attitudes" or "beliefs" not associated with mental illness. Presented first, it is designed to assess general comprehension, regardless of response style. The body of the test consists of 10 items of the S scale (genuine symptoms associated with schizophrenia) and 15 items on the M scale (bogus symptoms).

In the original scoring (Beaber et al., 1985), identification of malingering used either a C scale ≥ 3 or an M scale ≥ 4. The use of the S scale, however, was not recommended unless the participant endorsed "nearly all the items," because the use of the scale in combination with the other scales in the original validation work *reduced* classification accuracy.

The second scoring strategy was developed by Rogers, Bagby, and Gillis (1992) using Rule-Out/Rule-In scales. The Rule-Out scale is identical to the S scale. It is composed of 10 items

with the highest negative predictive power (NPP) values, which include symptoms sometimes observed with psychotic patients in an effort to "rule out" or eliminate those experiencing genuine symptoms and to retain respondents who may be indiscriminately endorsing symptoms. The Rule-In scale also consists of 10 items (i.e., 9 items from the M Scale and 1 C scale item); endorsement of these bogus symptoms is intended to "rule in" malingerers. The Rule-Out scale is applied first, followed by the Rule-In scale in a two-step procedure. Rogers and colleagues presented two alternatives: Option A for increased specificity and Option B for increased sensitivity. The essential difference between the two involves the Rule-In cut score for genuine patients (i.e., Option A < 2 and Option B = 0).

In the original validation study (Beaber et al., 1985), the M test was administered to undergraduates under honest and malingering instructions (i.e., "pretend you are in a situation where it would be to your advantage to look crazy"; Beaber et al., 1985, p. 1479). As a component of coaching for the feigned condition, participants read a description of the DSM-III criteria for schizophrenia to help them distinguish between genuine and malingering items. Their results were compared with those of male Veterans Administration (VA) hospital inpatients with a diagnosis of schizophrenia who completed the M Test under standard instructions.

Simulators (i.e., students feigning schizophrenia) scored consistently higher than inpatients on all three M Test scales. This finding suggests that simulators either did not effectively differentiate between scale items or adopted an indiscriminant pattern of endorsement. As noted in Table 19.1, the use of the M and C scales produced the best hit rate, though the authors did not provide the specificity and sensitivity for these individual scales. However, the M Test's high overall specificity using the combination of scales suggests that it may be used to screen out genuinely disordered individuals.

Gillis, Rogers, and Bagby (1991) attempted unsuccessfully to replicate the Beaber and colleagues (1985) results in a known-groups design, with sensitivity dropping precipitously to 40% for malingerers. This result was in marked contrast to those of simulators in the same study, for whom results yielded sensitivity rates (79.8%) very similar to those of Beaber and colleagues (78.2%). Alpha coefficients were excellent for the three scales: C (.87), S

TABLE 19.1. Design Features and Study Outcomes: M Test

| | | Groups | | | | | | Cut | Utility estimates | | | | |
| | | Experimental condition | | Criterion | | | | | PPP | NPP | Sens | Spec | d |
Study	Experimental population	Sim	Mal	Clin	Foren	Mixed							
Beaber et al. (1985)	College	104		65				M ≥ 4 C ≥ 3	.91	.71	78.2	87.3	M = 2.12 C = 1.94
Gillis, Rogers, & Bagby (1991)	Community, correctional, college	124				72		M ≥ 4 C ≥ 3	.91	.71	79.8	86.1	M = 3.08 C = 2.89
Gillis, Rogers, & Bagby (1991)	Forensic—pretrial		25[a]			72		M ≥ 4 C ≥ 3	.50	.81	40.0	86.1	M = 1.44 C = .74
Smith & Borum (1992)	Forensic—pretrial		23[f]		62			M ≥ 4 C ≥ 3	.43	.85	69.6	66.1	M = .38 C = .36
Hankins et al. (1993)[b]	Forensic—ITP		13[g]		66			M ≥ 4	.17	.84	30.8	69.7	—[c]
Schretlen, Neal, & Lesikar (2000)[b]	Forensic—pretrial		11[b]		86			M ≥ 4	.57	.96	72.7	93.0	M = 3.93
Rogers, Bagby, & Gillis (1992)	Forensic—pretrial		25[a]			72		Opt A Opt B	.61 .50	.93 .98	81.0 95.2	83.8 70.6	—[c]
Hankins et al. (1993)[d]	Forensic—ITP		13[g]		66			Opt A[d] Opt B	.25 .22	.89 .89	61.5 69.2	63.6 51.5	—[c]
Smith, Borum, & Schnika (1993)	Forensic—inmates		23[f]	62	62			Opt A Opt B	.43 .35	.85 .84	69.6 74.1	65.6 49.2	—[c]
Heinze (2003)	Forensic—inpatient ITST			66[e]				Rule out Rule in	—[c]	—[c]	88 85	52 60	—[c]

Note. Sim, simulators; Mal, malingerers; Clin, clinical; Foren, forensic; PPP, positive predictive power; Sens, sensitivity; Spec, specificity; ITP, incompetent to proceed; ITSP, incompetent to stand trial. [a]Based on 30- or 60-day inpatient evaluation and therapists' judgment of global malingering; [b]C scale omitted; [c]Means and SD not reported; [d]Item from the Rule-In scale was not administered; [e]Based on discharge diagnosis of malingering; [f]Based on independent forensic evaluation or strong indication of malingering in forensic report; [g]Based on judgment of a clinical interview with a forensic specialist; [h]Based on clinician's judgment with interview and review of records.

325

(.87), and M (.93). The factor structure of the M Test was also considered in this investigation. Results pointed to a three-factor solution, with the majority of the variance accounted for by a general malingering factor (i.e., 40.3%) and the other two factors essentially reflective of the other scales.

Three additional studies (Hankins, Barnard, & Robbins, 1993; Schretlen, Neal, & Lesikar, 2000; Smith & Borum, 1992) have evaluated the original scoring of the M Test (see Table 19.1) using known-groups comparisons. Results are markedly divergent, with sensitivity rates varying from 31 to 73%. Smith and Borum (1992) and Schretlen and colleagues (2000) had similar sensitivity rates (i.e., 69.6% and 72.7%, respectively), whereas Hankins and colleagues (1993) calculated sensitivity rates at only 30.8%.

The Rule-Out/Rule-In scoring has also produced varying results in four subsequent studies (Hankins et al., 1993; Heinze, 2003; Rogers, Bagby, & Gillis, 1992; Smith, Borum, & Schinka, 1993) using forensic samples in a known-groups comparison. Sensitivity for Option A ranged from 61.5 to 88%, whereas Option B was slightly better at 69.2 to 95.2%. Overall, specificity tended to be low, with most estimates ≤ 70%. These lower numbers decrease its usefulness as an effective screen.

What accounts for the marked variability in utility estimates for the two different M Test scoring methods? Likely explanations include the inherent differences between simulation and known-group designs, different scoring criteria, different base rates, within-group differences in the severity of psychiatric impairment, and demographic variable disparities between studies (e.g., gender, ethnicity, and educational levels). The importance of these variables extends beyond the M Test and is a consideration in evaluation of all screening measures for malingering.

The first potential explanation for the discrepancy in M Test results involves the inherent differences between simulation and known-groups design. A review of Table 19.1 reveals that studies with some of the highest sensitivity and specificity rates (e.g., Beaber et al., 1985; Gillis et al., 1991) used simulation designs. As noted, Gillis and colleagues (1991) found that the sensitivity for known groups was only half (i.e., 40%) of the simulation design. These same researchers note the risk of

relying solely on a simulation-design approach for the validation of screens.

Varying results might also be explained by differences in the application of the scoring criterion. Specifically, Schretlen and colleagues (2000) utilized only the M scale of the M Test, omitting the C scale. Similarly, Hankins and colleagues (1993) utilized the M scale, without the C scale and omitting one of the items from the M scale. In contrast, the two studies incorporating the original criteria, use of both C and M scales of the instrument (Gillis et al., 1991; Smith & Borum, 1992), had more similar results.

Different base rates are a third potential explanation for the discrepancy in M Test results. In forensic samples, base rates for malingering vary markedly. In surveying forensic experts, Rogers, Salekin, Sewell, Goldstein, and Leonard (1998) found major variations in base rates for forensic cases (M = 17.4%, SD = 14.4%). They also found considerable variability for nonforensic settings (M = 7.16%, SD = 7.09%). With reference to the M test, Hankins and colleagues' (1993) study, for example, had a base rate of malingering of 16.5% as compared with 27.1% for Smith and colleagues (1993). These variations in base rates have substantial effects on two utility estimates: positive predictive power (PPP) and negative predictive power (NPP). In fact, a consideration of PPP–NPP is crucial in considering the effectiveness of a screening measure in the context of such base rate variability. For a review of utility estimates, see Rogers, Chapter 2, this volume.

Another important methodological consideration potentially affecting the varying M Test results is differences across studies of the severity of psychological impairment in clinical comparison groups. For example, inpatients may provide higher scores on the M Test as a result of their impairment. Hankins and colleagues (1993), for example, noted that performance on the M Test was significant related to a discharge diagnosis of schizophrenia, as well as other administered clinical scales of "serious current psychopathology and current cognitive impairments" (p. 120). Likewise, Schretlen and colleagues (2000) found that genuine patients with moderate or severe impairment closely approximated suspected malingerers with M scale elevations. Endorsement of "bogus" symptoms by patients with severe impairment raises two issues: (1) whether these symptoms are truly bogus and (2) whether severe impairment compromises patients' comprehension (see Hankins et al., 1993). A third proposed explanation for the endorsement of "bogus" items might involve the fact that individuals with genuine psychopathology are endorsing an increased number of items as a demonstration of their degree of distress. In any event, these findings raise some questions about the use of the M Test for patients with severe impairment.

Finally, the demographic characteristics of different sample may affect M Test study results. Specifically, clinical comparison samples appear to be better educated than simulators and suspected malingerers. For example, Gillis and colleagues (1991) employed an outpatient clinic sample with a much higher level of education (i.e., 16.2 years) than suspected malingerers (i.e., 9.2 years). Similarly, Schretlen and colleagues (2000) and Heinze (2003) used clinical comparison samples with more years of education than feigning groups. These three studies yielded very positive results, which may have been affected by differences in educational level.

Race and gender are two other demographic variables that may be affecting the research on the M Test. Studies vary substantially in their minority representations, from 16.0% (Gillis et al., 1991) to 66% (Heinze, 2003). Smith and colleagues (1993) found that African American participants generally scored lower than European Americans. In addition, gender has been overlooked in M Test research. Studies have exclusively used only male participants, with the minor exception of Gillis and colleagues (1991) study. Even in this investigation, 96% of the malingering group was composed of males. The gender issue is particularly relevant because two M Test items are designated for men only. To avoid unnecessary complications, these items were intentionally omitted from Rule-Out/Rule-In scoring—something not addressed by Beaber and colleagues' (1985) original scoring.

Despite these potential threats to the external validity of the instrument, the M Test remains an important measure for the screening of malingering. Among the first of the generation of screening measures, the M Test has a body of research supporting its usefulness in selected settings. In addition, the M Test has utilized both known-groups and simulation de-signs. Its psychometric characteristics have been explored, demonstrating acceptable internal reliabilities and consistency. Furthermore, the M Test has guided the direction of subsequent investigations, from global "faking bad" to a more focused investigation of malingering of a particular condition. Finally, the instrument has demonstrated some utility in distinguishing malingerers of schizophrenia/psychosis in a forensic setting using the Rule-Out/Rule-In scoring system (Option B) for screening purposes only. Additional research with the instrument might explore the possible confounding factors of race, gender, education, and level of impairment on test scores.

M-FAST

The M-FAST (Miller, 2001) is a brief, 25-item structured interview designed to screen for malingered psychopathology in a forensic setting (Guriel et al., 2004; Guy & Miller, 2004; Miller, 2004). Miller (2001) described the M-FAST as rationally derived, with most detection strategies based on empirical research with the Structured Interview of Reported Symptoms (SIRS; Rogers, Bagby, & Dickens, 1992). Scales describing detection strategies are: Reported versus Observed (RO), Extreme Symptomatology (ES), Rare Combinations (RC), Unusual Hallucinations (UH), Unusual Symptom Course (USC), Negative Image (NI), and Suggestibility (S). The M-FAST items vary in the structure of their responses: 15 true–false questions, 5 frequency (i.e., always, sometimes, or never) items, and 2 yes or no questions. The remaining three items compare responses to observations. Items are scored as either 0 (i.e., false, never, no, or consistent) or 1 (i.e., true, always, sometimes, yes, or inconsistent). Miller recommended a cut score of ≥ 6 for suspected malingering, which is further evaluated with additional measures of malingering.

The M-FAST is intended for use in the assessment of malingered psychopathology and not feigned cognitive impairment, which requires entirely different detection strategies. Its use with certain diagnostic categories (e.g., anxiety disorders) is discouraged due to the "limited coverage of certain types of symptoms" (Miller, 2001, p. 5). The M-FAST was also designed for use with adults; no research has examined its potential usefulness in adolescent populations.

In the original development of the M-FAST, Miller (2001) conducted a series of investigations using both simulation and known-groups designs. An alpha coefficient of .93 was obtained for the M-FAST total score, with individual alphas ranging from .61 to .81. Test–retest reliability was also excellent for the total score ($r = .92$). Using known-groups comparisons based on SIRS scores, 29 suspected malingerers were compared with criminal and civil forensic patients and produced a very large effect size ($d = 3.32$). Receiver operator characteristic (ROC) analyses were calculated across the range of M-FAST scores for the instrument, demonstrating its relative effectiveness in distinguishing between malingerers and honest responders at an above-chance level. Miller (2004) provided additional analyses of the M-FAST's convergent and discriminant validity using the original validation sample. The M-FAST has moderate correlations with the Minnesota Multiphasic Personality Inventory (MMPI-2) F, Fb, and F(p) scales.

The M-FAST yielded generally good scale characteristics not only in the original study but also in subsequent research. Though somewhat variable, alpha coefficients for the individual scales were acceptable for four of the seven scales with multiple items. The lowest alpha coefficients in the Guy and Miller (2004) study were for the Extreme Symptomatology (ES = .53) and Reported versus Observed (RO = .29) subscales. Jackson, Rogers, and Sewell (2005) found slightly higher but consistent alpha coefficients in their sample for the RO (.63), as well as ES (.65), scale. These two scales were judged "marginal." The alpha coefficient ($\alpha = .91$) for the total score was impressive. Although the subscales are variable, the total score is key because it is used in the screening for possible feigned mental disorders. It remains excellent.

The convergent and discriminant validity of the M-FAST was supported by the research of Veazey, Hays, Wagner, and Miller (2005) in an acute psychiatric inpatient population using the Personality Assessment Inventory (PAI) validity scales. A high correlation was noted between the M-FAST total score and Negative Impression (NIM; $r = .76$) and a moderate negative correlation with Positive Impression (PIM; $r = -.55$). Limiting generalizability, rates of participation were low (i.e., 44 out of 150 consecutive referrals or 29.3%).

The effect of race on M-FAST results has been investigated. In the original validation study, Miller (2001) found that the sensitivity for European Americans dropped to .67 in the clinical sample. Issues of race were addressed by Guy and Miller (2004) via ROC curves; similar results were noted for African Americans (.90), European Americans (.93), and Hispanic American participants (1.00). These results are only indirectly related to clinical practice, as they assume that each M-FAST score will be used as a cut score. Sensitivities ranged from .86 (European Americans) to 1.00 (Hispanics). NPP measures were similarly high: .83 for African Americans to 1.00 for Hispanic Americans. Overall, these results suggest that the M-FAST is not substantially susceptible to race effects.

The potential confounding effect of gender also has been investigated, which was important because the original research used mostly males in the clinical samples. In contrast, two simulation samples were composed mostly of females (i.e., 68.1% and 72.3%). In subsequent research, Jackson and colleagues (2005) found no significant differences on the basis of gender.

In a small simulation study (Guriel et al., 2004), the M-FAST has demonstrated its resistance to the effects of coaching. Using undergraduates without any clinical comparison sample, these investigators examined the M-FAST in combination with the Trauma Symptom Inventory (TSI; Briere, 1995) to detect feigned PTSD. Without comparisons with genuine patients, most utility estimates have marginal significance. One exception is sensitivity. Providing information about PTSD symptoms *decreased* simulators' ability, apparently distracting them from the task of providing a credible performance. For uncoached and coached strategies conditions, the sensitivities were comparable but relatively low (.60 and .64, respectively).

The M-FAST as a screening tool has been investigated in several different populations, including correctional (Guy & Miller, 2004), acute psychiatric inpatient (Veazey et al., 2005), forensic/competency to stand trial (Jackson et al., 2005), and workers' compensation/personal injury (Alwes, Clark, Berry, & Granacher, 2006). Table 19.2 provides a summary of utility estimates and effect sizes.

In establishing suspected malingerers, several methodological concerns should be noted

TABLE 19.2. Design Features and Study Outcomes: M-FAST

Study	Population	Groups Experimental Sim	Mal	Criterion[g] Same population	ITST	Utility estimates Cut	PPP	NPP	Sens	Spec	d^a
Miller (2001, 2004)	Forensic—ITST		14[c]	36		6	.68	.97	.93	.83	3.32
Guy & Miller (2004)	Inmates seeking services		21[c]	29		6	.78	.89	.86	.83	2.06
Alwes et al. (2006)	Forensic—civil		23: Psy	172		6	.42[d]	.98	.83	.91	3.03
	Forensic—civil		75: Cog	172		6	.22	.95	.43	.88	.96
Jackson et al. (2005)	Forensic—inmates	43			41	6	—[f]	—[f]	—[f]	—[f]	1.47
			8[c]		41	6	—[f]	—[f]	—[f]	—[f]	2.80
Veazey et al. (2005)	Psychiatric— inpatients		7[e]	37		6	.40	.97	.80	.85	2.34[b]
						7	.50	.97	.80	.90	
						8	.57	.97	.80	.92	

Note. Sim, simulators; Mal, malingerers; ITST, incompetent to stand trial; PPP, positive predictive power; NPP, negative predictive power; Sens, sensitivity; Spec, specificity; Psy, psychiatric; Cog, cognitive; ^{a}Total score; ^{b}Effect size calculated by correlation between total score and PAI NIM scale; ^{c}Determined by responses to the SIRS; ^{d}Base rate of malingering = 7.5%; ^{e}Determined by PAI Malingering Index ≥ 3, within-groups design; ^{f}Not reported, insufficient data to calculate; ^{g}Unless indicated, criterion groups drawn from the same population as the experimental sample.

that affect the interpretation of Table 19.2. Miller (2001, 2004) and Guy and Miller (2004) did not use the standard classification for the SIRS (see Rogers, Chapter 18, this volume) but a broadened criterion (i.e., ≥ 2 elevations in the probable range), which introduces a false-positive rate of 18.2%. Veazey and colleagues (2005) used the PAI Malingering Index as a criterion for likely feigning, which has significant limitations (see Sellbom & Bagby, Chapter 11, this volume). These investigations are best considered bootstrapping comparisons (see Rogers, Chapter 1, this volume) rather than known-groups comparisons. Given their imprecision, utility estimates are not recommended for bootstrapping comparisons. They are included in Table 19.2 because there is only one small investigation that used a true known-groups comparison (Jackson et al., 2005), and it had a very small group.

The hallmark of a screen is to retain as many likely feigners as possible. Nearly all investigations used the standard cut score for the M-FAST: total score ≥ 6. Key utility estimates are NPP and sensitivity. Across six comparisons (see Table 19.2), NPP ranges from .83 to .91, with an unweighted mean of .87. This estimate

suggests that relatively few feigners (approximately 13%) are not retained for a full evaluation of malingering. Sensitivity values, though lower, are still very good. The one exception is Alwes and colleagues' (2006) examination of cognitive feigning. Because the M-FAST was not intended to screen for feigned cognitive impairment, this result is less relevant.

The M-FAST was developed and validated as a screen for feigned mental disorders. As such, it should not be used for the determination of malingering. Results in Table 19.2 confirm this. Excluding the less relevant comparison (cognitive feigning, PPP = .22), the PPP estimates are still highly variable, ranging from .40 to .78 (unweighted M = .60).

Effect sizes for the M-FAST total score are consistently very large. For relevant comparisons, they range from 1.47 to 3.32. These findings, as summarized in Table 19.2, provide excellent evidence of discriminant validity. Contrary to findings on the M Test, Jackson and colleagues (2005) found larger effect sizes for likely malingerers than for simulators.

Alwes and colleagues (2006) explored the possibility of using the M-FAST with workers' compensation and personal injury lawsuits. Using tests of neurocognitive effort (i.e., Test of Memory Malingering [TOMM], Victoria Symptom Validity Test [VSVT], and Letter Memory Test [LMT]), 75 likely feigners of neurocognitive symptoms were identified. Interestingly, they demonstrated a moderate effect size ($d = .96$). As noted in Table 19.2, the PPP (.22) was too low for practical use.

M-FAST: Summary and Future Directions

Future research might consider the effectiveness of the instrument in terms of its ability to detect malingering of mood and anxiety disorders; there has been some demonstration of the M-FAST's usefulness with these disorders (Alwes et al., 2006). The use of the M-FAST in the detection of other symptoms, including low intelligence and amnestic syndromes, as well as other neuropsychological deficits, is also recommended, as some researchers have noted the tendency for malingerers to adopt a "broad band" approach to malingering (e.g., Alwes et al., 2006; Heinze, 2003).

Several reviewed studies found significant differences between groups on education (e.g., Guy & Miller, 2004) in forensic samples, though this was not the case in an inpatient psychiatric setting (i.e., Veazey et al., 2005). Consequently, future research with the instrument might focus on balancing groups on this factor to eliminate this as a possible confounding variable, particularly in forensic settings.

The standard cut score for the M-FAST total score is ≥ 6 and was found to be the most effective in distinguishing group members. However, Veazey and colleagues (2005) indicated that a high cut score of 8 might be required in other settings, such as inpatient units. Different cut scores may reflect different levels of impairment at different settings. Future research might systematically examine how different levels of impairment (e.g., Global Assessment of Functioning [GAF] scores) affect the M-FAST's classifications.

In summary, the M-FAST has demonstrated good scale characteristics in its development and subsequent simulation research. Bootstrapping comparisons and known-groups comparisons have produced comparable results to those of simulation studies. The NPP has produced positive results for a feigning screen. The M-FAST total score is the most effective and produces large effect sizes. Its brevity and relative ease of administration are

two additional features that make this measure an attractive screening device. Clinicians should, therefore, consider the use of this instrument as a brief screening measure for the potential malingering of psychopathology, with a cut score of ≥ 6 on the total score as the most effective indicator. Though most of the research has been conducted in a correctional/forensic setting, the instrument will likely demonstrate its efficacy across other venues.

SIMS

The Structured Inventory of Malingered Symptomatology (SIMS; Widows & Smith, 2005) is a 75-item true–false, self-administered screen for the detection of malingering across a variety of clinical and forensic settings. With multiple scales, the SIMS evaluates the possibility of feigning a variety of psychiatric and neuropsychological symptoms. The SIMS is intended for use with individuals 18 years of age or older with at least a fifth-grade reading level. The SIMS is not recommended for persons with severe impairment who may be unable to attend to items. Finally, the SIMS should not be used beyond its stated purpose as a screen for malingering. The definitive classification of malingering requires more comprehensive measures (e.g., SIRS) and multiple sources of data (e.g., psychiatric and medical history).

SIMS items were developed using two separate methods. The first method involved the refinement of items selected from existing measures, such as the MMPI, SIRS, and Wechsler Adult Intelligence Scale—Revised (WAIS-R) that had demonstrated some utility in the detection of malingering. The second method involved the generation of additional items to reflect the qualitative characteristics of malingerers noted in previous research (e.g., Resnick, 1984; Rogers, 1984b; Seamons, Howell, Carlisle, & Roe, 1981). Expert raters served to confirm item placement in each scale. Detection strategies for feigned mental disorders include rare symptoms, improbable symptoms, and symptom combinations. Detection strategies for feigned cognitive impairment included Performance Curve and Magnitude of Error (i.e., approximate answers).

SIMS items are organized into five nonoverlapping scales of 15 questions each, designed to reflect commonly malingered conditions: Low Intelligence (LI), Affective Disorders (AF), Neurologic Impairment (N), Psychosis (P), and

Amnesia (AM). Items are scored as either "0" or "1" and summed for each scale and the total score. A cut score >14 on the total score identifies the need for a comprehensive assessment of malingering.

The initial validation of the SIMS (Smith, 1992; Smith & Burger, 1997) was conducted using 476 undergraduate students divided into developmental and cross-validational samples. These samples comprised predominantly females (71%) and European Americans (89.7%). Simulators were assigned to feign a specific diagnostic condition. For convergent validity, participants completed the MMPI F and K scales, the 16PF Faking Bad scale, and portions of the Malingering Scale (Schretlen & Arkowitz, 1990). Cut scores were developed for SIMS scales and total score that maximized the discrimination between each group and controls. These cut scores were then applied to the responses of the cross-validation sample.

The SIMS demonstrated good internal reliabilities for individual scales, ranging from .80 to .88. An exploratory factor analysis indicated a five-factor solution with each of the scales reflected. However, some N scale items crossloaded with P scale items. Alpha coefficients were calculated for each of the scales: P (.82), Am (.83), N (.83), Af (.86), and LI (.85). Univariate ANOVAs yielded expected differences between simulators and controls.

In the original research, the SIMS total score proved to be the most efficient screen of malingering. It accurately identified 95.6% of the simulators and 87.9% of the honestly responding participants. The other scales varied in terms of their sensitivity from a low of 74.6% using the Af to a high of 88.3% using the Am. Although very promising, a limitation of the original research was the lack of clinical comparison samples.

Subsequent research on the effectiveness of the SIMS falls into two distinct categories: simulation (analogue) designs and those that utilize known groups. Simulation designs have strong internal validity and can be used to test the effects of coaching. In contrast, known-groups comparisons are strong on external validity but limited on internal validity (see Chapter 1, this volume).

Four known-groups comparisons are reviewed involving criminal (i.e., Heinze & Purisch, 2001; Lewis, Simcox, & Berry, 2002; Poythress, Edens, & Watkins, 2001) and civil (i.e., Alwes, et al., 2006) forensic populations.

Of these studies, Heinze and Purisch (2001) was particularly impressive in its extensive study of 57 malingerers from a larger sample of 438 male inmates on which high agreement was independently reached for the determination of malingering (interrater agreement = .92). In the following paragraphs, known-group comparisons are examined first, followed by the simulation research.

As noted previously, the hallmark of a screen is its NPP and sensitivity. For the three relevant comparisons using known-group comparisons, the NPPs are .75, .99, and 1.00 (see Table 19.3). Superb NPPs are achieved when the cut score of 16 is used. Sensitivity estimates are outstanding, with a range from .85 to 1.00 for the four relevant comparisons; the unweighted average is excellent at .92. Taken together, the SIMS is very effective at retaining potential malingerers for a full assessment of malingering.

As a screen for feigned mental disorders, the SIMS is not expected to have high PPP values, because its purpose is to maximize NPP. As summarized in Table 19.3, its PPP tends to be only moderate, ranging from .28 to .55. These data suggest that practitioners should not go beyond the original purpose of the SIMS in attempting to make determinations of malingering.

A major strength of the SIMS is its impressive effect sizes. Using SIMS total scores produces exceptional effect sizes for known-groups comparisons of 2.06, 2.55, and 3.00. Even when applied to cognitive feigning, not its intended purpose, it still produces moderate effect sizes.

A limitation of several SIMS simulation studies is the absence of clinical comparison samples. As a result, utility estimates do not really capture the key distinction (i.e., the differentiation between malingered and genuine disorders). The results were important in the original development of the SIMS in demonstrating the potential usefulness of its scales. Thus the results of Smith (1992) were instrumental to the refinement of SIMS scales, although these utility estimates required further validation.

Research by Edens, Otto, and Dwyer (1999) is important in examining the effectiveness of the SIMS via a simulation design. Using a within-subjects design, they examined three conditions without clinical comparison samples (i.e., Psychosis, Depression, and Cognitive) and two conditions with clinical compar-

TABLE 19.3. Design Features and Study Outcomes: SIMS

| | | Groups | | | | | Utility estimates | | | | |
| | | | | Criterion[j] | | | | | | | |
Study	Population	Experimental simulators	Malingerers	Clin	Cont	Cut	PPP	NPP	Sens	Spec	d
Poythress, Edens, & Watkins (2001)	Forensic—inmates	29		30[c]	30[c]	14	.96	.91	.90	.97	—[d]
	Forensic—mental illness		26[c]			14	.55	.75	.85	.40	—[d]
Lewis et al. (2002)	Forensic—CTST		24[b]	31[b]		16	.54	1.00	1.00	.61	3.0
Heinze & Purisch (2001)	Forensic—CTST		57	59[e]		14	—[d]	—[d]	.87	—[d]	2.06
Alwes et al. (2006)	Forensic—civil		23[b] Disorders	172[b]		16	.28[f]	.99	.96	.67	2.55
	Forensic—civil		75[b] Cognitive	178[b]		16	.44[g]	.85	.75	.60	1.13
Smith (1992) Smith & Burger (1997)	College	208[i]			30	14	.98	.74	.96	.88	2.13
Rogers, Hinds, & Sewell (1996)	Forensic—adolescent	53		53[a]		16	.87	.62	.44	.94	—[d]
Edens et al. (1999)	College	196			196[a]	14	.92	.96	.96	.91	—[d]
		59 Psychosis			59[a]	14	.94	.98	.98	.93	3.14
		65 Depression			65[a]	14	.90	.92	.92	.89	2.48
		72 Cognitive			72[a]	14	.92	.99	.99	.92	3.52
		33 (prior MH)		33[a] (prior MH)		14	.91	.97	.97	.91	—[d]
		45 (current MH)		45[a] (current MH)		14	.82	1.00	1.00	.78	—[d]
Merckelbach & Smith (2003)[b]	College	57		10	231	16	.90	.98	.93	.98	2.12
Rogers, Jackson, et al. (2005)	Graduate students	14 Factitious Dependent			16	—[d]	—[d]	—[d]	—[d]	—[d]	1.09
		18 Factitious Demanding				—[d]					
		17 Simulators			16	—[d]	—[d]	—[d]	—[d]	—[d]	1.35
					16		—[d]	—[d]	—[d]	—[d]	1.45
Jelicic et al. (2006)[b]	College	45 Psychosis		15	15	14	1.00	.79	.91	1.00	1.71

Note. CTST, Competent to stand trial; Clin, clinical; Cont, control group; PPP, positive predictive power; NPP, negative predictive power; Sens, sensitivity; Spec, specificity; MH, mental health. [a]Within-subjects design; [b]Determined by responses to the SIRS; [c]Judgment by staff; [d]Not reported, insufficient data to calculate; [e]Sample from the Edens et al., 1999 study honestly responding; [f]Base rate of .075; [g]Base rate of .244; [b]Translation from Dutch; [i]Simulating low intelligence, depression, mania, psychosis, amnesia, neurological impairment, and faking bad; [j]Unless indicated, criterion groups drawn from the same population as the experimental sample.

isons: prior mental health history and current psychological distress. Both groups yielded impressive utility estimates that are comparable to those without clinical comparison samples. This finding lends support for examining these studies, at least as ancillary data.

SIMS studies have sought to extend research to adolescents and to factitious disorders. Using a within-subjects design, Rogers, Hinds, and Sewell (1996) sought to examine the SIMS with dually diagnosed adolescent forensic inpatients. With mostly substance abuse and mood disorders, the NPP was substantially lower than what was found with adult clinical samples. Further research is needed on its application to adolescent populations. In addition, Rogers, Jackson, and Kaminski (2004) conducted an initial study of the SIMS with two feigned factitious conditions and a feigned malingered condition. Without clinical comparison groups, their findings should be considered preliminary. Nevertheless, the SIMS total score produced a moderate effect size. The authors observed that those in the malingering condition scored higher than the control group on the N scale and that the factitious conditions scored higher than controls on the AF scale. In order to improve the effectiveness of the instrument, the researchers computed a new variable (AF – N). Applying a cut score on the new score of ≥ 1 resulted in a sensitivity and NPP of 1.00 with specificity of .31. The Rogers and colleagues (2004) study suggests that future feigning indicators may take into account the relationships between SIMS scales in maximizing clinical differentiation.

Edens and colleagues (1999) explored the potential impact of coaching or knowledge of particular mental disorders using the SIMS via a simulation design. The absence of clinical comparison samples for specific feigning conditions limits the practical usefulness of their findings. As a preliminary investigation, however, their findings suggest that the utility estimates for NPP and sensitivity appear to be robust, irrespective of the feigned condition.

Finally, simulation research has provided some initial evidence regarding the ability of the SIMS to act as an effective screening tool for malingering across cultures and languages and additional evidence regarding its resistance to coaching. For example, Merckelbach and Smith (2003) examined the psychometric properties of a Dutch translation of the SIMS. Using a small (n = 10) inpatient comparison

sample, undergraduates simulated several clinical conditions: amnesia, schizophrenia, or neurological conditions. Simulators were coached regarding each condition and provided with some incentive. Although preliminary, their results indicated strong discriminant validity (d = 2.12). ROC analysis produced very strong results, with an area under the curve (AUC) of .96. Jelicic, Hessels, and Merckelbach (2006) provided additional data on the Dutch SIMS, although interpretation of their results is constrained by the absence of a clinical comparison sample.

SIMS: Summary and Future Directions

The SIMS has demonstrated utility as a screening instrument for malingering. One of its strengths is its effectiveness within known-groups design, including both male and female patients (i.e., Alwes et al., 2006). As evidence of generalizability, the SIMS is effective with the same known groups, whether the sample was predominantly European American (93.2%, Alwes et al., 2006) or African American (60.9%, Poythress et al., 2001). Its application to adolescents would benefit from further research. The SIMS has demonstrated its relative resistance to coaching in simulation designs.

A major advantage of the SIMS is its low reading level (i.e., Fleisch–Kincaid Scale = 5.3), which makes it accessible to a wide range of respondents. The availability of a computerized administration and scoring program provides standardization in test administration, automation in scoring, efficient data storage, generation of multiple forms, and the creation of a less competitive testing environment (Guiterrez & Gur, 1998).

As a screening measure, the SIMS effectiveness across culture and language has received preliminary support, with additional research focused on the validation of additional translations, including German (e.g., Cima, Merckelbach, Hollnack, & Knauer, 2003).

Future research should examine further the optimal cut scores. Current research suggests a narrow range of ≥ 14 to ≥ 16. The role of settings and levels of psychological impairment should be addressed further. A potential concern is the possibility of false positives among severely impaired clinical populations.

The impact of age, culture, and education should also be addressed in future research. As noted previously, the SIMS was effective across diverse groups. As a screen for feigned mental disorders, its NPP and sensitivity should remain the focus of future investigations. Lewis and colleagues (2002) noted a "trend" toward differences in terms of race (nonwhites classified as malingering) and education (malingerers had a lower mean for years of education), suggesting that these factors may warrant closer scrutiny. Finally, research by Rogers and colleagues (2004; i.e., AF – N) suggests the possibility of other methods to enhance the clinical usefulness of the SIMS.

RECENTLY DEVELOPED SCREENING MEASURES

In addition to the screening devices reviewed, several more recently developed instruments have been investigated in the literature with regard to their effectiveness in the detection of malingered psychopathology. They include the Assessment of Depression Inventory (ADI), Malingering Detection Scale (MDS), African State Presidents' Detainee Scale (ASPDS), and the Morel Emotional Numbing Test (MENT).

Assessment of Depression Inventory

The ADI (Mogge & LePage, 2004) is a 39-item scale on which respondents indicate the nature of symptoms over a 2-week time frame using a 4-point Likert scale (i.e., *never, some, often,* or *always*). The ADI was developed in three separate investigations.

The first investigation established an initial item pool for the three scales: Depression (Dep), Feigning (Fg), and Random (Rd). Dep (27 items) utilized the DSM-IV criteria for major depressive episodes, three items for each of the nine inclusion criteria. The 65 items of the Fg were developed from "research literature on malingering styles . . . case studies, personal clinical experience with malingerers and depressed inpatients, and suggestions from colleagues" and resulted in those that were "extreme, bizarre, or atypical" of "real" depression (Mogge & LePage, 2004, p. 108). The Rd content includes simple questions that have "obvious" answers.

A simulation study (61 community simulators and 29 inpatients) was used to develop the final version of the ADI. Correlation (i.e., $\geq .5$) with the Beck Depression Inventory–II (BDI-II; Beck, Steer, & Brown, 1996) and effect sizes ($d > 1.2$) were the criteria for selecting the final 19 Dep items. Fg items were retained in a two-stage process. First, only those with a "medium" Cohen effect size ($d > .5$) were further analyzed. To minimize overlap with depressive items, only those 16 items that accounted for less than 5% of the variance on the BDI-II questions were retained. The final 4 questions on the Rd scale were answered in the expected direction by at least 60% of both samples.

The second investigation was a simulation design, with the final 39-item version of the ADI and the BDI-II administered to a patient group (39 inpatients and 11 outpatients), 39 naive feigners (not having worked in a mental health setting or experienced significant depression), and 38 "sophisticated feigners" (workers in a mental health facility). The feigning groups were instructed to "fake depression . . . to get out of trouble with the law . . . in a believable manner" (Mogge & LePage, 2004, p. 109). There were statistically significant differences between groups on Fg ($F[2,124] = 78.8$; $p < .001$), with feigning participants scoring higher than criterion group members. Rd results were nonsignificant. Fg was significantly higher for simulators than for patients. An Fg cut score of 15 yielded a sensitivity of .75 and a specificity of .98; it had a PPP of .98 and an NPP of .72.

The third simulation study cross-validated these results with 38 naive (nonpatients without mental health work experience or history of depression) and 35 sophisticated (nonpatients who worked in a mental health setting) simulators compared with those of a criterion group composed of 25 psychiatric inpatients and 33 VA outpatients. Using the same cut score on Fg (i.e., ≥ 15) yielded comparable findings (i.e., sensitivity of .84, specificity of .97, PPP of .98, and NPP of .97). For depression, a Dep cut score of ≥ 39 was established by combining both the initial and cross-validation sample, using the BDI-II scores (i.e., 20) as the criterion for moderate depression.

The ADI has demonstrated initial clinical utility in the screening within a psychiatric population attempting to feign depressive features. Its usefulness is enhanced by its low reading level (i.e., Flesch–Kincaid = 4.1). However, some scale characteristics for Fg were not discussed. Further investigations into the convergent and discriminant validity are recommended. Future investigators might consider the impact of incentives on responses and manipulation checks. Finally, research using a known-groups design (i.e., suspected malingerers) would further support the routine use of ADI in clinical populations.

Malingering Detection Scale

The MDS (Barkemeyer & Callon, 1989) is a 29-item, examiner-scored rating scale designed to distinguish between neurological patients with demonstrable organic disease and malingerers. The MDS is divided into two major sections: interview behaviors and apparent goals for patients' behavior. In the first section, items ask the professional to note the patient's manipulation attempts, specific responses to questions, and reactions to disagreement. The questions were developed based on their "high positive correlation with malingering" (Callon, Jones, Barkemeyer, & Brantley, 1990, p. 3) through the identification of some 26 recurring behaviors of malingering. Some of the items appear to be consistent with previously noted characteristics of malingerers. For example, Resnick (1984) notes that malingerers' presentations often fit no known diagnostic entity; this feature is captured by several of the MDS items.

In the second section, the examiner rates the potential goals of patients' behavior in terms of avoidance of normal responsibility and securing a concrete objective (e.g., monetary gain). The identification of motives for malingering also are considered in the form of "three general functions" that may point to malingering, such as the rejection of alternative explanations regarding the etiology of current difficulties.

Initially designed for use by physicians and psychologists, the MDS reportedly can be used by individuals without extensive professional training. However, two of the questions require some medical knowledge. Wymer, Barkemeyer, Jones, and Callon (2006, p. 37) reported a very brief administration time between "several seconds to several minutes." Positive responses are summed to calculate a total score. In the original validation study, Callon and colleagues (1990, p. 4) established a cut score ≥ 8 to be "associated with at least a 95% chance of malingering." As the MDS was specifically designed for a medical setting with neurology patients, its research is limited to that population (e.g., Callon et al., 1990; Wymer et al., 2006).

Two studies (Barkemeyer & Callon, 1989; Wymer et al., 2006) validate the MDS. The first validation study (Barkemeyer & Callon, 1989) consisted of an initial study and cross-validation. First, the MDS was completed by 122 adult patients at a neurology clinic. Thirty were classified in the malingering group based on at least two of three features (e.g., inconsistency between presenting complaints and defined symptoms complex, failure of the examination to support complaints, and failure of laboratory results to support the complaints). This design is best conceptualized as a bootstrapping comparison. As a scale, the MDS yielded an excellent internal consistency (.93).

Based on discriminant analysis, an MDS cut score of ≥ 8 yielded impressive utility estimates in terms of sensitivity (.90), specificity (.97), PPP (.90), NPP (.97), and effect size (3.95). Three malingerers (10.0%) and three genuine patients (3.3%) were misclassified. In the cross-validation, 17 malingerers and 49 genuine patients completed the MDS, with group designation determined by expert opinion of the senior investigator. Interrater reliabilities on the MDS between the two independent examiners (senior investigator and expert administering the MDS) was .94. Classification rates in this cross-validation work were reported to be similar in terms of sensitivity (.94), specificity (1.0), PPP (1.0), and NPP (.98). Wymer and colleagues (2006) confirmed specificity and discriminant validity of the MDS with 50 consecutive neurology patients with objective neurological findings. The MDS was completed by Wymer, who was blind to participants' medical information. Participants' scores ranged between 0 and 4. When a cut score of 8 was applied to the sample, a specificity rate of 100% was obtained.

Although the MDS does provide a relatively quick and unobtrusive assessment opportunity as suggested by the authors, the identified supportive research is limited. The key issue is whether its results will generalize to other clinical settings and professionals not closely involved in its development. In addition, further examination of specific neurological conditions and demographic variables (e.g., race) might help to eliminate the possibility of threats to internal and external validity. The use of standardized instructions for feigning (in the case of simulation designs) should be the focus of future investigations.

African State Presidents' Detainee Scale

The ASPDS (Bunnting, Wessels, Lasich, & Pillay, 1996) is a 20-item instrument designed to screen for malingering of general psychopathology. The authors derived test items from a review of the literature, as well as from "the author's personal clinical experience and from multi-disciplinary clinical meetings" (p. 242). The items are divided into two domains. The first involves pretrial behavior (e.g., claims to be mentally disordered), physical functioning (e.g., normal EEG), and family reports (e.g., unconfirmed reports of the individual's mental disorder). Other items relate more directly to malingering as outlined in DSM-IV (e.g., motive for the crime is found in the court records and psychiatric assessments). Items are scored as either positive or negative. A single score represents the total number of positive responses.

Bunnting and colleagues (1996) utilized a known-groups design to evaluate the ASPDS responses of (1) 50 forensic inpatients judged to be malingering and (2) 50 forensic patients evaluated as "mentally disordered or sick." Responses to the items were then divided into four categories based on their individual positive and negative predictive value. The three with the highest predictive value reportedly had an overall accuracy rate of classification ranging from 89 to 95%. The nature of these items appear to involve factors generally accepted in the literature as typical in malingerers (e.g., overt claims of mental illness across time, the atypical nature of the illness, and the presence of a clear motivation). However, the authors offered an additional 14 items judged to be effective in the differentiation of malingering. These additional items offer other intriguing content (e.g., "The crime is not against a close family member such as one's parents or one's own child"). Some items demonstrated a positive predictive value of 100%, though at the expense of lower negative predictive accuracy. Overall hit rates with these items ranged from 60 to 87%. Three items were not found to be clinically useful.

The investigation has a number of limitations, including lack of reports of scale characteristics and measures of convergent/discriminant validity, potential cultural confounds, lack of analyses of the impact of demographic characteristics (e.g., age, race, gender, and education), and the subjective nature of some rat-

ings (e.g., giving "silly" answers across situations). Furthermore, the ability of a screening instrument to "diagnose both malingering and sickness with a high degree of accuracy" does not appear to be (1) supported by the limited range of items endorsed or (2) corroborated via cross-validation research. At this point, the instrument cannot be recommended for routine use.

Morel Emotional Numbing Test for PTSD

The MENT (Morel, 1998) for PTSD is a 60-item instrument that is designed to assess simulated impairment in affect recognition. Items consist of photos of faces (both men and women) presented in a two-alternative forced-choice format across three sets. In Set I, the respondent is directed to circle the emotion corresponding to the photo (e.g., frustration, anger, fear). In Set II, one of two slides is selected that corresponds to the target word/emotion. In Set III, two slides and two words are matched. Other than matching the photo to the word, the only additional instruction occurs prior to Set I, when it is overtly suggested to the respondent that individuals with PTSD may have difficulty with the task. The author indicates that the threshold of difficulty is set sufficiently low so that those with intact neurocognitive functioning can expect "near-perfect accuracy." Testing requires approximately 5 to 15 minutes. A final score is derived from the total number of errors, with a cut score of ≥ 9 to minimize false positives. Test limitations involve the exclusion of individuals with neurological impairments that affect word recognition or visual acuity.

In the initial validation study, Morel (1998) used an F-K Index of ≥ 15 as a criterion to assess the effectiveness of the MENT in distinguishing between "veritable" and "suspect" disability claimants for PTSD. The suspect claimant group made significantly more errors on the MENT, 6 times the error rate compared with those already diagnosed with PTSD and 10 times the error rate compared with those from the inpatient substance abuse sample. The calculated sensitivity was .82 with a specificity of 1.0. The instrument also produced a PPP of 100% and an NPP of 94.4%. Though effective in distinguishing the suspect group, the study did note the apparent impact of age on MENT scores. Older participants produced more errors than younger participants with PTSD, which the author speculates may point to the susceptibility of the measure to right hemisphere decline with advancing age.

The MENT has also been used in investigations of the overreporting of recovered memories of childhood sexual abuse (Geraerts, Jelicic, & Merckelbach, 2006), as well as in a European clinical sample of combat-related PTSD (Geraerts et al., 2006).

CLINICAL RECOMMENDATIONS FOR THE USE OF SCREENING MEASURES

A key issue is how clinicians should select screening instruments to be used in the comprehensive assessment for malingering. The following factors should be considered:

- Does the screen have good scale characteristics? Psychometric properties should indicate good scale development.
- Does the screen have good reliability? Without good reliability, then any interpretation of the results is suspect.
- Is there solid evidence of convergent and discriminant validity?
- Do effect sizes and utility estimates support its intended use?
- In which settings and populations has it been tested and validated?

Feigning screens vary substantially in their focus and purpose. Some screens were designed to evaluate a particular set of symptoms or a particular condition (e.g., MENT for emotional numbing) but not others (e.g., M-FAST for neuropsychological symptoms). In contrast, the SIMS was designed to address an array of clinical conditions. Clinicians must choose between depth (MENT) and breadth (SIMS). When the nature of the clinical conditions being malingered is unclear, a screen that taps the broadest range of feigned difficulties is recommended. Table 19.4 provides an overview of the instruments reviewed in this chapter and the conditions for which they have demonstrated sensitivity.

Consideration should be given to the setting in which the screening measure is to be administered. Screens vary substantially in professional settings. Clinicians can clearly have greater confidence in their conclusions if the screen's validity was tested with similar populations. Most feigning screens are tested under general clinical conditions that support their general use. In some instances, the screens have been tested with specific disorders or clinical conditions. Data can assist in testing the sensitivity of the screen with that particular condition. In rare circumstances, relevant clinical comparison groups also allow clinicians to evaluate the specificity of the measure with a specific diagnosis or clinical condition. As an alternative, the use of diagnostic heterogeneous groups can assist in establishing specificity. When results are compared only with those of community controls, then estimates of specificity are not feasible. Table 19.4 provides initial data on clinical conditions that have been tested with feigning screens.

The method of administration should also be taken into account. Some clinicians may wish to take a multimodal approach that integrates interview-based (e.g., M-FAST) and self-report (e.g., SIMS) methods. An important question is whether examinees are more likely to dissimulate in face-to-face encounters versus paper-and-pencil or computer-based administrations.

Feigning screens are often applied in high-volume settings as an efficient method of prioritizing assessment methods. By themselves, they should not be used as the sole means of decision making except in those rare instances in which NPP has been cross-validated with similar populations and achieved exceptional levels (e.g., > .95). However, PPP must also be considered. When the base rate is hypothesized to be low and the PPP is also low (e.g., < .30), then the "gain" for a particular screen may be outweighed by its "cost."

The selection of an instrument and cut score with the highest sensitivity will enhance the probability that the *test* will identify malingerers as a group. The highest PPP improves the chances that an *individual score* does not misidentify as a malingerer. This is important both because the cost of high false positives (i.e., misidentifying genuine patients as malingerers) could potentially outweigh all other benefits of a feigning screen. To underscore a critical point, screening measures should not be used for the classification of malingering. Even comprehensive measures of feigning (e.g., the SIRS) require multimethod approaches to the determination of malingering. Table 19.5 provides

TABLE 19.4. Clinical Support for Screening Measures: An Examination of Populations and Clinical Conditions

Population	Clinical condition								
	General malingering	Psychosis/ schizophrenia	Cognitive/ neurocognitive symptoms	Amnesia	Neurological impairment	Factitious disorder	Depression	Low intelligence	PTSD
Forensic—criminal	M Test[a] M-FAST[a] SIMS[a]								
Forensic—civil	M-FAST[a] SIMS[a]		M-FAST[a] SIMS[a]						
Adolescent		SIMS[b]					SIMS[b]		
Inpatient psychiatric	M-FAST[a]						ADI[b]		
Outpatient clinical/simulation	M Test[a] M-FAST[a] SIMS[c]	M Test[b] SIMS[b]	SIMS[c]	SIMS[b]	MDS[a] SIMS[b]	SIMS[c]	SIMS[c]	SIMS[c]	M-FAST[c] MENT[a]

Note. PTSD, posttraumatic stress disorder; M-FAST, Miller Forensic Assessment of Symptoms Test; SIMS, Structured Inventory of Malingered Symptomatology; ADI, Assessment of Depression Inventory; MDS, Malingering Detection Scale; MENT, Morel Emotional Numbing Test. [a]Demonstrated effectiveness with likely malingerers; [b]Demonstrated effectiveness with simulators and a relevant clinical comparison group; [c]Possible effectiveness with simulators and a nonclinical control group.

TABLE 19.5. Feigning Screens and Best Cut Scores

Test	Cut scores
ADI	Fg Score ≥ 15
MDS	Total Score ≥ 8
MENT	Total Error Score ≥ 9
M-FAST	Total Score ≥ 6
M Test	Rule In/Rule Out—Option B
SIMS	Total Score ≥ 14

Note. ADI, Assessment of Depression Inventory; MDS, Malingering Detection Scale; MENT, Morel Emotional Numbing Test; M-FAST, Miller Forensic Assessment of Symptoms Test; SIMS, Structured Inventory of Malingered Symptomatology.

specific recommendations regarding test cut scores for use as screens.

DIRECTIONS FOR FUTURE RESEARCH

The purpose of this section is to highlight research needs related specifically to screening measures for malingering. The primary concerns follow.

1. *Specialized screens.* Initially, the M Test was constructed to tap malingering of one condition, schizophrenia. However, malingerers are likely not to limit their feigning to a single diagnostic entity. Instruments designed to tap a broader range (e.g., SIMS) have demonstrated success in this regard. Therefore, screening measures should attempt to represent a spectrum of feigned disorders, both in item development and subsequent validation.

2. *Irrelevant responding.* Random or irrelevant responding often results in a highly atypical response pattern that overlaps with malingering (see, e.g., the MMPI-2). Screening measures need to distinguish irrelevant responding from feigning, whether by design (e.g., inclusion of a subscale) or by patterns of responses. Only ADI offered such a scale among the instruments reviewed.

3. *Multiple detection strategies.* Screening measures have adopted a number of strategies for the detection of feigning that are summarized in Chapter 2 in this volume. The use of multiple strategies is justified based on the weight of evidence about the effectiveness of such instruments reviewed (e.g., M-FAST) in terms of detection. The next logical step is to assess the comparative utility of specific strategies across measures. The goals involve the investigation of (1) which strategies are robust and (2) which combinations of strategies are the most effective.

4. *Confounds to classification.* Demographic factors (e.g., race and educational status), as well as level of severity of psychiatric symptoms, should also be a focus of future research.

5. *Known-groups comparisons.* Results from simulation research need to be cross-validated using a variety of relevant clinical comparison samples. In addition, simulation research also should be validated with known-groups comparisons. In this case, results from suspected malingerers are compared with those from bona fide patients.

6. *Effects of coaching.* Several screens reviewed have initiated studies using coaching or sophisticated simulators. Further development of screens should consider the impact of coaching on their effectiveness, particularly in light of the increased availability of information via such avenues as the Internet.

7. *Computerized administration/reaction times.* Future investigations might also consider the utility of reaction times as a potential detection strategy. As more instruments offer the option of computerized administrations (e.g., SIMS), this option can be tested more fully.

V

Specialized Applications

20

Deception in Children and Adolescents

RANDALL T. SALEKIN, PhD
FRANZ A. KUBAK, MA
ZINA LEE, PhD

Children and adolescents increasingly constitute a significant portion of clinical cases seen in modern-day mental health clinics. Expansion of clinical cases with children stems from enhanced knowledge of child mental health problems and greater understanding of the importance of early intervention. School systems also contribute to the burgeoning number of cases, with frequent requests for intellectual, achievement, and vocational and diagnostic testing. In addition to these two streams of caseload activity, juvenile justice and family court systems have also evidenced pressing demands for evaluations and interventions with youths with conduct disorder or youths involved in custody and/or abuse and neglect cases. With the broadening of cases with children and adolescents, clinicians are frequently called on to provide psychological input on the child's personality and motivation in order to (1) determine the specific problem the child is experiencing, (2) generate an etiological explanation for the problem, and (3) provide a road map for change. Because many of the aforementioned cases are complex, the clinical issues at hand may also be complicated by children's and adolescents' dissimulation and deception.

Historically, children and adolescents have been viewed as candid reporters of their behavior. However, nearly all clinicians have evaluated children who deny disruptive behavior or claim an illness in the absence of genuine physiological symptoms. Although, for the most part, children and adolescents report in an honest manner, deceptive behavior may occur in the evaluation process. Therefore, clinicians are required to sift through psychosocial information to determine its accuracy. Over the past two decades, researchers and clinicians have become increasingly aware of the importance of examining what are commonly referred to as response styles in youths to determine the veracity of child reports.

The goal of this chapter is to provide a review of current research and knowledge on child and adolescent deception. This chapter first addresses six conceptual issues: (1) prevalence of childhood deception, (2) developmental patterns of deception, (3) types of response styles, (4) motivations for deception during the clinical assessment, (5) perceptions and influences on deception, and (6) personality and deception. In addition, we propose a new model for understanding child and adolescent deception that incorporates these conceptual issues. The final two sections of the chapter address assessment methods (e.g., interviews and psychological tests) and decision-making models to be applied in determining whether a youth is engaging in some form of deception. These sections discuss how to apply current knowledge toward a clinical understanding of dissimulation tendencies in children. We end with concluding comments and suggestions for future research on child and adolescent deception.

CONCEPTUAL ISSUES

Prevalence of Deception in Children and Adolescents

Data on the frequency of deceptive behavior in youths across settings are limited. The best information on nonclinical samples stems from two studies conducted in the mid-1980s. Achenbach (1985) noted that a large percentage of normal 4- to 5-year-old children engage in some form of lying. Similarly, Stouthamer-Loeber's (1986; Stouthamer-Loeber & Loeber, 1986) study estimated the prevalence of lying to be 19.4% in normal children, with a gradual decline to 15% in adolescents.

Data on malingering and specific response styles are also quite limited. Specifically, only two studies exist on this topic. First, Rogers, Hinds, and Sewell (1996) conducted a study of 53 dually diagnosed adolescent offenders and found a malingering prevalence rate of 15%, a rate similar to that found with adults (Rogers, 1997a; Yates, Nordquist, & Schultz-Ross, 1996). Second, Zahner (1991) investigated 138 preadolescents, 95 of whom were identified on the Child Behavior Checklist (CBCL; Achenbach, 1991) with elevated scale scores. Addressing the prevalence of other response styles in children, Zahner examined the quality of the responses to the Diagnostic Interview Schedule for Children—Revised (DISC-R) and found that 8.3% engaged in acquiescence ("yea saying"), whereas another 10.1% denied any problems ("nay-saying"). Some children were noted to have attempted to please the interviewer (8%), and some provided guarded responses (14%). In addition, according to Zahner (1991), 12% of the younger children (ages 6–8 years) tended to present themselves in an overly positive light (social desirability).

It is possible that the lack of epidemiological work and prevalence data on deception in children and adolescents may have been influenced by historical views of all children being candid responders. Such views would have necessarily deemphasized the need for studying, epidemiologically, deception in children. In addition, even as clinicians and researchers

became increasingly aware of deception in youths, difficulties were likely experienced by clinicians and scientists in conceptualizing childhood deception in relation to developmental stages. On this point, the Stouthamer-Loeber (1986) and Achenbach (1985) studies cast a wide net with respect to types of deception noted. In these studies, deceptive behaviors may range from denial and "white lies" to immodest and exaggerated reporting. In clinical and forensic practice, however, milder forms of lying should be distinguished from the more severe types of intentional deception, such as chronic lying, deliberate feigning, and false allegations. The latter examples are sometimes observed among externalizing youths with oppositional defiant disorder (ODD) and conduct disorder (CD), whereas the former might be considered a normal part of child and adolescent development. Clearly, the conceptualization of deception must take into consideration the types of deception and the developmental capabilities of children and adolescents. We discuss this issue in further detail next.

Developmental Capacity for Lying and Deception

Although the potential for deception and malingering is a salient concern in forensic settings, child and adolescent deception is thought to be common in everyday interactions (DePaulo, Kashy, Kirkendol, Wyer, & Epstein, 1996). Thus it is important to consider the developmental capacity for lying and the type of deception to ascertain when such behaviors are normative. Furthermore, consideration must be given to the frequency of deception from a developmental perspective. In other words, at what age is deception a cause for clinical concern?

Substantial evidence indicates that deception occurs in children as young as 3 years of age and that lying increases with age (Wilson, Smith, & Ross, 2003). Lewis, Stanger, and Sullivan (1989) found that 38% of 3-year-old children lied (i.e., denied peeking at a toy when instructed not to). When studies include slightly older children (ages 3 and 7 years), most denied either peeking or touching, with estimates ranging from 75% (Talwar & Lee, 2002) to 84% (Polak & Harris, 1999). Moreover, Talwar, Lee, Bala, and Lindsay (2002) found a significant age effect whereby only 37% of 3-year-olds lied as compared with 86% of 4- to 7-year olds. Although these studies suggest that children as young as 3 are capable of acting deceptively, these acts of deception are not necessarily intentional. Deception requires the ability to instill a false belief in the person being deceived. The denial of a transgression only requires representing a different belief, which has been termed a first-order false belief (Talwar & Lee, 2002). In contrast, the intent to deceive requires not only this first-order false belief but also instilling a false belief in the person being deceived (i.e., a second-order false belief representation). As noted by Talwar and Lee (2002), this second-order false-belief representation only begins to develop in children ages 6–7 years.

A number of studies demonstrate that although young children lie and engage in deception, they are not able to sustain this deception. Furthermore, second-order false-belief representations and the ability to sustain deception appear to increase with age. In a series of studies, Ruffman, Olson, Ash, and Keenan (1993) found that young children did not possess the conceptual knowledge that their deceptive behavior would result in a false belief in the person being deceived. Similarly, Polak and Harris (1999) found that children ages 3 and 5 years who engaged in false denials were not able to sustain these deceptions. Finally, studies comparing children between the ages of 3 and 5 suggested that older children are more likely to maintain deception by using strategies such as hiding their preferences (Peskin, 1992) and that they possess second-order false-belief representation skills (Sodian, 1991). However, more recent evidence from Talwar and Lee (2002) suggests that these abilities are more likely to occur at an older age (ages 6 and 7). Similarly, Talwar, Gordon, and Lee (2007) found that third and fifth graders were more likely than younger children to maintain their deceptions.

In summary, very young children may not engage in intentional acts of deception. Rather, what appears to be deceptive behavior may simply reflect the concealment of shame or the avoidance of punishment for a transgression. Furthermore, the existing body of literature suggests that intentional deception (i.e., the ability to instill false beliefs) begins to develop at about 6 to 7 years of age. Intentional decep-

tion is most relevant to clinical and forensic context; when attempting to deceive the evaluator, an individual must be successful in instilling a false belief in the examiner.

In addition to mastering the ability to instill false beliefs, other developmental considerations include verbal and nonverbal skills. It is unclear whether young children who engage in deceptive strategies are able to produce credible, deceptive statements (Bussey, 1992a, 1992b). For example, young children are not aware of inconsistencies during verbal communication (Talwar & Lee, 2002), which would betray attempts at intentional deception. Furthermore, children are less able to control and suppress facial and body cues associated with deception (Ekman, Roper, & Hager, 1980; Lewis, 1993). Evidence suggests that the ability to deceive emotions is associated with social skills that develop with maturity (Lewis, 1993). As children develop their verbal and nonverbal skills, they are likely to become increasingly skilled at deception. It is important to acknowledge that deception or malingering is likely due to a number of other factors in addition to developmental capacities, including motivation and situational demands. Despite a number of motivational and contextual factors that need to be considered in the evaluation of deception, the aforementioned research shows that mental health professionals can make rough demarcations regarding the developmental capabilities of youths with respect to dissimulation. Table 20.1 provides a general guideline for age-related deceptive capabilities.

Systematic research has yet to examine the nature of deception longitudinally across development. Cross-sectional data suggest that young children largely engage in denial and, with age, children develop the necessary skills for engaging in intentional forms of deception, such as second-order false beliefs, maintaining consistency during verbal communication, social skills, and monitoring facial expression and other nonverbal behavior. However, further research is needed on the developmental capacity to engage in deception. Importantly, the majority of studies examine deception outside of clinical and forensic settings and, as such, further research is needed on the deceptive capacities of youths in these settings. The next section examines the various types of deception observed among youths.

TABLE 20.1. A Developmental Guideline for Examining Deceptive Capabilities

Age	Expected deceptive capacities
< 3	Lack of evidence to support deception or dissimulation; lies that are told are likely denials of transgressions and the intention is likely to avoid punishment.
3–4	Able to tell very basic and unsophisticated lies (i.e., largely denials of transgressions). Perry (1995) notes that although very young children (i.e., about the age of 3) have difficulty understanding the concept of truth and lie based on beliefs, they can unintentionally deceive others by manipulating their behavior.
5–6	Can tell some lies, but they tend to be rather rudimentary (i.e., they are unable to sustain the deception over time).
6–12	Evidence that they are capable of intentional deception (i.e., instilling false beliefs in others and maintaining deception when probed). Increasingly able to tell sophisticated lies.
12–18	Capable of intentional deception and engaging in more sophisticated lies. Possibly malinger psychological problems and disorders; role playing and facial expressions under person's control and similar to those of adults.

Types of Deception in Children and Adolescents

Children and adolescents may deceive or dissimulate in a variety of ways and for a multitude of reasons. This subsection examines various types of deception, and the next subsection focuses more squarely on the potential reasons or motives for the deception. We begin with an examination of malingering and the specific case studies that exist in both forensic and nonforensic contexts.

A search of the literature indicates that written accounts of malingering among youths are quite rare. Quinn (1988) hypothesized that the low frequency of malingering among children may have to do with the considerable skill needed to malinger. Skills to malinger include the ability to role-play, to manage one's impression on others, and to effectively deceive others. As previously noted, the research thus far suggests that, for the most part, only adolescents have acquired these complex skill sets. Although this might explain why there are fewer cases of complex malingering in the literature on children and adolescents, it does not negate the possibility of less complex forms of deception and malingering in child and adolescent populations. Thus, although developmental abilities have implications for the prevalence of complex cases of malingering in younger populations, it does not speak to the prevalence of less sophisticated forms of dissimulation in children and adolescents. Several studies and clinical accounts have documented cases of malingering among youths in late childhood and adolescence (Faust, Hart, & Guilmette, 1988; Faust, Hart, Guilmette, & Arkes, 1988; Greenfeld, 1987; Stein, Graham, & Williams, 1995). Studies of malingering in younger children, however, are generally nonexistent in the published literature.

With respect to adolescent malingering, Greenfeld (1987) illustrated the case of a 14-year-old girl who became pregnant and malingered symptoms associated with psychosis. Her external incentive in this case was to remove herself from a household with very aversive conditions, including reports of sexual abuse. As a case of a younger child, Lu and Boone (2002) discuss a 9-year-old boy involved in litigation arising from a head injury sustained when he was struck by a car. A neuropsychological evaluation reportedly revealed feigned cognitive symptoms; specifically, the child displayed a noncredible performance on several specialized tests designed to assess effort and an atypical pattern of responses on standard cognitive measures. These results were reportedly further supported by marked discrepancies between the evaluation and testing specific to the litigation evaluation and tests previously administered in school and rehabilitation settings. This case study demonstrates that children as young as 9 may be capable of feigning cognitive impairment. As noted by these authors, the case highlights the need for routine evaluation of effort, irrespective of the age of the patient.

Conti (2004) noted that adolescents with CD may malinger attention-deficit/hyperactivity disorder (ADHD) symptoms to obtain unwarranted medication. Conti observed one definite and two probable cases of malingered ADHD at a detention center. According to Conti, one boy (age 16) searched the Internet and learned from his classes about the symptoms of ADHD. He later presented with ADHD symptoms. Once prescribed ritalin, the boy apparently sold and traded the medication to other youths. These cases of adolescents with CD emphasize the importance of third-party information and detailed record reviews.

Deception and malingering can also take place in general clinical practice. An example from clinical practice includes the fabrication of symptoms to avoid school attendance. Evans (2000) maintained that malingering might begin with the avoidance of an undesired event (e.g., bullying) but be maintained by external rewards (e.g., watching TV, playing video games, or sleeping late). From a developmental perspective, this case highlights how young children may feign symptoms for very different reasons (e.g., physical proximity to mother) than adolescents do (e.g., reduction of social embarrassment).

The malingering variant referred to as chronic school refusal, or "school phobia," is defined by Evans (2000, p. 185) as "the persistent and unadaptive attraction to positive, nonschool activities that result in the student missing school." Faked or exaggerated physical complaints are generally used to gain the desired nonschool activities. This feigning is thought to be under voluntary control and often unrelated to academic performance abilities or competency. Evans believed that this variant of malingering is more likely to occur with externalizing disorders such as CD or ODD. Bools, Foster, Brown, and Berg (1990) evaluated 100 English school refusals; 53 were classified as malingerers, many of whom also warranted a CD diagnosis. In contrast, Kearney and Beasley (1994) surveyed psychologists' ratings of school refusal; they found that only 7.8% were indicative of malingering.

These studies provide examples of deceptive behavior, especially malingering, in children and adolescents. Our literature search only revealed a handful of additional case studies of deception (see Bala, Lee, Lindsay, & Talwar, 2004; Bruns, Stein, Wells, & Wender, 2005; Franco, Goldfarb, Peebles, & Sabella, 2005; Kulaksizoglu, Polat, & Vatansever, 2002; Lennon, Pulos, & Rittner, 2005) in children or adolescents. However, the developmental literature

indicates that other forms of deception might include dissimulation and exaggeration or minimization of psychological problems. As summarized by Rogers in Chapter 1 of this volume, a range of response styles (e.g., honest, inconsistent, defensive, impression management, malingering) are all possible forms of deception that may be found in child and adolescent populations. In addition, it is possible that some children and adolescents may engage in a combination of response styles—what has been referred to as hybrid responding (see Chapter 1). Future studies are needed to delineate the potential types of deception that require consideration in child cases. Developmental trends may emerge from research studies that systematically investigate age-sensitive patterns.

In summary, the types of deception to consider in children and adolescents are similar to those found in adults. Defensiveness and denial are response styles that likely apply to youths of all ages. Cases of malingering have been documented in school-age children. More broadly, deceptive behavior in children and adolescents might be examined for its underlying motives, as well as the specific contexts in which the deception occurs. Likewise, truthfulness also involves several dimensions with respect to intent and context.

Motivations to Deceive

Youths may engage in deception based on various motivations. With adults, the motives to deceive are generally straightforward; examples include gaining unwarranted compensation, avoiding prosecution, and attaining a desirable position (Pope, Butcher, & Seelen, 1993). Clear-cut motivations are also observed in youths, such as the avoidance of being detained or the desire for more positive environments. In other cases, however, motivations are not readily apparent. The challenge for clinicians and researchers alike is to identify via clinical assessment both overt and less obvious motivations (e.g., attention and approval) that may be involved in child and adolescent deception.

The motives for deception in young children may vary. For example, Newton, Reddy, and Bull (2000) asked mothers of 3- and 4-year-olds to keep diaries of their children's deceptive behaviors. They found that young children engaged in a wide variety of deceptive behaviors that ranged in motivations, including amusement, the avoidance of physical and psychological discomfort, and material gain. Furthermore, all children had engaged in denial and had faked excuses to avoid or obtain something. Other common forms of deception included blaming others and spurious claims that they had completed chores. Wilson and colleagues (2003) found that one of the most common reasons for lying by both older (ages 4 and 5) and younger (ages 2 and 3) children was to avoid responsibility for a transgression. Taken together, it appears that the fear of punishment may be a large motivation underlying young children's deception.

Other motives to deceive (typically for older children and adolescents) were highlighted by Oldershaw and Bagby (1997) and McCann (1998). They include seeking medication, removal from school settings, or compensation and deception associated with custody or child abuse cases. Further examples include avoidance of detention centers and attempts to remain, or be placed, with the most desired parent following a divorce. Deception may also occur when youths present as more knowledgeable and/or mature, such as in the juvenile justice system (e.g., Miranda rights). Alternately, a youth might distort the amount of information that he or she knows in order to avoid being processed through the court system and/or to avoid responsibility and possible sanctions. To elaborate on this point, it is generally assumed that defendants in the criminal justice system are more prone to deliberately distort information or feign mental illness or some disability in order to obtain leniency in the form of a reduced sentence, acquittal, or other favorable treatment. Other response styles may also be elicited. Mental health professionals may be asked to address amenability to treatment, prospects for rehabilitation, and risk for violence (Salekin, 2004; Salekin, Salekin, Clements, & Leistico, 2005), and each of these clinical queries raises concerns about social desirability and impression management. As can be seen, a range of response styles may be observed when evaluating youths in juvenile courts.

The prevention of child physical and sexual abuse is a critical concern for the courts, which often must determine the veracity of abuse reporting. Reflecting the importance of this issue, research continues to examine the truthfulness of children's claims of sexual abuse (Gardner, 1992; Kuehnle, 1996; Myers, 1995; Ney, 1995; Schacter, Kagan, & Leichtman,

1995) and children's credibility and accuracy as witnesses in courtrooms (Ceci & Bruck, 1993; Goodman & Bottoms, 1993).

Sensitivity to the welfare of children is evident in child custody determinations. One consideration is the viewpoint of the child. The potential for deception is possible, based either on parental tactics (Mikkelsen, Gutheil, & Emens, 1992) or the child's own agenda. As an example of the latter, an adolescent may prefer a parent who is generally more permissive (McCann, 1998), but this parent may not be particularly effective at providing the child with proper supervision and monitoring or at giving the necessary warmth essential for healthy development.

This section discusses situations in which the motives to deceive are often clear; however, motivation in individual cases may be multidetermined and may include less obvious reasons for the deception. External incentives may include praise from friends, acceptance into a group, or greater acceptance by society at large. Motives may also include everyday positive activities (e.g., watching television or spending time with friends), key decision points for youths (e.g., minimizing contact with their parents), or attempts to be on equal footing with adults in terms of autonomy (e.g., presenting as overly brave and self-reliant). Table 20.2 summarizes different styles of presentation and representative motives and goals.

Efforts to link deception and its motives to general characteristics of youth have been largely unsuccessful. Research on the relationship between lying and basic demographic variables such as gender, socioeconomic status, and race are limited and inconclusive (Stouthamer-Loeber, 1986; Stouthamer-Loeber & Loeber, 1986). Data are also conflicting on the relationship between intelligence and deception (Ekman, 1989; Lewis, 1993; Stouthamer-Loeber, 1986). Practitioners are generally aware that such efforts to find links are too general to be clinically useful, although intelligence may be one factor that increases the complexity of the presentation (Lewis, 1993). Later in this chapter we also underscore how personality might be an important variable to consider.

Children's Perceptions and Deception

Oldershaw and Bagby (1997) noted that the youth's perception of the evaluation may be an important factor in his or her level of cooper-

TABLE 20.2. Presentation Style and Potential Motives for Deception

Presentation	Potential motives and goals
Defensive/healthy presentation	
Appear overly self-reliant	Desire for increased autonomy
Appear overly brave	Desire for increased autonomy and strong self-image
Present as nonsymptomatic	Not wanting to be seen as ill, different, or weak
Present as having a normal IQ	Avoid being ostracized by peers
Pathological/Faking Bad	
Present as uncaring	Protect self from other potentially harmful relationships
Present as highly dependent	Avoid responsibility/seek help
Present as callous	Appear tough and not in need of help
Present as mentally ill	Gain help from mental health or avoid responsibility

ation and overall presentation or response style to the clinician. Unlike most adults, it is possible that children may not have a realistic understanding of the assessment procedures and their purposes (see Evans & Nelson, 1977; Mash & Terdal, 1988). Oldershaw and Bagby (1997) recommend appraisal of children's perceptions, both at the beginning and periodically throughout the evaluation. This appraisal allows clinicians to better grasp potential motives to deceive or malinger. If youths know that they are being evaluated for potential abuse and foster care placement, they may overstate or understate past events, depending on their desire to live in a foster home or remain with their biological parents (Oldershaw & Bagby, 1997). If a gifted child holds the belief that superior performance on an intelligence test will lead to further alienation from peers, he or she may be motivated to intentionally underperform on the IQ test (Rim & Lowe, 1988). In summary, greater knowledge of the child's specific understanding of the assessment assists clinicians in remedying misperceptions and understanding the motives for dissimulation.

Children may also be influenced in the assessment by their perceptions of adults, especially those in authority. Clinicians should be aware of the possibility that they may be considerably more influential in directing children's responses than they are with adult clients. Some children may express whatever they believe adults will respond to positively, regardless of its truthfulness. For instance, Fuchs and Thelen (1988) found that expectancy of parental reactions strongly affected the likelihood of

emotional expression in children. Specifically, the more children believed that their parents would react negatively to a particular emotion, the less likely they were to express the emotion during assessment. Alternately, if a child believed that an adult examiner desired negative symptoms, he or she might comply with this perceived expectation (Oldershaw & Bagby, 1997).

Clinicians should attempt to learn more about their interviewing style and be aware of any subtle messages they may be displaying during the interview (e.g., acknowledgment or reinforcement of certain responses with a head nod or smile) and conduct questioning in a manner that minimizes these influences. As Oldershaw and Bagby (1997) note, acknowledgment can be an important aspect of the assessment that enhances rapport. However, they also caution that it may influence the child to continue talking, thereby increasing the chance of inadvertent reinforcement of specific content that may bias or even alter the child's presentation. Given that there are surprising cases of clinicians eliciting deceitful or dissimulated information, we provide some additional guidelines for how clinicians can avoid this in the assessment section of this chapter.

Research has yet to tackle the question of which youths are especially vulnerable to perceived adult expectations. However, there are likely some personality differences with respect to the willingness or desire of youths to be forthright or deceptive in their responses. Although there is not a great deal of research on this topic, Oldershaw and Bagby (1997) note that children may differ in their level of self-monitoring whereby some young children describe events without censoring their views, others may comply rigidly with adults (e.g., some children are taught not to disagree with persons in authority), and still others might be taught to be deceptive. Furthermore, some research demonstrates that highly anxious children are more sensitive to social reinforcement (Duffy & Martin, 1973; Zimmerman, 1970), raising the possibility that they may be more easily influenced by adults.

With respect to the interview process, research has shown that highly anxious children are more sensitive to social reinforcement because they have a strong fear of negative evaluations by others. Oldershaw and Bagby (1997) noted that such children may be affected by cues from the clinician because they fear criticism. Based on this research, highly anxious children may be more likely to give false information to clinicians if they are presented with positive reinforcement and less likely to deceive in an assessment in which these reinforcements are absent. There is a general clinical belief and some research to suggest that as a general rule children diagnosed with anxiety symptoms have been found to display a lower than average rate of lying in natural settings, likely because they recognize that falsehoods are not socially acceptable. However, youths with internalizing disorders may have a tendency to be defensive and minimize problems. In contrast, although children diagnosed with CD have a higher than average rate of lying (Stouthamer-Loeber, 1986), there are no data yet and perhaps no specific reason to speculate that they are especially influenced by their perceived expectations of adults with respect to the interview itself.

These points illustrate how personality can potentially influence the interview process. In addition, we have alluded to how personality and some forms of pathology might be more or less linked to deception. For instance, the case examples presented earlier in this chapter illustrated how personality likely correlates with different types of deception. This was most notable in the cases of CD and social phobia outlined by Bools and colleagues (1990) and Evans (2000) or the cases of CD reported by Conti (2004). In the next section, we discuss how personality might affect the interview process in greater detail and also discuss its potential connection to deception and malingering.

Personality and Deception

Personality in children and adolescents as it relates to deception is not well understood. In this section, we use the Big Five factor model of personality, given its importance in the field of psychology (Widiger & Trull, 2007), and DSM-IV childhood pathology to illustrate the potential significance of personality in the assessment of deception and malingering in youths. Although there is little research on personality and deception in children, one could easily conjure up images of how youths with varying degrees of Big Five personality characteristics (i.e., conscientiousness, extraversion, openness, neuroticism, and agreeableness) or DSM child psychopathology might perform differently with respect to lying and deception. For instance, children who are more open and conscientious might be less likely to engage in deceptive practices than extraverted, less agreeable, and less conscientious individuals.

There has recently been an effort to integrate the Big Five factors and the DSM-IV model for classifying disorders (see Krueger, 1999; Krueger, McGue, & Iacono, 2001; Krueger & Tackett, 2003; Tackett, 2006; Widiger & Trull, 2007), and we mention it here because we believe it may allow for greater clarity regarding the two systems and better help clinicians frame adolescent characteristics and deception from either a DSM or Big Five perspective or both. With regard to the DSM-IV child pathology model for disorders, it is important to note that these disorders can be distilled into two broad factors: internalizing and externalizing disorders. Externalizing disorders are characterized by more outward-directed behaviors, such as aggressiveness, noncompliance, overactivity, and impulsiveness, and include the DSM-IV categories of CD, ODD, and ADHD (also referred to as the disruptive behavior disorders). In contrast, internalizing disorders are characterized by more inward-focused experiences and behaviors such as anxiety, social withdrawal, and depression and include childhood disorders of anxiety and mood. One could surmise based on these descriptions that youths with externalizing disorders might be more likely to engage in deception and or malingering.

With regard to the integration, some researchers have suggested that internalizing groups can be understood in personality language as being low in extraversion and high in neuroticism. Externalizing youths can be understood in personality language as being high in extraversion, low in agreeableness, and low in conscientiousness. Personality models typically have a hierarchical structure composed of general "superfactors" and a number of narrower traits. At the apex of the hierarchy are the "big" traits that have been mentioned here and that constitute superfactor models such as the Big Five or Big Two (see Watson, Kotov, & Gamez, 2006). At the next lower level of the hierarchy, these traits can be decomposed into several distinct yet correlated subtraits or facets. These facets in turn can be further decomposed into even narrower traits and behavioral habits. Thus personality models allow both a broad look at characteristics and how they relate to malingering and a more specific and perhaps focused examination of specific traits. These models are potentially helpful because there may be important differences at the supertrait level, and there may also be noteworthy differences detected when one improves the resolution by examining more specific personality constellations. Within this hierarchical structure, case studies and some research suggest that youths with externalizing disorders might be more likely to be deceptive. However, with this hierarchical structure to personality, specific disorders such as CD and the more serious syndrome of psychopathy may be important to investigate, given their purported relation to deception. We briefly examine this specific personality style and its connection to malingering next.

Psychopathy and Malingering

Because the DSM model for malingering links this response style to antisocial personality disorder (APD), it is not surprising that CD is considered in malingering cases. More recently, researchers have been concerned that a variant of APD and CD, namely, psychopathy, might be more indicative of malingering. Because this personality style might have a special link to malingering, we explore current research on this issue. Psychopathy is a personality disorder characterized by a constellation of interpersonal (e.g., grandiosity), affective (e.g., callous), behavioral (e.g., irresponsible), and antisocial (e.g., criminal versatility) traits. As mentioned, these characteristics can also be understood via general models of personality, such as the Big

Five (Lynam et al., 2005; Salekin, Leistico, Trobst, Schrum, & Lochman, 2005).

Clinical accounts frequently describe individuals with psychopathy as especially adept at lying and deception, and several items in the Psychopathy Checklist—Revised (PCL-R; Hare, 1991, 2003) are related directly to deception, including pathological lying and conning or manipulative behavior. Despite much clinical lore about the deceptive abilities of individuals with psychopathy, results from empirical studies with adults are equivocal. Some researchers have found little to no evidence of an association between psychopathic traits and socially desirable responding, dissimulation, and exaggeration of psychopathological symptoms (e.g., Clark, 1997; Edens, Buffington, & Tomicic, 2000; Poythress, Edens, & Lilienfeld, 1998; Poythress, Edens, & Watkins, 2001). Likewise, Hare, Forth, and Hart (1989) concluded that the performance of offenders with psychopathy on self-report validity scales generally falls within acceptable ranges, suggesting that their response patterns are not necessarily deceptive. From a contrasting perspective, other researchers have found a positive relationship between psychopathic traits and malingering (e.g., Gacono, Meloy, Sheppard, Speth, & Roske, 1995; Kucharski, Duncan, Egan, & Falkenbach, 2006), and social desirability (Book, Holden, Starzyk, Wasylkiw, & Edwards, 2006).

Because of the equivocal results on this topic, it is difficult to determine whether individuals with psychopathy would be any more likely to malinger or have any special ability beyond those of youths with CD at deception. Part of the reason for equivocal findings on this topic may be that there are methodological flaws in the investigation of the relation between psychopathy and malingering. For instance, one potential problem may stem from the measurement of psychopathy. Specifically, the current indices of psychopathy are heterogeneous in content, polythetic in nature (see Rogers, 2001), and missing key traits that might be most highly linked to successful malingering (see Brinkley, Newman, Widiger, & Lynam, 2004; Salekin, 2002, 2006).

Only one study has examined the relationship between adolescent psychopathy and malingering. Rogers, Vitacco, and colleagues (2002) instructed juvenile offenders to simulate socially desirable or nonconformist roles to examine whether doing so influenced ratings of psychopathic traits. In the first session, adolescents were administered the Psychopathy Checklist: Youth Version (PCL:YV), the self-report Antisocial Process Screening Device (APSD), and the second edition of the Self-Report of Psychopathy (SRP-II) under standard instructions. In the second session, adolescents were instructed either to make a good impression (social desirability) or present a tough image (nonconformity). A second rater, masked to the original ratings, then readministered the three psychopathy measures. Rogers, Vitacco, and colleagues found that social desirability led to significant decreases and social nonconformity led to significant increases in psychopathic traits. Furthermore, the effect sizes were greater among adolescents with moderate levels of PCL:YV-assessed psychopathic traits (i.e., total scores $\geq$ 14). It should be noted that this study did not address whether or not individuals with psychopathy would be any more adept at deception or whether or not they would be more likely to lie and deceive. However, it does suggest that delinquent youths can increase or decrease their psychopathy scores based on their motives.

Taken together, existing research suggests that clinicians should not assume malingering when assessing individuals with psychopathy. Rather, individuals who exhibit psychopathic traits may be at an elevated risk for malingering, but this should be considered contextually in light of the purpose of the assessment and the nature of the charges. Also, we do not know whether individuals with psychopathy are any better at deception than other youths with externalizing disorders or those with no pathology. In addition, developmental considerations should outweigh evidence of psychopathic-like characteristics given that there remains some debate over whether such traits in juveniles are indicative of psychopathy later in life (Hart, Watt, & Vincent, 2002; Lynam, Caspi, Moffitt, Loeber, & Stouthamer-Loeber, 2007; Salekin, 2006; Salekin & Frick, 2005; Salekin, Neumann, Leistico, DiCicco, & Duros, 2004; Seagrave & Grisso, 2002).

Family Context and Response Styles

The family context plays an important role in assessing children (La Greca, 1983, 1990; Oldershaw & Bagby, 1997) for two primary reasons: (1) children are highly dependent on their parents for their growth and nurturance and

(2) parental pathology and communication style may affect perceptions of the youth's veracity in a particular case. To elaborate on this point, because children are dependent upon and receive guidance from others in their environment (Mash & Terdal, 1988), their actions are influenced by those who serve in a teaching and mentoring capacity. Although, in an ideal setting, the parents and the community work together in a synergistic fashion to raise children and adolescents with increasing levels of autonomy and socialization, these goals may not be met by everyone. Therefore, with respect to dissimulation, certain family variables appear to be related to children's lack of openness in clinical evaluations. Children tend to be more defensive during assessments when their home environments are characterized by parental rejection, inconsistent discipline, parental dishonesty, and parental pressure to perform, according to some research (Makaremi, 1992). Other research has suggested that children can be less than open when raised in highly religious families (Francis, Lankshear & Pearson, 1989), although the reason for this finding is unclear. Moreover, parental psychopathology and perhaps their degree of manipulativeness correlates with their children's ability to deceive others (Kraut & Price, 1976). Specifically, Cole, Barrett, and Zahn-Waxler (1992) found that children of depressed and anxious parents tend to minimize the expression of tension and frustration.

A second family factor that may affect perceptions of veracity is the parent's perceptions of the youth and the assessment. Assessment of children and adolescents includes not only children's self-reports but also parental reports about the child, which may also be distorted (Goodnow, 1988). Parental distortions are sometimes unintentional (e.g., parental depression resulting in negatively biased reports of their children). However, instances do occur in which parental reports about their children are deliberately distorted. For example, a parent involved in a child custody assessment may distort a child's symptomatology to reveal poor parenting on the part of the other spouse. Alternatively, a parent with temporary custody may intentionally minimize the child's psychological problems to portray an ideal custody placement (Oldershaw & Bagby, 1997). Use of parents as informants in the assessment of children is essential and helps with collateral source information. However, their inclusion adds an additional level of complexity to the assessment of dissimulation. As Oldershaw and Bagby (1997) observed, disparities in the reports could reflect (1) the child's deception, (2) honest differences between parents and their child, (3) testing and measurement differences, and (4) parental distortions about their child.

Up to this point, we have examined the prevalence of malingering, the developmental capability of adolescents to malinger, the types of deception they may engage in, and their motives for deception. In addition, we discussed some children's perceptions of the interview, as well as how personality and parental factors may affect deceptive practices. Next, we examine in greater detail the reasons for deception in adolescents and propose a new model for adolescent malingering. Following this, we provide specific data on tools frequently used to detect malingering and deception in youth.

Models of Deception and Malingering

Professionals should understand why individuals, and particularly children and adolescents, engage in dissimulation. There are various models for deception, ranging from the DSM-IV's definition of malingering to Rogers' (1997a) explanatory models (see Chapter 1, this volume). However, these models do not specifically address childhood and adolescent deception and malingering. We briefly note here that not all lying is necessarily problematic, because many children and adolescents are attempting to learn and survive in environments imposed on them. In addition, we argue that children learn, often from observing their parents or primary caretakers, that some deceptive behavior may be considered socially acceptable. In particular, children learn at very young ages that it is sometimes acceptable to tell "white lies" to protect the feelings of others (Ekman, 1989). This is a mild form of adaptational lying. More severe cases of lying may also be seen as adaptive if a youth is trying to improve his or her predominant environment from a negative to more positive one, such as the case example illustrated by Greenfeld (1998). According to Stouthamer-Loeber and Loeber (1986), however, the fact that lying is more often viewed as problematic behavior by adults has more to do with the connection made between lying and other antisocial behaviors (e.g., stealing or defying parental rules) and its

relationship to the context in which it occurs (e.g., lying to parents or teachers, as opposed to politeness toward casual friends).

Other forms of deception also serve the function of self-preservation for children and adolescents (Ekman, 1989). To be caught engaging in misbehavior or to admit unacceptable feelings or thoughts exposes the child to anxiety over potential disdain, scorn, or rejection from parents, caretakers, and the community more broadly. The emotional consequences of this rejection can be psychologically threatening to youths. In these contexts, lying and deception serve a self-protective function and, in some ways, can be viewed as adaptational (e.g., attempts to look self-reliant, brave, or autonomous). Nonetheless, some lying verges on being, or may be, pathological. Thus it could be said that childhood lying and deception ranges on a linear scale from being adaptive to maladaptive to, on the deepest end, pathological, such as the lying that is often linked to an antisocial personality disorder or CD and psychopathy (trait-based lying). However, it should be noted that CD and adaptation could be co-occurring. That is, even in cases in which youths have conduct problems and are faced with legal charges, they may attempt to minimize their negative actions (and focus on their prosocial strengths) or distort the truth to avoid being punished by their parents or the legal system. When the consequences are more severe, such as when adolescents face legal punishment before the court such as transfer to adult court, there is strong motivation to deny, minimize, or in some way distort self-reports. These motivations and the context are important assessment considerations and may also be generally representative of an adaptive style, although it is important not to disregard the possibility of highly maladaptive and characterological problems that indicate trait-based deception as opposed to environmentally and contextually based deception.

A New Model of Child and Adolescent Deception

We lack research examining the various characteristics of youths, their likelihood or ability to engage in deceptive behavior, and the interaction between individual characteristics and demands of the situation. Despite this limited knowledge, in this chapter we have highlighted the importance of considering developmental status, personality, context, and other important factors. Because we see many of these factors as critical to understanding deception in children and adolescents, we propose a new model for examining child and adolescent deception. An underlying theme of this model is that, for the most part, deception by children and adolescents is primarily a form of adaptation. It may be used to bring about more positive environments or to gain something that the youth believes is important (remaining with a parent that whom he or she views as more positive). However, this view is not to suggest that all deception by children and adolescents is adaptive, nor should all forms of children's deception be viewed less seriously. Manipulating the evaluative process can result in serious consequences, such as disrupting the institutional setting and compromising the ability of staff members to effectively manage youths. Thus one aspect of this model is to evaluate and acknowledge the adaptive nature of some deception but also to recognize more severe cases of deception in youths who may have histories of deceitful, manipulative, and exploitive behavior. The first described component of this model is a dimensional consideration of the adaptive, maladaptive, or pathological (trait-based) nature of the deception. A second and related aspect of this model is to examine key psychological concepts relevant

to deception in youths. We describe this model in further detail next.

Child and Adolescent Model of Deception

The child and adolescent model of deception, as illustrated in Figure 20.1, suggests that the evaluator take into account the developmental status (e.g., maturity) of the youth, his or her personality, and/or whether he or she has significant pathology (e.g., externalizing/internalizing), his or her particular situation (e.g., custody battle), and the context in which the deceptive practice occurs (e.g., the specific situation, such as minimizing the pathology of a parent they would like to remain with). This model allows an examination of deception through the frame of multiple chief childhood variables, including developmental status, personality, and contextual factors. As well, this model suggests that mental health professionals should also evaluate the potential adaptive nature of the deception, as mentioned earlier.

This model for child and adolescent deception and malingering may serve as a good starting point for conceptualizing and evaluating youths, with the overarching goal of attempting to define the problem, search for its underlying cause, and develop a treatment plan that would assist in the prosocial and healthy development

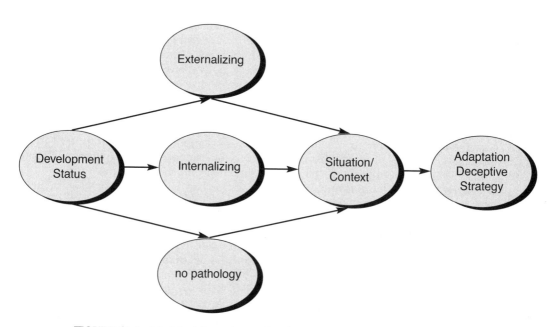

FIGURE 20.1. Model of deception and malingering for children and adolescents.

of the youth. However, this model requires further investigation, as it is early in its development. In the model illustrated in Figure 20.1, we use the two broad domains of internalizing and externalizing problems; however, researchers and clinicians alike may choose to use the five-factor model as a framework from which to evaluate the youth's situation and the deceptive strategy. The final sections of this chapter provide information on assessment procedures and threshold and clinical models to help discern whether dissimulation may be part of the youth's problem, which could then further help focus treatment.

CLINICAL ASSESSMENT OF DISSIMULATION

Traditionally, clinicians have attempted to extrapolate indicators of malingering and defensiveness from adults to youths. More recently, research has demonstrated substantive differences between children and adults in the nature of their feigned presentations and their subsequent detection. This chapter has highlighted important developmental differences to consider. It is necessary to examine the usefulness of detection strategies with youths at different levels of development and maturity.

Clinical Interviews

Traditional and structured interviews can provide comprehensive information on children's and adolescents' functioning, including the types and severity of symptoms and key information on dissimulation and deception. Information can be compared across interviews and sources. Child interviews alone may produce inconsistent information. Parent interviews, teacher interviews, and other collateral sources (e.g., school records) may show further inconsistencies; some of these inconsistencies are to be expected due to real differences that each reporter may see (e.g., setting variance, method variance, and reporter knowledge). For instance, some youths may vary greatly with respect to their behavior depending on the setting (e.g., school vs. home).

Clinical interviews offer an effective means to establish rapport and to have the youth report his or her symptoms without any restrictions. They can also help with the detection of dissimulation because would-be feigners must create a meaningful compilation of symptoms. These open-ended interviews can also examine the level of externalizing and internalizing symptoms. Structured interviews are probably best considered as a second step in the assessment process in that they offer very reliable and valid methods of assessing psychopathology and other clinical constructs.

With clinical and structured interviews, clinicians can evaluate the accuracy of general content provided in the interview format. Clinicians can determine whether (1) the information has a logical structure and (2) the child or adolescent was able to provide a meaningful unstructured account. Interviews also allow the clinician to examine the quality of details provided by youths. Clinicians could also look for spontaneous correction of inaccurate information, as well as a clients' ability to admit lack of memory for some events (Raskin & Esplin, 1991; Steller & Koehnken, 1989; Vrij, 2005; Vrij, Akehurst, Soukara, & Bull, 2002, 2004; Yuille, 1988).

Structured interviews that could help clinicians gather important diagnostic information on youths include: Dianostic Interview Schedule for Children–IV (DISC-IV; National Institute of Mental Health, 1991) and the Schedule of Affective Disorders and Schizophrenia for School-Age Children (K-SADS; Ambrosini, 1992). New measures such as the Missouri Assessment of Genetics Interview for Children (MAGIC; Reich & Todd, 2002) also offer some promise for the detection of malingering in youths. Again, these methods allow the examination of the coherence of the psychological problems reported and specifics about the symptoms being reported. Semistructured interviews would allow more probing of symptoms that seemed to need further clarification, as well as testing the limits on reported symptoms. In addition, structured interviews also provide for assessment of both the disruptive behavior disorders (externalizing disorders) and anxiety and depression (internalizing disorders), which may provide a valuable lens through which to examine deception and malingering.

An important prerequisite to structured interviewing is to ascertain whether the child understands the questions. Oldershaw and Bagby (1997) warn that what appears to be deceptive behavior may simply be the result of the child's misunderstanding of the structured inquiries. Children typically have less understanding of the words and phrases that adults use to describe the many nuances of human emotions (see Rogers, 2001). Several established practices of interviewing should be used to optimize cooperation and the quality of the interview data. First, open-ended questions minimize the possibility that the interviewer will lead the child to state conclusions that are suggested by the questions themselves. Overreliance on closed-ended questions, especially leading questions, may encourage acquiescence. Second, a number of clinicians and researchers have noted that "why" questions are generally nonproductive and lead to justifications (Rogers, 2001). Thus we recommend rephrasing questions that attempt to discern motivation (see LaGreca, 1990). Oldershaw and Bagby suggested that disclosures about the purpose of the evaluation will foster rapport and possibly reduce the motivation to deceive. Without such knowledge, children may assume the worst and modify their response styles accordingly. Nonetheless, children may still engage in some form of dissimulation when they realize that the objectives of the evaluation potentially differ from their own goals.

The next section examines psychological testing and its role in the detection of malingering and deception. We believe that clinical interviewing and a battery of assessment measures should be used to gather information about a youth. This comprehensive method for garnering information about a youth's functioning also allows multiple assessments across multiple sources of the youth's candor during the assessment process.

Psychological Testing and the Detection of Deception

Many psychological measures can be utilized to evaluate response styles. Nearly all the measures covered in this section have been discussed in earlier chapters. After a brief introduction to each measure, readers are referred to the appropriate chapters for background material. Most measures were originally developed and validated on adult populations. In some instances, measures are simply assumed to be effective with juvenile populations; however, they may not have been formally tested for their efficacy.

This section also provides an overview of assessment tools that have been used to examine child or adolescent response styles. It reviews data on multiscale inventories, cognitive measures, and a structured interview (i.e., the Structured Interview of Reported Symptoms [SIRS]). Table 20.4 provides the most recent studies that have examined dissimulation in child and adolescent populations. This table provides a brief description of the sample, the type of study design, and four estimates of diagnostic accuracy, including sensitivity, specificity, positive predictive power (PPP), and negative predictive power (NPP). With respect to the study design, various methods have been employed in the past to detect deception. For the most part, these can be summarized as simulated designs and natural setting designs. We begin by discussing the Minnesota Multiphasic Personality Inventory (MMPI) and its adolescent version, the MMPI-A.

Minnesota Multiphasic Personality Inventory—Adolescent Version

The MMPI-2 is the best known multiscale inventory, with extensive research on validity scales and response styles (see Greene, Chapter 10, this volume). For use with adolescents between 14 and 18 years of age, the MMPI—Adolescent Version (MMPI-A; Butcher et al., 1992) was developed as a 478-item inventory. Despite substantial changes in item content, the MMPI-A retains the same basic structure for clinical and validity scales. It is recommended that adolescents have a minimum of a sixth-grade reading level and at least low average verbal comprehension (Lezak, Howieson, & Loring, 2004). Very little data are available on the utility of the MMPI-A in detecting specific response styles. In a meta-analysis of the MMPI-2 examining malingering, Rogers, Sewell, Martin, and Vitacco (2003) identified specific detection strategies that were used with MMPI-2 validity scales. Examples include (see also Chapter 2, this volume) rare symptoms (Fp), quasi-rare symptoms (F and Fb) and erroneous stereotypes (Ds). For complete descriptions of standard and specialized MMPI-2 scales, see Chapter 10, this volume.

As a cautionary note for the MMPI-A, the Rogers and colleagues (2003) MMPI-2 meta-analysis uncovered a broad array of cut scores for most validity indicators. They warned against using cut scores without taking into account diagnostic issues and the risk of false positives. To maintain experimental rigor, we selected only those studies that attempted to

TABLE 20.3. MMPI and Adolescent Deception

First author(s)/date	Total N	Gender	Cut score	Utility estimates			
				Sens	Spec	PPP	NPP
Facing pathology							
Baer (1999)	89	Combined	F ≥ 79T	1.00	1.00	1.00	.98
			F − K >13	1.00	.93		
Lucio (2002)	292	Female	F ≥ 82 T	.76	.87	.86	.78
			F − K >27	.69	.91	.88	.75
		Male	F ≥ 66 T	.90	.80	.82	.89
			F − K >14	.80	.88	.87	.81
Rogers, Hinds (1996)	53	Combined	F ≥ 81 T			.66	.91
			F(p) ≥ 9			.45	.93
			F − K >20			.83	.91
Stein (1995)	276	Female	F ≥ 71 T	.99		.94	.89
Defensiveness							
Baer, Ballenger, & Kroll (1998)	44	Combined	L ≥ 64	.76	.91		
			K ≥ 60	.62	.74		
			F − K ≤ −10	.67	.44		
Stein & Graham (1999)	137	Female	L ≥ 60	.85	.82	.83	.84
			K ≥ 59	.72	.82	.80	.74
			L + K ≥ 19	.85	.81	.69	.91
		Male	L ≥ 56	.70	.78	.76	.73
			K ≥ 52	.67	.65	.60	.67
			L + K ≥ 20	.68	.76	.83	.58

Note. Sens, sensitivity; Spec, specificity; PPP, positive predictive power; NPP, negative predictive power.

distinguish specific response styles from relevant clinical samples (see Table 20.3).

When determining malingering, or "faking bad," one of the most common approaches has been to use the F-K index. Interestingly, this strategy has not been as successful as F or Fp alone in adult populations (Rogers et al., 2003).

Stein, Graham, and Williams's (1995) study found that a raw F cutoff score of ≥ 23 (i.e., 71T for girls, 66T for boys) was best for distinguishing fake-bad profiles from both honest clinical and community participants. This cutoff score produced almost perfect sensitivity rates and had exceptional PPP and NPP. In this study, the F scale was also able to distinguish between clinical participants with standard responses and fake-bad community responders, accurately capturing 100% of the clinical boys and 97% of clinical girls.

In a within-subjects study with 53 adjudicated, dually diagnosed adolescents, Rogers, Hinds, and Sewell (1996) found that the F scale was not as useful as the F-K index for detecting fake-bad profiles. With an F-K cutoff score >20, Rogers and colleagues found a clinically beneficial PPP of over 80% and NPP that surpassed 90%. Baer, Kroll, Rinaldo, and Ballenger (1999) compared the ability of the MMPI-A to distinguish between overreporting and random-responding profiles. They found that the F score was sensitive to both types of profiles, with a 79T score capturing all feigners and 95% of random responders, but not the clinical participants with standard instructions. When the cutoff score was increased to 90T, the F scale identified 96% of overreporters and none of the random reporters. The F-K index offered some utility as well, with a cutoff score of 13 identifying both overreported and random profiles, although it inaccurately identified 15% of clinical participants. Extending to Mexican adolescents, Lucio, Duran, Graham, and Ben-Porath (2002) found that the F and F-K index were able to differentiate between feigning and standard conditions, although a higher cutoff score was needed.

The F and F-K indexes appear to have clinical utility in detecting fake-bad profiles on the MMPI-A, although the data are still limited with adolescents. With a review of the combined data (see Table 20.3), it is recommended that youths be further evaluated for feigning if they exceed either of these two cutoff scores: F scale >70T or F-K >13. However, it is necessary to determine whether the adolescent is feigning or whether his or her level of clinical distress is in actuality extremely elevated. Fortunately, it appears that true clinical respondents do not typically score as highly as adolescents seeking to amplify their clinical presentation.

With regard to defensiveness, the L scale appears to be the standard validity scale that best distinguished between fake-good profiles and standard profiles for adolescents among the studies reviewed in this chapter. Baer and colleagues (1999) found that the L scale ≥ 64T was the most effective scale in distinguishing between defensive and honest conditions. Stein and Graham (1999) found similar results, with the L scale effectively distinguishing adolescents in a correctional and noncorrectional comparison. Stein and Graham used somewhat lower cutoff scores that were gender specific. The L scale was shown to have better identification than the K scale in both studies. Interestingly, the sum of L + K produced a very high NPP for girls (.91) and the highest PPP for boys (.83). Based on the current data, it is recommended that youths be further evaluated for defensiveness if they exceed the cutoff scores: L scale ≥ 60T for girls or ≥ 56 for boys. The indicator of L + K could be used as an ancillary indicator.

Millon Adolescent Clinical Inventory

The Millon Adolescent Clinical Inventory (MACI; Millon, Millon, & Davis, 1993) is a 160-item, true–false self-report measure designed to assess a broad range of psychological problems in adolescents between the ages of 13 and 19 (McCann, 1997; Salekin, Leistico, Schrum, & Mullins, 2005). The MACI consists of four validity scales: Disclosure (i.e., defensiveness), Desirability (i.e., social desirability), Debasement (i.e., exaggerated responding or feigning), and Reliability (item consistency). The validity scales evidence good internal consistency (i.e., alphas ranging from .73 to .87). One unique aspect of the MACI is that the scores are referred to as base rate scores (BR scores). BR scores below 75 suggest the profile is not very characteristic, whereas BR scores above 85 suggest the profile is very characteristic of the adolescent.

The Disclosure scale has a high positive correlation with the Debasement scale and a moderate negative correlation with the Desirability scale (McCann, 1997). These findings seem counterintuitive, and no explanation is provided for their associations (i.e., sample characteristics or methodology). As such, research is needed to provide greater insight into these relationships. A limitation of the Debasement scale is that elevations may indicate exaggerated responses, severe psychopathology, or both (Salekin et al., 2005). As summarized in Table 20.4, utility estimates are not available for the MACI validity scales.

The MACI Reliability scale is composed of only two items, which may not adequately assess inconsistent responding (Salekin et al., 2005). In an attempt to remedy this concern, Pinsoneault (2002) developed a new scale that reflects variable response inconsistency (M-VRIN), similar to the MMPI-2. The results are promising, with a specificity of .95 and sensitivity of .89.

McCann (1997) offers the following general guidelines for assessing the validity of MACI profiles. A single score is not sufficient to invalidate a MACI profile. Rather, a valid profile should exhibit Disclosure, Desirability, and Debasement BR scores below 75 and a Disclosure raw score above 200. Social desirability should be a concern when the Desirability BR score is above 75 and the Disclosure and Debasement BR scores are below 75. Exaggeration or overreporting should be a concern when Debasement BR scores are above 75 and Desirability BR scores are below 75. In addition, the manual recommends that a profile be considered invalid if both of the two reliability items are endorsed in opposite directions.

Despite these guidelines, there are no studies examining the ability of the existing MACI reliability and validity scales to accurately detect defensiveness or malingering. In other words, it is unclear whether the scales would detect defensiveness or malingering in simulation or known-groups research. Although Pinsoneault's (2002) study is promising, further independent research is necessary. In general, studies are needed that examine the ability of the MACI validity scales to accurately detect malingering, appropriate scores that maximize

TABLE 20.4. Self-Report Masures and Adolescent Deception

First author(s)/date	Total N	Gender	Cut score	Utility estimates			
				Sens	Spec	PPP	NPP
Behavior Assessment System for Children—2nd Ed.							
Reynolds & Kamphaus (2004)	13,000+	Combined Child	F = 7–15 L ≥ 13				
		Combined Adolescent	F = 7–15				
Millon Adolescent Clinical Inventory (MACI)							
Pinsoneault (2002)	108	Combined	M-VRIN ≥ 8 M-TRIN ≥ 10	.89 .88	.95 .93	.83 .75	.97 .97
Millon (1993)		Combined	Disclosure ≥ 85 Desirability ≥ 85 Debasement ≥ 85				
Personality Inventory for Youth (PIY)							
Wrobel (1999)	108	Combined	INC ≥ 64 T DEF ≥ 59 T VAL ≥ 2 (raw) FB = 70T to 79T				
Screening Inventory of Malingered Symptoms (SIMS)							
Rogers, Hinds (1996)	53	Combined	Total score ≥ 40	.49	.94		

Note. Sens, sensitivity; Spec, specificity; PPP, positive predictive power; NPP, negative predictive power.

specificity and sensitivity, and the generalizability of the scales across clinical groups, age groups, and ethnicity (see Table 20.4).

Personality Inventory for Youth

The Personality Inventory for Youth (PIY; Lachar & Gruber, 1995) is a 270-item true–false multidimensional instrument intended to index the emotional and behavioral adjustment of children and adolescents between the ages of 9 and 18 years with a third-grade reading level or above. The PIY contains four validity scales: (1) Validity (VAL) and (2) Inconsistency (INC) scales are sensitive to inconsistent responding; (3) the Dissimulation Scale (FB for "fake bad") addresses feigning; and (4) the Defensiveness Scale (DEF) identifies responders who deny problems or overly represent their virtues.

Wrobel and colleagues (1999) explored the ability of the PIY validity scales to detect re-

sponse styles. The usefulness of the Defensiveness scale was studied by asking adolescent psychiatric inpatients (ages 12–17 years) to "fake good." A separate study compared honest and random responses by high school psychology students with two feigning conditions: fake-moderate (i.e., pretending to be significantly disturbed to win a lawsuit, but not so severely disturbed to require hospitalization) and fake-severe.

Wrobel and colleagues (1999) reported that the four validity scales provided an accurate assessment of feigned, inconsistent, and defensive response styles. The fake-moderate, fake-severe, and random-response groups attained clinically elevated mean VAL and FB T scores when contrasted with the control condition. A VAL cutoff of > 2 (raw score) was able to correctly identify 88% of fake-severe responders and 79% of random responders, but only 20% of fake-moderate responders. An FB cutoff of > 69 (T score) correctly categorized 93% of fake-moderate responders, 100% of fake-severe responders, and 93% of random responders. A clinically elevated DEF score (> 59T) correctly classified 90% of the inpatient participants asked to fake good and remained low for all high school participants asked to fake bad. The INC cutoff (> 64T) correctly identified 96% of random responders but incorrectly elevated 30% of accurate responders. However, correct clinical elevations dropped to 0% for accurate responders and 89% for random responders when INC was combined with FB.

Although it appears that the PIY validity scales may assist practitioners in detecting potentially inaccurate responders, no other studies offer a cross-validation of these findings. From Wrobel and colleagues' (1999) study, FB scores that range from 70T to 79T may be used to identify exaggerated responders, but it is important to note that an isolated elevation of FB alone may reflect accurately severe emotional and social adjustment and not simple exaggeration. Importantly, more study is required to determine whether the PIY validity scales can effectively detect malingering across generalized populations.

Behavior Assessment System for Children—Second Edition

The Behavior Assessment System for Children—Second Edition (Reynolds & Kamphaus, 2004) is a multidimensional measure of emotional and behavioral disorders available in self-report, parent, and teacher format for several age ranges. The BASC-2 Self-Report of Personality contains five validity indexes: the F index (i.e., very negative behaviors), the Consistency index (i.e., divergent responses), the Response Pattern index (i.e., random responding), the L index (unrealistically positive), and the V index (nonsensical item endorsement). The general norms were gathered from over 13,000 cases from the ages of 2 through 18, and, when combined with the clinical norm samples, the overall sample came from over 375 sites across 40 states.

The BASC-2 manual (Reynolds & Kamphaus, 2004) offers raw-score ranges for cautionary or extreme cautionary endorsements for all of the BASC-2 validity indexes, although the Consistency and Response Pattern indexes can be identified only through the computer scoring program. Separate ranges are provided for their Self-Report—Child and Self-Report—Adolescent forms:

- For the Child self-report, the F index raw-score frequency is 4–6 (3.8% base rate) for Caution and 7–15 (.8%) for Extreme Caution.
- For the Adolescent self-report, the F index raw-score frequency is 4–6 (3.6%) for Caution and 7–15 (.6%) for Extreme Caution.
- For the Child self-report, the L index raw-score frequency for Caution is 10–12 (8.6%), and for Extreme Caution, 13 (.8%).
- For the Adolescent self-report, the L index raw-score frequency for Caution is 9–11 (4.9%), and for Extreme Caution, 12–15 (1.2%).

Interestingly, the BASC-2 manual does not provide internal-consistency alphas for the self-report validity indexes (Reynolds & Kamphaus, 2004). Regardless of the extensive normative data provided, no studies are available that evaluate the BASC-2 validity indexes and their abilities to accurately detect defensiveness or feigning. The absence of simulation or known-groups studies is a serious omission.

Structured Inventory of Malingered Symptomatology

The Structured Inventory of Malingered Symptomatology (SIMS; Smith, 1992) is a self-report questionnaire designed to detect faking across specific conditions (Smith, 1992; Smith & Burger, 1997). The SIMS can be completed with a fifth-grade reading level and contains 75 true–false items that map onto five nonoverlapping scales to detect feigned clinical conditions. A full description of its scales and their validation is included in Chapter 19 in this volume.

Rogers, Hinds, and Sewell (1996) examined the SIMS' utility with an adolescent inpatient population. Using a total cut score ≥ 16 and an Affective Disorder score ≥ 5, they achieved a promising PPP rate of .87. As an initial study, the SIMS was a moderately effective screen for adolescent feigning. However, Rogers and colleagues stressed several caveats. First, the SIMS' NPP rate was low, limiting its use in the determination of malingering. Second, the sample did not have an adequate representation of psychotic disorders; its use for adolescents within this diagnostic category is unknown. Additionally, the authors did not determine the SIMS' utility for detecting feigned cognitive disorders, although cognitive screening could be addressed by the Neurological and Low Intelligence scales. Intended as a feigning screen, the SIMS cannot be used to make any actual determinations of malingering. Elevations of one or more scales is an appropriate signal for further evaluation. With further cross-validation, the SIMS may be an effective and brief screen for adolescent malingering.

Psychological Tests and Feigned Cognitive Impairment

Feigned cognitive impairments are a growing concern, particularly during litigation. This section explores the use of several prominent cognitive-effort measures with children.

Raven's Standard Progressive Matrices

Raven's Standard Progressive Matrices (RPM; Raven, Raven, & Court, 2000) is a multiple-choice paper-and-pencil test composed of a series of visual pattern-matching and analogy problems and is recognized as a useful neuropsychological measure of cognitive reasoning and concept formation (Lezak, Howieson, & Loring, 2004). Examinees are required to conceptualize spatial, numerical, and design relationships that range from simple to very intricate and abstract patterns.

The RPM has successfully identified neuropsychological malingering in populations of adults using a simple formula based on a performance-curve detection strategy (Gudjonsson & Shackleton, 1986; see also Rogers, Chapter 2, this volume). It requires no additional administration procedures outside of its regular use. Within the adult standardization sample, the formula produced a cross-validated 26% false-negative rate and a 5% false-positive rate (Raven et al., 2000). Within a sample of children and adolescents, McKinzey, Prieler, and Raven (2003) found that using the same formula for detecting faked RPM profiles resulted in a false-positive rate of 7%, as well as a false-negative rate of 64%, which they attributed to their participants' inability to fake the test. However, they used Raven and colleagues' (2000) item difficulty analyses to guide the creation of a three-item scale (A3, A4, and B1) using the floor-effect strategy. It produced a 95% hit rate (see Table 20.5), with equal false positive and negative rates of 5% (McKinzey et al., 2003).

Test of Memory Malingering (TOMM)

The Test of Memory Malingering (TOMM; Tombaugh, 1996) is a simple forced-choice recognition-memory test. Its description and

TABLE 20.5. Measures for Detecting Cognitive Impairment

First author(s)/date	Total N	Gender	Cut score	Sens	Spec	PPP	NPP
				Utility estimates			
Raven's Standard Progressive Matrices (RPM)							
McKinzey (2003)	44	Combined	Failing A3, A4, or B1	.95	.95		
Test of Memory Malingering (TOMM)							
Word Memory Test (WMT)							
Courtney (2003)	111	Combined, Ages 6–9	Effort ≤ 96.0				
		Combined, Ages 10–17	Effort ≤ 74.5				
Green & Fiaro (2003)	135	Combined	Effort ≤ 82.5				

Note. Sens, sensitivity; Spec, specificity; PPP, positive predictive power; NPP, negative predictive power.

validation are provided in Chapter 14 in this volume. Its primary detection strategy is the floor effect: a cut of 90% accuracy on the second retention trial is the primary criterion for feigned cognitive impairment. Within a validation study using student simulators and controls, this cut score provided a sensitivity and specificity of 100% (Tombaugh, 1997).

Recently, several studies have examined the usefulness of the TOMM for children in cases of suspected feigning. Donders (2005) evaluated a sample of 97 children and adolescents referred for a wide range of clinical diagnoses, including attention-deficit/hyperactivity disorder, Asperger's disorder, brain tumor, fetal alcohol syndrome, and meningitis. Although the younger children (ages 6–8) did perform less competently than their older counterparts, more than 90% of the children were able to surpass the 90% criterion. Donders concluded that the TOMM could be used with school-age children to evaluate effort and possible feigning. Constantinou and McCaffrey (2003) found similar results across two separate populations of children, elementary and middle school students from both the United States and the city of Nicosia on the island of Cyprus. Overall, the children achieved a 98% accuracy rating on the TOMM Trial 2, greater than the adult cutoff score. These results suggest that the TOMM is not influenced by age, education, or gender. They provide promising data on the use of the TOMM in diverse cultures.

However, it has been suggested that some children are not detected for malingering with the TOMM but still perform below their abilities on other neuropsychological tests (Donders, 2005). Further cross-validation will be necessary to determine whether the TOMM is less sensitive to suboptimal effort than some other forced-choice tests. However, the evidence suggests that, when school-age children fail to meet the established cutoff score on the TOMM, inadequate test effort is likely.

Word Memory Test (WMT)

The Word Memory Test (WMT; Green, Allen, & Aster, 1996) assesses feigned impairment of verbal abilities. Clients are presented twice with a learning list of 20 word pairs that each share a strong semantic association (e.g., *pig–bacon; dog–cat*). After the two learning trials, participants are given a series of recognition

and recall tests (see Sweet et al., Chapter 13, this volume).

Differing from standard memory or neuropsychological tests, the WMT scores have been shown to be unrelated to age, intelligence, and level of education (Green, Lees-Haley, & Allen, 2002). According to Green and Flaro (2003), the WMT is generally unaffected by genuine cognitive deficits. Using a differential prevalence design, Green, Iverson, and Allen (1999) found that patients with identified brain injuries performed better on the WMT than patients with less severe brain injuries who were involved in litigation. Although the WMT has been extensively studied in adult populations (see Chapter 13), the data are limited with adolescents.

Green and Flaro (2003) studied WMT results for children of different age levels (means of 8, 11, 14, and 16 years of age) and found that younger children do not appear to score any lower on WMT subtests than older children. However, children with a reading level below third grade had difficulty with the computerized WMT and scored comparatively low on the WMT subtests.

Courtney, Dinkins, Allen, and Kuroski (2003) found that children's effort on the WMT was associated with reading ability and age; it is unclear whether reading ability or age contributed the most to this association. As a benchmark, however, children age 11 and older generated WMT scores comparable to adult normative data. Taken together, these findings suggest that when used with young children or those with a low reading ability, the WMT should be interpreted cautiously. For children age 10 or less, it is recommended that evaluation procedures include asking the children to read the words during WMT word list learning, followed by the evaluator correcting the reading if the child decoded the word incorrectly. With this method, the child is given every opportunity to succeed on this effort-based task.

Computerized Assessment of Response Bias

The Computerized Assessment of Response Bias (CARB; Allen, Conder, Green, & Cox, 1997) is a forced-choice memory test that capitalizes on a floor-effect strategy. Courtney and colleagues (2003) found that children age 11 years and older produced CARB scores that were comparable to those of adult disability claimants who achieved adequate effort. The 10-year-old children in the Courtney (2003) study produced CARB scores that were similar to those of children ages 11–14, but with twice the variability of the older children. Moreover, the average CARB total score for children age 9 and below was 7.1 *SD* below the average of the older children (Courtney et al., 2003). Based on these findings, the CARB should not be used with younger populations.

Structured Interviews

Structured Interview of Reported Symptoms

The Structured Interview of Reported Symptoms (SIRS) (Rogers, Bagby, & Dickens, 1992) is a well-validated structured interview for the assessment of feigned mental disorders. (See Rogers, Chapter 18, this volume, for the description of its scales and general validation.) Rogers, Hinds, and Sewell (1996) recruited adolescent participants from a court-referred residential treatment program. After examining participant responses in a within-subjects honest-feigning design, Rogers and colleagues recommend that the SIRS be used in collaboration with other measures rather than as the sole instrument for clinical classification. They found that lowering the cutoff score for primary SIRS scales from ≥ 3 to ≥ 2 in the probable-feigning range increased the PPP to .79, with the NPP remaining at .98. Although using other composite indexes increased the SIRS' PPP to .89, Rogers and colleagues cautioned against overfitting the data. The SIRS validation with children is lacking. For adolescents, it may provide ancillary data on feigning when limited to nonpsychotic clinical samples.

Combined Measures

Rogers, Hinds, and Sewell (1996) tested the combined effect of measures for detecting dissimulation in order to determine whether the SIRS and MMPI-A validity scales combined would perform better than either measure alone. The results indicated that for the SIRS the NPP was .98 and the PPP was .78, with the overall classification rate of 87.8%. As a group the MMPI-A validity scales and indicators alone produced an NPP of .85 and a PPP of .87,

with an overall classification rate of 85.8%. In combination, the SIRS and the MMPI-A produced an NPP of .94 and a PPP of .91, for an overall classification rate of 93%. These findings suggest that the use of the SIRS and MMPI-A together to assess malingering in adolescents enhances predictive capacity, whereas use of the MMPI-A alone may produce an unacceptable number of false positives. However, the SIRS requires a substantial time commitment, and therefore it may not be justified unless there is some indication of malingering. These results should be viewed as having more conceptual than clinical significance.

THRESHOLD AND CLINICAL DECISION MODELS

Despite 10 years of clinical practice and research since McCann (1998) and Oldershaw and Bagby (1997) wrote their respective works on child and adolescent deception, systematic research on juvenile response styles has made only modest advances. Defensiveness, for example, is likely prevalent in many child and adolescent clinical populations. However, the current research is insufficient to propose empirically validated threshold or clinical decision models.

Despite available scales on the MMPI-A, BASC, and MACI to assess defensiveness, the research has not established cutoff scores that are cross-validated. Also lacking are successful strides toward understanding the clinical relevance of particular scale elevations for specific age ranges. Similar to Oldershaw and Bagby (1997), we cannot make any specific recommendations, and we avoid any strong conclusions regarding defensiveness from these measures.

More research is available on malingering in adolescents, but this research is still very limited. Oldershaw and Bagby (1997) proposed a threshold model to determine when malingering should be fully evaluated. Although the classification rates were generally high for the SIRS and the MMPI-A, the lack of systematic cross-validation did not allow for the development of a clinical decision-making model at that time. With that caveat in mind, we suggest threshold models in Table 20.6 to help determine when feigning and defensiveness should be fully evaluated.

TABLE 20.6. Threshold Models for Adolescent Malingering and Defensiveness

Feigning of mental disorders should be fully assessed, if any of the following occur:
1. Clinical and structured interviewing indicative of a highly exaggerated pattern of reporting.
2. On the SIRS, any primary scale in the definite range or any two primary scales in the probable range.
3. On the MMPI-A, an F index of > 85 or an F-K index of > 20
4. On the SIMS, a total score > 40

Feigning of cognitive impairment should be fully assessed, if any of the following occur:
1. Clinical and structured interviewing indicative of feigned cognitive impairment.
2. On the TOMM, with children 9 and up, a total score on the 2nd trial > 44
3. On the WMT, with children 11 and up, Effort scores < 82.5

Defensiveness should be fully assessed, if any of the following occur:
1. Clinical and structured interviewing indicative of defensive response style.
2. On the MMPI-A, an L score ≥ 56
3. On the PIY, a DEF score > 59

The importance of clinical expertise is emphasized in each threshold model. As such, there is an emphasis on data from clinical and structured interviewing. For feigning, different detection strategies are required for each domain: feigned mental disorders and feigned cognitive impairment. For the former, a diverse set of detection strategies are available via the SIRS, MMPI-A, and SIMS. For the latter, research has been mostly limited to the floor effect. For defensiveness, denial of personal faults (L scale) appears to have the greatest potential.

CONCLUSIONS

Most of the literature on the assessment of malingering and deception has focused on adults (Rogers, 1997a). This chapter notes that there is an increasing need for applying reliable, valid, and practical methods for assessing malingering and deception among child and adolescent populations. The good news is that research has begun on these important issues, but there are so many more questions than answers at this point in time. These questions signal the need for research in several key areas.

This chapter elucidated several important considerations for both future research and practice. First, establishing the prevalence of different types of deception, categorized by gender and setting, is essential. Second, the role of developmental status and deception requires extensive longitudinal research. Third, the relationship of motivation to deception must be elucidated. Fourth, structured interviews, with their advantages over self-report measures, deserve additional investigation. Fifth, there is a need to examine personality and psychopathology and their relation to malingering. Research in this area could focus on the broad domains of internalizing and externalizing psychopathology. In addition, studies on personality, such as the Big Five factors, might shed more light on deception in youths. Sixth, with respect to clinical practice, we wonder whether the current state of knowledge indicates the importance of multiple-time point evaluations of functioning to determine the veracity of child and adolescent reports. Single-time point evaluations of youths are limiting in terms of their view and level of exaggeration on a topic. Finally, we believe research that focuses on the treatment of youths and that incorporates potentially deceptive practices is needed in order to further allow youths to develop in a healthy manner in their communities.

ACKNOWLEDGMENTS

We would like to thank David Berry for his help in providing us with data, as well as relevant studies on malingering and response styles with adolescents. We would also like to acknowledge a Social Sciences and Humanities Research Council of Canada (SSHRC) Postdoctoral Fellowship awarded to Zina Lee in support of this work.

21

Challenges and Advances in Assessment of Response Style in Forensic Examination Contexts

RANDY K. OTTO, PhD, ABPP

Given the many ways in which forensic evaluations differ from therapeutic evaluations, assessment of the examinee's response style is essential in the forensic assessment context. Litigants whose mental states are at issue in the legal proceedings in which they are involved typically have much at stake. In civil commitment and criminal proceedings, an examinee's liberty can be at risk. In custody and dependency proceedings, parents' access to their children is at issue. In guardianship proceedings, the rights of potential wards to control important personal matters, including managing finances and making health care decisions, can be restricted or removed. And in personal injury proceedings, plaintiffs may seek significant sums of money. Consequently, integral to assessing a litigant's legally relevant functioning or capacities is consideration of his or her response style and approach to the evaluation process more generally (Rogers & Bender, 2003; Melton et al., 2007; Heilbrun, 2001).

Discussed in this chapter are conceptual and practical challenges in the assessment of response style in forensic contexts. These challenges include: (1) the complicated nature of response styles; (2) significant limitations in consideration of response style included within the *Diagnostic and Statistical Manual of*

Mental Disorders (4th ed., text rev., American Psychiatric Association, 2000; hereinafter DSM-IV-TR); (3) appropriate use of assessment tools designed to assess response style; (4) appropriate presentation of findings and opinions regarding response style; and (5) use of third-party and collateral information in the assessment of response style.

CONCEPTUALIZATION OF RESPONSE STYLE

Preliminary Issues

The thinking and practices of mental health professionals who work in the forensic arena have been narrowly focused when it comes to matters of response style. Researchers and clinicians alike have historically emphasized person-centered explanations of response style and ignored situational and contextual factors. Paulhus (1991a) highlighted the importance of distinguishing between the two, noting the relative contributions of "response set" (i.e., a temporary and context-specific response style the examinee adopts) and "response style" (i.e., a more enduring, person-centered tendency to respond in a certain way across situations and over time). Forensic examiners must consider both individual and environmental contributions when describing the presentation and functioning of the examinee as they are related to some legal issue (Mischel, 1968, 1969).[1]

The overwhelming emphasis on one type of response style—malingering—is problematic insofar as it has resulted in deemphasis and neglect of other response styles. Examination of practitioners' websites and resumes reveals too many forensic psychologists and psychiatrists who identify expertise in "assessment of malingering," and a perusal of assessment journals makes clear that the bulk of research on response style has focused on malingering and related response styles such as symptom feigning. Finally, a cursory scan of test publishers' catalogs indicates that the large majority of response-style measures are devoted to identifying persons motivated to exaggerate or fabricate symptoms and impairments. Malingering (and related symptom and impairment feigning), however, are only one constellation of a myriad of response styles that forensic examinees might adopt.

Types of Response Style

Based on the preliminary work of Rogers (1997a; see also Chapter 1, this volume) six primary response styles can be identified that persons undergoing forensic psychological and psychiatric examinations may adopt: (1) symptom feigning, (2) guardedness/disavowal, (3) false presentation of positive traits, (3) irrelevant responding, (4) random responding, (5) honest/candid responding, and (6) hybrid responding. *Symptom feigning* is characterized by intentional exaggeration and/or fabrication of symptoms or impairments, without any assumptions about the examinee's intent, motivations, or goals. Malingering is the most frequently referenced type of symptom exaggeration/fabrication and, according to the DSM-IV-TR (American Psychiatric Association, 2000), is characterized by motivations other than to assume the sick role (also see later in the chapter). Factitious presentations (e.g., factitious disorder) are also subsumed within this category (see Hamilton et al., Chapter 8, this volume). *Guardedness/disavowal*[2] describes a response style characterized by intentional denial or disavowal of impairments or limitations. This response style is often, but not always, accompanied by *false presentation of positive traits* (i.e., intentionally misrepresent-

ing oneself as having positive attributes, traits, skills, or abilities that one does not possess). *Irrelevant responding* refers to a response style in which the examinee does not engage in the assessment process, whereas *random responding* connotes engagement in the process, but with random responses (Rogers, 1984b). Although examinees who adopt an *honest/candid* response style are motivated to offer accurate descriptions and accounts to the examiner, the information or test responses they provide may still not be accurate, because their accounts can be affected by a variety of other factors (e.g., perception, perspective, and memory). Finally, *hybrid responding* is characterized by two or more of any of the preceding described response styles and reflects the reality that examinees can adopt a number of different response styles during an examination. As the hypothetical cases presented next suggest, the response style that forensic examinees are most likely to adopt is a hybrid one.

Image a defendant, charged with battery on a law enforcement officer, who is motivated to do whatever necessary to gain an adjudication of not guilty by reason of insanity. This defendant might accurately recount a considerable amount of historical information (e.g., social, educational, vocational, medical and psychiatric histories); exaggerate or fabricate some symptoms (e.g., falsely report the experience of paranoid delusions and associated hallucinations resulting from an underlying psychotic disorder at and around the time of the offense); deny or minimize other relevant symptoms, impairments, or experiences (e.g., her anger and impaired judgment at and around the time of the offense resulting from alcohol intoxication; the emotional satisfaction she experienced during the offense); and portray herself as having positive attributes that she does not actually possess (e.g., empathy for those who are victimized by others; respect for law enforcement officers). Another example of how multiple response styles are likely to be observed in forensic contexts involves custody litigation and a father participating in a custody evaluation who seeks primary residential placement of and sole decision-making responsibility for his children in the context of a bitter divorce. This father may accurately recount a considerable amount of historical information (e.g., family, social, marital, educational, and medical histories); exaggerate some positive attributes (e.g., his desire to place his children's needs and desires before his own, his ability and willingness to shield his children from marital conflict and associated acrimony); fabricate some symptoms or impairments (e.g., the negative impact on his emotional well-being that his diminished contact with his children has caused); and deny or minimize other impairments (e.g., his alcohol dependence and associated emotional abuse of his wife and children). These examples should serve to make clear that, although specific response styles may be more common in some evaluation contexts than others, the modal response style in forensic examinations is probably a hybrid one.

Limitations of the DSM-IV-TR Conceptualization of Response Style

The conceptualization and discussion of response style offered in the DSM-IV-TR (American Psychiatric Association, 2000) and its previous iterations have been quite narrow. Response style is relevant to each DSM-IV-TR diagnosis insofar as all diagnoses are considered to be valid only if the reported symptoms or observed signs are genuine. Yet there are only three classifications in the 943-page volume that are directly relevant to response style, all of which are focused on symptom feigning: (1) the "V code" classification of malingering, (2) the diagnosis of factitious disorder, and (3) the provisional diagnosis of factitious disorder by proxy. Other response styles that are just as important to understanding a patient's or forensic examinee's functioning and presentation (e.g., disavowal/guardedness, irrelevant responding; also see Chapter 1, this volume) are not discussed or even identified in this important reference. Consequently, mental health professionals cannot rely solely on DSM-IV-TR for guidance in conceptualizing and assessing response style.

Malingering is defined in DSM-IV-TR as "the intentional production of falsely or grossly exaggerated physical or psychological symptoms, motivated by external incentives such as avoiding military duty, avoiding work, obtaining financial compensation, evading criminal prosecution, or obtaining drugs" (American Psychiatric Association, 2000, p. 739). The statement directing that "Under some circumstances, Malingering may represent adaptive behavior—for example, feigning illness while a captive of the enemy during wartime" (American Psychiatric Association, 2000, p. 739) suggests

an assumption that malingering is "nonadaptive" in most circumstances.

Because malingering is not a disorder but rather a "condition that may be a focus of clinical attention," there are no diagnostic criteria per se. The DSM-IV-TR identifies four factors, the presence of which should lead the examiner to "strongly suspect" malingering: (1) a medicolegal context of presentation, (2) a marked discrepancy between the person's claimed stress or disability and the objective findings, (3) a lack of cooperation during the diagnostic evaluation, and (4) the presence of antisocial personality disorder. Rogers (1997a) described this conceptualization of malingering as based on a "criminological" model that posits that there are a subset of "bad people" (i.e., those with antisocial traits) in "bad circumstances" (i.e., legal venues) who do "bad things" (i.e., are uncooperative), including misleading mental health professionals who are examining them. Rogers (1997a; see also Chapter 1, this volume) has provided ample support for his criticisms of the DSM model of malingering as poorly conceptualized and lacking empirical support.

Unlike malingering, factitious disorder (sometimes referred to as Munchausen syndrome) is classified in the DSM-IV-TR as a mental disorder, the criteria of which are: (1) the intentional production of physical or psychological signs or symptoms, (2) motivation to assume the sick role, and (3) the absence of external incentives (e.g., economic gain, improving physical well-being) for the behavior.[3] Comparison of the indicators for malingering and the diagnostic criteria for factitious disorder reveals that the DSM-IV-TR distinction between whether a particular individual suffers from a mental disorder (factitious disorder) or a "condition that may be a focus of clinical attention" (malingering) rests on the motivation for the symptom exaggeration or fabrication. Thus, if the mental health professional concludes that the person is feigning symptoms for purposes of assuming the sick role, then a mental disorder is considered to exist; but if symptom exaggeration or fabrication occurs for other reasons (including "external incentives"), then no disorder or impairment is considered to exist, although the behavior remains one that is worthy of attention and consideration. This distinction is based solely on the clinician's inferences regarding the motivation for the feigned symptoms. Because, by definition, external incentives exist in all forensic examination contexts (e.g., avoiding criminal sanctions, gaining a financial award or custody of one's child), forensic examiners may frequently find themselves in the uncomfortable position of attempting to defend their subjective impressions of their examinees' underlying motivations.

Although discussions about response style and its assessment have become more nuanced and sophisticated in the past 20 years, the current diagnostic system continues with a model that is lacking. The treatment and list of response styles should be expanded significantly in future versions of the DSM. Until such time, mental health professionals describing the response styles of their patients and examinees should not be constrained by the limited conceptualizations included in the DSM-IV-TR, but should consider the issue more broadly.

The Forensic Examiner's Challenge

The task of the mental health professional conducting a forensic examination is complex and multifaceted. In each case, the examiner must attempt to describe those aspects of the examinee's emotional, behavioral, and/or cognitive functioning that are relevant to a specific legal issue while considering the relative contributions of genuine and distorted reports. Table 21.1 provides a sampling of the various ways in which a forensic examinee's presentation of symptoms, impairments, and abilities can be affected by a variety of factors, including response style, memory, and unconscious factors.

Consider the case of a 27-year-old personal injury litigant with complaints of neck pain,

back pain, and symptoms of depression—all of which she attributes to an automobile accident that is the subject of the lawsuit. Further assume that the litigant has a preincident history of (1) multiple, diffuse, somatic complaints (including pain, gastrointestinal distress, sexual dysfunction, and conversion symptoms), (2) symptom fabrication designed to gain the attention of health care providers, (3) diffuse, significant symptoms of depression, and (4) fixed and enduring personality traits characterized by attention seeking, self-dramatization, shallow emotions, stormy relationships, a grandiose sense of self-importance, misperceptions of personal ability, arrogance, and a sense of entitlement. The forensic examiner needs to consider a broad array of diagnoses, classifications, and associated features and their contribution to the examinee's functioning. At a minimum, the following disorders and response styles, all of which may contribute to her presentation, must be considered: major depressive disorder, recurrent; somatization disorder; factitious disorder; personality disorder, not otherwise specified, with histrionic and narcissistic features; and malingering. When assessing and describing this plaintiff's emotional and behavioral functioning as it is related to the motor vehicle accident, the forensic examiner must consider the relative contributions of a variety of complex factors. These include whether the examinee's reports of symptoms, impairments, and abilities are affected by

1. Unconscious psychological processes (i.e., somatization features)
2. Limited memory and confusion (perhaps resulting from depression)

TABLE 21.1. A Sampling of Possible Presentations of Forensic Examinees

Type	Examples
Genuine effort	Genuine and accurately reported symptoms, impairments, or abilities
	Genuine and accurately reported symptoms or impairments, the cause of which is mistakenly identified due to factors such as memory limitations or confusion
	Genuine but inaccurately reported symptoms, impairments, and abilities, resulting from memory limitations, confusion, or unconscious processes
Distorted effort	Genuine but intentionally distorted symptoms, impairments, or abilities
	Genuine and accurately reported symptoms or impairments, the cause of which is intentionally misidentified (referred to as false imputation by Resnick, 1997)
	Intentionally distorted symptoms, impairments, or abilities
	Intentional misrepresentation of the degree to which genuine symptoms or impairments affect legally relevant capacities

3. Intentional exaggeration or fabrication of symptoms or impairments (i.e., malingering or factitious disorder)
4. False imputation of genuine or exaggerated symptoms or impairments (i.e., malingering)
5. Intentional misrepresentation of the degree to which symptoms or impairments affect legally relevant abilities (i.e., malingering)
6. Intentional denial of preexisting symptoms or impairments (i.e., disavowal)
7. False claims of positive attributes
8. A personality style characterized by dramatic presentation and feelings of entitlement (i.e., histrionic and narcissistic traits)

This assessment task is daunting, to say the least (Ekman & O'Sullivan, 2006).

CHALLENGES AND ADVANCES IN THE ASSESSMENT OF RESPONSE STYLE

Getting Beyond Feigning Assessments

As described previously, reviews of the professional literature make clear that test developers, researchers, and clinicians historically focused on assessment of exaggeration and fabrication of symptoms and impairment and have devoted considerably less effort to understanding and developing assessment tools focused on other types of response styles, including defensiveness/guardedness, presentation of positive attributes, random responding, and irrelevant responding. Examples of this emphasis are numerous. The title of this book, *Clinical Assessment of Malingering and Deception*, and the coverage of its chapters reveals this emphasis and the comparative lack of research on and attention to other response styles. A review of measures that have been designed for assessment of response style provides a similar picture. Whereas there are two well-known freestanding measures designed to assess denial and minimization (i.e., the Marlowe–Crowne Social Desirability Scale and the Paulhus Deception Scales [PDS]), many more measures are devoted to identification of persons motivated to exaggerate or fabricate symptoms and impairment (e.g., the Structured Interview of Reported Symptoms [SIRS], the Miller Forensic Assessment of Symptoms Tests [M-FAST], the Structured Inventory of Malingered Symptoms [SIMS], the Malingering

Probability Scale, the Validity Indicator Profile [VIP], the Portland Digit Recognition Test [PDRT], the Test of Memory Malingering [TOMM], the Victoria Symptom Validity Test [VSVT], the Computerized Assessment of Response Bias [CARB], the Word Memory Test [WMT], the Medical Symptom Validity Test, the Rey Memory for 15-Item Test [RMFIT], the Rey Dot Counting Test).

Further consideration of feigned cognitive impairment reveals a separate but related phenomenon. With rare exceptions (e.g., the VIP), most stand-alone feigning measures have focused only on feigned memory impairment. Although assessment of memory functioning is integral to most forensic neuropsychological assessments, many other aspects of neuropsychological functioning are relevant as well (e.g., intellectual functioning, attention, freedom from distractibility, executive functioning). Moving beyond stand-alone measures, embedded measures (see Iacono & Patrick, Chapter 15, this volume) represent an important advance in neuropsychological assessments. They are used to test a range of feigned cognitive abilities and can even be applied retrospectively to prior testing for a more comprehensive assessment of feigned cognitive impairment. Yet even more work can be accomplished with stand-alone measures, broadening their coverage beyond memory and application of detection strategies.

In contrast to feigned cognitive impairment, omnibus measures of emotional functioning and psychopathology, frequently employed by forensic examiners, reveal a greater balance. Although the majority of response style scales and indices of the Minnesota Multiphasic Personality Inventory-2 (MMPI-2) are devoted to identifying persons motivated to exaggerate and/or fabricate symptoms and impairments (e.g., F, F-K, Fp, FBS, Fptsd, Ds, Ds-r, O-S, and Md), a substantial number of scales and indices are designed to identify other response styles, including those of individuals motivated to deny or minimize symptoms (e.g., K, F-K, Mp, Wsd, and O-S), to present themselves as having positive attributes (e.g., L and S), or to respond randomly (i.e., VRIN and IR). Review of another frequently used omnibus measure—the Personality Assessment Inventory (PAI)—reveals similar findings (Edens, Cruise, & Buffington-Vollum, 2001; see also Sellbom & Bagby, Chapter 11, this volume). Four PAI scales or indices are designed to identify feigned psychopathology (NIM, MAL, INF, and RDF), three scales or indices focus on symptom denial and minimization (i.e., PIM, DEF, and CDF), and two scales are designed to assess randomly endorsed protocols (i.e., INC and INF). These accomplishments reflect an increasing appreciation of the complicated nature of response style and the need for its comprehensive assessment.

Appropriate Use of Psychological Tests without Embedded Measures of Response Style

Because response styles are typically of less concern in therapeutic settings, it is not surprising that many of the best validated psychological assessment tools were not developed with embedded scales or indices of response style (e.g., the Wechsler Adult Scale of Intelligence–III [WAIS-III], the Beck Depression Inventory–II, the Woodcock–Johnson Tests of Cognitive Ability–III, the NEO Personality Inventory—Revised [NEO-PI-R]). Demonstrating important advances in both clinical and forensic assessment is the development of such embedded scales or indices for measures such as the WAIS-III (see Berry & Schipper, Chapter 14, this volume) and the NEO-PI-R (see Chapter 11, this volume).

Use in forensic evaluations of psychological tests that do not include measures of response style is not problematic *providing* the examiner remains cognizant of their potential vulnerability to response style when interpreting and reporting test results and limitations. However, failure to consider the examinee's response style when completing the test and how it affects the test results (via use of freestanding measures of response style or other means) *is* problematic.

An important consideration in the development of specialized forensic measures is the inclusion of embedded scales for the assessment of response styles. The Evaluation of Competence to Stand Trial—Revised (ECST-R; Rogers, Tillbrook, & Sewell, 2004a, 2004b) is an example of a forensic assessment instrument that provides for explicit assessment of the examinee's response style. Those developing assessment tools for use in forensic examination contexts would do well to follow the example of Rogers and his colleagues and are urged to include scales or indices that provide some insight into the examinee's response style.

Appropriate Use of Response-Style Scales, Indices, and Measures

Tools and techniques that assess response styles are of assistance only if they are used appropriately. As described previously, some response-style tools are embedded within psychological tests (e.g., the MMPI-2, PAI, and ECST-R), whereas others are freestanding measures that do not assess other psychological constructs (e.g., the PDS, TOMM, SIMS, and SIRS).

Response-style scales or indices that are embedded within a more general measure can be used to inform the examiner's conclusions about the examinee's response style, as well as the meaningfulness and utility of the examinee's test performance more generally. Examiners should demonstrate more caution, however, when making inferences about performance and response style based on one measure and applying them to other measures, as doing so requires the inference that similar response styles were adopted by the examinee when completing both measures. Consider a forensic examination in which the plaintiff is administered, among other measures, the Wechsler Memory Scale–III (WMS-III), in order to gain normative-referenced data regarding the examinee's memory functioning, and the WMT, in order to inform conclusions about the examinee's response style and the meaningfulness of the examinee's performance on WMS-III. In this case it is important that the examiner appreciate and acknowledge that the response style the examinee adopted on one measure, the WMT, *could* be very different from the test-taking set adopted when completing the second measure, the WMS-III. Put more simply, although examinees might adopt similar response styles when completing multiple measures, this may not always be the case. In this example, the forensic clinician might also consider using response-style scales that are embedded within the WMS-III (see Sweet et al., Chapter 13, this volume). In general, forensic examiners should consider placement and ordering of measures carefully and indicate in their reports and testimony the inferential nature of conclusions drawn about an examinee's response style on one measure based on performance on another.

With rare exceptions (see, e.g., the SIMS) response-style measures are typically developed for the purpose of identifying a specific type of response style within a particular domain. For example, the M-FAST is designed to identify persons feigning psychotic spectrum symptoms, whereas the WMT, VSVT, and TOMM are designed to identify persons feigning memory impairment. Because of the specific focus of most freestanding measures of response style, examiners must choose their measures carefully and use test results only to inform opinions about the response style surrounding reports of the relevant symptom cluster. Consider the examination of a sexual harassment plaintiff who is seeking compensation for damages limited to symptoms of depression and generalized anxiety, impaired sexual desire and functioning, and alienation from his spouse. Integral to evaluating, understanding, and describing the examinee's emotional and behavioral functioning, of course, is assessment of his response style. Given the plaintiff's complaints, use of response-style measures designed to identify persons feigning symptoms that are not endorsed by this examinee (such as the TOMM, M-FAST, and WMT) is not indicated because elevations on any of these measures can only be interpreted as indicating that the examinee is not exaggerating or fabricating symptoms and impairments that he is not even reporting. Given the domains that these measures assess, it would be inappropriate to administer them and to interpret negative results as providing support for the claim that the examinee did not attempt to feign symptoms of depression, anxiety, and sexual dysfunction. How can an examinee be classified as feigning symptoms or a syndrome that he or she is not reporting? Instead, examiners should consider use of response-style measures carefully and select assessment tools based, in part, on the symptoms, impairments, disabilities, or abilities being reported.

In some evaluation contexts, forensic examiners can choose from a variety of response-style measures or scales to employ, many of which are highly related and produce similar scores and classifications. For example, when assessing the memory or other cognitive abilities of an examinee, there are a number of effort/response-style measures available for use, including the VIP, the WMT, and the TOMM. When multiple response-style measures or scales exist, the preferred approach is almost always to employ and interpret the results of the single most valid measure rather than using a number of highly correlated scales or measures. With rare exceptions (e.g., employing a "screen-first" approach), use of highly corre-

lated response-style measures does little to improve the accuracy of the examiner's conclusions, but it may inappropriately increase the examiner's confidence in such conclusions (see Borum, Otto, & Golding, 1991, for a more detailed discussion of this and other clinical decision-making errors in forensic assessment contexts). Consider the case of a female criminal defendant whose competence to proceed is in doubt based on her reports of significant memory impairment that, if genuine, could limit her ability to deliberate with counsel and understand and participate in the legal proceedings. In addition to formal assessment of the defendant's memory functioning using a structured measure of memory (such as the Memory Assessment Scales or the WMS-III), assessment of the examinee's response style using a measure such as the TOMM, VSVT, or WMT is indicated. Contraindicated, however, is use of more than one of these measures given their similar formats and high intercorrelations. Similarly, a large number of MMPI-2 scales are designed to identify symptom overreporting (e.g., F, Fp, Fptsd, FBS, Md, Ds, and Ds-r), some of which are highly correlated (see Greene, Chapter 10, this volume). Highly correlated measures may lead to increased confidence, with no associated increase in classification accuracy. Therefore, the forensic examiner would do best to identify and rely on the one or two response-style scales that are most accurate and show the lowest correlation. The need for this approach becomes all the more apparent when considering that the use of multiple measures can serve to *decrease* accuracy of response-style determinations if results from a less valid test or scale serve to temper opinions formed on the basis of results derived from a more valid test or scale. As a general rule, the examiner should administer and interpret the instrument that best assesses response style or, alternatively, administer the two best measures of response style *if* scores on the measures are not highly correlated (which suggests that they assess different constructs). Such an approach provides the most valid information about the examinee's response style while minimizing the risk of overconfidence (Borum et al., 1991; Garb, 1998).

As referenced earlier, examiners should be careful not to confuse the admonition against use of highly correlated measures of response style with appropriate use of multiple measures for purposes of screening and more detailed assessment. For example, one might administer the M-FAST to screen forensic examinees reporting psychotic spectrum symptoms and follow this with administration of the SIRS to assess in more detail those examinees who are identified by the M-FAST as possibly feigning such symptoms. Such a screen-detailed assessment approach using correlated measures is appropriate providing that the examiner relies primarily on results from the more valid measure (presumably the more detailed, time-intensive, and/or costly second measure) and guards against overconfidence should similar results on the two highly correlated measures be obtained.

Appropriate Interpretation and Presentation of Assessment Results

Examinees can exaggerate and/or fabricate symptoms or impairments for a variety of reasons. As previously described in more detail, malingering and factitious disorder are primarily distinguished in the DSM-IV-TR by the examinee's underlying motivations. Whereas malingering is defined as a response style that is characterized by feigning for purposes of external incentives, factitious disorder is characterized by production of symptoms for purposes of assuming the sick role. No measure of response style assesses the examinee's *motivation* for symptom exaggeration or fabrication, denial or minimization, or any other response style. Instruments or scales such as the SIMS, TOMM, and MMPI-2 validity scales are not measures of malingering but, rather, are tools designed to inform judgments about feigning (Otto, 2006; Rogers & Payne, 2006), as description of an examinee as malingering requires an inference about the examinee's motivations. Obfuscating this issue, several test developers have used the word *malingering* to title their measures (e.g., Structured Inventory of Malingered Symptomatology or Test of Memory Malingering) or scales (PAI Malingering Index or MMPI-2 Malingered Depression scale). Examiners should remain cognizant of the distinction between a particular response style and its underlying motivation and should make clear in their reports and testimony that no response-style test or scale provides information regarding the examinee's motivation.

Appropriate Use of and Reliance on Third-Party Information

Third-party information[4] is extremely useful in forensic examination contexts (e.g., Melton

et al., 2007; Simon & Gold, 2004). The Specialty Guidelines for Forensic Psychologists (Committee on Ethical Guidelines for Forensic Psychologists, 1991) advise, "Where circumstances reasonably permit, forensic psychologists seek to obtain independent and personal verification of data relied upon as part of their professional services to the court or a party to a legal proceeding" (p. 662), and the Ethical Guidelines for the Practice of Forensic Psychiatry (American Academy of Psychiatry and the Law, 1995) direct that "practicing forensic psychiatrists enhance the honesty and striving for objectivity of their work by basing their forensic opinions, forensic reports, and forensic testimony on all the data available to them" (p. 3). As a result, it is not uncommon for forensic examiners to access and rely on a variety of third-party data sources such as employment records, financial or tax records, military records, and accounts and perceptions of the examinee that are offered by neighbors, coworkers, witnesses, and victims (Otto, Slobogin, & Greenberg, 2006).

Just as they consider the response style of examinees, forensic examiners should consider the validity of collateral information that they have reviewed, whether such includes records or interviews with third parties (Otto et al., 2006). Little concrete guidance is available for forensic examiners who struggle with the issue of how to consider third-party accounts. The Specialty Guidelines for Forensic Psychologists (Committee on Ethical Guidelines for Forensic Psychologists, 1991) acknowledge that "forensic psychologists attempt to corroborate critical data that form the basis for their professional product. When using hearsay data that have not been corroborated, but are nevertheless utilized, forensic psychologists acknowledge the uncorroborated status of those data and their reasons for relying on such data" (p. 662). Similarly, the Ethical Guidelines for the Practice of Forensic Psychiatry (American Academy of Psychiatry and Law, 1995) direct that forensic psychiatrists "communicate the honesty and striving for objectivity of their work, efforts to obtain objectivity, and the soundness of their clinical opinion by distinguishing, to the extent possible, between verified and unverified information as well as among clinical 'facts,' 'inferences,' and 'impressions'" (p. 3). These provisions acknowledge that third-party data sources may be inaccurate due to a variety of factors and direct forensic examiners to seek multiple sources of information in an effort to assess the validity of reports offered by third parties as a result.

Austin (2002) offered a strategy for dealing with this issue that requires the forensic examiner to consider the utility of third-party data sources based on (1) the type of information provided and (2) the nature of the relationship between the informant and the parties in the litigation. The most helpful third-party observations, according to Austin, are those that are directly relevant to an issue at hand and that are offered by a person who is not aligned with anyone involved in the litigation. Less valuable and requiring greater corroboration are (1) accounts that support an examinee's claim or report that are offered by a collateral source who has a significant and positive relationship with that party (e.g., the spouse of a litigant alleging emotional harm stemming from age discrimination in the workplace) or (2) accounts that contradict the examinee's that are offered by a collateral who has or may be presumed to have a negative relationship with the examinee (e.g., the alleged victim of the criminal defendant raising an insanity defense). In contrast, observations that may be most helpful to the forensic examiner are those offered by individuals who are not aligned with any of the parties or whose accounts are contrary to what might be expected given the nature and valence of the relationship between the third party and those involved in the litigation.

Given concerns regarding the accuracy of third-party accounts offered by informants who have some personal relationship with the examinee, forensic examiners often rely on records documenting medical and mental health services provided to examinees. Although examiners may assume that the accounts offered in these records are accurate and unbiased because of the professional obligations of treatment providers, some research indicates that this may not be the case. Freeman, Rathore, Weinfurt, Schulman, and Sulmasy (1999) employed clinical vignettes to assess American physicians' attitudes about entering false information into patients' medical records in order to gain health insurance coverage for otherwise uncovered procedures. Of the 169 physicians surveyed, 58% sanctioned deception in order to bring about insurance coverage for treatment of a life-threatening condition, whereas only 2% reported that they would sanction such conduct to facilitate insurance reimbursement for cosmetic surgery. Of greater concern are data reported by Wynia, Cummins, VanGeest, and Wilson (2000). Of the 720 American physicians who responded to the investigators' anonymous survey about their actions when seeking insurance coverage for their patients, the following data were reported: 28% acknowledged exaggerating the severity of some patients' illnesses, 23% reported altering a billing report, and *10% indicated that they had written in the medical chart signs or symptoms that their patients did not evidence.*

Such patterns of deceptive behavior are not limited to physicians. Eighteen percent of 92 Illinois psychologists anonymously surveyed by Tubbs and Pomerantz (2001) reported "sometimes" altering a diagnosis to meet insurance criteria, and 44% of 108 mental health counselors surveyed by Danziger and Welfel (2001) reported that they had changed or would change a client's diagnosis in order to receive managed care reimbursement. More generally, Kielbasa, Pomerantz, Krohn, and Sullivan (2004) reported that psychologists were 10 times more likely to offer a formal diagnosis for clients whose services were reimbursed by third-party payers than for self-paying clients. These findings highlight the fact that, although third-party information sources have the potential to be helpful in forensic examination contexts, clinicians must be careful about making faulty assumptions regarding the validity of such collateral data.

LEGAL PARAMETERS

It is important that mental health professionals assessing response style in forensic examination contexts understand relevant rules of evidence and associated law regarding opinion testimony, as these authorities control what kind of evidence and opinions can be offered to the legal fact finder. A brief review of these issues and implications for assessment of and testimony about response style, structured around the Federal Rules of Evidence, is provided here. Although many states employ rules that are very similar to the Federal Rules of Evidence (FRE), readers should familiarize themselves with the law in the jurisdictions in which they practice.

Relevant Rules of Evidence

The first hurdle of admissibility is that of relevance (Ogloff, 1990). According to the Federal Rules of Evidence (FRE) 401, " 'relevant evidence' means evidence having any tendency to make the existence of any fact that is of consequence to the determination of the action more probable or less probable than it would be without the evidence" (p. 3). The relevance requirement is easily met by the argument that, integral to considering the forensic examiner's opinion about the examinee's mental state is an understanding of the examinee's response style and approach to the examination. Knowing whether the examinee was exaggerating, fabricating, denying, and/or minimizing impairments and/or abilities is crucial (and relevant) to understanding whatever aspect of the examinee's mental state is at issue in the legal proceeding.

FRE 702 requires that any expert opinions offered to the fact finder are based on "scientific, technical, or other specialized knowledge" and are the product of "reliable principles and methods" that the "witness has applied . . . to the facts of the case" (p. 13). This rule requires that expert opinions about response style be (1) based on knowledge that the fact finder does not possess (i.e., that such opinions flow from real expertise rather than common knowledge) and (2) derived from reliable principles and methods. This rule, for example, could be used to prevent a forensic examiner from offering an "expert opinion" that the examinee was exaggerating and/or fabricating psychiatric symptoms based on the fact that she made little eye contact when interviewed (because the belief that people who avoid eye contact are lying is general knowledge). In contrast, this rule would presumably allow testimony regarding the examinee's attempt to exaggerate and/or fabricate symptomatology based on elevations on a number of scales of the SIRS (because an understanding of how persons feigning severe and persistent mental disorder perform on this well-validated measure of response style is knowledge that is scientific, technical, or specialized).

According to FRE 403, relevant evidence may nonetheless be excluded if "its probative value is substantially outweighed by the danger of unfair prejudice" (p. 4). This rule has been cited in a string of appellate cases in which forensic examiners have couched their opinions and testimony about response style in terms of credibility or veracity. For example, in *Commonwealth v. Zamarripa* (1988), a male defendant appealed his sexual assault conviction in part on the grounds that the trial court allowed a psychologist to testify that the al-

leged victim's report that she did not consent to sexual contact with the defendant was truthful. In overturning the conviction, the appellate court ruled, "As the phenomenon of lying is within the ordinary capacity of jurors to assess, the question of witness credibility is reserved exclusively for the jury" (p. 980). A similar perspective is reflected in *Nicholson v. American National Insurance* (1998), in which a female sexual harassment plaintiff's appeal for a new trial was granted based on the trial court's failure to bar the defense psychiatrist from testifying about her "psychiatric credibility." The judiciary's discomfort with expert opinions about credibility and truthfulness is perhaps best summarized in *Bentley v. Carroll* (1998), in which a medical malpractice plaintiff's request for a new trial was granted in part as a result of the trial court's failure to strike expert testimony regarding his response style. At trial the defense expert—a psychiatrist—based his opinion that the plaintiff exaggerated emotional impairments on results of the MMPI, which he described as a measure that "gives you a profile of the validity and consistency of the individual answering it, sort of, I hate to use the word, mini truth, or lie detector, truth detector."

These decisions, insofar as they reflect the court's recognition that mental health professionals have no expertise with respect to determining the truthfulness of statements that have been offered by the examinee (see, e.g., Ekman & O'Sullivan, 1991), are largely accurate. Most important for forensic examiners to take from this line of decisions is that (1) *expert* opinions about response style should be based on scientific, technical, or specialized knowledge (i.e., *expertise*) rather than information that is available to, or conclusions that can just as easily be formed by, the decision maker, and that (2) descriptions of and opinions about an examinee's response style should be couched in language that emphasizes the specialized knowledge or techniques that were employed by the examiner.

Frye and *Daubert* Considerations

As indicated, FRE 702 requires that expert testimony, in addition to flowing from scientific, technical, or specialized knowledge, must be based on valid techniques. In some cases, the expert's opinion regarding response style may be challenged on the grounds that the technique from which the opinion was derived is not sufficiently valid. Historically, when considering this issue, trial courts employed a legal test that was developed by a federal circuit court in a 1923 case involving a precursor to the modern polygraph, specifically *Frye v. United States*. The *Frye* court held that, when considering the admissibility of expert testimony based on a particular technique, the court was to consider whether the technique "is sufficiently established to have gained general acceptance in the particular field in which it belongs" (*Frye v. United States*, 1923). In response to a string of criticisms about this legal standard, the Supreme Court, in *Daubert v. Merrell Dow Pharmaceuticals* (1993), replaced the "general acceptance" standard enunciated in *Frye* and with one that directed federal courts to consider a variety of factors when considering the admissibility of expert testimony—including but not limited to (1) the testability or falsifiabilty of the method employed, (2) the error rate of the method, if known, (3) whether the matter at issue has been subjected to peer review and publication, and (4) the general acceptance of the method in the relevant fields.

As a result, forensic examiners practicing in jurisdictions that continue to employ the *Frye* test or a variant should be prepared to demonstrate that the techniques they employ are "generally accepted" in the relevant scientific community, whereas those who practice in jurisdictions that employ the *Daubert* test or a variant of it should be prepared to discuss the validity, error rates, peer review, and general acceptance of the response-style assessment techniques that they employ.

SUMMARY

Given the complicated nature of response style, its assessment may be one of the most challenging aspects of forensic examinations. Although considerable gains in the understanding and assessment of response style have been made in the 20 years since the first edition of this book was published, much more work remains to be done. Researchers and clinicians alike need to move beyond their primary focus on symptom exaggeration and fabrication to address other response styles affecting forensic assessments. The efforts should take into account contextual and other factors (e.g., memory perspective) that can

TABLE 21.2. Checklist for Assessment of Response Style in Forensic Examination Contexts

1. Consider potential contribution of all response styles.
2. Avoid sole reliance on the examinee's self-report.
3. Select response-style scales, indices, or measures based on consideration of the examinee's reported symptoms, impairments, and abilities.
4. Carefully consider use of highly correlated scales, indices, or measures.
5. Do not overinterpret test findings and make clear any inferences and limitations in the report and testimony.
6. Ensure that all opinions offered regarding response style are "expert."

have significant effects on response style. And mental health professionals, when conducting forensic examinations, must consider the issue of response styles fully, use measures appropriately, and form and offer opinions regarding response style that flow from truly scientific and specialized knowledge (see Table 21.2).

NOTES

1. Inconsistent with Paulhus's definitions but consistent with common convention, the term *response style* is used throughout this chapter to refer to both individual and person-centered contributions and contextual contributions to examinees' presentations in forensic evaluations.
2. Although some use the term *defensiveness* to describe this response style (see Rogers, Chapter 1, this volume) this term is not employed here given that it is sometimes used to describe a lack of insight or accurate understanding that results from unconscious or psychic mechanisms.
3. Factitious disorder by proxy (sometimes referred to as Munchausen syndrome by proxy), which is identified in the DSM-IV-TR not as a formal diagnosis but as a concept deserving of further study, includes criteria essentially identical to those of factitious disorder but is applied in those cases in which the feigned signs or symptoms are produced in a person who is under the care of the individual who reports the impairments and is the subject of the diagnosis.
4. The term *third-party information* refers to all information obtained or sought during a forensic evaluation except testing completed by the examinee or statements made by the examinee to the forensic examiner.

22

Response Styles in the Assessment of Law Enforcement

REBECCA L. JACKSON, PhD
CODY CRAWFORD, BA

Selection of appropriate candidates to serve on municipal and state police forces is critical to the functioning of the police force and the safety of communities. The selection of appropriate individuals to serve our communities is necessarily a multifaceted endeavor, as successful officers must possess a variety of traits and abilities. For example, police officers must be in good physical health, be capable of engaging with the public, competent at administrative tasks, able to follow as well as give orders, and be capable of quickly judging situations and utilizing force or restraint as the situation demands. The demands on officers may further vary depending on the location of their departments. For example, Bartol (1991) notes that in small towns, officers may work for days without encountering any significant incidents. Therefore, certain departments may demand high boredom tolerance from their officers, whereas busy urban departments might prefer officers who enjoy constant activity.

Due to the variable demands on law enforcement officers, the job selection process is also multifaceted. Similar to other personnel selection settings, law enforcement selection makes use of traditional job selection methods such as interviews, letters of recommendation, and screening tests such as the civil-service examination. Unlike many other employment

settings, law enforcement selection also often includes physical examinations, drug testing, and criminal background checks (Hibler & Kurke, 1995). Law enforcement agencies have also been making greater use of assessment centers in their job selection procedures (More & Unsinger, 1987). Assessment centers generally involve large-scale job simulations that enable potential applicants to engage in job-related tasks while being scored on a variety of domains related to their performance. Assessment centers have demonstrated validity in predicting future job performance, but they are very expensive to launch and maintain (Coulton & Feild, 1995; McEvoy & Beatty, 1989). Despite their value, many departments cannot afford to adopt the use of assessment centers as part of routine job selection procedures.

A final element in law enforcement selection is the psychological assessment process. Under the umbrella of psychological assessment in preemployment screening reside two distinct activities. The first is assessing a candidate's personality to identify aspects that may or may not be suitable for law enforcement work. The second task is to identify potential psychopathology in applicants. Similar to other employers, law enforcement agencies must adhere to the Americans with Disabilities Act (ADA; 1990) when conducting preemployment screening. Most relevant to the current discussion is that the ADA allows medical evaluations to occur only after the individual has been tendered a conditional offer of employment. In terms of psychological assessment, measures that are designed to identify psychopathology are considered medical tests. Tests of "normal" personality are not, and therefore they are permissible even in the preoffer stage of the selection process.

Cochrane, Tett, and Vandecreek (2003) identified commonly used procedures in the selection of police personnel. Psychological testing was the fifth most commonly used procedure. Among the 155 departments that responded, psychological assessment was employed by 91.6% and was used only less frequently than background investigation (99.4%), medical exams (98.7%), interviews (98.1%), and application forms (95.5%). Psychological assessment in these departments was used more prominently than were procedures that are considered standard in law enforcement settings, such as drug testing (88.4%), or general personnel selection approaches, such as recommendation letters (46.5%) or tests of knowledge, skills, and abilities (46.5%). Bartol (1996) reported that police psychologists spend approximately one-third of their time engaged in preemployment screening activities.

The use of standardized psychological measures in law enforcement personnel selection has increased over the course of a decade. For example, in 1988, Delprino and Bahn reported that 52% of police agencies were conducting psychological screening, compared with 91% in 2003 (Cochrane et al., 2003). In 2004, the International Association of Chiefs of Police (IACP; 2004a) adopted guidelines for preemployment psychological evaluations. The guidelines outline which professionals are eligible to conduct assessments, the role of testing in the overall evaluation, and qualities that tests must possess. Specifically, the guidelines caution users to be familiar with the tests and the research related to their use, particularly in law enforcement candidate selection. Furthermore, they caution that tests should be "objective, job-related, and validated" (IACP, 2004a, p. 2).

In addition to the two uses of psychological assessment in law enforcement screening just discussed (i.e., to identify psychologically unstable candidates or personality characteristics unsuited for police work), psychological assessment is also used to evaluate officers who

have been found or are thought to be unfit for duty. The goals of this chapter are to examine standardized psychological measures that are frequently used during law enforcement assessment and identify the common response patterns and the relevance of these patterns to police selection and performance.

Common instruments used in police selection include the Minnesota Multiphasic Personality Inventory (MMPI; Hathaway & McKinley, 1940) and the revised MMPI-2 (Butcher, Dahlstrom, Graham, Tellegen, & Kaemmer, 1989), the Inwald Personality Inventory (IPI; Inwald, Knatz, & Shusman, 1982), and the California Psychological Inventory (CPI; Gough, 1987). These measures range in their focus and purpose. The MMPI-2 and IPI are considered to be primarily measures of psychopathology, although the MMPI-2 has a very general focus in comparison with the IPI's specialized application. In contrast, the CPI is considered a test of personality.

A more recent measure to be used in the assessment of law enforcement is the Personality Assessment Inventory (PAI) Law Enforcement, Corrections, and Public Safety Selection Report (Roberts, Thompson, & Johnson, 2004). Beyond the validation data reported in the manual, this version of the PAI has not been extensively tested or adopted for use in the assessment of law enforcement. Because of its clear relevance, however, a brief description of the measure is included, following our discussion of the three most commonly employed measures.

MMPI AND MMPI-2

Modal Profiles of Police Applicants

The MMPI and MMPI-2 are the longest standing assessment measures and are used by more than two-thirds of police departments (e.g., 71.6% of police departments recently endorsed its use; Cochrane et al., 2003). The MMPI-2 consists of three "traditional" validity scales and 10 primary clinical scales (see Greene, Chapter 10, this volume). In addition, supplementary scales, content scales, and dozens of specialized indices have been developed.

The MMPI-2 is by far the most common psychological assessment administered in law enforcement personnel testing (Cochrane et al., 2003). The majority of studies on police selection have been conducted on the original

MMPI. These original reports (e.g., Bernstein, Schoenfeld, & Costello, 1982; Matarazzo, Allen, Saslow, & Wiens, 1964) demonstrated that law enforcement applicants tend to respond in a defensive manner. Similar to other personnel selection settings, the law enforcement candidates tended to respond in a manner that puts them in the best possible light. As delineated by Rogers in Chapter 1 of this volume, this response pattern may reflect both defensiveness (i.e., minimization of psychological issues) and social desirability (i.e., emphasizing positive qualities and deemphasizing any shortcomings)

In an early analysis, Matarazzo and colleagues (1964) attempted to identify modal profiles of successful police applicants. In a male-only sample, he found that the typical profile has an elevated K (although not clinically significant). The clinical profiles were characterized by relatively low scales 2 (approximately 52T) and 0 (roughly 45T), with a slightly higher scale 3 (about 55T). Interestingly, scale 4 had the highest elevation, with an approximate average of 65T. Still, this elevation is lower than the 70T used with the MMPI as the benchmark for clinical interpretation.

Significant changes during the past two decades compel us to revisit the notion of a "normal" profile for law enforcement applicants. At least three important considerations play an important role. First, the Americans with Disabilities Act (ADA; 1990) triggered changes in preemployment psychological testing. Second, the increased diversity of police applicants and officers requires this profile to be further evaluated. Third and most important, MMPI-2 is a substantial revision of the MMPI, with changes in items, scale composition, and interpretation of clinical significance (i.e., 65T rather than 70T).

On the disability issue, the ADA declared it illegal to conduct psychological evaluations that would lead to the identification of a mental or emotional disorder or impairment until after the applicant has been tendered a conditional offer of employment. The practical importance of this change in legislation is that tests of psychopathology, such as the MMPI/MMPI-2 or IPI, may be administered only following a conditional offer of employment. Regarding diversity, more women and minorities are joining the law enforcement professions than was true 40 years ago. It is unknown how closely a "normal" law enforcement profile might fit minority and female applicants.

Since the MMPI-2's publication, the need for updated norms, and norms particularly for law enforcement applicants, has become clearly evident (Detrick, Chibnall, & Rosso, 2001; Kornfeld, 1995). Despite reports of general concordance between the MMPI and MMPI-2 (e.g., Ben-Porath & Butcher, 1989), at least two studies have demonstrated significant differences between MMPI and MMPI-2 scores (Chojnacki & Walsh, 1992; Munley, 1991). Although more than 17 years have passed since its publication in 1989, very little research is available on MMPI-2 normative data for police officer applicants (Detrick et al., 2001; Kornfeld, 1995).

ADA's requirements further diminish the relevance of the original MMPI studies. In particular, data from the original MMPI studies were obtained before the 1990 ADA; therefore, they include applicants from all stages of the employment pool. In contrast, MMPI-2 data have been mostly gathered after 1990. With the implementation of ADA, MMPI-2 data should eliminate the initial phase and focus only on those applicants who have passed the first rounds of screening and received conditional offers of employment. By itself, this substantially limits the generalizability of the original MMPI studies to current applicants.

Three studies of law enforcement candidates (Detrick et al., 2001; Devan, 2004; Kornfeld, 1995) are examined with an eye toward the development of an MMPI-2 modal profile. Summarized in Table 22.1, these studies are important in light of the significant changes in measurement (MMPI-2), law (ADA), and the recruitment pool. Table 22.1 includes descriptive data based on gender and minority status.

Kornfeld (1995) reported normative data for a group of police officer candidates that is comparatively smaller than those in the other two studies (total $N = 84$). As noted in Table 22.1, all applicants tended to score relatively low on the F scale (all means <40T) but evidenced some elevations of scale K, which suggests some defensiveness about psychological issues.

For clinical profiles, applicants generally had low scores on scales 2 and 0. Of particular interest, male samples tended to score low on scale 5, whereas females averaged a nearly clinically significant range (T = 64.20, SD = 4.50). Males with low scale 5 scores are described as

TABLE 22.1. Standard MMPI-2 Validity Scales for MMPI-2 Police Selection Studies

		Males		Females		
Scale	Study (author/date)	European American (n = 61[a], 395[b], 6207[c])	Minorities (n = 11[a], 35[b])	European American (n = 12[a], 34[b], 935[c])	Minorities (n = 3[b])	Weighted mean
L	Kornfeld (1995)	56.90 (11.71)	53.45 (8.83)	60.00 (10.50)		
	Detrick et al. (2001)	61.1 (11.5)	65.4 (13.4)	60.00 (11.00)	67.7 (7.4)	
	Devan (2004)	51.53 (9.46)		51.32 (10.09)		
	Weighted Mean (SD)	52.15 (9.62)	62.54 (12.80)	51.73 (10.13)	67.7 (7.4)	52.16 (9.71)
F	Kornfeld (1995)	39.79 (3.07)	38.27 (3.54)	39.50 (5.35)		
	Detrick et al. (2001)	41.3 (4.6)	43.6 (5.2)	43.3 (4.3)	45.7 (5.1)	
	Devan (2004)	43.72 (6.45)		45.96 (7.88)		
	Weighted Mean (SD)	43.54 (6.33)	42.33 (4.99)	45.79 (7.77)	45.7 (5.1)	43.82 (6.52)
K	Kornfeld (1995)	62.48 (6.23)	58.83 (8.09)	64.60 (5.43)		
	Detrick et al. (2001)	63.8 (7.2)	63.1 (7.6)	63.1 (7.7)	64.3 (9.6)	
	Devan (2004)	56.19 (9.47)		56.13 (9.74)		
	Weighted Mean (SD)	56.70 (9.32)	62.08 (7.90)	56.48 (9.65)	64.3 (9.6)	56.71 (9.36)

Note. Numbers in parentheses represent standard deviations. Devan reported means and standard deviations for male and female applicants, but reported ethnicity for only a subset of the sample; 93.7% of applicants were European American. [a] Kornfeld (1995), [b] Detrick, Chibnall, & Rosso (2001), [c] Devan (2004).

presenting themselves as extremely masculine, as having stereotypical masculine interests, and as being action oriented. In contrast, females with scale 5 elevations are described as typically rejecting the traditional female role and as having interests that are stereotypically more masculine than feminine. Kornfeld (1995) interpreted the high scale 5 scores of females as perhaps unique to, or especially relevant for, females entering a traditionally male-dominated profession. Females who reject the traditional feminine role may be more likely to gravitate to law enforcement and other male-dominant professions, but other interpretations are also possible. For example, Graham, Watts, and Timbrook (1991) reported that female students who were instructed to create a favorable impression of themselves also produced elevations on scale 5. It is possible, then, that women trying to create a favorable impression, such as in a personnel selection situation, will emphasize assertiveness, competitiveness, and an achievement orientation, which leads to elevations on scale 5 in female test takers.

Detrick and colleagues (2001) summarized mean scale scores for 467 police officer appli-

cants who had received conditional job offers. As Table 22.1 makes clear, the pattern of validity scores is similar to those reported by Kornfeld (1995), with moderately elevated K scores and moderately depressed F scores. Detrick and colleagues also reported low scores on scale 0 and a similar gender disparity on scale 5.

Devan (2004; discussed more fully in the following section) reported on a very large sample of police officer applicants (total N = 7,142). She reported that ethnicity data were available for only 3,411 participants. Of those, almost all (93.7%) were European Americans. Devan reported K scores that were less elevated (M = 56.18, SD = 9.51), with similarly low scores on scales 2 and 0.

Comparisons of ethnicity are stymied by (1) absence of data in the Devan (2004) study, (2) the minuscule number of minority females, and (3) the collapsing of all minorities into a single group, which could mask ethnic differences. Focusing on only male comparisons and excluding the Devan study, no clear patterns emerge across validity scales (see Table 22.1). Moreover, the effect sizes tend to be quite small. The largest difference was found on the K scale ($d = .56$; Kornfeld, 1995); however, the much larger study by Detrick and colleagues (2001) yielded a negligible difference ($d = .10$).

The majority of law enforcement applicants will produce clinical profiles within normal limits. Devan, Hungerford, Wood, and Greene (2001) conducted a review of the literature and identified 42 studies that utilized the MMPI or MMPI-2 for officer screening and selection. They found no MMPI or MMPI-2 scale that averaged in an elevated range (MMPI ≥ 70T; MMPI-2 ≥ 65T). Of course, averages can obscure both low and elevated scores for individual applicants. Taken together with the data in Table 22.1, these results suggest relatively few differences based on gender and ethnicity variation. As a whole, police applicants produce somewhat defensive, but valid, MMPI-2 profiles that describe psychologically healthy people who are relatively free of distress or worry, assertive and achievement oriented, and comfortable in the presence of others.

MMPI and MMPI-2 Response Styles among Police Officer Candidates

Psychologists involved in the selection of police officers are very concerned with the candor of the applicants. Presenting oneself in a positive light is expected of job applicants. For example, Devan (2004) reported that the mean MMPI-2 profile was within normal limits. However, the K scale was the most frequently elevated at 19.2%, followed by the L scale (11.9%). The question for the psychologist is whether this is "typical" defensiveness, associated with positive impression management and social desirability, or whether the response style represents an attempt at blatant deception. In the context of personnel selection, trying to present oneself in the most positive light (i.e., social desirability) may be different from concealing psychopathology (i.e., defensiveness). The first response style is typical of job applicants in general, and, in most respects, these individuals continue to be acceptable job candidates. The latter response from job applicants is potentially unacceptable.

Borum and Stock (1993) studied applicants for law enforcement positions who were found to be deceptive and who subsequently admitted during the clinical interview that they had intentionally lied in one or more areas of the application process ($n = 18$). The authors compared them with a group of police applicants who admitted no deception and for whom none could be detected ($n = 18$). They asked the following questions: Do these two groups differ on the validity indicators of the MMPI and the IPI? Do any of these scales or indexes effectively discriminate between the groups so that they could be used to identify candidates who need closer scrutiny? Beyond the standard validity scales, they used two specialized indicators (see Chapter 10, this volume): total O-S and Mp.

Of particular interest, Borum and Stock (1993) proposed the Es–K scale as a potential indicator of defensive responding. Ego Strength (Es) is believed to measure a general factor of capacity of personality integration or ego strength. High Es scores are indicative of an individual who is stable, reliable, responsible, and self-confident. High K scores are more indicative of defensiveness in an individual who is trying to give an appearance of adequacy, control, and effectiveness and who lacks self-insight and self-understanding. However, these two scores are considered to be related, and Caldwell (1988) suggested that interpretation of the Es scale is most effective when seen in comparison with the K scale. The positive characteristic of "personal organization" associated with high Es scores seems to be more prominent when Es is increasingly higher than K. To some extent, both scales measure psychological defenses against distress. Consequently, the comparison is made to differentiate the healthy defensiveness from the intentional effort to ignore or minimize difficulties. This is identified as the Es–K index.

The Es–K scale produced a very large effect size in the expected direction ($d = 1.85$; see Table 22.2); this effect size is more than double that computed for the K scale alone ($d = .74$). A cut score of −3 correctly classified 83.3% of the deceptive applicants with only a 5.5% false-positive rate. The Es–K scale outperformed cut scores for other MMPI indicators of impression management, including K, L, and MP, both in terms of false positives (44.4%, 38.9%, and 16.7%, respectively) and effect sizes (see Table 22.2). Unfortunately, Borum and Stock's (1993) investigation was limited to the original MMPI. To our knowledge, the Es–K scale has not been validated with the MMPI-2. In contrast to the MMPI-2, IPI's validity scale (i.e., Guardedness; $d = .73$) produced only a moderate effect size.

TABLE 22.2. Validity Scales for a Sample of Deceptive versus Candid Police Applicants

MMPI Scale	Deceptive (*n* = 18) M (SD)	Candid (*n* = 18) M (SD)	F	d
L	58.06 (8.67)	50.22 (5.40)	10.60**	1.09
K	66.94 (5.65)	62.11 (7.33)	4.91*	.74
Total O-S	−88.33 (33.19)	−71.89 (34.30)	2.14	.49
Mp Scale	18.39 (3.78)	15.72 (3.79)	4.48*	.71
F-K Index	−18.39 (3.48)	−15.89 (5.61)	2.58	.54
Es-K Index	−7.00 (4.31)	2.22 (5.59)	30.72***	1.85
IPI Scale				
GD	49.39 (8.71)	43.06 (8.59)	4.82*	.73

Note. From Borum and Stock (1993). Copyright 1993 by the American Psychological Association. Adapted by permission.
*p <.05; **p <.01; ***p <.001.

The notion of ego strength as a subtle construct distinct from more blatant efforts at self-distortion is similar to the distinction that has been made between self-deceptive enhancement and impression management (Paulhus & Reid, 1991).

Self-Deception versus Impression Management

Overly positive response sets can take one of two forms: self-deceptive enhancement (SDE) or impression management (IM). SDE is similar to ego strength, as defined earlier, in the sense that the individual engaging in this response style is exhibiting a healthy level of psychological defense and is responding in a way that he or she believes to be genuine. Paulhus and Reid (1991) characterized SDE respondents as honest in their responses despite inaccurate, overly positive views of themselves. In a sense, SDE can be said to occur outside the examinee's conscious awareness. Impression management, or IM, on the other hand, is a conscious attempt to distort one's presentation. To compare the two styles, SDE individuals who genuinely see themselves in a positive light and possess a healthy amount of psychological guardedness would be more suitable for police work than those individuals who consciously deny difficulties or blatantly lie. Therefore, the difference between SDE and IM within law enforcement evaluations may be a crucial distinction.

To illustrate SDE and IM, original work was conducted on the Balanced Inventory of Desirable Responding (BIDR) and later the Paulhus Deception Scales (PDS). Lautenschlager and Flaherty (1990) administered the BIDR to college students and found that BIDR–IM scores decreased in response to anonymous testing conditions and increased when students believed that their responses were being monitored. A similar pattern was not observed for the BIDR–SDE scale. These results demonstrated the relative sensitivity of IM and relative insensitivity of SDE to testing conditions of public versus anonymous disclosure. Furthermore, research suggests that SDE is a dimensional construct, whereas IM is taxonic. Essentially, IM will or will not be present in a particular protocol. SDE, on the other hand, is dimensional and assumed to be present to varying degrees within all individuals.

Devan (2004) divided her sample of 7142 police officer candidates into two taxon-based groups (IM present vs. IM absent) and found that the IM-present taxon group scored higher on all of the indices intended to measure intentional positive distortion (L, ODecp,[1] Sd, K, S, So). The differences were most pronounced for L (*d* = 2.98), ODecp (*d* = 1.32), and Sd (*d* = 1.02). Devan's findings partly support Bagby and colleagues' (1997b) recommendation that when assessing nonclinical individuals, such as job applicants, ODecp and S (*d* = .87) are useful to detect those normal individuals who might be presenting themselves in the most favorable light. These results suggest that the L and Sd scales may also be important in this population. The K ($d = .73$) and So ($d = .55$) scales were less discriminating between the groups.

The clinical scale profiles of the two groups were essentially identical. Devan (2004) reported that the IM-taxon respondents were found to be engaging in impression management through the use of specialized indices and would have gone undetected with only the traditional validity scales. Moreover, IM respondents scored significantly lower on six content scales (OBS, ANG, ASP, TPA, FAM, and WRK) and six supplementary scales (MT, PK, PS, AAS, APS, and HO) and significantly higher on two supplementary scales (O–H and Re) than those in the non-taxon group. These findings suggest that supplemental scales, content scales, and specialized validity indices may differentiate respondents engaging in IM in preemployment psychololgical screening of law enforcement applicants. Devan also estimated that about 33% of her sample were engaging in IM, which is similar to rates found in child custody cases (37%; Strong et al., 1999) and higher than estimates in general personnel screening (25%; Strong, Greene, & Kordinak, 2002). In her sample of law enforcement applicants, the items that contributed most to the IM taxon were items reflecting self-confidence, fearlessness, and bravery.

MMPI Response Styles and Future Job Performance

Although the majority of research with the MMPI suggests that police officer candidates often respond in a characteristically defensive manner, data regarding the predictive value of the response profile are mostly lacking. Isolated reports of slight defensiveness being predictive of better job performance (Bernstein, Schoenfeld, & Costello, 1982; Neal, 1986) are offset by results from larger analyses, including a meta-analysis. For example, Aamodt (2004) conducted a meta-analysis of personality inventories and job performance in law enforcement settings. Defensiveness on the MMPI (i.e., scales L and K) did not predict any of the included job performance outcomes, including (1) police academy grades, (2) supervisor ratings of performance, (3) discipline problems and complaints, (4) citizen and department commendations, or (5) absenteeism. On the contrary, Aamodt reports that elevations on scale F may be the most useful predictor of both poor academy performance and poor supervisor ratings.

With the exception of scale F, empirical evidence indicates no linear relationship between individual response-style scales and future job performance. However, these studies have not considered more sophisticated indices, such as the Es–K scale. Moreover, attempts have been made to identify predictors of performance that combine response-style information (via validity indicators) and clinical information.

For example, using the MMPI's Lie Scale as a centerpiece, Bartol (1991) developed what he termed the "immaturity index," which consisted of the combined raw scores of scales L, Pd, and Ma. Of 600 police officers, 44 eventually were dismissed or asked to resign due to failure to meet job performance requirements. Another 471 officers remained on the police force. Terminated officers scored significantly higher on each of the three scales than retained officers. Therefore, immaturity indexes were much higher for terminated officers ($M = 54.22$, $SD = 8.89$) than for retained officers ($M = 45.37$, $SD = 5.83$; $d = 1.44$). The officers in the terminated group were described by their supervisors as immature and inappropriate in their work. These officers engaged in irresponsible behavior, such as inappropriate use of firearms, frequent accidents in police vehicles, frequent tardiness and absenteeism, and failure to complete written work on time.

Using discriminant function analysis, the immaturity index correctly classified 74% of the officers. In addition, it correlated significantly with the MAC scale ($r = .38$). Bartol (1991) subsequently cross-validated the immaturity index on a small sample of 22 terminated and 22 retained officers. The overall classification rate was 81.2%.

Bartol (1991) also suggested immaturity index cut scores. Summing raw scores, 70% of officers terminated received immaturity scores of ≥ 49, compared with 23% of the retained group. Raising the cut score to ≥ 54 correctly identified 53% of the terminated group and 95% of the retained group. To date, the immaturity index has not been replicated with the MMPI-2 or by other police departments.

In sum, research with the MMPI-2 and law enforcement assessment suggests that law enforcement applicants, similar to job applicants in general, are likely to present themselves in a socially desirable and defensive manner. In terms of response styles, their validity scales are likely to be higher than average but not clinically significant (< 65T). T scores within the normal range on each of the MMPI's traditional validity scales are unlikely to be meaningful or to predict future job performance (Aamodt, 2004). However, combinations of scales (both validity scales and clinical scales) may be useful in identifying feigned protocols (Borum & Stock, 1993; Devan, 2004) and perhaps identifying individuals likely to perform poorly on the job (Aamodt, 2004; Bartol, 1991).

THE INWALD PERSONALITY INVENTORY

The Inwald Personality Inventory (IPI; Inwald, Knatz, & Shusman, 1982) is a 310-item true–false inventory designed to measure a variety of problematic characteristics thought to be relevant to law enforcement. Cochrane and colleagues (2003) reported that approximately 12% of police departments in their survey use the IPI for law enforcement selection. The IPI consists of 26 scales, including one validity scale (guardedness, or GD). The remaining 25 scales are organized around four content areas. The areas and representative scales are:

1. *Acting-out behaviors:* Alcohol use (AL), Drug use (DG), Driving Violation (DV), Job Difficulties (JD), Trouble with society and the Law (TL), and Absence Abuse (AA).
2. *Acting-out attitudes:* Substance Abuse (SA), Antisocial attitudes (AS), Hyperactivity (HP), Rigid Type (RT), and Type A (TA).
3. *Internalized conflict:* Illness Concerns (IC), Treatment Programs (TP), Anxiety (AN), Phobic personality (PH), Obsessive personality (OB), Depression (DE), Loner type (LO), Unusual experience and thoughts (EU).
4. *Interpersonal conflict:* Lack of Assertiveness (LA), Interpersonal Difficulties (ID), Undue Suspiciousness (US), Family Conflict (FC), Sexual Concerns (SC), and Spouse/mate conflicts (SP).

The Inwald Personality Inventory's (IPI; Inwald et al., 1982) GD scale was designed to detect socially desirable responding (Haaland & Christiansen, 1998; see also Rogers, Chapter 2, this volume) and to identify persons who

have minimized shortcomings and denied faults (Inwald et al., 1982).

Detrick and colleagues (2001) reported that the IPI's GD scale was more related to the MMPI-2's L scale ($r = .64$) than to K ($r = .30$). In addition, Borum and Stock (1993), in their previously described study of deceptive applicants, found that the GD scale produced a moderate effect size. Therefore, the GD scale may have some utility in detecting individuals engaged in less sophisticated impression management and/or deception (see Table 22.2).

Detrick and Chibnall (2002) investigated IPI profiles in newly hired police officers and found no differences on any IPI scales for officers retained after 1 year ($n = 108$) compared with those who dropped out ($n = 30$). These authors also utilized IPI scale scores to predict changes in performance ratings between evaluations conducted after 2 months of employment and evaluations conducted after 1 year of service. Performance ratings increased the most for officers who scored high in GD ($\geq$ T $= 60$) and low in DV ($\leq$ T $= 40$). Importantly, overall GD scores in this study were not significantly elevated and tended to be below the mean ($M = 43.6$). Detrick and Chibnall reported that these slightly elevated GD scores were related to higher levels of education and socioeconomic status. Thus slight but not clinically elevated GD scores may simply reflect greater psychological sophistication rather than overt defensiveness. Indirectly supporting this conclusion, Inwald and Shusman (1984) noted that police officers who demonstrated heightened awareness, discernment of others, and some wariness tended to be rated higher by supervisors and noted that these traits can be beneficial in police work.

Other researchers have not found a relationship between a candidate's GD score and job performance. For instance, Surrette and Serafino (2003) found a negative, though not significant ($r = -.23$), relationship to performance ratings at 1 year in a sample of 129 police officers in small towns in New Mexico. Perhaps reflecting the isolated environment, the only IPI scale that was significantly correlated with performance was LO ($r = .40$). Likewise, Kauder and Thomas (2003), utilizing a sample of 149 officers in Oregon, found that GD was unrelated to their three performance measures: Driving Performance, Performance in Dealing with People, and Overall Performance. Of the 26 IPI scales, only EU and FC were both positively and relatively strongly related to all three performance measures.

In his meta-analysis of personality inventories and police officer performance, Aamodt (2004) found across six studies that the mean-corrected correlation between GD and performance ratings was negligible ($M = -.04$). When grouped by outcome measures, defensiveness did not predict either performance ratings or discipline problems.

Haaland and Christiansen (1998) proposed that the lack of a consistent relationship between social desirability, as measured by the IPI GD scale, and performance may be due to the unique nature of the relationship between impression management and performance. Specifically, impression management may have a curvilinear relationship with job performance. Individuals higher in cognitive ability may be more successful in presenting in a socially desirable fashion. Cognitive ability is also predictive of job performance. To the extent that cognitive ability, job performance, and elevated (socially desirable) responses are correlated, validity of these personality tests to predict performance may not suffer. However, at the extreme end of the distribution, predictive validity may suffer when all the variance in personality scales is explained by social desirability.

Haaland and Christiansen (1998) tested the hypothesis utilizing the IPI in a sample of 442 law enforcement recruits. The authors constructed a personality composite scale of four IPI scales that were predictive of academy performance. The GD scale was adopted as the measure of social desirability. In the total sample, a positive relationship was observed between the personality composite and performance. However, in the top 12% of the distribution ($n = 53$), the relationship was actually negative. Among these individuals, higher scores on the personality composite were associated with lower performance scores. Furthermore, the relationship between personality and social desirability was strong in the upper 50% of the sample, but much stronger among top scorers. The authors concluded that recruits with scores in the uppermost range inflated their scores by endorsing only the most socially desirable items. Of interest, the mean GD score in highest group is 54.39 ($SD = 9.56$), which is about 1 standard deviation higher than the means reported in other studies (see Table 22.3) and nearly five T score

TABLE 22.3. Mean IPI Guardedness Scores in Three Samples of Law Enforcement Recruits

	n	Guardedness M
Detrick & Chibnall (2002)	138	44.16 ($SD = 11.25$)
Surrette & Serafino (2003)	30	47.47
Kauder & Thomas (2003)	149	42.01
Pooled Mean	*317*	*43.46*

Note. Surrette and Serafino (2003) and Kauder and Thomas (2003) did not report standard deviations.

points above the total sample in their study ($M = 50.00$, $SD = 9.58$).

Haaland and Christiansen's (1998) analysis demonstrates that validity scales within the normal range may in fact be clinically meaningful when assessing a high-functioning and motivated individual. Certainly, their findings must be replicated. To our knowledge, no researcher has replicated the analysis with the IPI or attempted to extend the findings to other multiscale inventories, such as the MMPI-2. To the extent that their results generalize to other samples, it appears that cut scores below what is considered clinically significant (e.g., 65T on the MMPI-2) might be meaningful in samples of law enforcement recruits.

CALIFORNIA PSYCHOLOGICAL INVENTORY

Personality tests such as the California Psychological Inventory are often used in law enforcement selection to help identify those potential officers who have personality characteristics similar to those of successful officers. The California Psychological Inventory (CPI; Gough, 1987) consists of 434 true–false items that assess a variety of personality characteristics. Cochrane and colleagues' (2003) survey indicated that approximately one-quarter (24.5%) of police departments reported utilizing the CPI. The CPI yields scores on 18 dimensions that are organized into four classes:

1. *Class I (Poise):* Dominance (Do), Capacity for status (Cs), Sociability (Sy), Social presence (Sp), and Self-acceptance (Sa).

2. *Class II (Normative Orientation and Values):* Well-being (wb), Responsibility (Re), Socialization (So), Self-control (Sc), Tolerance (To), Good impression (Gi), and Communality (Cm).
3. *Class III (Cognitive and Intellectual Functioning):* Achievement via conformance (Ac), Achievement via independence (Ai), and Intellectual efficiency (Ie).
4. *Class IV (Role and Interpersonal Style):* Psychological mindedness (Py), Flexibility (Fx), and Femininity (Fe).

The Good Impression Scale (Gi; a Class II variable) is used to detect positive impression management. It consists of 40 items that identified high school students who were instructed to endorse the items as if they were applying for an important job or trying to make a favorable impression. Similar to the IPI's GD scale, the Gi scale was intended as a measure of social desirability (Gough, 1987). T scores ≥ 69 (raw score 31) are thought to raise the issue that an individual may be "faking good" (Gough, 1987, p. 36).

In the CPI manual, Gough (1987) reports normative data on a variety of law enforcement samples, including parole and probation officers ($n = 65$), police officers ($n = 84$), and correctional officers ($n = 221$). Each of these occupational groups scored above the mean on Gi, though none of the averages were ≥ 69. Interestingly, police officers ($M = 62$T; raw = 26.18, $SD = 6.30$) scored significantly higher than both the parole and probation officer group ($M = 55$T; raw $M = 21.17$, $SD = 6.38$) and the correctional officers ($M = 55$T; raw $M = 21.45$, $SD = 6.23$). However, the magnitude of the difference is very small (ds of .11 and .16). Unfortunately, the manual does not report the number or percentage of individuals who exceeded the suggested cut score.

In addition to the Gi scale, Gough (1987) identified a raw score equation that was designed to improve on the sole use of the Gi scale in detecting invalid responding. The formula (44.67 + .15Do + .18Em + .35Gi − .11Wb − .13 to − .12Fx) makes prominent use of the Gi scale by weighing it heavily in the equation. A cut score of 56.65 was reported to detect those individuals who were "faking good." Among the 84 police officer applicants in the normative sample, this equation identified 10.7% ($n = 9$) of the sample as faking good. Police officers as a group achieved the

highest mean score on this index ($M = 53.54$, $SD = 2.38$). To our knowledge, this index has not been independently cross-validated in law enforcement samples.

Compared with the MMPI, considerably less attention has been given to law enforcement applicants' response styles on the CPI. Hogan (1971) suggested that the response styles of highly rated officers would emphasize self-assurance and functional intelligence. Hargrave and Hiatt (1989) determined that the primary difference between problem and nonproblem officers was found in the Class II variables of CPI. Class II variables, including the Gi scale, assess normative orientation and values. Nonproblem officers scored significantly higher than problem officers on these Class II variables, indicating that nonproblem officers present themselves on the CPI as socially desirable, mature, self-controlled, tolerant, and social.

Class II variables also factor into the CPI's social maturity index (Gough, 1966; Hogan & Kurtines, 1975). Using four Class II variables plus one Class I and one Class IV variable, the social maturity index was developed as a measure of responsible adaptation to the social environment. The six scales that compose the social maturity index are D, R, S, Gi, Cm, and Fx; it was first developed to discriminate between delinquent and nondelinquent youths. The point–biserial correlation between the social maturity index and the samples was .63. High scorers on this index were considered to be rational, idealistic, wholesome, clear thinking, and organized. Low scorers on the index were shallow, inconsiderate, intolerant, nervous, temperamental, and frivolous.

Hogan and Kurtines (1975) tested the social maturity index on two samples of law enforcement officers in Maryland and Oakland, CA. Both groups of police officers scored slightly, though not significantly, below the mean on social maturity. Social maturity scores failed to predict any of the performance criteria for the Oakland police officers.

Despite the popularity of the CPI in law enforcement selection (Cochrane et al., 2003) and its demonstrated validity in predicting job performance (Varela, Boccaccini, Scogin, Stump, & Caputo, 2004), little research has investigated the effects of response styles on the validity of the CPI profiles. Extant research suggests that candidates who present themselves in a positive light, along with showing a general orientation toward normative values, will be more successful in law enforcement tasks (Hargrave & Hiatt, 1989; Hogan, 1971; Hogan & Kurtines, 1975).

PAI Law Enforcement, Corrections, and Public Safety Selection Report

The PAI Public Safety Selection Report (Roberts et al., 2004) is a supplementary scoring system for the existing PAI Software Portfolio designed to display results specific to public safety employment screening (see Sellbom & Bagby, Chapter 11, this volume, for a more general description of the PAI). The PAI Public Safety Selection Report makes use of the full PAI, along with relevant demographic data that is collected from the examinee, in order to produce a detailed and tailored interpretation of the data. The authors report that it is appropriate for pre-employment screening, as well as fitness for duty evaluations and evaluations for special unit assignments, such as Special Weapons and Tactics (SWAT) or hostage negotiations.

The PAI Public Safety Selection Report is based on a normative sample of nearly 18,000 law enforcement officers, of whom 20% were female and 40% were minorities. All individuals in the normative group were hired and spent at least 1 year in that position. Profiles are generated against the full normative sample, the specific ethnic and gender sample, and the specific job type (e.g., police officer, corrections officer, or firefighter). For comparison, it also plots scores on the PAI community norms. The program, then, generates four different profiles.

Roberts and colleagues (2004) note that one of the main advantages of the PAI Public Safety Selection Report is that validity scales are sometimes elevated in law enforcement examinees when their scores are plotted against community norms. Validity scale elevations are not necessarily meaningful unless they are elevated when compared with those of similar individuals taking the test under similar conditions. For example, the authors include a profile illustration of a female applicant's scores with community norms compared with job-related norms. Her positive impression management (PIM) T score was elevated on community norms (70T) but average on law enforcement norms (56T). Also, by controlling for response bias in this fashion, Roberts and colleagues report that the clinical scales are

more often elevated on public safety norms than community norms. In a second example, the authors present a poorly suited male individual whose PIM and negative impression management (NIM) scores were within normal limits on community norms. Using job-specific norms, his NIM was highly elevated (T ≥ 90) and his PIM plummeted (T 37). The effect on the clinical scales was also remarkable. Previously normal scores (Ts <60) became highly significant (Ts ≥ 75), including paranoia, schizophrenia, alcohol problems, drug problems, aggression, and nonsupport.

Using job-specific norms, the PAI Public Safety Report also provides risk levels (low, moderate, high) for several problematic job-related behaviors, including substance abuse proclivity, illegal drug use concerns, alcohol use concerns, anger management problems, integrity problems, and job-related problems. It appears that the PAI Public Safety Report may be useful for law enforcement assessment purposes of both screening for psychopathology and identifying potentially effective (and ineffective) officers. The PAI Public Safety Report needs to be independently validated with peer-reviewed research. However, initial validation data is promising for its use in law enforcement assessment.

FITNESS-FOR-DUTY EVALUATIONS

The bulk of this chapter has focused on response styles and law enforcement applicant selection. It has evaluated the effects of positive impression management on test results and predictions of future performance. Whereas it can be reasonably assumed that individuals applying for work in law enforcement are motivated to minimize psychopathology in attempts to present themselves in the most favorable light, the same assumption cannot be made with respect to individuals presenting for fitness-for-duty evaluations. These officers may or may not be motivated to receive "a clean bill of health." Instead, they may have different motivations, including efforts to maximize the likelihood that they will be placed or remain on inactive or disability status. A full discussion of fitness-for-duty evaluations is beyond the scope of this chapter, but the issue is sufficiently important to warrant a brief discussion. A more comprehensive review of fitness-for-duty evaluations has been provided by Stone (1995).

Fitness-for-duty evaluations raise the possibility of at least two distinct response styles, depending on the examinee's motivation. Officers who wish to return to work would be expected to minimize psychopathology while presenting themselves most favorably. Officers wishing to be placed on disability or to remain on disability may maximize their presentations of impairment. Grossman, Haywood, Ostrov, Wasyliw, and Cavanaugh (1990) investigated the effects that these different motivations have on the MMPI validity scales. These authors compared two groups of fitness-for-duty examinees: (1) 20 officers who expressed a desire not to return to work and (2) 20 officers who wished to return to work. A control group (n = 20) was selected from active police officers who were not undergoing fitness evaluations.

The differences between the groups were in the predicted directions, but no mean T-score reached the 65 cut score on L, F, Ds, or Mp scales. Officers who did not wish to return to work produced significantly higher mean scores on the F scale (60.7T) and O-S index (25.0T) than the other two groups. No differences were observed for the L and Mp scales.

The range of clearly minimized profiles for the positive-motivation group was 20–85%, depending on the index used, and 15–45% for the negative-motivation group. Thus even the individuals who did not wish to return to work engaged in some minimization while taking the MMPI. Of the validity indices, Ds was most sensitive to exaggeration; 15% of the negative-motivation group showed evidence of exaggeration. None of the positive-motivation group showed exaggeration on any of the indices used (Ds, O-S, F-K, F). It appears that police officers in general were reluctant to admit psychological problems. Despite the minimization across all groups, a substantially greater degree of minimization was found for officers desiring to return to duty. The authors caution that the use of traditional validity scales is insufficient to detect response-style alterations in police officer examinees. The use of special scales and indices, such as the F-K index, the Ds scale, and the O-S index are recommended.

CONCLUSIONS

Psychological assessment is a cornerstone of law enforcement selection and fitness-for-duty evaluations. This chapter provides the reader with an introduction and overview of the specific effects that altered response styles may have on commonly used instruments. In most instances, assessment conducted under preemployment conditions will result in overly positive self-portrayals. The reviewed research indicates that a typical preemployment profile will have slight elevations on validity scales designed to detect positive impression management yet still be within normal limits.

Traditional approaches to test interpretation suggest that scores within the normal range are not meaningful and not interpretable (Greene, 1991). The review of research presented here demonstrates that subclinical elevations may be important when assessing high-functioning individuals who are motivated to present themselves in a particular fashion. It seems reasonable to suggest that desirable job candidates will be attempting to present in a positive fashion. The effort suggests that they are motivated to present well, indicating a desire to obtain the position. In contrast, candidates who do not attempt to present well may not be very invested in the position.

A more difficult challenge for the examiner is to separate the motivated individuals who are presenting well from the individuals who are engaging in blatant distortion or who are responding in a socially desirable fashion to the extent that all of their responses are saturated with social desirability. Several approaches to discriminating these groups were presented in this review (Borum & Stock, 1993; Devan, 2004; Haaland & Christiansen, 1998). Future research is likely to focus on distinguishing between self-deceptive enhancement and impression management with the MMPI-2 and other instruments (Devan, 2004). Haaland and Christiansen's (1998) finding that the effect of socially desirable responding on performance is curvilinear also deserves further research attention.

The MMPI and, more recently, the MMPI-2 continue to be the most commonly used psychological measures in law enforcement assessment (Cochrane et al., 2003), yet most of the validation research in this population was conducted with the original MMPI. Provided the MMPI-2 continues to be used routinely in selection decisions, validation is required. Furthermore, changes in the legal climate may have effects on assessment research. For example, because the ADA requires that psychopathology assessment be conducted only after the job offer, it is likely that the MMPI-2 or IPI will be given only to candidates who have already passed the rigorous prescreening procedures that are in place. Unstable or inappropriate candidates are less likely to survive the selection process to have the opportunity to participate in these assessments. As a result, the applicant who is taking the MMPI-2 in 2007 is not comparable with the pool of applicants who took the MMPI in the 1970s and 1980s, when much of the law enforcement research was conducted. Although extreme indicators of defensive responding and indicators of blatant deception remain applicable, it is

likely that the next generation of police selection researchers will focus more on normal personality traits indicative of highly effective police to enable departments to utilize psychological testing to choose the most promising applicants from among pools of acceptable applicants.

NOTE

1. ODecp replaced the Mp scale in the MMPI-2 (Nichols & Greene, 1991).

VI

Summary

23

Current Status of Clinical Methods

RICHARD ROGERS, PhD

Important advances in the clinical assessment of response styles have ensued between past and current editions of this book. One major contribution of this edition is to move beyond clinical correlates and isolated validity scale differences to the examination of detection strategies. As I outlined in Chapter 2 in this volume, detection strategies are *conceptually based and empirically validated* methods of evaluating a specific response style, as contrasted with its most relevant comparison groups. To be considered a detection strategy, validation must include multiple measures and multiple studies of relevant clinical populations. Statistical differences have only marginal relevance. Instead, the focus is on the magnitude of the differences (i.e., Cohen's *d*s) and their effectiveness at classifying individuals.

A major advance for this third edition was the inclusion of detection strategies in many chapters, with summaries of methods of validation, domains, and effect sizes. This systematic application of detection strategies is a major contribution of this text to both applied research and clinical practice. The chapter begins with an examination of feigning across three domains: mental disorders, cognitive impairment, and medical complaints.

DETECTION STRATEGIES FOR FEIGNING

Feigned Mental Disorders

Major strides have been accomplished in the development of detection strategies for per-

sons feigning general psychological impairment and specific disorders. In some instances, the detection strategy has been specifically tailored to address a specific disorder, such as posttraumatic stress disorder (PTSD; i.e., Fptsd; see Chapter 7, this volume). Does such a specialized focus represent an overrefinement? The simple answer is likely in the affirmative, considering the effectiveness of two broad-application scales, Fp and Ds, with populations with PTSD. However, specialized scales such as Fptsd could be clinically useful if they helped to differentiate feigned PTSD from other types of feigned disorders, such as malingered major depression. Though they are not yet available, determinations of the *type* of feigned disorders may be the first step in distinguishing feigned and genuine disorders in impaired examinees.

Table 23.1 summarizes the established detection strategies, with relevant information on validation designs and assessment methods. Of major importance, these established strategies have met rigorous standards with validation combining internal validity (i.e., simulation design) and external validity (i.e., known-groups comparisons supplemented with bootstrapping comparisons). In most instances, detection strategies have yielded large to very large effect sizes across multiple scales.

One exception, included in Table 23.1, exemplifies the need for such rigorous evaluations based on multiple types of validation and multiple methods. For "spurious patterns of psychopathology," the malingering (MAL) index produces generally large effect sizes across

TABLE 23.1. Detection Strategies for Feigned Mental Disorders

	Validation			Methods			
	Sim	KGC	BTS	Test	Interview	Effect size	Salient examples
Established strategies							
Rare symptoms	Y	Y	Y	Y	Y	Very large	SIRS RS, MMPI-2 Fp, and PAI NIM
Quasi-rare symptoms	Y	Y	Y	Y	Y	Very large	MMPI-2 F and Fb
Improbable symptoms	Y	Y	Y	Y	Y	Variable	SIRS IA and MCMI-III Validity Index
Symptom combinations	Y	Y	Y	N	Y	Very large	SIRS SC and MFAST RC
Spurious patterns of psychopathology	Y	Y	Y	Y	N	Large[a]	PAI MAL and RDF
Indiscriminant symptom endorsement	Y	Y	Y	Y	Y	Very large	SIRS SEL and SADS SEL
Symptom severity	Y	Y	Y	Y	Y	Very large	SIRS SEV and MMPI-2 LW
Obvious symptoms	Y	Y	Y	Y	Y	Very large	SIRS BL and MMPI-2 O-S
Reported versus observed symptoms	Y	Y	Y	N	Y	Variable[b]	SIRS RO and MFAST RO
Erroneous stereotypes	Y	Y	Y	Y	N	Very large	MMPI-2 Ds scale
Provisional strategies							
Close approximations to genuine symptoms	Y	N	N	Y	N	Unknown	MPS MAL scale
Overly specified symptoms	Y	Y	Y	N	Y	Moderate	SIRS OS scale

Note. Sim, simulation design; KGC, known-groups comparison; BTS, bootstrapping comparison. For scale names, please refer to relevant chapters.
[a]Consistently large for MAL; variable for RDF. Effect sizes are general estimates based on major studies.
[b]The SIRS RO has a very large effect size; the M-FAST RO has a moderate effect size (see Jackson et al., 2005).

simulation and known-groups comparisons (see Chapter 11, this volume, Table 11.5). As observed in the same table, the Rogers Discriminant Function (RDF) works well with simulation design but not known-groups comparisons, suggesting problems in its real-world applications to criminal–forensic settings. Following are recommendations to mental health professionals focused on the comprehensive assessment of feigned mental disorders.

1. The rare-symptoms strategy is the "workhorse" for the feigning of mental disorders. Clinicians may wish to adopt a multimethod approach using both test-based (e.g., Minnesota Multiphasic Personality Inventory [MMPI-2] Fp) and interview-based (e.g., Structured Interview of Reported Symptoms [SIRS] RS) methods for assessment. In addition to very large effect sizes, this strategy typically uses a narrow band of cut scores.

2. The quasi-rare-symptom strategy will continue to be popular, based more on tradition than accuracy for clinical classification. The scale development focused on an irrelevant contrast (feigned mental disorders vs. healthy controls). Genuinely disordered examinees often produce very high elevations, which is an expected finding because the key comparison (feigned vs. genuine disorders) was not used in scale development. Despite very large effect sizes, the cut scores are highly variable, thus vitiating classificatory accuracy. At best, clinicians should consider the quasi-rare-symptom strategy as a supplementary approach.

3. Improbable symptoms represent an extreme form of rare symptoms that have a fantastic or preposterous quality to them. Some feigners do not feel the need to simulate such extreme symptoms. Clinicians may wish to examine improbable symptoms as evidence of extreme feigning.

4. Two strategies (symptom combinations and spurious patterns of psychopathology) offer a sophisticated approach to feigning that addresses the relationships between symptoms and associated features. Their added complexity works against effective coaching. What easily absorbed information would assist feigners in avoiding atypical pairs of symptoms? It is recommended that at least one of these detection strategies be included in comprehensive assessments.

5. The domain of amplified detection strategies should also be included in assessments of feigning. Both "indiscriminant symptom endorsement" and "symptom severity" produce very large effect sizes. They are helpful in evaluating whether examinees are feigning the number and intensity of symptoms and psychopathology. The focus is not on the legitimacy of specific symptoms but, rather, the overall reporting. These strategies are a useful component in the evaluation of feigned mental disorders.

6. The final three strategies provide further insights into feigning. "Reported versus observed" adds a unique dimension to feigning assessment in comparing currently reported symptoms with concurrent observations. Although some inconsistencies are noted in genuinely disordered populations, feigners are detected by the regular pattern of reported symptoms in the absence of observations. The strategy of "erroneous stereotypes" produces very large effect sizes for the Ds scale. It is recommended for clinical practice because of its consistent cut score and effectiveness among sophisticated feigners. The Fake Bad Scale (FBS), which relies partly on erroneous stereotypes, has produced more mixed results (see Chapter 10, this volume; Rogers, Sewell, Martin, & Vitacco, 2003).

Two provisional strategies involve reported symptoms that differ qualitatively from most genuine symptoms. The Malingering Probability Scale (MPS; Silverton, 1999) uses the MAL scale to approximate genuine symptoms, whereas the SIRS Overly Specified Symptoms (OS) scale examines symptom endorsements that are unrealistically precise. These strategies are not as well validated as those described previously and should be used only in an ancillary capacity.

Detection strategies have been firmly established as a cornerstone for the comprehensive assessment of feigned mental disorders. Unlike research advances on structured interviews and multiscale interviews, the study of feigning on projective measures has remained essentially stalled during the past decade. One bright point highlighted by Sewell in Chapter 12 (this volume) is McDougall's (1996) work, which implicitly operationalizes two main detection strategies: rare symptoms and symptom combinations. Presently, the ability of feigners to produce impaired Rorschach protocols is well established. Future studies may be able to capitalize on McDougall's indicators of potential rare symptoms and symptom combinations. At present, independent measures of feigned mental disorders should be administered in conjunction with projective methods. When evidence of feigning is found, the Rorschach and other projective measures should not be interpreted.

In summary, mental health professionals can effectively evaluate feigned mental disorders and psychopathology. Because all measures are vulnerable to feigning, comprehensive assessments should include multiple detection strategies that integrate findings across test-based and interview-based methods.

Feigned Cognitive Impairment

Phenomenal growth has been experienced during the past decade in the development of assessment methods for feigned cognitive impairment. The implementation of detection strategies has not always been consistent in the development of new measures. Even among prominent researchers, construct drift has been observed. To maintain rigor in clinical practice and research, Chapter 2 (this volume) adheres closely to the operationalization of detection strategies by original researchers (see Rogers, Harrell, & Liff, 1993). As a specific example, symptom validity testing (SVT) should be used to designate below-chance performance (see Chapter 2, this volume). Practitioners must exercise considerable care, when citing research supporting their clinical practice, that terms are used accurately. Otherwise, slipshod definitions can undermine the credibility of assessment reports.

Neuropsychologists and other practitioners are also faced with a major challenge in generalizing across studies because research often uses different terms and criteria for establishing comparison groups. As a specific example,

Chapter 1 (this volume) lists *suboptimal effort* and *incomplete effort* as imprecise terms that should be avoided in clinical and forensic practice. Yet some studies continue to rely on these terms in designating criterion groups. Conceptually, problems in defining *optimal* effort and *complete* effort militate against the use of these terms for classification purposes. How do we ever know when an examinee is truly putting forth complete effort? In the forensic context, such imprecise terms may lack the Daubert (*Daubert v. Merrell Dow Pharmaceuticals*, 1993) criteria for falsifiability and attainable error rates (see Otto, Chapter 21, this volume). Moreover, the level of effort often omits key specifications. For example, what is the *expected* level of effort for a personal injury claimant experiencing major depression? Global inferences across all clinical conditions are clearly impermissible.

Most detection strategies for feigned cognitive impairment have been extensively cross-validated using multiple designs that capitalize on internal and external validity. Consistent with the Slick criteria (Slick, Sherman, & Iverson, 1999) for definite malingering, the SVT has been used as a good standard for establishing *known feigners* based on very high probabilities. A potential criticism of this very stringent criterion is that it may identify only extreme malingerers. Table 23.2 summarizes the established detection strategies for feigned cognitive impairment.

Traditionally, most cognitive feigning measures have focused on short-term memory to the exclusion of other cognitive abilities. A significant contribution of this book is its inclusion of Chapter 14 by Berry and Schipper, which examines feigned intelligence and neuropsychological deficits beyond memory. In selecting measures for feigned cognitive impairment, practitioners should select multiple detection strategies with scales that cover both memory and other domains. The following summarizes recommendations for mental health professionals on the comprehensive assessment of feigned cognitive impairment.

1. Two detection strategies (magnitude of error and performance curve) are sophisticated methods that address issues often overlooked by malingerers, who often attempt to get many items wrong without considering which items and which incorrect responses would be credible. In particular, the magnitude-of-error strat-

egy appears to produce large effect sizes even when simulators are coached (Bender & Rogers, 2004). It is recommended that practitioners include at least one of these strategies. Of note, "d" errors on the "b" test are very rare in diverse clinical populations.

2. The violation of learning principles strategy can be applied using both standard measures and clinical judgment. Most scales focus on memory functions and well-known principles (e.g., recognition should exceed recall). In contrast, the Dot Counting Test (DCT) compares concentration under differing conditions that facilitate or complicate counting. Beyond empirically tested comparisons, violations of learning principles can also be considered on an individualized basis. For example, substantially better performance on delayed than on immediate memory (e.g., Word Memory Test [WMT] or Test of Memory Malingering [TOMM]) violates a basic learning principle and can be used as evidence of feigning.

3. The floor effect is used in the majority of cognitive feigning measures. Its simplicity is both its intuitive appeal and its major limitation. It identifies test items that can be successfully passed by most persons with cognitive impairments. Especially with stand-alone measures, feigners can be easily coached to simply succeed when presented with questions in a specific format (e.g., Rey Memory for 15-Item Test [RFIT]). However, this strategy is strongly recommended for embedded measures.

4. SVT is the only detection strategy that can provide definite evidence of cognitive feigning. However, most feigners do not perform substantially below chance, thereby limiting SVT to demonstrating the presence, but not the absence, of feigned cognitive impairment. Requiring further study as an SVT is below-chance performance on the Category Test.

5. Forced-choice testing does not have a strong conceptual basis and simply refers to "lower than expected" performances. In some isolated cases, the clinical threshold has been established for cognitively compromised individuals, including those with comorbid Axis I disorders. In most instances, forced-choice testing should be avoided with preference given to principle-based detection strategies that yield robust results.

6. Pattern analysis is a valuable detection strategy using embedded measures. For example, disparities on the Wechsler Adult Intelligence Scale (WAIS) between Vocabulary and

TABLE 23.2. Detection Strategies for Feigned Cognitive Impairment

	Validation		Methods			
	Sim	External	Test	Embedded	Targeted abilities	Primary tests and scales
Established strategies						
Magnitude of error	Y	Y	Y	Y	Verbal, nonverbal	WMS-R, TOCA, "b" test ("d" errors)
Performance curve	Y	Y	Y		Verbal, nonverbal	VIP, TOCA
Violation of learning principles	Y	Y	Y	Y	Memory, concentration	CVLT-II CIA, 21-Item Test, WMT[a], DCT
Floor effect	Y	Y	Y	Y	Memory, concentration, Motor	WMT, DMT, TOMM, RFIT, LMT, WMS-RMI, RMT, WAIS-III digit span, RDS, TMT, FOT
Symptom validity testing (SVT)	Y	Y[b]	Y		Memory, verbal, nonverbal	DMT, TOMM, PDRT, VSVT, CARB, TOCA, Category Test
Forced-choice testing (FCT)	Y	Y	Y		Memory	PDRT
Pattern analysis	Y	Y		Y	Verbal, neuropsych.[c]	VDS, WMS-III (memory— WMI discrepancies) Severity indexing
Provisional strategies						
Consistency across comparable items	Y	Y	Y		Verbal, nonverbal	VIP
Atypical test pattern	Y	Y		Y	Neuropsych.[c]	HRB, WAIS, WCST, RMT
Symptom frequency	Y		Y		Cognitive symptoms	NSI

Note. Sim, simulation design; External, combines known-groups comparisons (KGC) with bootstrapping comparison (BTS) because some studies are difficult to categorize as either KGC or BTS; Test, a stand-alone specialized measure; Embedded, derived scale or indicator for a standardized cognitive or neuropsychological measure; TOCA, Test of Cognitive Abilities (a research measure that is not used in clinical practice). For test and scale names, please refer to relevant chapters.
[a]The WMT has significant potential (e.g., delayed vs. immediate recall) that has yet to be rigorously tested.
[b]Rather than known-groups designs, it uses binomial probability to establish a high likelihood of a known group of feigners.
[c]General abilities on neuropsychological test batteries.

Digit Span subtests have been used with some success to identify simulators. Feigners typically have a poor understanding of how WAIS-III subscales are affected by brain trauma. As noted by Bender in Chapter 5 (this volume), severity indexing can be used as a benchmark to evaluate whether the test findings are generally consistent with the purported brain trauma.

Beyond these detection strategies, clinicians often attempt to use symptom inconsistency as evidence of cognitive feigning. Fluctuating symptoms present a formidable challenge to "consistency across comparable items." For instance, patients with dementia may perform at varying levels throughout the day. However, the Validity Indicator Profile (VIP) has achieved

considerable success in examining the stability of performance across comparable items. This strategy is placed in the provisional category because it has not been rigorously tested with measures besides the VIP. "Symptom frequency" represents a unique perspective for feigned cognitive impairment. Practitioners may wish to consider a measure such as the Neuropsychological Symptom Inventory (NSI; Dean, 1982) for screening purposes (see Chapter 2, this volume).

Feigned Medical Complaints

The evaluation of medical symptoms and associated lab tests is limited to physician and other health care professionals skilled in their use. In

Chapter 9 (this volume), Granacher and Berry outline important indicators of feigned neurological deficits. For most mental health professionals, their work should be confined to examining the potential legitimacy of medical complaints. As consultants, these practitioners can provide valuable data for clinical decision making. Their results by themselves are rarely definitive. Instead, these findings can be used for screening purposes and for corroboration.

Chapter 2 (this volume) summarizes *potential* detection strategies for feigned medical complaints. Focusing on embedded measures, the MMPI-2 F_s (Infrequent Somatic Complaints) and overall elevations on the Symptom Checklist 90—Revised (SCL-90-R) may be used as preliminary screens for simulated medical and pain presentations. Deserving special attention is the Health Problem Overstatement (HPO) scale of the Psychological Screening Inventory (PSI; Lanyon & Cunningham, 2005); this scale produced a very large effect size ($d = 2.47$) between persons with health problems and those feigning health problems. Although it needs further testing with genuine medical inpatients and outpatients with severe conditions, the HPO scale shows substantial promise and should be considered for screening purposes.

DETECTION STRATEGIES FOR SIMULATED ADJUSTMENT

Most analogue studies of simulated adjustment do not provide multiple comparisons to distinguish specific response styles, such as defensiveness, social desirability, and impression management (see Rogers, Chapter 1, this volume). In general, studies of clinical populations tend to focus on defensiveness (i.e., the denial and minimization of symptoms and impairment). In contrast, research on job applicants emphasizes social desirability (i.e., an overly positive and prosocial presentation). However, practitioners need to review individual studies to ensure that relevant experimental conditions were used (e.g., social desirability vs. defensiveness). See Table 23.3.

Research on simulated adjustment is based almost entirely on simulation and differential prevalence designs. Independent classifications for known-groups comparisons are generally not possible, because defensiveness and social desirability are typically conceptualized as dimensional constructs. As noted in Chapters 1 and 24 (this volume), differential prevalence design has limited clinical relevance and provides only indirect evidence of response styles.

Most scales for evaluating simulated adjustment emphasize either (1) the denial of personal faults (i.e., L scale[1]) or (2) the blend of denied personal faults with the affirmation of virtuous behaviors (e.g., MMPI-2 S and Personality Assessment Inventory Positive Impression Management [PAI PIM]). In general, the blended approach produces stronger effect sizes than denial alone. However, both strategies are vulnerable to coaching that can greatly reduce their effectiveness. PAI research has capitalized on "spurious patterns of simulated adjustment" with mixed findings. The Defensiveness (DEF) index was rationally constructed

TABLE 23.3. Detection Strategies for Overly Positive Presentations

Established strategies	Effect sizes	Coaching	Primary examples
Deny personal faults	Moderate	Vulnerable	MMPI-2 L
Affirm virtuous behavior and deny personal faults	Moderate to large	Vulnerable	MMPI-2 S; PAI PIM; PDS IM and SDE; Marlowe–Crowne
Spurious patterns of simulated adjustment	Moderate to large[a]	Difficult to coach	PAI CDF and DEF
Denial of patient characteristics	Moderate	Variable	MMPI-2 K and Esd; SADS CRS
Social desirability	Large to very large	Remains effective	MMPI-2 Wsd[b] and ODecp

Note. Please refer to the individual chapters for the full names of measures and details about their effectiveness.
[a]Based on Morey (1996) and Sellbom and Bagby, Chapter 11, this volume: DEF typically has large effect sizes, whereas CDF are mostly moderate effect sizes.
[b]Wiggins social desirability scale, abbreviated as either Wsd or Sd.

and empirically tested to find patterns rarely observed among disclosing patients. It is very robust and difficult to coach because of its complexity. The Cashel Discriminant Function (CDF) was statistically derived and produces only moderate effect sizes.

Social desirability, as evaluated by the MMPI-2, appears to be the most effective detection strategy. Its two scales are closely correlated ($r = 85$; see Chapter 10, Table 10.9) and produce large to very large effect sizes. Of major significance, this strategy produces strong effect sizes even when participants have been coached. For evaluations of simulated adjustment, Wiggins social desirability (Wsd) and the Other Deception (O-Decp) scales should be the primary scales.

Defensiveness and Denied Substance Abuse

Significant progress has been made with the use of physiological markers for certain disavowed behaviors. Of these, the detection of denied substance abuse, especially through the application of hair analysis, has proven to be highly effective. In contrast, the use of global measures of defensiveness and deceit (e.g., polygraph and integrity testing) appear less accurate and more vulnerable to false positives (i.e., misclassifying an honest person as defensive or deceptive). In summary, the value of physiological markers is method-specific; atypical findings on physiological markers must be evaluated in light of the particular method and referral issue.

Detection strategies for denied substance abuse have advanced very little during the past decade. Despite the high prevalence of denied and minimized substance abuse, most screens and measures are content to ask face-valid questions (i.e., easy to deny or distort) without use of validity scales. When response-style scales are available, they typically either measure general social desirability (e.g., the Personal Experience Inventory [PEI]) or capitalize on clinical correlates, such as antisocial characteristics (e.g., Substance Abuse Subtle Screening Inventory [SASSI]). Given these limitations, practitioners need to rely heavily on collateral sources and laboratory testing to examine denials of substance abuse. As noted by Stein and Rogers Chapter 6 (this volume), disacknowledgement and honest misappraisals complicate the assessment of response styles. For example,

an individual may have purchased an illicit drug and may have been deceived about its psychoactive ingredients. This genuine misappraisal is very different from an intentional denial.

Denied Sexual Arousal

Formidable challenges continue to confront clinicians responsible for the evaluation and treatment of sex offenders. Sex offenders are typically placed in a double bind: (1) continued denial of sex offenses is generally viewed as a negative predictor of treatment potential and (2) openness about deviant sexual behaviors and ongoing sexual fantasies is likely to receive criminal and civil (e.g., sexually violent predator) sanctions. From a therapeutic perspective, one alternative is to acknowledge this double bind as part of a trust-building process. A very different alternative is the adoption of an adversarial role with the periodic use of polygraphs as an external incentive or threat for disclosures.

Mental health professionals are likely to avail themselves of most available methods, including polygraph and penile plethysmograph, despite their limited validity in assessing denied sexual deviance. Within a treatment context, the use of such measures as safeguards can assist clinicians, albeit modestly, in their therapeutic efforts. When used in an evaluative context with significant sanctions, these measures typically fall short of established standards for tests (see Lanyon & Thomas, Chapter 17, this volume) and may also be scrutinized via the Daubert criteria.

Denied or Minimized Cognitive Impairment

Persons with limited intellectual abilities sometimes minimize their cognitive deficits. One potentially adaptive approach is acquiescence, whereby persons simply "go along" with persons in authority, including mental health professionals (Gudjonsson, 1990, 2003). Such acquiescence is sometimes preferred by intellectually challenged persons rather than either acknowledging a lack of understanding or attempting to construct a different verbal response. The challenge for mental health professionals is to be aware of "yea-saying" and to minimize its effects on assessments. One approach is to ask questions that offer two simply stated alternatives. Even in this instance,

patterns sometimes emerge (e.g., consistent endorsement of the latter choice). Practitioners
must be able to differentiate acquiescence,
sometimes used as a method of defensiveness
(i.e., hiding cognitive deficits), from defensiveness per se.

Cognitive defensiveness is almost completely overlooked in clinical and personnel assessments. It is especially germane in employment settings in which sophisticated clinical
skills are essential to successful completion of
work-related tasks. Chapter 2 (this volume)
describes, for example, widespread defensiveness among airline pilots. Without standardized methods or established detection strategies, practitioners may wish to use cognitive
tasks with low face validity.

CRITERIA FOR EVALUATING
RESPONSE-STYLE MEASURES

Mental health professionals are often confronted with highly atypical or anomalous findings based on individual interviews and psychological measures. Of critical importance is the
relationship between these findings and response styles. This section provides a summary
of the principal findings for the use of specific
diagnostic methods.

Clinical methods can be conceptualized in
relationship to dissimulation on four levels:
susceptibility, detection, detection of coaching,
and interpretability.

1. *Susceptibility.* The most basic consideration is whether a particular method is vulnerable to dissimulation. For example, projective
methods once were viewed as inaccessible to
feigning, but this notion subsequently has been
disproved (see Chapter 12, this volume). When
methods are susceptible to feigning, then the
crucial issue is detection.

2. *Detection strategies and scales.* The second consideration is whether a measure includes empirically validated detection strategies that have been cross-validated across scales
and measures.

3. *Detection of coached dissimulators.* Practitioners and researchers are acutely aware that
dissimulating persons are not necessarily naive
and unprepared. On the contrary, some dissimulators have considerable knowledge of disorders, based on direct observation or on personal experiences. Some individuals also have

varying knowledge regarding the purpose and
design of assessment methods. Therefore, the
third consideration is whether the detection
strategies and scales remain effective despite
coaching and other forms of preparation.

4. *Interpretability.* Most early research designs implicitly assumed an "either/or" paradigm for response styles (e.g., malingering *or*
mental disorder). Given this simplistic dichotomization, researchers found no need to
investigate the interpretability of dissimulated
profiles. More recently, spurred by research on
the MMPI *K*-correction, investigators are beginning to explore the issue of interpretability:
What clinical conclusions can be rendered, despite the observed dissimulation?

Practitioners should consider the levels of
dissimulation in their selection of assessment
methods. As noted in Chapter 1 (this volume),
most clients are not completely forthright even
under seemingly optimal conditions. Moreover, research has convincingly demonstrated
that all measures are susceptible to response
styles. A circumscribed exception may be defensiveness on certain cognitive measures. Even
in this case, clients can prepare and enhance
their performances (see the discussion of cognitive defensiveness in Chapter 2, this volume).

Levels of dissimulation should be considered
across clinical domains and referral issues. Because of their complexity, this section features
common psychological measures used in the
assessment of reported symptoms and psychopathology. Table 23.4 summarizes major
trends across multiscale inventories, projective
measures, and structured interviews. First and
foremost, it should be unquestionably clear
that all measures of psychopathology are susceptible to response styles. To put it bluntly, decisions to simply neglect response styles likely
reflect professional naiveté.

As is obvious in Table 23.4, some major areas
of clinical assessment have not advanced in
their evaluation of response styles. Two major
areas of neglect have been structured interviews
and projective measures. Regarding the former,
clinical methods have been developed for comparing (1) client and collateral data and (2) the
client's structured and unstructured interview
data (see Rogers, Chapter 18, this volume). Not
to devalue these accomplishments, progress has
yet to be made on the implementation of detection strategies in the form of empirically validated scales. The outstanding exception is the

TABLE 23.4. Summary Table of Common Psychological Measures: Assessment of Malingering and Defensiveness

Measures	Response style	Susceptibility	Strategies	Effectiveness Scales	Scales—coached	Interpretability
MMPI-2	Malingering	Yes	Well developed	Effective	Effective	No
	Defensiveness	Yes	Well developed	Effective	Partial[a]	Partial[b]
PAI	Malingering	Yes	Well developed	Effective	Partial[c]	Partial[d]
	Defensiveness	Yes	Well developed	Effective	Partial	No
MCMI-III	Malingering	Yes	Developed[e]	Partially effective	No	No
	Defensiveness	Yes	Developed	Partially effective	No	No
NEO-PI-R	Malingering	Yes	Developed[f]	Effective	No	No
	Defensiveness	Yes	Developed[f]	Effective	No	No
Rorschach	Malingering	Yes	No[g]	No	No	No
	Defensiveness	Yes	No	No	No	No
Other projectives	Malingering	Yes	No	No	No	No
	Defensiveness	Yes	No	No	No	No
SADS	Malingering	Yes	Developed	Partially effective	No	No
	Defensiveness	Yes	Developed	Partially effective	No	No
Axis I interviews[h]	Malingering	Yes	No	No	No	No
	Defensiveness	Yes	No	No	No	No
Axis II interviews	Malingering	Yes	No	No	No	No
	Defensiveness	Yes	No	No	No	No
SIRS	Malingering	Yes	Well developed	Effective	Effective	Partial[i]
	Defensiveness	Yes	Developed	Partially effective	No	No

Note. Please refer to the individual chapters for the full names of measures and details about their effectiveness.
[a]Only specialized scales (i.e., Wiggins sd or Wsd, and ODecp) remain effective.
[b]Use of K-correction scales continues despite virtually no research in the past two decades.
[c]Very sophisticated users (doctoral students) can suppress NIM but not RDF.
[d]Recent research (Hopwood et al., 2007) attempts to identify which PAI scales are artificially elevated (see Chapter 24, this volume).
[e]The Debasement scale is a broader category than feigning, partially confounded by "personal unattractiveness."
[f]Postdevelopment scales were constructed by Schinka, Kinder, and Kremer (1997).
[g]Research suggests possible detection strategies but they remain to be validated.
[h]Excluding the SADS.
[i]A review of SIRS scales can give information about types of feigning (e.g., endorsement of symptoms with extreme severity), but not genuine disorders.

solid research on the Schedule of Affective Disorders and Schizophrenia (SADS) and its abbreviated version, the SADS-C (see Chapter 18, this volume). Regarding projective measures, researchers have largely neglected this critical component of clinical interpretation.

Multiscale inventories vary markedly in their sophistication with respect to response styles. Clearly, the MMPI-2 and PAI outstrip other measures in both their conceptualization of detection strategies and the breadth of their clinical research. In contrast, other inventories are comparatively limited in their usefulness. For example, a concern with the Millon Clinical Multiaxial Inventory (MCMI-III) is that its feigning scale (scale Z) is so highly correlated with clinical scales among presumably genuine populations ($rs \geq .75$ include 2B, 8A, C, A, H, D, R, SS, and CC; see Millon, Davis, & Millon, 1997, Table 3.6). For evaluations involving significant stakes for the examinees, a useful consideration is whether the measure has been tested and found to be effective with those individuals who are prepared (i.e., coached by others or self-coached).

The SIRS is commonly used in clinical and forensic evaluations. As a specialized measure, it has substantial advantages over more general assessment measures in the development of its scales and its extensive validation (see Chapter 18). The next section focuses briefly on forensic evaluations and specialized measures.

FORENSIC MEASURES AND RESPONSE STYLES

Forensic consultations place special demands on mental health professionals, given that the context is often perceived as adversarial and its conclusions are far-reaching. Therefore, the systematic evaluation of relevant response styles should be an integral component of forensic assessments. In using general measures, practitioners should familiarize themselves with the relevant literature. For example, clinicians must develop a thorough understanding of the MMPI-2 as it relates to child custody determinations before proceeding with these evaluations.

As discussed by Rogers and Shuman (2005), a major contribution to forensic psychology and psychiatry is the development of empirically validated forensic measures. Forensic measures (see, e.g., Chapters 18 and 21, this volume) provide specialized knowledge of legally relevant abilities. Unfortunately, many forensic measures have entirely neglected response styles, offering only lip service to their importance.

Interview-based competency-to-stand-trial measures represent the centerpiece of efforts to develop specialized forensic measures. Unfortunately, some test developers naively assumed that criminal defendants would not attempt to malinger despite the potentially grave consequences of proceeding to trial in felony cases. In other instances, however, considerable attention was paid to the development and testing of competency measures. Table 23.5 provides a summary of competency measures as they relate to feigning.

Forensic practitioners should consider a number of issues in selecting the best validated and most clinically relevant measures. Most competency measures are vulnerable to feigning. As a possible exception, Ryba, Sothmann, Arias, and Slavikova (2007) found that the Evaluation of Competency to Stand Trial—Revised (ECST-R) was difficult for simulators to feign incompetence. One advantage of the ECST-R

TABLE 23.5. A Summary Table for Competency to Stand Trial Measures and Feigning

Competency measure	Susceptibility	Strategies	Scales	Scales—coached	Interpretability
CAI	Yes	No	No	No	No
CAST-MR[a]	Yes	No	No	No	No
ECST-R	Limited[b]	Well developed	Multiple	Yes	Yes: feigned incompetence
GCCT	Yes	Developed	One	No	No
IFI	Yes	No	No	No	No
MacCAT-CA	Yes	No	No	No	No

Note. CAI, Competency to Stand Trial Assessment Instrument (McGarry & Curran, 1973); CAST-MR, Competence Assessment for Standing Trial for Defendants with Mental Retardation (Everington & Luckasson, 1992); ECST-R, Evaluation of Competency to Stand Trial—Revised (Rogers, Tillbrook, & Sewell, 2004); GCCT, Georgia Court Competency Test (Wildman et al., 1979); IFI, Interdisciplinary Fitness Interview (Golding, Roesch, & Schreiber, 1984); MacCAT-CA, MacArthur Competence Assessment Tool—Criminal Adjudication (Poythress et al., 1999).
[a]This is an orally administered measure.
[b]Ryba et al. (2007) found that nearly all (> 90%) uncoached and coached simulators were unable to produce a clinical profile consistent with incompetence.

is the low face validity of two of its three competency scales. Even with coaching, very few simulators were able to feign incompetence due to a mental disorder (7%) or cognitive impairment (2%).

As summarized in Table 23.5, only two competency measures systematically address the issue of feigning. The Georgia Court Competency Test (GCCT) is typically used as a screen for competency to stand trial. A malingering screen was added to the scale in 1995, which is moderately successful (see Chapter 18). More recently, the ECST-R was developed with several well-defined detection strategies that examine rare symptoms and symptom severity. For screening purposes, Ryba and colleagues (2007) found that most coached simulators were identified (> 90%) on a single scale, although a substantial number of nonfeigning controls were misclassified. In addition, the ECST-R also includes a screen for possible defensiveness. Of considerable interest, validated ECST-R cut scores can also be used to determine whether the feigning is likely to be associated with an effort to be found incompetent to stand trial.

CLINICAL RELEVANCE OF RESPONSE STYLES

The clinical relevance of dissimulation varies directly with the degree of distortion, the type of dissimulation, and the specific referral question. For example, a person with paranoid schizophrenia and an extensive history of auditory hallucinations may attempt to feign command hallucinations. The clinical relevance of such fabrications would depend greatly on the referral question and vary considerably in relevance depending on whether the patient is seeking voluntary hospitalization or attempting an insanity plea. Indeed, the relevance of any type of dissimulation can be established only with reference to a specific referral question.

Empirical data are incomplete on the prevalence of dissimulation by referral questions. For insanity evaluations, which often involve very high stakes, the prevalence of malingering was very low (4.5% of sane defendants; see Rogers, 1986). Interestingly, Rogers (1986) found that a broadened category (i.e., the spectrum from moderate deception to suspected malingering) more than quadrupled the numbers for sane defendants.

Regarding general forensic practice, large-scale surveys (Rogers, Salekin, Sewell, Goldstein, & Leonard, 1998; Rogers, Sewell, & Goldstein, 1994) of malingering found relatively small percentages (15.7% and 17.4%, respectively). In contrast, Mittenberg, Patton, Canyock, and Condit (2002) surveyed neuropsychologists and found estimates exceeding 30% when a broadened category (i.e., the spectrum from symptom exaggeration to suspected malingering) is used. The Rogers (1986) data are useful in explaining the disparities between Rogers, Sewell, and Goldstein (1994) and Rogers, Salekin, and colleagues (1996) and Mittenberg and colleagues (2002). When focused on definite cases, the prevalence of malingering remains relatively low. When a much broader categorization is used, the percentages are much greater. What is the clinical relevance of these disparities in prevalence rates?

1. Many researchers and practitioners are apparently confused by the Mittenberg and colleagues (2002) data and misuse these percentages in calculating base rates for malingering.
2. Misusing the higher percentages may mislead mental health and other professionals regarding the true prevalence of established malingering. The biasing effect in the overestimations of malingering is likely to be substantial but has not been formally investigated.

Prevalence estimates for nonforensic evaluations are surprisingly absent. Mental health professionals assigned to emergency rooms attest to both (1) malingering by voluntary patients seeking admission[2] and (2) defensiveness among involuntary patients denying or refusing to discuss their psychopathology, as well as the events precipitating their admission. Beyond these anecdotal data, a dearth of information is available on dissimulation in relation to inpatient or outpatient treatment. Survey data of forensic experts by Rogers, Sewell, and Goldstein (1994) and Rogers, Salekin, and colleagues (1996) produced estimates in the 5–7% range; these percentages may be overestimates of general clinical practice, given that forensic specialists often consult on high-stakes referrals.

Assessments in employment settings have the obvious potential for dissimulation. The determination of benefits as related to rehabil-

itation efforts may provide motivation in a minority of cases for feigned performances. In
contrast, some job applicants are likely to be
highly motivated to present themselves in the
best possible light. To address this issue with
law enforcement hires (see Jackson & Crawford, Chapter 22, this volume), the PAI examines validity indicators with reference to
specific norms (i.e., the population of job applicants). Such data provide a valuable reference point: Compared with other applicants, is
this person engaging in a larger-than-expected
level of defensiveness and social desirability?

Chapter 1 (this volume) briefly discussed the
potential effects of disclosing disabilities. Despite protection from the Americans with Disability Act (ADA), individuals may be motivated to hide or minimize their disabilities. In
other contexts, the motivation may be different. For example, increasing numbers of persons seek special accommodations in higher
education. Although many requests for special
accommodations appear unwarranted, the overall proportion of persons fabricating symptoms to circumvent academic requirements is
not likely to be large.[3] Special education placements often vary in the quality of services provided but almost always carry a social stigma.
We should, therefore, expect the proportion
of defensiveness to vary based on these two
parameters (i.e., quality of services and stigmatization).

A substantial number of forensic evaluations
yield atypical results that are possibly indicative of malingering. As noted in Chapter 1, clinicians must avoid the facile conclusion that
atypical results combined with putative external motivation and buttressed by DSM-IV
indices (e.g., antisocial personality disorder
[APD] and medicolegal evaluation) are tantamount to malingering. Our best available data
on malingering suggest that (1) forensic settings vary markedly in their prevalence rates
and (2) most forensic examinees, despite the
potential rewards, do not malinger. Moreover,
this hypothesis (i.e., atypical + APD + medicolegal = malingering) is convincingly refuted
when the range of forensic issues is properly
considered. For example, child custody is a
medicolegal issue for which the *opposite* outcome is commonly found. Parents, antisocial
or not, typically engage in defensiveness and
social desirability. Malingering would be totally counterproductive and is almost never
observed.

A commonsensical review of the forensic issues suggests that dissimulation is highly dependent on the legal issues and the specifics of
the case. Although plaintiffs in personal injury
cases may have something to gain from feigned
deficits, the amount of gain varies directly with
the degree of genuine disorder. For example, a
person with unequivocal memory impairment
coupled with major depression is not likely to
be compensated more for the fabrication of additional symptoms. Insanity cases may provide
an apparent motivation to malinger. However,
this apparent motivation may evaporate in
noncapital cases when the length and conditions of institutionalization (prison vs. maximum security hospital) are considered. In summary, Table 23.6 provides a heuristic framework for estimating the expected likelihood of
malingering, defensiveness, and social desirability by the type of assessment being conducted. Please note, however, that even a
"high" likelihood rarely exceeds 50%. These
designations are used for comparative purposes
only.

The relevance of dissimulation ranges widely
with the degree of distortion and the referral
question. One pivotal consideration underlying the analysis of clinical relevance is, If the
dissimulation were true, what appreciable
difference would it make to intervention or
disposition? For instance, a psychotically depressed woman who exaggerates her suicidal
ideation to ensure her hospitalization in a
crowded public facility should be hospitalized
irrespective of her malingering. Likewise, a job
applicant who minimizes past episodes of anxiety out of fear of stigmatization ought to be
considered for most positions, irrespective of
past anxiety episodes. In such cases, the dissimulation may have only a minor influence on
the professional opinion and subsequent decision making. Each case of suspected dissimulation must be evaluated thoroughly, as the clinician cannot determine *prior* to his or her
assessment what the potential relevance of a
specific response style is in an individual case.
The issue of relevance must be raised following each assessment in assigning the importance of the dissimulation to the overall evaluation of the patient.

Treatment Considerations

The majority of clinical assessments address related issues of treatment recommendations and

TABLE 23.6. Potential for Dissimulation by Types of Professional Evaluation

Domain	Referral issue	Likely response styles		
		Malingering	Defensiveness	Social desirability
Treatment	1. Voluntary outpatient	Low	Low	Variable[a]
	2. Voluntary inpatient	Variable[b]	Low	Low
	3. Involuntary inpatient	Low	Moderate	Low
Vocational	1. Rehabilitation assessments	Moderate	Low	Variable[c]
	2. Job placement/performance	Low	Variable[d]	Moderate to high[e]
School	1. Special education placement	Low	Variable[f]	Low
	2. Special accommodation under ADA	Variable[g]	Low	Variable
Forensic	1. Child custody	Low	Moderate	High
	2. Disability	High	Low	Variable[c]
	3. Insanity	High	Low	Low
	4. Presentence	Low	Variable[h]	High

[a]Outpatients often use presenting problems and do not discuss personally sensitive issues until trust and rapport have been developed.
[b]Where inpatient resources are scarce, voluntary patients may feel compelled to malinger in order to qualify for services.
[c]Overly virtuous presentations have been observed in vocational and disability assessments.
[d]For positions requiring emotional stability (e.g., pilots and police officers), defensiveness is commonly observed.
[e]This response style is common among job applicants and can be very frequent for competitive positions.
[f]Some persons with cognitive impairments have learned to avoid social stigma by "covering up" their deficits.
[g]Sometimes the issue involves the gross exaggeration of impairment rather than feigned symptoms.
[h]In minor offenses, defendants may hope for treatment alternatives to incarceration by appearing mentally disordered. In other cases, defendants may worry that the appearance of mental disorder will lead to a harsher sentence.

likely treatment outcomes. Little research exists on the relationship of specific styles of dissimulation to treatment response. Clinical interpretations based on the MMPI would suggest that a mild to moderate degree of defensiveness may be evidence of ego strength and positive treatment outcome (e.g., Marks, Seeman, & Haller, 1974). Paradoxically, some exaggeration of psychological impairment, as measured by the F scale of the MMPI, has been commonly labeled as a "cry for help" and a sign of increased motivation. As noted by Rogers in Chapter 24 of this volume, data by Krittman (2004) suggest that malingerers may show a greater investment than other patients in treatment, although their efforts may not be recognized by clinical staff.

Despite these clinical interpretations, little is known regarding the relationship of malingering, defensiveness, or irrelevant responding to the (1) type of treatment that should be recommended and (2) likelihood of treatment compliance and favorable outcome. Certainly,

patients with extreme presentations of dissimulation would appear to be poor treatment candidates. Individuals who either categorically deny any psychological difficulties or who unfalteringly malinger pervasive problems would not appear, on an intuitive basis, to be amenable to treatment. Mild to moderate degrees of malingering and defensiveness present a more complicated picture. With less severe dissimulation, therapists and clients may be able to establish a common ground for the treatment of "real" problems while trust and rapport are being established. Likewise, moderate levels of social desirability may suggest an implicit awareness of interpersonal needs that can be bridged by rapport and subsequent interventions.

A difficult issue to establish is the patient's motivation for dissimulation and the relevance of this motivation to treatment recommendations. A parent in a child custody dispute may have a strong motivation to deny problems prior to the child custody hearing but may manifest strong motivation for treatment if treatment is a condition of the custody. Similarly, an involuntary patient may be markedly defensive during the civil commitment proceedings, yet show at least some motivation to participate in treatment once the decision to hospitalize has been determined judicially. Simply put, any striking change in life circumstances signals the need to reevaluate the relationship of response styles to clinical interventions.

Treatment compliance is an important element in the assessment of treatment recommendations for malingering and defensive individuals. By definition, malingering and defensive individuals must be viewed as being at cross-purposes with their evaluators, although not necessarily with subsequent treatment. Without minimizing the confounding effects of dissimulation, many "presenting complaints" by generally forthright patients are deliberate gambits to test the trustworthiness and competence of the clinician. In other words, trust and the development of shared goals is a necessary component of most treatment interventions. From this perspective, the treating clinician may attempt to define a dissimulator's objectives and to assess to what extent the proposed treatment would assist the dissimulator in meeting these objectives. These objectives likely include the nature of the therapeutic relationship and concomitant feelings of vulnerability and dependency. The concerns underlying these objectives may extend beyond the therapeutic process and have real-world implications. An intrafamilial pedophiliac parent does have something to fear from therapy, specifically the loss of his or her children. An unskilled laborer, whether deserving of workers' compensation or not, is likely to be threatened by discussions about exaggerated symptoms of depression and his or her apparent impairment.

The question must also be considered of whether the client's response style should itself be the focus of therapy. Other obstacles to treatment, such as a lack of insight, are considered legitimate foci for therapy. Why not malingering and defensiveness? From an interpersonal perspective, a veneer of social desirability could be viewed as a problem of self-disclosure that could be addressed directly or indirectly. Likewise, malingering could be considered from a cognitive perspective as poor decision making with negative consequences.

Unfortunately, many clinicians view even the possibility of malingering as a reason not to attempt treatment (e.g., Pedroza, 2003). Instead, an important alternative is suggested: *Psychological interventions are heavily invested in overcoming obstacles to treatment by addressing them directly. Malingering and other forms of dissimulation are obstacles to treatment, not categorical excuses to avoid treatment.*

The assessment of treatability is at best an imprecise process, which relies heavily on trial and error (see Rogers & Webster, 1989). One fruitful approach would be to attempt a contractual arrangement with a dissimulating patient for an explicit treatment intervention over a specified time period. In cases in which treatment is deemed essential and nonoptional, enforced treatment would be strictly controlled by statutory requirements, with the treatment outcome often limited to the reduction of imminent dangerousness. In these latter cases, the focus is more on appropriate case management, with less attention paid to treatment compliance or outcome.

Nontreatment Considerations

Psychologists and other mental health professionals often engage in consultations that involve nontreatment decisions. In a classic study, Lorei (1970) surveyed Veterans Administration (VA) hospitals and found that the determination of malingering was second in importance only to dangerousness when assessing the potential dischargeability of inpatients. Patients in preparation for discharge may manifest a strong desire either to remain in the hospital or to receive a favorable community placement. Furthermore, outpatients may wish to present themselves as sufficiently impaired to warrant certain benefits (e.g., insurance reimbursement and worker's compensation) but not so impaired as to risk certain privileges (e.g., permanent loss of employment, hospitalization, or termination of parental rights; see Rogers & Cavanaugh, 1983). Military personnel may seek discharge from armed forces or noncombat placements (Carroll, 2003). Vocational, school, and forensic assessments frequently include such nontreatment dispositions. Such cases tend to be perceived as more adversarial than simple treatment decisions, because the clinician is likely to be seen as a means to an end (e.g., selection of the best candidate for a managerial position) and to have goals that differ from the client's (e.g., furthering the company's objectives, not the client's career).

The risk and potential benefits accrued from psychiatric and psychological assessment are often explicit and legally sanctioned. In nontreatment assessments, the clinician does not often have the luxury of a reassessment because a lasting determination must be rendered. As the potential benefits increase, the likelihood of dissimulation should also increase. The extent to which potential dissimulators weigh the risks of detection is not known, although awareness of risk should have a moderating effect on the probability of dissimulation.

Nontreatment dispositions typically require the clinician to examine a patient according to a specific legal or administrative standard within an adjudicative context. This standard reflects decisions, often made by agencies, schools, or the courts, which may not be perceived by the client as either beneficial or benevolent. Although the emphasis of such assessments is a particular standard, deception and dissimulation must also be considered. Within a nontreatment context, the use of corroborative data becomes increasingly important in making the appropriate recommendations or dispositions, because no prior or ongoing professional relationship exists.

Motivational Considerations

A final issue in considering the clinical relevance of dissimulation is to understand its adaptive functions for the dissimulator (see also the adaptational model in Chapter 1, this volume). Although clinicians frequently view dissimulation as a negative and complicating factor in clinical assessment, this same behavior may be viewed as positive and adaptive by the dissimulator. Goals of dissimulation may include the maintenance of an individual's sense of autonomy, securing of denied benefits, avoidance of painful circumstances, and avoidance of or disengagement from a difficult or involuntary process.

Such objectives, from the perspective of the dissimulator, may be viewed as attempts (successful or otherwise) to maintain a sense of worth or competency and to minimize avoidable pain or coercion. For example, patients who resist involuntary hospitalization or man-

datory treatment may be defending, whether correctly or not, their own right to self-determination. Individuals who deny disabling psychological disorders may be struggling to maintain their sense of competence either through work or through the continued custody of their children. Other dissimulators, who have experienced physical and/or psychological injuries through the negligence of others, may exaggerate their impairment from their own perspective of justice, believing that no financial compensation can ever equal the losses that they have incurred. Finally, dissimulators may be motivated by an understandable desire to avoid painful or coercive circumstances, which may be a factor in presentence evaluations or civil commitment proceedings.

A clinician's responsibility goes beyond the mere identification of dissimulators and extends to his or her understanding of their motivations for these deliberate distortions. Inquiry into the patients' perceived risks and benefits may be useful in understanding their motivations. In most cases, this motivation probably extends beyond tangible rewards and punishments of the immediate circumstances and is related to an individual's self-image. Simply presented as an inquiry, What are the different outcomes of this assessment and what do they mean to this individual's self-perception? For example, the acknowledgment of a severe mental disorder may well be devastating and unacceptable to a particular person's self-image of being strong and capable. Thus the role that motivation plays in dissimulation must be considered for each individual, addressed within a possibly adversarial context, and in relationship to a specific referral question.

An informal review of clinical reports suggests that some clinicians attempt to go one step further and make statements regarding an individual's personality on the basis of his or her specific dissimulative style. Reports may describe dissimulating patients as manipulative, self-serving, dishonest, uncooperative, and oppositional. Such inferences should never be generated on the basis of malingering and defensiveness alone. As a rule, such attempts to link response styles with personality characteristics should be avoided as an underlying premise of such often-pejorative interpretations is that only "bad" persons dissimulate. A preferable approach is to describe a patient's apparent motivation rather than to make unsupported inferences regarding character or personality.

CONFRONTATION OF SUSPECTED DISSIMULATION

An important and perhaps essential component in the clinical determination of dissimulation is to offer the patient some feedback regarding his or her presentation. This process might well include a summary of the patient's presentation and the difficulties or problems that the clinician has in accepting the patient's accounts at face value. Feedback on the patient's response style requires sensitivity, tact, and timing from the clinician.

As a general principle, clinicians should be parsimonious in their feedback and judicious in their confrontation of individuals seen for evaluation. The goals of providing feedback may include (1) informing the patient of the status of the evaluation, (2) asking the patient for assistance in clarifying incongruities, (3) eliciting more complete information, and (4) giving the patient an opportunity to change his or her self-report. Except under unusual circumstances, the purpose of such feedback or confrontation should not be to extract from the patient an "admission of dissimulation." The clinician should attempt to establish his or her conclusions prior to any discussion of dissimulation. Rather than extracting admissions, the purpose is to give the patient an opportunity to clarify areas of ambiguity and, more important, to offer insight into possible motivation for the dissimulation. An additional goal, which may be occasionally realized, is for the individual to spontaneously provide a more accurate description of his or her psychological impairment. Such revisions of self-reports must, of course, be carefully scrutinized because they may represent simply another attempt at malingering, defensiveness, or social desirability.

Confronting and giving feedback to a defensive patient typically require the use of corroborative data. Naturally, the clinician should attempt to present his or her observations in a straightforward and nonpejorative manner. The following are examples of feedback and confrontation with a defensive patient:

1. "Although you are telling me that everything is going fine, when I hear about . . .
   thing is going fine, when I hear about . . . [give description of current problems], I am having some trouble understanding this."
2. "I know how much you want me to believe that you have your problems well under control, but when I see you . . . [report clinical observations of the patient] I don't think this is the case."
3. "Life is not all black and white. Whenever someone tells me only the good side, I become interested in what is being left out. . . ."
4. "According to you, you are having no difficulty handling . . . [describe a specific problem], but according to . . . [name a reliable informant] you are experiencing. . . ."

Malingering patients, unlike their defensive counterparts, are commonly either inconsistent or improbable in their clinical presentation. Therefore, the clinician needs a wider range of probes in discussing dissimulation with malingerers. Representative probes include the following:

1. "Some of the problems you describe are rarely seen in patients with mental disorders. I am worried that you might be trying to make things seem worse than they are."
2. "Earlier in the evaluation you told me . . . ; now you are telling me. . . . I am having trouble putting this together."
3. "Although you have told me about . . . [description of current problems], when I observed you, you have not appeared. . . ."
4. "I don't want to hurt your feelings, but I just don't think things are quite as bad as you tell me they are."
5. "According to you, you have . . . [describe current problems], but according to . . . [name a reliable informant] you are. . . . Can you help me understand this?"

Irrelevant responders typically are disengaged from the assessment process. This disengagement makes feedback or confrontation particularly difficult because the patient is uninvolved and emotionally distant from the clinician. The clinician must weigh the merits of direct confrontation with irrelevant responders against the possibility that such confrontation may only further alienate the patient. Representative probes include:

1. "I don't think we got off on the right foot. Can we start again? Tell me in your words what you see as your problems."

2. "I know that you're not particularly pleased about being here. How can we make sure that this is not a waste of time for you?"
3. "I know you took these . . . [psychological tests] for me, but I don't think you paid much attention to how you answered them. What about . . . [point out specific test items], which you gave different answers to at different times?"

As discussed, the purpose of feedback and discussion is to provide a greater understanding of the patient's motivation. Experienced clinicians have found that matter-of-fact confrontation, with respect for the patient's personal dignity and efforts at dissimulation, often provides an avenue for further understanding of that patient. Not giving the patient an opportunity to address ambiguities and incongruities within the assessment process may well shortchange the evaluation itself.

An alternative to direct feedback is to offer the patient possible motivations for dissimulation. In a child custody case, the clinician might remark, "Many parents do themselves more harm than good by trying to appear perfect." For a chronic patient feigning hallucinations, the clinician might caution indirectly, "Sometimes patients make up symptoms to get special attention or more medication. The danger in doing this is that no one believes fakers, even when they are really in crisis." The indirect discussion of possible motivation has the advantage of providing a face-saving method of discussing and possibly changing dissimulation. The drawback is that the clinician's construal of motivation may impede further discussion of alternative motivations.

SYNTHESIS OF CLINICAL DATA

The clinician must integrate an array of clinical findings on the issue of dissimulation and discuss these findings in terms of both the referral question and clinical relevance. Such synthesis of dissimulation material requires the examination of the following dimensions: (1) the strength and consistency of results across psychological measures, (2) the absence of alternative explanations, (3) the possibility of hybrid styles of dissimulation, and (4) the methods of reporting dissimulation. Each of these dimensions is discussed individually.

Strength and Convergence of Findings

Among the dozens of standardized methods and specific techniques, the strength and robustness of measures must be considered in the determination of response styles. Several methods are particularly robust and produce very few false positives. For feigned psychopathology, the SIRS and occasionally the MMPI-2[4] provide highly robust findings. For feigned cognitive impairment, below-chance performance on SVT may furnish conclusive evidence. For defensiveness and deception, markedly anomalous findings on urinalysis, hair analysis, the Guilty Knowledge Test (GKT), and penile plethysmography can provide objective confirmation. Even with these robust findings, corroborative data should be actively sought and multiple methods employed.

Given the fallibility of individual diagnostic methods for the accurate identification of malingering and defensiveness, the degree of convergence among measures is crucial. If a clinician has ample data based on pencil-and-paper measures, clinical interviews, and corroborative sources regarding a patient's inconsistent or improbable presentation, then the determination of malingering, defensiveness, or irrelevant responding is a relatively straightforward matter. Sometimes, individuals will be tempted to feign on pencil-and-paper measures but respond forthrightly on interview-based approaches. What should the clinician do if the patient appears reliable on the basis of clinical and corroborative data and yet presents a malingered profile on the MMPI-2? At a minimum, such inconsistencies reduce the degree of certainty in the diagnostic conclusions (see also the subsequent section on hybrid styles of dissimulation). The absence of such convergence, depending on the particular clinical presentation, may argue for the general designation as an *unreliable* responder. Suffice it to say, highly consistent results from different sources of clinical investigation are invaluable in making definite conclusions regarding a specific dissimulative style.

Absence of Alternative Explanations

Specific indicators of dissimulation can be ranked on the degree to which they may be open to alternative interpretations. For example, rare symptoms are, by definition, infrequently seen in the clinical population; the presence of several such symptoms, although perhaps indicative of malingering, does not preclude other interpretations. In comparison, a large number of improbable symptoms or symptom combinations are extremely unlikely in bona fide patients.

As an illustration, an overly dramatic presentation has sometimes been described in case studies to signify feigning. Alternative explanations might include Axis I symptoms (e.g., grandiose delusions) or Axis II symptomatology (e.g., histrionic personality disorder). Other alternatives must be explicitly considered. Evaluations with conclusions about dissimulation are sometimes strengthened by the inclusion of these alternatives and the reasons that they are not compelling.

Standardized measures, such as the SIRS, can provide specific probability estimates that a particular presentation is feigned. For example, three or more SIRS primary scales in the probable range reflect a very high probability (e.g., 97%) of feigning. With such data, alternative explanations are unlikely to be viable. Although less clear with the MMPI-2 because of the variability in cut scores, extreme elevations on specialized indicators (e.g., raw Fp >9) with an unelevated variable response inconsistency (VRIN) can also signal a high likelihood of feigning.

Below-chance performance on SVT provides the most compelling evidence of feigning and the virtual exclusion of other explanations. When a sufficient number of trials are given and the scores are markedly below those of persons with *no* ability (i.e., chance performance), the likelihood of feigning is maximized. Although other factors may be present (e.g., fatigue and depression), they are insufficient to produce these abysmal results.

Hybrid Styles of Dissimulation

An important task in the clinical determination of dissimulation is whether a patient presenting with a mixed response style should be considered as a hybrid style or an ambiguous clinical presentation (see also Otto, Chapter 21, this volume). The clinician must be careful not to overinterpret contradictory findings, particularly when the indicators are gathered from distinct sources of clinical data. Two conditions under which diagnostic conclusions regarding hybrid styles may be justified are (1) on circumscribed issues and (2) within specified time periods. An example of circumscribed issues would be the assessment of a suspected child molester who appeared open and honest in the description of his day-to-day functioning with the notable exception of any discussion of pedophilia or other paraphilias. Depending on the quality of the clinical data, the clinician might well conclude that the patient has an honest–defensive response style and provide a thorough description of what is meant by this term.

The second condition would relate to specific time periods. Borrowing from forensic assessments, in occasional personal-injury evaluations, the patient is seen as defensive regarding his or her functioning prior to the injury (i.e., no problems at all) and malingering following the injury. Such clinical presentations would be characterized as a defensive–malingering response style requiring careful explanation to the referral source. However, many persons involved in personal injury cases appear to polarize their perspectives (i.e., the untroubled past versus the problem-ridden present; Rogers, 1995). Care must be taken to differentiate this common process of polarization from deliberate attempts to conceal past and fabricate current psychopathology.

The general guideline for addressing such clinical ambiguities is to label the case *unreliable* when any substantial doubt occurs about the specific response style. Furthermore, when the clinician is convinced that the patient is deliberately distorting his or her self-report but is not clearly malingering, defensive, or irrelevant, the clinician may characterize this style as *dissimulation*. The designation of hybrid response styles should be reserved for cases in which the clinical data are internally consistent and are understandable with respect to either circumscribed issues or specific periods.

Reporting Dissimulation

Response styles, such as malingering and defensiveness, can be conceptualized at three basic levels: mild, moderate, and severe. In synthesizing the clinical data, the clinician should attempt to describe the patient's malingering or defensiveness in terms of these levels. Table 23.7 presents the three gradations of malingering and defensiveness, with sample descriptions for their inclusion in clinical reports.

The clinician must decide, for the purposes of synthesizing clinical data into a relevant re-

TABLE 23.7. Reporting Dissimulation: A Sampling of Descriptive Statements

A. Mild dissimulation (malingering or defensiveness)

   1. Although minor distortions were observed in the patient's presentation, these are expected, given the context of the evaluation.

   2. Although the patient manifested a slight tendency to minimize (or amplify) his or her self-report, no major distortions were observed.

   3. Although some variations were noted in the patient's self-report, they have no (or little) bearing on diagnosis and treatment.

B. Moderate malingering

   1. Clinical findings clearly indicate that the patient was exaggerating (and/or fabricating) his or her psychological impairment. This was observed in . . . (descriptive examples).

   2. The patient has fabricated several important symptoms including . . . (descriptive examples); these symptoms have direct bearing on the patient's diagnosis and disposition.

   3. The patient has evidenced a moderate degree of malingering as observed in . . . (descriptive examples). This attempt to distort the evaluation raises some concern about motivation for treatment.

   4. The patient's self-report appears to be exaggerated (and/or fabricated) with . . . (descriptive examples). Difficulty in assessing the patient's motivation leaves unanswered what is his or her intended goal; the unresolved diagnosis is between factitious disorder and malingering.

C. Severe malingering

   1. The patient is attempting to present himself or herself as severely disturbed by fabricating many symptoms including . . . (descriptive examples).

   2. The patient has evidenced severe malingering by presenting . . . (strategies of malingering, e.g., "rare and improbable symptoms, uncorroborated by clinical observation"). Most notable examples of fabrication are . . . (descriptive examples).

D. Moderate defensiveness

   1. Clinical findings clearly indicate that the patient was minimizing (and/or denying) his or her psychological impairment. The defensiveness was observed in . . . (descriptive examples).

   2. The patient has denied several important symptoms, including . . . (descriptive examples); these denied symptoms have direct bearing on the patient's diagnosis and treatment.

   3. The patient has evidenced a moderate degree of defensiveness, as observed in . . . (descriptive examples). Such defensiveness is fairly common in patients being assessed for treatment.

E. Severe defensiveness

   1. The patient is attempting to present himself or herself as well adjusted by denying many observed symptoms, including . . . (descriptive examples).

   2. The patient has evidenced severe defensiveness by presenting . . . (strategies of defensiveness, e.g., "denial of everyday problems, endorsement of overly positive attributes, and denial of psychological impairment despite overwhelming clinical data to the contrary"). Most notable examples are . . . (descriptive examples).

   3. The patient's self-report includes the denial of any psychiatric difficulties, despite convincing evidence of . . . (DSM-IV diagnosis.) This severe defensiveness raises some concern about motivation for treatment.

port, what observations of the patient's response style should be included. As noted earlier, the clinical relevance of a patient's dissimulative style must be examined with reference to the referral question. With certain referral questions, discussion of the response style may have little direct bearing on the referral question, and therefore the clinician would have the option of briefly reporting or withholding his or her clinical observations. In the majority of cases, however, the patient's dissimulative style is relevant to the referral question, diagnosis, and capacity to form a therapeutic relationship. In such cases, the clinician should describe the patient's response style, including its severity. Although clinicians are encouraged to use the terms employed throughout this book, such terms are in no way a substitute for a thorough description of the patient's response style and its relevance to the assessment. The clinician must address the patient's deliberateness, type of distortion, and degree of distortion. In supporting his or her diagnostic conclusions, the clinician should provide specific examples, preferably employing direct quotes from the patient. In summary, the clinical report should include a detailed description of how the patient is responding and how this response style relates to both diagnostic issues and the referral question.

CONCLUSIONS

The strength of clinical assessment in the evaluation of malingering and defensiveness remains chiefly in the use of well-validated individual measures (see, e.g., Borg, Connor, & Landis, 1995). The synthesis of these measures must take into account their detection strategies and concomitant effectiveness. Although multiple measures do not always increase discrimination, the selective use of multiple detection strategies adds conceptual strength to the establishment of specific response style. A review of clinical methods by the four criteria of susceptibility, detection, detection of coach-

ing, and interpretability highlights the strengths and limitations in our current knowledge of dissimulation. Considerable advances have been realized during the past decade in the clinical assessment of response style. Further advances are needed, as delineated in the final chapter of this book.

NOTES

1. The L scale is traditionally viewed as employing idealized attributes; however, a content analysis readily reveals that it uses only the denial of personal shortcomings.
2. As indirect evidence, Logan, Reuterfors, Bohn, and Clark (1984) found that 14.3% of people who threatened the president were motivated by the desire for institutionalization. The involvement of the Secret Service apparently assisted inpatient hospitalization when feigned homicidal ideation toward ordinary citizens might not produce the desired result.
3. More often, students seeking accommodations at my university clinic openly state their objective (e.g., "I don't want to take math") but make no apparent attempt to feign.
4. Use of typical cutting scores on standard MMPI-2 validity scales frequently produce unacceptable numbers of false positives. However, high cut scores on specialized scales (Fp and Ds) can reduce false positives and increase confidence in feigning determinations.

24

Researching Response Styles

RICHARD ROGERS, PhD

Research methodology for the assessment of response styles has continued to evolve since the publication of the second edition of this book in 1997. However, the progress has been very uneven. Rapid and noteworthy advances are balanced by areas of virtual stagnation. Too often, research on response styles deemphasizes its conceptual underpinnings. Without explicitly operationalized detection strategies, assessment research on response-style measures remains largely an atheoretical enterprise that does not substantially contribute to our knowledge base. As a concrete example, previous chapters had variable success in determining detection strategies. They varied from post hoc extrapolations to well-defined, empirically validated strategies.

A major component of this chapter is the examination of five basic research designs that are often applied to the study of response styles. For the sake of simplicity, the term *dissimulators* is used to designate those individuals adopting any specific response style (e.g., malingering and defensiveness). In contrast, the term *deceivers* is reserved for nonspecific deception (e.g., lying and deceit). Before beginning this examination, I highlight the important linkages between theory and practice. The basic paradigm consists of three phases. First, competing models of deception can be explicitly tested. Second, these results will inform response-style researchers regarding basic principles and potential strategies. Third, the discriminant validity of these potential

strategies can be rigorously evaluated. This paradigm is illustrated in the next section concentrating on the valuable contributions of Sporer and Schwandt (2006, 2007).

LINKAGES BETWEEN THEORY AND PRACTICE

Response-style researchers can broaden their understanding of theory and practice by reading literature outside their own specialty areas. For example, Sporer and Schwandt (2007) provide a sophisticated analysis of general deception with testable hypotheses regarding different theoretical approaches. Although valuable in its own right, their analytical approach could be used as a model for the study of malingering, defensiveness, and other specific response styles.

Sporer and Schwandt (2006, 2007) identified four alternative models for understanding deception. They are described in an outline format with their concomitant predictions:

1. *Arousal theory.* Most persons engaging in deception will experience psychophysiological arousal. It is postulated that increased arousal will be observable in both nonverbal and paralinguistic cues (e.g., faster speech, more filled pauses, more nodding, and more limb movements).

2. *Affective theory.* Persons engaging in deception may experience a range of emotions,

from fear and guilt to "duping delight" (Ekman, 1988). Fear and guilt are postulated to have commonalities (e.g., decreased eye contact and greater limb movements) and differences (e.g., slower speech and decreased head movements with guilt but not fear).

3. *Attempted control theory.* Persons engaging in deception have beliefs about how deceivers are "caught" by others. They attempt to inhibit these telltale signs; unwittingly, these efforts may become their own cues to deception. It is postulated that many nonverbal and paralinguistic cues will be reduced in an effort to reduce detection.

4. *Cognitive theory.* Persons engaging in deception experience an increased cognitive load when constructing a coherent story that fits with past accounts. It is hypothesized that verbal output will be decreased (e.g., fewer words, slower speech, and increased pauses) as a result of this increased cognitive demand.

The value of the Sporer and Schwandt's work is that it presents a combination of competing and complementary hypotheses that can be empirically tested. Extrapolating to specific responses, researchers could examine whether impression management involving multiple decisions about socially appropriate responses places a greater cognitive load on simulators than more straightforward defensiveness. If it does, how can this information be used to develop an effective detection strategy?

The attempted control model provides a wealth of interesting hypotheses. It attempts to identify misconceptions about deceivers and to use the *absence* of these misconceptions as evidence of deception. This model for detection strategies is elegantly sophisticated in its use of deceivers' own countermeasures. MMPI-2 feigning research on the dissimulation scale capitalizes on neurotic stereotypes that may be reported by feigners. However, I am not aware of any studies regarding malingering stereotypes. Do they exist? Do feigners attempt to counteract them? Can their countermeasures be used as detection strategies? Does asking questions about malingering stereotypes improve their effectiveness?

According to Sporer and Schwandt (2007), the complexity of the task and level of involvement are important to the effectiveness of detection strategies. For instance, affective involvement can be minimized by simple responses to a written questionnaire (e.g., a Personality Assessment Inventory [PAI] administration). Their work would suggest that the active construction of a response-style presentation (e.g., malingering for worker's compensation) greatly increases physiological arousal and affective responses, especially when simulators realize that evaluators are considering the veridicality of their responses. Studies could be constructed to test the generalizability of these conclusions to specific response styles. For example, does an interview-based administration of the SIMS produce different levels of affect and arousal and more detectable responses than in its paper-and-pencil format? Does asking for a "free account" regarding mental health claims modify subsequent SIMS results, irrespective of format, for those feigning psychopathology?

Research on response styles often emphasizes assessment methods without sufficient attention to detection strategies or their overarching theoretical framework. For a more integrated body of knowledge, I propose that future studies should address at least two of the three phases of response-style research: theory, detection strategies, and empirical findings (e.g., scales or indicators). The next section examines the basic research designs used in response-style research.

RESEARCH DESIGNS

Table 1.1 in Chapter 1 (this volume), presents a succinct review of basic research designs and describes their comparative strengths and limitations. The large majority of studies are devoted to the simulation design, which uses analogue research to maximize internal validity. The remaining designs use quasi-experimental methods and examine aspects of external validity with varying degrees of success. Across all designs, a critical issue is the design's ability to establish discriminant validity using the most clinically relevant comparisons.

Two competing dimensions, important in reviewing these designs, are *clinical relevance* and *experimental rigor.* In certain respects, these dimensions are inversely related, so that it is often infeasible to achieve high levels of clinical relevance and experimental rigor within the same study. However, exceptions may occur, particularly when known-groups comparisons are augmented with sophisticated laboratory procedures (e.g., the use of hair analysis to verify denied substance abuse). Despite the likely trade-off between relevance and rigor, most research on dissimulation could be improved on one or both of these dimensions. Thus an objective of this section is to review current research designs and to offer recommendations with respect to both clinical relevance and experimental rigor.

Simulation Research

The vast majority of response-style research relies on simulation designs. Therefore, this chapter focuses on simulation studies, beginning with basic design issues.

Basic Design Issues

Simulation research is a subset of analogue research that includes relevant comparison samples. For example, feigning research must include clinical samples composed of individuals with genuine mental disorders and no evidence of feigning. The bulk of feigning studies use nonclinical participants who are randomly assigned to control groups (i.e., honest or standard conditions) and are compared with (1) one or more experimental groups with directions to simulate and (2) clinical samples of convenience. Within the experimental design, simulators and controls are compared; however, these results have only marginal relevance to malingering because they do not differentiate feigned from genuine disorders. In contrast, the quasi-experimental comparison of feigners to genuine patients provides the critical clinical data.

Analogue feigning research that does not include the relevant comparison groups is fatally flawed and should not be published. In particular, the exclusive use of student samples to study feigning produces confounded results. Do differences between simulators and nonclinical controls represent the effects of feigning, as the investigators desire? Alternatively, would these differences simply evaporate if simulators were compared with genuine patients? Because researchers have no data with which to address competing hypotheses, these findings are hopelessly confounded.

An instructive example regarding the dangers of omitting clinical samples is illustrated by the MMPI-2 F scale. Its items were selected based on infrequency of endorsement by *normative* and not *clinical* samples (i.e., a quasi-

rare strategy; see Chapter 2, this volume). Predictably, many F items are commonly endorsed by both feigners and genuine patients. For genuine diagnostic groups, average F scale elevations are 80.10 for schizophrenia and 86.31 for posttraumatic stress disorder (PTSD; see Rogers, Sewell, Martin, & Vitacco, 2003). For genuine patients one standard deviation (*SD*) above average, these elevations easily exceed 100T.

Researchers are tempted to rely only on college samples simply because of the ease of data collection. Ease of research at the expense of clinically relevant research is unwarranted. Recently, investigators have attempted to identify "clinical" groups in college populations. Again, the justification appears to be more expediency than experimental rigor. Although many students may experience mood (e.g., depression) and trauma-related (e.g., PTSD) symptoms, questions remain about the severity of these symptoms and their impact on day-to-day functioning. Studies relying solely on self-report measures (e.g., the PAI and Trauma Symptom Inventory [TSI]) may be using extrapolated diagnoses (see Chapter 18, this volume) as a poor proxy for accurate diagnosis. When structured interviews are used to confirm diagnoses, researchers must still grapple with their generalizability to more impaired clinical groups. Their interpretations and conclusions should still be confined to higher functioning clients, who are actively involved in pursuing long-term goals (e.g., college education). In contrast, forensic considerations of malingering often address different populations with severe symptoms and extensive impairment.

Elements of Simulation Research

Simulation studies share common elements that include instructions, preparation, incentives, standardization of measures, and manipulation checks (see Table 24.1). Each element is examined separately with an emphasis on improving the quality of response-style research.

Instructions

The clinical utility of simulation studies depends on the effectiveness of their experimental conditions to induce participants to "act as if" this condition were actually true (i.e., intrinsically motivated with real-world consequences). Efforts to achieve these related goals

TABLE 24.1. Checklist for Simulation Designs in the Evaluation of Response Styles

1. Relevant comparisons
   - ☐ Feigning vs. genuinely disordered?
   - ☐ Defensiveness vs. absence of mental disorders?
   - ☐ Impression management vs. socially adept?

2. Instructions for experimental conditions
   - ☐ Clear and comprehensible?
   - ☐ Sufficiently specific as to mirror real-world applications?
   - ☐ Familiar context with which participants may have had some experience?
   - ☐ Challenge participants as a method of motivation?
   - ☐ Underscore relevance as a method of motivation?
   - ☐ Caution about believable presentation?

3. Coaching
   - ☐ Inclusion of detection-based coaching?
   - ☐ Comorbidity vs. single disorder?

4. Incentives
   - ☐ Positive incentives for successful simulation?
   - ☐ Negative incentives for failed simulation?
   - ☐ Loss of credibility for failed simulation?

5. Optional considerations
   - ☐ Affective involvement: fear of consequences?
   - ☐ Affective involvement: anticipated pleasures for unwarranted gains?
   - ☐ Stereotypes about simulators?

are typically reduced to several written paragraphs that focus more on communication than involvement. In general, I would argue that experimental instructions should be improved. They need to invest participants with a sense of personal involvement (e.g., "Will *I* succeed or fail?") and their own beliefs about the study's relevance (e.g., containment of *my* rising insurance premiums because of bogus claims). An interesting empirical question is whether videotaped instructions might be more effective at involving participants, as contrasted to the relatively sterile written format.

Rogers and Cruise (1998) identified six basic elements that must be considered in construction of experimental instructions with respect to dissimulation. Additional elements (e.g., affective investment and stereotypes) should also be considered. This section examines each element separately.

Comprehensibility. The overriding issue is whether participants have a clear understanding of what is expected of them. Beyond verbal recall, can they grasp the true nature of the task and their role? Comprehension requires clear, simply written declarative sentences written at an easy reading level. Computer-based tools can assist in this endeavor. The WordPerfect program has both Flesch–Kincaid reading levels and estimates of sentence complexity. In contrast to WordPerfect, Microsoft Word has a truncated Flesch–Kincaid (i.e., ≤ grade 12; see DuBay, 2004).

Specificity. The instructions must be sufficiently explicit so that researchers will be able to make a meaningful interpretation of the resulting data. Of course, circumstances do occur in which a proportion of persons engage in a global response style (e.g., denial of all personal faults in contested child custody cases). In such cases, more global instructions may parallel real-world applications. With highly specific instructions, care must be taken so that participants can understand complex instructions and competently apply them in their research participation.

An important consideration in terms of external validity is whether researchers should ask participants to either feign or minimize a particular disorder. Some malingered disorders, such as feigned PTSD, may have specific benefits to malingerers (e.g., establishing proximate cause in personal injury cases or providing extended veterans' benefits). Such investigations are clearly warranted. In other cases, the feigning or denial of a particular disorder may be advantageous if a nonspecific feigning condition is also included. Specific disorders allow researchers to test whether the consideration of a particular disorder substantially affects the simulated condition.

Context. As part of an experimental design, most studies randomly assign participants to specific experimental conditions without considering the relevance of the assigned context to the individual participants. An alternative is to ask participants to choose which context or scenario they prefer in an effort to increase their investment in the simulation (see Elhai et al., 2005). However, this option violates the random assignment requirement of experimental designs.

Nearly all response styles occur in a specific context. As common examples, impression management is common among job applicants, and malingering is sometimes observed in disability cases. For purposes of external validity, specific contexts should be provided in simulation studies.

Rogers and Cruise (1998) provide a compelling argument that simulators should have some familiarity with the context being simulated. As a far-fetched analogy, researchers could never expect participants to effectively simulate a role in an entirely different culture (e.g., Inuit) from their own. It may be equally implausible to ask law-abiding college students to simulate an incarcerated murderer attempting to feign insanity as a legal defense. Researchers may wish to pilot-test their scenarios or contexts to ensure that participants have some familiarity. Alternatively, post hoc analyses may assist in systematically testing whether knowledge or experience affects the ability to effectively simulate.

Motivation and Incentives. Data from research participants may have limited generalizability

simply because these individuals trivialized their involvement as a necessary chore (e.g., extra credit for routine participation). Many simulation studies adopt a rather formulaic approach to motivation by simply offering nominal incentives and naively assuming that participants will be intrinsically motivated to perform their best. I would argue that investigators should use multiple methods in an effort to approximate real-world motivations. These methods include challenge, relevance, and positive and negative incentives (see Table 24.1).

One potentially useful approach is to *challenge* participants: "Can you beat the test?" or "Do you think you are *good enough* to beat the test?" This challenge can also be expressed in terms of success and failure:

> Most persons just aren't good enough to succeed. They fail at this task of ____ (e.g., feigning PTSD). They lack the skill and motivation to succeed. We are looking for those few who are willing to take the challenge. Can you handle it?

The goal is ego involvement. In real-world applications, persons are fully invested in the process and its outcome. Job applicants for a highly desirable position realize that only the "best" candidate will be offered the position. Nothing is gained by halfhearted efforts at simulation.

Participants may also be motivated if they understand the *relevance* of the research to their lives and the lives of their families. For example, spiraling insurance costs with decreased health care benefits are fueled, in part, by bogus and unnecessary claims. As a result, their parents may receive marginal or even substandard health care. As participants, do they want to try to help?

Motivation, while taking into account the relevance of the simulation task, must also grapple with external incentives that are frequently present in applied settings. For the job applicant, the incentive is readily apparent and heartfelt. How can studies of dissimulation mirror the importance and immediacy of securing a desirable position? Likewise, parents in child custody evaluations may dramatically limit their self-disclosure and attempt to enhance their social desirability in an effort to secure favorable custody decisions. The motivation to maintain one's family may well exceed any incentive available to researchers. Two aspects of incentives must be differentiated: the *type* of incentive and the *magnitude* of the incentive. Researchers are typically limited on both dimensions.

Credibility and the assumed motivation to appear credible are posited as powerful incentives for actual simulators. Not only is the loss of credibility likely to be associated with failure to achieve the goals of dissimulation, but this loss may also result in very negative social consequences. For example, a patient with borderline personality disorder who feigns a bogus suicide attempt (e.g., no drugs were ingested in an "overdose") not only loses the immediate goal (e.g., hospitalization and medical attention) but also may jeopardize future treatment, funding associated with disability status, and credibility among health care professionals and fellow patients. A criminal defendant feigning insanity places his or her future, if not life, at risk, as an insanity plea includes an admission of the crime.

Can research capture the negative social consequences of a bungled dissimulation? Designs might include some form of public disapproval (e.g., publishing failed attempts by research participants; see Patrick & Iacono, 1989). Rogers and Cruise (1998) found that the simulators were significantly influenced by the inclusion of negative consequences in experimental instructions. For external validity, simulation research should include both positive and negative incentives, because detected (i.e., "failed") simulation is likely to have severe consequences to the simulator.

Believability. More recent dissimulation research typically includes an admonition to the participants to make their presentations believable. Participants commonly are warned that the test or procedure has indicators of dissimulation. Thus the task becomes clearly defined: Dissimulation must be sufficiently believable to elude detection. In large-scale malingering research on the TSI, Elhai and colleagues (2007) found that cautionary instructions improved performance on both feigning and clinical scales.

Preparation and Participation

Studies on dissimulation are often limited in their clinical usefulness by minimal levels of preparation and questionable commitment by research participants. Persons are rarely given any preparation time or opportunities to plan

their strategy of deception. However, unstructured time will not necessarily be used for preparation. Researchers should structure this time so that participants are actively involved in preparation. They may offer choices about what materials could be reviewed and their potential value to the experimental condition. The provision of preparation materials may enhance participants' overall performance, including both their level of involvement and their effectiveness.

Preparation materials must be easy to comprehend and highly pertinent to the dissimulation task. For instance, presenting participants with unedited sections of DSM-IV is unlikely to enhance their understanding of a feigned disorder. Indeed, reading unfamiliar technical terms about sophisticated psychological constructs may lead to frustration and disaffection from the study's objectives. A recent innovation is to evaluate participants immediately following the preparation period regarding their understanding of the supplied materials. This testing helps to consolidate learned material and serves as a manipulation check for those with insufficient comprehension.

The level of participation by clinicians is often limited to the interpretation of isolated test data. Computer-based research could be used so that clinicians could request test data relevant to response styles and diagnoses. The sequential effects of additional data could be evaluated with reference to accuracy and confidence. An important consideration would be whether the presence of convergent data would lead to overconfidence and a confirmatory bias in estimations of deception (DePaulo, Charlton, Cooper, Lindsay, & Muhlenbruck, 1997).

Coaching

Coaching is an element of preparation. I have purposefully set coaching apart because of its importance to dissimulation. Coaching involves educating simulators to facilitate their avoidance of detection. As noted by Rogers, Bagby, and Chakraborty (1993), the unspoken assumption of most dissimulation research is that malingerers and defensive persons will *not* prepare and will remain naive to the purposes of testing. This assumption is untenable for two reasons. First, persons being evaluated must give informed consent based on the nature and goals of the evaluation. Second, these same persons have easy access to Internet resources and written materials that describe psychological tests, including descriptions of validity scales.

Two distinct procedures have been employed in coaching studies; they inform participants about either (1) mental disorders or other conditions to be simulated or (2) detection strategies. More commonly, studies inform about specific disorders and then administer standardized measures, such as multiscale inventories. Efforts at *disorder-based coaching* appear misguided because they are largely irrelevant to the assessment of response styles:

1. Many measures, such as multiscale inventories, are imprecise for diagnostic purposes. Therefore, feigners do *not* need to simulate a specific MMPI-2 2-point code to be considered as genuine patients with major depression. Hence, this type of coaching is mainly irrelevant.

2. Comorbidity is very common and can complicate the assessment of response styles (Elhai et al., 2007). Informing simulators about a single disorder completely omits issues of comorbidity.

3. Presentation of disorder-based coaching may actually mislead research participants. They can become preoccupied with creating a genuine disorder (e.g., clinical scales) rather than focusing on the primary task of avoiding detection on response-style scales (e.g., validity scales).

Predictably, studies have consistently found that the provision of irrelevant information (i.e., disorder-based coaching) has little or no effect on participants' ability to successfully simulate.

Researchers need to move away from the irrelevance of disorder-based coaching and embrace the more germane *detection-based coaching*. Rogers, Dolmetsch, and Cavanaugh (1983) compared the approaches and demonstrated the relevance and superiority of detection-based coaching.

Detection-based coaching informs participants in straightforward language about the use of detection strategies for the evaluation of response styles. This form of coaching assumes that actual malingerers will closely examine the purpose of psychological measures and attend to response-style measures, such as validity scales. Although some researchers might argue that this assumption is too stringent, the availability of Internet resources and malingering coaches suggests that such rigor is warranted. As an illustration of detection-based coaching, participants might be informed of the following: "The test has several indicators to identify persons faking disorders. For example, fakers sometimes fail very simple items that most brain-injured persons can successfully complete" (i.e., the floor effect). Current research on detection-based coaching emphasizes malingering. An interesting question is whether these findings generalize to defensiveness and impression management with the provision of relevant information on detection strategies.

Foiling Detection Strategies

A critical issue is whether detection strategies can remain professional secrets. This issue is especially important for those detection strategies that are easily neutralized by countermeasures. For example, the improbable-symptom strategy might be neutralized by simply avoiding far-fetched or fantastic symptoms. In contrast, the symptom-combination strategy would be difficult to foil based on the complexity of the task and the need for specialized knowledge. In the development of response-style measures, researchers should avoid easily foiled detection strategies.

An important alternative to easily foiled simple secrets (e.g., floor-effect detection strategy) and their vulnerability to coaching is the development of *intricate strategies*. Intricate strategies often involve the combination of multiple strategies. Rogers (1997b, p. 403) presented the following example:

> Please do your very best job on this test. For the test to be accurate, you have to try your best. *Warning:* Every now and then, someone tries to fool the test. They pretend to have problems in thinking that they really don't have. The test has safeguards against faking. First, the test keeps track of the answers you get wrong to see if they are easy items or hard items. Second, the test keeps track of how many seconds you use on items. If you take the same amount of time on easy and hard items, you are not trying your best. Third, the test looks at your wrong answers to see if you make the same kind of mistakes as people that really have problems.

This caution also addresses three additional safeguards for detecting feigned cognitive impairment (see Bender & Rogers, 2004).

What happens when simulators are informed proactively about intricate detection strategies? Bender and Rogers (2004) tested this question using the Test of Cognitive Abilities (TOCA; Rogers, 1996). Unlike with simple detection-based coaching, simulators appear to be unable to capitalize on this information and lower their scores on response-style measures to avoid detection. On the contrary, coached simulators did *slightly worse* than uncoached simulators. For example, coached simulators were 21% higher than uncoached simulators on the magnitude-of-error detection strategy.

The multiple tasks ask the simulator to consider two (or possibly more) detection strategies simultaneously. These strategies require the simulator to attempt to accommodate seemingly incompatible concepts. Attempts to focus on item difficulty (i.e., performance curve strategy) and plausibly incorrect responses (i.e., magnitude of error) may sacrifice response time and the product of response time × performance curve.

The idea of publicized intricate strategies was first described more than a decade ago. Unfortunately, research has been slow to test the effectiveness of this approach. Instead, simulation research continues to favor simple detection strategies based on the implicit, and likely naive, hope that feigners will remain uninformed. With burgeoning Internet resources, studies of publicized intricate strategies should become a high priority for malingering and other response styles.

Affective Involvement

Sporer and Schwandt (2006) suggest that different affective responses are likely to influence simulators' verbal and nonverbal presentations. They found differences between fear and guilt for deceptive persons. To my knowledge, affective involvement has not been considered in studies of specific response styles. In the consideration of malingering, studies are needed that focus on at least two general emotional responses: greed-based pleasure and fear. Analogous to gambling (e.g., decision affect theory; Mellers, Schwartz, & Ritov, 1999) and the deceptive goal of "duping delight," some malingerers are likely to experience pleasure at their anticipated and unwarranted gains. Alternatively, some malingerers may be motivated primarily by fear. In the criminal arena, this fear may correspond to a classic

avoidance–avoidance decision, with malingerers fearing the likely consequences if they do *not* feign (e.g., lengthy incarceration) or if they feign unsuccessfully (e.g., punitive actions as a result of being caught). Affective involvement represents a new and potentially important consideration in assessing response-style measures via simulation designs. Use of affective involvement may help to develop and refine detection strategies.

Response-Style Stereotypes

Simulation studies using response-style research typically ask participants to comply with experimental instructions and to provide their own convincing performances. A closely related method would be to ask participants to respond as a *typical* person in that experimental condition would. Using feigned mental disorders as an example, participants could be asked to respond as most malingerers would do. The purpose of these latter instructions would be to identify malingering stereotypes. Research using within-subjects designs could compare participants' own feigned performances with their stereotypical patterns. If successful, a new detection strategy might be developed based on response-style stereotypes.

Incentives

Rogers, Harrell, and Liff (1993) reviewed the role of incentives in malingering research. They found that few studies have directly compared the effect of incentives on simulators' performances. An unexpected finding by Wilhelm, Franzen, Grinvalds, and Dews (1991) was that undergraduates produced more extreme scores on several cognitive measures when offered a $20 incentive than did those participants without an incentive. Logically, the extremeness of scores increased the likelihood of detection. In other words, the desire for the award apparently increased the *motivation* to feign, possibly at the expense of believability.

Recent research on the magnitude of incentives has produced equivocal results. Shum, O'Gorman, and Alpar (2004) found that incentives ($20) produced more credible performances than no incentives, although classification rates remained largely unaffected. Elhai and colleagues (2007) attempted to provide higher incentives ($40 to $50) but made them available to only the top three performers in each group. When given instructions to be believable, the addition of the larger incentive appeared to increase motivation ($d = .47$; see Elhai et al., 2007, Table 1); however, its corresponding effect on lowering the TSI Atypical Presentation (ATP) elevation was modest ($d = .19$; see Table 2). The daunting challenge for simulation designs is provide rewards that approximate real-world incentives. Researchers have practical and ethical constraints on their abilities to offer large monetary incentives. Continued research is needed to evaluate competing hypotheses:

1. Are simulators more careful and potentially less detectable when incentives are increased?
2. Does simulators' increased motivation with larger incentives magnify their efforts to be impaired, thereby making them more detectable?

The effects of incentives on defensiveness remain unexplored. As noted previously, many of the potential rewards (e.g., securing a favorable position or custody of one's children) cannot be paralleled in dissimulation research. An interesting research possibility would be to assess the effects of incentives on defensiveness in comparison with social desirability and impression management. For example, job applicants attempting to make a favorable impression may be more detectable on measures of social desirability than defensiveness.

The previous discussion of motivation provides a practical overview of incentives and their potential role in dissimulation research. The following elements should be considered:

Magnitude of the Incentive

Simply put, is the incentive really an incentive? If the goal of winning is emphasized, then even symbolic rewards may suffice. Financially successful persons can become highly motivated by negligible rewards (e.g., penny poker) that have only symbolic value (e.g., "best" gambler). On the other hand, research sites do exist in which small monetary incentives are likely to represent a tangible reward. For example, correctional settings typically reimburse inmates at a nominal rate. In such settings, even a small $10.00 incentive may equal a week's pay.

Type of Incentive

Monetary incentives are the most easily implemented rewards in most research settings. Would offering nonmonetary rewards either (1) produce different results or (2) improve the external validity of the results? For example, would a weekend getaway at a nice hotel more closely approximate the "better life" sought in personal injury fraud than the typical financial incentive?

Probability of the Incentive

Dissimulation research is typically underfunded in terms of financial incentives. Although some researchers offer very modest incentives (e.g., $5.00) to each simulator, other investigators use a selection procedure (lottery system or "best" simulator) to provide more substantial rewards (e.g., $50.00 to $100.00) to a very small number of simulators. We simply do not know which alternative (high probability of a low incentive or low probability of a high incentive) provides the greater motivation.

Negative Incentives

A major omission in most simulation research is the use of any negative incentives. In real-world applications, simulators have (1) something to gain from successful deceptions and (2) something to lose from failed (i.e., detected) deceptions. Unfortunately, simulation studies tend to focus only on positive incentives at the expense of external validity. As an example of a simple design, researchers could offer credit simply for their participation in a series of studies. The credit would be "taken away" if the participants were detected. Naturally, informed consent would have to delineate these conditions, especially if more credit could be lost than gained from participation. A variation of this design with fewer ethical constraints would be research whereby participants select for themselves different conditions, ranging from high risk–high gain to low risk–low gain.

Rogers and Cruise (1998) studied the effects of negative incentives. They motivated student simulators by informing them that the names of failed simulators would be posted on the departmental bulletin boards. Simulators in the negative-incentive condition were more focused on their task of feigned depression and produced fewer irrelevant symptoms. Clearly, negative incentives should be considered as a core element for all response-style research. Using the Rogers and Cruise paradigm, possible ethical problems can be largely circumvented by posting fictitious names, thereby minimizing the potential discomfort to participants in the failed simulation group.

Manipulation Checks

Manipulation checks can be used to ensure that participants understood and complied with the experimental instructions. Three related elements must be considered: *recall, comprehension,* and *reported compliance.* More specifically, researchers must ascertain whether the participants remembered the instructions and understood what they meant. Although questions about compliance are vulnerable to social desirability, some effort should be made to determine the extent to which participants complied with the instructions. As a corollary to comprehension, researchers may also wish to discern the *relevance* of the instructions. If the instructions involve circumstances or psychological conditions completely alien to the participant, his or her performance is likely compromised. The manipulation check can also be applied to preparation materials supplied to research participants. As with the instructions, investigators can assess participants' recall and comprehension of these materials. If materials are not remembered or adequately understood, then this component of the experimental condition is compromised. As noted previously, some researchers test adequate knowledge immediately following the review of the preparation materials.

Beyond manipulation checks per se, post hoc questions can address (1) motivation to succeed and (2) limits on their participation (see Table 24.1). Participants' motivation may be affected by the incentive and the strength of their desire (depending on the instructions) to appear credible and elude detection. Other factors possibly limit involvement in the study. Participants may believe that they were unable to suppress their "true" selves or may have felt less capable of doing so for moral reasons (e.g., it is immoral to deceive; a good liar is a bad person) or because of psychological problems (e.g., emotional interference with following the instructions) or distrust of the experimenter (e.g., belief that the results will reflect negatively on the participant).

Researchers have also surveyed participants' beliefs about their success at dissimulation. Results have varied across studies. For example, Kropp (1992) found that 90% of simulators on the Structured Interview of Reported Symptoms (SIRS) believed they were successful; this belief was unrelated to their ability to elude detection. In contrast, Gothard (1993) found that 24% believed they had successfully feigned on the SIRS; again, the belief was unrelated to the performance. The relationship between perceived success and demonstrated effectiveness at detecting dissimulation deserves formal investigation across response styles and clinical domains.

Much more attention should be paid to the debriefing phase of dissimulation studies. Table 24.2 provides an elaborate model of manipulation checks that might serve to standardize specific inquiries. Researchers will need to be selective in their choice of what elements to include, although recall, comprehension, and reported compliance are essential. Moreover, some attention should be paid to participants' motivation to succeed and limits on their involvement.

Further Applications of Simulation Studies

Simulation studies of social desirability and defensiveness have typically been conducted with less care methodologically than corresponding research on malingering. Many studies have not included cautionary instructions on believability with information about the presence of scales to detect either social desirability or defensiveness. In addition, researchers apparently have assumed that participants would not need to be coached regarding the simulation of adjustment. Although this supposition probably has some justification in studies of nonclinical samples, it appears less defensible for persons with either severe disorders or chronic impairment. Moreover, malingering research clearly indicates that knowledge of detection strategies is a key element of successful feigning. Given this important finding, coached studies with knowledge of detection strategies clearly are needed for defensiveness and social desirability.

A second, virtually unexplored facet of simulation research is the interpretability of dissimulated results. For example, can we assume that a defensive person has psychological prob-

TABLE 24.2. An Overview of Manipulation Checks in Simulation Research

Facets of the research	Example questions
A. Instructional sets	
1. Recall of instructions	What were you told to do? What were your instructions?
2. Comprehension of instructions	What do these instructions mean to you?
3. Compliance with instructions	Some people always do what they are told whereas others prefer to improvise. . . . Which do you prefer? No one is perfect; what percentage of the time did you carefully follow instructions?
4. Relevance of the instructions	Have you ever been faced with a situation like the one described in the instructions? Could you relate to this scenario? Of course this was just an experiment; could you imagine yourself doing what you were asked to do if the situation warranted it?
B. Preparation	
1. Preparation effort	What did you do during the preparation time?
2. Knowledge of preparation materials	What do you remember from the preparation materials?
3. Relevance of preparation materials	How did the preparation materials help you?
C. Motivation to succeed	
1. Importance of the incentive	How hard did you try because you were challenged to succeed? . . . informed about its relevance?
2. Magnitude of the incentive	How much effort did you put forth? What would it take for you to put forward your very best effort?
3. Positive vs. negative incentives	What motivated you more: the reward (e.g., research credit) or fear of failure (e.g., posting of failed simulators)?
4. Detection of dissimulation	Were you aware that there were items on the _____ [name of test] designed to trip you up? Can you give us any specific examples?
D. Limits to participation	
1. Self-disclosure	Despite your efforts to appear different than you actually are, how much of the real you showed through?
2. Morality	Were there any moral or ethical reasons why you didn't participate fully in the study? What were they?
3. Emotional interference	Sometimes when people are going through a difficult time, they find it hard to really participate; did this happen to you?
4. Fear of success	Were you concerned that if you succeeded at fooling the test, this might mean that you are good at deceiving others?
5. Purpose of the study	Were you worried that the purpose of the study was something different from what you were told?
E. Other issues associated with deception	
1. Perceived success	How successful were you at fooling the _____ [name of test]?
2. Experience with dissimulation	How good are you at fooling others?
3. Types of deception	Some persons are better at hiding their feelings whereas others do a better job at keeping their past private; which fits you?

lems? If so, what are they? By the same token, can we conclude anything about a malingerer besides the simple fact that he or she is feigning? A frightening prospect is the assumption of mutual exclusivity: that the presence of feigning precludes a mental disorder (Rogers, 1984b). One solution is the development of correction formulas.

Earlier editions of this book have challenged response-style researchers to investigate methods for evaluating what is hidden by examinees. This challenge has gone largely unheeded. Critical needs for correction methods are twofold:

1. What genuine disorders are obscured by malingering?
2. What significant psychopathology is being obscured by defensiveness?

McKinley, Hathaway, and Meehl (1948) developed for the MMPI a "K-correction" formula to approximate the degree of impairment, taking into account the patient's degree of defensiveness. Now, more than four decades later, replication studies have yet to appear, although thousands of MMPI K-corrected profiles continue to be interpreted each year. Research is also needed to evaluate the merits of an F-correction to determine genuine disorders among those feigning.

What methods could be used to establish correction formulas? As an initial approach, the within-subjects simulation design appears well suited for the development of correction formulas. For malingering, genuine patients could be administered a measure such as the MMPI-2 under both standard and feigning instructions. For general diagnostic groups (e.g., samples with psychotic or mood disorders), specialized scales could be developed via empirical validation for the purposes of identifying genuine disorders among feigning patients. Naturally, such correction scales would require extensive cross-validation.

Work by Morey and his colleagues (see Hopwood, Morey, Rogers & Sewell, 2007) developed a different correction method for the PAI. First, Morey (2003) attempted to distinguish between two types of negative distortions: patients with a pessimistic overly pathologized response set and feigners. Because Negative Impression Management (NIM) is correlated with PAI clinical scales, he theorized that it would measure overly pathologized responses. In contrast, he observed that the

Rogers Discriminant Function (RDF; Rogers, Sewell, Morey, & Ustad, 1996) was highly effective at the classification of feigning but uncorrelated with PAI scales. Therefore, he categorized NIM-only elevations as overly pathologized responses and NIM-plus-RDF elevations as feigning.

Because NIM is correlated with clinical scales, Morey (1999) used different NIM scores to predict likely clinical scale elevations via simple linear regression. These NIM-predicted clinical elevations established the expected clinical scale scores. For individual cases, discrepancies between actual and NIM-predicted clinical elevations can be interpretable. Take the example of Depression being much higher than the NIM-predicted score; two different interpretations can be rendered:

- *Obscured depression.* When only NIM is elevated, a higher than predicted score is interpreted as genuine depression that may be obscured by the overly pathologized response set.
- *Feigned depression.* When RDF is also elevated, the higher than predicted score is interpreted as the examinee's attempt to appear depressed.

Hopwood and colleagues (2007) reanalyzed extensive data sets for Rogers, Ornduff, and Sewell (1993) and Rogers, Sewell, and colleagues (1996) to see whether discrepancy scores (actual vs. NIM-predicted) would be greatest for specific disorders being simulated (depression, generalized anxiety, and schizophrenia) than for other disorders. They found that simulators produced much greater discrepancy scores ($M = 13.94$) than genuine patients ($M = 6.51$) on the targeted PAI clinical scales.

The Hopwood and colleagues (2007) study suggests that new avenues can and should be explored in the development of correction methods. To simply conclude that a test is "invalid" is less than optimal. Original MMPI research and the Hopwood and colleagues approach should stimulate additional studies using these and alternative methods.

Most methodological improvements in simulation research focus primarily on improving its clinical relevance and overall generalizability. Current sampling techniques involve random samples of usually nonpsychiatric participants in both experimental and control groups.

This design can be augmented by the use of patients with mental disorders in experimental, control, and comparison groups. This modification would allow dissimulation research to address two important considerations: (1) How effectively can participants with mental disorders dissimulate? and (2) Do clinical decision rules work effectively for simulators with mental disorders?

Application of Simulation Design to Deception Research

Deception research, as illustrated by Sporer and Schwandt (2006, 2007), often uses simulation designs with specific attention to moderating variables. These studies are distinguished by their sophisticated designs. However, they are often limited in their clinical utility. For example, studies of paralinguistic cues require time-intensive coding of specific behaviors. Because of needed time and resources, this methodology is impractical for clinical assessments or other professional applications. The purpose of this brief section is twofold. First, deception studies can provide useful ideas for more applied research. Second, deception research should learn from the clinical literature how to develop efficient and effective methods for response-style appraisals.

The value of deception research is exemplified in the opening section of this chapter, which critically examines the linkage between theory, research, and practice. Sporer and Schwandt's meta-analyses are highlighted because they present multiple theories that are operationalized and rigorously tested. As a further example that was applied to work performance, Li and Bagger (2006) consider whether social desirability is best conceptualized as a single construct or whether it should be disaggregated into impression management and self-deception, in line with Paulhus's (1998) formulation. Although correlated with certain personality constructs, neither of the two constructs appeared particularly useful in predicting work performance (M $rs \leq .10$).

DePaulo and colleagues (1997) provided a critical examination of the relationship between accuracy and confidence in the detection of deception. Their work has important implications for the assessment of specific response styles. For example, they reviewed studies demonstrating that evaluators are more confident in their detection abilities based on the nature of the relationship. Applying this finding to professional practice, a testable hypothesis is whether the extensiveness of the assessment leads to unwarranted confidence in conclusions regarding malingering and defensiveness. DePaulo and colleagues also found that nonprofessionals had a "truthfulness bias" in assuming that most communications were honest, irrespective of their veracity. What biases do clinicians have regarding honesty, malingering, and defensiveness? How do these biases affect their accuracy?

The clinical relevance of deception research could be easily improved without substantively affecting its experimental rigor. The current practice of using only nonclinical participants could be augmented with clinical samples in both honest and deceptive conditions. Moreover, experimental conditions could include trained persons, such as mental health professionals and persons coached in dissimulation. These modifications would allow researchers to address more closely the applicability of research findings to clinical settings.

Known-Groups Comparisons

Known-groups comparisons are composed of two discrete and independent phases: (1) establishment of criterion groups (e.g., bona fide patients and malingerers) and (2) systematic analysis of similarities and dissimilarities between criterion groups. The primary challenge of known-groups comparisons is the first phase, namely, the reliable and accurate classification of criterion groups. Because of this challenge, such research is relatively rare in dissimulation studies.

Employment of known-groups comparisons addresses fully the clinical relevance of dissimulation research. First, the research typically is conducted in clinical or other professional settings in which dissimulation is expected to occur. Second and more important, the persons engaging in dissimulation are doing so for real-world reasons. The generalizability of their findings, at least to a portion of dissimulating persons, is well established; they obviously have the necessary background, antecedent events, personality variables, and motivation to participate in dissimulation. As with any design, researchers must consider the representativeness of one dissimulating sample to the total population of dissimulating persons. Although the combination of different samples dramatically improves the generalizability of known-groups comparisons, these investigations are limited to the unsuccessful (i.e., detected) persons.

The critical task of establishing criterion groups is generally reserved for highly trained experts (e.g., forensic psychologists and psychiatrists) and based on full evaluations (see, e.g., Viglione, Fals-Stewart, & Moxham, 1995). As an alternative, measures with stable cut scores and high levels of classification are sometimes used as a "gold standard" in known-groups comparisons. As outlined in Chapter 18 in this volume, the SIRS has been widely used in known-groups comparisons to establish independent groups. Its classification of feigned mental disorders has a very low false-positive rate. The SIRS is also accurate for classifying genuine patients when the indeterminate group is removed.

Known-groups comparisons must be distinguished from two other research designs that are examined in subsequent sections of this chapter:

1. Differential prevalence designs compare two samples, of which one sample is assumed to engage in the specific response style more frequently than the other. In the context of malingering, some researchers have assumed that persons engaged in litigation in a sample of convenience are more likely to be malingering than other clinical samples. However, both the identification of malingerers and the overall prevalence of malingering are not even attempted in research using differential prevalence designs. Therefore, its effectiveness cannot be established.

2. Bootstrapping designs use conservative decision rules, based on an independent measure or measures, to establish groups with a high probability of representing different criterion groups. Such use of decision rules must recognize the variability of cut scores and take into account the standard error of measurement.

Known-groups comparisons can be fundamentally flawed by use of questionable external criteria. This problem is exemplified by the use of questionable criteria or questionable experts:

• *Questionable criteria.* Hankins, Barnard, and Robbins (1993) adopted a very question-

able standard for the determination of malingering; *any* bogus symptom was deemed sufficient.

• *Questionable experts.* Edens, Poythress, and Watkins-Clay (2007) provided prison psychiatrists with rudimentary training and then considered them to be malingering experts. As described in Chapter 18 (this volume), they relied predominantly on an ineffective indicator of feigning (i.e., inconsistency) and produced poor results when compared with the SIRS.

The application of known-groups comparisons to individual response styles deserves specific comments. For easy reference, I have summarized each response style in the following paragraphs.

• *Malingering.* An avoidable problem with malingering research is the use of DSM indices to establish criterion groups. As noted in DSM-IV (American Psychiatric Association, 2000, p. 739), these indices are intended as a threshold model (i.e., "strongly suspected") and not a clinical decision model. The sole effort (Rogers, 1990b) to implement this threshold model resulted in very poor classification rates.

• *Deception.* A major weakness of polygraph research is the absence of an independent criterion for establishing deception. Most polygraph studies rely on the examiner, who administers the polygraph to extract a confession, which is then used to validate the efficacy of that procedure (Rogers, 1987). Such nonindependence unnecessarily confounds research findings on polygraph techniques.

• *Denied substance abuse.* A gold standard does exist for denied drug use, namely hair analysis. The highly reliable classification can be employed for both current (i.e., past month) and longitudinal (e.g., past year) substance abuse. As of yet, hair analysis has not been used in known-groups comparisons for denied or minimized drug abuse on psychological measures.

• *General defensiveness.* Researchers often have missed opportunities for known-groups comparisons with persons who minimize psychological problems. Circumstances occur in which documented evidence of denied psychopathology is available. Examples include mental health records in child custody determinations and review hearings for the release of involuntary patients. For child custody cases, a key issue is distinguishing relatively healthy parents engaging in impression management from those with significant psychopathology that may affect their parenting abilities. Known-groups comparisons have been virtually ignored for general defensiveness; this neglect should be remedied.

• *Defensiveness among sex offenders.* Studies have demonstrated that a high proportion of patients with paraphilias consciously minimize their aberrant sexual interests and activities (see Lanyon & Thomas, Chapter 17, this volume; see also Rogers & Dickey, 1991). Plethysmographic procedures have been somewhat useful in identifying comparative arousal patterns to a variety of erotic and aggressive stimuli. However, the relationship of these arousal patterns to subsequent sexual behavior requires further investigation. It is unclear, for example, whether individuals who have never engaged in deviant sexual behavior exist in the normal population, regardless of any anomalous phallometric results or unusual sexual interests they might have. More extensive work on nonreferred populations may be useful in establishing this relationship.

Research is also needed on laboratory methods to delineate their stability in a test–retest paradigm for clinical and nonclinical participants. Many clinicians treating sex offenders believe that the effectiveness of penile plethysmography as an assessment method attenuates over subsequent administrations. Of course, an alternative explanation is that treatment is successful. This conundrum could be explored by dividing patients with paraphilias into two groups, responsive and nonresponsive to treatment, and testing these two groups with the same or novel stimuli.

In summary, known-groups comparisons can provide unparalleled external validity when properly applied to response styles. Practitioners bear the responsibility of carefully reviewing design issues to avoid studies using slipshod methods based more on expediency than experimental rigor. The combination of known-groups comparisons (external validity) with simulation studies (internal validity) provides the strongest validation of response-style measures. The next section addresses differential prevalence designs, sometimes used as an inadequate substitute for known-groups comparisons.

Differential Prevalence Design

Rogers, Harrell, and Liff (1993) first described the differential prevalence design and carefully distinguished it from known-groups comparisons. In a differential prevalence design, the researcher *assumes* that two samples will have different proportions of dissimulating persons. The assumption is generally based on perceived incentives for deception; most commonly, persons involved in criminal proceedings or civil litigation are presumed more likely to dissemble than persons from other contexts.

The differential prevalence design, although offering indirect evidence of construct validity, has no practical value in establishing criterion-related validity and is inutile for clinical classification. Why such harsh criticism?

1. *Differences in prevalence rates are inferred, not measured.* Inferences are founded on commonsensical beliefs or general survey data rather than on estimates derived from the specific samples under investigation.

2. *Prevalence rates for individual response styles usually represent a minority of cases.* Looking across survey data for different referrals, typically less than one-third of the group membership can be classified with an individual response style. For example, Rogers (1997b) summarized extensive data from more than 500 forensic experts on the prevalence of malingering. Overall averages were about 7% in clinical settings and 15–17% in forensic settings.[1] Even when the stakes are very high (e.g., insanity evaluations; see Rogers, 1986), only a minority appear to feign or otherwise engage in deception.

3. *Elevated scores do not necessarily signify response styles.* This design prevents researchers from knowing which cases produced elevated scores. It is theoretically possible that every elevated score was produced by persons who were *not* engaged in the particular response style. Accuracy cannot be determined. Practitioners are often confused on this point. A prudent caveat might include the following: No useful conclusions can be drawn from this study about the accuracy of the response-style measures.

To recap these three points, we learn very little from differential prevalence designs about response styles. By design, we do not know *who* is dissimulating in each group. Logically, we do not know *how many* are dissimulating in each group. Even when groups yielded predicted differences, we do not know *what meaning* should be assigned to deviant or atypical scores. For all we know, every "deviant" or "atypical" score could be indicative of honest responding. We also do not know *how comparable* the different samples are on many important dimensions, beyond conjectured incentives.

Frederick (2000) made an interesting argument for the use of *mixed-group validation* to address the fundamental problems with differential prevalence design that were raised in the preceding paragraph (see also Rogers, 1997c). He argued that knowing which individuals were malingering was irrelevant; instead, knowledge of the proportion of malingerers could be used to calculate sampling error based on computer simulations. Although mathematically elegant, mixed-group validation is based on insupportable assumptions. First, it assumes that base rates are knowable. However, the base rate of malingering is highly variable. In surveying forensic experts, Rogers, Salekin, Sewell, Goldstein, and Leonard (1998) found marked variations in the prevalence of malingering, with a *SD* of 14.4%. Second, it assumes that the base rates are stable within the sample. Yet individual circumstances change, affecting the motivation to feign. Third, it appears to assume what needs to be tested, specifically the accuracy of the measure.

To illustrate the fundamental problems with mixed-group validation, take an absurd example. We could use head circumference as the feigning measure. We could reliably measure the circumferences and posit that individuals with the largest heads were feigning. Mixed-group validation would allow us to consider the sampling error and would generate utility estimates. Despite sophisticated statistics, this absurd example demonstrates the inherent fallacy of this approach.

Crawford, Greene, Dupart, Bongar, and Childs (2006) attempted to apply mixed-group validation to feigning on the MMPI-2. They made the unwarranted assumption that 7% of their inpatient sample was feigning. This percentage was derived from an entirely different reference point (i.e., forensic referrals to neuropsychologists). However, even if the samples shared general characteristics, this critical leap of faith is impermissible given the known variability across samples. Apparently without the

use of manipulation checks, they simply conjectured that 90% of highly atypical simulators (i.e., graduate students) were able to feign a presumably unfamiliar scenario (i.e., permanent and significant facial disfigurement). Despite these untenable suppositions, they reported effect sizes for the *total* samples. If they truly believed in mixed-group validation, they should eliminate 7% of inpatients and 10% of simulators. A series of random eliminations would allow the researchers to understand the potential variability in their utility estimates.[2]

In summary, differential prevalence designs are fundamentally flawed and carry the real risk that practitioners will be misled by their findings. Mixed-group validation cannot remedy its flaws. Therefore, it is recommended that differential prevalence designs be discarded as an unsound method for evaluating response styles.

Bootstrapping Design

Rogers and Bender (2003) described the use of a bootstrapping design to approximate a known-groups comparison. In the domain of feigned cognitive impairment, researchers have used multiple measures to identify suspected feigners. When properly applied, stringent rules are used to minimize false positives. In addition, marginal cases must be eliminated so that comparison groups (e.g., genuine patients) do not have false positives.

Bootstrapping designs can be useful in the development and validation of response-style measures. They should not take the place of known-groups comparisons, but they can provide helpful data that are especially relevant to external validity. For purposes of discriminant validity (see Chapter 2, this volume), bootstrapping designs are very helpful in examining effect sizes for different strategies, as applied to diverse samples. Because of uncertainties regarding group membership, bootstrapping designs should not be used for utility estimates or applied clinically for individual classifications.

As an example, Rogers, Payne, and colleagues (2007; see also Chapter 18, this volume) applied the bootstrapping design to a very large sample of disability referrals. Using this design, these investigators tested whether the SIRS produced similar effect sizes in its applications to different diagnostic groups. In addition, they examined the efficacy of the SIRS

IF scale as a screen for cognitive impairment. They used multiple indicators of feigned cognitive impairment and established likely feigning and likely genuine groups, eliminating those who fell into an indeterminate category. Although they established a cut score for the IF scale, it is used only for screening purposes.

Combined Research Models

Rogers (1995, 1997c) advocated the combination of simulation design and known-groups comparison in the validation of assessment methods for dissimulation. The respective strengths of both designs are complementary. Well-designed simulation studies address satisfactorily the need for experimental rigor (internal validity). Specific response styles can be investigated as they relate to assessment methods, characteristics and abilities of simulators, and incentives. Moreover, within-subject designs allow for the comparison of response styles and provide an opportunity to research correction formulas for dissimulation. In contrast, known-groups comparisons address sufficiently the need for clinical relevance (external validity). Dissimulating persons can be examined in the most relevant professional settings with all the external motivations in place.

Early research on the M Test (Beaber, Marston, Michelli, & Mills, 1985) illustrates the need for combined research models (i.e., simulation design plus known-groups comparison). The original simulation study appeared very promising, with initial classification rates approaching 90% (Beaber et al., 1985). A second study by different investigators (Gillis, Rogers, & Bagby, 1991) also yielded very positive results for the simulation design but not for the known-groups comparison (see Smith, Chapter 19, this volume). Indeed, cross-validation of the original rules suggests that they are not effective across both research designs (Hankins et al., 1993). As a result, Rogers, Bagby, and Gillis (1992) revised the decision rules based on a combined research design.

More recently, PAI feigning research underscores the importance of combining simulation designs with known-groups comparisons. Rogers, Sewell, and colleagues (1996) conducted an extensive simulation study comparing 166 naive and 80 sophisticated simulators with 221 patients with specific mental disorders. The RDF was carefully developed and cross-validated. Despite its sophisticated design and subsequent cross-validation, the RDF's results from the simulation design were not confirmed in a subsequent known-groups comparison with forensic patients (Rogers, Sewell, Cruise, Wang, & Ustad, 1998). Chapter 11 (this volume) discusses the merits of the RDF with simulation and known-groups comparisons.

The logical sequence is the development of an assessment method with simulation studies followed by known-groups comparisons. Simulation designs have two advantages in the validation of response-style measures: (1) the comparative availability of research participants for simulation research and (2) the ability to refine measures systematically based on simulation designs. In contrast, known-groups comparisons are challenging to implement for two reasons. First, some response styles occur infrequently, which means that extensive data collection is required. Second, experts in specific response styles are often not available. The substitution of any available clinicians (e.g., prison psychiatrists) undermines the value of known-groups comparisons. These experts must also be available to conduct extensive, research-quality evaluations. Given the research costs associated with known-groups comparisons, they are best used to cross-validate results of simulation studies.

The sine qua non of known-groups comparisons is use of the highest standards for independent classification. Use of measures with high levels of accuracy, such as the SIRS, standardizes this classification and reduces errors. When no gold standard is available, carefully selected experts in specific response styles are used. In establishing independent classification, researchers are cautioned against substituting expediency for experimental rigor. For example, Kucharski and Johnsen (2002) hypothesized that most criminal defendants referred for pretrial evaluations were malingering if their first documented symptoms occurred following their arrests. This is an interesting and testable hypothesis. These defendants could be administered the SIRS as a reliable and accurate method of independent classification. However, the mere assumption of malingering is insufficient. Likewise, brief routine assessments by available clinicians should not be equated with research-quality evaluations conducted by response-style experts (Edens et al., 2007). Again, the highest standards should be used in establishing the independent classifications.

Brennan and Gouvier (2006) compared results on the Slick criteria (Slick, Sherman, & Iverson, 1999) for suspected malingerers and simulators. One limitation of this study was its inclusion of the Slick criteria for "possible malingering," which are based largely on soft, nonempirical indicators that simply raise the possibility of feigning. Most research on feigned cognitive impairment avoids this category because of its imprecision. Interestingly, their data (Brennan & Gouvier, 2006, Figures 2 and 3) underscore the importance of combined research models. "Definite" malingering was categorized much more frequently among simulators (i.e., 12 of 48, or 25.0%) than among suspected malingerers (i.e., 1 of 54, or 1.9%). These findings strongly support the need for combined research capitalizing on the respective strengths of simulation designs and known-groups comparisons.

STATISTICAL AND METHODOLOGICAL APPLICATIONS

Research methodology for the assessment of deception and dissimulation increasingly has been standardized. Despite its obvious advantages, this standardization carries its own risk, namely, an unnecessary narrowing of research methods and a disinclination to explore alternative approaches. This brief section overviews several research methods, well established in other areas of psychological research, that are beginning to be applied to dissimulation research.

Receiver Operating Characteristic Analysis

Receiver operating characteristic (ROC) analysis was developed in the 1950s in research centering on signal detection across a range of applications (e.g., radar and memory vigilance tasks; see Swets, 1973). Although the potential applications of ROC analysis are relatively complex, a primary use in behavioral sciences is a plotting of sensitivity by the false-positive rate (Murphy et al., 1987). This graphical display allows the practitioner to immediately assess the accuracy of the measure in terms of sensitivity and specificity. As noted by Swets (1988), one early application of ROC analysis was in assessing the accuracy of polygraph examinations. Swets provided a penetrating

analysis of the measured values for the polygraph, with marked differences reported by the source of the study (e.g., commercial polygraphers versus university researchers). Swets also observed that the use of confessions as a criterion was likely to overestimate accuracy (e.g., data on confessing suspects are unlikely to generalize to nonconfessing suspects; nonconfessing suspects are likely to include an unknown percentage of deceptive persons).

Nicholson and his colleagues (Mouton, Peterson, Nicholson, & Bagby, 1995; Nicholson et al., 1997) championed the use of ROC analysis to evaluate feigned and defensive MMPI-2 profiles. They attempted to use "area under the curve" (AUC) to compare the relative usefulness of different validity scales. The limitation of this approach is that some scales are much more effective at lower or at higher ranges (see Nicholson et al., 1997, Figures 1–3), a fact that is obscured by AUC comparisons.

Although the late Robert Nicholson was a superb methodologist, I question the usefulness of ROC analysis as an effective method to evaluate the utility of response-style measures. A basic assumption of ROC analysis is that classifications should be rendered at every single possible score; otherwise, AUC is irrelevant. This assumption is controverted by clinical practice. Practitioners (and most researchers) use the best validated cut scores. Therefore, AUC comparisons are inapplicable. Moreover, clinical decisions may not seek the optimal classification (i.e., "elbow of the curve") but may wish to maximize sensitivity or specificity.

Utility estimates for response-style measures should not be limited to group accuracy (i.e., sensitivity and specificity) but should also take into account likelihood estimates for individual scores. For this purpose, utility estimates should also be considered in examining the probability of the presence (PPP) or absence (NPP) of a response style. For instance, clinicians need to know likelihoods: What is the likelihood that an Fp >9 signifies feigning?

Taxometric Analysis

Frederick (1995) is the first known investigator to apply taxometric analysis to dissimulation. He applied this analysis to the feigning of cognitive impairment on a large sample ($N = 774$) of honest and malingering participants. The value of taxometric analysis is the identification of underlying "taxons," or categories, that might not otherwise be observed by clinicians. This analysis requires very large samples and the administration of at least three related measures. Although ambitious, such efforts may assist in elucidating the "true" nature of specific response styles. Since Frederick's original work, taxometric analysis has been applied to different populations using the MMPI-2 validity scales (Strong, Greene, Hoppe, Johnston, & Olesen, 1999; Strong, Greene, & Schinka, 2000).

Strong, Glassmire, Frederick, and Greene (2006) applied taxometric analysis to the MMPI-2 Fp scale. Rather than using three separate measures, they chose to disaggregate Fp into three subscales that were rationally constructed based on higher correlations and similar content. These scales were used as uncorrelated and independent measures in the subsequent taxometric analysis. The Strong and colleagues approach provides an interesting method of examining taxonic latent structures for individual response-style scales.

Most recently, Walters and colleagues (2007) performed a taxometric analysis of SIRS data from 1,211 forensic examinees and compared these results to a subsample of 711 MMPI-2 protocols. Unlike Strong and colleagues (2006), their analyses strongly supported dimensional latent structure, indicating that the exaggeration and fabrication may represent a continuum. Interestingly, the Walters and colleagues results do not preclude the possibility of a taxon embedded with the dimensional structure. Taxometric analyses provide a fruitful avenue to explore categorical and dimensional models of malingering across different domains, such as feigned cognitive deficits and malingered medical complaints.

Item Response Theory

Zickar and Robie (1999) applied item response theory (IRT) to two models of faking: (1) "changing items" (deceivers perceive the test items differently) and "changing persons" (individuals consciously change their presentations for some desired outcome). Using a very large sample ($N = 1,424$) of military recruits, simulators and coached simulators clearly improved their scores over controls on target personality scales relating to emotional adjustment, work orientation, and nondelinquency. They tested and found large differences that were consistent with the "changing persons"

model of faking. Items functioned differently on both item (differential item functioning, or DIF) and scale (differential test functioning, or DTF) levels. They also examined which items and scales were the most vulnerable to defensiveness.

Stark, Chernyshenko, Chan, Lee, and Drasgow (2001) proposed that IRT is the method of choice for testing the effects of specific response styles on test scales (e.g., personality) because IRT goes beyond mean differences in examining latent trait distributions. Stark and colleagues found substantial differences using both differential prevalence (applicants vs. nonapplicants) and bootstrapping (high vs. low on impression management scores) designs. Of particular note, these differences could be minimized on the majority of scales with the elimination of several problematic items. Stark and colleagues' IRT applications show considerable promise in (1) testing the effects of a response style on clinical constructs and (2) eliminating items particularly vulnerable to response styles.

An initial review of IRT studies suggests that they have been used primarily to study the effects of defensiveness in employment situations. Clearly this work could be expanded to different settings and other response styles. My main reservation involves its application to measurement equivalence across samples with different response styles. According to Stark and colleagues (2001), the key issue to be tested is the comparability of item and scale parameters rather than mean differences between groups. They suggest that even large group differences are not problematic to evaluating measurement equivalence. Without questioning their IRT methodology, most clinical applications of psychological measures use cut scores. If simulators reduce their scores by 50%, the interpretation of this clinical construct will change significantly irrespective of its IRT equivalence. This issue of interpretability applies both to response-style measures and the effects of response styles on clinical measures.

FUNDAMENTAL QUESTIONS

The first and second editions of this book represent only a beginning in mapping out the future directions for dissimulation research. What is immediately apparent from a comprehensive review of the response-style literature

is the range of unresearched and underre-
searched topics. Little is known, for example,
about the background and characteristics of
dissimulators in clinical settings. Although the
motivation of dissimulators is often inferred,
the multidetermined nature of behavior belies
the simplicity of these inferences. Simply put,
the motivation of dissimulators is poorly understood. In addition, the influence of situational
and interactional variables on the frequency
and severity of dissimulation has not been adequately studied. Finally, virtually no studies
exist that examine the significance of dissimulation in the assessment of treatability and
legal issues. The following sections briefly outline fundamental questions in the study of dissimulation.

The Study of Dissimulators

Research has not addressed the sociodemographic variables, clinical characteristics, or
psychosocial backgrounds of defensive and
malingering persons. As a rare exception, Lees-
Haley (1992) examined the sociodemographic
backgrounds and clinical presentations of persons making spurious PTSD claims. Although
the consecutive sampling of 55 pseudo-PTSD
patients and 64 personal injury claimants as
controls is not ideal, the data suggest that
women may be represented more frequently
than thought by some clinicians (41.8%). Moreover, spurious claims, at least in this sample
drawn primarily from Los Angeles, were widely
distributed across ethnic groups (27.3% African
American, 52.7% European American, 16.4%
Hispanic American, and 3.6% other). Although
the data offer several tantalizing speculations
about differences between spurious PTSD
claims and genuine personal injury cases, the
sampling procedure does not allow their exploration.[3] Using a case-vignette approach,
Chibnall and Tait (1999) examined ethnic differences in clinician ratings of symptom illegit-
imacy for patients with low back pain complaints. The overall ratings of feigned symptoms
were very similar. Regarding estimates of
feigned pain when medical evidence did not
document a physical injury, clinicians appeared
to be much more influenced by litigation status
for European Americans than for African
Americans. Do these findings reflect ethnic biases by clinicians? Do they apply to other response styles?

Following is a sampling of related research
questions.

1. What is the prevalence of malingering and
   defensiveness, established by both clinical
   settings and referral questions?
2. What proportion of dissimulators has coexisting mental disorders?
3. Are there "pure" or "trait-based" dissimulators who consistently fake, regardless of
   the situation or any expected payoffs?
4. What are dissimulators' reported motivations for their intentional distortions?

Research on Decision Models

Most decision rules in dissimulation research
are very simple and typically dichotomous in
nature. For instance, the bulk of MMPI/
MMPI-2 research on defensiveness is consistent with this approach; such models do not
allow conclusions regarding gradations of defensiveness. Moreover, the lack of an indeterminant category means that misclassifications
are inevitable, because such decision rules do
not take into account (1) the capitalization on
chance variation or (2) the standard error of
measurement. One simple but fundamental
improvement was recommended by Rogers
(1997c, p. 423) but remains to be implemented:

• To avoid unnecessary and costly errors, response-style researchers should adopt a polychotomous classification with three groups:
  dissimulating, indeterminant, and non-dis-
  simulating.

All peer-reviewed research articles on the assessment of response styles should take into account the accuracy of measurement (e.g., standard error of measurement) in the creation of
cut scores and operationalization of response-
style groups. At a minimum, they should create
an indeterminate category or openly acknowledge the basic weakness of their research because an indeterminate category was not used.

A variation of decision rules is found in the
Malingering Probability Scale (MPS; Silverton,
1999). Silverton provided different decision
rules based on assumed base rates of malingering at 10, 20, and 50%. Although intellectually
appealing, the resulting classifications are likely
to be spurious simply because the base rates are

not known, either for specific settings or for particular referral questions.

Recent meta-analytic studies (e.g., Baer & Miller, 2002; Rogers, Sewell, Martin, & Vitacco, 2003) suggest that multiple decision rules are potentially useful depending on referral issues and settings. In many cases, an individual may exhibit moderately high elevations on some scales and extreme elevations on others. Research is needed to know which combinations of decision rules increase accuracy. Multiple decision rules can also be organized in a hierarchical order. In such cases, very large samples are required to test the permutations inherent in these models. For example, Rogers, Cashel, Johansen, Sewell, and Gonzalez (1997) found that two of the five Substance Abuse Subtle Screening Inventory (SASSI) steps did not appear to affect classification of undisclosed substance abuse.

Multivariate models, such as discriminant functions, have a potential to optimize classification. However, this advantage may prove to be a liability if not cross-validated on substantial samples because shrinkage in classification is very common, given the likelihood of capitalizing on chance variation. For example, Rogers, Sewell, Morey, and Ustad (1996) performed a two-stage discriminant analysis on 204 participants in the calibration sample and 199 participants in the cross-validation sample, with shrinkage in classification from 92.2 to 80.4%. Multivariate models often require extensive computations, ideally suited for computer scoring.

Many research questions emerge from the preceding discussion that are worthy of fuller inquiry.

1. What are the *misclassification* rates of response styles based on different types (e.g., dichotomous, polychotomous, or hierachical) of decision rules?
2. Can decision rules be developed to categorize gradations of dissimulation?
3. What are the advantages and disadvantages of multivariate models of classification?

Situational and Interactional Factors

Dissimulation within clinical and other applied settings is not an isolated event but an important element of an interactive process. The role of clinicians, for example, in unintentionally encouraging or discouraging dissimulation remains unknown. More to this point, the intensity of an adversarial situation as perceived by the potential dissimulator is likely to have an important influence on his or her presentation. Rogers and Payne (2006) described how some claimants may experience disability evaluations as an affront to their integrity and an attack on their financial security. Research is needed on whether these individuals experience a need to "prove their disability" and how such needs relate to malingering. As early evidence of situational effects, data from Audubon and Kirwin (1982) suggest that pretrial patients may tend to exaggerate their symptoms but that the same individuals, during a postacquittal assessment, may tend to minimize them. As part of an interpersonal process, clinicians are not exempt from inquiry; Rogers, Sewell and Goldstein (1994) found that psychologists' estimates of the prevalence of malingering ranged more than 50%. How much of this variability is accounted for by (1) differences among forensic settings or (2) the proclivities and presumptions of the psychologists remains to be investigated. Research questions that deserve empirical inquiry include the following:

1. What are mental health professionals' attitudes toward malingering and other specific response styles?
2. Are differences in professionals' attitudes reflected in either (1) the *actual* frequency of dissimulation or (2) the *perceived* frequency of dissimulation? Survey research with vignettes from actual cases may assist in this research.
3. Can environmental variables (e.g., a hostile or adversarial climate) be identified that significantly influence specific response styles? Simulation research with videotaped introductions (e.g., adversarial vs. cooperative) would be useful in addressing how environmental variables influence test data, including response-style measures.
4. How do separate components of forensic evaluations affect performance on clinical and response-style measures? Do cautions against dissimulation have their desired effect? Does an open discussion of examinees' other goals affect their clinical presentations, including response styles?

Dissimulation and Treatability

The role of specific response styles in the assessment of patients' treatability has been largely neglected. Krittman (2004) studied treatment compliance for patients in a residential treatment program, which included individuals deemed to be malingering. Unexpectedly, persons likely to be feigning evidence a *greater* involvement in treatment (i.e., more sessions attended) than their nonfeigning counterparts ($r = .32$). This greater involvement was not reflected in case managers' ratings, which indicated their perceptions that feigners were *less* involved. These findings raise several rival hypotheses. Are case managers biased by their knowledge of likely feigners? Alternatively, do the likely feigners attend more sessions but participate less?

An important issue is whether exaggeration of symptoms may be a "cry for help." Early research (Greene, 1988; Hale, Zimostrad, Duckworth, & Nicholas, 1986) has suggested that this interpretation may not have empirical support. Persons with marked elevations on MMPI validity scales often did not remain in treatment, raising questions about their treatment motivation. Berry and colleagues (1996) conducted a simulation study to examine specifically the effects of a "cry for help" condition on MMPI-2 validity and clinical scales. Simulators wanting immediate access to outpatient care reported very extreme scores (*M*s >100T) on F, Fb, Fp, and DS. Interestingly, their most common codetype was 6–8 (51.7%), which was far different from the clinical comparison sample (3.3%). Although simulators were not cautioned about the presence of validity scales, it seems unlikely that outpatients feeling desperate for immediate mental health care would engage in such preparation. In light of Berry and colleagues' findings, further studies are needed to separate those desperately seeking treatment (i.e., likely factitious disorders) from those with other motivations.

Rogers, Jackson, and Kaminski (2004) studied PAI validity scales for two groups of simulators who role-played factitious patients urgently seeking multiple therapy sessions each week. The simulators were sophisticated (i.e., advanced doctoral students) and asked to assume either a factitious-demanding or factitious-dependent role. Although hampered by modest group sizes (*n*s ranging from 14 to 18),

the factitious-demanding group appeared different from the factitious-dependent group on several PAI validity scales. Of most interest, *low* scores on the PAI defensiveness index distinguished both factitious groups from malingering and control conditions. An important implication of Rogers and colleagues' study is that treatment-seeking patients with factitious disorder should not be simply lumped together. Instead, meaningful subtypes of factitious and other response styles need to be investigated.

Viewing treatability from the perspective of occupational rehabilitation involving musculosketal injuries produces very different results. Alexy and Webb (1999) found that even mild elevations (> 60T) on scale L were associated with poor rehabilitation outcomes. Patients with elevated scores had a more than 300% greater likelihood (i.e., 39.1% vs. 10.3%) of remaining disabled. Overly virtuous presentations (see also Lanyon & Cunningham, 2005) may play an important role in determining treatment effectiveness. As demonstrated by Alexy and Webb, response styles and treatability need to be studied separately for different domains.

Denial and defensiveness are typically seen as obstacles to effective treatment. As an extreme example, nonadmitting sex offenders are typically seen as poor treatment candidates. For instance, Beyko and Wong (2005) found that denial and low motivation among sex offenders contributed to poor treatment completion. However, they saw these effects as limitations of the treatment program rather than shortcomings of the offenders. Their point is well taken. Without treatment safeguards to encourage such disclosures, most persons would not readily admit to behaviors that carry severe criminal sanctions and invidious stigmas.

Researchers may wish to consider the transtheoretical model (TTM; Prochaska & DiClemente, 1982) in examining the role of defensiveness and denial in the determination of treatment readiness. At the precontemplation stage, clients are not willing to acknowledge significant problems requiring treatment. An interesting research question is whether the TTM precontemplation stage should be viewed as a variant of defensiveness. A singular advantage of the TTM approach is that disacknowledgment is seen as an integral part of treatment, with its interventions and objectives

(Jordan & Rogers, 2004). In their review, DiClemente, Schlundt, and Gemmell (2004) openly discuss the challenges of applying the TTM model to alcohol and drug abuse. Nonetheless, they make a compelling argument that intervention programs must take into account the lack of motivation for change in the development of effective treatments.

Several research questions emerge on the relationship of dissimulation to patients' treatment responses.

1. To what extent do dissimulators comply with and follow treatment recommendations?
2. What are the treatment outcomes for dissimulating patients? In other words, do malingering or defensive patients with coexisting mental disorders respond as well as other patients with similar disorders?
3. Are TTM interventions, specific to the precontemplation stage, effective for different variants of denial and defensiveness?

Beyond TTM, researchers should consider whether the dissimulation itself should be treated or modified. From an adaptational model (see Chapter 1, this volume), a modification of the incentives for dissimulation should alter the response style. In the case of malingering, direct feedback on this response style may have a direct effect in changing the incentive from the desired goal (e.g., financial gain in a personal injury case) to the avoidance of further harm (e.g., social disapprobation and the possibility of fraud charges if the malingering is discovered). No research to date has examined the usefulness of direct or indirect interventions in modifying a response style.

Dissimulation and Legal Issues

The outcomes of forensic consultations may have far-reaching effects on examinees. However, researchers should not facilely assume that the presence of high stakes can be used as a proxy for malingering or defensiveness. In this regard, Rogers (1990a, 1990b) observed the potential dangers inherent in the DSM threshold model of malingering as applied to forensic cases. For instance, all criminal defendants with extensive antisocial histories being evaluated are likely to meet the threshold criteria (i.e., "two or more indices" are satisfied by antisocial personality disorder and medico-

legal evaluations). As a second example, some practitioners treat any complaint of intrafamilial sexual abuse as veridical and parents' subsequent disavowals as defensiveness. Research is urgently needed to test the effects of these assumptions on differences among mental health professionals and their decisions in clinical practice. Relevant investigations are required to address the role of dissimulation within forensic reports and legal outcomes. Research questions include the following:

1. In what proportion of forensic cases is the issue of dissimulation determinative of clinicians' psycholegal conclusions?
2. Given the far-reaching consequences of forensic evaluations, are different clinical criteria needed to differentiate specific response styles (malingering and defensiveness) from genuine responding?
3. What influences do descriptions of dissimulation within clinical reports have on the legal disposition?
4. In public policy terms, what errors (false positives or false negatives) are legal and mental health professionals willing to tolerate with respect to malingering and defensiveness?

CONCLUSION

Research on dissimulation can be roughly categorized in four phases: (1) early case studies, on which much of clinical practice is still based; (2) sustained interest in psychometric and social-psychological research that emphasizes group differences via simulation design; (3) the development of empirically validated detection strategies; and (4) the emphasis on individual classifications using combined research designs (e.g., simulation designs and known-groups comparisons). Valuable research has pursued two divergent paths. First, specialized measures (e.g., the SIRS) have been carefully constructed to evaluate specific response styles using sophisticated detection strategies. Second, embedded measures continue to be explored, with detection strategies being developed and validated within comprehensive measures (e.g., the Wechsler Adult Intelligence Scale–III; Wechsler, 1997).

Response-style research forms a complex matrix composed of specific response styles, detection strategies, and clinical domains. Important advances during the past decade have been acknowledged throughout this third edition. Although the refinement of assessment methods and the consolidation of response-style knowledge are critically important, pioneering research is needed for uncharted areas, such as detection strategies for feigned medical complaints.

NOTES

1. Mittenberg, Patton, Canyock, and Condit (2002) are sometimes erroneously reported to have rates of malingering exceeding 40%. This is not true; they used a much broader category that included suspected malingering and symptom exaggeration. In contrast, a large-scale study by Bianchini, Curtis, and Greve (2006) reported prevalence rates ranging from 16.3 to 26.7%. However, even these percentages are likely inflated by the inclusion of "probable" malingerers.

2. If they assumed that the Fp scale was a perfect measure of feigned mental disorders, then they could remove the most extreme elevations. However, assuming what needs to be proved would be a textbook example of circular reasoning.

3. Because the control group excluded all persons with PTSD, differences between the two samples may be attributable to either spurious or genuine PTSD.

References

Aamodt, M. G. (2004). *Research in law enforcement selection.* Boca Raton, FL: BrownWalker Press.

Abbey, S. (1996). Psychiatric diagnostic overlap in chronic fatigue syndrome. In M. Demitrack & S. Abbey (Eds.), *Chronic fatigue syndrome: An integrative approach to evaluation and treatment* (pp. 48–71). New York: Guilford Press.

Abel, G. G., Becker, J. V., Cunningham-Rathner, J., Mittelman, M., & Rouleau, J. (1988). Multiple paraphilic diagnoses among sex offenders. *Bulletin of the American Academy of Psychiatry and the Law, 16,* 153–168.

Abel, G. G., Blanchard, E. B., & Barlow, D. H. (1981). Measurement of sexual arousal in several paraphilias: The effects of stimulus modality, instructional set and stimulus content on the objective. *Behaviour Research and Therapy, 19,* 25–33.

Abel, G. G., Huffman, J., Warberg, B., & Holland, C. L. (1998). Visual reaction time and plethysmography as measures of sexual interest in child molesters. *Sexual Abuse: A Journal of Research and Treatment, 10,* 81–95.

Abrams, S. (1989). *The complete polygraph handbook.* Lexington, MA: Lexington Books.

Achenbach, T. M. (1985). *Assessment and taxonomy of child and adolescent psychopathology.* Thousand Oaks, CA: Sage.

Achenbach, T. M. (1991). *Integrative guide for the 1991 CBCL/4–18, YSR, and TRF profiles.* Burlington: University of Vermont, Department of Psychiatry.

Ackerman, M., & Ackerman, M. (1997). Custody evaluation practices: A survey of experienced professionals (revisited). *Professional Psychology: Research and Practice, 28,* 137–145.

Adamou, M., & Hale, A. (2003). PTSD and the law of psychiatric injury in England and Wales: Finally coming closer? *Journal of the American Academy of Psychiatry and the Law, 31*(3), 327–332.

Adshead, G., & Bluglass, K. (2005). Attachment representations in mothers with abnormal illness behaviour by proxy. *British Journal of Psychiatry, 187,* 328–333.

Aduan, R. P., Fauci, A. S., Dale, D. C., Herzberg, J. H., & Wolff, S. M. (1979). Factitious fever and self-induced infection: A report of 32 cases and review of the literature. *Annals of Internal Medicine, 90*(2), 230–242.

Ahlmeyer, S., Heil, P., McKee, B., & English, K. (2000). The impact of polygraphy on admissions of victims and offenses in adult sexual offenders. *Sexual Abuse: A Journal of Research and Treatment, 12,* 123–138.

Albert, S., Fox, H. M., & Kahn, M. W. (1980). Faking psychosis on the Rorschach: Can expert judges detect malingering? *Journal of Personality Assessment, 44,* 115–119.

Alexander, M. P. (1995). Mild traumatic brain injury: Pathophysiology, natural history, and clinical management. *Neurology, 45*(7), 1253–1260.

Alexy, W. D., & Webb, P. M. (1999). Utility of the MMPI 2 in work hardening rehabilitation. *Rehabilitation Psychology, 44*(3), 266–273.

Allen, J. J., & Iacono, W. G. (2001). Assessing the validity of amnesia in dissociative identity disorder: A dilemma for the DSM and the courts. *Psychology, Public Policy, and Law, 7,* 311–344.

Allen, J. J., Iacono, W. G., Laravuso, J. J., & Dunn, L. A. (1995). An event-related potential investigation of posthypnotic recognition amnesia. *Journal of Abnormal Psychology, 104,* 421–430.

Allen L. M., Conder, R. L., Green P., & Cox, D. R. (1997). *CARB '97: Computerized Assessment of Response Bias: Manual.* Durham, NC: CogniSyst.

Allen, L. M., & Green, P. (2001). Declining CARB failure rates over 6 years of testing: What's wrong with this picture? *Archives of Clinical Neuropsychology, 16,* 846.

Alliger, G. M., & Dwight, S. A. (2000). A meta-analytic investigation of the susceptibility of integrity tests to faking and coaching. *Educational and Psychological Measurement, 60,* 59–72.

Allport, G. W. (1937). *Personality: A psychosocial interpretation.* New York: Henry Holt.

Alpert, M., & Silvers, K. (1970). Perceptual characteristics distinguishing auditory hallucinations in schizophrenia and acute alcoholic psychoses. *American Journal of Psychiatry, 127,* 298–302.

Altshuler, L., Cummings, J., & Mills, M. (1986). Mutism: Review, differential diagnosis and report of 22 cases. *American Journal of Psychiatry, 143,* 1409–1414.

Alwes, Y. R., Clark, J. A., Berry, D. T. R., & Granacher, R. P. (2006). *Evaluation of brief malingering screening instruments in a civil forensic sample.* Manuscript submitted for publication.

Ambrosini, P. J. (1992). *Schedule of Affective Disorders and Schizophrenia for School-Age Children (6–18 years): Kiddie-SADS (K-SADS, Present State Version).* Philadelphia: Medical College of Pennsylvania.

American Academy of Psychiatry and the Law. (1991). *Ethical guidelines for the practice of forensic psychiatry.* Bloomfield, CT: Author.

American Congress of Rehabilitation Medicine. (1993). Definition of mild traumatic brain injury. *Journal of Head Trauma Rehabilitation, 8,* 86–87.

American Educational Research Association, American Psychological Association, & National Council on Measurement in Education. (1999). *Standards for educational and psychological testing.* Washington, DC: Author.

American Psychiatric Association. (1952). *Diagnostic and statistical manual of mental disorders.* Washington, DC: Author.

American Psychiatric Association. (1968). *Diagnostic and statistical manual of mental disorders* (2nd ed.). Washington, DC: Author.

American Psychiatric Association. (1980). *Diagnostic and statistical manual of mental disorders* (3rd ed.). Washington, DC: Author.

American Psychiatric Association. (1987). *Diagnostic and statistical manual of mental disorders* (3rd ed., rev.). Washington, DC: Author.

American Psychiatric Association. (1994). *Diagnostic and statistical manual of mental disorders* (4th ed.). Washington, DC: Author.

American Psychiatric Association. (2000). *Diagnostic and statistical manual of mental disorders* (4th ed., text rev.). Washington, DC: Author.

American Psychological Association. (1985). *Standards for educational and psychological testing.* Washington, DC: Author.

American Psychological Association. (2002). Ethical principles of psychologists and code of conduct. *American Psychologist, 57,* 1060–1073.

American Psychological Association Working Group on Investigation of Memories of Childhood Abuse. (1998). Final conclusions of the American Psychological Association Working Group on Investigation of Memories of Childhood Abuse. *Psychology, Public Policy, and Law, 4,* 933–940.

Americans with Disabilities Act of 1990, 42 U.S.C.A. §12101 *et seq.* (West 1993).

Amir, M., Kaplan, Z., & Kotler, M. (1996). Type of trauma, severity of posttraumatic stress disorder core symptoms, and associated features. *Journal of General Psychology, 123*(4), 341–351.

Anastasi, A. (1988). *Psychological testing* (6th ed.). New York: Macmillan.

Anderson, B. J., Gogineni, A., Charuvastra, A., Longabaugh, R., & Stein, M. D. (2001). Adverse drinking consequences among alcohol abusing intravenous drug users. *Alcoholism: Clinical and Experimental Research, 25*(1), 41–45.

Anderson, E. W., Trethowan, W. H., & Kenna, J. (1959). An experimental investigation of simulation and pseudo-dementia. *Acta Psychiatrica Neurologica Scandanavia, 34*(132), 1–42.

Andreyev, L. (1902). The dilemma. In L. Hamalian & V. Von Wiren-Garczyski (Eds.), *Seven Russian short novel masterpieces.* New York: Popular Library.

Applebaum, P., Jick, R., & Grisso, T. (1993). Use of posttraumatic stress disorder to support an insanity defense. *American Journal of Psychiatry, 150*(2), 229–234.

Arbisi, P. A., & Ben-Porath, Y. S. (1995). An MMPI-2 infrequent response scale for use with psychopathological populations: The infrequency-psychopathology scale, F(p). *Psychological Assessment, 7,* 424–431.

Arbisi, P. A., & Ben-Porath, Y. S. (1998). The ability of Minnesota Multiphasic Personality Inventory—2 validity scales to detect fake-bad responses in psychiatric inpatients. *Psychological Assessment, 10*(3), 221–228.

Arbisi, P. A., & Butcher, J. (2004). Failure of the FBS to predict malingering of somatic symptoms: Response to critiques by Greve and Bianchini and Lees Haley and Fox. *Archives of Clinical Neuropsychology, 19*(3), 341–345.

Archer, R. P., Buffington-Vollum, J. K., Stredny, R. V., & Handel, R. W. (2006). A survey of psychological test use patterns among forensic psychologists. *Journal of Personality Assessment, 87,* 84–94.

Archer, R. P., Gordon, R. A., & Kirchner, F. H. (1987). MMPI response set characteristics among adolescents. *Journal of Personality Assessment, 51,* 506–516.

Archibald, H. C., & Tuddenham, R. D. (1965). Persistent stress reaction after combat: A 20-year follow-up. *Archives of General Psychiatry, 12,* 475–481.

Ardolf, B. R., Denney, R. L., & Houston, C. M. (2007). Base rates of negative response bias and malingered neurocognitive dysfunction among criminal defendants referred for neuropsychological evaluation. *Clinical Neuropsychologist, 21*(6), 899–916.

Arnett, P. A., Hammeke, T. A., & Schwartz, L. (1995). Quantitative and qualitative performance on Rey's 15-item test in neurological patients and simulators. *Clinical Neuropsychologist, 9,* 17–26.

Arnold, D. W. (1991). To test or not to test: Legal issues in integrity testing. *Forensic Reports, 4,* 213–224.

Arnold, G., Boone, K. B., Lu, P., Dean, A., Wen, J., Nitch, W., et al. (2005). Sensitivity and specificity of finger tapping test scores for the detection of suspect effort. *Clinical Neuropsychologist, 19,* 105–120.

Arnold, I. A., de Waal, M. W., Eekhof, J. A., & van Hemert, A. M. (2006). Somatoform disorder in primary care: Course and the need for cognitive-behavioral treatment. *Psychosomatics, 47*(6), 498–503.

Arnold, M. M., & Lindsay, D. S. (2002). Remembering remembering. *Journal of Experimental Psychology: Learning, Memory, and Cognition, 28,* 521–529.

Arnold, M. M., & Lindsay, D. S. (2005). Remembrance of remembrance past. *Memory, 13,* 533–549.

Ashendorf, L., O'Bryant, S. E., & McCaffrey, R. J. (2003). Specificity of malingering detection strategies in older adults using the CVLT and WCST. *Clinical Neuropsychologist, 17,* 255–262.

Asher, R. (1951). Munchausen's syndrome. *Lancet, 1,* 339–341.

Ashlock, L., Walker, J., Starkey, T. W., Harmand, J., & Michel, D. (1987). Psychometric characteristics of factitious PTSD. *VA Practitioner, 4,* 37–41.

Assad, G. (1990). *Hallucinations in clinical psychiatry: A guide for mental health professionals.* New York: Brunner/Mazel.

Assad, G., & Shapiro, B. (1986). Hallucinations: Theoretical and clinical overview. *American Journal of Psychiatry, 143,* 1088–1097.

Association for Personnel Test Publishers. (1990). *Model guidelines for preemployment integrity testing programs.* Washington, DC: Author.

Atkinson, R., Henderson, R., Sparr, L., & Deale, S. (1982). Assessment of Vietnam veterans for post-traumatic stress disorder in Veterans Administration disability claims. *American Journal of Psychiatry, 139,* 1118–1121.

Audubon, J. J., & Kirwin, B. R. (1982). Defensiveness in the criminally insane. *Journal of Personality Assessment, 46,* 304–311.

Austin, J. S. (1992). The detection of fake good and fake bad on the MMPI-2. *Educational and Psychological Measurement, 52,* 669–674.

Austin, W. G. (2002). Guidelines for using collateral sources of information in child custody evaluations. *Family Court Review, 40,* 177–184.

Axelrod, B. N., Fichtenberg, N. L., Millis, S. R., & Wertheimer, J. C. (2006). Detecting incomplete effort with digit span from the WAIS-III. *Clinical Neuropsychologist, 20,* 513–523.

Axelrod, B. N., & Rawlings, D. B. (1999). Clinical utility of incomplete effort on the WAIS-R formulas: A longitudinal examination of individuals with traumatic brain injuries. *Journal of Forensic Neuropsychology, 1,* 15–27.

Ayoub, C. C., Alexander, R., Beck, D., Bursch, B., Feldman, K. W., Libow, J., et al. (2002). Position paper: Definitional issues in Munchausen by proxy. *Child Maltreatment, 7*(2), 105–111.

Ayoub, C. C., Schreier, H. A., & Keller, C. (2002). Munchausen by proxy: Presentations in special education. *Child Maltreatment, 7*(2), 149–159.

Babiak, P. (2000). Psychopathic manipulation at work. In C. Gacono (Ed.), *The clinical and forensic assessment of psychopathy* (pp. 287–312). Mahwah, NJ: Erlbaum.

Babikian, T., Boone, K. B., Lu, P., & Arnold, G. (2006). Sensitivity and specificity of various Digit Span scores in the detection of suspect effort. *Clinical Neuropsychologist, 20,* 145–159.

Babor, T. F., Stephens, R. S., & Marlatt, G. A. (1987). Verbal report methods in clinical research on alcoholism: Response bias and its minimization. *Journal of Studies on Alcohol, 48,* 410–424.

Backhaus, S. L., Fichtenberg, N. L., & Hanks, R. A. (2004). Detection of sub-optimal performance using a floor effect strategy in patients with traumatic brain injury. *Clinical Neuropsychologist, 18,* 591–603.

Baer, J. D., Baumgartner, W. A., Hill, V. A., & Blahd, W. H. (1991). Hair analysis for the detection of drug use in pretrial probation and parole populations. *Federal Probation, 55,* 3–10.

Baer, R. A., Ballenger, J., & Kroll, L. S. (1998). Detection of underreporting on the MMPI-A in clinical and community samples. *Journal of Personality Assessment, 71,* 98–113.

Baer, R. A., Kroll, L. S., Rinaldo, J., & Ballenger, J. (1999). Detecting and discriminating between random responding and over-reporting on the MMPI-A. *Journal of Personality Assessment, 72,* 308–320.

Baer, R. A., & Miller, J. (2002). Underreporting of psychopathology on the MMPI-2: A meta-analytic review. *Psychological Assessment, 14,* 16–26.

Baer, R. A., & Sekirnjak, G. (1997). Detection of underreporting on the MMPI-2 in a clinical population: Effects of information about validity scales. *Journal of Personality Assessment, 69,* 555–567.

Baer, R. A., & Wetter, M. W. (1997). Effects of information about validity scales on underreporting of symptoms on the Personality Assessment Inventory. *Journal of Personality Assessment, 68,* 402–413.

Baer, R. A., Wetter, M. W., & Berry, D. T. R. (1992). Detection of underreporting of psychopathology on the MMPI: A meta-analysis. *Clinical Psychology Review, 12,* 509–525.

Baer, R. A., Wetter, M. W., & Berry, D. T. R. (1995). Effects of information about validity scales on underreporting of symptoms on the MMPI-2: An analogue investigation. *Assessment, 2,* 189–200.

Baethge, C., Baldessarini, R. J., Freudenthal, K., Streeruwitz, A., Bauer, M., & Bschor, T. (2005). Hallucinations in bipolar disorder: Characteristics and comparison to unipolar depression and schizophrenia. *Bipolar Disorders, 7*(2), 136–145.

Bagby, R. M., Costa, P. T., McCrae, R. R., Livesley, W. J., Kennedy, S. H., Levitan, R. D., et al. (1999). Replicating the five factor model of personality in a psychiatric sample. *Personality and Individual Differences, 27,* 1135–1139.

Bagby, R. M., Gillis, J. R., & Dickens, S. (1990). Detection of dissimulation with the new generation of objective personality measures. *Behavioral Sciences and the Law, 8,* 93–102.

Bagby, R. M., Gillis, J. R., & Rogers, R. (1991). Effectiveness of the Millon Clinical Multiaxial Inventory Validity Index in the detection of random responding. *Psychological Assessment, 3,* 285–287.

Bagby, R. M., Gillis, J. R., Toner, B. B., & Goldberg, J. (1991). Detecting fake-good and fake-bad responding on the Millon Clinical Multiaxial Personality Inventory-II. *Psychological Assessment, 3,* 496–498.

Bagby, R. M., & Marshall, B. (2003). Positive impression management and its influence on the Revised NEO Personality Inventory: A comparison of analog and differential prevalence group designs. *Psychological Assessment, 15,* 333–339.

Bagby, R. M., & Marshall, M. B. (2005). Assessing response bias with the MCMI modifying indices. In R. J. Craig (Ed.), *New directions in interpreting the Millon Clinical Multiaxial Inventory* (pp. 227–247). New York: Wiley.

Bagby, R. M., Marshall, M. B., Bury, A., Bacchiochi, J. B., & Miller, L. (2006). Assessing underreporting and overreporting with the MMPI-2 validity scales. In J. B. Butcher (Ed.), *MMPI-2: A practitioner's guide* (pp. 39–69). Washington, DC: American Psychological Association.

Bagby, R. M., Nicholson, R. A., Bacchiochi, J. R., Ryder, A. G., & Bury, A. S. (2002). The predictive capacity of the MMPI-2 and PAI validity scales and indexes to detect coached and uncoached feigning. *Journal of Personality Assessment, 78,* 69–86.

Bagby, R. M., Rogers, R., & Buis, T. (1994). Detecting malingered and defensive responding on the MMPI-2 in a forensic inpatient sample. *Journal of Personality Assessment, 62,* 191–203.

Bagby, R. M., Rogers, R., Buis, T., & Kalemba, V. (1994). Malingered and defensive response styles on the MMPI-2: An examination of validity scales. *Assessment, 1,* 31–38.

Bagby, R. M., Rogers, R., Buis, T., Nicholson, R. A., Cameron, S. L., Rector, N. A., et al. (1997). Detecting feigned depression and schizophrenia on the MMPI-2. *Journal of Personality Assessment, 68,* 650–664.

Bagby, R. M., Rogers, R., Nicholson, R., Buis, T., Seeman, M. V., & Rector, N. (1997a). Does clinical training facilitate feigning schizophrenia on the MMPI-2? *Psychological Assessment, 9,* 106–112.

Bagby, R. M., Rogers, R., Nicholson, R., Buis, T., Seeman, M. V., & Rector, N. (1997b). Effectiveness of the MMPI-2 validity indicators in the detection of defensive responding in clinical and nonclinical samples. *Psychological Assessment, 9,* 406–413.

Baity, M. R., Siefert, C. J., Chambers, A., & Blais, M. A. (2007). Deceptiveness on the PAI: A study of naive faking with psychiatric inpatients. *Journal of Personality Assessment, 88,* 16–24.

Baker, A. (2007). Knowledge and attitudes about the parental alienation syndrome: A survey of custody evaluators. *American Journal of Family Therapy, 35*(1), 1–19.

Baker, A., Tabacoff, R., Tornusciolo, G., & Eisenstadt, M. (2003). Family secrecy: A comparative study of juvenile sex offenders and youth with conduct disorders. *Family Process, 42*(1), 105–116.

Baker, J. H. E., & Silver, J. R. (1987). Hysterical paraplegia. *Journal of Neurology, Neurosurgery and Psychiatry, 50,* 375–382.

Bala, N., Lee, K., Lindsay, R. C., & Talwar, V. (2004). Children's lie telling to conceal a parent's transgression: Legal implications. *Law and Human Behavior, 28,* 411–435.

Baldesserini, R. J., Finkelstein, S., & Arana, G. W. (1983). The predictive power of diagnostic tests and the effects of prevalence of illness. *Archives of General Psychiatry, 40,* 569–573.

Ballenger, J. F., Caldwell-Andrews, A., & Baer, R. A. (2001). Effects of positive impression management on the NEO Personality Inventory—Revised in a clinical population. *Psychological Assessment, 13,* 254–260.

Ballinger, B. R., Simpson, E., & Stewart, M. J. (1974). An evaluation of a drug administration system in a psychiatric hospital. *British Journal of Psychiatry, 125,* 202–207.

Bancroft, J., Jones, H. G., & Pullan, B. R. (1966). A simple transducer for measuring penile erections with comments on its use in the treatment of sexual disorders. *Behaviour Research and Therapy, 4,* 239–241.

Barbaree, H. E., & Marshall, W. L. (1989). Erectile responses among heterosexual child molesters, father–daughter incest offenders, and matched non-offenders: Five distinct age preference profiles. *Canadian Journal of Behavioural Science, 21,* 70–82.

Barbaree, H. E., Marshall, W. L., & Hudson, S. M. (1993). *The juvenile sex offender.* New York: Guilford Press.

Barkemeyer, C. A., & Callon, E. B. (1989). *Malingering Detection Scale.* Baton Rouge, LA: North Street Publishing.

Barlow, D. H., Becker, R., Leitenberg, H., & Agras, W. S. (1970). A mechanical strain gauge for recording penile circumference change. *Journal of Applied Behavioral Analysis, 3,* 73–76.

Barrash, J., Suhr, J. A., & Manzel, K. (2004). Detecting poor effort and malingering with an expanded version of the Auditory Verbal Learning Test (AVLTX): Validation with clinical samples. *Journal of the International Neuropsychological Society, 26,* 125–140.

Barrick, M. R., & Mount, M. K. (1991). The Big Five personality dimensions and job performance: A meta-analysis. *Personnel Psychology, 41,* 1–26.

Barth, J. T., Freeman, J., & Broshek, D. (2002). Mild head injury. In V. S. Ramachandran (Ed.), *Encyclopedia of the human brain* (pp. 81–92). New York: Elsevier.

Barth, J. T., Macciocchi, S., Boll, T., Giordani, B., & Rimel, R. (1983). Neuropsychological sequelae of minor head injury. *Neurosurgery, 13,* 529–533.

Bartol, C. R. (1991). Predictive validation of the MMPI for small-town police officers who fail. *Professional Psychology: Research and Practice, 22,* 127–132.

Bartol, C. R. (1996). Police psychology: Then, now and beyond. *Criminal Justice and Behavior, 23,* 70–89.

Bash, I., & Alpert, M. (1980). The determination of malingering. *Annals of the New York Academy of Science, 347,* 86–99.

Basso, M. R., Carona, F. D., & Lowery, N. (2002). Practice effects on the WAIS-III across 3-and 6-month intervals. *Clinical Neuropsychologist, 16,* 57–63.

Batchelder, K. (1995). Detecting malingered psychotic symptoms with the Rorschach Projective Technique. *Dissertation Abstracts International, 55*, 4099.

Bates, J. E. W. (2002). An examination of hangover effects on pilot performance. *Dissertation Abstracts International: Section B. The Physical Sciences and Engineering, 62*(9-B), 4257.

Bauer, K. A. (2004). Covert video surveillance of parents suspected of child abuse: The British experience and alternative approaches. *Theoretical Medicine and Bioethics, 25*(4), 311–327.

Bauer, L., & McCaffrey, R. J. (2006). Coverage of the TOMM, VSVT, and WMT on the Internet: Is test security threatened? *Archives of Clinical Neuropsychology, 21*, 121–126.

Bauer, L., Yantz, C. L., & Ryan, L. M. (2005). An examination of the California Verbal Learning Test II to detect incomplete effort in a traumatic brain-injury sample. *Applied Neuropsychology, 12*(4), 202–207.

Bauer, L., Yantz, C. L., Ryan, L. M., Warden, D. L., & McCaffrey, R. J. (2005). An examination of the California Verbal Learning Test II to detect incomplete effort in a traumatic brain-injury sample. *Applied Neuropsychology, 12*, 202–207.

Bauer, M., & Boegner, F. (1996). Neurological syndromes in factitious disorder. *Journal of Nervous and Mental Disease, 184*(5), 281–288.

Bauer, R., Grande, L., & Valenstein, E. (2003). Amnesic disorders. In K. Heilman & E. Valenstein (Eds.), *Clinical neuropsychology* (4th ed.). New York: Oxford University Press.

Bauer, R. M. (1984). Autonomic recognition of names and faces in prosopagnosia: A neuropsychological application of the Guilty Knowledge Test. *Neuropsychologia, 22*, 457–469.

Bauman, S., Merta, R., & Steiner, R. (1999). Further validation of the adolescent form of the SASSI. *Journal of Child and Adolescent Substance, 9*, 51–71.

Baumgartner, W. A., Hill, V. A., & Blahd, W. H. (1989). Hair analysis for drugs of abuse. *Journal of Forensic Sciences, 34*, 1433–1453.

Beaber, R. J., Marston, A., Michelli, J., & Mills, M. J. (1985). A brief test for measuring malingering in schizophrenic individuals. *American Journal of Psychiatry, 142*, 1478–1481.

Beaulieu, M. C. (2000). Stigma and legitimization in chronic fatigue syndrome: The role of social location. *Dissertation Abstracts International, 60*, 4267.

Beck, A. T., Steer, R. A., & Brown, G. K. (1996). *BDI-III: Manual.* San Antonio, TX: The Psychological Corporation.

Beck, J., & Harris, M. (1994). Visual hallucinations in non-delusional elderly. *International Journal of Geriatric Psychiatry, 9*, 531–536.

Beck, J. T., & Strong, S. R. (1982). Stimulating therapeutic change with interpretations: A comparison of positive and negative connotation. *Journal of Consulting Psychology, 29*, 551–559.

Becker, J. V., Hunter, J. A., Stein, R. M., & Kaplan, M. S. (1989). Factors associated with erection in adolescent sex offenders. *Journal of Psychopathology and Behavioral Assessment, 11*, 353–362.

Bender, S. D., Barth, J. T., & Irby, J. (2004). Historical perspectives. In M. Lovell, R. Echemendia, J. T. Barth, & M. W. Collins (Eds.), *Traumatic brain injury in sports: An international neuropsychological perspective* (pp. 1–21). Lisse, The Netherlands: Swets & Zeitlinger.

Bender, S. D., & Rogers, R. (2004). Detection of neurocognitive feigning: Development of a multi-strategy assessment. *Archives of Clinical Neuropsychology, 19*, 49–60.

Benke, T. (2006). Peduncular hallucinosis: A syndrome of impaired reality monitoring. *Journal of Neurology, 253*(12), 1561–1571.

Ben-Porath, Y. S. (1994). The ethical dilemma of coached malingering research. *Psychological Assessment, 6*, 14–15.

Ben-Porath, Y. S. (2003). Assessing personality and psychopathology with self-report inventories. In J. R. Graham & J. A. Naglieri (Eds.), *Handbook of psychology: Assessment psychology* (pp. 553–577). New York: Wiley.

Ben-Porath, Y. S., & Butcher, J. N. (1989). The comparability of MMPI and MMPI-2 scales and profiles. *Psychological Assessment, 1*, 345–347.

Ben-Porath, Y. S., & Waller, G. (1992). "Normal" personality inventories in clinical assessment: General requirements and the potential for using the NEO Personality Inventory. *Psychological Assessment, 4*, 14–19.

Ben-Shakar, G. (2002). A critical review of the control questions test (CQT). In M. Kleiner (Ed.), *Handbook of polygraph testing* (pp. 103–126). San Diego, CA: Academic Press.

Ben-Shakar, G., & Elaad, E. (2003). The validity of psychophysiological detection of information with the guilty knowledge test: A meta-analytic review. *Journal of Applied Psychology, 88*, 131–151.

Bentley v. Carroll, 734 A.2d 697 (Md. Ct. App., 1998).

Bernard, L., Houston, W., & Natoli, L. (1993). Malingering on neuropsychological memory tests: Potential objective indicators. *Journal of Clinical Psychology, 49*, 45–53.

Bernard, L. C. (1990). Prospects for faking believable memory deficits on neuropsychological tests and use of incentives in simulation research. *Journal of Clinical and Experimental Neuropsychology, 12*, 715–728.

Bernard, L. C., McGrath, M. J., & Houston, W. (1993). Discriminating between simulated malingering and closed head injury on the Wechsler Memory Scale—Revised. *Archives of Clinical Neuropsychology, 8*, 539–551.

Bernard, L. C., McGrath, M. J., & Houston, W. (1996). The differential effects of simulating malingering, closed head injury, and other CNS pathology on the Wisconsin Card Sorting Test: Support for the "pattern of performance" hypothesis. *Archives of Clinical Neuropsychology, 11*(3), 231–245.

Berney, T. (1973). A review of simulated illness. *South African Medical Journal, 47*, 1429–1434.

Bernstein, D. P., Kasapis, C., Bergman, A., & Weld, E. (1997). Assessing Axis II disorders by informant interview. *Journal of Personality Disorders, 11,* 158–167.

Bernstein, I. H., Schoenfeld, L. S., & Costello, R. M. (1982). Truncated component regression, multicollinearity and the MMPI's use in a police officer selection setting. *Multivariate Behavioral Research, 17,* 99–116.

Berrios, G. (1991). Musical hallucinations: A statistical analysis of 46 cases. *Psychopathology, 24,* 356–360.

Berry, C. M., Sackett, P. R., & Wiemann, S. (2007). A review of recent developments in integrity test research. *Personnel Psychology, 60,* 271–301.

Berry, D. T. R., Adams, J. J., Clark, C. C., Thacker, S. R., Burger, T. L., Wetter, M., et al. (1996). Detection of a cry for help on MMPI-2: An analogue investigation. *Journal of Personality Assessment, 67,* 26–36.

Berry, D. T. R., Baer, R. A., & Harris, M. J. (1991). Detection of malingering on the MMPI: A meta-analysis. *Clinical Psychology Review, 11,* 585–598.

Berry, D. T. R., Bagby, R. M., Smerz, J., Rinaldo, J. C., Caldwell-Andrews, A., & Baer, R. A. (2001). Effectiveness of NEO-PI-R research validity scales for discriminating analog malingering and genuine psychopathology. *Journal of Personality Assessment, 76,* 496–516.

Berry, D. T. R., & Granacher, R. P. (in press). Feigning of psychiatric symptoms in the context of documented severe head injury and preserved motivation on neuropsychological testing. In J. Morgan & J. Sweet (Eds.), *Neuropsychology of malingering casebook.* New York: Taylor & Francis.

Berry, D. T. R., Lamb, D. G., Wetter, M. W., Baer, R. A., & Widiger, T. A. (1994). Ethical considerations in research on coached malingering. *Psychological Assessment, 6,* 16–17.

Berry, D. T. R., & Schipper, L. J. (2007). Detection of feigned psychiatric symptoms during forensic neuropsychological examinations. In G. J. Larrabee (Ed.), *Assessment of malingered neuropsychological deficits* (pp. 226–263). New York: Oxford University Press.

Berry, D. T. R., Wetter, M. W., & Baer, R. A., (1995). Assessment of malingering. In J. N. Butcher (Ed.), *Clinical personality assessment: Practical approaches* (pp. 236–248). New York: Oxford University Press.

Berry, D. T. R., Wetter, M. W., Baer, R. A., Larsen, L., Clark, C., & Monroe, K. (1992). MMPI-2 random responding indices: Validation using a self-report methodology. *Psychological Assessment, 4,* 340–345.

Berry, D. T. R., Wetter, M. W., Baer, R. A., Widiger, T. A., Sumpter, J. C., Reynolds, S. K., et al. (1991). Detection of random responding on the MMPI-2: Utility of F, Back F, and VRIN scales. *Psychological Assessment, 3,* 418–423.

Bersoff, D. N. (Ed.). (2003). *Ethical conflicts in psychology* (3rd ed.). Washington, DC: American Psychological Association.

Betts, G. L. (1947). The detection of incipient army criminals. *Science, 106,* 93–96.

Beyko, M. J., & Wong, S. C. P. (2005). Predictors of *treatment* attrition as indicators for program improvement, not offender shortcomings: A study of *sex* offender *treatment* attrition. *Sexual Abuse: Journal of Research and Treatment, 17*(4), 375–389.

Bianchini, K., Love, J. M., Greve, K. W., & Adams, D. (2005). Detection and diagnosis of malingering in electrical injury. *Archives of Clinical Neuropsychology, 20,* 365–373.

Bianchini, K. J., Curtis, K. L., & Greve, K. W. (2006). Compensation and malingering in traumatic brain injury: A dose–response relationship? *Clinical Neuropsychologist, 20,* 831–847.

Bianchini, K. J., Greve, K. W., & Glynn, G. (2005). On the diagnosis of malingered pain-related disability: Lessons from the cognitive malingering research. *Spine Journal, 5,* 404–417.

Bianchini, K. J., Greve, K. W., & Love, J. M. (2003). Definite malingered neurocognitive dysfunction in moderate/severe traumatic brain injury. *Clinical Neuropsychologist, 17,* 574–580.

Bianchini, K. J., Houston, R. J., Greve, K. W., Irvin, T. R., Black, F. W., Swift, D. A., et al. (2003). Malingered neurocognitive dysfunction in neurotoxic exposure: An application of the Slick criteria. *Journal of Occupational and Environmental Medicine, 45,* 1087–1099.

Bianchini, K. J., Mathias, C. W., & Greve, K. W. (2001). Symptom validity testing: A critical review. *Clinical Neuropsychologist, 15,* 19–45.

Bigler, E. D. (1990a). Neuropsychology and malingering: Comment on Faust, Hart, and Guilmette. *Journal of Consulting and Clinical Psychology, 58,* 244–247.

Bigler, E. D. (1990b). *Traumatic brain injury: Mechanisms of damage, assessment, intervention, and outcome.* Austin, TX: Pro-Ed.

Bijttebier, P., & Vertommen, H. (1999). Antecedents, concomitants, and consequences of pediatric headache: Confirmatory construct validation of two parent-report scales. *Journal of Behavioral Medicine, 22*(5), 437–456.

Binder, L. M. (1993). Assessment of malingering after mild head trauma with the Portland Digit Recognition Test. *Journal of Clinical and Experimental Neuropsychology, 15,* 170–182.

Binder, L. M. (1997). A review of mild head trauma: Part II. Clinical applications. *Journal of Clinical and Experimental Neuropsychology, 19,* 432–457.

Binder, L. M., Kelly, M. P., Villaneuva, M. R., & Winslow, R. (2003). Motivation and neuropsychological test performance following mild head injury. *Journal of Clinical and Experimental Neuropsychology, 25,* 420–430.

Binder, L. M., & Rohling, M. (1996). Money matters: A meta-analytic review of the effects of financial incentives on recovery after closed head injury. *American Journal of Psychiatry, 153,* 7–10.

Binder, L. M., Rohling, M., & Larrabee, G. L. (1997). A review of mild head trauma: Part I. Meta-analytic review of neuropsychological studies. *Journal of Clinical and Experimental Neuropsychology, 19,* 421–431.

Bird, C. M., Papadopoulou, K., Ricciardelli, P., Rossor, M. N., & Cipolotti, L. (2004). Monitoring cognitive changes: Psychometric properties of six cognitive tests. *British Journal of Clinical Psychology, 43,* 197–210.

Bishop, E. R., & Holt, A. R. (1980). Pseudopsychosis: A reexamination of the concept of hysterical psychosis. *Comprehensive Psychiatry, 21,* 150–161.

Bitzer, R. (1980). Caught in the middle: Mentally disabled veterans and the Veterans Administration. In C. R. Figley & S. Leventman (Eds.), *Strangers at home: Vietnam veterans since the war* (pp. 305–323). New York: Praeger.

Blais, M. A., Benedict, K. B., & Norman, D. K. (1995). Concurrent validity of the MCMI-II modifier indices. *Journal of Clinical Psychology, 51,* 783–789.

Blanchard, D. D., McGrath, R. E., Pogge, D. L., & Khadivi, A. (2003). A comparison of the PAI and MMPI-2 as predictors of faking bad in college students. *Journal of Personality Assessment, 80,* 197–205.

Blanchard, K. A., Morgenstern, J., Morgan, T. J., Labouvie, E. W., & Bux, D. A. (2003). Assessing consequences of substance use: Psychometric properties of the inventory of drug use consequences. *Psychology of Addictive Behavior, 17,* 328–331.

Blanchard, R., Klassen, P., Dickey, R., Kuban, M. E., & Blak, T. (2001). Sensitivity and specificity of the phallometric test for pedophilia in nonadmitting sex offenders. *Psychological Assessment, 13,* 118–126.

Blanchard, R., Kolb, L. C., Pallmeyer, T. P., & Gerardi, R. J. (1982). A psychophysiological study of posttraumatic stress disorder in Vietnam vetereans. *Psychiatric Quaterly, 54,* 220–229.

Blanchard, R., Kuban, M. E., Blak, T., Cantor, J. M., Klassen, P., & Dickey, R. (2006). Phallometric comparison of pedophilic interest in nonadmitting sexual offenders against stepdaughters, biological daughters, other biologically related girls, and unrelated girls. *Sexual Abuse: A Journal of Research and Treatment, 18,* 1–14.

Blanchard, R., Racansky, I. G., & Steiner, B. W. (1986). Phallometric detection of fetishistic arousal in heterosexual male cross-dressers. *Journal of Sex Research, 22,* 452–462.

Blankenship, K., & Whitley, B. (2000). Relation of general deviance to academic dishonesty. *Ethics and Behavior, 10,* 1–12.

Blasingame, G. D. (1998). Suggested clinical uses of polygraphy in community-based sexual offender treatment programs. *Sexual Abuse: A Journal of Research and Treatment, 10,* 37–45.

Boccaccini, M. T., Murrie, D. C., & Duncan, S. A. (2006). Screening for malingering in a criminal-forensic sample with the Personality Assessment Inventory. *Psychological Assessment, 18*(4), 415–423.

Bogduk, N. (2004). Diagnostic blocks: A truth serum for malingering. *Clinical Journal of Pain, 20,* 409–414.

Bolter, T., Picano, J. J., & Zych, K. (1985). *Item error frequencies on the Halstead Category Test: An index of performance validity.* Paper presented at the annual meeting of the National Academy of Neuropsychology, Philadelphia, PA.

Book, A. S., Holden, R. R., Starzyk, K. B., Wasylkiw, L., & Edwards, M. J. (2006). Psychopathic traits and experimentally induced deception in self-report assessment. *Personality and Individual Differences, 41,* 601–608.

Bools, C., Foster, J., Brown, I., & Berg, I. (1990). The identification of psychiatric disorders in children who fail to attend school: A cluster analysis of a non-clinical population. *Psychological Medicine, 20,* 171–181.

Boone, K. B., & Lu, P. H. (1999). Impact of somatoform symptomatology on credibility of cognitive performance. *Clinical Neuropsychologist, 13,* 414–419.

Boone, K. B., & Lu, P. H. (2003). Noncredible cognitive performance in the context of severe brain injury. *Clinical Neuropsychologist, 17*(2), 244–254.

Boone, K. B., Lu, P., Back, C., King, C., Lee, A., Philpott, L., et al. (2001). Sensitivity and specificity of the Rey Dot Counting Test in patients with suspect effort and various clinical samples. *Archives of Clinical Neuropsychology, 17,* 1–19.

Boone, K. B., Lu, P., Sherman, D., Palmer, B., Back, C., Shamieh, E., et al. (2000). Validation of a new technique to detect malingering of cognitive symptoms: The b test. *Archives of Clinical Neuropsychology, 15,* 227–241.

Boone, K. B., Lu, P., & Wen, J. (2005). Comparison of various RAVLT scores in the detection of noncredible memory performance. *Archives of Clinical Neuropsychology, 20,* 301–320.

Boone, K. B., Salazar, X., Lu, P., Warner-Chacon, K., & Razani, J. (2002). The Rey 15-item recognition trial: A technique to enhance sensitivity of the Rey 15-Item Memorization Test. *Journal of Clinical and Experimental Neuropsychology, 24,* 561–573.

Borg, S., Connor, E. J., & Landis, E. E. (1995). *Impact of expertise and sufficient information on psychologists' ability to detect malingering.* Unpublished manuscript, Federal Bureau of Prisons, Butner, NC.

Borum, R., Otto, R. K., & Golding, S. (1991). Improving clinical judgment and decision making in forensic evaluation. *Journal of Psychiatry and Law, 21,* 35–76.

Borum, R., & Stock, H. (1993). Detection of deception in law enforcement applicants: A preliminary investigation. *Law and Human Behavior, 17,* 157–166.

Bow, J. N., Quinnell, F. A., Zaroff, M., & Assemany, A. (2002). Assessment of sexual abuse allegations in child custody cases. *Professional Psychology: Research and Practice, 33,* 556–575.

Brace, M. J., Scott Smith, M., McCauley, E., & Sherry, D. D. (2000). Family reinforcement of illness behavior: A comparison of adolescents with chronic fatigue syndrome, juvenile arthritis, and healthy controls. *Journal of Developmental and Behavioral Pediatrics, 21*(5), 332–339.

Bradford, J. M., & Smith, S. M. (1979). Amnesia and homicide: The Padola case and a study of thirty cases. *Bulletin of the American Academy of Psychiatry and the Law, 7,* 219–231.

Braginsky, B. M., & Braginsky, D. D. (1967). Schizophrenic patients in the psychiatric interview: An experimental study of their effectiveness at manipulation. *Journal of Consulting Psychology, 31,* 543–547.

Braham, L. G., Trower, P., & Birchwood, M. (2004). Acting on command hallucinations and dangerous behavior: A critique of the major findings in the last decade. *Clinical Psychology Review, 24*(5), 513–528.

Branaman, T. F., & Gallagher, S. N. (2005). Polygraph testing in sex offender treatment: A review of limitations. *American Journal of Forensic Psychology, 23,* 45–64.

Brand, B. L., McNary, S. W., Loewenstein, R. J., Kolos, A. C., & Barr, S. R. (2006). Assessment of genuine and simulated dissociative identity disorder on the Structured Interview of Reported Symptoms. *Journal of Trauma and Dissociation, 7,* 63–85.

Brandt, J. (1992). Detecting amnesia's impostors. In L. R. Squire & N. Butters (Eds.), *Neuropsychology of memory* (2nd ed., pp. 156–165). New York: Guilford Press.

Braverman, M. (1978). Post-injury malingering is seldom a calculated ploy. *Annals of the New York Academy of Sciences, 444,* 502–503.

Brems, C., & Johnson, M. E. (1991). Subtle–obvious scales of the MMPI: Indicators of profile validity in a psychiatric population. *Journal of Personality Assessment, 56,* 536–544.

Brennan, A. M., & Gouvier, W. D. (2006). Are we honestly studying malingering?: A profile and comparison of simulated and suspected malingerers. *Applied Neuropsychology, 13,* 1–11.

Breslau, N., & Davis, G. C. (1992). Posttraumatic stress disorder in an urban population of young adults: Risk factors for chronicity. *American Journal of Psychiatry, 149*(5), 671–675.

Breslau, N., Davis, G. C., Andreski, P., & Petersen, E. (1991). Traumatic events and post traumatic stress disorder in an urban population of young adults. *Archives of General Psychiatry, 156,* 908–911.

Breslau, N., & Kessler, R. (2001). The stressor criterion in DSM-IV posttraumatic stress disorder: An empirical investigation. *Biological Psychiatry, 50*(9), 699–704.

Breslau, N., Reboussin, B. A., Anthony, J. C., & Storr, C. L. (2005). The structure of posttraumatic stress disorder: Latent class analysis in 2 community samples. *Archives of General Psychiatry, 62,* 1343–1351.

Breuer, J., & Freud, S. (1955). Studies in hysteria. In J. Strachey (Ed. & Trans.), *The standard edition of the complete psychological works of Sigmund Freud* (Vol. 2, pp. 21–319). London: Hogarth Press. (Original work published 1895)

Brewin, C. R., Kleiner, J. S., Vasterling, J. J., & Field, A. P. (in press). Memory for emotionally neutral information in posttraumatic stress disorder: A meta-analytic investigation. *Journal of Abnormal Psychology.*

Briere, J. (1995). *Trauma Symptom Inventory professional manual.* Odessa, FL: Psychological Assessment Resources.

Briere, J., & Conte, J. (1993). Self-reported amnesia for abuse in adults molested as children. *Journal of Traumatic Stress, 6,* 21–31.

Brinkley, C. A., Newman, J. P., Widiger, T. A., & Lynam, D. R. (2004). Two approaches to parsing the heterogeneity of psychopathy. *Clinical Psychology: Science and Practice, 11,* 69–94.

Brittain, R. (1966). The history of legal medicine: The assizes of Jerusalem. *Medicolegal Journal, 34,* 72–73.

Brodey, B. B., Rosen, C. S., Brodey, I. S., Sheetz, B. M., Steinfeld, R. R., & Gastfriend, D. R. (2004). Validation of the Addiction Severity Index (ASI) for Internet and automated telephone self-report administration. *Journal of Substance Abuse Treatment, 26,* 253–259.

Brodey, B. B., Rosen, C. S., Winters K. C., Brodey, I. S., Sheetz, B. M., Steinfeld, R. R., et al. (2005). Conversion and validation of the Teen Addiction Severity Index (T-ASI) for Internet and automated-telephone self-report administration. *Psychology of Addictive Behaviors, 19*(1), 54–61.

Broughton, N., & Chesterman, P. (2001). Malingered psychosis. *Journal of Forensic Psychiatry, 12*(2), 407–422.

Brown, D., & Scheflin, A. W. (1999). Factitious disorders and trauma-related diagnoses. *Journal of Psychiatry and Law, 27*(3), 373–422.

Brown, D., Scheflin, A. W., & Hammond, D. C. (1998). *Memory, trauma treatment, and the law.* New York: Norton.

Brown, D., Scheflin, A. W., & Whitfield, C. L. (1999). Recovered memories: The current weight of the evidence in science and in the courts. *Journal of Psychiatry and Law, 27,* 5–156.

Brown, R. J. (2004). Psychological mechanisms of medically unexplained symptoms: An integrative conceptual model. *Psychological Bulletin, 130*(5), 793–812.

Brown, T. A., Campbell, L. A., Lehman, C. L., Grisham, J. R., & Mancill, R. B. (2001). Current and lifetime comorbidity of the DSM-IV anxiety and mood disorders in a large clinical sample. *Journal of Abnormal Psychology, 110,* 585–599.

Brownell, K. D., Hayes, S. C., & Barlow, D. H. (1977). Patterns of appropriate and deviant sexual arousal: The behavioral treatment of multiple sexual deviations. *Journal of Consulting and Clinical Psychology, 45,* 1144–1155.

Brozovich, R. (1970). Fakability of scores on the Group Personality Projective Test. *Journal of Genetic Psychology, 117,* 143–148.

Bruni, J. (2000). Episodic impairment of consciousness. In W. C. Bradley, R. B. Daroff, G. M. Fenichel, & C. D. Marsden (Eds.), *Neurology in clinical practice* (3rd ed., pp. 9–18). Boston: Butterworth Heinemann.

Bruns, B., Stein, M. T., Wells, R. D., & Wender, E. H. (2005). Scott: An 11-year-old boy with repetitive lying. *Journal of Developmental and Behavioral Pediatrics, 26,* 423–426.

Bruns, D., Disorbio, J. M., & Copeland-Disorbio, J. (1996). *Manual for the Battery for Health Improvement—2.* Minnetonka, MN: Pearson Assessments.

Buchan, B. J., Dennis, M. L., Tims, F. M., & Diamond, G. S. (2002). Cannabis use: Consistency and validity of self-report, on-site urine testing and laboratory testing. *Addiction, 97*(Suppl. 1), 98–108.

Buck, O. D. (1983). Multiple personality as a borderline state. *Journal of Nervous and Mental Disease, 171,* 62–65.

Buckhout, R. (1974). Eyewitness testimony. *Scientific American, 231,* 23–31.

Buckley, T. J., Pleil, J. D., Bowyer, J. R., & Davis, J. M. (2001). Evaluation of methyl tert-butyl ether (MTBE) as an interference on commercial breath-alcohol analyzers. *Forensic Science International, 123,* 111–118.

Bullard, P. L. (2003). Patients' intentional deceptions of medical professionals: Emphasizing concealment and under-reporting by purportedly healthy individuals. *Dissertation Abstracts International: Section B. The Physical Sciences and Engineering, 63*(10-B), 4891.

Bullman, R. J., & Wortman, C. B. (1977). Attributions of blame and coping in the real world: Severe accident victims and their lot. *Journal of Personality and Social Psychology, 33,* 351.

Bunnting, B. G., Wessels, W. H., Lasich, A. J., & Pillay, B. (1996). The distinction of malingering and mental illness in black forensic cases. *Medicine and Law, 15,* 241–247.

Burges, C., & McMillan, T. (2001). The ability of naive participants to report symptoms of post-traumatic stress disorder. *British Journal of Clinical Psychology, 40*(2), 209–214.

Burgoon, M., Callister, M., & Hunsaker, F. G. (1994). Patients who deceive: An empirical investigation of patient–physician communication. *Journal of Language and Social Psychology, 13,* 443–468.

Burkett, B., & Whitley, G. (1998). *Stolen valor: How the Vietnam generation was robbed of its heroes and history.* Dallas, TX: Verity Press.

Bursten, B. (1965). On Munchausen's syndrome. *Archives of General Psychiatry, 13,* 261–268.

Bury, A., & Bagby, R. (2002). The detection of feigned uncoached and coached posttraumatic stress disorder with the MMPI-2 in a sample of workplace accident victims. *Psychological Assessment, 14*(4), 472–484.

Bush, S., Ruff, R., Troster, A., Barth, J., Koffler, S., Pliskin, N., et al. (2005). Symptom validity assessment: Practice issues and medical necessity. *Archives of Clinical Neuropsychology, 20,* 419–426.

Bussey, K. (1992a). Children's lying and truthfulness: Implications for children's testimony. In S. J. Ceci, M. D. Leichtman, & M. Putnick (Eds.), *Cognitive and social factors in early deception* (pp. 89–109). Hillsdale, NJ: Erlbaum.

Bussey, K. (1992b). Lying and truthfulness: Children's definitions, standards, and evaluative reactions. *Child Development, 63,* 129–137.

Bustamante, J., & Ford, C. (1977). Ganser's syndrome. *Psychiatric Opinion, 14,* 39–41.

Butcher, J. N., Atlis, M. M., & Fang, L. (2000). Effect of altered instructions on the MMPI-2 profiles of college students who are not motivated to distort their responses. *Journal of Personality Assessment, 75,* 492–501.

Butcher, J. N., Dahlstrom, W. G., Graham, J. R., Tellegen, A. M., & Kaemmer, B. (1989). *MMPI-2: Manual for administration and scoring.* Minneapolis: University of Minnesota Press.

Butcher, J. N., Graham, J. R., Ben-Porath, Y. S., Tellegen, A., Dahlstrom, W. G., & Kaemmer, B. (2001). *Minnesota Multiphasic Personality Inventory—2: Manual for administration, scoring and interpretation* (Rev. ed.). Minneapolis: University of Minnesota Press.

Butcher, J. N., & Han, K. (1995). Development of an MMPI-2 scale to assess the presentation of self in a superlative manner: The S scale. In J. N. Butcher & C. D. Spielberger (Eds.), *Advances in personality assessment* (Vol. 10, pp. 25–50). Hillsdale, NJ: Erlbaum.

Butcher, J. N., Morfitt, R. C., Rouse, S. V., & Holden, R. R. (1997). Reducing MMPI-2 defensiveness: The effect of specialized instructions on retest validity in a job applicant sample. *Journal of Personality Assessment, 68,* 385–401.

Butcher, J. N., & Tellegen, A. (1966). Objections to MMPI items. *Journal of Consulting Psychology, 30,* 527–534.

Butcher, J. N., Williams, C. L., Graham, J. R., Archer, R. P., Tellegen, A., Ben-Porath, Y. S., et al. (1992). *MMPI-A: Minnesota Multiphasic Personality Inventory-A: Manual for administration, scoring, and interpretation.* Minneapolis: University of Minnesota Press.

Bylin, S., & Christianson, S. (2002). Characteristics of malingered amnesia: Consequences of withholding vs. distorting information on later memory of a crime event. *Legal and Criminological Psychology, 7,* 45–61.

Caine, S. L., Kinder, B. N., & Frueh, B. C. (1995). Rorschach susceptibility to malingered depressive disorders in adult females. In C. D. Spielberger & J. Butcher (Eds.), *Advances in Personality Assessment* (Vol. 10, pp. 165–174). Hillsdale, NJ: Erlbaum.

Caldwell, A. B. (1969). *MMPI critical items.* (Available from Caldwell Report, 5839 Green Valley Circle, Suite #203 Culver City, CA 90230)

Caldwell, A. B. (1988). *MMPI supplemental scale manual.* Los Angeles: Caldwell Reports.

Caldwell, A. B. (2003). [*MMPI-2 data research file for clinical patients.*] Unpublished raw data.

Caldwell-Andrews, A., Baer, R. A., & Berry, D. T. R. (2000). Effects of response sets on NEO-PI-R scores and their relations to external criteria. *Journal of Personality Assessment, 74,* 472–488.

Calhoun, P., Earnst, K., Tucker, D., Kirby, A., & Beckham, J. (2000). Feigning combat-related posttraumatic stress disorder on the Personality Assessment Inventory. *Journal of Personality Assessment, 75*(2), 338–350.

Callon, E. B., Jones, G. N., Barkemeyer, C. A., & Brantley, P. J. (1990, August). *Validity of a scale to detect malingering.* Paper presented at the annual meeting of the American Psychological Association, Boston.

Camara, W. J., Nathan, J. S., & Puente, A. E. (2000). Psychological test usage: Implications in professional psychology. *Professional Psychology: Research and Practice, 31,* 141–154.

Cantor, C., & Heads, N. (2004). Somatoform deception. *Australasian Psychiatry, 12*(4), 411.

Cantwell, J. B. (1981). Sexual abuse of children in Denver, 1979: Reviewed with implications for pediatric intervention and possible prevention. *Child Abuse and Neglect, 5,* 75–85.

Caradoc-Davies, G. (1988). Feigned alcohol abuse: A unique case report. *British Journal of Psychiatry, 152,* 418–420.

Carney, M. W., & Brown, J. P. (1983). Clinical features and motives among 42 artifactual illness patients. *British Journal of Medical Psychology, 56*(Pt. 1), 57–66.

Carp, A., & Shavzin, A. (1950). The susceptibility to falsification of the Rorschach psychodiagnostic technique. *Journal of Consulting Psychology, 14,* 230–233.

Carr, G. D., Moretti, M. M., & Cue, B. J. H. (2005). Evaluating parenting capacity: Validity problems with the MMPI-2, PAI, CAPI, and ratings of child adjustment. *Professional Psychology: Research and Practice, 36,* 188–196.

Carroll, M. F. (2003). Malingering in the military. *Psychiatric Annals, 33*(11), 732–736.

Carsky, M., Selzer, M. A., Terkelsen, K. G., & Hurt, S. W. (1992). The PEH: A questionnaire to assess acknowledgment of psychiatric illness. *Journal of Nervous and Mental Disease, 180,* 458–464.

Carter, D. M., Mackinnon, A., & Copoloy, D. (1996). Patients' strategies for coping with auditory hallucinations. *Journal of Nervous and Mental Diseases, 184*(3), 159–164.

Cashel, M. L., Rogers, R., Sewell, K. S., & Martin-Cannici, C. (1995). The Personality Assessment Inventory (PAI) and the detection of defensiveness. *Assessment, 2,* 333–342.

Cassel, R. N., & Brauchle, R. P. (1959). An assessment of the fakability of scores on the Group Personality Projective Test. *Journal of Genetic Psychology, 98,* 239–244.

Cattell, R. B., Eber, H. W., & Tatsuoka, M. M. (1970). *Handbook for the 16PF.* Champaign, IL: Institute for Personality and Ability Testing.

Ceci, S. J., & Bruck, M. (1993). Suggestibility of the child witness: A historical review and synthesis. *Psychological Bulletin, 113,* 403–439.

Cercy, S. P., Schretlen, D. J., & Brandt, J. (1997). Simulated amnesia and the pseudo-memory phenomena. In R. Rogers (Ed.), *Clinical assessment of malingering and deception* (2nd ed., pp. 85–107). New York: Guilford Press.

Chadwick, P., & Birchwood, M. (1994). The omnipotence of voices: A cognitive approach to auditory hallucinations. *British Journal of Psychiatry, 164*(2), 190–201.

Chaney, H. S., Cohn, C. K., Williams, S. G., & Vincent, K. R. (1984). MMPI results: A comparison of trauma victims, psychogenic pain and patients with organic disease. *Journal of Clinical Psychology, 40,* 1450–1454.

Chapman, S. L., & Brena, S. F. (1990). Patterns of conscious failure to provide accurate self-report data in patients with low back pain. *Clinical Journal of Pain, 6,* 178–190.

Cherepon, J., & Prinzhorn, B. (1994). Personality Assessment Inventory (PAI) profiles of adult female abuse survivors. *Assessment, 1*(4), 393–399.

Chibnall, J. T., & Tait, R. C. (1999). Social and medical influences on attributions and evaluations of chronic pain. *Psychology and Health, 14*(4), 719–729.

Chojnacki, J. T., & Walsh, W. B. (1992). The consistency of scores and configural patterns between the MMPI and MMPI-2. *Journal of Personality Assessment, 59,* 276–289.

Chouinard, M. J., & Rouleau, I. (1997). The 48-Pictures Test: A two-alternative forced-choice recognition test for the detection of malingering. *Journal of the International Neuropsychological Society, 3,* 545–552.

Christianson, S. A., & Bylin, S. (1999). Does simulating amnesia mediate genuine forgetting for a crime event? *Applied Cognitive Psychology, 13,* 495–511.

Cigrang, J. A., & Staal, M. A. (2001). Readministration of the MMPI-2 following defensive invalidation in a military job applicant sample. *Journal of Personality Assessment, 76,* 472–481.

Cima, M., Merckelbach, H., Hollnack, S., & Knauer, E. (2003). Characteristics of psychiatric prison inmates who claim amnesia. *Personality and Individual Differences, 35,* 373–380.

Cima, M., Merckelbach, H., Nijman, H., Knauer, E., & Hollnack, S. (2002). I can't remember, your honor: Offenders who claim amnesia. *German Journal of Psychiatry, 5,* 24–34.

Cima, M., Nijman, H., Merckelbach, H., Kremer, K., & Hollnack, S. (2004). Claims of crime-related amnesia in forensic patients. *International Journal of Law and Psychiatry, 27,* 215–221.

Clancy, S. A. (2005). *Abducted: How people come to believe they were kidnapped by aliens.* Cambridge, MA: Harvard University Press.

Clancy, S. A., & McNally, R. J. (2005–2006). Who needs repression?: Normal memory processes can explain "forgetting" of childhood sexual abuse. *Scientific Review of Mental Health Practice, 4,* 66–73.

Clancy, S. A., Schacter, D. L., McNally, R. J., & Pitman, R. K. (2000). False recognition in women reporting recovered memories of sexual abuse. *Psychological Science, 11,* 26–31.

Clark, C. R. (1997). Sociopathy, malingering, and defensiveness. In R. Rogers (Ed.), *Clinical assessment of malingering and deception* (2nd ed., pp. 68–84). New York: Guilford Press.

Clark, L. A. (1993). *The Schedule for Nonadaptive and Adaptive Personality: Manual for administration and scoring.* Minneapolis: University of Minnesota Press.

Clark, M. E., Gironda, R. J., & Young, R. W. (2003). Detection of back random responding: Effectiveness of MMPI-2 and Personality Assessment Inventory validity indices. *Psychological Assessment, 15,* 223–234.

Clements, R. (2000). Psychometric properties of the Substance Abuse Subtle Screening Inventory—3. *Journal of Substance Abuse Treatment, 23,* 419–423.

Clements, R., & Heintz, J. M. (2002). Diagnostic accuracy and factor structure of the AAS and APS scales of the MMPI-2. *Journal of Personality Assessment, 79*(3), 564–582.

Clevenger, S. V. (1889). *Spinal concussion*. London: Davis.

Cocco, K. M., & Carey, K. B. (1998). Psychometric properties of the Drug Abuse Screening Test in psychiatric outpatients. *Psychological Assessment, 10*(4), 408–414.

Cochrane, R. E., Tett, R. P., & Vandecreek, L. (2003). Psychological testing and the selection of police officers. *Criminal Justice and Behavior, 30*, 511–537.

Cofer, C. N., Chance, J., & Judson, A. J. (1949). A study of malingering on the MMPI. *Journal of Psychology, 27*, 491–499.

Cohen, J. (1962). The statistical power of abnormal–social psychological research: A review. *Journal of Abnormal and Social Psychology, 65*, 145–153.

Cohen, J. (1988). *Statistical power analysis for the behavioral sciences* (2nd ed.). Hillsdale, NJ: Erlbaum.

Cohen, M. A., Alfonso, C. A., & Haque, M. M. (1994). Lilliputian hallucinations and medical illness. *General Hospital Psychiatry, 16*, 141–143.

Cohen, S. (1984). Drugs in the workplace. *Journal of Clinical Psychiatry, 45*, 4–8.

Colby, F. (1989). Usefulness of the *K* correction in the MMPI profiles of patients and nonpatients. *Psychological Assessment, 1*, 142–145.

Cole, P. M., Barrett, K. C., & Zahn-Waxler, C. (1992). Emotion displays in two-year-olds during mishaps. *Child Development, 63*, 314–324.

Collie, J. (1971). *Malingering and feigned sickness*. London: Arnold.

Collinson, G. (1812). *A treatise on the law concerning idiots, lunatics, and other persons* non compos mentis. London: Reed.

Committee on Ethical Guidelines for Forensic Psychologists. (1991). Specialty guidelines for forensic psychologists. *Law and Human Behavior, 15*, 655–665.

Commonwealth v. Zamarripa, 549 A.2d 980 (1988).

Compton, W. M., & Cottler, L. B. (2004). *The Diagnostic Interview Schedule (DIS)*. St. Lois, MO: Washington University.

Connell, D. K. (1991). *The SIRS and the M Test: The differential validity of two instruments designed to detect malingered psychosis in a correctional sample*. Unpublished dissertation, University of Louisville.

Constantinou, M., Bauer, L., Ashendorf, L., Fisher, J., & McCaffrey, R. J. (2005). Is poor performance on recognition memory effort measures indicative of generalized poor performance on neuropsychological tests? *Archives of Clinical Neuropsychology, 20*, 191–198.

Constantinou, M., & McCaffrey, R. J. (2003). Using the TOMM for evaluating children's effort to perform optimally on neuropsychological measures. *Child Neuropsychology, 9*, 81–90.

Conti, R. P. (2004). Malingered ADHD in adolescents diagnosed with conduct disorder: A brief note. *Psychological Reports, 94*, 987–988.

Cook, D. M., & Meikle, A. W. (1985). Factitious Cushing's syndrome. *Journal of Clinical Endocrinology and Metabolism, 61*(2), 385–387.

Coons, P. M. (1993). Use of the MMPI to distinguish genuine from factitious multiple personality disorder. *Psychological Reports, 73*, 401–402.

Copoloy, D., Trauer, T., & Mackinnon, A. (2004). On the non-significance of internal versus external auditory hallucinations. *Schizophrenia Research, 69*(1), 1–6.

Cornelius, J., Mezzich, J., Fabrega, H., Cornelius, M., Myer, J., & Ulrich, R. (1991). Characterizing organic hallucinosis. *Comprehensive Psychiatry, 32*, 338–344.

Cornell, D. G., & Hawk, G. L. (1989). Clinical presentation of malingerers diagnosed by experienced forensic psychologists. *Law and Human Behavior, 13*(4), 375–383.

Costa, D. (2000). *Toronto Interview for Posttraumatic Symptoms (TIPS)*. Unpublished manuscript.

Costa, P. T., Bagby, R. M., Herbst, J. H., & McCrae, R. R. (2005). Personality self-reports are concurrently reliable and valid during acute depressive episodes. *Journal of Affective Disorders, 89*, 45–55.

Costa, P. T., & McCrae, R. R. (1992a). *NEO-PI-R and NEO-FFI: Professional manual*. Odessa, FL: Psychological Assessment Resources.

Costa, P. T., & McCrae, R. (1992b). " 'Normal' personality inventories in clinical assessment: General requirements and the potential for using the NEO Personality Inventory": Reply. *Psychological Assessment, 4*, 20–22.

Costa, P. T., Jr., & McCrae, R. R. (1985). *The NEO Personality Inventory Manual*. Odessa, FL: Psychological Assessment Resources.

Coulton, G. F., & Feild, H. S. (1995). Using assessment centers in selecting entry-level police officers: Extravagance or justified expense? *Public Personnel Management, 24*, 223–254.

Courtney, J. C., Dinkins, J. P., Allen, L. M., & Kuroski, K. (2003). Age related effects in children taking the Computerized Assessment of Response Bias and Word Memory Test. *Child Neuropsychology, 9*, 109–116.

Courtois, C. A. (1992). The memory retrieval process in incest survivor therapy. *Journal of Child Sexual Abuse, 1*, 15–31.

Craig, J. R. (1986). Personnel Selection Inventory. In D. J. Keyser & R. C. Sweatland (Eds.), *Test critiques* (Vol. 3, pp. 510–520). Kansas City, MO: Test Corporation of America.

Craig, R. J. (1999). Essentials of MCMI-III assessment. In S. Strack (Ed.), *Essentials of Millon Inventories assessment* (pp. 1–51). New York: Wiley.

Craig, R. J., Kuncel, R., & Olson, R. E. (1994). Ability of drug abusers to avoid detection of substance abuse on the MCMI-II. *Journal of Social Behavior and Personality, 9*, 95–106.

Craig, R. J., & Weinberg, D. (1992). Assessing drug abusers with the Millon Clinical Multiaxial Inventory: A review. *Journal of Substance Abuse Treatment, 9*, 249–255.

Cramer, B., Gershberg, M. R., & Stern, M. (1971). Munchausen syndrome. Its relationship to malingering, hysteria, and the physician–patient relationship. *Archives of General Psychiatry, 24*(6), 573–578.

Crawford, E., Greene, R., Dupart, T., Bongar, B., & Childs, H. (2006). MMPI-2 assessment of malingered emotional distress related to a workplace injury: A mixed group validation. *Journal of Personality Assessment, 86*, 217–221.

Crews, F. (1995). *The memory wars: Freud's legacy in dispute.* New York: New York Review of Books.

Croft, P. R., Racz, M. I., Bloch, J. D., & Palmer, C. H. (2005). Autopsy confirmation of severe pulmonary interstitial fibrosis secondary to Munchausen syndrome presenting as cystic fibrosis. *Journal of Forensic Science, 50*(5), 1194–1198.

Croft, R. D., & Jervis, M. (1989). Munchausen's syndrome in a 4 year old. *Archives of Diseases of Childhood, 64*(5), 740–741.

Cronbach, L. (1949). Statistical methods applied to Rorschach scores: A review. *Psychological Bulletin, 46,* 393–429.

Cross, T. P., & Saxe, L. (1992). A critique of the validity of polygraph testing in child sexual abuse cases. *Journal of Child Sexual Abuse, 1,* 19–33.

Cross, T. P., & Saxe, L. (2001). Polygraph testing and sexual abuse: The lure of the magic lasso. *Child Maltreatment, 6,* 195–206.

Cummings, J. L., & Miller, B. L. (1987). Visual hallucinations: Clinical occurrence and use in differential diagnosis. *Western Journal of Medicine, 146,* 46–51.

Cunnien, A. J. (1986). Alcoholic blackouts: Phenomenology and legal relevance. *Behavioral Sciences and the Law, 4,* 73–85.

Cunnien, A. J. (1997). Psychiatric and medical syndromes associated with deception. In R. Rogers (Ed.), *Clinical assessment of malingering and deception* (2nd ed., pp. 23–46). New York: Guilford Press.

Curtis, K. L., Greve, K. W., Bianchini, K. J., & Brennan, A. (2006). California Verbal Learning Test indicators of malingered neurocognitive dysfunction: Sensitivity and specificity in traumatic brain injury. *Assessment, 13,* 46–61.

Curtiss, G., & Vanderploeg, R. D. (2000). Prevalence rates for neuropsychological malingering indexes in traumatic brain injury. *American Psychological Association Division 40 Newsletter, 18,* 9–13.

Curwen, T. (2003). The importance of offense characteristics, victimization history, hostility, and social desirability in assessing empathy of male adolescent sex offenders. *Sexual Abuse: Journal of Research and Treatment, 15,* 347–364.

Cutter, F. (1964). Self-rejection distress: A new MMPI scale. *Journal of Clinical Psychology, 20,* 150–153.

Dahlstrom, W. G., Welsh, G. S., & Dahlstrom, L. E. (1972). *An MMPI handbook: Vol. I. Clinical interpretaion* (Rev. ed.). Minneapolis: University of Minnesota Press.

Dahlstrom, W. G., Welsh, G. S., & Dahlstrom, L. E. (1975). *An MMPI handbook: Vol. II. Research applications* (Rev. ed.). Minneapolis: University of Minnesota Press.

Dahmus, S., Bernardin, H. J., & Bernardin, R. (1992). Test review: Personal Experience Inventory. *Measurement and Evaluation in Counseling and Development, 25,* 91–94.

Dalla-Déa, H. R. F., De Micheli, D., & Formigoni, M. L. O. S. (2003). Effects of identification and usefulness of the Lie Scale of the Drug Use Screening Inventory (DUSI-R) in the assessment of adolescent drug use. *Drug and Alcohol Dependence, 72,* 215–223.

Dalzell, H. (2000). Whispers: The role of family secrets in eating disorders. *Eating Disorders: The Journal of Treatment and Prevention, 8,* 43–61.

Daniel, A. E., & Resnick, P. J. (1987). Mutism, malingering, and competency to stand trial. *Bulletin of the American Academy of Psychiatry and Law, 15*(3), 301–308.

Danziger, P. R., & Welfel, E. R. (2001). The impact of managed care on mental health counselors: A survey of perceptions, practices, and compliance with ethical standards. *Journal of Mental Health Counseling, 23,* 137–150.

Daubert, S. D., & Metzler, A. E. (2000). The detection of fake-bad and fake-good responding on the Millon Clinical Multiaxial Inventory—III. *Psychological Assessment, 12,* 418–424.

Daubert v. Merrell Dow Pharmaceuticals, 113 S. Ct. 2786 (1993).

Davidoff, D. A., Kessler, H. R., Laibstain, D. F., & Mark, V. H. (1988). Neurobehavioral sequelae of minor head injury: A consideration of post-concussive syndrome versus post-traumatic stress. *Cognitive Rehabilitation, 6,* 8–13.

Davidson, H. A. (1952a). *Forensic psychiatry* (2nd ed.). New York: Ronald Press.

Davidson H. A. (1952b). Malingered psychosis. *Bulletin of the Menninger Clinic, 14,* 157–163.

Davidson, J. (1993). Issues in the diagnosis of post-traumatic stress disorder. In J. M. Oldham, M. B. Riba, & A. Tasman (Eds.), *American Psychiatric Press review of psychiatry.* Washington, DC: American Psychiatric Press.

Davies, R., & McMillan, T. (2005). Opinion about post-concussion syndrome in health professionals. *Brain Injury, 19*(11), 941–947.

Davis, J. (2005). Victim narratives and victim selves: False memory syndrome and the power of accounts. *Social Problems, 52,* 529–548.

De Carteret, J. (1994). Occupational stress claims: Effects on worker's compensation. *American Association of Occupational Health Nurses Journal, 42,* 494–498.

De Fruyt, F., Van Leeuwen, K. G., Bagby, R. M., Rolland, J. P., & Rouillon, F. (2006). Assessing and interpreting personality change and continuity in patients treated for major depression. *Psychological Assessment, 18,* 71–80.

De Micheli, D., & Formigoni, M. L. O. S. (2000). Screening of drug use in a teenage Brazilian sample using the Drug Use Screening Inventory (DUSI). *Addictive Behaviors, 25*(5), 683–691.

De Micheli, D., & Formigoni, M. L. (2002). Psychometrics properties of the Brazilian version of DUSI (Drug Use Screening Inventory). *Alcohol Clinical and Experimental Research, 26*(10), 1523–1528.

de Wit, H., Uhlenhuth, E. H., Pierri, J., & Johanson, C. E. (1987). Individual differences in behavioral and subjective responses to alcohol. *Alcoholism: Clinical and Experimental Research, 11*(1), 52–59.

Dean, R. S. (1982). *Neuropsychological Symptom Inventory.* St. Louis, MO: Washington University School of Medicine.

Dearth, C. S., Berry, D. T., & Vickery, C. D. (2005). Detection of feigned head injury symptoms on the MMPI-2 in head injured patients and community controls. *Archives of Clinical Neuropsychology, 20*(1), 95–110.

Deb, S., Lyons, I., Koutzoukis, C., Ali, I., & McCarthy, G. (1999). Rate of psychiatric illness 1 year after traumatic brain injury. *American Journal of Psychiatry, 156,* 374–378.

Deese, J. (1959). On the prediction of occurrence of particular verbal intrusions in immediate recall. *Journal of Experimental Psychology, 58,* 17–22.

Delis, D., Kramer, J. H., Kaplan, E., & Ober, B. (2000). *The California Verbal Learning Test—Second edition.* San Antonio, TX: Psychological Corporation.

Dell, P. F. (1988). Professional skepticism about multiple personality. *Journal of Nervous and Mental Disease, 176,* 528–531.

Delprino, R. P., & Bahn, C. (1988). National survey of the extent and nature of psychological services in police departments. *Professional Psychology: Research and Practice, 19,* 421–425.

Demakis, G. J., Hammond, F., Knotts, A., Cooper, D. B., Clement, P., Kennedy, J., et al. (2007). The Personality Assessment Inventory in individuals with traumatic brain injury. *Archives of Clinical Neuropsychology, 22*(1), 123–130.

DeMyer, W. E. (2004). *Technique of the neurologic examination* (5th ed.). New York: McGraw-Hill.

Denney, R. L. (1996). Symptom validity testing of remote memory in a criminal forensic setting. *Archives of Clinical Neuropsychology, 11,* 589–603.

Denney, R. L., & Wynkoop, T. F. (2000). Clinical neuropsychology in the criminal forensic setting. *Journal of Head Trauma Rehabilitation, 15,* 804–828.

Dennis, M. L. (1999). *Global Appraisal of Individual Needs (GAIN): Administration guide for the GAIN and related measures (version 1299).* Bloomington, IL: Chestnut Health Systems.

Dennis, M. L., Chan, Y., & Funk, R. R. (2006). Development and validation of the GAIN Short Screener (GSS) for internalizing, externalizing and substance use disorders and crime/violence problems among adolescents and adults. *American Journal on Addiction, 15,* 80–91.

Dennis, M. L., Dawud-Noursi, S., Muck, R., & McDermett, M. (2003). The need for developing and evaluating adolescent treatment models. In S. J. Stevens & A. R. Morral (Eds.), *Adolescent substance abuse treatment in the United States: Exemplary models from a national evaluation study* (pp. 3–56). Binghamton, NY: Haworth Press.

Dennis, M. L., Funk, R., Godley, S. H., Godley, M. D., & Waldron, H. (2004). Cross-validation of the alcohol and cannabis use measures in the Global Appraisal of Individual Needs (GAIN) and Timeline Followback (TLFB; Form 90) among adolescents in substance abuse treatment. *Addiction, 99*(2), 120–128.

Dennis, M. L., Titus, J. C., Diamond, G., Donaldson, J., Godley, S. H., Tims, F., et al. (2002). The Cannabis Youth Treatment (CYT) experiment: Rationale, study design, and analysis plans. *Addiction, 97,* S16–S34.

Department of Veterans Affairs Office of the Inspector General. (2005). *Review of state variances in VA disability compensation payments (#05-00765–137).* Retrieved November 8, 2006, from *http://www.va .gov/oig/publications/efoia*

DePaulo, B. M., Charlton, K., Cooper, H., Lindsay, J. J., & Muhlenbruck, L. (1997). The accuracy-confidence correlation in the detection of deception. *Personality and Social Psychology Review, 1*(4), 346–357.

DePaulo, B. M., Kashy, D. A., Kirkendol, S. E., Wyer, M. M., & Epstein, J. A. (1996). Lying in everyday life. *Journal of Personality and Social Psychology, 70,* 979–995.

Derogatis, L. R. (1992). *SCL-90-R: Administration, scoring, and procedures manual II for the revised version.* Towson, MD: Clinical Psychometric Research.

Detrick, P., & Chibnall, J. T. (2002). Prediction of police officer performance with the Inwald Personality Inventory. *Journal of Police and Criminal Psychology, 17,* 9–17.

Detrick, P., Chibnall, J. T., & Rosso, M. (2001). Minnesota Multiphasic Personality Inventory—2 in police officer selection: Normative data and relation to the Inwald Personality Inventory. *Professional Psychology: Research and Practice, 32,* 484–490.

Deutsch, H. (1982). On the pathological lie (Pseudologia phantastica). *Journal of the American Academy of Psychoanalysis, 10,* 369–386.

Devan, J. L. (2004). *A taxometric analysis of impression management and self-deception on the MMPI-2 among law enforcement applicants.* Unpublished doctoral dissertation, Pacific Graduate School of Psychology.

Devan, J. L., Hungerford, L., Wood, H., & Greene, R. L. (2001, March). *Utilization of the MMPI/MMPI-2 as a personnel screening device for police officers: A meta-analysis.* Paper presented at the Society for Personality Assessment Midwinter Meeting, Philadelphia, PA.

DiClemente, C. C., Schlundt, D., & Gemmell, L. (2004). Readiness and stages of change in addiction treatment. *American Journal of Addictions, 13,* 103–119.

Dikmen, S. S., Machamer, J. E., Winn, H. R., & Temkin, N. R. (1995). Neuropsychological outcome at 1-year post head injury. *Neuropsychology, 9*(1), 80–90.

Dirks, J. F., Wunder, J., Kinsman, R., McElhinny, J., & Jones, N. F. (1993). A Pain Rating Scale and a Pain Behavior Checklist for clinical use: Development, norms, and the consistency score. *Psychotherapy and Psychosomatics, 59,* 41–49.

Dolan, K., Rouen, D., & Kimber, J. (2004). An overview

of the use of urine, hair, sweat and saliva to detect drug use. *Drug and Alcohol Review, 23,* 213–217.

Dollinger, S. J. (1985). Lightning-strike disaster among children. *British Journal of Medical Psychology, 58,* 375–383.

Donders, J. (2005). Performance of the TOMM in a mixed pediatric sample. *Child Neuropsychology, 11,* 221–227.

Donovan, D. M., Kivlahan, D. R., Doyle, S. R., Longabaugh, R., & Greenfield, S. F. (2006). Concurrent validity of the Alcohol Use Disorders Identification Test (AUDIT) and AUDIT zones in defining levels of severity among out-patients with alcohol dependence in the COMBINE study. *Addiction, 101*(12), 1696–1704.

Doren, D. M. (2002). *Evaluating sex offenders: A manual for civil commitment and beyond.* Thousand Oaks, CA: Sage.

Doss, R. C., Chelune, G. J., & Naugle, R. I. (1999). VSVT: Compensation-seeking versus non-compensation-seeking patients in a general clinical setting. *Journal of Forensic Neuropsychology, 1,* 5–20.

Drukteinis, A. (2003). Disability determination in PTSD litigation. In R. Simon (Ed.), *Posttraumatic stress disorder in litigation* (2nd ed.). Washington, DC: American Psychiatric Press.

DuBay, W. H. (2004). *The principles of readability.* Costa Mesa, CA: Impact Information. Retrieved September 23, 2006, from http://libproxy.library.unt.edu:5881/ERICDocs/data/ericdocs2/content_storage_01/0000000b/80/31/a4/7f.pdf.

Dubinsky, S., Gamble, D. J., & Rogers, M. L. (1985). A literature review of subtle–obvious items on the MMPI. *Journal of Personality Assessment, 49,* 62–68.

Duckworth, J. C., & Barley, W. D. (1988). Within-normal-limit profiles. In R. L. Greene (Ed.), *The MMPI: Use in specific populations* (pp. 278–315). San Antonio, TX: Grune & Stratton.

Duffy, J. B., & Martin, P. P. (1973). The effects of direct and indirect teacher influence student trait anxiety on the immediate recall of academic material. *Psychology in the Schools, 10,* 233–237.

Duncan, J. (1995). *Medication compliance in schizophrenic patients.* Unpublished doctoral dissertation, University of North Texas, Denton.

Duncan, S. A., & Ausborn, D. L. (2002). The use of Reliable Digits to detect malingering in a criminal forensic pretrial population. *Assessment, 9,* 56–61.

Dush, D. M., Simons, L. E., Platt, M., Nation, P. C., & Ayres, S. Y. (1994). Psychological profiles distinguishing litigating and nonlitigating pain patients: Subtle, and not so subtle. *Journal of Personality Assessment, 62,* 299–313.

Eakin, D. E. (2005). Detection of feigned posttraumatic stress disorder: A multimodal assessment strategy. *Dissertation Abstracts International: Section B. The Physical Sciences and Engineering, 65*(11-B), 6044.

Eakin, D. E., Weathers, F. W., & Benson, T. B. (2006). Detection of feigned posttraumatic stress disorder: A comparison of the MMPI-2 and PAI. *Journal of Psychopathology and Behavioral Assessment, 28*(3), 145–155.

East, N. (1927). *An introduction to forensic psychiatry in the criminal courts.* London: Churchill.

Easton, K., & Feigenbaum, K. (1967). An examination of an experimental set to fake the Rorschach test. *Perceptual and Motor Skills, 24,* 871–874.

Ebbinghaus, H. (1913). *Memory: A contribution to experimental psychology* (H. A. Ruger & C. E. Bussenius, Trans.). New York: Columbia University, Teachers College. (Original work published 1885)

Edelstein, B. (1999). *Hopemont Capacity Assessment Interview manual and scoring guide.* Unpublished manuscript, West Virginia University.

Edelstein, R. S., Luten, T. L., Ekman, P., & Goodman, G. S. (2006). Detecting lies in children and adults. *Law and Human Behavior, 30,* 1–10.

Edens, J. F., Buffington, J. K., & Tomicic, T. L. (2000). An investigation of the relationship between psychopathic traits and malingering on the Psychopathic Personality Inventory. *Assessment, 7,* 281–296.

Edens, J. F., Cruise, K. R., & Buffington-Vollum, J. K. (2001). Forensic and correctional applications of the Personality Assessment Inventory. *Behavioral Sciences and the Law, 19,* 519–543.

Edens, J. F., Otto, R., & Dwyer, T. (1998). Susceptibility of the Trauma Symptom Inventory to malingering. *Journal of Personality Assessment, 71*(3), 379–392.

Edens, J. F., Otto, R. K., & Dwyer, T. (1999). Utility of the Structured Inventory of Malingered Symptomatology in identifying persons motivated to malinger psychopathology. *Journal of the American Academy of Psychiatry and Law, 27,* 387–396.

Edens, J. F., Poythress, N. G., & Watkins-Clay, M. M. (2007). Detection of malingering in psychiatric unit and general population prison inmates: A comparison of the PAI, SIMS, and SIRS. *Journal of Personality Assessment, 88*(1), 33–42.

Edens, J. F., & Ruiz, M. A. (2005). *Personality Assessment Inventory Interpretive Report for Correctional Settings (PAI-CS) professional manual.* Odessa, FL: PAR.

Efendov, A. A., Sellbom, M., & Bagby, R. M. (2007). *The utility and comparative incremental validity of the MMPI-2 and Trauma Symptom Inventory Validity Scales in the detection of faked PTSD.* Manuscript submitted for publication.

Efendov, A. A., Sellbom, M., & Bagby, R. M. (in press). Incremental validity of the TSI Atypical Response Scale at detecting feigned post-traumatic stress disorder. *Psychological Assessment.*

Ehlers, W., & Plassmann, R. (1994). Diagnosis of narcissistic self-esteem regulation in patients with factitious illness (Munchausen syndrome). *Psychotherapy and Psychosomatics, 62*(1–2), 69–77.

Eisendrath, S. J. (1989). Factitious physical disorders: Treatment without confrontation. *Psychosomatics, 30*(4), 383–387.

Eisendrath, S. J., & McNiel, D. E. (2004). Factitious physical disorders, litigation, and mortality. *Psychosomatics, 45*(4), 350–353.

Eissler, K. (1951). Malingering. In G. B. Wilbur & W. Muensterberger (Eds.), *Psychoanalysis and culture* (pp. 218–253). New York: International Universities Press.

Ekman, P. (1988). Lying and nonverbal behavior: Theoretical issues and new findings. *Journal of Nonverbal Behavior, 12,* 163–176.

Ekman, P. (1989). Why lies fail and what behaviors betray a lie. In J. C. Yuille (Ed.), *Credibility assessment* (pp. 71–81). New York: Kluwer Academic/Plenum Press.

Ekman, P. (2001). *Telling lies: Clues to deceit in the marketplace, politics, and marriage.* New York: Norton.

Ekman, P., & O'Sullivan, M. (1991). Who can catch a liar? *American Psychologist, 46,* 913–920.

Ekman, P., & O'Sullivan, M. (2006). From flawed self-assessment to blatant whoppers: The utility of voluntary and involuntary behavior in detecting deception. *Behavioral Sciences and the Law, 24,* 673–686.

Ekman, P., Roper, G., & Hager, J. C. (1980). Deliberate facial movement. *Child Development, 51,* 886–891.

Elhai, J. D., Butcher, J. J., Reeves, A. N., Baugher, S. N., Gray, M. J., Jacobs, G. A., et al. (2007). Varying cautionary instructions, monetary incentives, and comorbid diagnostic training in malingered psychopathology research. *Journal of Personality Assessment, 88*(3), 328–337.

Elhai, J. D., Frueh, B., Gold, P., Gold, S., & Hamner, M. (2000). Clinical presentations of posttraumatic stress disorder across trauma populations: A comparison of MMPI-2 profiles of combat veterans and adult survivors of child sexual abuse. *Journal of Nervous and Mental Disease, 188*(10), 708–713.

Elhai, J. D., Gold, S., Sellers, A., & Dorfman, W. (2001). The detection of malingered posttraumatic stress disorder with MMPI-2 Fake Bad indices. *Assessment, 8*(2), 221–236.

Elhai, J. D., Gray, M. J., Naifeh, J. A., Butcher, J. J., Davis, J. L., Falsetti, S. A., et al. (2005). Utility of the Trauma Symptom Inventory's Atypical Response scale in detecting malingered post-traumatic stress disorder. *Assessment, 12,* 210–219.

Elhai, J. D., Kinder, B., & Frueh, B. (2004). Projective assessment of malingering. *Comprehensive handbook of psychological assessment: Vol. 2. Personality assessment* (pp. 553–561). New York: Wiley.

Elhai, J. D., Naifeh, J. A., Zucker, I. S., Gold, S. N., Deitsch, S. E., & Frueh, B. C. (2004). Discriminating malingered from genuine civilian posttraumatic stress disorder: A validation of three MMPI-2 infrequency scales (F, Fp, and Fptsd). *Assessment, 11*(3), 271.

Elhai, J. D., Ruggiero, K., Frueh, B., Beckham, J., & Gold, P. (2002). The Infrequency-Posttraumatic Stress Disorder Scale (Fptsd) for the MMPI-2: Development and initial validation with veterans presenting with combat-related PTSD. *Journal of Personality Assessment, 79*(3), 531–549.

Ellinwood, E. (1972). Amphetamine psychosis: Individuals, settings, and sequences. In E. H. Ellinwood, Jr. & S. Cohen (Eds.), *Current concepts on amphetamine abuse* (pp. 145–157). Rockville, MD: National Institute of Mental Health.

Ellis, A. (1946). The validity of personality questionnaires. *Psychological Bulletin, 43,* 385–440.

Ellis, A. (1953). Recent research with personality inventories. *Journal of Consulting Psychology, 17,* 45–49.

Ellis, A. P. J., West, B. J., Ryan, A. M., & DeShon, R. P. (2002). The use of impression management tactics in structured interviews: A function of question type? *Journal of Applied Psychology, 87,* 1200–1208.

Ellis, H. (1942). *Studies in the psychology of sex* (2 vols.). New York: Random House.

Ellison, M. L., Russinova, Z., MacDonald-Wilson, K. L., & Lyass, A. (2003). Patterns and correlated of workplace disclosure among professionals and managers with psychiatric conditions. *Journal of Vocational Rehabilitation, 18,* 3–13.

Emery, R. (2005). Parental alienation syndrome: Proponents bear the burden of proof. *Family Court Review, 43*(1), 8–13.

Emery, R. E., Otto, R. K., & O'Donohue, W. T. (2005). A critical assessment of child custody evaluations. *Psychological Science in the Public Interest, 6,* 1–29.

Enelow, A. (1971). Malingering and delayed recovery from injury. In J. Leedy (Ed.), *Compensation in psychiatric disability and rehabilitation.* Springfield, IL: Thomas.

Engel, G. L. (1970). Conversion symptoms. In C. M. MacBryde & R. S. Blacklow (Eds.), *Signs and symptoms* (5th ed.). Philadelphia: Lippincott.

English, K., Jones, L., Pasini-Hill, D., Patrick, D., & Cooley-Towell, S. (2000). *The value of polygraph testing in sex offender management* (Research report submitted to the National Institute of Justice, No. D97LBVX0034). Denver, CO: Department of Public Safety, Division of Criminal Justice, Office of Research and Statistics.

Epperson, D. L., Kaul, J. D., Huot, S., Goldman, R., & Alexander, W. (2003). *Minnesota Sex Offender Screening Tool—Revised.* St. Paul: Minnesota Department of Corrections.

Erickson, S. K., Lilienfeld, S. O., & Vitacco, M. J. (2007). A critical examination of the suitability and limitations of psychological tests in family court. *Family Court Review, 45*(2), 157–174.

Erlen, J., & Spillane, J. F. (2004). *Federal drug control: The evolution of policy and practice.* Binghamton, NY: Haworth Press.

Essig, S. M., Mittenberg, W., Petersen, R. S., Strauman, S., & Cooper, J. T. (2001). Practices in forensic neuropsychology: Perspectives of neuropsychologists and trial attorneys. *Archives of Clinical Neuropsychology, 16,* 271–291.

Etherton, J. L., Bianchini, K. J., Ciota, M. A., & Greve, K. W. (2005). Reliable Digit Span is unaffected by laboratory-induced pain: Implications for clinical use. *Assessment, 12,* 101–106.

Etherton, J. L., Bianchini, K. J., Ciota, M. A., Heinly, M. T., & Greve, K. W. (2006). Pain, malingering, and the WAIS-III Working Memory Index. *Spine Journal, 6,* 61–71.

Etherton, J. L., Bianchini, K. J., Greve, K. W., & Ciota, M. A. (2005). Test of memory malingering performance is unaffected by laboratory-induced pain: Implications for clinical use. *Archives of Clinical Neuropsychology, 20*(3), 375–84.

Etherton, J. L., Bianchini, K. J., Greve, K. W., & Heinly, M. T. (2005). Sensitivity and specificity of reliable digit span in malingered pain-related disability. *Assessment, 12*(2), 130–136.

Etherton, J. L., Bianchini, K. J., Heinly, M. T., & Greve, K. W. (2006). Pain, malingering, and performance on the WAIS-III Processing Speed Index. *Journal of Clinical and Experimental Neuropsychology, 28*(7), 1218–1237.

Etter, J. F. (2004). Asking about quantity and frequency of alcohol consumption before asking the CAGE questions produces lower ratings on the CAGE test. *Drug and Alcohol Dependence, 74,* 211–214.

Evans, F. I., & Nelson, R. O. (1977). Assessment of child behavior problems. In A. R. Ciminero, K. S. Calhoun, & H. E. Adams (Eds.), *Handbook of behavioral assessment* (pp. 603–681). New York: Wiley.

Evans, L. (2000). Functional school refusal subtypes: Anxiety, avoidance, and malingering. *Psychology in the Schools, 37,* 183–190.

Evans, R. G., & Dinning, W. D. (1983). Response consistency among high F scale scorers on the MMPI. *Journal of Clinical Psychology, 39,* 246–248.

Everington, C., & Luckasson, R. (1992). *Manual for Competence Assessment for Standing Trial for Defendants with Mental Retardation: CAST-MR.* Worthington, OH: IDS.

Everson, M. D., & Boat, B. W. (1989). False allegations of sexual abuse by children and adolescents. *Journal of the American Academy of Child and Adolescent Psychiatry, 28,* 230–235.

Evyapan, A. (2006). Pure mutism due to simultaneous bilateral lenticulostriate artery territory infarction. *CNS Spectrums, 11*(4), 257–259.

Exner, J. (1974). *The Rorschach: A comprehensive system.* New York: Wiley.

Exner, J. (1987). Computer assistance in Rorschach interpretation. In J. N. Butcher (Ed.), *Computerized psychological assessment: A practitioner's guide* (pp. 218–235). New York: Basic Books.

Exner, J. (1991). *The Rorschach: A comprehensive system: Vol. 2. Interpretation* (2nd ed.). New York: Wiley.

Exner, J. E. (1969). *The Rorschach systems.* New York: Grune & Stratton.

Exner, J. E., & Erdberg, P. (2005). *The Rorschach: A comprehensive system: Advanced interpretation* (3rd ed., Vol. 2). Hoboken, NJ: Wiley.

Fairbank, J. A., McCaffrey, R. J., & Keane, T. M. (1985). Psychometric detection of fabricated symptoms of posttraumatic stress disorder. *American Journal of Psychiatry, 142,* 501–503.

Falloon, I., & Talbot, R. (1981). Persistent auditory hallucinations: Coping mechanisms and implications for management. *Psychological Medicine, 11,* 329–339.

Fals-Stewart, W. (1995). The effect of defensive responding by substance-abusing patients on the Millon

Clinical Multiaxial Inventory. *Journal of Personality Assessment, 64,* 540–551.

Fals-Stewart, W. (1996). The ability of individuals with psychoactive substance use disorders to escape detection by Personality Assessment Inventory. *Psychological Assessment, 8,* 60–68.

Fals-Stewart, W., & Lucente, S. (1997). Identifying positive dissimulation by substance-abusing individuals on the Personality Assessment Inventory: A cross-validation study. *Journal of Personality Assessment, 68,* 455–469.

Fals-Stewart, W., O'Farrell, T. J., Freitas, T. T., McFarlin, S. K., & Rutigliano, P. (2000). The Timeline Followback reports of psychoactive substance use by drug-abusing patients: Psychometric properties. *Journal of Consulting and Clinical Psychology, 68*(1), 134–144.

Fang, F., Liu, Y., & Shen, Z. (2003). Lie detection with contingent negative variation. *International Journal of Psychophysiology, 50,* 247–255.

Fantoni-Salvador, P., & Rogers, R. (1997). Spanish versions of the MMPI-2 and PAI: An investigation of concurrent validity with Hispanic patients. *Assessment, 4*(1), 29–39.

Farber, B. A. (2003). Patient self-disclosure: A review of the research. *Journal of Clinical Psychology, 59,* 589–600.

Farber, B. A., & Hall, D. (2002). Disclosure to therapists: What is and is not discussed in psychotherapy. *Journal of Clinical Psychology, 58,* 359–370.

Faust, D., & Guilmette, T. J. (1990). To say it's not so doesn't prove that it isn't: Research on the detection of malingering. Reply to Bigler. *Journal of Consulting and Clinical Psychology, 58,* 248–250.

Faust, D., Hart, K., & Guilmette, T. J. (1988). Pediatric malingering: The capacity of children to fake believable deficits on neuropsychological testing. *Journal of Consulting and Clinical Psychology, 56,* 578–582.

Faust, D., Hart, K., Guilmette, T. J., & Arkes, H. R. (1988). Neuropsychologists' capacity to detect adolescent malingerers. *Professional Psychology: Research and Practice, 19,* 508–515.

Fay, P. J., & Middleton, W. C. (1941). The ability to judge truth-telling or lying from a voice transmitted over a public address system. *Journal of General Psychology, 24,* 211–215.

Feinn, R., Tennen, H., & Kranzler, H. R. (2003). Psychometric properties of the short index of problems as a measure of recent alcohol-related problems. *Alcoholism: Clinical and Experimental Research, 27*(9), 1436–1441.

Fekken, G. C., & Holden, R. R. (1987). Assessing the person reliability of an individual MMPI protocol. *Journal of Personality Assessment, 51,* 123–132.

Feldman, K. W., Feldman, M. D., Grady, R., Burns, M. W., & McDonald, R. (2007). Renal and urologic manifestations of pediatric condition falsification/Munchausen by proxy. *Pediatric Nephrology, 22*(6), 849–856.

Feldman, K. W., & Hickman, R. O. (1998). The central venous catheter as a source of medical chaos in Munchausen syndrome by proxy. *Journal of Pediatric Surgery, 33*(4), 623–627.

Feldman, M., & Graley, J. (1954). The effects of an experimental set to simulate abnormality on group Rorschach performance. *Journal of Projective Techniques, 18,* 326–334.

Feldman, M. D. (1994). Denial in Munchausen syndrome by proxy: The consulting psychiatrist's dilemma. *International Journal of Psychiatry in Medicine, 24*(2), 121–128.

Feldman, M. D. (1997). Canine variant of factitious disorder by proxy. *American Journal of Psychiatry, 154*(9), 1316–1317.

Feldman, M. D. (2000). Munchausen by Internet: Detecting factitious illness and crisis on the internet. *Southern Medical Journal, 93*(7), 669–672.

Feldman, M. D. (2001). Prophylactic bilateral radical mastectomy resulting from factitious disorder. *Psychosomatics, 42*(6), 519–521.

Feldman, M. D. (2004a). Munchausen by proxy and malingering by proxy. *Psychosomatics: Journal of Consultation Liaison Psychiatry, 45,* 365–366.

Feldman, M. D. (2004b). *Playing sick?: Untangling the web of Munchausen syndrome, Munchausen by proxy, malingering and factitious disorder.* New York: Brunner-Routledge.

Feldman, M. D., & Brown, R. M. (2002). Munchausen by proxy in an international context. *Child Abuse and Neglect, 26*(5), 509–524.

Feldman, M. D., Ford, C. V., & Stone, T. (1994). Deceiving others/deceiving oneself: Four cases of factitious rape. *Southern Medical Journal, 87*(7), 736–738.

Feldman, M. D., & Hamilton, J. C. (2006). Serial factitious disorder and Munchausen by proxy in pregnancy. *International Journal of Clinical Practice, 60*(12), 1675–1678.

Feldman, M. D., Hamilton, J. C., Deemer, H. N., & Phillips, K. A. (2001). Factitious disorder. In K. A. Phillips (Ed.), *Somatoform and factitious disorders* (pp. 129–166). Washington, DC: American Psychiatric Press.

Femina, D. D., Yeager, C. A., & Lewis, D. O. (1990). Child abuse: Adolescent records vs. adult recall. *Child Abuse and Neglect, 14,* 227–231.

Fendrich, M., & Vaughn, C. M. (1994). Diminished lifetime substance use over time: An inquiry into differential underreporting. *Public Opinion Quarterly, 58*(1), 96–123.

Fernandez, E., & McDowell, J. J. (1995). Response–reinforcement relationships in chronic pain syndrome: Applicability of Herrnstein's law. *Behaviour Research and Therapy, 33*(7), 855.

Ferrier, R. M. (2004). An atypical and significant hardship: The supermax confinement of death row prisoners based purely on status—A plea for procedural due process. *Arizona Law Review, 46,* 291–315.

Feucht, T. E., Stephens, R. C., & Walker, M. L. (1994). Drug use among juvenile arrestees: A comparison of self-report, urinalysis and hair assay. *Journal of Drug Issues, 24,* 99–116.

Fiedler, K., Schmod, J., & Stahl, T. (2002). What is the current truth about polygraph lie detection? *Basic and Applied Social Psychology,* 313–324.

Fink, P. (1992). Physical complaints and symptoms of somatizing patients. *Journal of Psychosomatic Research, 36,* 125–136.

Fink, P., Steen Hansen, M., & Sondergaard, L. (2005). Somatoform disorders among first-time referrals to a neurology service. *Psychosomatics, 46*(6), 540–548.

Firestone, P., Bradford, J. M., Greenberg, D. M., & Nunes, K. L. (2000). Differentiation of homicidal child molesters, nonhomicidal child molesters, and nonoffenders by phallometry. *American Journal of Psychiatry, 157,* 1847–1850.

First, M. B., Spitzer, R. L., Gibbon, M., & Williams, J. B. W. (2002a). *Structured Clinical Interview for DSM-IV-TR Axis I Disorders, Research Version, Patient Edition (SCID-I/P).* New York: Biometrics Research, New York State Psychiatric Institute.

First, M. B., Spitzer, R. L., Gibbon, M., & Williams, J. B. W. (2002b). *Structured Clinical Interview for DSM-IV-TR Axis I Disorders, Research Version, Patient Edition (SCID-I/NP).* New York: Biometrics Research, New York State Psychiatric Institute.

Firstman, R., & Talan, J. (1997). *The death of innocents.* New York: Bantam Books.

Fischer, C., Marchie, A., & Norris, M. (2004). Musical and auditory hallucinations: A spectrum. *Psychiatry and Clinical Neurosciences, 58*(1), 96–98.

Fischer, L., & Smith, G. (1999). Statistical adequacy of the Abel Assessment for Interest in Paraphilias. *Sexual Abuse: A Journal of Research and Treatment, 11,* 195–205.

Fishbain, D. A., Cole, B., Cutler, R. B., Lewis, J., Rosomoff, H. L., & Rosomoff, R. S. (2003). A structured evidence-based review on the meaning of nonorganic physical signs: Waddell signs. *American Academy of Pain Medicine, 4,* 141–181.

Fishbain, D. A., Cutler, R. B., Rosomoff, H. L., & Rosomoff, R. S. (2004). Is there a relationship between nonorganic physical findings (Waddell signs) and secondary gain/malingering? *Clinical Journal of Pain, 20,* 399–408.

Fisher, C., Gross, J., & Zuch, J. (1965). Cycle of penile erection synchronous with dreaming (REM) sleep. *Archives of General Psychiatry, 12,* 29–45.

Fisher, H. L., & Rose, D. (2005). Comparison of the effectiveness of two versions of the Rey Memory Test in discriminating between actual and simulated memory impairment, with and without the addition of a standard memory test. *Journal of Clinical and Experimental Neuropsychology, 27,* 840–858.

Fliege, H., Grimm, A., Eckhardt-Henn, A., Gieler, U., Martin, K., & Klapp, B. F. (2007). Frequency of ICD-10 factitious disorder: Survey of senior hospital consultants and physicians in private practice. *Psychosomatics, 48*(1), 60–64.

Fliege, H., Scholler, G., Rose, M., Willenberg, H., & Klapp, B. F. (2002). Factitious disorders and pathological self-harm in a hospital population: An interdisciplinary challenge. *General Hospital Psychiatry, 24*(3), 164–171.

Flynn, P. M., McCann, J. T., Luckey, J. W., Rounds-Bryant, J. L., Theisen, A. C., Hoffman, J. A., et al. (1997). Drug dependence scale in the Millon Clinical Multiaxial Inventory. *Substance Use and Misuse, 32*(6), 733–748.

Folks, D., & Freeman, A. (1985). Munchausen's syndrome and other factitious illness. *Psychiatric Clinics of North America, 8,* 263–278.

Folstein, M., Folstein, S., & McHugh, P. (1975). Minimental state: A practical method of grading cognitive state of patients for the clinician. *Journal of Psychiatric Research, 12,* 189–198.

Ford, C. V. (1996). *Lies!, lies!!, lies!!!: The psychology of deceit.* Washington, DC: American Psychiatric Press.

Ford, C. V., King, B. H., & Hollender, M. H. (1988). Lies and liars: Psychiatric aspects of prevarication. *American Journal of Psychiatry, 145*(5), 554–562.

Foreman, D. M. (2005). Detecting fabricated or induced illness in children. *British Medical Journal, 331*(7523), 978–979.

Forensic Research Incorporated. (1997). The validity and reliability of polygraph testing. *Polygraph, 26,* 215–239.

Forman, R. F., & McCauley, C. (1986). Validity of the positive control test using the field practice model. *Journal of Applied Psychology, 71,* 691–698.

Forrest, T. J., Allen, D. N., & Goldstein, G. (2004). Malingering Indexes for the Halstead Category Test. *Clinical Neuropsychologist, 18*(2), 334–347.

Forth, A. E., Kosson, D. S., & Hare, R. D. (2003). *Manual for the Hare Psychopathy Checklist—Youth Version.* Toronto, Ontario, Canada: Multi-Health Systems.

Fosberg, I. (1938). Rorschach reactions under varied instructions. *Rorschach Research Exchange, 3,* 12–31.

Fosberg, I. (1941). An experimental study of the reliability of the Rorschach psychodiagnostic technique. *Rorschach Research Exchange, 5,* 72–84.

Fosberg, I. (1943). How do subjects attempt to fake results on the Rorschach test? *Rorschach Research Exchange, 7,* 119–121.

Fowers, B. J. (1992). The Cardiac Denial of Impact Scale: A brief, self-report research measure. *Journal of Psychosomatic Research, 36,* 469–475.

Fowler, R. A., Butcher, J. N., & Williams, C. L. (2000). *Essentials of MMPI-2 and MMPI-A interpretation* (2nd ed.). Minneapolis: University of Minnesota Press.

Fox, D. D., Gerson, A., & Lees-Haley, P. R. (1995). Interrelationships of MMPI-2 validity scales in personal injury claims. *Journal of Clinical Psychology, 51,* 42–47.

Fox, D. D., Lees-Haley, P., Earnest, K., & Dolezal-Wood, S. (1995). Base rates of post-concussive symptoms in health maintenance organization patients and controls. *Neuropsychology, 9*(4), 606–611.

Francis, L. J., Lankshear, D. W., & Pearson, P. R. (1989). The relationship between religiosity and the short form JEPQ (JEPQ-S) indices of E, N, L and P among eleven year olds. *Personality and Individual Differences, 19,* 763–769.

Franco, K., Goldfarb, J., Peebles, R., & Sabella, C. (2005). Factitious disorder and malinger in adolescent girls: Case series and literature review. *Clinical Pediatrics, 44,* 237–243.

Frank, L. K. (1939). Projective methods for the study of personality. *Journal of Psychology, 8,* 389–413.

Frankfurter, D. (2006). *Evil incarnate: Rumors of demonic conspiracy and satanic abuse in history.* Princeton, NJ: Princeton University Press.

Franzen, M. D., Iverson, G. L., & McCracken, L. M. (1990). The detection of malingering in neuropsychological assessment. *Neuropsychology Review, 1,* 247–279.

Frederick, R., & Foster, H. (1991). Multiple measures of malingering on a forced-choice test of cognitive ability. *Psychological Assessment, 3,* 596–602.

Frederick, R. I. (1995, August). *Taxonometric analysis of malingering.* Paper presented at the annual meeting of the American Psychological Association, New York.

Frederick, R. I. (2000). A personal floor effect strategy to evaluate the validity of performance on memory tasks. *Journal of Clinical and Experimental Neuropsychology, 22,* 720–730.

Frederick, R. I., Carter, M., & Powel, J. (1995). Adapting symptom validity testing to evaluate suspicious complaints of amnesia in medicolegal evaluations. *Bulletin of the American Academy of Psychiatry and the Law, 23,* 231–237.

Frederick, R. I., & Crosby, R. (2000). Development and validation of the Validity Indicator Profile. *Law and Human Behavior, 24*(1), 59–82.

Frederick, R. I., Crosby, R. D., & Wynkoop, T. F. (2000). Performance curve classification of invalid responding on the Validity Indicator Profile. *Archives of Clinical Neuropsychology, 15,* 281–300.

Frederick, R. I., & Denney, R. L. (1998). Minding your "ps and qs" when using forced-choice recognition tests. *Clinical Neuropsychologist, 12,* 193–205.

Freeman, M. A., Hennessy, E. V., & Marzullo, D. M. (2001). Defensive evaluation of antismoking messages among college-age smokers: The role of possible selves. *Health Psychology, 20,* 424–433.

Freeman, V. G., Rathore, S. S., Weinfurt, K. P., Schulman, K. A., & Sulmasy, D. P. (1999). Lying for patients: Physician deception of third party payers. *Archives of Internal Medicine, 159,* 2263–2270.

Freud, S. (1953). Three essays on the theory of sexuality. In J. Strachey (Ed. & Trans.), *The standard edition of the complete psychological works of Sigmund Freud* (Vol. 7, pp. 123–243). London: Hogarth Press. (Original work published 1905)

Freud, S. (1962). The aetiology of hysteria. In J. Strachey (Ed. & Trans.), *The standard edition of the complete psychological works of Sigmund Freud* (Vol. 3, pp. 191–221). London: Hogarth Press. (Original work published 1896)

Freund, K. (1957). Diagnostika homosexuality u muszu. *Ceskoslovak Medicine, 53,* 382–393.

Freund, K. (1971). A note on the use of the phallometric

method of measuring mild sexual arousal in the male. *Behavior Therapy, 2,* 223–228.

Freund, K., Chan, S., & Coulthard, R. (1979). Phallometric diagnosis with nonadmitters. *Behaviour Research and Therapy, 17,* 451–457.

Freund, K., Langevin, R., & Barlow, D. (1974). Comparison of two penile measures of erotic arousal. *Behaviour Research and Therapy, 12,* 355–359.

Freund, K., Watson, R., & Rienzo, D. (1988). Signs of feigning in the phallometric test. *Behaviour Research and Therapy, 26,* 105–112.

Freund, K., & Watson, R. J. (1991). Assessment of the sensitivity and specificity of a phallometric test: An update of phallometric diagnosis of pedophilia. *Psychological Assessment, 3,* 254–260.

Freyd, J. J. (1996). *Betrayal trauma: The logic of forgetting childhood abuse.* Cambridge, MA: Harvard University Press.

Frick, P., Lahey, B., Loeber, R., & Stouthamer-Loeber, M. (1991). Oppositional defiant disorder and conduct disorder in boys: Patterns of behavioral covariation. *Journal of Clinical Child Psychology, 20*(2), 202–208.

Friedl, M. C., & Draijer, N. (2000). Dissociative disorders in Dutch psychiatric inpatients. *American Journal of Psychiatry, 157*(6), 1012–1013.

Friedman, A. F., Lewak, R., Nichols, D. S., & Webb, J. T. (2001). *Psychological assessment with the MMPI-2* (2nd ed.). Hillsdale, NJ: Erlbaum.

Friedman, L. S., Johnson, B., & Brett, A. S. (1990). Evaluation of substance-abusing adolescents by primary care physicians. *Journal of Adolescent Health Care, 11,* 227–230.

Friedman, M. J. (1981). Post-Vietnam syndrome: Recognition and management. *Psychosomatics, 22,* 931–943.

Friedman, M. J. (1997). Posttraumatic stress disorder. *Journal of Clinical Psychiatry, 58*(Suppl. 9), 33–36.

Friedrich, W. N. (1988). Child abuse and sexual abuse. In R. Greene (Ed.), *The MMPI: Use with specific populations* (pp. 246–258). Philadelphia: Grune & Stratton.

Frueh, B., Hamner, M., Cahill, S., Gold, P., & Hamlin, K. (2000). Apparent symptom overreporting in combat veterans evaluated for PTSD. *Clinical Psychology Review, 20*(7), 853–885.

Frueh, B., & Kinder, B. (1994). The susceptibility of the Rorschach inkblot test to malingering of combat-related PTSD. *Journal of Personality Assessment, 62,* 280–298.

Frueh, B. C., Elhai, J. D., Grubaugh, A. L., Monnier, J., Kashdan, T. B., Sauvageot, J. A., et al. (2005). Documented combat exposure of US veterans seeking treatment for combat-related post-traumatic stress disorder. *British Journal of Psychiatry, 186,* 467–472.

Frye v. United States, 293 F. 1013 (D.C. Cir. 1923).

Fuchs, D., & Thelen, M. (1988). Children's expected interpersonal consequences of communicating their affective states and reported likelihood of expression. *Child Development, 59,* 1314–1322.

Furnham, A., & Henderson, M. (1983). Response bias in self-report measures of general health. *Personality and Individual Differences, 4,* 519–525.

Gacono, C. B., Meloy, J. R., Sheppard, K., Speth, E., & Roske, A. (1995). A clinical investigation of malingering and psychopathy in hospitalized insanity acquittees. *Bulletin of the American Academy of Psychiatry and Law, 23*(3), 387–397.

Gaillard, Y., Vayssette, F., & Pepin, G. (2000). Compared interest between hair analysis and urinalysis in doping controls Results for amphetamines, corticosteroids and anabolic steroids in racing cyclist. *Forensic Science International, 107,* 361–379.

Gallucci, N. T. (1985). Influence of dissimulation on indexes of response consistency for the MMPI. *Psychological Reports, 57,* 1013–1014.

Gantner, A. B., Graham, J. R., & Archer, R.R . (1992). Usefulness of the MAC scale in differentiating adolescents in normal, psychiatric, and substance abuse settings. *Psychological Assessment, 4,* 133–137.

Garb, H. N. (1998). *Studying the clinician: Judgment research and psychological assessment.* Washington, DC: American Psychological Association.

Gardner, R. A. (1992). *True and false allegations of child sexual abuse.* Cresskill, NJ: Creative Therapeutics.

Garfield, P. (1987). Nightmares in the sexually abused female teenager. *Psychiatric Journal of the University of Ottawa, 12,* 93–97.

Gassen, M. D., Pietz, C. A., Spray, B. J., & Denney, R. L. (2007). Accuracy of Megargee's criminal offender infrequency (FC) scale in detecting malingering among forensic examinees. *Criminal Justice and Behavior, 34*(4), 493–504.

Gavin, D. R., Ross, H. E., & Skinner, H. A. (1989). Diagnostic validity of the drug abuse screening test in the assessment of DSM-III drug disorders. *British Journal of Addictions, 84,* 301–307.

Gavin, H. (1843). *On feigned and factitious diseases.* London: Churchill.

Geisser, M. E., Roth, R. S., Bachman, J. E., & Eckert, T. A. (1996). The relationship between symptoms of posttraumatic stress disorder and pain: Affective disturbance and disability among patients with accident- and non-accident-related pain. *Pain, 66,* 207–214.

Gelder, B. C., Titus, J. B., & Dean, R. S. (2002). The efficacy of neuropsychological symptom inventory in the differential diagnosis of medical, psychiatric, and malingering patients. *International Journal of Neuroscience, 112*(11), 1377–1394.

Geraerts, E. (2006). *Remembrance of things past: The cognitive psychology of remembering and forgetting trauma.* Unpublished doctoral dissertation, Maastricht University, The Netherlands.

Geraerts, E., Arnold, M. M., Lindsay, D. S., Merckelbach, H., Jelicic, M., & Hauer, B. (2006). Forgetting of prior remembering in people reporting recovered memories of childhood sexual abuse. *Psychological Science, 17,* 1002–1008.

Geraerts, E., Jelicic, M., & Merckelbach, H. (2006). Symptom overreporting and recovered memories of childhood sexual abuse. *Law and Human Behavior, 30,* 621–630.

Geraerts, E., Kozaric-Kovacic, D., Merckelbach, H.,

Peraica, T., Jelicic, M., & Candel, I. (2006). *Detecting deception of war-related posttraumatic stress disorder.* Manuscript submitted for publication.

Geraerts, E., Lindsay, D. S., Jelicic, M., Merckelbach, H., Raymaekers, L., Arnold, M. M., et al. (2007). *Cognitive mechanisms underlying recovered memory experiences of childhood sexual abuse.* Manuscript submitted for publication.

Geraerts, E., Schooler, J. W., Merckelbach, H., Jelicic, M., Hauer, B. J., & Ambadar, Z. (2007). The reality of recovered memories: Corroborating continuous and discontinuous memories of childhood sexual abuse. *Psychological Science, 18,* 564–568.

Geraerts, E., Smeets, E., Jelicic, M., van Heerden, J., & Merckelbach, H. (2005). Fantasy proneness, but not self-reported trauma, is related to DRM performance of women reporting recovered memories of childhood sexual abuse. *Consciousness and Cognition, 14,* 602–612.

Gervais, R., Rohling, M., Green, P., & Ford, W. (2004). A comparison of WMT, CARB, and TOMM failure rates in non-head injury disability claimants. *Archives of Clinical Neuropsychology, 19*(4), 475–487.

Gervais, R. O., Ben-Porath, Y. S., Wygant, D. B., & Green, P. (2007). Development and validation of a Response Bias Scale (RBS) for the MMPI-2. *Assessment, 14*(2), 196–208.

Gfeller, J. D., & Craddock, M. M. (1998). Detecting feigned neuropsychological impairment with the Seashore Rhythm Test. *Journal of Clinical Psychology, 54,* 431–438.

Gibbon, K. L. (1998). Munchausen's syndrome presenting as an acute sexual assault. *Medical Science and Law, 38*(3), 202–205.

Gierok, S. D., Dickson, A. L., & Cole, J. A. (2005). Performance of forensic and non-forensic adult psychiatric inpatients on the Test of Memory Malingering. *Archives of Clinical Neuropsychology, 20*(6), 755–760.

Gillis, J. R., Rogers, R., & Bagby, M. R. (1991). Validity of the M Test: Simulation design and natural group approaches. *Journal of Personality Assessment, 57*(1), 130–140.

Giza, C. C., & Hovda, D. A. (2004). The pathophysiology of traumatic brain injury. In M. R. Lovell, R. J. Echemendia, J. T. Barth, & M. W. Collins (Eds.), *Traumatic brain injury in sports: An international neuropsychological perspective* (pp. 45–70). Lisse, The Netherlands: Swets & Zeitlinger.

Glassmire, D. M., Bierley, R. A., Wisniewski, A. M., Greene, R. L., Kennedy, J. E., & Date, E. (2003). Using the WMS-III faces subtest to detect malingered memory impairment. *Journal of Clinical and Experimental Neuropsychology, 25,* 465–491.

Gleaves, D. H., Smith, S. M., Butler, L. D., & Spiegel, D. (2004). False and recovered memories in the laboratory and clinic: A review of experimental and clinical evidence. *Clinical Psychology: Science and Practice, 11,* 3–28.

Godley, M. D., Godley, S. H., Dennis, M. L., Funk, R., & Passetti, L. (2002). Preliminary outcomes from the assertive continuing care experiment for adolescents discharged from residential treatment. *Journal of Substance Abuse Treatment, 23,* 21–32.

Goebel, R. A. (1983). Detection of faking on the Halstead–Reitan neuropsychological test battery. *Journal of Clinical Psychology, 39,* 731–742.

Goldberg, J. O., & Miller, H. R. (1986). Performance of psychiatric inpatients and intellectually deficient individuals on a task that assesses validity of memory complaints. *Journal of Clinical Psychology, 42,* 792–795.

Goldberg, L. R., Grenier, J. R., Guion, R. M., Sechrest, L. B., & Wing, H. (1991). *Questionnaires used in the prediction of trustworthiness in preemployment selection decisions.* Washington, DC: American Psychological Association.

Golding, S. L., Roesch, R., & Schreiber, J. (1984). Assessment and conceptualization of competency to stand trial: Preliminary data on the Interdisciplinary Fitness Interview. *Law and Human Behavior, 8,* 321–334.

Goldstein, A. B. (1998). Identification and classification of factitious disorders: An analysis of cases reported during a ten-year period. *International Journal of Psychiatry in Medicine, 28*(2), 221–241.

Goldstein, H. (1945). A malingering key for mental tests. *Psychological Bulletin, 42,* 104–118.

Goodman, G. S., & Bottoms, B. L. (1993). *Child victims, child witnesses: Understanding and improving testimony.* New York: Guilford Press.

Goodness, K. R. (1999). *Retrospective evaluation of malingering: A validational study of the R-SIRS and CT-SIRS.* Unpublished doctoral dissertation, University of North Texas.

Goodnow, J. J. (1988). Parents' ideas, actions, and feelings: Models and methods from developmental and social psychology. *Child Development, 59,* 286–320.

Goodwin, D. W., Anderson, P., & Rosenthal, R. (1971). Clinical significance of hallucinations in psychiatric disorders: A study of 116 hallucinatory patients. *Archives in General Psychiatry, 24,* 76–80.

Goodwin, J., Sahd, D., & Rada, R. T. (1978). Incest hoax: False accusations, false denials. *Bulletin of the American Academy of Psychiatry and the Law, 6,* 269–276.

Goodyear, B. (2006). Diagnostic dilemmas in mild traumatic brain injury. *Advances in Medical Psychotherapy and Psychodiagnostics, 12,* 13–20.

Gorman, W. F. (1993). *Legal neurology and malingering: Cases and techniques.* St. Louis, MO: Green.

Gothard, S. (1993). *Detection of malingering in mental competency evaluations.* Unpublished dissertation, California School of Professional Psychology, San Diego.

Gothard, S., Rogers, R., & Sewell, K. W. (1995). Feigning incompetency to stand trial: An investigation of the GCCT. *Law and Human Behavior, 19,* 363–373.

Gothard, S., Viglione, D. J., Meloy, J. R., & Sherman, M. (1995). Detection of malingering in competency to stand trial evaluations. *Law and Human Behavior, 19*(5), 493–505.

Gottesman, I. I., & Prescott, C. A. (1989). Abuses of the MacAndrew MMPI alcoholism scale: A critical review. *Clinical Psychology Review, 9,* 223–258.

Gough, H. G. (1950). The *F* minus *K* dissimulation index for the MMPI. *Journal of Consulting Psychology, 14,* 408–413.

Gough, H. G. (1954). Some common misconceptions about neuroticism. *Journal of Consulting Psychology, 18,* 287–292.

Gough, H. G. (1966). Appraisal of social maturity by means of the CPI. *Journal of Abnormal Psychology, 71,* 189–195.

Gough, H. G. (1971). The assessment of wayward impulse by means of the Personnel Reaction Blank. *Personnel Psychology, 24,* 669–677.

Gough, H. G. (1987). *Manual for the California Psychological Inventory* (2nd ed.). Palo Alto, CA: Consulting Psychologists Press.

Gouvier, W., Uddo-Crane, M., & Brown, L. M. (1988). Base rates of postconcussional symptoms. *Archives of Clinical Neuropsychology, 3,* 273–278.

Grabe, H. J., Meyer, C., Hapke, U., Rumpf, H. J., Freyberger, H. J., Dilling, H., et al. (2003). Specific somatoform disorder in the general population. *Psychosomatics, 44*(4), 304–311.

Graber, R. A., & Miller, W. R. (1988). Abstinence or controlled drinking goals for problem drinkers: A randomized clinical trial. *Psychology of Addictive Behaviors, 2,* 20–33.

Graham, J. R. (2006). *MMPI-2: Assessing personality and psychopathology* (4th ed.). New York: Oxford University Press.

Graham, J. R., Watts, D., & Timbrook, R. E. (1991). Detecting fake-good and fake-bad MMPI-2 profiles. *Journal of Personality Assessment, 57,* 264–277.

Granacher, R. P. (2003). *Traumatic brain injury: Methods for clinical and forensic neuropsychiatric assessment.* New York: CRC Press.

Gray, B. T. (2001). A factor analytic study of the Substance Abuse Subtle Screening Inventory (SASSI). *Educational and Psychological Measurement, 61*(1), 102–118.

Gray, J., & Bentovim, A. (1996). Illness induction syndrome: Paper I—A series of 41 children from 37 families identified at the Great Ormond Street Hospital for Children NHS Trust. *Child Abuse Neglect, 20*(8), 655–673.

Grayson, H. M. (1951). *A psychological admissions testing program and manual.* Los Angeles: Neuropsychiatric Hospital, Veterans Administration Center.

Green, H., James, R. A., Gilbert, J. D., & Byard, R. W. (1999). Medicolegal complications of pseudologia fantastica. *Legal Medicine (Tokyo), 1*(4), 254–256.

Green, P. (2003). *Green's Word Memory Test for Microsoft Windows.* Edmonton, Alberta, Canada: Green's.

Green, P., Allen, L. M., & Astner, K. (1996). *The Word Memory Test: A manual for the oral and computerized forms.* Durham, NC: CogniSyst.

Green, P., Astner, K., & Allen, L. M., III. (1996). *The Word Memory Test: A manual for oral and computer-administrated forms.* Durham, NC: CogniSyst.

Green, P., Astner, K., & Allen, L. M., III. (1997, November). *Validation of the Word Memory Test in 400 consecutive compensation claimants, including 196 cases of head injury.* Paper presented at the National Academy of Neuropsychology, Las Vegas, Nevada.

Green, P., & Flaro, L. (2003). Word Memory Test performance in children. *Child Neuropsychology, 9,* 189–207.

Green, P., & Iverson, G. L. (2001). Validation of the Computerized Assessment of Response Bias in litigating patients with head injuries. *Clinical Neuropsychologist, 15,* 492–497.

Green, P., Iverson, G. L., & Allen, L. (1999). Detecting malingering in head injury litigation with the Word Memory Test. *Brain Injury, 13*(10), 813–819.

Green, P., Lees-Haley, P. R., & Allen, L. M. (2002). The Word Memory Test and the validity of neuropsychological test scores. *Journal of Forensic Neuropsychology, 2,* 97–124.

Greene, R. L. (1978). An empirically derived MMPI carelessness scale. *Journal of Clinical Psychology, 34,* 407–410.

Greene, R. L. (1980). *The MMPI: An interpretive manual.* New York: Grune & Stratton.

Greene, R. L. (1988). Assessment of malingering and defensiveness by objective personality measures. In R. Rogers (Ed.), *Clinical assessment of malingering and deception* (pp. 123–158). New York: Guilford Press.

Greene, R. L. (1988). Summary. In R. L. Greene (Ed.), *The MMPI: Use with specific populations* (pp. 316–321). Boston: Allyn & Bacon.

Greene, R. L. (1991). *The MMPI-2/MMPI: An interpretive manual.* Boston: Allyn & Bacon.

Greene, R. L. (1997). Assessment of malingering and defensiveness by multiscale inventories. In R. Rogers (Ed.), *Clinical assessment of malingering and deception* (2nd ed., pp. 169–207). New York: Guilford Press.

Greene, R. L. (2000). *The MMPI-2: An interpretive manual* (2nd ed.). Needham Heights, MA: Allyn & Bacon.

Greene, R. L., Weed, N. C., Butcher, J. N., Arredondo, R., & Davis, H. G. (1992). A cross-validation of MMPI-2 substance abuse scales. *Journal of Personality Assessment, 58,* 405–410.

Greenfeld, D. (1987). Feigned psychosis in a 14-year-old girl. *Hospital and Community Psychiatry, 38,* 73–75.

Gregory, R. J., & Jindal, S. (2006). Factitious disorder on an inpatient psychiatry ward. *American Journal of Orthopsychiatry, 76*(1), 31–36.

Greiffenstein, M. F. (2007). Motor, sensory, and perceptual–motor pseudoabnormalities. In G. J. Larrabee (Ed.), *Assessment of malingered neuropsychological deficits* (pp. 100–130). New York: Oxford University Press.

Greiffenstein, M., Baker, W., Axelrod, B., Peck, E., & Gervais, R. (2004). The Fake Bad Scale and MMPI-2 F-family in detection of implausible psychological trauma claims. *Clinical Neuropsychologist, 18*(4), 573–590.

Greiffenstein, M., Baker, W. J., & Gola, T. (1994). Validation of malingered amnesia measures with a large clinical sample. *Psychological Assessment, 6,* 218–224.

Greiffenstein, M., Baker, W. J., & Gola, T. (1996). Comparison of multiple scoring methods for Rey's malingered amnesia measures. *Archives of Clinical Neuropsychology, 11,* 283–293.

Greiffenstein, M. F., Baker, W. J., & Johnson-Greene, D. (2002). Actual versus self-reported scholastic achievement of litigating postconcussion and severe closed head injury claimants. *Psychological Assessment, 14*(2), 202–208.

Greiffenstein, M. F., Gola, T., & Baker, J. W. (1995). MMPI-2 validity scales versus domain specific measures in detection of factitious traumatic brain injury. *Clinical Neuropsychologist, 9,* 230–240.

Gresnigt, J. A. M., Breteler, M. H. M., Schippers, G. M., & Van den Hurk, A. A. (2000). Predicting violent crime among drug-using inmates: The Addiction Severity Index as a prediction instrument. *Legal and Criminological Psychology, 5,* 83–95.

Greub, B. L., & Suhr, J. A. (2006). The validity of the letter memory test as a measure of malingering: Robustness to coaching. *Archives of Clinical Neuropsychology, 21,* 249–254.

Greve, K. W., & Bianchini, K. J. (2004). Setting empirical cut-offs on psychometric indicators of negative response bias: A methodological commentary with recommendations. *Archives of Clinical Neuropsychology, 19,* 533–541.

Greve, K. W., & Bianchini, K. J. (2006). Classification accuracy of the Portland Digit Recognition Test in traumatic brain injury: Results of a known-groups analysis. *Clinical Neuropsychologist, 20,* 816–830.

Greve, K. W., Bianchini, K. J., Black, F. W., Heinly, M. T., Love, J. M., Swift, D. A., et al. (2006). The prevalence of cognitive malingering in persons reporting exposure to occupational and environmental substances. *Neurotoxicology, 27*(6), 940–950.

Greve, K. W., Bianchini, K. J., & Doane, B. M. (2006). Classification accuracy of the Test of Memory Malingering in traumatic brain injury: Results of a known-groups analysis. *Journal of Clinical and Experimental Neuropsychology, 28,* 1176–1190.

Griffin, M. L., Weiss, R. D., Mirin, S. M., Wilson, H., & Bouchard-Voelk, B. (1987). The use of Diagnostic Interview Schedule in drug-dependent patients. *American Journal of Drug and Alcohol Abuse, 13,* 281–291.

Griffith, J. L., & Slovik, L. S. (1989). Munchausen syndrome by proxy and sleep disorders medicine. *Sleep, 12*(2), 178–183.

Gripshover, D. L., & Dacey, C. M. (1994). Discriminative validity of the MacAndrew Scale in settings with a high base rate of substance abuse. *Journal of Studies on Alcohol, 55,* 303–308.

Grisso, T. (2003). *Evaluating competencies: Forensic assessments and instruments* (2nd ed.). New York: Kluwer Academic.

Grisso, T., & Appelbaum, P. S. (1998). *MacArthur Competence Assessment Tool for Treatment (MacCAT-T).* Sarasota, FL: Professional Resources Press.

Grossman, H. (2005). Amnestic disorders. In B. J. Sadock & V. A. Sadock (Eds.), *Kaplan and Sadock's comprehensive textbook of psychiatry* (8th ed., pp. 345–350). Philadelphia: Lippincott Williams & Wilkins.

Grossman, L. S., & Craig, R. J. (1995). Comparison of MCMI-II and 16 PF validity scales. *Journal of Personality Assessment, 64,* 384–389.

Grossman, L. S., Haywood, T. W., Ostrov, E., Wasyliw, O., & Cavanaugh, J. L. (1990). Sensitivity of MMPI validity scales to motivational factors in psychological evaluations of police officers. *Journal of Personality Assessment, 55,* 549–561.

Grossman, L. S., Wasyliw, O. E., Benn, A. F., & Gyoerkoe, K. L. (2002). Can sex offenders who minimize on the MMPI conceal psychopathology on the Rorschach? *Journal of Personality Assessment, 78,* 484–501.

Grossman, R., Buchsbaum, M. S., & Yehuda, R. (2002). Neuroimaging studies in post-traumatic stress disorder. *Psychiatric Clinics of North America, 25*(2), 317–340.

Grote, C. L., Kooker, E. K., Garron, D. C., Nyenhuis, D. L., Smith, C. A., & Mattingly, M. L. (2000). Performance of compensation seeking and non-compensation seeking samples on the Victoria Symptom Validity Test: Cross-validation and extension of a standardization study. *Journal of Clinical and Experimental Neuropsychology, 22,* 709–719.

Grubin, D., & Madsen, L. (2005). Lie detection and the polygraph: A historical review. *Journal of Forensic Psychiatry and Psychology, 16,* 357–369.

Guastello, S. J., & Rieke, M. L. (1991). A review and critique of honesty test research. *Behavioral Sciences and the Law, 9,* 501–523.

Gudjonsson, G., & Shackleton, H. (1986). The pattern of scores on Raven's matrices during "faking bad" and "non-faking" performance. *British Journal of Clinical Psychology, 25,* 35–41.

Gudjonsson, G. H. (1990). The relationship of intellectual skills to suggestibility, compliance and acquiescence. *Personality and Individual Differences, 11,* 227–231.

Gudjonsson, G. H. (2003). *The psychology of interrogations and confessions handbook.* London: Wiley.

Guilmette, T. J., Hart, K. J., & Giuliano, A. J. (1993). Malingering detection: The use of a forced-choice method in identifying organic versus simulated memory impairment. *Clinical Neuropsychologist, 7,* 59–69.

Gundez-Bruce, H., McMeniman, M., Robinson, D., Woerner, M., Kane, J., Schooler, N., et al. (2005). Duration of untreated psychosis and time to treatment response for delusions and hallucinations. *American Journal of Psychiatry, 162*(10), 1966–1969.

Guriel, J., & Fremouw, W. (2003). Assessing malingered posttraumatic stress disorder: A critical review. *Clinical Psychology Review, 23*(7), 881–904.

Guriel, J., Yañez, T., Fremouw, W., Shreve-Neiger, A., Ware, L., Filcheck, H., et al. (2004). Impact of coaching on malingered posttraumatic stress symptoms on the M-FAST and the TSI. *Journal of Forensic Psychology Practice, 4,* 37–56.

Gutierrez, J. M., & Gur, R. C. (1998). Detection of malingering using forced-choice techniques. In C. R. Reynolds (Ed.), *Detection of malingering during head injury litigation* (pp. 81–104). New York: Plenum Press.

Guy, L. S., & Miller, H. A. (2004). Screening for malingered psychopathology in a correctional setting: Utility of the Miller-Forensic Assessment of Symptoms

Test (M-FAST). *Criminal Justice and Behavior, 31*(6), 695–716.

Haaland, D., & Christiansen, N. D. (1998). *Departures in linearity in the relationship in applicant personality test score and performance and evidence of response distortion.* Paper presented at the 22nd annual International Personnel Management Association Assessment Council conference, Chicago.

Haidt, J., & Baron, J. (1996). Social roles and moral judgment of acts and omissions. *European Journal of Social Psychology, 26,* 201–218.

Haines, M. E., & Norris, M. P. (1995). Detecting the malingering of cognitive deficits: An update. *Neuropsychology Review, 5,* 125–149.

Haines, M. E., & Norris, M. P. (2001). Comparing student and patient simulated malingerer's performance on standard neuropsychological measures to detect feigned cognitive deficits. *Clinical Neuropsychologist, 15,* 171–182.

Hale, G., Zimostrad, S., Duckworth, J., & Nicholas, D. (1986, March). *The abusive personality: MMPI profiles of male batterers.* Paper presented at the 21st annual Symposium on Recent Developments in the Use of the MMPI, Clearwater, FL.

Hall, D. E., Eubanks, L., Meyyazhagan, L. S., Kenney, R. D., & Johnson, S. C. (2000). Evaluation of covert video surveillance in the diagnosis of Munchausen syndrome by proxy: Lessons from 41 cases. *Pediatrics, 105*(6), 1305–1312.

Hall, G. C. N. (1989). Sexual arousal and arousability in a sexual offender population. *Journal of Abnormal Psychology, 98,* 145–149.

Hall, G. C. N., Hirschman, R., & Oliver, L. I. (1995). Sexual arousal and arousability to pedophilic stimuli in a community sample of normal men. *Behavior Therapy, 26,* 681–694.

Hall, G. C. N., Proctor, W. C., & Nelson, G. M. (1988). Validity of physiological measures of pedophilic sexual arousal in a sexual offender population. *Journal of Consulting and Clinical Psychology, 56,* 118–122.

Hall, G. C. N., Shondrick, D. D., & Hirschman, R. (1993). The role of sexual arousal in sexually aggressive behavior: A meta-analysis. *Journal of Consulting and Clinical Psychology, 61,* 1091–1095.

Hall, H. (1982). Dangerousness predictions and the maligned forensic professional. *Criminal Justice and Behavior, 9,* 3–12.

Hall, H. P., & Poirer, J.G. (2001). *Detecting malingering and deception: Forensic distortion analysis* (2nd ed.). Boca Raton, FL: CRC Press.

Hall, R., Hall, R., & Chapman, M. (2006). Effects of terrorist attacks on the elderly: Part 2. Posttraumatic stress, acute stress and affective disorders. *Clinical Geriatrics, 14,* 17–24.

Hall, R. C. W., & Chapman, M. J. (2005). Definition, diagnosis and forensic implications of postconcussional syndrome. *Psychosomatics, 46*(3), 195–202.

Halligan, P. W., Bass, C., & Oakley, D. A. (2003). *Malingering and illness deception.* Oxford, UK: Oxford University Press.

Hamilton, J. (1985). Pseudo-posttraumatic stress disorder. *Military Medicine, 150,* 353–356.

Hamilton, J. C., & Feldman, M. D. (2006). *Munchausen syndrome.* Retrieved May 27, 2007, from *http://www.emedicine.com/med/topic3543.htm*

Hamilton, J. C., & Feldman, M. D. (2007). Factitious disorder and malingering. In G. O. Gabbard (Ed.), *Gabbard's treatments of psychiatric disorders* (4th ed., pp. 629–635). Washington, DC: American Psychiatric Press.

Hamilton, J. C., & Janata, J. W. (1997). Dying to be ill: The role of self-enhancement motives in the spectrum of factitious disorders. *Journal of Social and Clinical Psychology, 16*(2), 178–199.

Hamilton, J. E. (1906). *Railway and other accidents.* London: Bailliere, Tindall.

Hamsher, J., & Farina, A. (1967). "Openness" as a dimension of projective test responses. *Journal of Consulting Psychology, 31,* 525–528.

Hankins, G. C., Barnard, G. W., & Robbins, L. (1993). The validity of the M Test in a residential forensic facility. *Bulletin of the American Academy of Psychiatry and the Law, 21,* 111–121.

Hanson, R. K. (1997). *The development of a brief actuarial risk scale for sexual offense recidivism* (User Report No. 1997-04). Ottawa, Ontario, Canada: Department of the Solicitor General of Canada.

Hanson, R. K., & Morton-Bourgon, K. E. (2005). The characteristics of persistent sexual offenders: A meta-analysis of recidivism studies. *Journal of Consulting and Clinical Psychology, 73,* 1154–1163.

Hanson, R. K., & Thornton, D. (1999). *Improving actuarial risk assessments for sex offenders.* Ottawa, Ontario, Canada: Department of the Solicitor General of Canada.

Hanson, R. K., & Thornton, D. (2000). Improving risk assessments for sex offenders: A comparison of three actuarial scales. *Law and Human Behavior, 24,* 119–136.

Hapke, U., Schumann, A., Rumpf, H. J., John, U., & Meyer, C. (2006). Post-traumatic stress disorder: The role of trauma, pre-existing psychiatric disorders, and gender. *European Archives of Psychiatry and Clinical Neuroscience, 256*(5), 299–306.

Hare, R. D. (1991). *Manual for the Hare Psychopathy Checklist—Revised.* Toronto, Ontario, Canada: Multi-Health Systems.

Hare, R. D. (2003). *The Hare Psychopathy Checklist—Revised* (2nd ed.). Toronto, Ontario, Canada: Multi-Health Systems.

Hare, R. D., Forth, A. E., & Hart, S. D. (1989). The psychopath as prototype for pathological lying and deception. In J. C. Yuille (Ed.), *Credibility assessment* (pp. 25–49). Norwell, MA: Kluwer Academic.

Hargrave, G., & Hiatt, D. (1989). Use of the California Psychological Inventory in law enforcement officer selection. *Journal of Personality Assessment, 53*(2), 267–277.

Harrell, A. V., & Wirtz, P. W. (1989). *Adolescent Drinking Inventory professional manual.* Odessa, FL: Psychological Assessment Resources.

Harrow, M., Herbener, E. S., Shanklin, A., Jobe, T. H., Rattenbury, F., & Kaplan, K. J. (2004). Follow-up of psychotic outpatients: Dimensions of delusions and work functioning in schizophrenia. *Schizophrenia Bulletin, 30*(1), 147–161.

Harrow, M., O'Connell, E. M., Herbener, E. S., Altman, A. M., Kaplan, K. J., & Jobe, T. H. (2003). Disordered verbalizations in schizophrenia: A speech disturbance or thought disorder? *Comprehensive Psychiatry, 44*(5), 353–359.

Hart, S. D., Watt, K. A., & Vincent, G. M. (2002). Commentary on Seagrave and Grisso: Impressions of the state of the art. *Law and Human Behavior, 26,* 241–245.

Hartlage, S., Alloy, L. B., Vázquez, C., & Dykman, B. (1993). Automatic and effortful processing in depression. *Psychological Bulletin, 113,* 247–278.

Hartshorne, H., & May, M. A. (1928). *Studies in deceit.* New York: Macmillan.

Hartung, C. M., & Widiger, T. A. (1998). Gender differences in the diagnosis of mental disorders: Conclusions and controversies of the DSM-IV. *Psychological Bulletin, 123,* 260–278.

Harvey, A., & Bryant, R. (2000). Memory for acute stress disorder and posttraumatic stress disorder: A 2-year prospective study. *Journal of Nervous and Mental Disease, 188,* 602–607.

Harvey, A. G., & Bryant, R. A. (1998). Predictors of acute stress following mild traumatic brain injury. *Brain Injury, 12*(2), 147–154.

Hasin, D. S., & Grant, B. F. (1987). Assessment of specific drug disorders in a sample of substance abuse patients: A comparison of the DIS and SADS-L procedures. *Drugs and Alcohol Dependence, 19,* 165–176.

Hathaway, S. R., & McKinley, J. C. (1940). A multiphasic personality schedule (Minnesota): I. Construction of the schedule. *Journal of Psychology, 10,* 249–254.

Hausknecht, J. P., Trevor, C. O., & Farr, J. L. (2002). Retaking ability tests in a selection setting: Implications for practice effects, training performance, and turnover. *Journal of Applied Psychology, 87,* 243–254.

Hausotter, W. (1996). Expert assessment of railroad accidents at the beginning of the industrial age: A medical historical excursion with reference to current circumstances. *Versicherungsmedizin, 48*(4), 138–142.

Hay, G. G. (1983). Feigned psychosis: A review of the simulation of mental illness. *British Journal of Psychiatry, 143,* 8–10.

Hayes, J. S., Hale, D. B., & Gouvier, W. D. (1996, February). *Tests of malingering: Do they discriminate malingering in defendants with mental retardation?* Paper presented at the International Neuropsychological Society, Chicago.

Haywood, T. W., Grossman, L. S., & Cavanaugh, J. L. (1990). Subjective versus objective measurements of deviant sexual arousal in clinical evaluations of alleged child molesters. *Psychological Assessment, 2,* 269–275.

Heaton, R. K., Grant, I., & Matthews, C. G. (1991). *Comprehensive norms for an expanded Halstead–Reitan Battery: Demographic corrections, research findings and clinical applications.* Odessa, FL: Psychological Assessment Resources.

Heaton, R. K., Smith, H. H., Lehman, R. A. W., & Vogt, A. T. (1978). Prospects for faking believable deficits on neuropsychological testing. *Journal of Consulting and Clinical Psychology, 46,* 802–900.

Heilbrun, K. (2001). *Principles of forensic mental health assessment.* New York: Kluwer/Plenum Press.

Heinly, M. T., Greve, K. W., Bianchini, K. J., Love, J. L., & Brennan, A. (2005). WAIS Digit Span-based indicators of malingered neurocognitive dysfunction: Classification accuracy in traumatic brain injury. *Assessment, 12,* 429–444.

Heins v. Commonwealth of Pennsylvania, Unemployment Compensation Board of Review, 534 A.2d 592 (1987).

Heinze, M. C. (2003). Developing sensitivity and specificity to distortion: Utility of psychological tests in differentiating malingering and psychopathology in criminal defendants. *Journal of Forensic Psychiatry and Psychology, 14,* 151–177.

Heinze, M. C., & Purisch, A. D. (2001). Beneath the mask: Use of psychological tests to detect and subtype malingering in criminal defendants. *Journal of Forensic Psychology Practice, 1*(4), 23–52.

Helander, A., von Wachenfeldt, J., Hiltunen, A., Beck, O., Liljeberg, P., & Borg, S. (1999). Comparison of urinary 5-hydroxytryptophol, breath ethanol, and self-report for detection of recent alcohol use during outpatient treatment: A study on methadone patients. *Drug and Alcohol Dependence, 56,* 33–38.

Hellerstein, D., Frosch, W., & Koenigsberg, H. (1987). The clinical significance of command hallucinations. *American Journal of Psychiatry, 144,* 219–225.

Henly, G. A., & Winters, K. C. (1988). Development of problem severity scales for the assessment of adolescent alcohol and drug abuse. *International Journal of Addictions, 23,* 65–85.

Herman, J. L., & Schatzow, E. (1987). Recovery and verification of memories of childhood sexual abuse. *Psychoanalytic Psychology, 4,* 1–14.

Hermann, D. H. J. (1986). Criminal defenses and pleas in mitigation based on amnesia. *Behavioral Sciences and the Law, 4,* 5–26.

Hibler, N. S., & Kurke, M. I. (1995). Ensuring personal reliability through selection and training. *Police psychology into the 21st century* (pp. 55–91). Hillsdale, NJ: Erlbaum.

Hickey, S. E., Kasdan, M. L., & Stutts, J. T. (2003). Malingering by proxy: A form of pediatric condition falsification. *Journal of Developmental and Behavioral Pediatrics, 24,* 276–278.

Hilsabeck, R. C., & Gouvier, W. D. (2005). Detecting simulated memory impairment: Further validation of the Word Completion Memory Test (WCMT). *Archives of Clinical Neuropsychology, 20,* 1025–1041.

Hingson, R. W., Heeren, T., & Winter, M. R. (1999). Preventing impaired driving. *Alcohol Health and Research World, 23*(1), 31–39.

Hirayama, Y., Sakamaki, S., Tsuji, Y., Sagawa, T., Takayanagi, N., Chiba, H., et al. (2003). Fatality caused by self-bloodletting in a patient with factitious anemia. *International Journal of Hematology, 78*(2), 146–148.

Hirschel, J. D., & McCarthy, B. R. (1983). The TASC–drug treatment program connection: Cooperation, cooptation or corruption of treatment objectives? *Journal of Offender Counseling, Services and Rehabilitation, 8,* 117–131.

Hirshberg, B., Libutti, S. K., Alexander, H. R., Bartlett, D. L., Cochran, C., Livi, A., et al. (2002). Blind distal pancreatectomy for occult insulinoma, an inadvisable procedure. *Journal of the American College of Surgeons, 194*(6), 761–764.

Hiscock, M., & Hiscock, C. K. (1989). Refining the forced-choice method for the detection of malingering. *Journal of Clinical and Experimental Neuropsychology, 11,* 967–974.

Hofling, C. K. (1965). Some psychologic aspects of malingering, *General Practitioner, 31,* 115–121.

Hogan, J., & Brinkmeyer, K. (1997). Bridging the gap between overt and personality-based integrity tests. *Personnel Psychology, 50,* 587–599.

Hogan, R. (1971). Personality characteristics of highly rated policeman. *Personnel Psychology, 24,* 679–686.

Hogan, R., & Kurtines, W. (1975). Personological correlates of police effectiveness. *Journal of Psychology, 91,* 289–295.

Hoksbergen, R., & Laak, J. (2000). Adult foreign adoptees: Reactive attachment disorder may grow into psychic homelessness. *Journal of Social Distress and the Homeless, 9,* 291–308.

Holden, R. R., & Kroner, D. G. (1992). Relative efficacy of differential response latencies for detecting faking on a self-report measure of psychopathology. *Psychological Assessment, 4,* 170–173.

Hollander, E., & Simeon, D. (2002). Anxiety disorders. In R. E. Hales & S. C. Yudofsky (Eds.), *Textbook of clinical psychiatry* (4th ed.). Washington DC: American Psychiatric Press.

Hollrah, J. L., Schlottmann, R. S., Scott, A. B., & Brunetti, D. G. (1995). Validity of the MMPI subtle items. *Journal of Personality Assessment, 65,* 278–299.

Holstege, C. P., & Dobmeier, S. G. (2006). Criminal poisoning: Munchausen by proxy. *Clinical Laboratory Medicine, 26*(1), 243–253.

Holzer, H. M., & Hoolzer, E. (2003). *Fake warrios: Identifying, exposing, and punishing those who falsify their military service.* Philadelphia: Xlibris.

Hom, J., & Denney, R. L. (Eds.). (2002a). *Detection of response bias in forensic neuropsychology.* Binghamton, NY: Haworth Medical Press.

Hom, J., & Denney, R. L. (2002b). Detection of response bias in forensic neuropsychology: Part I. *Journal of Forensic Neuropsychology, 3,* 1–166.

Honts, C. R., Hodes, R. L., & Raskin, D. C. (1985). Effects of physical countermeasures on the physiological detection of deception. *Journal of Applied Psychology, 70,* 177–187.

Honts, C. R., Raskin, D., & Kircher, J. (1994). Mental and physical countermeasures reduce the accuracy of polygraph tests. *Journal of Applied Psychology, 79,* 252–259.

Hopwood, C. J., Morey, L. C., Rogers, R., & Sewell, K. W. (2007). Malingering on the Personality Assessment Inventory: Identification of specific feigned disorders. *Journal of Personality Assessment, 88*(1), 43–48.

Horn, J. L., Wanberg, K. W., & Foster, F. M. (1990). *Guide to the Alcohol Use Inventory.* Minneapolis, MN: National Computer System.

Howes, R. J. (1995). A survey of plethysmographic assessment in North America. *Sexual Abuse: A Journal of Research and Treatment, 7,* 9–24.

Howes, R. J. (2003). Circumferential change scores in phallometric assessment: Normative data. *Sexual Abuse: A Journal of Research and Treatment, 15,* 365–375.

Hoyert, D. L., Heron, M. P., Murphy, S. L., & Hsiang-Ching, K. (2006). Deaths: Final data for 2003. *National Vital Statistics Reports, 54,* 1–120.

Huba, G. J. (1986). The use of the runs test for assessing response validity in computer scored inventories. *Educational and Psychological Measurement, 46,* 929–932.

Huddleston, J. H. (1932). *Accidents, neuroses and compensation.* Baltimore: Williams & Wilkins.

Hughes, J., & Hill, C. (2006). Lying. In G. Bear & K. Minke (Eds.), *Children's needs: III. Development, prevention, and intervention* (pp. 159–169). Washington, DC: National Association of School Psychologists.

Hunsley, J., & Bailey, J. (1999). The clinical utility of the Rorschach: Unfulfilled promises and an uncertain future. *Psychological Assessment, 11,* 266–277.

Hunsley, J., & Bailey, J. (2001). Whither the Rorschach?: An analysis of the evidence. *Psychological Assessment, 13,* 472–485.

Hunter, J. E., & Schmidt, F. L. (1990). *Methods of meta-analysis: Correcting error and bias in research findings.* Newbury Park, CA: Sage.

Hurley, K. E., & Deal, W. P. (2006). Assessment instruments measuring malingering used with individuals who have mental retardation: Potential problems and issues. *Mental Retardation, 44*(2), 112–119.

Hurwitz, T. A. (2004). Somatization and conversion disorder. *Canadian Journal of Psychiatry, 49*(3), 172–178.

Iacono, W. G. (2007). Detecting deception. In J. T. Cacioppo, L. G. Tassinary, & G. Berntson (Eds.), *Handbook of psychophysiology* (3rd ed., pp. 688–703). New York: Cambridge University Press.

Iacono, W. G., Boisvenu, G. A., & Fleming, J. A. (1984). The effects of diazepam and methylphenidate on the electrodermal detection of guilty knowledge. *Journal of Applied Psychology, 69,* 289–299.

Iacono, W. G., & Lykken, D. T. (1997). The validity of the lie detector: Two surveys of scientific opinion. *Journal of Applied Psychology, 82,* 426–433.

Iacono, W. G., & Patrick, C. J. (1997). Polygraphy and integrity testing. In R. Rogers (Ed.), *Clinical assessment of malingering and deception* (2nd ed., pp. 252–281). New York: Guilford Press.

Iacono, W. G., & Patrick, C. J. (2006). Polygraph ("lie detector") testing: Current status and emerging trends. In I. B. Weiner & A. K. Hess (Eds.), *The handbook of forensic psychology* (pp. 552–588). Hoboken, NJ: Wiley.

Inabu, F. E., & Reid, J. E. (1967). *Criminal interrogation and confessions* (2nd ed.). Baltimore: Williams & Wilkins.

Inman, T. H., & Berry, D. T. R. (2002). Cross-validation of indicators of malingering: A comparison of nine neuropsychological tests, four tests of malingering, and behavioral observations. *Archives of Clinical Neuropsychology, 17,* 1–23.

Inman, T. H., Vickery, C. D., Berry, D. T. R., Lamb, D., Edwards, C., & Smith, G. T. (1998). Development and initial validation of a new procedure for evaluating adequacy of effort given during neuropsychological testing: The Letter Memory Test. *Psychological Assessment, 10,* 128–139.

International Association of Chiefs of Police. (2004a). *Pre-employment psychological evaluation services guidelines.* Retrieved from *http://www.theiacp.org/div_sec_com/sections/Pre-employmentPsychological Evaluation.pdf*

International Association of Chiefs of Police. (2004b). *Psychological fitness for duty evaluation guidelines.* Retrieved from *http://www.policepsych.com/fitforduty .html*

Inwald, R., E., Knatz, H., & Shusman, E. (1982). *Inwald Personality Inventory manual.* New York: Hilson Research.

Inwald, R. E., & Shusman, E. J. (1984). The IPI and MMPI as predictors of academy performance for police recruits. *Journal of Police Science and Administration, 12,* 1–11.

Iverson, G. (2005). Outcome from mild traumatic brain injury. *Current Opinion in Psychiatry, 18,* 301–317.

Iverson, G. (2006). Ethical issues associated with the assessment of exaggeration, poor effort, and malingering. *Applied Neuropsychology, 13,* 77–90.

Iverson, G. L. (2003). Detecting malingering in civil forensic evaluations. In A. M. Horton, Jr. & L. C. Hartlage (Eds.), *Handbook of forensic neuropsychology* (pp. 137–177). New York: Springer.

Iverson, G. L., & Binder, L. M. (2000). Detecting exaggeration and malingering in neuropsychological assessment. *Journal of Head Trauma Rehabilitation, 15,* 829–858.

Iverson, G. L., & Franzen, M. D. (1994). The Recognition Memory Test Digit Span and Knox Cube Test as markers of malingered memory impairment. *Assessment, 1,* 323–334.

Iverson, G. L., & Franzen, M. D. (1996). Using multiple objective memory procedures to detect simulated malingering. *Journal of Clinical and Experimental Neuropsychology, 18,* 38–51.

Iverson, G. L., Franzen, M. D., & Hammond, J. A. (1995). Examination of inmates' ability to malinger on the MMPI-2. *Psychological Assessment, 7,* 118–121.

Iverson, G. L., Franzen, M. D., & McCracken, L. M. (1991). Evaluation of an objective assessment technique for the detection of malingered memory deficits. *Law and Human Behavior, 15,* 667–676.

Iverson, G. L., Lange, R. T., Green, P., & Franzen, M. D. (2002). Detecting exaggeration and malingering with the Trail Making Test. *Clinical Neuropsychologist, 16,* 398–406.

Iverson, G. L., & McCracken, L. M. (1997). Postconcussive symptoms in persons with chronic pain. *Brain Injury, 11,* 783–790.

Iverson, G. L., & Tulsky, D. S. (2003). Detecting malingering on the WAIS-III: Unusual Digit Span performance patterns in the normal population and in clinical groups. *Archives of Clinical Neuropsychology, 18,* 1–9.

Iverson, G. L., Wilhelm, K., & Franzen, M. D. (1993). Objective assessment of simulated memory deficits: Additional scoring criteria for the 21 Items Test. *Archives of Clinical Neuropsychology, 8,* 235–236.

Jackson, D. N. (1971). The dynamics of structured personality tests: 1971. *Psychological Review, 78,* 229–248.

Jackson, D. N. (1976). *Basic Personality Inventory.* London, Ontario, Canada: Author.

Jackson, D. N. (1989). *Basic Personality Inventory manual.* Port Huron, MI: Sigma Assessment.

Jackson, R. L., Rogers, R., & Sewell, K. W. (2005). Forensic applications of the Miller Forensic Assessment of Symptoms Test (M-FAST): Screening for feigned disorders in competency to stand trial evaluations. *Law and Human Behavior, 29,* 199–210.

Jaffee, W. B., Trucco, E., Levy, S., & Weiss, R. D. (in press). Is this urine really negative?: A systematic review of tampering methods in urine drug screening and testing. *Journal of Substance Abuse Treatment.*

Jalazo, J., Steer, R. A., & Fine, E. W. (1978). Use of Breathalyzer scores in the evaluation of persons arrested for driving while intoxicated. *Journal of Studies on Alcohol, 39*(7), 1304–1307.

James, D. J., & Glaze, L. E. (2006). *Bureau of Justice Statistics special report: Mental health problems of prison and jail inmates.* Retrieved March 20, 2007, from *http://www.ojp.usdoj.gov/bjs/mhppji.pdf*

Janal, M., Ciccone, D., & Natelson, B. (2006). Sub-typing CFS patients on the basis of "minor" symptoms. *Biological Psychology, 73,* 124–131.

Janus, E. S. (2001). Sex offender commitments and the "inability to control": Developing legal standards and a behavioral vocabulary for an elusive concept. In A. Schlank (Ed.), *The sexual predator: Legal issues, clinical issues, special population* (Vol. 2, pp. 1–30). Kingston, NJ: Civic Research Institute.

Jason, L., Taylor, R., Stepanek, Z., & Plioplys, S. (2001). Attitudes regarding chronic fatigue syndrome: The importance of a name. *Journal of Health Psychology, 6*(1), 61–71.

Jelicic, M., Hessels, A., & Merckelbach, H. (2006). Detection of feigned psychosis with the Structured Inventory of Malingered Symptomatology (SIMS): A study of coached and uncoached simulators. *Journal of Psychopathology and Behavioral Assessment, 28*(1), 19–22.

Jelicic, M., Merckelbach, H., & van Bergen, S. (2004). Symptom validity testing of feigned amnesia for mock crime. *Archives of Clinical Neuropsychology, 19,* 525–531.

Jennett, B. (2002). The Glasgow Coma Scale: History and current practice. *Trauma, 4*(2), 91–103.

Jennett, B., & Bond, M. (1975). Assessment of outcome after severe brain damage. *Lancet, 1,* 480–484.

Jensen, T. K., Gulbrandsen, W., Mossige, S., Reichelt, S., & Tjersland, O. A. (2005). Reporting possible sexual abuse: A qualitative study on children's perspectives and the context for disclosure. *Child Abuse and Neglect, 29*(12), 1395–1413.

Johnson, J. A. (1986). PDI Employment Inventory. In D. J. Keyser & R. C. Sweatland (Eds.), *Test critiques* (Vol. 8, pp. 548–556). Kansas City, MO: Test Corporation of America.

Johnson, J. L., & Lesniak-Karpiak, K. (1997). The effect of warning on malingering on memory and motor tasks in college samples. *Archives of Clinical Neuropsychology, 12*(3), 231–238.

Johnson, L. D., O'Malley, P. M., & Bachman, J. G. (1994). *National survey on drug use from the Monitoring the Future study 1975–1993.* Rockville, MD: National Institute on Drug Abuse.

Johnson, M. K., Hashtroudi, S., & Lindsay, D. S. (1993). Source monitoring. *Psychological Bulletin, 114,* 3–28.

Johnson, R., Jr., Barnhardt, J., & Zhu, J. (2003). The deceptive response: Effects of response conflict and strategic monitoring on the late positive component and episodic memory-related brain activity. *Biological Psychology, 64,* 217–253.

Johnson, R., Jr., Barnhardt, J., & Zhu, J. (2004). The contribution of executive processes to deceptive responding. *Neuropsychologia, 42,* 878–901.

Jonas, J. M., & Pope, H. G., Jr. (1985). The dissimulating disorders: A single diagnostic entity? *Comprehensive Psychiatry, 26*(1), 58–62.

Jones, A., & Llewellyn, J. (1917). *Malingering.* London: Heinemann.

Jones, A. W. (1993). Pharmacokinetics of ethanol in saliva: Comparison with blood and breath alcohol profiles, subjective feelings of intoxication and diminished performance. *Advances in Clinical Chemistry, 39,* 1837–1844.

Jones'El v. Barge, 164 F. Supp. 2d 1096, 1101–1102 (W.D. Wis. 2001).

Jordan, M. J., & Rogers, R. (2004, March). *Creating therapeutic change in juvenile offenders: An application of the transtheoretical model.* Paper presented at the National Conference of the American Psychology–Law Society, Scottsdale, AZ.

Jourard, S. M. (1971). *Self-disclosure: An experimental analysis of the transparent self.* New York: Wiley Interscience.

Ju, D., & Varney, N. (2000). Can head injury patients simulate malingering? *Applied Neuropsychology, 7*(4), 201–207.

Judd, L. L., Hubbard, R. B., Huey, L., Attewell, P. A., Janowsky, D. S., & Takahashi, K. I. (1977). Lithium carbonate and ethanol induced "highs" in normal subjects. *Archives of General Psychiatry, 34,* 463–467.

Junginger, J. (1990). Predicting compliance with command hallucinations. *American Journal of Psychiatry, 147,* 245–247.

Junginger, J. (1995). Command hallucinations and the prediction of dangerousness. *Psychiatric Services, 46,* 911–914.

Junginger, J., & Frame, C. (1985). Self-report of the frequency and phenomenology of verbal hallucinations. *Journal of Nervous and Mental Disease, 173,* 149–155.

Jureidini, J. (1993). Obstetric factitious disorder and Munchausen syndrome by proxy. *Journal of Nervous and Mental Disease, 181*(2), 135–137.

Jureidini, J. N., Shafer, A. T., & Donald, T. G. (2003). "Munchausen by proxy syndrome": Not only pathological parenting but also problematic doctoring? *Medical Journal of Australia, 178*(3), 130–132.

Kahn, M., Fox, H., & Rhode, R. (1988). Detecting faking on the Rorschach: Computer versus expert clinical judgment. *Journal of Personality Assessment, 52,* 516–523.

Kalambokis, G., Konitsiotis, S., Pappas, D., & Tsianos, E. V. (2006). Akinetic mutism followed by a manic reaction on introduction of steroid replacement for Addison's disease. *Journal of Endocrinology Investigations, 29*(3), 257–260.

Kalmus, E., & Beech, A. R. (2005). Forensic assessment of sexual interest: A review. *Aggression and Violent Behavior, 10,* 193–217.

Kaminer, Y., Bukstein, O., & Tarter, R. E. (1991). The Teen-Addiction Severity Index: Rationale and reliability. *International Journal of Addictions, 26,* 219–226.

Kaminer, Y., Wagner, E., Plummer, B., & Seifer, R. (1993). Validation of the Teen-Addiction Severity Index (T-ASI): Preliminary findings. *American Journal of Addictions, 2,* 250–254.

Kanas, N., & Barr, M. A. (1984). Self-control of psychotic productions in schizophrenics [Letter to the editor]. *Archives in General Psychiatry, 41,* 919–920.

Kanin, E. J. (1994). False rape allegations. *Archives of Sexual Behavior, 23*(1), 81–92.

Kansagara, D. L., Tetrault, J., Hamill, C., Moore, C., & Olson, B. (2006). Fatal factitious Cushing's syndrome and invasive aspergillosis: Case report and review of literature. *Endocrinology Practice, 12*(6), 651–655.

Kansas v. Crane, 534 U.S. 407 (2002).

Kansas v. Hendricks, 521 U.S. 346 (1997).

Kapfhammer, H. P., Rothenhausler, H. B., Dietrich, E., Dobmeier, P., & Mayer, C. (1998). [Artifactual disorders—between deception and self-mutilation: Experiences in consultation psychiatry at a university clinic]. *Nervenarzt, 69*(5), 401–409.

Kaplan, B. J., & Sadock, V. A. (Eds.). (2003). *Synopsis of psychiatry* (9th ed.). Philadelphia: Lippincott, Williams, & Wilkins.

Kaplan, M., & Eron, L. (1965). Test sophistication and faking in the TAT situation. *Journal of Projective Techniques and Personality Assessment, 29,* 498–503.

Kapur, B. (1994). Drug testing methods and interpretations of test results. In S. MacDonald & P. Roman (Eds.), *Drug testing in the workplace* (pp. 103–120). New York: Plenum Press.

Kashluba, S., Casey, J., & Paniak, C. (2006). Evaluating the utility of ICD-10 diagnostic criteria for postconcussion syndrome following mild traumatic brain injury. *Journal of the International Neuropsychological Society, 12,* 111–118.

Kasper, M. E., Rogers, R., & Adams, P. A. (1996). Dangerousness and command hallucinations: An investigation of psychotic inpatients. *Bulletin of the American Academy of Psychiatry and Law, 24,* 219–224.

Kauder, B. S., & Thomas, J. C. (2003). Relationship between MMPI-2 and Inwald Personality Inventory (IPI) scores and ratings of police officer probationary performance. *Applied HRM Research, 8,* 81–84.

Kay, T. (1999). Interpreting apparent neuropsychological deficits: What is really wrong? In J. Sweet (Ed.), *Forensic neuropsychology: Fundamentals and practice* (pp. 145–183). Lisse, The Netherlands: Swets & Zeitlinger.

Keane, J. R. (1986). Wrong-way deviation of the tongue with hysterical hemiparesis. *Neurology, 36,* 1406–1407.

Keane, J. R. (1989). Hysterical gait disorders. *Neurology, 39,* 586–589.

Keane, T. M., Buckley, T., & Miller, M. (2003). Forensic psychological assessment in PTSD. In R. I. Simon (Ed.), *Posttraumatic stress disorder in litigation: Guidelines for forensic assessment* (2nd ed., pp. 119–140). Washington, DC: American Psychiatric Press.

Keane, T. M., Kolb, L. C., Kaloupek, D. G., Orr, S. P., Blanchard, E. B., Thomas, R. G., et al. (1998). Utility of psychophysiological measurement in the diagnosis of posttraumatic stress disorder: Results from a Department of Veterans Affairs Cooperative Study. *Journal of Consulting and Clinical Psychology, 66*(6), 914–293.

Kearney, C. A., & Beasley, J. F. (1994). The clinical treatment of school refusal behavior: A survey of referral and practice characteristics. *Psychology in the Schools, 31,* 128–132.

Keiser, L. (1968). *The traumatic neurosis.* Philadelphia: Lippincott.

Kelly, K., & Rogers, R. (1996). Detection of misreported drug use in forensic populations: An overview of hair analysis. *Bulletin of the American Academy of Psychiatry and Law, 24,* 85–94.

Kelly, R., & Smith, B. N. (1981). Posttraumatic syndrome: Another myth discredited. *Journal of the Royal Society of Medicine, 74,* 275–278.

Kendler, K. S., Prescott, C. A., Myers, J., & Neale, M. C. (2003). The structure of genetic and environmental risk factors for common psychiatric and substance use disorders in men and women. *Archives of General Psychiatry, 60,* 929–937.

Kennedy, B. P., & Minami, M. (1993). The Beech Hill Hospital/Outward Bound adolescent chemical dependency treatment program. *Journal of Substance Abuse Treatment, 10,* 395–406.

Kennedy, H., & Grubin, D. (1992). Patterns of denial in sex offenders. *Psychological Medicine, 22,* 191–196.

Kent, G., & Wahass, S. (1996). The content and characteristics of auditory hallucinations in Saudi Arabia and the UK: A cross-cultural comparison. *Acta Psychiatrica Scandinavica, 94*(6), 433–437.

Kessler, R., Sonnega, A., Bromct, E., & Hughes, M. (1995). Posttraumatic stress disorder in the National Comorbidity Survey. *Archives of General Psychiatry, 52*(12), 1048–1060.

Kessler, R. C., Chui, W. T., Dennier, O., Merikangas, K. R., & Walters, E. E. (2005). Prevalence, severity, and comorbidity of 12-month prevalence of DSM-IV disorders in the National Comorbidity Survey Replication. *Archives of General Psychiatry, 62*(6), 617–627.

Kessler, R. C., McGonagle, K. A., Zhao, S., Nelson, C. B., Hughes, M., Eshleman, S., et al. (1994). Lifetime and 12-month prevalence of DSM-III-R disorders in the United States. *Archives of General Psychiatry, 51*(1), 8–19.

Kewman, D. G., Vaishampayan, N., Zald, D., & Han, B. (1991). Cognitive impairment in musculoskeletal pain patients. *International Journal of Psychiatry in Medicine, 21,* 253–262.

Kielbasa, A. M., Pomerantz, A. M., Krohn, E. J., & Sullivan, B. F. (2004). How does clients' method of payment influence psychologists' diagnostic decisions? *Ethics and Behavior, 14,* 187–195.

Kiester, P. D., & Duke, A. D. (1999). Is it malingering, or is it "real"?: Eight signs that point to nonorganic back pain. *Postgraduate Medicine, 106,* 77–80, 83–84.

Kihlstrom, J. F., & Schacter, D. L. (2000). Functional amnesia. In F. Boller & J. Grafman (Eds.), *Handbook of neuropsychology* (2nd ed., Vol. 2, pp. 409–427). Amsterdam: Elsevier Science.

Killgore, W. D., & DellaPietra, L. (2000). Using the WMS-III to detect malingering: Empirical validation of the rarely missed index (RMI). *Journal of Clinical and Experimental Neuropsychology, 22,* 761–771.

Kim, C. H., Shin, H. C., & Won, C. W. (2005). Prevalence of chronic fatigue and chronic fatigue syndrome in Korea: Community-based primary care study. *Journal of Korean Medicine and Science, 20*(4), 529–534.

King, B. H., & Ford, C. V. (1988). Pseudologia fantastica. *Acta Psychiatrica Scandinavica, 77*(1), 1–6.

King, M. F., & Bruner, G. C. (2000). Social desirability bias: A neglected aspect of validity testing. *Psychology and Marketing, 17,* 79–103.

Kircher, J. C., Horowitz, S. W., & Raskin, D. C. (1988). Meta-analysis of mock crime studies of the control question polygraph technique. *Law and Human Behavior, 12,* 79–90.

Kirisci, L., Hsu, T. C., & Tarter, R. (1994). Fitting a two-parameter logistic item response model to clarify the psychometric properties of the Drug Use Screening Inventory for adolescent alcohol and drug abusers. *Alcohol Clinical and Experimental Research, 18,* 1335–1341.

Klein, S. (2000). Deception and substance abuse. *Dissertation Abstracts International, 60,* 5248.

Kleinman, S., & Stewart, L. (2004). Psychiatric–legal considerations in providing mental health assistance to disaster survivors. *Psychiatric Clinics of North America, 27*(3), 559–570.

Kleinmuntz, B. (1989). Review of the Phase II Profile Integrity Status Inventory and Addendum. In J. C. Conoley & J. J. Kramer (Eds.), *The tenth mental measurements yearbook* (pp. 635–638). Lincoln, NE: Buros Institute of Mental Measurements.

Kline, R. B., & Snyder, D. K. (1985). Replicated MMPI subtypes for alcoholic men and women: Relationship to self-reported drinking behaviors. *Journal of Consulting and Clinical Psychology, 53,* 70–79.

Klonoff, E. A., Youngner, S. J., Moore, D. J., & Hershey, L. A. (1983). Chronic factitious illness: A behavioral approach. *International Journal of Psychiatry in Medicine, 13*(3), 173–183.

Kluft, L. C. (1987). The simulation and dissimulation of multiple personality disorder. *American Journal of Clinical Hypnosis, 30,* 104–118.

Knight, K., Hiller, M. L., Simpson, D. D., & Broome, K. M. (1998). The validity of self-reported cocaine use in a criminal justice treatment sample. *American Journal of Drug Alcohol Abuse, 24*(4), 647–660.

Knoll, J. L. (2006a, October). *Real world challenges in correctional psychiatry.* Paper presented at the annual meeting of the American Academy of Psychiatry and the Law, Chicago.

Knoll, J. L. (2006b). A tale of two crises: Mental health treatment in corrections. *Journal of Dual Diagnosis, 3*(1), 7–21.

Knoll, J. L., & Resnick P. J. (1999). U.S. v. Greer: Longer sentences for malingerers. *Journal of the American Academy of Psychiatry and the Law, 27*(4), 621–625.

Koch, W., O'Neill, M., & Douglas, K. S. (2005). Empirical limits for the forensic assessment of PTSD litigants. *Law and Human Behavior, 29*(1), 121–149.

Kokish, R. (2003). The current role of post-conviction sex offender polygraph testing in sex offender treatment. *Journal of Child Sexual Abuse, 12,* 175–194.

Kokish, R., Levenson, J. S., & Blasingame, G. D. (2005). Post-conviction sex offender polygraph examination: Client-reported perceptions of utility and accuracy. *Sexual Abuse: Journal of Research and Treatment, 17,* 211–221.

Kokturk, N., Ekim, N., Aslan, S., Kanbay, A., & Acar, A. T. (2006). A rare cause of hemoptysis: Factitious disorder. *Southern Medicinal Journal, 99*(2), 186–187.

Kopelman, M. D. (1987). Crime and amnesia: A review. *Behavioral Sciences and the Law, 5,* 323–342.

Kopelman, M. D. (1994). The autobiographical memory interview (AMI) in organic and psychogenic amnesia. *Memory, 2,* 211–235.

Kopelman, M. D. (1995). The assessment of psychogenic amnesia. In A. D. Baddeley, B. A. Wilson, & F. N. Watts (Eds.), *Handbook of memory disorders* (pp. 427–448). New York: Wiley.

Kopelman, M. D., & Stanhope, N. (2002). Anterograde and retrograde amnesia following frontal lobe, temportal lobe, or diencephalic lesions. In L. R. Squire &

D. L. Schacter (Eds.), *Neuropsychology of memory* (3rd ed., pp. 47–60). New York: Guilford Press.

Koren, D., Hemel, D., & Klein, E. (2006). Injury increases the risk for PTSD: An examination of potential neurobiological and psychological mediators. *CNS Spectrums, 11*(8), 616–624.

Koren, D., Norman, D., Cohen, A., Berman, J., & Klein, E. M. (2005). Increased PTSD risk with combat-related injury: A matched comparison study of injured and uninjured soldiers experiencing the same combat events. *American Journal of Psychiatry, 162,* 276–278.

Kornfeld, A. D. (1995). Police officer candidate MMPI-2 performance: Gender, ethnic, and normative factors. *Journal of Clinical Psychology, 51,* 536–540.

Kortte, K. B., & Wegener, S. T. (2004). Denial of illness in medical rehabilitation populations: Theory, research, and definition. *Rehabilitation Psychology, 49,* 187–199.

Koss, M. P., & Butcher, J. N. (1973). A comparison of psychiatric patients' self-report with other sources of clinical information. *Journal of Research in Personality, 7,* 225–236.

Kozel, F. A., Johnson, K. A., Mu, Q., Grenesko, E. L., Laken, S. J., & George, M. S. (2005). Detecting deception using functional magnetic resonance imaging. *Biological Psychiatry, 58,* 605–613.

Kraemer, H. C. (1992). *Evaluating medical tests: Objective and quantitative guidelines.* Newberry Park, CA: Sage.

Krafft-Ebing, R. von (1965). *Psychopathia sexualis.* New York: Putnam. (Original work published 1886)

Krahn, L. E., Li, H., & O'Connor, M. K. (2003). Patients who strive to be ill: Factitious disorder with physical symptoms. *American Journal of Psychiatry, 160*(6), 1163.

Kranzler, H. R., Kadden, R. M., Babor, T. F., Tennen, H., & Rounsaville, B. J. (1996). Validity of the SCID in substance abuse patients. *Addiction, 91*(6), 859–868.

Kraus, A. (1994). Phenomenology of the technical delusion in schizophrenia. *Journal of Phenomenological Psychology, 25,* 51–69.

Kraut, R. E., & Price, J. D. (1976). Machiavellianism in parent and their children. *Journal of Personality and Social Psychology, 33,* 782–786.

Krieger, M., & Levin, S. (1976). Schizophrenic behavior as a function of role expectation. *Journal of Clinical Psychology, 32,* 463–467.

Krittman, S. W. (2004). *A longitudinal study of malingering and treatment compliance in a residential mental health program.* Dissertation Abstracts International: Section B. The Physical Sciences and Engineering, 64(8-B), 4046.

Kroenke, K., & Rosmalen, J. G. (2006). Symptoms, syndromes, and the value of psychiatric diagnostics in patients who have functional somatic disorders. *Medical Clinics of North America, 90*(4), 603–626.

Kroger, R. O., & Turnbell, W. (1975). Invalidity of validity scales: The case of the MMPI. *Journal of Consulting and Clinical Psychology, 43,* 48–55.

Kropp, P. R. (1992). *Antisocial personality disorder and malingering.* Unpublished doctoral dissertation, Simon Fraser University, Burnaby, BC, Canada.

Kropp, P. R., & Rogers, R. (1993). Understanding malingering: Motivation, method, and detection. In M. Lewis & C. Saarni (Eds.), *Lying and deception in everyday life* (pp. 201–216). New York: Guilford Press.

Krueger, R. B., Bradford, J. M. W., & Glancy, G. D. (1998). Report from the Committee on Sex Offenders: The Abel Assessment for Sexual Interest: A brief description. *Journal of the American Academy of Psychiatry and the Law, 26,* 277–280.

Krueger, R. F. (1999). Personality traits in late adolescence predict mental disorders in early adulthood: A prospective-epidemiological study. *Journal of Personality, 67,* 39–65.

Krueger, R. F., Hicks, B., Patrick, C. J., Carlson, S., Iacono, W. G., & McGue, M. (2002). Etiologic connections among substance dependence, antisocial behavior, and personality: Modeling the externalizing spectrum. *Journal of Abnormal Psychology, 111,* 411–424.

Krueger, R. F., McGue, M., & Iacono, W. G. (2001). The higher-order structure of common DSM mental disorder: Internalization, externalization, and their connection to personality. *Personality and Individual Differences, 30,* 1245–1259.

Krueger, R. F., & Tackett, J. L. (2003). Personality and psychopathology: Working toward the bigger picture. *Journal of Personality Disorders, 17,* 107–119.

Kucharski, L. T., Duncan, S., Egan, S. S., & Falkenbach, D. M. (2006). Psychopathy and malingering of psychiatric disorder in criminal defendants. *Behavioral Sciences and the Law, 24,* 633–644.

Kucharski, L. T., & Johnsen, D. (2002). A comparison of simulation and known groups in the detection of malingering on the MMPI-2. *Journal of Forensic Sciences, 47,* 1–5.

Kucharski, L. T., Ryan, W., Vogt, J., & Goodloe, E. (1998). Clinical symptom presentation in suspected malingerers: An empirical investigation. *Journal of American Academy of Psychiatry and Law, 26*(4), 579–585.

Kucharski, L. T., Toomey, J. P., Fila, K., & Duncan, S. (2007). Detection of malingering of psychiatric disorder with the Personality Assessment Inventory: An investigation of criminal defendants. *Journal of Personality Assessment, 88,* 25–32.

Kuehnle, K. (1996). *Assessing allegations of child sexual abuse.* Sarasota, FL: Professional Resource Exchange.

Kulaksizoglu, I. B., Polat, A., & Vatansever, S. (2002). An adolescent in Istanbul with Munchausen's syndrome. *International Journal of Psychiatry in Medicine, 32,* 311–315.

Kulik, J. A., Bangert-Drowns, R. L., & Kulick, C. C. (1984). Effective of coaching on aptitude tests. *Psychological Bulletin, 95,* 179–188.

Kulik, J. A., Kulick, C. C., & Bangert-Drowns, R. L. (1984). Effects of practice on aptitude and achievement test scores. *American Educational Research Journal, 21,* 435–447.

Kupers, T. A. (2004). Malingering in correctional settings. *Correctional Mental Health Report, 5*(6), 81–95.

Kurtz, J. E., Shealy, S. E., & Putnam, S. H. (2007). Another look at paradoxical severity effects in head injury with the Personality Assessment Inventory. *Journal of Personality Assessment, 88*(1), 66–73.

La Fontaine, J. S. (1998). *Speak of the devil: Tales of satanic abuse in contemporary England.* Cambridge, UK: Cambridge University Press.

La Greca, A. M. (1983). Interviewing and behavioral observations. In C. E. Walker & M. C. Roberts (Eds.), *Handbook of clinical child psychology* (pp. 109–131). New York: Wiley.

La Greca, A. M. (1990). Issues and perspectives on the child assessment process. In A. M. La Greca (Ed.), *Through the eyes of the child: Obtaining self-reports from children and adolescents* (pp. 3–17). Boston: Allyn & Bacon.

Labott, S., & Wallach, H. (2002). Malingering dissociative identity disorder: Objective and projective assessment. *Psychological Reports, 90,* 525–538.

Lacey, J. (1993). Self-damaging and addictive behaviour in bulimia nervosa: A catchment area study. *British Journal of Psychiatry, 163,* 190–194.

Lachar, D., & Gruber, C. P. (1995). *Manual for the Personality Inventory for Youth.* Los Angeles: Western Psychological Services.

Lachar, D., & Wrobel, T. A. (1974). Validating clinicians' hunches: Construction of a new MMPI critical item set. *Journal of Consulting and Clinical Psychology, 47,* 277–284.

Lacoursiere, R. B. (1993). Diverse motives for fictitious post-traumatic stress disorder. *Journal of Traumatic Stress, 6,* 141–149.

LaFond, J. Q. (2003). The costs of enacting a sexual predator law and recommendations for keeping them from skyrocketing. In B. J. Winick & J. Q. LaFond (Eds.), *Protecting society from sexually dangerous offenders.* Washington, DC: American Psychological Association.

Lally, S. (2003). What tests are acceptable for use in forensic evaluations?: A survey of experts. *Professional Psychology: Research and Practice, 34,* 491–498.

Lalumière, M. L., & Quinsey, V. L. (1993). The sensitivity of phallometric measures with rapists. *Annals of Sex Research, 6,* 123–138.

Lalumière, M. L., & Quinsey, V. L. (1994). The discriminability of rapists from non-sex offenders using phallometric measures: A meta-analysis. *Criminal Justice and Behavior, 21,* 150–175.

Lamb, D. G., Berry, D. T. R., Wetter, M. W., & Baer, R. A. (1994). Effects of two types of information on malingering of closed head injury on the MMPI-2: An analog investigation. *Psychological Assessment, 6,* 8–13.

Lamb, H., & Weinberger, L. (2005). The shift of psychiatric inpatient care from hospitals to jails and prisons. *Journal of the American Academy of Psychiatry and Law, 33,* 529–534.

Landre, N., Poppe, C. J., Davis, N., Schmaus, B., & Hobbs, S. E. (2006). Cognitive functioning and postconcussive symptoms in trauma patients with and without mild TBI. *Archives of Clinical Neuropsychology, 21,* 255–273.

Lang, P. J. (1985). The cognitive psychophysiology of emotion: Fear and anxiety. In A. H. Tuma & J. Maser

(Eds.), *Anxiety and the anxiety disorder* (pp. 131–170). Hillsdale, NJ: Erlbaum.

Lange, R. T., Iverson, G. L., Sullivan, K., & Anderson, D. (2006). Suppressed working memory on the WMS-III as a marker for poor effort. *Journal of Clinical and Experimental Neuropsychology, 28,* 294–305.

Lange, R. T., Sullivan, K., & Anderson, D. (2005). Ecological validity of the WMS-III rarely missed index in personal injury litigation. *Journal of Clinical and Experimental Neuropsychology, 27,* 412–424.

Langeluddecke, P. M., & Lucas, S. K. (2003). Quantitative measures of memory malingering on the Wechsler Memory Scale—Third Edition in mild head injury litigants. *Archives of Clinical Neuropsychology, 18,* 181–197.

Langevin, R. (1983). *Sexual strands: Understanding and treating sexual anomalies in men.* Hillsdale, NJ: Erlbaum.

Langevin, R. (1988). Defensiveness in sex offenders. In R. Rogers (Ed.), *Clinical assessment of malingering and deception* (pp. 309–327). New York: Guilford Press.

Langevin, R., & Paitch, D. (2005). *Clarke Sexual History Questionnaire for Males—Revised.* North Tonawanda, NY: Multi-Health Systems.

Langleben, D. D., Loughhead, J. W., Bliker, W. B., Ruparel, K., Childress, A. R., Busch, S. I., et al. (2005). Telling truth from lie in individual subjects with fast event-related fMRI. *Human Brain Mapping, 26,* 262–272.

Lanning, K. V. (1992). A law-enforcement perspective on allegations of ritual abuse. In D. K. Sakheim & S. E. Devine (Eds.), *Out of darkness: Exploring satanism and ritual abuse* (pp. 109–146). New York: Lexington Books.

Lanyon, R. I. (1993a). Assessment of truthfulness in accusations of child molestation. *American Journal of Forensic Psychology, 11,* 29–44.

Lanyon, R. I. (1993b). Development of scales to assess specific deception strategies on the Psychological Screening Inventory. *Psychological Assessment, 5,* 324–329.

Lanyon, R. I. (1993c). Validity of MMPI sex offender scales with admitters and nonadmitters. *Psychological Assessment, 5,* 302–306.

Lanyon, R. I. (2001). Psychological assessment procedures in sex offending. *Professional Psychology: Research and Practice, 32,* 253–260.

Lanyon, R. I. (2003). Assessing the misrepresentation of health problems. *Journal of Personality Assessment, 81,* 1–10.

Lanyon, R. I., & Cunningham, K. S. (2005). Construct validity of the misrepresentation scales of the Psychological Screening Inventory. *Journal of Personality Assessment, 85,* 197–206.

Lanyon, R. I., & Lutz, R.W. (1984). MMPI discrimination of defensive and nondefensive felony sex offenders. *Journal of Consulting and Clinical Psychology, 52,* 841–843.

Larrabee, G. J. (1997). Neuropsychological outcome, postconcussion symptoms, and forensic considerations in mild closed head trauma. *Seminars in Clinical Neuropsychology, 2,* 196–206.

Larrabee, G. J. (1998). Somatic malingering on the MMPI and MMPI-2 in litigating subjects. *Clinical Neuropsychologist, 12,* 179–188.

Larrabee, G. J. (2003a). Detection of malingering using atypical performance patterns on standard neuropsychological tests. *Clinical Neuropsychologist, 17,* 410–425.

Larrabee, G. J. (2003b). Detection of symptom exaggeration with the MMPI-2 in litigants with malingered neurocognitive deficit. *Clinical Neuropsychologist, 17,* 54–68.

Larrabee, G. J. (2003c). Exaggerated pain report in litigants with malingered neurocognitive dysfunction. *Clinical Neuropsychologist, 17,* 395–401.

Larrabee, G. J. (2005a). Assessment of malingering. In G. J. Larrabee (Ed.), *Forensic neuropsychology: A scientific approach* (pp. 115–158). New York: Oxford University Press.

Larrabee, G. J. (2005b). *Forensic neuropsychology: A scientific approach.* New York: Oxford University Press.

Larrabee, G. J. (2007). Identification of malingering by pattern analysis on neuropsychological tests. In G. J. Larrabee (Ed.), *Assessment of malingered neuropsychological deficits* (pp. 80–99). New York: Oxford University Press.

Larrabee, G. J., Millis, S. R., & Meyers, J. E. (2007, February). *Sensitivity to brain dysfunction of the Halstead–Reitan versus an ability-focused neuropsychological battery.* Paper presented at the annual meeting of the International Neuropsychological Society, Portland, OR.

Lasher, L. J., & Sheridan, M. S. (2004). *Munchausen by proxy: Identification, intervention, and case management.* Binghamton, NY: Haworth Press.

Laurenceau, J.-P., Barrett, L. F., & Rovine, M. J. (2005). The interpersonal process model of intimacy in marriage: A daily diary and multilevel modeling approach. *Journal of Family Psychology, 19,* 314–323.

Lautenschlager, G. J., & Flaherty, V. L. (1990). Computer administration of questions: More desirable or more social desirability? *Journal of Applied Psychology, 75,* 310–314.

Laws, D. R., & Holmen, M. L. (1978). Sexual response faking by pedophiles. *Criminal Justice and Behavior, 5,* 343–356.

Layden, M. (1966). Symptoms separate hysteric, malingerer. *Psychiatric Progress, 1,* 7.

Lazarus, A., & Kozinn, W. P. (1991). Munchausen's syndrome with hematuria and sepsis: An unusual case. *International Journal of Psychiatry in Medicine, 21*(1), 113–116.

Lazowski, L. E., Miller, F. G., Boye, M. W., & Miller, G. A. (1998). Efficacy of the Substance Abuse Subtle Screening Inventory—3 (SASSI-3) in identifying substance dependence disorders in clinical settings. *Journal of Personality Assessment, 71*(1), 114–128.

Leary, M. R., & Kowalski, R. M. (1990). Impression management: A literature review and two component model. *Psychological Bulletin, 107,* 34–47.

Lechner, D. E., Bradbury, S. F., & Bradley, L. A. (1998). Detecting sincerity of effort: A summary of methods and approaches. *Physical Therapy, 78,* 867–888.

Lee, K., Ashton, M. C., & de Vries, R. E. (2005). Predicting workplace delinquency and integrity with the HEXACO and five-factor models of personality structure. *Human Performance, 18*, 179–197.

Lees-Haley, P. R. (1992). Efficacy of MMPI-2 validity scales and MCMI-II modifier scales for detecting spurious PTSD claims: F, F-K, Faked Bad Scale, Ego Strength, Subtle–Obvious subscales, DIS, and DEB. *Journal of Clinical Psychology, 48*, 681–689.

Lees-Haley, P. R. (1997). Attorneys influence expert evidence in forensic psychological and neuropsychological cases. *Assessment, 4*, 321–324.

Lees-Haley, P. R., & Brown, R. S. (1993). Neuropsychological complaint base rates of 170 personal injury claimants. *Archives of Clinical Neuropsychology, 8*, 203–209.

Lees-Haley, P. R., & Dunn, J. (1994). The ability of naïve subjects to report symptoms of mild brain injury, posttraumatic stress disorder, major depression and generalized anxiety disorder. *Journal of Clinical Psychology, 50*, 553–556.

Lees-Haley, P. R., English, L. T., & Glenn, W. J. (1991). A fake bad scale on the MMPI-2 for personal-injury claimants. *Psychological Reports, 68*, 203–210.

Lees-Haley, P. R., Iverson, G. L., Lange, R. T., Fox, D. D., & Allen, L. M. (2002). Malingering in forensic neuropsychology: Daubert and the MMPI-2. *Journal of Forensic Neuropsychology, 3*(1–2), 167–203.

Lennon, R., Pulos, S., & Rittner, L. (2005). Pediatric condition of falsification in attention-deficit/hyperactivity disorder. *North American Journal of Psychology, 7*, 353–359.

LePage, J. P., & Mogge, L. (2001). Validity rates of the MMPI-2 and PAI in a rural inpatient psychiatric facility. *Assessment, 8*, 67–74.

Leroy, R. (1922). The syndrome of Lilliputian hallucinations. *Journal of Nervous and Mental Disorders, 56*, 325–333.

Letourneau, E. J. (2002). A comparison of objective measures of sexual arousal and interest: Visual reaction time and penile plethysmography. *Sexual Abuse: A Journal of Research and Treatment, 14*, 207–223.

Leudar, I., Thomas, P., McNally, D., & Glinski, A. (1997). What voices can do with words: Pragmatics of verbal hallucinations. *Psychological Medicine, 27*(4), 885–898.

Leung, A. (1992). Review of the Hogan Personnel Selection Series. In J. J. Kramer & J. C. Conoley (Eds.), *The eleventh mental measurements yearbook* (pp. 384–386). Lincoln, NE: Buros Institute of Mental Measurements.

Levin, H. S., Lilly, M. A., Papanicolau, A., & Eisenberg, H. M. (1992). Posttraumatic and retrograde amnesia after closed head injury. In L. R. Squire & N. Butters (Eds.), *Neuropsychology of memory* (2nd ed., pp. 290–308). New York: Guilford Press.

Levin, H. S., Mattis, S., Ruff, R. M., Eisenberg, H. M., Marshall, L. F., Tabaddor, K., et al. (1987). Neurobehavioral outcome following minor head injury: A three-center study. *Neurosurgery, 66*(2), 234–243.

Levinson, M. R., Aldwin, C. M., Butcher, J. N., De Labry, L., Workman-Daniels, K., & Boxxe, R. (1990). The MAC scale in a normal population: The meaning of "false positives." *Journal of Studies on Alcohol, 51*, 457–462.

Lewinsohn, P. M. (1970). An empirical test of several popular notions about hallucinations in schizophrenic patients. In W. Keup (Ed.), *Origin and mechanisms of hallucinations* (pp. 401–403). New York: Plenum Press.

Lewis, D. J. (1961). Lilliputian hallucinations in the functional psychoses. *Canadian Psychiatric Association Journal, 6*, 177–201.

Lewis, J. L., Simcox, A. M., & Berry, D. T. R. (2002). Screening for feigned psychiatric symptoms in a forensic sample by using the MMPI-2 and the structured inventory of malingered symptomatology. *Psychological Assessment, 14*(2), 170–176.

Lewis, M. (1993). The development of deception. In M. Lewis & C. Saarni (Eds.), *Lying and deception in everyday life* (pp. 90–105). New York: Guilford Press.

Lewis, M., Stanger, C., & Sullivan, M. W. (1989). Deception in 3-year-olds. *Developmental Psychology, 25*, 439–443.

Lezak, M. D., Howieson, D. B., & Loring, D. W. (2004). *Neuropsychological assessment* (4th ed.). New York: Oxford University Press.

Li, A., & Bagger, J. (2006). Using the BIDR to distinguish the effects of impression management and self-deception on the criterion validity of personality measures: A meta-analysis. *International Journal of Selection and Assessment, 14*(2), 131–141.

Libow, J. A. (1995). Munchausen by proxy victims in adulthood: A first look. *Child Abuse and Neglect, 19*(9), 1131–1142.

Libow, J. A. (2000). Child and adolescent illness falsification. *Pediatrics, 105*, 336–342.

Lidz, C. W., Banks, S., Simon, L., Schubert, C., & Mulvey, E. P. (2007). Violence and mental illness: A new analytic approach. *Law and Human Behavior, 31*, 23–31.

Liljequist, L., Kinder, B. N., & Schinka, J. A. (1998). An investigation of malingering posttraumatic stress disorder on the Personality Assessment Inventory. *Journal of Personality Assessment, 7*, 332–336.

Limosin, F., Loze, J. Y., & Rouillon, F. (2002). [Clinical features and psychopathology of factitious disorders]. *Annales Medicine Interne (Paris), 153*(8), 499–502.

Links, P. S., Steiner, M., & Mitton, J. (1989). Characteristics of psychosis in borderline personality disorder. *Psychopathology, 22*(4), 188–193.

Lipian, M. S., Mills, M. J., & Brantman, A. (2004). Assessing the verity of children's allegations of abuse: A psychiatric overview. *International Journal of Law and Psychiatry, 27*, 249–263.

Lipman, F. D. (1962). Malingering in personal injury cases. *Temple Law Quarterly, 35*, 141–162.

Lishman, W. A. (1988). Physiogenesis and psychogenesis in the "post-concussional syndrome." *British Journal of Psychiatry, 153*, 460–469.

Little, C. A., Williams, S. E., Puzanovova, M., Rudzinski, E. R., & Walker, L. S. (2007). Multiple somatic symptoms linked to positive screen for depression in pediatric patients with chronic abdominal pain. *Journal of Pediatric Gastroenterology and Nutrition, 44*(1), 58–62.

Lo, Y. L., Fook-Chong, S., & Tan, E. K. (2003). Increased cortical excitability in human deception. *Neuroreport, 14,* 1021–1024.

Loftus, E. F. (1979). *Eyewitness testimony.* Cambridge, MA: Harvard University Press.

Loftus, E. F., & Davis, D. (2006). Recovered memories. *Annual Review of Clinical Psychology, 2,* 469–498.

Loftus, E. F., & Loftus, G. R. (1980). On the permanence of stored information in the human brain. *American Psychologist, 35,* 409–420.

Loftus, E. F., Loftus, G. R., & Messo, J. (1987). Some facts about "weapon focus." *Law and Human Behavior, 11,* 55–62.

Logan, W. S., Reuterfors, D. L., Bohn, M. J., & Clark, C. L. (1984). The description and classification of presidential threateners. *Behavioral Sciences and the Law, 2,* 151–167.

Looman, J. (2000). Sexual arousal in rapists as measured by two stimulus sets. *Sexual Abuse: A Journal of Research and Treatment, 12,* 235–248.

Looman, J., Abracen, J., Maillet, G., & DiFazio, R. (1998). Phallometric nonresponding in sexual offenders. *Sexual Abuse: A Journal of Research and Treatment, 10,* 325–336.

Looman, J., & Marshall, W. L. (2001). Phallometric assessments designed to detect arousal to children: The responses of rapists and child molesters. *Sexual Abuse: A Journal of Research and Treatment, 13,* 3–13.

Looman, J., & Marshall, W. L. (2005). Sexual arousal in rapists. *Criminal Justice and Behavior, 32,* 367–389.

Lorei, T. W. (1970). Staff ratings of the consequence of release from or retention in a psychiatric hospital. *Journal of Consulting and Clinical Psychology, 34,* 46–55.

Loring, D. W. (Ed.). (1999). *INS dictionary of neuropsychology.* New York: Oxford University Press.

Louis, D. S., Doro, C., & Hayden, R. J. (2006). Factitious disorders. *Clinical, Occupational and Environmental Medicine, 5,* 435–443.

Lowensteien, L. F. (2001). Factors differentiating successful versus unsuccessful malingerers. *Journal of Personality Assessment, 77*(2), 333–338.

Lu, P. H., & Boone, K. B. (2002). Suspect cognitive symptoms in a 9-year-old child: Malingering by proxy. *Clinical Neuropsychologist, 16,* 90–96.

Lucio, E., Duran, C., Graham, J. R., & Ben-Porath, Y. S. (2002). Identifying faking bad on the Minnesota Multiphasic Personality Inventory—Adolescent with Mexican Americans. *Assessment, 9,* 62–69.

Lykken, D. T. (1959). The GSR in the detection of guilt. *Journal of Applied Psychology, 43,* 385–388.

Lynam, D. R., Caspi, A., Moffitt, T. E., Loeber, R., & Stouthamer-Loeber, M. (2007). Longitudinal evidence that psychopathy scores in early adolescence predict adult psychopathy. *Journal of Abnormal Psychology, 116,* 155–165.

Lynam, D. R., Caspi, A., Moffitt, T. E., Raine, A., Loeber, R., & Stouthamer-Loeber, M. (2005). Adolescent psychopathy and the Big Five: Results from two samples. *Journal of Abnormal Child Psychology, 33,* 431–443.

Lynn, E. J., & Belza, M. (1984). Factitious posttraumatic stress disorder: The veteran who never got to Vietnam. *Hospital and Community Psychiatry, 35*(7), 697–701.

Lynn, S. J., Lock, T. G., Myers, B., & Payne, D. G. (1997). Recalling the unrecallable: Should hypnosis be used to recover memories in psychotherapy? *Current Directions in Psychological Science, 6,* 79–83.

Lyons, D. (2003). Sex, God and greed. *Forbes, 171,* 66–72.

Maag, J. W., Irvin, D. M., Reid, R., & Vasa, S. F. (1994). Prevalence and predictors of substance abuse use: A comparison between adolescents with and without learning disabilities. *Journal of Learning Disabilities, 27,* 223–234.

MacAndrew, C. (1965). The differentiation of male alcoholic outpatients from nonalcoholic psychiatric outpatients by means of the MMPI. *Quarterly Studies of Alcohol, 47,* 161–166.

MacAndrew, C. (1981). What the MAC scale tells us about alcoholics: An interpretive review. *Journal of Studies on Alcohol, 42,* 604–625.

MacAndrew, C. (1986). Toward the psychometric detection of substance misuse in young men: The SAP scale. *Journal of Studies in Alcohol, 47,* 161–166.

Macciocchi, S. N., Seel, R. T., Alderson, A., & Godsall, R. (2006). Victoria Symptom Validity Test performance in acute brain injury: Implications for test interpretation. *Archives of Clinical Neuropsychology, 21,* 395–404.

Madrid v. Gomez, 899 F. Supp. 1146, 1228 (N.D. Cal. 1995).

Main, C. J. (1983). Modified Somatic Perception Questionnaire (MSPQ). *Journal of Psychosomatic Research, 27,* 503–514.

Maisto, S., Connors, G., Tucker, H., McCollam, H., & Adesso, V. (1980). Validation of the sensation scale, a measure of subjective psychobiological responses to ethanol. *Behavior Research Therapy, 18,* 37–41.

Maisto, S. A., Carey, M. P., Carey, K. B., Gordon, C. M., & Gleason, J. R. (2000). Use of the AUDIT and the DAST-10 to identify alcohol and drug use disorders among adults with a severe and persistent mental illness. *Psychological Assessment, 12*(2), 186–192.

Makaremi, A. (1992). Birth order, neuroticism, and psychoticism among Iranian children. *Psychological Reports, 71,* 919–922.

Mäkelä, K. (2004). Studies of the reliability and validity of the Addiction Severity Index. *Addiction, 99,* 398–410.

Malloy, L. C., Lyon, T. D., & Quas, J. A. (2007). Filial dependency and recantation of child sexual abuse allegations. *Journal of the American Academy of Child and Adolescent Psychiatry, 46*(2), 162–170.

Maloney, M. P., Duvall, S. W., & Friesen, J. (1980). Evaluation of response consistency on the MMPI. *Psychological Reports, 46,* 295–298.

Maloney, M. T., Glasser, A., & Ward, M. P. (1980). *Malingering: An overview*. Unpublished manuscript.

Manford, M., & Andermann, F. (1998). Complex visual hallucinations: Clinical and neurobiological insights. *Brain, 121*(10), 1819–1840.

Marcus, B., Lee, K., & Ashton, M. C. (2007). Personality dimensions explaining relationships between integrity tests and counterproductive behavior: Big Five, or one in addition? *Personnel Psychology, 60*, 1–34.

Marks, P. A., Seeman, W., & Haller, D. L. (1974). *The actuarial use of the MMPI with adolescents and adults*. Baltimore: Williams & Wilkins.

Marsh, J. T., Hilliard, J., & Liechti, R. (1955). A sexual deviation scale for the MMPI. *Journal of Consulting Psychology, 19*, 55–59.

Marshall, M. B., & Bagby, R. M. (2006). The incremental validity and clinical utility of the MMPI-2 Infrequency Posttraumatic Stress Disorder Scale. *Assessment, 13*(4), 417–429.

Marshall, W. L., Barbaree, H. E., & Eccles, A. (1991). Early onset and deviant sexuality in child molesters. *Journal of Interpersonal Violence, 6*, 323–336.

Marshall, W. L., & Fernandez, Y. M. (2000). Phallometric testing with sexual offenders: Limits to its value. *Clinical Psychology Review, 20*, 807–822.

Marshall, W. L., & Fernandez, Y. M. (2001). Phallometry in forensic practice. *Journal of Forensic Psychology Practice, 1*, 77–87.

Mart, E. (2002). Munchausen's syndrome (factitious disorder) by proxy: A brief review of its scientific and legal status. *Scientific Review of Mental Health Practice, 1*, 55–61.

Martin, C. S., Earleywine, M., Musty, R. E., Perrine, M. W., & Swift, R. M. (1993). Development and validation of the Biphasic Alcohol Effects Scale. *Alcohol Clinical and Experimental Research, 17*, 140–146.

Martin, M. J. (1970). Psychiatric aspects of patients with compensation problems. *Psychosomatics, 11*, 81–84.

Martin, T. A., Hoffman, N. M., & Donders, J. (2003). Clinical utility of the Trail Making Test ratio score. *Applied Neuropsychology, 10*, 163–169.

Martino, S., Grilo, C. M., & Fehon, D. C. (2000). Development of the Drug Abuse Screening Test for Adolescents (DAST-A). *Addictive Behaviors, 25*(1), 57–70.

Mash, E. J., & Terdel, L. G. (1988). Behavioral assessment of child and family disturbance. In E. J. Mash & L. G. Terdel (Eds.), *Behavioral assessment of childhood disorders* (2nd ed., pp. 3–65). New York: Guilford Press.

Mastrangelo, P. M., & McDonald, B. (2001). Defining "reasonable suspicion" of employee drug use: The Symptoms of Drug Impairment Checklist. *Applied HRM Research, 6*(1), 1–12.

Matarazzo, J. D., Allen, B. V., Saslow, G., & Wiens, A. N. (1964). Characteristics of successful policemen and firemen applicants. *Journal of Applied Psychology, 48*, 123–133.

Mathias, C. W., Greve, K. W., Bianchini, K. B., Houston, R. J., & Crouch, J. A. (2002). Detecting malingered neurocognitive dysfunction using the Reliable Digit Span in traumatic brain injury. *Assessment, 9*, 301–308.

Mayer, J., & Filstead, W. J. (1979). The Adolescent Alcohol Involvement Scale: An instrument for measuring adolescents' use and misuse of alcohol. *Journal of Studies on Alcohol, 40*, 291–300.

Mayfield, D., McLeod, G., & Hall, P. (1974). The CAGE questionnaire: Validation of a new alcoholism screening instrument. *American Journal of Psychiatry, 131*, 1121–1123.

McAllister, T. W. (1994). Mild traumatic brain injury and the postconcussive syndrome. In J. M. Silver, S. C. Yudofsky, & R. E. Hales (Eds.), *Neuropsychiatry of traumatic brain injury* (pp. 357–392). Washington, DC: American Psychiatric Press.

McCann, J., Flens, J., Campagna, V., Collman, P., Lazzaro, T., & Connor, E. (2001). The MCMI-III in child custody evaluations: A normative study. *Journal of Forensic Psychology Practice, 1*(2), 27–44.

McCann, J. T. (1997). The MACI: Composition and clinical applications. In T. Millon (Ed.), *The Millon inventories: Clinical and personality assessment* (pp. 363–388). New York: Guilford Press.

McCann, J. T. (1998). *Malingering and deception in adolescents: Assessing credibility in clinical and forensic settings*. Washington, DC: American Psychological Association.

McConaghy, N. (1999). Unresolved issues in scientific sexology. *Archives of Sexual Behavior, 28*, 285–318.

McCrae, R. R., Costa, P. T., & Dahlstrom, W. G. (1989). A caution on the use of the MMPI *K*-correction in research on psychosomatic medicine. *Psychosomatic Medicine, 51*, 58–65.

McCrae, R. R., & Terracciano, A. (2005). Personality profiles of cultures: Aggregate personality traits. *Journal of Personality and Social Psychology, 89*, 407–425.

McCusker, P. J., Moran, M. J., Serfass, L., & Peterson, K. H. (2003). Comparability of the MMPI-2 F(p) and F scales and the SIRS in clinical use with suspected malingerers. *International Journal of Offender Therapy and Comparative Criminology, 47*(5), 585–596.

McDougall, A. (1996). Rorschach indicators of simulated schizophrenia. *Dissertation Abstracts International, 57*, 2159.

McEvoy, G. M., & Beatty, R. W. (1989). Assessment centers and subordinate appraisals of managers: A seven-year examination of predictive validity. *Personnel Psychology, 42*, 37–52.

McEwen, B. S. (1997). Possible mechanisms for atrophy of the human hippocampus. *Molecular Psychiatry, 2*, 255–262.

McGarry, A. L., & Curran, W. J. (1973). *Competency to stand trial and mental illness*. Rockville, MD: National Institute of Mental Health.

McGaugh, J. L. (2003). *Memory and emotion: The making of lasting memories*. New York: Columbia University Press.

McGuire, B. E., & Shores, E. A. (2001). Simulation of pain on the Symptom Checklist 90—Revised. *Journal of Clinical Psychology, 57*, 1589–1596.

McKinley, J. C., Hathaway, S. R., & Meehl, P. E. (1948). The MMPI: K scale. *Journal of Consulting Psychology, 12*, 20–31.

McKinzey, R. K., Podd, M. H., Krehbiel, M. A., & Raven, J. (1999). Detection of malingering on the Raven Progressive Matrices: A cross-validation. *British Journal of Clinical Psychology, 38*, 435–439.

McKinzey, R. K., Prieler, J., & Raven, J. (2003). Detection of children's malingering on Raven's Standard Progressive Matrices. *British Journal of Clinical Psychology, 42*, 95–99.

McKinzey, R. K., & Russell, E. W. (1997). A partial cross-validation of the Halstead–Reitan Battery malingering formula. *Journal of Clinical and Experimental Neuropsychology, 19*, 484–488.

McLellan, A. T., Luborsky, L., Woody, G. E., & O'Brien, C. P. (1980). An improved diagnostic evaluation instrument for substance abuse patients: The Addiction Severity Index. *Journal of Nervous and Mental Disease, 168*, 26–33.

McNally, R. J. (2003). *Remembering trauma.* Cambridge, MA: Belknap Press/Harvard University Press.

McNally, R. J. (2005, December 9). E. T., where are you? [Letter to the editor]. *Chronicle of Higher Education, 52*(16), A43.

McNally, R. J. (2006). Applying biological data in the forensic and policy arenas. *New York Academy of Science, 1071*, 267–276.

McNally, R. J., & Clancy, S. A. (2005). Sleep paralysis, sexual abuse, and space alien abduction. *Transcultural Psychiatry, 42*, 113–122.

McNally, R. J., Clancy, S. A., & Barrett, H. M. (2004). Forgetting trauma? In D. Reisberg & P. Hertel (Eds.), *Memory and emotion* (pp. 129–154). Oxford, UK: Oxford University Press.

McNally, R. J., Clancy, S. A., Barrett, H. M., & Parker, H. A. (2005). Reality monitoring in adults reporting repressed, recovered, or continuous memories of childhood sexual abuse. *Journal of Abnormal Psychology, 114*, 147–152.

McNally, R. J., Perlman, C. A., Ristuccia, C. S., & Clancy, S. A. (2006). Clinical characteristics of adults reporting repressed, recovered, or continuous memories of childhood sexual abuse. *Journal of Consulting and Clinical Psychology, 74*, 237–242.

McNeil, D. E., Eisner, J. P., & Binder, R. L. (2000). The relationship between command hallucinations and violence. *Psychiatric Services, 51*(10), 1288–1292.

Meadow, R. (1977). Munchausen syndrome by proxy: The hinterland of child abuse. *Lancet, 2*, 343–345.

Medoff, D. (1999). MMPI-2 validity scales in child custody evaluations: Clinical versus statistical significance. *Behavioral Sciences and the Law, 17*, 409–411.

Meehl, P. E., & Hathaway, S. R. (1946). The K factor as a suppressor variable in the MMPI. *Journal of Applied Psychology, 30*, 525–564.

Megargee, E. I. (1972). *The California Psychological Inventory handbook.* San Francisco: Jossey-Bass.

Meisner, S. (1988). Susceptibility of Rorschach distress correlates to malingering. *Journal of Personality Assessment, 52*, 564–571.

Melberg, H. O. (2004). Three problems with the ASI composite scores. *Journal of Substance Use, 9*(3–4), 120–126.

Mellers, B., Schwartz, A., & Ritov, I. (1999). Emotion-based choice. *Journal of Experimental Psychology: General, 128*, 332–345.

Melton, G. B., Petrila, J., Poythress, N. G., Slobogin, C., with Lyons, P. M., Jr., & Otto, R. K. (2007). *Psychological evaluations for the courts: A handbook for mental health professionals and lawyers* (3rd ed.). New York: Guilford Press.

Melton, R. (1984). Differential diagnosis: A common sense guide to psychological assessment. *Vet Center Voice Newsletter, 5*, 1–12.

Mendelson, G. (1982). Not "cured by a verdict." *Medical Journal of Australia, 2*, 132–134.

Mendelson, G. (1985). Compensation neurosis. *Medical Journal of Australia, 142*, 561–564.

Menninger, K. A. (1934). Polysurgery and polysurgical addiction. *Psychoanalytic Quarterly, 3*, 173–199.

Merback, K. (1984). The Vet Center dilemma: Post-traumatic stress disorder and personality disorders. *Vet Center Voice Newsletter, 5*, 6–7.

Merckelbach, H., Hauer, B., & Rassin, E. (2002). Symptom validity testing of feigned dissociative amnesia: A simulation study. *Psychology, Crime and Law, 8*, 311–318.

Merckelbach, H., Smeets, T., Geraerts, E., Jelicic, M., Bouwen, A., & Smeets, E. (2006). I haven't thought about this for years! Dating recent recalls of vivid memories. *Applied Cognitive Psychology, 20*, 33–42.

Merckelbach, H., & Smith, G. P. (2003). Diagnostic accuracy of the Structured Inventory of Malingered Symptomatology (SIMS) in detecting instructed malingering. *Archives of Clinical Neuropsychology, 18*, 145–152.

Merrin, E. L., Van Dyke, C., Cohen, S., & Tusel, D. J. (1986). Dual factitious disorder. *General Hospital Psychiatry, 8*(4), 246–250.

Meyers, J. E., & Diep, A. (2000). Assessment of malingering in chronic pain patients using neuropsychological tests. *Applied Neuropsychology, 3*, 89–92.

Meyers, J. E., Morrison, A. L., & Miller, J. C. (2001). How low is too low, revisited: Sentence repetition and AVLT—Recognition in the detection of malingering. *Applied Neuropsychology, 8*, 234–241.

Midanik, L. (1982). Over-reports of recent alcohol consumption in a clinical population: A validity study. *Drug and Alcohol Dependence, 9*(2), 101–110.

Mieczkowski, T. (2002). Does Adam need a haircut?: A pilot study of self-reported drug use and hair analysis in an arrestee sample. *Journal of Drug Issues, 32*, 97–118.

Mieczkowski, T., Barzelay, D., Gropper, B., & Wish, E. (1991). Concordance of three measures of cocaine use in an arrestee population: Hair, urine and self-report. *Journal of Psychoactive Drugs, 23*, 241–249.

Mieczkowski, T., Landress, H. J., Newel, R., & Coletti, S. D. (1993, January). Testing hair for illicit drug use. *National Institute of Justice: Research in Brief,* 1–5.

Mieczkowski, T., Newel, R., & Wraight, B. (1998). Using hair analysis, urinalysis, and self-reports to estimate drug use in a sample of detained juveniles. *Substance Use and Misuse, 33*(7), 1547–1567.

Mikkelsen, E. J. (1985). Substance abuse in adolescents and children. In R. Michels, J. O. Cavenar, A. M. Cooper, S. B. Guze, L. L. Judd, G. L. Kelerman, et al. (Eds.), *Psychiatry* (Vol. 2). Philadephia: Lippincott.

Mikkelsen, E. J., Gutheil, T. G., & Emens, M. (1992). False sexual-abuse allegations by children and adolescents: Contextual factors and clinical subtypes. *American Journal of Psychiatry, 46,* 556–570.

Milani, M. (2006). Problematic client–animal relationships: Munchausen by proxy. *Canadian Veterinary Journal, 47*(12), 1161–1164.

Miles, A. (1989). The ability of informed fakers to simulate schizophrenia on the Rorschach. (Doctoral Dissertation, Oklahoma State University, 1989). *Dissertation Abstracts International, 49,* 4551.

Miller, G. A. (1985). *The Substance Abuse Subtle Screening Inventory—Revised (SASSI-R) manual.* Bloomington, IN: SASSI Institute.

Miller, G. A. (1990). *The SASSI—Adolescent manual.* Bloomington, IN: SASSI Institute.

Miller, G. A. (1994a). *The Substance Abuse Subtle Screening Inventory (SASSI) manual.* Bloomington, IN: SASSI Institute.

Miller, G. A. (1994b). *Supplement to the Substance Abuse Subtle Screening Inventory manual.* Bloomington, IN: Author.

Miller, G. A., & Lazowski, L. E. (1999). *The SASSI-3 manual.* Springville, IN: SASSI Institute.

Miller, G. A., & Lazowski, L. E. (2001). *Adolescent SASSI-A2 manual.* Springville, IN: SASSI Institute.

Miller, G. A., Roberts, J., Brooks, M. K., & Lazowski, L. E. (1997). *SASSI-3 user's guide: A quick reference for administration and scoring.* Bloomington, IN: Baugh Enterprises.

Miller, H. (1961). Accident neurosis. *British Medical Journal, 1,* 919–925.

Miller, H. A. (2001). *M-FAST: Miller Forensic Assessment of Symptoms Test professional manual.* Odessa, FL: Psychological Assessment Resources.

Miller, H. A. (2004). Examining the use of the M-FAST with criminal defendants incompetent to stand trial. *International Journal of Offender Therapy and Comparative Criminology, 48*(3), 268–280.

Miller, H. A. (2005). The Miller—Forensic Assessment of Symptoms Test (M-FAST): Test generalizability and utility across race, literacy, and clinical opinion. *Criminal Justice and Behavior, 32*(6), 591–611.

Miller, H. A., Amenta, A. E., & Conroy, M. A. (2005). Sexually violent predator evaluations: Empirical evidence, strategies for professionals, and research directions. *Law and Human Behavior, 29,* 29–54.

Miller, H. R., & Streiner, D. L. (1990). Using the Millon Clinical Multiaxial Inventory's Scale B and the MacAndrew Alcoholism Scale to identify alcoholics with concurrent psychiatric diagnoses. *Journal of Personality Assessment, 54,* 736–746.

Miller, L., O'Connor, E., & DiPasquale, T. (1993). Patients' attitudes toward hallucinations. *American Journal of Psychiatry, 150,* 584–588.

Miller, L., Ryan, J., Carruthers, C., & Cluff, R. (2004). Brief screening indexes for malingering: A confirmation of Vocabulary–Digit Span from the WAIS-III and the rarely missed index from the WMS-III. *Clinical Neuropsychologist, 18,* 327–333.

Miller, W. R. (1996). *Form 90: Structured Assessment Interview for Drinking and Related Behavior.* Washington, DC: Department of Health and Human Services.

Miller, W. R., Crawford, V. L., & Taylor, C. A. (1979). Significant others as corroborative sources for problem drinkers. *Addictive Behaviors, 4,* 67–70.

Miller, W. R., & Del Boca, F. K. (1994). Measurement of drinking behavior using the Form 90 family of instruments. *Journal of Studies on Alcohol, 12,* 112–118.

Miller, W. R., & Marlatt, G. A. (1984). *Manual for the Comprehensive Drinker Profile.* Odessa, FL: Psychological Assessment Resources.

Miller, W. R., Tonigan, J. S., & Longabaugh, R. (1995). *The Drinker Inventory of Consequences (DrInC): An instrument for assessing adverse consequences of alcohol abuse* (NIH Publication No. 95-3911, Vol. 4). Rock-ville, MD: U.S. Department of Health and Human Services, Public Health Service, National Institutes of Health, National Institute on Alcohol Abuse and Alcoholism.

Millis, S. R. (1992). The Recognition Memory Test in the detection of malingered and exaggerated memory deficits. *Clinical Neuropsychologist, 6,* 406–414.

Millis, S. R. (2002). Warrington Recognition Memory Test in the detection of response bias. *Journal of Forensic Neuropsychology, 2,* 147–166.

Millis, S. R., & Putnam, S. H. (1994). The Recognition Memory Test in the assessment of memory impairment after financially compensable mild head injury: A replication. *Perceptual and Motor Skills, 79,* 384–386.

Millis, S. R., Putnam, S., Adams, K., & Ricker, J. (1995). The California Verbal Learning Test in the detection of incomplete effort in neuropsychological evaluation. *Psychological Assessment, 7,* 463–471.

Millis, S. R., Rosenthal, M., Novack, T., Sherer, M., Nick, T. G., Kreutzer, J. S., et al. (2001). Long-term neuropsychological outcome after traumatic brain injury. *Journal of Head Trauma Rehabilitation, 16,* 343–355.

Millis, S. R., Ross, S. R., & Ricker, J. H. (1998). Detection of incomplete effort on the Wechsler Adult Intelligence Scale—Revised: A cross-validation. *Journal of Clinical and Experimental Neuropsychology, 20,* 167–173.

Millis, S. R., Wolfe, P., Larrabee, G., Hanks, R., Sweet, J. J., & Fichtenberg, N. (2007, February). *The California Verbal Learning Test—II in the detection of incomplete effort.* Paper presented at the annual meeting of the International Neuropsychological Society, Portland, OR.

Millon, T. (1983). *Millon Clinical Multiaxial Inventory.* Minneapolis: National Computer Systems.

Millon, T. (1987). *Millon Clinical Multiaxial Inventory—II manual.* Minneapolis, MN: National Computer Systems.

Millon, T. (1993). *Millon Adolescent Clinical Inventory.* Minneapolis, MN: National Computer Systems.

Millon, T. (1994). *Millon Clinical Multiaxial Inventory—III manual*. Minneapolis, MN: National Computer Systems.

Millon, T., Davis, R., & Millon, C. (1997). *The Millon Clinical Multiaxial Inventory—III manual* (2nd ed.). Minneapolis, MN: National Computer Systems.

Millon, T., Millon, C., & Davis, R. D. (1993). *Manual for the Millon Adolescent Clinical Inventory*. Minneapolis, MN: National Computer Systems.

Mischel, W. (1968). *Personality and assessment*. New York: Wiley.

Mischel, W. (1969). Continuity and change in personality. *American Psychologist, 24,* 1012–1018.

Mitchell, D., & Francis, J. P. (2003). A case of factitious disorder presenting as alcohol dependence. *Substance Abuse, 24*(3), 187–189.

Mitchell, J., & Vierkant, A. D. (1991). Delusions and hallucinations of cocaine abusers and paranoid schizophrenics: A comparative study. *Journal of Psychology, 125,* 301–310.

Mitrushina, M., Boone, K. B., Razani, J., & D'Elia, L. F. (2005). *Handbook of normative data for neuropsychological assessment*. New York: Oxford University Press.

Mittenberg, W., Aguila-Puentes, G., Patton, C., Canyock, E. M., & Heilbronner, R. L. (2002). Neuropsychological profiling of symptom exaggeration and malingering. *Journal of Forensic Neuropsychology, 3,* 227–240.

Mittenberg, W., Azrin, R., Millsaps, C., & Heilbronner, R. (1993). Identification of malingered head injury on the Wechsler Memory Scale—Revised. *Psychological Assessment, 5,* 34–40.

Mittenberg, W., DiGuilio, D., Perrin, S., & Bass, A. (1992). Symptoms following mild head injury: Expectation as aetiology. *Journal of Neurology, Neurosurgery, and Psychiatry, 55,* 200–204.

Mittenberg, W., Patton, C., Canyock, E. M., & Condit, D. C. (2002). Base rates of malingering and symptom exaggeration. *Journal of Clinical and Experimental Neuropsychology, 24,* 1094–1102.

Mittenberg, W., Rotholc, A., Russell, E., & Heilbronner, R. (1996). Identification of malingered head injury on the Halstead–Reitan Battery. *Archives of Clinical Neuropsychology, 11,* 271–281.

Mittenberg, W., Theroux, S., Aguila-Puentes, G., Bianchini, K., Greve, K., & Rayls, K. (2001). Identification of malingered head injury on the Wechsler Adult Intelligence Scale—3rd edition. *Clinical Neuropsychologist, 15,* 440–445.

Mittenberg, W., Theroux-Fichera, S., Zielinski, R. E., & Heilbronner, R. L. (1995). Identification of malingered head injury on the Wechsler Adult Intelligence Scale—Revised. *Professional Psychology: Research and Practice, 26,* 491–498.

Mizrahi, R., & Starkstein, S. E. (2006). Phenomenology and clinical correlates of delusions in Alzheimer disease. *American Journal of Geriatric Psychiatry, 14,* 573–581.

Modell, J. G., Mountz, J. M., & Ford, C. V. (1992). Pathological lying associated with thalamic dysfunction demonstrated by [99mtc]hmpao spect. *Journal of Neuropsychiatry and Clinical Neuroscience, 4*(4), 442–446.

Moeller, M. R., Fey, P., & Sachs, H. (1993). Hair analysis as evidence in forensic cases. *Forensic Sciences International, 63,* 43–53.

Mogge, N. L., & LePage, J. P. (2004). The Assessment of Depression Inventory (ADI): A new instrument used to measure depression and to detect honesty of response. *Depression and Anxiety, 20,* 107–113.

Moncho, R. (2004). Defensive responding on the Rorschach in a simulated child custody evaluation context (Doctoral dissertation, Pacific Graduate School of Psychology, 2004). *Dissertation Abstracts International, 65,* 1557.

Mooney, G., Speed, J., & Sheppard, S. (2005). Factors related to recovery after mild traumatic brain injury. *Brain Injury, 19*(12), 975–987.

Moore, B. A., & Donders, J. (2004). Predictors of invalid neuropsychological test performance after traumatic brain injury. *Brain Injury, 18,* 975–984.

Moore, R. A. (1972). The diagnosis of alcoholism in a psychiatric hospital: A trial of the Michigan Alcoholism Screening Test (MAST). *American Journal of Psychiatry, 128,* 1565–1569.

Moore, R. D., Bone, L. R., Geller, G., Mamon, J. A., Stokes, E. J., & Levine, D. M. (1989). Prevalence, detection, and treatment of alcoholism in hospitalized patients. *Journal of the American Medical Association, 261,* 403–407.

Moore, R. H. (1984). The concurrent and construct validity of the MacAndrews Alcoholism Scale among at-risk adolescent males. *Journal of Clinical Psychology, 40,* 1264–1269.

More, H. W., & Unsinger, P. C. (1987). *The police assessment center*. Springfield, IL: Thomas.

Morel, K. R. (1998). Development and preliminary validation of a forced-choice test of response bias for posttraumatic stress disorder. *Journal of Personality Assessment, 70*(2), 299–314.

Morey, L. C. (1991). *Personality Assessment Inventory professional manual*. Odessa, FL: Psychological Assessment Resources.

Morey, L. C. (1993, August). *Defensiveness and malingering indices for the PAI*. Paper presented at the annual convention of the American Psychological Association, Toronto, Ontario, Canada.

Morey, L. C. (1996). *An interpretive guide to the Personality Assessment Inventory*. Odessa, FL: Psychological Assessment Resources.

Morey, L. C. (1999). *PAI interpretive explorer module manual*. Odessa, FL: Psychological Assessment Resources.

Morey, L. C. (2003). *Essentials of PAI assessment*. New York: Wiley.

Morey, L. C., & Boggs, C. (2004). The Personality Assessment Inventory (PAI). In M. Hilsenroth & D. Segal (Eds.), *Comprehensive handbook of psychological assessment: Vol. 2. Personality assessment* (pp. 15–29). Hoboken, NJ: Wiley.

Morey, L. C., & Hopwood, C. J. (2004). Efficiency of a strategy for detecting back random responding on the

Personality Assessment Inventory. *Psychological Assessment, 16,* 197–200.

Morey, L. C., & Lanier, V. W. (1998). Operating characteristics of six response distortion indicators for the Personality Assessment Inventory. *Assessment, 5,* 203–214.

Morey, L. C., & Quigley, B. D. (2002). The use of the Personality Assessment Inventory (PAI) in assessing offenders. *International Journal of Offender Therapy and Comparative Criminology, 46,* 333–349.

Morey, L. C., Quigley, B. D., Sanislow, C. A., Skodol, A. E., McGlashan, T. H., Shea, M. T., et al. (2002). Substance or style?: An investigation of the NEO-PI-R validity scales. *Journal of Personality Assessment, 79,* 583–599.

Morgan, C. D., & Murray, H. H. (1935). A method for investigating fantasies: The Thematic Apperception Test. *Archives of Neurology and Psychiatry, 34,* 289–306.

Morgan, C. D., Schoenberg, M. R., Dorr, D., & Burke, M. J. (2002). Overreport on the MCMI-III: Concurrent validation with the MMPI-2 using a psychiatric inpatient sample. *Journal of Personality Assessment, 78,* 288–300.

Morgan, J., & Sweet, J. J. (in press). *Neuropsychology of malingering casebook.* New York: Psychology Press.

Morgan, J. P. (1984). Problems of mass urine screening for misused drugs. *Journal of Psychoactive Drugs, 16*(4), 305–317.

Mossman, D. (1994). At the VA, it pays to be sick. *Public Interest, 114,* 35–47.

Mott, R. H., Small, I. F., & Andersen, J. M. (1965). Comparative study of hallucinations. *Archives of General Psychiatry, 12,* 595–601.

Mouton, G. J., Peterson, S. A., Nicholson, R. A., & Bagby, R. M. (1995, August). *Detecting simulated malingering with the MMPI-2: Receiver operating characteristic analysis.* Paper presented at the annual convention of the American Psychological Association, New York, NY.

Munley, P. H. (1991). A comparison of MMPI-2 and MMPI-T scores for men and women. *Journal of Clinical Psychology, 47,* 87–91.

Munro, H. M., & Thrusfield, M. V. (2001). "Battered pets": Munchausen syndrome by proxy (factitious illness by proxy). *Journal of Small Animal Practice, 42*(8), 385–389.

Murphy, J. M., Berwick, D. M., Weinstein, M. C., Borus, J. F., Budman, S. H., & Klerman, G. L. (1987). Performance of screening and diagnostic tests: Application of receiver operating characteristic analysis. *Archives of General Psychiatry, 44,* 550–555.

Murphy, K. R. (1993). *Honesty in the workplace.* Pacific Grove, CA: Brooks-Cole.

Murphy, W. D., & Barbaree, H. E. (1994). *Assessments of sex offenders by measures of erectile response: Psychometric properties and decision making.* Brandon, VT: Safer Society Press.

Murphy, W. D., DiLillo, D., Haynes, M. R., & Steere, E. (2001). An exploration of factors related to deviant sexual arousal among juvenile sex offenders. *Sexual Abuse: A Journal of Research and Treatment, 13,* 91–103.

Murphy, W. D., & Peters, J. M. (1992). Profiling child sexual abusers: Psychological considerations. *Criminal Justice and Behavior, 19,* 24–37.

Myerholtz, L., & Rosenberg, H. (1997). *Screening college students for alcohol problems: Psychometric assessment of the SASSI-2.* Bethesda, MD: National Institute on Alcohol Abuse and Alcoholism.

Myerholtz, L. E., & Rosenberg, H. (1998). Screening DUI offenders for alcohol problems: Psychometric assessment of the Substance Abuse Subtle Screening Inventory. *Journal of Studies of Alcohol, 59,* 439–446.

Myers, J. E. B. (1995). New era of skepticism regarding children's credibility. *Psychology, Public Policy, and Law, 1,* 387–398.

Nakahara, Y., Shimamine, M., & Takahashi, K. (1992). Hair analysis for drugs of abuse: III. Movement and stability of methoxyphenamine (as a model compound of methamphetamine) along hair shaft with hair growth. *Journal of Analytic Toxicology, 16,* 253–257.

Nakao, M., & Yano, E. (2003). Reporting of somatic symptoms as a screening marker for detecting major depression in a population of Japanese white-collar workers. *Journal of Clinical Epidemiology, 56*(10), 1021–1026.

Nakayama, M. (2002). Practical use of the concealed information test for criminal investigation in Japan. In M. Kleiner (Ed.), *Handbook of polygraph testing* (pp. 49–86). San Diego, CA: Academic Press.

Nampiaparampil, D. E., & Shmerling, R. H. (2004). A review of fibromyalgia. *American Journal of Managed Care, 10*(11, Pt. 1), 794–800.

National Alliance on Mental Illness. (2006). *Grading the states: A report on America's healthcare system for serious mental illness.* Arlington, VA: Author. Available at *http://www.nami.org/gtstemplate.cfm?section= grading_the_states*

National Institute of Mental Health. (1991). *NIMH Diagnostic Interview for Children, Version 2.3.* Rockville, MD: Author.

National Research Council. (2003). *The polygraph and lie detection.* Washington, DC: National Academies Press.

Nayani, T., & David, A. (1996). The auditory hallucination: A phenomenological survey. *Psychological Medicine, 26*(1), 177–189.

Neal, B. (1986). The K scale (MMPI) and job performance. In J. Reese & H. Goldstein (Eds.), *Psychological services for law enforcement* (pp. 83–90). Washington, DC: U.S. Government Printing Office.

Needle, R., McCubbin, H., Lorence, J., & Hochhauser, M. (1983). Reliability and validity of Adolescent Self-Reported Drug Use in a family-based study: A methodological report. *International Journal of the Addictions, 18,* 901–912.

Nelson, N. W., Boone, K., Dueck. A., Wagener, L., Lu, P., & Grills, C. (2003). Relationships between eight measures of suspect effort. *Clinical Neuropsychologist, 17,* 263–272.

Nelson, N. W., Sweet, J. J., Berry, D. T., Bryant, F. B., & Granacher, R. P. (2007). Response validity in forensic neuropsychology: Exploratory factor analytic evidence of distinct cognitive and psychological constructs. *Journal of the International Neuropsychological Society, 13*(3), 440–449.

Nelson, N. W., Sweet, J. J., & Demakis, G. J. (2006). Meta-analysis of the MMPI-2 Fake Bad Scale: Utility in forensic practice. *Clinical Neuropsychologist, 20*, 39–58.

Netter, B., & Viglione, V. (1994). An empirical study of malingering schizophrenia on the Rorschach. *Journal of Personality Assessment, 62*, 45–57.

Newman, A. (2002, April 13). Analyze this: Vincent Gigante, not crazy after all those years. *New York Times.* Retrieved March 20, 2007 from query.nytimes.com/gst/fullpage.html?sec=health&res=9E06E5D6153B F930A25757C0A9659C8B63.

Newton, P., Reddy, V., & Bull, R. (2000). Children's everyday deception and performance on false-belief tasks. *British Journal of Developmental Psychology, 18*, 297–317.

Ney, T. (1995). *True and false allegations of child sexual abuse: Assessment and case management.* New York: Brunner/Mazel.

Nichols, D. S. (2001). *Essentials of MMPI-2 assessment.* New York: Wiley.

Nichols, D. S., & Greene, R. L. (1991, March). *New measures for dissimulation on the MMPI/MMPI-2.* Paper presented at the 26th annual Symposium on Recent Developments in the Use of the MMPI (MMPI-2/MMPI-A), St. Petersburg Beach, FL.

Nichols, D. S., Greene, R. L., & Schmolck, P. (1989). Criteria for assessing inconsistent patterns of endorsement on the MMPI: Rationale, development, and empirical trials. *Journal of Clinical Psychology, 45*, 239–250.

Nichols, H. R., & Molinder, I. (1984). *Multiphasic Sex Inventory.* Tacoma, WA: Nichols & Molinder Assessments.

Nichols, H. R., & Molinder, I. (1996). *Multiphasic Sex Inventory II handbook.* Tacoma, WA: Nichols & Molinder Assessments.

Nicholson v. American National Insurance, 154 F.3d 875 (1998).

Nicholson, K., & Martelli, M. F. (2007). Malingering: Traumatic brain injury. In G. Young, A. W. Kane, & K. Nicholson (Eds.), *Causality of psychological injury* (pp. 427–475). New York: Springer.

Nicholson, S. D., & Roberts, G. A. (1994). Patients who (need to) tell stories. *British Journal of Hospital Medicine, 51*(10), 546–549.

Nies, K., & Sweet, J. (1994). Neuropsychological assessment and malingering: A critical review of past and present strategies. *Archives of Clinical Neuropsychology, 9*, 501–552.

Nimnuan, C., Hotopf, M., & Wessely, S. (2001). Medically unexplained symptoms: An epidemiological study in seven specialties. *Journal of Psychosomatic Research, 51*(1), 361–367.

Nitch, S., Boone, K. B., Wen, J., Arnold, G., & Alfano, K. (2006). The utility of the Rey Word Recognition Test in the detection of suspect effort. *Clinical Neuropsychologist, 20*, 873–887.

Nochajski, T. H., & Wieczorek, W. F. (1998). Identifying potential drinking–driving recidivists: Do non-obvious indicators help? *Journal of Prevention and Intervention in the Community, 17*(1), 69–83.

Norris, M. P., & May, M. C. (1998). Screening for malingering in a correctional setting. *Law and Human Behavior, 22*, 315–323.

Noyes, R., Jr., Stuart, S., Langbehn, D. R., Happel, R. L., Longley, S. L., & Yagla, S. J. (2002). Childhood antecedents of hypochondriasis. *Psychosomatics, 43*(4), 282–289.

Noyes, R., Jr., Stuart, S. P., Langbehn, D. R., Happel, R. L., Longley, S. L., Muller, B. A., et al. (2003). Test of an interpersonal model of hypochondriasis. *Psychosomatic Medicine, 65*(2), 292–300.

Nunes, K. L., Firestone, P., Bradford, J. M., Greenberg, D. M., & Broom, I. (2002). A comparison of modified versions of the Static-99 and the Sex Offender Risk Appraisal Guide. *Sexual Abuse: A Journal of Research and Treatment, 4*, 253–269.

O'Bannon, R. M., Goldinger, L. A., & Appleby, G. S. (1989). *Honesty and integrity testing.* Atlanta, GA: Applied Information Resources.

O'Bryant, S. E., Hilsabeck, R. C., Fisher, J. M., & McCaffrey, R. J. (2003). Utility of the Trail Making Test in the assessment of malingering in a sample of mild traumatic brain injury litigants. *Clinical Neuropsychologist, 17*, 69–74.

O'Donohue, W. T., & Letourneau, E. (1992). Psychometric properties of the penile tumescence assessment of child molesters. *Journal of Psychopathology and Behavioral Assessment, 14*, 123–174.

O'Farrell, T. J., & Langenbucher, J. (1988). Timeline drinking behavior interview. In M. Hersen & A. Bellack (Eds.), *Dictionary of behavioral assessment techniques* (pp. 477–479). Elmsford, NY: Pergamon Press.

O'Malley, P. M., Johnston, L. D., Bachman, J. G., & Schulenberg, J. (2000). A comparison of confidential versus anonymous survey procedures: Effects on reporting of drug use and related attitudes and beliefs in a national study of students. *Journal of Drug Issues, 30*(1), 35–54.

O'Neill, B., Williams, A. F., & Dubowski, K. M. (1983). Variability in blood alcohol concentrations: Implications for estimating individual results. *Journal of Studies on Alcohol, 44*, 222–230.

Ogloff, J. R. P. (1990). The admissibility of expert testimony regarding malingering and deception. *Behavioral Sciences and the Law, 8*, 27–43.

Oksol, E. M., & O'Donohue, W. T. (2003). A critical analysis of the polygraph. In W. T. O'Donohue & E. R. Levensky (Eds.), *Handbook of forensic psychology: Resource for mental health and legal professionals.* San Diego, CA: Academic Press.

Oldershaw, L., & Bagby, R. M. (1997). Children and deception. In R. Rogers (Ed.), *Clinical assessment of malingering and deception* (pp. 153–166). New York: Guilford Press.

Olio, K. A. (1989). Memory retrieval in the treatment of

adult survivors of sexual abuse. *Transactional Analysis Journal, 19,* 93–100.

Olio, K. A. (2004). The truth about "false memory syndrome." In P. Caplan & L. Cosgrive (Eds.), *Bias in psychiatric diagnosis* (pp. 163–169). Boston: Aronson.

Olson, W. K. (1991). *The litigation explosion.* New York: Dutton.

Ones, D. S. (1993). *The construct validity of integrity tests.* Unpublished doctoral dissertation, University of Iowa.

Ones, D. S., Mount, M. K., Barrick, M. R., & Hunter, J. E. (1994). Personality and job performance: A critique of the Tett, Jackson, and Rothstein (1991) meta-analysis. *Personnel Psychology, 47,* 147–156.

Ones, D. S., Schmidt, F. L., & Viswesvaran, C. (1994a, April). Do broader personality variables predict job performance with higher validity? In R. Page (Chair), *Personality and job performance: Big Five versus specific traits.* Symposium conducted at the annual meeting of the Society for Industrial and Organizational Psychology, Nashville, TN.

Ones, D. S., Schmidt, F. L., & Viswesvaran, C. (1994b, April). Examination of construct validity with linear composites and generalizability coefficient constructed correlations. In F. L. Schmidt (Chair), *What is new in construct-based research methodology?* Symposium conducted at the annual meeting of the Society for Industrial and Organizational Psychology, Nashville, TN.

Ones, D. S., & Viswesvaran, C. (1998a). Gender, age, and race differences on overt integrity tests: Results across four large-scale job applicant data sets. *Journal of Applied Psychology, 83,* 35–42.

Ones, D. S., & Viswesvaran, C. (1998b). Integrity testing in organizations. In S. B. Bacharach, A. O'Leary-Kelly, J. M. Collins, & R. W. Griffith (Eds.), *Dysfunctional behavior in organizations: Violent and deviant behavior* (pp. 243–276). London: JAI Press.

Ones, D. S., Viswesvaran, C., & Reiss, A. D. (1996). Role of social desirability in personality testing for personnel selection: The red herring. *Journal of Applied Psychology, 81,* 660–679.

Ones, D. S., Viswesvaran, C., & Schmidt, F. L. (1993a). Comprehensive meta-analysis of integrity test validities: Findings and implications for personnel selection and theories of job performance. *Journal of Applied Psychology, 78,* 679–703.

Ones, D. S., Viswesvaran, C., & Schmidt, F. L. (1993b, August). *Integrity tests predict substance abuse and aggressive behavior at work.* Paper presented at the American Psychological Association Convention, Toronto, Ontario, Canada.

Ones, D. S., Viswesvaran, C., & Schmidt, F. L. (2003). Personality and absenteeism: A meta-analysis of integrity tests. *European Journal of Personality, 17,* S19–S38.

Orey, S. A., Cragar, D. E., & Berry, D. T. R. (2000). The effects of two motivational manipulations on the neuropsychological performance of mildly head injured college students. *Archives of Clinical Neuropsychology, 15,* 335–348.

Ossipov, P. V. (1944). Malingering: The simulation of psychosis. *Bulletin of the Menninger Clinic, 8,* 31–42.

Ostfeld, B. M., & Feldman, M. D. (1996). Factitious disorder by proxy: Awareness among mental health practitioners. *General Hospital Psychiatry, 18*(2), 113–116.

Otis, J. D., Pincus, D. B., & Keane, T. M. (2006). Comorbid chronic pain and posttraumatic stress disorder across the lifespan: A review of theoretical models. In G. Young, A. W. Kane, & K. Nicholson (Eds.), *Psychological knowledge in court: PTSD, pain, and TBI* (pp. 242–268). New York: Springer.

Otto, R. K. (2006, June). *Assessment of response style in forensic examination contexts.* Workshop held at the American Academy of Forensic Psychology meetings, San Juan, Puerto Rico.

Otto, R. K., & Edens, J. F. (2003). Parenting capacity. In T. Grisso (Ed.), *Evaluating competencies: Forensic assessments and instruments* (2nd ed., pp. 229–307). New York: Kluwer.

Otto, R. K., & Hall, J. E. (1988). The utility of the Michigan Alcoholism Screening Test in the detection of alcoholics and problems drinkers. *Journal of Personality Assessment, 52,* 499–505.

Otto, R. K., Lang, A. R., Megargee, E. I., & Rosenblatt, A. I. (1988). Ability of alcoholics to escape detection by the MMPI. *Journal of Consulting and Clinical Psychology, 56,* 452–457.

Otto, R. K., & Petrila, J. (2006). Admissibility of expert testimony regarding recidivism risk in sexually violent predator proceedings. In A. Schlank (Ed.), *The sexual predator: Law and public policy, clinical practice* (Vol. 3, pp. 2-1–2-11). Kingston, NJ: Civic Research Press.

Otto, R. K., Slobogin, C., & Greenberg, S. (2006). Legal and ethical issues in accessing and utilizing third party information. In A. Goldstein (Ed.), *Forensic psychology: Emerging topics and expanding roles* (pp. 190–205). Hoboken, NJ: Wiley.

Oulis, P., Mavreas, V., Mamounas, J., & Stefanis, C. (1995). Clinical characteristics of auditory hallucinations. *Acta Psychiatrica Scandinavica, 92*(2), 97–102.

Ozer, E. J., Best, S. R., Lipsey, T. L., & Weiss, D. S. (2003). Predictors of posttraumatic stress disorder and symptoms in adults: A meta-analysis. *Psychological Bulletin, 129,* 52–73.

Palmer, R. F., Dwyer, J. H., & Semmer, N. (1994). A measurement model of adolescent smoking. *Addictive Behaviors, 19,* 477–489.

Pankratz, L. (1985, May). *The spectrum of factitious post-traumatic stress disorder.* Paper presented at the annual meeting of the American Psychiatric Association, Dallas, TX.

Panton, J. H. (1979). *Validation of the Aggravated Sex (Asx) Scale for the MMPI.* Unpublished manuscript. Raleigh: North Carolina Department of Social Rehabilitation and Control.

Parker, N. (1979). Malingering: A dangerous diagnosis. *Medical Journal of Australia, 1*(12), 568–569.

Parker, P. E. (1996). Factitious psychological disorders. In M. D. Feldman & S. J. Eisendrath (Eds.), *The spec-*

trum of factitious disorders (pp. 37–49). Washington, DC: American Psychiatric Press.

Parks, T. E. (1999). On one aspect of the evidence for recovered memories. *American Journal of Psychology, 112,* 365–370.

Patrick, C. J., Hicks, B. M., Krueger, R. F., & Lang, A. R. (2005). Relations between psychopathy facets and externalizing in a criminal offender sample. *Journal of Personality Disorders, 19,* 339–356.

Patrick, C. J., & Iacono, W. G. (1989). Psychopathy, threat, and polygraph test accuracy. *Journal of Applied Psychology, 74,* 347–355.

Patrick, C. J., & Iacono, W. G. (1991). Validity of the control question polygraph test: The problem of sampling bias. *Journal of Applied Psychology, 76,* 229–238.

Patterson, E., Taylor, L., & Wells, C. (2005). A guide to overt and covert surveillance. *Journal of Healthcare Protection Management, 21*(1), 90–96.

Paulhus, D. L. (1991). Balanced Inventory of Desirable Responding (BIDR). In J. P. Robinson, P. R. Shaver, & L. S. Wrightsman (Eds.), *Measures of personality and social psychological attitudes* (pp. 17–59). San Diego, CA: Academic Press.

Paulhus, D. L. (1998). *Paulhus Deception Scales (PDS).* North Tonawanda, NY: Multi-Health Systems.

Paulhus, D. L., Bruce, M. N., & Trapnell, P. D. (1995). Effects of self-presentation strategies on personality profiles and their structure. *Personality and Social Psychology Bulletin, 21,* 100–108.

Paulhus, D. L., & Reid, D. B. (1991). Enhancement and denial in socially desirable responding. *Journal of Personality and Social Psychology, 60,* 307–317.

Pavlidis, I., Eberhardt, N. L., & Levine, J. A. (2002). Seeing through the face of deception: Thermal imaging offers a promising hands-off approach to mass security screening. *Nature, 415,* 35.

Pearlson, G., Kreger, L., Rabins, R., Chase, G., Cohen, B., Wirth, J., et al. (1989). A chart review study of late-onset and early-onset schizophrenia. *American Journal of Psychiatry, 146,* 1568–1574.

Pedroza, G. L. (2003). Attitudes and beliefs of psychologists toward the workers' compensation system. *Dissertation Abstracts International: Section B. The Physical Sciences and Engineering, 63*(8-B), 3933.

Peebles, J., & Moore, R. J. (1998). Detecting socially desirable responding with the Personality Assessment Inventory: The Positive Impression Management scale and the Defensiveness index. *Journal of Clinical Psychology, 54,* 621–628.

Perkins, D. C. (2006). Employee fraud and embezzlement. *The Business Owner, 30*(4), 1–10.

Perry, G. G., & Kinder, B. N. (1992). Susceptibility of the Rorschach to malingering: A schizophrenia analogue. In C. D. Spielberg & J. N. Butcher, *Advances in personality assessment* (Vol. 9, pp. 127–140). Hillsdale, NJ: Erlbaum.

Perry, N. W. (1995). Children's comprehension of truths, lies, and false beliefs. In T. Ney (Ed.), *True and false allegations of child sexual abuse: Assessment and case management* (pp. 73–98). New York: Brunner/Mazel.

Persinger, M. (1994). Elicitation of "childhood memories" in hypnosis-like settings is associated with complex partial epileptic-like signs for women but not for men: Implications for the false memory syndrome. *Perceptual and Motor Skills, 78*(2), 643–651.

Persinger, M. A. (1992). Neuropsychological profiles of adults who report "sudden remembering" of early childhood memories: Implications for claims of sex abuse and alien visitation/abduction. *Experiences Perceptual and Motor Skills, 75,* 259–266.

Peskin, J. (1992). Ruse and representations: On children's ability to conceal information. *Developmental Psychology, 28,* 84–89.

Peterson, E., & Viglione, D. (1991). *The effect of psychological knowledge and specific role instruction of MMPI malingering.* Unpublished manuscript, California School of Professional Psychology, San Diego, CA.

Pettigrew, C., Tuma, J., Pickering, J., & Whelton, J. (1983). Simulation of psychosis on a multiple-choice projective test. *Perceptual and Motor Skills, 57,* 463–469.

Petzel, T., Johnson, J., & McKillip, J. (1973). Response bias in drug surveys. *Journal of Consulting and Clinical Psychology, 40,* 427–439.

Pfohl, B., Blum, N., & Zimmerman, M. (1995). *The Structured Interview for DSM-III-E Personality: SIDP-III-R.* Iowa City: University of Iowa.

Pfohl, B., Blum, N., & Zimmerman, M. (1998). *The Structured Interview for DSM-IV Personality: SIDP-IV.* Iowa City: University of Iowa.

Phillips, M. R., Ward, N. G., & Ries, R. K. (1983). Factitious mourning: Painless patienthood. *American Journal of Psychiatry, 140*(4), 420–425.

Piazza, N. J. (1996). Dual diagnosis and adolescent psychiatric inpatients. *Substance Use and Misuse, 31,* 215–223.

Piedmont, R. L., McCrae, R. R., Riemann, R., & Angleitner, A. (2000). On the invalidity of validity scales: Evidence from self-reports and observer ratings in volunteer samples. *Journal of Personality and Social Psychology, 78,* 582–593.

Pierre, J., Wirshing, D., & Wirshing, W. (2003). "Iatrogenic malingering" in VA substance abuse treatment. *Psychiatric Services, 54,* 253–254.

Pinsoneault, T. B. (2002). A variable response inconsistency scale and a true response inconsistency scale for the Millon Adolescent Clinical Inventory. *Psychological Assessment, 14,* 320–330.

Pittman, R. K., Saunders, L. S., & Orr, S. P. (1994, April). Psychophysiologic testing for posttraumatic stress disorder. *Trial,* 22–26.

Pittman, R. K., & Sparr, L. (1998). PTSD and the law. *PTSD Research Quarterly, 9*(2), 1–6.

Pittman, R. K., Sparr, L. F., Saunders, L. S., & McFarlane, A. C. (1996). Legal issues in posttraumatic stress disorder. In B. A. van der Kolk, A. C. MacFarlane, & L. Weisaeth (Eds.), *Traumatic stress: The effects of overwhelming experience on mind, body, and society* (pp. 378–397). New York: Guilford Press.

Plassmann, R. (1994). Inpatient and outpatient long-term psychotherapy of patients suffering from factitious disorders. *Psychotherapy and Psychosomatics, 62*(1–2), 96–107.

Polak, A., & Harris, P. L. (1999). Deception by young children following noncompliance. *Developmental Psychology, 35,* 561–568.

Pole, N. (2006). Moderators of PTSD-related psychophysiological effect sizes: Results from a meta-analysis. *Annals of the New York Academy of Science, 1071,* 422–424.

Pollack, S. (1982). Dimensions of malingering. In B. H. Gross & L. E. Weinburger (Eds.), *New directions for mental health services: The mental health professional and the legal system* (pp. 63–75). San Francisco: Jossey-Bass.

Pollina, D. A., Dollins, A. B., Senter, S. M., Krapohl, D. J., & Ryan, A. H. (2004). Comparison of polygraph data obtained from individuals involved in mock crimes and actual criminal investigations. *Journal of Applied Psychology, 89,* 1099–1105.

Pollock, P., Quigley, B., Worley, K., & Bashford, C. (1997). Feigned mental disorder in prisoners referred to forensic mental health services. *Journal of Psychiatric Mental Health Nursing, 4*(1), 9–15.

Pollock, P. H. (1998). Feigning auditory hallucinations by offenders. *Journal of Forensic Psychiatry, 9,* 305–327.

Poole, D. A., & Lamb, M. E. (1998). *Investigative interviews of children: A guide for helping professionals.* Washington, DC: American Psychological Association.

Pope, H. G., & Hudson, J. I. (1995). Can memories of childhood sexual abuse be repressed? *Psychological Medicine, 25,* 121–126.

Pope, H. G., Jonas, J. M., & Jones, B. (1982). Factitious psychosis: Phenomenology, family history, and long-term outcome of nine patients. *American Journal of Psychiatry, 139,* 1480–1483.

Pope, K. S., Butcher, J. N., & Seelen, J. (1993). *The MMPI, MMPI-2 & MMPI-A in court: A practical guide for expert witnesses and attorneys.* Washington, DC: American Psychological Association.

Popkin, C. L., & Wells-Parker, E. (1994). A research agenda for the specific deterrence of DWI. *Journal of Traffic Medicine, 22,* 1–14.

Popli, A. P., Masand, P. S., & Dewan, M. J. (1992). Factitious disorders with psychological symptoms. *Journal of Clinical Psychiatry, 53*(9), 315–318.

Porter, S., Birt, A. R., Yuille, J. C., & Herve, H. F. (2001). Memory for murder: A psychological perspective on dissociative amnesia in legal contexts. *International Journal of Law and Psychiatry, 24,* 23–42.

Potter, B. A., & Orfali, J. S. (1990). *Drug testing at work: A guide for employers and employees.* Berkeley, CA: Ronin.

Powell, K. E. (1991). *The malingering of schizophrenia.* Unpublished doctoral dissertation, University of South Carolina, Columbia.

Poythress, N. G., Edens, J. F., & Lilienfeld, S. O. (1998). Criterion-related validity of the Psychopathic Personality Inventory in a prison sample. *Psychological Assessment, 10,* 426–430.

Poythress, N. G., Edens, J. F., & Watkins, M. M. (2001).

The relationship between psychopathic personality features and malingering symptoms of major mental illness. *Law and Human Behavior, 25*(6), 567–581.

Poythress, N., G., Nicholson, R., Otto, R. K., Edens, J. F., Bonnie, R. J., Monahan, J., et al. (1999). *Professional manual for the MacArthur Competence Assessment Tool—Criminal Adjudication.* Odessa, FL: Psychological Assessment Resources.

Pragst, F., & Balikova, M. A. (2006). State of the art in hair analysis for detection of drug and alcohol abuse. *Clinica Chimica Acta, 370,* 17–49.

Price, K. P. (1994). Posttraumatic stress disorder and concussion: Are they incompatible? *Defense Law Journal, 43,* 113–120.

Prigatano, G., & Amin, K. (1993). Digit Memory Test: Unequivocal cerebral dysfunction and suspected malingering. *Journal of Clinical and Experimental Neuropsychology, 15,* 537–546.

Prigatano, G., Smason, I., Lamb, D., & Bortz, J. (1997). Suspected malingering and the digit memory test: A replication and extension. *Archives of Clinical Neuropsychology, 12,* 609–619.

Prins, J. B., van der Meer, J. W., & Bleijenberg, G. (2006). Chronic fatigue syndrome. *Lancet, 367,* 346–355.

Prior, L., & Wood, F. (2003). Characteristics of the sick role. In P. W. Halligan, C. Bass, & D. A. Oakley (Eds.), *Malingering and illness deception* (pp. 122–131). Oxford, UK: Oxford University Press.

Prochaska, J. O., & DiClemente, C. C. (1982). Transtheoretical therapy: Toward a more integrative model of change. *Theory, Research and Practice, 19*(3), 276–288.

Putzke, J. D., Williams, M. A., Daniel, F. J., & Boll, T. J. (1999). The utility of K-correction to adjust for a defensive response set on the MMPI. *Assessment, 6,* 61–70.

Pyszora, N. M., Barker, A. F., & Kopelman, M. D. (2003). Amnesia for criminal offenses: A study of life sentence prisoners. *Journal of Forensic Psychiatry and Psychology, 14,* 475–490.

Quinn, K. M. (1988). Children and deception. In R. Rogers (Ed.), *Clinical assessment of malingering and deception* (pp. 104–119). New York: Guilford Press.

Quinsey, V. L., & Chaplin, T. C. (1988a). Penile responses of child molesters and normals to descriptions of encounters with children involving sex and violence. *Journal of Interpersonal Violence, 3,* 259–274.

Quinsey, V. L., & Chaplin, T. C. (1988b). Preventing faking in phallometric assessments of sexual preference. *Annals of the New York Academy of Sciences, 528,* 49–58.

Quinsey, V. L., Chaplin, T. C., & Carrigan, W. F. (1979). Sexual preferences among incestuous and nonincestuous child molesters. *Behavior Therapy, 10,* 562–565.

Rabin, L. A., Barr, W. B., & Burton, L. A. (2005). Assessment practices of clinical neurophysiologists in the United States and Canada: A survey of INS, NAN, and APA Division 40 members. *Archives of Clinical Neuropsychology, 20,* 33–65.

Radley, A., & Green, R. (1987). Illness as adjustment: A

methodology and conceptual framework. *Sociology of Health and Illness, 9,* 179–207.

Rahilly, P. M. (1991). The pneumographic and medical investigation of infants suffering apparent life threatening episodes. *Journal of Paediatric and Child Health, 27*(6), 349–353.

Raitt, F., & Zeedyk, M. (2003). False memory syndrome: Undermining the credibility of complainants in sexual offences. *International Journal of Law and Psychiatry, 26*(5), 453–471.

Rand, D. C., & Feldman, M. D. (1999). Misdiagnosis of Munchausen syndrome by proxy: A literature review and four new cases. *Harvard Review of Psychiatry, 7*(2), 94–101.

Raskin, D. C. (1989). *Psychological methods in criminal investigation and evidence.* New York: Springer.

Raskin, D. C., & Esplin, P. W. (1991). Statement Validity Assessment: Interview procedures and content analysis of children's statements of sexual abuse. *Behavioral Assessment, 13,* 265–291.

Raskin, D. C., & Honts, C. R. (2002). The comparison question test. In M. Kleiner (Ed.), *Handbook of polygraph testing* (pp. 1–47). San Diego, CA: Academic Press.

Rathus, S. A., Fox, J. A., & Ortins, J. B. (1980). The MacAndrew scale as a measure of substance abuse and delinquency among adolescents. *Journal of Clinical Psychology, 36,* 579–583.

Rauch, J. (2005). If Paul Shanley is a monster, the State didn't prove it. *National Journal, 37,* 746–747.

Raven, J., Raven, J. C., & Court, J. H. (2000). *Manual for Raven's Progressive Matrices and Vocabulary Scales: Section 3. The standard progressive matrices.* Oxford, UK: Oxford Psychologists Press.

Rea, J. A., DeBriere, T., Butler, K., & Saunders, K. J. (1998). An analysis of four sexual offenders' arousal in the natural environment through the use of a portable penile plethysmograph. *Sexual Abuse: A Journal of Research and Treatment, 10,* 239–255.

Reber, K. (1996). Children at risk for reactive attachment disorder: Assessment, diagnosis, and treatment. *Progress Family Systems Research and Therapy, 5,* 83–98.

Rebok, G. W., Li, G., Baker, S. P., Grabowski, J. G., & Willoughby, S. (2002). Self-rated changes in cognition and piloting skills: A comparison of younger and older airline pilots. *Aviation, Space, and Environmental Medicine, 73,* 466–471.

Rees, L. M., Tombaugh, T. N., & Boulay, L. (2001). Depression and the Test of Memory Malingering. *Archives of Clinical Neuropsychology, 16,* 501–506.

Rees, L. M., Tombaugh, T. N., Gansler, D. A., & Moczynski, N. P. (1998). Five validation experiments of the Test of Memory Malingering (TOMM). *Psychological Assessment, 10,* 10–20.

Reich, P., & Gottfried, L. A. (1983). Factitious disorders in a teaching hospital. *Annals of Internal Medicine, 99,* 240–247.

Reich, W., & Todd, R. D. (1999). *MAGIC—Missouri Assessment of Genetics Interview for Children: Specifications Manual.* St. Louis, MO: Washington University School of Medicine.

Reid-Seiser, H. L., & Fritzsche, A. (2001). The usefulness of the NEO PI-R Positive Presentation Management Scale for detecting response distortion in employment contexts. *Personality and Individual Differences, 31,* 639–650.

Reinert, D. F., & Allen, J. P. (2002). The Alcohol Use Disorders Identification Test (AUDIT): A review of recent research. *Alcoholism, Clinical and Experimental Research, 26*(2), 272–279.

Reitan, R. M., & Wolfson, D. (1985). *The Halstead–Reitan Neuropsychological Test Battery.* Tucson, AZ: Neuropsychology Press.

Resnick, P. (1984). The detection of malingered mental illness. *Behavioral Sciences and the Law, 2*(1), 20–38.

Resnick, P. J. (1997). Malingering of posttraumatic disorders. In R. Rogers (Ed.), *Clinical assessment of malingering and deception* (2nd ed., pp. 130–152). New York: Guilford Press.

Resnick, P. J. (2002). Malingering. In R. Rosner (Ed.), *Principles and practice of forensic psychiatry* (2nd ed., pp. 543–554). New York: Chapman & Hall.

Retzlaff, P., Sheehan, E., & Fiel, A. (1991). MCMI-II response style and bias: Profile and validity scales analyses. *Journal of Personality Assessment, 56,* 466–477.

Rey, A. (1941). L'examen psychologique dans le cas d'encephalopathie tramatique. *Archives de Psychologie, 28,* 286–340.

Rey, A. (1964). *L'examen clinique en psychologie.* Paris: Presses Universitaires de France.

Reynolds, C. R. (1998). *Detection of malingering during head injury litigation.* New York: Plenum Press.

Reynolds, C. R., & Kamphaus, R. W. (2004). *Behavioral Assessment for Children, Second Edition (BASC-2).* Shoreview, MN: AGS Publishing.

Reznek, L. (2005). The Rey 15-Item Memory Test for malingering: A meta-analysis. *Brain Injury, 19,* 539–543.

Richards, H., & Pai, S. (2003). Deception in prison assessment of substance abuse. *Journal of Substance Abuse Treatment, 24,* 121–128.

Richman, J., Green, P., Gervais, R., Flaro, L., Merten, T., Brockhaus, R., et al. (2006). Objective tests of symptom exaggeration in independent medical examinations. *Journal of Occupational and Environmental Medicine, 48,* 303–311.

Rim, S. B., & Lowe, B. (1988). Family environments of underachieving gifted students. *Gifted Child Quarterly, 32,* 353–359.

Risberg, R. A., Stevens, M. J., & Graybill, D. F. (1995). Validating the adolescent form of the Substance Abuse Subtle Screening Inventory. *Journal of Child and Adolescent Substance Abuse, 40,* 25–41.

Ritson, B., & Forest, A. (1970). The simulation of psychosis: A contemporary presentation. *British Journal of Medical Psychology, 43,* 31–37.

Roberto, L. (1993). Eating disorders as family secrets. In I. B. Evan (Ed.), *Secrets in families and family therapy* (pp. 160–177). New York: Norton.

Roberts, M. D., Thompson, J. A., & Johnson, M. (2004). *PAI law enforcement, corrections, and public safety se-*

lection report. Lutz, FL: Psychological Assessment Resources.

Robins, L. N., Helzer, J. E., Cottler, L. B., Works, J., Goldring, E., McEvoy, L., et al. (1985). *The DIS Version III: A training manual.* St. Louis, MO: Washington University School of Medicine.

Roediger, H. L., III, & McDermott, K. B. (1995). Creating false memories: Remembering words not presented in lists. *Journal of Experimental Psychology: Learning, Memory, and Cognition, 21,* 803–814.

Rogers, R. (1984a). *Rogers Criminal Responsibility Assessment Scales (R-CRAS) and test manual.* Odessa, FL: Psychological Assessment Resources.

Rogers, R. (1984b). Towards an empirical model of malingering and deception. *Behavioral Sciences and the Law, 2,* 93–112.

Rogers, R. (1986). *Conducting insanity evaluations.* New York: Van Nostrand Reinhold.

Rogers, R. (1987). The assessment of malingering within a forensic context. In D. N. Weisstub (Ed.), *Law and psychiatry: International perspectives* (Vol. 3). New York: Plenum Press.

Rogers, R. (1988a). Researching dissimulation. In R. Rogers (Ed.), *Clinical assessment of malingering and deception* (1st ed., pp. 309–327). New York: Guilford Press.

Rogers, R. (1988b). Structured interviews and dissimulation. In R. Rogers (Ed.), *Clinical assessment of malingering and deception* (1st ed., pp. 250–268). New York: Guilford Press.

Rogers, R. (1990a). Development of a new classificatory model of malingering. *American Academy of Psychiatry and Law, 18,* 323–333.

Rogers, R. (1990b). Models of feigned mental illness. *Professional Psychology, 21,* 182–188.

Rogers, R. (1992). *Structured Interview of Reported Symptoms.* Odessa, FL: Psychological Assessment Resources.

Rogers, R. (1995). *Diagnostic and structured interviewing: A handbook for psychologists.* Odessa, FL: Psychological Assessment Resources.

Rogers, R. (1996). *Test of Cognitive Abilities.* Unpublished test, University of North Texas.

Rogers, R. (Ed.). (1997a). *Clinical assessment of malingering and deception* (2nd ed.). New York: Guilford Press.

Rogers, R. (1997b). Introduction. In R. Rogers (Ed.), *Clinical assessment of malingering and deception* (2nd ed., pp. 1–19). New York: Guilford Press.

Rogers, R. (1997c). Researching dissimulation. In R. Rogers (Ed.), *Clinical assessment of malingering and deception* (2nd ed., pp. 398–426). New York: Guilford Press.

Rogers, R. (1997d). Structured interviews and dissimulation. In R. Rogers (Ed.), *Clinical assessment of malingering and deception* (2nd ed., pp. 301–327). New York: Guilford Press.

Rogers, R. (1998). Assessment of malingering on psychological measures: A synopsis. In G. P. Koocher, J. C. Norcross, & S. S. Hill, III (Eds.), *Psychologist's desk reference* (pp. 53–57). New York: Oxford University Press.

Rogers, R. (2003). Standardizing DSM-IV diagnoses: The clinical applications of structured interviews. *Journal of Personality Assessment, 81,* 220–225.

Rogers, R. (2004). Diagnostic, explanatory, and detection models of Munchausen by proxy: Extrapolations from malingering and deception. *Child Abuse and Neglect, 28*(2), 225–238.

Rogers, R., Bagby, R. M., & Chakraborty, D. (1993). Faking schizophrenic disorders on the MMPI-2: Detection of coached simulators. *Journal of Personality Assessment, 60,* 215–226.

Rogers, R., Bagby, R. M., & Dickens, S. E. (1992). *Structured Interview of Reported Symptoms (SIRS) and professional manual.* Odessa, FL: Psychological Assessment Resources.

Rogers, R., Bagby, R. M., & Gillis, J. R. (1992). Improvements in the M Test as a screening measure for malingering. *Bulletin of the American Academy of Psychiatry and the Law, 20*(1), 101–104.

Rogers, R., Bagby, R. M., & Vincent, A. (1994). Factitious disorders with predominantly psychological signs and symptoms: A conundrum for forensic experts. *Journal of Psychiatry and Law, 22,* 91–106.

Rogers, R., Cashel, M. L., Johansen, J., Sewell, K. W., & Gonzalez, C. (1997). Evaluation of adolescent offenders with substance abuse: Validation of the SASSI with conduct-disordered youth. *Criminal Justice and Behavior, 24,* 114–128.

Rogers, R., & Cavanaugh, J. L. (1983). "Nothing but the truth" . . . A re-examination of malingering. *Journal of Psychiatry and Law, 11,* 443–460.

Rogers, R., & Cruise, C. R. (1998). Assessment of malingering with simulation designs: Threats to external validity. *Law and Human Behavior, 22,* 273–285.

Rogers, R., & Cruise, K. (2000). Malingering and deception among psychopaths. In C. B. Gacono (Ed.), *The clinical and forensic assessment of psychopathy: A practitioner's guide* (pp. 269–284). Mahwah, NJ: Erlbaum.

Rogers, R., & Dickey, R. (1991). Denial and minimization among sex offenders: A review of competing models of deception. *Annals of Sex Research, 4,* 49–63.

Rogers, R., Dolmetsch, R., & Cavanaugh, J. L., Jr. (1983). Identification of random responders on MMPI protocols. *Journal of Personality Assessment, 47,* 364–368.

Rogers, R., Duncan, J. C., & Sewell, K. W. (1994). Prototypical analysis of antisocial personality disorder: DSM-IV and beyond. *Law and Human Behavior, 18,* 471–484.

Rogers, R., Gillis, J., Turner, R., & Frise-Smith, T. (1990). The clinical presentation of command hallucinations. *American Journal of Psychiatry, 147,* 1304–1307.

Rogers, R., Harrell, E. H., & Liff, C. D. (1993). Feigning neuropsychological impairment: A critical review of methodological and clinical considerations. *Clinical Psychology Review, 13,* 255–274.

Rogers, R., Hinds, J. D., & Sewell, K. W. (1996). Feigning psychopathology among adolescent offenders: Validation of the SIRS, MMPI-A, and SIMS. *Journal of Personality Assessment, 67,* 244–257.

Rogers, R., & Jackson, R. L. (2005). Sexually violent predators: The risky enterprise of risk assessment. *Journal of the American Academy of Psychiatry and the Law, 33,* 523–528.

Rogers, R., Jackson, R. L., & Kaminski, P. L. (2004). Factitious psychological disorders: The overlooked response style in forensic evaluations. *Journal of Forensic Psychology Practice, 3,* 115–129.

Rogers, R., Jackson, R. L., Salekin, K. L., & Neumann, C. S. (2003). Assessing Axis I symptomatology on the SADS-C in two correctional samples: The validation of subscales and a screen for malingered presentations. *Journal of Personality Assessment, 81,* 281–290.

Rogers, R., Jackson, R. L., Sewell, K. W., & Harrison, K. S. (2004). An examination of the ECST-R as a screen for feigned incompetency to stand trial. *Psychological Assessment, 16,* 139–145.

Rogers, R., Jackson, R. L., Sewell, K. W., & Salekin, K. L. (2005). Detection strategies for malingering: A confirmatory factor analysis of the SIRS. *Criminal Justice and Behavior, 32*(5), 511–525.

Rogers, R., & Kelly, K. S. (1997). Denial and misreporting of substance abuse. In R. Rogers (Ed.), *Clinical assessment of malingering and deception* (2nd ed., pp. 108–129). New York: Guilford Press.

Rogers, R., Kropp, P., Bagby, R., & Dickens, S. (1992). Faking specific disorders: A study of the Structured Interview of Reported Symptoms (SIRS). *Journal of Clinical Psychology, 48*(5), 643–648.

Rogers, R., & Mitchell, C. N. (1991). *Mental health experts and the criminal courts: A handbook for lawyers and clinicians.* Toronto, Ontario, Canada: Carswell.

Rogers, R., & Neumann, C. S. (2003). Conceptual issues and explanatory models of malingering. In P. W. Halligan, C. Bass, & D. A. Oakley (Eds.), *Malingering and illness deception: Clinical and theoretical perspectives* (pp. 71–82). Oxford, UK: Oxford University Press.

Rogers, R., Ornduff, S. R., & Sewell, K. W. (1993). Feigning specific disorders: A study of the Personality Assessment Inventory (PAI). *Journal of Personality Assessment, 60,* 554–560.

Rogers, R., Payne, J., & Granacher, R. P. (2007). *Use of the SIRS in a disability context: An examination of validity and generalizability.* Manuscript submitted for publication.

Rogers, R., & Payne, J. W. (2006). Damages and rewards: Assessment of malingered disorders in compensation cases. *Behavioral Sciences and the Law, 24,* 645–658.

Rogers, R. Payne, J. W., Berry, D. T. R., & Granacher, R. P., Jr. (2007). *Use of the SIRS in compensation cases: An examination of its validity and generalizability.* Manuscript submitted for publication.

Rogers, R., & Reinhardt, V. (1998). Conceptualization and assessment of secondary gain. In G. P. Koocher, J. C. Norcross, & S. S. Hill (Eds.), *Psychologist's desk reference* (pp. 57–62). New York: Oxford University Press.

Rogers, R., Salekin, R. T., Sewell, K. W., Goldstein, A., & Leonard, K. (1998). A comparison of forensic and nonforensic malingerers: A prototypical analysis of explanatory models. *Law and Human Behavior, 22,* 353–367.

Rogers, R., Sewell, K., & Goldstein, A. (1994). Explanatory models of malingering: A prototypical analysis. *Law and Human Behavior, 18,* 543–552.

Rogers, R., & Sewell, K. W. (2006). MMPI-2 at the crossroads: Aging technology or radical retrofitting? *Journal of Personality Assessment, 87,* 175–178.

Rogers, R., & Sewell, K. W. (2007). *Base rates and diagnostic efficiency statistics: An initial investigation of feigning on the PAI.* Unpublished manuscript, University of North Texas.

Rogers, R., Sewell, K. W., Cruise, K. R., Wang, E. W., & Ustad, K. L. (1998). The PAI and feigning: A cautionary note on its use in forensic-correctional settings. *Assessment, 5,* 399–405.

Rogers, R., Sewell, K. W., & Goldstein, A. (1994). Explanatory models of malingering: A prototypical analysis. *Law and Human Behavior, 18,* 543–552.

Rogers, R., Sewell, K. W., Grandjean, N. R., & Vitacco, M. J. (2002). The detection of feigned mental disorders on specific competency measures. *Psychological Assessment, 14,* 177–183.

Rogers, R., Sewell, K. W., Martin, M. A., & Vitacco, M. J. (2003). Detection of feigned mental disorders: A meta-analysis of the MMPI-2 and malingering. *Assessment, 10,* 160–177.

Rogers, R., Sewell, K. W., Morey, L. C., & Ustad, K. L. (1996). Detection of feigned mental disorders on the Personality Assessment Inventory: A discriminant analysis. *Journal of Personality Assessment, 67,* 629–640.

Rogers, R., Sewell, K. W., & Salekin, R. T. (1994). A meta-analysis of malingering on the MMPI-2. *Assessment, 1,* 227–237.

Rogers, R., Sewell, K. W., & Ustad, K. L. (1995). Feigning among chronic outpatients on the MMPI-2: A systematic examination of fake-bad indicators. *Assessment, 2,* 81–89.

Rogers, R., & Shuman, D. (2000). *Conducting insanity evaluations* (2nd ed.). New York: Guilford Press.

Rogers, R., & Shuman, D. W. (2005). *Fundamentals of forensic practice: Mental health and criminal law.* New York: Springer.

Rogers, R., Tillbrook, C. E., & Sewell, K. W. (2004a). *Evaluation of Competency to Stand Trial—Revised (ECST-R) and professional manual.* Odessa, FL: Psychological Assessment Resources.

Rogers, R., Tillbrook, C., & Sewell, K. (2004b). *Professional manual for the Evaluation of Competency to Stand Trial-Revised.* Odessa, FL: Psychological Assessment Resources.

Rogers, R., Ustad, K. L., & Salekin, R. T. (1998). Forensic applications of the PAI: A study of convergent validity. *Assessment, 5,* 3–12.

Rogers, R., & Vitacco, M. J. (2002). Forensic assessment of malingering and related response styles. In B. Van Dorsten (Ed.), *Forensic psychology: From classroom to courtroom* (pp. 83–104). New York: Kulwer Academic.

Rogers, R., Vitacco, M. J., Jackson, R. L., Martin, M., Collins, M., & Sewell, K. W. (2002). Faking psychopathy?: An examination of response styles with antisocial youth. *Journal of Personality Assessment, 78,* 31–46.

Rogers, R., & Webster, C. D. (1989). Assessing treatability in mentally disordered offenders. *Law and Human Behavior, 13,* 19–29.

Rohling, M. L., Meyers, J. E., & Millis, S. R. (2003). Neuropsychological impairment following traumatic brain injury: A dose–response analysis. *Clinical Neuropsychologist, 17*(3), 289–302.

Rohsenow, D. J. (1982). The Alcohol Use Inventory as predictor of drinking by male heavy social drinkers. *Addictive Behaviors, 7,* 387–395.

Root, J. C., Robbins, R. M., Chang, L., & van Gorp, W. G. (2006). Detection of inadequate effort on the California Verbal Learning Test—Second Edition: Forced choice recognition and critical item analysis. *Journal of the International Neuropsychological Society, 12,* 688–696.

Rosanoff, A. J. (1920). *Manual of psychiatry.* New York: Wiley.

Rosen, G. M. (1995). The Aleutian Enterprise sinking and posttraumatic stress disorder: Misdiagnosing in clinical and forensic settings. *Professional Psychology: Research and Practice, 26,* 82–87.

Rosen, G. M., Sawchuk, C. N., Atkins, D. C., Brown, M., Price, J. R., & Lees-Haley, P. R. (2006). Risk of false positives when identifying malingered profiles using the Trauma Symptom Inventory. *Journal of Personality Assessment, 86,* 329–333.

Rosenberg, C. (1968). *The trial of the assassin Guiteau.* Chicago: University of Chicago Press.

Rosenberg, D. A. (1987). Web of deceit: A literature review of Munchausen syndrome by proxy. *Child Abuse and Neglect, 11*(4), 547–563.

Rosenhan, D. (1973). On being sane in insane places. *Science, 172,* 250–258.

Ross, H. E., Gavin, D. R., & Skinner, H. A. (1990). Diagnostic validity of the MAST and the alcohol dependence scale in the assessment of DSM-III alcohol disorders. *Journal of Studies on Alcohol, 51,* 506–513.

Ross, S. R., Millis, S. R., Krukowski, R. A., Putnam, S. H., & Adams, K. M. (2004). Detecting incomplete effort on the MMPI-2: An examinations of the FBS in mild head injury. *Journal of Clinical and Experimental Neuropsychology, 26,* 115–124.

Ross, S. R., Putnam, S. H., & Adams, K. M. (2006). Psychological disturbance, incomplete effort, and compensation-seeking status as predictors of neuropsychological performance in head injury. *Journal of Clinical and Experimental Neuropsychology, 28,* 111–125.

Ross, S. R., Putnam, S. H., Millis, S. R., Adams, K. M., & Krukowski, R. A. (2006). Detecting insufficient effort using the Seashore Rhythm and Speech-Sounds Perception Tests in head injury. *Clinical Neuropsychologist, 20,* 798–815.

Rothke, S. E., Friedman, A. F., Dahlstrom, W. G., Greene, R. L., Arredondo, R., & Mann, A. W. (1994). MMPI-2 normative data for the F – K index: Implications for clinical, neuropsychological, and forensic practice. *Assessment, 1,* 1–15.

Rounsaville, B. J., Cacciola, J., Weissman, M. M., & Kleber, H. D. (1981). Diagnostic concordance in a follow-up study of opiate addicts. *Journal of Psychiatric Research, 16,* 191–201.

Rowan, C. (1982, June 21). *Cleveland Plain Dealer,* p. 10B.

Rowley, G., & Fielding, K. (1991). Reliability and accuracy of the Glasgow Coma Scale with experienced and inexperienced users. *Lancet, 337,* 535–538.

Rubinsky, E. W., & Brandt, J. (1986). Amnesia and criminal law: A clinical overview. *Behavioral Sciences and the Law, 4,* 27–46.

Ruff, R. (1996). Miserable minority: Emotional risk factors that influence the outcome of a mild traumatic brain injury. *Brain Injury, 10*(8), 551–565.

Ruff, R. (2005). Two decades of advances in our understanding of mild traumatic brain injury. *Journal of Head Trauma Rehabilitation, 20*(1), 5–18.

Ruff, R. M., & Richardson, A. M. (1999). Mild traumatic brain injury. In J. J. Sweet (Ed.), *Forensic neuropsychology: Fundamentals and practice* (pp. 313–338). Lisse, The Netherlands: Swets & Zeitlinger.

Ruffman, T., Olson, D. R., Ash, T., & Keenan, T. (1993). The ABCs of deception: Do young children understand deception in the same way as adults? *Developmental Psychology, 29,* 74–87.

Ruffolo, L. F., Guilmette, T. J., & Willis, W. G. (2000). Comparison of time and error rates on the Trail-Making Test among patients with head injuries, experimental malingerers, patients with suspect effort on testing, and normal controls. *Clinical Neuropsychologist, 14,* 223–230.

Ruiz, M. A., Drake, E. B., Glass, A., Marcotte, D., & van Gorp, W. G. (2002). Trying to beat the system: Misuse of the Internet to assist in avoiding the detection of psychological symptom dissimulation. *Professional Psychology: Research and Practice, 33,* 294–299.

Rumans, L. W., & Vosti, K. L. (1978). Factitious and fraudulent fever. *American Journal of Medicine, 65*(5), 745–755.

Ryan, A. M., & Sackett, P. R. (1987). Pre-employment honesty testing: Fakability, reactions of test takers, and company image. *Journal of Business and Psychology, 1,* 248–256.

Ryba, N. L., Sothmann, F. C., Arias, E., & Slavikova, M. (2007, August). *Usefulness of the ECST-R in determining competence and detecting feigning.* Paper presented at the American Psychological Association convention, San Francisco.

Sachs, M. H., Carpenter, W. T., & Strauss, J. S. (1974). Recovery from delusions. *Archives of General Psychiatry, 30,* 117–120.

Sackett, P. R., Burris, L. R., & Callahan, C. (1989). Integrity testing for personnel selection: An update. *Personnel Psychology, 42,* 491–529.

Sackett, P. R., & Harris, M. M. (1984). Honesty testing for personnel selection: A review and critique. *Personnel Psychology, 37,* 221–246.

Sackett, P. R., & Waneck, J. E. (1996). New developments in the use of measures of honesty, integrity, conscientiousness, dependability, trustworthiness, and reliability for personnel selection. *Personnel Psychology, 49,* 787–829.

Sadock, B. J., & Sadock, V. A. (2003). *Kaplan and Sadock's synopsis of psychiatry* (9th ed.). Philidelphia: Lippincott Williams & Wilkins.

Salekin, R. T. (2002). Psychopathy and therapeutic pessimism: Clinical lore or clinical reality? *Clinical Psychology Review, 22,* 79–112.

Salekin, R. T. (2004) *The Risk Sophistication Treatment Inventory (RSTI).* Odessa, FL: Psychological Assessment Resources.

Salekin, R. T. (2006). Psychopathy in children and adolescents: Key issues in conceptualization and assessment. In C. J. Patrick (Ed.), *Handbook of psychopathy* (pp. 389–414). New York: Guilford Press.

Salekin, R. T., & Frick, P. J. (2005). Psychopathy in children and adolescents: The need for a developmental perspective. *Journal of Abnormal Child Psychology, 33,* 403–409.

Salekin, R. T., Leistico, A.-M. R., Schrum, C. L., & Mullins, J. (2005). Millon Adolescent Clinical Inventory. In T. Grisso, G. Vincent, & D. Seagrave (Eds.), *Mental health screening and assessment in juvenile justice* (pp. 253–264). New York: Guilford Press.

Salekin, R. T., Leistico, A.-M. R., Trobst, K. K., Schrum, C. L., & Lochman, J. E. (2005). Adolescent psychopathy and personality theory—the interpersonal circumplex: Expanding evidence of a nomological net. *Journal of Abnormal Child Psychology, 33,* 445–460.

Salekin, R. T., Neumann, C. S., Leistico, A.-M. R., DiCicco, T. M., & Duros, R. L. (2004). Psychopathy and comorbidity in a young offender sample: Taking a closer look at psychopathy's potential importance over the disruptive behavior disorders. *Journal of Abnormal Psychology, 113,* 416–427.

Salekin, R. T., Salekin, K. L., Clements, C. B., & Leistico, A.-M. R. (2005). Risk–Sophistication–Treatment Inventory (RST-I). In T. Grisso, G. Vincent, & D. Seagrave (Eds.), *Mental health screening and assessment in juvenile justice* (pp. 341–356). New York: Guilford Press.

Salvo, M., Pinna, A., Milia, P., & Carta, F. (2006). Ocular Munchausen syndrome resulting in bilateral blindness. *European Journal of Ophthalmology, 16*(4), 654–656.

Samenow, S. (1984). *Inside the criminal mind.* New York: Times Books.

Samra, J., & Koch, W. J. (2002). The monetary worth of psychological injury. In J. R. P. Ogloff (Ed.), *Taking psychology and law into the twenty-first century* (pp. 285–322). New York: Kluwer Academic/Plenum Press.

Sansone, R. A., Weiderman, M. W., Sansone, L. A., & Mehnert-Kay, S. (1997). Sabotaging one's own medical care. *Archives of Family Medicine, 6*(6), 583–586.

Santor, D. A., Bagby, R. M., & Joffe, R. J. (1997). Evaluating stability and change in personality and depression. *Journal of Personality and Social Psychology, 73,* 1354–1362.

Saroka vs. Dayton Hudson Corp.,. 18 Cal. App. 4th 1200 (1991).

Saunders, J. B., Aasland, O. G., Babor, T. F., De La Fuents, J. R., & Grant, M. (1993). Development of the Alcohol Use Disorders Identification Test (AUDIT): WHO collaborative project on early detecting of persons with harmful alcohol consumption: II. *Addiction, 88,* 791–804.

Savino, A. C., & Fordtran, J. S. (2006). Factitious disease: Clinical lessons from case studies at Baylor University medical center. *Proceedings (Baylor University Medical Center), 19*(3), 195–208.

Saxe, L., Dougherty, D., & Cross, T. (1985). The validity of polygraph testing: Scientific analysis and public controversy. *American Psychologist, 40,* 355–366.

Scandell, D. J. (2000). Development and initial validation of validity scales for the NEO-Five Factor Inventory. *Personality and Individual Differences, 29,* 1153–1162.

Schacter, D. L. (1986). On the relation between genuine and simulated amnesia. *Behavioral Sciences and the Law, 4,* 47–64.

Schacter, D. L. (1996). *Searching for memory: The brain, the mind, and the past.* New York: Basic Books.

Schachter, D. L., Kagan, J., & Leichtman, M. D. (1995). True and false memories in children and adults: A cognitive neuroscience perspective. *Psychology, Public Policy, and Law, 1,* 411–428.

Schagen, S., Schmand, B., de Sterke, S., & Lindeboom, J. (1997). Amsterdam Short-Term Memory Test: A new procedure for the detection of feigned memory deficits. *Journal of Clinical and Experimental Neuropsychology, 19,* 43–51.

Schinka, J. A., Kinder, B. N., & Kremer, T. (1997). Research validity scales for the NEO-PI-R: Development and initial validation. *Journal of Personality Assessment, 68,* 127–138.

Schlank, A. (2001). *The sexual predator: Legal issues, clinical issues, special populations* (Vol. 2). Kingston, NJ: Civic Research Institute.

Schmidt, F. L., Viswesvaran, V., & Ones, D. S. (1997). Validity of integrity tests for predicting drug and alcohol abuse: A meta-analysis. In W. J. Bukowski (Ed.), *Meta-analysis of drug abuse prevention programs* (pp. 69–95). Rockville, MD: NIDA Press.

Schmitt, N. (1985). Review of London House Attitude Inventory. In J. V. Mitchell, Jr. (Ed.), *The ninth mental measurement yearbook* (pp. 868–870). Lincoln, NE: Buros Institute of Mental Measurement.

Schneck, J. (1970). Pseudo-malingering and Leonid Andreyev's *The Dilemma. Psychiatric Quarterly, 44,* 49–54.

Schneider, S., & Wright, R. (2004). Understanding denial in sexual offenders: A review of cognitive and motivational processes to avoid responsibility. *Trauma, Violence, and Abuse, 5*(1), 3–20.

Schoenberg, M. R., Dorr, D., & Morgan, C. D. (2003). The ability of the Millon Clinical Multiaxial Inventory—Third Edition to detect malingering. *Psychological Assessment, 15,* 198–204.

Schoenberg, M. R., Dorr, D., Morgan, C. D., & Burke, M. (2004). A comparison of the MCMI-III personality disorder and modifier indices with the MMPI-2 clinical and validity scales. *Journal of Personality Assessment, 82,* 273–280.

Schooler, J. W. (2001). Discovering memories of abuse in the light of meta-awareness. In J. J. Freyd & A. P. DePrince (Eds.), *Trauma and cognitive science: A meeting of minds, science, and human experience* (pp. 105–136). New York: Haworth.

Schooler, J. W., Bendiksen, M., & Ambadar, Z. (1997). Taking the middle line: Can we accommodate both fabricated and recovered memories of sexual abuse? In M. A. Conway (Ed.), *Recovered memories and false memories* (pp. 251–292). Oxford, UK: Oxford University Press.

Schouten, P. G., & Simon, W. T. (1992). Validity of phallometric measures with sex offenders: Comments on the Quinsey, Laws, and Hall debate. *Journal of Consulting and Clinical Psychology, 60,* 812–814.

Schreier, H. A. (1996). Repeated false allegations of sexual abuse presenting to sheriffs: When is it munchausen by proxy? *Child Abuse and Neglect, 20*(11), 1135–1137.

Schreier, H. A. (2000). Factitious disorder by proxy in which the presenting problem is behavioral or psychiatric. *Journal of the American Academy of Child and Adolescent Psychiatry, 39*(5), 668–670.

Schretlen, D., & Arkowitz, H. (1990). A psychological test battery to detect prison inmates who fake insanity or mental retardation. *Behavioral Sciences and the Law, 8,* 75–84.

Schretlen, D., Neal, J., & Lesikar, S. (2000). Screening for malingered mental illness in a court clinic. *American Journal of Forensic Psychology, 18*(1), 5–16.

Schretlen, D. J. (1988). The use of psychological tests to identify malingered symptoms of mental disorder. *Clinical Psychology Review, 8,* 451–476.

Schretlen, D. J. (1990). A limitation of using the Wiener and Harmon obvious and subtle scales to detect faking on the MMPI. *Journal of Clinical Psychology, 46,* 782–786.

Schretlen, D. J. (1997). Dissimulation on the Rorschach and other projective measures. In R. Rogers (Ed.), *Clinical assessment of malingering and deception* (2nd ed., pp. 208–222). New York: Guilford Press.

Schretlen, D. J., Brandt, J., Krafft, L., & van Gorp, W. (1991). Some caveats in using the 15-Item Memory Test to detect malingered amnesia. *Psychological Assessment, 3,* 667–672.

Schwan, R., Albuisson, E., Malet, L., Loiseaux, M., Reynaud, M., Schellenberg, F., et al. (2004). The use of biological laboratory markers in the diagnosis of alcohol misuse: An evidence-based approach. *Drug and Alcohol Dependence, 74,* 273–279.

Schwartz, J. A. (1998). Adapting and using the Substance Abuse Subtle Screening Inventory—2 with criminal justice offenders: Preliminary results. *Criminal Justice and Behavior, 25,* 344–365.

Scragg, P., Bor, R., & Mendham, M. (2000). Feigning post-traumatic stress disorder on the PAI. *Clinical Psychology and Psychotherapy, 7,* 155–160.

Seagrave, D., & Grisso, T. (2002). Adolescent development and the measurement of juvenile psychopathy. *Law and Human Behavior, 26,* 219–239.

Seamons, D., Howell, R., Carlisle, A., & Roe, A. (1981). Rorschach simulation of mental illness and normality by psychotic and nonpsychotic legal offenders. *Journal of Personality Assessment, 45,* 130–135.

Seibel, M., & Parnell, T. (1998). The physician's role in confirming the diagnosis. In T. Parnell & D. Day (Eds.), *Munchausen by proxy syndrome: Misunderstood child abuse* (pp. 68–94). Thousand Oaks, CA: Sage.

Seigel, R., & West, L. (Eds.). (1975). *Hallucinations: Behavior, experience and theory.* New York: Wiley.

Selzer, M. L. (1971). Michigan Alcoholism Screening Test: The quest for a new diagnostic instrument. *American Journal of Psychiatry, 127,* 1653–1658.

Selzer, M. L., Vinokur, A., & van Rooijen, M. A. (1975). A self-administered short Michigan Alcohol Screening Test (SMAST). *Journal of Studies on Alcohol, 36,* 117–126.

Servan-Schreiber, D., Tabas, G., & Kolb, R. (2000). Somatizing patients: Part II. Practical management. *American Family Physician, 61*(5), 1423–1428, 1431–1432.

Seto, M. C. (2001). The value of phallometry in the assessment of male sex offenders. *Journal of Forensic Psychology Practice, 1,* 65–75.

Seto, M. C., Lalumière, M. L., & Blanchard, R. (2000). The discriminative validity of a phallometric test for pedophilic interests among adolescent sex offenders against children. *Psychological Assessment, 12,* 319–327.

Sewell, K. W., & Rogers, R. (1994). Response consistency and the MMPI-2: Development of a simplified screening scale. *Assessment, 1,* 293–299.

Sewell, K. W., & Salekin, R. T. (1997). Understanding and detecting dissimulation in sex offenders. In R. Rogers (Ed.), *Clinical assessment of malingering and deception* (2nd ed., pp. 328–350). New York: Guilford Press.

Shane, P., Jasiukaitis, P., & Green, R. S. (2003). Treatment outcomes among adolescents with substance abuse problems: The relationship between comorbidities and post-treatment substance involvement. *Evaluation and Program Planning, 26,* 393–402.

Sharland, M. J., & Gfeller, J. D. (2007). A survey of neuropsychologists' beliefs and practices with respect to the assessment of effort. *Archives of Clinical Neuropsychology, 22,* 213–223.

Shear, M. K., Greeno, C., Kang, J., Ludewig, D., Frank, E., Swartz, H. A., et al. (2000). Diagnosis of nonpsychotic patients in community clinics. *American Journal of Psychiatry, 157*(4), 581–587.

Sheridan, M. S. (2003). The deceit continues: An updated literature review of Munchausen syndrome by proxy. *Child Abuse and Neglect, 27*(4), 431–451.

Sherman, D. S., Boone, K. B., Lu, P., & Razani, J. (2002). Re-examination of a Rey Auditory Verbal Learning Test/Rey Complex Figure discriminant function to detect suspect effort. *Clinical Neuropsychologist, 16,* 242–250.

Sherman, J. J., Turk, D. C., & Okifuji, A. (2000). Prevalence and impact of posttraumatic stress disorder-like symptoms on patients with fibromyalgia syndrome. *Clinical Journal of Pain, 16,* 127–134.

Sherman, M., Trief, P., & Sprafkin, Q. R. (1975). Impression management in the psychiatric interview: Quality, style and individual differences. *Journal of Consulting and Clinical Psychology, 43,* 867–871.

Shields, A. L., & Caruso, J. C. (2003). Reliability generalization of the Alcohol Use Disorders Identification Test. *Educational and Psychological Measurement, 63*(3), 404–413.

Shobe, K. K., & Schooler, J. W. (2001). Discovering fact and fiction: Case-based analyses of authentic and fabricated memories of abuse. In G. M. Davies & T. Dalgleish (Eds.), *Recovered memories: Seeking the middle ground* (pp. 95–151). Chichester, UK: Wiley.

Shum, H. K., O'Gorman, J. G., & Alpar, A. (2004). Effects of incentive and preparation time on performance and classification accuracy of standard and malingering-specific memory tests. *Archives of Clinical Neuropsychology, 19,* 817–823.

Sigal, M., Gelkopf, M., & Meadow, R. S. (1989). Munchausen by proxy syndrome: The triad of abuse, self-abuse, and deception. *Comprehensive Psychiatry, 30*(6), 527–533.

Sigall, H., & Page, R. (1971). Current stereotypes: A little fading, a little faking. *Journal of Personality and Social Psychology, 18,* 247–255.

Silverberg, N., & Barrash, J. (2005). Further validation of the expanded Auditory Verbal Learning Test for detecting poor effort and response bias: Data from temporal lobectomy candidates. *Journal of Clinical and Experimental Neuropsychology, 27,* 907–914.

Silverton, L. (1999). *The Malingering Probability Scale (MPS) manual.* Los Angeles: Western Psychological Services.

Simon, R. (Ed.). (2003). *Posttraumatic stress disorder in litigation: Guidelines for forensic assessment* (2nd ed.). Washington, DC: American Psychiatric.

Simon, R. L., & Gold, L. H. (2004). *American Psychiatric Publishing textbook of forensic psychiatry.* Washington, DC: American Psychiatric Press.

Simpson, G. (1987). Accuracy and precision of breath-alcohol measurements for a random subject in postabsorptive state. *Clinical Chemistry, 32,* 261–268.

Sivec, H. J., Hilsenroth, M. J., & Lynn, S. J. (1995). Impact of simulating borderline personality disorder on the MMPI-2: A cost–benefits model employing base rates. *Journal of Personality Assessment, 64,* 295–311.

Sivec, H. J., Lynn, S. J., & Garske, J. P. (1994). The effect of somatoform disorder and paranoid psychotic disorder role-related dissimulations as a response set on the MMPI-2. *Assessment, 1,* 69–81.

Skinner, H. A. (1982). The Drug Abuse Screening Test. *Addictive Behaviors, 7,* 363–371.

Skopp, G., Potsch, L., & Moeller, M. R. (1997). On cosmetically treated hair—aspects and pitfalls of interpretation. *Forensic Science International, 84,* 43–52.

Slick, D. J., Hopp, G., Strauss, E., & Spellacy, F. J. (1996). Victoria Symptom Validity Test: Efficiency for detecting feigned memory impairment and relationship to neuropsychological tests and the MMPI-2 validity scales. *Journal of Clinical and Experimental Neuropsychology, 18,* 911–922.

Slick, D. J., Hopp, G., Strauss, E., & Thompson, G. B. (1997). *Victoria Symptom Validity Test.* Odessa, FL: Psychological Assessment Resources.

Slick, D. J., Iverson, G. L., & Green, P. (2000). California Verbal Learning Test indicators of suboptimal performance in a sample of head-injury litigants. *Journal of Clinical and Experimental Neuropsychology, 22,* 569–579.

Slick, D. J., Sherman, E. M. S., & Iverson, G. L. (1999). Diagnostic criteria for malingered neurocognitive dysfunction: Proposed standards for clinical practice and research, *Clinical Neuropsychologist, 13,* 545–561.

Slick, D. J., Tan, J. E., Strauss, E., & Hultsch, D. (2004). Detecting malingering: A survey of experts' practices. *Archives of Clinical Neuropsychology, 19,* 465–473.

Slick, D. J., Tan, J. E., Strauss, E., Mateer, C. A., Harnadek, M., & Sherman, E. M. S. (2003). Victoria Symptom Validity Test scores of patients with profound memory impairment: Nonlitigant case studies. *Clinical Neuropsychologist, 17,* 390–394.

Slovenko, R. (1994). Legal aspects of posttraumatic stress disorder. *Psychiatric Clinics of North America, 17,* 439–446.

Small, I. F., Small, J. G., & Andersen, J. M. (1966). Clinical characteristics of hallucinations of schizophrenia. *Diseases of the Nervous System, 27,* 349–353.

Smart, R. G., & Jarvis, G. K. (1981). Do self-report studies of drug use really give dependable results? *Canadian Journal of Criminology, 23,* 83–92.

Smith, B. H. (1967). A handbook of tests to unmask malingering. *Consultant, 7,* 41–47.

Smith, G., & Fischer, L. (1999). Assessment of juvenile sexual offenders: Reliability and validity of the Abel Assessment for Interest in Paraphilias. *Sexual Abuse: A Journal of Research and Treatment, 11,* 207–216.

Smith, G. P. (1992). *Deception of malingering: A validation study of the SLAM test.* Unpublished doctoral dissertation, University of Missouri, St. Louis.

Smith, G. P., & Borum, R. (1992). Detection of malingering in a forensic sample: A study of the M Test. *Journal of Psychiatry and Law, 20*(4), 505–514.

Smith, G. P., Borum, R., & Schinka, J. A. (1993). Rule-Out and Rule-In scales for the M Test for malingering: A cross-validation. *Bulletin of the American Academy of Psychiatry and the Law, 21*(1), 107–110.

Smith, G. P., & Burger, G. K. (1997). Detection of malingering: Validation of the Structured Inventory of Malingered Symptomatology (SIMS). *Journal of the American Academy of Psychiatry and the Law, 25,* 183–189.

Snowdon, J., Solomons, R., & Druce, H. (1978). Feigned bereavement: Twelve cases. *British Journal of Psychiatry, 133,* 15–19.

Sobell, L. C., & Sobell, M. B. (1996). *Timeline Followback user's guide: A calendar method for assessing alcohol and drug use.* Toronto, Ontario, Canada: Addiction Research Foundation.

Sobell, M. B., Sobell, L. C., & VanderSpek, R. (1979). Relationships among clinical judgment, self-report, and breath-analysis measurements of intoxication in alcoholics. *Journal of Consulting and Clinical Psychology, 47,* 204–206.

Sodian, B. (1991). The development of deception in young children. *British Journal of Developmental Psychology, 9,* 173–188.

Sokol, M. C., McGuigan, K. A., Verbrugge, R. R., & Epstein, R. S. (2005). Impact of medication adherence on hospitalization risk and healthcare cost. *Medical Care, 43,* 521–530.

Sokol, R. G., Ager, J. W., & Martier, S. S. (1992). Methodological issues in obtaining and managing substance abuse information from prenatal patients. In M. M. Kilbey & K. Asghar (Eds.), *Methodological issues in epidemiological, prevention and treatment research on drug-exposed women and their children* (Research Monograph 117, pp. 80–97). Rockville, MD: National Institute on Drug Abuse.

Soniat, T. L. (1960). The problem of "compensation" neurosis. *South Medical Journal, 53,* 365–368.

Sorin, A., April, M. M., & Ward, R. F. (2006). Recurrent periorbital cellulitis: An unusual clinical entity. *Otolaryngology and Head and Neck Surgery, 134,* 153–156.

Sosin, D. M., Sniezek, J. E., & Thurman, D. J. (1996). Incidence of mild and moderate brain injury in the United States. *Brain Injury, 10,* 47–54.

Sparr, L. (1990). Legal aspects of posttraumatic stress disorder: Uses and abuses. In M. Wolf & A. Mosnaim (Eds.), *Posttraumatic stress disorder: Etiology, phenomenology and treatment* (pp. 238–264). Washington, DC: American Psychiatric Press.

Sparr, L., & Pankratz, L. D. (1983). Factitious posttraumatic stress disorder. *American Journal of Psychiatry, 140*(8), 1016–1019.

Sparr, L. F., & Atkinson, R. M. (1986). Post-traumatic stress disorder as an insanity defense: Medicolegal quicksand. *American Journal of Psychiatry, 140,* 1016–1019.

Spiegel, D. (1997). Foreword. In D. Spiegel (Ed.), *Repressed memories* (pp. 5–11). Washington, DC: American Psychiatric Press.

Spiegel, D., & Fink, R. (1979). Hysterical psychosis and hypnotizability. *American Journal of Psychiatry, 139,* 431–437.

Spiro, H. R. (1968). Chronic factitious illness: Munchausen's syndrome. *Archives of General Psychiatry, 18*(5), 569–579.

Spitzer, M. (1992). The phenomenology of delusions. *Psychiatric Annals, 22,* 252–259.

Spitzer, R. L., & Endicott, J. (1978). *Schedule of affective disorders and schizophrenia.* New York: Biometric Research.

Spitzer, R. L., Williams, J. B. W., Gibbon, M., & First, M. B. (1990). *Structured Clinical Interview for DSM-IIII-R (SCID).* Washington, DC: American Psychiatric Press.

Sporer, S. L., & Schwandt, B. (2006). Paraverbal indicators of deception: A meta-analytic synthesis. *Applied Cognitive Psychology, 20*(4), 421–446.

Sporer, S. L., & Schwandt, B. (2007). Moderators of nonverbal indicators of deception: A meta-analytic synthesis. *Psychology, Public Policy, and Law, 13*(1), 1–34.

Sreenivasan, S., Kirkish, P., Garrick, T., Weinberger, L. E., & Phenix, A. (2000). Actuarial risk assessment models: A review of critical issues related to violence and sex-offender recidivism assessments. *Journal of the American Academy of Psychiatry and the Law, 28,* 438–448.

Stark, S., Chernyshenko, O. S., Chan, K. Y., Lee, W. C., & Drasgow, F. (2001). Effects of the testing situation on item responding: Cause for concern. *Journal of Applied Psychology, 86*(5), 943–953.

Steffan, J. S., Clopton, J. R., & Morgan, R. D. (2003). An MMPI-2 scale to detect malingered depression (*Md* scale). *Assessment, 10,* 382–392.

Steffan, J. S., Morgan, R. D., Cicerello, A. R., & Birmingham, D. L. (2005). Utility of the MCMI-III in detecting response bias by forensic patients. *American Journal of Forensic Psychology, 23,* 43–58.

Stein, L. A. R., Colby, S. M., Barnett, N. P., Monti, P. M., & Lebeau, R. (2006). [Admitted under- and overreported alcohol and marijuana use in incarcerated adolescents.] Unpublished raw data, University of Rhode Island.

Stein, L. A. R., Colby, S. M., O'Leary, T. A., Monti, P. M., Rohsenow, D. J., Spirito, A., et al. (2002). Response distortion in adolescents who smoke: A pilot study. *Journal of Drug Education, 32*(4), 271–286.

Stein, L. A. R., & Graham, J. R. (1999). Detecting fake-good MMPI-A profiles in a correctional facility. *Psychological Assessment, 11,* 386–395.

Stein, L. A. R., & Graham, J. R. (2001). Use of the MMPI-A to detect substance abuse in a juvenile correctional setting. *Journal of Personality Assessment, 77*(3), 508–523.

Stein, L. A. R., & Graham, J. R. (2005). Ability of substance abusers to escape detection on the Minnesota Multiphasic Personality Inventory—Adolescent (MMPI-A) in a juvenile correctional facility. *Assessment, 12*(1), 28–39.

Stein, L. A. R., Graham, J. R., Ben-Porath, Y. S., & McNulty, J. L. (1999). Using the MMPI-2 to detect substance abuse in an outpatient mental health setting. *Psychological Assessment, 11,* 94–100.

Stein, L. A. R., Graham, J. R., & Williams, C. L. (1995). Detecting fake-bad MMPI-A profiles. *Journal of Personality Assessment, 65,* 415–427.

Stein, L. A. R., Lebeau-Craven, R., Martin, R., Colby, S. M., Barnett, N. P., Golembeske, C., Jr., et al. (2005). Use of the Adolescent SASSI in a juvenile correctional setting. *Assessment, 12*(4), 384–394.

Steinberg, C. E. (1993). The *Daubert* decision: An update on the Frye rule. *Newsletter of the American Academy of Psychiatry and the Law, 8,* 66–99.

Steinweg, D. L., & Worth, H. (1993). Alcoholism: The keys to the CAGE. *American Journal of Medicine, 94,* 520–523.

Steller, M., & Koehnken, G. (1989). Criteria-based statement analysis. In D. C. Raskin (Ed.), *Psychological methods in criminal investigation and evidence* (pp. 217–245). New York: Springer.

Stermac, L. (1988). Projective testing and dissimulation. In R. Rogers (Ed.), *Clinical assessment of malingering and deception* (pp. 159–168). New York: Guilford Press.

Stinchfield, R., & Winters, K. C. (2003). Predicting adolescent drug abuse treatment outcome with the Personal Experience Inventory (PEI). *Journal of Child and Adolescent Substance Abuse, 13*(2), 103–120.

Stone, A. (1993). Post-traumatic stress disorder and the law: Critical review of the new frontier. *Bulletin of the American Academy of Psychiatry and the Law, 21*, 23–36.

Stone, A. V. (1995). Law enforcement psychological fitness for duty: Clinical issues. In M. I. Kurke & E. M. Scrivner (Eds.), *Police psychology into the 21st century* (pp. 109–131). Hillsdale, NJ: Erlbaum.

Stone, D. C., Boone, K. B., Back-Madruga, C., & Lesser, I. M. (2006). Has the rolling uterus finally gathered moss?: Somatization and malingering of cognitive dysfunction in six cases of "toxic mold" exposure. *Clinical Neuropsychologist, 20*, 766–785.

Stone, J., Carson, A., & Sharpe, M. (2005). Functional symptoms and signs in neurology: Assessment and diagnosis. *Journal of Neurology, Neurosurgery and Psychiatry, 76*(Suppl. 1), 2–12.

Stone, J., & Sharpe, M. (2006). Functional symptoms in neurology: Case studies. *Neurologic Clinics, 24*(2), 385–403.

Stone, J., Zeman, A., & Sharpe, M. (2002). Functional weakness and sensory disturbance, *Journal of Neurology, Neurosurgery and Psychiatry, 73*, 241–245.

Storm, J., & Graham, J. R. (2000). Detection of coached general malingering on the MMPI-2. *Psychological Assessment, 12*, 158–165.

Story, D. L. (2000). *Validation of a short form of the Structured Interview of Reported Symptoms (SIRS).* Unpublished doctoral dissertation, Carlos Albizu University, Miami, FL.

Stouthamer-Loeber, M. (1986). Lying as a problem behavior in children: A review. *Clinical Psychology Review, 6*, 267–289.

Stouthamer-Loeber, M., & Loeber, R. (1986). Boys who lie. *Journal of Abnormal Child Psychology, 14*, 551–564.

Strauss, E., Hultsch, D. F., Hunter, M., Slick, D. J., Patry, B., & Levy-Benchton, J. (2000). Using intraindividual variability to detect malingering in cognitive performance. *Clinical Neuropsychologist, 14*, 420–432.

Streiner, D. L. (2003). Diagnosing tests: Using and misusing diagnostic and screening tests. *Journal of Personality Assessment, 81*, 209–219.

Strong, D. R., Glassmire, D. M., Frederick, R. I., & Greene, R. L. (2006). Evaluating the latent structure of the MMPI-2 Fp scale in a forensic sample: Taxometric analysis. *Psychological Assessment, 18*, 250–261.

Strong, D. R., Greene, R. L., Hoppe, C., Johnston, T., & Olesen, N. (1999). Taxometric analysis of impression management and self-deception on the MMPI-2 in child-custody litigants. *Journal of Personality Assessment, 73*, 1–18.

Strong, D. R., Greene, R. L., & Kordinak, S. T. (2002). Taxometric analysis of impression management and self-deception in college student and personnel evaluation settings. *Journal of Personality Assessment, 78*, 161–175.

Strong, D. R., Greene, R. L., & Schinka, J. A. (2000). A taxometric analysis of MMPI-2 Infrequency Scales [F and F(p)] in clinical settings. *Psychological Assessment, 12*(2), 166–173.

Stuart, S., & Noyes, R., Jr. (1999). Attachment and interpersonal communication in somatization. *Psychosomatics, 40*(1), 34–43.

Stuart, S., & Noyes, R., Jr. (2006). Interpersonal psychotherapy for somatizing patients. *Psychotherapy and Psychosomatics, 75*(4), 209–219.

Stutts, J. T., Hickey, S. E., & Kasdan, M. L. (2003). Malingering by proxy: A form of pediatric condition falsification. *Journal of Developmental and Behavioral Pediatrics, 24*(4), 276–278.

Substance Abuse and Mental Health Services Administration. (1996, August). *Advance Report No. 18: Preliminary estimates from the 1995 national household survey on drug abuse.* Rockville, MD: Office of Applied Studies.

Suhr, J. A., & Boyer, D. (1999). Use of the Wisconsin Card Sorting Test in the detection of malingering in student simulator and patient samples. *Journal of Clinical and Experimental Neuropsychology, 21*, 701–708.

Suhr, J. A., & Gunstad, J. (2002). "Diagnosis threat": The effect of negative expectations on cognitive performance. *Journal of Clinical and Experimental Neuropsychology, 24*, 448–457.

Suhr, J. A., Gunstad, J., Greub, B., & Barrash, J. (2004). Exaggeration Index for an expanded version of the Auditory Verbal Learning Test: Robustness to coaching. *Journal of Clinical and Experimental Neuropsychology, 26*, 416–427.

Suhr, J. A., Tranel, D., Wefel, J., & Barrash, J. (1997). Memory performance after head injury: Contributions of malingering, litigation status, psychological factors, and medication use. *Journal of Clinical and Experimental Neuropsychology, 19*, 500–514.

Sullivan, K., Deffenti, C., & Keane, B. (2002). Malingering on the RAVLT: Part II. Detection strategies. *Archives of Clinical Neuropsychology, 17*, 223–233.

Sullivan, M. J. (2006). Psychological methods of pain control: Basic science and clinical perspectives. *Journal of Nervous and Mental Disease, 194*(5), 388.

Sumanti, M., Boone, K. B., Savodnik, I., & Gorsuch, R. (2006). Noncredible psychiatric and cognitive symptoms in a workers' compensation "stress" claim sample. *Clinical Neuropsychologist, 20*, 754–765.

Summit, R. C. (1983). The child sexual abuse accommodation syndrome. *Child Abuse and Neglect, 7*, 177–193.

Surrette, M. A., & Serafino, G. (2003). Relationship between personality and law enforcement performance. *Applied HRM Research, 8*, 89–92.

Svanum, S., & McGrew, J. (1995). Prospective screening

of substance dependence: The advantages of directness. *Addictive Behaviors, 20*, 205–213.

Sweet, J. J. (Ed.). (1999a). *Forensic neuropsychology: Fundamentals and practice.* Exton, PA: Swets & Zeitlinger.

Sweet, J. J. (1999b). Malingering: Differential diagnosis. In J. Sweet (Ed.), *Forensic neuropsychology: Fundamentals and practice.* Lisse, The Netherlands: Swets & Zeitlinger.

Sweet, J. J., Ecklund-Johnson, E., & Malina, A. (2007). Overview of forensic neuropsychology. In J. Morgan & J. Ricker (Eds.), *Textbook of clinical neuropsychology.* New York: Taylor & Francis.

Sweet, J. J. & King, J. H. (2002). Category Test validity indicators: Overview and practice recommendations. *Journal of Forensic Neuropsychology, 3*, 241–274.

Sweet, J. J., King, J. H., Malina, A. C., Bergman, M. A., & Simmons, A. (2002). Documenting the prominence of forensic neuropsychology at national meetings and in relevant professional journals from 1990 to 2000. *Clinical Neuropsychologist, 16*, 481–494.

Sweet, J. J., Nelson, N., & Heilbronner, R. (2005, June). *Relative lack of correspondence of individual MMPI-2 validity scales with individual measures of cognitive effort.* Paper presented at the annual meeting of the American Academy of Clinical Neuropsychology, Minneapolis, MN.

Sweet, J. J., Wolfe, P., Sattlberger, E., Numan, B., Rosenfeld, J. P., Clingerman, S., et al. (2000). Further investigation of traumatic brain injury versus insufficient effort with the California Verbal Learning Test. *Archives of Clinical Neuropsychology, 15*, 105–113.

Swenson, W. M., & Morse, R. M. (1975). The use of Self-Administered Alcoholism Screening Test (SAAST) in a medical center. *Mayo Clinic Proceedings, 50*, 204–208.

Swets, J. A. (1973). The relative operating characteristic in psychology. *Science, 182*, 990–999.

Swets, J. A. (1988). Measuring the accuracy of diagnostic systems. *Science, 240*, 1285–1293.

Swift, R. M., & Swette, L. (1992). Assessment of ethanol consumption with a wearable, electronic ethanol sensor/recorder. In R. Litten & J. Allen (Eds.), *Measuring alcohol consumption.* Totowa, NJ: Humana Press.

Tackett, J. L. (2006). Evaluating models of the personality-psychopathology relationship in children and adolescents. *Clinical Psychology Review, 26*, 548–599.

Talwar, V., Gordon, H. M., & Lee, K. (2007). Lying in elementary school years: Verbal deception and its relation to second-order belief understanding. *Developmental Psychology, 43*(3), 804–810.

Talwar, V., & Lee, K. (2002). Development of lying to conceal a transgression: Children's control of expressive behaviour during verbal deception. *International Journal of Behavioral Development, 26*, 436–444.

Talwar, V., Lee, K., Bala, N., & Lindsay, R. C. L. (2002). Children's conceptual knowledge of lying and its relation to their actual behaviors: Implications for court competence examinations. *Law and Human Behavior, 26*, 395–415.

Tan, L., & Ward, G. (2000). A recency-based account of the primacy effect in free recall. *Journal of Experimental Psychology: Learning, Memory, and Cognition, 26*, 1589–1625.

Tarter, R. E., & Hegedus, A. M. (1991). The Drug Use Screening Inventory: First applications in evaluation and treatment of alcohol and other drug use. *Alcohol Health and Research World, 15*, 65–75.

Tearnan, B. H., & Lewandowski, M. J. (1997). *The Life Assessment Questionnaire (LAQ).* Unpublished manuscript (availabel from Pendrake, Inc., Reno, NV).

Teasdale, G., & Jennett, B. (1974). Assessment of coma and impaired consciousness: A practical scale. *Lancet, 2*, 81–84.

Teichner, G., & Wagner, M. T. (2004). The Test of Memory Malingering (TOMM): Normative data from cognitively intact, cognitively impaired, and elderly patients with dementia. *Archives of Clinical Neuropsychology, 19*, 455–464.

Tellegen, A. (1982). *Manual for the Multidimensional Personality Questionnaire.* Unpublished manuscript, University of Minnesota, Minneapolis.

Tellegen, A. (in press). *Manual for the Multidimensional Personality Questionnaire.* Minneapolis: University of Minnesota Press.

Tenhula, W. N., & Sweet, J. J. (1996). Double cross-validation of the Booklet Category Test in detecting malingered traumatic brain injury. *Clinical Neuropsychologist, 10*, 104–116.

Terracciano, A., & McCrae, R. R. (2006). National character does not reflect mean personality traits levels in 49 cultures: Reply. *Science, 311*, 777–779.

Terre, L., Poston, W. S., Foreyt, J., & St. Jeor, S. T. (2003). Do somatic complaints predict subsequent symptoms of depression? *Psychotherapy and Psychosomatics, 72*(5), 261–267.

Tett, R. P., Jackson, D. N., & Rothstein, M. (1991). Personality measures as predictors of job performance: A meta-analytic review. *Personnel Psychology, 44*, 703–742.

Thakur, M., Hays, J., Ranga, K., & Krishnan, R. (1999). Clinical, demographic and social characteristics of psychotic depression. *Psychiatry Research, 86*(2), 99–106.

Thomann, K., & Rauschmann, M. (2003). "Post-traumatic stress disorder": Historical aspects of a "modern" psychiatric illness in the German language areas. *Medizinhistorisches Journal, 38*(2), 103–138.

Thomann, K., & Rauschmann, M. (2004). Whiplash injury and "railway spine." *Versicherungsmedizin, 56*(3), 131–135.

Thompson, C. R., & Beckson, M. (2004). A case of factitious homicidal ideation. *Journal of the American Academy of Psychiatry and the Law, 32*(3), 277–281.

Thompson, G. B. (2002). The Victoria Symptom Validity Test: An enhanced test of symptom validity. In J. Hom & R. L. Denney (Eds.), *Detection of response bias in forensic neuropsychology* (pp. 43–67). New York: Haworth Press.

Thompson, J. S., Stuart, G. L., & Holden, C. E. (1992). Command hallucinations and legal insanity. *Forensic Reports, 5*, 29–43.

Thompson, J. W., LeBourgeois, H. W., & Black, F. W. (2004). Malingering. In R. Simon & L. Gold (Eds.),

The American Psychiatric Publishing textbook of forensic psychiatry (pp. 427–448). Washington, DC: American Psychiatric Press.

Thompson, L. L., & Cullum, C. M. (1991). Pattern of performance on neuropsychological tests in relation to effort in mild head injury patients. *Archives of Clinical Neuropsychology, 6*, 231.

Thornton, B., Audesse, R. J., Ryckman, R. M., & Burckle, M. J. (2006). Playing dumb and knowing it all: Two sides to an impression management coin. *Individual Differences Research, 4*, 37–45.

Thornton, D. (2002). Constructing and testing a framework for dynamic risk assessment. *Sexual Abuse: A Journal of Research and Treatment, 14*, 139–153.

Timbrook, R. E., Graham, J. R., Keiller, S. W., & Watts, D. (1993). Comparison of the Wiener–Harmon Subtle–Obvious scales and the standard validity scales in detecting valid and invalid MMPI-2 profiles. *Psychological Assessment, 5*, 53–61.

Timmons, L., Lanyon, R., Almer, E., & Curran, P. (1993). Development and validation of Sentence Completion Test indices of malingering during examination for disability. *American Journal of Forensic Psychology, 11*, 23–38.

Tombaugh, T. N. (1996). *Test of Memory Malingering (TOMM)*. Toronto, Ontario, Canada: Multi-Health Systems, Inc.

Tombaugh, T. N. (2002). The Test of Memory Malingering (TOMM) in forensic psychology. In J. Hom & R. Denney (Eds.), *Detection of response bias in forensic neuropsychology*. Binghamton, NY: Haworth Press.

Tonigan, J. S., & Miller, W. R. (2002). The Inventory of Drug Use Consequences (InDUC): Test–retest stability and sensitivity to detect change. *Psychology of Addictive Behaviors, 16*(2), 165–168.

Toobert, S., Bartelme, K., & Jones, E. S. (1959). Some factors related to pedophilia. *International Journal of Social Psychiatry, 43*, 272–279.

Toth, E. L., & Baggaley, A. (1991). Coexistence of Munchausen's syndrome and multiple personality disorder: Detailed report of a case and theoretical discussion. *Psychiatry, 54*(2), 176–183; discussion, 184–186.

Trabucchi, M., & Bianchetti, A. (1996). Delusions. *International Psychogeriatrics, 8*(Suppl. 3), 383–385.

Travin, S., Cullen, K., & Melella, J. T. (1988). The use and abuse of erection measurements: A forensic perspective. *Bulletin of the American Academy of Psychiatry and the Law, 16*, 235–250.

Travin, S., & Protter, B. (1984). Malingering and malingering-like behavior: Some clinical and conceptual issues. *Psychiatry Quarterly, 56*, 189–197.

Trichter, J. G., McKinney, W. T., & Pena, M. (1995). DWI demonstrative evidence: Show and tell the easy way. *Voice, 24*(3), 34–47.

Trimble, M. (1982). *Post-traumatic neurosis from railway spine to whiplash.* Chichester, UK: Wiley.

Trueblood, W., & Schmidt, M. (1993). Malingering and other validity considerations in the neuropsychological evaluation of mild head injury. *Journal of Clinical and Experimental Neuropsychology, 15*, 578–590.

Trull, T. J. (1992). DSM-III-R personality disorders and the Five Factor model of personality: An empirical comparison. *Journal of Abnormal Psychology, 101*, 553–560.

Trull, T. J., & Sher, K. J. (1994). Relationship between the Five-Factor model of personality and Axis I disorders in a nonclinical sample. *Journal of Abnormal Psychology, 103*, 350–360.

Truman, T. L., & Ayoub, C. C. (2002). Considering suffocatory abuse and Munchausen by proxy in the evaluation of children experiencing apparent life-threatening events and sudden infant death syndrome. *Child Maltreatment, 7*(2), 138–148.

Tubbs, P., & Pomerantz, A. M. (2001). Ethical behaviors of psychologists: Changes since 1987. *Journal of Clinical Psychology, 57*, 395–399.

Turk, D. C., & Burwinkle, T. M. (2005). Clinical outcomes, cost-effectiveness, and the role of psychology in treatments for chronic pain sufferers. *Professional Psychology: Research and Practice, 36*(6), 602.

U.S. Congressional Office of Technology Assessment. (1990). *The use of integrity tests for pre-employment screening* (Report No. OTA-SET-442). Washington, DC: U.S. Government Printing Office.

Uomoto, J. M., & Esselman, P. C. (1993). Traumatic brain injury and chronic pain: Differential types and rates by head injury severity. *Archives of Physical Medicine and Rehabilitation, 74*, 61–64.

Ustad, K. L. (1997). *Assessment of malingering in a jail referral population: Screening and comprehensive evaluation.* Unpublished doctoral dissertation, University of North Texas.

Vagnini, V. L., Sollman, M. J., Berry, D. T. R., Granacher, R. P., Clark, J. A., Burton, R., et al. (2006). Known-groups cross-validation of the Letter Memory Test in a compensation-seeking mixed neurologic sample. *Clinical Neuropsychologist, 20*, 289–304.

Vallabhajosula, B., & Van Gorp, W. G. (2001). Post-Daubert admissibility of scientific evidence on malingering of cognitive deficits. *Journal of the American Academy of Psychiatry and the Law, 29*, 302–315.

Van Gorp, W. G., Humphrey, L. A., Kalechstein, A., Brumm, V. L., McMullen, W. J., & Stoddard, N. A. (1999). How well do standard clinical neuropsychological tests identify malingering?: A preliminary analysis. *Journal of Clinical and Experimental Neuropsychology, 21*, 245–250.

Van Iddekinge, C. H., Raymark, P. H., Eidson, C. E., & Putka, D. J. (2003). *Applicant-incumbent differences on personality, integrity, and customer service measures.* Poster presented at the 18th annual convention of the Society for Industrial and Organizational Psychology, Orlando, FL.

Van Oorsouw, K., & Merckelbach, H. (2004). Feigning amnesia undermines memory for mock crime. *Applied Cognitive Psychology, 18*, 505–518.

Van Oorsouw, K., & Merckelbach, H. (2006). Simulating amnesia and memories of a mock crime. *Psychology, Crime and Law, 12*, 261–271.

Veazey, C. H., Hays, J. R., Wagner, A. L., & Miller, H. A. (2005). Validity of the Miller Forensic Assessment of

Symptoms Test in psychiatric patients. *Psychological Reports, 96,* 771–774.

Vickers-Douglas, K. S., Patten, C. A., Decker, P. A., Offord, K. P., Colligan, R. C., Islam-Zwart, K. A., et al. (2005). Revision of the Self-Administered Alcoholism Screening Test (SAAST-R): A pilot study. *Substance Use and Misuse, 40,* 789–812.

Vickery, C. D., Berry, D. T., Dearth, C. S., Vagnini, V. L., Baser, R. E., Crager, D. E., et al. (2004). Head injury and the ability to feign neuropsychological deficits. *Archives of Clinical Neuropsychology, 19,* 37–48.

Vickery, C. D., Berry, D. T. R., Inman, T. H., Harris, M. J., & Orey, S. A. (2001). Detection of inadequate effort on neuropsychological testing: A meta-analytic review of selected procedures. *Archives of Clinical Neuropsychology, 16,* 45–73.

Victor, T. L., & Abeles, N. (2004). Coaching clients to take psychological and neuropsychological tests: A clash of ethical obligations. *Professional Psychology: Research and Practice, 35,* 373–379.

Viglione, D. J., Fals-Stewart, W., & Moxham, E. (1995). Maximizing internal and external validity in MMPI malingering research: A study of a military population. *Journal of Personality Assessment, 65,* 502–513.

Vitacco, M. J., Neumann, C. S., & Jackson, R. (2005). Development of a four-factor model of psychopathy: Associations with ethnicity, gender, violence, and intelligence. *Journal of Consulting and Clinical Psychology, 73,* 466–476.

Vitacco, M. J., & Rogers, R. (2005). Assessment of malingering in correctional settings. In C. Scott & J. Gerbasi (Eds.), *Handbook of correctional mental health* (pp. 133–153). Washington, DC: American Psychiatric Press.

Vitacco, M. J., Rogers, R., Gabel, J., & Munizza, J. (2007). An evaluation of malingering screens with competency to stand trial patients: A known-groups comparison. *Law and Human Behavior, 31,* 249–260.

Volbrecht, M. E., Meyers, J. E., & Kaster-Bundgaard, J. (2000). Neuropsychological outcome of head injury using a short battery. *Archives of Clinical Neuropsychology, 15,* 251–265.

von Hahn, L., Harper, G., McDaniel, S. H., Siegel, D. M., Feldman, M. D., & Libow, J. A. (2001). A case of factitious disorder by proxy: The role of the healthcare system, diagnostic dilemmas, and family dynamics. *Harvard Review of Psychiatry, 9*(3), 124–135.

Vrij, A. (2005). Criterion-based content analysis: A qualitative review of the first 37 studies. *Psychology, Public Policy, and Law, 11,* 3–41.

Vrij, A., Akehurst, L., Soukara, S., & Bull, R. (2002). Will the truth come out?: The effect of deception, age, status, coaching, and social skills on the CBCA scores. *Law and Human Behavior, 26,* 261–283.

Vrij, A., Akehurst, L., Soukara, S., & Bull, R. (2004). Let me inform you how to tell a convincing story: CBCA and reality monitoring scores as a function of age, coaching, and deception. *Canadian Journal of Behavioral Science, 36,* 113–126.

Wachpress, M., Berenberg, A. N., & Jacobson, A. (1953). Simulation of psychosis. *Psychiatric Quarterly, 27,* 463–473.

Wakefield, H., & Underwager, R. (1992). Recovered memories of alleged sexual abuse: Lawsuits against parents. *Behavioral Sciences and the Law, 10,* 483–507.

Waldman, I. D., Singh, A. L., & Lahey, B. B. (2006). Dispositional dimensions and the causal structure of child and adolescent conduct problems. In R. R. Krueger & J. L. Tackett (Eds.), *Personality and psychopathology* (pp. 112–152). New York: Guilford Press.

Walker, F. O., Alessi, A. G., & Digre, K. B. (1989). Psychogenic respiratory distress. *Archives of Neurology, 46,* 196–200.

Waller, N. D. (1992). Review of the Inwald Personality Inventory. In J. J. Kramer & J. C. Conoley (Eds.), *The eleventh mental measurements yearbook* (pp. 418–419). Lincoln, NE: Buros Institute of Mental Measurements.

Walsh, K. W. (1985). *Understanding brain damage: A primer of neuropsychological evaluation.* Edinburgh, UK: Churchill Livingstone.

Walters, G. D. (1988). Assessing dissimulation and denial on the MMPI in a sample of maxium security male inmates. *Journal of Personality Assessment, 52,* 465–474.

Walters, G. D., Rogers, R., Berry, D. T. R., Miller, H. A., Duncan, S. A., McCusker, P. J., et al. (2007). *Malingering as a categorical or dimensional construct: The latent structure of feigned psychopathology as measured by the SIRS and MMPI-2.* Manuscript submitted for publication.

Walters, G. D., White, T. W., & Greene, R. L. (1988). Use of the MMPI to identify malingering and exaggeration of psychiatric symptomatology in male prison inmates. *Journal of Consulting and Clinical Psychology, 56,* 111–117.

Walters, G. L., & Clopton, J. R. (2000). Effect of symptom information and validity scale information on the malingering of depression on the MMPI-2. *Journal of Personality Assessment, 75,* 183–199.

Wanberg, K. W., Horn, J. L., & Foster, F. M. (1977). A differential assessment model for alcoholism: The scales of the Alcohol Use Inventory. *Journal of Studies on Alcohol, 38,* 512–543.

Wanberg, K. W., Lewis, R. A., & Foster, F. M. (1978). Alcoholism and ethnicity: A comparative study of alcohol use patterns across ethnic groups. *International Journal of the Addictions, 13,* 1245–1262.

Wanek, J. E., Sackett, P. R., & Ones, D. S. (2003). Towards an understanding of integrity test similarities and differences: An item-level analysis of seven tests. *International Journal of Selection and Assessment, 7,* 35–45.

Wang, E. W., Rogers, R., Giles, C. L., Diamond, P. M., Herrington-Wang, L. E., & Taylor, E. R. (1997). A pilot study of the Personality Assessment Inventory (PAI) in corrections: Assessment of malingering, suicide risk, and aggression in male inmates. *Behavioral Sciences and the Law, 15,* 469–482.

Ward, T., Gannon, T., & Keown, K. (2006). Beliefs, values, and action: The judgment model of cognitive distortions in sexual offenders. *Aggression and Violent Behavior, 1,* 323–340.

Warriner, E. M., Rourke, B. P., Velikonja, D., & Metham, L. (2003). Subtypes of behavioral and emotional sequelae in patients with traumatic brain injury. *Journal of Clinical and Experimental Neuropsychology, 25,* 904–917.

Wasyliw, O. E., Benn, A. F., Grossman, L. S., & Haywood, T. W. (1998). Detection of minimization of psychopathology on the Rorschach in cleric and noncleric alleged sex offenders. *Assessment, 5,* 389–397.

Watson, C. G. (1975). Impression management ability in psychiatric hospital samples and normals. *Journal of Consulting and Clinical Psychology, 43,* 540–545.

Watson, D., Kotov, R., & Gamez, W. (2006). Basic Dimensions of temperament in relation to personality and pathology. In R. Krueger & J. Tackett (Eds.), *Personality and psychopathology* (pp. 7–38). New York: Guilford Press.

Wechsler, D. (1981). *Manual for the Wechsler Adult Intelligence Scale—Revised.* San Antonio, TX: Psychological Corporation.

Wechsler, D. (1987). *Manual for the Wechsler Memory Scale—Revised.* San Antonio, TX: Psychological Corporation.

Wechsler, D. (1997). *Manual for the Wechsler Adult Intelligence Scale—Third Edition.* San Antonio, TX: Psychological Corporation.

Weed, N. C., Ben-Porath, Y. S., & Butcher, J. N. (1990). Failure of Wiener and Harmon MMPI Subtle scales as personality descriptors and as validity indicators. *Psychological Assessment, 2,* 281–285.

Weed, N. C., Butcher, J. N., McKenna, T., & Ben-Porath, Y. S. (1992). New measures for assessing alcohol and drug abuse with the MMPI-2: The APS and AAS. *Journal of Personality Assessment, 58,* 389–404.

Weed, N. C., Butcher, J. N., & Williams, C. L. (1994). Development of MMPI alcohol/drug problem scales. *Journal of Studies on Alcohol, 55,* 296–302.

Weinborn, M., Orr, T., Woods, S. P., Conover, E., & Feix, J. (2003). A validation of the Test of Memory Malingering in a forensic psychiatric setting. *Journal of Clinical and Experimental Neuropsychology, 25,* 979–990.

Weingartner, H., Cohen, R., Murphy, D., Martello, J., & Gerdt, C. (1981). Cognitive processes in depression. *Archives of General Psychiatry, 38*(1), 42–47.

Weintraub, M. I. (Ed.). (1995). Malingering and conversion reactions [Special issue]. *Neurological Clinics, 13.*

Weintraub, M. I. (2006). Psychogenic injuries and the law. In M. Hallet, S. Fahn, S. Jankovic, & J. Lang (Eds.), *Psychogenic movement disorders: Neurology and neuropsychiatry* (pp. 319–322). Philadelphia: Lippincott Williams & Wilkins.

Weissfeld, J. L., Holloway, J. J., & Kirscht, J. P. (1989). Effects of deceptive self-reports of quitting on the results of treatment trials for smoking: A quantitative assessment. *Journal of Clinical Epidemiology, 42,* 231–243.

Weissman, H. B. (1990). Distortions and deceptions in self-presentation: Effects of protracted litigation on personal injury cases. *Behavioral Sciences and the Law, 8,* 67–74.

Wertham, F. (1949). *The show of violence.* Garden City, NY: Doubleday.

Wessely, S., Chalder, T., Hirsch, S., Wallace, P., & Wright, D. (1997). The prevalence and morbidity of chronic fatigue and chronic fatigue syndrome: A prospective primary care study. *American Journal of Public Health, 87*(9), 1449–1455.

Weston, W. A., & Dalby, J. T. (1991). A case of pseudologia fantastica with antisocial personality disorder. *Canadian Journal of Psychiatry, 36*(8), 612–614.

Wetter, M. W., Baer, R. A., Berry, D. T. R., & Reynolds, S. K. (1994). The effect of symptom information on faking on the MMPI-2. *Assessment, 1,* 199–207.

Wetter, M. W., Baer, R. A., Berry, D. T. R., & Robison, L. (1993). MMPI-2 profiles of motivated fakers given specific symptom information: A comparison to matched patients. *Psychological Assessment, 5*(3), 317–323.

Wetter, M. W., Baer, R. A., Berry, D. T. R., Robison, L. H., & Sumpter, J. (1993). MMPI-2 profiles of motivated fakers given specific symptom information: A comparison to matched patients. *Psychological Assessment, 5,* 317–323.

Wetter, M. W., Baer, R. A., Berry, D. T. R., Smith, G. T., & Larsen, L. H. (1992). Sensitivity of MMPI-2 validity scales to random responding and malingering. *Psychological Assessment, 4,* 369–374.

Wetter, M. W., & Corrigan, S. (1995). Providing information to clients about psychological tests: A survey of attorney's and law students' attitudes. *Professional Psychology: Research and Practice, 26,* 474–477.

Wheeler, K. G. (1985). Review of The Stanton Inventory. In J. V. Mitchell, Jr. (Ed.), *The ninth mental measurements yearbook* (pp. 1469–1470). Lincoln, NE: Buros Institute of Mental Measurements.

White, H. R., & Labouvie, E. W. (1989). Towards the assessment of adolescent problem drinking. *Journal of Studies on Alcohol, 50,* 30–37.

Whitfield, C. (2001). The "false memory" defense: Using disinformation and junk science in and out of court. *Journal of Child Sexual Abuse, 9,* 53–78.

Widiger, T. A., & Trull, T. (2007). Plate tectonics in the classification of personality disorder. *American Psychologist, 62,* 71–83.

Widom, C. S., & Morris, S. (1997). Accuracy of adult recollections of childhood victimization: Part 2. Childhood sexual abuse. *Psychological Assessment, 9,* 34–46.

Widows, M., & Smith, G. P. (2005). *Structured Inventory of Malingered Symptomatology (SIMS) and professional manual.* Odessa, FL: Psychological Assessment Resources.

Wiener, D. N. (1948). Subtle and obvious keys for the MMPI. *Journal of Consulting Psychology, 12,* 164–170.

Wierzbicki, M. (1993). Use of the MCMI Subtle and Obvious subscales to detect faking. *Journal of Clinical Psychology, 49,* 809–814.

Wierzbicki, M. (1997). Use of Subtle and Obvious scales to detect faking on the MCMI-II. *Journal of Clinical Psychology, 53,* 421–426.

Wiggins, E. C., & Brandt, J. (1988). The detection of simulated amnesia. *Law and Human Behavior, 12,* 57–78.

Wiggins, J. S. (1959). Interrelationships among MMPI measures of dissimulation under standard and social desirability instructions. *Journal of Consulting Psychology, 23,* 419–427.

Wildman, R., Batchelor, E., Thompson, L., Nelson, F., Moore, J., Patterson, M., et al. (1979). The Georgia Court Competency Test [Abstract]. *Newsletter of the American Association of Correctional Psychologists, 2,* 4.

Wiley, S. (1998). Deception and detection in psychiatric diagnosis. *Psychiatric Clinics of North America, 21*(4), 869–893.

Wilhelm, K. L., Franzen, M. D., Grinvalds, V. M., & Dews, S. M. (1991, November). *Do people given knowledge and offered money fake better?* Paper presented at the annual conference of the National Academy of Neuropsychology, Dallas, TX.

Wilkinson, C. B. (1983). Aftermath of a disaster: The collapse of the Hyatt Regency Hotel skywalks. *American Journal of Psychiatry, 140,* 1134–1139.

Wilkinson, L., & Task Force on Statistical Inference. (1999). Statistical methods in psychology journals: Guidelines and explanations. *American Psychologist, 54,* 594–604.

Williams, J. B. W., Gibbon, M., First, M. B., Spitzer, R. L., Davies, M., Borus, J., et al. (1992). The structured clinical interview for DSM-III-R (SCID): II. Multisite test-retest reliability. *Archives of General Psychiatry, 49,* 630–636.

Williams, L. M. (1994). Recall of childhood trauma: A prospective study of women's memories of child sexual abuse. *Journal of Consulting and Clinical Psychology, 62,* 1167–1176.

Williams, M. A., Putzke, J. D., LaMarche, J. A., Bourge, R. C., Kirklin, J. K., McGiffin, D. C., et al. (2000). Psychological defensiveness among heart transplant candidates. *Journal of Clinical Psychology in Medical Settings, 7,* 167–174.

Williams, R. J., & Nowatzki, N. (2005). Validity of adolescent self-report of substance use. *Substance Use and Misuse, 40,* 299–311.

Williams, V. L. (1995). Response to Cross and Saxe's "A critique of the validity of polygraph testing in child sexual abuse cases." *Journal of Child Sexual Abuse, 4,* 55–71.

Willis, C. G. (1986). Reid Report/Reid Survey. In D. J. Keyser & R. C. Sweatland (Eds.), *Test critiques* (Vol. 2, pp. 631–636). Kansas City, MO: Test Corporation of America.

Wilson, A. E., Smith, M. D., & Ross, H. S. (2003). The nature and effects of young children's lies. *Social Development, 12,* 21–45.

Wilson, D. B. (2001). Effect size determination program [Computer software]. Retrieved from mason.gmu .edu/%7Edwilsonb/ma.html (see es_calculator.zip).

Wilson, J. P. (1981). *Cognitive control mechanisms in stress response syndromes and their relation to different forms of the disorder.* Unpublished manuscript, Cleveland State University.

Wilson, J. P. (2004). PTSD and complex PTSD: Symptoms, syndromes, and diagnoses. In J. P. Wilson & T. M. Keane (Eds.), *Assessing psychological trauma and PTSD* (2nd ed., pp. 7–44). New York: Guilford Press.

Wilson, J. P., & Zigelbaum, S. D. (1983). The Vietnam veteran on trial: The relation of posttraumatic stress disorder to criminal behavior. *Behavioral Sciences and the Law, 1,* 69–83.

Wilson, R. J. (1998). Psychophysiological signs of faking in the phallometric test. *Sexual Abuse: Journal of Research and Treatment, 10,* 113–126.

Wilson, S. L. (2001). Attachment disorders: Review and current status. *Journal of Psychology, 135,* 37–51.

Winters, K. C. (1991). *Personal Experience Screening Questionnaire (PESQ) manual.* Los Angeles: Western Psychological Services.

Winters, K. C. (1992). Development of an adolescent alcohol and other drug abuse screening scale: Personal Experiences Screening Questionnaire. *Addictive Behaviors, 17,* 479–490.

Winters, K. C. (1999). A new multiscale measure of adult substance abuse. *Journal of Substance Abuse Treatment, 16*(3), 237–246.

Winters, K. C., Anderson, N., Bengston, P., Stinchfield, R. D., & Latimer, W. W. (2000). Development of a parent questionnaire for use in assessing adolescent drug abuse. *Journal of Psychoactive Drugs, 32*(1), 3–13.

Winters, K. C., & Henly, G. A. (1989). *The Personal Experience Inventory (PEI) test and manual.* Los Angeles: Western Psychological Services.

Winters, K. C., Latimer, W. W., Stinchfield, R. D., & Henly, G. A. (1999). Examining psychosocial correlates of drug involvement among drug clinic-referred youth. *Journal of Child and Adolescent Substance Abuse, 9*(1).

Winters, K. C., Stinchfield, R. D., & Henly, G. A. (1993). Further validation of new scales measuring adolescent alcohol and other drug abuse. *Journal of Studies on Alcohol, 54,* 534–541.

Winters, K. C., Stinchfield, R. D., Henly, G. A., & Schwartz, R. H. (1991). Validity of adolescent self-report of alcohol and other drug involvement. *International Journal of the Addictions, 25,* 1379–1395.

Winters, K. C., Stinchfield, R., & Latimer, W. W. (2004). Clinical assessment of adolescent drug abuse with the Personal Experience Inventory (PEI). In M. E. Maruish (Ed.), *The use of psychological training for treatment planning and outcomes assessment: Vol. 2. Instruments for children and adolescents* (3rd ed., pp. 371–404). Mahwah, NJ: Erlbaum.

Wolf, A. W., Schubert, D. S. P., Patterson, M., Grande, T., & Pendleton, L. (1990). The use of the MacAndrew Alcoholism Scale in detecting substance abuse and antisocial personality. *Journal of Personality Assessment, 54,* 747–755.

Wolfe, P. L., Millis, S. R., Hanks, R., Larrabee, G., Sweet, J. J., & Fichtenberg, N. (in submission) *California Verbal Learning Test—II: Variables for detection of insufficient effort.* Manuscript submitted for publication.

Wood, J., Nezworski, M., Garb, H., & Lilienfeld, S. (2001). The misperception of psychopathology: Problems with norms of the Comprehensive System for the Rorschach. *Clinical Psychology: Science and Practice, 8,* 350–373.

Wood, R. (2004). Understanding the "miserable minority": A diathesis–stress paradigm for postconcussional syndrome. *Brain Injury, 18*(11), 1135–1153.

Woolley, R. M., & Hakstian, A. R. (1992). An examination of the construct validity of personality-based and overt measures of integrity. *Educational and Psychological Measurement, 52,* 475–489.

Wooten, A. J. (1984). Effectiveness of the *K* correction in the detection of psychopathology and its impact on profile height and configuration among young adult men. *Journal of Consulting and Clinical Psychology, 52,* 468–473.

World Health Organization. (1992). *International statistical classification of diseases and related health problems* (10th ed.). Geneva, Switzerland: Author.

World Health Organization. (1994). *Schedules for Clinical Assessment of Neuropsychiatry (SCAN).* Geneva, Switzerland: Author.

Wrobel, T. A., Lachar, D., Wrobel, N. H., Morgan, S. T., Gruber, C. P., & Neher, J. A. (1999). Performance of the Personality Inventory for Youth validity scales. *Assessment, 6,* 367–376.

Wydra, A., Marshall, W. L., Earls, C. M., & Barbaree, H. E. (1983). Identification of cues and control of sexual arousal by rapists. *Behaviour Research and Therapy, 21,* 469–476.

Wygant, D. B., Ben-Porath, Y. S., Berry, D. T. R., & Arbisi, P. A. (2006, March). *An MMPI-2 validity scale designed to detect somatic overreporting in civil forensic settings.* Paper presented at the American Psychology–Law Society conference, St. Petersburg Beach, FL.

Wymer, J. H., Barkemeyer, C. A., Jones, G. N., & Callon, E. B. (2006). Validation of the Barkemeyer-Callon-Jones Malingering Detection Scale. *American Journal of Forensic Psychology, 24*(1), 33–43.

Wynia, M. K., Cummins, D. S., VanGeest, J. B., & Wilson, I. B. (2000). Physician manipulation of reimbursement rules for patients: Between a rock and a hard place. *Journal of the American Medical Association, 283,* 1858–1865.

Wynkoop, T. F., & Denney, R. L. (1999). Exaggeration of neuropsychological deficit in competency to stand trial. *Journal of Forensic Neuropsychology, 1,* 29–53.

Wynkoop, T. F., Frederick, R. I., & Hoy, M. (2006). Improving the clinical utility of the SIRS cognitive items: Preliminary reliability, validity, and normative data in pretrial and clinical samples. *Archives of Clinical Neuropsychology, 21,* 651–656.

Wypijewski, J. (2004). The passion of Father Paul Shanley. *Legal Affairs, 3,* 34–41.

Yates, B. D., Nordquist, C. R., & Schultz-Ross, R. A. (1996). Feigned psychiatric symptoms in the emergency room. *Psychiatric Services, 47*(9), 998–1000.

Yildiz, M., & Torun, F. (2003). [A case report of factitious disorder with hallucinations]. *Turkish Journal of Psychiatry, 14*(3), 239–244.

Yorker, B. C. (1996). Hospital epidemics of factitious disorder by proxy. In M. D. Feldman & S. J. Eisendrath (Eds.), *The spectrum of factitious disorders* (pp. 157–174). Washington, DC: American Psychiatric Press.

Young, M. S., & Schinka, A. (2001). Research validity scales for the NEO-PI-R: Additional evidence for reliability and validity. *Journal of Personality Assessment, 76,* 412–420.

Young, S. E., Stallings, M. C., Corley, R. P., Krauter, K. S., & Hewitt, J. K. (2000). Genetic and environmental influences on behavioral disinhibition. *American Journal of Medical Genetics (Neuropsychiatric Genetics), 96,* 684–695.

Youngjohn, J. R. (1995). Confirmed attorney coaching prior to neuropsychological evaluation. *Assessment, 2,* 279–283.

Youngjohn, J. R., Davis, D., & Wolf, I. (1997). Head injury and the MMPI-2: Paradoxical severity effects and the influence of litigation. *Psychological Assessment, 9,* 177–184.

Yuille, J. C. (1988). The systematic assessment of children's testimony. *Canadian Psychology, 29,* 247–262.

Yutzy, S. (2002). Somatoform disorders. In R. E. Hales & S. C. Yudofsky (Eds.), *Textbook of clinical psychiatry* (4th ed.). Washington, DC: American Psychiatric Press.

Zahner, G. E. (1991). The feasibility of conducting structured diagnostic interviews with preadolescents: A community field trial of the DISC. *Journal of the American Academy of Child and Adolescent Psychiatry, 30,* 659–668.

Zalewski, C., Thompson, W., & Gottesman, I. (1994). Comparison of neuropsychological test performance in PTSD, generalized anxiety disorder, and control Vietnam veterans. *Assessment, 1,* 133–142.

Zickar, M. J., & Robie, C. (1999). Modeling fake-good personality items: Item-level analysis. *Applied Psychology, 85,* 551–563.

Zilberstein, K. (2006). Clarifying core characteristics of attachment disorders: A review of current research and theory. *American Journal of Orthopsychiatry, 76,* 55–64.

Zimmerman, B. J. (1970). The relationship between teacher, class, behavior and student school anxiety levels. *Psychology in the Schools, 7,* 89–93.

Zimmerman, M., & Mattia, J. I. (1999). Psychiatric diagnosis in clinical practice: Is comorbidity being missed? *Comprehensive Psychiatry, 40,* 182–191.

Zisook, S., Byrd, D., Kuck, J., & Jeste, D. V. (1995). Command hallucinations in outpatients with schizophrenia. *Journal of Clinical Psychiatry, 56*(10), 462–465.

Zitelli, B. J., Seltman, M. F., & Shannon, R. M. (1987). Munchausen's syndrome by proxy and its professional participants. *American Journal of Diseases of Childhood, 141*(10), 1099–1102.

Zuckerman, M. (1999). *Vulnerability to psychopathology: A biosocial model.* Washington, DC: American Psychological Association.

Author Index

Subject Index